THE MAX PLANCK HANDBOOKS
IN EUROPEAN PUBLIC LAW

General Editors
ARMIN VON BOGDANDY
PETER M HUBER
SABRINA RAGONE

Constitutional Foundations

The Max Planck Handbooks in European Public Law

Constitutional Foundations

VOLUME 2

Edited by
ARMIN VON BOGDANDY
PETER M HUBER
SABRINA RAGONE

MAX-PLANCK-GESELLSCHAFT

Great Clarendon Street, Oxford, OX2 6DP,
United Kingdom

Oxford University Press is a department of the University of Oxford.
It furthers the University's objective of excellence in research, scholarship,
and education by publishing worldwide. Oxford is a registered trade mark of
Oxford University Press in the UK and in certain other countries

© The several contributors 2023

The moral rights of the authors have been asserted

First Edition published in 2023

All rights reserved. No part of this publication may be reproduced, stored in
a retrieval system, or transmitted, in any form or by any means, without the
prior permission in writing of Oxford University Press, or as expressly permitted
by law, by licence or under terms agreed with the appropriate reprographics
rights organization. Enquiries concerning reproduction outside the scope of the
above should be sent to the Rights Department, Oxford University Press, at the
address above

You must not circulate this work in any other form
and you must impose this same condition on any acquirer

Public sector information reproduced under Open Government Licence v3.0
(http://www.nationalarchives.gov.uk/doc/open-government-licence/open-government-licence.htm)

Published in the United States of America by Oxford University Press
198 Madison Avenue, New York, NY 10016, United States of America

British Library Cataloguing in Publication Data

Data available

Library of Congress Control Number is on the file at the Library of Congress

ISBN 978–0–19–872642–5

DOI: 10.1093/oso/9780198726425.001.0001

Printed and bound by
CPI Group (UK) Ltd, Croydon, CR0 4YY

Links to third party websites are provided by Oxford in good faith and
for information only. Oxford disclaims any responsibility for the materials
contained in any third party website referenced in this work.

Preface

Five years ago, we published the first volume of the Max Planck Handbooks in European Public Law. Entitled *The Administrative State*, it explored key concepts of constitutional and administrative law in many of the countries that together make up the European legal space. We then published two volumes on constitutional adjudication: one on institutions, the other with comparative analysis. The current volume adds deep analysis of the foundations of fourteen constitutional orders, complementing the other three volumes.

Many colleagues helped bring this volume to fruition through comments and feedbacks on previous versions of the text. In particular, Martin Jarrett and Naomi Shulman polished a significant number of country reports; Angelika Schmidt, Jana Kirchberg, and Hajar Kasmi provided invaluable help in formatting the texts and completing the footnotes. The publication was made possible, finally, by the *Deutsche Forschungsgemeinschaft*, whose Gottfried Wilhelm Leibniz Prize provided the funding for the Max Planck Handbooks series and thus enables us to pursue a truly European research project.

Bologna, Heidelberg, and Munich, August 2022
Armin von Bogdandy
Peter M Huber
Sabrina Ragone

Contents

List of Contributors	xv

1: The Evolution and *Gestalt* of the Austrian Constitution — 1
Ewald Wiederin

A. Origins of the Current Constitution — 3
   1. External Cause and Driving Forces — 4
   2. Models and Influences — 7
   3. Original Solutions — 9
   4. Insurmountable Dissent — 11
B. The Evolution of the Constitution — 12
   1. Flexibility and Rigidity of the Constitution — 12
   2. The Development of the Constitution in the First Republic — 17
   3. The Development of the Constitution in the Second Republic — 20
   4. Contributions of Jurisprudence and Doctrine — 23
C. Basic Structures and Concepts — 25
   1. Constitution, Simple Law, and Politics — 25
   2. Democracy — 26
   3. Federalism — 32
   4. Rule of Law — 36
   5. Separation of Powers — 40
   6. Fundamental Rights — 46
   7. Terms for the Entity — 50
D. Constitutional Identity — 51
   1. Continuity between the First and the Second Republic — 51
   2. Permanent Neutrality — 52
   3. The Basic Constitutional Order — 52

2: The Evolution and *Gestalt* of the Czech Constitution — 55
David Kosař and Ladislav Vyhnánek

A. Introduction — 56
B. The Origins of the Current Constitution — 58
   1. Sources of Inspiration — 60
   2. Between Klaus and Havel: Drafting the Constitution — 61
   3. The Final Product: A Fragile Compromise — 63
C. The Evolution of the Constitution (Post-1993 Development of the Czech
   Constitutional *Gestalt* and Major Challenges) — 65
   1. Dealing with the Past and Building the Material *Rechtsstaat* — 65
   2. The 1998 Opposition Agreement and the Growing Distrust in Traditional
      Political Parties — 67
   3. Accession to the European Union — 68
   4. Economic Crisis and the Constitutional Dimension of Social Conflicts — 73
   5. The Two-Headed Executive: Weak Governments and Trouble-Making
      Presidents — 75
   6. An Over-Judicialized Constitution — 77

viii CONTENTS

	7. Where Are the People?	80
	8. A Danger of Democratic Backsliding	80
D.	Basic Structures and Concepts	82
	1. Formal Aspects of the Czech Constitutional *Gestalt*	82
	2. Substantive Aspects of the Czech Constitutional *Gestalt*	88
E.	Constitutional Identity	99
F.	Conclusion	107

3: The Evolution and *Gestalt* of the French Constitution — 109
Guillaume Tusseau

A.	Origins of the Current Constitution	109
B.	The Evolution of the Constitution	114
	1. High-Energy Constitutionalism	114
	2. Low Juridicity Constitutionalism	122
C.	Basic Structures and Concepts	131
	1. Delegative Constitutionalism	132
	2. Human Rights Constitutionalism	141
D.	Constitutional Identity	146
	1. A New (Im)balance of Powers	147
	2. The Judicialization of the French Constitutionalism	153
	3. The (Lethal?) Internalization of Political Conflict	158

4: The Evolution and *Gestalt* of the German Constitution — 163
Susanne Baer

A.	Origins of the Current Constitution	163
	1. Sources, Theories, Texts	164
	2. Framing, Drafting	165
	3. Commitments, Ideologies, People	166
	4. Between Global, Local, and Comparative	166
	5. Consensus and Controversies	169
B.	The Evolution of the Constitution	171
	1. The First Fan: Karlsruhe	172
	2. A Slow Start, the 'Never Again', and 'One of You We Are'	175
	3. Post-1968	177
	4. Post-1989	179
	5. EU Integration	180
	6. Globalization	181
	7. Changes of the Text	181
	8. Changes in Society	184
C.	Basic Structures and Concepts	191
	1. Position, Standing, Significance	191
	2. Fundamental Rights and Proportionality	193
	3. Foundational Principles of the State	195
	4. Democracy, Elections, Parliament	196
	5. Defensive Democracy	200
	6. Federalism, Form of State, Units, Territory	201
	7. *Rechtsstaat*	203
	8. Welfare State, Protective and Social Dimensions of Fundamental Rights	205
	9. Secularism	208
	10. Constitutionalization	210
D.	Constitutional Identity	211

5: The Evolution and *Gestalt* of the Hungarian Constitution
Gábor Halmai

217

A. Origins of the Current Constitution	217
1. The 1989 Constitution	217
2. Two Decades of Constitutional Democracy?	219
3. Hungary's Fundamental Law	222
B. The Evolution of the Constitution	223
1. Cardinal Laws and Amendments to the Fundamental Law	223
2. The Fourth and Fifth Amendments	226
3. The Sixth, Seventh, Ninth, Tenth, and Eleventh Amendments	231
4. No Judicial Review of Constitutional Amendments	236
C. Basic Structures and Concepts	245
1. Government without Checks	245
2. Identity of the Political Community	246
3. Intervention into the Right to Privacy	248
4. Weakening of the Protection of Fundamental Rights	249
5. Constitutional Entrenchment of Political Preferences	251
6. A Populist Illiberal Constitutional System	254
D. Constitutional Identity	257
1. The Abuse of the Concept	257
2. The Instrumental Role of Religion in National Identity	266

6: The Evolution and *Gestalt* of the Italian Constitution
Sabrina Ragone and Giacomo D'Amico

269

A. Origins of the Current Constitution	269
1. Historical Experiences Affecting the Constitution	269
2. Foreign Influence and Use of Comparative Law	274
3. Main Critical Points	276
4. Political Equilibria in the Constituent Assembly and their Impact on the Outcome	279
B. The Evolution of the Constitution	283
1. The Evolution of the Form of Government	283
2. The Evolution of Regionalism	286
3. The Evolution of Constitutional Adjudication	289
4. Critical Features and Junctures	292
5. The Development of the Constitution as a Source Subject to Interpretation and Implementation	296
6. Rigidity and Amendability	298
C. Basic Structures and Concepts	302
1. The Value of the Constitution and the Constitutionalization of the Legal System	302
2. Democracy and Sovereignty	304
3. Rule of Law and Protection of Constitutional Rights	307
4. Separation and Distribution of Powers among Constitutional Bodies and Territorial Entities	309
D. Constitutional Identity	316

7: The Evolution and *Gestalt* of the Lithuanian Constitution
Irmantas Jarukaitis

319

A. Origins of the 1992 Constitution of Lithuania	319

x CONTENTS

1. The Early Origins of the Lithuanian Constitutionalism	319
2. Evolution of the Lithuanian Constitutionalism during the Interwar Period	324
3. Re-establishment of the Independence and Adoption of the 1992 Constitution	327
B. The Evolution of the 1992 Constitution: Between the Rigidity and the Flexibility	333
1. Central Role of the CC in Developing the Constitution	333
2. Lithuania's Integration into Trans-Atlantic Structures and its Impact on the Constitution	340
C. Basic Principles and Structures of the 1992 Constitution	352
1. Main Features of the 1992 Constitution and its Role in the National Legal Order	353
2. Basic Constitutional Principles Describing the Republic of Lithuania	356
3. Rule of Law and Fundamental Rights	361
4. Constitutional Organs and Separation of Powers	365
D. The Lithuanian Constitutional Tradition and the Constitutional Identity	376

8: The Evolution and *Gestalt* of the Dutch Constitution — 381
Leonard F M Besselink

A. Introduction	382
B. Origins of the Current Constitution	384
1. What is the Constitution?	384
2. National Constitutional Development: International Parameters and National Causes	384
3. The Great Transformations	385
4. The Adaptations	394
5. The Minor Amendments	399
6. Perennial Controversies	400
C. The Evolution of the Constitution: The Institutional Parameters of Constitutional Development	401
1. Constitution-Making Power: The Rigidity of the Constitution	401
2. The Role of the Government in Constitution Making	403
3. The Role Played by Parliament	404
4. The Role of Courts: The Unwritten Rules and Principles of Constitutional Law	405
5. The Role of Foreign Constitutional Law	408
D. Basic Structures and Concepts	409
1. The Relation of the Constitution to Other Parts of the Legal Order	410
2. The Relation of the Constitution to Politics and Democracy	415
3. *Rechtsstaat*: Fundamental Rights and Legality	420
4. Horizontal and Vertical Division of Powers	424
5. The Absence of an Overarching Concept of Political Unity	427
E. Constitutional Identity	428

9: The Evolution and *Gestalt* of the Polish Constitution — 431
Michal Szwast, Marcin Szwed, and Paulina Starski

A. The Origins of the Constitution	433
1. Poland's Constitutional Past: Polish Constitutionalism throughout the Centuries	433
2. 'Constitutional Moment' in Times of Transition: The Path to the 1997 Constitution and its Substance	438
B. The Constitution, its Rigidity, and Evolution	444

1. Constitutional Rigidity	444
2. The Constitutional Tribunal as a Catalyst of Constitutional Evolution and a Forum for the Resolution of Constitutional Conflicts	449
C. The Caesura: The Dismantlement of the Constitutional Order	457
D. The Axiology of the Constitution of 1997: Basic Structures and Concepts	463
1. The Constitution and its Supremacy	464
2. The Constitutional Concept of Sovereignty, the 'Nation', and the 'Common Good'	469
3. The Constitution and the 'Democratic State Ruled by Law'	471
4. The Constitutional Protection of Human Rights: Dignity of the Person, Equality, and Freedom	476
5. The Constitution and the Separation of Powers	481
6. The Constitution and the Form of the State	486
7. The Constitution and its Identity	488
E. Conclusions and Outlook	490
Epilogue	490

10: The Evolution and *Gestalt* of the Romanian Constitution   493
Bogdan Iancu

A. Origins of the Current Constitution	493
1. Constitutionalism in Romania: Continuities and Discontinuities	493
2. The Genesis of Constitutionalism in Romania	496
3. Return or New Beginning? The Constitution of 1991	508
B. The Evolution of the Constitution	515
1. Shifting Contexts: New Conflicts, New Vocabularies	515
2. The 'Euro-Amendments'	516
3. Constitutional Conflicts	521
4. Anticorruption as a Quasi-constitutional Meta-discourse	524
C. Basic Structures and Concepts	531
1. The Constitutionalization of Romanian Law	531
2. Fundamental Rights and the Rule of Law	536
3. Separation of Powers	542
D. Constitutional Identity	545

11: The Evolution and *Gestalt* of the Spanish Constitution   549
Victor Ferreres Comella

A. Origins of the Current Constitution	549
1. Historical Background	549
2. The Constitutional Spirit: The Politics of '*Consenso*'	553
3. Foreign Influences and the Impact of Constitutional Scholars	558
B. The Evolution of the Constitution	560
1. Constitutional Rigidity: The Amendment Procedure	560
2. Procedural Dualism and Substantive Limits to Amendments	562
3. Interpretation	564
4. Influential Personalities in the Development of the Constitution	565
C. Basic Structures and Concepts	565
1. The Position of the Constitution in the Legal and Political System	565
2. Democracy	566
3. The Rule of Law: General Principles	569
4. Recognition and Protection of Fundamental Rights	570

xii   CONTENTS

5. Constitutional Organs and Separation of Powers	575
6. Political Unity and the Sovereignty of the Spanish People	594
D. Constitutional Identity	597

12: The Evolution and *Gestalt* of the Swedish Constitution

601

Thomas Bull and Ian Cameron

A. Origins of the Current Constitution	601
1. The Four Constitutional Documents in Sweden	601
2. Historical Experiences Influencing the Current Instrument of Government	602
3. Major Critical Points During the Constituent Phase of the Instrument of Government and Political Factors Influencing the Outcome	605
4. Issues Explicitly Left Open at the Time of the Adoption of the New Instrument of Government and Subsequent Development of These	608
B. The Evolution of the Constitution	611
1. Major Features of the Constitutional Order	611
2. Foreign Influence and Common Features of Nordic Constitutions	614
3. What Personalities (Judges, Academics, Politicians) and Which Legal Texts have had a Special Importance in the Development of the Constitution?	617
4. The Balance Between Rigidity and Flexibility in the Constitution	618
C. Basic Structures and Concepts	619
1. The Position of the Constitution within the Legal System	619
2. Democracy	622
3. Relationship Between Constitutional Law and International Law	624
4. Relationship Between Constitutional Law and EU Law	626
5. Rights and the Rule of Law	628
6. Constitutional Organs, the Separation of Powers, the Organization of the Courts, and the Independence of the Judiciary	630
7. The Organization of the State	633
8. Citizenship and the 'Political Unity'	635
D. Constitutional Identity	635

13: The Evolution and *Gestalt* of the Swiss Constitution

639

Giovanni Biaggini

A. Origins of the Swiss Constitutional System: The Creation of the Federal Constitutions of 1848, 1874, and 1999	640
1. Foundation of the Confederation: The Federal Constitution of 1848	641
2. Expansion of the Constitutional Order of the Confederation: The Fully Revised Constitution of 1874	645
3. Constitutional Renewal: The Federal Constitution of 1999	647
B. The Evolution of the Constitution: Milestones and Formative Factors	653
1. Main Types of Procedure of Constitutional Amendment	653
2. Milestones in the Development of the Constitution	656
3. Actors and 'Neglected Issues' of Constitutional Development	661
C. Basic Structures and Concepts	663
1. The Federal Constitution as a Basis for and Object of Politics	663
2. On the Significance of Structure-establishing Constitutional Principles	664
3. Democracy and the Understanding of Democracy	665
4. The Rule of Law and the Understanding of Fundamental Rights	670
5. Organ Make-up and Understanding of the Separation of Powers	673
6. Federalism and the Understanding of Federalism	680

D.	Constitutional Identity: Characteristics and Identity-creating Elements	685
	1. Citizens and People, Nation and State in the Light of the Federal Constitution	685
	2. Balancing Out of Equality and Inequality as a Never-ending Task	687

14: The Evolution and *Gestalt* of the British Constitution 689
Martin Loughlin

A.	Introduction	689
B.	Origins of the Current Constitution	692
	1. Historical Experiences	692
	2. International Influences	695
	3. Major Debating Points	697
	4. Defining Moments	699
	5. Influential Texts	701
C.	The Evolution of the Constitution	704
	1. The Evolving Constitution	704
	2. Main Controversies	709
	3. Flexibility of the Constitution	717
D.	Basic Structures and Concepts	719
	1. Constitutional Law and Politics	719
	2. Sovereignty and Democracy	721
	3. Institutions of Government	727
	4. State, Nation, and Citizen	731
E.	Constitutional Identity	733

Index 737

List of Contributors

Susanne Baer is a Professor of Public Law and Gender Studies at Humboldt University of Berlin, Germany.

Leonard F M Besselink is a Professor Emeritus of Constitutional Law at the University of Amsterdam and Professor at the LUISS School of Law in Rome, Italy.

Giovanni Biaggini is a Professor of Constitutional Law, Administrative Law, and European Law at the University of Zurich, Switzerland.

Thomas Bull is a Judge at the Swedish Supreme Administrative Court.

Ian Cameron is a Professor of International Law at the University of Uppsala, Sweden.

Giacomo D'Amico is a Professor at the University of Messina, Italy.

Victor Ferreres Comella is a Professor of Constitutional Law at Pompeu Fabra University of Barcelona and Visiting Professor at the University of Texas in Austin, United States of America.

Gábor Halmai is a Professor of Comparative Constitutional Law at the European University Institute, Italy.

Bogdan Iancu is an Associate Professor at the University of Bucharest, Romania.

Irmantas Jarukaitis is an Associate Professor at Vilnius University, Lithuania.

David Kosař is an Associate Professor and Director of the Judicial Studies Institute at Masaryk University, Czechia.

Martin Loughlin is a Professor of Public Law at the London School of Economics & Political Science, United Kingdom.

Sabrina Ragone is an Associate Professor of Comparative Public Law at the University of Bologna and Senior Research Affiliate at the Max Planck Institute for Comparative Public Law and International Law in Heidelberg, Germany.

Paulina Starski is a Professor of German and Comparative Public Law, European Law, and International Law at Albert Ludwig University of Freiburg, and Senior Research Affiliate at the Max Planck Institute for Comparative Public Law and International Law in Heidelberg, Germany.

Michał Szwast is an Assistant Professor at the University of Warsaw, Poland.

Marcin Szwed is an Assistant Professor at the University of Warsaw, Poland.

Guillaume Tusseau is a Professor of Public Law at Science Po and member of the Institut universitaire de France.

Ladislav Vyhnánek is an Assistant Professor of Constitutional Law at Masaryk University, Czechia.

Ewald Wiederin is a Professor of Public Law at Vienna University, Austria.

1

The Evolution and *Gestalt* of the Austrian Constitution

Ewald Wiederin[*]

A. Origins of the Current Constitution	3	c) Parliamentary Debate	6
1. External Cause and Driving Forces	4	2. Models and Influences	7
a) The Disintegration of the Habsburg		a) The Austrian December Constitution of	
Monarchy	4	1867	7
b) The Draft Constitutions	5	b) The Weimar Constitution of 1919	8

[*] Translated by Claudia Priewasser, reviewed by Martin Jarrett.

1. Citation of the constitution as common in Austria:
   Federal Constitutional Law (*Bundes-Verfassungsgesetz; B-VG*), BGBl. 1920/1, republished in BGBl. 1930/1, last amended by Federal Constitutional Law BGBl. I 2021/235.
   Besides the Federal Constitutional Law (*B-VG*) there are about a hundred more Federal Constitutional Laws (*Bundesverfassungsgesetze*, abbreviated to *BVG*) and several hundreds of constitutional provisions in federal statutory laws (G) or state treaties (StV). An enumeration is therefore unfeasible. A part of the ancillary constitutional law is listed in 2.

2. List of related laws:
   Basic Law on the General Rights of Nationals (*Staatsgrundgesetz über die allgemeinen Rechte der Staatsbürger*), RGBl. 1867/142 as amended by BGBl. 1988/684, cited as StGG.
   State Treaty for the Re-establishment of an Independent and Democratic Austria (*Staatsvertrag betreffend die Wiederherstellung eines unabhängigen und demokratischen Österreichs*), BGBl. 1955/152 as amended by BGBl. I 2008/2, cited as State Treaty of Vienna.
   Federal Constitutional Law on the Regulation of Financial Relations between the Federation and the other Territorial Entities (Financial Constitutional Law; *Bundesverfassungsgesetz über die Regelung der finanziellen Beziehungen zwischen dem Bund und den übrigen Gebietskörperschaften; Finanz-Verfassungsgesetz 1948–F-VG 1948*), BGBl. 1948/45 as amended by BGBl. I 2012/51.
   Federal Constitutional Law on the Protection of Personal Liberty (*Bundesverfassungsgesetz über den Schutz der persönlichen* Freiheit), BGBl. 1988/684 as amended by BGBl. I 2008/2, cited as PersFrG.
   Convention for the Protection of Human Rights and Fundamental Freedoms (*Konvention zum Schutze der Menschenrechte und Grundfreiheiten*), BGBl. 1958/210 as amended by BGBl. III 2021/68, cited as ECHR, and its Additional Protocols ratified by Austria (ZP)).
   Federal Law concerning the Protection of Personal Data (*Bundesgesetz über den Schutz personenbezogener Daten; Datenschutzgesetz 2000–DSG 2000*), BGBl. I 1999/165 as amended by BGBl. I 2021/148, cited as DSG 2000.

3. Collection of laws:
   Federal Law Gazette (*Bundesgesetzblatt*), abbreviated to BGBl. The BGBl. has been published by the Federal Chancellery since 1920 as the official collection of federal law. Until the end of 2003, it was published in paper form. Since 2004, it has been published on the internet at www.ris.bka.gv.at. Since 1997, it has consisted of three parts: Part I is for statutory laws, Part II for ordinances, and Part III for state treaties. The legal norms are being cited according to part, year and number of the publication.
   Land Law Gazette (*Landesgesetzblatt*), abbreviated as LGBl. The LGBl. are being published as the official collections of *Länder* law by the *Länder* partly in paper form and partly via the internet.

4. Judicial decisions:
   Collection of Decisions and most important Resolutions of the Constitutional Court (*Sammlung der Erkenntnisse und wichtigsten Beschlüsse des Verfassungsgerichtshofes*), abbreviated as VfSlg., is the official collection published on behalf of the Constitutional Court since 1921. Decisions are cited according to number and year.
   Collection of Decisions and Resolutions of the Supreme Administrative Court (*Sammlung der Erkenntnisse und Beschlüsse des Verwaltungsgerichtshofes*), abbreviated to VwSlg., is the official collection published on behalf of the Administrative Court. It consists of an old series (1900–1934) and a new series starting 1946, and is divided into a part on administrative law (A) and a part on financial law (F). Decisions are cited according to number, part, and year.

Ewald Wiederin, *The Evolution and* Gestalt *of the Austrian Constitution* In: *The Max Planck Handbooks in European Public Law*. Edited by: Armin von Bogdandy, Peter M Huber, and Sabrina Ragone, Oxford University Press. © Ewald Wiederin 2023.
DOI: 10.1093/oso/9780198726425.003.0001

c) The Federal Constitution of the Swiss
    Confederation of 1874 — 9
3. Original Solutions — 9
    a) The Constitutional Judiciary — 9
    b) The Concept of Democracy — 10
    c) Transformation of the Unitary State
        into a Federal State — 10
4. Insurmountable Dissent — 11
    a) Fundamental Rights — 11
    b) The Organization of General Public
        Administration — 11
    c) Federal Allocation of Competences — 11

B. **The Evolution of the Constitution** — 12
1. Flexibility and Rigidity of the
    Constitution — 12
    a) The Provisions on Constitutional
        Amendments — 12
        i)   Quorum of the National Council — 12
        ii) Designation of Constitutional
             Amendments As Such — 12
        iii) The Status of the Federal Council
             in the Constitutional Amendment
             Procedure — 13
        iv) The Differentiation between
             Partial and Total Revision of the
             Constitution — 14
    b) Effects on Constitutional Practice
        and Interpretation — 15
        i)   Technical Approach to
             Constitutional Law — 16
        ii) Fragmentation of
             Constitutional Law — 16
        iii) Rejection of Constitutional
             Customary Law — 17
2. The Development of the Constitution
    in the First Republic — 17
    a) 1925: Constitutional Reform for
        Simplification of the Administration — 17
    b) 1929: Reconstruction of the
        Constitution to Prevent the Civil War — 18
    c) 1933/34: Collapse during the Crisis — 19
3. The Development of the Constitution
    in the Second Republic — 20
    a) Restoration of the Constitutional
        Order of 1920/29 — 20
    b) Termination of Allied Control and
        Neutrality — 20
    c) Closing Gaps inside the Federal
        Constitutional Law — 21
    d) Rehabilitation of Treaties — 21
    e) Strengthening the *Länder* — 22
    f) Extension and Modification of Legal
        Remedies — 22
    g) Accession to the European Union — 23
4. Contributions of Jurisprudence
    and Doctrine — 23
    a) First Phase: Dominance of Practice — 23
    b) Second Phase: Self-Assurance
        of Doctrine — 24
    c) Third Phase: Principles — 24

C. **Basic Structures and Concepts** — 25
1. Constitution, Simple Law, and Politics — 25
    a) The Constitution as a Framework — 25

b) Limitations on the Constitutionalisation
    of the Legal System — 25
c) The Constitutional Court's Perception
    of its Role — 26
2. Democracy — 26
    a) 'Its Law Emanates From the People':
        The Democracy Model of the Federal
        Constitutional Law — 27
    b) Homogeneity by Substantiation
        (*Konkretisierungen*) — 29
    c) Influence of the Principle of
        Democracy — 30
3. Federalism — 32
    a) Strict Parity of the Feeble *Länder*: The
        Model of Federalism of the Federal
        Constitutional Law — 32
    b) Fixed Separation of Legislative
        Competences with Predominance
        of the Federation — 33
    c) Cooperative Federalism in
        Administration with Predominance
        of the *Länder* — 34
    d) Dominance of the Federation in the
        Judiciary — 35
    e) Dominance of the Federation in the
        Financial Constitution — 35
4. Rule of Law — 36
    a) Conformity with Legal Acts of a
        Higher Level: The Concept of Rule
        of Law of the Federal
        Constitutional Law — 36
    b) Independence of the Judiciary — 38
    c) Legal Protection against Administrative
        Acts with a Focus on the Legal Form — 38
    d) The Concept of the Rule of Law as a
        Principle — 39
5. Separation of Powers — 40
    a) Legislation and Enforcement: The
        Supremacy of Parliament — 40
    b) The Concern for a '*Verwaltungsbruch*':
        Separation of Powers in the Federal
        Constitutional Law — 41
    c) The Interrelation between Parliament,
        Federal President, and Federal
        Government — 43
    d) Control by the Court of Audit and
        Control by the Ombudsman — 45
6. Fundamental Rights — 46
    a) The Older Layer of Fundamental
        Rights — 46
    b) The European Convention on Human
        Rights — 48
    c) Recent Safeguards of Fundamental
        Rights — 49
    d) Extent and Binding Force of
        Fundamental Rights — 50
7. Terms for the Entity — 50
    a) Law instead of *Gewalt* — 51
    b) Republic Instead of *Staat* — 51

D. **Constitutional Identity** — 51
1. Continuity between the First and the
    Second Republic — 51
2. Permanent Neutrality — 52
3. The Basic Constitutional Order — 52

A. Origins of the Current Constitution

'*L'Autriche, c'est ce qui reste.*' (The rest is Austria). These words of Clemenceau are at the origin of Austrian statehood. The fall of the Danube Monarchy and its fragmentation into national states resulted in the necessity to draw up a genuine constitution for the German-speaking territories of the former Cisleithania. The original plan was to formulate a constitution that would serve as a mere transitory constitution for a subsequent integration of Austria into the German *Reich*. This plan, however, failed due to the opposition of the Allies. Initially, Austrian statehood was merely a dictate (*Oktroy*) and it was perceived as such. Decades passed before the Austrians came to terms with the first undesired course, after which they were able to find their own identity.

However, the constitution of this young and fragile structure, which was adopted in 1920, had a clear profile and a strong identity. This identity was influenced much more by the constitution of the former monarchical state, particularly when compared with the constitutions of the other successor states emerging from the Austro-Hungarian Empire. The Federal Constitutional Law (*Bundes-Verfassungsgesetz, B-VG*) of 1920 took inspiration from the Basic Laws of 1867, both in its rejection and in its reception of the concepts included therein. The constitutional monarchy was replaced by a democratic republic, the unitary state of Cisleithania was transformed into a federal state without undergoing fundamental changes, and the system of rule of law as set up by the monarchy was adopted and further developed by adding a constitutional judiciary.

Not only does the legacy of the monarchy live on in the rules of the new constitution, but it has also significantly characterized the way in which this constitution is dealt with. In an era of national states, the attempt to maintain the cohesion of a multilingual and multinational structure by pointing to its common history and the legitimacy of a ruling dynasty was doomed to failure. Because of this, at least from the date of the Austro-Hungarian Compromise of 1867 (*Ausgleich*), the monarchy emphasized the stipulation of spheres of competence and the setting up well-ordered legal procedures: a multi-ethnic state was not to be kept alive by common values. As the central administration of the Habsburg Empire had had its seat in Vienna and Vienna was taken over by the young republic, this cultural experience lingered on in Austria—Hans Kelsen's Pure Theory of Law (*Reine Rechtslehre*) elevated it into theory and powerfully reinforced in its effects. Until today, they dominate the ambiance in which the constitutional law is being lived, cultivated, and taught. The Austrian constitutional tradition is a tradition of exact separations with a preference for formal ways of conflict resolution and based on the conviction that the constitutional discourse must be strictly distinguished from the political discourse, because it could otherwise not be a common language for the political opponents. It is a positivist tradition with a sceptical view towards weighting considerations, mistrusting both practical reason and justness and thus focusing on decisions pursuant to well-ordered proceedings.[1]

These basic attitudes have an influence on the doctrines of legal sources and interpretation. As regards the theory of legal sources, Adolf Merkl's theory of the hierarchy of norms (*Stufenbau der Rechtsordnung*)[2] is the uncontested leading theory which is successfully

---

[1] For details see Alexander Somek, '§ 33 Wissenschaft vom Verfassungsrecht: Österreich', in Armin von Bogdandy, Pedro Cruz Villalón, and Peter M Huber (eds), *Handbuch Jus Publicum Europaeum Vol II* (CF Müller, Heidelberg, 2008) 639 ff.

[2] For references and acknowledgment see Martin Borowski, 'Die Lehre vom Stufenbau des Rechts nach Adolf Julius Merkl', in Stanley Paulson and Michael Stolleis (eds), *Hans Kelsen. Staatsrechtslehrer und Rechtsphilosoph des 20. Jahrhunderts* (Mohr Siebeck, Tübingen, 2005) 122, 124 ff.

applied as a universal formula to explain the legal world in the most different contexts. As regards interpretation, there is a preference for measuring instruments rather than explanatory instruments: topoi and figures serving to justify results are secondary to methods to explore meanings and reconstruct intentions. This explains the high significance of historical interpretation which may be unfamiliar to external observers.

1. External Cause and Driving Forces

a) The Disintegration of the Habsburg Monarchy

The disintegration of the Dual Monarchy was the external cause for the creation of the Federal Constitutional Law. After the catastrophe of the First World War, the formerly unified nations declared their independence. On 21 October 1918 the *Reichsrat* (Imperial Council) members of the 'German' parties assembled to prepare for the establishment of a German–Austrian state and subsequently, proclaimed the Republic of German-Austria as a state on 30 October 1918.[3] Emperor Karl paved the way to this proclamation[4] by his abdication on 11 November 1918.[5]

On the basis of its first decision, which was largely drafted by Karl Renner, the Provisional National Assembly (*Provisorische Nationalversammlung*) step by step adopted a preliminary constitution which established German–Austria as a democratic republic, and summoned a Constituent National Assembly (*Konstituierende Nationalversammlung*).[6] This National Assembly first convened on 4 March 1919 and reaffirmed that German–Austria was a democratic republic and that it was an integral part of the German Reich.[7] However, the project of integration into the German Reich as a *Bundesland*,[8] which was supported by all major

---

[3] Decision of the Provisional National Assembly for German Austria of 30 October 1918 on the Basic Institutions of Public Authority (*Beschluss der Provisorischen Nationalversammlung für Deutschösterreich vom 30.10.1918 über die grundlegenden Einrichtungen der Staatsgewalt*), State Law Gazette (*Staatsgesetzblatt*, abbreviated hereafter as StGBl.) 1918/1.

[4] The founding of the state with this proclamation took place in breach of legal continuity; the young republic did not draw its sovereignty from the monarchy. *Pars per toto* Adolf Merkl, *Die Verfassung der Republik Deutschösterreich* (Deuticke, Vienna, 1919) 2; 'German Austria is therefore a new entry among the states.'

[5] Special edition of *Wiener Zeitung* of 11 November 1918, No 261. Karl later revoked his abdication and refused to renounce to the throne.

[6] Most important steps: Law of 12 November 1918 on the Form of State and Government of German-Austria (*Gesetz vom 12.11.1918 über die Staats- und Regierungsform von Deutschösterreich*), StGBl. 1918/5; Law of 14 November 1918 relating to the acquisition of public authority in the *Länder* (*Gesetz vom 14.11.1918, betreffend die Übernahme der Staatsgewalt in den Ländern*), StGBl. 1918/24; Law of 22 November 1918 on the Extent, Borders and Relations of the State Territory of German-Austria (*Gesetz vom 22.11.1918 über Umfang, Grenzen und Beziehungen des Staatsgebietes von Deutschösterreich*), StGBl. 1918/40; Law of 18 December 1918 on the Convocation of the Constituent National Assembly (*Gesetz vom 18.12.1918 über die Einberufung der konstituierenden Nationalversammlung*), StGBl. 1918/114; Law of 19 December 1918 Amending or Complementing Several Provisions of the Decision of the Provisional National Assembly on the Basic Institutions of Public Authority of 30 October 1918 (*Gesetz vom 19.12.1918, womit einige Bestimmungen des Beschlusses der Provisorischen Nationalversammlung über die grundlegenden Einrichtungen der Staatsgewalt vom 30.10.1918 [...] abgeändert oder ergänzt wurden*), StGBl. 1918/139.

[7] Law of 12 March 1919 on the Form of State (*Gesetz vom 12.3.1919 über die Staatsform*), StGBl. 1919/174.

[8] The Weimar Constitution of 1919 had made arrangements for that in art 61 para 2 and provided for the participation of the German-Austrian members of the *Reichsrat* (first with an advisory vote, and with full voting rights after the union was established). In a note of 2 September 1919 the allied and associated powers under the threat of force demanded that Germany repeal art 61 para 2 Weimar Constitution. With a note of 5 September 1919 the Federal government conceded the inapplicability of this Paragraph and with Protocol of 22 September 1919 even acknowledged its invalidity (see Gerhard Anschütz, *Die Verfassung des Deutschen Reichs* (14th edn, Stilke, Berlin, 1933) 340 with further references). These governmental acts, however, had no derogatory effect due to the lack of

political forces, was rejected by the Entente: Austria was condemned to statehood. After the conclusion of the peace treaty,[9] the Constituent National Assembly had to change the name of the state from 'German-Austria' to 'Austria' in autumn 1919.[10] Because of this, the decision was made to elaborate the constitution of a sovereign state instead of a constitution of a member state of Germany.

b) The Draft Constitutions

The preparation of a new constitution from several parties was subject to various influences.[11] Which influences were the decisive factors has been subject of controversy. There are as many founding legends as there were driving forces.

The first initiatives came from the central administration.[12] As early as 1918, Renner had established reform departments inside the State Chancellery (*Staatskanzlei*). He appointed Hans Kelsen as a consultant and—in May 1919—commissioned him to prepare a constitutional draft. In summer 1919, Kelsen finalized the draft, adding several alternatives from his own initiative in order to respond to 'various political options'.[13]

In October 1919, the newly appointed State Secretary Michael Mayr took over the task of coordinating the work on the constitution. He first debated the basic points of the new constitution, especially the federal allocation of competences, with the State Offices (*Staatsämter*) of the central administration[14] and then made contact with the *Länder*. As a result of his intermediation, he published a first draft, which was based on Kelsen's fifth version, in February 1920.[15] Shortly before that, Tyrol had tabled a federalist alternative draft.[16]

On 15 February 1920, Mayr presented his draft at the Länder-*Conference* in Salzburg (*Salzburger Länderkonferenz*). While the conservative parties signalled their approval, the Social Democrats voiced reservations: the conference was adjourned on 17 February 1920 without tangible results. For the *Länder*-Conference in Linz from 20 to 23 April 1920 (*Linzer Länderkonferenz*), Mayr revised his draft.[17] The Greater German People's Party

---

publication in the Imperial Law Gazette (*Reichsgesetzblatt*, abbreviated hereafter as RGBl.). Art 61 para 2 Weimar Constitution therefore remained in force.

[9] Treaty of St Germain-en-Laye of 10 September 1919, StGBl. 1920/303.

[10] Law of October 21, 1919 on the Form of State, StGBl. 1919/484.

[11] See the descriptions by Klaus Berchtold, *Verfassungsgeschichte der Republik Österreich*, vol I: 1918–1933 (Springer, Vienna, 1998) 189 ff (with further references), and Christian Neschwara, 'Zur Entwicklung des Verfassungsrechts nach 1918', in Herbert Schambeck (ed), *Parlamentarismus und öffentliches Recht in Österreich*, vol 1 (Duncker & Humblot, Berlin, 1993) 83, 96 ff.

[12] They are documented by Felix Ermacora, *Die Entstehung der Bundesverfassung 1920. Dokumente der Staatskanzlei über allgemeine Fragen der Verfassungsreform* (Braumüller, Vienna, 1989).

[13] See the report of the Constitutional Committee, '991 Beilagen zu den Stenographischen Protokollen der Konstituierenden Nationalversammlung 3' (citation); and Hans Kelsen, *Österreichisches Staatsrecht – Ein Grundriss, entwicklungsgeschichtlich dargestellt* (Mohr, Tübingen, 1923) 160 ff. All six drafts set up by Kelsen can be found in Felix Ermacora, *Die Entstehung der Bundesverfassung 1920: Die Sammlung der Entwürfe zur Staats- bzw. Bundesverfassung* (Braumüller, Vienna, 1990) 62 ff. See also the analysis by Georg Schmitz, *Die Vorentwürfe Hans Kelsens für die österreichische Bundesverfassung* (Manz, Vienna, 1981) 44 ff.

[14] Documentation by Felix Ermacora, *Die Entstehung der Bundesverfassung 1920. Materialien und Erläuterungen (III): Die Aufgabenverteilung zwischen Bund und Ländern* (Braumüller, Vienna, 1986) 4 ff, 10 ff.

[15] *Reichspost* of 10 February 1920. In order not to prejudice the state government, the draft was termed a private paper.

[16] The draft prepared by Falser on behalf of the *Landtag* circulated in two versions which can be found in Felix Ermacora, *Die Entstehung der Bundesverfassung 1920: Die Sammlung der Entwürfe zur Staats- bzw. Bundesverfassung* (n 13) 503 ff. However, Tyrol was not able to present this draft as the basis for consultations before the Conference of the *Länder* held in Salzburg (*Salzburger Länderkonferenz*).

[17] So-called first '*Linzer Entwurf*' (draft of Linz), printed in Felix Ermacora, *Quellen zum österreichischen Verfassungsrecht (1920)* (Ferdinand Berger und Söhne, Vienna, 1967) 106.

('*Großdeutsche*') and the Social Democrats equally presented their ideas. Both the Mayr draft supported by the Christian Socials and the draft of the Social Democrats prepared by Robert Danneberg were based on the systematic structure created by Kelsen and on the wording he had used; as for content, they barely differed from each other in large parts.[18] The consultations held in Linz led to a further approximation of the positions.[19] The attempt to reconcile the remaining differences in point of view and to issue a common government bill[20] failed due to the collapse of the coalition. The parties submitted their drafts as legislative proposals to the Constituent National Assembly.[21]

c) Parliamentary Debate

In July 1920, the Constitutional Committee of the Constituent National Assembly elected a subcommittee composed of seven members, whereof three belonged to the Christian Socials, three to the Social Democrats, and one to the German Nationalists. Otto Bauer of the Social Democrats was chairman; the other members and substitute members to be named for their outstanding roles were Ignaz Seipel, Robert Danneberg, and Heinrich Clessin. The subcommittee decided to make the drafts of Linz and the Danneberg draft for their basis of deliberations. It consulted Kelsen, Mayr, and other officials of the State Chancellery like Georg Froehlich, Egbert Mannlicher, and Adolf Merkl, heard respondents on selected issues and sought expert opinions from public law scholars and judges of the high courts.[22] After a first intensive phase of deliberations during twelve sessions, which was completed on 26 August 1920, the subcommittee published a provisional draft.[23] The negotiations between the Social Democrat Party and the Christian Democrat Party, which were conducted to remove the remaining differences of opinion between 1 and 18 September 1920, ended in a compromise which would exclude a number of controversial issues from the discussions on the constitution. The second phase of work in the subcommittee started on 13 September 1920 and served the purpose of thoroughly deliberating the draft article by article. It ended on 23 September 1920. During the following days, the Constitutional Committee convened for debate; it made only minor modifications to the draft and adopted its report as early as 26 September 1920.[24] On 29 September 1920, Seipel opened the plenary debate as rapporteur, and on 1 October 1920 the Constituent National Assembly finalized its work on the constitution by unanimous decisions on the 'Federal Constitutional Law'

---

[18] See for a comparison of the two drafts Felix Ermacora, *Die Entstehung der Bundesverfassung 1920: Die Sammlung der Entwürfe zur Staats- bzw. Bundesverfassung* (n 13) 290 ff.

[19] The Conferences of the *Länder* in Linz and Salzburg are documented by Felix Ermacora, *Materialien zur österreichischen Bundesverfassung (I). Die Länderkonferenzen und die Verfassungsfrage* (Braumüller, Vienna, 1989) 93 ff, 201 ff.

[20] See the Renner-Mayr draft finalized on 8 June 1920, subsequently published by Renner in the *Wiener Zeitung* of 8 July 1920, printed in Felix Ermacora, *Quellen zum österreichischen Verfassungsrecht (1920)* (n 17) 188 ff.

[21] Draft of the Christian Social Party of 25 June 1920, 888 Beilagen zu den Stenographischen Protokollen der Konstituierenden Nationalversammlung = Felix Ermacora, *Quellen zum österreichischen Verfassungsrecht (1920)* (n 17) 141 ff; draft of the Social Democrat Party of 7 July 1920, 904 Beilagen zu den Stenographischen Protokollen der Konstituierenden Nationalversammlung = Felix Ermacora, *Quellen zum österreichischen Verfassungsrecht (1920)* (n 17) 152 ff. Before that, the Greater German Association had tabled its proposal on 18 May 1920: see 842 Beilagen zu den Stenographischen Protokollen der Konstituierenden Nationalversammlung = Felix Ermacora, *Quellen zum österreichischen Verfassungsrecht (1920)* (n 17) 78 ff.

[22] For detailed references see Christian Neschwara, 'Entwicklung des Verfassungsrechts nach 1918' (n 11) 105 ff.

[23] *Wiener Zeitung* of 29 August 1920, No 198, printed in Felix Ermacora, *Quellen zum österreichischen Verfassungsrecht (1920)* (n 17) 379 ff.

[24] 991 Beilagen zu den Stenographischen Protokollen der Konstituierenden Nationalversammlung = Felix Ermacora, *Quellen zum österreichischen Verfassungsrecht (1920)* (n 17) 547 ff.

(*Bundes-Verfassungsgesetz*)[25] and on a Law on Constitutional Transition (*Verfassungsüberg angsgesetz*).[26]

2. Models and Influences

The key figure in all of these processes is Hans Kelsen: the two constitutional proposals submitted by the two leading parties to the parliament trace back to his drafts and he was involved in the parliamentary debate as a permanent advisor. His intention was, by his own account, to 'maintain everything useful from the previous constitution, preserve the continuity of constitutional institutions to the extent possible', but to 'lean on the Swiss, and even more the new German Imperial Constitution'.[27]

This exhaustively designates the formative models. In broad terms, it can be said that the constitutional institutions were largely taken over from the monarchy, whereas the parts dedicated to the principles of democracy and federalism attempt to follow a middle course between the monarchy and the Weimar Constitution. The Swiss example is reflected in the systematic structure and in the denomination of certain bodies, rather than in content.

a) The Austrian December Constitution of 1867

The fact that the December Constitution of 1867 served as a model is particularly apparent in the provisions on the judiciary. Some of the rules on the judicial guarantees and the separation of judiciary and administration have been adopted directly from the Basic Law on the Judiciary; the provisions on the review of promulgations (*Kundmachungsprüfung*) and public liability (*Amtshaftung*) were obviously inspired by it.[28] The articles on the administrative judiciary are based on the Law on the Establishment of an Administrative Court (*Ver waltungsgerichtshofsgesetz*; RGBl. 1876/36). The articles relating to the organization and to the jurisdiction of the constitutional judiciary draw inspiration from the provisions of the *Reichsgericht*.[29] The legality principle vested in the new constitution, though considerably tightened, is also part of the Austrian tradition and can already be found in the December Constitution.[30]

---

[25] Law of 1 October 1920 establishing the Republic of Austria as a Federal State (*Gesetz vom 1. Oktober 1920, womit die Republik Österreich als Bundesstaat eingerichtet wird—Bundes-Verfassungsgesetz*), StGBl. 1920/450, issued on 5 October 1920; taking into account the corrigendum for typographical errors StGBl. 1920/501 newly printed in Federal Law Gazette (*Bundesgesetzblatt*, abbreviated hereafter as BGBl.) BGBl. 1920/1, issued on 10 November 1920.

[26] Constitutional Law of 1 October 1920 Relating to the Transition to the Federal Constitution (*Verfassungsgesetz vom 1. Oktober 1920, betreffend den Übergang zur bundesstaatlichen Verfassung*), StGBl. 1920/451, BGBl. 1920/2 (hereafter abbreviated as ÜG 1920).

[27] Hans Kelsen, *Österreichisches Staatsrecht—Ein Grundriss, entwicklungsgeschichtlich dargestellt* (n 13) 161; 'alles Brauchbare aus der bisherigen Verfassung beizubehalten, die Kontinuität der verfassungsrechtlichen Institutionen möglichst zu wahren' but 'an die schweizerische, aber noch mehr an die neue deutsche Reichsverfassung anzulehnen'.

[28] See arts 6, 7, 9, and 14 Basic Law on the Judiciary (*Staatsgrundgesetz über die richterliche Gewalt*), RGBl. 1867/144.

[29] See for composition and appointment art 5, for the jurisdiction on demarcation conflicts (*Kompetenzgerichtsbarkeit*); art 2, for jurisdiction on pecuniary claims (*Kausalgerichtsbarkeit*); art 3 lit a for jurisdiction on complaints of infringement of fundamental rights (*Grundrechtsgerichtsbarkeit*); art 3 lit b Basic Law Establishing a Supreme Court of the Empire (*Staatsgrundgesetz über die Einsetzung eines Reichsgerichts*), RGBl. 1867/143.

[30] See art 11 Basic Law on the Executive (*Staatsgrundgesetz über die Ausübung der Regierungs- und Vollzugsgewalt*), RGBl. 1867/145.

The provisions on the status of the members of the National Council (*Nationalrat*) and the Federal Council (*Bundesrat*) were obviously modelled on the Basic Law on the Representation of the Empire (*Reichsvertretung*; RGBl. 1867/141).[31] As for the federal allocation of competences, the general clause which favours the *Länder* is taken over together with some individual competences,[32] and the responsibilities of the Federal President are comparable to those of the monarchs.[33]

b) The Weimar Constitution of 1919

The Constitution of the German Reich of 11 August 1919 (*Weimarer Reichsverfassung*, *WRV*) strongly influenced the setup of the democratic parts of the new Austrian constitution. The proclamation of democracy, which heads the German Constitution, has been adopted nearly verbatim in article 1 Federal Constitutional Law, and, in its structuring, the Federal Constitutional Law equally follows the Weimar example in large parts: the provisions relating to uniform election principles for all forms of popular representation (articles 17 and 22 WRV), to the duration of the legislative period and the assembly of the first chamber (article 23 WRV), and to investigative committees (article 34 WRV), significantly influenced the wording of the parallel provisions of the Federal Constitutional Law. The same applies to the rules on the status of the delegates and legislative procedures: the provisions on free mandate (article 21 WRV), on parliamentary immunity in connection with the exercise of the members' mandate in parliament (indemnity; article 30 WRV) and on the rights of members who are public officials or soldiers (article 39 WRV) may, in a modified form, be found in the Federal Constitutional Law as well; the provisions of the Weimar Constitution concerning legislative proposals (article 69 WRV), the signing and publication of laws by the *Reichspräsident* (article 70 WRV), the objection of the *Reichsrat* and the resolution of the *Reichstag* against this objection (insistence, *Beharrungsbeschluss*; article 74 WRV) and amendments to the constitution (article 76 WRV) were, at very least, inspiring examples.

There are also similarities in the field of federalism. Like the Weimar Constitution, the Federal Constitutional Law avoids calling the *Länder* member states or assigning sovereignty to them. Some provisions on competences and the model of framework legislation, i.e. federal laws establishing legislative principles (*Grundsatzgesetzgebung*; article 10 WRV) are copied; the right of the Federal government to object to laws of the *Länder* is based on article 12 para 2 WRV, the obligation to newly establish the number of delegates of the *Länder* (*Bundesräte*) after every general census follows article 61 para 3 WRV; the wording of article 3 Federal Constitutional Law can be traced back to the articles on the state territory and the transfer of state territory within the *Reich* (articles 2, 18 WRV); finally, the provisions on the constitutional judiciary might have indirectly been influenced by the provisions on the judicial settlement of federal disputes (articles 13 para 2, 19 WRV). Another zone of influence is the regulation of the status of general principles of international law in domestic law: article 9 Federal Constitutional Law is a literal copy of article 4 WRV.

---

[31] See notably section 16 (immunity), section 8 (public officials and functionaries) Basic Law on the *Reichsvertretung* (*Staatsgrundgesetz über die Reichsvertretung*).

[32] See sections 11 and 12 Basic Law on the *Reichsvertretung*, RGBl. 1867/141.

[33] See art 3 to 6 Basic Law on the Executive.

c) The Federal Constitution of the Swiss Confederation of 1874

There is scarcely of any concrete evidence for the influence of the Federal Constitution of the Swiss Confederation of 1874 (*Bundesverfassung der Schweizerischen Eidgenossenschaft vom 29. Mai 1874*; BV). If there is such influence at all, it affected more the general concept of the constitution than individual institutions. The most important idea taken over from the Swiss federal constitution is definitely the differentiation between total revision and partial revision of the federal constitution,[34] on which the Austrian rules on '*Gesamtänderung*' and '*Teiländerung*' were modelled.[35] The Swiss influence on the denomination of the highest bodies of the Federation is clearly visible: *Nationalrat* (National Council), *Bundesrat* (Federal Council), *Bundesversammlung* (Federal Assembly), and *Bundespräsident* (Federal President) are terms which are also known by the BV 1874.[36] Moreover, the title of the first chapter headed 'General Provisions' is apparently taken over from the BV 1874.[37]

3. Original Solutions

a) The Constitutional Judiciary

The Federal Constitutional Law may certainly claim originality regarding the rules on the constitutional judiciary.[38] It is the keystone holding together both the concept of the rule of law and the concept of federalism of the new constitution.[39]

First, the abundance of competences assigned to the Constitutional Court (*Verfassungsgerichtshof, VfGH*) is astonishing: besides the competences of the former *Reichsgericht*,[40] it also has jurisdiction to review the legality of ordinances (article 139), the constitutionality of statutory laws (article 140), the lawfulness of elections (article 141), the prosecution of certain public officials in impeachment procedures (*staatsrechtliche Anklage*) (article 142 f), and on violations of international law (article 145). The ensemble of these provisions resulted in the Constitutional Court being competent to review *ex officio* each general legal norm to be applied in a case pending with it both concerning the legality of the enactment procedure and its compliance with superordinate law. The provisions on the review of statutory laws were also helpful for federalism: both the *Länder* governments (*Landesregierungen*) and the Federal government (*Bundesregierung*) could challenge each

---

[34] See art 118 to 121 BV 1874.

[35] The earlier drafts reflected even more clearly its role as a model than does the effective art 44 para 2 Federal Constitutional Law.

[36] See art 72 (National Council), art 95 (Federal Council), art 71 (Federal Assembly, consisting of both Councils), art 98 (Federal President) BV 1874.

[37] See also the parallelism between art 1 BV and art 2 Federal Constitutional Law, art 4 BV and art 7 Federal Constitutional Law, art 3 BV and art 15 para 1 Federal Constitutional Law, art 43 BV and art 6 Federal Constitutional Law.

[38] See e.g. Heinz Schäffer, 'Der Beitrag Österreichs zur europäischen Rechtskultur' (2004) 52 Jahrbuch des öffentlichen Rechts der Gegenwart 51, 53 ff. For details on its genesis see Herbert Haller, *Die Prüfung von Gesetzen* (Springer, Vienna, 1979) 30 ff, 45 ff; Theo Öhlinger, 'The Genesis of the Austrian Model of Constitutional Review of Legislation' (2003) 16 Ratio Juris 206, 209 ff; Ewald Wiederin, 'Der österreichische Verfassungsgerichtshof als Schöpfung Hans Kelsens und sein Modellcharakter als eigenständiges Verfassungsgericht', in Thomas Simon and Johannes Kalwoda (eds), *Schutz der Verfassung. Normen, Institutionen, Höchst- und Verfassungsgerichte* (Duncker & Humblot, Berlin, 2014) 283, 284 ff.

[39] Hans Kelsen, *Österreichisches Staatsrecht—Ein Grundriss, entwicklungsgeschichtlich dargestellt* (n 13) 208.

[40] See art 137 (pecuniary claims), art 138 (demarcation conflicts), and art 144 (complaints of infringement of fundamental rights) Federal Constitutional Law.

other's laws before the Constitutional Court at any time and thus effectively take a stand against violations of the federal allocation of competences.

As for its judicial review of legal norms, the Constitutional Court is designed to be a 'negative legislator' (*negativer Gesetzgeber*): in its decision, it does not establish the invalidity of a norm *ex tunc*, but it repeals a statutory law (*einfaches Gesetz*) or an ordinance (*Verordnung*). From the time of the adoption of the Federal Constitutional Law in its original version, the Constitutional Court has had the power to order that its repeal become effective *pro futuro*, thereby tolerating the situation where the unlawful general norm remains in force for a transition period in the interest of legal certainty.[41] This concept has become known as Austrian model of constitutional review and was adopted by many other states first after the Second World War and—in a second stage—after the fall of the Iron Curtain.

b) The Concept of Democracy

The concept of democracy endorsed by the new constitution grants parliament a predominant position and makes it the hub of public decision-making processes.[42] Initially, the head of state was elected and sworn in by the Federal Assembly which consists of the National Council and the Federal Council (article 60), the members of the Constitutional Court were elected and sworn in half by the National Council, half by the Federal Council (article 147 para 3). Both in the Federation and in the *Länder*, the administration was subordinate to 'people's commissioners' (*Volksbeauftragte*; article 19), who were elected by the National Council and the *Landtag* (*Land* parliament) respectively and were controlled by and accountable to it.

This supremacy of legislation, which deviates from the traditional separation of powers regime, expands into other provisions as well. Article 18 subordinates the entire public administration to a legal reservation (*Gesetzesvorbehalt*) and installs a principle of legal certainty (*Bestimmtheitsgebot*), which obliges parliament to take all essential decisions itself. The new constitution also permits the use of authoritarian elements to serve its concept of democracy: article 20 lays down the right of the *Volksbeauftragte* to issue instructions (*Weisung*) and the binding force of their instructions on public administration officials as a constitutional precept.

c) Transformation of the Unitary State into a Federal State

A third original solution is the gentle transformation of the unitary state into a federal state in a way which would maintain the traditional structures to a large extent. This way, the general dissent between the Christian Socials and the Social Democrats as to whether the republic was to be constituted as a federal state or as a unitary state, could be bridged. The monarchy had already been a highly decentralized unitary state, which had a *Land* legislation next to a *Reich* legislation and which knew an autonomous *Land* administration next to the *Reich* administration. The specific features of Austrian federalism can be explained from the acceptance of this legacy.[43]

---

[41] See art 140 para 3 Federal Constitutional Law.

[42] Hans Kelsen, *Österreichisches Staatsrecht—Ein Grundriss, entwicklungsgeschichtlich dargestellt* (n 13) 164, therefore classifies the Austrian constitution as the 'extreme type of a parliamentary republic'.

[43] See Hans Kelsen, *Österreichisches Staatsrecht—Ein Grundriss, entwicklungsgeschichtlich dargestellt* (n 13) 165 ff.

4. Insurmountable Dissent

The Federal Constitutional Law has remained a torso because consensus could not be reached on several points which were controversial in terms of ideology. Merely an agreement on ad-hoc solutions was achieved, which prevented failure of the whole project.

a) Fundamental Rights

In the establishment of fundamental rights, the relevant drafts aligned closely with the catalogue of the Weimar Constitution. However, the gap between the approach of the Christian Socials, whose draft had entirely omitted fundamental rights, and that of the Social Democrats was unbridgeable concerning the matters of fundamental social rights and freedom of religion.[44] Therefore, everything was left as it was: with the final provisions of the new constitution (article 149) the monarchy's catalogue of fundamental rights was taken over as a constitutional law.

b) The Organization of General Public Administration

The organization of the bodies of general public administration in the *Länder* was a second point of dissent. The Social Democrats attached great importance to the democratization of the administration on all levels. They succeeded in codifying the establishment of territorial municipalities in accordance with the principle of self-administration (*Selbstverwaltung*) in articles 115 to 119; however, the provisions remained wishful thinking at first. Until the federal constitutional law envisaged in article 120 should come into force, the existing authoritarian structures of district administration (*Bezirksverwaltung*) were preserved.[45] They remain in existence to this day.

c) Federal Allocation of Competences

There was a standstill as to the constitutional regulation of the educational system (*Schulverfassung*), which was not bridged by reception of the status quo, but by agreement to an unfortunate compromise: article 14 left open the allocation of competences in the fields of school, education, and adult education, and promised the adoption of a separate constitutional law to regulate the powers of the Federation and the *Länder*. The transitional provisions stipulated the existing laws in these fields could only be amended by way of corresponding laws of the Federation and the *Länder* (so-called '*paktierte Gesetzgebung*').[46]

Apart from that, the constitution generally provided for an allocation of legislative and enforcement responsibilities in articles 10 to 15. However, according to a transitory regulation, these provisions should only come into effect on the day when first, the constitutional law on the financial equalization between the territorial entities (*Verfassungsgesetz über die finanzielle Auseinandersetzung zwischen den Gebietskörperschaften*), second, the constitutional law envisaged in article 14 on the allocation of responsibilities in the fields of school, education, and adult education, and third, the constitutional law promised in article 120 on the organization of the general public administration in the *Länder* should come into force.

---

[44] The section on fundamental rights of the new constitution was at first left blank and finally deleted in the last meeting of the Constitutional Subcommittee: see Felix Ermacora, *Quellen zum österreichischen Verfassungsrecht (1920)* (n 17) 492.

[45] Section 34 ÜG 1920.

[46] Section 42 para 2 lit f ÜG 1920.

12 EWALD WIEDERIN

Until then, the distribution of responsibilities was maintained as stipulated in the Basic Law on the *Reichsvertretung* of 1867.[47]

B. The Evolution of the Constitution

1. Flexibility and Rigidity of the Constitution

a) The Provisions on Constitutional Amendments

The Federal Constitutional Law does not contain a separate provision on its revision: the provisions on constitutional amendments are integrated into the section on the federal legislative procedure (articles 41 to 49b Federal Constitutional Law). The amendment of the constitution is therefore regarded as a part of legislative procedure. Unless special provisions are in place, the general regulations apply. This means that the bodies which are entitled to submit legislative proposals to the National Council may also submit proposals on constitutional amendments. These bodies are the members of the National Council,[48] the Federal Council in whole or one-third of the members of the Federal Council, as well as the Federal government (article 41 para 1 Federal Constitutional Law). Moreover, 100,000 persons who are entitled to vote or one-sixth each of the voters of three *Länder* may present motions (article 41 para 2 Federal Constitutional Law).[49]

i) Quorum of the National Council

Constitutional law may be enacted by the National Council in the presence of at least half of its members. A motion for change must be carried by a two-thirds majority (article 44 para 1 Federal Constitutional Law). The higher quorums for presence and for consensus are meant to impede constitutional amendments and to protect the parliamentary minority, which is in opposition, against a simple majority. Moreover, a qualified minority can initiate a consultation with the people: if a third of the members of the National Council so demands, constitutional amendments must be submitted to a referendum in which the federal people vote (*Bundesvolk*) (article 44 para 3 Federal Constitutional Law).

ii) Designation of Constitutional Amendments As Such

Article 44 para 1 Federal Constitutional Law makes clear that constitutional amendments may be enacted both by way of constitutional laws and by constitutional provisions which are contained in 'ordinary' statutory federal laws (*einfache Bundesgesetze*). Constitutional law need not be concentrated within a single document, nor does it have to have a specific form. Instead, any statutory federal law may contain individual provisions—articles, sections, paragraphs, or even individual sentences[50]—which enjoy constitutional status.

In order to make constitutional law externally identifiable, article 44 para 1 Federal Constitutional Law asks for an explicit denomination as constitutional law

---

[47] See section 42 para 1 and para 2 lit a ÜG 1920.

[48] The Federal Law on the Rules of Procedure of the National Council (*Geschäftsordnungsgesetz*), BGBl. 1975/410 as amended by BGBl. I 2021/178, knows private member's motions (*Selbständige Anträge von Abgeordneten*; section 26 para 1), and committee motions (*Selbständige Anträge von Ausschüssen*; section 27 para 1).

[49] It is contested whether petitions for referenda aiming at constitutional amendments may also be tabled in the form of general suggestions (i.e. the prevailing opinion) or if a formal legislative proposal is mandatory so Heinz Mayer and Gerhard Muzak, *B-VG Bundesverfassungsrecht. Kommentar* (5th edn, Manz, Vienna, 2015) 224.

[50] See Hans Kelsen, Georg Froehlich and Adolf Merkl, *Die Bundesverfassung vom 1. Oktober 1920* (first published 1922, reprint Verlag Österreich, Vienna, 2003) 123.

('*Verfassungsgesetz*') or as a constitutional provision ('*Verfassungsbestimmung*').[51] This denomination is a constitutive element: if it is omitted, it will be statutory legislation, even if a provision may have been intended to be a constitutional provision and may have reached the quorums required for the enactment of constitutional law.

Constitutional provisions in statutory laws and the requirement of explicit denomination of constitutional law as 'constitutional law' are Austrian specifics: the external unity of the constitution is not achieved by singularity of the document, but by labelling. The chosen course might seem unusual today but was to be expected when we consider the historic context. Even the constitutional law of the monarchy had not been contained in a single document, but was spread over five Basic Laws.[52] In addition, it had been common practice to accept provisions deviating from the Basic Laws set out in ordinary laws of the *Reich*, provided that the quorums required for amendments of the Basic Laws had been met.[53] This resulted in changes in the constitution which were not detectable as such, unless one read through the protocols of the deliberations in the *Reichsrat*.[54] The introduction of an obligation of denomination (*Bezeichnungspflicht*) was intended to make this form of derogation from the constitution in the form of constitutional provisions visible.[55] It was presumably inspired by the hope to complicate political agreement on such provisions in future.

iii) *The Status of the Federal Council in the Constitutional Amendment Procedure*

Taking into account its status as a second chamber, the Federal Council has a comparatively weak position in the procedure for amendment of the constitution. In general, amendments of the constitution do not differ from other laws.[56] Enactments of the National Council must be transmitted to the Federal Council immediately according to article 42 para 1 Federal Constitutional Law; however, its consent is not required. According to article 42 para 2 Federal Constitutional Law, it can only raise a reason-based objection against the enactment of a law, and it must be conveyed to the President of the National Council by the chairman of the Federal Council in writing within eight weeks of the enactment being received by the Federal Council pursuant to article 42 para 3 Federal Constitutional Law. Such an objection requires a simple majority of the votes cast. It has merely suspensive effect: if the National Council in the presence of at least half its members confirms its original resolution

---

[51] These denominations are to be taken in a literal sense, but not literally. In practice, federal constitutional laws are usually denominated as '*Bundesverfassungsgesetz*' in order to distinguish them from constitutional law of the *Länder* in the title. Constitutional law contained in statutory federal laws is referred to as '*Verfassungsbestimmung*' (and not as '*Bundesverfassungsbestimmung*').

[52] See the references in nn 2–33.

[53] On this issue Gerald Stourzh, 'Qualifizierte Mehrheitsentscheidungen in der Entwicklung des österreichischen Verfassungsstaats 1848–1918', in Anna Gianna Manca and Luigi Lacchè (eds), *Parlament und Verfassung in den* konstitutionellen Verfassungssystemen Europas (Duncker & Humblot, Berlin, 2003) 29, 36 ff.

[54] On the comparable practice in the German Empire and in the Weimar Republic see Ulrich Hufeld, *Die Verfassungsdurchbrechung - Rechtsproblem der Deutschen Einheit und der europäischen Einigung. Ein Beitrag zur Dogmatik der Verfassungsänderung* (Duncker & Humblot, Berlin, 1997) 39 ff.

[55] Art 1 para 2 of the Law on the Introduction of the Constitution of the Czechoslovak Republic (*Gesetz betreffend die Einführung der Verfassungsurkunde der tschechoslowakischen Republik vom 29.2.1920*), stipulating an obligatory denomination for constitutional laws, seems to have been an immediate model. This assumption is supported by the fact that the introduction of an obligatory denomination was proposed at a very late stage of deliberations: see Felix Ermacora, *Quellen zum österreichischen Verfassungsrecht (1920)* (n 17) 483. The earlier drafts merely referred to an 'amendment of the federal constitution'.

[56] See Hans Kelsen, Georg Froehlich, and Adolf Merkl, *Bundesverfassung vom 1. Oktober 1920* (n 50) 124: 'The difference between ordinary and constitutional laws is irrelevant for the Federal Council's procedure.'

by a majority of at least two-thirds of the votes cast,[57] the way is paved for signature and publication of the constitutional amendment.

Apart from the objection, the Federal Council has another, more effective instrument at its disposal. Amendments to the constitution must be submitted to a national referendum if one-third of the members of the Federal Council so demands (article 44 para 3 Federal Constitutional Law). Such an appeal to the people may also be demanded simultaneously with an objection.

There are two situations only where the Federal Council has a true right of assent: first, if the provisions relating to its status in articles 34 and 35 Federal Constitutional Law are being amended (articles 35 para 4 Federal Constitutional Law), and second, if by constitutional law or a constitutional provision the competences of the *Länder* in the fields of legislation or enforcement are being restricted (article 44 para 2 Federal Constitutional Law). In the first case, a resolution is carried by a simple majority of the members, provided that a majority of the members from at least four *Länder* also approve the amendment. In the second case, the presence of at least half the members and a majority of two-thirds of the votes cast are required.

iv) *The Differentiation between Partial and Total Revision of the Constitution*

According to article 44 para 3 Federal Constitutional Law, any total revision of the constitution must be submitted to a national referendum upon conclusion of the parliamentary procedure, but before authentication of the revision by the Federal President. This is also the case for a partial revision if one-third of the members of the National Council or the Federal Council so demands.

At first, there were two competing approaches to interpret the notion of 'total revision' in this provision, which had already been included in the original version of the Federal Constitutional Law as article 44 para 2. According to the formal interpretation, a total revision was considered to mean replacing the Federal Constitutional Law of 1920 by a new constitutional document, whereas the content-related, material interpretation focused on the extent to which the basic features of the state were to be changed and demanded an obligatory referendum for radical and significant amendments of the fundamental principles of the constitution.[58] After the Second World War, the material approach prevailed.[59] The question as to which constitutional precepts are of an essential character making them 'fundamental principles' (*Grundprinzipien* or *Baugesetze*) and thus protecting them from significant amendments, has been controversial until today. The Constitutional Court, which has the final say on this question, holds that the principles of the democratic republic (article 1 Federal Constitutional Law) and of federalism (article 2 Federal Constitutional Law), which have been put at the head of the constitution, as well as the principle of the rule of law, which is unwritten yet a pervasive force throughout the entire constitution, represent the basic constitutional order which may not be significantly impaired without the consent of the sovereign.[60]

---

[57] The quorums for constitutional amendments laid down in art 44 para 1 Federal Constitutional Law are also applicable to such insistence resolutions (*Beharrungsbeschlüsse*).

[58] Hans Kelsen, Georg Froehlich and Adolf Merkl, *Bundesverfassung vom 1. Oktober 1920* (n 50) 124.

[59] The formal interpretation which was considered an alternative, though not prevailing, interpretation during the inter-war period is not even mentioned in current textbooks.

[60] Collection of Decisions and most important Resolutions of the Constitutional Court (*Sammlung der Erkenntnisse und wichtigsten Beschlüsse des Verfassungsgerichtshofes*, abbreviated hereafter as VfSlg.) 2455/1952.

Another controversy revolves around which body has to decide within the current procedure whether a constitutional amendment has to be submitted to a referendum because it constitutes a total revision. Pursuant to one approach, it is the exclusive competence of the National Council.[61] If the National Council erroneously considers an amendment to be a partial revision, the constitutional amendment will be unconstitutional, but this mistake can only be corrected by the Constitutional Court by repealing the constitutional amendment as unconstitutional. According to the prevailing counterview, the Federal President also has to assess the character of a constitutional amendment and order a referendum if necessary.[62] However, his order requires a recommendation by the Federal government pursuant to the general rules (article 67 para 1 Federal Constitutional Law).

In case of a total revision, article 44 para 3 Federal Constitutional Law requires a procedural step to be taken which would otherwise be merely optional. Although this step is only a procedural matter, an opportunity has been taken in legal doctrine relating to it to contrast 'ordinary' constitutional law with the basic constitutional order and assign to the latter a higher rank.[63] This differentiation was obviously influenced by the theory of hierarchy of norms.

b) Effects on Constitutional Practice and Interpretation

In global comparison, these rules for constitutional amendment make the Federal Constitutional Law a rather flexible constitution. As it knows no eternal content,[64] amendments may be made in any direction, provided that the procedural rules are complied with. The quorums of the National Council and the participation of the federal people are within the internationally accepted usual range. However, the possibilities of the Federal Council to intervene fall behind the competences of other second chambers.

The constitutional provisions are overlaid by conventions which give the *Länder* a strong influence. By way of politics, the National Council makes its resolutions on constitutional amendments subject to the consent of the *Konferenz der Landeshauptleute* (Conference of the state governors). If this body, which is a legally unregulated, purely informal coordination board, gives its consent, then the way is paved for the Federal Council to give its consent to a constitutional amendment in general. Therefore, until today, there has not been a case where the Federal Council has opposed a constitutional amendment by requesting a referendum or refusing to grant consent; the last cases of objection[65] date back over more than fifty years.

Only on one occasion has a national referendum been held pursuant to article 44 para 3 Federal Constitutional Law: the constitutional bases for the Accession of Austria to the European Union (BGBl. 1994/744) were unanimously considered to be a total revision in

---

[61] Heinz Mayer, 'Verfahrensfragen der direkten Demokratie', in Johannes Hengstschläger and others (eds), *Festschrift für Herbert Schambeck* (Duncker & Humblot, Berlin, 1994) 511, 520 ff; Theo Öhlinger and Harald Eberhard, *Verfassungsrecht* (12th edn, Facultas, Vienna, 2019) recital 444.

[62] Klaus Berchtold, *Der Bundespräsident* (Springer, Vienna, 1969) 185, 246; Kurt Ringhofer, *Die österreichische Bundesverfassung* (Verlag des österreichischen Gewerkschaftsbundes, Vienna, 1977) 153; Andreas Janko, *Gesamtänderung der Bundesverfassung* (Verlag Österreich, Vienna, 2004) 250 ff.

[63] See Robert Walter, 'Der Stufenbau nach der derogatorischen Kraft im österreichischen Recht' (1965) Österreichische Juristenzeitung 169, 170; Theo Öhlinger and Harald Eberhard, *Verfassungsrecht* (n 61) recital 10 ff, 62 ff.

[64] See Markus Vašek, *Unabänderliches Verfassungsrecht und Revisionsschranken in der österreichischen Bundesverfassung. Dargestellt am demokratischen, republikanischen und bundesstaatlichen Prinzip* (Verlag Österreich, Vienna, 2013), and Martin Hiesel, 'Gibt es in Österreich unabänderliches Verfassungsrecht?' (2002) Österreichische Juristenzeitung 121, 123 ff, both criticizing the opposing views.

[65] See Christian Neschwara, 'Zur Entwicklung des Verfassungsrechts nach 1918' (n 11) 179 ff.

substance. In another case, the Constitutional Court repealed a provision of the Federal Public Procurement Law as unconstitutional. This provision, which had been adopted without the necessary referendum, was considered a total revision because it amounted to a breach of fundamental standards of the rule of law.[66]

i) Technical Approach to Constitutional Law

Total revisions being a rare exception, partial amendments are countless. The Austrian constitution has been amended more often than any other constitution in the world.[67] And its core—the Federal Constitutional Law of 1920—is a document that is susceptible to amendment.[68] Formally, constitutional legislation is made harder to change compared to simple legislation; but, in substance, it is an everyday phenomenon. The constitution is neither sacrosanct nor is it immune to the interference of politics. Therefore, the constitution can hardly fulfil its function of laying down binding rules for politics and setting legal limits. This task is increasingly performed by the basic constitutional order.[69]

The reasons for this are primarily of a political nature. Over long periods of time, specifically from 1945 to 1966, 1987 to 1994, 1995 to 2000, and 2007 to 2008, a coalition government consisting of the two major parties ÖVP (Austrian People's Party) and SPÖ (Social Democrat Party of Austria) held a two-thirds majority in parliament and could change the constitution 'when necessary'. This was frequently the case for trivial, short-term political reasons. The possibility to establish compromises within the form of constitutional law was used to protect them in many respects: against review of its content by the Constitutional Court, against cessation of the coalition before or after upcoming elections, against the loss of influence of one's own political camp in the future, even after a move to the opposition.

ii) Fragmentation of Constitutional Law

As a result, the constitution has been amended on many occasions. The explanation for this high frequency of amendments lies in the constitution itself because it provides for the possibility to integrate constitutional provisions into federal statutory law. This possibility has encouraged the thoughtless handling of the constitution. It is not easy to keep track of the Austrian constitution in its entirety. Its core is a document which has been amended more than a hundred times. Next to it, there are about a hundred Federal Constitutional Laws (*Bundesverfassungsgesetze*), containing ancillary constitutions for specific areas, then about five hundred constitutional provisions in federal statutory laws, more than a dozen treaties enjoying constitutional rank, and finally, around twenty constitutional provisions in treaties.[70] The current publications of constitutional law have good reasons to refrain from printing the whole *corpus constitutionalis* and settle for a more or less extensive selection of constitutional provisions.[71]

---

[66] VfSlg. 16.327/2001.

[67] The number of constitutional amendments has not been surveyed yet; it is in the thousands.

[68] Until 15 February 2019 there were 133 amendments (including republications and corrigendua for typographical errors).

[69] Theo Öhlinger, 'Braucht Österreich eine Verfassung?' (2000) juridikum 4, 5 ff.

[70] A complete yet by now outdated compilation can be found in the report of the second committee of the Austrian Convention (*Österreich-Konvent*) of 9 July 2004, available at www.konvent.gv.at (last accessed 31 March 2022).

[71] The only exception was the text volume edited by Andrea Martin of the commentary by Karl Korinek, Michael Holoubek, and others (eds), *Österreichisches Bundesverfassungsrecht. Kommentar* (loose-leaf edn, Verlag Österreich, Vienna, 1999 and ff). It has not been continued since the eleventh edition 2013.

Because of this fragmentation, it has become common practice to compare the Austrian constitution to a ruin.[72] The lack of external unity corresponds to a lack of internal closedness of the constitution. The sheer mass of constitutional law is comparable to excessive regulation which does not stop at minor details. As a result, a simple majority in parliament often does not have the necessary freedom to reform politically controversial areas.

There have been many attempts to avoid the trap of constitutional interlocking. After preliminary studies of the scientific community,[73] the Austrian Convention (*Österreich-Konvent*) had finalized a clearing up strategy in 2004,[74] which was implemented in 2008. More than a thousand constitutional provisions were repealed, declared to have ceased to be in force or deprived of their constitutional rank in the First Federal Constitutional Law on the Clearing up of the Federal Constitution (*Erstes Bundesverfassungsbereinigungsgesetz*).[75] At the same time, and even more importantly, an amendment to the constitution removed the causes of non-functional constitutional law by empowering statutory legislation to alter borders, delegate public powers, and render administrative bodies independent from instructions. Since then, the fragmentation of constitutional law has not been eliminated, but it has been considerably reduced.

iii) Rejection of Constitutional Customary Law
There is unanimous agreement that this dense network of constitutional law leaves no room for constitutional customary law.[76] Austrian constitutional law is entirely codified. It should not be overlooked, however, that with the basic constitutional order, derived from the meaningless word 'total revision', a normative layer has been established that comes close to customary law in its mode of operation.

2. The Development of the Constitution in the First Republic

a) 1925: Constitutional Reform for Simplification of the Administration
In order to restore the ailing public finances and to keep its commitments given to the League of Nations, the government set about merging the apparatus of the federal administration in the *Länder* with that of the autonomous *Land* administration. This administrative reform was linked to a constitutional reform.[77] At the same time, the Constitutional Court's decision VfSlg. 328/1924, that repealed a federal social security law for a violation of the regulations

---

[72] This image originates from Hans R Klecatsky. As an example from his wide range of publications see Hans R Klecatsky, 'Bundes-Verfassungsgesetz und Bundesverfassungsrecht', in Herbert Schambeck (ed), *Das österreichische Bundes-Verfassungsgesetz und seine Entwicklung* (Duncker & Humblot, Berlin, 1980) 83 ff, 94 ff.

[73] Highlights include the studies of Robert Walter, *Überlegungen zu einer Neukodifikation des österreichischen Bundesverfassungsrechts*, vol 2 (Verlag Österreich, Vienna, 1994); and Richard Novak and Bernd Wieser, *Zur Neukodifikation des österreichischen Bundesverfassungsrechts* (Verlag Österreich, Vienna, 1994).

[74] Bericht des Österreich-Konvents. Teil 3: Beratungsergebnisse, vol 1, 2005 33 ff.

[75] BGBl. I 2008/2.

[76] Ludwig K Adamovich, Bernd-Christian Funk, Gerhart Holzinger, and others, *Österreichisches Staatsrecht*, vol 1 (2nd edn, Verlag Österreich, Vienna, 2011) recital 04.017; Andreas Hauer, *Staats- und Verwaltungshandeln. Studienbuch* (5th edn, Pedell, Linz, 2017) 282; Heinz Mayer, Gabriele Kucsko-Stadlmayer, and Karl Stöger, *Grundriss des österreichischen Bundesverfassungsrechts* (11th edn, Manz, Vienna, 2015) recital 105; Bernhard Raschauer, *Allgemeines Verwaltungsrecht. Lehrbuch* (5th edn, Verlag Österreich, Vienna, 2017) recital 465.

[77] For a detailed illustration of motives, process and content of the reform see Klaus Berchtold, *Verfassungsgeschichte der Republik Österreich* (n 11) 369 ff. The documents and *travaux préparatoires* are printed in ibid, *Die Verfassungsreform von 1925* (Braumüller, Vienna, 1992) 79 ff.

on the allocation of competences reminded the political sphere that it must overcome the political impasse from the year 1920: the distribution of responsibilities from the year 1867, which had been provisionally left in force, was no longer up to date. The constitutional reform of 1925 was devoted to these purposes. The amendment to the Federal Constitutional Law BGBl. 1925/268 brought into force the allocation of competences that was provided for in the Federal Constitutional Law of 1920 by untying it from the question of competences in the field of education. It transferred several competences to the Federation[78] and adapted the regulations on indirect federal administration (*mittelbare Bundesverwaltung*), on control by the Court of Audit (*Rechnungskontrolle*) and on the public law judiciary (*Gerichtsbarkeit des öffentlichen Rechts*). Accompanying legislation eliminated the duplicity of administrative bodies by transforming the district commissions (*Bezirkshauptmannschaften*) into administrative authorities of the *Länder* (BGBl. 1925/269) and by establishing offices of the *Länder* governments (*Ämter der Landesregierungen*) as central departments of *Länder* administration in all *Länder* save Vienna (BGBl. 1925/289). The procedural reform, which was carried out simultaneously, endowed Austria with the internationally pioneering Administrative Procedure Acts (*Verwaltungsverfahrensgesetze*),[79] which have remained in force until today.

b) 1929: Reconstruction of the Constitution to Prevent the Civil War

Following the elections in the year 1927 and the burning of the Palace of Justice on 15 July 1927, the internal political climate came more prominently into public focus.[80] The Social Democrats called a (largely unsuccessful) public transport strike, established a municipal protection guard (*Gemeindeschutzwache*) in Vienna, and rearmed the *republikanischer Schutzbund* (Republican Protection League). The government militarized the *Heimwehr* (Home Guard) and sought various means to weaken the Social Democrats, which were already weak outside the National Council, as well as inside parliament. Moreover, the Constitutional Court was a thorn in its side because it had decided against the government in politically sensitive matters.[81] Reform proposals of the *Landbund* (Rural League) and the *Heimwehr* set the ball rolling in early autumn 1929. The new government under Schober took advantage of the opportunity and submitted a legislative proposal to the National Council.[82] The Social Democrats were ready for talks. In the parliamentary negotiations, they succeeded in defusing the corporative and autocratic parts of the draft and finally gave their consent.

The amendment of the Federal Constitutional Law BGBl. 1929/392 pursued four main objectives. The first priority was the weakening of parliament by the strengthening of the executive: following the Weimar model,[83] it provided for the election of the Federal President

---

[78] This concerned among others the areas of security (aliens, police, and registration of residence, legislation on weapons), environment (forestry, water legislation), traffic (automotive technology), and culture (federal theatres).

[79] BGBl. 1925/273–276. See from contemporary literature Egbert Mannlicher and Emmerich Coreth, *Die Gesetze zur Vereinfachung der Verwaltung* (Verlag der Österreichischen Staatsdruckerei, Vienna, 1926).

[80] See Klaus Berchtold, *Verfassungsgeschichte der Republik Österreich* (n 11) 442 ff, 463 ff.

[81] See on second marriage following dispense from the *Landeshauptmann* (*Dispensehe*) VfSlg. 878/1927, 951/1928, 1001/1928 and 1059/1928; on cinemas VfSlg. 720/1926; on road police VfSlg. 1030/1928; on the Vienna Law on Expulsion VfSlg. 1119/1928.

[82] The documents and *traveaux préparatoires* on the reform are printed in Klaus Berchtold, *Die Verfassungsreform von 1929*, vol 2 (Braumüller, Vienna, 1979). For a reference to the process see also Christian Neschwara, 'Zur Entwicklung des Verfassungsrechts nach 1918' (n 11) 143 ff.

[83] See arts 25, 41, 47, 53, WRV.

by universal suffrage. It authorized him to dissolve the parliament and issue emergency decrees (*Notverordnungen*), and it conferred on him the supreme command of the military and the competence to form the Federal government. The vote of no confidence was reasonably modified as compared with Weimar, while the right to issue emergency decrees was restrained by concessions to parliament. The further strengthening of the Federation in the area of internal security was another concern. The Federation was endowed with pertinent competences; it enforced the dissolution of the paramilitary protection associations of the *Länder* and was granted the right of participation in the exercise of the remaining competences of the *Länder* in security issues. These amendments particularly affected the *Land* Vienna, which was traditionally socialist and which, in addition, had to tolerate amendments to its internal organization. Under the heading of 'de-politicization', the amendment further reorganized the Constitutional Court and secured a decisive influence on its composition to the executive (the incumbent judges—among them Hans Kelsen—were removed from office as of 15 February 1930). The last objective, the realization of 'true democracy' by implementation of the corporate concept remained conceptual: the transformation of the Federal Council into a 'state and corporate Council' (*Länder- und Ständerat*) had been resolved but was never brought into effect.

c) 1933/34: Collapse during the Crisis

In the years 1932/33, the government majority in the National Council dwindled, meaning that every vote counted. The position of chair thus became a burden because the chairman had no right to vote. On 4 March 1933, a dispute over the rules of internal procedure after a mishap in voting resulted in Renner resigning from his office as President of the National Council. Ramek and Straffner as second and third Presidents followed his lead. The government took the view that the National Council had eliminated itself. It fought attempts to reconvene the National Council and made use of the Wartime Economy Authority Law of 1917 (*Kriegswirtschaftliches Ermächtigungsgesetz*) to issue ordinances which were challenged before the Constitutional Court by the *Land* Vienna. In order to prevent these ordinances from being repealed, it first persuaded affiliated members of the Constitutional Court to resign (with the assurance that they be reappointed); consequently, it issued an ordinance which entitled the members recommended by parliament to attend sittings of the court only when all of these members were in office (BGBl. 1933/191). Following the resignation of government-affiliated members, this was not the case anymore. The Constitutional Court started a review procedure relating to this ordinance but held that it did not have the necessary quorum to take a decision. It addressed the Federal President with the request that the vacancies be filled as soon as possible. However, the government refrained from submitting recommendations. After the National Council, the Constitutional Court was eliminated as well. The government prepared a corporate authoritarian constitution in spring 1934 and published it in BGBl. 1934/239 as Constitution of the Austrian Federation (*Verfassung des Bundesstaates Österreich*).[84] Thus, the democratic republic of Austria, which was not yet fourteen years old, was history for the time being.

---

[84] To keep up the appearance of constitutional continuity the parliament was convened on 30 April 1934 after the opposition members had been removed from the National Council. On this day it adopted a Federal Constitutional Law on Extraordinary Measures in the Field of the Constitution ('*Bundesverfassungsgesetz über außerordentliche Maßnahmen im Bereich der Verfassung*') on the basis of which the Federal government resolved the constitution of 1934 a second time. Four years later another Federal government ordered the *Anschluss* of Austria to the German *Reich* on the basis of this very Federal Constitutional Law.

3. The Development of the Constitution in the Second Republic

a) Restoration of the Constitutional Order of 1920/29

The declaration of independence (*Unabhängigkeitserklärung*) 1945, StGBl. 1, proclaimed by the political parties restored the democratic republic of Austria and promised to 'establish it in the spirit of the constitution of 1920'. Accordingly, article 1 of the Constitution Transition Law (*Verfassungs-Überleitungsgesetz*), StGBl. 1945/4, which was resolved by the provisional state government chaired by Karl Renner, reinstated the 1929 version of the Federal Constitutional Law and all the other formal federal constitutional law according to the status of legislation as it stood on 5 March 1933. At the same time, article 4 stipulated that these provisions must be replaced by the provisions of the Provisional Constitution (*Vorläufige Verfassung*), StGBl. 1945/5 (establishing a unitary state incorporating all powers) until the date of expiration of a six-month period from the first assembly of the National Council. The newly elected National Council convened on 19 December 1945 and passed a Transition Law (*Übergangsgesetz*) to shorten the duration of this period. It was, however, not published due to the absence of approval from the Allied Council. Despite Allied opposition, the approach established by Werner, according to which the Federal Constitutional Law re-entered into force on 19 December 1945, prevailed in state practice.[85] The following amendments were limited to integrating the measures adopted in 1945 into the Federal Constitutional Law or rehabilitating them by amending the constitutional standards.[86] The fact that constitutional amendments required the written approval from the Allied Council according to article 6 of the Second Control Agreement (*2. Kontrollabkommen*) of 28 June 1946[87] is one reason for this reticent attitude.

b) Termination of Allied Control and Neutrality

The signing of the State Treaty of Vienna in 1955 ended the era of Allied control. After regaining sovereignty, Austria declared 'permanent neutrality of its own accord' (*immerwährende Neutralität*, BGBl. 1955/211), thereby meeting a commitment given to the Soviet Union in the Moscow Memorandum (*Moskauer Memorandum*) of 15 April 1955.[88] The grand coalition government of the ÖVP and the SPÖ, which had been in existence since 1945 and which enjoyed wide parliamentary support, transferred its decision-making power to a coalition committee, including the interest groups of the economy and of the workforce into the decision-making process and degraded parliament to a voting machine. Moreover, these parties allocated the leading positions in the administration, in state-affiliated companies and partly also in the judiciary among themselves. These proportional agreements (*Proporzabkommen*) were often also adhered to during the periods of one-party

---

[85] See Leopold Werner, 'Vorläufige Verfassung—oder Bundesverfassung?' (1946) Österreichische Juristenzeitung 277 ff. On this issue with further references Johannes Schnizer, 'Österreichische Verfassungsmythen und Erkenntnis des Rechts' (2004) Journal für Rechtspolitik 16, 20 ff; Klaus Berchtold, 'Verfassungsentwicklung seit 1945', in Österreichische Parlamentarische Gesellschaft (ed), *Festschrift 75 Jahre Bundesverfassung* (Verlag Österreich, Vienna, 1995) 139, 143 ff; Christian Neschwara, 'Zur Entwicklung des Verfassungsrechts nach 1918' (n 11) 176.

[86] See Christian Neschwara, 'Zur Entwicklung des Verfassungsrechts nach 1918' (n 11) 179 ff; Klaus Berchtold, 'Verfassungsentwicklung seit 1945' (n 85) 146 ff.

[87] Printed in Ludwig Adamovich, *Die Bundesverfassungsgesetze* (8th edn, Verlag der Österreichischen Staatsdruckerei, Vienna, 1953) 6–15.

[88] On the genesis of the State Treaty of Vienna see the standard reference by Gerald Stourzh, *Um Einheit und Freiheit* (4th edn, Böhlau, Vienna, 1998), in the documentary annex of which the Moscow Memorandum is printed 66–70.

governments between 1966 and 1987 or 'small coalitions' until the year 2000. This consensus culture was able to bridge the rifts which had been torn open between the two political camps in the interwar years and had saved Austria from constitutional crises. The only 'crisis' of the post-war period is not worthy of its name: the Habsburg case attracted the attention of the scientific community as there were attempts to correct the jurisdiction of the Administrative Court (*Verwaltungsgerichtshof, VwGH*)[89] by constitutional legislation.[90]

The coalition government made use of its broad majority to adopt constitutional amendments, most of which were made outside the Federal Constitutional Law and thus overlapped and replaced the provisions of the original document in its normative nature. Legal doctrine read the regained sovereignty into the provisions of the Federal Constitutional Law on the state territory, thereby raising constitutional objections against the transfer of sovereign rights inside international agreements. State practice reacted to this concern by regarding the disputed provisions as constitutional amendments and passing corresponding resolutions. In this way, the mass of constitutional law lacking steering-effect further increased. Both trends still continue to this day. However, substantial amendments may also be identified which have developed the torso 'Federal Constitutional Law' toward a full constitution and re-determined its relation to the community of states under international law, to the *Länder* and to the European Union.

c) Closing Gaps inside the Federal Constitutional Law

In 1962, two gaps which were poorly resolved by provisional regulations were closed. With the amendment BGBl. 1962/205 on the 'Basic Principles of Municipal Law', the concept of an abstract unitary municipality (*abstrakte Einheitsgemeinde*) was introduced into the Federal Constitutional Law. Vested with a high degree of autonomy and their own sphere of competences (*eigener Wirkungsbereich*), the municipalities enjoyed protection against the interference of the *Länder* whose competence to impose legislation on municipalities was rendered de facto meaningless. In the amendment BGBl. 1962/215, a regulation on the 'competences in the matters of schools, education and adult education' was achieved, while the requirement of corresponding laws of the Federation and the *Länder* was eliminated. The downside was the introduction of a qualified majority requirement for future amendments and the establishment of special administrative bodies for schools which were staffed proportionally according to political majorities (article 81a Federal Constitutional Law). In the amendment BGBl. 1975/316, a regulation on the agricultural and forestry school system, which had first been left out, was added. The constitutional regulation of the party system and of public service broadcasting was equally accomplished, albeit outside the Federal Constitutional Law. The work on the catalogue of fundamental rights, which was still missing, had begun with much enthusiasm, dragged on over many years and was finally discontinued after the adoption of the Federal Constitutional Law on the Protection of Personal Liberty (*Bundesverfassungsgesetz über den Schutz der persönlichen Freiheit*) in 1988.

d) Rehabilitation of Treaties

It had become settled practice to adopt constitutional provisions in treaties by a qualified majority, but to refrain from denominating them as such. In its decision VfSlg. 4049/1961

---

[89] Collection of Decisions and Resolutions of the Supreme Administrative Court (*Sammlung der Erkenntnisse und Beschlüsse des Verwaltungsgerichtshofes*, hereafter abbreviated as VwSlg.) 6035 A/1963.

[90] See Gustav E Kafka, 'Der Fall Dr. Otto Habsburg' (1963) 88 AöR 451, 452 ff with further references, and BGBl. 1963/172.

relating to the ECHR, the Constitutional Court withdrew the legal basis of this practice, thereby providing the basis for a readjustment of the status of treaties in the domestic law. The amendment BGBl. 1964/59 implemented a flexible model: the National Council may in its decision on ratification both determine the rank of the treaty in the hierarchy of norms and decide whether to implement the treaty exceptionally by a special transformation instead of its adoption. Provisions enjoying the status of constitutional law must be denominated as constitutional amendments (*verfassungsändernd*) in the resolution on ratification. At the same time, treaties which had been regarded as constitutional amendments in state practice earlier were given constitutional status retroactively. However, the possibility to give constitutional status to treaty provisions was made use of so often that it was abolished in 2008 without any replacement.

e) Strengthening the *Länder*

The development of the constitution had eclipsed the *Länder*. Their range of competences had been small from the beginning, and they were repeatedly curtailed. According to VfSlg. 3134/1956, their constitutions were regarded as implementing laws of the Federal Constitutional Law and their parliaments had sunken into lethargy. The 1960s brought about a change:[91] the *Länder* started to demand more competences. Federalism resurged and found expression in the scientific work of Koja and Pernthaler, who called for a reorientation of the understanding of federalism.[92] In 1974 the *Länder* scored a first success: the amendment on federalism ('*Föderalismusnovelle*') BGBl. 1974/444 in part met the demands by transferring competences to the *Länder*, strengthening their position in indirect federal administration and incorporating the signing of agreements between the Federation and the *Länder* (*Gliedstaatsvertrag*) as an instrument of federal cooperation in the constitution. Ten years later, the requirement of the Federal Council's assent for the transfer of competences to the Federation was introduced (BGBl. 1984/490), thereby granting the *Länder* a share in the competence for decision-making on competences ('*Kompetenz-Kompetenz*') which had been reserved for the National Council until then. In 1988, they were granted the long-desired status as subjects of international law (*Völkerrechtssubjekt*; BGBl. 1988/685), albeit only to a limited extent. Finally, the capacity of the Federal government to veto *Länder* laws for compromising federal interests (*Gefährdung von Bundesinteressen*) was abolished in 2012 (BGBl. I 2012/51).

f) Extension and Modification of Legal Remedies

The showpiece section of the Federal Constitutional Law, the parts relating to Constitutional Jurisdiction, had equally lost its splendour over the years. The amendment to the Federal Constitutional Law BGBl. 1975/302 introduced an individual application (*Individualantrag*) for challenging statutory laws, ordinances, and treaties as a subsidiary means of remedy and dispelled a longstanding divergence in the jurisdiction of the Constitutional Court and the Administrative Court by adding to the list of objects of complaint the 'exercise of direct administrative command or compulsion' (*unmittelbare verwaltungsbehördliche Befehls- und Zwangsgewalt*).

---

[91] On this Richard Novak, 'Bundes-Verfassungsgesetz und Landesverfassungsrecht', in Schambeck, *Bundes-Verfassungsgesetz* (n 72) 111, 124 f; and Klaus Berchtold, 'Verfassungsentwicklung seit 1945' (n 85) 152 ff.

[92] See above all Friedrich Koja, *Das Verfassungsrecht der österreichischen Bundesländer* (1st edn, Springer, Vienna, 1967) 17 ff ('relative constitutional autonomy', *relative Verfassungsautonomie*), and Peter Pernthaler, 'Der österreichische Bundesstaat im Spannungsfeld von Föderalismus und formalem Rechtspositivismus' (1969) 19 Zeitschrift für öffentliches Recht 361–379.

In order to complement the classical forms of legal protection, the Ombudsman Board (*Volksanwaltschaft*) was established first as a temporary body and was then integrated into the Federal Constitutional Law in 1981 (BGBl. 1981/350). In 1999, a Human Rights Advisory Council (*Menschenrechtsbeirat*) was established with the Federal Ministry of the Interior, whose task was to counsel the department in human rights issues and accompany and monitor the exercise of coercive measures by police forces. In 2012, the Human Rights Advisory Council was integrated into the Ombudsman Board and was given a mandate to control the entire federal administration.

The jurisprudence of the ECtHR relating to article 6 ECHR led to a half-hearted reform of the system of legal protection in 1988. Instead of true administrative courts, independent administrative tribunals were established in the *Länder* (*unabhängige Verwaltungssenate in den Ländern*). These tribunals were administrative bodies but operated with reference to quasi-judicial guarantees to meet with the requirements for tribunals set up by the ECHR. In 1997, they were supplemented by the Federal Asylum Senate (*Bundesasylsenat*), which was an equally designed independent federal body responsible for review of complaints in asylum matters, and which was transformed into the Asylum Court (*Asylgerichtshof*) in 2008.

In 2012, the completion of the reform was achieved. The amendment introducing the administrative judiciary (*Verwaltungsgerichtsbarkeits-Novelle*) BGBl. I 2012/51 established true administrative courts of first instance below the level of the Administrative Court which has existed since 1876: one administrative court in each of the nine *Länder* for control of the administration of the *Länder* and of indirect federal administration (*mittelbare Bundesverwaltung*), one Federal Administrative Court (*Bundesverwaltungsgericht*) for control of direct federal administration (*umittelbare Bundesverwaltung*), and one Federal Finance Court (*Bundesfinanzgericht*) for taxation and financial criminal law. On this occasion, about a hundred special administrative bodies which were formerly responsible for review of the administration alongside the Administrative Court were dissolved.

The Constitutional Court was also endowed with further competences. As of 2013, the parties to proceedings before the ordinary courts may submit an application for review of a legal norm if they have doubts on the lawfulness of a legal provision applied by a court of first instance in its decision. Since 2014, the Constitutional Court has acted as an arbitration body for certain parliamentary disputes and as an authority for review of complaints against the conduct of investigating committees.

g) Accession to the European Union

The Accession to the European Union was the deepest cut in the constitutional structure. A special Federal Constitutional Law on the Accession of Austria to the European Union (*Ermächtigungs-BVG*; BGBl. 1994/744), which was subject to a referendum because it amounted to a total revision, paved the way for signing the accession treaty. An amendment to the Federal Constitutional Law provided for the necessary complementing and adjusting regulations (BGBl. 1994/1013).

4. Contributions of Jurisprudence and Doctrine

a) First Phase: Dominance of Practice

The development of the constitution was accompanied and also promoted by jurisprudence and legal doctrine. In the interwar period, the Constitutional Court assumed a clearly dominant role. It took the new constitution seriously and filled it with life in its decisions. Even if its decisions had far-reaching implications, it kept a verbal distance from politics, especially focusing on 'formal' questions and leaving the 'content' to the democratic process.[93] The more a constitutional guarantee was formal, the better its development opportunities. The (highly political) jurisprudence pertaining to the legality principle and the fine-spun case law on the federal allocation of competences are particularly remarkable. The commentaries from this era kept records of its decisions without condensing or systemizing them.[94] Only the standard commentary by Kelsen, Froehlich, and Merkl[95] stood the test of time and is still being consulted to this day. The textbooks were basically limited to communicating the basic structures of the constitution close to its text and depicting the origin of its institutions;[96] among them, the *Grundriss* by *Adamovich*,[97] which aims to establish the underlying system, stands out. After the Second World War, the picture barely changed: not only did the Constitutional Court show the way, it also provided the theoretical framework itself. Well-known theories like the *Versteinerungstheorie* ('petrification theory'), the *Überschattungstheorie* ('overshadow theory'), or the *Herzog-Mantel-Theorie* ('duke-coat-theory') were generated inside the Constitutional Court. One reason for the simultaneous reticence shown by legal doctrine was the role perception of contemporary scholars, which limited themselves to reconstructing the framework set up by the case-law. Another reason was the double role of the prominent protagonists (i.e. Kelsen, Adamovich, Werner, Antoniolli).

b) Second Phase: Self-Assurance of Doctrine

In the 1960s, doctrine caught up with practice. Disciples of Walter Antoniolli and Adolf Merkl intensified their critical analysis of jurisprudence and confronted the Constitutional Court with integrated alternative concepts. Among the then-emerging manuals, the work by Walter on organizational structures[98] and the manual on human rights by Ermacora[99] should be highlighted. They addressed postulates to the Constitutional Court, such as the call for an efficient implementation of the review of the respect of fundamental rights in relation to fundamental rights containing a formal legal reservation (*formeller Gesetzesvorbehalt*).

c) Third Phase: Principles

In the mid-eighties, the Constitutional Court responded to this call and again took the lead. After the realignment of jurisprudence on human rights by applying a test of proportionality (*Verhältnismäßigkeit*) of interferences, the Constitutional Court brought out the principle of the rule of law and developed a jurisprudence on the system of state organization which was aligned with the principle of democracy. All these major guidelines are based on a more substantive understanding of the notion of constitution on the one hand, and a

---

[93] See e.g. VfSlg. 1396/1931, where the Constitutional Court refuses 'to review a law adopted in accordance with the constitutional procedure for its content and its appropriateness', 295.

[94] See Ludwig Adamovich and Georg Froehlich, *Die österreichischen Verfassungsgesetze* (1st edn, Verlag der Österreichischen Staatsdruckerei, Vienna, 1925, 2nd edn, 1930).

[95] Hans Kelsen, Georg Froehlich and Adolf Merkl, *Die Bundesverfassung vom 1. Oktober 1920* (n 50).

[96] See Hans Kelsen, *Österreichisches Staatsrecht—Ein Grundriss, entwicklungsgeschichtlich dargestellt* (n 13), Hans Frisch, *Lehrbuch des österreichischen Verfassungsrechtes* (Springer, Vienna, 1932).

[97] Ludwig Adamovich, *Grundriß des österreichischen Staatsrechtes* (2nd edn, Verlag der Österreichischen Staatsdruckerei, Vienna, 1932).

[98] Robert Walter, *Österreichisches Bundesverfassungsrecht. System* (Manz, Vienna, 1972).

[99] Felix Ermacora, *Handbuch der Grundfreiheiten und der Menschenrechte* (Manz, Vienna, 1963).

strong focus on principles on the other.[100] Every now and then, the constitutional legislator corrected unwanted decisions by adopting amendments to the constitution.[101] In return, the Constitutional Court sounded a note of warning: if adopted repeatedly, such measures of merely partial effect may constitute a total revision of the federal constitution.[102]

C. Basic Structures and Concepts

1. Constitution, Simple Law, and Politics

a) The Constitution as a Framework

The common system of reference for the relation between constitutional law and 'ordinary' or 'primary' law (*einfaches Gesetz*), is the doctrine of hierarchy of norms (*Stufenbau der Rechtsordnung*). The constitution is the source from which the whole legal system must derive because it authorizes the enacting of law.

The constitution has the highest rank because it determines the content of ordinary law (*Stufenbau nach der rechtlichen Bedingtheit*) and because it prevails in case of a conflict of norms (*Stufenbau nach der derogatorischen Kraft*). In order to avoid such conflicts, ordinary law must be interpreted in conformity with the constitution in case of doubt. Still the constitution remains only the rule of the game; its function is basically limited to the distribution of spheres of authority, influence, and freedom, while the definition of the content is left to the policy-maker. Accordingly, the constitution is conceived as a framework, which aims at leaving room for discretion to the democratic process and which deliberately evades providing a final answer to every single question.

b) Limitations on the Constitutionalisation of the Legal System

The said understanding of 'constitution' is adequate for the Federal Constitutional Law because it concentrates on regulating institutions, competencies, and procedures, while it omits state purposes or national objectives. Although Austria is a highly developed social state, the term 'social state' is not mentioned in the constitution. Recent constitutional developments have accumulated a handful of national objectives;[103] on the whole, however, these national objectives neither establish a coherent system nor do they show a representative view of governmental functions. In summary, there is no sufficient spectrum of constitutional values from which to deduct a correct solution by way of weighing of interests. In consequence, fundamental rights (similarly lacking structural unity) are conceived rather as guarantees of freedoms in their capacity as laws limiting state power ('*negative Kompetenznormen*'), as opposed to values designed to be granted extensive implementation and optimization which

---

[100] For a critique, see Richard Novak, 'Demokratisches Prinzip und Verfassungswandel', in Hedwig Kopetz and others (eds), *Festschrift für Wolfgang Mantl*, vol 1 (Böhlau, Vienna, 2004) 117, 128 ff: '*Der Wandel vom 'Formalen' zum 'Materiellen', um die Schlagworte zu wiederholen, ist unverkennbar. Das Verfassungsverständnis ist in Gefahr, von einem Extrem ins andere zu fallen.*' (To repeat the key terms, the transition from 'formal' to 'substantial' is obvious. The concept of constitutionality runs the risk of going from one extreme to the other.)

[101] See only BGBl. 1986/106 (in reaction to VfSlg. 9950/1984—ban on self-incrimination); BGBl. 1987/125 (VfSlg. 10.932/1986—economic needs test for taxi ranks); BGBl. 1991/627 (VfSlg. 12.568/1990—retirement age); BGBl. I 2002/45 (VfSlg. 16.400/2001—securities supervision).

[102] VfSlg. 11.829/1988. See Heinz Mayer and Gerhard Muzak, *B-VG Bundesverfassungsrecht. Kommentar* (n 49) 231 ff with further references.

[103] For references see Theo Öhlinger and Harald Eberhard, *Verfassungsrecht* (n 61) recital 91 ff.

would therefore have to be respected by the policy-maker even beyond their mere content as a ban or an imperative.

Apart from these content-related reasons setting limitations on the constitutionalization of the legal system, procedural obstacles also persisted at first. Whereas a judicial review of decisions of civil and criminal courts (*ordentliche Gerichtsbarkeit*) is provided for, a complaint before the Constitutional Court—which may be filed against a decision of an administrative court—is excluded. This made it easier for justices to cultivate criminal and civil law as autonomous parts of the legal system, thereby making them detached from constitutional influences. The accession to the ECHR and the introduction of an individual complaint has triggered a change. Recently, the Supreme Court has consistently referred to fundamental rights in its jurisprudence.[104]

c) The Constitutional Court's Perception of its Role

Consistently, the Constitutional Court itself defines its role until today with great reservation. Its aim is neither to bind the legislator to the solution it deems best in the sense of the constitution, nor to anticipate the policy-maker's decision.[105] Its self-conception is best characterized by the following guiding principle: the respect of the constitution is paramount to the extent as it speaks and just as much as when it remains silent. However, today there is no longer any judicial self-restraint in its jurisprudence anymore: after having adopted a positivist approach in the beginning, the Constitutional Court has long renounced this approach. It plays its role in a manner which secures its place among the activist constitutional courts.

2. Democracy

'Austria is a democratic republic' (*Österreich ist eine demokratische Republik.*) This commitment to democracy and republic is at the top of the constitution. In the first place, it renounces monarchy. This rejection is reinforced by the reception of the '*Habsburgergesetz*'[106] as a constitutional law and by the exclusion of members of (former) reigning families from holding the office of Federal President (article 60 para 3 Federal Constitutional Law). However, it is also programmatic. Although the term is only used as an adjective and its use is limited to only a small number,[107] democracy is the common thread which runs through the Federal Constitutional Law.[108]

The constitution has opted for a tolerant democracy, which can be explained by looking at the context of its creation: it does not know irrevocable content and even allows for the abolition of democracy by way of a total revision ('*Gesamtänderung*').[109] However,

---

[104] See Lamiss Khakzadeh-Leiler, *Die Grundrechte in der Judikatur des Obersten Gerichtshofs* (Verlag Österreich, Vienna, 2011).

[105] VfSlg. 13.038/1992, 13.661/1993.

[106] Law on the Banishment and Expropriation of the House Habsburg-Lothringen (*Gesetz betreffend die Landesverweisung und die Übernahme des Vermögens des Hauses Habsburg-Lothringen*), StGBl. 1919/209. Today, no one is subject to banishment, following declarations of renunciation of the right to succeed to the throne.

[107] In addition to art 1 see also art 9a para 1 and 79 para 2 no 2 lit a Federal Constitutional Law, which were not included in the original version of the Federal Constitutional Law and which assign the protection of the democratic freedoms of the inhabitants to national defence authorities.

[108] Adolf Merkl, 'Die Baugesetze der österreichischen Bundesverfassung', in Hans Klecatsky (ed), *Die Republik Österreich* (Herder, Vienna, 1968) 77, 81.

[109] Heinz Peter Rill and Heinz Schäffer, 'Art. 1 B-VG', in Benjamin Kneihs and Georg Lienbacher (eds), *Rill-Schäffer-Kommentar Bundesverfassungsrecht* (loose-leaf edn, Verlag Österreich, Vienna, 2001 and ff) recital 22,

Austria responded to its experience following the *Anschluss* (1938) by tabooing National Socialism.[110] Its uncompromising rejection and combating of this ideology is a fundamental characteristic of the restored republic, with which any state action must align.[111]

a) 'Its Law Emanates from the People': The Democracy Model of the Federal Constitutional Law

The second sentence in article 1 of the Federal Constitutional Law ('*Ihr Recht geht vom Volk aus*') combines democracy and the rule of law: it is the law that emanates from the people, not the authority of the democratic republic. The constitutive people (*demos*) do not rule by authoritarian decision.[112] They speak through law, treating all nationals equally and granting all nationals an equal part in its enacting.[113] Thus, the rule of the people and the rule of law are 'connected at the roots'.[114]

The people's influence is exerted by various channels. The core chain of legitimacy is parliamentarian:[115] the people elect representatives both in the Federation and in the *Länder*, thereby delegating legislative power to them. The legal acts passed by the delegates provide ways and means to the administration, thus making it substantively dependent on parliament. This dependence is cemented by the fact that administration is subject to an examination of its affairs by parliament. Apart from these instruments of substantive control, the parliaments exercise powers to create and remove administrative bodies so that they have an influence on the composition of the highest administrative authorities. In the *Länder*, parliamentary interference is direct by virtue of the federal constitution: the members of the state governments *(Landesregierung)* are elected and removed from office by the *Landtag*. At the federal level, the National Council's power is limited to passing a vote of no confidence against the members of the Federal government, thereby initiating their dismissal indirectly.[116]

This differentiation is caused by the amendment of the Federal Constitutional Law of 1929 which introduced a presidential chain of legitimacy complementing and—at the same time—restricting the parliamentarian chain of legitimacy. According to article 60 Federal Constitutional Law, the federal people (*Bundesvolk*) elect a Federal President

---

34; dissenting Peter Oberndorfer, 'Art. 1 B-VG', in Karl Korinek, Michael Holoubek, and others, *Österreichisches Bundesverfassungsrecht. Kommentar* (n 71) recital 10.

[110] See National Socialism Prohibition Act 1947 (VerbotsG 1947), StGBl. 1945/13 as amended by BGBl. 1992/148. It is complemented by art 9 of the State Treaty of Vienna (1955) obliging Austria to dissolve all organizations which are national socialist, fascist, or hostile to the United Nations and to sanction membership and activity in such organizations.

[111] VfSlg. 10.705/1985. See Klaus Zeleny, 'Enthält die österreichische Bundesverfassung ein antinationalsozialistisches Grundprinzip?' (2004) juridikum 182–188; Klaus Zeleny, 'Enthält die österreichische Bundesverfassung ein antinationalsozialistisches Grundprinzip?' (2005) juridikum 22–27.

[112] Hans Kelsen, *Allgemeine Staatslehre* (Springer, Vienna, 1925) 99: '*Sinn der Staatsgewalt [ist] nicht der, daß ein Mensch anderen Menschen, sondern dass Menschen Normen unterworfen sind, wenn es auch Menschen sind, die— dabei selbst wieder Normen unterworfen—diese Normen setzen*' ['It is not the spirit of state authority to subject one human being to another, but to subject human beings to law, albeit it is human beings who pass the law and—in doing so—are bound by law'].

[113] Kurt Ringhofer, *Die österreichische Bundesverfassung* (n 62) 13 f.

[114] So the conventional wording by René Marcic, 'Die Sache und der Name des Rechtsstaates', in Max Imboden (ed), *Gedanke und Gestalt des demokratischen Rechtsstaates* (Herder, Vienna, 1965) 54: '*Demokratie und Rechtsstaat sind in der Wurzel eins*' (Democracy and rule of law are one at the roots).

[115] See Theo Öhlinger and Harald Eberhard, *Verfassungsrecht* (n 61) recital 332; Heinz Peter Rill and Heinz Schäffer, 'Art 1 B-VG' (n 109) recital 20.

[116] See art 74; art 147 para 2 Federal Constitutional Law (conferring the right to nomination of six members and six substitute members of the Constitutional Court).

(*Bundespräsident*) who will appoint the Federal government, the civil servants of the federation (*Bundesbeamte*), and all other federal officials (*Bundesfunktionäre*). Being responsible for the conclusion of treaties, he also has a role in making legislation.

The Federal government's continuance depends on the confidence of both organs enjoying direct democratic legitimacy. In case of irreconcilable differences between the Federal President and the National Council, each party is free to appeal to the people and prompt a decision: the Federal President can force a new election for National Council, while the National Council can request a referendum on the removal of the Federal President and thus prevent his further exercise of the office. However, both parties must rely on the assistance of another body. Before the Federal President can dismiss the National Council, a recommendation by the Federal government is required. The National Council's request must be transferred into a decision of the Federal Assembly (*Bundesversammlung*). If the *Bundesvolk* confirms the Federal President in office, it will simultaneously pave the way for a new election for parliament: according to article 60 para 6 Federal Constitutional Law, the rejection of the motion to depose the Federal President results in the dissolution of the National Council.

The constitution equally designs its other '*direct-democratic*' (i.e. *populist*) elements in a manner to allow the initiation or the correction of decision-making in parliament, but not its substitution.[117] The *Bundesvolk* may have the final say on matters of substance now and then, but it is not in the driver's seat. In the Constitutional Court's view, the fact that a referendum may only be initiated by parliament and not by the people is even a fundamental element of the democratic concept of the Federal Constitutional Law.[118]

As the law is the key instrument of democratic governance of the enforcement power (*Vollziehung*), the constitution takes precautions against malfunctions by obliging the parliament to provide efficient guidance when enacting legislative acts. According to article 18 para 1 Federal Constitutional Law, the entire public administration shall be based on law. This unobtrusive phrase, which is supplemented by a concurrent provision on the issuing of ordinances in the second paragraph,[119] has developed into the central norm of democratic rule of law.[120] It establishes an absolute legal reservation (*Gesetzesvorbehalt*) which has, from the beginning, been broadly interpreted and strictly applied.[121] The prevailing doctrine uses the terms 'enforcement' and 'administration' synonymously.[122] It includes self-administration in the scope of application of these terms[123] and deduces from this legal provision a principle called principle of legality (*Legalitätsprinzip*). It is a universal imperative of significance (*universelles Wesentlichkeitsgebot*) which obliges parliaments to render all essential decisions

---

[117] See art 41 para 2 (petition for a referendum, *Volksbegehren*), art 44 para 3 (referendum on federal laws, *Volksabstimmung über Bundesgesetze*), art 49b (consultation of the people, *Volksbefragung*) Federal Constitutional Law. See also Heinz Peter Rill and Heinz Schäffer, 'Art 1 B-VG' (n 109) recital 27 ff.

[118] See VfSlg. 16.241/2001 referring to the historical development. Yet the Constitutional Court is going too far in its interpretation of the historic sources.

[119] '*Jede Verwaltungsbehörde kann auf Grund der Gesetze innerhalb ihres Wirkungsbereiches Verordnungen erlassen.*' ['Every administrative authority can on the basis of law issue ordinances within its sphere of competence.']

[120] As sole example Heinz Peter Rill, 'Art. 18 B-VG' in Benjamin Kneihs and Georg Lienbacher (eds), *Kommentar* (n 109) recital 1 ff.

[121] For a fundamental statement see VfSlg. 176/1923; VfSlg. 5240/1966 regarding discretion; VfSlg. 8280/1978 regarding the admissibility of target programmes (*finale Programmierung*).

[122] Heinz Mayer, Gabriele Kucsko-Stadlmayer and Karl Stöger, *Grundriss des österreichischen Bundesverfassungsrechts* (n 76) recital 569; Kurt Ringhofer, *Die österreichische Bundesverfassung* (n 62) 81.

[123] VfSlg. 2828/1955, 5438/1966, 7837/1976; Robert Walter, *Österreichisches Bundesverfassungsrecht. System* (n 98) 391; Heinz Peter Rill, 'Art 18 B-VG' (n 120) recital 24.

in a statutory form.[124] To put it into the Austrian legal perspective, which brings the rule of law angle forward: Article 18 Federal Constitutional Law establishes a principle of legal certainty (*Determinierungsgebot*) which is addressed to the law-maker and which obliges the law-maker to grant a sufficient degree of predetermination of acts of the enforcement and prohibits delegation of decisions to the administration.[125] Should the law leave too much room for manoeuvre to the administration, it must be repealed as unconstitutional. The same applies to a statutory authorization to issue ordinances (*Verordnungsermächtigung*): if a statutory authorization does not exactly predetermine the regulatory purpose, means and core content of a regulation, it is equally condemned for being a merely 'formal delegation' (*formalgesetzliche Delegation*).[126]

b) Homogeneity by Substantiation (*Konkretisierungen*)

The election of the general representative bodies in the Federation (National Council, *Nationalrat*), in the *Länder* (state parliament, *Landtag*) and in the municipalities (Municipal Council, *Gemeinderat*) is meticulously designed by the same basic principles. In a departure from the monarchy's majority voting system (*Mehrheitswahlrecht*), the constitution imposes proportional representation (*Verhältniswahlrecht*) and the principles of universal, equal, direct, personal, free, and secret suffrage for all three levels.[127]

The right to vote for the members of the National Council is conferred to citizens who have completed their sixteenth year of life on the day of the election, the age limit for eligibility for office being eighteen years. Exclusion from the right to vote or from eligibility may only be a consequence of a final verdict by a court. Due to homogeneity requirements (*Homogenitätsgebote*), these specifications also influence the elections for the state parliaments and the Municipal Councils.[128] In addition, the census-based system (*Bürgerzahlprinzip*) provides for the uniformity of elections: the seats to be allocated are divided among the constituencies in proportion to the number of nationals, *Länder* citizens or municipal citizens, who in accordance with the result of the last census, had their principal domicile in a particular constituency.[129] On municipal level, Union citizens are equally entitled to vote and stand as candidate next to Austrian nationals.[130] After the Constitutional Court had declared postal voting (*Briefwahl*) incompatible with the principles of secret and personal suffrage,[131] the constitutional legislator first declared postal vote admissible for

---

[124] See VfSlg. 16.921/2003, with reference to Kurt Ringhofer, *Die österreichische Bundesverfassung* (n 62) 82. According to the Constitutional Court the necessary degree of predetermination is dependent on the subject matter of an ordinance (see VfSlg. 13.785/1994, 16.911/2003—'*differenziertes Legalitätsprinzip*' ['differentiated principle of legality']). Demonstrating the tautology Heinz Peter Rill, 'Art 18 B-VG' (n 120) 51–57.

[125] See e.g. Theo Öhlinger and Harald Eberhard, *Verfassungsrecht* (n 61) recital 601.

[126] See VfSlg. 11.859/1988 regarding the authorization to issue provisions on constructional engineering.

[127] See art 26 para 1, art 95 para 1, art 117 para 2 Federal Constitutional Law, art 8 of the State Treaty of Vienna.

[128] According to art 95 para 2 Federal Constitutional Law the State parliament electoral regulations (*Landtagswahlordnung*) may not impose more stringent conditions for suffrage and electoral eligibility than does the Federal Constitutional Law for elections to the National Council; of course, the conditions for eligibility may not be wider than those laid down in federal legislation on the elections to the National Council. According to art 117 para 2 Federal Constitutional Law the same accounts for the Municipal Council electoral regulations (*Gemeindewahlordnung*) in relation to the State parliament electoral regulations.

[129] See with minor modifications art 26 para 2, art 95 para 3, art 117 para 2 Federal Constitutional Law. As a result of this regulation which favours constituencies with more children, the Austrian People's Party (*ÖVP*) won more seats in the National Council elections in 1953 and 1959 than the Social Democrat Party of Austria (*SPÖ*), although it received fewer votes.

[130] See art 22 para 1 Treaty on the Functioning of the European Union; Council Directive 94/80/EC.

[131] VfSlg. 10.412/1985.

votes cast abroad. In 2007, it was also admitted for votes cast in the domestic territory in the event of voters being prevented on the day of election from casting their vote.

According to section 1 of the Political Parties Act (*ParteienG*),[132] the existence and diversity of political parties are key elements of the democratic order. They may be freely established, unless the Federal Constitutional Law provides otherwise, and they are granted subsidies for their activities from public funds. Since election proposals may not only be brought forward by political parties, other loose associations also frequently take part in elections as well. The position of the members of parliament (*Abgeordnete*) is characterized by the independence of the mandate (*Freiheit des Mandats*) and by parliamentary immunity (*Immunität*) on both the federal and state levels.[133]

The National Council as the representative of the federal people stands alongside with the Federal Council (*Bundesrat*) as representative of the *Länder*. Its members are appointed by the *Länder* and elected by the state parliaments; again, the distribution of the seats among the *Länder* is based on the number of citizens (*Bürgerzahlprinzip*) and the principle of proportional representation.[134] For the *Länder*, the single-chamber system (*Einkammersystem*) is binding. On municipal level, the Municipal Council is the highest enforcement body which is authorized to elect the mayor, unless the *Länder* constitutions provide for election by the municipal people (*Gemeindevolk*) and to which all other municipal bodies are accountable.[135]

The participation of the people in the judiciary as jurors (*Geschworene*) or as lay judges (*Schöffen*) is provided for by article 91 Federal Constitutional Law. In the administrative branch, however, authoritarian elements prevail, even though article 120 Federal Constitutional Law has been mentioning the democratization of district administration (*Bezirksverwaltung*) as (an unrealized) concept for eighty years. According to article 20 para 1 Federal Constitutional Law, administrative bodies are bound to the instructions (*Weisungen*) of the administrative institutions superior to them and are accountable to them regarding the fulfilment of their official duties. The Austrian tradition views these rules and the civil service system (*Berufsbeamtentum*) to be basic features of the concept of a democracy focused on law,[136] and the hierarchic model of administration is seen to be the correlative of parliamentary control of the highest administrative bodies: the interrelation between the administrative bodies regarding responsibility and accountability, which is established by the 'instruction', allows for the highest administrative bodies to be held liable for the activities of subordinate administrative authorities and departments.[137]

c) Influence of the Principle of Democracy

In the beginning, it was deemed unnecessary to resort to democracy as a principle, given all these detailed clarifications: it seemed sufficient to interpret and apply the regulations of the Federal Constitutional Law in the light of the programmatic democratic promises. In order to make accountability to parliament as flawless as possible, the Constitutional Court held that article 19 Federal Constitutional Law prohibits the conferral of the highest

---

[132] BGBl. I 2012/56 as amended by BGBl. I 2021/247.

[133] See arts 56–58, art 96 Federal Constitutional Law.

[134] See arts 34 and 35 Federal Constitutional Law.

[135] See art 117 para 6, art 118 para 5 Federal Constitutional Law.

[136] Classical text: Adolf Merkl, *Demokratie und Verwaltung* (Perles, Vienna, Leipzig, 1923) 16 ff; more recent Heinz Peter Rill and Heinz Schäffer, 'Art 1 B-VG' (n 109) recital 21.

[137] Theo Öhlinger and Harald Eberhard, *Verfassungsrecht* (n 61) recital 510.

administrative tasks onto bodies other than the highest administrative bodies.[138] The obligation to comply with instructions of superior bodies (*Weisungsbindung*), as laid down by article 20 para 1 Federal Constitutional Law, was elevated to a principle which would permeate and characterize the entire administration and distinguish it from the judiciary.[139] Thus, non-territorial self-administration (*nichtterritoriale Selbstverwalt-ung*) was put under pressure: there seemed to be no place for it among the comprehensive principle of the 'instruction' on the one side and the explicit entrenchment and safeguard of the autonomy of the municipalities on the other, even though it had been postulated as unobjectionable in some of the provisions on the allocation of competences of the Federal Constitutional Law. The doctrine took a differing approach regarding the assessment of the admissibility of non-territorial self-governing bodies, with one strain of doctrine holding that the existence of a constitutional provision on competences (*Kompetenztatbestand*) would be the relevant criterion, while the second train held the existence of the self-governing body on the date of the adoption of the Federal Constitutional Law should be the relevant criterion.[140] Meanwhile, the Constitutional Court approved the establishment of self-governing bodies at large, provided that a number of conditions are met.[141] The primary focus is the safeguard of democratic principles in the context of internal organization.[142] The constitutional legislator confirmed the jurisdiction and added a general frame for the establishment of non-territorial self-administration in the year 2008.[143]

In its recent jurisprudence, the Constitutional Court has set strict boundaries on the delegation of public powers to private individuals (*Beleihung*) and the establishment of special administrative bodies. In substance, it once again drew on the principle of democracy. According to the Constitutional Court, the assignment of official duties (*Hoheitsgewalt, imperium*) to private individuals and the establishment of outsourced special administrative bodies (i.e. bodies not subordinate to the highest administrative bodies; *Ausgliederung*) are only allowed if core matters of state responsibility (*staatliche Kernaufgaben*) are not restricted and if a high administrative body, which is accountable to the parliament, is endowed with those steering mechanisms necessary to effectively ensure the lawfulness of enforcement activities.[144] This jurisprudence is obviously influenced by the prevailing German theory on democracy which attaches importance to a continuous chain of legitimacy to be maintained between the electorate and the official decision makers.[145]

---

[138] VfSlg. 2323/1952, 12.506/1990; Friedrich Koja, *Das Verfassungsrecht der österreichischen Bundesländer* (2nd edn Springer, Vienna, 1988) 276; Heinz Mayer, Gabriele Kucsko-Stadlmayer, and Karl Stöger, *Grundriss des österreichischen Bundesverfassungsrechts* (n 76) recital 657, 823, with further references.

[139] VfSlg. 1641/1948, 3134/1956, 4648/1964, 14.473/1996; Heinz Mayer and Gerhard Muzak, *B-VG Bundesverfassungsrecht. Kommentar* (n 49) 155 f; Bernhard Raschauer, 'Art. 20 Abs. 1 B-VG', in Karl Korinek, Michael Holoubek, and others, *Österreichisches Bundesverfassungsrecht. Kommentar* (n 71) recital 11 ff. See also VfSlg. 16.400/2001, where a difference is made between a direct and an indirect scope of application of art 20 para 1 Federal Constitutional Law, following Ludwig K Adamovich, Bernd-Christian Funk and Gerhart Holzinger, *Österreichisches Staatsrecht*, vol 2 (Verlag Österreich, Vienna, 1998) recital 27.051.

[140] Karl Korinek, *Wirtschaftliche Selbstverwaltung* (Springer, Vienna, 1970) 41; Robert Walter, *Österreichisches Bundesverfassungsrecht. System* (n 98) 611 ff.

[141] VfSlg. 8215/1977, 17.023/2003.

[142] VfSlg. 8466/1970, 17.023/2003.

[143] Art 120a–120c Federal Constitutional Law. For an in-depth commentary see Harald Eberhard, *Nichtterritoriale Selbstverwaltung* (Verlag Österreich, Vienna, 2014).

[144] VfSlg. 14.473/1996, 16.400/2001 (citation), 17.421/2004.

[145] For a commentary on the étatist bias of this concept see Helmuth Schulze-Fielitz, 'Grundsatzkontroversen in der deutschen Staatsrechtslehre nach 50 Jahren Grundgesetz' (1999) 32 Die Verwaltung 241, 256 ff.

3. Federalism

Austrian Federalism bears almost paradoxical features. Although underdeveloped in practice, it presents itself powerfully in theory. The competences of the *Länder* in the field of legislation are sparse; their autonomy in constitution-making is severely restricted.[146] The *Länder* may take comfort in the fact that they formally face the Federation as equal partners.

The federalist institutions have been designed neither according to the example of American dual federalism (*Trennungsföderalismus*) nor the cooperative federalism (*Verbundföderalismus*) of German origin. Austrian federalism is both at the same time. As regards legislation, competences are fixed rigidly and firmly. In the administrative branch, the framework conditions are exquisitely flexible. The judiciary (*Gerichtsbarkeit*) is the exclusive domain of the Federation.

a) Strict Parity of the Feeble *Länder*: The Model of Federalism of the Federal Constitutional Law

To the astonishment of many foreign spectators, federal laws and the laws of the *Länder* rank equally in Austria: the undisputed theory interprets the reticence of the constitution as a deliberate rejection of the principle 'Bundesrecht bricht Landesrecht' (federal law overrides state law). However, it is contested whether conflicting laws would override one another following the principle of '*lex posterior derogat priori*' or whether emerging conflicts must be dissolved by way of the Constitutional Court's cassation of those statutory regulations which were issued in defiance of the provisions on the division of powers.[147] Likewise, ordinances generally have equal rank. The Federation precedes only on the level of the constitutions: according to article 99 para 1 Federal Constitutional Law, amendments to the constitutions of the *Länder* are only admissible in so far as the federal constitution is not affected by them. The result is a paradoxical double role of the Federation: on the one hand, it is an equal partner of the *Länder* within the federal state; on the other hand, it is the superordinate source of the whole ensemble's constitution. In laying down the division of powers, the federal constitution serves as an umbrella by which and under which the Federation and the *Länder* have an equal position and legal orders of equal rank.

Another particularity can be seen in the lack of provisions which would allow the Federation to take action against the *Länder* if they did not comply with their constitutional duties. The Federal Constitutional Law has done away with settling disputes within the federal state politically by confederal enforcement (*Bundesexekution*). It favours settling disputes by legal action. If the Federation comes to the conclusion that the *Länder* have exceeded their sphere of powers, it must refer the case to the Constitutional Court. Only the Federal President, on whom the execution of the Constitutional Court's decisions is incumbent, may resort to federal military intervention according to article 146 para 2 Federal Constitutional Law.

However, a certain compensation for the lack of powers of direct intervention by the Federation may be seen in provisions which arrange for the transfer of competences to the Federation should the *Länder* unlawfully let their competences lie idle. For instance, any failure of the *Länder* to take the measures necessary for the implementation of state treaties

---

[146] See Friedrich Koja, *Das Verfassungsrecht der österreichischen Bundesländer* (n 138) 29 ff, 99 ff, 269 ff.

[147] See Ewald Wiederin, *Bundesrecht und Landesrecht* (Springer, Vienna, 1995) 70 ff with further references.

will result in the transfer of competence for such measures to the Federation according to article 16 para 4 Federal Constitutional Law. Similar transfer provisions apply to the adoption of legislation implementing legislative principles of the Federation (*Ausführungsgesetze zu Grundsatzbestimmungen des Bundes*) and to the transposition of European law.[148]

The tendency to subject disputes to legal regulation has shaped the design of federal supervisory powers (*Bundesaufsicht*). Although the Federal Constitutional Law does not entirely waive supervision of the Federation over the *Länder*, its supervision is consistently designed to be dependent on certain requirements. According to article 15 para 8 Federal Constitutional Law, the Federation is only entitled to control the observance of the regulations it has issued in matters in which the Federation is responsible for legislation while the *Länder* are responsible for the execution of those laws. Thus, the Federation is limited to an observant form of supervision. In principle,[149] the constitution does not allow the Federation to prevent shortcomings in the measures of the *Länder* by passing instructions. According to Article 132 para 1 No 2 Federal Constitutional Law, the Federation is limited to taking action against administrative decisions (*Bescheide*) issued by the administrative bodies of the *Länder* before the Administrative Courts for unlawfulness of the content.

b) Fixed Separation of Legislative Competences with Predominance of the Federation

The federal division of powers is a matter of nearly unmanageable complexity. Four articles of the Federal Constitutional Law are central and form the main types of the general allocation of powers: article 10 assigns the responsibility for legislation and enforcement of certain matters to the Federation; article 11 provides that, in some matters, legislation is the responsibility of the Federation, while the enforcement of those laws is the responsibility of the *Länder*; pursuant to article 12, the Federation is responsible for legislation as regards principles, while the *Länder* are responsible for implementing legislation and enforcement. According to article 15, all matters which are not expressly assigned to the Federation remain within autonomous sphere of competence of the *Länder*. These provisions form the so-called general division of powers (*allgemeine Kompetenzverteilung*). It is accomplished by further regulations for specific areas—from taxation via the school system to public procurement— in articles 13, 14, 14a, and 14b Federal Constitutional Law, which are predominantly oriented toward the four main types, but also add another dozens of special types,[150] thereby further increasing systematic diversity. But if that were not enough, all these regulations are occasionally overlapped by a shadow regime on competences outside the Federal Constitutional Law consisting of temporary or permanent exceptions, of provisions derogating from the allocation of competences, of constitutional regulations covering responsibilities for certain statutory laws in their precise form and of clarifications of competences assigned to the *Länder*. Finally, more than eighty rules of law (*Rechtssätze*) issued by the Constitutional

---

[148] See art 15 para 6, art 23d para 5 Federal Constitutional Law. According to the first provision the Federation must have set a (specific) deadline for the *Länder* to take action; according to the latter the European Court of Justice must have issued a decision against Austria establishing an infringement.

[149] Exceptions are provided for by art 14 para 8, art 14a para 6 Federal Constitutional Law for school administration, by art 15 para 2 Federal Constitutional Law for local security police and by art 16 para 5 Federal Constitutional Law for the implementation of state treaties in such matters as belong to the autonomous sphere of competence of the *Länder*.

[150] For an oversight see Ludwig K Adamovich and Bernd-Christian Funk, *Österreichisches Verfassungsrecht* (3rd edn Springer, Vienna, 1985) 177, and Theo Öhlinger and Harald Eberhard, *Verfassungsrecht* (n 61) recital 250 ff.

Court are attributed a formal constitutional rank by the prevailing legal doctrine.[151] In this way, almost another hundred constitutional provisions acting as regulations on competences are added to almost 150 regulations on competences inside the Federal Constitutional Law.

Altogether, these regulations provide the Federation with an excessively powerful position as regards legislation. In Austria, even powers traditionally vested with the federated states, like internal security, school, and cultural issues, are the responsibility of the Federation. As for important fields of competence, only the areas of building law and regional planning, nature conservation, event administration, and tourism remain with the *Länder*.

The constitutional allocation of competences for legislation is generally firm and rigid. Although regulations on competences for 'legislation on demand' (*Bedarfskompetenzen*) have gained ground in recent years,[152] they are still marginally represented. Article 10 para 2 Federal Constitutional Law allows for delegation of legislative competences in just a few matters; for the rest, it is the narrow exception that proves the rule. Due to the lack of concurrent legislative powers, it is impossible for the Federation and the *Länder* to decide politically on an ad hoc basis, depending on their interest and ability to deal with tasks, which of them should deal with a novel problem or implement legal acts of the European Union. Therefore, amendments in the allocation of powers are day-to-day business.

In interpreting the provisions on competences, the Constitutional Court has been oriented more towards traditionally established rights than towards the purpose of a regulation. Until today, the most important method of interpretation has been the 'doctrine of petrification' (*Versteinerungstheorie*), which requires constitutional terms generally and provisions on competences, in particular, to be interpreted as defined by the 'simple' legislation at the time of their creation.[153] Terms as implied powers or competences by virtue of the nature of the matter (*Kompetenzen kraft Natur der Sache*) did not gain ground in the jurisprudence. This way, depletion of the remaining powers of the *Länder* was averted. In combination with some selective adjustments, however, a segmentation of the federal heart of the constitution was caused which is without equal.

c) Cooperative Federalism in Administration with Predominance of the *Länder*

In the administrative branch, the *Länder* have a comparably strong position. The most important matters of public authority are listed in article 10 Federal Constitutional Law, therefore the enforcement of legislation is assigned to the Federation. However, the emerging impression of a prevalence of the Federation is misleading. The federalist principle that every entity shall perform its own duties through its own bodies[154] is virtually disrupted by article 102 Federal Constitutional Law with regard to the federal administration. According to article 102 para 1 Federal Constitutional Law, in so far as no federal authorities exist, the executive power of the Federation is exercised by the *Landeshauptmann* (State Governor) and the state authorities are subordinated to him. The administrative tasks of the Federation are fulfilled indirectly by the administrative bodies of the *Länder* without there being any transition in competences. The Federation is only involved in enforcement on the highest

---

[151] For an in-depth analysis see Ulrich E Zellenberg, 'Art 138 para 2 B-VG', in Karl Korinek, Michael Holoubek, and others, *Österreichisches Bundesverfassungsrecht. Kommentar* (n 71) recital 26 ff.

[152] See art 11 para 2 Federal Constitutional Law (administrative procedure), art 10 para 1 No 12 (waste management), art 11 para 1 No 7 Federal Constitutional Law (approval of projects which require an environmental impact assessment where material effects on the environment are to be anticipated).

[153] See VfSlg. 2721/1954, 3666/1959, 9336/1982, 10.831/1986, 13.322/1992, 14.972/1997. See also Heinz Schäffer, *Verfassungsinterpretation in Österreich* (Springer, Vienna, 1971) 97 ff, and Ludwig K. Adamovich and Bernd-Christian Funk, *Österreichisches Verfassungsrecht* (n 150) 44 ff, 190 ff.

[154] See VfSlg. 4413/1963.

administrative level via its (well-staffed) ministries. This model of enforcement is called 'indirect federal administration' (*mittelbare Bundesverwaltung*)[155] by the Federal Constitutional Law, a term coined by Karl Renner. It contrasts 'direct federal administration' (*unmittelbare Bundesverwaltung*) which applies inter alia to the key matters of external affairs, public finance, military affairs, and the administration of security issues (*Sicherheitsverwaltung*).

Indirect federal administration is the rule, not the exception. The Federation may only make use of its own administrative bodies to execute matters listed in article 102 para 2 Federal Constitutional Law. For the establishment of federal authorities for other matters, the consent of the *Länder* concerned is required, in accordance with article 102 para 4 Federal Constitutional Law. According to article 102 para 1 Federal Constitutional Law, the same applies if the Federation wishes to entrust federal bodies, which are subordinate to the State Governor, with enforcement duties instead of the authorities of the *Länder* originally subordinate to him.

The execution of state administration is designed in a similarly flexible way. The *Länder* may stipulate by statutory law that Federal bodies can participate in state administration, if the Federal government gives its consent according to article 97 para 2 Federal Constitutional Law. In matters listed in article 11 Federal Constitutional Law, however, where legislation falls within the responsibility of the Federation and enforcement falls within the responsibility of the *Länder*, there is no general authorization to entrust administrative bodies of another territorial entity with duties of one's own. Correspondingly, there are numerous special provisions permitting deviations in specific matters.[156]

d) Dominance of the Federation in the Judiciary

In the beginning, the *Länder* did not have any share in jurisdiction. In ordinary jurisdiction (*ordentliche Gerichtsbarkeit*), this is still the case to this day: according to Article 82 para 1 Federal Constitutional Law, it emanates from the Federation. Consistently, the enforcement in civil and criminal matters is assigned to the Federation by Article 10 para 1 No. 6 Federal Constitutional Law. The *Länder* are only authorized to issue provisions in the field of criminal and civil law insofar as this is necessary to regulate a matter within the scope of their legislation (article 15 para 9 Federal Constitutional Law).

The amendment of 2012 on the administrative judiciary has granted the *Länder* a share of some administrative jurisdiction: since the implementation of the reform in 2014, they have each had one administrative court facing two administrative courts of first instance on the side of the Federation. The two public law high courts, the Supreme Administrative Court and the Constitutional Court, have naturally remained federal courts.

e) Dominance of the Federation in the Financial Constitution

The financial constitution (*Finanzverfassung*) equally assigns a dominant role to the Federation. According to section 3 para 1 Financial Constitutional Law (*Finanz-Verfassungsgesetz, F-VG*), legislation relating to 'taxation and the distribution of revenues from taxes between the Federation and the *Länder* (municipalities)' falls under

---

[155] The introduction of indirect federal administration was aimed at eliminating the 'duplication of administration' (*Doppelgleisigkeit der Verwaltung*) which existed until then. This is comprehensible as it is a measure of administrative reform, but it is nonetheless a federal curiosity: during transition from a unitary to a federal state, the existing duality of administrative bodies in the *Länder*—viceregents (*Statthaltereien*) and district commissions (*Bezirkshauptmannschaften*) on one side, autonomous administrative bodies of the *Länder* on the other—was abolished and replaced by a uniform system of administrative bodies which is responsible both for federal and for Land administration.

[156] See art 15 para 4 Federal Constitutional Law and constitutional provisions in statutory laws.

the responsibility of the Federation. This makes the *Länder* dependent on the allocation of funds by the Federation. The distribution is settled in the Fiscal Equalization Act (*Finanzausgleichsgesetz*). The *Länder* may well delay the adoption of this federal law by way of the Federal Council (*Bundesrat*), but they cannot prevent it.

It is a political custom that the adoption of the Fiscal Equalization Act is preceded by negotiations between the territorial entities (Federation, *Länder*, and municipalities) and that it is to expire after four years. Only a few types of taxes fall within the exclusive competence of the *Länder* or the municipalities by virtue of the current Fiscal Equalization Act.[157] This is not only the Federation's responsibility. The *Länder* have explicitly refused to be endowed with genuine fiscal autonomy.

According to section 2 Financial Constitutional Law, each territorial entity must cover the expenses arising from the fulfilment of its duties. This principle is disrupted firstly by sections 2 and 4 Financial Constitutional Law. These provisions empower the legislator in charge to provide otherwise, insofar as this is done in compliance with burden-sharing (*Lastenverteilung*) and as long as the limits of the financial capacity of the territorial entities involved are not exceeded. Secondly, it is overlaid by the Federal Constitutional Act BGBl. I 1998/61, which authorizes the territorial entities to enter into agreements on a consultation mechanism (*Konsultationsmechanismus*) and a stability pact (*Stabilitätspakt*). According to the agreement on the consultation mechanism BGBl. I 1999/35 made on this basis, the allocation of additional costs is subject to negotiations in a consultation body;[158] if an agreement cannot be reached there, the final responsibility for coverage of the costs remains with the territorial entity by which the costs were incurred (*Bestellerprinzip*).

4. Rule of Law

The principle of rule of law (*Rechtsstaat*) is not expressly proclaimed by the Federal Constitutional Law. However, it is the basis of the constitution's institutions and it is indirectly made reference to by the proclamation of the principle of democracy in article 1 Federal Constitutional Law. The fact that it is not the public authority but the law that emanates from the people demonstrates the necessity to issue a legal constitution and to impose constraints on public authority.

a) Conformity with Legal Acts of a Higher Level: The Concept of Rule of Law of the Federal Constitutional Law

In its decision VfSlg. 2929/1955, the Constitutional Court held for the first time that the spirit of the rule of law is that 'all acts of state bodies must be rooted in law and eventually in the constitution and that a system of legal protection guarantees that the legal existence only of such acts may be regarded as secured, which were issued in conformity with the acts of a higher level by which they are determined'. This statement, which was originally borrowed from a textbook[159] and condensed into a formula in further case law,[160] is obviously referring

---

[157] See sections 16 and 17 Fiscal Equalisation Act 2017, BGBl. I 2016/116 as amended by BGBl. I 2022/10.
[158] See for further information Heinz Schäffer, 'Konsultationsmechanismus und innerstaatlicher Stabilitätspakt' (2001) 56 Zeitschrift für öffentliches Recht 145, 201 ff, and Peter Bußjäger, 'Rechtsfragen zum Konsultationsmechanismus' (2000) Österreichische Juristenzeitung 581, 583 ff.
[159] Ludwig Adamovich, *Grundriß des österreichischen Verfassungsrechts* (4th edn, Springer, Vienna, 1947) 71.
[160] For validations see VfSlg 11.196/1986, 13.223/1992, 13.699/1994, 13.834/1994.

to the theory of the hierarchy of norms (*Stufenbau der Rechtsordnung*).[161] Therefore, it is not surprising that the rule of law is understood in a formal sense in the first place.

Primacy of law (*Vorrang des Gesetzes*) and legal reservation (*Vorbehalt des Gesetzes*), as stipulated by article 18 para 1 Federal Constitutional Law, are the core of the principle of the rule of law.[162] 'The entire public administration shall be based on law.' In the view of prevailing doctrine, this provision stipulates that any act of public administration, including self-administration (*Selbstverwaltung*), must find a legal basis in a formal statutory law. The responsibilities of administrative bodies, the external organizational structure of these bodies, and the procedures to be applied must equally be laid down by statutory law. The absolute legal reservation is only disrupted by the authorization to provide otherwise and to issue ordinances, which are both based directly on the constitution. As a principle of legal certainty (*Bestimmtheitsgebot*), article 18 para 1 Federal Constitutional Law ensures that the target group addressed by a statutory law can reliably assess the consequences of their acts. At the same time, it implicitly rejects a legal system formed by judges (*Richterstaat*).[163] Moreover, it demands standards as to the accessibility and comprehensibility of legal norms which are deduced from the principle of the rule of law, insofar as they are not explicitly incorporated in the constitution.

However, the Austrian '*Rechtsstaat*' is not only a state of law—it is also a constitutional state and a state of legal protection.[164] As enforcement is bound by law, so must the law respect the constitution. The legislator must obey the regulations on legislative procedure, it must observe the federal distribution of competences and, above all, it must respect the content-related restrictions imposed by fundamental rights. There are gradual but no essential differences between the binding effect of legislation on enforcement and the binding effect of the constitution on legislation. The adoption of any legal act requires compliance with the acts of a higher rank determining this adoption. Accordingly, even the adoption of constitutional laws is legally bound. All state authority must be legally constituted—and whatever is legally constituted is also legally bound.

The last element of the formula deployed by the Constitutional Court shows the way this binding force comes into effect: the state under the rule of law as established by the Federal Constitutional Law is not least a state of legal protection. By screening the mechanisms of legal protection stipulated by the constitution, the image of the hierarchy of norms is affirmed, as the judicial control by the Administrative Court and the Constitutional Court conforms to the legal sources (*Rechtsquellen*). According to article 130 para 1 Federal Constitutional Law, the administrative courts scrutinize administrative decisions (*Bescheide*) as well as the exercise of direct administrative command and compulsion (*Maßnahmen*) for unlawfulness. The Constitutional Court examines ordinances for conformity with statutory laws (article 139 Federal Constitutional Law) and statutory laws for conformity with the constitution (article 140 Federal Constitutional Law). Both the supremacy of the law and the supremacy of the constitution are protected by independent courts in different ways.

---

[161] See Peter Pernthaler, *Österreichisches Bundesstaatsrecht* (Verlag Österreich, Vienna, 2004) 558.

[162] The earlier doctrine basically identified the rule of law with this provision. Most recent Walter Antoniolli and Friedrich Koja, *Allgemeines Verwaltungsrecht* (3rd edn, Manz, Vienna, 1996) 125 ff.

[163] Heinz Peter Rill and Heinz Schäffer, 'Art. 44 B-VG', in Benjamin Kneihs and Georg Lienbacher, *Kommentar* (n 109) recital 32. See for constitutional restrictions on the further development of the law by judicial interpretation (*richterliche Rechtsfortbildung*) VfSlg. 11.500/1987.

[164] The triad '*Gesetzesstaat, Verfassungsstaat und Rechtsschutzstaat*' traces back to Robert Walter, *Österreichisches Bundesverfassungsrecht. System* (n 98) 112 ff; by now, it is generally accepted; see Heinz Peter Rill and Heinz Schäffer, 'Art. 44 B-VG' (n 109) recital 29.

b) Independence of the Judiciary

The independence of judges is highly valued by the Federal Constitutional Law and is established in a high level of detail.[165] The ideal is a professional judge holding civil servant status: once appointed, a judge will remain in office until the retirement age which has been laid down by law. As a basic rule, judges are independent and cannot be removed or transferred from office. They can only be subject to instructions in matters of judiciary administration which are not to be settled by collegiate bodies; a transfer from office requires a formal decision by a judge, unless it was necessary for reasons of changes in the organization of the judiciary. Business is to be allocated among the judges in advance. A matter devolving upon a judge in accordance with this allocation may be removed from his jurisdiction only by decree of a chamber of judges because either, one, he is prevented from properly discharging his responsibilities or, two, he is unable to cope with his duties, due to their extent, within a reasonable time.

The (ordinary) judges are appointed by the Federal President upon proposal for appointment by the Federal government or, by reason of his authorization, by the Minister of Justice. The administrative judges of the *Länder* are appointed by the state government, while the administrative judges of the Federation by the Federal President upon proposal by the Federal government. Prior to that, the competent personnel chambers of the courts must submit proposals for appointment which shall comprise at least three names and at least twice as many names as there are judges to be appointed. Such proposals for appointment are regularly respected in practice, but they are not binding. This is different for the Supreme Administrative Court, where the plenary assembly retains the right to appoint the judges by virtue of article 134 para 3 Federal Constitutional Law (*Recht der Selbstergänzung*).

c) Legal Protection against Administrative Acts with a Focus on the Legal Form

Upon a second glance at the chapter on Constitutional and Administrative Guarantees, another particularity of the Federal Constitutional Law is disclosed which further limits legal protection rather than granting comprehensive access. Similar to the *edictum* of the Roman *praetor*, the system of legal protection strictly follows an approach governed by *actiones*. The jurisdiction of both the Constitutional Court and the administrative courts is linked to the legal form of an act. In order for a complaint to be admissible, the complainant must claim an infringement of his rights, with that infringement taking the form of an administrative decision. This way, the administrative decision is the bottleneck through which every person wishing to complain about the administration before the courts must pass. A complaint may also be filed against the exercise of direct administrative command and compulsion (*Akte unmittelbarer verwaltungsbehördlicher Befehls- und Zwangsgewalt*), which expands the scope of legal protection and proves its dependency on the legal form. To be able to seize the institutions responsible for safeguarding legal conformity, it is not enough that there has been an infringement of rights. It is obvious that any further requirement would adversely affect the effectivity of judicial control: a systematic assessment shows that a formal access criterion, which is added to the requirement of there being an infringement in rights, can only mean curtailing legal protection, even though rights may have been curtailed.

In the beginning, there were attempts to fill the gaps that showed up in legal protection with a newly developed principle which required infringements to take a specific form: if the administration touches on the rights of citizens, it must act either by way of

---

[165] See art 86 to art 88a Federal Constitutional Law. See also Heinz Mayer, Gabriele Kucsko-Stadlmayer and Karl Stöger, *Grundriss des österreichischen Bundesverfassungsrechts* (n 76) recital 769 ff.

an administrative decision or by way of the exercise of direct administrative command and compulsion.[166] In contrast, legal doctrine suggested that any infringement of rights which is not caused by an administrative decision should be considered exercise of direct administrative command and compulsion.[167] Both methods have shown to be inappropriate because the real-world phenomenon of 'simple sovereign administrative action' (*schlicht-hoheitliches Verwaltungshandeln*) cannot reasonably be deemed unconstitutional nor can it be regarded as command or compulsion. Meanwhile, due to the legal amendments introduced into the administrative judiciary in 2012, legal protection against such simple sovereign administrative action is at least allowed for where access to the administrative court is granted by statutory law.[168] There was, however, no agreement on the introduction of a comprehensive system of legal protection against all acts of public power.

d) The Concept of the Rule of Law as a Principle

The successful concept of the legal protection system as it was applied by the Roman *praetor* was already guided by an approach which considered the rule of law as a principle. In recent jurisprudence, the Constitutional Court explicitly affirmed this approach and drew substantial inferences from it. Since its decision VfSlg. 11.196/1986, the Constitutional Court has consistently demanded that institutions that grant legal protection must have a minimum level of factual efficiency of such protections (*Mindestmaß an faktischer Effizienz*). Therefore, it is deemed to be inadmissible to unilaterally impose all consequences of a possibly unlawful decision upon the appellant, as long as the appeal is not finally decided upon. A number of provisions entirely excluding the possibility to grant suspensive effect to an appeal were repealed for this reason.[169] For the same reason, time limits for legal remedy which were too short, procedural rules that adversely affected efficiency or the exclusion of any recourse to legal remedies were considered to be contrary to the principle of the rule of law.[170] Furthermore, the Constitutional Court deduces from the principle of the rule of law that judicial decisions must be made available to the public,[171] that an administrative authorization may not be withdrawn without giving reasons,[172] and that legal norms must display a minimum degree of accessibility and comprehensibility.[173] At the turn of the millennium, it even repealed a constitutional provision as unconstitutional because it stipulated that *Land* legislation in a certain area of public procurement was not subject to review for conformity with the federal constitution.[174]

---

[166] VfSlg. 13.223/1992. For the underlying theory of the 'closedness of the system of legal sources' (*Geschlossenheit des Rechtsquellensystems*) Ludwig K Adamovich and Bernd-Christian Funk, *Österreichisches Verfassungsrecht* (n 150) 50, 254.

[167] See Franz Merli, "Normativität' und Begriff der Maßnahme nach Art. 129a Abs. 1 Ziff. 2 B-VG' (1993) Zeitschrift für Verwaltung 251, 255.

[168] Art 130 para 2 No. 2 Federal Constitutional Law. See Martin Lenzbauer, *Schlichte Hoheitsverwaltung* (Verlag Österreich, Vienna, 2018) 67 ff.

[169] VfSlg. 11.196/1986, 12.683/1991, 13.003/1992, 13.305/1992, 15.218/1998.

[170] VfSlg 13.493/1993, 15.529/1999, 16.245/2001, 16.460/2002.

[171] VfSlg. 12.409/1990.

[172] VfSlg. 12.184/1989.

[173] See VfSlg. 12.420/1990, concerning legal norms which may 'only be comprehended on the basis of a subtle expertise, extraordinary methodical skills and a certain pleasure in solving brain teasers' (*mit subtiler Sachkenntnis, außerordentlichen methodischen Fähigkeiten und einer gewissen Lust am Lösen von Denksportaufgaben;* 776) with reference to VfSlg. 3130/1956 ('archival diligence', *archivarischer Fleiß*); see also VfSlg. 14.968/1997, 16.317/2001, 16.381/2001, 16.852/2003.

[174] VfSlg. 16.327/2001.

5. Separation of Powers

In contrast to other constitutions, the Federal Constitutional Law neither proclaims its commitment to the principle of separation of powers and nor is Montesquieu's triad of legislature, executive, and judiciary a central feature of its structure. However, by establishing an organizational framework of institutions to which delimited duties are assigned, it acknowledges a separation of powers in substance. The influence of the concept is also evident in the system of the Federal Constitutional Law.[175] Instead of the traditional division into three elements, there are two partitions into two which characterize the separation of powers as provided for by the Federal Constitutional Law. First, legislative power is separated from its execution, namely both on federal and state levels: the second chapter concerns 'Federal Legislation', the third chapter concerns 'Federal Enforcement', and the fourth chapter concerns 'Legislation and Enforcement of the *Länder*'. The third chapter on federal enforcement further differentiates between administration and ordinary jurisdiction.

The acceptance of control as a fourth power is another deviation from the traditional tripartite structure. Next to the aforementioned chapters, there are three more chapters concerning legislation and enforcement on federal and state levels with different aspects of control: The seventh chapter includes provisions on 'Control of Public Accounts and Administration of Public Funds' (*Rechnungs- und Gebarungskontrolle*), the current ninth chapter relates to 'Control by the Ombudsman' (*Missstandskontrolle)*, while the eighth chapter on 'Constitutional and Administrative Guarantees' comprises the provisions on the administrative courts, the Administrative Court, and the Constitutional Court. Hence, the provisions on public law judiciary are not incorporated into the chapter on federal enforcement but are juxtaposed with it inside a separate chapter. This results in a curious hybrid status: constitutional and administrative jurisdiction is covered in a separate chapter, although it is part of the judiciary in terms of organization; as an instrument of control over the administration it is a counterpoint to the enforcement of the Federation, although it must be attributed to the enforcement of the Federation according to the provisions on the allocation of competences.

a) Legislation and Enforcement: The Supremacy of Parliament

The differentiation between making legislation and its enforcement is perceived as a strict formal separation: the legislative bodies are limited to legislative activities, while the enforcement bodies are limited to enforcement activities. The participation of the parliament in enforcement and the participation of the executive power in legislation are both only admissible where the constitution deviates from the principle of separation of powers. The most important exceptions are covered in section E of the second chapter relating to the 'Participation of the National Council and of the Federal Council in the Enforcement of the Federation'.

According to the prevailing opinion, the formal separation knows no equivalent principle of content-related, 'material' separation of powers. Apart from a few exceptions,[176] the parliament neither has to respect a field reserved for the administration, nor does it have to limit

---

[175] See Günther Winkler, 'Das österreichische Konzept der Gewaltentrennung in Recht und Wirklichkeit' (1967) 6 Der Staat 293, citation by Günther Winkler, *Orientierungen im öffentlichen Recht* (Springer, Vienna, 1979) 229, 234 ff.

[176] According to art 83 para 1 Federal Constitutional Law districts of circuit courts, as an example, are established by an ordinance issued by the Federal government; a statutory law would be deemed unconstitutional.

itself to issuing 'general-abstract' norms. It may therefore regulate individual cases and take measures, as long as the action takes the form of statutory law.[177] The parliament is strictly barred from making use of a legal form which is reserved for the enforcement bodies, as, for instance, when adopting ordinances or issuing administrative decisions.[178]

Apart from that, the relation between legislation and its enforcement is determined by the principle of legality laid down by article 18 Federal Constitutional Law: the enforcement power is bound by law. Any form of exercise of public power must be based on a statutory law, unless the constitution, by way of exception, provides an authorization to act. The parliament sets the direction by statutory law; those who apply the law must comply in enforcing the law. Only the Constitutional Court stands outside the scope of the enforcement power because of its competence to examine statutory laws for their conformity with the constitution and repeal them in case of violation.

As a consequence of this understanding of the notion of separation, legislation is formally at the same level as enforcement, although, from a substantive point of view, it enjoys primacy. Since the enforcement branch is subject to law, it may not be subordinate, but is certainly subsequent to parliament.

b) The Concern for a '*Verwaltungsbruch*': Separation of Powers in the Federal Constitutional Law

The enforcement branch, once separated out from the legislature, is further divided into administration and judiciary. The Federal Constitutional Law establishes different organizational structures and declares in its article 94 para 1 that the judiciary and the administration shall be separate at all levels of proceedings.

This second fundamental separation is equally perceived as formal organizational separation of powers. First, article 94 para 1 Federal Constitutional Law is a ban on hybrid organization and prohibits the establishment of bodies which are administrative bodies and courts at the same time; second, it is an obligation to allocate enforcement duties rigorously either to the administration or to the judiciary upon objective criteria; third, it precludes regulations which allow administrative and judicial bodies to give instructions to one another;[179] and fourth, it prohibits the introduction of interrelating appeal procedures (*Instanzenzüge*) or of other forms of procedural interdependence.[180] However, a principle of content-related separation of powers may not be deduced from article 94 para 1 Federal Constitutional Law: in principle, the legislature is free to choose whether it wishes to allocate a matter to the administration or to the judiciary. Even article 6 ECHR could not alter that fact because the right to an independent and impartial tribunal may also be preserved if the competent administrative authority is given judicial character. As the sole exception, the Constitutional Court held that the imposition of severe sentences must be reserved to the ordinary judiciary.[181] By now, it has given up this view.[182]

---

[177] For the general admissibility of measures by statutory law see VfSlg. 3118/1956, 13.738/1994; Theo Öhlinger and Harald Eberhard, *Verfassungsrecht* (n 61) recital 620; Peter Pernthaler, *Österreichisches Bundesstaatsrecht* (n 161) 567, 571.

[178] See Leopold Werner, 'Kann der Nationalrat Verordnungen erlassen?' (1951) Juristische Blätter 353, 355 ff; VfSlg. 2320/1952, 5436/1966.

[179] VfSlg. 7882/1976. The same accounts for binding statements: see VfSlg. 6278/1970, 10.300/1984.

[180] VflSlg. 13.273/1992.

[181] VfSlg. 12.151/1989, 14.361/1995, under reference to art 91 Federal Constitutional Law. For dissenting legal doctrine and further references see Manfred Burgstaller, 'Art. 91 Abs. 2–3 B-VG', in Karl Korinek, Michael Holoubek and others, *Österreichisches Bundesverfassungsrecht. Kommentar* (n 71) recital 42 ff.

[182] VfSlg. 20.231/2017; VfGH 4. 10. 2018, G 62/2018; 26. 11. 2018, G 219/2018.

The consequences of this approach to the principle of separation of powers are difficult to explain to Austrian criminal law experts and generate feelings of surprise, if not bewilderment, in foreign observers.[183] Since article 94 para 1 Federal Constitutional Law explicitly prohibits appeal procedures from the administration to the judiciary and vice versa, it also categorically rejects judicial control of administrative acts.[184] This form of review will only be admissible if the constitution provides for it with exceptional provisions. The provisions on the administrative judiciary stipulated in article 94 para 1 Federal Constitutional Law are such *leges speciales*. Their concept was created during the monarchy in a way which would subject administration to judicial control in a manner that preserved its autonomy as extensively as possible. The administrative judiciary was to control administration, but not to administer in its place. The latter was execrated as an 'administrative breach' (*Verwaltungsbruch)* and was deemed important to avoid.[185] The administrative judiciary created in the nineteenth century was strictly structured with a view to achieving this aim. The Supreme Administrative Court, firstly, had to respect the margin of discretion accorded to the administration; secondly, it only had the power to annul the administrative act, but not to take a decision on the merits of the case; thirdly, it was bound to the findings on the facts of the case as established by the relevant administrative authority; finally, a complaint submitted to the Administrative Court had no suspensive effect, neither could it be granted by the Administrative Court—suspensive effect could only be granted by the administrative authority. This detail regarding the concept of suspensive effect expresses the underlying concern that the Constitutional Court might 'co-govern' inside the administrative branch instead of contenting itself with its role as a controller. Some of the elements of this concept were codified by the Federal Constitutional Law, others were tacitly approved by it.[186]

The administration is even more strongly insulated from control exerted by the ordinary judiciary: article 94 para 1 Federal Constitutional Law generally leaves no room for it.[187] This principle even applies where the administrative authority is in the position of reconciling conflicting interests of private parties. The Constitutional Court, however, has accepted legal devices by which the parties may turn to an ordinary court once the matter has been decided upon by the administrative body, provided that the administrative decision is invalidated *ex lege* by virtue of the application to the court. Moreover, the court must have the right to entirely reassess the matter without being prejudged by the previous decision.[188]

---

[183] See Otto Lagodny, 'How the Austrians or Germans do without it?', in Christian Grafl and others (eds), *Festschrift für Manfred Burgstaller* (NWV Verlag, Vienna, 2004) 409, 416 ff; Stefan Storr, 'Die österreichische Bundesverfassung—eine Hausbesichtigung' (2009) Zeitschrift für Verwaltung 530, 536.

[184] For an in-depth commentary see Christian Kopetzki, *Unterbringungsrecht* (Springer, Vienna, 1995) 212 ff; for a critique see Ewald Wiederin, 'In allen Instanzen getrennt. Zum Verhältnis von Justiz und Verwaltung am Beispiel des strafprozessualen Vorverfahrens', in *Vienna Law Inauguration Lectures—Antrittsvorlesungen an der Rechtswissenschaftlichen Fakultät der Universität Wien*, vol 2 (Manz, Vienna, 2010) 41, 49 ff.

[185] For this key to understanding the characteristics of the Austrian administrative judiciary see Günther Winkler, 'Die Entscheidungsbefugnis des österreichischen Verwaltungsgerichtshofes im Lichte der Gewaltentrennung', cited by: Günther Winkler, *Orientierungen im öffentlichen Recht* (n 175) 105, 111 ff.

[186] See the standard textbook by Peter Oberndorfer, *Die österreichische Verwaltungsgerichtsbarkeit* (Trauner, Linz, 1983) 33 ff.

[187] This is different where fundamental rights require a judicial order (see e.g. art 10 Basic Law on the General Rights of Nationals (*Staatsgrundgesetz über die allgemeinen Rechte der Staatsbürger*, hereafter abbreviated as StGG)) or accept judicial review (see e.g. art 6 para 1 Federal Constitutional Law on the Protection of Personal Liberty (*Bundesverfassungsgesetz über den Schutz der persönlichen Freiheit*, hereafter abbreviated as PersFrG).

[188] VfSlg. 3121/1956, 3236/1957, 10.452/1985, 13.824/1994. Examples can be found in the areas of social security law, tenancy law and in expropriation law.

The constitutionality of these 'successive competences' (*sukzessive Kompetenzen*) were questioned in legal doctrine for being an inadmissible circumvention.[189]

The amendments of 2012 that introduced the administrative judiciary have shifted powers significantly. On the one hand, the newly established administrative courts of first instance are largely obliged to decide on the merits of the case by virtue of the constitution.[190] In this respect, they are not only controlling the administration, but they are also taking its place. On the other hand, the newly adopted article 94 para 2 Federal Constitutional Law authorizes the legislator to provide for a possibility of an appeal against an administrative decision before an ordinary court. The traditional understanding of the principle of separation of powers has thereby been both confirmed and eroded.

c) The Interrelation between Parliament, Federal President, and Federal Government

In view of the sheer magnitude of Austrian constitutional law and its attention to detail, it is common to find the legal existence of certain public institutions provided for in the constitution: the main features of public security authorities, school authorities, and district administrative authorities (*Bezirksverwaltungs-behörden*) are laid down in the constitution to protect them from being abolished or reorganized by a simple majority in parliament. Other bodies are only honoured with incorporation into the constitution to remove obstacles opposing their establishment, such as provisions on competences or organization. It may not be wrong to denote all these bodies as 'constitutional bodies in a formal sense' (*Verfassungsorgane im formellen Sinn*), but it does not make sense in a substantial way.

Among the constituted bodies, article 19 para 1 Federal Constitutional Law emphasizes the Federal President, the Federal Ministers, the State Secretaries and the Members of the *Länder* Governments, referring to them as supreme authorities (*oberste Organe*). These bodies may certainly be called 'constitutional bodies in a substantive sense' (*Verfassungsorgane im materiellen Sinn*). The constitution includes finely nuanced provisions on their interaction with parliament.

The *Länder* are bound to a parliamentary system of government by article 101 Federal Constitutional Law: the members of the Land Government are elected by the *Landtag* and are dependent on its confidence. The *Landeshauptmann* is a member of the state government and is *primus inter pares*. However, the federal constitution allocates the exercise of indirect federal administration to the *Landeshauptmann*. It endows him with competences rendering him head of state and the central hub in the relation between the Federation and the *Länder*.[191]

In 1929, the once parliamentary system of government was supplemented by elements of a presidential system originating from the Weimar Constitution on federal level. The result is a combined system which is, at the same time, plebiscitary-presidential and parliamentarian.[192] The Federal President and the members of the National Council are elected by universal suffrage (article 60 Federal Constitutional Law). The Federal Chancellor and, on his recommendation, the other members of the Federal government are appointed and removed from office by the Federal President (article 70 Federal Constitutional Law). If the

---

[189] See Richard Novak, 'Quasi-Instanzenzüge im österreichischen Recht' (1976) Zeitschrift für Verwaltung 53, 54 ff.

[190] Art 130 para 4 Federal Constitutional Law.

[191] See art 16 para 2, art 98 para 1, art 102 para 1, art 103, art 104 para 2, art 105 Federal Constitutional Law, and section 1 Federal Constitutional Act BGBl. 1925/289.

[192] For a different accentuation see Theo Öhlinger and Harald Eberhard, *Verfassungsrecht* (n 61) recital 336, in whose opinion it is at best a parliamentary government system with a presidential element.

National Council passes a vote of no confidence against the Federal government or its individual members, the Federal President will have to remove them from office (article 74 para 1 Federal Constitutional Law). Each single member of the Federal government must therefore enjoy the confidence of both bodies directly elected by the people. The responsibility to issue the acts of creation and dismissal, however, lies exclusively with the Federal President.

Apart from the right to appoint the government, the Federal President possesses the traditional powers of a head of state and the right to issue emergency decrees (*Notverordnungen*) limited by participation rights of a parliamentary committee.[193] Moreover, he can dissolve the National Council according to article 29 Federal Constitutional Law. All his acts, however, require a recommendation from the Federal Government or a Federal Minister authorized by it, unless otherwise provided by constitutional law. In this way, his discretion is limited. His power mainly lies in the competence to form a government.

The Federal President may be accused before the Constitutional Court of a violation of the constitution and may be removed from office by referendum. Parliamentary decisions to assert these forms of legal and political accountability are to be taken by a majority of at least two-thirds of the votes cast.[194] So long as the Federal President has the support of a qualified minority in the National Council, he can temporarily keep a government, which is not approved by a majority in the National Council, in office and he can replace it by a government that adheres to the same policy line. In the circumstance where there is a dwindling support of a parliamentary majority, he can use public opinion to make way for new elections by dissolving the National Council.[195]

In reality, these considerable powers were never used.[196] After the Second World War, the Federal President acted as state notary far removed from political life for half a century and only made use of his powers in accordance with settled political customs. In the recent past, his competence to form a government has gained in significance.

The Federal government, which is entrusted with the highest administrative business, is composed of the Federal Chancellor and the Federal Ministers according to article 69 para 1 Federal Constitutional Law. The Federal Chancellor presides, but he does not have the right to issue guidelines nor any other privileges. Governmental decisions require unanimity. Next to the Federal government as a collegiate body, the Federal Ministers also constitute ('monocratic') supreme administrative bodies, without priority being assigned to either of them; rather, the allocation of business is to be agreed upon by the legislator.[197] According to article 77 Federal Constitutional Law, the Federal Ministers are entrusted with the direction of the respective Federal Ministries which are established to assist in the performance of the business of the federal administration.[198] Federal Ministers without portfolios may be appointed exceptionally. In order to assist the Federal Ministers and to deputize them in

---

[193] For an overview see Robert Walter, *Österreichisches Bundesverfassungsrecht. System* (n 98) 448–466, and Theo Öhlinger and Harald Eberhard, *Verfassungsrecht* (n 61) recital 483–487.

[194] See art 60 para 6 Federal Constitutional Law on the motion to convene the Federal Assembly with a view to hold a referendum on the deposition of the Federal President, see art 68 Federal Constitutional Law on the decision of the Federal Assembly on a charge before the Constitutional Court.

[195] For a closer look see Robert Schick, 'Die Rolle des Staatsoberhaupts', in Walter Berka and others (eds), *Verfassungsreform* (NWV, Vienna, 2004) 11, 25 ff.

[196] The National Council was only dissolved once in 1930 (see BGBl. 1930/294). The new election, however, did not produce the desired result, but resulted in the resignation of the Federal government.

[197] See Heinz Mayer, Gabriele Kucsko-Stadlmayer, and Karl Stöger, *Grundriss des österreichischen Bundesverfassungsrechts* (n 76) recital 654; for a different view VfSlg. 2323/1952 on the ministries system (*Ministerialsystem*).

[198] See VfSlg. 4117/1961.

parliament, State Secretaries (*Staatssekretäre*), who are bound to instructions by the Federal Ministers, may be attached to them (article 78 Federal Constitutional Law).

The National Council is entitled to examine the administration of affairs by the Federal government.[199] As a means of political control, the National Council has at its disposal all the traditional instruments: the 'right to citation' (*Zitationsrecht*, i.e. the right to call for the presence of a minister at deliberations), the right of interpellation (*Fragerecht*), the 'right of resolution' (*Resolutionsrecht*, i.e. the right to pass resolutions expressing its wishes regarding the exercise of the executive power), and the right to set up investigative committees (*Enqueterecht*). It is supported by two powerful subsidiary bodies (*Hilfsorgane*) in the form of the Court of Audit and the Ombudsman Board. Standing sub-committees are established to supervise the activities of the intelligence services of police and the Federal Armed Forces.

d) Control by the Court of Audit and Control by the Ombudsman

The Federal Constitutional Law devotes an entire chapter each to the control of public accounts and administration of public funds (*Rechnungs- und Gebarungskontrolle*) by the Court of Audit and to the control by the Ombudsman Board (*Missstandskontrolle*). The prominent position in which they are placed shows their high significance, which is provided for in the constitution, but this status is also due to the fact that the Court of Audit and the Ombudsman Board are not only responsible at the federal level, but also at the *Länder* level. Since they assist parliament in exercising political control as subsidiary bodies, both are allocated to the legislature inside the traditional scheme of separation of powers.[200]

The Court of Audit's task is to examine the administration of public funds by the territorial entities, by business enterprises over which the public authority has a controlling influence and by selected self-administration bodies for proper accounting, regularity, economy, efficiency, and expediency.[201] It is in part an institution of the National Council, but also in part an institution of the *Landtag*. It is directed by a president who is elected by the National Council for a twelve-year term of office. Within their sphere, the *Länder* are free to establish similar institutions alongside the Court of Audit.

The Ombudsman Board is modelled on the Scandinavian example and has the task of scrutinizing the Federation for maladministration *ex officio* and upon complaint by citizens alleging such maladministration.[202] The commissions appointed by it are responsible to visit and inspect detention facilities and institutions and programmes for handicapped persons and to examine acts of exertion of administrative power and compulsion of the administrative bodies for compliance with human rights. The Ombudsman Board can issue recommendations to which the administration has to react; it must annually render a report on its activity to the National Council and the Federal Council. It consists of three members

---

[199] See arts 52–53 Federal Constitutional Law. For a commentary on these provisions see Heinz Mayer, Gabriele Kucsko-Stadlmayer, and Karl Stöger, *Grundriss des österreichischen Bundesverfassungsrechts* (n 76) recital 500–559, and Andreas Nödl, *Parlamentarische Kontrolle* (Böhlau, Vienna, 1995).

[200] See VfSlg. 1454/1932; Theo Öhlinger and Harald Eberhard, *Verfassungsrecht* (n 61) recitals 329, 572, 586; Karl Korinek, 'Art. 121 B-VG', in Karl Korinek, Michael Holoubek, and others, *Österreichisches Bundesverfassungsrecht. Kommentar* (n 71) recital 15 ff; Rudolf Thienel, 'Art. 148a B-VG', in Benjamin Kneihs and Georg Lienbacher (eds), *Kommentar* (n 109) recital 3. This allocation to legislature is questioned by a minority in legal doctrine which argues for the executive.

[201] See art 121 and arts 126b to art 127b Federal Constitutional Law and section 31a para 1 Federal Act on the Austrian Broadcasting Corporation (ORF Act, *ORF-G*), BGBl. 1984/531 as amended by BGBl. I 2021/247. On the Court of Audit Johannes Hengstschläger, *Rechnungshofkontrolle* (Manz, Vienna, 2000).

[202] See art 148a–148j Federal Constitutional Law and the comments on these provisions by Gabriele Kucsko-Stadlmayer in Karl Korinek, Michael Holoubek, and others, *Österreichisches Bundesverfassungsrecht. Kommentar* (n 71), and by Rudolf Thienel, 'Art. 148a B-VG' (n 200).

elected by the National Council for a six-year term of office on the basis of a joint recommendation for which each of the three parties with the largest number of mandates in the National Council may nominate one member. The Ombudsman Board is generally responsible for monitoring the sphere of the Federation; it can be declared competent for the sphere of the *Länder* by the constitutional laws of the *Länder*. The *Länder* are also free to establish similar institutions for their own sphere. *Tirol* and *Vorarlberg* made use of this option.

6. Fundamental Rights

Since Austrian constitutional law lacks a uniform document, fundamental rights are equally spread over a variety of legal sources.[203] But they can at least be sorted according to different layers. The first (historic) layer consists of those fundamental rights which were integrated into the Federal Constitutional Law in 1920 or which the Federal Constitutional Law took notice of. The second layer is the European Convention on Human Rights, which has constitutional status in Austria, including its Additional Protocols. The two layers are complemented by selected additions to the *acquis* of fundamental rights adopted in the recent past. The differences in seniority and origin set limits on how these fundamental rights can be understood as a uniform system. In case of variances between genuinely national fundamental rights and the safeguards of the ECHR, the favourability principle (*Günstigkeitsprinzip*) applies.[204]

a) The Older Layer of Fundamental Rights

The main source of the older layer of fundamental rights is the Basic Law of 1867 on the General Rights of Nationals (*StGG*, RGBl. 142). It further refers to the Law on the Protection of the Rights of the Home (*Gesetz zum Schutze des Hausrechtes*) of 1862 (RGBl. 88) and is supplemented by a Decree of the Provisional National Assembly of 1918 (StGBl. 3) and by some articles of the Treaty of Saint-Germain (StGBl. 1920/303). According to article 149 para 1 Federal Constitutional Law, these documents are regarded as constitutional laws. The Federal Constitutional Law itself does not incorporate a catalogue of fundamental rights, but it contains individual safeguards: the right to equality before the law (*Gleichheit vor dem Gesetz*) and the right to 'one's lawful judge' (*Recht auf den gesetzlichen Richter*) were deemed so important by the constitutional legislator that they were integrated into the Federal Constitutional Law irrespective of the repetition caused.

Following nineteenth-century tradition,[205] the StGG 1867 safeguards the rights to equality, liberty, and property, but neglects rights to security, subsistence, or procedural rights. In detail, the following rights are granted: equality before the law (article 2); free access to public office (article 3); freedom of movement of persons and of possessions (article 4); inviolability of property (article 5); freedom of residence and employment (article 6); inviolability of the rights of the home (article 9); privacy of letters (article 10); secrecy of telecommunications added in 1974 (article 10a); right to petition (article 11); freedom of assembly and association (article 12); freedom of expression (article 13); freedom of conscience and creed (article 14);

---

[203] For a chronological overview see Walter Berka, *Verfassungsrecht* (7th edn, Verlag Österreich, Vienna, 2018) recital 1177.
[204] See art 53 ECHR and art 8 para 3 PersFrG.
[205] It was inspired by the catalogue of fundamental rights of the March Constitution 1849, RGBl. 1849/151, and the Belgian Constitution 1831.

THE EVOLUTION AND *GESTALT* OF THE AUSTRIAN CONSTITUTION   47

freedom of science (article 17); freedom of art, added in 1982 (article 17a); and freedom to choose vocation and training (article 18). Moreover, it declares abolished 'every liege bond and thraldom' (*jeden Unterthänigkeits- und Hörigkeitsverband*) in perpetuity (article 7) and secures privileges for legally recognized churches and religious communities (article 15). The other provisions are considered to have ceased to be in force.[206]

Its wording is short and straightforward. The safeguards are in part absolute guarantees; in part they are subject to restrictions because of statutory reservations (*Gesetzesvorbehalte*). These are considered to be either requirements for the enactment of a statutory law to give effect to a fundamental right (*Ausgestaltungsvorbehalte*) or requirements for enactment of a statutory law to restrict a fundamental right (*Eingriffsvorbehalte*).[207] When restrictions are permitted, a statutory law basis is always required. Occasionally, a judicial order is asked for in addition.

In the interwar period, case law had still taken these formal requirements at their word and refused to question the existence of a public interest or to examine the proportionality of an interference. A leading decision passed in 1928 states the following: 'The common welfare or the common best are terms which cannot be defined by juridical means, it is exclusively for the legislator to assess the fulfilment of these conditions ... The Constitutional Court must categorically refuse to issue an opinion on this matter.'[208]

Contrary to a widespread prejudice, however, the refusal to examine the proportionality of the legal basis of an infringement did not result in a complete ineffectiveness of fundamental rights. It has to be noted that the Constitutional Court took the formal requirements for restrictions stated in the StGG even more seriously: the existence of a statutory basis and its sufficient predetermination and the existence of a judicial order were meticulously examined.[209] Moreover, the right to equality before the law (article 7 Federal Constitutional Law) was brought to life and interpreted as a ban on arbitrariness (*Willkürverbot*), right from the beginning.[210] There was never a doubt that, in general, parliament is also bound by fundamental rights and that laws issued by it may violate such rights.[211]

After the Second World War the Constitutional Court gradually abandoned this restrained position. On the one hand, it further developed the right to equality before the law into a general principle of objectivity (*Sachlichkeitsgebot*)—first relating to differentiations between two regulated subjects, later for legal provisions as such.[212] It thereby had the opportunity to establish different objectivity requirements for different areas which became

---

[206] For a commentary on art 20 StGG (possibility to suspension of fundamental rights) see art 149 para 2 Federal Constitutional Law; on art 8 StGG see BGBl. 1988/684. As regards art 1, art 16, and art 19 StGG, theory and practice predominantly assume the existence of material derogation: for evidence see Christoph Lanner, *Kodex Verfassungsrecht* (22th edn, Lexis Nexis 2005) 156, 158.

[207] This differentiation primarily has procedural consequences for the Constitutional Court.

[208] VfSlg. 1123/1928, 370.

[209] See VfSlg. 775/1927, 797/1927, 943/1928, 1074/1928, 1338/1930. It is along this line that the right to one's lawful judge was gradually extended by the Constitutional Court to be a constitutional guarantee of legally stipulated responsibilities and application rights: see Norbert Schopf, *Das Recht auf ein Verfahren vor dem gesetzlichen Richter* (Verlag Österreich, Vienna, 2000) 45 ff.

[210] See VfSlg. 216/1923, 287/1924 (violation of the right to equality by disciplinary measures for a marriage below social status); VfSlg. 449/1925 (exclusion from appointment to the office of head of school for reasons of religious denomination); VfSlg. 651/1926 (violation for the exclusion of a woman from the occupation as a taxi driver according to business regulations); VfSlg. 1231/1929 (exclusion of teachers from eligibility for the municipal executive board).

[211] See VfSlg. 259/1924, 1123/1928, 1230/1929, 1304/1930; Ludwig Adamovich, *Grundriß des österreichischen Staatsrechtes* (2nd edn, Verlag der österreichischen Staatsdruckerei, Vienna, 1932) 98; for the derogation of legal provisions by fundamental rights see e.g. VfSlg. 449/1925, 617/1926.

[212] For a critique see Alexander Somek, *Rationalität und Diskriminierung* (Springer, Vienna, 2001) 109 ff, 211 ff.

more stringent in time and to scrutinize all kinds of restrictions of freedom for proportionality under article 7 Federal Constitutional Law. In this way, the right to equality before the law has become a kind of catch-all fundamental law capable of closing gaps in the catalogue of fundamental rights. On the other hand, the Constitutional Court moved from a mere formal examination over to a substantive control of infringements and limitations in respect of fundamental freedoms: first in the 1950s as regards property, applying a strict proportionality test to expropriations;[213] later in the 1980s as regards the freedom of employment in claiming a public interest for restrictions and asking if the restrictive means were suitable and adequate.[214]

Then the spell was broken. Now, the Constitutional Court is testing infringements for proportionality in respect of all other freedom-based rights as well.[215] This development has widely evened out systematic differences between fundamental rights: the absolute guarantees appear to enclose an unwritten legal reservation and a balancing test has to be conducted with regard to the public interest.[216] The only absolute ban that has resisted the demands of a balancing of interests until today is the ban on censorship.[217]

Importance was attached to the historical interpretation of the rights enshrined in the StGG.[218] In its decision VfSlg. 7400/1974, the Constitutional Court even deduced from their origin in the liberal era that their effect was limited to repelling state interventions.[219] More recently, the Constitutional Court has committed to an interpretation meeting the needs of current risks. In the examination of interferences with economic rights, it applies stringent conditions in accordance with international standards.

b) The European Convention on Human Rights

The second key source of fundamental rights is the ECHR. Following the accession of Austria to the ECHR in 1958, the National Council approved the treaty by a majority sufficient for a constitutional amendment. Due to a lack of denomination as a constitutional amendment, however, the Constitutional Court denied it had constitutional status in its decision VfSlg. 4049/1961. Moreover, it held that the treaty was not directly applicable.[220] A constitutional act passed in 1964 retroactively ascertained its constitutional status.[221] Still, the Constitutional Court first maintained its rejection of direct applicability.[222] The reason for this approach, which came in for much criticism, was its concern that large parts of criminal and civil law might have ceased to be in force because they were in conflict with the

---

[213] First signs shown in VfSlg. 1809/1949, 1853/1949; a breakthrough was achieved in VfSlg. 3666/1959. This era also generated the postulate of an (absolute) limitation on restrictions of the essence of fundamental rights (*Wesensgehalt*; VfSlg. 3118/1956, 3505/1959, 8195/1977), which gained no importance in practice.

[214] For the first time VfSlg. 10.179/1984 (control of the trade of metal scrap). For a commentary on the overturn in case-law and its implications see Walter Berka, *Die Grundrechte* (Springer, Vienna, 1999) 263 ff with further references; Manfred Stelzer, *Das Wesensgehaltsargument und der Grundsatz der Verhältnismäßigkeit* (Springer, Vienna, 1991) 143 ff.

[215] See on the freedom of art VfSlg. 11.737/1988; on the freedom to choose vocational training VfSlg. 13.845/1993; on the right to real property VfSlg. 14.701/1996.

[216] See Michael Holoubek, *Die Struktur der grundrechtlichen Gesetzesvorbehalte* (Orac, Vienna, 1997) 28.

[217] See VfSlg. 6615/1971, 8461/1978, 12.394/1990.

[218] On the right to real property see also VfSlg. 13.603/1993 with further references.

[219] In doctrine there has been opposition to this assessment and has partly pointed to the findings of historical research which deem the liberal theory of fundamental rights to be a projection of the twentieth century.

[220] See also VfSlg. 4260/1962, 4433/1963; on the lack of direct applicability see prior to that VfSlg. 3767/1960. The Constitutional Court's position follows Günther Winkler: see Günther Winkler, 'Der Verfassungsrang von Staatsverträgen', citation following Günther Winkler, *Orientierungen im öffentlichen Recht* (n 175) 51, 58 ff, and Günther Winkler, 'Zur unmittelbaren Anwendbarkeit von Staatsverträgen', ibid, 83, 93 ff.

[221] See the amendment to the Federal Constitutional Law BGBl. 1964/59.

[222] VfSlg. 4795/1964, 4885/1964.

provisions of the ECHR. After this concern had been dispelled,[223] the Constitutional Court made use of the ECHR in a manner that treated it the same as all other constitutional norms. It never doubted that its provisions ensured constitutionally guaranteed rights.[224] In recent jurisprudence, a fundamental opposition against the ECHR was hinted at in only one decision: in VfSlg. 11.500/1987 it comments on the notion of 'civil rights' in article 6 ECHR as 'almost overthrowing consequences of the recent case-law of the European Court of Human Rights' which was based on frank development of the law by judge and from which the Constitutional Court had to withdraw its support because it was bound 'by the constitutional principles of state organization'. In other respects, the Constitutional Court closely followed the steps in the development of Strasbourg case law.[225] Occasionally, it added its own original contributions by emphasizing new aspects and deduced from the ECHR higher standards of protection.[226]

The ECHR enriched the existing *acquis* of fundamental rights with security rights, rights of due process, and further freedoms. By granting rights, which are guaranteed only to nationals in the StGG 1867, as universal rights, it also enlarged the circle of persons entitled to a series of constitutional safeguards. Finally, and with respect to the substantial reservations it stipulates for statutory law to impose restrictions, it served as a catalyst for a change in the approach to national fundamental rights.[227]

c) Recent Safeguards of Fundamental Rights

The two catalogues of fundamental rights, the StGG and the ECHR, are framed by more recent fundamental rights which are in part codified in separate federal constitutional laws, in part integrated into statutory laws or state treaties. The provisions of this third layer of fundamental rights secure rights for the Slovenian and Croatian minorities;[228] they enshrine the freedom of political parties (section 1 ParteienG), data protection (section 1 DSG 2000), protection from extradition,[229] and a right to conscientious objection;[230] they enlarge and deepen the principle of equality;[231] they guarantee specific rights to children by way of a separate federal constitutional law;[232] and finally, the PersFrG is another separate federal constitutional law safeguarding the right to personal liberty. The PersFrG is characteristic of the recent safeguards of fundamental rights in many respects. First, it seeks to translate the demands of the ECHR into the Austrian fundamental rights tradition in a modern way. Second, it contains an explicit principle of proportionality which is further subdivided.[233]

---

[223] By way of acceptance of the formerly repudiated concept of 'invalidation': see Robert Walter, 'Derogation oder Invalidation?', in Felix Ermacora and others (eds), *Hundert Jahre Verfassungsgerichtsbarkeit, fünfzig Jahre Verfassungsgerichtshof in Österreich* (Europa Verlag, Munich, 1968) 209, 213 ff.

[224] VfSlg. 4706/1964, 4792/1964.

[225] See Heinz Schäffer, 'Der Beitrag Österreichs zur europäischen Rechtskultur' (n 38) 57.

[226] See the decisions VfSlg. 11.506/1987, 11.776/1988, in which severe disciplinary sanctions are qualified as criminal charge in the sense of art 6 ECHR. As a consequence, it is a guarantee of a legal remedy by way of art 2 of Protocol No 7 to the ECHR.

[227] Walter Berka, *Verfassungsrecht* (n 203) recital 1173.

[228] See the provisions art 7 No 2 to 4 State Treaty of Vienna passed in 1955, section 7 Minority School Act for *Carinthia* (BGBl. 1959/101 as amended by BGBl. 2021/170), section 1 Minority School Act for *Burgenland* (BGBl. 1994/641 as amended by BGBl. 2018/101).

[229] See sections 12 and 44 Extradition and Mutual Assistance Act, BGBl. 1979/529.

[230] Section 1 Conscientious Objection Act (*ZivildienstG*), BGBl. 1986/679 as amended by BGBl. I 2020/16.

[231] See the Federal Constitutional Act on the Elimination of All Forms of Racial Discrimination (*BVG zur Durchführung des Internationalen Übereinkommens über die Beseitigung aller Formen rassischer Diskriminierung*), BGBl. 1973/390; art 7 para 1 cl 3 and 4, para 2 and para 3 Federal Constitutional Law.

[232] See the Federal Constitutional Act on the Rights of Children (*BVG über die Rechte von Kindern*), BGBl. I 2011/4.

[233] See art 1 para 3 and 4 PersFrG.

Third, its safeguards occasionally go into great detail and significantly surpass article 5 ECHR in terms of their sophistication.

d) Extent and Binding Force of Fundamental Rights

Fundamental rights are binding on the state in all its forms: legislation is equally submitted to them as is the executive, and both public administration and acts of administrative authorities under private law are measured against them. Private individuals, however, are only bound by fundamental rights if they are either exercising public duties (*Beliehene*) or if the relevant fundamental rights provision explicitly orders so. This is only the case with the fundamental right to data protection.

The complaint to the Constitutional Court for violations of constitutionally guaranteed rights (article 144 para 1 1st alternative Federal Constitutional Law) is specifically designed to enforce fundamental rights. It may only be lodged against decisions and orders of the administrative courts, not against decisions and orders of civil and criminal courts. The effect of this specific characteristic of the Austrian constitutional jurisdiction is that neither the ordinary courts nor the Supreme Administrative Court are subject to control for a violation of fundamental rights by the Constitutional Court. The possibility to lodge an application against decisions of the courts after exhaustion of domestic remedies with the European Court of Human Rights is a functional substitute for this deficiency.

The second significant mechanism to enforce fundamental rights is the competence of the Constitutional Court to review statutory laws according to article 140 Federal Constitutional Law. As the violation of constitutionally guaranteed rights is a violation of the constitution, it can and it must result in the repeal of the reviewed statutory law by the Constitutional Court. The fact that all courts may challenge legislation ensures that their decisions are taken on constitutionally unobjectionable bases: as far as concerns are raised and relevant reasons are given against the constitutionality of a statutory law, the courts are obliged to appeal to the Constitutional Court, even where they are not convinced of its unconstitutionality.[234] In ordinary jurisdiction, where a complaint against a decision is not admissible, the parties to a proceeding may at least challenge the legal provisions applied by the court in the first instance proceedings before the Constitutional Court. Finally, private individuals can challenge statutory laws by which they are directly and actually affected in their rights and where the use of a legal remedy against the concrete act of enforcement of the law would constitute an unacceptable resort (*Individualantrag*).[235] Broadly equivalent instruments are available to challenge ordinances (article 139 Federal Constitutional Law), re-enactments (article 139a Federal Constitutional Law), and state treaties (article 140a Federal Constitutional Law).

7. Terms for the Entity

In its terminology, the Federal Constitutional Law follows an unemotional approach. It does not include a preamble; the terms used are technical-legal; everything pathetic or political is evaded as far as possible. To give an example, it speaks of 'constitutionally guaranteed rights' instead of fundamental rights or fundamental freedoms. With this tenor, a distinction is made in the constitution between state authority (*Staatsgewalt*) and the state as a whole.

---

[234] Heinz Mayer, Gabriele Kucsko-Stadlmayer, and Karl Stöger, *Grundriss des österreichischen Bundesverfassungsrechts* (n 76) recital 1111 with further references.

[235] See Theo Öhlinger and Harald Eberhard, *Verfassungsrecht* (n 61) recital 1019 ff with further references.

a) Law instead of *Gewalt*

The Federal Constitutional Law is a largely non-violent constitution. In contrary to the December Constitution of 1867,[236] it strictly abstains from any terminology referring to *Gewalt* or power.[237] Instead of legislative, executive and judicial power, it uses the terms legislation (*Gesetzgebung*), enforcement (*Vollziehung*), and jurisdiction (*Gerichtsbarkeit*). The constitution even renounces the expression separation of powers. It rather relies on the allocation of competences and regulation of relations between legal bodies. This emphasis on legal instead of political concepts reflects the influence of the Pure Theory of Law (*Reine Rechtslehre*), which largely views state and law as identical.

b) Republic Instead of *Staat*

It is along this line that the term state is used sparingly by the Federal Constitutional Law. It knows the terms *Bundesstaat* (federal state), *Staatsbürgerschaft* (citizenship), *Staatssprache* (national language), *Staatsvertrag* (state treaty), *Staatssekretär* (state secretary), *Staatswirtschaft* (state economy), and *Staatsschuld* (public debt), and it even stipulates *staatliche Verwaltung* (public administration). The mere word '*Staat*', however, is only used to refer to foreign states.[238] If its own state entity is to be addressed, the constitution regularly refers to the Republic of Austria[239] or the Republic.[240] The decisions of the courts are equally pronounced and issued 'in the name' of the Republic (article 82 para 2 Federal Constitutional Law). Recent legislation often shows that the word *Republik* is being used for the entity by explicitly naming the territorial entities Federation, *Länder*, and municipalities in brackets.[241]

D. Constitutional Identity

Identities are a cultural construct designed to hold an entity together. Those who seek to create them are reacting to threats to the entity. And as the threats change, so the identities are subject to continuous change. For the Austrian state and its constitutional law, three narratives can be identified which were able to build unity and convey uniqueness.

1. Continuity between the First and the Second Republic

After a phase of hesitation, restored Austria decided after 1945 to slip back into the constitution it had put away two eras earlier like an ill-fitting suit. The identity of the constitution was to emphasize the identity of the state and to support the thesis of the occupation of Austria

---

[236] The terms '*richterliche Gewalt*' (judicial power) and '*Regierungs- und Vollzugsgewalt*' (government and executive power) were used by two Basic Laws (*Staatsgrundgesetze*) even in their titles.

[237] See Hans Kelsen, Georg Froehlich, and Adolf Merkl, *Bundesverfassung vom 1. Oktober 1920* (n **50**) 65: '*Für die Sphäre des Rechtes und der juristischen Betrachtung kommen eben nicht Gewalten, sondern nur Rechtsnormen, die Kompetenz statuieren, in Betracht*'. ['For the sphere of law and legal consideration not powers, but only legal norms stating competency, are to be considered'].

[238] See art 9 para 2 Federal Constitutional Law (foreign states), art 16 para 1 Federal Constitutional Law (neighbouring states).

[239] See e.g. art 6 para 1, 8a para 1 and 2, 23a para 1 Federal Constitutional Law; see also the Declaration of Independence, StGBl. 1945/1.

[240] See e.g. art 8 para 1, 62 para 1, 65 para 1, 82 para 2 Federal Constitutional Law.

[241] See e.g. art 7 para 1, 8 para 2 Federal Constitutional Law; sections 1–6 Federal Constitutional Act on National Objectives, BGBl. I 2013/111.

by the German *Reich*.[242] However, another decisive fact for the return was that there was not much left, apart from the mothballed old clothes, which could have conveyed republican identity. The Federal Constitutional Law of 1920 was never able to arouse emotions or even constitutional patriotism, still: in the beginning, the Republic of Austria was not much more than this constitution. Therefore, there is an inner logic in the fact that, despite the reluctance of the Allies, the Second Republic reclaimed the constitution in which the First Republic had been established. To reach this aim, even a break with formal legal continuity was accepted in 1946.

It may well be that the life-lie of new beginning, which helped to blank out the era of Austrofascism 1933–1938 and the membership of Austria in the national socialist German *Reich* 1938–1945, was an invitation to exaggerate the construction of continuity and identity. In the practice of public law of the Second Republic, the original context of the Federal Constitutional Law of 1920 became more present and decisive than it had ever been in the First Republic.

2. Permanent Neutrality

With the end of the allied occupation, neutrality became an identity-creating constitutional principle. It was a code for liberation and a sign for Austria's regained sovereignty. From the beginning, it bore mythical elements. The first myth was that Austria declared neutrality 'of its own accord without external obligation': in truth, Austria followed an obligation under international law. The second myth was the fact that neutrality was to be 'permanent': to make this commitment to neutrality properly permanent would have implied a total revision and would therefore have required a referendum.[243] By now, as a result of the membership to the UN and the accession to the European Union, neutrality has entirely transcended into myth. Special provisions on constitutional level (articles 23 ff Federal Constitutional Law) establish obligations which cannot be reconciled with a classical form of neutrality; a fundamentally modified approach to neutrality further reduced the remaining substance.[244] Still, neutrality remains an important element of the emotional identity of Austrians.

3. The Basic Constitutional Order

From the perspective of constitutional law, identity aligns with the basic constitutional order, which has entered public awareness on the occasion of the referendum on access to the EU. As portrayed, jurisprudence and doctrine deduce from the constitutional revision norm, which subjects 'any total revision of the federal constitution' to an obligatory referendum (article

---

[242] Leopold Werner, 'Das Wiedererstehen Österreichs als Rechtsproblem' (1946) Juristische Blätter 85–93, 105–8; 'Nachwort' (1947) Juristische Blätter 137–45, 161–64; looking back: Felix Ermacora, *Österreichische Verfassungslehre* (Braumüller, Vienna, 1970) 61 ff.

[243] For details see Rainer Lippold, 'Strukturfragen der Verfassung am Beispiel der immerwährenden Neutralität Österreichs' (1991) 42 Austrian Journal of Public and International Law (Zeitschrift für Öffentliches Recht) 295–318.

[244] See Stefan Griller, 'Vom Wandel der immerwährenden Neutralität', in Österreichische Parlamentarische Gesellschaft (ed), *Festschrift 75 Jahre Bundesverfassung* (Verlag Österreich, Vienna, 1995) 729–753.

44 para 3 Federal Constitutional Law), 'building laws' (*Baugesetze*) or fundamental principles which constitute the whole order. This basic constitutional order is the layer of norms which actually fulfils constitutional functions; according to theory and jurisprudence, it is established without involvement of the parliament. According to jurisprudence, democracy (article 1 Federal Constitutional Law), federalism (article 2 Federal Constitutional Law), and the rule of law are constitutional principles (VfSlg. 2455/1952). Doctrine distinguishes democracy from republic and further subdivides the rule of law into three principles: rule of law in a narrower sense, separation of powers, and fundamental rights (so-called 'liberal' principle).[245] Postulates which go beyond these and seek to recognize also permanent neutrality, social welfare, participation in European integration, state secularism, sovereignty, or municipal self-government (and many others) as fundamental principles have remained marginal positions.[246]

The specifically Austrian facets of democracy, republic, federalism, rule of law, separation of powers, and safeguards of fundamental rights are illustrated in Section C. Of course, not all of these details on the concrete design of these fundamental principles form part of the basic constitutional order, which is beyond the reach of parliament as a constitutional legislator (with the power to partially amend the constitution). It is not the intention of the following summary to explore the core of the constitution which may only be amended under arduous conditions. It rather seeks to place emphasis on the particularities which might surprise foreign observers.

With regard to the concept of democracy, it is remarkable that jurisprudence and doctrine have consistently developed its tie with the concept of rule of law and have inaugurated law enacted by parliament as the centre of democratic government. Moreover, authoritarian elements like the hierarchy inside the administration system exist alongside the democratic essentials. It is a characteristic of the republican feature of the constitution that it bans the use of titles of nobility[247] and that it took precautions against a restoration of monarchy until 2011 by refusing the right to assume to the position of head of state to members of (former) ruling dynasties.

The characteristics of federalism are the principle of parity of Federation and *Länder* (rejecting the traditional supremacy of federal law over the law of the *Länder*), the restriction of federal supervisory powers to legal supervision, the preference given to judicial settlement of conflicts, the monopoly of the federation in criminal and civil judiciary, the importance of administration being executed by authorities of the *Länder* on behalf of the federation (indirect federal administration, *mittelbare Bundesverwaltung*), and the limited range of competences enjoyed by the *Länder*.

The approach to the notion of '*Rechtsstaat*' (rule of law) is oriented to the theory of the hierarchy of norms and places emphasis on legal certainty. As a consequence of this approach, legislation seems to be superior to enforcement. The principle of separation of judiciary and administration is understood in a formal way and is interpreted as a ban on reciprocal influence. As a result, it is not only the courts which are protected from interference

---

[245] Robert Walter, *Österreichisches Bundesverfassungsrecht. System* (n 98) 103; Heinz Peter Rill, and Heinz Schäffer, 'Art 44 B-VG' (n 109) 21; Theo Öhlinger and Harald Eberhard, *Verfassungsrecht* (n 61) recital 63; Heinz Mayer, Gabriele Kucsko-Stadlmayer, and Karl Stöger, *Grundriss* (n 61) recital 146.

[246] For references and a critique see Heinz Peter Rill and Heinz Schäffer, 'Art 44 B-VG' (n 109) recital 22 ff.

[247] The ECtHR held this to be part of the national identity of the Republic of Austria in the sense of Art 4 (2) EU Treaty in its decision *Sayn-Wittgenstein*, Case C-208/09, Slg. 2010 I-13718.

by the administration, but also the administration, which is protected from judicial control, unless special constitutional provisions (like the stipulations of the Federal Constitutional Law on the administrative judiciary) pave the way for examination of administrative acts. The structure of the rule of law is finalized by the constitutional judiciary watching over both the constitutionality of laws and the legality of ordinances.

2

The Evolution and *Gestalt* of the Czech Constitution

David Kosař and Ladislav Vyhnánek[*]

A. Introduction	56	6. An Over-Judicialized Constitution	77
B. The Origins of the Current Constitution	58	7. Where Are the People?	80
1. Sources of Inspiration	60	8. A Danger of Democratic Backsliding	80
2. Between Klaus and Havel: Drafting the Constitution	61	D. Basic Structures and Concepts	82
3. The Final Product: A Fragile Compromise	63	1. Formal Aspects of the Czech Constitutional *Gestalt*	82
C. The Evolution of the Constitution (Post-1993 Development of the Czech Constitutional *Gestalt* and Major Challenges)	65	a) The Polycentric Constitution and Sources of Constitutional Law	83
		b) A Rigid Constitution	85
1. Dealing with the Past and Building the Material *Rechtsstaat*	65	2. Substantive Aspects of the Czech Constitutional *Gestalt*	88
2. The 1998 Opposition Agreement and the Growing Distrust in Traditional Political Parties	67	a) Human Rights Constitutionalism	88
		b) Democratic Principle and Popular Sovereignty	90
3. Accession to the European Union	68	c) The *Rechtsstaat* Principle	91
4. Economic Crisis and the Constitutional Dimension of Social Conflicts	73	d) Separation of Powers	95
		e) Unity and Decentralization	97
5. The Two-Headed Executive: Weak Governments and Trouble-Making Presidents	75	E. Constitutional Identity	99
		F. Conclusion	107

Abbreviations

BVerfG	*Bundesverfassungsgericht* (German Federal Constitutional Court)
CCC	Czech Constitutional Court
CEE	Central and Eastern Europe
Charter	Czech Charter of Fundamental Rights and Freedoms
CJDCC	Collection of Judgments and Decisions of the Constitutional Court
CJEU	Court of Justice of the European Union
EU	European Union
EU Charter	Charter of Fundamental Rights of the European Union

[*] Rulings of the Czech Constitutional Court: Important rulings (all judgments and some decisions) of *Ústavní soud České republiky* (the Czech Constitutional Court) are published in the printed publication called the 'Collection of Judgments and Decisions of the Constitutional Court'. All rulings (judgments, decisions as well as opinions) of the Czech Constitutional Court are available at its website: http://www.usoud.cz/.

David Kosař and Ladislav Vyhnánek, *The Evolution and* Gestalt *of the Czech Constitution* In: *The Max Planck Handbooks in European Public Law.* Edited by: Armin von Bogdandy, Peter M Huber, and Sabrina Ragone, Oxford University Press.
© David Kosař and Ladislav Vyhnánek 2023. DOI: 10.1093/oso/9780198726425.003.0002

ECHR European Convention for the Protection of Human Rights and Fundamental Freedoms
ECtHR European Court of Human Rights
FCCC Constitutional Court of the Czech and Slovak Federal Republic
ICCC Interwar Czechoslovak Constitutional Court
LCC Law on the Constitutional Court of 16 June 1993 (see below).

A. Introduction

In 2018, Czechia celebrated twenty-five years of its own statehood and a century since Czechoslovakia came into being. The latter anniversary was by far the more important as all Czech leaders, unlike their Slovak counterparts,[1] have always considered Czechoslovakia as their own state[2] and viewed Czechia as a natural successor state.[3] In fact, the number '8' has a special place in Czech history.[4] In 1918, Czechoslovakia gained independence from Austria-Hungary in the wake of the First World War. In 1938, the Western powers (France, Britain, and Italy) met Hitler in Munich and eventually consented to the annexation of Czechoslovakia's *Sudetenland* (mostly Western Bohemia) by Hitler's Germany.[5] A few days later, German troops marched into the *Sudetenland*, which became officially a part of the Third Reich. This marked an end to democratic statehood in the Czech lands for almost fifty years, as in February 1948 the Communist Party successfully completed a coup d'état and in 1968, when the Czechs wanted to liberalize their communist regime, the Soviet Union and its allies invaded Czechoslovakia. All of these events left a deep imprint on the Czech constitutional *Gestalt*.

---

[1] It is telling that Vladimír Mečiar, the first Slovak Prime Minister (1992–1998), deleted 28 October—the most important national holiday in Czechoslovakia and in the Czech Republic, which marks the beginning of an independent Czechoslovak state in 1918—from the list of national holidays (see Law No. 241/1993 Z. z., on National Holidays, Days of Rest, and Memorial Days). 28 October was reinstated to the list of National Holidays in Slovakia only in 2020.

[2] Czechoslovakia has historically been seen by a significant proportion of Slovak society as a 'Czech project' and the 1992 Slovak Constitution builds more on the ethnic understanding of the Slovak nation. See Juraj Marušiak, 'Ústavy SR a ČR a ich úloha v procese konštruovania národných identít', in Vladimír Goněc (ed), *Česko-slovenská historická ročenka* (Stredoeurópska vysoká škola v Skalici, Bratislava, 2013) 96. In Czechia, there is an overwhelming consensus that views Czechoslovakia as a basis for modern Czech statehood. Generally, see also Eric Stein, *Czecho/Slovakia: Ethnic Conflict, Constitutional Fissure, Negotiated Breakup* (Michigan University Press, Ann Arbor, MI, 1997).

[3] Even though this view is not a correct one under public international law as both new states, Czechia and Slovakia, had to undertake a procedure of admission (as new member states) to international organizations Czechoslovakia had been a member prior to dissolution. For further details, see e.g. Tomáš Dumbrovský and Kristýna Urbanová, 'From Velvet Revolution to Purple Dissolution: Dismantling of Czechoslovakia From Above', in Sara McGibbon, Lea Raible, and Jure Vidmar (eds), *Research Handbook on Secession* (Edward Elgar, Northampton, MA, 2020); Mahulena Hofmann, 'Czechoslovakia, Dissolution of', in Rüdiger Wolfrum (ed), *Max Planck Encyclopedia of Public International Law (MPEPIL)* https://opil.ouplaw.com/view/10.1093/law:epil/978019 9231690/law-9780199231690-e1024 (last accessed on 13 March 2022); and Patrick Dumberry, *A Guide to State Succession in International Investment Law* (Edward Elgar, Northampton, MA, 2018) 143–155.

[4] The importance of the years ending with '8' is generally accepted in the Czech popular literature, see e.g. František Emmert, *Osudové osmičky v našich dějinách* (Computer Press, Prague, 2008). On the other hand, many important events took place also in other years and many historians have warned against overemphasizing and oversymbolizing the years ending with '8' (see e.g. František Šulc, 'Osudové české osmičky' (Lidovky.cz, 29 December 2007) https://www.lidovky.cz/noviny/osudove-ceske-osmicky.A071229_000110_ln_noviny_sko (last accessed on 13 March 2022); and Martin Janda, 'České osudové osmičky 20. století' (21.stoleti.cz, 19 March 2008) https://21stoleti.cz/2008/03/19/ceske-osudove-osmicky-20-stoleti/ (last accessed on 13 March 2022).

[5] See the Munich Agreement (30 September 1938), the settlement reached by Germany, Great Britain, France, and Italy that permitted German annexation of the Sudetenland in Western Czechoslovakia.

This chapter provides a condensed look at the Czech constitutional *Gestalt*.[6] It argues that, in order to understand it, it is necessary to go beyond the text of the 1993 Czech Constitution and view it also as a historical, political, and social phenomenon. More specifically, we show that the Czech constitutional system has been built on liberal democratic values and on the legacy of the first Czechoslovak Republic. The key institutions and the general constitutional design have followed well-tested constitutional patterns and the early experience with the functioning of the new constitutional system lent themselves to optimistic interpretations. At the same time, we stress some dangerous subtones of the Czech constitutional development that are often neglected by constitutional law scholars.

While the system still seems to be in a relatively good shape, its future is hard to predict and even the evaluation of constitutional-political and social developments within the last decade is a difficult task. Even though the Czech constitutional landscape has not been subject to changes and challenges of the same magnitude as some of its Visegrád counterparts (Slovakia[7] in the 1990s and Hungary[8] and Poland[9] in the 2010s), there are clear signs of its fragility and susceptibility to democratic backsliding. The reasons of the fragility do not lie in the structure of the constitutional system itself, but rather in the social underpinning of the key constitutional values. This makes Czechia a particularly interesting case as it is arguably an outlier among the Visegrád countries, but we do not know for how long.

We may thus ask what explains the differences between the Visegrád countries when just sixteen years ago, when they joined the European Union, they were seen as a bloc and as the good pupils of democratic transition. Are the Czech constitutional values rooted deeply enough to withstand a real earthquake? Will Czechia follow the path that Hungary and Poland now seem to be taking? Are the recent events in Czechia just a necessary child illness of the constitutional system taken out of proportion by their observers and the outlier status of Czechia as a democratic outpost in Central Europe still holds? We cannot claim that we know the answers, but a careful analysis of the Czech constitutional *Gestalt* can bring us closer to them.

The structure of this chapter is as follows. Section B analyses the historical, political, and social context of the 1993 Constitution with an emphasis on the drafting process and the sources that inspired the new Czech constitutional system. Section C then identifies critical junctures of the post-1993 constitutional development as well as the new challenges that the Czech constitutional system faces. These two sections are crucial building blocks for understanding the Czech constitutional *Gestalt* as they explain key constitutional narratives. The following two sections zero in on constitutional doctrines and theories: Section D analyses the basic structural aspects of the Czech constitutional system and its key principles. Section E then critically analyses the Czech constitutional identity. Section F concludes.

---

[6] By 'Czech constitutional *Gestalt*' we mean an overall picture of the Czech constitutional landscape that encompasses constitutional doctrines, normative constitutional theories, as well as constitutional narratives.

[7] See e.g. Herbert Kitschelt, *Post-Communist Party Systems: Competition, Representation, and Inter-Party Cooperation* (CUP, Cambridge, 1999) 42; and Valerie Bunce and Sharon Wolchik, 'The 1998 Elections in Slovakia and the 2000 Elections in Croatia: The Model Solidifies and Is Transferred', in Valerie Bunce and Sharon Wolchik (eds), *Defeating Authoritarian Leaders in Post-Communist Countries* (CUP, Cambridge, 2011) 53–84.

[8] See e.g. Gábor Halmai, 'From the "Rule of Law Revolution" to the Constitutional Counter-Revolution in Hungary', in Wolfgang Bedenek (ed), *European Yearbook of Human Rights* (Intersentia, Cambridge, 2012) 367; Renáta Uitz, 'Can you tell when an illiberal democracy is in the making? An appeal to comparative constitutional scholarship from Hungary' (2015) 13 International Journal of Comparative Law 279.

[9] See Wojciech Sadurski, *Poland's Constitutional Breakdown* (OUP, Oxford, 2019); and Fryderyk Zoll and Leah Wortham, 'Judicial independence and accountability: Withstanding political stress in Poland' (2019) 42 Fordham International Law Journal 875.

B. The Origins of the Current Constitution

The 1993 Constitution came into being as a direct consequence of the dissolution of Czechoslovakia,[10] but the context of its origins is much more complex. Four direct factors have arguably influenced the drafting process and the future constitutional system more than anything else. Besides that, some older indirect sources of inspiration have to be mentioned in order to fully appreciate the complex nature of the Czech constitutional thought.

First, even though it is, strictly speaking, not a revolutionary constitution,[11] the 1993 Czech Constitution has several revolutionary features. The process of its drafting and its resulting content were inevitably shaped by the 1989 Velvet Revolution. At the time of the drafting of the 1993 Constitution, the communist regime and its injustices were still fresh in the memories of the key stakeholders as the Velvet Revolution had taken place less than three years before. The deeply rooted desire that power should be exercised in a different way from in the past reflected 'the fears originating in, and related to, the previous political regime',[12] in which power was monopolized by Communists. This reflection on the communist past became so imprinted on the Czech Constitution's DNA that it shaped not only the constitutional text itself, but its further development and constitutional practice. The 1993 constitutional system thus should be understood as a reaction to the totalitarian past of the Czech nation. This was, of course, most clearly visible in the initial phases of the Czech constitutional development in the 1990s, but it has remained a strong factor influencing the functioning of the constitutional system until today.

Second, the division of Czechoslovakia surprised many, including constitutional drafters and scholars, and resulted in a hasty drafting process within a rather narrow circle of experts. Unlike in Poland (1997) and Hungary (2011), the Czech constitutional drafters thus had little time to scrutinize the most institutional choices, some of which were made 'on the way' and without much consideration. While the major political parties of that time had their say in the final shape of the 1993 Czech Constitution, they often had to defer to the expert drafting group. There was simply not enough time to come up with alternative solutions, as virtually all the work had to be done within less than six months (between July and December 1992).

Third, Czechs have always viewed the First Czechoslovak Republic (1918–1938) as the golden era of Czech constitutionalism,[13] and hence the 1920 Czechoslovak Constitution served as a template for drafting the new one. While the golden era view might be considered an idealization of an imperfect political community and constitutional system,[14] it was still the only era which could reasonably provide a historical foundation for Czech modern democratic statehood.[15]

---

[10] For a concise description of the negotiated break-up of Czechoslovakia see Eric Stein, *Czecho/Slovakia* (n 2).

[11] A series of amendments of the Czechoslovak socialist federative constitution was adopted as an immediate reaction to the 1989 Velvet revolution.

[12] András Sajó, *Limiting Government* (CEU Press, Budapest, 1999) 2.

[13] This view dates to the First Czechoslovak Republic. Tellingly, first two Czechoslovak Presidents, Tomáš Garrigue Masaryk and Edvard Beneš, portrayed Czechoslovakia as the 'Switzerland of the East', see Andrea Orzoff, *Battle for the Castle: The Myth of Czechoslovakia in Europe, 1914–1948* (OUP, Oxford, 2009).

[14] This is not an isolated view. See for example Mary Heiman, *Czechoslovakia: The State that Failed* (Yale University Press, New Haven, CT, 2009); and Andrea Orzoff, *Battle for the Castle* (n 13).

[15] For further details see Eric Stein, *Czecho/Slovakia* (n 2); Abby Innes, *Czechoslovakia: The Short Goodbye* (Yale University Press, New Haven, CT, 2001); Veronika Svoboda, *Vznik Ústavy České republiky* (PhD thesis 2018) 107, available at:140066181.pdf (cuni.cz) (last accessed on 13 March 2022); and David Kosař, Jiří Baroš, and Pavel Dufek, 'The twin challenges to separation of powers in Central Europe: Technocratic governance and populism' (2019) 15 EuConst 427, 442–443.

Last but not least, following decades of isolation from the Western world in terms of values, economy, and even very basic interpersonal relationships, there was a strong sense of 'coming back to Europe', to the cultural space where Czech society thought it belonged and from which it was violently torn. Czechoslovakia thus soon after the Velvet Revolution became a member of the Council of Europe. Czechia then yearned to join the NATO and the European Union. To make the latter happen, it even happily embraced the 1993 Copenhagen Criteria[16] and initiated the cumbersome accession process.[17]

In sum, each of these four major factors has left a mark, each in its own way, on the constitutional *Gestalt* of newly independent Czechia.[18] However, the process of drafting the Czech Constitution was affected also by foreign sources, the practical exigencies, and the politics of the day. In particular, the tensions between Czechoslovak President Václav Havel and the Czech Prime Minister Václav Klaus framed the drafting as well as the implementation of the Czech Constitution for more than a decade. We will discuss these influences in more depth in the subsections that follow.

Besides these rather direct influences, the origins of the Czech Constitution (and even more the origins of some later tensions) cannot be fully understood without appreciating some older crossroads of the Czech statehood. These are still represented in the Czech popular conscience and represent—in the minds of many—the main determinants of the Czech constitutional project. The impact on popular conscience of the Hussite movement and the following Czech branch of reformation (especially the Czech Brethren) cannot be understated. The evaluation of the Hussite movement and the values it represented was at the very heart of the later identity-defining debates of twentieth century. These debates raged especially during the first Czechoslovak Republic, but even the Communist regime 'borrowed' the Hussite movement in order to justify its identity and trace its roots to the defining moments of the Czech statehood. Even though seemingly forgotten history, the Hussite movement (or often its modern and often self-serving interpretations) has not lost its ties to the Czech statehood. On the one hand, it can be used to argue that equality and social justice have always been key Czech national values. On the other hand, the value of independence or even nationalist arguments and distrust towards foreign elements can also be tied to the interpretation of the Hussite period. One cannot forget that after the end of the fifteenth century, the Czech lands were gradually integrated into the Habsburg monarchy (the important dates being 1526 and 1620). The perception of subjugation to foreign powers (sometimes referred to as 'The Darkness Period') has also persisted in the Czech popular conscience. The notion of the Czech 'Hussite statehood' was thus a semi-direct predecessor of the first Czechoslovak Republic. Czechia—willingly or not—has inherited perceptions and debates about 'the purpose of the Czech history'. Is the purpose of existence

---

[16] The Copenhagen criteria (after the European Council in Copenhagen in 1993 which defined them) are the essential conditions all candidate countries must satisfy to become EU member states (see Presidency Conclusions, Copenhagen European Council 1993).

[17] For further details see Dimitry Kochenov, *EU Enlargement and the Failure of Conditionality: Pre-Accession Conditionality in the Fields of Democracy and the Rule of Law* (Kluwer Law International, Alphen aan den Rijn, 2008).

[18] The name 'Czechia' is new, approved in 2016 by the Czech Cabinet as the official short name of the Czech Republic. We use the name Czechia to describe the Czech Republic (1993–today) and the Czech part of Czechoslovakia (1918–1992) in order to avoid confusion as the term 'Czech Republic' meant different things in Czech modern history. In 1918–1968 the 'Czech Republic' did not officially exist (a more common term in that era was 'Czech lands' [*České země*]), after the federalization of Czechoslovakia the term 'Czech Republic' referred to the Czech subunit in the federation (1969–1992), and only after the division of Czechoslovakia did it become the official title of the independent Czech state.

of the Czech(oslovak) state simply to pursue the ideals of humanity, as Masaryk claimed?[19] Or should we define our statehood in nationalist terms and search for the specific values of the *Czech* nation? Conflicting attitudes towards this central problem are still at the heart of Czech constitutional-political tensions.[20]

1. Sources of Inspiration

One must concede that the Czech constitutional system is not an entirely original one. Even though it possesses a few distinctive features, it is still rather a mixture of several historical and foreign sources of inspiration. While a pinnacle position amongst these sources belongs arguably to the 1920 Czechoslovak Constitution,[21] foreign and international sources were also very significant. In particular, the European Convention on Human Rights[22] and the German constitutional system deserve a special mention as they heavily influenced the final shape of the Czech constitutional system.

In fact, German influence can be traced in many areas. Entrenchment of the Eternity Clause in article 9 para 2 of the Constitution,[23] many features of the original position of the President,[24] and the aforementioned strong position and extensive competences[25] of the Czech Constitutional Court (hereinafter: the 'CCC') are amongst the most important examples. Czech post-communist political leaders also intended to create a short and general constitution, and in this regard they were heavily influenced by the US Constitution.[26] The position of the Senate and its features, in particular the model of the partial replacement of a third of the senators every two years, are clearly inspired by the US and French constitutions.[27] A specific inspiration from the US model can also be traced in the procedure for the appointment of CCC Justices, which copies the US federal judges' appointment procedure.[28]

Jan Filip, a prominent Czech constitutionalist and CCC Justice, emphasizes that besides the often mentioned 'grand ideas' sources (such as the ECHR, Germany, and the United States of America), some 'lesser known' constitutions served as sources of inspiration. He mentions that some parliamentary rules of procedure were influenced by the Spanish and the then Polish constitutions.[29]

---

[19] Tomáš G Masaryk, *Česká otázka* (MKP, Praha, 2013) 250.

[20] See Section E.

[21] Veronika Svoboda, *Vznik Ústavy České republiky* (n 15) 107. It is important to note that even the 1920 Constitutional Charter was not an entirely original document as it had been partially inspired by the constitution of the Third French Republic.

[22] The UN International Covenants (ICCPR66 and ICESCR66) should also be mentioned.

[23] A more detailed account of the Eternity Clause and its importance is provided in Sections C and D.

[24] Cyril Svoboda, 'Komentář k čl. 54', in Cyril Svoboda and Dušan Hendrych (eds), *Ústava České republiky: komentář* (C.H. Beck, Praha, 1997) 82.

[25] Including—unlike many other CEE constitutional systems—the existence of a constitutional complaints procedure.

[26] Veronika Svoboda, *Vznik Ústavy České republiky* (n 15) 107. It is important to note that even the 1920 Constitutional Charter was not an entirely original document as it had been partly inspired by the constitution of the third French Republic.

[27] Jan Filip, 'Zapomenuté inspirace Ústavy ČR: k 10. výročí přijetí Ústavy ČR' (2002) 10 Časopis pro právní vědu a praxi 295, 300–301.

[28] See David Kosař and Ladislav Vyhnánek, 'The Constitutional Court of Czechia', in Armin von Bogdandy, Peter Huber, and Christoph Grabenwarter (eds), *The Max Planck Handbooks in European Public Law, Vol. III: Constitutional Adjudication: Institutions* (OUP, Oxford, 2020) 119–182.

[29] Jan Filip, 'Zapomenuté inspirace Ústavy ČR' (n 27) 300–301.

While the influence of foreign sources is indisputable, foreign international experts had very little impact on the drafting process and the final product.[30] The foreign inspiration was thus provided mainly by domestic experts with ties to or extensive knowledge of other constitutional systems,[31] by direct use of translated constitutional documents, and by trips to other countries and consultations.

2. Between Klaus and Havel: Drafting the Constitution

The drafting process itself has not until recently been comprehensively documented[32] and some of its aspects acquired an almost mythological dimension. Some partial accounts have been published in commentaries on the Constitution and several law review articles.[33] The most comprehensive document is probably the unpublished diary of Miroslav Sylla, one of the drafters. Parts of this diary have been quoted in other publications,[34] but many aspects of the drafting process have remained in the realm of oral history.[35] Very recently, Veronika Svoboda finalized her dissertation which offers the most comprehensive account of the Constitution's creation.[36]

As we have already mentioned above, the drafting process was marked by its haste and relative secrecy. Unlike in some other CEE countries, which were drafting their constitutions at roughly the same time, there was no constitutional assembly (such as in Romania[37]) nor referendum (such as in Estonia or Lithuania).[38] Instead, the major portion of drafting the Czech Constitution was done in executive-style commissions.

The governmental commission that was entrusted with drafting the constitutional proposal was established by a decision of the government in July 1992. The creation of this commission was initiated by the Prime Minister, Václav Klaus, and is considered one of his most important contributions to the drafting process. The members of the commission represented the relevant political parties,[39] the expert community and the government itself. Besides the formally appointed members, other experts, and members of the Czech National

---

[30] Veronika Svoboda, *Vznik Ústavy České republiky* (n 15) 89–90.

[31] Future Justices of the CCC Vladimír Klokočka and Vojtěch Cepl were particularly important in this regard. Vladimír Klokočka was academically active in Germany and Vojtěch Cepl provided his knowledge of US law and other common law sources. This tendency to rely on comparative materials can also be traced in their subsequent judicial activities.

[32] The most comprehensive set of the relevant documents is Jindřiška Syllová and Miroslav Sylla, *Ústava České republiky 1992: Dokumenty a ohlasy* (Wolters Kluwer, Alphen aan den Rijn, 2018).

[33] The texts by Jan Broz (Jan Broz, 'Vznik návrhu Ústavy ČR pohledem členů vládní a parlamentní komise', in Jan Broz and Jan Chmel (eds), *Pohled za oponu: studie o vzniku Ústavy České republiky a o kontextu její interpretace* (Leges, Prague, 2017) 11) and Miloslav Výborný (Miloslav Výborný, 'K okolnostem přípravy Ústavy ČR z parlamentní perspektivy', in Jan Kysela (ed), *Deset let Ústavy ČR: Východiska, stav, perspektivy* (Senát Parlamentu České republiky 2003) 60 deserve a special mention.

[34] See e.g. Jindřiška Syllová and Miroslav Sylla, *Ústava České republiky 1992* (n 32).

[35] See e.g. interviews with and biographies of influential CCC Justices: Tomáš Němeček, *Vojtěch Cepl: Život právníka ve 20. století* (Leges, Prague, 2010); Tomáš Němeček, *Diskrétní zóna* (Vyšehrad, Prague, 2012); Tomáš Němeček, *Padni komu padni: Život a případy Elišky Wagnerové* (Leges, Prague, 2014); Jiří Baroš (ed), *Vladimír Čermák: člověk – filozof – soudce* (Masaryk University, Brno, 2009); Antonín Procházka, *V boji za ústavnost: Ze vzpomínek bývalého ústavního soudce* (Centrum pro studium demokracie a kultury, Brno, 2008).

[36] Veronika Svoboda, *Vznik Ústavy České republiky* (n 15).

[37] See Anneli Albi, *EU Enlargement and the Constitutions of Central and Eastern Europe* (CUP, Cambridge, 2001) 21.

[38] Ibid, 22.

[39] Interestingly enough, future Justices of the CCC Vojtěch Cepl and Miloslav Výborný were amongst the members, representing two small political parties.

Council (the then Czech Chamber of the Federal Czechoslovak Parliament) attended the commission's meetings, despite opposition from Václav Klaus.[40]

At the same time, there was a parliamentary commission[41] whose task was to reflect the development of the governmental commission's work and provide it with recommendations and general feedback. The Constitution itself, after all, had to be eventually adopted by the parliament. The constitutional committee of the Czech National Council intervened in the process as well.

Finally, President Václav Havel was indirectly involved in the drafting process. His influence was mainly channelled through his personal relationships with many members of the respective commissions (e.g. Václav Benda and Vojtěch Cepl).[42] In addition, he authored several texts that he sent to the commissions in which he made clear his opinions on several constitutional issues.[43] Some people from the close circle of Havel's advisors, such as the future CCC Justice Vladimír Klokočka, exerted their influence through these channels as well.

The drafters of the Constitution unanimously agree that public opinion and the media had little to no impact on their work. Even the broader community of experts (lawyers, political scientists, and other scholars) had virtually no say in the drafting process, although some state institutions and non-governmental organizations sent their suggestions to the Czech National Council.[44] Frankly speaking, the Czech Constitution was drafted in a hasty manner by a small number of constitutional lawyers within a few weeks in 1992. This hastiness and under-inclusiveness have been criticized ever since[45] and it arguably still has a noticeable impact on the Constitution, its limited social acceptance and even on less tangible phenomena such as constitutional sentiments and constitutional identity.[46]

It is well beyond the scope and ambitions of this text to discuss all the debates and clashes surrounding the drafting of the Constitution. Therefore, we will focus only on the most significant and far-reaching ones. Moreover, it is important to emphasize that the drafters themselves have conceded that, in order to make sure that the Constitution would be adopted, many controversial issues have been omitted from the final text or intentionally addressed only vaguely.

The sources of inspiration discussed above in Section B provided a set of limits for the drafters. It was thus reasonably clear that the new constitutional system must be a standard democratic one. More specifically, the model of a parliamentary republic was an obvious choice. But beyond that, serious discussions were dedicated to many of the Constitution's features that we now consider axiomatic. Issues such as the existence of an upper legislative chamber (bicameralism), the electoral system (majoritarian or proportionate) to be used, the position of a constitutional court and the protection of fundamental rights (whether to have an 'incorporated' charter of rights or a separate charter) generated heated debates between the participants in the drafting process.

One of the important sources of the disagreements was the growing tension between (then Czechoslovak President) Václav Havel and (then Czech Prime Minister) Václav Klaus and their conflicting visions of society, politics, and law. Václav Klaus is an economist

---

[40] Veronika Svoboda, *Vznik Ústavy České republiky* (n 15) 58.
[41] It was actually established just three days after the governmental commission.
[42] Veronika Svoboda, *Vznik Ústavy České republiky* (n 15) 58.
[43] Brigita Chrastilová and Petr Mikeš, *Prezident republiky Václav Havel a jeho vliv na československý a český právní řád* (Aleš Čeněk, Ostrava, 2003) 371.
[44] Veronika Svoboda, *Vznik Ústavy České republiky* (n 15) 89.
[45] Jiří Malenovský, 'O legitimitě a výkladu české ústavy na konci století existence moderního českého státu' (2013) 152 Právník 745.
[46] See Parts C.7 and E.

who believes in the free market. He did not have much belief in legal institutions and consequently he underestimated their importance.[47] At the same time, he viewed democracy in narrow Schumpeterian terms and thus he was hostile towards certain constitutional institutions and principles, such as the separation of powers, the protection of fundamental rights, and constitutional review, as they, in his opinion, unnecessarily complicate democratic procedures.[48] On a more pragmatic level, his goal was to weaken the position of the President. While Václav Klaus succeeded in reducing the power of the President,[49] even his influence was not great enough to prevent the inclusion of the aforementioned key principles of modern constitutionalism.

After roughly five months, in November 1992, the government proposal was finalized. On 16 December 1992, the proposal was to be discussed in the Czech National Council. Following a crucial political agreement, in accordance with which the representatives of the coalition parties promised not to propose or support any kind of amendment,[50] the Constitution was adopted by a convincing majority: 172 out of 198 MPs present voted in its favour.

3. The Final Product: A Fragile Compromise

Thus, despite all the tensions and conflicting opinions, a compromise was reached. The drafters as well as MPs preferred the model of multiple constitutional documents. The Constitution itself consists of eight parts: (1) Basic Provisions; (2) Legislative Power; (3) Executive Power; (4) Judicial Power; (5) the Supreme Auditing Office; (6) the Czech National Bank; (7) Territorial Self-Government; and (8) Final and Inter-Temporal Provisions. In addition, the Constitution contains a Preamble which refers to its value inspirations and provides helpful assistance in interpreting it. Interestingly, the drafters of the Czech Constitution decided to omit fundamental rights from the Constitution and entrenched in a separate constitutional document, the Charter (see below Sections C and D.2.a).

The first part of the Constitution, despite Václav Klaus's aforementioned scepticism, emphasized liberal democratic values, such as democracy, the separation of powers, the rule of law, and fundamental-rights protection. The principle of the separation of powers was adopted in its classical tripartite form, but the Constitution also created two specific independent institutions, namely the Supreme Auditing Office and the Czech National Bank. In addition, it defined Czechia as a sovereign and unitary state. Interestingly, the basic provisions also include environmental protection, one of the traceable legacies of Václav Havel. Some of those basic principles were further entrenched by the Eternity Clause.[51]

---

[47] Václav Benda, a member of the governmental commission, recounted a funny and symptomatic story in this regard. Václav Klaus, unimpressed by the commission's progress and not appreciating the importance of its constitutional discussions, repeatedly 'threatened' (not as a joke) that he would clear one weekend in his schedule and draft the constitution on his own: Veronika Svoboda, *Vznik Ústavy České republiky* (n 15) 70.

[48] Ibid.

[49] Most importantly, the Constitution does not give the President the competence to propose legislation (*legislative initiative*).

[50] Veronika Svoboda, *Vznik Ústavy České republiky* (n 15) 123–124. Some minor amendments were proposed and accepted, though (and numerous other amendments were proposed and rejected).

[51] Art 9 para 2 of the Czech Constitution. A further analysis of the basic principles and the Eternity Clause follows in Section D.

After heated debate, the concept of a two-chamber parliament won out. However, the upper chamber, the Senate, is significantly weaker. The weakness lies in the fact that it can be outvoted in cases of ordinary laws, even though an absolute majority in the Chamber of Deputies is necessary for that to happen. The Senate's consent is necessary only in the case of constitutional laws, organic laws in accordance with article 40 of the Constitution, and international treaties.[52] On the other hand, the Senate's practical significance is heightened by its asymmetrical composition. While elections to the Chamber of Deputies take place every four years[53] on the basis of a proportionate electoral system, senators are elected in staggered elections (one-third of the Senate every two years) for a six-year mandate in a two-round, first-past-the-post voting system. This often leads to the two chambers being made up of contrasting proportions of the political spectrum. As a result, the governing coalition rarely enjoys a safe majority in both houses. This institutional feature, coupled with the notoriously unstable position of governments in the Czech constitutional system,[54] makes the Senate stronger than the constitutional text would suggest. Additionally, the Senate has been entrusted with the important competence of confirming the appointment of CCC Justices.

The executive branch consists of the government, which is considered the highest executive body, and the President, who is the Head of State.[55] On paper, the President is much weaker, but in practice that is not necessarily so, especially since the introduction of the direct election of the President in 2012. In fact, the relatively strong position of the President,[56] the notorious instability of the governments and their mutual relationship have always posed a significant institutional challenge.[57] Moreover, the President has a major say in staffing the Constitutional Court as he is the only body that can nominate its Justices.[58]

Judicial power was entrusted to the ordinary courts and the Czech Constitutional Court. The very strong position of the CCC is one of the most important features of the Czech constitutional *Gestalt*, as several parts of this chapter will make clear.[59] Interestingly, from the comparative perspective, the Czech Constitution prohibits establishment of any special court[60] and explicitly abolished military justice in perpetuity.[61]

Finally, the Constitution also includes a basic framework of territorial self-government. The position of self-governmental units has been one of the more dynamic aspects of the Czech constitutional system, in terms of both legislative activity and the CCC's case law. Most importantly, the Czech parliament created Higher Self-Governmental Units in 1997 and the CCC has gradually empowered municipal authorities vis-à-vis the central state organs.[62]

---

[52] There are additional non-legislative areas in which the Senate's consent is required.

[53] Even though snap elections have been quite common in the short Czech constitutional history.

[54] See also Section C.5.

[55] Prosecutors' Offices are also mentioned as part of the executive branch (art 80 of the Constitution), but constitutional regulation has little normative significance.

[56] Which was later boosted by the introduction of the direct election of the President.

[57] For further details see Section C.5.

[58] The Senate then affirms the Justices. Czechia thus adopted the American model of selecting Justices, which is rather unusual for a parliamentary democracy. For more details, see David Kosař and Ladislav Vyhnánek, 'The Constitutional Court of Czechia' (n 28).

[59] See Sections C.6 and D.1.

[60] Art 91 para 1 of the Constitution.

[61] Art 110 of the Constitution.

[62] For further details see Section C.5.

C. The Evolution of the Constitution (Post-1993 Development of the Czech Constitutional *Gestalt* and Major Challenges)

The previous parts have sketched the origins, sources of inspiration and the final shaping of the 1993 Czech constitutional system. Before we turn to the substantive features of the Czech constitutional *Gestalt*, we must discuss the milestones of the post-1993 constitutional history and the main challenges that the young Czech constitutional system has faced. In fact, reflection on these challenges by the Czech constitutional actors has been at least as important for the resulting constitutional system as the context of its creation.

We have identified eight major post-1993 challenges that affected the Czech constitutional *Gestalt*. First, the new Czech state had to deliver on its constitutional promises. It had to establish in practice a new liberal democratic legal system, deal with the past injustices and create the institutions envisaged by the Constitution. Second, the 1998 Opposition Agreement between the two then dominant political parties (Civic Democratic Party and the Social Democratic Party) challenged the Czech electoral system and led to disillusionment of the people with traditional political parties and politics more generally. Third, Czechia had to prepare for accession to the European Union and cope with the internal legal effects of EU law. Fourth, the financial crisis forced the government to adopt controversial austerity measures and subsequently brought a new kind of cases concerning social and economic issues before the CCC. These cases, which reflected the unequal wealth distribution and other deep tensions in Czech society, turned what had been until then purely political issues into constitutional questions. Now, the genie was out of the bottle and the CCC has inevitably been drawn into the political clashes. Fifth, the introduction of the direct election of the President in 2012 further divided Czech society and weakened an already fragile government. Sixth, the CCC arguably over-judicialized the Constitution. It adopted the 'unconstitutional constitutional amendment' doctrine, judicialized issues that had been left to the political process in the 1990s (such as intraparty democracy) and started to impose its value solutions in a more aggressive way. Seventh, the rise of populism in Central Europe did not leave Czechia untouched. The ordinary people felt that they had little say about the direction of the country and thus they started to call for strong leaders, improving direct democracy and curtailing experts and technocratic institutions. As a result, there is an inherent danger of democratic backsliding in Czechia, even though this eighth challenge has not materialized yet.

1. Dealing with the Past and Building the Material *Rechtsstaat*

As mentioned above, one of the important aspects that influenced the nature of the 1993 Czech constitutional system was the relationship of the new regime with its communist, non-democratic past. It is important to note, however, that this influence did not stop on 1 January 1993. On the contrary, much of the 1990s 'everyday constitutional work' consisted of dealing with the past in one way or another.

Most of the legislative work in this regard was completed during the federal intermezzo between 1989 and 1992. In this period, the Federal Assembly adopted numerous laws aimed at dealing with past injustices. These included laws concerned restitution,[63]

---

[63] A notable exception was—until recently—the question of church restitutions. The process of restitution of church property began only in 2013, after the adoption of Law N. 428/2012 Coll. The delay may be explained by the

lustration,[64] and rehabilitation.[65] Secondly, it adopted extensive new fundamental rights legislation, including laws concerning the right to peaceful assembly,[66] the right to associate in political parties,[67] the right to petition,[68] and significant reforms of criminal and civil law.

While the legislative work was not over, much of it was done already during the federal democratic period, especially in 1991 and 1992. However, implementation of these federal laws, and thus also the responsibility for dealing with the past and building the *Rechtstaat*, became a major task of the new Czech state and the CCC in particular.[69] Consequently, the first decade of the CCC's operation is generally viewed as an era in which the CCC fought firmly to establish the basic constitutional values in the Czech legal order and to remedy past injustices. It is important in this regard that the CCC was, with a few exceptions,[70] not involved in first-order political battles with the executive and legislative branches. Instead, most of its hard 'transitional justice' work consisted of dealing with constitutional complaints against the decisions of ordinary courts.[71]

In this regard, the CCC adopted[72] and developed several constitutional doctrines and introduced them into Czech legal practice. The principle of proportionality, indirect horizontal application of fundamental rights (*Drittwirkung*), the priority of human rights-friendly interpretation (*in dubio pro libertate*),[73] and prohibition of 'excessive formalism' in statutory interpretation, are among the most important principles that the CCC fought to establish. On many occasions, it had to overcome the stiff resistance of the ordinary courts, and the Supreme Court in particular.

The contrast between the CCC's purposive and value-laden reasoning and the rather strict formalist Supreme Court's interpretation techniques even led to the so-called 'war of the courts' (*válka soudů*). The major battleground turned out to be the interpretation of article 269 para 1 of the Criminal Code concerning the conscientious objector status of Jehovah's Witnesses. While the Supreme Court held that every single evasion of military service was

---

fact that this question was—and still remains—a rather explosive politically sensitive one. This can be illustrated *inter alia* by the recent (2019) adoption of a law that introduces a new tax on property transferred during church restitutions and thus limits the church restitutions' effect.

[64] In detail, see David Kosař, 'Lustration and lapse of time: "dealing with the past" in the Czech Republic' (2008) 4 EuConst 460.

[65] N. 119/1990 Coll.

[66] N. 84/1990 Coll.

[67] N. 424/1991 Coll.

[68] N. 85/1990 Coll.

[69] See Francesco Biagi, *European Constitutional Courts and Transitions to Democracy* (CUP, Cambridge, 2020).

[70] The most important exceptions include some of the CCC judgments concerning electoral law and the financing of political parties. In the 2001 *Grand Election* judgment (judgment of 24 January 2001, Pl. ÚS 42/2000) the CCC declared unconstitutional some changes in the electoral system of the parliament's lower chamber because they introduced too many majoritarian elements into the Czech 'system of proportional representation'. In a similar vein, the CCC has generally supported equality of the chances of smaller political parties in issues like campaign or political party financing—much to the chagrin of the two major political parties led by Václav Klaus and Miloš Zeman.

[71] See Francesco Biagi, *European Constitutional Courts and Transitions to Democracy* (n 69).

[72] Many of these doctrines were 'borrowed' from the case law of the German Constitutional Court. Two of the most influential Justices of the CCC in the 1990s, Vladimír Klokočka and Pavel Hollländer, were particularly keen on searching for inspiration in Germany. As a result, there are more than sixty references to the BVerfG's jurisprudence in the CCC's case law. Moreover, the significance of the BverfG's case law is greater than the mere number of references suggests, as it shaped key constitutional doctrines in the early phases of the CCC's existence. The CCC has transplanted, among other things, the German proportionality test, and has been heavily inspired by the German approach to basic constitutional principles, such as democracy and the *Rechtsstaat*.

[73] A special variation of this principle is the preference for interpretation that favours an individual entitled to restitution of property (*in favorem restitutionis*); see for example judgment of the CCC of 21 June 2017, III. ÚS 1862/16.

a new criminal act, the CCC found this position unconstitutional for violation of freedom of conscience and the principle of *ne bis in idem*.[74] The Supreme Court refused to follow the CCC's judgments until 1999, when it eventually buckled under the growing pressure.[75] The scars have remained though, and the relationship between these two courts has always been tense.

While the CCC assumed its intended role as the guardian of the Constitution with vigour and emerged as the key player in substantive transition to democracy,[76] the involvement of other institutions was rather mixed. The executive and legislative branches obviously did their part in the continuous reform of the Czech constitutional order, but they also ignored some constitutional promises made by the 1993 Constitution.

The Senate's position is particularly important in this regard. The inclusion of the upper chamber in the Constitution was not universally applauded by politicians.[77] The resentment towards the Senate postponed its creation until 1996. Thus, for almost four years, the lower chamber of the parliament (the Chamber of Deputies) was unchecked and even assumed the specific powers of the Senate, such as the confirmation of CCC Justices.[78]

The Supreme Administrative Court shared a similar fate. The Constitution, inspired by the First Czechoslovak Republic as well as by Austria and Germany, envisaged the Supreme Administrative Court as a top court in administrative law matters and implicitly expected that a fully fledged system of administrative justice would be established. Despite this clear textual guidance, the Supreme Administrative Court came into being only in 2003. Moreover, politicians fulfilled this constitutional promise only after the CCC held that the previous incomplete system of administrative justice was unconstitutional, because it did not offer a 'full review' of administrative acts within the meaning of article 6 ECHR.[79] Without this nudge by the CCC, the creation of the Supreme Administrative Court could have taken even longer.

2. The 1998 Opposition Agreement and the Growing Distrust in Traditional Political Parties

The so-called 'Opposition Agreement'—a political pact between the two dominant political parties in the 1990s—has had a great and long-lasting impact on the Czech political and constitutional landscape. While the events leading to the conclusion of the Opposition Agreement are very complex, few moments stand out.

Following an internal split in the then ruling Civic Democratic Party in 1997, the Czech party system was rewritten. Next to the two dominant parties (Civic Democratic Party 'CDP' and the Social Democratic Party 'SDP'), a new and potentially powerful bloc of four smaller centre-right parties—the 'Coalition of Four'.[80] The new coalition, heavily supported by the

---

[74] See, for example, judgment of the CCC of 18 September 1995, IV. ÚS 81/95, and judgment of the CCC of 4 March 1998, I. ÚS 400/97.

[75] Including pressure from the newly appointed President of the Supreme Court (and a future Vice-President of the CCC), Eliška Wagnerová.

[76] See Francesco Biagi, *European Constitutional Courts and Transitions to Democracy* (n 69).

[77] The most important opponent was Václav Klaus, whose political power in the 1990s cannot be overstated. The members of the lower chamber of the parliament, especially the members of the parliamentary majority, also had little reason to support the Senate, as it limits their power by definition.

[78] The first wave of Justices in 1993 was thus confirmed by the Chamber of Deputies.

[79] Judgment of the CCC of 27 June 2001, Pl. ÚS 16/99.

[80] The 'Coalition of Four' included also two parliamentary parties at the time—Christian Democrats and the Freedom Union.

then President Václav Havel, came into being after the 1998 parliamentary elections as a counterweight to the so-called 'Opposition Agreement'. The 1998 elections resulted in a political deadlock. Neither the CDP nor the SDP could form a government on its own and neither could, nor wanted,[81] to form a coalition with other parliamentary parties. Thus, the idea of the Opposition Agreement was born. SDP and CDP, who are natural ideological opponents, formed an agreement with the following major consequences. First, the SDP managed form a minority government supported by the CDP. But, even more importantly, attempts were made to rewrite the Czech political landscape in order to allow the two biggest parties to form strong governments in the future, weaken smaller parties and curtail some of the pluralistic aspects of the Czech political system.[82]

Perhaps the most important constitutional challenge of the Opposition Agreement was the attempt to change the electoral system by introducing many majoritarian elements to the previously very proportional system. This attempt was halted by the CCC, which found most majoritarian elements of the electoral reform to be unconstitutional.[83] The boldest reform by the parties to the Opposition Agreement was thus unsuccessful. However, the legacy of the agreement itself is still alive in the public political consciousness and manifests the split between the 'pragmatic' political forces vying for strong and effective governments and the 'idealistic, Havelian' forces (the latter often being referred to scornfully as 'truth-and-lovers' or 'snowflakes'). Some authors even claim that the Opposition Agreement betrayed the voters of both parties and contributed to the growing distrust in traditional political parties and politics in general.[84] This disillusionment in turn planted the seed for the meltdown of both CDP and SDP in the 2010s and the rise of business parties and populist political movements,[85] which may, in the future, present a danger for the Czech constitutional democracy.[86] One may object that CDP and SDP were still at the peak of their power after the 2006 parliamentary elections, but the distrust in politics and traditional parties was already there.

3. Accession to the European Union

Few factors, if any, have had a greater impact on the Czech constitutional landscape than Czechia's accession to the EU, as this was arguably a once-in-a-lifetime constitutional moment. Even though the accession to the NATO was considered a key political goal of the 1990s, the European Union was considered a practically more important step. As some contemporary commentators put it, the NATO was the silver, the EU was the gold.[87]

---

[81] Especially the relationship between the later Coalition of Four member (the Freedom Union) and the CDP was soured by the internal split. The head of the CDP (future President Václav Klaus) saw it as a betrayal and the Freedom Union had great reservations concerning Václav Klaus.

[82] Among other things, the two biggest parties tried to exert their influence by controlling the Council of the Czech Television (Česká televize).

[83] Judgment of the CCC of 24 January 2001, Pl. ÚS 42/2000, *Grand Election* judgment. For further details on this judgment see below in n 133.

[84] See Lukáš Linek, *Zrazení snu?* (SLON, 2010). See also a journalistic account of this Agreement: Erik Tabery, *Vládneme, nerušit: opoziční smlouva a její dědictví* (Paseka, Prague, 2006).

[85] See Sean Hanley, 'Dynamics of new party formation in the Czech Republic 1996–2010: Looking for the origins of a "political earthquake"' (2012) 28 East European Politics 119 (see as well Tim Haughton, Vlastimil Havlik, and Kevin Deegan-Krause, 'Czech elections have become really volatile. This year was no exception' (Washington Post, 24 October 2017).

[86] See Sean Hanley and Milada Anna Vachudová, 'Understanding the illiberal turn: democratic backsliding in the Czech Republic' (2018) 34 East European Politics 8, 276. See also Sections C.7 and C.8 below.

[87] Václav Bartuška, 'Jsme členem NATO, alliance má nyní 19 členů' (iDNES.cz, 14 March, 1999) https://www.idnes.cz/zpravy/domaci/jsme-clenem-nato-aliance-ma-nyni-19-clenu.A_990311_200409_domaci_jkl (last accessed on 13 March 2022).

The EU's constitutional importance can be traced in at least four relatively separate dimensions. First, as already mentioned, the political goal of 'coming back to Europe' was an important factor that influenced the drafting process of the Czech constitutional documents. While the adoption of liberal democratic values by the Czech constitution is not exclusively attributable to the EU and the prospect of accession, it surely played a role.

At a more specific level, the Czech government and parliament had to negotiate, prepare, and adopt extensive changes to legislation as well as some structural constitutional changes (the so called 'Euro-Amendment' of the Constitution) that were supposed to prepare Czechia for accession and the subsequent operation of EU law within the domestic legal order. The most important constitutional changes in this regard concerned revising article 10 of the Constitution (concerning the status of international treaties in the Czech constitutional order) and adding a new article 10a (which allows the transfer of power to international organization such as the EU). These changes made Czechia a fully monist state and created constitutional conditions for the direct effect of EU law in cases where EU law calls for it.

Third, the Constitution had to account for the act of accession itself. A special constitutional law was adopted which provided that a referendum must take place.[88] The actual referendum, which is the only referendum so far in Czech history, took place on 13 and 14 June 2003. A decisive majority (77 per cent of the voters) eventually supported accession to the EU.

Finally, the fourth dimension concerns the specific position of EU law within the Czech legal order. It is this fourth dimension that has generated the most controversy and has been hotly debated right up until today. It was again the CCC that played the most active role in determining the relationship between domestic law and EU law. The opportunity came quite early. In 2006, less than two years after the accession, the CCC issued its *Solange*-like judgment, *Sugar Quotas III*.[89] While generally accepting the supremacy of EU law, it explicitly rejected the possibility of its *unconditional* supremacy.[90] More specifically, it opined that:

> There is no doubt that the Czech Republic's accession to the European Communities (EC), or European Union (EU), brought about a fundamental change within the Czech legal order, as, at that moment, the Czech Republic incorporated into its national law the entire mass of European law. This undoubtedly caused a shift in the legal environment formed by sub-constitutional legal norms, and this shift must necessarily influence the understanding of the entire existing legal order, including its constitutional principles and maxims, naturally on the condition that the factors influencing the national legal environment are not, in and of themselves, in conflict with the principle of a democratic state based on the rule of law, or, in other words, that the interpretation of these factors must not endanger this democratic state based on the rule of law. Such a shift would come into conflict with article 9 para 2 or article 9 para 3 of the Constitution of the Czech Republic.

---

[88] Constitutional Law N. 515/2002 Coll.

[89] Judgment of the CCC of 8 March 2006, Pl. ÚS 50/04, *Sugar Quotas III*.

[90] Due to this aspect the *Sugar Quotas III* judgment is considered the Czech cousin of the famous judgments of the German Federal Constitutional Court in *Solange I*, *Solange II*, and *Maastricht*. See Pavel Holländer, 'Soumrak moderního státu' (2013) 152 Právník 1. In English, see Darinka Piqani, 'Constitutional Courts in Central and Eastern Europe and their attitude towards European integration' (2007) 1 EJLS 213.

In the event that the European Union and its legal order ceased to fulfil the 'conditions of conferral', the CCC hinted that it would feel obliged to reel back in the competences previously conferred to the European Union:

> The Czech Republic has conferred these powers upon EC institutions. In the Constitutional Court's view, this conferral of a part of its powers is naturally a conditional conferral, as the original bearer of sovereignty, as well as the powers flowing therefrom, still remains the Czech Republic, whose sovereignty still stems from article 1 para 1 of the Constitution of the Czech Republic. In the Constitutional Court's view, the conditional nature of the delegation of these powers is manifested on two planes: the formal and the substantive plane. The first of these planes concerns the power attributes of state sovereignty itself, the second plane concerns the substantive component of the exercise of state power. In other words, the delegation of a part of the powers of national organs may persist only so long as these powers are exercised in a manner that is compatible with the preservation of the foundations of state sovereignty of the Czech Republic, and in a manner which does not threaten the very essence of the substantive law-based state. In such determination, the Constitutional Court is called upon to protect constitutionalism (article 83 of the Constitution of the Czech Republic). According to article 9 para 2 of the Constitution of the Czech Republic, the essential attributes of a democratic state governed by the rule of law, remain beyond the reach of the Constituent Assembly itself.[91]

This warning did not remain isolated in the case law of the CCC. In the *Lisbon I* judgment, the Court reiterated that in the event of a clear conflict between the Czech Constitution and EU law that could not be overcome by any reasonable interpretation, the constitutional order of the Czech Republic, in particular its substantive core,[92] had to take precedence.[93] The CCC thus held that the core parts of the constitutional order (basically the Eternity Clause[94]) are absolutely protected not only from domestic interferences, but also from changes stemming from international and European obligations. Thus, for the CCC, at least rhetorically, the obligation to respect the primacy of EU law was never considered an unconditional one.[95]

Despite these vociferous warnings, the CCC's practical stance towards EU law has been rather welcoming and accommodating. In the European Arrest Warrant judgment,[96] the CCC held that there is an obligation[97] to interpret domestic law in a manner consistent with EU law which applies even with regard to the constitutional rules. The compatibility of the European Arrest Warrant with the Charter of Fundamental Rights and Freedoms was objectively questionable, because article 14 para 4 of the Charter explicitly guarantees that no citizen may be forced to leave her homeland. The outcome of the case was to a great extent

---

[91] Judgment of the CCC of 8 March 2006, Pl. ÚS 50/04, *Sugar Quotas III*.

[92] It is not entirely clear whether the CCC used the term 'substantive core' as an equivalent to the more developed (by the CCC) Eternity Clause, but we believe that that is the case, as Pavel Holländer, the (then future) judge-rapporteur in *Melčák*, published an influential law review article which connected art 9 para 2 of the Czech Constitution with the concept of 'substantive core'. See Pavel Holländer, 'Materiální ohnisko ústavy a diskrece ústavodárce' (2005) 144 Právník 313.

[93] Judgment of the CCC of 26 November 2008, Pl. ÚS 19/08 *Lisbon I*, para 85.

[94] See below Section D.1.b.

[95] See below Section E.

[96] Judgment of the CCC of 3 May 2006, Pl. ÚS 66/04, *European Arrest Warrant*.

[97] The Czech Constitutional Court drew the obligation not only from art 1 para 2 of the Czech Constitution but also from the former art 10 of the EC Treaty; see judgment of the CCC of 3 May 2006, Pl. ÚS 66/04, para 61.

influenced by the way the Czech Constitutional Court formulated the starting point of its approach:

> If the Constitution ... can be interpreted in several ways, only certain of which lead to the attainment of an obligation which the Czech Republic undertook in connection with its membership of the EU, then an interpretation must be selected which supports the carrying out of that obligation, and not an interpretation which precludes it.[98]

In accordance with this attitude, the CCC went to great lengths to find an interpretation of the Charter that would be compatible with the European Arrest Warrant framework decision or, more precisely, with the law implementing it. This approach is all the more noteworthy in view of the fact that other European constitutional courts did not adopt an interpretation that was as euro-friendly as the Czech one.[99] This led even foreign authors to note that 'in contrast to its Polish (and especially German) counterpart, the CCC tried to minimize any kind of possibility of a clash between its constitutional fundamentals and the European legal order' and that 'it did not engage in any kind of sovereignty discourse, which would be typical in the context of extradition procedures that usually trigger serious concerns for the protection by the state of its own citizens'.[100]

In its subsequent case law, the CCC applied the welcoming and accommodating 'EU friendly' approach to interpretation, even with regard to the basic principles of the Czech Constitution. The interpretation of 'sovereignty' in the *Lisbon I* judgment[101] may serve as a good example of this trend. In this case, the Czech President claimed, *inter alia*, that the Lisbon Treaty (or rather the Treaties after its ratification) called into question the basic meaning of state sovereignty and thus threatens the very nature of the Czech Republic as a sovereign state. The CCC once again showed its readiness to accept paradigmatic changes brought about by European integration. It claimed that—paradoxically—the key expression of state sovereignty is the ability to dispose of one's sovereignty (or part of it), or temporarily or even permanently to cede certain competences.[102] It followed that finding up by emphasizing that the concept of sovereignty can no longer be understood in a traditional sense as 'a rigid legal concept, but also as a concept with a practical, moral, and existential dimension'.[103] The Court also appreciated that the EU's integration process was not changing the nature and understanding of sovereignty in a radical manner and that it was 'an evolutionary process and, among other things, a reaction to the increasing globalization in the world'.[104]

Still, the CCC did not completely let go of the 'national' dimension of sovereignty. It emphasized that article 10a of the Czech Constitution does not permit the transfer of all the state's powers to the European Union. In other words, an 'unlimited transfer of sovereignty' cannot take place. However, the CCC has shown some judicial restraint in stating that

---

[98] Judgment of the CCC of 3 May 2006, Pl. ÚS 66/04, *European Arrest Warrant*.

[99] Germany and Poland, for example, had to find other (legislative) ways to accept the effects of the framework decision. See e.g. Jan Komárek, 'European Constitutionalism and the European Arrest Warrant: In search of the limits of "contrapunctual principles"' (2007) 44 CMLR 9; and Oreste Pollicino, 'European Arrest Warrant and Constitutional Principles of the Member States: a case law-based outline in the attempt to strike the right balance between interacting legal systems' (2008) 9 GLJ 1313, 1353.

[100] Darinka Piqani, 'Constitutional Courts in Central and Eastern Europe' (n 90) 225 (both citations).

[101] For a succinct commentary on this judgment see Petr Bříza, 'The Czech Republic: The Constitutional Court on the Lisbon Treaty Decision of 26 November 2008' (2009) 5 EuConst 143.

[102] *Lisbon I* judgment, para 104.

[103] Ibid, para 107.

[104] Ibid, para 108.

the limits of this transfer are predominantly a political question, and judicial interference should come into consideration only in the event of clear violation of the core constitutional principles.[105]

Similar conclusions can be made as regards the CCC's approach to the concept of democracy. In its *Lisbon II* judgment, the Court rejected the idea that representative democracy, as protected by the Eternity Clause, is by definition tied to the level of nation states. It affirmatively quoted the opinion of Advocate General Maduro in Case C-411/06 *Commission v Parliament and Council*[106] and held that the democratic processes on the Union level and the domestic level supplement each other and are mutually dependent. Therefore, the CCC does not view European integration and the strengthening of democratic processes at the EU level as a prima facie challenge to democracy at the national level: '[T]he principle of representative democracy is one of the standard principles for the organisation of larger entities, both inter-state and non-state organisations. The existence of elements of representative democracy on the Union level does not rule out implementation of those same elements presupposed by the constitutional order of the Czech Republic, nor does it mean exceeding the limits of the transfer of powers established by article 10a of the Constitution.'[107]

The only clear exception to the generally euro-friendly attitude of the CCC is the judgment in the *Holubec* case.[108] In this case, the CCC held that the CJEU acted *ultra vires* when it issued its ruling in the *Landtová* case.[109] This ruling impugned the previous case law of the CCC relating to the pension benefits of people adversely affected by the dissolution of Czechoslovakia.[110] However, the importance of this judgment for the future evolution of the case law should not be overestimated. It can be argued that this exception was motivated by predominantly domestic reasons and not by an aspiration to take on the Court of Justice of the European Union. The CCC's act of defiance was merely a flashpoint in its long-lasting and somewhat bitter struggle with the Supreme Administrative Court, which refused to follow the Constitutional Court's case law and, in the end, decided to drag the Court of Justice into the battlefield.[111] The two courts have fought over the outcome of the Slovak pensions saga for many years and the intensity (one could even say 'emotional charge') is evident in many of the Constitutional Court's actions over the years.[112]

---

[105] Ibid, para 109.

[106] Opinion of Advocate General Maduro in *Commission v Parliament and Council* C-411/06 [2009] ECLI:EU:C:2009:189.

[107] Judgment of the CCC of 3 November 2009, Pl. ÚS 29/09, *Lisbon II*, para 139.

[108] Judgment of the CCC of 31 January 2012, Pl. ÚS 5/12, *Holubec*.

[109] Court of Justice of the European Union, Case C-399/09, *Landtová* [2011], ECLI:EU:C:2011:415.

[110] For further details of this complex problem see Jan Komárek, 'Playing with matches: The Czech Constitutional Court declares a judgment of the Court of Justice of the EU ultra vires' (2012) 8 EuConst 323; Robert Zbíral, 'Czech Constitutional Court, Judgment of 31 January 2012, Pl. ÚS 5/12: A legal revolution or negligible episode? Court of Justice decision proclaimed ultra vires' (2012) 49 CMLRev 1475; Michal Bobek, 'Landtová, Holubec, and the problem of an uncooperative court: Implications for the preliminary rulings procedure' (2014) 10 EuConst 54; and Zdeněk Kühn, 'Ultra vires review and the demise of constitutional pluralism: The Czecho-Slovak pension saga, and the dangers of state courts' defiance of EU law' (2016) 23 MJECL 185.

[111] As Zbíral puts it, '[the Constitutional Court's] prime target was the SAC, and the ECJ was used as a mere accessory, whose exemplary rebuke was necessary in order to sentence the main culprit' (Robert Zbíral, 'Czech Constitutional Court, judgment of 31 January 2012' (n 110) 1488).

[112] Only the unique nature of this case can explain the fact that the Czech Constitutional Court harshly criticized the Supreme Administrative Court for triggering the preliminary reference procedure before the CJEU (judgment of the CCC of 12 August 2010, III. ÚS 1012/10). In other cases, the Constitutional Court chastised ordinary courts for doing the opposite (as not asking a preliminary question, where it was appropriate, violates the principle of a 'legal judge') and sometimes even forced them to ask a preliminary question (see e.g. judgment of the CCC of 8 January 2009, II. ÚS 1009/08).

Despite being interesting for both EU and constitutional scholars, this unique case can hardly be seen as a true reflection of the Czech Constitutional Court's attitude towards EU law. Moreover, this struggle and its personal dimension were strongly tied to the composition of the so-called 'second'[113] Czech Constitutional Court (2003–2012), while the 'third' Czech Constitutional Court (2013–now) has so far taken up only the more euro-friendly aspects of the second CCC's case law.[114] However, from the comparative perspective, this judgment is no longer an outlier case or material for 'footnotes of EU law textbooks', as suggested by some commentators.[115] The recent case law of the executive-captured Polish Constitutional Tribunal,[116] the Danish Supreme Court's *Ajos* judgment[117] and especially the *PSPP* ruling of the German Federal Constitutional Court[118] show that the *ultra vires* doctrine is no longer a dormant nuclear weapon in the domestic constitutional courts' arsenal. The CCC's *Holubec* judgment, however inconsequential in the European space, was the first *ultra vires* ruling by an apex court at the domestic level which started the debate that will surely continue for quite some time.

4. Economic Crisis and the Constitutional Dimension of Social Conflicts

An important feature of Central and Eastern constitutionalism in general, and the Czech constitutional system in particular, is the inclusion of an extensive list of social, economic, and cultural rights. It should be noted, however, that the Czech constitutional order, unlike that in Germany, does not include an explicit entrenchment of the 'welfare state' principle.[119] Nevertheless, social rights protection in the Charter can be interpreted as indirect constitutionalization of this principle. The extensive protection of economic, social, and cultural rights can be attributed both to the time of the Charter's adoption and to the sentiments of the Czech people, who have traditionally placed a lot of emphasis on social rights and equality. In fact, Czechia is one of the most economically egalitarian countries in the world. The World Bank currently ranks Czechia as the second most income-egalitarian country in the world, which—especially when coupled with a relatively high level of GDP per capita— suggests that social and economic equality is considered an important value. Despite this,

---

[113] This term is used to describe the members of the CCC between 2003 and 2013. See David Kosař and Ladislav Vyhnánek, 'The Constitutional Court of Czechia' (n 28) 119.

[114] Even though the recent changes in the composition of the CCC cannot serve as conclusive evidence of this presumption, some of them may prove important. For example, Pavel Holländer (judge rapporteur of the CCC's opinions in the Melčák and Landtová cases and a strong proponent of an expansive interpretation of the Eternity Clause) left the CCC in 2013, whereas Jiří Zemánek (a prominent advocate of the euro-friendly attitude of the CCC) was appointed in 2014. Zemánek's euro-friendliness became clear in particular in his majority opinion in the *EP Threshold* judgment, in which he vigorously defended the 5 per cent threshold in the European Parliament elections. See also Hubert Smekal and Ladislav Vyhnánek, 'Equal voting power under scrutiny: Czech Constitutional Court on the five per cent threshold in the 2014 European Parliament Elections' (2016) 12 EuConst 148, 149 and 163.

[115] Robert Zbíral, 'Czech Constitutional Court, Judgment of 31 January 2012' (n 110) 1490.

[116] See Wintold Zontek, 'You can't forbid judges to think' (Verfassungsblog, 5 February 2020) verfassungsblog.de/you-cant-forbid-judges-to-think (last accessed on 13 March 2022).

[117] See Mikael Rask Madsen, Henrik Palmer Olsen, and Urška Šadl, 'Competing supremacies and clashing institutional rationalities: The Danish Supreme Court's decision in the Ajos case and the national limits of judicial cooperation' (2017) 23 European Law Journal 140.

[118] German Federal Constitutional Court, Judgment of the Second Senate of 5 May 2020, 2 BvR 859/15.

[119] Unlike—for example—art 20 para 1 of the German Basic Law.

social justice and equality has faced considerable challenges in the last decades, as we will show in the following paragraphs.

The inclusion of these rights attracted significant criticism from foreign scholars,[120] but in the Czech case, the social rights clauses remained mostly dormant in the 1990s and early 2000s. It was only in the wake of the financial and economic crisis of the late 2000s that the question of social rights rose to prominence.

After the Topolánek government (2006–2009) adopted a series of legislative austerity measures, the political battle between the left and the right was transferred to the CCC. The CCC had to take a stance on vexing issues such as the justiciability of social rights, their scope, and the degree of deference to be given to the legislature in these issues. The resulting case law can be seen as a compromise. The CCC adopted a deferential 'rationality test'[121] and it left wide room for manoeuvre for the legislature, but, having said this, it did not hesitate to annul several statutes that excessively limited the scope or the core of social rights.[122] However, the CCC has not hitherto delivered a judgment such as the German *Hartz IV*, which made comments on the actual number of benefits from the social welfare system.

While the constitutional dimension of socio-economic issues rose to prominence around the time of the economic crisis, the constitutionalization of socio-economic issues should not be seen as a closed chapter of the Czech constitutional development. First, the legacy of the economic crisis is still evident. The last decade of the CCC's functioning has been marked by reviews of socio-economic legislation. Both legislation limiting the extent of the welfare state and legislation regulating the economic activity of individuals now form a major part of political and, consequently, often legal battles.

Second, other constitutional issues concerning social problems are on the horizon. Most importantly, as of 2021 around 750,000 (almost a tenth of the adult population) people in Czechia are affected by writs of execution and find themselves in bankruptcy or close to a debt-trap. This issue offers more than one constitutional challenge. Besides the obvious constitutional dimension of the problem, there is an undeniable political dimension. People affected by these problems may quickly lose, or in the worst-case scenario have already lost, trust in the constitutional system's ability to address their problems. Under such conditions, it is challenging, one, to promote any meaningful version of constitutional patriotism[123] and, two, to expect that a decisive majority of the people will identify with the basic constitutional values.[124] The consequences are already discernible. The Czech constitutional system suffers from a relatively low level of trust,[125] and, at the same time, populist and authoritarian parties, such as the Freedom and Direct Democracy movement and the Communist Party,

---

[120] See *inter alia* Sunstein, who called constitutionalization of positive socio-economic rights a big mistake, possibly a catastrophe: Cass R Sunstein, 'Against Positive Rights', in András Sajó (ed), *Western Rights? Post-Communist Application* (Kluwer Law International, Alphen aan den Rijn, 1996) 225.

[121] See, for example, judgment of the CCC of 20 May 2008, Pl. ÚS 1/08, *Healthcare fees*; or see e.g. Marek Antoš, 'The Czech Constitutional Court and Social Rights: Analysis of the Case Law', in Pavel Šturma and Narciso Leandro Xavier Baez (eds), *International and Internal Mechanisms of Fundamental Rights Effectiveness* (RW&W Science & New Media, Passau, Berlin, Prague, 2015) 187.

[122] See, most notably, judgment of the CCC of 27 November 2012, Pl. ÚS 1/12, *Public service*. Here, the legislator established an obligation for unemployed people to work in the so-called 'public service' in order to retain the corresponding social benefits.

[123] In general, we understand constitutional patriotism as a sense of civic attachment to constitutional values and principles—a sense that those values and principles are essential for forming and upholding a political community. For further details see Jürgen Habermas, *Between Facts and Norms: Contribution to a Discourse Theory of Law and Democracy* (MIT Press, Cambridge, MA, 1996) 491–515 and 566–567; and Jan-Werner Müller, *Constitutional Patriotism* (Princeton University Press, Princeton, NJ, 2007).

[124] See Section D.1.

[125] For further details see Sections C.6 and D.1.

are enjoying strong support among the people most affected. This challenge, however, is not a secret one. It is a hotly debated topic and, for example, the government's Human Rights Council has recently identified the problem of debt-traps and property repossessions as a top human rights priority.[126]

5. The Two-Headed Executive: Weak Governments and Trouble-Making Presidents

As emphasized in Section B, Czechia was from the start of the drafting process envisaged as a parliamentary republic. The basic outline of the executive branch thus followed the established model. The government, headed by a Prime Minister, was responsible to the parliament and this office was put at the top of the executive branch. The President was elected by the parliament, held few purely executive powers, and served as a representative Head of State.

From the very outset, however, the structure of the executive branch and the position of the President became contested issues. On the one hand, some scholars have argued that the President is not actually part of the executive branch, but rather a constitutional body *sui generis*, a *pouvoir neutre*. This opinion, advocated for example by Václav Pavlíček,[127] was based on the analysis of the President's powers, but it was obviously also formed on the basis of comparative influences. While this position had a certain logic, it was difficult to defend the assertion that the President is not an executive body, because the Constitution explicitly puts the President in the part entitled 'The Executive Power'. On the other hand, some authors have put forward arguments which could move the position of the President closer to the semi-presidential model.[128] One of the main arguments in this regard was that the President, unlike the stereotypically weak presidents in many parliamentary models, enjoyed numerous powers that could be used without countersignature. Still, if nothing else, the indirect election of the President at a joint session of both chambers of the parliament prevented the Czech model being labelled as semi-presidential.

These discussions were not purely academic. The position of the President was contested in practical political life and it also became an important question in several CCC cases. In the case concerning the appointment of the Governor of the Czech National Bank, the CCC had to decide whether such appointment required a countersignature. The majority of the Court preferred the interpretation that left the matter entirely in the President's hands. Their key argument was that a neutral and non-partisan President better serves the purpose of protecting the Czech National Bank's independence. The dissenting minority, in retrospect quite fittingly, countered that the majority accorded with the position of the then President Václav Havel too much and that the neutrality and non-partisan nature of the office of President was wishful thinking rather than an objective reading of the Constitution. Interestingly, the notion of a non-partisan and neutral President was dealt a blow just a few years later in the midst of President Václav Klaus's clash with Iva Brožová, the President of

---

[126] See the Human Rights Council of the Czech Government, *2018 Report on the State of Human Rights in Czechia* at https://www.vlada.cz/cz/ppov/rlp/dokumenty/zpravy-lidska-prava-cr/zprava-o-stavu-lidskych-prav-v-ceske-republice-v-roce-2018-175718/ (last accessed on 13 March 2022).

[127] See Marek Antoš, 'Pravomoci prezidenta republiky po zavedení přímé volby' (2011) 57 Acta Universitatis Carolinae 30.

[128] Jan Kysela and Zdeněk Kühn, 'Presidential elements in government: the Czech Republic' (2007) 3 EuConst 91.

the Supreme Court. After the first direct election of the President in 2013, which immediately split Czech citizens into two halves, this notion was definitely abandoned.

The peculiar position of the President has also had an important political dimension. The office was always held by a significant political figure. In fact, the three Czech Presidents so far have been members of the 'triumvirate' of the most important politicians of modern Czech history: Václav Havel, Václav Klaus, and Miloš Zeman. Not surprisingly, once they assumed presidential office, they often used their authority at the expense of weak and unstable governments. This is nothing new in the Czech lands though. The special position of the President, which is de facto much stronger than the Constitution would suggest, dates back to the First Czechoslovak Republic. Although the 1920 Czechoslovak Constitution contained a nuanced system of separation of powers,[129] this principle was sidelined in national political life. Most importantly, the first President of the country and a towering figure of the entire interwar period, Tomáš Garrigue Masaryk, was deeply distrustful of political parties, parliamentary leaders, and the parliament itself. He created an informal political organization known as *Hrad* ('The Castle'), a powerful coalition of intellectuals, journalists, businessmen, religious leaders, and First World War veterans.[130] Due to his charisma, the fractured political scene and support of the *Hrad*, Masaryk *de facto* set the country's political agenda until his death in 1937.[131]

Governmental weakness and resulting instability are the second important piece of the puzzle, an understanding of which is necessary for one properly to assess the functioning of the Czech executive branch. There have been no fewer than fifteen governments in the relatively short (1993–2019) Czech constitutional history. Out of these, three were so-called 'caretaker governments', three were minority governments tolerated by (at least nominally) opposition parties and many others have governed with just a very small majority, so that just a handful (even as few as one or two) of rebellious coalition members of the Chamber of Deputies could put the government under pressure or even cause its fall.[132]

Many politicians and several academics have attributed governmental weakness to an electoral system that does not consistently produce stable majorities in the Chamber of Deputies, to which the government is responsible. However, all attempts to significantly change the electoral system have failed, partly also due to the CCC which put a halt to introducing majoritarian elements into the election of the Chamber of Deputies. Most importantly, in the 2001 *Grand Election* judgment, the CCC declared unconstitutional the Election Law amendment that increased the number of voting districts, introduced a modified D'Hondt method and abolished the second scrutiny.[133] It did so because, according to the CCC's Justices, that amendment introduced too many majoritarian elements into the Czech 'system of proportional representation' in the Chamber of Deputies,[134] which is explicitly entrenched in the Czech Constitution.[135]

---

[129] Some commentators of that time even claimed that it was too nuanced and contained so many checks and balances that it could hardly function in practice. See the discussion in Jana Osterkamp, 'Ústavní soudnictví v meziválečném Československu' (2007) 146 Právník 585, 616.

[130] Andrea Orzoff, *Battle for the Castle* (n 13).

[131] This has significant repercussions for the interwar separation of powers. See David Kosař et al, 'The Twin Challenges to Separation of Powers' (n 15) 442–443.

[132] Attempts to negotiate with these rebels have at times caused further political and legal problems, such as the 2012/2013 attempted criminal prosecution of coalition MPs who had been promised well-paid positions in exchange for their resignations from the parliament.

[133] Judgment of the CCC of 24 January 2001, Pl. ÚS 42/2000, *Grand Election* judgment.

[134] Ibid.

[135] The CCC used a similar 'cumulative effects doctrine' again in 2021, when it annulled the legal threshold for the coalitions and, much more importantly, held that the combination of fourteen districts and the system of

Further half-hearted attempts to strengthen the governments by changing the electoral system were made later. In the period between 2006 and 2009, the government considered introducing some elements which would favour the winner of the elections, such as a certain form of winner's bonus. These ideas have never materialized, however. Similarly, a subsequently proposed solution introducing some German elements of rationalized parliamentarism[136] never got past the rhetorical stage.[137] On the other hand, the CCC—in a judgment strongly resembling the *Grand Election* judgment—even declared some features of the post-2002 electoral system unconstitutional for keeping too many majoritarian elements. These included mainly the electoral formula coupled with uneven size of electoral districts (which tended to overrepresent the strongest political parties) and a higher electoral threshold for coalitions.[138]

Ironically, instead of rationalizing Czech parliamentarism, the 2012 Constitutional Amendment[139] did the opposite. It introduced, among other things, direct election of the President. This step has weakened the government even further, as the directly legitimated President, who has historically enjoyed a special status in Czech society,[140] can exert even greater pressure on an unstable government and use his political resources to submit it to his will. This was clearly shown during the 'co-habitation' of President Miloš Zeman and the 2014–2017 Sobotka government.

6. An Over-Judicialized Constitution

Drafters of the Czech Constitution vested broad powers in the CCC.[141] It is generally assumed that 'when drafting the provisions concerning the Constitutional Court in 1992, [they] were also significantly inspired by the German Basic Law and constitutional system'.[142] With a certain degree of simplification, it is possible to say that the jurisdiction of the CCC mirrors that of the German Federal Constitutional Court (hereinafter: the 'BVerfG'). The CCC has almost all the powers a Constitutional Court can think of. It decides on (1) abstract constitutional review, (2) concrete constitutional review, (3) individual constitutional complaints, (4) horizontal as well as vertical separation of powers disputes, and (5) conformity of international treaties with the Czech constitutional order before their ratification.[143]

In addition, the CCC has various ancillary powers covering electoral disputes, the dissolution of political parties, removal of the President, and the implementation of decisions of international tribunals.[144] The CCC has also been very creative in searching for its 'implied

---

allocation of seats (D'Hondt formula used at the level of electoral districts) causes unequal and disproportional (Judgment of the CCC of 2 February 2021, sp. zn. Pl. ÚS 44/17, *Grand Election II* judgment).

[136] Such as the constructive vote of no confidence.

[137] No proposal to amend the Constitution in this regard has ever materialized and the attempts to install 'the chancellor system' have stopped after a couple of roundtables with experts in the Chamber of Deputies.

[138] Judgment of the CCC of 2 February 2021, Pl. ÚS 44/17, *Grand Election II* judgment.

[139] Constitutional Law N. 71/2012 Coll.

[140] See the discussion of the position of Masaryk, Havel, Klaus, and Zeman above.

[141] For further details see David Kosař and Ladislav Vyhnánek, 'The Constitutional Court of Czechia' (n 28).

[142] Jiří Přibáň, 'Judicial Power vs. Democratic Representation: The Culture of Constitutionalism and Human Rights in the Czech Legal System', in Wojciech Sadurski (ed), *Constitutional Justice, East and West: Democratic Legitimacy and Constitutional Courts in Post-Communist Europe in a Comparative Perspective* (Kluwer Law International, Alphen aan den Rijn, 2002) 374, 379.

[143] See art 87 of the Czech Constitution. For further details see David Kosař and Ladislav Vyhnánek, 'The Constitutional Court of Czechia' (n 28).

[144] Ibid.

powers'. In this vein, it has embraced the doctrine of unconstitutional constitutional amendment[145] and suggested that it might review even amnesties.[146] As a result, there are very few acts (if any) that escape review by the CCC.[147] The only competence which the CCC has lost, in comparison to its federal predecessor, is the power to issue advisory opinions. Furthermore, as should become clear from the following paragraphs, the CCC has not hesitated to interpret its powers extensively.[148] Still, it would be hasty to label the CCC as a very activist court. Its rise as an important political actor, which everybody must take seriously, was incremental and its activism is often more of a verbal or symbolic nature rather than real political landscape-changing brushstrokes. On the one hand, the CCC invented the power to review constitutional amendments and ruled that the ECJ has ruled *ultra vires* in the *Holubec* case.[149] On the other hand, it has shown restraint in other cases (e.g. in social rights cases and in reviewing the presidential amnesty[150]) and generally has not rendered bold substantive judgments that would attract wide international interest such as the Hungarian death penalty judgment.[151] Put differently, the CCC has been creative and activist in expanding its jurisdiction, but rather reluctant to exploit it to pursue substantive policies against the will of the political majority.

In terms of its impact on Czech society, the CCC has steadily risen to prominence. While it delivered several important judgments in the 1990s, few of them shook up the political establishment in Prague. The CCC started showing its teeth only in the early 2000s. In the abovementioned 2001 *Grand Election* judgment[152] it de facto prevented the creation of a two-party state.[153] A year later, in the 2002 *Euro-Amendment* judgment,[154] it extensively re-interpreted a major part of constitutional amendment adopted by the parliament.

The proverbial big bang came only a few years later. In the 2009 *Melčák* judgment,[155] the CCC adopted the doctrine of unconstitutional constitutional amendments and annulled the constitutional law shortening the fifth term of office of the Chamber of Deputies, which was adopted in order to find the quickest way to hold snap elections. By doing so, it effectively postponed the parliamentary elections and reshuffled the cards in Prague. In 2010–2012 it struck down several austerity measures adopted by the centre-right coalition in the wake of the global financial crisis. Finally, in 2012 the CCC showed its teeth also towards the Court of Justice of the EU as it found the CJEU's *Landtová* judgment *ultra vires*.[156]

The series of these judgments in 2009–2012 makes clear that the CCC has become a powerful institution to be taken seriously by all political and judicial actors, on both the domestic and European levels. However, in order to understand the position of the CCC properly, one must look at several dimensions, including the CCC's relationship with the ECtHR and the CJEU and even at the CCC's own self-image.

---

[145] Judgment of the CCC of 10 September 2009, Pl. ÚS 27/09, *Melčák*.
[146] Judgment of the CCC of 5 March 2013, Pl. ÚS 4/13, *Amnesty of Václav Klaus*, para 42.
[147] The Czech constitutional law does not know any form of *actio popularis* though.
[148] See, e.g. Marek Antoš, 'The Czech Constitutional Court and Social Rights' (n 121).
[149] See also Section E.
[150] Decision of the CCC of 5 March 2013, n. Pl. ÚS 4/13.
[151] See judgment of the Hungarian Constitutional Court of 24 October 1990 (Decision 23/1990 (X.31) AB).
[152] See judgment of the CCC of 24 January 2001, Pl. ÚS 42/2000, *Grand Election* judgment.
[153] This was an attempt by the two (then) strongest parties (the Social Democratic Party and the centre-right Civic Democratic Party) to entrench their positions during the so-called 'Opposition Agreement' period. For further details on the Opposition Agreement see Section C.2.
[154] Judgment of the CCC of 25 June 2002, Pl. ÚS 36/01, *Euro-Amendment*.
[155] Judgment of the CCC of 10 September 2009, Pl. ÚS 27/09, *Melčák*.
[156] Judgment of the CCC of 31 January 2012, Pl. ÚS 5/12, *Holubec* (in the Czech context this judgment is often referred to also as *Slovak Pensions XVII* to show that it is a part of the much longer 'Slovak Pension Saga').

More specifically, the position of the CCC in the Czech political and constitutional system is determined not only by its institutional design, but also by the dynamics of its relationship with other constitutional bodies, the public, and with supranational and international courts. Given its broad array of powers, the CCC has had ideal conditions for shaping the evolution of the constitutional and political landscape of Czechia since the 1990s. The fact that the CCC has enjoyed considerable public support—especially for a country where state institutions are generally viewed with suspicion[157]—surely helped too.

The relationship between the CCC and the parliament is quite intensive. Besides the obvious fact that the CCC reviews laws adopted by the parliament, the abstract review of legislation might be initiated by a group of members of the parliament (usually opposition members) which influences the political dynamics of the use of these proceedings.[158] However, over the last twenty-five years, the relationship between the CCC and the parliament has obviously evolved beyond what is discernible from the constitutional text. Regarding this relationship, several developments stand out.

First, the already mentioned *Melčák* case made clear that the CCC has claimed the competence to review constitutional amendments[159] and the parliament has not stood up to this assertion of power. This has shifted the balance between the CCC and the parliament quite significantly, since the CCC has effectively proclaimed itself the Czech '*Grenzorgan*'[160] that has the last word in questions of constitutional order.

However, the *Melčák* case, although important, concerned an exceptional problem. The CCC's relationship with the parliament has been shaped primarily by day-to-day issues. While it is not surprising that the CCC—when reviewing legislation—places some substantive constitutional limits on the legislature, it has become involved in the legislative process as well. There is now an established doctrine according to which the CCC can review the internal procedure in the parliament and annul statutory law for failing to follow the correct procedure. Especially in the 2000s, the CCC has attempted to stop the use of so-called 'legislative riders'[161] and to set rules for the use of procedures that limit the ability of a parliamentary minority to 'obstruct' the legislative process.[162] However, this case law has not been settled yet[163] and thus it is still not entirely clear what are the constitutional limits of 'purity' of the legislative process.

---

[157] For example, in 2012, while the CCC enjoyed the strong or moderate support of approximately 60 per cent of the population (which reflected the general trend from previous years), the political institutions such as the parliament or the government received much lower numbers (even below 20 per cent, hardly ever exceeding 40 per cent). See empirical research available at https://www.stem.cz/duvera-nejvyssim-soudnim-institucim/ and https://www.stem.cz/duvera-v-nejvyssi-politicke-instituce-prosinec-2012/ (both last accessed on 13 March 2022).

[158] Petrov and Kopeček have shown that the ability to initiate review is an important political tool of the opposition, especially when the government enjoys a stable majority: see Lubomír Kopeček and Jan Petrov, 'From parliament to courtroom: Judicial review of legislation as a political tool in the Czech Republic' (2016) 30 East European Politics and Societies and Cultures 120.

[159] For further analysis see also Yaniv Roznai, 'Legisprudence limitations on constitutional amendments? Reflections on the Czech Constitutional Court's declaration of unconstitutional Constitutional Act' (2014) 8 ICL Journal 29; and Ivo Šlosarčík, 'Czech Republic 2009–2012: On unconstitutional amendment of the Constitution, limits of EU law and direct presidential elections' (2013) 3 EPL 435.

[160] By this we refer to the Verdross/Kelsen concept of 'border organs'. See Alfred Verdross, *Völkerrecht* (2nd edn, Springer, Berlin, Heidelberg, 1950). See also Franz C Mayer, 'Europäische Verfassungsgerichtsbarkeit', in Armin von Bogdandy (ed), *Europäisches Verfassungsrecht: Theoretische und dogmatische Grundzüge* (Springer, Berlin, Heidelberg, 2003) 260–261; and Theodor Schilling, 'Alec Stone Sweet's "Juridical Coup d'État" revisited: Coups d'état, revolutions, grenzorgane, and constituent power' (2012) 13 GLJ 287.

[161] See Judgment of the CCC of 15 February 2007, Pl. ÚS 77/06.

[162] Judgment of the CCC of 1 March 2011, Pl. ÚS 53/10, available in English at Decisions | The Constitutional Court (usoud.cz) (last accessed on 13 March 2022).

[163] The judge rapporteur of the *Legislative riders* judgments, Eliška Wagnerová, has even opined that one of the following judgments (judgment of the CCC of 31 January 2008, Pl. ÚS 24/07) effectively overruled some of the

7. Where Are the People?

While the CCC has—at least so far—enjoyed a very strong position, there is one institutional element that is strangely lacking in the Czech constitutional practice: namely the people. This statement is obviously and intentionally quite provocative and deserves a more detailed explanation.[164]

While the Constitution is based on the principle of popular sovereignty, the 'operational sovereignty' of the people is kept to the minimum and the Czech people are thus a perfect example of the 'dormant sovereign'. Czechia is actually one of the few European Union countries that has no general regulation of referenda. The only existing example was the ad hoc constitutional law concerning a referendum on the Czech Republic's accession to the European Union.[165]

Furthermore, the prioritization of legal over political[166] and civic constitutionalism, and the consequent limitation of participatory elements in democratic government, are blamed by some authors as a cause of political and constitutional crises in Czechia as well as in other CEE countries.[167] While this is a rather abstract and debatable statement, there are certainly indicators of the detachment of the people from constitutional institutions and basic values. Relatively low voters' turnouts,[168] a lack of trust in key institutions (including parliament), and the rise of populist political parties[169] hint that the level of the people's identification with the constitutional and political system is quite low and that constitutional patriotism in the Czech case is more a theoretical idea than lived reality.[170]

8. A Danger of Democratic Backsliding

So far in this section, we have addressed only issues and events that happened or have been happening for quite some time. But given the youth of the Czech constitutional system, it would be a mistake to overlook certain challenges that have appeared only recently. Even though it is too soon for a definitive evaluation, it begs the question whether some of the developments of the last five or six years cannot be interpreted as signs or forewarnings of some form of backsliding from the liberal democratic nature of the Czech constitutional system.[171] The question becomes even more pressing if we put the Czech development in the context of the developments in the Visegrád countries or—even more broadly—in the CEE region.[172]

main principles stemming from *Legislative riders*. See Wagnerová's dissenting opinion to this judgment, available in English at Decisions | The Constitutional Court (usoud.cz) (last accessed on 13 March 2022).

[164] See also Sections D and E.
[165] Constitutional Law N. 515/2002 Coll., on the Referendum on the Accession to the European Union.
[166] The best analysis of the differences between legal and political constitutionalism can be found in Richard Bellamy, *Political Constitutionalism: A Republican Defence of the Constitutionality of Democracy* (CUP, Cambridge, 2007).
[167] See Paul Blokker, *New Democracies in Crisis? A Comparative Constitutional Study of the Czech Republic, Hungary, Poland, Romania and Slovakia* (Routledge, London, 2013).
[168] Especially in the case of institutions with a low level of diffuse support such as the Senate.
[169] See Section C.8.
[170] See David Kosař and Ladislav Vyhnánek, 'Constitutional Identity in the Czech Republic: A New Twist on An Old Fashioned Idea', in Christian Calliess and Gerhard van der Schyff (eds), *Constitutional Identity in a Europe of Multilevel Constitutionalism* (CUP, Cambridge, 2019) 85. On constitutional patriotism see also n 123.
[171] This subsection should be read in conjunction with the previous parts (especially the 'Where are the people?' subsection 7), but we also develop these issues in Section E dedicated to constitutional identity and in the conclusion.
[172] See David Kosař et al, 'The Twin Challenges to Separation of Powers' (n 15).

The possible forewarnings of backsliding can be divided in two categories. The first one is simply a matter of instability of the party system and the rise in importance of populist parties.[173] This process is not specifically a Czech problem or even a problem of Central and Eastern Europe. In the Czech context, however, this is coupled with convictions of substantial parts of population[174] that democracy is not important for them or that undemocratic regimes are or may be better than democratic.[175] Still, a stable majority of people considers democracy important and is generally content with the political system. The bigger problem thus may be that a strong majority of the Czech population seems to think that 'politicians do not care about the opinions of ordinary people' and that it is not possible for the ordinary people to influence political decision-making.[176] Furthermore, the targets of populist or downright anti-system parties are not only those people who do not identify with (liberal) democratic. As the Visegrád experience shows, people who support democracy, but who are disillusioned by its current form, may be susceptible to promises of 'another form of democracy' in the style of Viktor Orbán. Still, we present these phenomena more as a potential breeding ground for future development rather than signs of backsliding in themselves.

The second category includes more tangible signs of disagreement with the course of constitutional development in the first two decades of the modern Czech constitutional history. In this regard, we can refer to attacks by the winner of the 2017 parliamentary elections and current Prime Minister Andrej Babiš[177] and current President Miloš Zeman on the upper chamber of the parliament, the Senate. Both of them have expressed their desire to abolish the Senate, because it—in their opinion—unnecessarily complicates the process.[178] Andrej Babiš went even further. He has also pledged, one, to reduce the number of MPs in the lower chamber from 200 to 101[179] and, two, abolish municipal assemblies.[180] He openly prefers to 'run the state like a firm',[181] implying that any checks and balances as well as complex procedural rules are but a nuisance.[182] The vision of Andrej Babiš and Miloš Zeman thus seems

---

[173] See Sean Hanley, 'Dynamics of new party formation in the Czech Republic' (n 85); Vlastimil Havlík, 'Populism as a threat to liberal democracy in East Central Europe', in Jan Holzer and Miroslav Mareš (eds), *Challenges to Democracies in East Central Europe* (Routledge, London, 2016) 36–55; Vlastimil Havlík and Petr Kaniok, 'Populism and Euroskepticism in the Czech Republic: Meeting friends or passing by' (2016) 16 Romanian Journal of European Affairs 20.

[174] See also Section E.

[175] In the polls conducted by a branch of the Sociological Institute of the Czech Academy of Science in the last fifteen years, it is shown that roughly 20–30 per cent of the respondents support the 'undemocratic regimes may be better' thesis and roughly 15–25 per cent of the respondents do not think the regime matters. See the document from 5 March 2020, available at https://cvvm.soc.cas.cz/media/com_form2content/documents/c2/a5155/f9/pd200305.pdf (last accessed on 13 March 2022).

[176] See another set of polls by the same institute from March 2020, available here: https://cvvm.soc.cas.cz/media/com_form2content/documents/c2/a5169/f9/pd200313.pdf (last accessed on 13 March 2022).

[177] See Tim Haughton et al, 'Czech elections have become really volatile' (n 85).

[178] Andrej Babiš has even incorporated this idea (and other ideas) in his book *O čem sním když náhodou spím [What do I dream about when I am accidentally asleep]* (Czech Print Center, Ostrava, 2017), available here https://www.anobudelip.cz/file/edee/2017/o-cem-snim-kdyz-nahodou-spim.pdf (last accessed on 13 March 2022).

[179] This change would seriously skew the electoral rules against smaller political parties. Viktor Orbán did actually the same in Hungary (see Miklós Bánkuti et al, 'Hungary's illiberal turn: Disabling the Constitution', 23 Journal of Democracy (2012) 138).

[180] See Andrej Babiš, *O čem sním když náhodou spím* (n 178).

[181] See e.g. Jan Jandourek, 'Babiš chce řídit stat jako firmu. To asi nepůjde, stát není firma' (Reflex on-line, 6 September 2013) www.reflex.cz/clanek/info-x/51716/babis-chce-ridit-stat-jako-firmu-to-asi-nepujde-stat-neni-firma.html (last accessed on 13 March 2022). For a scholarly analysis of Babiš's entrepreneurial party see Lubomír Kopeček, 'I'm paying, so I decide – Czech ANO as an extreme form of a business-firm party' (2016) 30 East European Politics and Societies 725; Vít Hloušek and Lubomír Kopeček, 'Entrepreneurial parties: A basic conceptual framework' (2017) 24 Czech Journal of Political Science 83.

[182] See e.g. Rick Lyman, 'The Trump-like figures popping up in Central Europe' (New York Times, 24 February 2017) www.nytimes.com/2017/02/24/world/europe/zbigniew-stonoga-andrej-babis.html (last accessed on 13 March 2022).

follow the 'pragmatic' and 'strong and effective governments' narratives that we have mentioned when discussing the Opposition Agreement.[183]

More recently, we have also witnessed more specific warning signs of democratic decay in terms of actions of individual office holders. For instance, a recently elected Ombudsman openly denies the existence of discrimination and questions the CCC's case law as well as meaningfulness of 'new rights' such as the right of fathers to be present at childbirth.[184] Even more importantly, several judges of the Czech Constitutional Court and the Supreme Administrative Court alleged that the Chancellor of President Miloš Zeman attempted to persuade judges of these two courts to decide high-profile political cases in line with Zeman's preferences.[185] Such events were simply unheard of in the 1990s and 2000s and their emergence should not be underestimated. If such actions become numerous and go unpunished legally or politically, they may gradually erode the current Czech constitutional *Gestalt* and, in the worst-case scenario, pave the way for the Hungarian or Polish paths.[186]

D. Basic Structures and Concepts

In the last two parts, we discussed the broader political and social context of drafting the Czech Constitution in the early 1990s and the major critical junctures and challenges of the Czech constitutional *Gestalt*. In this part we will identify and analyse the basic structural aspects of the Czech constitutional system and its key concepts that have arisen from the aforementioned processes.

1. Formal Aspects of the Czech Constitutional *Gestalt*

In order to understand the key substantive concepts of the Czech constitutional *Gestalt* and the dynamics of the constitutional system's evolution, it is necessary to understand the more technical and formal aspects of the Czech constitutional system which shape its structure. Therefore, we will first explain the polycentric nature of the Czech Constitution, identify the complex web of sources of Czech constitutional law, and discuss the repercussions of the rigidity of the Czech Constitution.

---

[183] See Section C.2 above.

[184] See Ivana Svobodová, 'Přes 300 právníků apeluje na ombudsmana, aby se přestal řídit dojmy' (Respekt.cz, 14 April 2020) https://www.respekt.cz/agenda/pres-300-akademiku-apeluje-na-ombudsmana-aby-se-prestal-ridit-dojmy (last accessed on 13 March 2022); and Tereza Kučerová, 'Právníci zaslali Křečkovi otevřený dopis. Neplníte svou funkci řádně, míní' (iDNES.cz, 14 April 2020) https://www.idnes.cz/zpravy/domaci/otevreny-dopis-pravn ici-ombudsman-stanislav-krecek.A200414_093505_domaci_kuce (last accessed on 13 March 2022).

[185] See Ondřej Kundra and Andrea Procházková, 'Mynář se pokusil ovlivnit vysoce postavené soudce' (Respekt, 6 January 2019) https://www.respekt.cz/politika/mynar-se-pokusil-ovlivnit-vysoce-postavene-soudce (last accessed on 4 January 2021); Renata Kalenská, 'Soudcova výpověď o Zemanově útoku na justici: Dával mi jasně najevo, jak máme rozhodnout, říká Baxa' (Deník N, 16 January 2019) https://denikn.cz/54570/soudcova-vypo ved-o-zemanove-utoku-na-justici-daval-mi-jasne-najevo-jak-mame-rozhodnout-rika-baxa/ (last accessed on 4 January 2021); and Ondřej Kundra, 'Mynář prozradil před poslanci o kontaktech se soudci víc, než chtěl' (Respekt, 23 January 2019) https://www.respekt.cz/politika/hradni-pokus-o-ovlivnovani-soudcu-mynar-prozradil-vic-nez-chtel (last accessed on 4 January 2021).

[186] See also David Kosař et al, 'The Twin Challenges to Separation of Powers' (n 15).

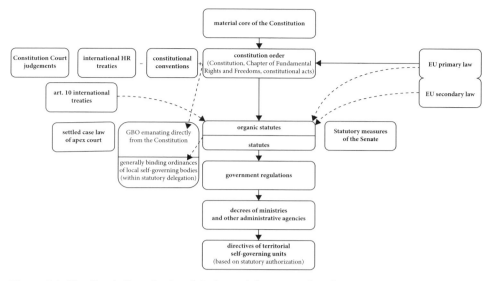

Figure 2.1 The Czech Constitutional Order and the Hierarchy of Norms

a) The Polycentric Constitution and Sources of Constitutional Law

As we have already mentioned above, the value clash between the proponents and opponents of an entrenched charter of rights has resulted in the division of the constitutional text into two basic documents, the Constitution itself and the Charter of Rights and Freedoms (Figure 2.1).

This fact is reflected by the Constitution itself in its article 112, which creates the concept of 'constitutional order'. According to this provision, the constitutional order of the Czech Republic consists of:

> This Constitution, the Charter of Fundamental Rights and Basic Freedoms, constitutional acts adopted pursuant to this Constitution, and those constitutional acts of the National Assembly of the Czechoslovak Republic, the Federal Assembly of the Czechoslovak Socialist Republic, and the Czech National Council defining the state borders of the Czech Republic, as well as constitutional acts of the Czech National Council adopted after the sixth of June 1992.

The Czech Constitution thus consists of a set of constitutional laws rather than a single comprehensive document. Besides the Constitution,[187] the Charter,[188] and the constitutional laws defining the state borders of the Czech Republic there are currently three other constitutional laws. First, there is the Constitutional Law on the Security of the Czech Republic[189] which contains a basic regulation of states of emergency. Second, there is a Constitutional Law Establishing the Higher Self Governmental Units.[190] Finally, the Constitutional Law on the Referendum on the Accession to the European Union[191] is a rather peculiar part of the

---

[187] Constitutional Law N. 1/1993 Coll.
[188] Decision N. 2/1993 Coll.
[189] Constitutional Law N. 110/1998 Coll.
[190] Constitutional Law N. 347/1997 Coll.
[191] Constitutional Law N. 515/2002 Coll.

constitutional order within the meaning of article 112 para 1 of the Constitution. Its peculiarity lies in the fact that it is an ad hoc Constitutional Law that—though still formally valid—became normatively exhausted after the actual referendum had taken place.

It is, however, crucial to mention that the concept of constitutional order—or rather its precise content—has been contested. Most importantly, the CCC has interpreted it in an extensive manner. In the so-called '*Euro-Amendment* judgment',[192] it has ruled that *international human rights treaties*, a category that is not explicitly mentioned in the Constitution after 2001, also form part of the constitutional order, and it has treated them as such ever since.[193] At the same time, ECtHR case-law is considered to have normative precedential power.

After this judgment, it is important to distinguish between international human rights treaties meeting the requirements of article 10 of the Czech Constitution on the one hand, and 'other' article 10 treaties. The former have constitutional rank and belong to the Czech constitutional order, while the latter have merely application priority before statutory law.[194] This constitutionalization of international human rights treaties has had a far-reaching impact on the Czech legal system and has significantly shaped the Czech human rights jurisprudence.

Some CCC rulings[195] and constitutional conventions[196] are also considered binding sources of constitutional law, even though the exact extent of their importance remains slightly unclear. Of these two supplementary sources, the position of the CCC's judgments has been analysed more thoroughly.

The key constitutional provision regulating the effects of the CCC's rulings can be found in article 89 para 2 of the Constitution which reads as follows: 'enforceable rulings of the Constitutional Court are binding on all authorities and persons'. However, this provision gives very few answers to practical questions and various issues surrounding the rulings' effects.

On the one hand, interpretation of the term 'enforceable' has caused few problems so far. According to article 89 para 1 of the Constitution, rulings of the CCC are enforceable as soon as they are announced in the manner provided for by statute unless the CCC decides otherwise. On the other hand, two general questions concerning article 89 para 2 have been particularly controversial. First, it has been debated which rulings (and which parts of an individual ruling) are considered binding. Second, there are various opinions on the nature and extent of the binding power itself.

The direct effects of the CCC's rulings are less controversial and generally accepted. Even though article 89 para 2 of the Constitution mentions 'rulings' generally, only judgments can have any meaningful direct effects (i.e. annulment of a piece legislation or an ordinary court's decision).[197] In contrast, the debate on precedential effects has not yet been settled. The main issue is which part of the CCC's judgment exactly has the *erga omnes* effect (*are binding on all authorities and persons*) anticipated by article 89 para 2 of the Constitution. An 'anti-precedential' part of literature suggested, mainly in the 1990s,[198] that only the operative part of a ruling and not its reasoning could have *erga omnes* effects. However, the case law of the Constitutional Court soon asserted that the main reasons (*tragende Gründe*) for the ruling

---

[192] Judgment of the CCC of 25 June 2002, Pl. ÚS 36/01 *Euro-Amendment*.
[193] The context and analysis of this decision follows in Section D.1.b.
[194] See the text after the semi-colon in art 10 of the Czech Constitution.
[195] See for example judgment of the CCC of 13 November 2007, IV. ÚS 301/05.
[196] See for example judgment of the CCC of 20 June 2001, n. Pl. ÚS 14/01.
[197] A decision does not even create *res iudicata* (art 35 para 1 LCC *a contrario*).
[198] See the debate reproduced in Jiří Přibáň, 'Judicial Power vs. Democratic Representation' (n 142) 381.

have certain precedential effects.[199] According to the CCC, the ordinary courts,[200] as well as other state organs, have a constitutional duty to follow the main reasoning of the CCC's rulings in similar cases.[201] The other constitutional actors have gradually accepted the notion of precedential effect,[202] even though in some cases we may still encounter some resistance from the ordinary courts.[203]

The status of constitutional conventions is perhaps the most contested aspect of the Czech constitutional system. Even though the binding nature of constitutional conventions has been confirmed by the Czech courts on several occasions,[204] not all of the relevant constitutional actors have internalized this position. Quite recently, for example, Czech President Miloš Zeman has labelled the concept of constitutional convention as 'idiotic' and made clear that he will not let himself be bound by unwritten rules.[205]

To complete the picture, the Constitution also defines the hierarchy of sub-constitutional sources of law. The status of statutes (*zákony*), the Senate's statutory measures (*zákonná opatření*), government regulations (*nařízení vlády*),[206] ministerial decrees (*vyhlášky ministerstev*),[207] and directives of territorial self-governing units issued in the area of assigned public administration (*nařízení obce* or *nařízení kraje*)[208] is clear as these sources of law follow a clear hierarchical order.[209] Regarding statutes, it is also important to emphasize that those statutes that must be passed by both chambers of the parliament[210] and those that directly implement the Czech Constitution, such as the Municipalities Act, are often referred to as 'organic laws'.[211]

b) A Rigid Constitution

The Czech Constitution is a rigid one and this choice has never been seriously questioned. The notion of an entrenched constitution protected by procedural rules against hasty change and guarded by a strong specialized Constitutional Court is, of course, an important aspect of the German constitutionalism which was a crucial source of inspiration for the Czech Constitution.[212] This being said, the Czech constitutional order is not amongst the most rigid constitutions in the world. First, Czechia, being a unitary state, obviously lacks the

---

[199] Judgment of the CCC of 13 November 2007, IV. ÚS 301/05, paras 55 ff.
[200] In the individual constitutional complaints proceeding the 'precedential' binding power vis-à-vis the legislature is yet another issue.
[201] This obviously gives rise—though indirectly—to an obligation to know the CCC's case law.
[202] See the discussion in Ladislav Vyhnánek, 'Judikatura v ústavním právu', in Michal Bobek and Zdeněk Kühn (eds), *Judikatura a právní argumentace* (Auditorium, Prague, 2013) 353.
[203] Perhaps the best example of such resistance is the 'Slovak pensions' saga which involved a conflict between the Supreme Administrative Court and the CCC. See Robert Zbíral, 'Czech Constitutional Court, Judgment of 31 January 2012' (n 110) and other literature cited above in n 110. Both the civil and the criminal branch of the Supreme Court had similar encounters with the CCC (*ne bis idem*, reception of the judgment of the CCC of 19 September 1995, IV. ÚS 81/95).
[204] For example, in the judgment of 20 June 2000, Pl. ÚS 14/01, *Appointment of the CNB Governor*.
[205] See Lukáš Werner and Jan Wirnitzer, 'Pojem ústavní zvyklosti je idiotský, řekl Zeman. Němcové nechal naději' (iDNES.cz, 11 July 2013) https://www.idnes.cz/zpravy/domaci/zeman-sance-na-vladu-pro-cssd-a-byva lou-koalici.A130711_071534_domaci_wlk (last accessed on 13 March 2022).
[206] See art 78 of the Czech Constitution.
[207] See art 79 para 3 of the Czech Constitution.
[208] See art 79 para 3 in conjunction with art 105 of the Czech Constitution.
[209] Note that in order to avoid unnecessary confusion in English I depart from literal translation and use a different term for each of these sources of law, even though the original Czech wording of the Czech Constitution employs the same term 'nařízení' for several sources of law.
[210] See art 40 of the Constitution.
[211] Karel Klíma, *Odpovědnost územní samosprávy* (Metropolitan University Prague Press, Prague, 2014) 25.
[212] See Section B.1.

safeguards known from federal countries, such as ratification by states or lands. Second, the people are not included in the process of constitutional change.

The formal aspect of rigidity thus consists only of (1) the heightened three-fifths majorities required in the two chambers of the parliament to adopt a constitutional law,[213] (2) the mandatory consent of the Senate, which cannot be overruled by the Chamber of Deputies in the case of constitutional laws, and (3) the Eternity Clause.[214]

The Czech Constitution is thus rigid, but not overly so. The practical rigidity of the constitutional order is yet another issue. In addition to the constitutional laws listed above,[215] the parliament has adopted six constitutional laws that amended the Constitution and one that amended the Charter.[216] While several of these amendments have been rather minor,[217] two of them have had significant repercussions for the Czech constitutional *Gestalt*. The 2002 Euro-Amendment,[218] aimed at preparing the Czech constitutional system for accession to the European Union, reshaped the Czech constitutional system and arguably also its material core. The 2012 Amendment, which introduced the direct election of the President and modified other elements of President's constitutional status, has brought Czechia closer to a semi-presidential system.[219]

Other possible changes in the Czech constitutional order have so far remained only in the rhetorical realm. Proposals to introduce referenda to the Czech constitutional system and thus widen the area of popular participation are prominent in this regard,[220] but significant discussion has also taken place as regards the effectiveness of the executive branch and the position of the government.

The Czech Constitution also includes the so-called 'Eternity Clause' in its article 9 para 2, which provides that 'any changes in the essential requirements of a democratic state governed by the rule of law are impermissible'. This Eternity Clause has been interpreted as having supra-constitutional status and cannot be changed even by a constitutional amendment. Thus, it adds another ultra-rigid layer to the constitutional structure.

Despite earlier uses of the Eternity Clause in the CCC's case law,[221] it was its *Euro-Amendment* judgment[222] that identified the full potential of the Eternity Clause in the Czech Constitution. In this case, the CCC effectively reinterpreted a key aspect of the 2001 constitutional amendment and interpreted the Czech Constitution as if such an amendment had never been made—all of this based on article 9 para 2 of the Czech Constitution.

In this case, the CCC was confronted with constitutional changes introduced by Constitutional Law No. 395/2001.[223] Prior to the Law's adoption, the Czech Constitution had basically adhered to the dualist concept of the relationship between international and

---

[213] According to art 39 para 4 of the Constitution a three-fifths majority of *all* deputies and *present* senators is necessary to adopt a constitutional law.

[214] On the Eternity Clause see Section E.

[215] See Section D.1.

[216] There have been several amendments of the constitutional laws defining the state's borders or the Constitutional Law on Higher Self-Governing Units, but these have been rather technical and not of great importance.

[217] Such as the amendment limiting the immunities of members of the parliament and Constitutional Justices or the one that increased the maximum length of detention under art 8 para 3 of the Charter from twenty-four to forty-eight hours.

[218] Constitutional Law N. 395/2001 Coll.

[219] Constitutional Law N. 71/2012 Coll.

[220] On the problem of popular participation see also Sections C.7 and F.

[221] Judgment of the CCC of 21 December 1993, Pl. ÚS 19/93.

[222] Judgment of the CCC of 25 June 2002, Pl. ÚS 36/01.

[223] The so-called 'Euro-Amendment'; this name is derived from the fact that this amendment was meant to prepare the Czech Constitution for the Czech Republic's accession to the European Union.

national law. At the same time, it recognized one important exception, namely so-called 'international human rights treaties'. This category of international treaties enjoyed direct effect in national law[224] and the CCC had the authority to annul legislation that was not in conformity with such international human rights treaties.

Following the aforementioned constitutional amendment, the situation changed considerably. First, the Czech Constitution adopted a monist approach to international treaties, declaring that all promulgated treaties to the ratification of which parliament has given its consent and by which the Czech Republic is bound form a part of the Czech legal order and take precedence over statutes (article 10 of the Czech Constitution). Second, since international human rights treaties have ceased—from the constitutional point of view—to form a special category of international treaties, the CCC has lost its authority to review whether national legislation conforms to standards set by them. This competence of the CCC was functionally replaced by the authority of general courts directly to apply any international treaty (including, but not limited to, international human rights treaties) in cases where it conflicted with a domestic statute.

However, the CCC refused to acknowledge the effects of the *Euro-Amendment* and interpreted the Czech Constitution as if the CCC was still allowed to review domestic legislation from the point of view of its conformity with international human rights treaties. It claimed that such a change would lower the procedural level of human rights protection and that it would—as such—contradict the very basic constitutional principles protected by the Eternity Clause. This heavily criticized[225] judgment indicated the resolve of the CCC to draw very concrete practical implications from the Eternity Clause.

Therefore, few experts were genuinely surprised when—in 2009—the CCC in the *Melčák* judgment[226] took yet another step and made it clear that it has, or thinks it has, the authority to annul constitutional laws. The constitutional law in question[227] was adopted in the middle of a political crisis and was supposed to solve the crisis by a once-and-for-all shortening of the fifth term of office of the Chamber of Deputies, thus finding the quickest way to arrive at snap elections. Even though article 35 of the Czech Constitution provided for several opportunities to dissolve the Chamber of Deputies, the deputies did not find them acceptable and opted for an ad hoc constitutional law that allowed this singular shortening of the electoral term. Most scholars considered this solution to be in conformity with the Czech Constitution as the same solution had been successfully employed in a similar political impasse in 1998.[228] However, the CCC thought otherwise and annulled the constitutional law in question because it was a one-time solution that contravened the principle of generality of law and the prohibition of retroactivity.[229]

---

[224] See art 10 of the Czech Constitution prior to changes introduced by Constitutional Law No 395/2001: '*ratified and promulgated international human rights treaties, by which the Czech Republic is bound, are directly binding and take precedence over statutes*'.

[225] Cf Zdeněk Kühn and Jan Kysela, 'Je ústavou vždy to, co Ústavní soud řekne, že ústava je?' (2002) 10 Časopis pro právní vědu a praxi 199; and Jan Filip, 'Nález č. 403/2002 Sb. jako rukavice hozená ústavodárci Ústavním soudem' (2002) 11 Právní zpravodaj 11.

[226] Judgment of the CCC of 10 September 2009, Pl. ÚS 27/09, *Melčák*. For further analysis see also Yaniv Roznai, 'Legisprudence limitations on constitutional amendments? Reflections on the Czech Constitutional Court's declaration of unconstitutional Constitutional Act' (2014) 8 Vienna Journal on International Constitutional Law 29; and Ivo Šlosarčík, 'Czech Republic 2009–2012: On unconstitutional amendment of the Constitution, limits of EU law and direct presidential elections' (2013) 3 European Public Law 435.

[227] Constitutional Law N. 195/2009 Coll.

[228] See Constitutional Law N. 69/1998 Coll. of 19 March 1998, on Shortening the Term of the Chamber of Deputies.

[229] See n 226.

Both the aforementioned examples show that the CCC is not shy of using the Eternity Clause to drastically reinterpret or even annul constitutional laws. Moreover, it has not exercised much restraint and has done so in cases where the violation of the Eternity Clause was far from obvious.[230]

2. Substantive Aspects of the Czech Constitutional *Gestalt*

Having explained the polycentric nature and rigidity of the Czech Constitution, we may turn our attention to the substantive aspects of the Czech constitutional system, namely human rights constitutionalism, the principle of democracy, the principle of (material) *Rechtsstaat*, the principle of separation of powers and the principle of territorial self-governance.

a) Human Rights Constitutionalism

Fundamental rights and their protection hold a special place in the Czech constitutional *Gestalt*. Even Charter 77, the most important dissident project of the communist era,[231] was actually a project concerning human rights, challenging the communist regime's failure to deliver on its promises after the ratification of the ICCPR. Hence, the new Czech post-1989 and post-1993 constitutional project put significant emphasis on the effective protection of human rights.[232]

There are several important questions in this regard. First, the Charter is a very ambitious document that contains virtually all human rights protected by the ECHR as well as an extensive list of social, economic, and cultural rights. Second, the Constitution has created a robust system of fundamental rights protection. Its article 4 stipulates that 'fundamental rights and basic freedoms shall enjoy the protection of judicial bodies'. Apart from that, a very strong CCC has been established with an extensive set of powers, including the power to review individual decisions in the constitutional complaints procedure.[233]

The CCC, soon after its creation, adopted important fundamental rights doctrines that have created a doctrinal framework of fundamental rights protection. Three of the most influential Justices of the CCC in the 1990s and 2000s, Vladimír Klokočka, Pavel Holländer, and Eliška Wagnerová, were particularly keen on searching for inspiration in Germany. As a result, there are more than sixty references to the BVerfG's jurisprudence in the CCC's case law.[234] Moreover, the significance of the BVerfG's case law is greater than the mere number of references suggests, as it shaped key constitutional doctrines in the early phases of the CCC's existence. The CCC has transplanted, among other things, the German proportionality test,[235] the doctrine of 'fundamental rights as objective values', and the concept of *Drittwirkung*.[236]

---

[230] For a more sober application of the Eternity Clause, see *Lisbon I* judgment, para 93.

[231] See Jonathan Bolton, *Worlds of Dissent: Charter 77, The Plastic People of the Universe, and Czech Culture under Communism* (Harvard University Press, Cambridge, MA, 2012).

[232] Despite the aforementioned scepticism of some important political figures, such as Václav Klaus.

[233] See Section C.6.

[234] See Ladislav Vyhnánek, 'Judikatura v ústavním právu' (n 202) 349; and Jana Ondřejková, Kristina Blažková and Jan Chmel, 'The Use of Foreign Legal Materials by the Constitutional Court of the Czech Republic', in Giuseppe Franco Ferrari (ed), *Judicial Cosmopolitanism The Use of Foreign Law in Contemporary Constitutional Systems* (Brill, Leiden, 2019) 599 ff.

[235] See judgment of the CCC of 12 October 1994, Pl. ÚS 4/94.

[236] Judgment of the CCC of 14 July 2004, I. ÚS 185/04.

Another layer of the Czech human rights constitutionalism concerns the importance of international human rights law. The CCC has been considered a champion in the application of the ECHR in Czechia and relied heavily on the ECtHR's case law when interpreting the Constitution and the Charter.[237] It quotes the Strasbourg jurisprudence on a regular basis and in an extensive manner.[238] This trend is not surprising since the catalogue of human rights adopted in Czechia was, to a significant degree, influenced by the ECHR. In fact, several definitions of human rights in the Czech Charter mirror almost word for word their equivalents in the ECHR.[239]

In general, the case law of the CCC has been very 'ECHR-friendly'.[240] It has been heavily influenced by the Strasbourg Court's jurisprudence in areas such as freedom of speech, the right to privacy[241] and positive obligations under articles 2, 3, and 4 ECHR.[242] It can be argued that the CCC acts as the ECHR's ally in that helps to enforce the ECHR jurisprudence domestically, especially vis-à-vis the ordinary courts and the parliament.[243]

Due to its 'ECHR-friendly' approach, the CCC also carefully avoided or brushed aside any potential conflict between the Czech constitutional laws and the ECHR. Instead, it tried to read the ECHR into the Czech constitutional order and, if necessary, stretched the human rights provisions in the Czech Charter of Fundamental Rights to their limits. For instance, the CCC sometimes quashed the decisions of the ordinary courts with the use of highly contestable conclusions based on a very expansive reading of the ECHR and the ECtHR's case law. For instance, the CCC[244] literally 'created' the right to monetary relief for non-pecuniary injuries.[245] This is not an uncommon move for a European constitutional court.[246] However, the CCC did not rely on the Czech Charter of Fundamental Rights at all. Instead, it arrived at this conclusion *solely* on the ground of interpretation of article 5 para 5 ECHR[247] and argued that the notion of 'an enforceable right to compensation' (*droit à réparation*) in article 5 para 5 ECHR has an autonomous meaning which entails the right to compensation for

---

[237] See, for example, Michal Bobek and David Kosař, 'The Application of European Union Law and the Law of the European Convention of Human Rights in the Czech Republic and Slovakia: An Overview', in Giuseppe Martinico and Oreste Pollicino (eds), *National Judges and Supranational Laws: A Comparative Overview on the National Treatment of EU Law and the ECHR* (Europa Law Publishing, 2010) 157; Lubomír Majerčík, 'Czech Republic: Strasbourg Case Law Undisputed', in Patricia Popelier, Sarah Lambrecht, and Koen Lemmens (eds), *Criticism of the European Court of Human Rights* (Intersentia, Cambridge, 2016) 131 ff; and Ladislav Vyhnánek, 'A holistic view of the Czech Constitutional Court approach to the ECtHR's case law' (2017) 77 ZaöRV 715.

[238] David Kosař et al, *Domestic Judicial Treatment of European Court of Human Rights Case Law: Beyond Compliance* (Routledge, London, 2020).

[239] See David Kosař, 'Conflicts between Fundamental Rights in the Jurisprudence of the Czech Constitutional Court', in Eva Brems (ed), *Conflicts Between Fundamental Rights* (Intersentia, Cambridge, 2008) 349.

[240] For this reason, we could not trace any opposition to the more activist approach shown recently by the ECtHR. Both constitutional courts seem to be 'touchy' only if the ECtHR criticizes *their* practice. See e.g. the reaction of the CCC to the ECtHR's ruling in *Krčmář and Others v the Czech Republic* (App no 35376/97, 3 March 2000), described in Jiří Malenovský, 'Obnova řízení před ústavním soudem v důsledku rozsudku Evropského soudu pro lidská práva' (2001) 140 Právník 1241, 1242.

[241] Judgment of the CCC of 15 March 2005, I. ÚS 367/03.

[242] See e.g. judgment of the CCC of 2 March 2015, I. ÚS 1565/14.

[243] See David Kosař and Jan Petrov, 'The Architecture of the Strasbourg System of Human Rights: The Crucial Role of the Domestic Level and the Constitutional Courts in Particular' (2017) 77 ZaöRV 585.

[244] Judgment of the CCC of 13 July 2006, Pl. ÚS 85/04, available in English at 1-85-04.pdf (usoud.cz) (last accessed on 13 March 2022).

[245] Judgment of the CCC of 13 July 2006, Pl. ÚS 85/04. For a detailed discussion of this judgment see Michal Bobek, 'Ústavní soud: Má srovnávací argumentace přednost před českým zákonodárcem, judikaturou i doktrínou anebo je císař nahý?' (2006) 12 Soudní rozhledy 415.

[246] See e.g. the famous *Princess Soraya* case of the German Federal Constitutional Court (34 BVerfGE 269, 1973). Cf. Donald Kommers, *The Constitutional Jurisprudence of the Federal Republic of Germany* (Duke University Press, Durham, NC, 1997) 124–128.

[247] And with the use of comparative argument 'read into' art 5 para 5 ECHR.

both pecuniary and non-pecuniary injury. Unfortunately, the ECtHR has, to our knowledge, never held so.

The CCC has also addressed the relationship between the ECHR and other non-human rights, international treaties. For instance, when it faced a conflict between the obligations stemming from the ECHR on the one hand and the European Convention on Extradition on the other, it relied on its earlier *Euro-Amendment* judgment[248] and held that the ECHR must prevail as it is a human rights treaty.[249] In sum, the CCC again confirmed its generous 'pro-ECHR stance'. However, the CCC has not yet had to deal with more difficult cases such as conflicts between the ECHR and UN Security Council Resolutions. Under the logic of the CCC reasoning, the ECHR should prevail over *any* 'non-human rights treaty', which is not only a problematic position vis-à-vis article 103 of the UN Charter, but also a more generous reading of the ECHR than the one provided by the ECtHR itself.[250]

b) Democratic Principle and Popular Sovereignty

The principle of popular sovereignty is not explicitly mentioned in the Constitution, but it is still implicitly protected by article 2 para 1 which states that the people are 'the source of all power in the State'. In other words, in the Czech Republic there is no source of state power other than the people and state power can be exercised only through bodies of the state which are derived from the people either directly or indirectly, and thereby legitimized to exercise the power. The only exception is the direct exercise of state power by the people in accordance with the provisions of article 2 para 2 of the Constitution, which reads as follows: 'a Constitutional Law may define when the people exercise state power directly'. The only existing example of this is constitutional law on a referendum on the Czech Republic's accession to the European Union.[251]

This constitutional principle is strongly attached to the principle of democracy as articulated mainly in article 1 para 1 of the Constitution and Article 2 para 1 of the Charter: '(1) The State is founded on democratic values and must not be bound either by an exclusive ideology or by a particular religion.' The principle of democracy is also mirrored in Article 23 of the Charter. It sets out the right to resistance and which reads as follows: 'citizens have the right to resist anybody who would do away with the democratic order of human rights and fundamental freedoms, established by the Charter, if the work of the constitutional organs and an effective use of legal means are frustrated'.

The principle of consensus is implicitly stated in article 5 of the Constitution. According to it, all participants in political competition must accept basic democratic precepts and reject violence as a means of asserting their interests, otherwise this non-violent, open, and pluralistic competition would not be possible at all. This is safeguarded in the Political Parties Act[252] with its mechanism of dissolution of political parties and movements disregarding these basic consented-to principles of democracy, non-violence, and respect for the human rights of all.

---

[248] Judgment of the CCC of 25 June 2002, Pl. ÚS 36/01 *Euro-Amendment*.
[249] Judgment of the CCC of 15 April 2003, Pl. ÚS 752/02. For further details see Eliška Wagnerová, 'The Direct Applicability of Human Rights Treaties', in Venice Commission, *The status of international treaties on human rights* (Council of Europe Press, 2006) 117.
[250] See *Behrami v France* (App no 71412/01), and *Saramati v France, Germany and Norway* (App no 78166/01), admissibility decisions of the ECtHR (GC) of 2 May 2007.
[251] Constitutional Law N. 515/2002 Coll., on the Referendum on the Accession to the European Union. See also Section C.3.
[252] Law N. 424/1991 Coll., on Political Parties.

The principle of majority is stated in article 6 of the Constitution together with the closely connected principle of the protection of minorities: 'political decisions shall proceed from the will of the majority, expressed by free vote. Majority decisions shall respect the protection of minorities'. Another important aspect of the principle of democracy is the time-limited terms of office of the government, the President, and parliament, and consequently the regular holding of elections.[253]

The principle of democracy must be respected not only during the law-making process, but also when laws are interpreted. The rules maintaining democracy and prohibiting the misuse of interpretation are contained in article 9 para 3 of the Constitution which provides that 'legal norms may not be interpreted so as to authorize anyone to remove or jeopardize the democratic foundations of the state'.

The protection of political rights and safeguards of plurality are inseparably linked to the principle of democracy. The principle of plurality is understood to mean that the State is not bound by any concrete ideology or religion,[254] and conflicts of opinions are solved by discussion and voting or elections. The free competition of political forces is set out in article 22 of the Charter and in article 5 of the Constitution.[255] This plurality is represented by a wide variety of mass media, civic associations, and especially political and election parties, which can challenge each other in free and fair elections in which at least two parties must take part. Additionally, the protection of, *inter alia*, the freedom of expression and information, the freedoms of assembly, association in political parties or equal access to public offices are considered basic building blocks of the democratic principle and often invoked by the CCC.

On the other hand, the Czech constitutional system embraces the concept of 'militant democracy'.[256] This is discernible even from statutory law that allows for the dissolution of political parties[257] and criminalization of hate speech. Furthermore, both the ordinary courts and the CCC seem to accept the militant democracy approach. Important cases in this regard include the dissolution of the Workers' Party by the Supreme Administrative Court[258] and the CCC's approach to verbal crimes.[259]

c) The *Rechtsstaat* Principle

The Constitution explicitly embraces the *Rechtsstaat* principle in its very first article.[260] What is more, the essential requirements of that principle are protected by the Eternity Clause.[261] That makes the *Rechtsstaat* principle, along with the democratic principle arguably one of the two most important principles of Czech constitutionalism.

As a result, conceptualization of this principle is crucial. Before we delve into the CCC's understanding of the *Rechtsstaat* principle and the doctrine, we must add three caveats. First, the Constitution defines neither the principle nor its essential components. This de facto left significant room for the CCC to pad this vague principle with more precise content. Second,

---

[253] Art 21 para 1 of the Charter.

[254] See art 2 para 1 of the Charter.

[255] 'The political system is based on free and voluntary formation of and free competition between political parties respecting the basic democratic precepts and rejecting violence as a means of asserting their interests.'

[256] Judgment of the Supreme Administrative Court of 17 February 2010, Pst 1/2009-348. For a broader context see Miroslav Mareš, 'Czech militant democracy in action dissolution of the Workers' Party and the wider context of this Act' (2012) 26 East European Politics and Societies: and Cultures 33.

[257] Law N. 424/1991, paras 12–16a.

[258] Judgment of the Supreme Administrative Court of 17 February 2010, Pst 1/2009-348.

[259] Notably the Judgment of the CCC of 28 February 2011, IV. ÚS 2011/10 that explicitly invokes the concept of militant democracy and declares it a constitutional principle.

[260] Art 1 para 1 of the Constitution.

[261] Art 1 para 2 of the Constitution.

the Czech Constitution explicitly refers to the '*Rechtsstaat*' (*právní stát*) and not to the 'rule of law' (*vláda práva*).[262] While these concepts are often used interchangeably, there are significant differences between them. Most importantly, '*Rechtsstaat* rests on some sort of connection of between the legal system and the state, [whereas] the rule of law is a quality of, or theory about, a legal order.'[263] The choice of the wording in the Czech Constitution thus implies a strong connection between the state and the legal system and makes clear that the state (not just the legal norms) must be of a certain quality to qualify as *Rechtsstaat*. It also explains a peculiar understanding of the Czech *Rechtsstaat* principle, which is very broad and includes several procedural and organizational principles of constitutionalism. Finally, the Czech *Rechtsstaat* principle is a reactive and value-laden concept, because it reflects the Czech totalitarian past and perhaps also the constitutional identity of Czechia.[264]

Now we can move to the conceptualization of the *Rechtsstaat* principle. Early on, the CCC rejected the purely formal reading of the principle and made clear that the Constitution presupposes a material *Rechtsstaat*. In its understanding of material *Rechtsstaat*, the CCC built on the reasoning of its federal predecessor which spelled out its perception of the material *Rechtsstaat* in the *Lustration I* judgment:[265]

> In contrast to the totalitarian system, which was founded on the basis of the goals of the moment and was never bound by legal principles, much less principles of constitutional law, a democratic state proceeds from quite different values and criteria.
>
> …
>
> Each state, or rather those which were compelled over a period of forty years to endure the violation of fundamental rights and basic freedoms by a totalitarian regime, has the right to [en]throne democratic leadership and to apply such legal measures as are apt to avert the risk of subversion or of a possible relapse into totalitarianism, or at least to limit those risks.
>
> …
>
> As one of the basic concepts and requirements of a law-based state [*Rechtsstaat*], legal certainty must, therefore, consist [of] certainty with regard to its substantive values. Thus, the contemporary construction of a law-based state [*Rechtsstaat*], which has for its starting point a discontinuity with the totalitarian regime as concerns values, may not adopt … criteria of formal-legal and material-legal continuity, which is based on a differing value system, not even under the circumstances that the formal normative continuity of the legal order makes it possible. Respect for continuity with the old value system would not be a guarantee of legal certainty but, on the contrary, by calling into question the values of the new system, legal certainty would be threatened in society

---

[262] On the differences between the principle of the rule of law and the *Rechtsstaat* principle see Rainer Grote, 'Rule of law, Rechtsstaat and 'État de droit', in Christian Starck (ed), *Constitutionalism, Universalism, and Democracy: A Comparative Analysis* (Nomos, Baden-Baden, 1999) 270; Michael Rosenfeld, 'Rule of Law Versus Rechtsstaat', in Peter Häberle and Jörg P Müller (eds), *Menschenrechte und Bürgerrechte in einer vielgestaltigen Welt* (Helbing & Lichtenhahn, Basel, 2000) 49; Nicholas W Barber, 'Review: The Rechtsstaat and the Rule of Law' (2003) 53 The University of Toronto Law Journal 443, 444.

[263] Nicholas W Barber, 'Review: The Rechtsstaat and the Rule of Law' (n 262) 444.

[264] On the Czech constitutional identity see David Kosař and Ladislav Vyhnánek, 'Ústavní identita České republiky' (2018) 157 Právník 854.

[265] Pl. 03/92 *Lustration I*. This judgment has been widely cited in comparative constitutional law casebooks. For further details see also Zdeněk Kühn, 'České lustrační rozhodnutí – role srovnávacího práva a nedostatky v soudcovské argumentaci', in Oto Novotný (ed), *Pocta Vladimíru Mikule k 65. Narozeninám* (Aleš Čeněk, Ostrava, 2002) 361, 369.

and eventually the citizens' faith in the credibility of the democratic system would be shaken.[266]

The CCC accepted this conceptualization of material *Rechtsstaat* in its first judgment concerning the Act on the Lawlessness of the Communist Regime:

> However, the [pre-Second World War] positivist tradition ... in its later development many times exposed its weakness. ... in Germany, the National Socialist domination was accepted as legal, even though it gnawed out the substance and, in the end, destroyed the basic foundations of the Weimar democracy. After the war, this legalistic conception of political legitimacy made it possible for Klement Gottwald [the first Communist Czechoslovak president] to 'fill old casks with new wine'. Then in 1948 he was able, by the formal observance of constitutional procedures, to 'legitimate' the February Putsch. In the face of injustice, the principle that 'law is law' revealed itself to be powerless.[267]

Since then, the CCC has repeatedly invoked the material reading of *Rechtsstaat* and this reading is supported by virtually all scholars.[268]

There is much less agreement regarding the individual components of the *Rechtsstaat* principle. As mentioned above, the concept of *Rechtsstaat* is understood broadly and its components can be divided into five categories: (1) formal *Rechtsstaat* safeguards; (2) procedural *Rechtsstaat* safeguards; (3) organizational *Rechtsstaat* safeguards; (4) rights oriented *Rechtsstaat* safeguards; and (5) other substantive *Rechtsstaat* safeguards.[269] In what follows we will discuss the most important ones.

The formal dimension of the *Rechtsstaat* principle stems from explicit provisions of the Constitution as well as from the general *Rechtsstaat* clauses in articles 1 and 2 of the Constitution and articles 1 to 4 of the Charter. The formal *Rechtsstaat* includes basically all eight of Fuller's formal-rule-of-law principles,[270] but it goes well beyond that. More specifically, the CCC held that legal rules must be general,[271] publicly promulgated,[272] prospective,[273] sufficiently clear and intelligible,[274] free of inconsistencies,[275] relatively stable,[276] non-arbitrary and thus obeyable,[277] and administered in a way that does not wildly diverge from their obvious or apparent meaning.[278] Of these eight principles, the CCC is particularly

---

[266] English translation of the judgment available at: *czechoslovakia_lustration_1992.pdf (csic.es), specifically pages 12 f (last accessed on 13 March 2022).

[267] Judgment of 21 December 1993, Pl. ÚS 19/93, *Lawlessness of the Communist Regime*.

[268] For an overview of the relevant case law and literature, see Maxim Tomoszek, *Podstatné náležitosti demokratického právního státu* (Leges, Prague, 2015) 40–45 and 56–94.

[269] We build on the categorization provided by Tomoszek (Maxim Tomoszek, *Podstatné náležitosti demokratického právního státu* (Leges, Prague, 2015) 72–80), but we categorize the *Rechtsstaat* principles slightly differently for the international audience.

[270] Lon L Fuller, *The Morality of Law* (Yale University Press, New Haven, CT, 1969) 33–94.

[271] See, for example, judgment of the CCC of 17 March 2009, Pl. ÚS 24/08, *Prague Airport*, and the aforementioned *Melčák* case.

[272] Judgment of the CCC of 3 June 3009, I. ÚS 420/09, para 25.

[273] *Melčák* case; and judgment of the CCC of 12 August 2014, I. ÚS 3849/11, para 28.

[274] Judgment of the CCC of 16 June 1997, IV. US 167/97, and judgment of the CCC of 12 November 2013, Pl. ÚS 22/13, para 24.

[275] Judgment of the CCC of 6 February 2007, IV. ÚS 38/06, Part IV, and judgment of the CCC of 20 May 2014, II. ÚS 2560/13, para 28.

[276] Judgment of the CCC of 6 March 2014, II. ÚS 3764/12, para 23.

[277] Judgment of the CCC of 19 June 2014, III. ÚS 980/13, para 29.

[278] Judgment of the CCC of 6 March 2014, II. ÚS 3764/12, paras 23–24, and judgment of the CCC of 31 March 2015, Pl. ÚS 1/14, para 62.

vigilant in guarding the prohibition of retroactivity and legal certainty. In addition to these well-established formal rule of law principles, the CCC's conception of *Rechtsstaat* also encompasses a general principle of legality which contains several safeguards: state authority may be asserted only if it is provided for by law and in the manner prescribed by law;[279] everyone may act in a way that is not prohibited by law, nobody may be compelled to do what is not imposed on them by statutory law, and only statutory law may define what constitutes a crime and the penalties that may be imposed for committing it;[280] and the prohibition of the excessive or superfluous application of otherwise rationally and non-arbitrarily selected instruments of regulation.[281]

In addition, the CCC spelt out several procedural *Rechtsstaat* safeguards that roughly correspond to what Jeremy Waldron refers to as the procedural characteristics of the rule of law.[282] These safeguards develop the guarantees in the Constitution and Charter[283] and include in particular the right to an effective judicial protection of fundamental rights and freedoms,[284] the right to access a court,[285] the right to a lawful judge,[286] the right to a fair trial[287] before an independent[288] court, the presumption of innocence,[289] and reasonable length of the judicial proceedings.[290] Moreover, it also includes a principle that compensation for damages may be demanded from the state if such damage is caused by the unlawful decision of a court or a public administrative authority, or as the result of an incorrect official procedure.[291]

As mentioned above, the Czech concept of *Rechtsstaat* requires a certain quality from the State, and thus it also encompasses several safeguards that belong to the framework-of-government part of the Constitution. These organizational *Rechtsstaat* safeguards include the separation of powers,[292] territorial self-government,[293] the democratic nature of the legislative process,[294] an independent[295] judiciary, the democratic accountability of political decision-making and free competition of political parties,[296] the enforceability of rights,[297] and maintaining an effective system of the investigation and prosecution of crime.[298] Some

[279] Judgment of the CCC of 5 November 1996, Pl. ÚS 14/96, art 2 para 3 of the Constitution and art 2 para 2 of the Charter.

[280] Judgment of the CCC of 23 October 2008, III. ÚS 487/07, Part IV. See also arts 39 and 40 para 6 of the Charter.

[281] Judgment of the CCC of 1 August 2005, IV. ÚS 31/05.

[282] Jeremy Waldron, 'The rule of law and the importance of procedure', in James E Fleming (ed), *Nomos L: Getting to the Rule of Law* (New York University Press, New York, NY, 2011) 3–31.

[283] See in particular art 3 para 3 of the Charter, art 4 of the Constitution, art 36 para 1 of the Charter, arts 36 para 1 and 37 of the Charter, art 81 of the Constitution, art 38 para 1 of the Charter, arts 1, 3, 36 para 1 and 37 para 3 of the Charter.

[284] See, for example, the *Euro-Amendment* judgment of the CCC.

[285] Judgment of the CCC of 26 April 2005, Pl. ÚS 11/04.

[286] Judgment of the CCC of 18 October 2001, III. ÚS 29/01.

[287] Judgment of the CCC of 26 April 2005, Pl. ÚS 11/04, judgment of the CCC of 21 February 2007, II. ÚS 490/04 and many others.

[288] Judgment of the CCC of 18 June 2002, Pl. ÚS 7/02, or Judgment of the CCC of 29 September 2009, Pl. ÚS 33/09.

[289] Judgment of the CCC of 12 January 2009, II. ÚS 1975/08.

[290] Judgment of the CCC of 22 January 2004, IV. ÚS 475/03.

[291] Judgment of the CCC of 6 December 2011, Pl. ÚS 35/09.

[292] Judgment of the CCC of 15 February 2007, Pl. ÚS 77/06.

[293] Judgment of the CCC of 2 April 2013, Pl. ÚS 6/13, *Klatovy*, para 27. For further details see Section D.2.e.

[294] Judgment of the CCC of 15 February 2007, Pl. ÚS 77/06. See also art 59 para 2, art 69 para 2, arts 78 and 79, art 87, art 95 paras 1, 2, art 105, arts 39–52 of the Constitution.

[295] Judgment of the CCC of 18 June 2002, Pl. ÚS 7/02. See also arts 87 and 95 para 1, arts 81 and 82 para 1 of the Constitution, art 36 para 1 of the Charter.

[296] Judgment of the CCC of 10 September 2009, Pl. ÚS 27/09, *Melčák*.

[297] Judgment of the CCC of 12 October 2009, IV. ÚS 380/09.

[298] Judgment of the CCC of 28 June 2011, Pl. ÚS 17/10, para 62.

authors argue that the organizational dimension of the *Rechtsstaat* includes even the exist-ence of a specialized 'Kelsenian' Constitutional Court, respect for the international obliga-tions of the Czech Republic and the incorporation of all international treaties ratified by the parliament into the domestic law with priority application over domestic laws.[299]

The remaining two dimensions of the *Rechtsstaat* principle concern, with a certain degree of simplification,[300] what is in common law often referred to as substantive rule of law. We decided to divide these substantive *Rechtsstaat* safeguards into two categories, substantive *Rechtsstaat* safeguards aimed at protecting fundamental rights (rights-oriented substantive *Rechtsstaat* safeguards) and other substantive *Rechtsstaat* safeguards that reflect moral and specific Czech constitutional values.

Rights-oriented *Rechtsstaat* safeguards include respect of the State towards fundamental rights and freedoms, the protection of individual autonomy, equality and the prohibition of discrimination, the prohibition of arbitrariness, the principle of proportionality. Other substantive *Rechtsstaat* safeguards include value discontinuity with the communist regime, human dignity, liberty, and fairness. These very broad substantive values serve as a potential safety net that the CCC can rely on in addressing apparent injustice that cannot be remedied by a more specific *Rechtsstaat* component.

In sum, the *Rechtsstaat* principle is a crucial principle of Czech constitutionalism. It en-compasses not only a broad set of formal, procedural, and organizational principles, but also envisages a state based on substantive values such as fundamental rights and fairness. Therefore, it has an undeniable moral dimension.[301] Its breadth has both advantages and drawbacks. On the one hand, it is a flexible concept that can serve as a trump card that the CCC can use if a clear violation of a more specific provision is not apparent. On the other hand, it might be so broad that it loses analytical clarity and separate meaning. If the rule of law encompasses almost everything in the Constitution, then it may well be nothing. Therefore, it would be better if the CCC used it more sparingly in future and prevented the inflation of the uses of this concept in its case law.

d) Separation of Powers

The principle of the separation of powers is a cornerstone of the Czech Constitution. Some scholars even claim that it is the 'jolly joker' of Czech constitutionalism.[302] The principle of horizontal separation of powers stems from article 2 para 1 of the Czech Constitution, which reads as follows: 'all state authority emanates from the people; they exercise it through legis-lative, executive, and judicial bodies', whereas the principle of vertical separation of powers is enshrined in article 8 of the Czech Constitution, which stipulates that '[t]he right of self-governing territorial units to self-government is guaranteed'.

The key organ that decides on most separation of powers issues is the CCC.[303] It decides on both intra-branch[304] and inter-branch[305] competence conflicts. It conceives its power to

---

[299] See e.g. Vojtěch Šimíček, 'Komentář k čl. 1', in Lenka Bahýlová et al, *Ústava České republiky – komentář* (Linde, Prague, 2010) 28.

[300] Rainer Grote, 'Rule of law, Rechtsstaat and 'État de droit'' (n 262); Michael Rosenfeld, 'Rule of Law Versus Rechtsstaat' (n 262); Nicholas W Barber, 'Review: The Rechtsstaat and the Rule of Law' (n 262) 444.

[301] See e.g. judgment of the CCC of 19 January 2017, I. ÚS 3308/16.

[302] Jan Grinc, 'Rozhodování sporů o rozsah kompetencí jako žolík čl. 87 Ústavy' (2014) 23 Jurisprudence 5.

[303] For the sake of brevity, I leave aside the potential delegation of competence to decide some separation of powers issues to the SAC (as envisaged by art 87 para 3 of the Czech Constitution) and peculiar disputes under Law N. 131/2002 Coll., on Deciding Selected Competence Disputes.

[304] See judgment of the CCC of 20 June 2001, Pl. ÚS 14/01, *Appointment of the Governor and the Vice-Governor of the Czech National Bank*.

[305] See e.g. judgment of the CCC of 28 June 2005, Pl. ÚS 24/04, *Elbe Weirs*.

96   DAVID KOSAŘ AND LADISLAV VYHNÁNEK

decide on the competence disputes[306] broadly as to cover not only (1) disputes about the competence to issue the decision (classical competence disputes), but also (2) disputes about taking other measures, and (3) the so-called 'joint competence' disputes.[307]

The classical competence conflicts include both positive[308] and negative[309] conflicts about competence to hand down a decision. The CCC also held, building on the German doctrine, that conflicts of competence can be initiated also by the part of the constitutional organ (*Teilorgan*)[310] which significantly broadened the standing in this type of proceedings before the CCC. The disputes about taking other measures vary from territorial disputes between municipalities[311] to negative competence conflicts regarding the provision of first aid.[312] The CCC also decides on vertical separation of powers disputes between the central organs and the territorial self-governing units.[313]

According to the CCC, the principle of separation of powers is part of the concept of the rule of law. This applies both to horizontal separation of powers[314] as well as to vertical.[315] The basic tenets of the rule of law are protected by the Czech Eternity Clause, which reads as follows: 'any changes in the essential requirements for a democratic state governed by the rule of law are impermissible'.[316] As mentioned above,[317] the CCC found this provision justiciable[318] and adopted the doctrine of unconstitutional constitutional amendments.[319] In other words, the Czech Eternity Clause has supra-constitutional status and it thus prevails over 'ordinary constitutional law'.

Several scholars have argued that the principle of horizontal separation of powers as well as basic features of territorial self-government are protected by the Czech Eternity Clause. For instance, Karel Klíma argues that territorial self-government is an 'essential requirement for a democratic state governed by the rule of law',[320] which means that it has supra-constitutional status. Other constitutional scholars and judges concur.[321]

Importantly, it is generally accepted in the CCC's case law that separation of powers is a legitimate constitutional limitation to fundamental rights.[322] Even if we assume for now that

---

[306] Art 87 para 1(k) of the Czech Constitution.
[307] For further details see Jan Filip, Pavel Holländer, and Vojtěch Šimíček (eds), *Zákon o Ústavním soudu: Komentář* (2nd edn, C H Beck, München, 2007) 765 ff; and Jan Grinc, 'Rozhodování sporů o rozsah kompetencí jako žolík čl. 87 Ústavy' (n 302).
[308] See e.g. judgment of the CCC of 20 June 2001, Pl. ÚS 14/01.
[309] See e.g. judgment of the CCC of 27 September 2007, Pl. ÚS 5/04, *Emergency Health Care*.
[310] See e.g. judgment of the CCC of 28 July 2009, Pl. ÚS 9/09.
[311] See e.g. judgment of the CCC of 11 March 1999, IV. ÚS 361/98, and judgment of the CCC of 3 June 2008, Pl. ÚS 18/08.
[312] See e.g. *Emergency Health Care* (n 309).
[313] On territorial self-governance see below Section D.2.e.
[314] See e.g. judgment of the CCC of 28 June 2005, Pl. ÚS 24/04, *Elbe Weirs*, and judgment of the CCC of 17 March 2009, Pl. ÚS 24/08, *Airport Ruzyně*.
[315] See e.g. judgment of the CCC of 30 September 2002, IV. ÚS 331/02; judgment of the CCC of 7 May 2013, III. ÚS 1669/11; judgment of the CCC of 2 April 2013, Pl. ÚS 6/13, *Klatovy*, para 27; judgment of the CCC of 22 November 2016, III.ÚS 2200/15, para 16; and judgment of the CCC of 20 February 2018, Pl. ÚS 6/17, para 82.
[316] Art 9 para 2 of the Czech Constitution.
[317] See n 221 above and the text that follows.
[318] See e.g. judgment of the CCC of 25 June 2002, Pl. ÚS 36/01, *Euro-Amendment*; judgment of the CCC of 10 September 2009, Pl. ÚS 27/09, *Melčák*.
[319] See e.g. Yaniv Roznai, 'Legisprudence Limitations on Constitutional Amendments?' (n 226).
[320] Karel Klíma, *Odpovědnost územní samosprávy* (n 211) 20–21.
[321] Vojtěch Šimíček, 'Komentář k čl. 9', in Lenka Bahýlová et al, *Ústava České republiky—komentář* (Linde, Prague, 2010) 156 ff; Pavel Molek, *Materiální ohnisko jako věčný limit evropské integrace?* (MUNI Press, Brno, 2014) 138; and Pavel Rychetský et al, *Ústava České republiky: ústavní zákon o bezpečnosti České republiky. Komentář* (Wolters Kluwer, Alphen aan den Rijn, 2015) 87.
[322] See e.g. judgment of the CCC of 2 April 2013, Pl. ÚS 6/13, *Klatovy* (striking down the linked slot machines statutory regulation on the vertical separation of powers grounds); and Decision of the CCC of 13 January 2015, Pl.

separation of powers is not a part of the Czech Eternity Clause,[323] it is a constitutional value and thus the principles of separation of powers and fundamental rights are legal norms of the same legal force. If there is a conflict between two constitutional values, it requires careful balancing, a task which is vested primarily in the CCC.

e) Unity and Decentralization

Even though Czechia is a unitary and not a federative state, it has a territorial structure and self-governmental units. The principle of territorial self-government is a cornerstone of the Czech constitutional order. It is explicitly mentioned among the 'fundamental principles' in Chapter One of the Czech Constitution (article 8) and the Constitution then devotes the whole of its Chapter Seven (articles 99–105) to territorial self-government. Territorial self-governing units are sometimes referred to as the 'sixth power' (the self-governing power) of the State.[324] Several scholars have even argued that the principle of territorial self-government is protected by the Czech Eternity Clause.[325]

The key provisions of the Czech Constitution concerning territorial self-government are the following. Article 8 stipulates that '[t]he right of self-governing territorial units to self-government is guaranteed'. Article 100 para 1 provides that 'territorial self-governing units are territorial communities of citizens with the right to self-government'. Finally, article 104 para 3 stipulates that 'representative bodies [of territorial self-governing units] may, within the limits of their jurisdiction, issue generally binding ordinances'.

The power of self-governing units has increased since 1993, both quantitatively and qualitatively. First, besides the already existing municipal self-government, higher self-governing units (regions) were established by the Constitutional Law Establishing Higher Territorial Self-governing Units,[326] which came into force on 1 January 2000. In the Czech territory, fourteen higher territorial self-governing units were established. One of them is Prague, which is a higher self-governing unit, as well as a municipality and the capital of the Republic.[327] The Constitutional Law Establishing Higher Territorial Self-governing Units delimits the territory of regions according to the territory of districts[328] and builds on administrative division of the State.[329] However, the newly established fourteen self-governing regions differ territorially and organizationally from the eight administrative regions in which the Regional National Committees operated until 1990, and which even now are the territorial districts for a number of specialized authorities of the state administration.[330] From the territorial point of view, regions established by the 1997 Constitutional Law closely follow the regions that existed in 1949–1960, and thus generally respect all the regional centres at the medium level.

ÚS 17/14, *Senator Dryml*, paras 45–51 (which ruled out judicial review of a disciplinary decision of the parliament on the horizontal separation of powers grounds).

[323] See n 215 above and the text that follows.
[324] Karel Klíma, 'Územní samospráva jako 'šestá' moc podle Ústavy ČR?', in Stanislav Kadečka (ed), *Pocta Petru Průchovi* (Vysoká škola aplikovaného práva, Prague, 2009) 103.
[325] Vojtěch Šimíček, 'Komentář k čl. 9' (n 321) 156 ff; Pavel Molek, *Materiální ohnisko jako věčný limit evropské integrace?* (n 321); and Pavel Rychetský et al, *Ústava České republiky* (n 321) 87.
[326] Law N. 347/1997 Coll.
[327] Art 13 of the Constitution and a special Law on the Capital City of Praha No. 131/2000 Coll.
[328] Formerly the basic type of division of the state, recently only some state authorities have been organized on a district basis, e.g. tax offices and labour offices.
[329] Law N. 36/1960 Coll. on Territorial Division of the State.
[330] The most important example is the structure of ordinary courts in accordance with the Law on Courts and Judges No. 6/2002 Coll.

Furthermore, the scope of self-governing power has been gradually increased, mainly through judicial interpretation of the Constitution. Importantly, entrenchment of territorial self-government in the Czech Constitution was an antidote to the communist doctrine of centralization of state power and marked a clear discontinuation with the communist regime.[331] The 1993 Czech Constitution clearly opted for the decentralization of state power and treated territorial self-government as one of the cornerstones of the new democratic regime. By doing so, it emphasized the subsidiarity of the state power in the matters of local interest.[332]

Until the creation of the regions and the adoption of the new Municipalities Act,[333] the principle of territorial self-government was unfulfilled and often neglected by the central organs. Given the fact that the first term of regional councils (2000–2004) was the era of learning by trial and error and of 'regional and municipal institution-building', the territorial self-governing units (both the municipalities and the regions) started to be truly assertive and challenge the encroachment of the central authorities upon the constitutional principle of territorial self-government only in 2004–2008. This in turn led to the significant development in the CCC's case law on vertical separation of powers and the scope of municipal authority.

The CCC's early case law was relatively restrictive regarding the autonomy of territorial self-governing units and the scope of municipal authority. However, the CCC gradually expanded the scope of municipal authority in a series of judgments in 2005–2007[334] in which the CCC developed the four-step test for review of generally binding ordinances. It has applied this four-step test ever since.[335] It consists of the following prongs: (1) whether the municipality had the competence to issue a given generally binding ordinance; (2) whether the municipality, by issuing a given generally binding ordinance, exceeded its material competence stipulated by law (that is whether it acted *ultra vires*); (3) whether the municipality, by issuing a given generally binding ordinance, abused its competence entrusted to it by the statute; and (4) whether a given generally binding ordinance is manifestly unreasonable.[336]

The CCC confirmed and explicitly explained this decisive shift[337] in its case law in its *Jirkov* judgment,[338] where it held, among other things, that (1) the municipal independent (self-governing) competence flows directly from the Constitution and thus municipalities do not require express authorization by the statute to issue a generally binding ordinance,[339]

---

[331] See judgment of the CCC of 11 December 2007, Pl. ÚS 45/06, *Jirkov*, para 24; Pavel Zářecký, 'Kněkterým otázkám ústavního zakotvení územní samosprávy' (2008) 51 Správní právo 14, in particular at 14–16.

[332] See also judgment of the CCC of 7 May 2013, Pl. ÚS 20/16, para 15.

[333] Law N. 128/2000 Coll.

[334] See judgment of the CCC of 22 March 2005, Pl. ÚS 63/04, *Prostějov*; judgment of the CCC of 13 September 2006, Pl. ÚS 57/05, *Nový Bor*; judgment of the CCC of 22 May 2007, Pl. ÚS 30/06, *Ostrov*.

[335] See Pavel Rychetský et al, *Ústava České republiky* (n 321) 1073 ff (and especially para 8 of the commentary on art 104); Lenka Bahýlová et al, *Ústava České republiky—komentář* (Linde, Prague, 2010) 1427 ff, and in particular 1435 (commentary on art 104); Vladimír Sládeček et al, *Ústava České republiky. Komentář.* (2nd edn, C. H. Beck, München, 2016) 1222 ff.

[336] See judgment of the CCC of 22 March 2005, Pl. ÚS 63/04, *Prostějov*; judgment of the CCC of 13 September 2006, Pl. ÚS 57/05, *Nový Bor*; judgment of the CCC of 22 May 2007, Pl. ÚS 30/06, *Ostrov*.

[337] Several commentators have discussed and approved this shift in the CCC's case law. See Pavel Holländer, 'Otazníky ústavnosti obecně závazných vyhlášek' (2008) 16 Právní rozhledy 693; Tomáš Langášek, 'Obrat v nazírání Ústavního soudu na obecně závazné vyhlášky' (2008) Právní rozhledy 356; Ivo Pospíšil, 'Nejnovější judikatura Ústavního soudu k obecně závazným vyhláškám' (2010) 18 Časopis pro právní vědu a praxi 51; Ivo Pospíšil, 'Regulace hazardu jako rukavice hozená před Ústavním soudem: ústavní limity 'kontroly' územních samosprávných celků a jejich dotváření judikaturou Ústavního soudu' (2012) 20 Časopis pro právní vědu a praxi 111; and Jan Brož, 'Obecně závazné vyhlášky (veřejný pořádek deset let od jirkovského nálezu)' (2018) 26 Právní rozhledy 310.

[338] Judgment of the CCC of 11 December 2007, Pl. ÚS 45/06, *Jirkov*.

[339] Ibid, paras 26–27 (referring to the CCC's earlier case law).

and that (2) municipalities may issue a generally binding ordinance even in the area already regulated by the statute, if the object and purpose of the given ordinance is different from the object and purpose of a statute.[340] Since then, it has become a settled case law.

The CCC later held that territorial self-government units are key elements of the separation of powers, which guarantees greater liberty to individuals,[341] and that 'self-governing municipalities guarantee the principle of subsidiarity [of state power], according to which decision-making and responsibility in public matters should be executed at the lowest level of public authority, which is the nearest one to the citizens'.[342] In defining the scope of the constitutional right to territorial self-government, it is thus 'impossible to proceed solely from the wording of the statute, since the right to self-government also has a material aspect (or its own constitutional content) [and ...] the implementing statute cannot empty or in effect eliminate the content of the constitutionally guaranteed right to territorial self-government'.[343] This has two repercussions. First, the scope of territorial self-government 'cannot be dependent just on the legislation, because it could lead to arbitrariness of the legislature and the violation of the principle of territorial self-government itself, which is one of the basic values of a democratic state based on the rule of law'.[344] Second, any limitations to the constitutional principle of territorial self-government must be applied restrictively.[345]

The CCC actually upheld several generally binding ordinances adopted under article 10(a) of the Municipalities Act which regulated matters of public order that were regulated by a statute. More specifically, the CCC upheld generally binding ordinances concerning regulation of lottery terminals and linked slot machines,[346] regulation of the use of pyrotechnics,[347] the regulation of prostitution,[348] the consumption of alcohol in public spaces,[349] and accepted the generally binding ordinance regulating the opening hours of restaurants and bars.[350]

E. Constitutional Identity

In the previous part we aimed to introduce the basic structural substantive features of the Czech constitutional system. The question remains, however, what is the pure essence of the Czech constitutional *Gestalt*, what is its identity[351] and how was it formed. Thus, in this section, we are attempting to present the substantive essence of the Czech constitutional system. In order to do that, we will build on the theoretical concept of constitutional

---

[340] Ibid, para 34 (referring to the CCC's earlier case law).

[341] Judgment of the CCC of 9 August 2016, Pl. ÚS 20/16, para 15.

[342] Ibid.

[343] Judgment of the CCC of 20 February 2018, Pl. ÚS 6/17, para 82.

[344] Judgment of the CCC of 7 May 2013, III.ÚS 1669/11. See also judgment of the CCC of 22 November 2016, III.ÚS 2200/15, para 16–18.

[345] Judgment of the CCC of 22 November 2016, III.ÚS 2200/15, para 16.

[346] See judgment of the CCC of 14 June 2011, Pl. ÚS 29/10 *Chrastava*; judgment of the CCC of 7 September 2011, Pl. ÚS 56/10 *Františkovy Lázně*; Judgment of the CCC of 27 September 2011, Pl. ÚS 22/11 *Kladno* (even though the CCC eventually decided all three judgments on the ground of express statutory authorization under art 10(d) of the Municipalities Act); judgment of the CCC of 2 April 2013, Pl. ÚS 6/13, *Klatovy*.

[347] Judgment of the CCC of 13 September 2006, Pl. ÚS 57/05, *Nový Bor*.

[348] See judgment of the CCC of 13 March 2007, Pl. ÚS 10/06, *Plzeň*.

[349] See judgment of the CCC of 7 September 2010, Pl. ÚS 11/09, *Jeseník*.

[350] See judgment of the CCC of 2 November 2010, Pl. ÚS 28/09, *Břeclav*, paras 33–41. Note that the CCC eventually struck down this ordinance for another reason.

[351] We published our earlier thoughts on this subject in David Kosař and Ladislav Vyhnánek, 'Constitutional Identity in the Czech Republic' (n 170).

identity[352] and try to discern the Czech constitutional identity. Afterwards, we will offer a closer look at the very basic substantive principles that are tied to the Czech constitutional identity and form the core of the Czech constitutional project.

The single most important actor in defining the contours of the Czech constitutional identity in the public sphere is the CCC. Even though it has not used the 'constitutional identity' language explicitly, it has built a considerable amount of 'identity fabric' over the last two decades that we can draw from. For this reason, we will first discuss the relevant provisions of the Czech Constitution that served as a point of departure for the CCC. Then, we will explain how the CCC interprets the Eternity Clause and what implications this may have for the construction of the Czech constitutional identity. However, we will also show that the legal conception(s) of the Czech constitutional identity may clash with its popular conception(s).

The logical point of departure in the search for constitutional identity is the constitutional text. However, the Czech Constitution does not explicitly mention the concept of constitutional identity. Nevertheless, it contains two provisions that are quite useful for constructing one: (1) the set of basic principles that define the nature of Czech statehood in article 1 para 1, and (2) the 'Eternity Clause' in article 9 para 2 which immunizes some of those principles. As von Bogdandy and Schill note, the very fact of deep entrenchment of eternity clauses can be understood as evidence of their importance in the context of national constitutional identity.[353] We will thus first analyse the content of the Eternity Clause and then try to extrapolate from it the concept of Czech constitutional identity.

According to article 1 para 1, '*the Czech Republic is a sovereign, unitary*, and *democratic* state governed by the *rule of law* [[354]], founded on respect for the *rights and freedoms of men and of citizens*'. Article 9 para 2 then further entrenches some of the principles set out in article 1 para 1. More specifically, the Eternity Clause provides that, 'any changes in the essential requirements of a *democratic* state governed by the *rule of law* are impermissible'.[355] Even a quick glance at the text of these provisions reveals that article 1 para 1 of the Czech Constitution and the Eternity Clause are interrelated and have two concepts in common, namely the principles of democracy and the rule of law. The other principles mentioned in article 1 para 1 of the Czech Constitution (unitary state, sovereignty and respect for human rights) are not explicitly protected by the Eternity Clause, but that does not necessarily mean that they are not significant for its interpretation.

---

[352] Specifically, we refer to the understanding of identity of Gary Jacobsohn who stresses the identity 'beyond text' and who influenced our attempts to see potential rifts between the 'legal story' and the 'people's story' of identity. Jacobsohn claims that 'A constitution acquires an identity through experience; this identity exists neither as a discrete object of invention, nor as a heavily encrusted essence embedded in a society's culture, requiring only to be discovered. Rather, identity emerges dialogically and represents a mix of political aspirations and commitments that are expressive of a nation's past, as well as the determination of those within the society who seek in some ways to transcend that past.' See Gary J Jacobsohn, 'The formation of constitutional identities', in Rosalind Dixon and Tom Ginsburg (eds), *Comparative Constitutional Law* (Edward Elgar, Northampton, MA, 2011) 129–130.

[353] Armin von Bogdandy and Stephan Schill, 'Overcoming absolute primacy: Respect for national identity under the Lisbon Treaty' (2011) 48 CMLRev 1417, 1432.

[354] More precisely, neither provision mentions the 'rule of law' in the proper sense. It is based on the notion of 'právní stát', which is the literal translation of the German '*Rechtsstaat*'. There are some conceptual differences between '*Rechtsstaat*' and 'rule of law', mostly related to the substantive aspects of the respective concepts. See n 262.

[355] The Eternity Clause could obviously (as a matter of fact) be replaced or modified by a revolution, i.e. outside the existing constitutional system. As a matter of law (within the existing constitutional system), the Eternity Clause is arguably untouchable by any institution acting within the Constitution (judgment of the CCC of 10 September 2009, Pl. ÚS 27/09, *Melčák*). In theory, both Orbán's (brand new constitution) and Erdoğan's (ad hoc constitutional referendum) scenarios are thus possible, but they would be considered extra-constitutional, and it is unclear how the CCC would react to such change if it were to touch the Eternity Clause.

Unlike some other constitutions,[356] the Czech Constitution does not include a more detailed list of values and principles entrenched in the Eternity Clause. Therefore, in order to understand the substantive content and meaning of this clause we must analyse the relevant case law of the CCC as well as the doctrinal efforts to make sense of it.

Before doing that, however, it is important to understand the logic and consequences of inclusion of the aforementioned abstract principles in the very core of the Czech constitutional project. First, these principles are not unique or specific to the Czech Republic as a political community. The concept of sovereignty (notwithstanding the disputes about its content and evolution) has been a definitional sign of a state ever since the Westphalian consensus.[357] Democracy, the rule of law and respect for human rights are considered core principles of Western liberal democracies. Even the principle of a unitary state is hardly something that would make the Czech Constitution specific and recognizable.

The Eternity Clause, or at least its abstract textual expression, thus emphasizes not the 'unique features' of the Czech Republic and its aspirations, but rather the values and aspirations it shares with other states, especially with the Western and Central European ones.[358] The preamble to the Czech Constitution bolsters this understanding by referring to the Czech Republic as 'a part of the family of democracies in Europe and around the world'.

Such a concept should not come as a surprise if we consider the origins of the Czech constitutional project. As we have already emphasized above, after the fall of the communist regime and the short intermezzo before the dissolution of Czechoslovakia, the Czech Republic aimed to deal with its past and then 'return to Europe'[359] where it thought it belonged. The constitutional emphasis on the shared values of liberal democracies was a logical choice from both points of view.

As we have suggested above, the more precise content of the Eternity Clause and its relation to article 1 para 1 of the Constitution were developed in the CCC's case law. In fact, the CCC has been the single most important player in both developing the content of the Eternity Clause and giving it some bite and practical effect.

First, the CCC does not limit the extent of the Eternity Clause to the values and principles explicitly mentioned in the text of article 9 para 2 of the Czech Constitution. Relying on article 1 para 1 of the Czech Constitution, the Court recognized protection of the fundamental rights[360] and state sovereignty[361] as integral parts of the Eternity Clause and thus expanded its scope.

Furthermore, the CCC had several opportunities to concretize the meaning of the principles protected by the Eternity Clause. It interpreted the rule of law principle as including several more specific components such as the prohibition of the arbitrary overruling of previous case law,[362] the prohibition of retroactivity,[363] and the principle of the generality of

---

[356] See, for example, art 79 para 3 of the German Basic Law; and art 288 of the Portuguese Constitution.

[357] See e.g. José E Alvarez, 'State Sovereignty Is Not Withering Away: A Few Lessons for the Future', in Antonio Cassese (ed), *Realizing Utopia: The Future of International Law* (OUP, Oxford, 2012) 26.

[358] A similar trend is recognizable even in the case law of the Czech Constitutional Court, which seems to be quite open to foreign and supranational inspirations. See also Ladislav Vyhnánek, 'A Holistic View' (n 237).

[359] The main Czech political goals of the 1990s were to finish the political transformation (i.e. to establish a liberal democracy), economic transformation (to entrench free market economy) and to join the 'Western structures' such as the EU, the Council of Europe and NATO. For the popular reflection of this phenomenon see Pavel Maršálek, 'Evropská integrace, unijní občanství a česká národní identita' (2014) 60 Acta Universitatis Carolinae 73, 77.

[360] Judgment of the CCC of 29 May 1997, III. ÚS 31/97.

[361] *Lisbon I* judgment, in particular paras 93 and 97.

[362] Judgment of the CCC of 11 June 2003, Pl. ÚS 11/02.

[363] Judgment of the CCC of 10 September 2009, Pl. ÚS 27/09, *Melčák*.

law.[364] The democratic principle then includes popular sovereignty and representative democracy[365] as well as some basic principles of electoral law.[366] As regards the protection of fundamental rights, the CCC has even held that 'limiting an already achieved procedural level of protection of fundamental rights and freedoms' is inconsistent with the Eternity Clause.[367]

A similar—but slightly wider—understanding of the Eternity Clause can be found in some doctrinal literature. In the commentary on the Constitution, Šimíček included the following principles within the scope of the Eternity Clause: the sovereignty of the people, the entrenchment and protection of fundamental rights, the rule of law, free competition among political parties, majority rule complemented by the protection of minorities, limited terms of office, basic principles of election law, judicial independence, the separation of powers, and basic features of self-government.[368]

Some authors have suggested that the Czech Constitution—just like any other constitution—has a certain 'substantive core' that reflects its inner logic and integrity and that the existence and importance of these core principles is not dependent on the Eternity Clause.[369] In the event of a change or a removal of the substantive core, the integrity of the affected constitution would be destroyed and consequently the old constitution would be replaced by a new one with a new substantive core.[370] Molek argues that the Czech Eternity Clause is an attempt to express the Constitution's substantive core but that it fulfils this aim (like any other such attempt) only approximately. He claims that the scope of the Eternity Clause is in some respects narrower than the substantive core. For example, the republican form of government forms a part of the Czech Constitution's substantive core even though it is not covered by the Eternity Clause.[371] In other words, substantive core is an ideal compressed essence that each constitution logically possesses, whereas the Eternity Clause is just an explicit prohibition on altering certain basic principles of the Czech Constitution. Despite significant overlaps between the two concepts, they are not identical. Preuss[372] further develops the concept of substantive core and links it to that of constitutional identity. At the same time, he advises against frequent practical use of these concepts as they are not sufficiently defined by any authority, and we lack meaningful criteria for establishing such a definition.[373]

On a general level, these judicial and doctrinal lists of values and principles protected by the Eternity Clause and the substantive core seem to support our previous argument that the Czech constitutional project is centred around the shared values of European liberal democracies. Still, it would be hasty to conclude that the Czech constitutional conception of these principles and values does not include anything unique. This is mainly due to the fact that the aforementioned formative historical events (or rather the constitutional engagement

---

[364] In ibid.

[365] Judgment of the CCC of 21 December 1993, Pl. ÚS 19/93.

[366] Judgment of the CCC of 6 February 2001, Pl. ÚS 42/2000.

[367] Judgment of the CCC of 25 June 2002, Pl. ÚS 36/01.

[368] Vojtěch Šimíček, 'Komentář k čl. 9' (n 321) 156 ff.

[369] See Pavel Molek, *Materiální ohnisko jako věčný limit evropské integrace?* (n 321).

[370] In ibid. The concept of the substantive core is very similar to the understanding of the eternity clause in the Norwegian constitution (the 'spirit' and 'principles' of the Norwegian constitution cannot be amended). See Eivind Smith, 'Old and protected? On the "supra-constitutional" clause in the Constitution of Norway' (2011) 44 Israeli Law Review 369.

[371] Pavel Molek, *Materiální ohnisko jako věčný limit evropské integrace?* (n 321) 91.

[372] Ondřej Preuss, 'Demokratický právní stát tesaný do pískovce' (2016) 24 Časopis pro právní vědu a praxi 365. Preuss for example claims that the nature of the Czech Republic as a unitary state as opposed to a federation might be understood as a part of the Constitution's substantive core despite not being mentioned by art 9 para Czech Constitution.

[373] In ibid 367.

with those events) gave the CCC as well as the political bodies opportunities to shed some light on their understanding of the basic constitutional principles, such as the rule of law, equality, and protection of fundamental rights.

Perhaps the most significant judgment in this regard was issued in the *Dreithaler* case.[374] In this judgment, the CCC refused to annul a decree of President Beneš[375] that provided for the confiscation of enemy (mainly German and Hungarian) property after the Second World War based on the principle of collective guilt. The CCC opined that, given the extraordinary nature of the Second World War and its aftermath, it was impossible to look at the legal problems arising purely through the lens of a modern liberal democracy and impose the current values on a problem that was half a century old. The judgment's reasoning also clearly reflects a notion of collective responsibility of the German (and to a lesser extent the Hungarian) people that is very problematic from the point of view of the contemporary understanding of individual responsibility and the dignity of a human being. It is not without interest that the aftermath of the Second World War and the Beneš decrees have played a role in yet another episode of the Czech constitutional identity. The fear—realistic or not—that the EU Charter of Fundamental Rights might jeopardize the Beneš decrees was arguably the reason for the Czech insistence on joining Protocol No 30 to the Lisbon Treaty.[376]

We can thus feel an inherent tension in the conception of the Czech constitutional identity. The normative Eternity Clause and substantive core emphasize the shared values of European liberal democracies. On the other hand, the last two examples have shown that the Czech constitutional institutions may be willing to adjust the interpretation and acceptance of these values, especially if they threaten to influence the status quo that was brought about by the formative historical events of the modern Czech constitutional history.

Still, the question remains—in the absence of an authoritative definition—whether we should base our tentative conception of the Czech constitutional identity (1) on the Eternity Clause (as developed by the CCC), or (2) on the less defined, yet theoretically founded, concept of substantive core, or (3) develop the Czech constitutional identity as a completely distinct concept. Each of these three approaches has its own merit. Unamendable provisions surely have something to do with polity's identity, and according to some scholars form 'the genetic code of the Constitution'.[377] Thus, the Eternity Clause is a natural starting point for the construction of constitutional identity, if only for practical reasons.[378] At the same time, several Czech scholars have argued persuasively that the Eternity Clause does not contain the entire basic structure of the Czech Constitution, and hence it provides an incomplete picture of the Czech constitutional identity.[379] Faced with these two options, we are inclined to link the Czech constitutional identity to the broader of these conceptions: that is to the conception of 'substantive core'. In our opinion, it paints a more complete picture of the foundational values and principles of the Czech constitutional *Gestalt*.

There is, however, yet another approach to the Czech constitutional identity that goes beyond the mere normative concept of the Eternity Clause and substantive core and that

---

[374] Judgment of the CCC of 8 March 1995, Pl. ÚS 14/94, *Dreithaler*.

[375] Decree No 108/1945, on the confiscation of enemy property and the National Restoration Fund.

[376] For more information and the importance of this episode for the Czech constitutional identity see Pietro Faraguna, 'Taking constitutional identities away from the courts' (2016) 41 Brooklyn Journal of International Law 492, 548 ff.

[377] See Yaniv Roznai, *Unconstitutional Constitutional Amendments: The Limits of Amendment Powers* (OUP, Oxford, 2017) 15–39.

[378] As we show in the next part, the CCC intends to protect the Eternity Clause against all possible threats and has equipped it with far-reaching effects.

[379] See in particular Ondřej Preuss, 'Demokratický právní stát tesaný do pískovce' (n 372) 366.

leads from the 'shared European values of democracy, rule of law and human rights' to something with a more specific 'Czech flavour'. Besides the *Dreithaler* case and the *Lisbon* saga, it is supported by a short dictum in the *Holubec* judgment in which the CCC opined that seventy years of the Czechoslovak statehood and the subsequent peaceful dissolution of Czechoslovakia are building blocks of the Czech constitutional identity.[380] Interestingly, this approach goes beyond the text and legal values of the Czech Constitution and incorporates a reflection of the Czech nation's past into the concept of constitutional identity.

From this point of view, it begs the question whether the strictly normative and aspirational approach to the concept of constitutional identity, based almost exclusively on the text of the Czech Constitution and further refined by the CCC, is soundly rooted in Czech society and shared by the people. The answer to this question has no direct or immediate normative consequences for the Czech Constitution and its identity. It is however crucial for the longevity and stability of the Czech constitutional identity in the long run.

In the ideal scenario, the normative concept of the substantive constitutional core and 'constitutional sentiments' of the Czech people would converge and forge a strong sense of constitutional patriotism[381] and consequently a robust and hopefully long-lasting constitutional identity.[382] However, given the exclusion of the people and even of most of the political institutions from the formation of Czech constitutional identity,[383] there is limited interaction between these two dimensions of constitutional identity. The lack of these dynamic factors may stall the process of the development of the Czech constitutional identity shared by the wider public and even increase the gap between the constitutional values and the socio-political reality, which in turn may alienate the legal elites from their people.

As we have already suggested, domestic institutions, other than the CCC, have remained rather passive in shaping Czech constitutional identity, even though there are some notable exceptions. Apart from President Václav Klaus's aforementioned insistence on joining Protocol No 30 to the Lisbon Treaty, the biggest contributions by other institutions to the development of the constitutional identity are probably the petitions of the Senate and senators in the *Lisbon I* and *Lisbon II* cases. The petitioners in these cases formulated a list of questions concerning the content of the Eternity Clause and its effects, which in turn pushed the CCC to formulate its own position. Yet another example of the political institutions engaging with the formative events of Czech constitutional history and thus attempting to contribute to the formation of the Czech constitutional identity, was the adoption of the so-called 'Lex Beneš'.[384] The legislative intent of this law was not only to acknowledge the accomplishments of Edvard Beneš prior to and during the Second World War, but also partly to legitimize the controversial choices made in the wake of that war, in particular the expulsion of Sudeten Germans and Hungarians from the then Czechoslovak territory. However, the 'identity-forming' importance of Lex Beneš is reduced by the fact that both the Senate and the President rejected the bill, and it was adopted only once the Chamber of Deputies overrode the Senate's and President's vetoes.[385]

---

[380] Judgment of the CCC of 31 January 2012, Pl. ÚS 5/12, *Holubec*.

[381] For our understanding of constitutional patriotism see n 123.

[382] See David Kosař and Ladislav Vyhnánek, 'Ústavní identita České republiky' (n 264).

[383] And from the formation of the Czech constitution—see Section C.7.

[384] Law N. 292/2004 Coll. The only provision (except that governing its entry into force) of Lex Beneš is section 1 which reads as follows, 'Edvard Beneš has made contributions towards the State.'

[385] As Lex Beneš was an ordinary statute, the Chamber of Deputies could override the Senate's position as well as the presidential veto.

Similarly, legal scholars have, until recently,[386] also devoted little attention to the identity issues and the concepts of the Eternity Clause and the material core of the Constitution. Only since the *Melčák* judgment has the academic literature caught up and, recently, several academics have helped to map the existing conceptual framework and developed it further.[387]

Thus, the people and even the political institutions have so far generally been left out of the process of formation of constitutional identity.[388] Even the dissolution of Czechoslovakia itself was prepared in a non-transparent manner by the executive leaders without a referendum or any substantial involvement of the people whose country was being prepared for burial. The ever-strengthening voices that support the traditional understanding of state sovereignty[389] or the calls for strengthening the role of the 'nation' in the Czech Constitution[390] might soon be the driving force of a process that 'takes the Constitution away from courts' and reshapes the understanding of the Czech constitutional identity. Even though constitutional scholars view these recent proposals with suspicion, they struck a chord with many people and exposed significant tensions between the elites and the rest of society. These tensions have been present since the very beginning of the independence of the Czech Republic,[391] but they were, to a large extent, hidden behind the post-Velvet euphoria, joining the European Union and 'catching up' with the West.[392] Only the financial and migration crises exposed them fully.

This brings us back to the importance of popular feelings and their reflection of the formative events of Czech history. Since the people have been excluded from the formation of the Czech normative aspects of constitutional identity and there has been no discussion on the extent to which this elitist view of constitutional identity reflects the public's view of constitutional identity, social acceptance of the main constitutional values and principles—and consequently of the normative construction of constitutional identity—is uncertain.

We cannot delve into all the details of the Czech formative historical and social events that still influence the popular conscience. However, the basic overview includes the Hussite movement, the following Germanization and Catholicization politics as well as suppression of the autonomy of Czech lands under the Austrian Empire (1620–1918), the creation of an independent Czechoslovakia in 1918, the Great Depression in the late 1920s and early 1930s,

---

[386] The most important exception is perhaps an article by Pavel Holländer, Justice of the CCC in 1993–2003, the vice-president of the CCC in 2003–2013 and a judge-rapporteur in the *Melčák* case concerning the constitutional core and its effects. See Pavel Holländer, 'Materiální ohnisko ústavy' (n 92).

[387] See e.g. Pavel Molek, *Materiální ohnisko jako věčný limit evropské integrace?* (n 321); and Ondřej Preuss, 'Demokratický právní stát tesaný do pískovce' (n 372).

[388] See also Section B.2.

[389] A typical proponent of such view is Václav Pavlíček, a Professor of Constitutional Law at the Charles University; see Václav Pavlíček, 'Kdo je v České republice ústavodárcem a problém suverenity', in Marie Vanduchová and Jaromír Hořák (eds), *Na křižovatkách práva: pocta Janu Musilovi k sedmdesátým narozeninám* (C.H. Beck, München, 2011) 21–38, and, more recently Jan Kovařík, 'Ústavní právník k migrační krizi: Stát rozhoduje, komu umožní vstup' (Novinky.cz, 11 July 2016).

[390] Such an idea was proposed by Aleš Gerloch, the former Dean and Head of the Constitutional Law Department at the Charles University: see Jindřich Ginter, 'Ústavní právník Gerloch chce vrátit do ústavy národ' (Novinky.cz, 14 November 2016). It is important in this regard that the Czech Constitution, unlike the Slovak one, has consciously opted for the 'citizen-based' rather than 'ethnic/nation-based' approach to the people. See also Juraj Marušiak, 'Ústavy SR a ČR' (n 1).

[391] Note that the Czech people were not given an opportunity to express their opinion on the dissolution of Czechoslovakia in a referendum, played no role in the drafting of the Czech Constitution, and many of them had a limited understanding of the nature of the capitalist regime they ended up in. A recently published oral history of the Velvet Revolution is telling in this respect: see Miroslav Vanek and Pavel Mücke, *Velvet Revolutions: An Oral History of Czech Society* (OUP, Oxford, 2016).

[392] However, 'catching up' is not a natural development; see e.g. Jan Komárek, 'The struggle for legal rform after Communism: Zdeněk Kühn, the judiciary in Central and Eastern Europe: mechanical jurisprudence in transformation? (Martinus Nijhoff, 2011)' (2015) 63 AJCL 285.

the Munich Treaty of 1938 and the subsequent annexation of Czech lands by the Third Reich in 1939, the 1946 semi-free parliamentary elections and the subsequent communist coup d'état in 1948, the Prague Spring of 1968, the Velvet Revolution of 1989, and the dissolution of Czechoslovakia in 1993.

Even though these historical milestones as such do not form part of the constitutional identity,[393] they translated into specific constitutional narratives that cannot easily be discerned from the constitutional text. For instance, the Great Depression and communist rule resulted in a strong emphasis on eradicating socio-economic inequalities, but significantly less so on socio-cultural inequalities.[394] Even though this has been translated 'only' into the protection of social and economic rights in the Czech Charter of Fundamental Rights and Freedoms and not into the Eternity Clause (unlike in Germany), the principle of the welfare state is arguably one of the key components of Czech society's understanding of what the basic functions of the constitution and the state are. Yet another example concerns the evaluation of the 'general humanist' heritage of Tomáš Garrigue Masaryk (and perhaps dating even back to the Hussite movement and its interpretations)[395] and revolves around the question: 'What is the purpose of the Czech Constitution?' Is its purpose to protect the Czech nation specifically? Or is the 'Czech question' simply a question of humanity and morality, as Masaryk claimed? These questions are not rhetorical and do not raise purely abstract debates. Solutions of practical constitutional dilemmas[396] depend on the answers to these questions. Quite interestingly, this identity question has even been considered by Václav Havel, who was the figurehead of an informal post-Velvet movement that had its roots in certain parts of the dissent during the communist era. This pro-Havel humanist movement was eventually labelled by its opponents and detractors as the 'truth-and-lovers'. This label is a clear reference to Havel's famous quotation, 'Truth and love shall prevail over lies and hatred.'[397] An emphasis on universal values, such as human rights and universal morality (clearly building on Masaryk's legacy), was typical for this stream of Czech politics. Zeman's and Klaus's contrasting approach has been more pragmatic, nation-state and state-interest oriented. In other words, these three men significantly contributed to the emergence of two distinct camps in emerging Czech politics. Despite Havel's death, these camps are clearly present even today and shape some of the most important cleavages in Czech constitutional politics. Their conflicting legacies are still shaping the search for Czech constitutional identity.

These examples show that the Czech popular approach to constitutional identity may have a different pedigree from the normative conception developed by the CCC and based on the constitutional text. However, the main point is that the lack of any discourse between proponents of legal and popular constitutional identity deprives this concept of the dynamic aspect that could reduce the gap between these conceptions and forge a widely shared conception of constitutional identity that stands on firm ground. This neglect of the popular input is in fact a typical trait of Czech constitutionalism. Legal constitutionalism has been prioritized over political constitutionalism,[398] which undermined popular constitutionalism and severely

---

[393] But cf Václav Pavlíček who claims that the guarantees of Czech statehood must be found in the historical context and experiences Czech society has lived through (see Václav Pavlíček, *O české státnosti: úvahy a polemiky, část 3., Demokratický a laický stát* (Karolinum, Prague, 2009).

[394] See Barbara Havelková, 'Resistance to anti-discrimination Law in Central and Eastern Europe—a post-Communist Legacy?' (2016) 17 GLJ 627.

[395] See Section B.

[396] These dilemmas include various topics such as sovereignty and independence vs international cooperation and the EU; refugees' rights; but also, generally the emphasis on the liberal democratic values.

[397] This quotation itself is a wordplay on 'The truth prevails' from the Czech Presidential Flag.

[398] The best analysis of the differences between legal and political constitutionalism can be found in Richard Bellamy, *Political Constitutionalism* (n 166).

limited participatory elements in democratic government.[399] As a result, Czechia does not have a developed understanding of its constitutional identity and its constitution does not seem to be as important to its self-understanding as those in Germany or France.[400]

Therefore, the main task for the elites in the coming years is to initiate the discussion about the Czech constitutional identity and to find common ground, not necessarily in the lowest common denominator, but between the legalistic approaches and the popular constitutional narratives. This debate should ideally, in the long run, develop into the sense of political belonging and constitutional patriotism that would complement the ethnic and religious (in the Czech context largely atheist) identities of the Czech people. Unfortunately, Czech public intellectuals have so far failed to even start reconciling these two positions and forging them into the constitutional identity that would find robust support among Czech citizens.[401] This is a pity since constitutional identity is a double-edged sword. If grasped properly, it is an opportunity to build a new foundation of Czech statehood and glue the polarized segments of Czech society together. However, constitutional identity can also be abused, as we can see in Viktor Orbán's disingenuous attempts at nurturing national constitutional identity as a counter-concept to European constitutional identity.[402]

F. Conclusion

Throughout this chapter we have shown that the Czech constitutional system is still in relatively good shape. However, it is also very fragile and susceptible to democratic backsliding.[403] In fact, Czechia went close to 'Visegrád backsliding scenario' in the 2017 parliamentary elections. Had the three established political parties, which barely passed the 5 percent hurdle, finished beneath the electoral threshold, Czechia could have followed Poland and Hungary and might have celebrated another dark year with the number '8' in 2018.[404] Fortunately, that did not happen.

However, the sources of discontent in Czech society have not disappeared and the upcoming 2021 parliamentary elections can end up differently. Intensifying internal social conflicts (such as growing income disparity, the debt-trap of one-tenth of Czech citizens which indirectly affects a quarter of society and increasing cultural differences between cosmopolitan urban population and conservative majority in smaller cities and villages), animosity towards foreigners caused by the migration crisis, and growing disagreement with the overly fast liberalization of values imposed by the European Union and the Council of Europe, still present a danger for the current Czech constitutional *Gestalt*. Several recent events such as the alleged attempts to influence the outcome of judicial proceedings by politicians[405] already show that this danger is real.

---

[399] See Paul Blokker, *New Democracies in Crisis?* (n 167).

[400] For a succinct study of the German conception of *Verfassungsidentität* and its French equivalent of *identité constitutionnelle de la France* see Jan-Herman Reestman, 'The Franco-German constitutional divide. Reflections on national and constitutional identity' (2009) 5 EuConst 374.

[401] See David Kosař and Ladislav Vyhnánek, 'Ústavní identita České republiky' (n 264).

[402] See Renáta Uitz, 'National Constitutional identity in the European Constitutional Project: A recipe for exposing cover ups and masquerades' (VerfassungsBlog, 11 November 2016), http://verfassungsblog.de/national-constitutional-identity-in-the-european-constitutional-project-a-recipe-for-exposing-cover-ups-and-masquerades/ (last accessed on 13 March 2022).

[403] See Section C.8.

[404] To be sure, the Senate, a stronghold of traditional parties, could have blocked constitutional amendments, but we know from Poland that strong majorities in the lower chamber can, with the help of President, adopt major policy changes even without changing the Constitution.

[405] See Section C.8.

In other words, Czechia has not yet reached the safe zone. The successful development of the Czech constitutional *Gestalt* is thus dependent on many endogenous and exogenous factors. But, in our opinion, by far the most important challenge is the debt-trap that paralyses a significant segment of Czech society. These people see no bright future. And if they do not have a future, they do not care about taking the right decisions. These have-nots may simply want to punish the haves and vote for an authoritarian leader who will go after the liberal and allegedly 'rotten' elite.

However, at the time of writing this chapter, Czechia seems to be more resistant to an illiberal turn than its Visegrád neighbours. In fact, very few political scientists included Czechia among 'backsliders' in Central and Eastern Europe and the 'Hungarian' or 'Polish' paradigm can be made to fit only very loosely as the major challenge so far has not been creeping capture of existing institutions, but the entrenchment of private interests in the state and in party politics.[406] But the reasons for a different Czech trajectory are more sociological than legal. In contrast to some other Central European countries, Czechia has not witnessed significant depopulation.[407] In fact, the elites stay in the Czech lands and contribute to Czech public life rather than fleeing to the United Kingdom or Germany. Moreover, Czechia, unlike Hungary and Poland, lacks a powerful nationalist narrative or another unifying ideology that would operate as a mobilizing factor for the insurgence against the current constitutional system.

Hence, Czechia is not on the verge of democratic collapse. It is rather in the state of 'democratic careening', as the democratic game has changed in decisive ways since the 1990s even as democracy neither collapsed nor more firmly consolidated in the process.[408] So far, it has been swaying towards the consolidated democracies. Yet this state cannot be taken for granted. Only the future will tell us whether liberalism became 'the god that failed'[409] in Czechia as well.

---

[406] See Sean Hanley and Milada Vachudová, 'Understanding the illiberal turn: democratic backsliding in the Czech Republic', East European Politics 34, no. 3 (2018) 276–296.

[407] Ivan Krastev and Stephen Holmes, 'How liberalism became "the god that failed" in Eastern Europe' (The Guardian, 24 October 2019) https://www.theguardian.com/world/2019/oct/24/western-liberalism-failed-post-communist-eastern-europe?CMP=Share_iOSApp_Other&fbclid=IwAR2qQzavjnBy-UxjNys2UBVEr9lg271C QNR4PEZy2HdjifkPOYklKfhsnjU/ (last accessed on 13 March 2022).

[408] Dan Slater, 'Democratic cdareening', World Politics 65, no. 4 (2013) 729–763. See also Licia Cianetti and Seán Hanley, 'The end of the backsliding paradigm', Journal of Democracy 31(1) 66–80.

[409] Ivan Krastev and Stephen Holmes (n 407).

3

The Evolution and *Gestalt* of the French Constitution

Guillaume Tusseau

A. Origins of the Current Constitution	109	a) The Unsupersedeable Heritage of 1789	141
B. The Evolution of the Constitution	114	i. The Civil and Political Rights of 1789	141
1. High-Energy Constitutionalism	114	ii. Supraconstitutional Principles?	142
a) Sieyès Illustrated and Enacted	114	b) The Temptation of Economic and Social Enrichment	144
b) The Practice of Constitutional Drafting	116	**D. Constitutional Identity**	146
i. Constitutional Constructivism	116	1. A New (Im)balance of Powers	147
ii. The Quandary of Entrenching Constitutional Self-Government	118	a) Parliament as a Constitutional Minor	147
2. Low Juridicity Constitutionalism	122	b) The President of the Republic as the Keystone of the New Regime	149
a) The Political Enforcement of Constitutions	123	c) The People as a Constitutional Actor	151
i. The Hostility to Judicial Review	123	2. The Judicialization of the French Constitutionalism	153
ii. A Constitution for a Class of Experts	126	a) The Introduction of Constitutional Review	154
b) The Legislative Fabric of the French Polity	128	i. The Development of the Conseil Constitutionnel	154
C. Basic Structures and Concepts	131	ii. Towards a Fully Developed Constitutional Court	156
1. Delegative Constitutionalism	132	b) The Constitutionalization of the French Polity	157
a) The Representative Principle	132	3. The (Lethal?) Internalization of Political Conflict	158
i. Severing the People from its Representatives	132	a) Inhabiting the Regime	158
ii. Unification of the Polity	133	b) A Harmonious Combination of Liberal and Social Values	160
b) The Illusions of Semi-Direct Democracy	137		
c) The Separation of Powers	138		
2. Human Rights Constitutionalism	141		

A. Origins of the Current Constitution

Is the Constitution of the Fifth Republic the final constitution? In a few years from now, it will have outlived all its predecessors. This is not to say that the institutions set up in 1958 have not had hard times. They were born out of the collapse of the Fourth Republic. They immediately gave the government the means to face the Algerian crisis. Aside from exceptional circumstances, they ensured a peaceful and regular transmission of power. Contrary to former constitutions, they restored 'State power'[1] and reinforced its control, while allowing

---

[1] Georges Burdeau, 'La conception du pouvoir dans la Constitution française du 4 octobre 1958' (1959) 9 Revue française de science politique 87.

Guillaume Tusseau, *The Evolution and* Gestalt *of the French Constitution* In: *The Max Planck Handbooks in European Public Law.* Edited by: Armin von Bogdandy, Peter M Huber, and Sabrina Ragone, Oxford University Press. © Guillaume Tusseau 2023. DOI: 10.1093/oso/9780198726425.003.0003

the internalization of political disagreement. They permitted massive economic, social, and societal reforms and favoured an active foreign policy as well as the integration into an unprecedented regional organization. Moreover, it is truly exceptional that they managed to evolve through two dozen constitutional amendments instead of a total reversal. Having considered the failures of the preceding regimes, the Constitution of the Fifth Republic seems to have avoided regime crisis, political crisis, and institutional crisis.

The Fifth Republic emerged in a time of crisis. The institutions and the politicians of the preceding regime were not able to meet the needs of the time, mainly because it was impossible to form stable and coherent governmental majorities. Under the threat of a military coup, President Coty asked De Gaulle to become *président du Conseil*. It was clear to De Gaulle that he would lead the last government of the Fourth Republic. Pursuant to the Constitutional Act of 3 June 1958 that amended the procedure for constitutional amendment, his government was empowered to draft a project that would be prepared in consultation with a committee where parliamentarians would sit. The text would be submitted to the people. In its very inception, the Fifth Republic marginalized the representatives who had ruled France since the 1870s. For the first time, a Republican constitution was drafted by a small committee, much like an authoritarian constitution. The final say on the text would belong to the people.

Paradoxically, if there is any crisis, it may lie precisely in how successfully the Fifth Republic has dominated the course of political history. This dominance has favoured the formation of a political class perceived as homogeneous and distant from the people. It enjoys efficient institutional means to govern, to such an extent that it may appear closed off from social demand.[2] The crisis, leading to calls for a Sixth Republic, would then result from the very absence of crisis.

This is why one wonders, within the more general contemporary context of economic, social, cultural, political, and legal turmoil, what kind of path has led to the current constitution. In order to address the Fifth Republic's singularity, one must also understand what perspective on constitutional law it embodies. Did it manage to adapt the French State to changing circumstances because its drafters capitalized on a rich previous constitutional experience? Or does it owe its stability to a crucial break with the past?

Since the Revolution of 1789, France's tormented history has consisted in an impressive succession of legal norms, institutional settings, and political projects, which have been enshrined in formal constitutions.[3] Whether it allows identifying 'a thick layer'[4] so as to reach 'deep structural knowledge'[5] and a more lasting *Gestalt* that would cast light on a 'French way' to conceive of the constitution is debatable, however. In a non-technical way, the idea of *Gestalt* refers to the way the mind organizes an individual's experience and perception. The example of Ludwig Wittgenstein's image of the Duck-Rabbit[6] makes clear that, depending

---

[2] Presenting the most important issues to be debated, see e.g. Groupe de travail sur l'avenir des institutions, *Refaire la démocratie* (Assemblée nationale, Paris, 2015).

[3] For a general presentation, see e.g. Michel Troper and Lucien Jaume (ed), *1789 et l'invention de la Constitution* (LGDJ, Paris, 1994); Pascal Jan, *Les Constitutions de la France*, vol III (LGDJ, Issy-les-Moulineaux, 2017); Marcel Morabito, *Histoire constitutionnelle de la France de 1789 à nos jours* (first puplished 2012, 16th edn, LGDJ, Paris, 2020); Jean-Jacques Chevallier and others (eds) *Histoire de la Ve République: 1958-2015* (16th edn, Dalloz, Paris, 2017).

[4] Armin von Bogdandy, 'The Idea of European Public Law Today', in Armin von Bogdandy, Sabino Cassese, and Peter M Huber (eds), *Max Planck Handbooks in European Public Law*, vol I (OUP, Oxford, 2017) chapter 1 Section A.3.

[5] Armin von Bogdandy, ibid, Section A.2.c.

[6] Ludwig Wittgenstein, *Philosophische Untersuchungen/Philosophical Investigations* (Wiley-Blackwell, Malden MA, 2009) Part II, s XI.

on the kind of conceptual frame individuals use to process their visual perception, they do not see the same thing. As philosophy of science teaches, observation is governed by theory and depends on the intellectual frame one decides to apply to the flow of the raw materials of perception.[7] Similarly, regarding a possible *Gestalt* of French constitutionalism, one may investigate how a specific way to imagine constitutional governance has become increasingly entrenched.

As Philippe Ardant puts it:

> One of the characteristics of our constitutional history is that it cannot be analyzed as the persevering search for perfection or for ideal institutions. It owes very little to theories and it cannot be understood in terms of progress. It is above all a series of answers given, often in a hurry, to concrete problems that confronted a power seeking to secure its foundations. Its richness is due first of all to its continual adaptation to a constantly renewed conjuncture.

Is this to say that no conceptual matrix ever determined and limited, first, which problems could be envisioned as requiring an answer and, second, what those answers might be? This is unlikely, so that it is worth investigating French constitutionalism in order to look for continuity behind the apparent discontinuities,[8] so as to try and identify what other authors have suggested regarding as the 'constitutional patrimony'[9] or the 'genetic code of French constitutions'.[10] From this perspective, one may insist on the similarities between the concept of *Gestalt* and certain definitions of the concept of culture.[11]

As conceptualized by Paul W Kahn, the study of constitutional cultures aims to reveal the intellectual framework that defines one's legal and political reality. 'A cultural study of law [...] seeks to bring to self-consciousness those background structures of meaning that are always already in place and which make possible the particular regulatory schemes over which we argue.'[12] Beyond the explicit norms and behaviours, it specifically addresses:

> implicit or incompletely explicit *assumptions*, or more or less *unconscious mental habits*, operating in the thought of an individual or a generation. It is the beliefs which are so much a matter of course that they are rather tacitly presupposed than formally expressed and argued for, the ways of thinking which seem so natural and inevitable that they are not scrutinized with the eye of logical self-consciousness, that often are most decisive of the character of a philosopher's doctrine, and still oftener of the dominant intellectual tendencies of an age.[13]

---

[7] See especially Willard Van Orman Quine, *Ontological Relativity and other Essays* (Columbia University Press, New York, 1969); Wilfrid Sellars, *Empiricism and the Philosophy of Mind* (Harvard University Press, Cambridge MA, 1997).

[8] Association française des constitutionnalistes, *La continuité constitutionnelle en France de 1789 à 1989* (Presses universitaires d'Aix-Marseille, Aix-en-Provence, 1990).

[9] Pascal Jan, *Les Constitutions de la France*, vol 1 (n 3) 9.

[10] Stéphane Mouton, 'Le 'code génétique' des constitutions françaises', in Henry Roussillon (ed), *Demain, la sixième République?* (Presses de l'Université des sciences sociales, Toulouse, 2007) 75.

[11] Mirosław Wyrzykowski (ed), *Constitutional Cultures* (Institute of Public Affairs, Warsaw, 2000); Silke Hensel and others, *Constitutional Cultures: On the Concept and Representation of Constitutions in the Atlantic World* (Cambridge Scholars publishing, Newcastle upon Tyne, 2012).

[12] Paul W Kahn, *The Cultural Study of Law: Reconstructing Legal Scholarship* (The University of Chicago Press, Chicago, 1999) 92. See also Peter Häberle, *Verfassungslehre als Kulturwissenschaft* (2nd edn, Duncker & Humblot, Berlin, 1998).

[13] Arthur Oncken Lovejoy, *The Great Chain of Being: A Study of the History of an Idea* (Harvard University Press, Cambridge MA, 1964) 7.

Constitutional culture or *Gestalt* thus appears as a background precondition for positive constitutional rules. Consequently, identifying it is a challenge in an interpretive enterprise that attempts to offer an orderly portrayal of the structure with which a specific society gives meaning to its own reality.[14] In order to identify such an intellectual environment, one does not need any explicit strong theory regarding how *Gestalt* or culture may be defined.[15] As Jeremy Webber puts it:

> The concept of culture is not so much a way of identifying highly specified and tightly bounded units of analysis, then, as a heuristic device for suggesting how individual decision-making is conditioned by the language of normative discussion, the set of historical reference points, the range of solutions proposed in the past, the institutional norms taken for granted, given a particular context of repeated social interaction. The integrity of cultural explanations does not depend upon the 'units' being exclusive, fully autonomous, or strictly bounded. Rather, it depends upon there being sufficient density of interaction to generate distinctive terms of evaluation and debate.[16]

According to such a perspective, constitutional law can be understood as a symbolic system that structures the political imagination as a whole, establishing the intellectual and practical patterns which use the community's past as a starting point for its future.[17] Legal rules, including constitutions, have been described not as merely reflecting an outside reality but as possessing a more active, 'constitutive', dimension.[18] As Clifford Geertz wrote, 'The point here is that the "law" side of things is not a bounded set of norms, rules, principles, values, or whatever from which jural responses to distilled events can be drawn, but part of a distinctive manner of imagining the real.'[19]

Understood in this way, culture is a complex set of (not necessarily convergent) ideas, beliefs, legends, practices, actions, attitudes, understandings, expectations, mentalities, representations, sensibilities, symbols, myths, references, purposes, values, rules, institutions,

---

[14] See e.g. Clifford Geertz, *The Interpretation of Cultures* (Basic Books, New York, 1973) 3–30.

[15] On this topic, see Alfred L Kroeber and Clyde Kluckhohn, *Culture* (Vintage Books, New York, 1952); Louis Schneider and Charles M Bonjean (eds), *The Idea of Culture in the Social Sciences* (CUP, Cambridge, 1973); Lawrence M Friedman, 'Legal culture and social development' (1969) 4 Law & Society Review 29; Lawrence M Friedman and Rogelio Pérez-Perdomo (eds), *Legal Culture in the Age of Globalization. Latin America and Latin Europe* (Stanford University Press, Stanford, 2003); Lawrence M Friedman and Harry N Scheiber (eds), *Legal Culture and the Legal Profession* (Westview Press, Boulder CO, 1996); José Ramón Narváez Hernández, *La cultural jurídica. Ideas e imágenes* (Porrúa, México, 2010); Giorgio Rebuffa and Erhard Blankenburg, 'Culture juridique', in André-Jean Arnaud (ed), *Dictionnaire encyclopédique de théorie et de sociologie du droit* (2nd edn, LGDJ, Paris, 1993) 139; Roger Cotterrell, 'The Concept of Legal Culture', in David Nelken (ed), *Comparing Legal Cultures* (Brookfield, Vt, Aldershot, 1997) 13; Lawrence M Friedman, 'The Concept of Legal Culture: A Reply', in David Nelken (ed), *Comparing Legal Cultures* (Brookfield, Vt, Aldershot, 1997) 33; David Nelken, 'Defining and Using the Concept of Legal Culture', in Esin Örücü and David Nelken (eds), *Comparative Law: A Handbook* (Hart, Oxford, 2007) 109; David Nelken, 'Legal Cultures', in David S Clark (ed), *Comparative Law and Society* (E Elgar, Cheltenham, 2012) 310; Melba Luz Calle Meza, 'A propósito de la cultura constitucional' (2010) 25 Revista Derecho del Estado 221; Denys Cuche, *La notion de culture dans les sciences sociales* (4th edn, La découverte, Paris, 2010).

[16] Jeremy Webber, 'Culture, legal culture, and legal reasoning: A comment on Nelken' (2004) 25 Australian Journal of Legal Philosophy 27, 32.

[17] Paul W Kahn, 'Comparative constitutionalism in a new key' (2003) 101 Michigan Law Review 2677.

[18] Alan Hunt, *Explorations in Law and Society: Towards a Constitutive Theory of Law* (Routledge, London, 1993).

[19] Clifford C Geertz, 'Fact and law in comparative perspective', http://hypergeertz.jku.at/GeertzTexts/Local_Knowledge.htm (last accessed 21 March 2022).

habits, etc., which allows specific questions to be asked, specific answers to be imagined, and specific choices to be made, while ruling out others. It defines which experiences are possible and which are not. To borrow from Nelson Goodman, what is investigated is a 'way of worldmaking'[20] that accounts for the specific ways a given polity experiences itself as a historical agent.[21]

Since the advent of legal modernity, the constitution has been understood as a point of reification for the group, as it is the specific vehicle for the sovereign's self-expression, self-establishment, and self-continuance. Not only does it have a normative dimension, which makes it 'the supreme law of the land',[22] but it is also endowed with a symbolic,[23] expressive,[24] emotive,[25] and totemic,[26] meaning, as it belongs to the foundational narrative of the polity.[27]

From this perspective, two main lines of enquiry must be distinguished in order to describe the evolution and *Gestalt* of the French constitution: 'Genealogy traces the history of the central concepts of a legal order; architecture looks at the structure of those concepts and their relationships to each other.'[28] The two are not disconnected, as it is through history that several concepts appear and come to fit more or less easily with one another, so as to give a sort of organic integrity to the constitutional *Gestalt*.

Accordingly, Section B deals with the structural aspects of the French constitutional *Gestalt*. It tries to elucidate what kind of political message and legal tool a constitution is thought to be. Section C addresses the substantive aspects of French constitutional culture, i.e. the content that is embedded in the previously identified formal vehicle. The last part of this chapter demonstrates how the coherent picture that emerged from the two previous sections after a century and a half of constitutional government has been called into question. Although they heavily relied on French history and thus situated themselves within the established *Gestalt*, the drafters of the constitution of 1958 explicitly purported to transform it. Section D asks whether the basic elements so far mapped out can still account for the current state of constitutional culture or whether France has experienced a transformation of its constitutional identity as defined thus far.

---

[20] Nelson Goodman, *Ways of Worldmaking* (Harvester Press, Hassocks, 1978).

[21] Anne Norton, 'Transubstantiation: The dialectic of Constitutional authority' (1988) 55 The University of Chicago Law Review 458; Marcel Gauchet, *L'avènement de la démocratie II: La crise du libéralisme (1880-1914)* (Gallimard, Paris, 2007) 201.

[22] See Guillaume Tusseau, 'Deux dogmes du constitutionnalisme', in Wanda Mastor (ed), *Penser le droit à partir de l'individu. Mélanges en hommage à Elisabeth Zoller* (Dalloz, Paris, 2018) 835.

[23] Bernard Lacroix, 'Les fonctions symboliques des constitutions: bilan et perspectives', in Jean-Louis Seurin (ed), *Le constitutionnalisme aujourd'hui* (Economica, Paris, 1984) 186; Marcelo Neves, *A constitucionalização simbólica* (3rd edn, WMF Martins Fontes, São Paulo, 2011).

[24] Cass R Sunstein, 'On the expressive function of law' (1996) 144 University of Pennsylvania Law Review 2021; Mark V Tushnet, 'The possibilities of comparative Constitutional law' (1999) 108 Yale Law Journal 1225.

[25] Gerardo Eto Cruz, *El desarrollo del Derecho Procesal Constitucional a partir de la jurisprudencia del Tribunal Constitucional peruano* (Centro de Estudios Constitucionales, Lima, 2008) 72.

[26] Carlos R G Cichello, *Teoría totémica del derecho* (Circulo argentino de jusfilosofia intensiva, Buenos Aires, 1986).

[27] Hans Vorlander, 'Constitutions as Symbolic Orders: The Cultural Analysis of Constitutionalism', in Paul Blokker and Chris Thornhill (eds), *Sociological Constitutionalism* (CUP, Cambridge, 2017) 209; Paulo Ferreira da Cunha, *Direito constitucional geral* (2nd edn, Quid Juris, Lisboa, 2013) 227–247; Paul W Kahn, 'Freedom, Autonomy, and the Cultural Study of Law', in Austin Sarat and Jonathan Simon (eds), *Cultural Analysis, Cultural Studies, and the Law: Moving Beyond Legal Realism* (Duke University Press, Durham, 2003) 154.

[28] Paul W Kahn, *The Cultural Study of Law* (n 12) 91. See also Paul W Kahn, *Political Theology: Four New Chapters on the Concept of Sovereignty* (Columbia University Press, New York, 2011) 103, 120.

B. The Evolution of the Constitution

Terms ending with '–tion', like 'constitution', are affected by the process-product ambiguity. It makes it difficult to know whether one is mentioning the process through which something is created or the created thing once the process is completed. From a structural viewpoint, these two dimensions help elucidate the French *Gestalt*. Whereas great amounts of energy have been devoted to drafting constitutions and to making them the backbone of political life, once they have been enacted, the constitutions faded away in the practice of self-government. Borrowing from Roberto M Unger, the French 'high-energy'[29] conception of constitution-making (1) seems to devolve into a certain 'low juridicity' constitutionalism (2).

1. High-Energy Constitutionalism

The French constitutional *Gestalt* relies on a specific conception of what it means for the French people to confer a constitution upon themselves. Its fundamental aspects were captured by Emmanuel Joseph Sieyès (1748–1836). He was elected to the *États Généraux* in 1789, participated in several assemblies during the Revolution, and finally joined Bonaparte's endeavour, always exerting considerable influence on the constitutional debates.[30] His seminal *Qu'est-ce que le Tiers-État?*, which circulated by November 1788 (a), set the stage for the French conception of constitution-making (b).

a) Sieyès Illustrated and Enacted

For Sieyès, the Nation is the fundamental and sovereign actor of constitutional life: 'The nation is prior to everything. It is the source of everything. Its will is always legal; indeed, it is the law itself.'[31] He insists that even though modern political societies have entered the age of indirect rule,[32] the community never surrenders its power. In his own words:

> The community does not cast aside its right to will: this is inalienable; it can only delegate the exercise of that right. [...] Nor can it delegate the full exercise of it. It delegates only that portion of its total power which is needed to maintain order. [...] it is no longer the *real* common will which is in operation, but a *representative* common will. It has two ineffaceable characteristics which we must repeat. 1) This will which resides in the body of representatives is neither complete nor unlimited; it is a mere portion of the grand, common, national will. 2) The delegates do not exercise it as a right inherent in themselves, but as a right pertaining to other people; the common will is confided to them in trust.[33]

This implies a sharp distinction between two types of powers. The Nation exercises its power by making constitutions, thus appearing as the *pouvoir constituant*. It delegates

---

[29] Roberto M Unger, *The Left Alternative* (Verso, London, 2009).
[30] See e.g. Paul Bastid, *Sieyès et sa pensée* (Hachette, Paris, 1970); Pasquale Pasquino, *Sieyès et l'invention de la constitution en France* (Odile Jacob, Paris, 1998); Raymond Kubben, 'L'Abbé de Sieyès. Champion of National representation, Father of Constitutions', in Denis J Galligan (ed), *Constitutions and the Classics: Patterns of Constitutional Thought from Fortescue to Bentham* (OUP, Oxford, 2014) 290.
[31] Emmanuel-Joseph Sieyès, *What is the Third Estate?* (M Blondel tr, Pall Mall Press, London, 1963) 124.
[32] See Section C.1.a.
[33] Emmanuel-Joseph Sieyès, *What is the Third Estate?* (n 31) 122–123.

the day-to-day exercise of political power to the representative *pouvoirs constitués*. 'Neither aspect of the constitution is the creation of the constituted power, but of the constituent power. No type of delegated power can in any way alter the conditions of its delegation.'[34] Whereas the bodies that act as the Nation's representatives must comply with the conditions which the sovereign has imposed on their action, the Nation remains totally free. As the origin of everything, the Nation is explicitly free from any constitutional constraint:

> [T]he constitution [...] relates only to the government. It would be ridiculous to suppose that the Nation itself could be constricted by the procedures or the constitution to which it had subjected its mandatories. [...] The Nation owes its existence to *natural* law alone. The government, on the contrary, can only be a product of *positive* law. Every attribute of the Nation springs from the simple fact that it exists.[35]

Worldwide, Sieyès' theory is a landmark piece of constitutional thought.[36] These principles were almost fully enshrined in the first text of French constitutional history, which ushered in the new era of constitutional rule, distinct from the *Ancien Régime*,[37] and left a considerable imprint on the French constitutional *Gestalt*. For example, article 3 of the Declaration of the Rights of Man and of the Citizen reads, 'The principle of all sovereignty resides essentially in the Nation. No body nor individual may exercise any authority which does not proceed directly from the Nation.' The principle of sovereignty is distinguished from the exercise of sovereignty.[38] Whereas the former is invariably and intrinsically located in the Nation, the latter can be delegated. The constitution of 1791 (Title III) implements the institutional consequences of these principles:

> Art.1. Sovereignty is one, indivisible, inalienable, and imprescriptible. It appertains to the Nation; no section of the people nor any individual may assume the exercise thereof.
> Art. 2. The Nation, from which alone all powers emanate, may exercise such powers only by delegation.
> The French Constitution is representative; the representatives are the legislative body and the King.

As for the *pouvoir constituant*, the final Title of the same document provides that 'The National Constituent Assembly declares that the Nation has the imprescriptible right to change its Constitution.'[39] From a metaphysical viewpoint, this doctrine highlights the religious dimension of the French Revolution. As Ulrich K Preuss puts it:

---

[34] Ibid, 124–125.

[35] Ibid, 125–126.

[36] See e.g. Egon Zweig, *Die Lehre vom Pouvoir constituant. Ein Beitrag zum Staatsrecht der französischen Revolution* (J.C.B. Mohr, Tübingen, 1909); Claude Klein, *Théorie et pratique du pouvoir constituant* (PUF, Paris, 1996).

[37] See Pierre Duclos, *La notion de constitution dans l'œuvre de l'assemblée constituante* (Dalloz, Paris, 1932); Association française des constitutionnalistes, *1791, la première Constitution française* (Economica, Paris, 1993); François Furet and Ran Halévi, *La monarchie républicaine: la Constitution de 1791* (Fayard, Paris, 1996); Michel Troper, 'La Constitution de 1791 aujourd'hui' (1992) 9 Revue française de droit constitutionnel 3.

[38] See also Section C.1.a.i.

[39] The sequel of this provision is not totally coherent with this principle. See Section B.1.b.ii.

The Constituent power is the secularized version of the divine power to create the world *ex nihilo*, to create an order without being subject to it. The will of the constituent power aims at transforming itself into an objective and enduring incarnation, a constitution, but it cannot simultaneously submit itself to its own creation without losing its character as the supreme secular power.[40]

France's tormented constitutional history has confirmed the Nation's almightiness time and time again.

b) The Practice of Constitutional Drafting

This vision of the Nation's power implied strong constructivism (i). This led to problems that commonly occur when constitutional drafters rely on the doctrine of the *pouvoir constituant* to create a constitution intended to last forever, thus denying the same faculty to future actors. But unlike in the United States, the French conception of sovereignty prevented any problem of transgenerational self-government from arising (ii).

i. Constitutional Constructivism

Since 1789, it has appeared that setting (1791, Year I–1793, Year III–1795, 1848, 1875, 1946, and 1958), stabilizing (Year VIII–1799) or restoring (as with the 1814 Charter) a legal, political, administrative, social, civil, and moral order should necessarily find expression in constitution-making. In the *cahiers de doléances*, the monarchy was reproached for not having a constitution.[41] The Revolution began on 17 June 1789, when the deputies of the Third Estate, following Sieyès' contention that the Third Estate is the Nation, proclaimed themselves an *Assemblée nationale*. It continued when they swore not to depart until they had given the Realm a constitution. Finally, on 9 July they proclaimed themselves an *Assemblée nationale constituante*, thus largely overstepping the purpose for which the King had convened the *États Généraux*.

Since that moment, it has become indispensable for any political project to be embodied in a constitution. Even in 1814, the 'Restoration', which was so hostile to the Revolution's principles and institutions, could not escape from the new paradigm its enemies had established. Even though it was not the Nation but divine Providence which advocated for the (re-)establishment of the monarchy, even though it was not a constitution which the people imposed on the King *qua pouvoir constitué*, even though it was not a constitution in the strict sense but a 'constitutional charter', a flexible rather than a rigid document[42]—nevertheless, a text establishing the regime's basic institutions and fundamental values seemed necessary. It became unthinkable for the French polity to be without a written document stabilizing the major principles for the State's organization.

As a consequence, the French legal *Gestalt* is based on a kind of constructivism. Analysing the idea of a constitution, Paul Bastid noticed a fundamental ambiguity:

---

[40] Ulrich K Preuss, 'Constitutional Powermaking for the New Polity: Some Deliberations on the Relations Between Constituent Power and the Constitution', in Michel Rosenfeld (ed), *Constitutionalism, Identity, Difference, and Legitimacy: Theoretical Perspectives* (Duke University Press, Durham, 1994) 143, 144.

[41] Debating the existence of a constitution under the Old Regime, see Arnaud Vergne, *La notion de constitution d'après les cours et assemblées à la fin de l'Ancien régime, 1750–1789* (De Boccard, Paris, 2006).

[42] See James Bryce, *Studies in History and Jurisprudence*, vol 1 (OUP, New York, 1901) 124–215.

Sometimes it applies to an act, most often voluntary and free, which transforms an existing situation; sometimes, on the contrary, it designates a given fact, alien to the intervention of man. [...] Is the constitution a spontaneous product of nature, that is to say, in this case of social reality, in which the share of human genius, of individual initiative, is nil? On the contrary, is it a work of art, a voluntary creation in which the ingenuity of the mind is reflected? In a nutshell, is it natural or artificial?[43]

French constitutionalism embodies the second alternative. The constitution was never thought to be a pre-existing document nor was it expected to emerge spontaneously. A constitution's function is to devise a deliberate and rational ordering of the whole social sphere. The hostility to customary, unwritten, unsystematic constitutionalism led by tradition implied a kind of 'constitutional superstition',[44] i.e. a faith in the causal power of the constitutional word, equated with the divine word. One can hardly imagine a constitutional *Gestalt* more opposed to that of Edmund Burke.[45] It trusts in the artificial creation of the will, based on abstract reason.[46] Mitigating this form of constitutional demiurgism, Madame de Staël once remarked that '[t]he constituent Assembly always thought [...] there was something magic in its decrees'.[47]

This shared understanding of what it meant to draft a constitution endured. In 1958, De Gaulle was called to take power because of the Algerian crisis, which the Fourth Republic was incapable of handling, mainly due to governmental instability.[48] He announced that his first act would be to draft a new constitution. Even though some fundamental principles remain the same, there is thus a habit of 'new formal constitutional departures' in French politics.

Because of the great value placed on abstract ideals in French political life,[49] a culture of constitutional *tabula rasa* emerged, requiring that the Revolution be repeated. In 1789, the *pouvoir constituant* seemed first to de-constitute the *Ancien Régime* and then to reconstitute an entirely new order.[50] This is why several constitutions were quite long and contained many provisions on the detailed political, social, administrative, and legal order to be

---

[43] Paul Bastid, *L'idée de constitution* (Economica, Paris, 1985) 9–10. See also Olivier Beaud, 'L'histoire du concept de constitution en France. De la constitution politique à la constitution comme statut juridique de l'État' (2010) 2 Jus politicum 31; Michel Ganzin, 'Le concept de constitution dans la pensée jusnaturaliste (1750–1789)', in *La constitution dans la pensée politique* (Presses universitaires d'Aix-Marseille, Aix-en-Provence, 2001) 167–201.

[44] Paul Bastid, ibid, 186.

[45] See Edmund Burke, *Reflections on the Revolution in France* (first published 1791, The Liberal Arts Press, New York, 1955).

[46] Alexis de Tocqueville, *The Old Regime and the Revolution*, vol 1 (AS Kahan tr, The University of Chicago Press, Chicago, 1998) 195–202; Paul Bastid, n 43, 145; Martin Loughlin, 'The Constitutional imagination' (2015) 78 The Modern Law Review 1; Albrecht Korshorke and others, *Der fiktive Staat. Konstruktionen des politischen Körpers in der Geschichte Europas* (Fischer, Frankfurt-am-Main, 2007); Hannah Pitkin, 'The idea of a Constitution' (1987) 37 Journal of Legal Education 167; Keith M Baker, 'Constitution', in François Furet and Mona Ozouf (eds), *Dictionnaire critique de la Révolution française*, vol 3 (Flammarion, Paris, 2017) 179.

[47] Germaine de Staël, *Considérations sur la Révolution française*, vol 1 (first published 1818, Charpentier, Paris, 1862) 325.

[48] See Emmanuel Cartier and Michel Verpeaux (eds), *La Constitution du 27 octobre 1946: nouveaux regards sur les mythes d'une constitution 'mal aimée'* (Mare & Martin, Paris, 2017).

[49] Theodore Zeldin, *Histoire des passions françaises (1848–1945)*, vol 4 (Le Seuil, Paris, 1979) 82–125.

[50] Ran Halévi, 'La déconstitution de l'Ancien Régime. Le pouvoir constituant comme acte révolutionnaire' (2010) 2 Jus Politicum 7; Michel Pertué, 'La notion de constitution à la fin du 18e siècle', in Jacques Guilhaumou and Raymonde Monnier (eds), *Des notions-concepts en révolution: Autour de la liberté politique à la fin du 18e siècle* (Société des études robespierristes, Paris, 2003) 39.

established.[51] They were clear inaugural moments and resembled political platforms as well as new catechisms.

This explains why, to a great extent, French political history is the history of struggles to establish, preserve, and change constitutions. Political conflict could hardly be accommodated in existing institutions. It could not be incorporated into a given constitutional setting but was necessarily expressed in terms of a constitutional ambition. As René Rémond explained:

> Constitutions, instead of being an element of national cohesion and its reference have all been issues of controversy: being the expression of a dogma, the application of a philosophical system, they asked, beyond simple conformity to their practical dispositions, for an almost religious adherence to their inspiration. For those who did not adhere to their truth, only one possible solution: outright refusal. [...] If the devotees of the Constitution in force require an unconditional adherence, its opponents are not less intransigent: their opposition is also flawless and denounces any attempt at acceptance, even a conditional one: all rallying is held for a denial.[52]

Many constitutions were drafted and planned. Yet not so many were adopted or put into force, ranging from 34 (1875) to 377 (Year III) articles, and even less have functioned concretely. Several types of regimes have been established: monarchy, republic, empire, parliamentarianism, dualist parliamentarianism, monist parliamentarianism, plebiscitarianism, conventionalism, etc. Several institutional combinations have been tested: bicameralism, polycameralism, and monocameralism; single-seated executive, bicephal executive, and collective executive; strict separation of powers, checks and balances, etc.

This frenetic activity testifies to a shared belief that constitutional change is the natural means to achieve political change. This is still evident in the call for a Sixth Republic, regularly voiced by political reformers during the Fifth Republic.[53] How did such constitutionalism face the problem of the constitutional establishment of self-government?

ii. The Quandary of Entrenching Constitutional Self-Government

How can a Nation claiming full sovereignty establish a lasting new political order for its own self-government without contradicting itself? How can the *pouvoir constituant* provide for its own silencing by establishing a stable legal order while simultaneously basing the validity of this silencing on its own almightiness, which then implies the reversibility of this legal order?[54]

---

[51] See Section B.2.b.

[52] René Rémond, 'Les Français et leur Constitution', in Jean-Claude Colliard and Yves Jégouzo (eds), *Le nouveau constitutionnalisme. Mélanges en l'honneur de Gérard Conac* (Economica, Paris, 2001) 23, 26.

[53] See e.g. Arnaud Montebourg and Bastien François, *La Constitution de la 6e République. Réconcilier les Français avec la démocratie* (Odile Jacob, Paris, 2005); Bastien François, *La 6e République: pourquoi, comment?* (Les Petits matins, Paris, 2015); *L'avenir en commun: le programme de la France insoumise et son candidat Jean-Luc Mélenchon* (Le Seuil, Paris, 2016); Henry Roussillon, 'Le mythe de la 'VIe République" (2002) 52 Revue française de droit constitutionnel 707; Henry Roussillon (ed), *Demain, la sixième République?* (n 10).

[54] Jed Rubenfeld, 'Legitimacy and Interpretation', in Larry Alexander (ed), *Constitutionalism. Philosophical Foundations* (CUP, Cambridge, 1998) 194. See also Anne Norton, 'Transubstantiation: The Dialectic of Constitutional Authority' (n 21); Martin Loughlin and Neil Walker (eds), *The Paradox of Constitutionalism: Constituent Power and Constitutional Form* (OUP, Oxford, New York, 2007); Keith M Baker, 'Constitution' (n 46).

The French constitutional *Gestalt* perfectly illustrates this difficulty. There is a tension between the principle of the supremacy of the *pouvoir constituant*, on the one hand, and the minuteness of most of the devices provided by constitutions for constitutional amendment, i.e. for the sovereign to organize its own survival after the revolution, on the other.[55] The last title of the first French constitution is symptomatic of precisely this tension. It provided for the Nation's right to change its constitution but immediately added that it should comply with a complex process. Three consecutive legislatures needed to express a uniform wish for the constitutional amendment. Then, a fourth legislature, augmented by 249 specific members, would constitute an Assembly of Revision which would vote on the amendment. The members of the third legislature could not be elected to the Assembly of Revision. Moreover, the three legislatures in charge after 1791 could not propose any amendment to the constitution. This would not have allowed for a constitutional amendment until 1801.

In this respect, the French constitutional *Gestalt* illustrates the paradoxes of self-obligation and of self-amendment.[56] When entrenching a new vision of the polity, the French sovereign usually drafts a constitution and tries to make it last.[57] It thus limits the power in the name of which it often allowed itself to get rid of the preceding constitutional order. This kind of performative contradiction demonstrates how difficult it is for any revolution to establish itself as the source of a new order: 'A successful revolution must deny the revolutionary experience to all who succeed the founders' generation. The paradox of revolution is that it cannot preserve its own achievements without destroying the very experience of political freedom that makes it valuable.'[58]

This is one of the structural characteristics of the French constitutional *Gestalt*. With the exception of the Constitution of Year I—which, proclaiming that '[a] people has always the right to review, to reform, and to alter its constitution' and that '[o]ne generation cannot subject to its law the future generations',[59] established a relatively flexible amendment procedure (articles 115 to 117)[60]—and of the royal Charters of 1814 and 1830, which were truly flexible documents, the Constitution of 1791 set the pattern for the entrenchment of the *pouvoir constituant*.[61] The Constitution of Year III,[62] which confirmed the sovereignty of the Nation (article 2), was extremely rigid (Title XIII), some deputies even considering prohibiting constitutional amendment and applying the death penalty to any such proposal.[63]

From a practical viewpoint, the tension was rapidly resolved. The sovereign *pouvoir constituant* systematically modified pre-existing constitutions in defiance of the amendment procedure.

---

[55] See for a general discussion Edouard Bédarrides, *Réviser la constitution. Une histoire constitutionnelle française* (Th. Droit public, Université de Bourgogne, 2004).

[56] See Alf Ross, 'On Self-Reference and a Puzzle in Constitutional Law' (1969) 78 Mind 1; Peter Suber, *The Paradox of Self-Amendment: A Study of Logic, Law, Omnipotence, and Change* (P Lang, New York, 1990).

[57] Philippe Ségur, 'Temps et illusion en droit constitutionnel', in Henry Roussillon (ed), *Etudes en l'honneur du professeur Jean-Arnaud Mazères* (Litec, Paris, 2009) 741.

[58] Paul W Kahn, *The Reign of Law: Marbury v. Madison and the Construction of America* (Yale UP, New Haven, 1997) 55.

[59] Declaration of the Rights of Man and of the Citizen of Year I, art 28.

[60] Association française des constitutionnalistes, *La Constitution du 24 juin 1793: l'utopie dans le droit public français?* (Editions universitaires de Dijon, Dijon, 1997); Julien Boudon, *Les Jacobins. Une traduction des principes de Jean-Jacques Rousseau* (LGDJ, Paris, 2006).

[61] See e.g. art 111 of the Constitution of 1848.

[62] See Roger Dupuy and Marcel Morabito (eds), *1795, pour une République sans révolution* (Presses universitaires de Rennes, Rennes, 1996); Michel Troper, *Terminer la Révolution. La Constitution de 1795* (Fayard, Paris, 2006).

[63] Paul Bastid, *L'idée de constitution* (n 43) 167.

Thus, the Constitution of 1791 failed to be in force for even one year. It was abandoned after the King vetoed several bills. In September 1792, the Republic was proclaimed and a new assembly, the Convention, began to draft a new constitution, which was never applied. The Constitution of Year III only lasted for four years and was abolished by Bonaparte's *coup d'état* in Year VIII (1799). The *Restauration* in 1814 eliminated the entire Napoleonic constitutional system. In 1830, the July Revolution resulted not in the amendment of the Charter but in its total replacement with a new Charter. When Louis-Napoléon Bonaparte became the President of the Second Republic, under the constitutional text of 1848,[64] he could not be re-elected (article 45). He attempted to have this constitutional provision modified but did not manage to secure the required qualified majority. The difficulties of constitutional amendment imposed on the sovereign resulted once more in a *coup d'état*, on 2 December 1851, and in the abolition of the constitution.

In the end, the quest for constitutional entrenchment was expressed in complex amendment formulas. Yet these proved totally ineffective because the constitution itself was abolished. It is accepted that the sovereignty of the Nation—whose will is 'always legal by the simple fact that it is', regardless of its form of expression—is able to find a way to express itself, i.e. to create constitutional law, including against positive norms. As Sieyès put it, 'It would be ridiculous to suppose that the Nation itself could be constricted by the procedures or the constitution to which it had subjected its mandatories.'[65] For most of French constitutional history, constitutional change did not signify change within the constitution but always change of the (entire) constitution itself.

The French polity does not seem to renounce politics, as opposed to law, as easily as Americans, who have secured the establishment and continuance of one and the same document, leading to a form of constitutional worship.[66] The French often make a fresh start in constitutional politics instead of trying to enforce a fixed set of principles by means of institutional devices. Progressively, though, distinct constitutional traditions have emerged and have inspired constitution-making: authoritarian Bonapartism, monarchical parliamentarianism, solidarist enlightened republicanism, etc.

Paradoxically, the more the sovereign entrenched its will, the less the constitution endured. By contrast, the two *Chartes* of 1814 and 1830 were flexible documents. Nevertheless, they stabilized the French polity for more than three decades, a feat no other regime after the Revolution had achieved. This is all the more evident for the Third Republic, the regime that lasted the longest.[67] First, under the three Constitutional Acts of 1875, the distinction between constitutional norms and ordinary legislation was practically abolished.[68] After 1848, and contrary to what had happened during the Revolution, there were no more ad hoc assemblies of constitutional revision. This resulted in a 'resorption of the constituent power into the legislative power'.[69] After 1875, the sovereign, embodied in parliament,[70] was totally unlimited. National sovereignty had developed into representative and parliamentary

---

[64] See Paul Bastid, *Doctrines et institutions politiques de la Deuxième République* (Hachette, Paris, 1945); François Luchaire, *Naissance d'une constitution: 1848* (Fayard, Paris, 1998).

[65] Emmanuel-Joseph Sieyès, *Préliminaire de la constitution. Reconnaissance et exposition raisonnée des Droits de l'Homme et du Citoyen* (Ph-D Pierres, Versailles, 1789) 12–13. See Section B.1.a.

[66] See e.g. Henry P Monaghan, 'Our perfect Constitution' (1981) 56 New York University Law Review 353; Sanford Levinson, *Constitutional Faith* (Princeton University Press, Princeton, 2011); Jack M Balkin, *Constitutional Redemption. Political Faith in an Unjust World* (Harvard University Press, Cambridge MA, 2011).

[67] See Jean-Félix de Bujadoux, *La Constitution de la IIIe République* (LGDJ, Issy-les-Moulineaux, 2015).

[68] Raymond Carré de Malberg, *La loi, expression de la volonté générale* (Sirey, Paris, 1931).

[69] Paul Bastid *L'idée de constitution* (n 43) 187.

[70] See also Section C.1.a.

sovereignty. Possibly because it had refrained, in accordance with the dominant paradigm in the French *Gestalt*, from entrenching the constitution, the Third Republic was able to achieve 'the miracle of a lasting Republic'.[71]

Second, this regime did not flow from any systematic political ideology, nor did it purport to design a new order. Mostly, it codified common political practice.[72] It was born out of a compromise between legitimist monarchists, Orleanist monarchists and republicans. This is why the constitution, which was easily convertible from a republic to a monarchy, was short. It was not committed to any political project. Contrary to the other constitutions, it could absorb political conflict without being abolished to allow for ideological change. After the insurrectional episode of *la Commune* in 1871, according to one author, 'There will be no more popular uprising in Paris. It is the end of the romantic Paris of the nineteenth century revolutions. There is no other way now than the political struggle',[73] i.e. disagreement within the constitution itself.

Consequently, a lasting constitution must depart from 'high-energy' constitution-making.

Under the Fifth Republic, article 89 of the Constitution deals with constitutional amendment to the classical conception of the *pouvoir constituant* that is embedded in the French constitutional *Gestalt*.[74] The *Conseil constitutionnel* expressly refused to join other constitutional courts (Germany, Italy, Turkey, Colombia, Romania, India, etc.) in admitting the constitutional review of constitutional amendments.[75] It thus opposed any supraconstitutional limitations resembling a basic structure or an 'eternity clause' that would restrict the *pouvoir constituant*. It maintained that the *pouvoir constituant* was always free to amend the constitution and thus remained sovereign.[76] As the *Conseil* decided in 2003:

> Article 61 of the Constitution gives the Constitutional Council the task of reviewing the conformity with the Constitution of organic acts and, when they are referred to it under the conditions laid down in this article, ordinary acts […]. The Constitutional Council does not have the power to rule on a constitutional amendment pursuant to article 61, article 89, or any other provision of the Constitution.[77]

It also granted that its decisions that strike down unconstitutional statutes be superseded by constitutional amendments.[78]

As a consequence, the sovereign always remains a full-fledged constitutional actor able to change the constitution, be it within the constitutional forms or outside them.[79] Whatever the product's intended substance, durability, etc., the producer's power remains. This faith can be an element accounting for the apparent absence, denial, or scotomization of Europe

---

[71] Claude Nicolet, *L'idée républicaine en France (1789–1924). Essai d'histoire critique* (Gallimard, Paris, 1982) <159.

[72] Claude Nicolet, ibid, 164, 187–248; Adhémar Esmein, *Eléments de droit constitutionnel français et comparé* (6th edn, Sirey, Paris, 1914) 626.

[73] Marcel Gauchet, *L'avènement de la démocratie II* (n 21) 168.

[74] See Section D.1.c.

[75] See Sabrina Ragone, *I controlli giurisdizionali sulle revisioni costituzionali. Profili teorici e comparative* (Bononia University Press, Bologna, 2011); Guillaume Tusseau, *Contentieux constitutionnel compare. Une introduction critique au droit processuel constitutionnel* (LGDJ, Issy-les-Moulineaux, 2021) 749–754, 790-7.

[76] See e.g. Denis Baranger, 'The language of eternity: Judicial review of the amending power in France (or the absence thereof)' (2011) 44 Israel Law Review 389.

[77] Decision no 2003-496 DC. See also Decision no 92-312 DC.

[78] See e.g. Decision no 2000-429 DC.

[79] See also Section D.1.c.

in the deepest layers of the French constitutional *Gestalt*, in spite of its evident presence in the current constitutional document (Title XV). The ideas of a divided sovereignty, of an irreversible transfer of sovereign rights to a supranational entity, and of the development of a supranational constitutional order are alien to French legal culture, which remains centred on the idea of the Nation's imprescriptible and inalienable sovereignty. Even when constitutional identity, as understood by the *Conseil constitutionnel*, proves to be an obstacle to European integration, the *pouvoir constituant* is allowed to remove the obstacle.[80]

The French effort resembles an unsuccessful crusade to entrench constitutional values. In addition to overly rigid amendment procedures, rejecting the judicial review of statutes contributed to this failure.

2. Low Juridicity Constitutionalism

In French legal culture, the constitution seems far less important than the statute. '*La loi*' (not '*la constitution*', nor '*le droit*') is the crucial concept of legal thought and legal representation, especially for ordinary citizens. John Bell aptly points out that '[a]mong these constitutional values [in the various branches of the French legal system], the respect for *loi* is central'.[81] According to Rousseau,[82] only the *loi* is 'the expression of the general will' (article 6 of the Declaration of the Rights of Man and of the Citizen). According to traditional mythology, the statute starts with all people, envisions only general objects, and applies to all. As one cannot be unjust towards oneself, the statute is necessarily the expression of political autonomy and justice. This is why there is no need to review statutes. The first constitution clearly expressed this 'legicentrism' in the following terms: 'There is no authority in France superior to that of the law; the King reigns only thereby, and only in the name of the law may he exact obedience.'[83] Strikingly enough, the constitution, whose functions include establishing a system of legal sources, itself contended that it was not the supreme law of the land. As Karl Marx aptly noticed, 'The legislative power made the French Revolution.'[84] Simultaneously, 'all the Revolutions project relied on statutes'.[85] The centrality of *la loi* has deep roots in the pre-revolutionary theory of sovereignty. Jean Bodin, in his *Six livres de la République*, contended that:

> The first attribute of the sovereign prince therefore is the power to make law binding on all his subjects in general and on each in particular. But to avoid any ambiguity one must add that he does so without the consent of any superior, equal, or inferior being necessary. If the prince can only make law with the consent of a superior, he is a subject; if of an equal he shares his sovereignty; if of an inferior, whether it be a council of magnates or the people, it is not he who is sovereign.[86]

---

[80] Decision no 2006-540 DC.

[81] See John Bell, *French Legal Cultures* (Butterworths, London, 2001) 255, vi–vii, 53–58, 243–245.

[82] Jean-Jacques Rousseau, *Du contrat social* (first published 1762, GF Flammarion, Paris, 1966). See David Fonseca, *La rhétorique constitutionnaliste. Généalogie du discours doctrinal sur la loi* (Thèse Droit public University Paris Ouest Nanterre La Défense, 2009).

[83] Constitution of 1791, art 3, section 1, chapter II, Title III.

[84] Karl Marx, *Critique du droit politique hégélien* (Albert Baraquin tr, Editions sociales, Paris, 1975) 104.

[85] Denis Baranger, *Penser la loi. Essai sur le législateur des temps modernes* (Gallimard, Paris, 2018) 52.

[86] Jean Bodin, *Six Books of the Commonwealth* (first published 1576) Book I, Chapter X, http://www.yorku.ca/comninel/courses/3020pdf/six_books.pdf (last accessed on 21 March 2022).

In the French constitutional *Gestalt*, it is a well-established principle that the legislature—not a court—is the institution that speaks for the community.[87] This explains the legal impact of constitutions on the French legal order. Constitutions seem to play an important role in voicing political projects, but respect for this form of discourse is low once it is enacted. First of all, legicentrism accounts for the difficulties that French constitutions had in devising enforcement mechanisms for themselves (a). Second, because of constitutional volatility, much of what is of fundamental importance, i.e. 'constitutive' or 'constitutional' in some sense of this term, is not contained in the constitutional document but rather in ordinary statutes (b).

a) The Political Enforcement of Constitutions

The French *Gestalt*'s reluctance to allow the judiciary to intervene in legislative and political matters (i) meant that the people were excluded from the constitutional sphere (ii).

i. The Hostility to Judicial Review

According to a common paradigm of juridicity, a rule is a legal rule if it can be enforced by a specific institution called a 'judge'. In this respect, French constitutional law appears as a kind of *lex imperfecta*.[88]

Due to widespread hostility towards parliaments, which served as the courts of the *Ancien Régime* and blocked reforms seeking to diminish their privileges, the revolutionaries refused to grant the judiciary any power apart from that of applying the statutes in a mechanical way. Montesquieu, who expressed the dominant view, argued that since their function was limited to producing legal syllogisms, 'The national judges are no more than the mouth that pronounces the words of the law, mere passive beings, incapable of moderating either its force or rigour.'[89] The judicial functions were strictly separated from the legislative and executive ones.[90] Pursuant to the Statute of 16-24 August 1790 (Title II), several provisions of which remain in force today:

> Art. 10. The courts may not directly or indirectly take any part in the exercise of the legislative power, nor prevent or suspend the execution of the decrees of the legislature, sanctioned by the King, on pain of forfeiture.
>
> Art. 13. The judicial functions are distinct and will always remain separate from the administrative functions. The judges cannot, on pain of forfeiture, disturb in any way whatsoever, the operations of the administrative bodies, nor call before them the administrators in relation to the performance of their functions.

Article 3 of Chapter V of Title III of the 1791 Constitution similarly read:

---

[87] See Section C.1.

[88] See e.g. Roger Latournerie, conclusions on Conseil d'État, 6 November 1936 *Arrighi* et *Coudert*, Dalloz, 1938.3.1.

[89] Montesquieu, *The Spirit of Laws* (first published 1748) Book XI, Chapter VI. On the conception of the judiciary at the time of the French Revolution, see Michel Troper, 'La séparation des pouvoirs et le pouvoir judiciaire en 1791', in *1791, la première Constitution française* (n 37) 355.

[90] See Jacques Chevallier, *L'élaboration historique du principe de séparation de la juridiction administrative et de l'administration active* (LGDJ, Paris, 1970). On the cultural dimension of this design, see e.g. Guillaume Tusseau, 'Article 2. Le dualisme juridique', in Jean-Jacques Bienvenu, Jacques Petit, Benoit Plessix, and Bertrand Seiller (eds), *La constitution administrative de la France* (Dalloz, Paris, 2012) 35.

The courts may not interfere with the exercise of the legislative power, suspend the execution of laws, encroach upon administrative functions, or summon administrators before them for reasons connected with their duties.

Such distrust, still discernible in the fact that the Constitution of 1958 only accepts a 'judicial authority'[91] instead of a proper 'judicial power', precluded judicial review of the constitutionality of statutes[92] as it had developed in the United States.[93] It would have been reminiscent of the practice of parliaments, which claimed a right to control the King's acts by referring to the 'fundamental laws' of the realm.[94] When judges had any difficulty in interpreting a statute, they were obligated to refer the matter to the legislature instead of solving the difficulty for themselves (article 21, Chapter V, Title III of the 1791 Constitution).

As Dicey aptly commented:

> The restrictions placed on the action of the legislature under the French constitution are not in reality laws, since they are not rules which in the last resort will be enforced by the Courts. Their true character is that of maxims of political morality, which derive whatever strength they possess from being formally inscribed in the constitution and from the resulting support of public opinion.[95]

This is not to say that there was no proposal in this respect. Twice in the 1790s, Sieyès presented the project of a *'jurie constitutionnaire'*, which would be empowered to review the constitutionality of public action. In two discourses of two and eighteen Thermidor Year III, he imagined a system which would make the constitution establish enforceable obligations, like ordinary law.[96] Because judges were barred from encroaching on the legislative and executive functions, an ad hoc body had to be established. Sieyès declared:

> I ask three services of the constitutional jury:
> 1) That it faithfully guard the constitutional deposit;
> 2) That it concern itself, free from fatal passions, with all the views that may serve to improve the constitution;
> 3) Finally, that it offer civil liberty a resource of natural equity on those serious occasions when the tutelary law has forgotten its just guarantee.

> In other words, I consider the constitutional jury:
> 1) A court of cassation in the constitutional order;
> 2) A workshop to propose the constitutional amendments that time might require;
> 3) Finally, a complement of natural justice to the shortcomings of positive jurisdiction.[97]

---

[91] Title VIII of the Constitution.

[92] Julien Bonnet, *Le juge ordinaire français et le contrôle de la constitutionnalité des lois. Analyse critique d'un refus* (Dalloz, Paris, 2009).

[93] *Marbury v Madison* 5 U.S. 137 (1803).

[94] See e.g. Roger Bickart, *Les Parlements et la notion de souveraineté nationale au XVIIIᵉ siècle* (F. Alcan, Paris, 1932); Philippe Pichot-Bravard, *Conserver l'ordre constitutionnel (XVIᵉ – XIXᵉ siècle). Les discours, les organes et les procédés juridiques* (LGDJ, Paris, 2011).

[95] Albert Venn Dicey, *Introduction to the Study of the Law of the Constitution* (first published 1915, 8th edn, Liberty Fund, Indianapolis, 1992) 70.

[96] *Réimpression de l'ancien Moniteur*, vol 25 (H Plon, Paris, 1862) 442–452. On this project, see Michel Troper, *Terminer la Révolution* (n 62) 197–220; Jörg Luther, *Idee e storie di giustizia costituzionale nell'ottocento* (G. Giappichelli, Torino, 1990) 39–48; Marco Fioravanti, 'Sieyès et le jury constitutionnaire: perspectives historico-juridiques' (2007) 349 Annales historiques de la Révolution française 87.

[97] *Réimpression de l'ancien Moniteur*, ibid, t. XXV, 442.

The jury would have consisted of 108 former MPs, of whom one third would change every year. The thirty-six new members would have been chosen by the jury itself from among the 250 MPs who were leaving the legislative houses each year. The two legislative houses and the citizens could have referred petitions to the jury.[98] Acts declared unconstitutional would have been regarded as null and void.[99] But the Convention rejected this project. Similar proposals only surfaced anew under the Constitution of the Fourth Republic and, more successfully, under the Fifth Republic with the *Conseil constitutionnel*.[100]

American constitutionalism sought to provide a check on the omnipotent legislature and relied on the judiciary to enforce the constitution. By contrast, the *Gestalt* of French constitutionalism articulated political mistrust vis-à-vis the King and the judiciary. Accordingly, it promoted the reign of the statute rather than that of the law in general or the constitution in particular.[101] Understood as a political platform that was not directly applicable, the constitution needed to be enforced first and foremost by the legislature. The judiciary needed to be understood as a guarantee for the statute's supremacy much more than a device to ensure that the representatives respect the will of the people as it was enshrined in the constitution.[102]

Nevertheless, one should not conclude that the French constitutional *Gestalt* was totally insensitive to the enforcement of constitutions.[103] But instead of conferring constitutional guardianship to judges, this function was attributed to other institutions, thus exemplifying several forms of political review.[104]

First, there could be an ad hoc body, which would not belong to the traditional legal institutions, such as the *jury constitutionnaire*, the *Comité constitutionnel* in 1946 or the *Conseil constitutionnel* since 1958.[105]

Second, a legislative body could be entrusted with seeing to it that the other institutions respected the constitution. In the Constitution of Year III, two houses were established, the *Conseil des Cinq-Cents* and the *Conseil des Anciens*. Legislative initiative belonged to the former, whereas the latter could only accept or refuse the *Cinq-Cents'* resolutions (article 95). One of the grounds for refusal was the violation of the constitution (article 88). If it vetoed the resolution, the *Conseil des Anciens* expressed its decision with the following formula: 'The Constitution annuls' (article 97), which is similar to what a judge exercising judicial review could have said. Under Napoléon Bonaparte's rule, constitutional review was in the hands of a *Sénat conservateur*. Pursuant to article 21 of the Constitution of Year VIII, one of its functions was to '[maintain] or [annul] all acts which were referred to it as unconstitutional by the Tribunat or by the government'. Because of its loyalty to Napoléon, this

---

[98] *Réimpression de l'ancien Moniteur*, ibid, t. XXV, 451 (Art VI).

[99] *Réimpression de l'ancien Moniteur*, ibid, t. XXV, 451 (Art VIII).

[100] See Section D.2.

[101] Paul W Kahn, *The Reign of Law* (n 58).

[102] For a detailed discussion, see Roberto Luis Blanco Valdés, *El valor de la constitución. Separación de poderes, supremacía de la ley y control de constitucionalidad en los orígenes del Estado liberal* (Alianza, Madrid, 1998). See also Edouard Laboulaye, *Histoire des États-Unis* (5th edn, Charpentier, Paris, 1870) 479; Bartolomé Clavero, *Happy Constitution. Cultura y lengua constitucionales* (Trotta, Madrid, 1997) 75.

[103] See Section B.1.b.ii.

[104] See Guillaume Tusseau, 'El control político de constitucionalidad en Francia', trad. in José Luís Prado Maillard (ed), *El control político en el Derecho comparado* (Comares, Granada, 2010) 31; Guillaume Tusseau, 'Enfrentar el panjudicialismo epistémico: la escotomización de formas políticas de control de constitucionalidad' (2017) 18 Parlamento y constitución 9.

[105] See Section D.1.

assembly never accomplished its function properly. This further decreased the legitimacy of constitutional review.

Third, it could behove executive bodies to review the constitutionality of other institutions' behaviour. Such is, for example, one of the justifications for the King's partial veto under the 1791 Constitution. A remnant of that idea remains in article 5 of the Constitution of 1958, which provides that, 'The President of the Republic shall ensure due respect for the Constitution.'

The fourth and last possibility was for 'the people themselves'[106] to exercise constitutional review. According to article 123 of the Constitution of Year I, 'The French Republic respects loyalty, courage, age, filial love, misfortune. It places the constitution under the guaranty of all virtues.' The following constitution, in article 377, explicitly stated that 'The French people entrust the present constitution to the fidelity of the Legislative Body, the Executive Directory, the administrators, and the judges; to the vigilance of fathers of families, to wives and mothers, to the affection of young citizens, to the courage of all Frenchmen.'

Whatever the institutional imagination in order to protect the constitution, judicial review of legislation was excluded from the French constitutional *Gestalt*. Enforcing the will of the sovereign was left to political institutions. This made constitutional law the province of a few experts.

ii. A Constitution for a Class of Experts

When one attempts to reconstruct the *Gestalt* of French constitutionalism, one puzzling question relates to whose conceptions are targeted. Lawrence M Friedman classically distinguished between the 'internal' culture of legal professionals and the 'external' culture of the population and the 'lay' members of the community at large.[107]

In this respect, it is noteworthy that there is no teaching of law as such before higher education. This prevented any popular culture of law from emerging. Elementary courses of 'civic instruction' can provide basic elements regarding their legal and constitutional environment to schoolchildren, such as the Declaration of the Rights of Man and of the Citizen, the flag, the national anthem, the figure of Marianne, the republican ideal, or the motto '*liberté, égalité, fraternité*'. But this can hardly be sufficient for the law to have any important part in the individual's basic understandings and representations of social life.

The absence of judicial review contributed to a specific (lack of) relationship between the people and their constitutions. In the United States, the ordinary citizen *qua* litigant has a direct means to ask for the enforcement of the constitution to her benefit. Such is also the case in systems where constitutional complaints like *Verfassungsbeschwerde*, *amparo*, and their progeny exist: here, ordinary people also have direct access to the judicial enforcement of the constitution. One specificity of the French constitutional *Gestalt*, after 1789, is that the constitution is not routinely available to ordinary citizens. Until 1 March 2010,[108] there was no means for a popular activation of the constitutional documents. 'This largely

---

[106] Larry D Kramer, *The People Themselves: Popular Constitutionalism and Judicial Review* (OUP, Oxford, 2004).

[107] Lawrence M Friedman, *The Legal System: A Social Science Perspective* (Russell Sage Foundation, New York, 1975) 194, 223. See also Max Weber, *Sociologie du droit* (Jacques Grosclaude tr, PUF, Paris, 2017) 181–206; John Ferejohn, Jack Rakove, and Jonathan Riley, 'Editors' Introduction', in John Ferejohn, Jack Rakove, and Jonathan Riley (eds), *Constitutional Culture and Democratic Rule* (CUP, Cambridge, 2001) 1, 10; Nestor P Sagüés, 'Cultura constitucional y desconstitucionalización' (2010) Anuario de derecho constitucional latinoamericano 97.

[108] See Section D.2.

explains why there is still no constitutional culture in France: the constitution is made for the governors, not for the governed.'[109]

As a consequence, popular constitutional claims could only be expressed in terms of changing the constitution[110] and hardly in terms of enforcing the existing constitution. There could be no grass-roots development of a popular constitutional culture. To adapt the title of a book by Cass R Sunstein, French constitutionalism is definitely a 'constitution of a few minds'.[111] Only political public authorities daily apply, enforce, interpret, invoke, disregard, or violate the constitutions, which remain out of the citizens' reach.

One can hardly imagine novels or movies concentrating on famous real or fictitious constitutional cases or on the resignation or assassination of a constitutional judge. The constitution is not part of popular culture. First Amendment-, Second Amendment-, Miranda-talks and the like are inconceivable. The constitution is not a spontaneous means of expressing one's discontent, claims, etc. Activist circles hardly make any civic use of the constitution because until recently, the layman had no access to the *Conseil constitutionnel*.

The fact that the constitution remained the province of public authorities can be regarded as a remnant of Catholic tradition. Tocqueville contended that French constitutionalism developed as a new civic religion. As is evident from the words of the Declaration of the Rights of Man and of the Citizen,[112] it valued an abstract and universal vision of humankind, purported to usher in a new era for the whole world, and adopted a proselyte tone, dividing the nationals and seducing foreigners just like a religion.[113] The values the Declaration expresses are universal in three respects. They are not addressed to a specific people but to all humankind; they flow from natural law and reason, which are universal; the rights they entrench belong to each man *qua* human being.[114] But as a substitute for religion, French constitutional culture does not allow the citizen a personal reading of the sacred texts which the constitutions represent. On the contrary, the necessity of a constitutional clergy that has sole direct access to constitutional law is crucial to the self-understanding of the French polity.

The constitution belongs to the culture of political actors, MPs, ministers, civil servants working in the legislative houses and administrations, etc. Practices and traditions have become established in these spheres and have outlived many political regimes and constitutional documents, thus ensuring the continuance of a specific understanding of constitutional rule. For example, the political staff which had ruled and begun to implement parliamentary practice under the Charters of 1814 and 1830 was still in office during the Second Empire. It managed to restore parliamentary practices in France by the 1860s. These remained firmly established during the Third Republic and to the present day.

A telling example is Eugène Pierre's *Traité de droit politique, électoral et parlementaire*.[115] Under the Third Republic, it was as famous as many other books actually entitled 'constitutional law', and it was much more useful for understanding the institutions. Pierre was not a law professor, however, but the Secretary General of the presidency of the *Chambre des députés* from 1885 to 1925. First of all, his example is symptomatic of the extent to which the constitutional sphere was the province of a few specialists deeply involved in the political

---

[109] Marie-Claire Ponthoreau, *Droit(s) constitutionnel(s) comparé(s)* (Economica, Paris, 2010) 261–262.

[110] See Section B.1.b.i.

[111] Cass R Sunstein, *A Constitution of Many Minds. Why the Founding Document Doesn't Mean What it Meant Before* (Princeton University Press, Princeton, 2009).

[112] See Section C.2.

[113] Alexis de Tocqueville, *The Old Regime and the Revolution* (n 46) 99–101.

[114] Florent Guénard, *La démocratie universelle. Philosophie d'un modèle politique* (Le Seuil, Paris, 2016) 167–175.

[115] Eugène Pierre, *Traité de droit politique électoral et parlementaire* (2nd edn, Motteroz, Paris, 1902).

machinery. Secondly, concerning its practical importance, constitutional law was displaced by infraconstitutional norms, as Pierre was mainly interested in the standing orders of parliament and not in the Constitutional Acts of 1875.

b) The Legislative Fabric of the French Polity

Due to the volatility of constitutional documents, crucial aspects of the organization of the French polity were consolidated by other means after the Revolution. The documents called 'constitutions' appeared to be mere 'vestiges':[116] Those in power only paid them lip service before concentrating on what proved crucial for the structure and operation of self-government. This is why constitutional provisions such as amendment procedures were disregarded. To mention another example, what is known as the 'Grévy constitution', after one of the Third Republic's first Presidents, resulted from a customary[117] limitation or abolition of the sweeping presidential powers, and especially of the President's right to dissolve the lower house of parliament. Rather than implementing the Constitutional Acts of 1875, it did the exact opposite.

Marx identified this practical downgrading of constitutional documents early on. He understood that, in spite of appearances, the revolution that abolished the monarchy and established the republic in 1848 did not alter crucial elements:

> The new constitution was at bottom only the republicanized edition of the constitutional Charter of 1830. [...] The old organization of the administration, the municipal system, the judicial system, the army, etc., continued to exist inviolate, or, where the constitution changed them, the change concerned the table of contents, not the contents; the name, not the subject matter.[118]

Where does the constitutional *Gestalt* locate the building blocks and operational framework of the French polity? French legicentrism offers a clue. As is evident from the Declaration of the Rights of Man and of the Citizen, the constituents trusted the legislative power to achieve enlightened political reform.[119] Accordingly, the organization of French self-government depended on several subconstitutional elements, which had an impact on the structure and functioning of the institutions. Significantly, they led authors to identify several 'constitutions' apart from the formal constitution. Using this term in this context is justifiable, as Daniel Villey proposes. He 'prefers, in order to define the idea of a constitution, to see in the constitution the permanent, the durable, as opposed to the decrees or even the statutes produced by these temporary circumstances'.[120] This use of the term 'constitution' to denote the most important and lasting elements of French society, even though they do not appear in the constitutional document strictly so called, is not only metatheoretical. As Michel Pertué contends, at the time of the French Revolution, the term 'constitution' was widely

---

[116] Georges Burdeau, 'Une survivance: la notion de constitution', in *Mélanges Mestre* (Sirey, Paris, 1956) 53.

[117] On constitutional custom, see especially René Capitant 'La coutume constitutionnelle' (21 décembre 1929) Gazette du Palais.

[118] Karl Marx, *The Eighteenth Brumaire of Louis Bonaparte* (first published 1852) Chapter 2 http://www.marxists.org/archive/marx/works/1852/18th-brumaire/ (last accessed 22 March 2022).

[119] See e.g. Jean Morange, *La Déclaration des droits de l'homme et du citoyen* (PUF, Paris, 2002) 66; Gustavo Zagrebelsky, *Le droit en douceur. Il diritto mite* (Michel Leroy tr, Economica, Paris, 2001) 49–52.

[120] Daniel Villey, 'L'idée de constitution' (January-March 1961) Politique. Revue internationale des doctrines et des institutions 299.

used because after the destruction of the *Ancien Régime*, everything needed to be created anew, by means of reason and law:

> The fact of leaving nothing of what existed before, of irremediably rejecting everything, required the opening of an immense site of reconstruction, *constitution* and *reconstitution*. Then the word bursts, in both senses of the word, because the word constitution resonates and shines in the new discourse, but also because it loses its precise and integral meaning to connote the 'revolutionarity' of all the great laws adopted by the *Constituante*. [...] At the time, one spoke of the *constitution* of the Assembly, the *constitution* of the legal order, the municipal *constitution* or [the *constitution* of] the municipalities, the *constitution* of the departments, the *constitution* of the army, the naval *constitution*, the *constitution* of the finances, the *constitution* of the colonies, the civil *constitution* of the clergy, etc. [...] Very widely used, beyond the limits of the constitutional field [i.e. the organization of political power *stricto sensu*], to qualify a general enterprise of regeneration and re-composition, the word constitution, when it designates the fundamental law and thus has its specialized meaning, indicates a text that initially describes the State in all its aspects and that takes the dimensions of a general code of public law where referrals to the ordinary statute are few. Many articles deal with public contributions, the National Treasury and accounting, the National Guard, education, assistance, the electoral system, and so on. Moreover, 'civil society is at the same time at the head and heart of the text'. The basic principles of social organization are indeed at the beginning of the revolutionary texts in which one then meets all the components of society: fathers, mothers, wives and widows, brothers and cousins. Constitutions respond to the fears and the hopes of landlords, tenants, usufructuaries, as well as farmers and sharecroppers, creditors and debtors: severe for nobles and emigrants, they are concerned with old people and abandoned children. [...] This constitutional overflow reveals instead the totalizing ambition of the French Revolution.[121]

A new world was to be established, in the form of new '*a priori* forms of sensibility'.[122] New spaces were created, such as uniform and regular *départements* instead of *baillages*, *pays*, and *provinces*. The revolutionary calendar established a new time. New popular events and the elimination of traditional corporations and intermediary bodies, instilled by means of a novel educational project, promoted a new sociability between equals.[123]

In the political order, for example, under parliamentary regimes, the houses' standing orders contain crucial norms. As Eugène Pierre contended:

> The standing orders are apparently only the internal law of the assemblies, a collection of prescriptions designed to methodically carry out a meeting in which many opposing aspirations meet and contradict one another. In reality, it is a formidable instrument in the hands of the parties; it often has more influence than the constitution itself on the running of public affairs.[124]

---

[121] Michel Pertué, 'La notion de constitution à la fin du 18ᵉ siècle' (n 50) 48–49.
[122] Immanuel Kant, *Kritik der reinen Vernunft* (3rd edn, Raymund Schmidt, Heiner Klemme (ed), F. Meiner, Hamburg, 1990).
[123] See Mona Ozouf, *L'homme régénéré. Essais sur la Révolution française* (Gallimard, Paris, 1989) 116–157.
[124] Eugène Pierre, *Traité de droit politique électoral et parlementaire* (n 115) 490.

In the civil order, many of the Church's functions were transferred to the State. The constitutive elements were enshrined in such monuments as the Civil code. Unchanged for a long time, this text, which is no more than a statute, determined the basic principles of social interaction in the form of marriage, inheritance, property, contract, responsibility, etc. It established a civil order which proved reliable and stable despite great volatility in the political field and especially at the constitutional level. According to Jean Carbonnier:

> In less than two centuries, the country has watched, phlegmatically, as more than ten political constitutions came and went [...]. Its true constitution is the Civil code. [...] Materially, sociologically, if one prefers, it has the meaning of a constitution, because in it are recapitulated the ideas around which the French society was constituted after the Revolution and still continues to be constituted in our days.[125]

In the administrative order,[126] fully independent from the judiciary,[127] a highly qualified and professionalized civil service, and especially the 'grands corps', contains the constitutive elements. The role of the *Conseil d'État* since 1799 is especially noteworthy. This body firmly established itself at the beginning of the nineteenth century and still exists today. It acted alternatively as a legislative assembly, an advisor for the government, and an administrative judge ensuring the administration's submission to the law.[128] Its members play a crucial role in the drafting of statutes and the functioning of ministries. As Georges Vedel puts it:

> Perhaps most important was that this [constitutional] discontinuity, far from undermining the function and image of the Council of State, underlined more clearly the authority of an institution that remained unshakable as political regimes and constitutional moods came and went, like a solid rock in the midst of the whirlwinds of change. Thus, France's 'administrative constitution' seems much more certain and settled than its political constitutions.[129]

A second aspect of the administrative organization is local government. It was rapidly set up in the immediate years following the Revolution. The '*communes*' were established on the basis of parishes; the cantons and departments[130] were created in 1789–1790. The '*préfet*', created by the statute of 28 Pluviose Year VIII, exercised the central state's control over local administration. Most of this system has remained in place, with changes towards greater decentralization, increased local powers, and more democratic institutions during the nineteenth and twentieth centuries.[131] But never was it seriously considered possible to restore

---

[125] Jean Carbonnier, 'Le Code civil', in Pierre Nora (ed), *Les lieux de mémoire*, vol 2 (Gallimard, Paris, 1986) 293, 309. See similarly Yves Gaudemet, 'Le Code civil, "constitution civile de la France"', in *1804–2004. Le Code civil, un passé, un présent, un avenir* (Dalloz, Paris, 2004) 297.

[126] See Jean-Jacques Bienvenu and others (eds), *La constitution administrative de la France* (n 90).

[127] See Section B.2.a.i.

[128] See e.g. Jean-Jacques Gleizal, *Le droit politique de l'État. Essai sur la production historique du droit administrative* (PUF, Paris, 1980) 18.

[129] Georges Vedel, 'Discontinuité du droit constitutionnel et continuité du droit administratif: le rôle du juge', *Mélanges offerts à Marcel Waline*, vol 2 (LGDJ, Paris, 1974) 777, 793. See also Alexis de Tocqueville, *The Old Regime and the Revolution* (n 46) 240; Maurice Hauriou, *Précis élémentaire de droit administratif* (Sirey, Paris, 1925) 2.

[130] Act of 22 December 1790.

[131] See Jean-Bernard Auby, Jean-François Auby, and Rozen Noguellou, *Droit des collectivités locales* (6th edn, PUF, Paris, 2015).

the unsystematic territorial organization of the *Ancien Régime* nor to disregard the benefit of having so powerful a local agent as the *préfet*. Moreover, just as the institutional structure was preserved, so the persons in power frequently remained the same despite constitutional disruptions.

Tocqueville, Maurice Hauriou, and Georges Vedel all argued that, contrary to the political constitution, the 'administrative constitution' would endure, ensuring the institutional stability that was out of reach at the formal constitutional level.

Remarkably enough, in France, it was not the formal constitution but infraconstitutional institutions, and mostly statutes, that had the most enduring impact on self-government and popular culture.

Describing the evolution of the constitutions' substance, Philippe Ardant[132] underlines how all matters linked to the ordinary universe of the citizens progressively disappeared: the organization of local government, local assemblies, nationality, marriage, family, accountancy, judges, public agents, public forces, election law, '*poids et mesures*', army, election law, etc. By contrast, the first constitutions were full-fledged 'codes of public law writ small'.[133] Despite objections to redefining as 'constitutional' what had proved to be lasting, this demonstrates how the building blocks of the French polity, purportedly established by constitutional documents, were progressively transferred to ordinary statutes. Paradoxically, this kind of 'subconstitutionalism' was precisely the means that allowed the statutes to outlive the constitutional document in force when they were adopted. For the French practice of self-government, such was the 'ruse of [constitutional] reason'.[134] Even though somewhat paradoxical, a constitutional *Gestalt*, understood as a way to structure political power after the *Ancien Régime*, emerged from the chaos of constitutional history and gave specific shape to the understanding of self-government.

C. Basic Structures and Concepts

After elucidating what creating a constitution means in the French *Gestalt*, the question arises what kind of political project this vehicle conveys. Since the French Revolution, two components have been included in the concept of the constitution that form part of the French culture. French constitutional history may be perceived as a series of variations on the competing conceptions of these concepts, which have rapidly become part of the constitutional *Gestalt*. Following article 16 of the Declaration of the Rights of Man and of the Citizen, 'Any society in which the guarantee of rights is not assured, nor the separation of powers determined, has no constitution.' Two main dimensions emerge from this canonical definition of a constitution. The first is related to the principles that regulate the machinery of the State, i.e. the institutional devices that aim at enabling and disciplining the Nation's self-government (1). The second consists of the values that underlie the law to be enacted on behalf of the Nation, both as an inspiration and as a limit (2). Both define the *pouvoir constituant*'s goals, purposes, and justifications in the ongoing process of French constitution-making.

---

[132] Philippe Ardant, 'Le contenu des Constitutions: variables et constantes' (1989) 50 Pouvoirs 31.
[133] Paul Bastid, *L'idée de constitution* (n 43) 23–24, 154; Smilarly, see Michel Pertué, 'La notion de constitution à la fin du 18ᵉ siècle' (n 50) 48–49.
[134] Georg W F Hegel, *La Raison dans l'histoire* (Kostas Papaioannou tr, UGE, Paris, 1965) 129.

1. Delegative Constitutionalism

The succession of conflicting regimes testifies to a wavering between two major ways to envision self-government. Following Sieyès, French culture appears deeply committed to a representative form of (self-)government (a). But it simultaneously insists on the people's direct participation in the political sphere (b). Both conceptions are to be applied in a system of separation of powers (c).

a) The Representative Principle

According to *Qu'est-ce que le Tiers-État?*, political societies have entered the age of representative government. Self-government implies that the people are ruled by individuals they choose, not that they rule themselves. Loosening the principle of self-government (i) proved crucial for the constitutional *Gestalt* and for the unity of the polity (ii).

i. Severing the People from its Representatives

Indirect rule could be perceived as a practical result of the empirical fact that, due to the large population in France, direct rule was impossible. But there is more. When in 1791 Malouet proposed to allow the people to ratify the drafted constitution, he faced strong objections. Since the Declaration of 1789, the principle or essence of sovereignty had been distinguished from its exercise.[135] While the first belonged to the Nation, the second could—and had to—be delegated. By stating that 'The Nation, from which alone all powers emanate, may exercise such powers only by delegation. The French constitution is representative; the representatives are the legislative body and the King', the Constitution of 1791 (Title III, article 2) paved the way for the constitutions to come.

This distinction provided a justification for the political power to be exercised on behalf of the people, without necessarily implying their right to participate, especially the right to vote. This is why, for example, the Constitution of 1791 (Title III, Chapter I, Section II, article 2) established the indirect vote and a poll tax (*suffrage censitaire*) to distinguish passive citizens from active ones. Only the latter were allowed to vote. Voting was regarded not so much as a human right but as a kind of social function, exercised on behalf of the community by those who were eligible to do so. The Constitution of Year III (articles 8 and 16) established suffrage on the basis of property and intellectual capacity (*suffrage capacitaire*).

This was consistent with the fact that many members of the first constituent assemblies thought that the people were well suited to choose those who would govern but unfit to govern themselves. As Montesquieu wrote:

> The people, in whom the supreme power resides, ought to have the management of everything within their reach: that which exceeds their abilities must be conducted by their ministers. [...] The people are extremely well qualified for choosing those whom they are to entrust with part of their authority. [...] As most citizens have sufficient ability to choose, though unqualified to be chosen, so the people, though capable of calling others to an account for their administration, are incapable of conducting the administration themselves.[136]

---

[135] See Section B.1.
[136] Montesquieu, *The Spirit of Laws* (n 89) Book II, Chapter II. See also ibid, Book XI, Chapter VI.

While they are undoubtedly vested in the essence of sovereignty, its exercise could be delegated: 'On the one hand, it was necessary to promote the idea that the foundation of power had to be located in the country, but on the other hand, it was just as important to divest the said country of the political decision.'[137] For Sieyès, it was perfectly clear that 'we want a *representative* constitution, not a *democratic* one.'[138] Only the idea of representation could make it possible to speak of self-government. But this elitist self-government was also a means to ensure that public reason, and not crude popular will or interest, ruled. As Guizot wrote in his study of the history of representation:

> It is a question of discovering all the elements of legitimate power dispersed in society and of organizing them into actual power, that is, to concentrate, to realize public reason, public morals. What is called representation is nothing but the means of arriving at this result. It is not an arithmetic machine designed to collect and count individual wills. It is a natural process for extricating from society public reason, which alone has the right to govern it.[139]

As a consequence, the representative principle is neither simply a principle of division of labour nor an institutional second best due to practical constraints, but rather a central element in an articulated conception of the best regime. It also implies a specific relationship between those Bentham called the 'subject many' and the 'ruling few'.[140] French constitutional law has always rejected the imperative mandate, according to which the representatives are appointed to slavishly follow their electors' political will rather than to express their own visions of the common good. As Condorcet once put it, 'My electors have chosen me not to defend their ideas, but mine!' For example, article 35 of the Constitution of the Second Republic explicitly forbade the members of the National Assembly to receive any binding mandate. Article 27 of the Constitution of 1958 similarly reads: 'No Member [of parliament] shall be elected with any binding mandate.'

Refusing the imperative mandate was also a way to avoid any fragmentation of the political will. These elements thus contributed to making the constitutional domain the province of a specialized and autonomous class of experts.[141] Simultaneously, they permitted the establishment of a unified political subject.

ii. Unification of the Polity
According to the representative mandate, deputies never represent only their constituents or their province but always the whole Nation. As article 34 of the Constitution of 1848 put it, 'The members of the National Assembly are the representatives, not of the department which nominates them, but of the whole of France.' The *Conseil constitutionnel* confirmed this deeply rooted conception, stating that, 'If deputies and senators are elected by universal suffrage, directly for

---

[137] Stéphane Rials, 'Constitutionnalisme, souveraineté et représentation (La représentation: continuité ou nécessité?)', in Association française des constitutionnalistes, *La continuité constitutionnelle en France de 1789 à 1989* (n 8) 49.

[138] Emmanuel-Joseph Sieyès, *Quelques idées de constitution, applicables à la ville de Paris en juillet 1789* (Baudoin, Versailles, 1789) 18–19. See also Emmanuel-Joseph Sieyès, 'Sur l'organisation du pouvoir législatif et la sanction royale', 7 September 1789, in François Furet and Ran Halévi (eds), *Orateurs de la Révolution française. I. Les constituants* (La Pléiade, Paris, 1989) 1018.

[139] François Guizot, *Histoire des origines du gouvernement representatif en Europe*, vol 2 (Didier, Paris, 1851) 150.

[140] See e.g. Jeremy Bentham, *First Principles Preparatory to Constitutional Code*, in Philip Schofield (ed), *The Collected Works of Jeremy Bentham* (Clarendon Press, Oxford, 1989) 68–70.

[141] See Section B.2.a.ii.

the former, indirectly for the latter, each of them represents the whole Nation in Parliament and not the population of her own constituency.[142]

The real people are thus excluded from the daily operations of the political institutions. *Qua pouvoir constituant*, they are immediately tied to strict rules of constitutional amendment.[143] *Qua pouvoir constitué*, they do not appear except indirectly, as the entity in the name of which 'representatives' freely exercise their own power.

In light of Thomas Hobbes's philosophy, the representation of unity goes hand in hand with the unity of representation.[144] According to Hobbes:

> A multitude of men are made one person when they are by one man, or one person, represented […]. For it is the unity of the representer, not the unity of the represented, that maketh the person one. And it is the representer that beareth the person, and but one person: and unity cannot otherwise be understood in multitude.[145]

Making every MP represent the Nation instead of only her constituents secures the Nation's unity. This unity does not antedate the political process. Contrary to a traditional representation of German constitutionalism, which is based on the people's pre-existing characteristics, such as ethnicity, language, culture, social ties, religion, etc., the *Gestalt* of French constitutionalism testifies, once again, to artificiality and constructivism. It is not based on ethnos but on demos, i.e. on the active construction of a people consisting of equal individuals, whose common characteristic is precisely that they are represented by specific bodies.[146] Constitutional texts are endowed with a performative dimension, allowing them to create the collective political subject that proclaims them.[147]

In order to allow for such uniform representation, the empirical differences among the real people had to be erased. An abstract and homogeneous 'society of equals',[148] however fictitious it might seem, had to be established. This was one of the functions of French universalism in the proclamation of human rights, and one of the main rationales for the refusal of any representation of interests, privileges (as *leges privatae*), derogatory personal statuses, and rights which would benefit specific identities or groups instead of similar, interchangeable individuals.[149] Whereas the people under the Old Regime were concrete, local, multiple, and diverse, living in distinct social contexts, professional corporations, and religious communities, the French Revolution created a unified and abstract image of the people.[150] From the French Revolution onwards for approximately a century, this legitimized the fact that groups, associations, professional corporate organizations, and trade unions were held in high suspicion and even prohibited. According to a term coined by Sieyès, the Nation needed to be 'made one' through a process of 'adunation'.[151]

---

[142] Decision no 99-410 DC.

[143] See Section B.1.b.ii.

[144] Pierre Brunet, *Vouloir pour la Nation. Le concept de représentation dans la théorie générale de l'État* (LGDJ, Paris, 2004).

[145] Thomas Hobbes, *Leviathan* (first published 1651) Chapter XVI, https://www.gutenberg.org/files/3207/3207-h/3207-h.htm (last accessed on 22 March 2022).

[146] See e.g. Michel Rosenfeld, *The Identity of The Constitutional subject. Selfhood, Citizenship, Culture, and Community* (Routledge, London, 2010) 149–183.

[147] See e.g. Judith Pryor, *Constitutions. Writing Nations, Reading Difference* (Birkbeck Law Press, Abingdon, 2008).

[148] See Pierre Rosanvallon, *La société des égaux* (Le Seuil, Paris, 2011) ; Pierre Rosanvallon, *Le peuple introuvable. Histoire de la représentation démocratique en France* (Gallimard, Paris, 1998) 16, 33–83.

[149] See Section C.2.a.i.

[150] Paolo Grossi, *Mitologie giuridiche della modernità* (3rd edn, A. Giuffrè, Milano, 2007) 201–208.

[151] See Jacques Guilhaumou, 'Nation, individu et société chez Sieyès', (1997) 26 Genèses 4.

In this perspective, the representative principle is connected to legicentrism. It justifies the statute's centrality, *qua* expression of the general will as proclaimed by the representatives. It is the object of a religious faith,[152] which in other places takes the constitution for its object. Legislative fetishism also testifies to a new conception of the sources of law. In the Middle Ages, specialists could discover the law from among a wide variety of materials (texts, customs, doctrinal opinions, decisions, practices, etc.). By contrast, after the French Revolution, legislation emerged as the only source of law. Especially in the form of the code, the statute purports to be a unified and exclusive source, reflecting the unity of the State and the sovereign.[153] It is also the privileged instrument of voluntarist political reconstruction.[154]

Representation must also be linked to the mythology of the unity of the polity, be it a monarchy or a republic.[155] 'Jacobinism'[156] is a characteristic element of French territorial organization. For example, article 1 of Title II of the Constitution of 1791 reads, 'The kingdom is one and indivisible; its territory is distributed into eighty-three departments, every department into districts, every district into cantons.' This reorganization was part of the revolutionary *tabula rasa*. The administrative divisions that had emerged under the *Ancien Régime* gave way to a rational system that made the whole territory more easily manageable. Based on personal and territorial equality, it allowed for the uniform application of the legislated legal system, which replaced a complex mix of local customs and special laws. As it is sovereign and the same for all, *la loi* ensures that no other intermediary form of sociability exists between the abstract individual and the State.[157] Many constitutions contain similar provisions. In the texts adopted in Year I, Year III, and Year VIII, article 1 of the constitutions reads, 'The French Republic is one and indivisible.' A similar provision existed in 1848 (Preamble, article I). Article 2 of the current Constitution maintains that 'France shall be an indivisible, secular, democratic and social Republic'.

Nevertheless, centralization progressively loosened during the nineteenth century and has done so even more clearly since the 1980s. Greater powers have been delegated to the *communes* and the *départements*. New territorial collectivities such as the *régions* have been created. The central State's control has become less stringent.[158] In 2003, the constitution was amended to affirm the 'decentralized' character of the Republic.[159] The latest version of article 1 reads:

> France shall be an indivisible, secular, democratic and social Republic. It shall ensure the equality of all citizens before the law, without distinction of origin, race, or religion. It shall respect all beliefs. It shall be organised on a decentralised basis.

---

[152] See Georges Burdeau, 'Le déclin de la loi' (1963) 8 Archives de philosophie du droit 35; Georges Burdeau, 'Essai sur l'évolution de la notion de loi en droit français' (1939) 9 Archives de philosophie du droit et de sociologie juridique 7. See also Jean-Claude Bécane, Michel Couderc, and Jean-Louis Hérin, *La loi* (2nd edn, Dalloz, Paris, 2010).

[153] Paolo Grossi, *Mitologie giuridiche della modernità* (n 150) 19–26, 34, 97, 99–100, 134–137, 175, 208–215, 225.

[154] See Section B.2.b.

[155] Roland Debbasch, 'Unité et indivisibilité', in Association française des constitutionnalistes, *La continuité constitutionnelle en France de 1789 à 1989* (n 8)7; Roland Debbasch, *Le principe révolutionnaire d'unité et d'invisibilité de la République. Essai d'histoire politique* (Economica, Paris, 1988); Gérard Marcou, 'Le principe d'indivisibilité de la République' (2002) 100 Pouvoirs 45.

[156] Lucien Jaume, *Le discours jacobin et la démocratie* (Fayard, Paris, 1989).

[157] Claude Nicolet, *L'idée républicaine en France (1789-1924)* (n 71) 461; Jean-Jacques Gleizal, *Le droit politique de l'État* (n 128) 33-5, 128; Paolo Grossi, *Mitologie giuridiche della modernità* (n 150) 208–215.

[158] See Jean-Bernard Auby, Jean-François Auby, and Rozen Noguellou, *Droit des collectivités locales* (n 131).

[159] Constitutional Act no 2003-276 of 28 March 2003.

136 GUILLAUME TUSSEAU

> Statutes shall promote equal access by women and men to elective offices and posts as well as to position of professional and social responsibility.

More precisely, article 72 of the Constitution provides that:

> Territorial communities may take decisions in all matters arising under powers that can best be exercised at their level.
>
> In the conditions provided for by statute, these communities shall be self-governing through elected councils and shall have power to make regulations for matters coming within their jurisdiction.
>
> In the manner provided for by an Institutional Act, except where the essential conditions for the exercise of public freedoms or of a right guaranteed by the constitution are affected, territorial communities or associations thereof may, where provision is made by statute or regulation, as the case may be, derogate on an experimental basis for limited purposes and duration from provisions laid down by statute or regulation governing the exercise of their powers.
>
> No territorial community may exercise authority over another. However, where the exercising of a power requires the combined action of several territorial communities, one of those communities or one of their associations may be authorized by statute to organise such combined action.
>
> In the territorial communities of the Republic, the State representative, representing each of the members of the Government, shall be responsible for national interests, administrative supervision and compliance with the law.

In spite of this evolution, which certainly does not establish a right to local self-rule, it is evident that the French constitutional *Gestalt* is hostile, in principle, to conferring any rights to specific groups or to acknowledging the existence of communities apart from one national community, which is the product of the process of representation.[160] This is why the *Conseil constitutionnel* declared unconstitutional a statute on affirmative action for women in the political domain,[161] its ruling being superseded only by constitutional amendment.[162] This is also why the *Conseil* struck down a statute that intended to recognize the existence of a 'Corsican people, component of the French people'.[163] There is currently a debate concerning a wider right to differentiation for territorial collectivities in the context of President Macron's initiatives to amend the constitution.

In the French constitutional *Gestalt*, self-government thus appears as an all-encompassing and artificial operation, as opposed to one allowing pre-existing diversities to express themselves at the political level.[164] A deliberate constitutional blindness erases the concrete dimension of 'real' citizens, aiming to construct a unified people made of uniform citizens. Only in times of constitutional crisis was it expected that the people could intervene—most of the time only to support the revolutionary elite. Nevertheless, this is only part of the story.

---

[160] See Section C.1.a.ii.

[161] Decision no 82-146 DC.

[162] Constitutional Act no 99-569 of 8 July 1999. See Section B.1.b.

[163] Decision no 91-290 DC. Similarly, the *Conseil* barred the adoption of the European Charter for Regional or Minority Languages in its Decision no 99-412 DC. Art 75-1 of the Constitution was inserted in 2008 to supersede this decision. But to date, the convention has not been ratified.

[164] Comparing several concepts of representation involved, see Hannah F Pitkin, *The Concept of Representation* (University of California Press, Berkeley, 1967).

Due to the shadow of Rousseau's conception of self-government,[165] this tendency met with some criticism and an opposite trend—or even a kind of subculture or counter-culture—over the course of constitutional history.

b) The Illusions of Semi-Direct Democracy

Several devices have been conceived in order to make the real people an active part of the machinery of self-government, not merely a means of justification. Since the French Revolution and with the exception of the royal Charter of 1814, the idea that the essence of sovereignty lay in the people was never called into question. What was debated was whether (and how) the people could exercise their sovereignty.[166] The proposed devices never seemed fully convincing nor practically viable as forms of direct self-government.

For example, the Convention expressly stated in article 2 of the Constitution of Year I, drafted by an assembly and adopted by referendum, that, 'The French people, for the exercise of its sovereignty, is distributed in primary assemblies of canton.' In practical terms, the *corps législatif* could itself adopt 'decrees' (*décrets*) in several fields (article 55). As far as 'statutes' (*lois*) were concerned (articles 56 ff), the *corps législatif* could only propose a text, which was sent to the *communes*. The procedure was as follows:

> Art. 59. If, forty days after the sending in of the proposed law, of the absolute majority of departments, one-tenth of all the primary assemblies, legally assembled by the departments, have not protested, the bill is accepted and becomes a law.
> Art. 60. If protest be made, the Legislative Body calls together the primary assemblies.

Regarding constitutional amendments, article 115 provided that:

> If, in one-half of the departments plus one, one-tenth of the regularly constituted primary assemblies requests the revision of a Constitutional Act or the amendment of some of its articles, the Legislative Body shall be required to convoke all the primary assemblies of the Republic to ascertain if there are grounds for a National Convention.

This pioneering constitution was the only one to provide for the popular exercise of sovereignty. But it was never applied. It nevertheless remains symptomatic—both in its adoption, by referendum, and in its failure—of an important tendency in the French constitutional *Gestalt*.

Other devices related to direct democracy were conceived under Napoleon Bonaparte's rule. '*Plébiscites*' were electoral consultations by which the people accepted or refused Bonaparte's, and later Napoléon I's and Napoléon III's, proposals. These never worked fairly and were used as a means for an authoritarian rule to claim legitimacy out of popular support. No direct popular consultation ever led to a negative result before the refusal of the first project of a constitution for the Fourth Republic in 1946.[167]

Plebiscite remained highly criticized for maintaining the authoritarian apparatus. In fact, it did not really operate as a device which lessened the delegative aspect of French constitutionalism. It was only a way to have the people accept ever greater delegations of power to a single man. The direct political presence of the people was thus a mere illusion. Like under the *Ancien Régime*, it allowed one individual to embody all of society. As Arthur de La

---

[165] See Julien Boudon, *Les Jacobins* (n 60).
[166] See Section B.1 and C.1.a.
[167] See Sections C.1.c and D.3.b.

Guéronnière once wrote, 'The emperor is not a man, he is a people.'[168] Representation was thus understood as a kind of embodiment rather than as a series of mandates.

The direct political presence of the people was regarded as a threat from many sides. After the Terror and Napoleonic rule, conservative opinion identified the people and its *pouvoir constituant* mainly with insurrection, usurpation, rebellion, and disorder. Those who favoured the people were also reluctant to institutionalize its political role because they regarded doing so as an elimination of the people's natural right to insurrection.[169]

Nevertheless, direct democracy resurfaced. A two-pronged referendum was held in 1945 in order to decide whether or not to restore the Third Republic and how to draft the new constitution in case the Third Republic was rejected. Two referenda took place in 1946 in order ratify the new constitution and another in 1958 when the Constitution of the Fifth Republic was accepted on 28 September. Though it was suppressed for most of constitutional history, the French *Gestalt* has never abandoned the temptation of directly involving the people. Article 3 of the Constitution of 1958 tries to synthesize the competing trends:

> National sovereignty shall vest in the people, who shall exercise it through their representatives and by means of referendum.
>
> No section of the people nor any individual may arrogate to itself, or to himself, the exercise thereof.

The link between representation and direct involvement can be interpreted in two conflicting ways. According to one perspective, the Fifth Republic was able to achieve a good balance between these two trends thanks to the legislative (article 11), local (article 72-1) and constitutional (article 89) referenda. From another perspective, the practice of referenda essentially remained plebiscitarian.[170] This was quite clear under De Gaulle's rule because the Head of State explicitly stated, whenever consulting the people, that he would resign if he lost—which he actually did in 1969. The personal dimension of referenda was also clear when the French people rejected the Treaty establishing a constitution for Europe in 2005. Many observers claimed that this outcome resulted more from disapproval vis-à-vis those who were asking the question than from what the treaty stipulated. This raises great concern regarding the appropriate use of this tool, which President Macron was considering in order to insert environmental concern in article 1 of the Constitution before the amendment failed in the Senate.

The tension between these adversarial tendencies within the French constitutional *Gestalt* still persist, even though the people now undoubtedly participate in self-government in a more genuine way. Nevertheless, it remains the case that referenda can only take place provided ordinary representatives decide it. There is no formal, constitutional way for the people to step in *proprio motu* in the political field. Currently, there are debates concerning the introduction of the popular initiative.[171]

c) The Separation of Powers

In 1789, the separation of powers was considered so evident as to be part of the definition of a constitution.[172] This principle, classically said to be borrowed from Montesquieu, was

---

[168] Arthur de La Guéronnière, *Portraits politiques contemporains. Napoléon III* (Aymot, Paris, 1853) 92.

[169] See Pierre Rosanvallon, *La démocratie inachevée. Histoire de la souveraineté du peuple en France* (Gallimard, Paris, 2000) 74–90.

[170] See Jean-Marie Denquin, *Référendum et plébiscite. Essai de théorie générale* (LGDJ, Paris, 1976).

[171] See also Section D.1.c.

[172] Michel Troper, 'L'interprétation de la Déclaration des droits; l'exemple de l'article 16' (1988) 8 Droits 111.

not understood as defining any specific institutional organization. In order to avoid despotism, as it appeared under the absolute monarchy, and to preserve freedom, the *pouvoir constituant* had to separate the powers, no matter by what means.[173] As the judiciary was neglected or despised,[174] two powers had to be established: the legislative and the executive.

Initially, the executive function was understood in rather strict terms as being in charge of the mere material execution of the legislature's will. Pursuant to the Constitution of 1791, for example (Title III, Chapter IV, Section I, article 6), 'The executive power cannot make any law, even temporary, but only proclamations that conform with the laws, in order to impose or to remind of their application.' Progressively, the body in charge of the executive function was endowed with broader functions, such as the power to adopt general administrative acts (*pouvoir réglementaire*)[175] and the power to deal with foreign affairs. This led to the emergence of the larger 'governing function'.[176] It also incorporated or shared some elements of the legislative function, especially regarding legislative initiative or veto.

It was clear that, when understood as normative functions, the legislative and the executive power could not be equal. Execution was conceptually subordinate to legislation.[177] In accordance with the recommendation that the powers be separated, two main institutional designs were possible. The first one sought to establish a balance of powers by splitting the legislative function among several bodies, one of which also exercised the executive function. This was the model that England and the United States adopted. The constitution of 1791 followed this example, with the *Corps législatif* and the King, who was granted a veto power, sharing the legislative power. According to the drafters of this text, the fact that the consent of two co-authors was necessary to adopt a statute guaranteed political moderation. No specialized bodies were established. Moreover, the bodies' independence was limited by the responsibility of the ministers, who had to ensure that the King executed the legislation he had agreed to adopt. Although this first constitution was short-lived, the institutional dynamics seemed to lead to a form of parliamentary regime. This tendency was revived after the First Empire. Parliament managed to hold the King's ministers politically responsible. This legacy of the Charter of 1814 was not lost. It became more evident under the Charter of 1830.[178] After 1860, it contributed to the Second Empire's evolution towards a more liberal regime and has remained a stable principle of French constitutional practice. It appeared to be so crucial to the French constitutional *Gestalt* as to be imposed on De Gaulle's government for the drafting of the current constitution.[179]

The second main possibility, which was favoured by the democrats and entered the Constitution of Year I, strictly divided a legislative body from an executive one. Because of the supremacy of legislation, the representative parliament's power would not be limited by

---

[173] Michel Troper, *La séparation des pouvoirs et l'histoire constitutionnelle française* (LGDJ, Paris, 1972).

[174] See Section B.2.a.

[175] Michel Verpeaux, *La naissance du pouvoir réglementaire: 1789-1799* (PUF, Paris, 1991).

[176] Michel Troper, 'La théorie de la fonction gouvernementale chez Georges Burdeau', in Bernard Chantebout (ed), *Le pouvoir et l'État dans l'œuvre de Georges Burdeau* (Economica, Paris, 1993) 73; Michel Troper, 'Responsabilité politique et fonction gouvernementale. Mutation des conceptions de l'exécutif sous la Révolution française', in Olivier Beaud and Jean-Michel Blanquer (eds), *La responsabilité des gouvernants* (Descartes & cie, Paris, 1999) 33; Michel Troper, *Terminer la Révolution* (n 62) 163–180. See more generally Nicolas Roussellier, *La force de gouverner. Le pouvoir exécutif en France, XIXᵉ-XXIᵉ siècles* (Gallimard, Paris, 2015).

[177] Raymond Carré de Malberg, *Contribution à la théorie générale de l'État spécialement d'après les données fournies par le droit constitutionnel français*, 2 vol (Sirey, Paris, 1920–1922); Charles Eisenmann, 'L'*Esprit des lois* et la spération des pouvoirs', in *Mélanges Raymond Carré de Malberg* (Sirey, Paris, 1933) 163.

[178] Alain Laquièze, *Les origines du régime parlementaire en France (1814-1848)* (PUF, Paris, 2002).

[179] See Section C.2.a.ii.

any other power, and the executive body would be maintained in a subordinate position.[180] The Constitution of Year III intended to mix the two systems.[181] It instituted specialized missions for the executive *Directoire* and the *Corps législatif*. But by stating that 'The *Corps législatif* is composed of a *Conseil des Anciens* and a *Conseil des Cinq-Cents*', article 44 established an internal balance between the two houses of parliament, thus inaugurating the first French bicameral system. Napoleonic regimes went further and established polycameral systems, which were in fact subject to personal rule. This tradition has been maintained, except by the Constitution of the Second Republic, which intended to revive the idea that because a united Nation is sovereign, it should find its institutional embodiment in a single body. Bicameralism, which also existed under the Restoration, the July Monarchy, and the Third and Fourth Republic, seems to be so entrenched in the French constitutional *Gestalt* that one of the reasons why the people rejected the first constitutional draft of 1946 appeared to be an attempt to suppress the Senate. Similarly, when De Gaulle asked the people if they consented to a constitutional reform in 1969, the vote against the reform prevailed. This is sometimes explained by the fact that the proposed amendment would have diminished the powers of the Senate.

The principle of the separation of powers is not unambiguous. This is due to the limited scope of Montesquieu's recommendation as well as to the fact that institutional, functional, legal, and political separations have never been fully distinguished. One may debate the inclusion of this principle in the French constitutional *Gestalt*. So many institutional solutions and political practices have been explored that this element has been affected by the greatest discontinuity.[182] Depending on the predominance of the legislative or of the executive organ, Maurice Hauriou has tentatively identified recurring '*cycles*' in French constitutional history. Each cycle is composed of a first phase of parliamentary domination, a second phase of executive reaction, and a third phase of equilibrium. The first cycle includes the revolutionary constitutions dominated by the legislative assemblies (1791 to Year VIII–1799), the executive reaction of the Napoleonic regimes (Year VIII–1799 to 1814), and the parliamentary equilibrium of the Charters (1814 to 1848). The second cycle begins with the revival of the republican and revolutionary spirit of the Second Republic (1848 to 1851), followed by the dictatorship of the Second Empire (1852 to 1870), and concludes with the parliamentary Third Republic.[183]

Nevertheless, according to Jacques Chevallier:

Beyond what divides them, these two versions share a certain number of common postulates, which testify to the permanence of revolutionary achievements: the purely formal definition of functions and the idea of the supremacy of the statute; the interweaving in the exercise of powers; the conception of justice in general, whose status has not been affected in any way by constitutional vicissitudes, and of administrative justice in particular, whose connection to the executive power has not been called into question.[184]

---

[180] See Guillaume Glénard, *L'exécutif et la Constitution de 1791* (PUF, Paris, 2010).

[181] Michel Troper, 'La séparation des pouvoirs dans la Constitution de l'an III', in Gérard Conac and Jean-Pierre Machelon (eds), *La Constitution de l'an III. Boissy d'Anglas et la naissance du libéralisme constitutionnel* (PUF, Paris, 1999) 51.

[182] Jacques Chevallier, 'La séparation des pouvoirs', in Association française des constitutionnalistes, *La continuité constitutionnelle en France de 1789 à 1989* (n 8) 113; Jean-Marie Denquin, 'La séparation des pouvoirs', in Simone Goyard-Fabre (ed), *L'État au XXᵉ siècle: regards sur la pensée juridique et politique du monde occidental* (Vrin, Paris, 2004) 141.

[183] See Maurice Hauriou, *Précis de droit constitutionnel* (2nd edn, Sirey, Paris, 1929) 293–331.

[184] Jacques Chevallier, 'La séparation des pouvoirs' (n 37) 133.

In the French constitutional *Gestalt*, this conception of the institutional setting went hand in hand with political morality. It was meant to protect specific substantive values, which were simultaneously presupposed for the operation of self-government.

2. Human Rights Constitutionalism

Several principles are so deeply entrenched in French constitutional culture that no regime has been able to abandon them[185] (a). From the start, these principles were only called into question in relation to their development, improvement, and enrichment (b).

a) The Unsupersedable Heritage of 1789

The civil and political rights proclaimed during the French Revolution (i) appear to be so deeply rooted in the constitutional *Gestalt* as to be sometimes considered supraconstitutional principles (ii).

i. *The Civil and Political Rights of 1789*

The Declaration of the Rights of Man and of the Citizen approved by the National Assembly of France on 26 August 1789 set the stage for the society that would replace the *Ancien Régime*. Although royalist circles may have planned to go back to the old order, this was never a serious practical perspective. This text takes the form of a catechism for a new political era, in which the revolutionaries, *qua* 'representatives of the French people, organized as a National Assembly', 'have determined to set forth in a solemn declaration of the natural, unalienable, and sacred rights of man, in order that this declaration, being constantly before all the members of the Social body, shall remind them continually of their rights and duties'.

Expressing universal and evident truths, the most basic principles were rights which any individual was granted *qua* human being:

> Art. 1. Men are born and remain free and equal in rights. Social distinctions may be founded only upon the general good.
> Art. 2. The aim of all political association is the preservation of the natural and imprescriptible rights of man. These rights are liberty, property, security, and resistance to oppression.

Tocqueville suggested a religious reading of this text, understood as a declaration of pre-existing principles and a message for all of humankind.[186] This religious dimension explains why the Revolution 'civilized' many religious aspects of social life and thus tended to make it more secular.[187]

> France is a people-Christ, and the Revolution is a universal symbolic fact in which the fate of humanity is at stake. Like the Christian incarnation, it creates an irreversible point of reference in time, two radically different before and after. [...] In short, the Revolution, a totally human event on the one hand—since it is precisely men's control of their destiny—is,

---

[185] See Section B.2.b.
[186] Alexis de Tocqueville, *The Old Regime and the Revolution* (n 46) 99–101.
[187] Claude Nicolet, *L'idée républicaine en France (1789–1924)* (n 71) 329–330.

on the other hand, out of reach, and in any case out of any comparison, even with the Reformation, even with the Glorious Revolution, even with the American Declarations.[188]

Principles such as equality, liberty, property, and security have been repeated constantly ever since. There were undoubtedly several ways to express them, in a more or less optimistic, voluntarist, or conservative fashion. But they became so intrinsic to the constitutional *Gestalt* as to appear in almost every constitutional document, be it in a declaration of human rights at the beginning of the constitution, within the constitution itself, or both.

For example, the Declaration of the Rights of Man and the Citizen was placed before the Constitution of 1791. The latter began with a Title I dedicated to the 'Fundamental provisions guaranteed by the constitution'. It listed several rights similar to those of the Declaration. Article 2 of the Declaration of Year I provided that, 'These [natural and imprescriptible] rights are equality, freedom, security, and property.'

While the Constitution of Year III dealt not with 'natural rights' but with the 'rights of man in society' and adopted more restrictive definitions, the principles remained the same: liberty, equality, security, and property. The Constitution of Year VIII did not contain any declaration of rights but only much briefer 'general provisions'. But article 12 of the Act of Brumaire 19, Year VIII, after Bonaparte's *coup d'état*, provided that changes in the constitutional realm could only aim to 'consolidate, guarantee and inviolably consecrate the sovereignty of the French people, the one and indivisible Republic, the representative system, the division of powers, liberty, equality, security and property'. Reviving the revolutionary tradition, the constitutional preamble of the Second Republic similarly acknowledged the existence of liberty, equality, fraternity, family, labour, property, and public order. The preambles of the constitutions of 1946 and 1958 expressly paid homage to the principles of 1789 and recalled the French people's attachment to them.

Yet more revealing, even the Charter of the *Restauration* of 1814 contained a title devoted to the 'Public law of the French', which guaranteed equality, liberty, freedom of opinion, property, etc. Even the constitutional projects of Vichy's government, which was so hostile to much of French constitutional heritage, mentioned them. According to Jean Rivero:

> Even if there is a lot of hypocrisy in these consecrations [by regimes that have misapplied them], all these regimes are aware of the impossibility of not reminding the French that their 'public law' includes the essential liberties of 1789. In this way, they remember them over generations, and this memorized continuity, this memory that something happened in 1789, which marks a break with the archaic regime where these freedoms did not exist, is what prepares the future.[189]

Could these rights be so crucial that, in contrast to other tenets of the French constitutional *Gestalt*,[190] not even the *pouvoir constituant* could alter them?

ii. Supraconstitutional Principles?

The principles of 1789 were so crucial to the French polity's self-understanding that their cultural status was disconnected from their legal status. The Declaration of the Rights of

---

[188] Claude Nicolet, *L'idée républicaine en France (1789–1924)* (n 71) 106. See also Pierre Bouretz, *La République et l'universel* (Gallimard, Paris, 2002).

[189] Jean Rivero, 'Les libertés', in Association française des constitutionnalistes, *La continuité constitutionnelle en France de 1789 à 1989* (n 8) 152, 158.

[190] See Section B.1.b.ii.

Man and the Citizen was not in force anymore three years after its adoption. It remained excluded from positive law until 1971.[191] But instead of downgrading human rights in the constitutional imagination, this loss of validity and bindingness rapidly helped them acquire a kind of mythical presence. Legislatures refused to re-enact the Declaration and grant it a constitutional value that might have been used by courts to establish constitutional review. Nevertheless, on 28 March 1901, parliament mandated that the Declaration be exposed in schools. In this constitutional *Gestalt*, the fundamental guarantee of rights was not dependent on the judiciary but on civic education, on the one hand, and on political participation through the election of representatives who would express the general will, on the other hand.[192] Even when these principles were not part of positive law under the Third Republic, where only three formal Constitutional Acts were in force, authors like Maurice Hauriou regarded them as the 'social constitution' of France, as opposed to its (at that time brief) 'political constitution'.[193]

Twice in French history, these principles have been presented as guidelines that the *pouvoir constituant* had to follow while drafting the constitutional document.

This was the case in 1851, when Louis-Napoléon Bonaparte decided to overthrow the constitution he could not amend by regular means.[194] In the proclamation with which he announced his *coup d'état*, on 2 December 1851, he enumerated five principles the future constitution had to respect:

> 1°—A responsible chief appointed for ten years;
> 2°—Ministers dependent on the executive power alone;
> 3°—A Council of State composed of the most distinguished men, preparing the laws and supporting their discussion before the legislative body;
> 4°—A legislative body discussing and voting on the laws, appointed by universal suffrage, without a list vote which falsifies the election;
> 5°—A second assembly, composed to represent the country in all its diversity, functioning as a moderating power, a guardian of the fundamental pact and public liberties.

More explicitly, in 1958, when De Gaulle became *président du Conseil* in order to implement constitutional change, the Constitutional Act of 3 June 1958 established several principles.[195] It provided that:

> The Government of the Republic prepares a draft constitutional bill implementing the following principles:

> 1° Only universal suffrage is the source of power. It is from universal suffrage or the bodies elected by it that the legislative power and the executive power derive;
> 2° The executive power and the legislative power must be effectively separated so that the Government and Parliament each assume for its part and under its own responsibility the full extent of their powers;
> 3° The Government must be responsible before Parliament;

---

[191] See Section D.2.a.i.
[192] Claude Nicolet, *L'idée républicaine en France (1789–1924)* (n 71) 55–58.
[193] See Maurice Hauriou, *Précis de droit constitutionnel* (n 183) 611–735.
[194] See Section B.1.b.ii.
[195] See Section D.

4° The judicial authority must remain independent to be able to ensure the respect of the essential freedoms as defined by the preamble of the constitution of 1946 and by the Declaration of Human Rights to which it refers;

5° The Constitution must make it possible to organize the relations of the Republic with the peoples associated with it.

In this very peculiar example of a total revision of the constitution by means of an amendment to the revision procedure, the *pouvoir constituant* had to enforce several principles, which can be regarded as a condensed version of the French constitutional *Gestalt*. Although the *pouvoir constituant* is traditionally understood as totally free,[196] some constitutional possibilities seemed to be ruled out from the beginning. Restrictions on what has become thinkable and practically feasible follow from this *Gestalt*. As Georges Vedel suggests:

> What is remarkable [in French constitutional history] is that every push towards democracy [1791, 1848 and 1875], even if it ultimately failed, was incorporated into French political experience and psychology as an irreversible achievement, as though, in France, democracy had progressed in waves, each of which retreats after having rolled in but also starts higher than the preceding one.[197]

However deeply they were entrenched in the French *Gestalt*, the principles of 1789 have been sharply criticized by conservatives, traditionalists, and Marxists alike.[198] The latter contended that these were only formal rights for the *bourgeois*, abstract rights for an abstract citizen, individual rights for people whose concrete social situation was unduly ignored. Indeed, this claim far predated the leftist critique. There have been several attempts to enrich the economic and social dimensions of human rights.

b) The Temptation of Economic and Social Enrichment

From the outset, social concerns have been important, thus implying an internal tension between the various objectives of French constitutionalism. The process of creating and unifying the self-governing polity involved abstract concepts.[199] Constructing the citizen implied disregarding anything that might distinguish one individual from another. The human rights declaration of 1789 helped shape this character by endowing it with abstract prerogatives that uniformly applied to anyone. This was part of the destruction of the multiple personal statuses that had existed under the *Ancien Régime*. On the contrary, the idea of economic and social rights implies paying attention to the diversity of empirical conditions in which the citizens live. For example, it involves considering their genders, ages, health, wealth, education, condition in life, social status, etc., thus introducing a new tension to the substance of the *Gestalt*.

For example,[200] Title I of the Constitution of 1791 provided that:

> A general establishment for *public relief* shall be created and organized to raise foundlings, relieve the infirm poor, and furnish work for the able-bodied poor who have been unable to procure it for themselves.

---

[196] See Section B.1.
[197] Georges Vedel, *Manuel élémentaire de droit constitutionnel* (Sirey, Paris, 1949) 71.
[198] See e.g. Bertrand Binoche, *Critiques des droits de l'homme* (PUF, Paris, 1989).
[199] See Section C.1.a.ii.
[200] See Section C.1.

Public instruction for all citizens, free of charge in those branches of education which are indispensable to all men, shall be constituted and organized, and the establishments thereof shall be apportioned gradually, in accordance with the division of the kingdom.

The Constitution of Year I is commonly identified as a prominent source of economic and social rights in France. It has been a constant reference for the Left under the Third Republic. Its Declaration of the Rights of Man and of the Citizen provided that:

Art. 21. Public relief is a sacred debt. Society owes maintenance to unfortunate citizens, either in procuring work for them or in providing the means of existence for those who are unable to labour.

Art. 22. Education is needed by all. Society ought to favour with all its power the advancement of the public reason and to put education at the door of every citizen.

As the result of popular '*journées*', the Constitution of 1848 also had an important social dimension. Since that time, the Republic's motto has been '*liberté, égalité, fraternité*'.[201] Article VIII of its preamble reads:

The Republic must protect the citizen in his person, his family, his religion, his property, his work, and make available to everyone the education that is indispensable to all men; it must, by fraternal assistance, ensure the subsistence of citizens in need, either by providing them with work within the limits of its resources, or, in the absence of familial support, by giving aid to those who cannot work.

This trend has been enshrined in French constitutionalism most recently and at the same time most clearly in the preamble of the Constitution of 27 October 1946, which was largely inspired by the deliberations of the *Conseil national de la Résistance* and was deeply influenced by socialist ideals, at a time when the Communist party was the leading party in France.[202] After the disaster of The Second World War, the preamble reaffirmed the sacred and inalienable rights of 1789. But, with due attention to modern circumstances, it 'further proclaim[ed], as being especially necessary to our times, [various] political, economic and social principles'.

Among these are equality between women and men, the right of asylum, the right to employment, the right to participate in trade unions, the right to strike, the right to health and rest, the right to social benefits for several groups of people, the right to instruction, etc.

Instead of liberal, civil, and political fundamental rights or fundamental rights of the 'first generation', granted to abstract and, as such, unreal individuals, socio-economic rights, or fundamental rights of the 'second generation', are conferred on real, concrete human beings. These new rights do not only impose restrictions on the State's action so as to preserve a private sphere of action. They also compel it to act positively in order to secure minimal conditions of well-being for every individual. In this context, an individual is envisioned in his or her social dimension. A 'material' democracy seems to emerge after or along with the merely 'formal' democracy proclaimed with the French Revolution.

---

[201] See Michel Borgetto, *La devise 'Liberté, égalité, fraternité'* (PUF, Paris, 1997).
[202] See e.g. *Le préambule de la Constitution de 1946. Antinomies juridiques et contradictions politiques* (PUF, Paris, 1996); Gérard Conac, Xavier Prétot, and Gérard Teboul (eds), *Le préambule de la Constitution de 1946. Histoire, analyse et commentaires* (Dalloz, Paris, 2001); Yves Gaudemet (ed), *Le préambule de la Constitution de 1946* (Editions Panthéon-Assas, Paris, 2008).

One should notice that the preamble of 1946 by no means intends to supersede the Declaration of 1789 but mainly to complement it and update it.[203] Enriching human rights constitutionalism is connected to the evolutions and tensions of delegative constitutionalism. The revival of direct democracy devices after the Second World War becomes comprehensible from the perspective of self-government and its institutional setting.[204] As the people have become progressively less fictitious, it was easier to make them participate directly in self-government and to abandon what Georges Burdeau called 'governed democracy' for 'governing democracy' and 'political democracy' for 'social democracy'.[205]

During the more than two centuries that have elapsed since the beginning of the constitutional era, a specific *Gestalt*, with several salient features, has emerged and stabilized:

> The conception that one feeds on the Constitution and its role changes [in 1789]. The Constitution does not only aim to define the rules of accession to power and of its exercise. Its mission is also to transform society, to change mentalities, to make the faithful and obedient subject of the Very Christian King a virtuous citizen, committed to equality, free from any commitment to the Church, useful to his country, aware of his rights and his duties towards public affairs. The Constitution is now an act of the general will, nourished by a new conception of humanity and society, a text proclaiming human rights and guaranteeing political freedom through a learned mechanism of the separation of powers, which distinguishes the field of the legislature and that of the executive power.[206]

One crucial issue is whether this culture is definitely fixed in its structure, substance, and dynamics or whether it is open to changes.

D. Constitutional Identity

To what extent does the current French constitution[207] correspond to the constitutional *Gestalt* described above? It appears to combine three competing traditions: the revolutionary (national sovereignty, centrality of *la loi*, human rights); the caesarean (strong executive power, direct link between the Head of State and the people); and the parliamentary (representative houses of parliament, separation of powers, responsible government, political equilibrium).[208] Whereas the first tradition is a legacy of the first constitutional debates, the second comes from the Empires, and the last one from the Monarchies.

Is the fact that the Fifth Republic lasted so long evidence of a successful synthesis? Or did it radically break away from the French constitutional *Gestalt* and open a new path? Can

---

[203] See also Section D.3.b.

[204] See Section C.1.b. On the ambiguities and tensions between the 'real people' and the 'legal people', see Pierre Rosanvallon, *Le peuple introuvable* (n 148); Pierre Rosanvallon, *La démocratie inachevée* (n 169).

[205] Georges Burdeau, *La démocratie* (Le Seuil, Paris, 1966).

[206] Philippe Pichot-Bravard, *Conserver l'ordre constitutionnel* (n 94) 335.

[207] For a general presentation, see e.g. François Luchaire, Gérard Conac, and Xavier Prétot (dir.), *La Constitution de la République française: analyses et commentaires* (3rd edn, Economica, Paris, 2008); Charles Waline, Marc Thoumelou, and Samir Hammal, *Les institutions de la France en questions* (La Documentation française, Paris, 2013); Guillaume Tusseau, *Droit constitutionnel et institutions politiques* (6th edn, Le Seuil, Paris, 2021); Guy Carcassonne and Marc Guillaume, *La Constitution* (15th edn, Le Seuil, Paris, 2019); Philippe Raynaud, *L'esprit de la Ve République. L'histoire, le régime, le système* (Perrin, Paris, 2017); Francis Hamon and Michel Troper, *Droit constitutionnel* (42nd edn, LGDJ, Issy-les-Moulineaux, 2021).

[208] Marcel Morabito and Daniel Bourmaud, *Histoire constitutionnelle et politique de la France (1789-1958)* (5th edn, Montchrestien, Paris, 1998) 6.

these two possibilities not go hand in hand, so that the constitution's disruptive appearance was in fact a means to give shape to the deepest elements of the *Gestalt*? The text of 1958 undoubtedly intended to establish an unprecedented balance of powers (1). Departing even more evidently from the established culture, France seems to have joined the worldwide trend towards judicialized constitutionalism[209] (2). Finally, just like the Third Republic with which they share so little, the current constitutional norms and institutions seem to have internalized political conflict[210] to such an extent that the constitutional debate may be weakening and may lead to a dead end (3).

1. A New (Im)balance of Powers

The fundamental change introduced in 1958 was related to political representation. Under the Third and Fourth Republics, the sovereignty of the Nation had degenerated into that of the representatives, i.e. that of parliament. There were no checks on the parliament's normative productions, while the government was entirely subject to the parliament's control. This led to political instability and inefficiency. The drafters of the constitution wanted to put an end to this malfunctioning of democracy. Whereas parliament's classic form of representation now plays a lesser role (a), the Head of State has emerged as a new kind of representative (b). Both coexist with the possible political presence of the people (c).

a) Parliament as a Constitutional Minor
The MPs' participation in the drafting of the Constitution was limited. Some MPs only belonged to the Consultative Committee that offered advice on the Government's draft. Once the constitution was approved, parliament, whose bicameral structure was preserved, was institutionally downgraded. Whereas it appeared first in the Constitution of 1946, it now appears after the President of the Republic (Title II) and after the Government (Title III). Its functions are defined by article 24 of the Constitution, which reads, 'parliament shall pass statutes. It shall monitor the action of the Government. It shall assess public policies.' Regarding the legislative function, under the Third and Fourth Republics, parliament could address all topics and even freely decide to delegate its own power to the government, but now articles 34 and 37 limit its scope of intervention to specifically enumerated topics. All the remaining issues are handled by the Government, whose autonomous *pouvoir réglementaire* has thus become the normal source of law, contrary to the common legicentrism of the French constitutional *Gestalt*. This was understood as a revolution, and a major *capitis diminutio* for parliament, whose action was moreover subject to review by the newly created Constitutional Council.[211]

Even within its devolved sphere of intervention, parliament's autonomy was diminished. The constitution predetermined the rhythm of its sessions. The *Conseil constitutionnel* exercised a mandatory review of its influential standing orders[212] so as to ensure that the assemblies could not bypass the constitutional limitations. As far as the adoption of legislation was concerned, parliament seemed heavily constrained. Several instruments were used

---

[209] For a critical discussion, see Guillaume Tusseau, 'Deux dogmes du constitutionnalisme' (n 22).
[210] See Section B.1.b.ii.
[211] See Section D.2.
[212] See Section B.2.b. For a general presentation, see Pierre Avril, Jean Gicquel, and Jean-Eric Gicquel, *Droit parlementaire* (6th edn, LGDJ, Issy-les Moulineaux, 2021).

in order to 'rationalize' French parliamentarianism. Progressively, as the electoral system based on the majority vote in a double ballot seemed to guarantee a strong majority to support the government (*fait majoritaire*), the constraints loosened. But several limitations on parliament's autonomy remain.

Today, for example, parliament only decides half of its agenda (article 48). Most of the bills result from a governmental initiative (article 39). The government exerts extraordinary influence on legislative procedure. Pursuant to article 40, 'Private Members' Bills and amendments introduced by Members of Parliament shall not be admissible where their enactment would result in either a diminution of public revenue or the creation or increase of any public expenditure.' Bills are normally read twice by each house of parliament. Nevertheless, article 42 allows the government to hasten the procedure and to limit the process to one reading in each house. If the National Assembly and the Senate are unable to agree on a common version of the bill, the government is allowed to let the National Assembly decide in last resort (article 45). Article 44 creates the procedure of '*vote bloqué*': 'If the Government so requests, the House before which the Bill is tabled shall proceed to a single vote on all or part of the text under debate, on the sole basis of the amendments proposed or accepted by the Government.' Finally, pursuant to article 49 of the constitution:

> The Prime Minister may, after deliberation by the Council of Ministers, make the passing of a Finance Bill or Social Security Financing Bill an issue of a vote of confidence before the National Assembly. In that event, the Bill shall be considered passed unless a resolution of no-confidence, tabled within the subsequent twenty-four hours, is carried as provided for in the foregoing paragraph [i.e. solely votes cast in favour of the no-confidence resolution being counted and the latter not being passed unless it secures a majority of the Members of the House]. In addition, the Prime Minister may use the said procedure for one other Government or Private Members' Bill per session.

If all these instruments are combined, the government can require parliament to pass bills quickly, with limitations on the issues to be discussed, and sometimes without a vote. The constitutional amendment of 2008 tried to restore the balance between the executive and the legislative power, while taking into account the Fifth Republic's mistrust of parliament.[213] The debate initiated in 2018 by President Macron aimed to reform the legislative procedure so as to make it more efficient, for example by turning the accelerated procedure into the normal procedure or by allowing legislative committees to adopt statutes. Some feared that this may again reduce the power of the two assemblies, and this project was abandoned.

Regarding political responsibility, which is a characteristic of parliamentary regimes, the drafters of the constitution wanted to avoid short-lived governments, such as those at the end of the Third Republic and during the entire Fourth Republic. Political instability was detrimental to the authority of the State and to its decision-making power. It led to inefficiency and deprived the people of any real control over its representatives.

The government's responsibility was rationalized as well. Whereas governments could be voted down by both houses of parliament under the Third Republic, only the National Assembly, which is directly elected by the people, now has that power (articles 20, 49 and

---

[213] For a general assessment, see Olivier Rozenberg, 'Un petit pas pour le Parlement, un grand pas pour la Ve République. L'évaluation de la révision constitutionnelle du 23 juillet 2008' (2016) 61 LIEPP Working Paper, http://spire.sciencespo.fr/hdl:/2441/5jdbpj7sbb9njan70s9btil7d9/resources/wp-61-revision-constitutionnelle-rozenberg-v2.pdf (last accessed 22 March 2022).

50). But it is not totally free. If a form of *konstruktive Misstrauensbewegung* is not established, confidence and diffidence votes are only possible under strict conditions. Pursuant to article 49:

> The Prime Minister, after deliberation by the Council of Ministers, may make the Government's programme or possibly a general policy statement an issue of a vote of confidence before the National Assembly.
>
> The National Assembly may call the Government to account by passing a resolution of no-confidence. Such a resolution shall not be admissible unless it is signed by at least one-tenth of the Members of the National Assembly. Voting may not take place within forty-eight hours after the resolution has been tabled. Solely votes cast in favour of the no-confidence resolution shall be counted and the latter shall not be passed unless it secures a majority of the Members of the House. Except as provided for in the following paragraph, no Member shall sign more than three resolutions of no-confidence during a single ordinary session and no more than one during a single extraordinary session.

Prime Ministers have interpreted this provision to mean that no explicit confidence vote is needed before they act. Where motions of no-confidence are concerned, the chronology and majorities required make them quite hard to use. Although 59 spontaneous motions have been tabled to date, only one was adopted. It targeted Prime Minister Pompidou because of De Gaulle's use of article 11 to amend the constitution.[214] Pompidou duly resigned. But De Gaulle refused his resignation. He dissolved the National Assembly, won the legislative elections with a comfortable majority, accepted Pompidou's resignation and reappointed him as Prime Minister.

This episode made it evident that, contrary to traditional parliamentary practice, government—thanks to rationalized parliamentarism—was able to circumvent parliament, thus relying instead on another constitutional figure, which had not played a central role under a Republican regime.

b) The President of the Republic as the Keystone of the New Regime

The President of the Republic was immediately presented by Michel Debré, one of the drafters of the constitution, as the 'keystone'[215] of the new regime. The President is the first post to appear in the constitution, which assigns him broad missions. Pursuant to article 5, 'The President of the Republic shall ensure due respect for the constitution. He shall ensure, by his arbitration, the proper functioning of the public authorities and the continuity of the State. He shall be the guarantor of national independence, territorial integrity and due respect for Treaties.'

Whereas under the Third and Fourth Republics, the President was elected by parliament, the new constitution broadened the electorate. Eighty thousand MPs, mayors, general counsellors, and delegates from the territorial collectivities voted to elect the President, thus increasing his institutional independence from the traditional representatives. But this is not sufficient to explain the famous 'presidentialist' character of the Fifth Republic. In 1962, De Gaulle decided to change the electoral process so as to allow the people to elect the President

---

[214] See Section D.1.c.
[215] Michel Debré, 'Discours devant le Conseil d'État', 27 August 1958, http://mjp.univ-perp.fr/textes/debre1958.htm (last accessed on 22 March 2022).

directly. This change was extremely important for the regime. As Marx had understood when such an election was established under the Second Republic:

> While the votes of France are split up among the seven hundred and fifty members of the National Assembly, they are here, on the contrary, concentrated on a single individual. While each separate representative of the people represents only this or that party, this or that town, this or that bridgehead, or even only the mere necessity of electing someone as the seven hundred and fiftieth [...], he is the elect of the Nation and the act of his election is the trump that the sovereign people plays once every four years. [...] The National Assembly, indeed, exhibits in its individual representatives the manifold aspects of the national spirit, but in the President this national spirit finds its incarnation. As against the Assembly, he possesses a sort of divine right; he is President by the grace of the people.[216]

The amendment to article 6 of the constitution established a direct link between the people and the Head of State. Except for the short-lived Constitution of 1848, which ended in a *coup d'état*,[217] this conflicted with the Republican tradition. Thus, the Fifth Republic belongs to the category of presidential regimes, which are characterized by the dualism of bodies directly legitimized by popular vote.[218] To this first element of political and institutional dis-intermediation were added, from a functional viewpoint, powerful constitutional tools such as the right to call a referendum (articles 11 and 89),[219] the right to dissolve the National Assembly (article 12), and the right to use emergency powers (article 16). Regarding the other institutions, the President alone appoints the Prime Minister. Pursuant to article 19, 'Instruments of the President of the Republic, other than those provided for under articles 8 (paragraph one), 11, 12, 16, 18, 54, 56 and 61, shall be countersigned by the Prime Minister and, where required, by the ministers concerned.' The main decisions connecting the President directly to the people (articles 11, 12 and 16) or the most important institutions (article 8 regarding the appointment of the Prime Minister; article 18 regarding the right to communicate with the two houses of parliament, article 56 regarding the appointment of members of the *Conseil constitutionnel*; articles 54 and 61 regarding the right to activate the *Conseil*'s control) are designed as '*pouvoirs propres*'. As they are not countersigned, the President is allowed to use them freely.

Despite executive bicephalism and article 20 mentioning that, 'The Government shall determine and conduct the policy of the Nation', the President is in fact in charge, due to a form of constitutional convention.[220]

Carl Schmitt opposed two forms of representation, namely *Stellvertretung* and *Repräsentation*. The former belongs to the domain of material, plural, and limited private interests. It is expressed in parliaments, where different perspectives can be presented and debated, and exposes the division of the social body. By contrast, the latter form of representation belongs to a loftier, more spiritual sphere. *Repräsentation* makes a transcendent

---

[216] Karl Marx, *The Eighteenth Brumaire of Louis Bonaparte* (n 118).
[217] See Section B.1.b.ii.
[218] See Juan J Linz, 'Presidential or Parliamentary Democracy: Does it Make a Difference?', in Juan J Linz and Arturo Valenzuela (eds), *The Failure of Presidential Democracy*, vol 1 (Johns Hopkins University Press, Baltimore, 1994) 3.
[219] See Section D.1.c.
[220] Pierre Avril, *Les conventions de la constitution. Normes non écrites du droit politique* (PUF, Paris, 1997).

and unitary body, the people, visible in the public sphere.[221] De Gaulle's conception of his function may be interpreted in these terms. The Fifth Republic not only downgrades what was the traditional form of representation according to the French constitutional *Gestalt*. It simultaneously promotes another kind of embodiment of the people.

The combination of direct presidential election and governmental responsibility led to many discussions about the exact nature of the Fifth Republic's regime. Whereas the first device is characteristic of presidential regimes, the second, imposed by the Constitutional Act of 3 June 1958, is characteristic of parliamentary ones. While the former was tested once in 1848 with unfortunate results, French political history seemed to impose the second in the long run. The strange combination was puzzling for taxonomic enterprises, which alternatively classified the Fifth Republic as semi-presidential,[222] semi-parliamentary,[223] 'neither parliamentary nor presidential',[224] monarchic-republican,[225] or 'demonarchic'.[226]

There are proposals that offer a kind of synthesis, distinguishing the regime, which is semi-presidential, from the system, which is presidentialist. The constitutional regime may be defined as a legal structure, a set of rules concerning the allocation and exercise of power. This subset relates to the political forces, the electoral majorities, the practices of the actors—in a nutshell, to 'political life'. The global political system can be considered as the whole formed by these two interacting subsets.[227] Regarding the regime, the constitution combines the direct election of the President with the existence of a responsible government, which shares the executive power with the President. As to the political system, it is dominantly presidential, since the President has important powers that he actually uses, especially when the President's party also has a majority in the National Assembly, thus eclipsing the role of the Prime Minister. Sometimes, a kind of parliamentary corrective appears during periods of 'cohabitation', when the internal balance within the executive branch favours the Prime Minister who enjoys, contrary to the President, the National Assembly's support.[228] Since 2002, the President's and the National Assembly's mandates have been aligned. Since the former is elected first, the latter is made dependent. The MPs' legitimacy mostly resides in their commitment to apply the President's platform. The *quinquennat* increased the presidentialization of the regime, although since 2022, being supported by a relative majority only in the National Assembly de facto limited the President's influence.

The Fifth Republic's longevity may be due partly to this idiosyncratic combination. More originally, the Constitution of 1958 set the stage for a new constitutional actor.

c) The People as a Constitutional Actor

Pursuant to article 3 of the Constitution, 'National sovereignty shall vest in the people, who shall exercise it through their representatives and by means of referendum'. For the first time,

---

[221] Carl Schmitt, *Verfassungslehre* (Duncker und Humblot, München, 1928) 204–216. See Olivier Beaud, '*Représentation* et *Stellvertretung*: sur une distinction de Carl Schmitt' (1987) 6 Droits 11.

[222] Maurice Duverger, *Institutions politiques et droit constitutionnel*, vol 1 (18th edn, PUF, Paris, 1990) 188–192; Arend Lijphart (ed), *Parliamentary versus Presidential Government* (OUP, Oxford, 1992) 8.

[223] Louis Favoreu, *Les cours constitutionnelles* (3rd edn, PUF, Paris, 1996) 16.

[224] Jacques Robert, 'Le président de la République en France: ni parlementaire ni présidentiel?', in Jean-Louis Seurin (ed), *La présidence en France et aux États-Unis* (Economica, Paris, 1986) 333.

[225] See Charles de Gaulle, quoted by Alain Peyrefitte, *Le mal français* (Plon, Paris, 1976) 56–57.

[226] Jacques Georgel, *La cinquième République: une démonarchie* (LGDJ, Paris, 1990).

[227] Guillaume Tusseau, *Droit constitutionnel et institutions politiques* (n 207) 671–668; Olivier Duhamel, 'Une démocratie à part' (2008) 126 Pouvoirs 17.

[228] See e.g. Jean-Marie Denquin, *La monarchie aléatoire. Essai sur les constitutions de la Ve République* (PUF, Paris, 2001).

it became possible for the people not merely to delegate their sovereignty to representatives but to exercise it directly.[229]

Since 1958, two main types of national referenda have existed. The first permits constitutional amendments. Pursuant to article 89, only the President of the Republic, on the recommendation of the Prime Minister, and Members of Parliament are authorized to initiate amendments. In fact, only executive initiatives have succeeded. The two Houses must pass the bill to amend the constitution on identical terms, which gives the Senate a veto power. The normal way is to have the amendment approved by referendum. This is mandatory for parliamentary initiatives, for which the direct intervention of the people themselves provides a safeguard against their representatives' possibly misplaced intentions. For executive initiatives, two options exist: the amendment may be adopted either by referendum or by parliament convened in Congress, with a three-fifths majority of the votes cast. Only one constitutional amendment was adopted by referendum, in 2000, regarding the reduction of the President's mandate from seven to five years. President Macron intended to have another one adopted pursuant to this procedure. It would have amended article 1 of the constitution and imposed to 'guarantee the preservation of the environment and biological diversity and the fight against climate change'. But it failed because of persisting disagreement between the two houses of parliament.

The second type of national referendum allows for the adoption of ordinary legislative norms. Originally, pursuant to article 11, the President of the Republic could submit to referendum a government bill dealing with the organization of the public authorities, approving a Community agreement, or providing for the authorization to ratify a treaty. The scope of the possible referendum has been extended to include 'reforms relating to the economic, social or environmental policy of the Nation, and to the public services contributing thereto'. It has been used eight times, mostly when De Gaulle was in power. What is remarkable, this procedure was used twice to amend the constitution. In 1962, De Gaulle persuaded the people ratify the direct election of the President of the Republic. But in 1969, after failing to have his reform of the territorial organization of the country and of the Senate adopted, he resigned.

Resorting to article 11 to amend the constitution was highly controversial. Many actors and scholars considered it unconstitutional. Nevertheless, De Gaulle argued that because the organization of the 'public authorities' is a possible object of a referendum, this also includes constitutional amendment. After he became President, François Mitterrand stated that, 'The established use, approved by the people, can now be considered as one of the procedures of amendment, concurrently with article 89.'[230] Moreover, it may be deemed appropriate that there is a means to bypass a possible veto of the Senate and have the people themselves decide. Finally, from the viewpoint of the French constitutional *Gestalt*, one may surmise, in a Sieyesian vein, that the French people are sovereign and so can change their constitution by whatever means they choose.[231]

The *Conseil constitutionnel*'s review of the text adopted in 1962 fits this logic. It decided that:

> If article 61 of the constitution gives the Constitutional Council the mission to assess the conformity with the constitution of Institutional Acts and ordinary acts which must or

---

[229] See Jean-Baptiste Roche, *Les mutations de la démocratie directe en France depuis 1945* (Th. Droit public, Université Rennes I, 2017).

[230] François Mitterrand, 'Sur les institutions' (1988) 45 Pouvoirs 138.

[231] See Section B.1.

may be submitted for its review, without specifying whether this competence extends to all texts of a legislative nature, regardless of whether they have been adopted by the people following a referendum or have been voted by Parliament, or if, on the contrary, it is limited only to the latter category, it follows from the spirit of the constitution, which made the Constitutional Council a regulating body of the activity of the public authorities, that the acts that the constitution intended to cover in its article 61 are only the acts voted by Parliament and not those which, adopted by the people following a referendum, constitute the direct expression of national sovereignty.[232]

The constitutional justice thus favours the direct expression of popular sovereignty. Although risky for the authority that initiates it, the referendum offers a privileged means for the people to declare and impose their will. From this viewpoint, there is a stark contrast between parliamentary legislation and popular legislation.[233]

Although the referendum is frequently equated with the plebiscite, especially in the Gaullist practice, the Fifth Republic allowed for a fair process, to which several negative results testify. It made the people a direct constitutional actor. Nevertheless, whereas the people could answer questions that were asked by referendum, they did not have any real possibility to ask questions for themselves. In other words, they had no right of constitutional or legislative initiative. In 2008, article 11 was amended to provide that:

A referendum […] may be held upon the initiative of one fifth of the Members of Parliament, supported by one tenth of the voters enrolled on the electoral register. This initiative shall take the form of a Private Member's Bill and shall not be applied to the repeal of a statutory provision promulgated for less than one year.

The process appears quite cumbersome. One-fifth of parliament (185 MPs) and one-tenth of the voters (4.7 million) are high thresholds. The public has nine months to voice its support. It is quite easy for the houses to make the process fail merely by 'examining' the proposed bill within six months. It was used once in 2019 and failed, only 1.1 million voters supporting the initiative. A second and a third attempt failed in 2021 and 2022, respectively, as the Constitutional Council considered the proposal unconstitutional. This is why many people currently demand reform, which would increase the possibilities for the people to bypass their representatives. Under the Fifth Republic, and somehow conflicting with the French constitutional *Gestalt*, these appear to have lost their monopoly on the adoption of legal norms. In addition, they are submitted to unprecedented control.

2. The Judicialization of the French Constitutionalism

France progressively abandoned its traditional legicentrism, thanks to the incremental development of the *Conseil constitutionnel* (a). The enrichment of constitutional case law helped to profoundly modify the fabric of the French polity. Progressively, French legislative infraconstitutionalism was formally constitutionalized (b).

---

[232] Decision no 62-20 DC.
[233] See Section D.2.

a) The Introduction of Constitutional Review

The creation of the *Conseil constitutionnel* was quite unnatural, as it meant the abolition of the doctrine of the legislature's infallibility.[234] Nevertheless, the creature outgrew what its creators imagined (i) and appeared as the embryo of a constitutional court properly so called (ii).

i. *The Development of the Conseil Constitutionnel*

Significantly, the new body was not named 'Constitutional Court'. The *Conseil* consists of the former Presidents of the Republic—which is currently highly criticized—and nine appointed members. The latter serve non-renewable terms of nine years. One-third of them are appointed every three years. Three—among them the president of the *Conseil*—are appointed by the president of the Republic, three by the president of the National Assembly, and three by the president of the Senate. Until 2008, these nominations were not subject to control. Since that date, parliament's commissions have been allowed to veto a proposition with a supermajority of three-fifths. No specific qualification is required, especially in terms of professional expertise.

The main purpose of this institution was to bar the Houses of Parliament from intruding on the normative power that the new constitution had conferred on the government. It was deemed 'a watchdog' before the 'parliamentary jail' of article 34.[235] The device was thus part of a major blow to traditional legislative and parliamentary sovereignty.[236] As Michel Debré explained:

> The creation of the Constitutional Council manifests the will to subordinate the statute, that is to say the will of Parliament, to the superior rule laid down by the constitution. It is neither in the spirit of the parliamentary system, nor in the French tradition, to give judges, that is to say to give every litigant, the right to question the value of the law. The project has therefore devised a special institution that can only be set in motion by four authorities: the President of the Republic, the Prime Minister, and the Presidents of the Houses of Parliament. […] The constitution thus created a weapon against the deviation of the parliamentary system.[237]

The *Conseil*'s missions include monitoring presidential and parliamentary elections and referenda (articles 7, 11, 58, 59, and 60), advising political authorities (article 16), solving conflicts of constitutional interpretation (articles 39 and 41), reviewing international norms (article 54), and performing the mandatory review of the Institutional Acts and the standing orders of the *Assemblée nationale* and the *Sénat* (articles 46 and 61). As these two categories of norms directly implement the constitution, it was impossible to allow the traditional representatives any margin by which they might imperil the constitutional construction. The main characteristic of the constitutional review thus established was that the *Conseil* could

---

[234] See Loïc Philip, 'Le Conseil constitutionnel', in Didier Maus, Louis Favoreu, and Jean-Luc Parodi (eds), *L'écriture de la Constitution de 1958* (Economica, Paris, 1992) 467. For a general presentation, see Guillaume Tusseau, 'Constitutional Council of France (*Conseil constitutionnel*)', in Rüdiger Wolfrum, Rainer Grote, and Frauke Lachenmann (eds), *Max Planck Encyclopedia of Comparative Constitutional Law* (2017) http://oxcon. ouplaw.com/home/mpeccol (last accessed February 15, 2019); Dominique Rousseau, Pierre-Yves Gahdoun, and Julien Bonnet, *Droit du contentieux constitutionnel* (12th edn, LGDJ, Issy-les-Moulineaux, 2020); Guillaume Drago, *Contentieux constitutionnel français* (5th edn, PUF, Paris, 2020).

[235] See Section D.1.a.

[236] See Sections B.2 and C.1.a.

[237] Michel Debré, 'Discours devant le Conseil d'État' (n 215).

only review an ordinary statute after it had been adopted by the two houses of parliament but before it was promulgated by the President of the Republic. As initially imagined, the *Conseil* would not review the texts against the fundamental rights provisions alluded to in the preamble of the constitution. It would only preserve the separation of powers between the legislature and the government.

Progressively, the institution underwent an autonomous development. The main explanation for this change is the advancement of the rhetoric of the rule of law in France and the international spread of judicial review more generally, in other States as well as at the supranational level.

One could intuitively state that the standard of constitutional review is the constitution—i.e. the constitutional text *stricto sensu*. However, this standard has become a wider 'constitutionality block'. In its 70–39 DC and its more famous 71–44 DC rulings, the *Conseil* used the preamble to the constitution as a source of constitutional law. Since this preamble mentions the French people's attachment to the Declaration of the Rights of Man and of the Citizen of 1789, 'confirmed and complemented' by the Preamble to the constitution of 1946, these two texts have also been given formal constitutional value. As a result, civil and political rights as well as economic and social rights have been granted fundamental legal value. Because the 1946 Preamble uses the expression 'fundamental principles acknowledged in the laws of the Republic' (PFRLR), this undefined category has also been constitutionalized. It has allowed the *Conseil* to establish unwritten constitutional norms, such as the principle of judicial independence, freedom of association, the specificity of juvenile justice, etc. The *Conseil* has also identified other principles and objectives with constitutional value (e.g. the fight against tax evasion, the protection of the public order, the pluralism of ideas, thoughts, and opinions). The *Conseil* no longer merely preserved competences, rather, it also guarded substantive values, especially fundamental rights. By this act of self-assertion, which was France's *Marbury v Madison*, the *Conseil* incorporated the main legacies of French constitutionalism into formal constitutional law. In 2005, the Charter for the Environment was added to the standards of constitutional review.

A major change was the introduction in 1974 of the right for 60 MPs, i.e. political minorities, to refer a statute to the *Conseil constitutionnel*. This resulted in more frequent '*saisines*' of the *Conseil* and in a more detailed case law, especially when political '*alternances*' took place in 1981, 1986, 1988, 1993, 1997, 2002, and 2012. Both the Left and the Right allowed the *Conseil* to review the most important aspects of the other camp's political platform. This also contributed to the *Conseil*'s legitimacy and acceptance on both sides of the political spectrum, as it seemed to exercise review in a similar fashion and to implement identical principles, irrespective of the statute's author.

Three competing and not necessarily incompatible representations of the *Conseil* emerged, portraying it as a body that controls parliament, contributes to the political minority's constitutional status, and guarantees fundamental human rights.

French constitutional culture became less political and more juridified. Constitutional law approached the paradigm of judicially enforced law. Whereas the statute *qua* expression of the general will had previously reigned supreme, the *Conseil constitutionnel* clearly stated in 1985 that 'a statute only expresses the general will provided it respects the constitution'.[238]

Until the development of constitutional review, constitutional law as a discipline was undervalued. Legal doctrine focused on private law. Paradigmatically, private law jurists

---

[238] Decision no 85-197 DC.

had a text—the Civil Code—and the rulings of the *Cour de Cassation* to comment upon and study. In the sphere of public law, only specialists of administrative law could engage in similar academic work. Although there was no administrative code, the case law of the *Conseil d'État* also provided material for legal commentary. Conversely, since there was nothing upon which to comment in legal terms, constitutional doctrine was more or less absorbed by political science, the only field of studies that could describe how constitutional institutions actually functioned. As the *Conseil Constitutionnel* began to play a more important role, a new, sanctioned constitutional law emerged. Thus, constitutional scholars, like their counterparts in private and administrative law, now had a real law and a proper case law to study, following the type of legal scholarship most prevalent in France. As an academic discipline, constitutional law laid claim to more attention in legal education. New journals—such as the *Revue française de droit constitutionnel*, first published in 1990—, new handbooks, and new courses appeared.

From the perspectives of both positive law and scholarship, constitutional law increased its own juridicity.[239] This normalization of constitutional scholarship, especially under the influence of Louis Favoreu,[240] has led to a form of *Isolierung* that is not without its shortcomings.[241] Another reform removed the current constitution from constitutional culture.

ii. Towards a Fully Developed Constitutional Court

The system of constitutional justice remained incomplete in at least two respects. First, in 1975, the *Conseil* refused to enforce article 55 of the Constitution.[242] Pursuant to this provision, 'Treaties or agreements duly ratified or approved shall, upon publication, prevail over Acts of Parliament, subject, with respect to each agreement or treaty, to its application by the other party.' The *Conseil* distinguished 'constitutionality review' from 'conventionality review'. It considered only the first within its powers. Ordinary judiciary and administrative judges had to review whether statutes respected international norms and to exclude their application in case of a contradiction. The *Cour de cassation*[243] and the *Conseil d'État*[244] accepted this new function, thus implying that domestic legislation, which was once sovereign, is now judicially limited by constitutional as well as supranational norms.

Any ordinary judge can set aside a statute if she holds that it violates an international norm. Prominent among them are the European Convention for the Protection of Human Rights and Fundamental Freedoms and the European Union treaties. These texts contribute to the protection of human rights, which, from a substantive point of view, are similar to those protected by the constitution. A kind of imbalance appeared between the *Conseil constitutionnel* and the ordinary courts. Thanks to the conventionality review, the latter can exercise a function quite similar to constitutional review. Moreover, conventionality review is procedurally

---

[239] Bastien François, 'Du juridictionnel au juridique. Travail juridique, construction jurisprudentielle du droit et montée en généralité', in CURAPP, *Droit et politique* (PUF, Paris, 1993) 201; Bastien François, 'La constitution du droit? La doctrine constitutionnelle à la recherche d'une légitimité juridique et d'un horizon pratique', in CURAPP, *La doctrine juridique* (PUF, Paris, 1993) 210.

[240] Louis Favoreu, *La constitution et son juge* (Economica, Paris, 2014).

[241] See Guillaume Tusseau, 'La Vᵉ République et l'évitement (provisoire?) de la crise: du droit constitutionnel à la science du droit constitutionnel', in Dominique Chagnollaud de Sabouret and Benoît Montay (eds), *Les soixante ans de la Constitution 1958-2018* (Dalloz, Paris, 2018) 45.

[242] Decision no 74-54 DC.

[243] Cour de cassation, Chambre mixte, May 24, 1975, *Société des cafés Jacques Vabre*, pourvoi n° 73-13556.

[244] Conseil d'État, Assemblée, October 20, 1989 *Nicolo*, req. n° 108243.

more efficient because judges can exclude a statute after its promulgation. Besides, as the two most important international systems also allow for individual petitions to a supranational court, the *Conseil's* guarantee for human rights seemed comparatively weak.

Secondly, the *Conseil's* a priori review had intrinsic limitations. An unconstitutional statute could only be quashed before it was promulgated, whereas some difficulties might appear when the statute was applied to concrete cases. Only a few political actors, whose determination to protect the constitution could not always be taken for granted, could refer a statute to the *Conseil*. As a result, problematic statutes were not reviewed. Moreover, as ordinary citizens could directly invoke supranational rights before ordinary courts and supranational courts, it seemed odd—although congruent with the constitutional *Gestalt*—that they were prevented from availing themselves of the rights that the constitution conferred on them.

After two failed attempts in 1990 and 1993, the 'question prioriaire de constitutionnalité' was introduced in 2008. It is now possible for ordinary citizens to question the validity of their representatives' actions. Once a statute has been enacted, it is no longer immune to review. Concretely, '[i]f, during proceedings in progress before a court of law, it is claimed that a legislative provision infringes the rights and freedoms guaranteed by the constitution, the matter may be referred by the *Conseil d'État* or by the *Cour de Cassation* to the *Conseil Constitutionnel*'. The litigant needs to prove that the statute applies to the suit, that it has never been declared constitutional, and that the question is not devoid of seriousness. If the judge is satisfied that these conditions are met, she transfers the file to the supreme court, which acts within three months as a second filter for the demand. After a period of three months, the *Conseil* is automatically seized. Once the question has been transferred, the *Conseil* has three months to decide, following a truly adversarial procedure. As of 1 December 2022, more than 1,000 QPC decisions have been handed down. Whereas a declaration of unconstitutionality impedes the enactment of the statute within the framework of *ex ante* review, in the case of *ex post* review, it results in the derogation of the pre-existing norm. The *Conseil* is allowed to postpone the effects of the derogation it pronounces. This preserves legal certainty while granting the legislature sufficient time to remedy unconstitutionalities without creating a legal vacuum. Decisions are final and binding on all authorities.

The reform points to a more 'judicialized' environment, where ordinary people become familiar with popular constitutional culture instead of constitutional law remaining the province of a class of experts.

b) The Constitutionalization of the French Polity

The development of constitutional justice contributed to the constitutionalization of the law.[245] First, there was a major change in the production of constitutional law. Until the Fifth Republic, constitutions were created in heated moments of political demiurgism.[246] The *Conseil constitutionnel* has allowed for the continuous and incremental development of a 'living' constitutional law. Constitutional norms are more numerous. They are not expressed once and for all in a restrictive document but emerge ceaselessly from judicial interpretation. Thanks to constitutional review, constitutional law is no longer a mere parchment

---

[245] Michel Troper, 'Le constitutionnalisme entre droit et politique', in CURAPP, *Droit et politique* (PUF, Paris, 1993) 82; Bertrand Mathieu and Michel Verpeaux (eds), *La constitutionnalisation des branches du droit* (Economica, Paris, 1998).

[246] See Section B.1.

barrier. Since it is effectively enforceable, it 'has become a true [sanctioned] law',[247] whose 'revenge'[248] or 'resurrection'[249] can be observed.

Secondly, the scope of constitutional rules has increased. The *Conseil* endows principles that were traditionally part of other branches of the law (civil law, labour law, tax law, criminal law, education law, commercial law, etc.) with a formal constitutional value. When a statute is referred to it, the *Conseil* needs to identify the basic constitutional principles that govern its field of intervention. As a consequence, all the branches of the law seem more unified. They are rooted in common basic principles. Simultaneously, the living constitutional law is given a more concrete substance. The *Conseil* thus makes existing principles binding in an unprecedented way.

A significant change impacts the fabric of the polity. Enduring ordinary legislation had previously established several of its crucial elements.[250] Because of the creeping constitutionalization of the various branches of the law, several infraconstitutional elements identified earlier have been given formal constitutional value, for example when the *Conseil* admitted the existence of a PFRLR such as freedom of association, resulting from the statute of 1 July 1901, or the independence of the judiciary, resulting from the statute of 24 May 1872. The metaphorical civil, administrative, political, economic, and social constitutions have now become part of constitutional normativity.

Whereas the balance of power between the executive and the legislative branches remains highly debated, mostly to limit presidentialism and revive the role of parliament, constitutional review is not called into question. Most constitutional actors and constitutional scholars seem to accept the new configuration of French constitutionalism. Could this mean, as Kahn suggests in another context, 'the end of constitutional theory'?[251]

3. The (Lethal?) Internalization of Political Conflict

In accordance with De Gaulle's ambition to 'endow the State with institutions which restore, in a form appropriate to modern times, the stability and continuity of which it has been deprived for a hundred and sixty-nine years',[252] one of the peculiarities of the Constitution of 1958 is its duration. Thanks to the regular practice of constitutional amendment (a) and the conciliation between the traditions of 1789 and 1946 (b), the Fifth Republic has gained support from all political sides.

a) Inhabiting the Regime

The Fifth Republic has discovered constitutional amendment. The constitution was itself born out of a (total) constitutional amendment.[253] The existence and the fundamental principles of the regime are no longer called into question, except by more or less marginal

---

[247] Jean Rivero, 'Rapport de synthèse', in Louis Favoreu (ed), *Cours constitutionnelles européennes et droits fondamentaux* (Economica, Paris, 1982) 528–529; Pierre Avril, 'Enchantement et désenchantement constitutionnels sous la Vᵉ République' (2008) 126 Pouvoirs 5, 6.

[248] Pierre Avril, 'Une revanche du droit constitutionel?' (1989) 49 Pouvoirs 5.

[249] Dominique Rousseau, 'Une résurrection: la notion de constitution' (1990) Revue du droit public 5.

[250] See Section B.2.b.

[251] Paul W Kahn, *Legitimacy and History. Self-Government in American Constitutional Theory* (Yale University Press, New Haven, 1992) 210.

[252] Charles De Gaulle, *Mémoires d'espoir*, vol 1 (Plon, Paris, 1970) 23.

[253] See Section B.1.b.i.

parties. This is the result of a successful internalization of political conflict. De Gaulle was the first President. He exercised most of the powers he had devised for himself. Using the emergency powers of article 16 in 1961, dissolving the National Assembly in 1962, and resorting to referendum in 1961, 1962, and 1969, he shaped the foundational interpretations of the most salient constitutional innovations.[254] This helped restore the authority of the State and the decision-making and problem-solving capacities of the political process.

Significantly, the most radical opponent of these institutions, François Mitterrand, became President of the Republic in 1981. He confirmed: 'The institutions were not made for me. But they work well for me.'[255] Whereas the Left was hostile to De Gaulle's institutions and political practice, which it criticized as a '*permanent coup d'état*',[256] it accepted them, first by intending to modify them and then by participating in them, especially in the legislative and presidential elections. Eventually, 'It appear[ed] possible to change politics and society without changing the regime.'[257]

This is a major change in a culture where any political vision had to be expressed in a constitution.[258] The institutions survived political '*alternance*' between the Right and the Left and then the Left and the Right undamaged.[259] What is more, the constitution has accommodated situations of '*cohabitation*', where a President and a National Assembly (and consequently a government) from two opposing sides were simultaneously in charge (1986–1988, 1993–1995, 1997–2002).

As a consequence of the almost general consensus on the framework for political competition, there is no incentive to get rid of the constitution, which has now lasted for more than sixty years.[260] This does not mean that the document or its interpretation has not changed. But voices demanding a radical overthrow of the constitutional order appear isolated.

Constitutional changes now take the form of constitutional amendments rather than attempting to alter the entire constitution. Modifying the constitution is no longer a sacrilege.[261] The constitution has been amended no less than twenty-four times since 1958, the rhythm of modifications recently accelerating, especially due to European integration.[262] The last modification in 2008 affected more than fifty articles involving the President of the Republic, parliament, the *Conseil constitutionnel*,[263] the *Défenseur des droits*, etc. As part of a vast project of institutional reform, President Macron recently intended to amend the constitution again so as to promote a more representative, responsible, and efficient democracy. Among other things, the number of MPs as well as the number of their terms would have been reduced. The parliamentary procedure would have been modernized in order to allow for the faster adoption of statutes and to improve parliament's functions of controlling and

---

[254] See Guillaume Tusseau, 'Le présidentialisme de la Ve République: la part de l'autosuggestion dans la culture constitutionnelle française contemporaine', in Olivier Duhamel and others (eds), *La Ve République démystifiée* (Presses de Sciences Po, Paris, 2019) 27.

[255] François Mitterrand, *Le Monde*, 2 July 1981.

[256] François Mitterrand, *Le coup d'État permanent* (Plon, Paris, 1964).

[257] Olivier Duhamel, *La gauche et la Ve République* (PUF, Paris, 1993) 473.

[258] See Section B.1.b.i.

[259] On the political traditions in France, see Sudhir Hazareesingh, *Political Traditions in Modern France* (OUP, Oxford, 1994).

[260] Guy Carcassonne, 'Immuable Ve République' (2008) 126 Pouvoirs 27.

[261] René Rémond, 'Les Français et leur Constitution' (n 52) 30.

[262] See e.g. Marc Guillaume, 'Les révisions constitutionnelles: une Constitution moins procédurale et plus fondamentale', (2018) 166 Pouvoirs 27; Julien Jeanneney, 'Le réformisme constitutionnel sous la Ve République', in Philippe Blachèr (ed), *La Constitution de la Cinquième République: 60 ans d'application (1958-2018)* (LGDJ, Paris, 2018) 135.

[263] See Section D.2.

assessing public policies. The powers of the High Council of the Judiciary would have been increased in order to secure judicial independence more effectively. However, as a result of political tensions, debates on these projects have been postponed. Only a modification of article 1 of the constitution to provide for the protection of the environment was still contemplated in 2021. But even that failed.[264]

The concept of constitutional amendment is undoubtedly a major change. But it simultaneously confirms one aspect of legicentrism.[265] It reinforces the idea that the more sacred and unchangeable a constitution is in France, the less enduring it is, while the less sacred and rigid it is, i.e. the more it resembles a statute, the more it is able to embody the stabilizing fundamental law of the land. Agreement about the basic institutional structure goes hand in hand with agreement about the values of self-government.

b) A Harmonious Combination of Liberal and Social Values

Today, both the Declaration of 1789 and the preamble of 1946[266] have constitutional value.[267]

The attachment to the principles of 1789 is evident from the fact that whenever a new drafting was proposed, it was not accepted. In 1946, a first constitutional draft contained a modernized bill of rights, consisting, for one, of liberties and, for another, of social and economic rights. For the first time in history, the referendum's result was negative. By contrast, the second constitutional draft may have been approved, at least in part, because it did not aim to supersede the Declaration of 1789 but only to complement it with 'political, economic, and social principles especially necessary to our times'. One may interpret these two votes as a resistance of the constitutional *Gestalt*.

In 2008, President Sarkozy appointed a Commission to determine whether it was necessary or advisable to modify, complement, and update the old texts to which the preamble referred in order to reflect today's societal condition, especially regarding equality between men and women, bioethics, human dignity, pluralism, privacy, etc. The Commission tellingly refused to suggest any change and entitled its report '*redécouvrir* [rediscover] *le préambule de la constitution*'.[268] This illustrates once again how powerfully the substance of the texts of 1789 and 1946 are present in the French constitutional *Gestalt*.

The ambiguity between the two texts appears sufficient at the same time to embody the past of French constitutionalism and to sustain the future dynamics of self-government. By bridging the gap between the more or less conflicting perspectives of these two sets of fundamental principles, especially thanks to the *Conseil constitutionnel*'s case law,[269] the Fifth Republic has once again internalized ideological and political conflict.

The Declaration mostly protects individual civil and political rights that safeguard against the state's interference. The *Conseil* has duly implemented and expanded equality,[270] liberty, property,[271] and safety. As well as proportionality in punishment, the presumption of innocence,

---

[264] See Section D.1.c.
[265] See Section B.2.
[266] See Section C.2.
[267] See Section D.2.a.i.
[268] Available at http://lesrapports.ladocumentationfrancaise.fr/BRP/084000758/0000.pdf (last accessed on 22 March 2022). See e.g. Denys de Béchillon and others, 'Faut-il actualiser le préambule de la Constitution?', (2012) 2 Constitutions 247.
[269] See Section D.2.a.
[270] See e.g. Decision n° 87–232 DC and 2010–1 QPC.
[271] See e.g. Decisions n° 82–139 DC and 2016–540 QPC.

freedom of opinion, expression, and communication,[272] and the right to fair trial[273] have been secured. Although the 1946 preamble purports to 'confirm and complement' these rights, its inspiration is quite different. The economic and social rights it proclaims are more sensitive to their context of implementation and to the identities of their holders. They tend to impose positive obligations on the state. Such is, for example, the case of the duty to work and the right to employment, the right to unionize,[274] the right to strike,[275] the rights of workers to participate in the collective determination of their working conditions and in the management of the workplace,[276] the Nation's obligation to provide the individual and family with the conditions necessary for their development[277]—including the right to a family life, to social security, and to education—and to guarantee to all the protection of their health, material security, rest, and leisure.

It is not possible to clearly identify a specific hierarchy among the fundamental rights, a 'double standard' of review, or whether some rights have a higher rank than others. Most of the time, the *Conseil* tries to balance rights against each other in order to ensure an acceptable equilibrium, so that none of the rights involved suffer an unreasonable or disproportionate disadvantage. Simultaneously, the conflicting sources of the parameters of review contribute to increasing the *Conseil*'s discretionary power when assessing the validity of political authorities' actions.

Recently, the *Conseil* resorted to the notion of fraternity,[278] from the Republic's maxim of 'Liberty, Equality, Fraternity', to strike down a statute.[279] Whereas the first two elements have been widely used, the last one has not. This ruling testifies to the *Conseil*'s sensitivity to the entire constitutional heritage. The Constitution of 1958 was strongly committed to restoring the 'power of the state'.[280] As is evident from the Constitutional Act of 3 June 1958,[281] it chose not to exclude any of the opposing substantive values.

One may then generalize the conclusion put forward regarding the Left and the Fifth Republic. There seems to be widespread agreement on both the structure of self-government and the substance of the political inputs it starts with and the outputs it produces. As a result, one may be right in considering that France is witnessing the 'disappearance of coherent constitutional ideologies, which are replaced by what could be called, without any pejorative connotation, constitutional opportunism'.[282]

This does not mean that there is no more French constitutional *Gestalt*. But it no longer seems to be defined by passionate controversies prompting frenetic constitutional drafting. One explanation for this may be that the major stakes of constitutional debates are no longer at the national but rather at the supranational level. Some contend that national

---

[272] See e.g. Decision n° 84–181 DC.

[273] See e.g. Decision n° 96–373 DC.

[274] See e.g. Decisions n° 80–127 DC and 2010–42 QPC.

[275] See e.g. Decision n° 79–105 DC.

[276] See e.g. Decisions n° 77–79 DC and 2010–42 QPC.

[277] See e.g. Decision n° 93–325 DC.

[278] Michel Borgetto, *La notion de fraternité en droit public français. Le passé, le présent et l'avenir de la solidarité* (LGDJ, Paris, 1993).

[279] Decision n° 2018–717/718 QPC. See Guillaume Tusseau, 'Le Conseil constitutionnel et le 'délit de solidarité': de la consécration activiste d'une norme constitutionnelle sous-appliquée à la révélation d'une stratégie contrainte de communication juridictionnelle?' (2019) Revue critique de droit international privé 35.

[280] Georges Burdeau, 'La conception du pouvoir dans la Constitution française du 4 octobre 1958' (1959) 9 Revue française de science politique 87.

[281] See Section C.2.a.ii.

[282] Olivier Duhamel, *La gauche et la Ve République* (n 257) 29.

constitutionalism is definitely outdated and superseded by 'global constitutionalism', especially in the European Union.[283] Nevertheless, in most of French legal doctrine, and especially among constitutionalists, let alone in popular perception, the reflection on global constitutionalism has not substantially developed.[284] The French *Gestalt* still appears intrinsically national.

The argument still holds that:

> Law is a symbolic system that structures the political imagination. The 'rule of law' is a shorthand expression for a cultural practice that constructs a particular understanding of time and space, of subjects and groups, as well as of authority and legitimacy. It is a way of projecting, maintaining, and discovering meaning in the world of historical events and political possibilities.[285]

One needs to be cautious with the contemporary 'burial of the constitutional debate'.[286] The withering away of explicit constitutional ideologies and debate falls short of eliminating implicit ones, which prove all the more difficult to identify and discuss. One may suggest that a critical aspect of the Fifth Republic, which may lead to a crisis, lies precisely in the fact that it seems to have escaped from any crisis.[287] The *Gestalt* concerns the issue of how a specific framework, as it results from a particular context and history, allows for certain thoughts or radically silences others by removing them from sight and discussion. Consequently, the *Gestalt* is about acceptance, resistance, resignation, and subordination.[288] The constraints and limits it places on political imagination must be highlighted and scrutinized: By doing so, the solidification of a constitutional *Gestalt* does not become synonymous with the sort of lethal 'constitutional fatigue'[289] which would rule out the idea that another constitutionalism remains possible.

---

[283] See e.g. Koen Lenaerts and Piet Van Nuffel, *Constitutional Law of the European Union* (3rd edn, Sweet & Maxwell, London, 2011); Armin von Bogdandy and Jürgen Bast (eds), *Europäisches Verfassungsrecht. Theoretische und dogmatische Grundzüge* (2nd edn, Springer, Berlin, 2009).

[284] See e.g. Guillaume Tusseau, 'Un chaos conceptuel qui fait sens: la rhétorique du constitutionnalisme global', in Jean-Yves Chérot and Benoit Frydman (eds), *La science du droit dans la globalisation* (Bruylant, Bruxelles, 2012) 182; Guillaume Tusseau (ed), *Debating Legal Pluralism and Constitutionalism: New Trajectories for Legal Theory in the Global Age* (Cham, Springer, 2020).

[285] Paul W Kahn, 'Comparative Constitutionalism in a New Key' (n 17).

[286] Olivier Duhamel, *La gauche et la Ve République* (n 257) 545.

[287] See e.g. Guillaume Tusseau, 'La Ve République et l'évitement (provisoire?) de la crise: du droit constitutionnel à la science du droit constitutionnel' (n 241).

[288] See Armand Mattelart and Erik Neveu, *Introduction aux* Cultural Studies (La découverte, Paris, 2008) 36.

[289] Carlos de Cabo Martín, *Pensamiento crítico, constitucionalismo crítico* (Trotta, Madrid, 2014) 10.

4

The Evolution and *Gestalt* of the German Constitution

Susanne Baer

A. Origins of the Current Constitution	163	c) Reproductive Rights, Medical Ethics	186
1. Sources, Theories, Texts	164	d) Data, Technology, Surveillance	187
2. Framing, Drafting	165	e) Religious Pluralism	188
3. Commitments, Ideologies, People	166	f) Economic Justice, Poverty	189
4. Between Global, Local, and Comparative	166	g) Private Actors	189
5. Consensus and Controversies	169	h) Environmental Justice	190
B. The Evolution of the Constitution	171	**C. Basic Structures and Concepts**	191
1. The First Fan: Karlsruhe	172	1. Position, Standing, Significance	191
2. A Slow Start, the 'Never Again', and		2. Fundamental Rights and Proportionality	193
'One of You We Are'	175	3. Foundational Principles of the State	195
3. Post-1968	177	4. Democracy, Elections, Parliament	196
4. Post-1989	179	5. Defensive Democracy	200
5. EU Integration	180	6. Federalism, Form of State, Units,	
6. Globalization	181	Territory	201
7. Changes of the Text	181	7. *Rechtsstaat*	203
8. Changes in Society	184	8. Welfare State, Protective and Social	
a) Proportionality: Liberal		Dimensions of Fundamental Rights	205
Constitutionalism Replaces		9. Secularism	208
Authoritarian States of Law	184	10. Constitutionalization	210
b) Gender Equality, Gender	185	**D. Constitutional Identity**	211

A. Origins of the Current Constitution

The story of today's German constitutionalism is mostly told as reacting to fascism and the Second World War, building upon German constitutional traditions of the *Paulskirchenverfassung* of 1848/49 and the Weimar Constitution of 1919 (*Weimarer Reichsverfassung*). With this double reference,[1] German constitutionalism also deliberately departed from the Weimar Constitution by making constitutional law enforceable, no mere promise, 'declamation, declaration or directive', with a separate federal constitutional court, and setting out with fundamental rights based on the 'general clause for the whole catalogue of fundamental rights' (Carlo Schmid), inviolable human dignity (article 1), to eventually also design democratic decision making and the organs of the state, in later chapters. As such,

---

[1] Horst Dreier, 'Grundlagen und Grundzüge staatlichen Verfassungsrechts: Deutschland', in Armin von Bogdandy, Sabino Cassese, and Peter M Huber (eds), *Handbuch Ius Publicum Europaeum* I (CF Müller, Heidelberg, 2014) s 1 n 6–77; see also Peter Unruh, *Der Verfassungsbegriff des Grundgesetzes* (Mohr Siebeck, Tübingen, 2002) evolutionary category; Michaela Hailbronner, 'Rethinking the rise of the German Constitutional Court: From anti-Nazism to value formalism', (2014) 12 (3) International Journal of Constitutional Law 626–649.

Susanne Baer, *The Evolution and* Gestalt *of the German Constitution* In: *The Max Planck Handbooks in European Public Law*. Edited by: Armin von Bogdandy, Peter M Huber, and Sabrina Ragone, Oxford University Press. © Susanne Baer 2023.
DOI: 10.1093/oso/9780198726425.003.0004

the Basic Law is rooted in a notion of constitutionalism that incorporates a specific liberal notion of fundamental rights. This dates back to the Magna Carta of 1215, the Virginia Bill of Rights of 1776 as well as the French declaration of 1789; its main influence however seems to be the concept of the enlightened rational subject described by philosopher Immanuel Kant and some, although not all, constitutional thinkers from the early twentieth century.[2]

However, there is also a somewhat competing and not least revisionist story told. According to it, the Basic Law is an *oktroi*, a constitution imposed by the Allied Forces after the Second World War. Even today, historical accounts of Germany's constitutionalism feature ambivalent repercussions, either perceiving the Allied Forces as defeating and occupying Germany, or as liberating and redirecting a people. Finally, there is a perception of German constitutionalism as a successful and indispensable instrument to organize and inform a democratic, rule and value-based way of life.

Politically, German constitutionalism grew out of, as most German legal scholars tend to call it, a 'catastrophe' or 'collapse'. Depending on perspective, the defining trauma was a lost war and overall defeat, yet it seems that the constitutional moment rather defined this as liberation. It was a deliberate 'no' to the past, but it was an imperfect new beginning, limited to the Western zones with a constitution drafted and passed into a 'Basic Law' without Soviet involvement and not applicable in the GDR, the Eastern German socialist state. Therefore, the Basic Law was a 'provisionary' or 'transitory' text,[3] specifically to allow for a constitution for all of Germany at some later time.

This East/West divide, which informed the ideological Cold War between communism and socialism on the one side and liberal capitalism on the other, also produced an impasse in German constitutional history. Since the Basic Law was not meant to foreclose a future for all of Germany, it did not define a certain economic system as 'the' economic system for Germany. Therefore, different from German state constitutions from the same time, the Basic Law did not promote social rights, but it does feature some rather socialist notions, specifically in that article 14 para 2 states that 'property entails obligations. Its use shall also serve the public good'. Article 14 para 3 permits expropriation for the public good, and article 15 allowed for a transfer of 'land, natural resources and means of production […] or the purpose of nationalization […] to public ownership or other forms of public enterprise'. It has never been used, but it signals the early commitment not to have the constitution define the economy. Instead, that matter was left to the politicians. Their job was to implement the 'principle of the social state', as laid down in article 20 para 1.

1. Sources, Theories, Texts

German constitutionalism has many sources. Not least, the American, British and French Military Government had a say in reestablishing constitutional law in Germany after 1945. But it was the eleven framers on the island *Herrenchiemsee* in Bavaria and the sixty-five

---

[2] One prominent voice is Georg Jellinek, but not Carl Schmitt, the Nazi 'crown jurist', who ran an influential intellectual circle after 1945. On Weimar, see Peter C Caldwell, *Popular Sovereignty and the Crisis of German Constitutional Law* (Duke University Press, Durham, 1997). Historically, liberal constitutionalism excluded women based on gender, and some men based on racism and class.

[3] The term is primarily attributed to Theodor Heuss, *Der Parlamentarische Rat 1948–1949, Akten und Protokolle* (Bundesarchiv, Walter de Gruyter, Berlin 2010); Christian Bumke, Andreas Voßkuhle. *Casebook Verfassungsrecht* (Mohr Siebeck, Tübingen, 2015) 1, describe the process of creating the constitution as rather technical, due to the transitional character of the document, which may underrate some actors' and the public's commitment.

drafters commissioned by the German *Länder*, or states, in Bonn, as well as those who eventually accepted the Basic Law as the highest law of the land, that are now seen as parenting the Basic Law. As academics and politicians, who were traumatized by the immediate past, they wanted a legal text, not a mere aspirational document. Looking for inspiration, they primarily referred to German sources, such as the Weimar Constitution. Yet, they did not to copy it. They rather sought to heal what was destroyed, like federalism,[4] and do better, specifically as a 'defensive democracy'. Also, there were civil society demands to respond to, namely regarding women's rights and the right to refuse the draft. In addition, the framers and drafters actively engaged with the fresh global consensus on human rights by referring to the Universal Declaration, proclaimed in Paris in 1948. In passing, they also indulged in some comparative considerations. Eventually, they endorsed a concept of constitutionalism associated with Austrian legal philosopher Hans Kelsen, although they also had regard to some predecessors in German history, most particularly an independent and specialized constitutional court.

It was the Western Allies who most powerfully called for constitutionalism. The London—or mostly Frankfurt—Documents[5] contained their key considerations, including a reservation clause that left it to them to approve the draft. Specifically, and a matter that was repeatedly emphasized during deliberations, the US military government insisted on a vertical version of separated powers via federalism, which contrasted with the centralization of the fascist Nazi state. This approach meant that a 'Parliamentary Council' of drafters was formed, with its delegates being appointed by state governments. By comparison, for the Weimar constitution, a 'National Convention' had been established in Weimar. Accordingly, this new approach was a rather unique way to organize a constitutional moment.[6]

2. Framing, Drafting

The original text of the German Basic Law, then, was framed during a few days on the island of *Herrenchiemsee*, and drafted in September 1948 until May 1949, in the *Pädagogische Akademie zu Bonn*, in the Rhine valley's new West German capital, far from Hitler's capital, now in the middle of the Soviet zone, Berlin.[7] The text was a deliberately modest attempt to regain standing after defeat and amidst destruction, in the global community of democracies, specifically understood as republican forms of government under the rule of law, namely in the preamble, article 1 and the list of principles to inform the state in article 20, forever, guaranteed in article 79 para 3. For the drafting assembly, state parliaments had delegated sixty-one men and four women. There was no popular movement behind the

---

[4] See Hans Maier, 'Der Föderalismus - Ursprünge und Wandlungen' Archiv des öffentlichen Rechts (1990) 115, 213; Hans-Jochen Vogel, 'Die bundesstaatliche Ordnung des Grundgesetzes', in Ernst Benda, Werner Maihofer, and Hans-Jochen Vogel (eds), *Handbuch des Verfassungsrechts der Bundesrepublik Deutschland* (De Gruyter, Berlin, 2011) 1041–1102.

[5] The documents were handed to the eleventh Presidents of the German states, see n 1 'Frankfurter Dokumente' (1951) Jahrbuch des öffentlichen Rechts Neue Folge 1, 2.

[6] Dreier, IPE I, n 1: 'Unikat'; Christian Bumke and Andreas Voßkuhle, *German Constitutional Law* (OUP, Oxford, 2019) 1.

[7] Influential persons were Bergsträßer, Süsterhenn, Dehler, and Greve, maybe even more so Theodor Heuss and Carlo Schmid, next to Hans Nawiasky, Hermann von Mangoldt. Elisabeth Selbert was one of the four women, and she had suffered from discrimination based on gender and her Jewish family, while Theodor Maunz had made a case for the Nazi regime before, but became a member of a state government and a still renowned scholarly commentator on the Basic Law.

constitution, but the public participated by media attention and by sending postcards, notably to include an equal-rights provision to ensure gender equality for women.[8]

3. Commitments, Ideologies, People

Clearly, the commitment to join what was the community of Western liberal democracies included a commitment to adhere to international law and human rights, as prominently stated in the preamble and article 1 para 2. Also, this new Germany did not want to wage war, and listed the individual right to refuse the draft in its new constitution. In addition, the lesson of Weimar was to weaken autocratic as well as populist temptation. This resulted in designing a representative democracy, with parties mediating the public's will and almost no plebiscite decisions,[9] a decidedly weak president and a strong chancellor, who was to be elected by the *Bundestag* alone (article 63), to be removed only by constructive vote (article 67), and to be a leader of the cabinet (articles 64, 65, 69 para 2), which is why some labelled the period of Chancellor Konrad Adenauer in particular a 'chancellor's democracy' (*Kanzlerdemokratie*). In addition, German constitutionalism features a primacy of legislation, yet all legislation is bound to constitutional limits that are reviewed by a specialized court responding to any citizen's complaints (article 93). Further, it provides for few options to leave decisions to the executive (article 80). This results in an obligation of parliament to take responsibility, a notion that strongly informs the constitutional perspective on European integration as well.

4. Between Global, Local, and Comparative

In such a situation, at least three venues may offer some orientation. While constitution-making in Eastern and Central Europe after 1989, in African postcolonial transitional settings, and in some Asian states often 'went comparative', the Germans oscillated between going global and staying local. The story mostly told is local, but inspiration was also taken from global sources and there are pinches of both French and US constitutionalism. As may be expected in a nation framing the story of its highest law of the land, German constitutional history is more often told as a local reaction to the 'catastrophe' of 1945, again, invoking ambivalence between defeat and destruction. Putting the German Basic Law in a local frame, the story is then either a break with the dehumanization of the Holocaust and the cruelty of the war, or it is a continuation of the longue durée of Weimar and before. Both versions exist. And certainly, the rich history of German constitutionalism itself was the predominant inspiration as well as the warning flag on what to avoid or do better.

Specifically, the priority on fundamental rights, with article 1 on dignity, and the whole first chapter on liberties and equalities, differ from the traditional architecture of German state constitutions. It was to be understood as a 'never again' to the cruelty of the immediate past, despite the fact that German's colonial history was not part of this national story, nor were all Nazi atrocities, most particularly the crimes against people with disabilities, with a non-discrimination clause added as late as 1994, while homosexuals are still not explicitly protected against discrimination despite persecution and murder before 1945. In addition,

---

[8] Barbara Böttger, *Das Recht auf Gleichheit und Differenz* (Westfälisches Dampfboot, Münster, 1990).
[9] Otmar Jung, *Grundgesetz und Volksentscheid* (Springer, Heidelberg, 1994); Christopher Schwieger, *Volksgesetzgebung in Deutschland* (Duncker und Humblot, Berlin, 2005).

article 16 para 1 established a right to abstain from military service, which was in fact driven by families who had lost men in the war and wrote to the Council to call for such a pacifist right.[10] Beyond fundamental rights, rejecting fascist Germany meant rejecting a strong presidency, establishing parliament as the central organ that must not delegate legislative powers to the executive (article 80), creating a court with the power of judicial review, and, as also mandated by the Allied interventions, committing to federalism.

Finally, the eternity clause in article 79 para 3 was meant to 'strip the mask of legality from the face of a revolution' (Dehler[11]). Since the coming to power of the Nazis has been seen as a legal coup, the clause prohibits amendments to the constitution that modify the very meaning of dignity (in article 1) or touch upon the fundamental principles of the state (in article 20). Overall, the explicit statement of constitutionalism as such, in article 1 para 3, highlights the non-authoritarian, non-populist, non-majoritarian commitment of the German constitution, in that it states: 'The following basic rights shall bind the legislature, the executive and the judiciary as directly applicable law.' In addition, article 19 para 4 ensures legal protection against all acts of authority, and article 19 para 3 extends legal standing to also cover collective actors.

In addition, the Basic Law was deliberately designed as a constitution for a 'defensive' or 'militant' democracy, to fight its enemies if needed. By now, it is a known fact that the Weimar Republic did not collapse because the Constitution was wrongly designed. However, the Basic Law is understood to at least protect a status quo,[12] while it may also be described as protecting a democratic future.

Then, there is the global aspect. The orientation of the drafters of the Basic Law towards a global commitment to human rights is indeed well documented. At the very moment of framing a new foundational contract for the country that started and lost the Second World War, the framers engaged in some form of 'globalization'. This happened long before the term got popular, with the international norms that were negotiated at the same time as the Universal Declaration of Human Rights, a standard for the national frame. To be clear, this was not the commitment of the traditionally influential German public law professors' guild, not few of whom had actively been part of or supported the Nazi regime.[13] Rather, it was the commitment of the 'parents' drafting that constitution.

By going global, many clauses of the *Grundgesetz* were discussed with reference to the non-binding, but nonetheless globally respected, Universal Declaration of Human Rights from 10 December 1948, with its predecessors in the UN Charter.[14] During the proceedings, conservative member Adolf Süsterhenn, a later member of the European Commission of Human Rights of Strasbourg (1954–1974), was the first to explicitly refer to a then draft of the UDHR 8 September 1948, in the plenary. Even more influentially, social democrat

---

[10] Dreier, n 1 (note 14).

[11] Dreier, IPE § 1, n 28.

[12] Dreier, IPE § 1, n 2 '*Bestandssicherung*'.

[13] A famous example is *Theodor Maunz*, who published the first study treatise on the Basic Law in 1951 and became the renowned co-editor of a lead commentary of the *Grundgesetz*. See Horst Dreier and Walter Pauly, *Die deutsche Staatsrechtslehre in der Zeit des Nationalsozialismus*, in VVDStRL 60 (De Gruyter, Berlin, 2011); Ingo Müller, *Furchtbare Juristen – die unbewältigte Vergangenheit unserer Justiz* (Kindler, Munich, 1987); Ingo Müller, *Hitler's Justice: The Courts of the Third Reich* (Deborah Lucas Schneider tr, Harvard University Press, Cambridge MA, 1992). The conceptual changes among academics describes Frieder Günther, *Denken vom Staat her* (Oldenbourg, Munich, 2004).

[14] Charter of the United Nations (signed 26 June 1945, entered into force 24 October 1945) Preamble, Art 1 n 3, Art 13, 55, 56, 62, 76. See *Der Parlamentarische Rat*, vol 2 (2014) (n 3); Heinrich Wilms, *Ausländische Einwirkungen auf die Entstehung des Grundgesetzes* (Kohlhammer, Stuttgart, 1999); Horst Dreier, Kontexte des Grundgesetzes (1999) *Deutsches Verwaltungsblatt* 667–679.

168   SUSANNE BAER

Ludwig Bergsträsser presented an exhaustive list of fundamental rights, to orient the discussion, and included a translation of six clauses of the UDHR, all in all referred to eighteen times.[15] In addition, he embedded the Basic Law with the Western tradition of constitutionalism, most particularly referring to the Magna Charta from 1215, the Virginia Declaration, the French Declaration, the German *Paulskirchenverfassung*, Weimar Constitution, and to the UN.

Specifically, the starting point of dignity, article 1 of the Basic Law, is understood as a commitment to a global norm.[16] Drafting the dignity clause, the head of sub-committee Hermann von Mangoldt explained the relationship between dignity and liberties by referring to the preamble of the draft Declaration.[17] Yet even more clearly, the reference to human rights in article 1 para 2 points directly to the UDHR. The argument was that 'if they can do it, we should be able to do it as well'.[18]

The specific rights to equality and against discrimination in article 3 para 2 and para 3 are, then, primarily understood as a 'never again' to the antisemitism and racism under the NS regime. In fact, the list of dubious characteristics that signify discrimination as a violation of the right to equality is almost fully identical to article 2 UDHR, to which the Germans added 'language', to cover more forms of inequality.[19] Yet notably, neither the UN nor the Germans acknowledged the persecution of gay men in Nazi Germany, and thus did not counter homophobia by not including sexuality in the list. In later attempts to update article 3 para 3, the majority argued that this was unnecessary, since covered by the general clause,[20] while the small revision of the Basic Law from 1994, after the German reunification in 1989/ 1990, opened a window of opportunity for disability-rights activists to add a specific equality clause there.

In addition, the drafters explicitly copied the UN draft by adding a right not to be stripped of one's national citizenship, in article 16 para 1.[21] More generally, the UN draft was referred to in order to destroy scepticism about the broad wording of some clauses. Also, references were made to more global standards to back up political preference, as when conservatives re-institutionalized marriage and the family in article 6, which had already been an element in the Weimar Constitution, but needed additional global back-up now.[22] In another instance, they rejected a version of the right to liberty that contained a commitment to 'brotherhood' based on the argument not to draft a non-enforceable programme but truly legal rights.[23] Similarly, the guarantee of religious freedom is deliberately broader than its UN counterpart,[24] while the limitation clause relating to the freedom of occupation or

---

[15] *Der Parlamentarische Rat*, vol 5 (2010) 16 ff (n 3).

[16] Stephan Hobe, 'Der Einfluss der Allgemeinen Erklärung der Menschenrechte vom 10. Dezember 1948 auf das Grundgesetz und die verfassungsrechtliche Staatspraxis der Bundesrepublik Deutschland', in Klaus Dicke (ed), *Zur Wirkungsgeschichte der Allgemeinen Erklärung der Menschenrechte in Verfassungsrecht und Politik* (UNO, Bonn, 2004) 7–26; Thilo Rensmann, *Wertordnung und Verfassung* (Mohr Siebeck, Tübingen, 2007).

[17] *Der Parlamentarische Rat*, vol 5 (2010) (n 3), Ausschuß für Grundsatzfragen, 568.

[18] 'Aber wenn die das können, müssten wir es eigentlich auch können.' 22. Sitzung des Ausschusses für Grundsatzfragen, 18 November 1948, *Der Parlamentarische Rat*, vol 5 (2010), 593 (n 3).

[19] One of the few mothers of the GG, social democrat *Friederike Nadig*, proposed a version even closer to the UN draft which was not accepted; in *Der Parlamentarische Rat*, vol 2 (2014), 742 (n 3).

[20] The Court now consistently applies a similarly strict standard to justify inequalities to sexual orientation, based on the general equality clause of para 1 interpreted as close to the specific non-discrimination clause of para 3.

[21] Hauptausschuss, 18. Sitzung, 4 December 1948, *Der Parlamentarische Rat*, vol 14 (2010), 216 ff (n 3).

[22] Daniel Eberhardt, 'Der Einfluss der Allgemeinen Erklärung der Menschenrechte auf die Grundrechtsberatung des Grundgesetzes im Parlamentarischen Rat', (2009) 14 MenschenRechtsMagazin 162, 169.

[23] Ausschuss für Grundsatzfragen, 22. Sitzung, 18 November 1948, *Der Parlamentarische Rat*, vol 5 (n 3) 596.

[24] Ausschuss für Grundsatzfragen, 24. Sitzung, 23. November 1948, *Der Parlamentarische Rat*, vol 5 (n 3) 621 ff.

profession is framed more narrowly.[25] Regarding other rights—freedom of information, the home, property—UN law was referred to in passing, but it was not particularly influential.

While some UN rights were deliberately rejected as unfit for the German context, like the right to participation in cultural life or the right of parents in article 26 UN, some global human rights were subject to controversial debate, like a right to a secular education, which was debated at length. Other human rights were deemed unfit for a liberal constitution, like the right to work or the right to health, while some German state constitution's make provision for these rights. But on the federal level, many social concerns were considered to be provided for by more general clauses, like the right to equal pay as a dimension of the right to equality and non-discrimination. Interestingly, considering the context of poverty, destruction and despair, the right to existential social needs from article 25 para 1 UN was first included as a fundamental right, then moved towards the end of the text, and then eventually dropped altogether. All in all, there are forty-two references to UN drafts in the plenary, and fifty-five references in the Committee of Fundamental Questions (*Grundsatzfragen*).

Next to the UN references, there are some very basic transnational and global commitments of the German Basic Law that gained prominence much later. Namely, the preamble declares that constitution to be 'inspired by the determination to promote world peace as an equal partner in a united Europe'. Article 2 para 2 states that 'the German people therefore acknowledge inviolable and inalienable Human Rights as the basis of every community, of peace and of justice in the world'. Article 25 enshrines the primacy of international law, and article 24 immediately allowed for a transfer of sovereign powers, and specifically, joining a system of collective security.

Last, but not least, there was a comparative calling, although on a much smaller scale than the call to endorse Global Human Rights. However, framers and drafters also sought ideas for the Basic Law from foreign constitutions, most particularly from countries that had won the war, had liberated, and now engaged in rebuilding Germany as a constitutional democracy. In addition, the rich variety of German state constitutions, some of them passed earlier than the Basic Law itself, inspired the draft.

5. Consensus and Controversies

The commitment to 'never again' was highly consensual during the constituent phase, while many other issues were not. Eventually, the final draft of the new constitution was accepted by a large majority of fifty-three to twelve votes, and later ratified by all but the Bavarian state parliament. In the process, some proposals were simply dropped, others quite fervently rejected, and some highly controversial ones lead to lasting compromise.

From the outset, it is obvious that the German Basic Law prioritizes liberties as equal rights, grounded in dignity. It does not frame a grand social commitment, in that it does not feature social rights as promises, but there is an emphasis on the welfare state as a foundational principle in article 20 para 1, repeated in article 28 para 1, and there was an understanding that liberal rights also carry affirmative commitments. Eventually, the Court thus interpreted the right to human dignity as a guarantee of the state to enable every human being to live a dignified life.

---

[25] Heuss, *Der Parlamentarische Rat* (n 3) 100.

Considering the histories of secular constitutionalism, it does also not come as a surprise that religion was a polarizing force in the Council. This informs the legal take on marriage and on families, eventually enshrined as institutions in article 6. Different religious politics also inform the equilibrium between parenting and public education, and public versus private as well as secular versus denominational schools, in article 7. In addition, the very status of religion and religious associations gave rise to considerable controversy. Eventually, the German post-1945 constitution largely endorses a Weimar compromise, namely integrating Weimarian state–church relations found in article 139.[26]

Next to fundamental rights and secularism, federalism was controversial as well.[27] While all agreed on such a model of separating powers, details of the make-up, powers, and proceedings of the second chamber, the Bundesrat, were sharply contested, as were the details of the financial constitutional, in chapter X. Last, but not least, revisions of that part of the constitution, which organizes finance, yet in fact largely defines federalism, have been rather abundant to date. Since 1949, there have been around two hundred amendments of the Basic Law, with an increase of fifty percent of the text. While often seen as an indicator of instability, German constitutional scholars tend to treat this as an indication of commitment, in that changes of the text indicate that the text is taken seriously.[28] In substance, amendments did not touch the basic structure.

Several decisions were taken against the backdrop of a somewhat skewed narrative of the Weimar constitution. Often, that document was portrayed as a list of principles rather than enforceable rights. Opposed to that, the framers and the drafters of the Basic Law wanted the text to have practical meaning, enforceable in court as rights, not mere principles. Therefore, the first chapter lists fundamental rights as liberties to be protected against state action, while social rights did not figure prominently, despite the pressing needs of the people at the time. Different from later drafting processes in Eastern or Southern Europe, and different from many constitutions in South America or Africa, the German drafters did not want to promise anything the court, or state, would not be able to deliver. However, the inviolability of human dignity in article 1 and the principle of the welfare state in article 20 para 1 for the federation, and article 28 para 1 for the states, do frame the specifics in articles 2 to 19. Also, the right to freely choose an occupation or profession, place of work and place of training at least addresses the prime source of social security.

In addition, the failure of the Weimar Constitution figured as a political trauma,[29] which informed some more decisions on the political make-up of Germany after 1945. The prime example is the outright refusal to install referenda, including the decision to not even put the constitution itself in front of the people for approval. Additional post- and anti-Weimar Constitution features are clauses on political parties as mediators of the people's will, yet bound to constitutional loyalty (article 21), election law, federalism, courts and judges, state–church relations, etc.[30]

Finally, the framers and drafters wanted strong judicial review. It was rather uncontroversial to install a Kelsenian court, prominently proposed in 1929 by Heinrich Triepel, not

---

[26] On church lobbying Gerhard Besier, *Die Rolle der Kirchen im Gründungsprozeß der Bundesrepublik Deutschland* (Lüneburg Unibuch, Lüneburg, 2000).

[27] A rare original voice from the Court in English is Gerhard Leibholz, The Federal Constitutional Court in Germany and the 'Southwest Case' (1952) 46 American Political Science Review 723–731.

[28] Dreier, IPE § 1, n 45.

[29] Michael Stolleis, *Geschichte des Öffentlichen Rechts in Deutschland*, vol 4 (CH Beck, Munich, 2012) 124.

[30] More in Christoph Gusy (ed), *Weimars lange Schatten—"Weimar" als Argument nach 1945* (Nomos, Baden-Baden, 2003).

a '*Staatsgerichtshof*' to decide conflicts among state organs only, but an independent and specialized institution for the whole spectrum of constitutional law, next to an independent judiciary. The Federal Constitutional Court, in articles 93 and 94, even appears first, with the Supreme Courts, specialized as such, to follow suit in article 95, and a guarantee of independent judges in articles 97 and 98, accompanied by individual procedural due process rights, in articles 101 to 104. The first draft of the constitution vested broad powers in the Court, yet the individual constitutional complaint, which is now the prime access route of citizens to the Basic Law, was introduced by legislation later. Thus, there was a founding document, as law, and an institution willing to implement it.[31]

B. The Evolution of the Constitution

Regarding public and political attention, the early days of the *Grundgesetz* were rather solemn. There was no referendum because of a post-Weimar and post-NS scepticism as to the wisdom of 'the people' and based on an understanding of the Basic Law as a proclamation for the Western zones only, rather than all of Germany. However, there was also scepticism and there were some outright attacks. Namely, key figures in constitutional law, predominantly labelled *Staatsrecht* by a conservative mainstream,[32] as well as politicians, were no fans of constitutionalism with enforceable rights and a strong court with the power of judicial review.

While the statistics conceptualized constitutionalism as the state of law and order, the Basic Law's architecture called for putting fundamental rights first and emphasized democracy. Early challenges followed established lines. Some complained that the people were put as creators (in article 20 para 2 clause 1), while God should figure as the only one, and more prominently. Others opposed what they considered overly modern changes in the law, such as in the gender equality clause now applicable to their marriage and their families as well. At the same time, the organized left, and specifically voices from East Germany, criticized the Basic Law's inherent capitalism, joined by conservative sceptics, some former Nazis included, with a rather broad fascination for Russia, close to the German 'soul', but also authoritarian, and religious.[33] Overall, most conservatives refused to go either East nor West, in refusing Allied 'Occupation', and opted for a 'Europe of Fatherlands' (de Gaulle),[34] a concept still influential behind the scenes of European integration. All in all, the new German Basic Law saw rather prominent academics not much cherish but rather attack the new constitution, while others, often new to the scene, somewhat timidly publicized the text and explained its meaning.[35]

---

[31] Stolleis, *Geschichte,* 145 ff (n 29).

[32] The canonical conservative treatise on German constitutional law is a Handbook of the Law of the State (*Handbuch des Staatsrechts*), while a liberal version was named the Handbook of Constitutional Law (*Handbuch des Verfassungsrechts*), now joined by a Handbook of Fundamental Rights (*Handbuch der Grundrechte*). The progressive 'alternative' commentary of the Basic Law (*Alternativkommentar*) only saw two editions.

[33] See Stolleis, *Geschichte,* 126 ff (n 29).

[34] An ambivalent sceptic was *Rudolf Smend*, first calling for 'silent resistance' (Stolleis, *Geschichte,* 129 (n 29)), then actively engaged in the new democratic order, different from NS-head jurist *Carl Schmitt*, who pitied the 'poor little men in Bonn' and despised the *Grundgesetz*, sharing that with his famous disciples, Forsthoff, Weber, ER Huber and others.

[35] A known attack came from Werner Weber, *Weimarer Verfassung und Grundgesetz*, 1949, with a call for the traditional civil servant, but opposed to party politicians and the priority on parliament and opposed to the strong position of the judiciary and the Constitutional Court. A prominent defender is *Hans Peter Ipsen*, in his inaugural speech as president of the University of Hamburg: *Über das Grundgesetz* (1949).

As with all legal history, the evolution of German constitutional law does not follow an easy route of linear progress. The dominant narrative emphasizes that the constitution is law, and not mere symbolism or ideology or decorum. It is taken for granted that this law evolves over time, both by way of (in Germany, many) amendments to the text and by interpreting its meaning in new cases, thus: by way of application. However, it is also clear, and it is an explicit guarantee in the text, that this evolutionary change of meaning has its limits, to not undo the very foundation democratic constitutionalism is built upon. Since the Basic Law was the 'never again' to the failings before, the 'eternity clause' in article 79 para 3 marks the red line not to cross. Notably, this evolutionary drive is also slowed down and channelled significantly by German legal culture, which may be described as deeply committed to the Kantian idea of critical rationality. This informs a strong commitment to the rule of law, stability and foreseeability, and a logically consistent order of good law. Thus, German constitutional lawyers often refer to the concept of the 'silent change of the constitution' (*stiller Verfassungswandel*) to describe changed understandings of text in interpreting it. In fact, the concept captures nothing but the application of the Basic Law to new sets of facts. As such, German constitutional law may not be rooted in one constitutional moment, and its birth has been described as 'irregular constitutional genesis'.[36]

However, German constitutionalism has evolved through several transitions. Post-1945 meant building a democracy that respected human rights, with follow-ups on the military question and federalism; post-1968 meant modernizing society, post-1989 meant integrating two people, politics, societies into one; and 1992 meant joining a larger and closer European Union. In the twenty-first century, Europeanization and globalization are opportunities and challenges, with the simultaneous intensification of connections and overlap, as well as divide and erosion of multilateral commitments.

1. The First Fan: Karlsruhe

Yet at the start, the Basic Law did not have many fans. In fact, rather prominent legal scholars are on record in opposing it. However, the Basic Law had one fan that was strong and willing to make it work: the Federal Constitutional Court.[37] The framers drafted a model, conceptualized by Austrian jurist Hans Kelsen, to create a centralized and specialized system of judicial review, based in Karlsruhe, next to the regular traditional Supreme Court.[38] The first set of judges consisted of twenty-three men and one woman, diverse in age and professional background, most from politics or judgeships, a few from the academy, one from the administration and one from the diplomatic corps. In particular, and very different from the German civil and criminal law Supreme Court (*Bundesgerichtshof*), this first set of Justices had some distance to the Nazi regime, including some who had been persecuted and exiled and they were still

---

[36] Dreier, IPE § 1, n 2.

[37] Also see Justin Collings, *Democracy's Guardians: A History of the German Federal Constitutional Court 1951-2001* (OUP, Oxford, 2015); Donald Kommers, Russel Miller, 'Das Bundesverfassungsgericht: Procedure, Practice and Policy of the German Federal Constitutional Court' (2008) 3 Journal of Comparative Law 194; Martin Borowski, 'The Beginnings of Germany's federal constitutional court' (2003) 16 Ratio Juris 155; regarding comparative perspectives: Susanne Baer, 'Comparing Courts', in Anna Kaiser, Niels Petersen, Johannes Saurer (eds), *The U.S. Supreme Court and Contemporary Constitutional Law* (Routledge, Abingdon, 2018) 253.

[38] Kommers and Miller argue that it is also the continental belief in constitutional law as genuine political law and the unfamiliarity of regular judges with constitutional law that prompted this decision; Donald Kommers and Russel Miller, *The Constitutional Jurisprudence of the Federal Republic of Germany* (Duke University Press, Durham, 2012), 3. However, removing high courts from the political centre is a German tradition, i.e. with the *Reichsgericht* in Leipzig, not Berlin.

under attack from the right.[39] But, as is known today, and as an exception to this rule, one Nazi prosecutor did serve on the court. However, the Court had been removed from the scene of a capital, as a smaller sibling of the 'real' Supreme Court in Karlsruhe. Decision by decision, that Federal Constitutional Court turned German constitutionalism into an item most trusted by the people, according to annual polls on trust in institutions.[40]

There are many factors that may contribute to such good standing. Regarding trust, and hopefully resilience, the way of judging seems to be an important feature. When you read the German judgments, there are the shorter decisions by the Chambers, composed of three Justices. These are meant to specify what the Senates, each with eight Justices, have agreed upon as standards, in significantly longer rulings. They are designed as a comprehensive treatise of all relevant aspects. They do expose the facts including the history of the legal conflict, rephrase all arguments by third parties and experts, explain and specify and eventually refine the constitutional standards (in Section C.1), and apply them in the 'Subsumtion' (always C.2), to then explain what follows (Section D). All rulings come in that order, some numbering one hundred pages or more. Regularly, the judgments are criticized as overly complicated and detailed, and thus hard and too long to read. Yet to date, the Court insists that big questions need refined answers, but also publishes a summary for the press, in German and English, right away.

Certainly, length is not everything. In the Court's rulings, the style is usually seen and meant to be systematic, 'doctrinal' ('*dogmatisch*'), and somewhat scholarly, rather different from jurisprudential styles in many common law cultures, a bit more like the ECHR, yet quite different from the ECJ that presents short and condensed answers to very specific questions, often without any background information. In German constitutional jurisprudence, there are also, beyond the rare event of concurring or dissenting opinions, no individual authors, and no references to an individual perspective: consensus is considered key. Also, the Chambers must decide in full consensus, without a right to dissent, or move the case to the Senate if the three Justices disagree, while the Senate delivers rulings as a collegiate body. It may expose a numerical disagreement,[41] yet usually acts as one. After all, this is considered to be an important factor that strengthens the Court as an institution, with a collegial body deliberately composed as politically diverse, yet beyond political and personal preference in its decisions. Also, decisions often present rich empirical data, researched by the Court itself and collected via expert options that are called for in the proceedings, sometimes based on targeted questions that are also sent out to the government and all parties that are invited to join the proceedings.[42] Sometimes, they are also discussed in the rare public hearings of a case.[43]

---

[39] Details in Stolleis, *Geschichte*, 146–155.

[40] A comparative assessment is provided by Sascha Kneip, 'Rolle und Einfluss des Bundesverfassungsgerichts in international vergleichender Perspektive' (2012) Zeitschrift für Politik 72–89.

[41] Senate rulings may, at the very end, declare the decision to be taken unanimously, which signals consensus where it is not expected, or declare a 5:3, 6:2 or 7:1 vote, without any names given. In an extremely rare 4:4 decision, the Act in question is considered constitutional (thus, an *in dubio* for the legislature), and reasons of both sides are published side by side. One example is the Spiegel-ruling in 1962 (BVerfGE 15, 77), in which the Court rejected the complaint of the publisher Augstein, responsible for the most influential liberal-left weekly 'Der Spiegel', who sought protection against a massive police and security forces search, detention of seven journalists, and four-week blockage of its press offices, based on allegations of treason, which were eventually never put to trial for lack of evidence. However, the four Justices who clearly denounced such state action as a violation of freedom of the press found more resonance in the long run.

[42] The Federal Constitutional Court Act (available in English and French on the Court's website) provides for such measures. In s 77 and s 94 para 1, 2, the Court is obliged to invite statements by all relevant organs of the federation and the states, may add the Supreme Courts and State Courts (s 82 para 3), consult the parties to the case from which the constitutional controversy arose (s 82 para 2).

[43] The Federal Constitutional Court Act understands public hearings as the norm, in s 25 para 1, yet allows the parties to refrain from it, and differentiates between different types of proceedings. Since over 90 percent of the

Another factor that informs the style of German constitutional jurisprudence is the community of scholars that act as fervent, fast, and critical additional interpreters of the constitution.[44] They closely follow every move of the Court, and of political initiatives, and scholars regularly appear in front of the Court as counsel to the parties, more often than lawyers. Despite a critique that challenged the 'fixation' of scholars on the Court, there is a quality to such close academic feedback. In Germany, such feedback is not considered 'purely academic' in a negative sense, as removed from practice, because around half the Justices come from and return to that community of scholars, and they remain colleagues during their tenure on the bench.[45] Certainly, with changes in the composition of the Court, the style of judging will change.

To date, the Court is however at the centre of an academic and political culture that monitors constitutionalism and its development in every decision closely. In a Roman civil law tradition that generally privileges a judges' perspective on cases, systematic commentaries (*Kommentare*) of each clause of the Constitution do not only expose the history and underlying concepts, but also discuss every ruling. Systematic treatises, often written for law schools and very different from casebooks used in other legal cultures, intensely engage with the Court's jurisprudence. Finally, rather short, and doctrinally focused, reviews of rulings are swiftly and constantly published in law journals, which are not edited by students and published by universities, but commercially published and edited by publishing houses, lawyers, and law professors, and meant to be used by courts and lawyers alike. In addition, in preparing a case for the collegiate of the two Senates, reporting Justices present rather academic treatises that take all academic writings into account. As such, Germany still features a comparatively academic constitutional culture.

Beyond the procedural aspects, substance matters to build or sustain the standing of a constitutional court, and the variety of constitutionalism. Today, the German Basic Law is perceived as 'the epicenter of Germany's constitutional democracy',[46] and generally considered a success, and the Court is its prime exponent. It must not be disregarded that the times are changing, in that the autocratic legalists of right-wing nationalist populism do challenge that consensus, and directly attack the Court's legitimacy and standing.[47] But still, the Court is

---

cases are individual complaints, public hearings are rare (around ten per year, based on s 894 para 5 cl 2), yet—again very different from many other legal cultures—long and intense, usually lasting one or two days, resembling a colloquium and a restaging of the legislative process allowing all things to be heard and considered.

[44] Häberle described an even larger 'open community of interpreters of the constitution' ('Die offene Gesellschaft der Verfassungsinterpreten') (1975) Juristenzeitung, 297–305, including media and civil society; for more, see Markus Kotzur, *Peter Häberle on constitutional theory* (Nomos, Baden-Baden, 2018). From a comparative perspective, the standing of public law scholarship in Germany is rather unique, and adds to its predominant conceptual approach, sorting cases systematically into *Dogmatik*. However, the difference may be more approach and style than substance; i.e. German scholarship has been criticized to be overly focused on court decisions, usually a signature of common law cultures, and rulings from constitutional and supreme courts around the world often reach similar results.

[45] According to s 3 para 4, Justices may remain professors at a German university, albeit the duties at the Court take precedence over any academic activity. Otherwise, political positions are incompatible with serving at the Court: s 3 para 3.

[46] Donald Kommers, Russel Miller, *The Constitutional Jurisprudence,* 38 (n 38).

[47] In Germany, this is one element of the strategy of the political party '*Alternative für Deutschland*', or '*AfD*', which both attacks individual members of the Court, denounces rulings, and launches cases to expose the Court as a collaborator in the corrupt and elitist 'system parties', a concept taken from Nazi rhetoric in the 1930s. On the rule of law crisis that tries to enlist classic sceptics of judicial review. See Susanne Baer, 'The Rule of—and not by any—Law. On Constitutionalism' (2018) 71.1 Current Legal Problems 335–368; Nicola Lacey, 'Populism and the Rule of Law' (2019) 15 Annual Review of Law and Social Science 79–96.

generally understood as a bulwark against arbitrary abuse, political excess, and a protector of a middle-ground consensus, and eventually, justice. Comparatively speaking, it enjoys neither the majestic yet somewhat removed standing of the French Conseil, nor does it occupy a public position of fame and heroism, like the US or Canadian Supreme Court or the Inter-American Court of Human Rights at times. Depending on the conceptual background, it is rather seen as a factor of 'the integration of society',[48] often referred to as a 'guardian'[49] of fundamental rights, even a guiding light with its 'order of values' (*Werteordnung*), and finally a safety belt for democracy and sometimes emergency brake, specifically regarding European and international integration.

A strong constitutional court is, then, always at risk. Right from the start, the Court, while not free in taking or rejecting a case but for reasons defined by the Act on the Constitutional Court that defines the details of the procedures listed in article 93, was confronted with highly political questions, with strong political actors involved, the public engaged, and media attention present. Early controversies around an attempt to have the Court allow the Chancellors move to rearm Germany, with rather aggressive disrespect shown from members of government towards the Court,[50] as well as decisions on federalism or when the Court rejected the attempt to create a government-controlled TV station, may thus best be understood as important evolutionary moments in implementing the system itself. When the government did neither properly fund the Court, nor showed adequate respect to follow its rulings, the Court made an eminent declaratory move to establish itself as a supreme constitutional organ. To gain the standing it did not yet have, the Court did not only issue bold decisions, in that it confronted the government and political majority within its constitutional limits. In addition, facing outright rejection and dismissal by key politicians, the Court issued a memorandum (*Denkschrift*), authored by Justice Gerhard Leibholz, in 1952. It now officially described itself as the 'guardian of the constitution' (*Hüter der Verfassung*) and claimed equal standing in the arrangement of political power, next to President, Chancellor, Parliament (*Bundestag*) and Second Chamber (*Bundesrat*). This meant a budget of one's own to be negotiated directly with parliament rather than allocated by government. It resulted in a new building and in modern transparency. It was very different from the old palaces of justice of regular courts. And it allowed the Court to become a key player in public affairs.

2. A Slow Start, the 'Never Again', and 'One of You We Are'

The Court, as the key proponent of Germany's new constitutionalism, did not come to its recent standing easily. Early decisions signalled a rather conservative stance. The Court did not expose much sympathy for minorities and their fundamental rights. Namely, homosexual

---

[48] Rudolf Smend, *Verfassung und Verfassungsrecht* (Duncker & Humblot, Berlin, 1928).

[49] The concept goes back to authoritarian as well as committed Nazi legal thinker Carl Schmitt, 'Der Hüter der Verfassung' (1929) 55 Archiv des öffentlichen Rechts 161–237, with a response in 1932, by Hans Kelsen, in *Wer soll der Hüter der Verfassung sein?* (Nomos, Baden-Baden, 2008) 1873–1922. See also Oliver Lembcke, *Hüter der Verfassung* (Mohr Siebeck, Tübingen, 2007); Günter Frankenberg, 'Hüter der Verfassung einer Zivilgesellschaft' (1996) Kritische Justiz 1–14.

[50] BVerfGE 2, 79—*Plenargutachten Heuß (Plenary Report, 1952)* describes and discusses how politics may attempt to manipulate a court. For an in depth study of the history see Heinz Laufer, *Verfassungsgerichtsbarkeit und politischer Prozess* (Mohr Siebeck, Tübingen, 1968). A history of the Court that focuses on the personalities at work is Rolf Lamprecht, *Das Bundesverfassungsgericht* (bpb, Bonn, 2011).

men, despite their suffering from Nazi persecution, had their attempt to not be further stigmatized as criminals rejected. This rejection was founded on a striking mix of references to medical, psychological and other academic findings at the time, sheer prejudice and stereotype, and moral and theological considerations unabashedly used to justify discrimination.[51] In 2013, the Court at least confirmed that this ruling was outdated.[52] In addition, the early Court did cling to another somewhat problematic tradition, in protecting the traditions of the executive. In 1958, the Court interpreted article 33 para 5 to privilege members of the civil service, which laid the ground for a long line of rulings that regulate specific aspects from selection and promotion to pay schemes, yet also serves to justify the prohibition of a strike to call for better working conditions, i.e. by public school teachers, and was referred to in striking down more flexible working time schemes, i.e. part-time positions, in higher ranks.[53]

Eventually, German constitutionalism was however also detailed in decisions that said, 'never again'. Primarily, this is based on the Courts decision to allow for a prohibition of the then Nazi-revisionist political party of the SRP.[54] Yet note that this was quickly followed by the prohibition of the communist political party, the KPD.[55] The rulings have been and are still referred to as an emphatic 'yes' to a liberal democracy, as part of the commitment to join the European and global community of such states, to be accepted after the catastrophe before. Until the Court revisited the issue in 2017, it was, notably, the KPD ruling that provided the canon of the basic concepts of the meaning of constitutional democracy, updated and reformed, by also considering the jurisprudence of the ECHR, in the substantive NPD ruling.[56]

More importantly, there were early signs of a willingness to strengthen individual liberties, including a critical civil society, as a key feature of a democracy that deserves its name. Somewhat surprisingly, a ruling on professional liberties of pharmacists was used to denounce a patriarchal authoritarian state.[57] However, the Justices were less courageous when they were asked to protect the many young men who refused the draft for pacifist reasons.[58] Yet they refused to accept Chancellor Adenauer's plan to run a government TV station.[59] Namely, it was the Senate with, at the time, mostly conservative Justices that blocked the Chancellor himself, who then is famously on record to declare that '[t]he whole cabinet unanimously understands the ruling of the GFCC to be wrong', which provoked a political storm of protest, and the conservative President of the Court officially stated that 'Each and every one is free in assessing rulings by the Federal Constitutional Court or also consider them to be wrong. Yet according to the constitutional order, no constitutional organ may decide or officially declare that a ruling by the Federal Constitutional Court is not in line with the law.'[60] Eventually, the government was happier with rulings in the years to follow, but the

---

[51] BVerfGE 6, 389—*Homosexualität* (*Homosexuality, 1957*).

[52] BVerfGE 133, 59, 57—*Sukzessivadoption* (*Successive Adoption, 2013*).

[53] BVerfGE 107, 218 and 107, 258—*Beamtenbesoldung Ost I and Lippeverband* (*East German Civil Service Salary I and II, 2003*); BVerfGE 148, 296—*Streikverbot für Beamte* (*No Right to Strike for Civil Servants, 2018*); BVerfGE 149, 1—*Hochschulkanzler Brandenburg* (*University Chancellor, 2018*).

[54] BVerfGE 2, 1—*SRP-Verbot* (*Prohipition of Socialist Reichs Party, 1952*). The case is excerpted and discussed in Donald Kommers, Russel Miller, *The Constitutional Jurisprudence*, Chapter V (n 38). See also Peter Niesen, 'Anti-extremism, negative republicanism, civic society: Three paradigms for banning political parties' (2002) 3/7 German Law Journal.

[55] BVerfGE 5, 85—*KPD-Verbot* (*Prohibition of KPD, 1956*).

[56] BVerfGE 144, 20—*NPD-Verbotsverfahren* (*NPD Ban Proceedings, 2017*).

[57] BVerfGE 7, 377—*Apotheken-Urteil* (*Pharmacy, 1958*).

[58] BVerfGE 12, 45—*Kriegsdienstverweigerung I* (*Conscientious Objection, 1960*).

[59] BVerfGE 12, 205—*Rundfunkentscheidung I* (*State TV, 1961*).

[60] Declared 16 March 1961, reprinted in Rolf Lamprecht, *Das Bundesverfassungsgericht* (bpb, Bonn, 2011) 82.

Court had, publicly, won a fight, and established its standing to guard the constitution, whatever political power wants.

In another version of 'never again', the Court declared pension rights for Nazi civil servants unconstitutional. The long ruling exposed the guilt of a German elite at the heart of 'the state', a 'perverted civil service', now trying to appear 'neutral'. That '131-judgement' opposed attempts to reintegrate such 'professionals', based on an understanding of the past to allow for a new beginning. Authored by a mix of people formerly excluded from such ranks, this was a bold move. To no surprise, the Court faced strong and fervent opposition from many sides, including, again, lead legal academics.[61]

However, German constitutionalism continued to be informed by 'politics of the past', responding to questions of transitional justice, and directly confronting a fascist autocracy with an aspiring democracy, based on fundamental rights protected by the rule of law. In 1994, the Court stated that the prohibition of a rally at which the persecution of Jewish people in the 'Third Reich' will be denied is compatible with constitutional requirements.[62] In 2009, the Court stated that criminal law specifically targeting antisemitism and racist hatred is not a 'general law' that may limit free speech, according to article 5, but nonetheless an immanent exception from the rule of content neutrality, 'in view of the injustice and the horror which National Socialist rule inflicted on Europe and large parts of the world, defying general categories, and of the establishment of the Federal Republic of Germany which was understood as an antithesis of this'.[63] Notably, responding to two requests from Parliament, the Court did not outlaw the neo-fascist party NPD because, one, it either refused to hear a case on parties without the state withdrawing its undercover agents or, two, it emphasized a prohibition of a party to be the *ultima ratio* of a defensive democracy not to be used when there is no real threat to the system, because the party is too weak. However, in these rulings, as in the foundational exposure of its notion of a constitutional democracy in the *KPD*-case,[64] the Court reminded everyone that the 'never again' informs the constitution.

3. Post-1968

In Germany, as in many other countries, '1968' has become the code for students protesting authority, women demanding self-determination and equality, and, as student organizer Rudi Dutschke famously demanded, 'march through the institutions', setting out for reform. If society changes that much, constitutionalism changes as well, yet often slowly, and not in one sweeping move. Indeed, the student protest against former Nazis teaching at universities, and uncritical academic traditions, reached the Court in the early 1970s. In the first of now many 'university rulings', 398 professors protested reform legislation, joined by another 600, because a German state had mandated all public university bodies to comprise a 'three-third parity' of professors, assistants, and students. This in fact took the majority away from professors and redefined the group of academics to be more than those with the 'Habilitation', a post-doc procedure to filter academic achievement. In a 6:2 decision, the Court accepted that students and assistants might have a vote, but restored the professor's majority in academic matters, which the dissenters criticized as judicial overreach.[65]

---

[61] Stolleis, *Geschichte*, 161–164 (n 29).
[62] BVerfGE 90, 241—*Auschwitzlüge (Lie, 1994)*.
[63] BVerfGE 124, 300—Rudolf Heß Gedenkfeier *(Wunsiedel, 2009)*.
[64] BVerfGE 5, 85—*KPD-Verbot (Prohibition of the KPD, 1956)*.
[65] BVerfGE 35, 79—*Hochschul-Urteil (Universities I, 1973)*.

In fact, many issues of 1968 are closely related to fundamental rights, and the Court has decided some of them, yet not always in what may be a progressive mode. How do new ways of thinking informed by a pluralist and participatory vision of a vibrant democracy, by active citizens that engage in critical conversations, and by a rejection of patriarchy and serious demands for gender equality, inform constitutionalism? Its academic proponents seemed to remain largely untouched, 'structurally conservative'. The Court has largely been an educator in demanding 'freedom for those who think differently' (*Freiheit der Andersdenkenden*), a phrase from socialist theorist Rosa Luxemburg. This applies to decisions restricting police power, and demanding reforms of marriage and family law. At the time, some rulings certainly boldly moved against a mainstream. However, there is also the other side, as in the university decision. Another example is the ruling on the emergency amendment of article 13 to allow for larger than ever surveillance of the home without prior judicial control was declared constitutional, the first decision in which three Justices used the newly introduced option to publish their reasons to dissent.[66] Overall, the Court is still remembered to be a defender of individual civil rights, including religious freedom and, in a seminal step in securing rights for all, individual rights for those imprisoned.[67] In 1977, the Court also demanded clear and consistent rules for life long imprisonment, which must ensure that there remains 'hope to regain one's freedom',[68] a predecessor of the later 'right to hope' in ECHR jurisprudence.

During the 1970s, fundamental rights of freedom of speech, press and the arts (article 5) and freedom of assembly (article 8) were defined as key components of a democratic society, with what may be called a republican vision of citizenship. In addition, the Court used the principle of proportionality to require police and protesters to negotiate,[69] which may have contributed to build a constitutionalism of middle ground. Yet at the same time, all state governments started in 1972 to test the loyalty of all civil servants, including schoolteachers, to the constitutional order, in what was called 'radicals order' (*Radikalenerlass*). This move, in fact, led to a denial of access to their profession, specifically a prohibition of their profession (*Berufsverbot*) to around 130 young educators. Prominent intellectuals protested, like Sartre, Russell, or Mitterand from France, but in 1975, the Court accepted this practice, again a bulwark in defending the traditions of the German civil service,[70] which for many ignored German history itself. Three Justices dissented, sharply. By now, the ruling is largely seen as an exception to the rule rather than its emanation.

Also, the Court strengthened public broadcasting as a critical source of information. Politically, this also legitimizes a general fee, and mandates pluralist, not exclusively party-driven boards to govern the programme. However, and to be eventually developed as a strong line of jurisprudence in the years to come, the Court first emphasized the rights of personality as an individual right to protect the private lives even of prominent people, and, as in the *Lüth* case, reemphasized its power to control the application of law between private parties.[71] In addition, the Court explained, in another 'never again', that courts may move beyond the wording of a statute if there is a higher calling of justice, namely, constitutional law,

---

[66] BVerfGE 30, 1—*Abhörurteil* (*Eavesdropping*, 1970).

[67] In 1972, the GFCC dropped the concept of a special relationship between individuals and the state that would allow for unlimited uses of power (*besonderes Gewaltverhältnis*), in demanding the power in prison to be based on law (*Gesetzesvorbehalt*), BVerfGE 33, 1—*Strafgefangene* (*Prison, 1972*). The case arose around controlling mailings from prisoners, which the Court considered to be protected as free speech; the law was passed in 1976.

[68] BVerfGE 45, 187—*Lebenslange Freiheitsstrafe* (*Lifelong Imprisonment, 1977*).

[69] BVerfGE 69, 315—*Brokdorf* (*Brokdorf, 1985*).

[70] BVerfGE 39, 334—*Extremistenbeschluß* (*Prohibition of Profession, 1975*).

[71] BVerfGE 7, 198—*Lüth* (*Lüth, 1958*).

THE EVOLUTION AND *GESTALT* OF THE GERMAN CONSTITUTION   179

that calls for it. So when the overwhelmingly powerful Springer press, the main publisher of highly influential tabloids and weekly journals, published a fake interview with the then wife of the Shah of Iran, Soraya, and the civil courts had issued damages without a basis in statutory law, the Court upheld the ruling: 'Law and statutes do usually fall into one, but not necessarily and always.'[72] In light of German history, this may be read as another 'no' to the positivist stance mandating the application of laws even when they are utterly unjust.

4. Post-1989

However, German constitutionalism was still a scarred affair. The framers and drafters deliberately named the constitution a 'Basic Law' at a time at which Germany was not united, and thus insisted on what seemed to be a Cold War dream that would never come true, the reunification of East and West. The Court followed that route in a decision to uphold the politically very controversial Basic Relations Treaty with East Germany, in which then social-democrat Chancellor Brandt was attacked as bowing to Communism and selling out on the constitutional commitment to never legally recognize the GDR as a state. However, the Court exposed the 'dual nature' of the compromise, and, in what it explicitly called judicial restraint, in fact allowed a rather controversial politics to move on.[73]

As such, the Basic Law had always envisioned a real constitution for all of Germany, to be passed by referendum, in article 146, and allowed to add new states, in article 23. When the wall between East and West Germany fell in 1989, one would have expected another wave of changes, if not the end of the provisional Basic Law. Some call it the biggest challenge to the Basic Law ever.[74] In a civil society-driven democratic moment, many expected the passing by referendum of a now truly national constitution. However, this was not the chosen path.[75] Rather, and despite significant efforts in civil society to discuss a new Basic Law, micro surgical adjustments were agreed upon. Politicians in charge decided to use article 23 to add states to the federation. While some saw this as a rather colonial takeover, with deep ramifications in German politics, it was organized in the Unification Treaty between the GDR and West Germany of 1990 and may be described as a constitutional amendment by ratifying legislation, an exception from the rule accepted as historically singular by the Court.[76] Again, and typical for a political culture committed to the rule of law, namely constitutionalism, the Court was called upon to decide on the issue in many cases. Basically, it saw 'the German question' to have been properly answered,[77] giving way to political compromise.

In substance, the Treaty recommended a discussion on necessary changes of the Basic Law in article 5. A Commission formed by thirty-two members of parliament and state governments decided on rather small changes of the text. They added a state obligation to

---

[72] BVerfGE 34, 269—*Soraya (Soraya, 1973)*.

[73] BVerfGE 36, 1—*Grundlagenvertrag (East-West Basic Treaty, 1973)*. Shortly after the Treaty was ratified, both states joined the United Nations. The Court emphasized that, 'The principle of judicial self-restraint is aimed at keeping open the leeway for political action guaranteed by the Constitution for the other constitutional organs. It also declared Germans to be more than citizens of the Federal Republic, thus incorporating East Germans.

[74] Dreier, IPE § 1, n 58.

[75] The treaty recommended an assessment of the necessity of constitutional amendments; a 32-member Commission, with delegates from both chambers, thus all-party politicians.

[76] BVerfGE 84, 90—*Bodenreform I (Land Reform I, 1991)*, on expropriation in the GDR as dealt with in the Unification Treaty.

[77] Internationally, the corresponding act was the '2 plus 4 Treaty', with both German states and the Allied states France, Britain, Russia and the US, 12 September 1990.

implement gender equality (article 3 para 2 clause 2), disability as a non-discrimination clause (article 3 para 3 clause 2) and environmental protection as a state goal (article 20a). All of these are not unification specifics but entered through this window of opportunity driven by long time feminist efforts to clarify the legitimacy of positive action to end sex discrimination, and international efforts to secure rights against disabling societal standards and facts, most prominently resulting in the Convention on the Rights of Persons with Disabilities, eventually passed in 2006, and driven by, among others, German legal scholar and activist Theresia Degener.[78] In fact, the focus was to adjust federalism to the enlargement in the East.

5. EU Integration

As in any other member state of the EU, European integration[79] has been and continues to be an evolutionary force in national constitutional law. Maybe a constitution like the Basic Law that opts for 'open statehood'[80] has an easier way to meet such challenges. However, this does not do away with the substantive challenge to conceptualize multi-level constitutionalism, and the institutional challenge of one national court ruling on a transnational governance structure. Yet where the core commitment is not a vision of the nation, which had been corrupted by the fascist regime, nor sovereignty as independence, but rather 'the determination to promote world peace as an equal partner in a united Europe', as stated in the Preamble of the Basic Law, European integration poses a specific set of questions. By now, several clauses specifically address Europe, like article 28 para 2 clause 3 on local voting rights, article 88 on the European Central Bank or articles 45 and 52 para 3a on institutions for European politics. More broadly, the European question in German constitutional law became and is still a quest for basic standards of fundamental rights, and of democracy, albeit specifically defined.[81]

As an immediate reaction to unification, article 23 was removed, but, only two years later, it was turned into the clause that constitutionalized European integration. The European constitutional scheme also consists of article 28 para 1 clause 3, which extends municipal voting rights to EU citizens, and article 88, which covers the European Central Bank, while articles 45 and 52 para 3a establish committees for European Affairs in both chambers. This resulted in the rather late need for constitutional amendments when the EU became a political union in 1992. In one exceptional case, even the Basic Law itself was swiftly amended to implement an ECJ ruling, on access of women to the military.[82]

Yet, as elsewhere, EU integration is often controversial, depending on one's idea of the nation and European solidarity, as well as one's attitude towards specific developments in

---

[78] See Gerard Quinn and Theresia Degener, *Human rights and disability* (OHCHR, UN, New York and Geneva, 2002).

[79] Karl-Peter Sommermann, s 14, in Armin von Bogdandy, Pedro Cruz Villalón and Peter M Huber (eds), *Handbuch Ius Publicum Europaeum* (CF Müller, Heidelberg, 2008).

[80] Christian Bumke, Andreas Voßkuhle, *Casebook on German Constitutional Law* (OUP, Oxford, 2019) 16 ff.

[81] For a critical account, see Daniel Halberstam and Christoph Möllers, 'The German constitutional court says "Ja zu Deutschland!"' (2009) 10 German Law Journal 1241–1258.

[82] *Tanja Kreil v Bundesrepublik Deutschland* [2000] ECLI:EU:C:2000:2, which followed *Angela Maria Sirdar v The Army Board and Secretary of State for Defence* [1999] ECLI:EU:C:1999:523. The ECJ held the broad exclusion of women from all military service with weapons to be discrimination based on sex, yet accepts exceptions under specific circumstances, i.e. on submarines. The ruling was met with 'wild protest' (Werner Heun, 'Art 12a', in Horst Dreier, *Kommentar zum Grundgesetz* (3rd ed. CH Beck, Munich, 2013), with reference to eminent jurist *Rupert Scholz* who saw this as an act '*ultra vires*') yet was also widely accepted. The relevant clause in art 12a on military service was introduced in 1968 and amended in 2000.

or driven by EU law. There is a strong German commitment towards the EU, and politicians are deeply dedicated to Europe. Yet academic EU law experts are also often seen as overly post-national, idealistic pro-EU integrationists. The German *Staatsrechtslehrer* (professor of national constitutional law) works in a tradition of a belief in the nation-state, engaged in methodological nationalism. Thus, for some, the Basic Law is by now a paradox as a 'European constitution'.[83] For others, it is one version of 'embedded constitutionalism'.[84] According to the Court's jurisprudence, the national constitution safeguards what should remain German while being a member of the EU.

6. Globalization

Germany, and German constitutionalism, has not only become European, but also went global. Certainly, a constitutional history specifically meant to reintegrate a nation that had brought so much horror to the world is bound to go international. However, to embed a national constitution in an international legal environment poses challenges, nonetheless.

When it comes to fundamental rights, Germany is first and foremost a member state of the Council of Europe, the larger and more clearly political Europe when compared to the EU. Global developments like the Declaration of Human Rights inspired the framers and the drafters, which may be one reason why German constitutionalism developed with a sense of always being already in tune with global standards. For a long time, German constitutional law thus remained rather unaffected by international norms. However, this changed with the growing importance of the Council system. Starting out with a Commission, to be eventually replaced by a fully developed international court, the ECtHR in Strasbourg, it is now a beacon of a strong commitment to human rights stretching from Russia to Portugal.

The commitment to Strasbourg paved the way to an integration of UN law. Beyond cases in which international law is a matter of fact, as in international tax relations, or regarding the recognition of degrees, or dealing with international relationships and families, or child abduction and international crime, German constitutional jurisprudence now integrates ratified UN law into its interpretation of the Basic Law.[85]

7. Changes of the Text

Generally, the development of German constitutional law is largely attributed to the Court, backed up and inspired by the academic field of constitutional law. However, there have also been changes of the text of the Basic Law. This amendment procedure is governed by article 79 that allows for amendments, which must be incorporated in the text (para 1), a transparency rule. Yet more importantly, amendments must not ever violate the eternal guarantees of human dignity and the governing principles of the state, as defined in article 20, because of the 'eternity clause' in article 79 para 3. It is a barrier to constitutional change and has become an important building block of German constitutionalism in the EU.[86]

---

[83] Dreier, IPE § 1, n 65, with more references to academic positions on the issue.

[84] Another element is the conversation among courts. See Susanne Baer, 'Comparing Courts,' in Anna-Bettina Kaiser, Niels Petersen and Johannes Saurer (eds), *The U.S. Supreme Court and Contemporary Constitutional Law* (Nomos, Baden-Baden, 2018) 253–271.

[85] For more details, see below, Section D.

[86] Below Section D.

182 SUSANNE BAER

Beyond this 'eternity' limit, amendments must be based on what seems like a large majority of two-thirds in both houses, but the practice of German politics proves otherwise. The two large parties have been able to meet this requirement (and regularly so). Thus, more than half the text has seen changes, which have there by added 50 percent to its volume. Two significant moves may be understood as follow-ups to 1949. Otherwise, amending activities are not perceived as a sign of weakness, but understood to indicate the vitality of the constitution, a document that counts in politics.[87]

Within ten years of the Second World War, Germany was ready to reintroduce military power in its *Wehrverfassung* (Military Constitution) in 1956. This is a follow-up action to the original drafting of the Basic Law. Since 1950, the German conservative government under Adenauer tried to rearm the country, partly considering the crisis of Korea and the presence of the Russian Army in the GDR that actively fought a civil uprising on 17 June 1953. However, many Germans, including the Protestant church, the unions and prominent intellectuals refused the move to militarize again, while the Social Democrats were afraid it would inhibit reunification. A pacifist manifesto was passed in 1955 at the historical site of German constitutionalism, the *Paulskirche* (Paul's church) in Frankfurt, but it did not prevent the changes.[88] While article 24 para 2 made it conditional to be part of a collective system of security, namely NATO, joined in 1955, the supermajority added to the list of federal powers in article 73 n 1 'defense, including conscription'. For them, building a national army was another step to become part of 'the West'. Yet the controversies indicated deep cleavages in the German society. However, this also laid ground for a constitutionalism that includes the military, a power not beyond that law.

Discussions of German military involvement now often invoke the Basic Law. The constitution does not only grant powers, but is interpreted to organize their use as well, even in military matters. Considering this, it is not as surprising that in 1994, the Court created a 'parliament's army'. It held that every out-of-area mission of German Armed Forces must be mandated by a majority in the German federal parliament, the *Bundestag*.[89] Thus, the constitution even subjects a classic site of exclusively executive power to democratic deliberation and approval.

The second follow-up, by amending the Basic Law, dates from 1968. The revolutionary sixties were the time of protest when the governing parties set out to prepare for the state of emergency, in the Emergency Constitution, or '*Notstandsverfassung*'. In Germany, there was much reason to protest even beyond the general mood of '68, in another version of 'never again'. Many feared an authoritarian state with secret police, after the Nazi terror regime had merged police and military forces to carry out domestic operations. All of this came at a time of loud protest about former Nazi traditions in universities, including law schools, and a time of international protest about the Shah regime in Iran, and against the US war in Vietnam. Despite being highly controversial in substance as well as in style, the political majority nonetheless inserted twenty-eight new articles into the Basic Law. Changes ranged from new limitations to fundamental rights (articles 9, 10, 11) to a whole new chapter on national self-defence (article 115a–115l). Namely, these amendments created options to react to domestic crises that later became the focus of the 'German 9/11' question, when the Court was asked whether an 'Aviation Security Act' may ever allow a civil plane to be shot if captured by terrorists and likely to be used as their weapon. After the First Senate had held that

---

[87] Dreier, IPE § 1, n 45-6.
[88] Dreier, IPE § 1, n 73.
[89] BVerfGE 90, 286, 1672 ff—*Out-of-area-Einsätze (Out-of-area Operations, 2001)*.

no human being can ever be sacrificed for anything, because of the eternal guarantee of the inviolability of human dignity in article 1 para 1 of the Basic Law, the Second Senate called for a rare Plenary decision of the whole court, to ensure the coherence of both senates, and upheld a law that allowed the government, yet not one cabinet member alone, to decide that military forces may be deployed domestically in certain limited times of crisis.[90]

Also, the emergency constitution amended the fundamental right in article 10 to detail the conditions of wiretapping, including the replacement of judicial review with *ex post* political oversight. Since then, there have been and are influential voices that call this amendment unconstitutional itself[91] because it violates the eternity clause of article 79 para 3. The Court was split but upheld the changes in a (rare) 5:3 ruling.[92] By now, the Court has called for proportionality of security measures again and again. This is based on a jurisprudence that gives standing to individuals to directly challenge legislation, based on the fact that security measures are designed so that people do not know whether they are subject to surveillance or not. Then, the Court mandated the legislature to install effective mechanisms of control and oversight, to compensate for the impossibility of judicial review in an actual case. In addition, the Court repeatedly emphasized that the collection of personal data must be restricted, and strictly limited to legitimate goals that outweigh the privacy interests at hand, in each case.[93] Yet in 1998, police powers to fight organized crime motivated a similarly substantial—and controversial—amendment of article 13 to now allow for wiretapping in the home. In a controversial ruling, the Court upheld the change, rejecting an eternity clause challenge.[94] And in 1993, which were the early days of threats of terrorism, another controversial amendment was passed, based on a compromise by the then grand coalition of social democrats and Christian conservatives, to article 16a regarding the then largely restricted right to asylum. Claims that the restrictions violated the eternity clause that protects dignity in article 1 were rejected by the Court.[95]

Regarding changes of the text of the Basic Law, there was another set of less controversial moves. These amendments, in various reform efforts, were meant to repair the unsatisfactory state of financial affairs. A large reform in 1969, also reacting to the recession in 1966/67, in fact remodelled federalism by replacing a system of dualism with cooperation. At the time, the tendency was in fact to centralize power, while later, the wish became to re-empower the states. Several grand efforts were made in Commissions on Federalism Reform. Yet they were not as ideological as at other times in the long history of German federalisms. This mode of distributing power was always subject to modifications, but largely not charged with substantive questions of fundamental rights.

---

[90] There are three decisions on the Aviation Security Act: BVerfGE 115, 118—*Luftsicherheitsgesetz (First Senate, 2006)*, BVerfGE 132, 1—*Luftsicherheitsgesetz (Plenary Ruling, 2012)*, BVerfGE 133, 241—*Luftsicherheitsgesetz (Second Senate, 2014)*. See Kai Moller, 'On treating persons as ends: The German Aviation Security Act, Human Dignity, and the German Federal Constitutional Court' (2006) Public Law 457–466; Russell A Miller, 'Balancing security and liberty in Germany' (2010) 4 J Nat'l Sec L & Pol'y 369.

[91] Among them was influential scholar and commentator of the Basic Law Günter Dürig, in Hans Spanner and others (eds), *Festgabe für Theodor Maunz* (CH Beck, Munich, 1971) 41.

[92] However, the Court accepted this, with proportionality requirements. See BVerfGE 30, 1—*Abhörurteil (Wiretapping, 1970)*; BVerfGE 93, 181—*Rasterfahndung (Investigation, 1995)*, updated in BVerfGE 100, 313—*Telekommunikationüberwachung I (Telecommunications I,* 1998). The commission is called the G-10-Commission, since it controls the implementation of the law that implements art 10.

[93] There is a long line of rulings, the most significant of which are published by the Court in a special collection in English. Today's doctrinal standards are consolidated in BVerfGE 141, 220—*BKA (BKA, 2016)*.

[94] BVerfGE 109, 279, 315 ff—*Großer Lauschangriff (Grand Acoustic Surveillance, 2004)*.

[95] BVerfGE 94, 49, 103—*Sichere Drittstaaten (Safe Third Country, 1996)*.

Also, in 1993, the *pouvoir constitué* amended article 16 to article 16a, which basically did away with the formerly broadly granted fundamental right to asylum. It is also one of several articles in the Basic Law that were not just amended but detailed like a statute. According to many, this is considered to be at least a sin in style, as well as an example of over-constitutionalization, thereby hindering future 'politics of compromise'.[96]

8. Changes in Society

German constitutionalism had a slow start, then developed an emphatic 'never again' to the past and added a clear commitment to the future. To explain a more than purely positivist legal practice, there is the concept of 'silent constitutional change' (*stiller Verfassungswandel*), which in fact is not more than applying the constitution to new sets of facts. However, in a legalistic and academic legal culture, this is defined as a distinct 'method' in German legal thinking and has never been very controversial. As such, German constitutionalism is clearly devoted to what has been otherwise metaphorically described as a 'living tree': the present and the future. And certainly, when major social, cultural, and economic as well as political developments become an item of constitutional law, controversies and conflict abound.

a. Proportionality: Liberal Constitutionalism Replaces Authoritarian States of Law
First and foremost, German constitutionalism is one factor to build a society based on fundamental respect of each and every one, namely: dignity, and equal liberties, as guaranteed in articles 1, 2 and 3, which may be read as a basic triangle of fundamental rights.[97] Yet to overcome authoritarian, patriarchal and illiberal traditions, another feature of German constitutionalism seems crucial: proportionality. Today, proportionality is a well-known and widely discussed doctrine in fundamental rights law, a backbone of a deep commitment to civil liberties as such. It entered the constitutional scene, coming from longer trajectories in administrative law, in an economic context of market liberties. Namely, when a pharmacist complained that he was prohibited from opening a pharmacy because the local government considered one to be enough, the Court took a sweeping move to denounce such measures, unknown to 'other countries with a comparable civilisatory standard'. In fact, the Court reversed the old order, and prioritized individual liberties over a general state interest. It voted for a society comprised of individuals. The state may only limit in their self-determination based on law (*Gesetzesvorbehalt*), thus with the legitimation of the political process, and if it pursues legitimate aims (*legitime Ziele*), employs suitable (*geeignet*) means, that are necessary (*erforderlich*), in the sense of being the least intrusive, and impose a bearable (*zumutbar*) burden considering all relevant interests, are proportional.[98] Eventually, then, proportionality became one indispensable component to rationally adjudicate whether an interference of any fundamental right amounts to a violation, in that it cannot be justified as

---

[96] Dieter Grimm, 'Wie man eine Verfassung verderben kann', in Dieter Grimm, *Die Verfassung und die Politik: Einsprüche in Störfällen* (CH Beck, Munich, 2001) 126.

[97] Susanne Baer, 'Dignity, liberty, equality: A fundamental rights triangle of Constitutionalism' (2009) 4 University of Toronto Law Journal, 417–468.

[98] BVerfGE 7, 377—*Apotheken-Urteil* (*Pharmacy Case, 1958*). In that ruling, the Court used a 'gradation' scheme (*Stufentheorie*) like levels of scrutiny. Recently, the Court does not rigidly define such levels, but differentiates, as always and to allow for more precision to capture the meaning and effects of a legislative act, but also to allow for more flexibility, the type and intensity of an interference, the weight of corresponding legitimate interests, and additional relevant factors.

a proportionate means to reach legitimate aims. By now, it is applied to rights of liberty and equality alike.

b. Gender Equality, Gender

Equality, and namely, gender equality, does not come naturally to constitutional democracies. In drafting the Basic Law, it needed thousands of postcards to pass an explicit equal rights clause, to address sex inequality in article 3 para 2, amended by adding emphasis after 1989 to honour gender equality efforts in East Germany. Yet in 1948, statutory law and culture was patriarchal, with a rigid ideology of the good German mother, which informs the special emphasis on protecting mothers in article 6 para 4, and with hegemonic masculinity deeply injured by defeat in the war, which may be one way to look at the low level of protection for children born to unwed mothers, in article 6 para 5. The Basic Law itself postponed the implementation of gender equality, but only for a few years to 1953, according to article 117 para 1.

Yet when politics did not even intend to move then, it was left to the Court to insist on gender equality. Driven by what must be rather courageous and exceptional individual complaints by women, some backed up by the non-partisan German Female Lawyers Association DJB, but in conservative political times of the 'Adenauer years', the Court was required to say that this right indeed applied throughout the legal system, thus to marriage and family law as well. There was one female Justice at the time, yet with colleagues willing to take fundamental rights seriously, and indeed apply them. A long line of gender equality rulings started with striking down the patriarchal rule that the father decides if parents disagree (*Stichentscheid*), defended by the government as protection of 'marriage and the family in its Christian-occidental tradition'.[99] The tone was soft, calling upon the 'natural consensus among rational human beings', and the focus was the well-being of the child. Grudgingly, relevant actors followed suit.

Starting as early as 1978, the Court held, and reemphasized in a consistent series of cases, that individuals who change their gender, as transsexuals, have a right to be recognized as such, and be protected against prejudice by issuing papers that do not reveal their past.[100] Less complicated, yet socially at least as unusual, the Court also held that individuals medically defined as neither male nor female, but born intersexual, must be given the right of recognition in personal status laws, based on the protection of one's identity, according to the right to self-determination (article 2 para 1) and the right to human dignity (article 1 para 1) combined.[101] Interestingly, this ruling got a lot of attention at the time of its pronouncement. It managed to overcome stereotypes of femininity and masculinity, although the extreme political right rallied, and continues to rally, against 'abnormalities' to advocate for a patriarchal restoration of 'the family'. Additionally, after years of fighting for gender equality in job searches without much success, such advertisements swiftly started to address 'male, female or third gender candidates' ('m/w/d'). However, some also started to question

---

[99] BVerfGE 10, 59—*Elterliche Gewalt* (*Paternal Preference, 1959*). Contextual information may be found in Rolf Lamprecht, *Das Bundesverfassungsgericht* (bpb, Bonn, 2011) 73 ff. The ruling inspired then lawyer and now Justice of the US Supreme Court, Ruth Bader Ginsburg in her argument to strike down gender-based classifications, in *Reed v Reed* 404 US 71 (1971); as she describes in the Foreword to the third edition of Donald Kommers, Russel Miller, *The Constitutional Jurisprudence* (n 38).

[100] BVerfGE 49, 286—*Transsexuelle* (*Transsexuals I, 1978*); followed by BVerfGE 60, 123; 88, 87; 115, 1; 116, 243; 121, 175; 128, 109—*Junge Transexuelle* (*Young Transexualls, 1982, 1993, 2005, 2006, 2008, 2011*).

[101] BVerfGE 147, 1—*Geschlechteridentität/ Das Dritte Geschlecht* (*Gender Identity/Third Option, 2017*).

whether affirmative action to secure equal opportunities for women must now be modified or dropped entirely, in yet another attempt of rollback.

In the twenty-first century, the Court also insisted that homosexual relationships and families have fundamental rights and shall be protected against discrimination. Different from some other countries, however, it was not the Court that implemented this change. Notably, the Basic Law does not feature sexual orientation or identity as a listed inequality in article 3 para 3, despite the history of Nazi persecution of gay men.[102] However, the Court has explained that discrimination on the basis of sexual orientation is prohibited, at least implicitly, because it resembles those inequalities the text mentions.[103] Yet again, this was designed to be incremental rather than revolutionary. For example, in the ruling on equal rights to adopt a partner's child, the issue was framed as one about protecting children from insecurity first, and the discriminatory character of the statute was not considered. With references to the legal developments in other countries, such socially controversial and morally loaded questions are answered in a sober tone, with a systematic analysis of the law, in style that is as doctrinal as can be.

c. Reproductive Rights, Medical Ethics

Socially, other questions are even more controversial, in that they are loaded with moral as well as religious preconceptions. In a constitutional culture deeply committed to learning from history, medical ethics have not only foundational status, but also carry histories. In Germany, these histories are the horror of medical experiments in the Concentration Camps associated with medical doctor Mengele, the Nazi violence of forced sterilization to prevent 'unworthy life', and population politics with a rigid regimen to produce 'Aryan Germans', including criminal sanctions for abortion. However, self-determination (not framed as 'choice') was also a key demand of women's movements both in the early twentieth century as well as around 1968 (*Mein Bauch gehört mir*), and abortion is a specifically controversial case in many countries.[104] In addition, a growing movement of disabled persons protested against medical intervention to produce 'healthy' children, which is another example of 'never again'. Also, the more recent demand for self-determination to end one's life, against the prohibition of assisted suicide, was supported and fought across the social and political spectrum, and swiftly turned into a question of fundamental rights for the Court to answer.

In such controversies, the Court is usually a late, never proactive but always a responsive and decisive player. When it was confronted with challenges to the hard-won legislative compromise to liberalize the strict abortion regime in the 1970s, it issued what may be, by comparison, a Solomonic ruling: there is dignity in unborn life, and rights of the mother as well, and the legislature enjoys some latitude in designing a comprehensive scheme to recognize both.[105] For those who wanted women to decide, it was a disappointment, yet for

---

[102] With further references see Susanne Baer, 'Gleichberechtigung revisited. Zur Interpretation des art 3 GG und internationaler Gleichbehandlungsgebote' (2013) NJW 3145–3150.

[103] The lead decision is BVerfGE 124, 199—*Gleichbehandlung eingetragener Lebensgemeinschaft (Equal Treatment of Registered Partnerships, 2009)*, followed by BVerfGE 126, 400—*Steuerliche Diskriminierung eingetragener Lebenspartnerschaften (Inheritance Tax Equality for Registered Partners, 2010)*; 131, 239—*Lebenspartnerschaft von Beamten (Equality of Marriage and Registered Partnership in 'Family benefits' in Public Service, 2012)*: 133, 59 – *Sukzessivadoption (Successive Adoption by Same-sex Parents, 2013)*; 133, 377 – *Ehegattensplitting (Equal Tax Benefits for Different and Same-sex Couples, 2013)*.

[104] For a comparative analysis, see Norman Dorsen and others, *Comparative Constitutionalism*, (3rd edn, West, Eagan, 2016) Chapter 7 B; see as well Reva Siegel, 'The Constitutionalization of Abortion', in Rebecca Cook, Joanna Erdman and Bernard Dickens (eds), *Abortion Law in Transnational Perspective* (2014).

[105] BVerfGE 39, 1—*Schwangerschaftsabbruch I (Abortion, 1975)*.

those rigidly opposed to any abortion ever, it was also a loss. In 1993, the Court revisited the issue. Again, it balanced competing interests and employed a scheme to protect unborn life, yet also allow women to end pregnancy after being advised of all options.[106] And in 1997, the Court blocked the application of overly rigid regulations of doctors that perform abortions.[107] All these decisions put the Court under pressure and were handed down to pacify sharp controversies in society, at least for a while. In 2019 however, the issues returned because of right-wing campaigns to criminalize gynaecologists who informed women about abortion online. They resulted in a complaint that asked the Court whether this was compatible with the constitution.

A somewhat historical, yet also moral and often religious, sensitivity around medical ethics also informed controversies around another ruling: child as damage. In 1997, the Court upheld the civil courts' assessment that doctors may be held liable for false information about the genetic risks of having children.[108] The ruling became known as 'child as damage', an evidently cruel label, and was not conceived well.

More recently, the Court had to decide additional cases around medical ethics. Confronted with harsh personal tragedies, as well as complicated medical matters, and appealing to very basic understandings of personhood, individual liberties, self-determination, life and death, the Court issued rulings on forced medical treatment of people in detention[109] as well as people under legal care.[110] It emphasized that the state has an obligation to care for those unable to do so themselves, based on the right to life and health (article 2 para 2 clause 1, and with a reference to the UN Convention of Rights of Persons with Disabilities), and may thus even allow for such treatment, albeit, because of the proportionality requirement, as ultima ratio. In 2020, the Court then issued its ruling on assisted suicide, which crushed a hard-won political compromise and thus resulted in a long period of stasis, in which the legislature did not act.[111]

d. Data, Technology, Surveillance

Dynamic change is a feature of medicine, as it is the characteristic of technology. In an effort to apply constitutional law to new phenomena, this led to one of the most internationally renowned contributions of German constitutionalism to the protection of fundamental rights, the doctrine of 'informational self-determination'. This line of jurisprudence started with the Census Case in 1983.[112] In what may seem almost trivial at times when big data is scanned in systems using algorithms, the Court responded to widespread protest of a census that collected demographic data on paper with a reminder that 'under conditions of modern data processing, protection of the individual against unlimited use of data' must be a fundamental right. Therefore, any restrictions of this liberty must be based on a law compatible with constitutional requirements. And since data processing is usually a practice out of sight from those affected, the clarity (*Normenklarheit*) of such law is more important than usual, as are organizational and procedural safeguards of proportionality. Until today, these are the

---

[106] BVerfGE 88, 203—*Schwangerschaftsabbruch II (Abortion, 1993)*.
[107] BVerfGE 96, 120—*Bayerisches Schwangerenhilfegesetz e.A (Injunction against Bavarian Abortion Law, 1997)*; BVerfGE 98, 265—*Bayerisches Schwangerenhilfegesetz (Bavarian Abortion Law, 1998)*.
[108] BVerfGE 96, 375—*Kind als Schaden (Child as Damage, 1997)*.
[109] BVerfGE 128, 282—*Zwangsbehandlung im Maßregelvollzug (Forced Treatment in Detention, 2011)*.
[110] BVerfGE 142, 313—*Zwangsbehandlung (Forced Treatment, 2016)*.
[111] BVerfGE 153, 182—*Sterbehilfe (Assisted Suicide, 2020)*.
[112] BVerfGE 65, 1—*Volkszählung (Census, 1983)*.

188 SUSANNE BAER

starting points and foundational standards to assess whether security and police laws do violate fundamental rights.

Over the years, the Court reminded the legislature again and again to pay more respect to what is called privacy in other legal contexts, and informational self-determination in German constitutional law. In 2008, the Court added an application of these standards to hardware, in framing a 'right to the confidentiality and integrity of information systems'.[113] However, this social and technological change did not only inspire court rulings. As mentioned, the text of the Basic Law was not just amended, but de facto legislated in detail in article 10 as well as in article 13. Eventually, this jurisprudence on surveillance measures refined proportionality requirements to a degree that motivated the legislature to copy and paste what the Court said, which then in turn motivated the Court to synthesize established standards.[114] With changes in society, the Court attributed more weight to the legitimate aim to fight terrorism and organized crime.[115] However, it also bound German authorities to their fundamental rights commitments when dealing with other countries in times of globalization,[116] despite the growing pressure to allow for more security technology. Again, German jurisprudence must be read in light of history, be it the totalitarian fascist state before 1945, or the surveillance practices by the 'Stasi' in the GDR, or the repressive atmosphere in the 1970s when the state fought the terror from the 'RAF'. At the time, like early developments in German constitutional law, the traditions of the civil service read into article 33 para 5 conflicted with more liberal commitments to fundamental rights even for those who served in public functions. When the states ran background checks on teachers on whether they adhered to the 'democratic basic order' in the 1970s, they were backed up by the Court, yet the Strasbourg Court eventually declared this practice a violation of human rights by the ECHR.[117]

e. Religious Pluralism

As regards religion, German constitutionalism features a rather unique model, and with the social dynamics that affect the issue as well as the need to find a European consensus in areas in which EU law applies, there are also intense conflicts. Right from the start, it was highly controversial whether the constitution should address the issue at all; the framers did not propose anything, and the drafters almost fell apart over proposals.[118] Last, but not least, the Weimar compromise from the early twentieth century was transferred to the Basic Law via article 140, more compromise than promise. It was not until German unification, which added a secularized East to a society formerly seen as mostly Christian, with a Catholic south and a Protestant north, and it was not until the visible rise of religious pluralism, with smaller Jewish and fast-growing Muslim communities, and with the demise of membership in the formerly dominant, state-registered, and state-privileged Catholic and Lutheran-protestant

---

[113] BVerfGE 120, 274, 358 ff—*Online-Durchsuchung* (*Online Search Case, 2008*).

[114] Namely: BVerfGE 141, 220—*Bundeskriminalamtsgesetz* (*Federal Police Agency BKA, 2016*). Key decisions are BVerfGE 30, 1—Abhörurteil (*Surveillance Case, 1970*); BVerfGE 109, 279—*Großer Lauschangriff* (*Grand Acoustic Surveillance, 2003*); BVerfGE 125, 260—Vorratsdatenspeicherung (*Data Storage, 2010*).

[115] BVerfGE 133, 277—*Antiterrordateigesetz* (*Counter-Terrorism Database Act, 2013*).

[116] BVerfGE 141, 220, 328—*Bundeskriminalamtsgesetz* (*Federal Police Agency BKA, 2016*): 'In no case may Germany lend its hand to violations of human dignity.'

[117] *Vogt v Germany*, App no 15851/91, 26 September 1995 (violation of art 10). This at least modified the ruling in BVerfGE 39, 334—*Extremistenbeschluss (Resolution on Extrimists, 1975)*. The practice ended between 1985 and 1991, when Bavaria stopped the checks. However, it resurfaced in the twenty-first century with the growing presence of right-wing extremists in German politics.

[118] Dreier, IPE § 1, n 36.

churches, that conflicts arose. Today, German constitutionalism is considered a secular concept, but it emphasizes equal religious freedom and the right of religious communities to basically run their own affairs.

f. Economic Justice, Poverty

Changes in society that may affect constitutionalism are also of an economic nature. In West Germany, and during the Cold War, German constitutionalism developed a strong anti-communist stance, which was, however, more anti-authoritarian than directed against re-distribution of economic gains. Thus, article 20 para 1 declares Germany to be a 'social' state, which article 28 transfers to the *Länder*. Certainly, this has been and still tends to be considered less important than the equally foundational principles of democracy, federalism, and the rule of law. However, a social dimension is an ingredient of German constitutionalism as well.

This may not be surprising. In Germany, there is a long tradition of social security and healthcare law, some fought for by workers' movements and social democrats as solidarity, some based on Catholic concepts of welfare, and some introduced in large reforms of the nineteenth and early twentieth century. After 1945, poverty was again an issue in a destroyed country hosting many refugees, when Germans who had settled in Eastern and Central Europe had to return home. During economic recessions, employment matters and social security came back to the Court, and the harsh effects of a reform of the system known as 'Hartz IV' forced the Court on several occasions to address the 'conditions of a minimum dignified existence', before eventually declaring that the guarantee of human dignity, in article 1, obliges politics to care.[119] Later, it was specified that this applies to every human being, irrespective of migration policy rationales.[120] In addition, the Court declared cutting welfare (because the welfare-recipient failed to comply with 'try-to-find-employment' obligations) unconstitutional because such measures were not based on solid data that showed that people are really able to get back to caring for themselves when stripped of state support.[121]

Beyond those principled decisions, including the mandate to care for dignified existence, German constitutionalism also acknowledges that every liberty is based on the ability to make use of it. Therefore, individual rights may, under certain conditions, also be raised with their 'protective content' (*Schutzgehalt*), in their 'objective dimension' and then even amount to direct claims for benefits.

g. Private Actors

The late twentieth and early twenty-first century has also been a time of significant changes in constellations and forms of power. While liberal constitutionalism is based on the idea that 'negative' rights limit state action, these changes raise the question of whether fundamental rights also protect against private actors. The German Court addressed this issue as early as 1958, when a man named *Lüth* called for a boycott of a former Nazi-filmmaker, and the civil courts were called upon to adequately address such private quarrels based on the Constitution, because fundamental rights have such a 'third-party effect'. Later, the privatization of state functions also posed the question of whether constitutional law addresses private actors, such as private companies who control the internet.

---

[119] BVerfGE 125, 175—*Hartz IV (Social Security I, 2010).*
[120] BVerfGE 132, 134—*Asylbewerberleistungsgesetz (Asylum Seekers Benefits, 2012).*
[121] BVerfGE 152, 68—*Sanktionen im Sozialrecht (sanctions in welfare law, 2019).*

The Court started to develop an answer in what may seem like much smaller cases: an airport, a flash mob[122] or a soccer game. In 2011, there was the question of whether there is a right to stage political protest in the Frankfurt airport. The airport had been privatized and was being run as a company, yet it was still half state-owned. With a comparative reference to the North American notion of a 'public forum', the Court held that the Basic Law does indeed apply. Thus, fundamental rights need to be respected by a private corporation, at least when it serves a public function. The decision to ban any political expression in the airport was held to violate the complainant's fundamental rights to freedom of expression under article 5 para 1 clause 1 and to freedom of assembly under article 8 para 1.[123] As had been accepted widely before, but had not ever been applied, the Court explained that the use of private-law forms of organization does not exempt state authority from being bound by fundamental rights. Rather, and like public enterprises that are in the sole ownership of the state and are organized in the forms of private law, enterprises owned both by private owners and the state, in which the public authority has a controlling influence, are directly bound by the constitution. The ruling was based on article 1 para 3, which the Court explained to be based on a fundamental distinction: as a matter of principle, the citizen is free, and the state is bound. The state, it stated, assumes its responsibilities in a fiduciary capacity on behalf of the citizens and is accountable to them, the constitution comprehensively and directly commits the state's activities to the fundamental rights, and this also applies where the state makes use of civil law when assuming its responsibilities.

In 2018, the Court added, in the case of a soccer fan banned from seeing a game live at the stadium, thus in the cultural context in which soccer is of national significance, that at least the right to equal treatment needs to be respected by private parties when they offer services to the general public.[124] Therefore, if soccer associations grant admission without distinction to anyone, and where exclusion from a game has a considerable impact on the ability of the persons concerned to participate in social life, the associations are bound to basic legal guarantees and soccer fans may not be banned without sufficient factual reasons, a fair hearing and reasons given to allow for legal redress.

h. Environmental Justice

In the twenty-first century, constitutional courts are or will be confronted with, again, new questions. One of them reacts to pollution and technological risk and other forms of harm that affect the environment, and thus, humans. In Germany, there are constitutional assessments of both high-risk technology when introduced, and of the political decision to put an end to using it, namely atomic energy after the catastrophe in Fukushima (*Atomausstieg*). Regarding risk, German constitutional law understands the right to life and health to have a positive dimension in that it obliges the state, and legislator, to adhere to an obligation to protect (*Schutzpflicht*), and thus properly assess risk and take care of avoidable danger.[125] Regarding the decision to stop using dangerous technology, the Court explained that this is the business of politics, that business expectations are not property, but that investments based on a state of law that are then worthless must be compensated as expropriation (article

---

[122] In a preliminary injunction, a Chamber (three Justices) applied the standards established by the Senate in Fraport to a case in which people were fined for consumption of alcohol in a city square that was open to the public yet owned and controlled by a private party; see BVerfG, 3. Chamber of the First Senate, 18 July 2015—1 BvQ 25/15.
[123] BVerfGE 128, 226—*Fraport (Fraport, 2011)*.
[124] BVerfGE 148, 267—*Stadionverbot (Soccer Stadium, 2018)*.
[125] BVerfGE 49, 89—*Kalkar I (Kalkar I, 1978)*.

14 para 2).[126] In 2021, the Court then held that climate law must take the liberty and rights of future generations into account, since inaction would lead to a situation in which they would be unduly burdened.[127] This was a surprise to many who had considered this to be a question of state obligations, but the Court reframed it to fit the classic notion of negative rights, albeit 'intertemporal'.

C. Basic Structures and Concepts

1. Position, Standing, Significance

When the German Basic Law turned seventy in 2019, the country celebrated with pride and joy, including a three-day fair with all democratic institutions around the Court in Karlsruhe, yet no central solemn state function was organized. That same year, a prominent few were invited to a memorial function commemorating one hundred years of the Weimar Constitution from 1919, in Weimar. Both events may illustrate the status of the Basic Law in Germany today: it is a beacon of democracy, and an endorsement of the civil values all are at least expected to agree upon, but toned down to public reason, a hopefully solid glue for society.

Year after year, opinion polls asking for trust in institutions find the constitution on the podium, and the Court well in front of parliament or politicians. To a degree, this shows that throughout German history, the rule of law tended to be a more promising principle than democracy, with politics as 'dirty business' and law as the shining light of reason. Yet German constitutionalism is not a civil religion. Rather, in Germany the constitution is a normative basis referred to as common ground, as mere rationality, more prosaic than charismatic. As such, it is an important dimension of the 'we', a collectivist notion Germans tend to see as a question rather than embrace as identity, which allows for a version of non-nationalistic pride in what has been labelled 'constitutional patriotism'.[128]

As such, the Basic Law starts with fundamental rights, and constitutes and organizes the state second, to have the state serve the person, rather than the person ever serving the state again. Therefore, it is entirely clear, and explicitly stated in article 1 para 3 and article 20 para 3, that the constitution takes precedence over statutory law.[129] Judicial review is not a problem, but a mandate of the Court to eventually declare legislation null and void. Also, everyone is guaranteed access to raise a claim that parliament or any other 'public force' has violated fundamental rights (article 19 para 4). At the same time, the Court regularly emphasizes a preponderance of politics, leeway for legislative assessments and decisions, prognostic space, room for compromise, and allows for time to reregulate while an unconstitutional law remains valid. The tension between applying the law and intervening in politics is, then, subject to extensive scholarly and political debate.[130]

---

[126] BVerfGE 143, 246—*Atomausstieg (Nuclear Phase-out, 2016).*

[127] BVerfG Order of the First Senate, 24 March 2021—1 BvR 2656/18—*Klimaschutz (climate protection).*

[128] See Jan-Werner Muller, *Constitutional patriotism* (Princeton UP, Princeton, 2009); Jan-Werner Muller, Kim Lane Scheppele, 'Constitutional patriotism: an introduction' (2008) 6 ICON 67–71.

[129] In German constitutional history, this *Verfassungsvorrang* is associated with Georg Jellinek, *Allgemeine Staatslehre* (3rd ed, O. Häring, Berlin, 1914).

[130] More on the critique of constitutionalization below. On judicial review, see Donald Kommers, Russel Miller, *The Constitutional Jurisprudence*, 33 (n 38); for a comparative assessment, see Norman Dorsen and others, *Comparative Constitutionalism*, Chapter 3 (n 104). Recent critics of the German Court are Matthias Jestaedt and others, *Das entgrenzte Gericht* (Jeff Seitzer tr, Suhrkamp, Berlin, 2011); Matthias Jestaedt and others, *The German Federal Constitutional Court: The Court Without Limits* (OUP, Oxford, 2019).

Regarding Europe, and despite some rather snotty predictions that national constitutionalism would become much less significant, and 'Karlsruhe' a merely local institution, the German story may be the example for another trend which I call 'embedded constitutionalism', and the intense transnational discourse in an 'association of courts' (*Gerichtsverbund*).[131] The Basic Law already featured the visionary preamble after 1945 to allow Germany to come back to the international community, and this longing was revitalized in a mix of national and post national, rather narrow or broader, commitments to understandings of democracy, based on the rule of law. Certainly, where law itself becomes a European or global field, as in employment relations or financial transactions, national constitutional law loses its grip. Yet in all other fields, it is no surprise that in a constitutional system with a strong court and a wide range of access routes to mobilize it, constitutionalism has become a key factor in meeting the demands of the time.

As in all constitutional democracies that deserve the name, German constitutionalism is driven by a variety of actors. In a context that emphasizes rationality and methodologically refined doctrine, academics play quite an important role. There was not such a strong presence among framers and drafters, but there is tradition to elect constitutional law professors to the Karlsruhe bench, who then keep in touch with the communities they come from and return to, after the fixed term of twelve years on the Court. According to the Court rules of procedure, law professors—who must have two law degrees, including the one to practice—may also act as lawyers in constitutional cases, and they regularly do, commissioned both by those that raise complaints and by the government.

In addition, political debates in public and parliament engage constitutionalism regularly, but 'Karlsruhe' certainly occupies a central position. The Court is itself driven, based on the many access routes, by political parties of the opposition and states, as much as by citizens, which still, comparatively speaking, engage in limited strategic litigation alliances. While it could plausibly describe itself as the 'guardian of the constitution' for a while, the Court is now more often seen as an umpire, sometimes to remove a political impasse, and often a reminder to not sell the basics under pressure, as in the fight against terrorism or in trans- and international relations.

The framers and drafters deliberately designed the German constitution to be more than a collection of empty promises or principles as mere guidelines. Human dignity comes first, in article 1 para 1, and exceptional courts, the death penalty, and abuse in detention are outlawed in articles 101, 102, 104 para 1 clause 2. A commitment to human rights as the foundation of global peace follows suit in para 2, and a bold clarification that this constitution is 'directly enforceable law', in article 1 para 3. Enforceability was one key lesson taken from the Weimar Constitution, and this required a specialized constitutional court established in article 94, with considerable power of judicial review, accessible by state organs, the parties, and individual constitutional complaints. This defined the Court as a cornerstone of the system to back up the grand promises of the Basic Law that cannot be touched in essence, according to article 19 para 2, and may not be amended, according to article 79 para 3. The Court has since been called a citizen's court, the constitution's 'guardian', and lately the 'umpire'.[132] Famously, early German Chancellor Konrad Adenauer was rather surprised when that new

---

[131] BVerfGE 140, 317, 44—*Identitätskontrolle* (*Identity Review I, 2015*). See Ingolf Pernice, *Das Verhältnis europäischer zu nationalen Gerichten im europäischen Verfassungsverbund* (De Gruyter, Berlin, 2006); Andreas Voßkuhle, 'Multilevel cooperation of the European constitutional courts: Der Europäische Verfassungsgerichtsverbund (2010) 6 European Constitutional Law Review 175.

[132] See Christian Bumke, Andreas Voßkuhle, *Casebook on German Constitutional Law*, 9–11 (n 80).

institution in fact used its power and stopped his plan to start a government TV station.[133] As with all such courts, 'Karlsruhe' has faced, and again and again faces, more or less harsh comments, has more or less fans with a public voice, and is more or less careful to stay within its bounds. Oftentimes, the 'sound' colours the reactions at least as much as the decisions, and the sound is mostly an echo, in the media and from academics. Here, the Court, like all such institutions, also faces challenges to gain respect in a world of fast and short communication, since complex rulings do not fit social media formats. In fact, successful constitutional complaints are rare: the success rate is only below 2 percent. Moreover, few rulings go against the political majority, in legislation and government, but they are the most prominent. As such, the Court is a loud but rare voice, yet the constitution is a factor of everyday political life.

In such a context, it is again essential that the constitution and constitutional jurisprudence are, after all, regarded as law, not politics. Historically, the task was rather clear: in Germany after 1945, democracy should not only never again be the unlimited rule of a majority cheering a charismatic leader, but also be a rational organization of political power, separated along functions and federalism, based on the rule of law, with courts to protect the rights of individuals, clearly distinguished from the principles that should inform state action and politics. Yet in the twenty-first century, commitments vary, and boundaries multiply. Some basic features of constitutionalism may be taken for granted, or may be underrated, which contributes to the risk of disrespect of constitutionalism at times when the rule of law, and thus, a human rights-based democracy, are under severe pressure.[134]

2. Fundamental Rights and Proportionality

In German constitutional law, the first part of the Basic Law emphatically starts with dignity, the '*Grundnorm*' of article 1 para 1, which has been activated in several decisions by the Court to, one, guarantee a meaningful existence beyond mere survival, two, establish the guilt principle in criminal law, three, guard against extradition to a country with the risk of torture or other degrading treatment, or death, and, four, eventually limit speech when it turns to hate.[135] Then, there is the general right to liberty (article 2) and equality (article 3 para 1), both of which are then detailed, from non-discrimination (article 3 para 2, para 3) to religious freedom (article 4), free speech, freedom of the media, of research and of the arts (article 5), right to assembly (article 8) and association (article 9), secrecy of communication (article 10) and privacy of the home (article 13), rights to and in marriage and a family (article 6), to the profession one chooses (article 12), to property (article 14) and eventually although weakened by referenda, with access to asylum (article 16). Each right is complemented by specific rules of when and how to justify their limitation, different from constitutions with a general limitation clause. In addition, there are individual rights to organize the state not based on race, or creed, or gender, but based on equal access to public office (article 33 para 2). There is also a clause to organize democracy based on the right to vote (article 38).

---

[133] BVerfGE 12, 205—*Rundfunkentscheidung (State TV, 1961)*. Regarding EU law on TV programmes BVerfGE 92, 203—*EG-Fernsehrichtlinie (EU Television Directive, 1995)*.

[134] Susanne Baer, 'Grundrechte unter Druck', in Matthias Ruffert (ed), *Europa-Visionen* (Nomos, Baden-Baden, 2019) 169–192; Susanne Baer, 'Democracy in peril' (2019) 10 Transnational Legal Theory, 140–162.

[135] Dreier IPE § 1, n 143–148. Early on, the GFCC characterized dignity as the 'highest value' and 'essential constitutive principle' of the Basic Law, i.e. in BVerfGE 5, 85, 204—*KPD-Verbot (Prohibition of the KPD, 1956)*. On the 'existential minimum', see below welfare state, on the guilt principle, see BverfGE 133, 168—*Verständigungsgesetz (No 'Deal' in Criminal Trials, 2013)*; on protection of refugees, interpreting the Basic Law in line with the Geneva Refugee Convention and the ECHR, BverfGE 94, 49—*Sichere Drittstaaten (Safe Third Countries, 1995)*.

Regarding the justice system, due process and fair trial, there is the fundamental right to be heard in court (article 103 para 1), and to have a judge decide on any deprivation of liberty (article 104 para 2 clause 1). This is seen as a rather extensive and comparatively modern list, which also inspired, as many German scholars like to emphasize, the European Charter of Fundamental Rights of the EU, passed in 2000. This perception also informs an assumption that international human rights guarantees will usually guarantee less. But with seminal rulings that delivered many such promises early on, namely on free speech, freedom of the press, freedom of association, as well as gender equality in marriage and the family, German constitutionalism is understood to be a guarantee, first and foremost, of fundamental rights.

In German constitutionalism, fundamental rights are unthinkable without proportionality, or as some still say, the *Übermaßverbot*. *Verhältnismäßigkeit* or proportionality is a core element of all rulings on fundamental rights, and it became a German export item picked up by many other jurisdictions around the world.[136] Although sometimes treated as merely a doctrinal tool, or as just another term for balancing, proportionality is, in German constitutional law, a central and rather refined substantive feature of utmost importance to German constitutionalism. It was developed in German administrative law to limit the reach of a patriarchal state. It became a way to organize and systematically address all aspects relevant to a given case and evaluate legislative choice considering its direct and indirect effects, to in fact limit balancing to a last stage assessment of how much may be asked of citizens to bear in order to reach a legitimate goal. Also, proportionality started as the doctrinal test to justify intrusions into protected liberties, but eventually travelled to equality jurisprudence as well. In what has been called the 'newest' formula to test equality claims, the Court now discusses whether an unequal burden or disadvantage may be justified as sufficiently proportional to a legitimate aim.

Applicable in all fundamental rights contexts, the area in which proportionality started most prominently may be freedom of speech and the press, guaranteed by article 5 para 1. It was the early case law of the Karlsruhe court that showed the people that they had a voice, and that attempts to silence them would be controlled, and eventually declared illegal. At least, this informed one of the most prominent German rulings, in the case of *Lüth*, in 1958, in what now may seem like a paradigmatic conflict. At the time, the Court was asked to intervene in a conflict between formally private parties. It was a conflict over the fascist past, particularly around the showing of a movie that was a key antisemitic propaganda product for the Nazis in Hamburg. A civil servant called for a boycott of this film. In a social context in which many did not denounce the recent past, and many had been involved themselves in problematic roles and who had sentenced opposition figures to death, as well as in the 1950s context of silencing and taboo rather than robust debate, the Court opted for the latter. The Court explained that to form public opinion on relevant questions of the common good, the private economic interest may have to stand back in order to allow for all to participate in such controversies equally. Since then, the Court has built its reputation as a citizen's court partly by protecting free speech, a critical press, political art, and performance, as well as

---

[136] Dreier, IPE § 1, n 130-2. A seminal treatise is Peter Lerche, *Übermaß und Verfassungsrecht* (Duncker & Humblot, 1961). In English, see Gertrude Luebbe-Wolff, 'The principle of proportionality in the case-law of the German Federal Constitutional Court' (2014) 12 Human Rights Law Journal; Dieter Grimm, 'Proportionality in Canadian and German Constitutional Jurisprudence' (2007) University of Toronto Law Journal 383; Bernhard Schlink, 'Proportionality in constitutional law: why everywhere but here' (2011) 22 Duke J Comp & Int'l L 291; Niels Petersen, *Proportionality and judicial activism* (CUP, Cambridge, 2017); with comparative material see Norman Dorsen and others, *Comparative Constitutionalism*, Chapter 3 C (n 104).

rights of associations and assembly to protest, and care for a proportional consideration of the protection of one's personality.

More recently, this logic of proportionality has also been applied in equality cases. German constitutionalism originally followed a traditional interpretation of equality rights first, specifically that people in the same situations should be treated similarly. But it moved on from there. It eventually applied, beyond the basic prohibition of arbitrariness (*Willkürkontrolle*), a 'new' and then a 'newest' formula to address inequalities as disproportional violations of equal rights.[137] In short, when there is unequal treatment, the burden to justify it is the higher, one, the more a constitutional liberty interest is affected, two, the more the criteria to differentiate resemble the list of prohibited grounds of discrimination in article 3 para 3, and, three, the more the factor that triggers the inequality cannot be influenced by those affected.[138]

In the area of fundamental rights, there is another feature of German constitutionalism worth mentioning. Based on the grand promise of inviolable human dignity in article 1, yet with the rather typical comprehensive view of the constitution, German constitutional law also prominently features, and thus protects, a general right to personality and self-determination, with the general liberty clause in article 2 para 1 read in conjunction with dignity. It is an 'unnamed' fundamental right.[139] It covers constitutive aspects of the self that are neither protected by liberty rights nor moments in each social context but offers protection against specific endangerments of the self-determined development and preservation of one's personality. For example, one such aspect is information about one's existence, or the recognition of one's chromosomal makeup as female, male, or intersexual.[140]

3. Foundational Principles of the State

Beyond rights, German constitutionalism organizes politics. Therefore, the second part of the Basic Law is dedicated to 'the federation and the states', but it starts, more importantly, with the grand foundational principles, namely in article 20. They are not enforceable as individual rights but guaranteed 'forever' (article 79 para 3), or at least until a new constitution would replace this catalogue. Namely, German constitutionalism rests on democracy, as a 'militant' democracy, on federalism and more separation of powers, on the rule of law, and is a social state, as well as a secular one. Added later, article 20a proclaims the state to protect, in its responsibility to future generations, natural resources and animals, albeit as framed by law.[141] Also, 'openness towards Europe' (article 23) and 'friendliness towards international

---

[137] Important rulings that moved in this direction are BVerfGE 55, 72—*Präklusion I (Preclusion in Civil Proceedings, 1980)*; BVerfGE 87, 234, 255—*Einkommensanrechnng (Unemployment Benefits, 1992)*; BVerfGE 88, 87—*Transsexuelle (Transexuals, 1993)*; BVerfGE 85, 191—*Nachtarbeitsverbot (Nightshift Prohibition, 1992)*.

[138] Examples are: BVerfGE 126, 400, 416—*Steuerliche Diskriminierung eingetragener Lebenspartnerschaften (Tax Discrimination of Registered Partners, 2010)*; BVerfGE 130, 131—*Rauchverbot in Restaurants (Smoking Ban in Restaurants, 2012)*; 133, 59—*Sukzessivadoption (Successive Adoption, 2013)*.

[139] A recent summary of the development is provided by BVerfGE 141, 186—*Isolierte Vaterschaftsanfechtung (Isolated Paternity Claim, 2016)*, under B I.

[140] BVerfGE 147, 1—*Option des dritten Geschlechts (Third Gender Option, 2017)*. According to the Court, art 2 in conjunction with art 1 protect a 'gender identity', including one beyond male and female (in that case: intersexual). The Court also based its ruling on a violation of art 3 para 3 cl 1 which protects people that are not to be attributed to male or female from discrimination based on sex. See also Peter Dunne, Jule Mulder, 'Beyond the binary: Towards a third sex category in Germany' (2018) 19/3 German Law Journal 627.

[141] In German constitutional law, such principles are understood as 'normative goals of the state' (*Staatszielbestimmungen*) and may constitute legitimate goals that justify limitations of rights.

law' (article 1 para 2, article 25) must be added to the list of grand principles of German constitutionalism overall.

4. Democracy, Elections, Parliament

The German Basic Law features a list of core principles of constitutionalism in article 20 para 1, which are protected 'forever' against amendments by article 79 para 3. Next to defining Germany as a federal republic based on the rule of law, it highlights the democracy principle, operationalized as representative democracy primarily, yet based on the idea of 'self-determination of all citizens'[142]. The third part of the Basic Law then organizes democratic decision-making. It adds substance to the principle in article 20 para 1.[143] Again trying to learn from history, the framers and drafters did thus start out with several 'political rights' for an active citizenry,[144] opted against much presidential power and regulated for a parliamentary-representative system. They emphasized democratic parties, in a 'party state democracy',[145] protected as and bound by article 21, and essentially did not allow for plebiscites (the exception is redrawing state borders, in article 29 para 2).

According to constitutional design, parliament is central, with general, direct, free, equal, and secret elections (article 38 para 1 clause 1), the principle of publicity and majority vote (article 42). It has the power to call on the government to appear in front of the plenary (article 43) and install investigative committees (article 44). Its members are protected from persecution (article 46) and supported in their democratic efforts (article 48). Last but not least, parliament has the power to replace the chancellor (article 67),[146] and certainly, the power to legislate, a process defined in articles 76 to 79 and 82, with the option of exceptional executive decrees, according to articles 80 and 81.

Here, power is bound to the principle of democratic legitimation, which needs to be operational, in what was first described as a strict chain of legitimacy (*Legitimationskette*),[147] to eventually become a minimum overall 'level of legitimation' (*Legitimationsniveau*), in a more flexible approach.[148] It is also applied to the appointment of judges,[149] or the status of

---

[142] BVerfGE 44, 125, 142—*Öffentlichkeitsarbeit* (*Public Information Campaigns I, 1977*).

[143] For comparative material see Norman Dorsen and others, *Comparative Constitutionalism,* Chapter 12 (n 104). German constitutionalism draws on older notions of democracy, Hans Kelsen, *Vom Wesen und Wert der Demokratie* (2nd ed, Mohr Siebeck, Tübingen, 1929); Hermann Heller, *Staatslehre* (Sijthoffs, Leiden, 1934). After 1945, a key thinker was Konrad Hesse, *Grundzüge des Verfassungsrechts der Bundesrepublik Deutschland* (20th ed, CF Müller, Heidelberg, 1995).

[144] This has been emphasized again and again by the GFCC, i.e. BVerfGE 20, 56, 99—*Parteienfinanzierung I* (*Party Financing,* 1966); 44, 125, 140—*Öffentlichkeitsarbeit* (*Public Relation,* 1977); 69, 315, 346—*Brokdorf* (*Brokdorf, 1985*). Specifically, freedom of speech has been labelled as 'utterly constitutive' of democracy, in the famous *Lüth* ruling, BVerfGE 7, 198, 208—*Lüth* (*Lüth, 1958*).

[145] See Dieter Grimm, 'Politische Parteien', in Ernst Benda, Werner Maihofer and Hans-Jochen Vogel (eds), *Handbuch des Verfassungsrechts der Bundesrepublik Deutschland* (De Gruyter, Berlin, 2011), s 14.

[146] This 'constructive vote' has been used in 1982 to install chancellor Kohl. It is attributed to concepts by Ernst Fraenkel, 'Verfassungsreform und Sozialdemokratie' (1932) 9 Die Gesellschaft 109–124.

[147] BVerfGE 93, 37, 41, 75 ff—*Mitbestimmungsgesetz Schleswig-Holstein* (*Limits of Labor Participation in Public Administration, 1995*).

[148] BVerfGE 107, 59—*Lippeverband* (*Functional Autonomy of the Executive, 2002*); BVerfGE 130, 76 (*Delegation of Forensic Treatment Facilities to Private Operators, 2012*); BVerfGE 136, 194—*Weinsteuer* (*Wine Fee, 2014*).

[149] BVerfGE 143, 22—*Bundesrichterwahl* (*Federal Judges, 2016*); BVerfGE 148, 69—*Vereinbarkeit der Ernennung von Beamten zu Richtern auf Zeit* (*Temporary Administrative Judges, 2018*).

prosecutors,[150] which tends to be controversial, and up for a comparative assessment under European law.[151]

In German constitutional law, the concept of democracy is also closely linked to the nation-state, and primarily informs the legitimation mechanisms of state power, as in article 20 para 2: 'All state authority is derived from the people. It shall be exercised by the people'. Certainly, there are those that call for a 'democratization of society',[152] but the majority rejects this claim. In addition, democracy has been interpreted as based on membership, as in nationality. To accommodate European integration (Article 22 TFEU), municipal voting rights were extended to EU member state nationals via article 28 para 1 clause 3 in 1992. But the attempt of some municipalities to also integrate other non-Germans residents failed when the Court held, in 1990, that 'the people' that the constitution refers to is not those persons affected by the polity, but a 'unified group', determined by nationality, thus German as defined in article 116 para.[153] The ruling disappointed those in favour of a more integrated society, which is a clear minority in German constitutional scholarship,[154] and thus applauded by most.

Again, informed by Germany's history of mass mobilization and manipulation, German constitutionalism cares about will-formation. First and foremost, article 21 highlights political parties as key mediators of the will of the public, in a representative democracy. German constitutionalism features the 'party state' envisioned by Gerhard Leibholz,[155] drawing on the idea of party competition by Max Weber.[156] Parties are defined by law, backed up by the Court, to organize to participate in elections, and actively pursue this goal, based on internal membership democracy. And while there is the freedom to find a party, there is also the option, exclusively reserved to a special proceeding in the Court, to declare a party unconstitutional and dissolve it, as an element of a 'defensive democracy'. In the early years, the decisions to dissolve parties on the extreme right and left—SRP and KPD—were opportunities to define the notion of Germany's liberal democratic order (*freiheitlich demokratische Grundordnung* or *fdGO*[157]) and limit a prohibition to those that have an 'actively militant and aggressive attitude' towards it, to not just radically disagree, but to 'destroy the order itself'.[158] In addition, as the Court clarified in 2017 when it rejected the attempt to prohibit

---

[150] German prosecutors in criminal cases are subject to orders by the responsible member of the government, which has been declared a violation of their necessary independence, by the ECJ, Decision of 27 May 2019, joined cases C 508/18 and C-82/19 PPU, OG, PI, ECLI:EU:C:2019:456.

[151] In cases of extradition, it is decisive to assess whether the rule of law is still in place. There are controversies in the EU around the independence of the justice system. When comparative arguments are used to defend violations of the principle, context is key. On constitutional requirements in appointing judges, based on equal and merit-based access to public office (art 33 para 2), yet in a procedure in which political actors participate, see BVerfGE 143, 22—*Bundesrichterwahl (Federal Judge Election, 2016)*.

[152] Ekkehart Stein and others, *Alternativkommentar zum Grundgesetz* (Luchterhand, Munich, 2001) art 20 para 61 ff.

[153] BVerfGE 83, 37—*Ausländerwahlrecht I (Municipal Elections and Foreigners, 1990)*.

[154] For a sweeping critique of election jurisprudence, see Hans Meyer, *Die Zukunft des Bundestagswahlrechts* (Nomos, Baden-Baden, 2010). See also then Justice on the Court Brun-Otto Bryde, 'Ausländerwahlrecht und grundgesetzliche Demokratie' (1989) 44 Juristenzeitung 257–262, who was the first judge proposed by the Green Party. From the other side, prominent conservative scholar published the proceedings, Josef Isensee, *Das Ausländerwahlrecht vor dem Bundesverfassungsgericht: Dokumentation der Verfahren* (CF Müller, Heidelberg, 1993).

[155] *Der Parteienstaat des Bonner Grundgesetzes* (1951).

[156] Max Weber, *Economy and Society* (University of California Press, Berkeley, 1978) 284.

[157] BVerfGE 2, 1, 12—*SRP-Verbot (Prohibition of SRP, 1952)*. Excerpted and contextualized in Norman Dorsen and others, *Comparative Constitutionalism*, Chapter 12 A 2 (n 104).

[158] BVerfGE 5, 85, 141—*KPD-Verbot (Prohipition of KPD, 1956)*.

the at the time small radical right party NPD,[159] a party must 'actively seek' such destruction with at least an option of success.[160] The Court emphasized that the prohibition of a party is a double-edged sword a democratic state may use against its organized enemies (headnote 1). Therefore, parties can question constitutionalism yet may not—or 'never again'—disregard the foundational dignity of every human being, as in ideologies of racism. Democracy, then, 'is the rule of free and equal persons', and racism denies that rule. In addition, democracy is a multi-party system, and the democratic state based on the rule of law, including 'the state's monopoly on force', and parties may be prohibited if they actively seek a one-party rule and endorse force as a means of politics.

While these rulings define the basics of German constitutional democracy, the principle of democracy and the party clause are also understood to guarantee for party competition and equal opportunities of parties, again based on articles 20 and 21, and on the general guarantee of equal treatment in article 3 para 1. The right to equal opportunities applies to party financing as well as campaigning, in that the state must open its facilities to all parties equally. As always, equality does not mean identical or symmetrical. Therefore, the Court has held that there is no right of access to public broadcasting, but a right to distribution of airtime based on electoral success.[161]

While the Basic Law emphasizes parties, the Court clarified early on that the notion of democracy (article 20), rooted in the guarantee of equal elections (article 38), and including equality in general (article 3), also empowers individual MPs. Such cases were in fact brought by individuals against the parties,[162] and, in fact, are signs of protest the 'factions' discipline', which is exercised to shut down internal protest. If there are no 'compelling reasons of confidentiality', all political groups have the same rights.[163] In fact, the de facto rise of the 'party state', albeit in a multi-party setting with coalition governments as the norm, informed warnings, which is rather plausible in a country that had lived through party dictatorship, yet also a sign of a liberal strain in an otherwise rather statist mainstream.

As a principle, democracy is not a fundamental right like those listed in articles 1 to 19. Usually, this would result in an inability of raising a citizen's complaint to the Court designed and understood to be the 'guardian' of individual rights. However, and in a move that consolidates its key position in German politics, the Court interpreted the right to vote guaranteed in article 38 to be right to democracy, both on the level of states and in federal matters, as well as international affairs. In what has been seen as a bold move regarding European integration, the Court accepts direct complaints by any citizen that the principle of democracy was violated.

Article 38 states that members of parliament shall be elected in general, direct, free, equal, and secret elections. This is understood to require election law itself to comply with the principle of democracy, including a specifically strict notion of equality. The Court found this to be guaranteed in article 3 para 1 as well, which thereby opened the door to use the power of judicial review in respect of state election laws.[164] In addition, the Court interprets the clause

---

[159] In 2017, the NPD had 5000 members, and not represented in legislatures in Germany. Notably, the first attempt to prohibit it failed because the informants of the security agencies that had infiltrated the party were not removed, BVerfGE 107, 339—*NPD-Verbot (Prohibition I, 2003)*.

[160] BVerfGE 144, 20—*NPD-Verbot II (NPD Prohibition II, 2017)*.

[161] BVerfGE 14, 121—*FDP-Sendezeit (FDP Airtime, 1962)*; BVerfGE 47, 198, 237—*Wahlwerbesendungen (Election Advertising, 1978)*.

[162] BVerfGE 80, 188, 221—*Wüppesahl (Independent Bundestag Member, 1989)*.

[163] BVerfGE 70, 324—*Haushaltskontrolle der Nachrichtendienste (Oversight of Intelligence Agencies, 1986)*.

[164] Not yet in BVerfGE 99, 1, 8 ff—*Bayerische Kommunalwahlen (Minimum Signatures to Participate in Elections, 1998)*, overruled BVerfGE 34, 81, 98 ff—*Wahlgleichheit (Electoral Equality, 1972)*.

on political parties in article 21 to guarantee their equal standing.[165] Thus, every vote must have the same value. However, German election laws do establish a threshold that requires parties to gain more than 5 percent of the vote to enter the German *Bundestag*. In fact, this renders votes for small parties worthless. Responding to a challenge of the threshold, the Court added that the constitution also safeguards the 'functional effectiveness' of elected bodies, and prevents fragmentation into many small groups, which can hinder or prevent the formation of a stable majority.[166] Therefore, the 5 percent threshold in national elections results in an unequal value of votes but is justified as a proportionate measure to reach a highly important legitimate aim. Somewhat surprisingly, the same threshold for European elections did not survive a challenge in 2009.[167] There, the Court did accept the resulting inequality of votes, because it saw no danger of fragmentation that could result in political instability. The key consideration was the difference the Senate saw between the European Parliament and the German *Bundestag*, in that the latter forms a government, while the former influences politics defined by member states. Some merely feared their seats would be endangered by small parties now geared towards success, and critics argued that a national idea of democracy shall not be applied to Europe.

More generally, the fear of those in power to lose their seats renders rulings on election laws particularly controversial. One may say that such decisions are about politicians themselves, and they react with heightened sensitivity, yet may also consider that political consensus that is necessary to re-legislate when rules are struck down is very hard to reach. Therefore, election law decisions are among the most criticized, and any change mandated by the constitution, yet asked for by the Court, endangers the standing of the Court as a recognized referee in politics more than most other demands. When the Court remanded a change to limit so-called overhang seats,[168] it resulted in a long impasse in parliament, risking non-compliance with the Court order itself.[169]

Interference with the activities of parties and members of parliament are similarly sensitive. Here again, the Court focuses on the guarantee of free, equal, secret etc. elections, in article 38. It emphasizes that the vote must be, by all means, free from mistakes, and prohibited the use of election computers not fit to do so.[170] Also, the vote shall be based on the citizen's ability 'to form opinions and make judgments in a free, open process', which is why state institutions are allowed to inform the public but forbidden to exert influence on elections.[171] Yet when elected, representatives of the people must also remain free from pressure, be it from the state or from their political parties as a powerful social group, which informs compensation schemes[172] as well as side-income regulations.[173] However, this was extremely controversial, with four Justices (out of eight) rejecting any measure that leads to monitoring, because any deficit should be subjected to political decisions, and thus, the vote. This rare deep split that divided the Court was again seen in the aftermath of 1989.

---

[165] BVerfGE 82, 322, 337—*Gesamtdeutsche Wahl (Post-Reunification all of Germany Elections, 1990)*.

[166] BVerfGE 82, 322, 338—*Gesamtdeutsche Wahl (Post-Reunification all of Germany Elections, 1990)*.

[167] BVerfGE 129, 300—*Fünf-Prozent-Sperrklausel EuWG (Five Percent Threshold for European Parliament Election, 2011)*.

[168] BVerfGE 131, 316—*Landeslisten (Overhang Seats II, 2012)*.

[169] Regarding the size of electoral districts, see BVerfGE 95, 335, 363—*Überhangmandate II (Overhang Seats I, 1997)*.

[170] BVerfGE 123, 39—*Wahlcomputer (Election Computer, 2009)*.

[171] BVerfGE 44, 125, 139–140—*Öffentlichkeitsarbeit (Public Information Campaigns I, 1977)*.

[172] BVerfGE 40, 296, 313—*Abgeordnetendiäten (Legislative Salaries, 1975)*.

[173] BVerfGE 118, 277—*Verfassungsrechtlicher Status der Bundestagsabgeordneten (Constitutional Status of Bundestag Members, 2007)*.

Then, a member of parliament who had previously worked for the East German secret police (*Staatssicherheit* or '*Stasi*') complained about an investigation run against him, and the subsequent extensive reports that would be published. He lost, with four Justices upholding transparency regulations, and four others rejecting such far-reaching exposure.[174] However, such an observation must be based on the consent of parliament itself.[175] Therefore, when the *Bundestag* lifts immunity to investigate tax evasion, it may do so.[176]

5. Defensive Democracy

The notion of a 'militant', in literal translation a 'quarrelling democracy', and better termed a 'defensive' one, is a key element of German constitutionalism. It is, again, a 'never again' to autocrats taking over by electoral means, a concept crafted by political theorists Karl Loewenstein and Karl Mannheim, both exiled from Germany by the Nazis, while reflecting on fascism taking over.[177] In the Basic Law, it has several dimensions. One is that amendments must be incorporated in the main text (article 79 para 1), and some things can never be changed, according to the 'eternity clause' in article 79 para 3. In addition, article 9 para 2 allows for the prohibition of associations whose aims, or activities contravene the criminal laws, or that are directed against the constitutional order or the concept of international understanding, while article 21 para 2 allows the Court to prohibit a political party that, by reason of their aims or the behaviour of their adherents, seeks to undermine or abolish the free democratic basic order or to endanger the existence of the country. Finally, article 18 defines who may forfeit their basic rights because of abuse of rights to combat the free democratic basic order. Again, this is a matter that has to be declared by the Federal Constitutional Court, but at least to date, it is a weapon that has been seen as too lethal to ever use.

These options are not only negative rejections, but also offer opportunities to state what is wanted and what deserves protection. In the early days of German Basic Law constitutionalism, the young Court did not only ban one party on the right (1952, a de facto follow up of the NSDAP, SRP) and one on the left (1956 KPD), which may exemplify its effort to appear unbiased; the guardian of the constitution and the umpire of the political game. In these rulings, the Court also defined the very meaning of the 'free democratic basic order', the values of the Basic Law, the notion of citizenship and democracy. In the 1960s, the Court however also accepted the screening of teachers as to their ideological commitments, which the ECHR later considered a violation of fundamental rights as a defensive democracy that went too far.

In the twenty-first century, and before the global rise of right-wing autocratic nationalism that reached Germany a bit later that its neighbouring countries, an effort to prohibit the, at the time, weak right-wing NPD was unsuccessful. In a first decision, the Court refused to take the case because the government could not guarantee it had removed all infiltrated secret agents from the scene. In a second decision on the merits, the Court later did not find the party to have the 'potential' to ever achieve its goals.[178] Quickly, the constitution was

---

[174] BVerfGE 99, 19—*Gysi III (Gysi III, 1998)*.
[175] BVerfGE 134, 141—*Beobachtung von Abgeordneten (Observation of Members of Parliament—Ramelow, 2013)*.
[176] *BVerfGE 104, 310 – Pofalla II (Pofalla II, 2001)*.
[177] Karl Mannheim, *Diagnosis of Our Time: Wartime Essays of a Sociologist* (Kegan Paul Trench, Trubner & Co, London, 1943); Karl Loewenstein, 'Militant Democracy and Fundamental Rights' (1937) 31 American Pol Sci Rev 417, 638. Excerpts and comparative context in Norman Dorsen and others, *Comparative Constitutionalism*, Chapter 12 B 2 (n 104).
[178] BVerfGE 144, 20, 1518 ff—*NPD II (NPD Prohibition Procedure, 2017)*.

amended to allow for a termination of party funding in such a case, in article 21 para 3. Yet the ruling itself also clearly marked, and indeed condemned, the intolerable nature of racism and autocratic ideologies, thus reemphasizing the very core ideas the Basic Law stands for. Similarly, when the Court was asked to assess the constitutionality of decisions of the Federal Ministry of the Interior to prohibit an association that supported, what Germans call *Neo-Nazis* in prison, to prohibit a motorcycle gang engaged in organized crime, and to outlaw an Islamic Charity that funded Hamas activities in Palestine, it did not only uphold these executive decisions. In addition, it explained that German constitutionalism is meant to defend democracy and the rule of law, including in international relations, itself. And in what may seem particularly German, the Court also took a side in a politically charged controversy in legal scholarship and obliged such acts to be proportional.[179] As such, German constitutionalism is meant to defend itself when needed.

6. Federalism, Form of State, Units, Territory

Another foundational principle of German constitutionalism is, according to article 20, federalism. It cannot ever be amended (article 79 para 3). Both driven by the long story of German 'small statehood' (*Kleinstaaterei*), and the Allies' demand for a vertical separation of powers, the framers and drafters clearly defined the form of state as a federation. To date, these are sixteen states (*Länder*) ranging from cities like Hamburg, Bremen, or Berlin to large territorial states like North-Rhine Westphalia, from the rich Southern regions Bavaria, or Baden-Württemberg, to traditionally poor Northern Schleswig-Holstein, and from old Western ones to the new Eastern Saxony etc., each with their own constitution, constitutional court, parliament, government etc. On the central level, federalism is operative in the second chamber, the *Bundesrat*, as defined in Part IV of the Basic Law, followed by the President, with notary functions (Part V), and the government (Part VI). In those parts, the focus is institutions, defining and distributing their powers.

As regards the power to make legislation, as well as taxes, the centrifugal reality of German politics however sharply contradicts constitutional design. According to article 30, all legislative power rests with the States if not otherwise defined, which is then done in often amended and now long catalogues of federal power in articles 70 to 74. In fact, education and culture are left to the states, although often rely on huge federal 'programmes', which combine funding with policy, and employ intense mechanisms of governmental coordination, i.e. setting educational standards to access to higher education. Rarely is the Court called upon to limit federal intervention, as was the case in the politically charged, and structurally conservative, decision that prohibited the federal government from reforming traditional (and hierarchical, very status-sensitive) conditions to become a university professor.[180] In addition, there is the norm of *Bundestreue* which obliges the states not to contradict federal policies, but stay 'faithful' to the federation.[181] Similarly, article 107 para 2 forces the federation to distribute tax income to all states fairly, which results in the always controversial horizontal compensatory scheme of the *Finanzausgleich* in which more affluent states

---

[179] BVerfGE 149, 160—*Vereinsverbot (Prohibition of Associations, 2018)*. In the ruling, the Court summarizes the rather authoritarian history of such prohibitions, to then state proportionality requirements that force the executive to choose less intrusive means before the ultima ratio of prohibiting a '*Verein*', based on art 9 para 2.

[180] BVerfGE 111, 226—*Juniorenprofessur (Professorship, 2004)*.

[181] The principle was already mentioned in the very early rulings BVerfGE 1, 299, 315—*Wohnungsbauförderung (Housing Promotion, 1952)*, but figures in many decisions always.

202 SUSANNE BAER

sponsor the poorer ones, although it is limited by the principle to neither weaken the strong states nor totally equalize all of them.[182]

The separation of powers that matters politically is the horizontal separation between legislative, the executive and the judiciary, which is a separation provided for in the foundational clause of article 20 para 2 clause 2. In German constitutional law, this is a core ingredient of the rule of law,[183] and the clause is interpreted to ensure mutual oversight of the organs of state over one another, to exercise a moderating influence, yet to also safeguard an efficient delivery of state functions. As regards this efficiency point, it specifically means that decisions shall be taken by the organ most suited for it. While law is a tool that the legislator is best placed to design and use, and administration is the suitable task for the executive, planning was controversial in that it is a decision somewhere between normative rulemaking and application to a specific place. As such, it involves wide-scale and prognostic assessments as well as option for a preference.[184]

Also, the German constitutional governance scheme insists on a right to information between state organs. It wants the separated powers to be acquainted with each other and work together for the common good. Specifically, the Court developed a line of jurisprudence to strengthen the right of parliament to be sufficiently informed by the government. This includes information on highly sensitive matters of foreign policy, like arms exports,[185] or complicated and urgent international matters, like European reactions to a financial crisis.[186] And specifically, this is a right for minorities in parliament, particularly the political opposition. They have the right to set up investigative committees, based on article 44,[187] and the Court held early on that such committees have the right to gather evidence in order to fulfil their task.[188] This includes access to government files, yet not to private documents.[189]

Yet more recently, the Court also clarified that information does not come for free. Rather, the principle of 'separated yet interacting powers' informs a notion of constitutional responsibility. The organ that has the power has a right to get information, but is also obliged to then decide, and face the political consequences. In several rulings, the Court therefore reminded parliament itself that it needs to live up to its calling. International relations are also a mandate with a responsibility,[190] namely an 'integration responsibility' parliament must carry to implement EU integration according to article 23.

---

[182] For more, see commentaries on art 20. See also Christina Federer-Meyer, *Finanzielle Solidarität* (Mohr Siebeck, Tübingen, 2017). From a comparative perspective, see Norman Dorsen and others, *Comparative Constitutionalism*, Chapters 5 (n 104).

[183] Christian Bumke, Andreas Voßkuhle, *Casebook on German Constitutional Law*, 1403 (n 80).

[184] With references to the line of jurisprudence, BVerfGE 95, 1, 15—*Südumfahrung Stendal (Stendal South Bypass, 1996)*.

[185] BVerfGE 137, 185—*Rüstungsexport (Arms Exports, 2014)*.

[186] BVerfGE 129, 124—*EFS (Greece and Euro Rescue Package, 2011)*. The Court held that the Euro Stabilization Mechanism Act must be interpreted in conformity with the constitution, to the effect that the Federal Government is obliged to obtain prior approval by the Budget Committee before giving guarantees within the meaning of the Act.

[187] A right of minorities in parliament was first stated in BVerfGE 67, 100—*Flick-Untersuchungsausschuss (Committee of Inquiry, 1984)* and restated in BVerfGE 105, 197—*Minderheitsrechte im Untersuchungsausschuss (Party Contributions Committee of Inquiry, 2002)*. In both cases, a majority did not want to touch key German industrials as well as, more importantly, the sources of money that the parties gathered as donations.

[188] BVerfGE 49, 70—*Untersuchungsgegenstand (Committee of Inquiry, 1978)*.

[189] BVerfGE 124, 78, 114—*Untersuchungsausschuss (Federal News Agency Committee of Inquiry, 2009)*; BVerfGE 77, 1—*Neue Heimat (New Home, 1987)*.

[190] BVerfGE 142, 123—*OMT-Programme (OMT-Programme, 2016)*. For details, see below.

7. *Rechtsstaat*

Finally, it is the *Rechtsstaatsprinzip*, literally the law's state, the *État de Droit*, or *Estado de Derecho*, eventually inspired by an ancient idea of the 'Law's Empire',[191] now internationally known, yet differently understood and implemented as the rule of law,[192] that informs German constitutionalism. The concept is considered distinctly German,[193] and the term is used in article 28 para 1, to align the States with the federation as defined in article 20. In addition, the *Rechtsstaat* is, according to article 23 para 1, a principle to govern European integration.

To define its content, the German Basic Law offers article 20 para 2 clause 2. It states that all state power derives from the people, such power shall be articulated in elections, and it shall be executed via specific organs of legislation, the executive, and the judiciary, thus setting the ground for a horizontal separation of powers. Also, article 20 para 3 binds all public authority to the law, as the 'hard historical core' meaning[194], to cover both the *Vorrang* (primacy) of statutory law, primarily directed at the executive to not act without or against a decision by parliament, thus: democratic legitimation, as well as, albeit implicitly, the *Vorbehalt* (requirement) of statutory law. Indeed, it is the principle of the primacy of statutory law, guaranteed in article 20 para 3, with predictability and certainty, and based on democratic legitimacy, that informs German constitutionalism's idea of horizontal distribution of powers. A prime example is the insistence that any decision that touches upon fundamental rights must be taken by parliament, rather than the executive alone. The doctrine is called *Wesentlichkeitstheorie*, or 'essential matter theory', which also implies that non-essential matters may very well be dealt with by competent authority alone. Thus, when the state runs schools, it does not only educate or 'care for' future citizens, but also interferes with fundamental rights, which, the Court decided, calls for decisions taken by parliament, thus: democratic deliberation and political responsibility.[195] Such rulings broke with the until then dominant idea that there are sites of special relations between state and people (*besondere Gewaltverhältnisse*) in schools, prisons, or civil service, where the state is not bound by fundamental rights.[196] Also, when nuclear power facilities clearly involve a risk for the health of people, the Court agreed with the claim that a law passed by parliament is required to fix the basics of such a procedure, because of a duty to protect people's health and lives.[197] As in

---

[191] An early concept came from English philosopher James Harrington 1611–1677. The German history of ideas draws on philosopher Immanuel Kant, but more prominently in liberal administrative law reformer Robert von Mohl, *Die Polizei-Wissenschaft nach den Grundsätzen des Rechtsstaats* (Heinrich Laupp, Tübingen, 1832), following ideas of the southern German liberals Welcker, Rotteck and others. A prominent contribution to today's understanding is Georg Jellinek, *Allgemeine Staatslehre* (O. Häring, Berlin, 1900).

[192] The German notion of *Rechtsstaat* and the Anglo-American as well as the international understanding of the rule of law may not be as different anymore. See, i.e. Neil MacCormick, 'Der Rechtsstaat und die rule of law' (1984) Juristenzeitung 65. On the German concept Ernst-Wolfgang Böckenförde, 'Entstehung und Wandel des Rechtsstaatsbegriffs', in Festschrift für Adolf Arndt zum 65. *Geburtstag* (Europäische Verlagsanstalt, Hamburg 1969) 53; Philipp Kunig, *Das Rechtsstaatsprinzip* (Mohr Siebeck, Tübingen, 1986); Katharina Sobota, *Das Prinzip Rechtsstaat* (Mohr Siebeck, Tübingen, 1996).

[193] A comprehensive account is given by Wolfgang Böckenförde, *State Society and Liberty* (JA Underwood tr, St Martin's Press, New York, 1991) 47–70.

[194] Dreier, IPE § 1, n 121, who refers to Jesch and Böckenförde.

[195] BVerfGE 47, 46, 78—*Sexualkundeunterrricht (Sex Education, 1977)*; 58, 257, 268 – *Schulentlassung (School Suspension, 1981)*; see also BVerfGE 84, 212, 226—*Aussperrung (Worker's lockout, 1991)*. An earlier case dealt with fairness requirements in administration of the justice system, BVerfGE 40, 237, 248 *Justizverwaltungsakt (Administrative Order in Prison, 1975)*.

[196] A seminal ruling is BVerfGE 33, 1—*Strafgefangene (Prison, 1972)*.

[197] BVerfGE 49, 89—*Kalkar I (Kalkar I, 1978)*; see also BVerfGE 83, 130, 142—*(Mutzenbacher, 1990)*, different from BVerfGE 68, 1, 108—*Atomwaffenstationierung (NATO Double Track Decision, 1984)*, rejecting an absolute requirement of parliamentary decision. See also BVerfGE 104, 151—*NATO Konzept (NATO Conzept, 2011)*.

most constitutional settings, and very much in favour of the power of parliament, there is a 'preponderance of parliament'.[198] Here, the Court opted for a functional approach to decide which organ and procedure may be best suited for a particular type of state action.[199] For example, there is then a requirement of judicial supervision of state intelligence measures to scan private data, to protect fundamental rights, but informed by a functional understanding of judicial authorization. Similarly, courts then are required to decide on physical restraints on patients confined under public law in psychiatric hospitals, because courts are best designed to fulfil that function.[200]

Article 20 para 3 also supplements article 1 para 3 in that binds all state power to fundamental rights. In addition, article 19 para 4 guarantees access to judicial review for anyone whose rights have been violated by public power, which has also been called a 'foundational norm' by the Court early on.[201] It is understood to be much more than a mere guarantee of access to a court, but also covers the right to fair and efficient judicial review of state— and nowadays, also of powerful state-like, yet formally private—action. Also, it established the right to judicial decisions within a reasonable time, which the ECtHR also recognizes as a European fundamental right. Finally, the guarantee of access to justice is backed up in the section of the Basic Law that covers the judiciary by the so-called 'judicial fundamental rights', in articles 101, 102, 104 para 1 clause 2. In Germany, rule of law is always also rule of courts.[202] In a somewhat controversial ruling on the right to ride a horse in the forest, the Court even accepted what the dissent considered a 'petty' claim to be brought to court, because even 'small' interferences with basic rights do violate the constitution.[203] Thus, it is also clearly not for the Court or anyone else to decide what matters, how much, and to who.

In German constitutionalism, the *Rechtsstaat* did not only precede democracy. There is also a particular emphasis on lawfulness and legal control of administrative action, which informed EU founding father Walter Hallstein's emphasis on the 'community of law' (*Rechtsgemeinschaft*) in the 1960s, forming the European Community.[204] In Germany, the rule of law also implies an emphasis on proportionality, reaching beyond its key function in limiting interferences with fundamental rights. Its background is liberal protest against the paternalistic state, and the rule-of-law idea of controlling the administration yet accepting its expertise and functional adequacy to run public affairs. The genealogy of proportionality traces back to German administrative police law. It requires that the state pursue legitimate goals, employ useful and necessary means only, and consider all rights involved to eventually act so that it (the relevant exercise of power) is reasonable in the sense of not asking too much of anyone. It is understood as a key ingredient of lawfulness. Here again, German constitutionalism insists on rationality as a factor of justice. Even without any anchor in the text of the constitution, and some disagreement as to what it should be based on, proportionality is thus completely accepted as a key ingredient of the rule of law.[205]

---

[198] Roman Herzog, cited by Dreier, IEP § 1, n 119.

[199] This has been called for prominently by Konrad Hesse, *Grundzüge des Verfassungsrechts der Bundesrepublik Deutschland* (20th ed, CF Müller, Heidelberg, 1995) 482.

[200] BVerfGE 141, 220, 172 ff—*BKA (Federal Criminal Agency, 2015)*; BVerfGE 149, 293—*Fixierungen (Physical Restraint in Psychiatric Institutions, 2018)*.

[201] BVerfGE 58, 1, 40—*Eurocontrol I (Eurocontrol I, 1981)*, citing to a lead commentary of the Basic Law by Hermann, von Mangoldt, Friedrich Klein, *Das Bonner Grundgesetz* (2nd ed Vahlen, Munich, 1957).

[202] Dreier, IPE § 1, n 125.

[203] BVerfGE 80, 137—*Reiten im Walde (Horse Riding in the Forest, 1989)*, with a dissent.

[204] Walter Hallstein, *Die europäische Gemeinschaft* (Econ, Düsseldorf, 1973); Trs by Charles Roetter, *Europe in the Making* (Allen & Unwin, Crows Nest, 1972).

[205] Dreier, IPE § 1, n 130-2.

Also, the rule of law implies a foundational perspective on reliability which includes a requirement of legal clarity or determinacy (*Bestimmtheitsgebot*). It again allows the citizen to understand what they are asked to do or not to do. Specifically, this became an important part of security laws that allow the state to act in secrecy and make it even more important for the law to define very clearly what may happen there.[206]

Thus, and early on, the Court has treated the principle as a mix of demands.[207] There are ongoing controversies as to its meaning,[208] which have intensified considering the crisis of the rule of law, and specifically attacks on judicial independence and judicial review in Europe in the twenty-first century.[209] Recent conflicts in the European Union raise the question of compliance with Article 2 TEU,[210] and there are dangerous ideological claims of a 'crisis of the rule of law' from nationalist populists fighting migration, who sometimes even enlist the rather pragmatic criticism of deficits in legal protection and overly burdensome demands of legal procedures. In Germany, such a controversy was a paradigmatic post-1968 conflict between former Nazis and committed democrats. Then, a formal understanding of the rule of law was prominently advocated by conservative *Staatsrechtslehrer* Ernst Forsthoff, while socialist jurist and political scientist Wolfgang Abendroth[211] advocated a holistic understanding of the rule of law and the welfare state principle, both listed in article 20 of the Basic Law. In the twenty-first century, the Venice Commission, as the key advisory body formed by the Council of Europe, insists on a substantive notion. It comprises both legal redress and court supervision, particularly in the form of due process and fair trial guarantees. It also comprises substantive protection against disadvantage, and abuse also belongs to the package.[212] Regarding the *Rechtsstaat*, German constitutionalism has opted to agree with those that do not limit the rule of law to a formal promise, but understand its material content as definitive, particularly in its emphasis on the substantive meaning of fundamental rights.

8. Welfare State, Protective and Social Dimensions of Fundamental Rights

Finally, a foundational principle explicitly guaranteed in article 20 para 1 is the 'social' or welfare state. Again, concepts differ and the German notion of the *Sozialstaat* has a specific genealogy and, thus, meaning.[213] It reaches back to municipal reforms by Lorenz von

---

[206] Regularly, the GFCC requires security regulation to be specifically clear on the powers of the executive, defining thresholds (i.e. a 'concrete danger' rather than a broad assumption) to collect and use personal data. See BVerfGE 113, 348, 375 ff; 120, 378, 407 ff; 141, 220, 265, 94—*Vorbeugende Telekommunikationsüberwachung (Preventive Telecommunication Surveillance, 2005)*.

[207] BVerfGE 7, 89, 92—*Hamburgisches Hundesteuergesetz (Hamburg Dog Tax, 1957)*.

[208] Dreier, IPE § 1, n 116, warns of an 'inflational plague'.

[209] Susanne Baer, 'The Rule of—and not by any—Law' (2019) 71/1 Current Legal Problems 335–368; Nicola Lacey, 'Populism and the Rule of Law' (2019) LSE Working Papers.

[210] Kim Lane Scheppele 'Autocratic legalism' (2018) 85 Univ Chicago Law Review 545.

[211] Ernst Forsthoff, *Rechtsstaat im Wandel* (2nd ed, CH Beck, Munich, 1976); for his early work *Der totale Staat* (Hanseatische Verlagsanstalt, Hamburg, 1933), and the opponent Wolfgang Abendroth, 'Zum Begriff des demokratischen und sozialen Rechtsstaats im Grundgesetz der Bundesrepublik Deutschland', in Michael Buckmiller, Joachim Perels, and Uli Schöler (eds), *Gesammelte Schriften*, vol 2 (Offizin, Zürich, 2008) 338. For comparative perspectives, see Norman Dorsen and others, *Comparative Constitutionalism*, Chapter 11 B (n 104).

[212] Venice Commission, 'Rule of Law Checklist', CDL-AD(2016)007-e, 2016, published on www.venice.coe.int (last accessed 28 March 2022).

[213] For European developments, see Eberhard Eichenhofer, *Geschichte des Sozialstaats in Europa* (CH Beck, Munich, 2007).

Stein, who was inspired by French political philosophy that discussed the social state of humans as different from the state of nature, which Stein synthesized with the State. A true liberal as early as 1850, he wanted the State to care for the social state of workers, not just to keep them going, but to 'further their freedom'. Later, chancellor of the monarchy, Otto von Bismarck, introduced social legislation that served to stabilize the regime and fight the demands of workers movements. Eventually, such ideas were constitutionalized in the Weimar Constitution in articles 151 to 165. Then, some post-Second World War constitutions named the welfare state as an important component of constitutionalism, like France or Spain, as well as several German states. They were later to be followed by Portugal, Romania, or Estonia. It also became an element of article 20.

However, as a foundational principle, the social state is much less prominent in constitutional law than the other ones.[214] This may be reminiscent of the Cold War rejection of communism. Also, there are no 'social rights' in the Basic Law, because these were taken by the drafters and framers to result in 'empty promises'. Not least, the scepticism towards redistribution via constitutional law is in line with structurally conservative notions of merely 'negative rights', which German constitutional law focuses on as the 'defensive function' (*Abwehrfunktion*) of liberty rights. However, German constitutionalism also features a 'positive dimension' of fundamental rights that amounts to 'protective obligations' (*Schutzpflichten*) of the state. In rulings on abortion as well as on the shooting an airplane to prevent a terrorist attack, the Court has insisted on the duty of the state to actively 'protect and promote' fundamental rights.[215] Often, this results in an obligation to take precautions when people are in danger, but this also gives the legislature a wide margin of appreciation on how to exactly do that. When an eminent German industrialist was kidnapped by the left radical 'Red Army Faction' in 1977, the Court refused to step in, which may be one of the most tragic moments for the Court, as well as an indicator of the limited reach of 'positive' protective rights.[216]

Also, a comparative reading of the Basic Law does offer several such social guarantees, i.e. in article 6 regarding motherhood, article 7 on education, article 9 para 3 protecting unions, article 14 para 2 and para 3 on expropriation, and article 15 on socializing means of production, as well as—if interpreted as such—article 3 para 2 and para 3 against discrimination. However, the welfare state principle is predominantly interpreted from a liberal point of view.[217]

With the preponderance of liberty, there have been few cases that focus on the social dimensions of constitutionalism. Yet economic justice and questions of poverty have been aspects of cases around social security and labour law, as well as issues of healthcare or

---

[214] See Dreier, IPE § 1, n 97. Donald Kommers and Russel Miller, *The Constitutional Jurisprudence* (n 38), treat it as an element of basic rights and liberties, yet not an element of the structure of German constitutionalism. For an extensive discussion see Ernst Benda, ‚Der soziale Rechtsstaat', in Ernst Benda, Werner Maihofer and Hans-Jochen Vogel (eds), *Handbuch des Verfassungsrechts* (De Gruyter, Berlin, 1994) 719, compared to the doyen of German social law, Hans Zacher, 'Das soziale Staatsziel', in Josef Isensee and Paul Kirchhof (eds), *Handbuch des Staatsrechts der Bundesrepublik Deutschland II* (CF Müller, Heidelberg, 1987) s 28.

[215] Seminal decisions are BVerfGE 39, 1, 42—*Schwangerschaftsabbruch (Abortion I, 1974)*, with an important dissent by Rupp von Brünneck and Simon, at 68 ff; BVerfGE 115, 118—*Luftsicherheitsgesetz (Aerial Security Act, 2006)*. Other rulings were concerned with environmental protection, i.e. BVerfGE 79, 174—*Straßenverkehrslärm (Street Noise, 1988)*.

[216] BVerfGE 46, 160—*Schleyer (Schleyer Kidnapping, 1977)*.

[217] Hans Michael Heinig, *Der Sozialstaat im Dienst der Freiheit* (Mohr Siebeck, Tübingen, 2008); Klaus-Peter Sommermann, 'art 20 para 1', in Hermann von Mangoldt, Friedrich Klein, Christian Starck, *Grundgesetz*, (CH Beck, Munich, 2018), para 108–114. Alternative accounts are rare. One is Helmut Ridder, *Die soziale Ordnung des Grundgesetzes* (Opladen, Leverkusen, 1975). See also Nikolaus Marsch, Laura Münkler, Thomas Wischmeyer (eds), *Apokryphe Schriften* (Mohr Siebeck, Tübingen, 2018).

education. As one example, when students from out-of-state argued that a higher fee for university studies would violate their rights, the Court explained that federalism may well allow for such distinctions, but that other constitutional principles and rights would limit what can be asked of who. Namely, equal access to a higher education that is de facto organized across states cannot easily distinguish based on people's home addresses, and equal opportunities based on merit and not on the economic status of parents do limit the option to ask students to pay. Also, the prohibition of discrimination on several grounds must be adhered to, thus resulting in differentiated schemes that take family responsibilities or other challenges to mobility into account.[218] Thus, German constitutionalism features a holistic interpretation of several constitutional guarantees that limit the legislature's options to burden citizens financially.

Finally, since 2010, social questions have been addressed by the Court in the name of dignity, read in conjunction both with the welfare state principle and the principle of democracy. The latter gives responsibility to parliament, and thus requires politicians to properly address human needs and assess the adequate number of benefits required to live a dignified life. As such then, the inviolable right to human dignity becomes a guarantee that Germany will not leave anyone behind. When people living on basic benefits asked the Court in 2010 that what they got was not enough, the Court prominently stated that such a guarantee is indeed enforceable, and ordered the legislature to recalculate, in a plausibly rational way that addresses needs realistically, and not 'out of the blue' (ins Blaue hinein).[219] This disappointed those who had asked for more money, since they had to wait for politicians to act, but this has also been seen as a rather bold move in constitutionalizing welfare. In 2012, asylum seekers asked whether this guarantee was theirs to claim as well, and the Court again answered in the affirmative. However, the decision came as no surprise since the benefits for foreigners, mostly asylum-seeking refugees, had been set low from the start, and had never been altered to accommodate inflation. Thus, the government defended its very low benefits rates weakly, and the Court held that they were 'evidently' insufficient to secure a dignified life. In the ruling, the Court stated that dignity may not be relativized, and specifically not for reasons of migration policy.[220] When thousands of refugees came to Germany in 2015, that sentence gained a meaning that was unforeseeable before. However, to date, the Court has not revisited the many changes to regulations that are for the benefit of foreigners.

Regarding Germans and EU citizens, it allowed the state to charge the family first before subsiding someone's life.[221] But does the constitution also allow the state to withdraw benefits when people do not comply with administrative expectations to get back to paid work? At a time of public controversies over new forms of poverty and precariat, experiments with an 'unconditioned basic income', worries about long-time unemployed, even at times when employers cannot fill all positions, and calls for an end to being 'overly generous' (demanding a clear distance between low salaries and state benefits), the Court was looked at as the actor to solve a puzzle that the political majority are not likely to touch. In the 2019 ruling on sanctions, the Court insisted upon the inviolability of dignity, even when people fail. Yet at the same time, it allowed the state to establish cooperation obligations, thus asking people to at least try to sustain themselves, and to back such legitimate obligations up with sanctions if people refuse for no reason. The welfare state may ask for some action

---

[218] BVerfGE 134, 1—*Studiengebühren Bremen (Student Fees, 2013)*.
[219] BVerfGE 125, 175, 221 ff—*Hartz IV (Minimum Existence Benefits I, 2012)*.
[220] BVerfGE 132, 134—*Asylbewerberleistungsgesetz (Asylum Seekers Benefits, 2012)*.
[221] BVerfGE 142, 353—*Bedarfsgemeinschaft (Community of Need in Social Security, 2016)*.

from welfare recipients before giving tax money away. But if the state chooses the sanction of benefit withdrawals, it must adhere to strictest proportionality requirements, namely, to be sure that both the obligations as well as the sanctions function properly, at all times be ready to pay, end sanctions when people cooperate, take care of exceptional needs etc.[222] The even more controversial question of what this means for foreigners who are required to return to the country they left, including asylum seekers who were not granted asylum in Germany, or people forced to return to countries still partly at war or very poor, has not yet been addressed by the Court. However, it is somewhat foreseeable that this question will be posed in constitutional terms in the future.

9. Secularism

According to the compromise of the framers and drafters of the Basic Law, German constitutionalism features a 'state church law' (*Staatskirchenrecht*). It is not the law of a state church, as in England or Sweden. Indeed, as per the stipulations laid down in article 140, Germany has no state church. In turn, this provision was inspired by article 137 para 1 of the Weimar Constitution. Structurally, German law does also not mandate a strict separation of state and church, as in the US, nor *laïcité*, as in France, but organizes a cooperative coexistence. Thus, 'state church law' is all regular, secular law that is applicable to the churches, and this law is ultimately based on articles 137 to 141 Weimar Constitution.

For a long time, this cooperative scheme that privileged registered religions in several ways primarily applied to two churches, Lutheran-protestant and catholic. Therefore, changes in the religious composition of society present challenges. Socially, there have been significant losses in church membership, even though the German state treats everyone who has been baptized as a member and deducts a tax for transfer to the church, thereby meaning that leaving a church requires an activity, rather than joining as an adult. Beyond the demise of religious belief in society, there is the rebirth of Jewish communities, there were upcoming 'new religions', and there is a growing number of Muslims in Germany, all of whom also put the older scheme under pressure.

Not all such controversies reach the Court, but some do. Constitutional conflicts arose early. Although not entirely progressive at the time, the Court protected Jehovah's Witnesses, particularly their freedom of conscience.[223] They were formerly persecuted by the Nazis. They refused to perform military service and they were regularly, and harshly, sentenced by the lower courts. But when the recognition of religious communities as such becomes a constitutional question, the Court also allowed the state to not register Jehovah's Witnesses for lack of adherence to the law.[224] Also, it did not accept a community primarily active in an economic sense, like Scientology,[225] or because it is organized in ways that would allow for a simple extension of the cooperative scheme, like Muslim associations.[226] Prominently, the Court also had to address non-Christian religious practices like butchering and religious

---

[222] BVerfG, Judgment of 5 November 2019, 1 BvL 7/16—*Sanktionen im Sozialrecht (Sanctions in Social Law, 2019)*.

[223] BVerfGE 23, 127—*Zeugen Jehovas (Jehovah's Witnesses I, 1968)*. In that same year, the complaint by a communist local politician who had survived a Nazi Concentration Camp was rejected, because of his support for a prohibited party; BVerfGE 23, 191—*Dienstflucht (Hey, 1968)*.

[224] BVerfGE 102, 370—*Körperschaftsstatus der Zeugen Jehovas (Jehovah's Witnesses II, 2000)*.

[225] BVerfGE 99, 185—*Scientology (Scientology, 1998)*.

[226] On requirements, see BVerfGE 83, 341—*Ba'hai (Ba'hai, 1991)*.

clothing, namely the Muslim headscarf. In a predominantly Christian or secular society, the Court was more rarely called upon to strike down tradition yet did so regarding the silence requirement in Bavarian law on Good Friday (*Karfreitag*), which resulted in a disproportionally strict festivity ban.[227]

While the Basic Law guarantees the right of parents to decide whether their children take religious education in school (article 7 para 2), article 7 para 3 also establishes religion to be a regular subject in public schools and it should be offered in accordance with religious communities, with a special clause for the traditionally secular state of Bremen in article 141. This did fit society for a long time, but it does not easily accommodate religious pluralism and organizations that are very different from the Vatican.

One rather paradigmatic issue shedding light on the demographic changes of Germany is the headscarf worn by Muslim women for reasons of their religious belief, a case that had to be decided in many versions and contexts around the world.[228] The first cases were brought by a Muslim who sought public employment in education and childcare. In 2003, the Court decided that a decision by parliament is needed for such decisions, based on the well-established doctrine of essential questions (*Wesentlichkeitstheorie*), namely all intrusions into fundamental rights require statutory law (*Gesetzesvorbehalt*), thus: in a narrower sense, democratic political responsibility and legitimation.[229] In 2015, the Court's First Senate held that such a statute may not discriminate between religions, and namely not privilege a Christian belief. Also, it ruled that teachers have fundamental rights even when publicly employed, including religious freedom (article 4), and an interference with that right can only be justified in exceptional cases and, of course, any interference must be proportionate. Thus, teachers may wear a headscarf for religious reasons. They might be asked to transfer if this causes trouble no one can handle anymore, yet they must leave only if there is a clear danger to security at school.[230] In several Chamber rulings, this was also applied to employees in day-care facilities and more broadly to social workers. However, in 2020, the Second Senate clarified that there may be positions in which religious freedom has to cede to an interest of state neutrality. When asked about the right to wear a headscarf as a trainee judge or state prosecutor, the Court said no. It should be noted, however, there is still the right to wear a headscarf during legal education, that is, while working towards a qualification as a lawyer.[231]

Similarly, in a country in which welfare and healthcare facilities are largely run by organizations that belong to or are owned by the Catholic or Protestant Church, social as well as demographic change produces challenges and gives rise to constitutional conflict. In the case of a doctor who divorced and remarried to practice in a church-run hospital, the Court held that he must forego his right to religious self-determination, while the Federal Supreme Labor Court held otherwise and mobilized the European Court of Justice to support its view.[232] Here, constitutional conflicts are not anymore just disagreements, but move in a

---

[227] BVerfGE 143, 161—*Karfreitag (Good Friday, 2016).*

[228] For comparative analysis, see Norman Dorsen and others, *Comparative Constitutionalism*, Chapter 10 (n 104).

[229] BVerfGE 108, 282—*Kopftuchverbot I (Headscarf of Teachers I, 2003).*

[230] BVerfGE 138, 296—*Kopftuchverbot II (Headscarf of Teachers II, 2015).*

[231] BVerfG, Order of the Second Senate, 14 January 2020—2 BvR 1333/17 (*Headscarf Ban for Trainees serving as Judges or Prosecutors, 2020*).

[232] BVerfGE 137, 273—*Katholischer Chefarzt (Chief Doctor, 2014)*; after a preliminary question from the Federal Labour Court, by ECJ, *IR v JQ*, 11 September 2018, ECLI:EU:C:2018:696; to then be decided in BAG, 20 February 2019—2 AZR 746/14.

complicated network of actors in employment relations[233] and courts which do not work in a hierarchy. In a related constellation, a job applicant was rejected because she was not a member of the church that wanted expertise in human rights reporting. The ECJ issued a ruling that allows the state to give leeway to churches yet calls upon the legal system to provide for proper judicial review.[234] While this may look like a compromise to some, and while those fighting for protection against discrimination appreciated the small step forward in not leaving any church-related activity untouched by equality standards, German constitutional lawyers were mostly outraged. And, as usual, the Court was asked upon to decide whether the ECJ went too far, in disregard of the specificities of German state–church-relations.

10. Constitutionalization

As much as the standing of the Basic Law and the Court as its speaker indicate the success of post-Second World War democratization in Germany, there has been and is a concern of over-constitutionalization.[235] The concept, as applied to a national legal order, appears in different versions. While early criticism came from conservatives,[236] the warnings directed at the Court more recently are informed by very different segments of the political spectrum. Sometimes, the allegation of over-constitutionalism is a cover-up for a sheer interest in the outcome. The more interesting discussion focuses on the gagging effect of constitutional law on politics. The more the constitution, and the constitution as interpreted by the Constitutional Court, defines the limits or even obligations of 'the state', the more politics are limited in choosing their ways, and the less political diversity there is to vote for in elections.

Regarding substance, there seem to be three areas in which warnings against too much constitutional guidance are a recurring theme. One such area is civil law. German legal culture is based on a Roman law—inspired German tradition of civil law in which the Civil Code from 1900 is still often cherished for its (early) consistency informing beauty. When constitutional law challenges that code, it tends to be perceived as a usurpation,[237] the invader, and the 'other', by some civil law scholars.

Also, and until today, the expansion of judicial review to control the regular courts' adherence to the constitution, which in fact allows the Court to control private law controversies as well, thus creating what is often called 'horizontal review', is controversial. Yet notably, this happened in the conflict over a call for boycott of a movie by famous Nazi propaganda filmmaker Veit Harlan, by the noble democratic civil servant *Lüth*.[238] Thus, even that self-empowering move of the Court is deeply rooted in German history. In later moves, the Court

---

[233] There are many rulings on church-related employment, privileged as a matter of the church alone, i.e. BVerfGE 70, 138—*Loyalitätspflicht (Loyalty Obligations, 1985)*.

[234] *Vera Egenberger v Evangelisches Werk für Diakonie und Entwicklung eV*, Decision of 17 April 2018, ECLI:EU:C:2018:257. The ruling responds to a preliminary question by the Federal Labour Court (BAG), 17 March 2016—8 AZR 501/14 (A), which then decided based on the ECJ ruling in BAG, 25 October 2018—8 AZR 501/1. In early 2020, the case was pending at the GFCC.

[235] Gunnar Folke Schuppert, Christian Bumke, *Die Konstitutionalisierung der Rechtsordnung* (Nomos, Baden-Baden, 2000).

[236] Prominently Carl Schmitt, 'Die Tyrannei der Werte', in *Festgabe für Ernst Forsthoff zum 65. Geburtstag* (CH Beck, Munich, 1967) 60; Ernst Forsthoff, 'Zur heutigen Situation einer Verfassungslehre', in *Epirrhosis: Festgabe für Carl Schmitt* (Duncker & Humblot, Berlin, 1968) 185.

[237] Prominent civil law scholars criticize the GFCC control of the Supreme Court, since the GFCC would not have the mandate to become the 'super revision court' (*Superrevisionsinstanz*). See Uwe Diederichsen, 'Das Bundesverfassungsgericht als oberstes Zivilgericht' (1998) 198 Archiv für zivilistische Praxis 171.

[238] BVerfGE 7, 198——*Lüth (Lüth, 1958)*.

eventually granted access to fundamental rights protection also to non-Germans, both from the EU as from other countries.[239] In light of more recent developments, the Court has expanded its scope of review again. As mentioned, the Court held in 2011 that even when an airport is mostly privatized, fundamental rights to political protest may still apply in such de facto public fora.[240] In 2019, the Court held that, in a society in which soccer is a sport of enormous cultural significance, stadium owners must adhere to basic procedural rights and ensure equal treatment if they ban a fan from going to the games.[241]

Specifically, when the Court held that contracts signed in situations of 'disturbed parity', the courts are obliged to counter such inequality, many civil law scholars were, and still are, up in arms. This line of jurisprudence started in a case in which a freelancer was banned from working in a field close to his former prime contractor, which was considered overly harsh.[242] A little later, the Court struck down loan contracts regularly issued by banks to husbands or fathers with signatures by their wife or daughter, without checking whether they would ever profit from the loan or be able to repay it.[243] Eventually, European legislation added to the trend by passing rules against discrimination that required member states to pass laws that cover rent and housing and mass contracts, thus touching the basics of civil law, which is why the whole 'problem' tends to now be attributed to the EU alone.

D. Constitutional Identity

Article 4 TEU refers to the 'national identity' of the EU member states. What exactly does this mean? At least for Germans, this is a tricky question. Historically, the 'German question' was a troubling one for national and international relations during the nineteenth and twentieth century. It called for a definition of the territory (division or unity) and asked about the power of that rich country in the middle of the continent.[244] After 1945, philosopher Karl Jaspers raised the question of 'German guilt',[245] while liberal political thinker Dolf Sternberger directly addressed *Die deutsche Frage* ('The German Question') as a challenge to international politics post-Second World War, and defined it as Germans not knowing who they are,[246] while in the midst of the protests around 1968, cultural theorist Theodor Adorno

---

[239] The Basic Law explicitly grants some fundamental rights to Germans, while others are granted for everyone. Foreigners may however always rely on the general right to self-determination as the fundamental human right of liberty in art 2 para 1, which results in lower requirements to justify a limitation of that right. Legal entities may claim rights according to art 19 para 3, if they are in a situation that typically deserves rights protection, while public legal entities may only claim those rights that constitute such institutions in deliberate distance to the state, as in the case of universities (art 5 para 3) or public broadcasting, in as much they need such protection (BVerfGE 78, 101—*Eigentumsrecht von Rundfunkanstalten (Property Rights, 1988)*, as in all procedural matters. Also, the CFCC has allowed a foreign EU member state company to claim property rights, in BVerfGE 143, 246, 196— *Atomausstieg (Atomic Energy Plant Phase Out, 2016)*.
[240] BVerfGE 128, 226—*Fraport (Fraport, 1991)*.
[241] BVerfGE 148, 267—*Stadionverbot (Soccer Stadion Ban, 2018)*.
[242] BVerfGE 81, 242—*Handelsvertreter (Sales Agent, 1990)*.
[243] BVerfGE 89, 214—*Bürgschaftsverträge (Bank Bail, 1993)*.
[244] A prominent account of Germany's historical development is provided by Heinrich August Winkler, *Der lange Weg nach Westen*, (2nd edn, CH Beck, Munich, 2000). See also Dirk Verheyen, *The German Question* (2nd edn, Routledge, Abingdon, 2018); and the comment by Robert Kagan, 'The New German Question' (2019) *Foreign Affairs* May/June 2019. See also Bernhard Giesen, 'National Identity as Trauma. The German Case', in Bo Strath (ed), *Myth and Memory in the Construction of Community* (Peter Lang, Bern, 2000) 227.
[245] Karl Jaspers, *The Question of German Guilt*, (EB Ashton tr, Fordham UP, New York City, 2000), originally published as '*Die Schuldfrage*' (Piper, Munich, 1947).
[246] Dolf Sternberger, 'Die deutsche Frage' (1949) 8/9 Der Monat.

pondered 'What is German?'[247] On the one hand, then, German national identity refers to a country in which masses applauded men marching into two world wars, and that had so many participate in, and never even protest, persecution and murder, which culminated in the Holocaust. This also informs the fear of new German power, both in other countries and among Germans, which led to visible controversies around German unification, German military engagement, and a leadership role in the EU. On the other hand, 'made in Germany' is a marker of market strength, signalling endurance and innovation. More specifically, German constitutionalism is considered a success story, and it has remarkable comparative standing. Between affirmation and scepticism, political debates remain rather controversial. Specifically in light of globalization, including global migration, and European integration as well as diverging trends, and in times of worrying political gains by authoritarian nationalist populism, there seems to be a need to (re-) define national identity, i.e. as the 'lead culture' (*Leitkultur*) all newcomers have to submit to, or as 'constitutional patriotism', a concept presented in the 1970s and revived in the twenty-first century, or as post-national identity 'being European' and other versions of cosmopolitanism. Thus, historically, often religiously or culturally grounded constructs of 'German' compete with more sober and sometimes in fact constitutional ideas.

The Basic Law itself lists foundational principles, such as republic, democracy, federalism, rule of law, welfare state (article 20), and defines them as unamendable (article 79 para 3). Also, it obliges all German states to act accordingly, to be 'homogenous' (article 28 para 1). In addition, the guarantee of dignity as inviolable (article 1 para 1) and the commitment to human rights (article 1 para 2), as well as access to judicial review (articles 1 para 3, 19 para 4), are considered key ingredients of German constitutionalism today. Although there is a distinction between rights for Germans and rights for everyone in the Basic Law itself, the list of fundamental rights is considered a guarantee of human rights,[248] and thus informs less of a nationalistic and more of a humanistic vision of 'us'.

However, the nation certainly has its constitutional limits, namely when it comes to political voice and power. In 1990, the Court struck down a state law that allowed foreigners to participate in local and municipal elections. 224 conservative members of the federal parliament had lodged proceedings to stop policies that resulted in more inclusionary local politics. They succeeded because the Court interpreted article 20 para 1 ('All state power emanates from the people') not only to constitutionalize the principle of democratic sovereignty, but to also define the subject of such democracy, the people. In principle, then, article 116 para 1 defines German nationality, which is the legal prerequisite for one's civil status and informs who can vote. Deductively, it also defines who is not German.[249]

In German constitutionalism, national identity and democracy are deeply intertwined in even more ways. Namely, 'constitutional identity' is the concept used by the Court to address the limits of democratic power in an international environment. It is important to note that

---

[247] Theodor W Adorno, 'On the question: "What is German?"', Thomas Y Levin tr (1985) 36 New German Critique 121.

[248] Angelika Siehr, *Die Deutschenrechte des Grundgesetzes* (Duncker & Humblot, Berlin, 2001). Based on the concept of 'open statehood' and European integration, rights explicitly guaranteed to Germans are also applied to European member state citizens, while non-EU citizens are at least protected by the general rights to liberty and equality. thus with more options to justify limitations.

[249] BVerfGE 88, 37, 51 ff—*Ausländerwahlrecht I (Foreigners' Voting Rights, 1990)*. There is an abundance of scholarly literature on the issue. See, i.e. Rolf Grawert, 'Staatsangehörigkeit und Staatsbürgerschaft' (1994) 23 Der Staat 179; Joseph H Weiler, 'Demos, Telos and the German Maastricht Decision' (1995) 1 European Law Journal 219.

this is not a fuzzy idea of 'national identity',[250] but a conceptual understanding of several guarantees of the German constitution. However, it has and does inform intense controversies over the role of national constitutionalism, and the power of national constitutional courts, in Europe.

German constitutional jurisprudence on the topic of Europe started early,[251] and eventually intensified, keeping up with the political decision for integration. The concept of 'constitutional identity' was presented in a case in which someone asked not to be extradited to another member state, despite EU law on the European Arrest Warrant, because basic conditions of dignity were not met.[252] Then, the Court explained what the national constitution defines as its very core, in the Basic Law itself, and what that means in the overall context of national constitutional and EU law, in its ruling on the Lisbon treaty in 2009.[253] Eventually, the Court explained in, what is by now, a series of decisions that, according to article 23 para 1 clause 1, Germany contributes to and participates in the EU, which also results in the precedence of application (*Anwendungsvorrang*) of EU law in Germany. EU law ranks even higher than national constitutional law itself. However, the Court also said, such precedence 'only extends as far as the Basic Law and the relevant Act of Approval permit or envisage the transfer of sovereign powers'.[254] Thus, EU law may only cover what the Basic Law or the statute that transposes EU law allows for. 'Limits to the opening of German statehood thus derive, pursuant to article 23 para 1 clause 3 GG, from the constitutional identity of the Basic Law', which the Court identifies as laid down in the eternity clause of article 79 para 3 as well as in the EU integration clause of article 23 para 1 clause 2. In fact, the Court considers the self-determination of the people by way of majority decisions in elections and votes to be constitutive for what it calls 'the state order of the Basic Law', which is based on the concept of the value and dignity of the human being as a 'personality', as 'a human rights core to the principle of democracy', rooted in human dignity. Therefore, even well-meaning paternalistic care would not be enough, but citizens shall responsibly participate as much as possible in making decisions for the entire community. In a move that also opens the door to individual constitutional complaints, the Court understands the right to vote in article 38 para 1 clause 1 to 'protect the voters from a loss in substance of their sovereign power (a power that is crucial for the constitutional order)' that may be brought about by considerable curtailment or substantial erosion of the rights of parliament or an excessive use of powers by EU organs.[255]

---

[250] Different from that, there are comparative discussions. Michel Rosenfeld distinguishes German, French, British, US and European and postcolonial constitutional identities, in Michel Rosenfeld and András Sajó (eds), *The Oxford Handbook of Comparative Constitutional Law* (OUP, Oxford, 2012).

[251] See BVerfGE 2, 143—*EVG-Vertrag (European Defence Treaty, 1953)*.

[252] BVerfGE 113, 273, 296—*Europäischer Haftbefehl (European Arrest Warrant, 2005)*, a 5:3 decision motivating a strong dissent.

[253] BVerfGE 123, 267, 348—*Vertrag von Lissabon (Lissabon Treaty, 2009)*.

[254] See BVerfGE 73, 339, 375 and 376—*Solange (As long as II, 1986)*; BVerfGE 89, 155, 190—*Maastricht Treaty, 1993)*; BVerfGE 123, 267, 348 ff—*Vertrag von Lissabon (Lissabon Treaty, 2009)*; BVerfGE 126, 286, 302—*Ultra-Vires-Kontrolle (Honeywell, 2010)*; BVerfGE 129, 78, 99 – *Anwendungserweiterung (Application of German Fundamental Rights to EU Legal Entities, 2011)*; 129, 124—*EFS (EFS, 2011)*; BVerfGE 132, 195—*Europäischer Stabilitätsmechanismus (European Stability Mechanism, 2012)*; 134, 366, 384, 26—*OMT-Beschluss (OMT Programme, 2014)*; BVerfGE 135, 317 *ESM-Vertrag (ESM Treaty)*; BVerfGE 140, 317—*Identitätskontrolle (Identity Control, 2015)*; BVerfGE 142, 123—*OMT Programme (OMT Programme, 2016)*, after a preliminary reference to the ECJ BVerfGE 134, 366—*OMT-Beschluss (OMT Programme, 2014)*. In the 1970s, the Court retained the power to decide in BVerfGE 37, 271—*Solange I (As Long as, 1974)*.

[255] Next to fundamental rights review, the GFCC employs two types of review regarding EU law. Identity review (*Identitätskontrolle*) asks the question of whether acts of the EU affect the principles of art 1 and 20, while ultra vires review (*Ultra-vires-Kontrolle*) addresses the boundaries of democratically legitimated EU integration not to be exceeded in a manifest and structurally significant manner and thereby violate the principle of the sovereignty

Regarding fundamental rights, German constitutionalism has bound itself to international human rights, particularly as guaranteed in the ECHR and specified in the jurisprudence of the ECtHR in Strasbourg. This does not mean that there is automatic acceptance of anything said there, but simply means that the interpretation of the national constitution will take into account international guarantees. This does not result in automatic consensus, either but informed famous 'dialogues' between these courts. One such 'dialogue' concerned a famous princess, Caroline von Monaco (then: Hannover), who complained about invasive press coverage. The German Court insisted on more respect for privacy, while the international court emphasized freedom of the press. Eventually, both moved towards the other.[256] Also, when the Court basically upheld a system of lifelong incarceration next to limited prison sentences, the ECtHR disagreed, the case went back and forth, before eventually reaching a consensus.

The structure of EU law differs from international human rights law, but the Court envisions a similar consensus-oriented relationship with the ECJ. While scholars as well as media reports tend to scandalize a 'war of the judges', most issues are not controversial in a world of embedded constitutionalism, in which a member state constitution usually accepts the political decision to transfer power to a multilateral institution like the EU. In fact, however, the decisive element of the current understanding of constitutional law is the discursive 'dialogue of courts', the 'mobile' of judicial bodies, framed as a *Verfassungsgerichtsverbund* (an association or union of constitutional courts): i.e. assessing the European Banking Union, the Court did not simply accept EU law, but engaged in a dialogue with the ECJ by submitting preliminary questions, before then interpreting EU law itself. It eventually declared that, so interpreted, this law was in line with German constitutional law.[257] Yet in the controversial PSPP ruling in 2020, the Second Senate disagreed with the ECJ and considered it to act beyond its competencies, not by overstepping its bounds, but by underperforming judicial control of the European System of Central Banks.[258]

However, it is a challenge, and a question frequently asked, how national constitutionalism shall survive, or what it should look like, in a highly integrated legal regime. German constitutional jurisprudence has evolved. In 1986, the Court was convinced that Europe had established fundamental rights protection, at the time without a human rights catalogue of its own.[259] This was restated in the pivotal Maastricht Treaty decision in 1993, the Banana Market decision in 2000, and the Lisbon Treaty ruling in 2009. In 2019, the Court joined EU efforts to really protect fundamental rights, now based on both member states' constitutions and the Charter of Fundamental Rights, in a shared commitment to the European Convention.

That year, the Court responded in two cases on one's right to one's data. It was confronted with the claim of whether someone also has the right to be forgotten, particularly via taking data out of a search engine, and a media archive, eventually. Again, German fundamental rights jurisprudence proudly features an elaborate scheme of 'informational

---

of the people. The latter was the focus of the Judgment of the Second Senate of 5 May 2020—2 BvR 859/15—that calls on the ECJ to consistently control the legality of actions of the European Central Bank.

[256] BVerfGE 101, 361—*Caroline II*; *von Hannover v Germany*, App No 59320, Chamber ruling of 24 June 2004; App No 40660/08, Grand Chamber ruling of 7 February 2012.

[257] BVerfGE, Decision of the Second Senate 30 July 2019—2 BvR 1685/14—(*Bankenunion*). The Press Release stated: 'If interpreted strictly, the framework for the European Banking Union does not exceed the competences of the European Union.'

[258] BVerfGE 154, 17—*PSPP, 2020*.

[259] BVerfGE 73, 339, 1565 ff—*Solange II (As Long as II, 1986)*.

self-determination', which obviously also inspired both EU legislation as well as ECJ rulings in cases brought against big search engines.[260] Eventually, the Court was asked by a man to block access to old media reports. For a long time, he had been released from a prison sentence for murder on a sailboat that had raised media attention at the time and feared reputational damage and social harm in times in which anyone would be able to find these old reports via a name search only. Also, an employer asked the Court to protect her right to have an interview that she once gave over quarrels with personnel to be removed from press archives because it had no significance in present times and damaged her employer reputation. In one case, the applicable EU Directive covered the issue fully, while in the other one, it applied, but left room for member states to find their own ways. Should a national constitutional court now refuse to take at least the first case because EU law was to be applied, or insist on a 'national identity' and judge it according to its national constitution? Or should the Court refer one or both cases to the ECJ? Or should the national constitution be applied in a manner that considers EU law like international human rights?

In 2019, the Court addressed the challenge. In what may be understood as another contribution to the conversation among courts, a floating and interdependent arrangement meant to further the protection of fundamental rights was developed, what both the Court and ECtHR Justice Renate Jaeger once called a 'mobile'. Regarding the right to be forgotten, the Court applies the national constitution in cases affected, but yet not fully determined, by EU law,[261] while it applies the Charter of Fundamental Rights of the EU in cases fully determined by EU law as long as this is in line with national constitutional requirements, which may mean that preliminary questions are sometimes referred to the ECJ.[262] Key arguments in this respect are the existence of a common ground of European constitutionalism, namely in the ECHR, as well as the respect for member state pluralism according to Article 6 TEU, as much as Germany's commitment to European integration, namely in article 23. Again, national constitutionalism is, in Germany, deeply embedded in transnational and international legal orders.

Regarding the EU, it seems that the more controversial European integration came to be, the more the Court became an influential European integration actor in both insisting on national democratic legitimacy for any international cooperation, yet also backing up European integration as consistent with the 'open statehood' (*offene Staatlichkeit*) that German constitutionalism endorses. Several national constitutional or supreme courts in Europe have argued along similar lines. To be clear, the concept of 'constitutional identity' is not applied if it is abused by courts who do not further democracy and fundamental rights, as the core components of the idea in German constitutional law, but rather use it to limit both European integration and the ECHR consensus by removing or eroding such protection. In German constitutional debates, controversies focus on other issues.

Not all questions have been answered, and some will be revisited in time. That is, it is controversial that the Court gives standing to challenges of European integration measures to any citizen based on her right to vote (article 38). This allows the Court to review much EU law, yet it also places a responsibility on a national constitutional court that it some think it is not designed to carry. Often, conservative nationalists use this venue to protest

---

[260] *Google Spain v AEPD & Gonzalez*, Dec of 13 May 2014, ECLI:EU:C:2014:317.
[261] BVerfG, Order of the First Senate, 6 November 2019—1 BvR 16/13—*Recht auf Vergessen (Right to be Forgotten I)*.
[262] BVerfG, Order of the First Senate, 6 November 2019—1 BvR 276/17—*Recht auf Vergessen (Right to be Forgotten II)*.

further integration, which also invokes the risk that the Court is instrumentalized to echo that ideology. Such complaints did not only force the Court to control mayor segments of EU law, but also to jump right into the financial crisis and its aftermath, which in addition raised the broader question of economic competences of courts as such. In these discussions, much depends on what the EU is seen as, and is meant to be. However, when national constitutional law binds all organs of the state when acting beyond national borders, difficult questions arise.

Eventually, 'Karlsruhe' has become a code for national constitutional limits of EU law-making and politics, although the Court emphasizes again and again that nationalism is not its calling. In fact, the Court rarely intervened in European matters, which prompted some critics to call it 'a dog that barks but does not bite', or a 'toothless tiger'.[263] In 2016, the Court held that a criminal court decision to hand a US citizen over to Italian authorities was a violation of Germany's constitutional identity. The man had been charged and sentenced with a crime in absentia, and Italian law did not offer a second chance to challenge that decision, and thus be heard in person with a competent court revisiting his case. This is a fact that the criminal court failed to properly take into account. It was eventually found to violate the guilt principle (*Schuldprinzip*) of criminal sanctions that is based in the inviolability of human dignity, article 1 para 1, and the principle of the rule of law, article 20 para 3, both listed in the eternity clause in article 79 para 3: 'The German state cannot lend its hand to violations of human dignity by other countries.' And this fundamental, and considering article 1, this very German statement has been used again, in limiting the federal police powers cooperate with non-German agencies. Thus, the areas in which German constitutionalism limits international affairs to date are basic standards of criminal law, i.e. when German authorities send a person, or send personal data, to other countries.[264] Also, with the 'right to be forgotten' rulings in 2019, the Court set out on a new path of collaboration with the European institutions to work on a lasting consensus on fundamental rights.

In a world with borders that change or erode, because of strong drifts towards globalization and regional transnationalism, national constitutional law must, according to German constitutionalism, change as well. The German tradition of a strong commitment to the state, sometimes even in its classic Westphalian form, is not easy to align with such callings. At the same time, the German commitment to 'never again' accept fascism or any other populist dictatorship, and the denial of human dignity to anyone, both inspires a defensive stance of a paradigmatic post-Second World War 'never again'-constitution, and a strong international commitment, which is also not always easy to align. German constitutional law has embedded itself in both European human rights and European Union law as well as in international legal commitments. There is much at stake after what is seen as, all in all, successful efforts to rebuild a national democracy committed to federalism and the rule of law, to the welfare state and to fundamental rights. In Germany, constitutional law, in an intense exchange between the Court and the academy, conceptually focused, and driven by cases randomly brought, seems dedicated to find a way that is as much German as it is European and international.

---

[263] Namely, these were reactions to the ruling on the European Banking Union in 2019. However, they seem to be driven by a particular political stance towards EU politics, rather than by doctrinal disagreement.

[264] Key elements of criminal law are considered essential to human dignity in Germany like the principle that there shall not be a sanction without individual guilt, or the requirement that prisoners must be guaranteed basic living conditions like a minimum size of prison cells, or the guarantee of legal limits to gathering and using personal data, including the prohibition to support a system that employs torture.

5

The Evolution and *Gestalt* of the Hungarian Constitution

Gábor Halmai

A. Origins of the Current Constitution	217	**C. Basic Structures and Concepts**	245
1. The 1989 Constitution	217	1. Government without Checks	245
2. Two Decades of Constitutional Democracy?	219	2. Identity of the Political Community	246
		3. Intervention into the Right to Privacy	248
3. Hungary's Fundamental Law	222	4. Weakening of the Protection of Fundamental Rights	249
B. The Evolution of the Constitution	223		
1. Cardinal Laws and Amendments to the Fundamental Law	223	5. Constitutional Entrenchment of Political Preferences	251
2. The Fourth and Fifth Amendments	226	6. A Populist Illiberal Constitutional System	254
3. The Sixth, Seventh, Ninth, Tenth, and Eleventh Amendments	231	**D. Constitutional Identity**	257
		1. The Abuse of the Concept	257
4. No Judicial Review of Constitutional Amendments	236	2. The Instrumental Role of Religion in National Identity	266

A. Origins of the Current Constitution

The parliament passed the current constitution, entitled the Fundamental Law of Hungary, on 18 April 2011.[1] The Fundamental Law, which entered into force on 1 January 2012, supersedes the previous constitution (hereinafter: the 1989 Constitution), which, in keeping with the requirements of democratic constitutionalism during the 1989–1990 regime change, comprehensively amended the first written Constitution of Hungary (Act XX of 1949).

1. The 1989 Constitution

In 1989, the illegitimate legislature, which had not been democratically elected, formally enacted the comprehensive modifications of the 1949 Constitution after peaceful negotiations between the representatives of the Communist regime and their democratic opposition. In scholarship, this process is called 'post-sovereign' or 'pacted constitution-making',[2] and it also took place in Spain at the end of the 1970s and in South Africa from the beginning

---

[1] For the English translation of the Fundamental Law, see The Fundamental Law of Hungary (www.njt.hu) (last accessed on 10 April 2022).

[2] See respectively Andrew Arato, *Post Sovereign Constitutional Making. Learning and Legitimacy* (OUP, Oxford, 2016), and Michel Rosenfeld, *The Identity of the Constitutional Subject: Selfhood, Citizenship, Culture, and Community* (Routledge, London, 2009).

Gábor Halmai, *The Evolution and* Gestalt *of the Hungarian Constitution* In: *The Max Planck Handbooks in European Public Law.* Edited by: Armin von Bogdandy, Peter M Huber, and Sabrina Ragone, Oxford University Press. © Gábor Halmai 2023.
DOI: 10.1093/oso/9780198726425.003.0005

through the middle of the 1990s. In 1989, during the so-called 'round-table negotiations', the participants of the Opposition Round-table (OR) and the representatives of the state party (the Hungarian Socialist Workers' Party) set forth the concepts of transforming the 1949 Rákosi-Constitution, which was inspired by Stalin, into a rule of law document. Afterwards, the illegitimate parliament only annexed the comprehensive amendment to the Constitution, which entered into force on 23 October, the anniversary of the 1956 Revolution, and which was, with lesser or greater changes, the basic document of the 'constitutional revolution' until 2011.

Immediately preceding the establishment of the OR in March 1989, the Hungarian Socialist Worker's Party (Magyar Szocialista Munkáspárt—MSZMP) had written a new (draft) Constitution and submitted it to the parliament. Thus, the opposition was afraid that those in power would create the 'new' constitutional framework themselves. During the Round Table negotiations, which started in mid-June, the OR tried to prevent this by maintaining that it would be the task of the new parliament, set up after the parliamentary elections, to adopt the new constitutional order. For example, they refused to negotiate about creating the institution of the President of the Republic. Instead, they recommended that the speaker of parliament should be vested temporarily with the powers of the President. Moreover, the participants of the OR had agreed on establishing the Constitutional Court prior to the new Constitution only three days before the negotiations ended.

Various factors contributed to the abandonment of the idea that the new, democratically elected parliament would adopt a new Constitution. These certainly included the fact that the opposition could not be sure that the MSZMP would not win by absolute majority against its rivals, which were far less known among the voters. But several signs indicate that, even if they obtained a relative majority, they could not prevent the MSZMP's ability to form a government. Of course, the MSZMP could not be sure of its success either. Thus, its members could not ignore the possibility of 'advance constitution-making', certainly in exchange for promises to guarantee some of their positions. Such a promise could take the shape of the parties ultimately signing the agreement to directly elect the President before the parliamentary elections, a solution that would have favoured the communist reformer, Imre Pozsgay. This was prevented by the success of the referendum initiated by the Alliance of Free Democrats (Szabad Demokraták Szövetsége—SZDSZ) and the Federation of Young Democrats (Fiatal Demokraták Szövetsége—FIDESZ), at the time a liberal party. Consequently, the President was elected by the new parliament only after the first democratic elections.

This shows that both the state party and the opposition were motivated not to leave the establishment of the transition's constitutional framework to a new Constitution by the fear that they could lose the democratic elections. Thus, the 1989 constitutional amendment introduced new substantive material to the 1949 framework. It can be considered a rule of law document, even though the Rákosist-Kádárist skeleton emerges sometimes, especially concerning the unchanged chapter structure, which begins with the state organization and is followed by the fundamental-rights parts. Apparently, the negotiation-based drafting explains why the old-new Constitution principally followed the model of a consensual democracy widely accepted in the continental European systems. The system of government, which assumed the presence of more than two parties in parliament and a coalition governance, meant that the parties knowingly rejected both the semi- or full presidential regime, preferred by the MSZMP and applied in many post-communist countries even today, and the English Westminster-type of two-party parliamentarism. When compared to the Western European solutions, the decision-making process set up in 1989–1990 had other distinctive characteristics clearly explained by the legacy of the forty-year totalitarian regime: not only was it based on the consensus among the coalition parties, but in some cases, it required the involvement of the opposition, and it significantly strengthened the checks on the governmental powers.

As regards the acts requiring a two-thirds majority, in their original form as 'acts with the force of the Constitution', the support of the opposition practically called for a two-thirds quorum in all questions concerning government structure and fundamental rights. In 1990, the 'pact' between the largest governing and opposition party radically reduced the number of qualified acts. In exchange for this and for accepting the constructive vote of confidence, the SZDSZ was granted the right to nominate a 'moderately weak' President of the Republic. In 1989, the OR was able to prevent including the institution of a 'moderately strong' President—a position designed for Imre Pozsgay—and so a semi-presidential system in the Constitution. But the presidential powers of Árpád Göncz were undeniably stronger than those set out in the Act No I of 1946, with its purely representational presidency. The President's 'neutral' powers meant that he belonged neither to the executive nor to the legislative branch but rather had an equilibrating role between the two. The powers of the Constitutional Court, which were extremely broad compared to other European solutions, and the complicated system of parliamentary commissioners also stemmed from the idea of limiting the executive.

The parties of the OR accepted the MSZMP's plan to set up the Constitutional Court as an institution counterbalancing the executive, as is prevalent in the consensual democracies of Europe, even for the temporary period prior to the elections. However, instead of a body for preserving the state party's power, the opposition insisted on a Court which radically limited the parliament and the government, whose decisions could not be overturned by the parliament (as initially proposed by the MSZMP), and where everyone was entitled to submit a petition to review the constitutionality of a piece of legislation (so-called 'popular action').

2. Two Decades of Constitutional Democracy?

In the second democratic term (1994–1998), the two new governing parties, the Hungarian Socialist Party (MSZP), successor of the MSZMP with an absolute majority of the seats alone, and its liberal coalition partner (SZDSZ) had more than two-thirds of the parliamentary seats and revived the threat that the governing parties could monopolize the making of the Constitution. This danger, however, was warded off by the governing coalition itself, which demonstrated restraint. They decided that the parliamentary committee set up to draft the Constitution could only adopt a resolution if it was supported by five out of the six parties, and if the committee rejected proposed passages, the provisions of the existing Constitution would prevail. In principle, this policy could have guaranteed the consensual drafting of a new, up to date Constitution. But in the summer of 1996 the new draft of the Constitution did not receive two-thirds of the votes in parliament because a part of the MSZP did not support it. The leftist wing of the government's stronger party prevented the approval of the draft because it did not include the declaration of the social character of the state and mechanisms for reconciling interests.

In the parliamentary period of 1998–2002, it seemed that the government would have gladly restricted the constitutional institutions of the consensus-based exercise of governmental powers, above all that of the parliament's means to control the executive. For instance, the first FIDESZ-led government decreased the frequency of the plenary sessions to every third week and prevented the establishment of any ad-hoc investigating committee of the parliament. However, they had neither the courage nor the necessary support to carry out the required constitutional amendments.

Many scholars criticized the Hungarian making of the Constitution of 1989. In his book published in 1992, the American law professor Bruce A Ackerman states, 'The constitutional guarantees of a liberal rule of law state can be established only if a new Constitution is adopted, and the possibility to adopt a new basic law fades as the time passes.'[3] He maintains that there would have been an opportunity, and indeed a need, to adopt a new Constitution in Hungary at the beginning of the political transition, which would have solved the legitimacy deficit of the 'system change', as with the German Basic Law (*Grundgesetz*) of 1949.

Even before the 2010 parliamentary elections and the subsequent illiberal turn, certain developments already raised the questions whether the constitutional values were widely recognized and if the Hungarian constitutional democracy could be considered consolidated two decades after the regime change. As a result of losing constitutional consensus among the political players, a large segment of these political actors, or their successors, no longer subscribed to the constitutional values accepted at the time of the regime's transition. Partly owing to this development, their supporters and a significant portion of society also no longer held the principles underlying constitutional democracy in high regard. In other words, it appears that the Constitutional Court's vision, expressed early in the transition process, never materialized: 'It is not only legal statutes and the operations of state organs that need to be in strict compliance with the Constitution, but the Constitution's conceptual culture and values need to fully suffuse society.'[4]

Indeed, the Constitutional Court led by László Sólyom aimed to construct such a constitutional culture by interpreting the Constitution in an activist way. This approach was expressed in the concept of the 'invisible Constitution', elaborated in Sólyom's concurring opinion to the decision on the death penalty: 'The Constitutional Court must continue its effort to explain the theoretical bases of the Constitution and of the rights included in it and to form a coherent system with its decisions, which as an "invisible Constitution" provides for a reliable standard of constitutionality beyond the Constitution, which nowadays is often amended out of current political interest; therefore this coherent system will probably not conflict with the new Constitution to be adopted or with future Constitutions.'[5] Therefore, Sólyom and many scholars argued that the text of the 1989 Constitution and the jurisprudence of the Constitutional Court make a new Constitution unnecessary.

FIDESZ's first term in power between 1998 and 2002 was followed by eight years of the Socialist–Liberal coalition government of MSZP and SZDSZ. This period was characterized by corruption as well as by the economic and moral failures of the governing parties. Prime Minister Ferenc Gyurcsány's speech to his Socialist Party fraction members in May 2006, weeks after his governing coalition won the parliamentary elections, was a symbolic event. In this speech, broadcasted on Hungarian Public Radio on 17 September 2006, Gyurcsány admitted that his party had made a mess of Hungary's economy and that '[w]e lied morning, noon and night'. There were immediate protests, organized by the main opposition party FIDESZ, who had lost the elections in April. Thanks to this situation, the governing coalition

---

[3] Bruce Ackerman, *The Future of Liberal Revolution* (Yale University Press, New Haven, 1992). Andrew Arato also claims that the constitution-making process in Hungary was incomplete. See Andrew Arato, 'What I have learned: Concluding remarks' (2010) 26 South African Journal on Human Rights 134–138.
[4] Decision 11/1992. (III. 5.) AB.
[5] Decision 23/1990. (XII. 31.) AB.

suffered large setbacks in the nationwide municipal elections held in October, after which the Prime Minister—following the President's wish—requested the vote of confidence to re-inforce political support for his austerity package and the transformation of the inefficient public sector. Even as parliament voted, tens of thousands of people gathered on Kossuth Square just outside the parliament and demanded Gyurcsány's dismissal. But lawmakers from Hungary's two coalition parties signalled their near-unanimous support for the Prime Minister in the confidence vote. After the opposition failed to dismiss the government, both in parliament and on the streets, it initiated national referendums on issues related to the budget and to the government's programme on certain reforms of health care and the higher education system. According to the Constitution, these questions cannot be subject to a referendum. Nevertheless, the majority of the Constitutional Court approved them. With a success rate of more than 80 per cent, the referendum held in 2008 finally destroyed the popularity of the governing parties. Even though they decided, in 2009, to replace Gyurcsány with Gordon Bajnai, another Socialist politician, by means of another vote of confidence, it was too late.

Before the 2010 elections, the majority of voters were already dissatisfied not only with the government but also with the transition itself, more so than in any other East Central European country.[6] FIDESZ reinforced these feelings by claiming that there was no real transition from 1989 to 1990, that the previous elite had merely converted its lost political power to an economic one. It cited as evidence the last two prime ministers of the Socialist Party, who both became rich after the transition due to the privatization process.

Disappointment with the regime transition was obviously exacerbated by the perfunctory nature of confronting the past, specifically the fact that for the most part, the new regime failed to hold the leaders of the state party accountable or to screen for people who had co-operated with the clandestine services of the old regime. Many of those who fell into these categories managed to convert their previous political influence into economic clout under the new regime, while the restitution provided to the victims of the former regime, be it in material or informational terms, was largely symbolic. Unlike the Czech, Slovak, and Polish parliaments in the early 2000s, the Hungarian legislature did not offer access to the docu-ments of the former secret services, although doing so would have recognized everyone's right to learn about public-interest documents stored in archives and enabled society to learn about its own history.

Populism, nationalism, anti-Europeanism, and anti-secularism spread more easily among those who were disillusioned with regime transition, as did racism, anti-Semitism, and homophobia, especially since certain political forces, in an effort to maximize votes, failed to reject the support of those who held such views. The fact that the establishment of the constitutional system in Hungary, as in other Central European regime transitions, was also concluded rapidly gave hope that the process of consolidation would be considerably quicker here. In light of the current situation in Hungary, however, one might well conclude that the current political and social consensus regarding democratic values is considerably more fragile than two decades ago in the early stages of regime transition. The state of demo-cratic and human rights culture and the lack of trust in democratic institutions—especially parliament and the political parties—make it harder to avoid the road that leads back to a

---

[6] In 2009, 51 per cent of Hungarians disagreed with the statement that they were better off since the transition, while only 30 per cent agreed. (In Poland 14 per cent and in the Czech Republic 23 per cent detected worsening, and 70 per cent and 75 per cent respectively perceived improvement.) See Eurobarometer, 2009, Microsoft Word—EB71StandardFullReport230909TCA.doc (www.europa.eu) (last accessed on 11 April 2022).

totalitarian regime. In part, the underlying reason is that the Hungarian institutions created at the beginning of the regime transition, including the Constitutional Court, are no longer substantial guarantees for asserting constitutionalism, as we will see in more detail below. But another reason is that the international and above all the European environment no longer appears fully willing and able to enforce international democratic standards.

The constitutional system without the second step of a post-sovereign constitution-making process, namely a final Constitution, seemed to work for more than twenty years, until FIDESZ's overwhelming electoral victory in 2010. How was the stage set for FIDESZ to win such a high percentage of the votes and change the entire constitutional setting without much resistance from the citizens? In addition to the unsuccessful and unpopular policy of the Socialist–Liberal governments, it also required FIDESZ's populism. The two key characteristics of this populism are anti-elitism and anti-liberalism. FIDESZ's anti-elitism—an unusual attribute for a key representative of the transition elite—rests on the assumption that society's wise majority is behind the 2010 electoral victory and that through the 'revolution at the voting booths', this majority has delegated its power to the government representing it. Consequently, no other mediating institution—banks, multinational corporations, political parties, or civic organizations—can authentically express the popular will. The 'National System of Cooperation' rather than elite bargains manifest that will. This populist version of conservative politics is also anti-liberal, which is rather surprising seeing as it comes from a party that used to consider itself liberal. This anti-liberalism puts great faith in the state's central organizing role in the economy, education, and culture.[7]

3. Hungary's Fundamental Law

FIDESZ's populism was directed against all elites, including those who had designed the 1989 constitutional system (a process in which FIDESZ had also participated). The party claimed that it was time for a new revolution and described the results of the 2010 elections as a 'revolution of the ballot boxes'. Viktor Orbán's intention with this revolution was to eliminate all checks and balances and even the parliamentary rotation of governing parties. In a speech held in September 2009, Orbán predicted that there was 'a real chance that politics in Hungary will no longer be defined by a dualist power space. Instead, a large governing party will emerge in the centre of the political stage [that] will be able to formulate national policy, not through constant debates but through a natural representation of interests'. Orbán's vision for a new constitutional order—one in which his political party occupies centre stage in Hungarian political life and puts an end to debates over values—has now been entrenched in a new Constitution, enacted in April 2011. The new constitutional order was built with the votes of his political bloc alone, and it aims to keep the opposition at bay for a long time. The new constitutional order of the Fundamental Law and the cardinal laws perfectly fulfils this plan: it does not separate powers or guarantee fundamental rights. Therefore, the new Hungary (not even a Republic in name anymore) cannot be deemed a state governed by the rule of law.

Together with its tiny Christian democratic coalition partner, the centre-right government of FIDESZ, or the Alliance of Young Democrats, received more than 50 per cent of the actual votes and so, due to the disproportionate election system, two-thirds of the seats in the

---

[7] See FIDESZ's populist conservatism in more detail: Umut Korkut, *Liberalization Challenges in Hungary: Elitism, Progressivism, and Populism* (Palgrave and Macmillan, Basingstoke, 2012) 162–176.

2010 parliamentary elections. With this overwhelming majority, they were able to enact a new Constitution without the votes of the weak opposition parties. But this constitutionalist exercise aspired to illiberal constitutionalism.[8]

The Fundamental Law was drafted without taking any of the elementary political, professional, scientific, and social debates into account. These considerations stem from the applicable constitutional norms and those parliamentary rules that one would expect to be met in a debate concerning a document that will define the life of the country over the long term. Effectively, only the representatives of the governing political parties participated in the debate. In its opinion approved at its plenary session of 17–18 June 2011, the Council of Europe's Venice Commission also expressed its concerns about the document, which was drawn up in a process that excluded the political opposition and professional and other civil organizations.[9] The document—according to the declaration set forth in article B)—seeks to maintain that Hungary is an independent, democratic state governed by the rule of law and furthermore—according to article E)—that Hungary contributes to the creation of European unity. However, in many respects it does not comply with standards of democratic constitutionalism and the basic principles set forth in article 2 of the Treaty on the European Union.

B. The Evolution of the Constitution

1. Cardinal Laws and Amendments to the Fundamental Law

Before 1 January 2012, when the new Constitution entered into force, the Hungarian parliament had been preparing a plethora of so-called cardinal—or two-third majority—laws, changing the shape of virtually every political institution in Hungary and diminishing the guarantee of constitutional rights. These cardinal laws included the laws on freedom of information, the Constitutional Court, criminal prosecution, citizenship, family protection, the independence of the judiciary, the status of churches, and elections to parliament. In the last days of 2011, parliament had also enacted the so-called 'transitory provision' to the Fundamental Law, claiming that it had constitutional status. This provision partly supplemented the new Constitution even before it went into effect.

These new laws have been uniformly detrimental to the political independence of state institutions, the transparency of law-making, and the future of human rights in Hungary.

---

[8] In an interview on Hungarian public radio on 5 July 2013, Prime Minister Viktor Orbán responded to European Parliament critics regarding the new constitutional order by admitting that his party did not aim to produce a liberal constitution. He said, 'In Europe, the trend is for every constitution to be liberal; this is not one. Liberal constitutions are based on the freedom of the individual, and they subdue welfare and the interest of the community to this goal. When we created the Constitution, we posed questions to the people. The first question was the following: What would you like? Should the Constitution regulate the rights of the individual and create other rules in accordance with this principle, or should it create a balance between the rights and duties of the individual? As I recall, more than 80 per cent of the people responded by saying that they wanted to live in a world where freedom existed but where welfare and the interest of the community could not be neglected, and that these elements need to be balanced in the Constitution. I received an order and mandate for this. For this reason, the Hungarian Constitution is a constitution of balance, and not a side-leaning constitution, which is the fashion in Europe, as there are plenty of problems there'. See A Tavares, *jelentés egy baloldali akció* (The Tavares report is a leftist action), Interview with PM Viktor Orbán on 5 July 2013, Kossuth Rádió.

[9] FIDESZ's counter-argument was that the other parliamentary parties excluded themselves from the decision-making process with their boycott, with the exception of Jobbik, which voted against the document.

Ignoring serious warnings from then European Commission President José Barroso,[10] the FIDESZ government recently pushed through two cardinal laws on financial matters. The new law[11] on the central bank (the Magyar Nemzeti Bank or MNB) gives the Prime Minister the right to appoint all vice-presidents of the bank, while previously, the president of the central bank initiated the nominations process himself. The law creates a new third vice-president for the bank, and Prime Minister Viktor Orbán can appoint one of these vice-presidents immediately. The new law also expands the number of members on the monetary council. The monetary council, which sets monetary policy and interest rates, will grow to nine members, of which six already were or soon will be put into office by the FIDESZ government.

On the same day it passed this law, parliament passed a constitutional amendment that also affects the status of the central bank. According to this amendment, parliament may merge the central bank with the existing Financial Supervisory Authority to create a new agency within which the central bank would be just one division. The government would then be able to name this new agency's head, who would effectively become the boss of the president of the central bank, thus reducing the bank president to a mere vice-president in the new agency. The constitutional amendment does not actually complete the merger—it just lays the constitutional groundwork for the later disappearance of the independent bank. The new Economic Stability Law—also a target of EU criticism—creates a permanent flat tax, requiring all personal wage income to be taxed at the same rate, starting in January 2013.

The constitutional amendment that also passed on 30 December, the last day of the parliamentary session, dealt with the independence of the judiciary. In it, both the head of the National Judicial Office and the public prosecutor, two people very close to the governing party and elected by the FIDESZ parliamentary supermajority, can choose which judge hears each case. In a prior decision, the Constitutional Court had declared a law unconstitutional that permitted political officials to assign cases in this way. To avoid constitutional questions, the government simply included the new powers to assign cases in the Constitution itself.

The constitutional reforms have also seriously undermined the independence of the ordinary judiciary by changing the judicial appointment and reassignment process. According to the Cardinal Acts on the Structure of the Judiciary and the Legal Status of Judges,[12] the Head of the National Judicial Office can select either any judge from among the top three candidates recommended by the judicial council of the court where the appointment would be made or none of them at all. If she decides against the top candidate, or against any of the candidates listed, she must only report the reasons to the National Judicial Council, a new body that has a mere advisory role in this matter. While formally, the President of the Republic must sign off on all new judicial appointments, only the decision of the Head of the National Judicial Office is needed to promote or demote a judge presently sitting anywhere in the judiciary. The new law contains no procedures through which a sitting judge can contest such a reassignment. The nomination process for new judges became quite salient because the Transitory Provisions to the Fundamental Law, an omnibus constitutional addendum

---

[10] On Barroso's letter to Orbán see Edith Balázs, 'Baroso Calls on Hungary's Orbán to Withdraw Laws, Origo Says' (Bloomberg, 20 December 2011) http://www.bloomberg.com/news/2011-12-20/barroso-calls-on-hungarys-orban-to-withdraw-laws-origo-says.html (last accessed on 18 January 2021).

[11] For the contents of the new national bank law see Bloomberg News, 'Hungary Passes Central Bank Rules Despite Risk to Bailout' (The New York Times, 30 December 2011) http://www.nytimes.com/2011/12/31/business/global/hungary-passes-central-bank-rules-despite-risk-to-bailout.html?_r=2 (last accessed on 18 January 2021).

[12] Act CLXI of 2011 on the Organization and Administration of the Judiciary and Act CLXII of 2011 on the Legal Status and Remuneration of Judges.

also passed at the very end of 2011, reduced the retirement ages for judges on ordinary courts from 70 to 62, starting on the day the new Constitution went into effect. This change forced 274 judges into early retirement. Those judges included six of the twenty court presidents at the county level, four of the five appeals-court presidents, and twenty of the eighty Supreme Court judges. In July 2012, the Constitutional Court declared the suddenly lowered retirement age for judges unconstitutional.[13] But by the time the Court ruled, the 274 judges had already been fired. President Áder said he would not withdraw the orders firing the judges, and the Head of the National Judicial Office said that the newly hired and promoted judges would not be removed from office, even if the unconstitutionally fired judges were reinstated by order of the labour courts. The European Commission requested that the European Court of Justice expedite its decision in the infringement proceeding initiated to redress this issue, and in November 2012, the Court ruled that Hungary's reduced retirement age for judges is discriminatory.[14] Despite these decisions, the fired judges were not reinstated.[15]

Many other cardinal laws were passed in the last two weeks before the Fundamental Law entered into force. According to the cardinal law on the status of the churches as well as a separate law on the Transitional Provisions of the Fundamental Law—both enacted with a two-thirds majority at the end of 2011—the power to designate legally recognized churches is vested in parliament itself. The law has listed fourteen legally recognized churches and required all other previously registered churches (some 330 religious organizations in total) to either re-register under considerably more demanding new criteria or continue to operate as religious associations without the legal benefits offered to the recognized churches (like tax exemptions and the ability to operate state-subsidized religious schools). As a result, only eighteen have been able to re-register, so the vast majority of previously registered churches have been deprived of their status as legal entities. Because registration requires an internal democratic decision-making structure, the majority of previously registered churches were not able to continue to operate with any legal recognition under the new regime. Non-traditional and non-mainstream religious communities, which had not confronted any legal obstacles between 1989 and 2011, are now facing increasing hardships and discrimination as a result.

On 23 December 2011, parliament was also set to vote on the controversial election law with its gerrymandered electoral districts, making the electoral system even more disproportionate and so giving the current governing party an advantage in future elections. The main changes in the system were as follows: a shift to the majoritarian principle by increasing the proportion of single-member constituency mandates, eliminating the second round, replacing the absolute majority with a relative-majority system, and introducing 'winner-compensation'.

In late 2012, the parliament amended the Fundamental Law and passed a new cardinal law on election procedures, introducing a new system of voter registration. The most important change was the abolition of the system of automatic voter registration. Now, Hungarian citizens are no longer automatically entitled to vote but must register every four years to be allowed to vote. This is extremely unusual in European comparison, but even the very few countries that require registration strive to facilitate this process for their citizens. While the

---

[13] Decision 33/2012 (VII.17) AB.

[14] Case C-186/12 *Commission v Hungary* [2012] ECJ/CJEU.

[15] See the details of the case in Gábor Halmai, 'The Early Retirement of the Hungarian Judges', in Fernanda Nicola and Bill Davis (eds), *EU Law Stories: Contextual and Critical Histories of European Jurisprudence* (CUP, Cambridge, 2017) 471–488.

original bill contained a provision giving citizens in Hungary proper a brief window of two weeks to register by mail, the version finally adopted eliminated this option. Only citizens abroad were entitled to register by mail. The new law also limited both the time for campaigning and advertising spaces, thus placing even greater restrictions on the opposition's already limited channels of communication with the public. Even those matters that were anticipated to be slight progress, i.e., the number of signatures necessary for placing candidates on the ballot, ultimately turned out to be far less generous than originally suggested.

2. The Fourth and Fifth Amendments

On 11 March 2013, the Hungarian parliament added the Fourth Amendment[16] to the country's 2011 Constitution, re-enacting a number of controversial provisions that had been annulled by the Constitutional Court and rebuffing requests by the European Union, the Council of Europe, and the US government that urged the Hungarian government to seek the opinion of the Venice Commission before enacting the amendment. The Fourth Amendment also added new restrictions to the Constitutional Court, inserted provisions that limit the application of constitutional rights, and raised questions about whether concessions that Hungary made to European bodies in the previous year in order to comply with European law are themselves now unconstitutional. These moves rekindled serious doubts about the state of liberal constitutionalism in Hungary and Hungary's compliance with its international commitments under the Treaties of the European Union and under the European Convention on Human Rights.

This amendment was submitted to parliament as a 'private member's bill'. According to Hungarian parliamentary procedure, government bills must go through a stage of social consultation before the bill is put up for a vote. Social consultation requires the government to determine how interested civil society groups and relevant government ministries view the effects of the proposed law. But private member's bills skip that requirement and can go straight to the floor of the parliament for a vote. The Fourth Amendment was introduced by all of the MPs in the government's parliamentary fraction and the vote followed strict party lines, with every member of the governing party's bloc voting yes and everyone else either voting no or boycotting the vote. Yet the government avoided open political debate on the bill by using the private member's bill procedure.

The government declared that this fifteen-page comprehensive amendment to the still-new Constitution was necessary because of previous decisions by the Hungarian Constitutional Court, in particular a ruling issued at the very end of 2012. This decision held that those parts of the Transitional Provisions of the Fundamental Law that are not transitional in nature could not be deemed part of the Constitution and were therefore invalid.[17] (The Venice Commission had previously reviewed and criticized some elements of the Transitional Provisions.[18]) In his letter to Mr Thorbjørn Jagland, Secretary General of the Council of Europe, dated 7 March 2013, Mr Tibor Navracsis, the Hungarian Minister of Public Administration and Justice, argued that the Fourth Amendment's main objective was

---

[16] See the 'official' English text of the amendment provided by the government here: http://www.venice.coe.int/webforms/documents/?pdf=CDL-REF%282013%29014-e (last accessed on 10 April 2022).

[17] Decision 45/2012. (XII. 29.).

[18] See Opinion 664/2012 on the Act CCVI of 2011 on the Right to Freedom of Conscience and Religion and legal Status of Churches, Denominations and Religious Communities.

to formally incorporate into the text of the Fundamental Law itself the provisions annulled for formal procedural reasons. He argued that the amendment is therefore, 'to a great extent, merely a technical amendment to the Fundamental Law, and most of its provisions do not differ from the former text of the Transitional Provisions or they are directly linked thereto. Accordingly, the significance and novelty of this proposal should not be overestimated'. Mr József Szájer, the FIDESZ member of the European Parliament who served as the official representative of the Hungarian government at the hearing before the Commission on Security and Cooperation in Europe (US Helsinki Commission) on 19 March 2013, went even further, claiming that the amendment was 'basically a copy-paste exercise of a purely technical nature' done at the request of the Court itself.[19]

These statements are misleading. In its decision of 28 December 2012, the Constitutional Court did not review the substance of the Transitional Provisions, since the ombudsman had not requested such a review in his petition. Instead of asking that the nullified provisions be reinserted into the Constitution as an amendment, the Court only said that if the parliament wanted a provision to be part of the Constitution, it was not enough to declare that the Transitional Provisions had constitutional status. Instead, the parliament had to use the formal procedure laid out in the Constitution to make a constitutional amendment. The Court did not tell the government to reinsert the annulled provisions in the Constitution.

In fact, the ruling on the Transitional Provisions enabled the Constitutional Court to review the substance of some of the cardinal laws that were identical to the corresponding parts of the Transitional Provisions. Most of the provisions struck down by the Constitutional Court when it reviewed the Transitional Provisions were also embedded in cardinal laws that the parliament had passed previously. With these provisions now 'demoted' from constitutional status by the Court's ruling, the Court then undertook to review the almost identical provisions in the cardinal laws. Among these reviewed and annulled laws was one on voter registration, which the Court found unconstitutional on substantive grounds because it constituted an unnecessary barrier to voting.[20]

When the Fourth Amendment was submitted to the parliament, a decision was also expected on the constitutionality of the cardinal law on the status of churches. The Court did in fact issue its ruling on 26 February 2013,[21] declaring parts of the law that regulated the parliamentary registration of churches unconstitutional. These provisions had first been enacted as law on 12 July 2011, were struck down by the Constitutional Court on procedural grounds in December 2011,[22] and then reinserted in the Transitional Provisions one week after the Constitutional Court struck down the law. This section of the Transitional Provisions was then struck down by the Court again in December 2012 because the provision failed to guarantee procedural fairness in the parliamentary process by which churches were certified. Within a week, the annulled provisions were again added to a constitutional amendment, the Fourth Amendment, which included a section prohibiting the Constitutional Court from substantively evaluating constitutional amendments, thus shielding it from the Court's review.

The fact that the government was defeated in the voter registration and church registration cases shows that even though the FIDESZ government had elected seven of the fifteen

---

[19] Mr Szájer's testimony can be found at Testimony Szajer_0.pdf (www.csce.gov) (last accessed on 11 April 2022).

[20] Decision 1/2013. (I. 5.). AB.

[21] Decision 6/2013. (III. 1.) AB.

[22] Decision 164/2011. (XII. 20.) AB.

judges with the votes of their own parliamentary bloc by that time, these judges still did not hold a reliable majority in the Court.[23] That may have provided a reason for the government to want to limit the Court's influence even further.

In response to these decisions, the Fourth Amendment elevated the annulled permanent provisions of the Transitional Provisions into the main text of the Fundamental Law, with the intention of excluding further constitutional review. At the same time, it prohibited the Constitutional Court from reviewing the substantive constitutionality of constitutional amendments. The Fourth Amendment therefore contained all of the annulled sections of the Transitional Provisions except the section on voter registration. Even though the Constitutional Court argued that the parliament's registration of churches does not provide a fair procedure for the applicants, this procedure will be constitutional in the future. For the Fourth Amendment includes this procedure, previously declared unconstitutional, in the Constitution itself, thus putting it beyond the Constitutional Court's reach. Effectively, this gravely restricts the freedom to establish new churches in Hungary.

The Fourth Amendment also included in the Constitution and so put beyond the Constitutional Court's reach the power of the President of the National Judicial Office (NJO) to move cases from the court to which they are assigned by law to a different, less crowded court anywhere in the country. While the Constitutional Court did not have the opportunity to review the substance of this provision for constitutionality, it had previously struck down a similar provision giving that power to the Prosecutor General.[24] The Venice Commission had criticized the NJO President's power to move cases,[25] and the Hungarian government had added some restrictions on this power by amending the relevant cardinal law in summer 2012.

A number of statutory provisions previously annulled by the Constitutional Court have also become part of the Fourth Amendment. One of them authorizes the legislature to set conditions for state support in higher education, such as requiring graduates of state universities to remain in the country for a certain period of time after graduation if the state has paid for their education. The Constitutional Court had declared this unconstitutional in December 2012 because it violates both the right to free movement and the free exercise of occupation. The European Commission had expressed its concern over this restriction on the movement of Hungarian students in an 'EU Pilot' letter to the government of Hungary in November 2012.[26]

Another reversal of a declaration of unconstitutionality is the authorization for both the national legislature and local governments to declare homelessness unlawful in order to protect 'public order, public security, public health and cultural values'.[27] The Constitutional Court had declared it unconstitutional to prohibit homelessness as a status because it violated

---

[23] When it came to power in 2010, the FIDESZ government changed the rules for nominating judges to the Court so that all of the recently elected judges were elected by the FIDESZ two-thirds majority in parliament without needing (and generally without receiving) the support of any opposition parties. The government increased the number of judges on the Court from eleven to fifteen so that they would have even more seats to fill. When the Court struck down the Transitional Provisions and the Law on the Status of Churches in December 2012 and February 2013 respectively, seven of the fifteen judges had been named by FIDESZ since 2010. In February 2013, an eighth judge was added, and in April 2013, a ninth FIDESZ judge joined the bench.

[24] Decision 166/2011 (XII. 20.) AB.

[25] See Opinion 663/2012 on Act CLXII of 2011 on the Legal Status and Remuneration of Judges and Act CLXI of 2011 on the Organization and Administration of Courts.

[26] Amicus Brief to the Venice Commission on the Fourth Amendment to the Fundamental Law of Hungary, 44-50, http://fundamentum.hu/sites/default/files/amicus_brief_on_the_fourth_amendment.pdf (last accessed on 11 April 2022).

[27] Art 8 of the Fourth Amendment to the Fundamental Law.

the human dignity of people who could not afford a place to live.[28] But since the power to declare homelessness unlawful has now been included in the Constitution and placed beyond the reach of the Constitutional Court, it cannot be reviewed again.

In late 2012, the Court had annulled the definition of the family in the law on the protection of families because it was too narrow and excluded all families other than very traditional ones consisting of married different-sex parents with children.[29] Now the Fundamental Law defines marriage as permissible only between men and women. It also establishes the parent–child relationship as the basis of the family, excluding not only same-sex marriage but also all non-marital partnerships. The Fourth Amendment therefore overruled yet another Constitutional Court decision.

Under the old Constitutional Court jurisprudence, group libel laws were found to be an unconstitutional restriction on free speech.[30] The Fourth Amendment entrenched in the Constitution those parts of the new Civil Code that permit private actions to remedy group libel, not only in the case of the protection of racial, religious, and other minorities, but also where offenses are committed 'against the dignity of the Hungarian nation'. Since the Fourth Amendment annulled all of the Constitutional Court's case law from 1990 to 2011, the addition of this provision to the Constitution does not directly contradict a recent case, but it is a jarring reversal of something that had been taken for granted in Hungarian constitutional law.

As part of the Fourth Amendment to the Fundamental Law, a new article U has been adopted, which supplements detailed provisions on the country's communist past and statute of limitations in the body text of the Constitution. This new article, passed after twenty-three years of solid democracy and a working system of the rule of law, revisits the settlements made during the immediate transition from communist dictatorship to democracy by reopening possible cases against former communist officials. While the law could possibly serve the aim of accountability, in the only case opened so far (the *Biszku* case),[31] it in fact represents victors' justice by weakening the ruling party FIDESZ's political rival, the Socialist Party (the successor of the Communist Party).

Article U(1) states that the pre-1989 Communist Party (the Hungarian Socialist Workers' Party) and its satellite organizations that supported communist ideology were 'criminal organizations', whose leaders were liable 'without a statute of limitations'. In sections 7 and 8, however, that broad statement is contradicted by provisions that define a mechanism for

---

[28] Decision 38/2012. (XI. 14.) AB.

[29] Decision 43/2012. (XII. 20.) AB.

[30] Decision 96/2008. (VII. 3.) AB.

[31] Béla Biszku, who had played a key role as Minister of Interior between 1957 and 1961 in the reprisals against the participants of the 1956 revolution, was charged with crimes, which were subject to the statute of limitations. Therefore, the parliament enacted a law, called in the media 'Lex Biszku', which translated the definition of crimes against humanity of the Nuremberg Statute into Hungarian and explicitly authorized the Hungarian courts to prosecute them, without defining the contextual elements of crimes against humanity and also criminalizing the violation of common Article 3 of the Geneva Conventions in contravention to the *nullum crimen* principle. Moreover, the law introduced the category of 'communist crimes' and declared that the commission or aiding and abetting of serious crimes such as voluntary manslaughter, assault, torture, unlawful detention and coercive interrogation is not subject to a statute of limitations when committed on behalf, with the consent of, or in the interest of the party state. This provision clearly replicates the one that was found unconstitutional by the Constitutional Court in 1992. Based on the new law Béla Biszku was the only person convicted for being a member of the interim executive committee of the communist party which set up a special armed force in order to 'maintain order' and act with force against civilians if need be. The court acquitted the defendant regarding the most serious charge and found him guilty only of complicity and two unrelated petty crimes: abuse of ammunition and the denial of the crimes of the communist regime. For these minor crimes, he was sentenced for two years imprisonment suspended for three years. The verdict was still not final, because the prosecution appealed for a heavier judgment, while the defendant asked for total acquittal, but after the verdict was made public the defendant died.

interrupting and tolling the statute of limitations for as yet unprosecuted communist-period crimes.

Furthermore, the Fundamental Law includes a very broad and general liability for a number of past acts, including destroying post-Second World War Hungarian democracy with the assistance of Soviet military power, the unlawful persecution, internment, and execution of political opponents, the defeat of the 1956 October Revolution, destroying the legal order and private property, creating national debt, 'devastating the value of European civilization', and all criminal acts that were committed with political animus and had not been prosecuted by the criminal justice system for purely political motives.

Articles U(2) and U(3) call for remembrance of the communist past and create a new national committee to document national memory in this regard. New article U(4) provides that former communist leaders are public persons with respect to their past political actions and as such must tolerate public scrutiny and criticism, except for deliberate lies and untrue statements, as well as disclosure of personal data linked to their functions and actions. New article U(5) provides grounds for new legislation reducing the pensions and other benefits of specific leaders of the communist dictatorship. This provision appears to contradict Constitutional Court decision 43/1995, which held that people could not be denied pension payments after they had paid into the state pension scheme as they were required to do. But that decision, together with all others made before the Fundamental Law entered into force, has been annulled by the Fourth Amendment.

Articles U(6) through (8) relate to the tolling and interruption of the statute of limitations for specific serious crimes that article U(1) seems to say are not time-barred. There is as yet no law that defines which crimes are serious enough to justify the removal of all time limitations on prosecutions and which are subject to the newly reset clock for prosecutions. These provisions contradict the Constitutional Court's declaration in its decision 11/1992 that this sort of extension of the statute of limitations is unconstitutional. Yet article U(9) bars victims of the communist period from compensation by ruling out the passing of any new laws that might provide such compensation to individuals for harms caused them during the period that individual cases would re-examine. To reverse course after twenty-three years puts those who may be prosecuted long after the fact at a distinct disadvantage. More than two decades is a very long period of time after which to question the legal framework of the statute of limitations for the types of criminal acts in question. Such provisions may not run afoul of the time-honoured doctrine of *nullum crimen sine lege*, but they may nonetheless constitute violations of rights to due process of law.

Following international pressure, the Hungarian government finally made some cosmetic changes to its Fundamental Law, doing little to address concerns voiced by the Council of Europe and the European Parliament. The changes left provisions in place that undermine the rule of law and weaken human rights protection. The Hungarian parliament, with a majority of its members from the governing party, adopted the Fifth Amendment on 16 September 2013.[32] Hungary's reasoning stated that the amendment aims to 'conclude the constitutional debates in an international forum'. The Prime Minister's Office issued a

---

[32] Both foreign and Hungarian Human Rights NGOs said that the 'amendments show the government is not serious about fixing human rights and rule of law problems in the Constitution'. See the assessment of Human Rights Watch from 18 September 2013; http://www.hrw.org/news/2013/09/17/hungary-constitutional-change-falls-short (last accessed on 11 April 2022) and the joint opinion of three Hungarian NGOs; http://helsinki.hu/oto dik-alaptorveny-modositas-nem-akarasnak-nyoges-a-vege (last accessed on 11 April 2022).

THE EVOLUTION AND *GESTALT* OF THE HUNGARIAN CONSTITUTION 231

statement that 'The government wants to do away with those … problems that have served as an excuse for attacks on Hungary.' The major elements of the amendment are as follows:

a) Regarding political campaigns on radio and television, commercial media broadcasters are allowed to air political ads, but they must operate similarly to public media channels—i.e., distribution of airtime for political ads should not be discriminatory and should be provided free of charge. But since commercial media cannot be obliged to air such ads, it is unlikely that commercial outlets would agree to run campaign ads without charge.

b) Regarding recognition of religious communities (in line with the relevant cardinal law), the amendment emphasized that all communities are entitled to operate freely, but that parliament must still vote on whether those who seek further cooperation with the state (the so-called 'established churches') receive that status. This means that the amendment did not address discrimination against churches not recognized by the government. Parliament, rather than an independent body, confers recognition, which is necessary for a church to apply for government subsidies.

c) The provision enabling the government to levy taxes to settle unforeseen financial expenses that occur after a court, such as the European Court of Justice, rules against the country was also removed. But the reasoning added that the government is always free to levy new taxes, and this amendment will cost Hungarian taxpayers at least six billion Forints in the next five years.

d) The amendment allowed for the merger of the central bank (MNB) and the financial watchdog institution (PSZÁF).

e) Although the amendment elevated some provisions of a self-governing supervisory body, the National Judicial Council, to the level of the Constitution, and slightly strengthened the Council's powers, it still left key tasks of administering the courts to the National Judicial Office.

f) One positive amendment removed the power of the National Judicial Office's President to transfer cases between courts—a change already made at the statutory level, but since the Head of the Office was already able to appoint new judges loyal to the government all over the country, the transfer power was no longer needed to find politically reliable judges.

3. The Sixth, Seventh, Ninth, Tenth, and Eleventh Amendments

In June 2016, as part of the Hungarian government's anti-migration policy, the National Assembly representatives of the FIDESZ-KDNP governing alliance and the radical-nationalist opposition party Jobbik approved the Sixth Amendment to the Fundamental Law. This amendment authorizes the National Assembly to declare, at the government's initiative, a 'terrorism state of emergency' (*terrorveszélyhelyzet*) in the event of a terrorist attack or the 'significant and direct danger of a terrorist attack' (*terrortámadás jelentős és közvetlen veszélye*). In March 2017, the Hungarian parliament passed an amendment to the Asylum Act that forced all asylum seekers into guarded detention camps. While their cases are being decided, asylum seekers, including women and children over the age of fourteen, will be herded into shipping containers surrounded by a high razor-wire fence on the Hungarian side of the border.[33]

---

[33] On 14 March 2017, the European Court of Human Rights found that the detention of two Bangladeshi asylum-seekers for more than three weeks in a guarded compound without any formal, reasoned decision

With these legislative measures adopted, the government began a campaign against the EU's relocation plan. First, it initiated a referendum. On 2 October 2016, Hungarian voters went to the polls to answer one referendum question: 'Do you want to allow the European Union to mandate the relocation of non-Hungarian citizens to Hungary without the approval of the National Assembly?' Although 3.3 million Hungarians, 98 per cent of those who cast votes and 92 per cent of all the valid votes (6 per cent were spoiled ballots) were in agreement with the government and thus answered no, the referendum was invalid because the turnout was only around 40 per cent instead of the required 50 per cent.

Because of the failure of the referendum, Prime Minister Orbán introduced the Seventh Amendment to defend Hungarian constitutional identity and to politically legitimize non-compliance with EU law in this area. In the Foundation section, the draft-amendment touched upon the National Avowal, the Europe clause, and the provision on the interpretation of the Fundamental law. In the section on Freedoms and Responsibilities, it dealt with the provision on prohibition of expulsion of Hungarian citizens and the collective expulsion of foreigners.[34]

The proposal was to add a new sentence to the National Avowal, following the sentence, 'We honour the achievements of our historical Constitution, and we honour the Holy Crown, which embodies the constitutional continuity of Hungary's statehood and the unity of the nation.' The new sentence would read, 'We hold that the defence of our constitutional self-identity, which is rooted in our historical Constitution, is the fundamental responsibility of the state.'

Paragraph 2 of the Europe clause (article E) of the Fundamental Law would be amended to read, 'Hungary, as a Member State of the European Union and in accordance with the international treaty, will act sufficiently in accordance with the rights and responsibilities granted by the founding treaty, in conjunction with powers granted to it under the Fundamental Law together with other Member States and European Union institutions. *The powers referred to in this paragraph must be in harmony with the fundamental rights and freedoms established in the Fundamental Law and must not place restrictions on the Hungarian territory, its population, the state, or its inalienable rights'*. [The new sentence is in italics.]

A new paragraph 4 would be added to article R: '(4) It is the responsibility of every state institution to defend Hungary's constitutional identity.'

The following new paragraph 1 was planned to be added to article XIV: '(1) No foreign population can settle in Hungary. In accordance with the procedures established by the National Assembly for Hungarian territory, foreign citizens, not including the citizens of countries in the European Economic Area, may have their documentation individually evaluated by Hungarian authorities.'

All 131 MPs of the FIDESZ-KDNP governing coalition voted in favour of the proposed amendment, while all sixty-nine opposition MPs either did not vote (sixty-six representatives) or voted against the amendment (three representatives). The proposed amendment

and without appropriate judicial review had amounted to a de facto deprivation of their liberty (Art 5 of the Convention) and right to effective remedy (Art 13). The Court also found a violation of Art 3 on account of the applicants' expulsion to Serbia insofar as they had not had the benefit of effective guarantees to protect them from exposure to a real risk of being subjected to inhuman and degrading treatment (judgment of 14 March 2017 in the case of *Ilias and Ahmed v Hungary*, Application no 47287/15). We should take into account that this unlawful detention of the applicants in the transit zone was based on less restrictive rules enacted in 2015.

[34] The National Avowal is the preamble of the 2011 Fundamental Law of Hungary, and the Foundation section contains the main principles, while the section on Rights and Responsibilities contains the fundamental rights and obligations.

thus fell two votes short of the two-thirds majority required to approve amendments to the Fundamental Law. Although in principle, Jobbik supported the proposed Seventh Amendment, the party's MPs did not participate in the vote because the government had failed to satisfy Jobbik's demand that the Hungarian Investment Immigration Program, which grants citizens of foreign countries who purchase 300,000 Euros in government 'residency bonds' permanent residence in Hungary, be repealed.[35]

After the failed constitutional amendment, the Constitutional Court, loyal to Orbán, came to the rescue of his constitutional identity defence of the government's policies on migration. The Court carved out an abandoned[36] petition of the equally loyal Commissioner for Fundamental Rights, filed a year earlier, before the referendum was initiated. In his motion, the Commissioner asked the Court to deliver an abstract interpretation of the Fundamental Law in connection with the Council Decision 2015/1601 of 22 September 2015.[37] (For a more detailed analysis of the Constitutional Court's decision see below, under Section D.)

After the April 2018 parliamentary elections, with FIDESZ having regained its two-thirds majority, the government finally enacted the Seventh Amendment on 20 June, this time with Jobbik's votes. In addition to the failed provisions on constitutional identity, the amendment contains other topics, ranging from freedom of assembly to establishing special administrative courts and to the entrenchment of 'Christian culture', all to be protected by state authorities.

One of the issues of the amendment is that it continues the fight against immigration by forbidding foreigners from settling in the country en masse: 'No alien population shall be settled in Hungary' (new article XIV section (1) of the Fundamental Law). Therefore, the 'Stop Soros' legislative package, named after Hungarian-American philanthropist George Soros and enacted together with the amendment, criminalizes NGOs and activists aiding 'illegal migrants in any way'.[38] According to Justice Minister László Trócsányi, migration threatens Hungarians' 'self-identity', a concept that the Seventh Amendment added to the preamble of the Constitution. Entitled National Avowal, it states, 'We hold that it is a fundamental obligation of the state to protect our self-identity rooted in our historical Constitution.'[39] Also, article R was supplemented with the following section (4): 'All bodies of the State shall protect the constitutional identity of Hungary.' In order to make any further European Union joint effort, similar to the Council's relocation plan to solve migration, constitutionally questionable, section (2) of article E (the so-called EU clause) was replaced with the following wording: 'The joint exercise of certain powers with the EU shall not limit

---

[35] During the vote on the amendment, Jobbik MPs displayed a sign, which referred to the program and read, 'He [or she] Is a Traitor Who Lets in Terrorists for Money!'

[36] The Constitutional Court has no deadline to decide on petitions.

[37] The petition was based on section 38 para 1 of the Act CLI of 2011 on the Constitutional Court, which reads, 'On the petition of Parliament or its standing committee, the President of the Republic, the Government, or the Commissioner for Fundamental Rights, the Constitutional Court shall provide an interpretation of the provisions of the Fundamental Law regarding a concrete constitutional issue, provided that the interpretation can be directly deduced from the Fundamental Law.'

[38] In its Opinion, adopted on 22–23 June 2018, two days after the enactment of the 'Stop Soros' bill, but leaked to the BBC prior to the vote in the Hungarian Parliament, the Council of Europe's Venice Commission recommended to repeal the provision of the law on illegal migration because it 'criminalizes organizational activities not directly related to the materialization of illegal migration.' CDL-AD(2018)013-eHungary—Joint Opinion on the Provisions of the so-called 'Stop Soros' draft Legislative Package which directly affect NGOs (in particular Draft Art 353A of the Criminal Code on Facilitating Illegal Migration), adopted by the Venice Commission at its 115th Plenary Session (Venice, 22–23 June 2018).

[39] As I will show in Section D, the Hungarian historical Constitution did not follow the English example, which was the model of an organic, progressively reformed basic law. Instead, its dominant approach was authoritarian.

Hungary's inalienable right of disposal related to its territorial integrity, population, form of government, and governmental organization.'

The original provision of article R section (3) already prescribed that 'The provisions of the Fundamental Law shall be interpreted in accordance with their purposes, the National Avowal contained therein and the achievement of our historical constitution.' Due to the Seventh Amendment, constitutional self-identity and Hungary's Christian culture will already be binding elements of constitutional interpretation, but the new text of article 28 commits the courts to reflect the purpose of the laws and their amendments in their reasoning. Since providing reasons for the drafts falls not to the legislature itself but to those who initiate the bills—generally the government—their reasoning binds the Courts' interpretation of the Fundamental Law.

The amended text of article VI limits freedom of assembly and freedom of expression by defending the private and family life of others: 'Everyone has the right to respect for his or her private and family life, home, communication, and good reputation. The exercise of freedom of expression and the right of assembly shall not harm others' private and family life and their homes.' Shortly after the adoption of the amendment, the parliament also enacted a new law on the Protection of Private Life. A planned demonstration in front of Prime Minister Orbán's residency in December 2014, by a group of people dissatisfied with the government's action regarding the losses of those who had taken mortgages in foreign currencies, preceded these limitations. Despite the fact that the law did not explicitly proscribe demonstrations in front of politicians' houses, both the ordinary and the Constitutional Court concurred with the police's ban. However, in its decision, the Constitutional Court instructed parliament to harmonize regulations of privacy and freedom of assembly.[40]

Due to a last-minute addendum to the draft Seventh Amendment by a group of FIDESZ MPs, another new provision of the Fundamental Law makes homelessness illegal: 'It is forbidden to live in public places on a permanent basis.' The provision explains that the state 'must safeguard the use of public places' and that the municipalities 'will attempt to offer accommodation to all homeless persons'. This provision also has a special precedent in the history of FIDESZ' illiberal agenda. After a Budapest city council led by a FIDESZ majority enacted a local ordinance that banned homelessness from public places, the Orbán government extended the ban to the entire country. In November 2012, the Constitutional Court found the law unconstitutional.[41] The abovementioned Fourth Amendment added the following section 3 to article XXII of the Fundamental Law: 'In order to protect public order, public security, public health and cultural values, an Act or a local government decree may, with respect to a specific part of public space, provide that staying in public space as a habitual dwelling shall be illegal.' The new provision even authorizes national bodies to criminalize homelessness in a country of 'Christian culture'.

In the future, as established by the Seventh Amendment to the Fundamental Law, administrative courts will handle all cases concerning demonstrations and homelessness as well other issues important to the government, such as access to information of public interest or electoral disputes. The Seventh Amendment establishes the Administrative High Court as a new supreme court for administrative cases, parallel to the Curia, the supreme judicial body of regular courts. Instituting a parallel judicial structure for administrative issues is not unprecedented, of course. But the actual cause of the change and the increased likelihood, made possible by a ministerial decree from 2017, that former civil servants will be appointed

[40] Decision 13/2016. (VII. 18.) AB.
[41] Decision 38/2012. (XI. 14.) AB.

as administrative court judges casts doubts on the government's true intentions. During the 2018 election campaign, Prime Minister Orbán harshly criticized one of the Curia's judgments on electoral law as being disadvantageous to FIDESZ, claiming that 'the Curia was not up to its task intellectually'.[42]

The Ninth Amendment to the Hungarian Fundamental Law, introduced in November 2020, announces FIDESZ's new target: gender ideology and the rights of LGBTIQ people. While the 2011 Fundamental Law already defined marriage as the union of a man and a woman, the new constitutional amendment extends conventional gender norms to parenthood by inscribing in the Constitution that 'The mother is a woman, the father is a man.' In addition, the amendment fixes children's gender identity at birth so that later gender changes can never be reflected in the birth register.[43] This new provision reads, 'Every child shall have the right to the protection and care necessary for his or her proper physical, mental and moral development. Hungary shall protect the right of children to a self-identity[44] corresponding to their sex at birth and shall ensure an upbringing for them that is in accordance with the values based on the constitutional identity and Christian culture of our country' (article XVI (1), as amended). In an essay published in one of the government's newspapers, Prime Minister Viktor Orbán explained this change by calling the Fundamental Law 'our national Christian Constitution' and arguing that 'Christian democrats also expect schools to reinforce the sex identity that the Creator has conferred on each child at birth: to help girls become fine and admirable women and to help boys become men able to provide security and support for their families. Schools should protect the ideal and values of the family and should keep minors away from gender ideology and rainbow propaganda.'[45]

Together with the draft of the Ninth Amendment to the Fundamental Law, the government also introduced an amendment to the Civil Code, stating that only married couples are eligible to adopt children. Not only will this exclude single people, but because the Constitution already bars same-sex marriage, the government's anti-LGBTIQ ideology even more importantly bars same-sex couples from adopting a child. According to the Act's official reasons, this serves the 'interest of the child,' who should have both a mother and a father. An exception to this rule will be made only if the Minister responsible for family policies gives personal permission to single parents.[46]

Of course, these provisions will immediately conflict with both existing European human rights law and existing European Union law. Under the European Court of Human Rights' decision *Christine Goodwin v UK* (2002), states must make it possible to change birth registers if a person's gender identity changes, and under *EB v France* (2008), the state may not discriminate on the basis of sexual orientation when considering whether a person is eligible to adopt. And it is not just European human rights law that has been expanding its protection

---

[42] See Daniel G Szabó, 'Criminalizing Migrants' Helpers and Establishing Special Administrative Courts in Hungary' (2018) *Diritti Comparati Working Paper*, 1, 5 (article is available to read online at https://www.dirittico mparati.it/criminalizing-migrants-helpers-establishing-special-administrative-courts-hungary/ (last accessed 11 April 2022)).

[43] See Gábor Halmai, Gábor Mészáros, and Kim Lane Scheppele, 'So It Goes', Part II. *Verfassungsblog*, 20 November 2020. https://verfassungsblog.de/so-it-goes-part-ii/ (last accessed on 22 March 2021).

[44] In an interesting but telling way, the English translation provided by the Ministry of Justice uses the self-identity instead of the literal translation of gender identity presumably to avoid the hated term of gender.

[45] Orbán, Viktor, 'Together We Will Succeed Again', *Magyar Nemzet*, 21 September 2020, https://magyarnem zet.hu/english/together-we-will-succeed-again-8695452/ (last accessed 11 April 2022).

[46] The details of these changes, and the way that they fit into a long-running campaign against gender nonconformity are well described in Eszter Polgári and Tamás Dombos, 'A New Chapter in the Hungarian Government's Crusade Against LGBTQI People', *Verfassungsblog*, 18 November 2020, https://verfassungsblog.de/ a-new-chapter-in-the-hungarian-governments-crusade-against-lgbtqi-people/ (last accessed 11 April 2022).

of the principle of non-discrimination on the basis of sexual orientation and sexual identity. Since 1996, discrimination on the basis of sexual identity has constituted a violation of EU law. The European Commission's new LGBTIQ initiative is designed to expand protection of gender identity even further.

At the parliamentary election on 3 April 2022 six opposition parties united for the first time against the incumbent governing party, but paradoxically FIDESZ's victory against the united opposition was the biggest ever since 2010, gaining 135 out of the 199 seats. After the election the government submitted the Tenth Amendment to the Fundamental Law, re-writing the rules of article 53 of the Constitution on the state of danger (and rule by decree as it happened during the previous two years). According to the new rules, the government will also be able to declare this kind of emergency 'in the event of armed conflict, war or humanitarian catastrophe in a neighbouring country'. In other words, the new Orbán government, using the pretext of the Ukraine War, continues to govern by decree.

On 19 July 2022 again exclusively with the votes of the governing FIDESZ Party, the Parliament adopted the Eleventh Amendment to the Fundamental Law, which referring to 'historical self-identity, the preservation of traditions and the strengthening of the national character of democracy' from 1 January 2023 changed the name of the 'megye' (county) to 'vármegye' (verbatim translation: 'castle-county'), returning to the administrative designation used before 1945. Citing cost-effectiveness considerations, the amendment also changed the timing of the local elections to fall on the same day as European parliamentary elections. This means the local mayors and councillors who obtained their mandates in 2019 will stay in their position till 1 October 2024.

4. No Judicial Review of Constitutional Amendments

In July 2010, the new Hungarian government elected in April adopted a law[47] that imposed a so-called 'special tax' on severance, bonuses, and other rewards for state employees who left the public service and received such financial benefits in excess of two million forints (~$9,000). The tax rate was set at 98 per cent and was to be retroactively applied to all money paid out over the preceding year. The government argued that its predecessor had used severance payments as an instrument for rewarding political loyalists in the public service. At the same time, the punitive tax rate applied not only to the presumed target group of high-level former civil servants but also to teachers, doctors, and other professional groups who had received such benefits after decades of service.

In October, the Constitutional Court struck down the special tax in a unanimous decision.[48] Noting that justice demands the measure, the government, on the very day of the decision, introduced amendments to the Constitution allowing retroactive legislation in certain cases and removing the Constitutional Court's jurisdiction to review laws pertaining—among other things—to budgetary and tax policy. According to the latter amendment, the Constitutional Court judges can only review these financial laws from the perspective of those rights (the right to life and human dignity, protection of personal data, freedom of thought, conscience and religion, or the right to Hungarian citizenship) that they typically cannot breach. This withdrawal of the right to review financial laws created a solution found

---

[47] Act XC on the creation or amendment of certain economic and financial laws (2010. XC. tv. Egyes gazdasági és pénzügyi tárgyú törvények megalkotásáról, illetve módosításáról).
[48] Constitutional Court decision 184/2010. (X. 28.).

nowhere else in the world, since there is no other institution functioning as a Constitutional Court whose right of review has been restricted based on the object of the legal norms to be reviewed. Therefore, in the case of laws that are not reviewable by the Court, the requirement that the Constitution be a fundamental law, and that it be binding on everyone, is not fulfilled.

Together with the constitutional amendment, the government also reintroduced the nullified law with unchanged provisions, even expanding its retroactive application to the preceding five years.[49] In response to various petitions seeking to invalidate both of the government's constitutional amendments, the Court soon confronted the question of whether these measures were unconstitutional and if it had the authority to review them. It issued a decision in July 2011, a year after the retroactive special tax was first adopted.

The opinion of the majority decision issued by the Hungarian Constitutional Court and written by Judge Mihály Bihari first presents the wide-ranging package of petitions and of constitutional amendments impugned by the petitioners as well as the legal and constitutional provisions that the petitions cited in support of their arguments. Then, it sets forth the Constitutional Court's jurisdiction to review constitutional amendments. The reasoning on this issue is introduced by a comparative analysis that is meant to buttress the majority position but is in fact tendentious, one-sided, and lacks any scientific foundation.[50] The examples in the comparative framework are selective, as is best demonstrated by the fact that even though the analysis focuses on the 'Constitutional Courts of countries following the so-called European model of (centralized) judicial review', it conveniently 'forgets' to mention the Italian and Czech Constitutional Courts and, from outside Europe, also the Indian Supreme Court, which—as we have seen—has the most expansive jurisprudence in this area, as well as the South African and Columbian Constitutional Courts, and the Peruvian, Brazilian, Sri Lankan, and Nepalese Supreme Courts. But the analysis also might have mentioned Azerbaijan, Kyrgyzstan, Moldova, and Ukraine among the successor states of the USSR.[51] If the judge who delivered the opinion had understood the concept of unconstitutional constitutional amendments and the closely related issue of the function of eternal constitutional clauses, he would have realized that it makes more sense to look for examples in those Asian, African, Latin American, and European countries that—like Hungary—seek to prevent the return of a totalitarian regime by limiting total sovereignty when it comes to amending or drafting a Constitution. (That is why it should hardly be surprising to find that

---

[49] Ultimately, the Court found a 'loophole' in the constitutional amendment limiting its jurisdiction and nullified the Act again in May 2011, citing a violation of human dignity. At the same time, in the context of many other laws, its diminished jurisdiction did stop the Court from intervening. Ultimately, the retroactive effect of the law was greatly reduced, since it only applied to the beginning of 2010 rather than to 2005, as the government's second proposal on the issue intended (Constitutional Court decision 37/2011. (V. 10.)). One of the civil servants also filed a petition with the European Court of Human Rights, complaining that the imposition of a 98 per cent tax on part of her severance pay, under a legislation that had entered into force ten weeks before her dismissal, amounted to an unjustified deprivation of property. In its Chamber judgment of 14 May 2013 in the case of *NKM v Hungary* (application no 66529/11), the European Court of Human Rights unanimously held that the 98 per cent tax on part of the severance pay of a Hungarian civil servant violated her right to peaceful enjoyment of property and therefore constituted a violation of Art 1 of Protocol No 1 (protection of property) of the European Convention on Human Rights.

[50] This is not the first time that the Constitutional Court has employed selective comparisons to bolster its position. The same happened in decision 154/2008 (XII. 17.), which struck down registered partnership for heterosexual partners. For a critical analysis, see Gábor Halmai and others, 'Távol Európától. Kiemelt védelem alacsony színvonalon' ['Far from Europe. A low level of preeminent protection'] (2009) 1 Fundamentum 89–108.

[51] On the solutions employed by the successor states of the former USSR, see the Venice Commission's report: *Report on Constitutional Amendment*. Adopted by the Venice Commission at its 81st Plenary Session (Venice, 11–12 December 2009), Venice Commission: Council of Europe (www.coe.int) (last accessed on 11 April 2022).

such legacies are absent in those Western European states fortunate enough not to have such a historical background).

The second serious distortion in the comparative analysis is the argument meant to substantiate the majority position, according to the judge delivering the opinion. This argument holds that the German Federal Constitutional Court has never reached a conclusion of unconstitutionality as a result of judicial review, while the others also have only rarely arrived at such a determination. This is certainly not true with regard to the Indian Supreme Court, which goes unmentioned in this analysis, but which has found Prime Minister Indira Gandhi's comprehensive constitutional reforms antithetical to the basic structure of the Indian Constitution. Beyond this, however, it is also irrelevant with regard to examining the issue of jurisdiction. Even if no constitutional amendment had ever been nullified, the underlying constitutional issue to be decided would still be whether and how to substantiate the judicial limitation of the power to amend the Constitution. Obviously, the Court would not need to 'strain' to investigate this issue if the Constitution were to expressly grant it such powers. But in the absence of these powers—as in the Hungarian Constitution, for instance—the body performing judicial review must solve this dilemma itself by interpreting the Constitution.[52] The simplest method for doing so—a possibility available to the Constitutional Court judges—is the Austrian solution, which posits that the Constitutional Court clearly has jurisdiction because its right of review extends to all laws and because laws of a constitutional rank (and, in the Hungarian domestic context, acts amending the Constitution) are also laws.

The majority opinion on the merits begins by examining procedural validity, in other words by investigating the potential failures of the law-making process. In doing so, the Constitutional Court sharply criticized the constitutional amendment practices of the parliament constituted on 14 May 2010. Up to the point when the Court handed down the decision in question, parliament had adopted ten constitutional amendments within thirteen months (and nine of these within seven months), which affected thirty-three provisions of the Constitution. (In other words, it would be no exaggeration to say that even before adopting the Fundamental Law (i.e., the new Constitution) on 18 April 2011, and in fact partially even subsequently, parliament substantially transformed the state's constitutional order.) Of these amendments, only two were proposed by the government, or rather the Minister for Public Administration and Justice acting in the government's name. The rest—including the restriction of the Constitutional Court's powers, the special tax with retroactive effect covering a five-year period, the reduction in the number of MPs, and the elevation of the National Media and Info-communications Authority to a constitutional level—were adopted in response to bills presented by individual MPs and were passed with high priority in several cases, resulting in a shorter than usual law-making procedure.

As far as the legal basis for the jurisdiction to determine the unconstitutional nature of the constitutional amendment process is concerned, the majority reasoning does not offer any detailed explanation of why it has—felicitously—changed its hitherto generally negative attitude toward reviewing constitutional amendments. It merely notes, '[I]t is not possible to rule out the Constitutional Court's jurisdiction with regard to the review of the procedural

---

[52] That is why it is difficult to understand why the opinion of the majority decision says, 'it needs to be emphasized, however, that in all these cases it is either the given state's Constitution that determines the Constitutional Court's right to undertake constitutional (amendment) review, or the judicial body protecting the Constitution itself expands—without express constitutional authorization to do so—its jurisdiction to include constitutional review.' Indeed. *Tertium non datur.*

invalidity of constitutional provisions, since unlawfully or even unconstitutionally adopted legal provisions that suffer from constitutional invalidity are considered automatically void, as if they had never been created in the first place'.

The only question the opinion fails to clarify is the following: if a constitutional amendment is considered a law from a procedural angle, then why is it not considered a law in terms of substance, that is to say, if it may be reviewed as a law in one respect, then why not in the other? Two opposing voices point out this contradiction, or more specifically this lack of real reasoning. In his concurring opinion, Judge István Stumpf, together with the Court's president, Péter Paczolay, recommends abolishing the review of both procedure and merits, while András Bragyova proposes in his dissent that both should be undertaken.

In the examination of procedural unconstitutionality, the majority notes that the amendment procedures raise 'problems of legitimacy' because the necessary consultations (for example with the Constitutional Court regarding the consequences of limiting its powers) failed to take place. It even goes as far as to say that the successive amendment of the Constitution, performed with the objective of realizing current political interests and ends, is an alarming development in light of the requirements of the democratic rule of law because it jeopardizes the stability of the Constitution. Based on the above, the majority notes that the procedure 'obviously fails to fully satisfy the requirements of the democratic rule of law'. This formulation is reminiscent of Mikhail Bulgakov's 'sturgeon of the second freshness' at the buffet in *The Master and Margarita*. According to the majority of the Hungarian Constitutional Court's judges, however, this fish is edible, as the final verdict states that 'formally, the procedure has met the procedural rules laid out in the Constitution and the Act on Legislation'. Hence, the judicial body denied the petition seeking to obtain a judgment of invalidity on procedural grounds. As far as satisfying the requirements of the Act on Legislation, for instance, the opinion itself states that the consultations prescribed by said Act have failed to take place. Thus, a more thorough, circumspect reasoning might have at least touched upon the question of why the procedural requirements of the Act on Legislation are not constitutional requirements. For example, in a rather extreme situation in which an MP introduced a constitutional amendment on a Wednesday without a preliminary process, without previous consultations or an impact study, etc., the amendment was adopted in a vote on Thursday, was promulgated on Friday, and entered into effect on Monday.

This lack of intellectual depth also extends to substantive constitutional review, which is based on the fallacious thesis that since the Hungarian Constitution does not contain any immutable provisions, the Constitutional Court does not have a standard against which to assess the substance of the constitutional amendments. Only few constitutions contain explicit 'eternal clauses,' however. The most famous is undoubtedly the German Basic Law (*Grundgesetz*) with its article 79 para 3, but as we saw above, even this provision lacks an explicit jurisdictional rule that would authorize the Federal Constitutional Court to protect the immutable constitutional provisions during the process wherein constitutional amendments are enacted. It was the judges of the Court in Karlsruhe who endowed themselves with this power by construing the *Grundgesetz* accordingly. The same was true of most judicial bodies, which—acting as guardians of their respective constitutions—derived this jurisdiction for themselves in the process of reviewing constitutional amendments, even without an 'eternal clause'. The most prominent example is the Indian Supreme Court's doctrine on the 'basic structure' of the Constitution, which the Court used in order to provide a basis for conducting a review even without an unchangeable rule and without express constitutional authorization to do so. Naturally, those who use the instrument of comparative law selectively from the start—like the author of the majority opinion—by acknowledging only

240 GÁBOR HALMAI

solutions that buttress their thesis could easily arrive at the conclusion, completely divorced from the facts, that 'Constitutional Courts generally tend to refrain from establishing for themselves the jurisdiction to review the Constitution.' (Another distortion is manifest in the terminology employed in the majority reasoning, which consistently refers to reviewing the Constitution rather than reviewing constitutional amendments, even though a review is possible before these amendments enter into effect. Indeed, it is even conceivable to defer their entry into effect in the interest of conducting a review.) Thus, despite the fact that the petitioners offered several standards for review, ranging from the 'invisible Constitution'[53] to the essence and the fundamental values of the democratic state on the rule of law to the *ius cogens* norm (a fundamental—and generally recognized—legal principle of international law), the majority has adhered to its previous jurisprudence, at least in the context of reviewing the substance of the amendments. They dismissed the petitions, even though the Court's reasoning contains the following passages: 'Based on the principles enshrined in international agreements, the Hungarian Constitution contains immutable parts, whose immutability is based not on the will of the Constitution's creators but rather on *ius cogens* and those international agreements to which the Republic of Hungary is party. [...] The norms, principles, and fundamental values of *ius cogens* together constitute a standard that all future constitutional amendments and constitutions need to satisfy.'

With these words, the majority binds not only the constitutional amendments reviewed here to these standards but even the Fundamental Law adopted on 18 April 2011. At the same time, it appears that the majority believes that it is not within the Constitutional Court's powers to ensure that constitutional amendments (or the new Constitution) satisfy these standards, meaning that there is effectively no way to enforce them. Yet Judge Péter Kovács— joined by Mihály Bihari, the Constitutional Court judge who delivered the decision—notes that if the constitutional amendment were to contravene or grossly violate an international legal obligation that Hungary had assumed, from which it was impossible to withdraw due to the legal or political significance of the obligation in question, and if this conflict could not be resolved by constitutional interpretation, then the Constitutional Court would be entitled to

---

[53] The concept of an 'invisible Constitution' was developed by the former president of the Constitutional Court, László Sólyom. Its underlying idea is that the Court's jurisprudence offers a theoretical framework for evaluating the question of constitutionality, thus complementing the text of the Constitution and, in fact, superseding it when the latter is amended in a way that violates crucial constitutional values. Introducing the notion, Sólyom wrote the following in his concurring opinion on the death penalty in 23/1990. (X. 31.): 'The Constitutional Court must continue the work of laying down the theoretical foundations of the Constitution and the rights enshrined therein, and it must create a coherent system through its decisions. This system may stand above the Constitution—which is still often amended to satisfy current political interests—as an "invisible Constitution", serving as a stable measure of constitutionality. In doing so, the Constitutional Court enjoys a certain latitude as long as it remains within the conceptual confines of constitutionality.' While Sólyom did not repeat the comments irritating politicians, he also did not negate their substance. In an interview, he stated, 'I have never denied that our constitutional jurisdiction, especially in "the hard cases", .. is at the borderline of constitution-writing.' (Gábor A Tóth, 'A "nehéz eseteknél" a bíró erkölcsi felfogása jut szerephez. Beszélgetés Sólyom Lászlóval, az Alkotmánybíróság elnökével' ['In "difficult cases", the judge's moral views come into play. A conversation with László Sólyom, the president of the Constitutional Court'] (1997) 1 Fundamentum, 37). This was emphasized in another interview that he gave in 1998, before his term ended, he emphasized this issue as well. He was elaborating on the misinterpretation of the term 'invisible Constitution' when the journalist confronted him with the question whether the metaphor should be unsaid altogether. His response was, 'No, what I have written is there. In those days, the Constitution was amended month by month, depending on the political climate. Therefore, I wanted to point out that the Constitution is of a higher nature: a firm system based not only on technical rules but on values too. Our decisions were meant to express this value system, to clarify, to expose, to implement, because from the one-line paragraphs and brief sentences one cannot see it. Some focus purely on the letter in their constitutional adjudication; I have seen it both in Europe and in Asia.' (Cs. Mihalicz, Interjú Sólyom Lászlóval, az Alkotmánybíróság volt elnökével [Interview with László Sólyom, former President of the Constitutional Court] (1998) Budapesti Könyvszemle (BUKSZ) 438).

review it. What the opinion fails to address or answer, however, is whether, for example, the requirements concerning the democratic rule of law in article 2 of the Treaty on the European Union constitute such obligations and whether the impugned constitutional amendments violate these requirements. In his concurring opinion, even Judge István Stumpf—who evidently believes that the right course would have been to dismiss all petitions—points out the contradiction between the operative part of the decision dismissing the petition and the above-cited reasoning. If that was not his view—if he thought, in fact, that a substantive review of the constitutional amendments was warranted—then at least as far as this particular issue was concerned, he would have attached a dissenting rather than a concurring opinion to the majority stance.

Nevertheless, despite dismissing the petition for lack of jurisdiction, the majority opinion does reserve for the Court a signalling right—or rather obligation—which is just as absent from the Constitution as the possibility of judicial review. Indeed, even the standard formulated as the constitutional basis for this obligation is nowhere to be found in the written text of the Constitution. (In describing 'constitutional protection through signalling' as a phenomenon that is beyond the 'Constitutional Court's normative jurisdiction', Judge András Holló evinces a keen appreciation of the fact that signalling is situated outside the Constitution. In other words, it appears that there are indeed jurisdictions outside the Constitution.) This standard states, '[T]he attained level of constitutional protection of rights and its system of guarantees may not be diminished.' By way of example, the opinion invokes a scenario wherein the limitation of the Constitutional Court's jurisdiction goes so far as to upset the system of the separation of powers, which is based on checks and balances. It fails to address, however, when such a point is reached, nor does it explain whether the present amendment has upset said balance. The only example given is a situation in which the constituent power wishes to adopt a legal provision, previously nullified by the Constitutional Court, by including it in the Constitution. As discussed above, that is exactly what happened in 1990 with the restrictions on suffrage, which the Constitutional Court had declared unconstitutional without indicating as much to the constituent power.

With regard to the two principal constitutional amendments impugned by petitions, the restriction of the Constitutional Court's jurisdiction and the retroactive special tax, the majority informed the constituent power that there are contradictions between the new provisions and some of the Constitution's existing provisions, especially the requirements of the rule of law and legal security in article 2 para 1. According to the majority, these contradictions require the constituent power to intervene. Another distortion emerges here, namely that this signalling is akin to that which the judicial body indicated in its decision 23/1990 (X. 31.) on the unconstitutionality of the death penalty. In this decision, the Court called attention to the contradiction between article 8 para 2, which provides the basis for the unconstitutionality of the death penalty, and article 54 para 1, which fails to categorically rule out the most severe penalty. However, the vast difference between the two cases is that in 1990, the majority of the Court's judges resolved the contradiction by offering a constitutional interpretation—specifically in favour of article 8 para 2—while at this later point, the majority opinion did not see this as a workable solution.

The majority also dismissed the petitions seeking a determination that the Constitution's articles 32/A and 70/I (2) are in breach of international agreements. The dismissal rightly holds that the petitions were not filed by someone entitled to make such a submission. After all, pursuant to the law, only the National Assembly, a permanent committee thereof, or any member of parliament, the President of the Republic, the government or any of its members, the president of the State Audit Office, the president of the Supreme Court, or the prosecutor general were entitled to file such a petition. What is wrong, however, is the argument that the Constitutional Court did not wish to exercise its right to proceed *ex officio* because the issue 'whether or not it has jurisdiction may be disputed in this case'. Yet would it not be self-evident to clarify such controversies in the framework of an *ex officio* proceeding? In his concurring opinion, István Stumpf, too, points out this contradiction in the reasoning. Of course, he does so only in order to express his support for dismissing the petition. Had he not believed that dismissal was the right course of action but thought instead that a substantive review was necessary with regard to the constitutional omission, he would have written a dissent rather than a concurring opinion in this respect as well.

The majority decision also rejects the petitions that request a review of how the restriction of the Constitutional Court's jurisdiction is transposed into the Act on the Constitutional Court, arguing that such a review would indirectly examine the constitutional provisions with similar content. Here, the majority proved unable to resolve a contradiction, which was a necessary consequence of its wrong decision regarding the constitutional amendment. What is at issue here is that the judicial body failed once again to substantively review the impugned legal provision, a review that should have resulted in a dismissal rather than a rejection according to longstanding practice. Yet invoking lacking jurisdiction, which always manifests itself in dismissal, would obviously have been difficult to defend in the context of a law.

The Court created a very bad precedent when the majority of Constitutional Court judges voluntarily signed the death sentence of judicial review. Taking the allegory further, one might of course object that even a decision that would have declared the constitutional amendments unconstitutional, consequently nullifying them, could not have averted the demise of judicial review, neither in the short term in the context of the Constitution in force nor in the long run in the context of the Fundamental Law passed on 18 April 2011, which entered into force on 1 January 2012.[54]

A committed German critic of the constitutional amendments and the Fundamental Law claims, in his excellent blog, that it would not have served the interests of constitutionalism if the Court judges had chosen to change their previous jurisprudence on this question precisely when their own powers were at stake.[55] But does the question of the restriction of their powers not point to a larger issue whose significance goes beyond protecting the Court's interests, narrowly understood, and does this issue not concern Hungarian constitutionalism in its entirety? And did not Chief Justice Marshall's opinion in *Marbury v Madison*, which introduced the previously unknown practice of judicial review into the Court's constitutional jurisprudence, thereby revolutionizing constitutionalism across the globe, pertain directly to the Court's powers? The greatest problem of most of the judges on the Hungarian Constitutional Court is precisely that they gave up on the ideal of constitutionalism.

In the final days of 2011, parliament enacted the so-called Act on the Transitional Provisions to the Fundamental Law with self-proclaimed constitutional status, which partly supplemented the new Constitution even before it went into effect. In late 2012,

---

[54] The Fundamental Law considerably restricts the Constitutional Court's ex-post review of the challenged amendment for as long as state debt exceeds half of what is referred to in the Hungarian text as 'entire domestic product', the content of which is uncertain. For a detailed critique of the Fundamental Law, see Zoltán Fleck and others, *Opinion on the Fundamental Law of Hungary* (2011). Available in English from the Law and Public Affairs page, Princeton University: http://lapa.princeton.edu/hosteddocs/amicus-to-vc-english-final.pdf (last accessed on 11 April 2022).

[55] Maximilian Steinbeis, 'Ungarn: Orbán verdoppelt seinen Einsatz' (Verfassungsblog.de, 16 July 2011) http://verfassungsblog.de/ungarn-orbn-verdoppelt-seinen-einsatz (last accessed on 11 April 2022).

in the decision 45/2012. (XII. 29.), the Constitutional Court ruled that those parts of the Transitional Provisions of the Fundamental Law that are not transitory in nature cannot be considered part of the Constitution and are therefore invalid. While this decision did not go into the substance of the constitutionality of the Transitional Provisions, since the ombudsman's petition requested only a formal review, the majority of the judges this time emphasized in the reasoning that in order to preserve the unity of the Constitution they may consider reviewing the substance of a constitutional amendment.

Reacting to this decision in March 2013, the MPs of the governing parties enacted the Fourth Amendment to the Fundamental Law. One part of this long amendment simply elevates the annulled non-transitory provisions of the Transitional Act into the main text of the Fundamental Law, in some cases in a somewhat modified formulation and in others with unchanged wording. The following provisions were elevated to constitutional rank without any alteration: the rules on citizenship, the endowment of mayors with administrative competences, the authorization of both the Chief State Prosecutor and the President of the Judicial Council to select another court if they think that the competent one is overburdened with cases, as well as the extension of the restriction of the Constitutional Court's review power in financial matters, even after state debt does not exceed half of the entire domestic product, for laws which were enacted in the period when the debt did exceed the limit.

The amendments include some that were not part of the Transitional Provisions but are also consequences of a previous Constitutional Court's annulment. One of them is the authorization of the legislature to set conditions for state support in higher education, for instance to prescribe, that graduates of state universities remain in the country for a certain period of time after graduation. (Without a prior Constitutional Court decision, the amendment also limits the autonomy of universities by allowing the government to supervise their financial management.) Authorizing both the legislature and municipal governments to criminalize homelessness is another act of revenge for a declaration of unconstitutionality. In a recent decision, the Court also banned political advertisements in electoral campaigns. In reaction to this, the amended text of the Fundamental Law has allowed a cardinal law to limit political ads. In late 2012, the Court annulled the very definition of the family in the law on the protection of families on the grounds that it was too exclusive. Now, the Fundamental Law defines marriage and the parent-children relationship as the basis of family relationships, without mentioning extra-marital relations and parenting. Also, the Constitutional Court expressed constitutional concerns about private-law limitations on hate speech, which violates the dignity of certain groups. The new amendment allows such limitations, not only to protect racial and other minorities, but also the dignity of the members of the Hungarian nation, who make up the overwhelming majority of the population.

Finally, a further set of amendments, related to the power of the Constitutional Court itself, directly reacts to the judges' recent unwelcome decisions. The new text of the Fundamental Law indirectly reacts to the Court's readiness to review the substance of constitutional amendments, expressed in its decision on the unconstitutionality of the Transitional Provisions' non-transitory elements, prompted an indirect reaction in the new text of the Fundamental Law: while it allows the review of an amendment's procedural aspects, it specifically excludes any substantive review.

In his letter to Mr Thorbjørn Jagland, Secretary General Council of Europe, Mr Tibor Navracsis, Minister of Public Administration and Justice, explains, 'The Proposal states that the Constitutional Court may review, from a procedural point of view, the constitutionality of the Fundamental Law itself and any amendments thereof, in order to check their compliance with procedural law requirements regulated in the Fundamental Law. This is a new competence for the Constitutional Court, because, under the Fundamental Law so far, it had no legal options whatsoever for reviewing the amendments to the Fundamental Law. The provision is in accordance with the Court's jurisprudence based on the former Constitution, under which, for the last time in decision 61/2011, the Constitutional Court explicitly reinforced the notion that it had no power to review in merits the amendments to the Constitution. The decision of 45/2012 on the Transitional Provisions also did not overrule this former practice.'

As we have seen, unfortunately, none of these arguments are correct. In the reasoning of its abovementioned decision 45/2012 (XII. 29.), the Constitutional Court emphasized that it has the constitutional responsibility to protect the unity of the Constitution and to ensure that the text of the Constitution can be clearly identified. The justices added that an amendment of the Constitution cannot create an irresolvable inconsistency in the constitutional text. Therefore, they argued, 'In certain cases, the Constitutional Court can review the continued realization of the substantive constitutional requirements, guarantees and values of the democratic state governed by the rule of law and their incorporation into the Constitution.'

In this decision, therefore, the Court concluded that it had the theoretical power to review constitutional amendments for their substantive constitutionality.

As we can see, the formal review power in the case of constitutional amendments is not a new competence for the Constitutional Court, since it has derived this from its competences under both the old and the new Constitution. While the Court had stated, in the past, that it did not have the power to review amendments to the Constitution on substantive grounds, it changed its opinion in its decision 45/2012, claiming the power to review future constitutional amendments for their substantive conflict with basic constitutional principles. Therefore, the Fourth Amendment's ban on substantive review of constitutional amendments is a direct reaction to this Constitutional Court decision from December 2012. The real reason for this ban is to prevent the Court from evaluating the Fourth Amendment or any subsequent amendment on substantive grounds. Thus, the Fourth Amendment's ban on substantive review of constitutional amendments has allowed the government to escape review by including any provision previously declared unconstitutional directly in the Constitution. This move abolished the difference between ordinary and constitutional politics, between statutory legislation and constitution-making. Now, the government's two-thirds majority is above any power that might constrain it. Constitutionally speaking, it can now do anything it wants to do.

A decision on the constitutionality of the Fourth Amendment, which the Constitutional Court issued on 21 May 2013, demonstrates this situation. In his petition, the ombudsman argued that by failing to discuss parts of the suggested modification to the amendment at the plenary session, the parliament violated the formal requirements of the amendment procedure. Moreover, he maintained that some of the amendment's provisions that contradict provisions of the Fundamental Law endanger the unity of the Constitution, which is also a formal requirement of the amendment procedure in his view. The majority of the judges did not find any formal mistake in the amendment procedure and therefore rejected the first part of the petition. Arguing that they lacked competence, they did not review the contradictions between constitutional provisions on the basis of the ombudsman's argument about constitutional unity. Furthermore, they argued that there is no substantial limit to the amendment power and that the Constitutional Court consequently has no jurisdiction for such a review.

C. Basic Structures and Concepts

In this section, I address some of the flaws in the structures and concepts of the Fundamental Law of Hungary that are suspected of permitting exceptions to the European requirements of democracy, constitutionalism, and the protection of fundamental rights, and whose application, it is feared, could conflict with Hungary's international obligations.

1. Government without Checks

The 2011 Constitution appears to still contain the key features of constitutional constraint imposed by checked and balanced powers. But those constraints are largely illusory because key veto points have been abolished or seriously weakened.[56] Appointments to key offices, like Constitutional Court judgeships, ombudsmen, the Head of the State Audit Office, and the public prosecutor, no longer require minority party input. Independent boards regulating crucial institutions necessary for democracy, such as the election commission and the media board, no longer ensure multiparty representation. The Constitutional Court itself has been packed and weakened because its jurisdiction has been limited.

The constitutional reforms have seriously undermined the independence of the ordinary judiciary by changing the judicial appointment process. The Head of the National Judicial Office can select any judge from among the top three candidates recommended by the judicial council of the court where the appointment is to be made. The retirement age for judges on ordinary courts was reduced from seventy to sixty-two, beginning on the day the new Constitution went into effect. This change forced around 10 per cent of the Hungarian judges into early retirement. Those judges included six of the twenty court presidents at the county level, four of the five appeals court presidents, and twenty of the eighty Supreme Court judges. The Head of the National Judicial Office, who is close personal friends with the Prime Minister and married to the chief author of the new Constitution, and the public prosecutor, also a FIDESZ loyalist, can assign specific cases to specific courts according to their assessment of the courts' relative workloads.

The old ombudsman system has also been seriously weakened. In place of four separate ombudsmen with separate staffs and independent jurisdictions, the new system has only one general 'parliamentary commissioner for human rights' with two deputies operating under his direction and a greatly reduced staff. The old data protection ombudsman's office has been eliminated and its functions have been transferred to a new office that is part of the government and no longer an independent body.

The State Audit Office, once a bastion of independent expertise, has been given additional powers in the new constitutional order to launch serious investigations into the misuse of public funds. But the new Head of the State Audit Office, elected for twelve years by a two-thirds vote of the parliament, has no professional auditing experience. Instead, he was a former FIDESZ MP.

The new Constitution created a new Budget Council with the power to veto any budget that the parliament may produce that adds even a single Forint to the national debt. The

---

[56] See a more detailed analysis of the lack of checks and balances in Miklós Bánkuti, Gábor Halmai, and Kim Lane Scheppele, 'From Separation of Powers to a Government without Checks: Hungary's Old and New Constitutions', in Gábor A Tóth (ed), *Constitution for a Disunited Nation. On Hungary's 2011 Fundamental Law* (CEU Press, New York, Budapest 2012) 237–268.

Budget Council consists of three officials, two elected by a two-thirds vote of the parliament and one appointed by the President of the Republic. The Constitution says that if parliament fails to agree on a budget by 31 March of each year, the President may dissolve the parliament and call new elections. Obviously, if the Budget Council, dominated by FIDESZ loyalists, vetoes the budget on the eve of the deadline, the constitutional trigger may be pulled for new elections. Should another party come to power in a future election, this provision will hang over its term in office like the Sword of Damocles.

The Constitution also made it possible to increase the government's influence over monetary policy by raising the number of vice-presidents from two to three and giving the Prime Minister the authority to select individuals for these positions.

The constraints on power included in the new Constitution are also illusory because the individuals who occupy crucial positions can be appointed for extraordinarily long terms, thus maintaining the current government's control over any foreseeable future government. Loyalists to the current government can remain in power through multiple election cycles, thereby making it almost impossible for a future government dominated by other political parties to carry out new policy initiatives. Offices such as that of the public prosecutor (nine years), the president of the Supreme Court of Justice (named the 'Kúria', nine years), the president of the National Judicial Office (nine years), the Head of the Budget Council (six years), the Head of the State Audit Office (twelve years), constitutional judges (twelve years), the commissioner for fundamental rights (six years), and the president of the National Media and Communications Authority (nine years) were filled by the FIDESZ government, but the people in those powerful offices—all party loyalists—will remain through multiple election cycles.

2. Identity of the Political Community

An important criterion for a democratic constitution is that everybody living under it can regard it as his or her own. The Fundamental Law breaches this requirement on multiple counts.

a) Its lengthy preamble, entitled National Avowal, defines the subjects of the Constitution not as the totality of people living under Hungarian law but as the Hungarian ethnic nation: '*We, the members of the Hungarian Nation* ... hereby proclaim the following'. A few paragraphs later, the Hungarian nation returns as 'our nation torn apart in the storms of the last century'. The Fundamental Law defines this nation as a community whose binding fabric is 'intellectual and spiritual', not political but cultural. There is no place in this community for the nationalities living within the territory of the Hungarian state. At the same time, there is a place in it for Hungarians living beyond the state's borders.

The elevation of the 'single Hungarian nation' to the status of constitutional subject suggests that the scope of the Fundamental Law somehow extends to all of historical, pre-First World Warr Hungary, and certainly to those places where Hungarians still live today. This suggestion is not without its constitutional consequences: the Fundamental Law makes the right to vote accessible to those members of the 'united Hungarian nation' who live outside the territory of Hungary. It gives people who are not subject to the laws of Hungary a say in who should make up the Hungarian legislature. In the 2014 elections, when FIDESZ gained two-thirds of the seats, 95.5 per cent of voters living outside the country voted for the party that had provided them with the new citizenship, while FIDESZ received only 43.5 per cent of the votes within Hungary. The votes of non-resident citizens were needed for FIDESZ' two-thirds majority. In 2018, the percentage of votes for FIDESZ from voters outside state borders even increased to 96.2 per cent, but this time, the party got the two-thirds majority anyway, regardless of the votes of citizens living outside Hungarian borders.[57] This outcome clearly resulted from the appreciation these extraterritorial citizens have for FIDESZ.[58]

b) The Fundamental Law characterizes the nation referred to as the subject of the Constitution as a Christian community, narrowing even further the range of people who can claim to belong to it. 'We recognize the role of Christianity in preserving nationhood', it declares, not as a statement of historical fact but also with respect to the present. And it expects everyone who wishes to identify with the Constitution to identify with its opening entreaty as well: 'God bless the Hungarians'. As mentioned earlier, the Seventh Amendment supplemented these provisions by referring to Christian culture as a good to be protected by all state authorities.

c) The preamble of the Fundamental Law also claims the 'continuity' of Hungarian statehood, which it describes as lasting from the country's beginnings until the German occupation of the country on 19 March 1944, when it was interrupted only to be restored on 2 May 1990, the day of the first session of the freely elected parliament. Thus, it rejects not only the communist dictatorship but also the Temporary National Assembly convened at the end of 1944, which split with the fallen regime. It rejects the National Assembly election of December 1945. Today's democracy watchers would classify the parliamentary election of December 1945 as 'partly free', adding that it was the freest in Hungary's entire history up until that time. It also rejects the progressive legislation of the National Assembly: the 'little Constitution' of the Republic, approved in early 1946, which the Round Table was able to draw on in 1989, as well as the abolition of noble titles and the Upper House of Parliament.

The historical dividing lines drawn by the preamble of the Fundamental Law obscure the fact that war crimes and crimes against humanity were committed not only by foreign occupying forces and their agents but also, between 1920 and 1944, by extreme right-wing 'free troops' and the security forces of the independent Hungarian state, and not only against 'the Hungarian nation and its citizens' but also against other peoples. Nor does the Fundamental Law acknowledge that Hungary's statehood was not interrupted on 19 March 1944. While the government agencies' freedom to act was restricted, they were not shut down. The Regent remained in his office, and the parliament sat and regularly passed the bills introduced by the government. The Hungarian state leadership did not declare the termination of legal continuity but instead cooperated with the occupying powers.

The Fundamental Law only recognizes the (pre-1944) glorious pages of Hungarian history but does not acknowledge the acts and failures that give cause for self-criticism. It only holds to account the—reputed or genuine—injuries inflicted on the Hungarian people by foreign powers and does not acknowledge the wrongs committed by the Hungarian state against its own citizens and other peoples.

Paul Shapiro of the US Holocaust Memorial Museum, in his testimony at 'The Trajectory of Democracy—Why Hungary Matters' hearing before the Commission on Security & Cooperation in Europe: The US Helsinki Commission, held on 19 March 2013 in Washington, DC, said the following about the continuity of Hungary's statehood and the

---

[57] Balázs Majtényi, Aliz Nagy and Péter Kállai, ''Only FIDESZ'—Minority Electoral Law in Hungary' (Verfassungsblog.de, 31 March 2018) https://verfassungsblog.de/only-fidesz-electoral-law-in-hungary/ (last accessed on 11 April 2022).

[58] About this feeling of honour, see Szabolcs Pogonyi, *Extra-Territorial Ethnic Politics, Discourses and Identities in Hungary* (Springer, Heidelberg, 2017), 166–169.

Hungarian government's shared responsibility in the Hungarian Holocaust: 'Under Regent and Head of State Miklós Horthy, foreign Jews resident in Hungary were deported to their deaths. Jewish men were forced into labour battalions, where tens of thousands died. And over 400,000 Hungarian Jews and at least 28,000 Romani citizens of the country were deported from Hungary to Auschwitz. During the months that followed the removal of Horthy from power in October 1944, the Arrow Cross Party of Ferenc Szálasi committed additional atrocities. The record is one of immense tragedy: 600,000 Hungarian Jews murdered out of a total Jewish population of over 800,000; at least 28,000 Romani victims and significant participation and complicity in the crime by Hungarian authorities from the Head of State down to local gendarmes, police and tax collectors in tiny villages.'[59]

As Gary Jeffrey Jacobsohn observes, the language of constitutions, and especially of their preambles, is exceptionally informative in conveying the authors' underlying meaning and may indicate a commitment on their part to establish a constitutional identity. But until confirmed in the accumulated practice of the constitutional community, this goal will remain unfulfilled.[60] The attempt to establish a constitutional identity seems to have failed after the transition in 1989–1990, but it also remains to be seen whether this new attempt will be successful.

3. Intervention into the Right to Privacy

The Fundamental Law breaks with a distinguishing feature of the constitutions of states under the rule of law, namely, that they comprise the methods of exercising public authority and the limitations on such authority on the one hand and the guarantees of the enforcement of fundamental rights on the other. Instead, the text brings several elements of private life under its regulatory purview in a manner that is not doctrinally neutral but rather based on a Christian-conservative ideology. By establishing the individual's obligations towards the community, it prescribes, for the community's members, a life model whose normative preferences correspond to this ideology. These values are already enshrined in the Fundamental Law's preamble, entitled National Avowal:

'We recognize the role of Christianity in preserving nationhood'.
'We hold that individual freedom can only be complete in cooperation with others.'
'We hold that the family and the nation constitute the principal framework of our coexistence, and that our fundamental cohesive values are fidelity, faith and love'.
'Our Fundamental Law ... expresses the nation's will and the form in which we want to live'.
Particularly considering that according to article R), the provisions of the Fundamental Law must also be interpreted in keeping with the National Avowal, and that according to article I para 3, fundamental rights may be restricted in the interest of protecting a constitutional value, this provision could serve as the basis for a restriction of fundamental rights.

[59] See the transcript of the hearing at: https://www.csce.gov/international-impact/events/trajectory-democracy-why-hungary-matters (last accessed on 11 April 2022).
[60] Gary J Jacobsohn, 'The Formation of Constitutional Identity', in Tom Ginsburg and Rosalind Dixon (eds), *Comparative Constitutional Law* (Edward Elgar, Cheltenham, 2011) 131.

Certain provisions of the Fundamental Law pertaining to fundamental rights intervene in questions of marriage and the family, the prohibition on same-sex marriage, and the protection of embryonic and foetal life, prescribing ideologically based normative value preferences in private relationships.

a) According to article L) of the Fundamental Law:

'(1) Hungary shall protect the institution of marriage as the union of a man and a woman established by voluntary decision, and the family as the basis of the nation's survival.

(2) Hungary shall encourage the commitment to have children.

(3) The protection of families shall be regulated by a cardinal Act'.

The Fundamental Law's conception of marriage—which, incidentally, follows the definition serving as the basis for the Constitutional Court's decision 154/2009 (XII. 17.) AB on the constitutionality of registered domestic partnerships—corresponds roughly to the Catholic natural-law interpretation of marriage, which regards faithfulness, procreation, and the indestructible sanctity of the spousal relationship as the most important elements of marriage. This constitutional regulation, founded on natural-law principles, protects those interests of the people that not everyone attributes to themselves and with which they do not necessarily wish to identify themselves, and thus it breaches their autonomy. When defining marriage and evaluating the role of the family, a modern, living constitution—especially a new Fundamental Law—should accommodate the societal changes that increase the individual's range of choices. This should have required the Fundamental Law to regulate the institution of marriage and family along with fundamental rights, guaranteeing the self-determination of the individual and the principle of equality.

b) With the constitutional ban on same-sex marriage, the framers of the Constitution have ruled out the future ability of the Hungarian legislature to follow the worldwide tendency and allow same-sex marriage. In keeping with this, article XV of the Fundamental Law does not mention discrimination based on sexual orientation and gender identity in its list of prohibited forms of discrimination. This means that the Hungarian framers of the Constitution do not prohibit the state from supporting or discriminating against a way of life—based on sexual orientation alone. This solution runs counter not only to the European Union's Charter of Fundamental Rights and the case law of the European Court of Justice (for the latest example, see judgment C-147/08 in the case of *Jürgen Römer v Freie und Hansestadt Hamburg*) but also to the provisions of Hungary's Act CXXV of 2003 on the Promotion of Equal Treatment and Equal Opportunities, which remains in force.

While it is almost impossible for the Constitution to be completely neutral, these provisions greatly challenge the autonomy of those who do not accept the normative life models defined on the basis of the Fundamental Law's ideological values—as the preamble puts it, 'the form in which we want to live'—and can even exclude such individuals from the political community.

4. Weakening of the Protection of Fundamental Rights

It is not only the substantive provisions of the Fundamental Law pertaining to fundamental rights that significantly contribute to the decline in the level of fundamental-rights protection. A further factor is the weakening of institutional and procedural guarantees that could otherwise uphold those rights that remain under the Fundamental Law. The most important instance of such weakening is a change to the review power of the Constitutional Court, diminishing its ability to perform its tasks related to the protection of fundamental rights. Added to this is the change, prior to the Fundamental Law's entry into force, in the composition of the Constitutional Court, which will further impede it in fulfilling its function as protector of fundamental rights.

a) The considerable restriction on *ex post* review has caused great controversy in Hungary and abroad because the withdrawal of the right to review financial laws was unprecedented worldwide, since there is no other institution functioning as a Constitutional Court whose right of review has been restricted based on the object of the legal norms to be reviewed. The Constitutional Court justices can only review these laws from the perspective of those rights (the right to life and human dignity, protection of personal data, freedom of thought, conscience and religion, or the right to Hungarian citizenship) that they typically will not breach. The restriction remains in effect for as long as state debt exceeds half of what the Hungarian text refers to as 'entire domestic product', the content of which is uncertain. Therefore, in the case of laws that are not reviewable by the Court, the requirement that the Constitution be a Fundamental Law that is binding on everyone is not fulfilled. This also clearly represents a breach of the guarantees, set out in article 2 of the TFEU, relating to respect for human dignity, freedom, equality, and the respect of human rights—including the rights of persons belonging to a minority.

With regard to the Constitutional Court's powers of ex-post review, the effectiveness of the protection of fundamental rights is reduced not only by the limitation of their objective scope but also by a radical restriction of the range of persons that may initiate a Constitutional Court review. This restriction results from the fact that one of the peculiarities of the Hungarian regime change was abolished: the institution of the *actio popularis*, which allows any individual to submit a petition claiming the ex-post judicial review of statutes, regardless of their personal involvement or injury. Over the past two decades or more, this unique institution has provided not only private individuals but also non-governmental organizations and advocacy groups with the opportunity to contest those legal provisions that they consider unconstitutional before the Constitutional Court, for the public good. Of course, it could be argued that this institution has never existed in any other democratic state, but it has nevertheless undoubtedly contributed substantially to ensuring the previously achieved level of fundamental-rights protection, which is now diminishing.

In future, abstract *ex post* judicial review of statutes, under point e) paragraph 2 of section 24 of the Fundamental Law, may only be initiated by the government, a quarter of the votes of members of parliament, or the Commissioner for Fundamental Rights. Given the balance of power in the current parliament, this makes any such petitions much more difficult, since the government is hardly about to make use of this opportunity against their own bills, while a quarter of MPs' votes would assume a coalition between the two democratic opposition parties and the extremist right-wing party, which supports the government.[61]

The cardinal Act on the Constitutional Court, passed in October 2011, decided on the fate of the several hundred petitions already submitted to the Court in the form of an *actio*

---

[61] Indeed, in 2012 it was only the ombudsman, who filed such petitions in thirty-five cases (twelve petition files were still pending earlier, and there were twenty-three new ones). The Constitutional Court decided on eleven of these cases, six cases in favour of the petitions, and five rejections. There are still twenty-four petitions pending. See Ombudsmani indítványok az Alkotmánybíróság előtt. (Petitions of the ombudsman before the Constitutional Court) http://www.jogiforum.hu/hirek/28922 (last accessed on 10 April 2022).

popularis by private individuals who were entitled to do so prior to the entry into force of the Fundamental Law but who will be subsequently divested of this right. The *in malam partem* retroactive effect, so willingly applied by the present government in other cases, also came into play here, with the result that the Constitutional Court does not pass judgment on previously submitted petitions.

b) Private individuals or organisations may only turn to the Constitutional Court in future if they themselves are the victims of a concrete breach of law and this has already been established in a civil-administration or a final court decision. In this case, the legal remedy offered by the Constitutional Court will naturally only affect them. In other words, the extension of opportunities to submit constitutional complaints is no substitute whatsoever for the widely available right of private individuals and organisations to file petitions.

c) There is no doubt that the widely available opportunity to submit complaints could be beneficial to the judging of cases involving fundamental rights, as has been the case in Germany, Spain, and the Czech Republic. A prerequisite for this, however, is a Constitutional Court committed to fundamental rights and independent from the government. Yet the present government has done all it can to prevent this since taking office in May 2010. This process began with the alteration of the system for nominating Constitutional Court justices, giving the governing parties the exclusive opportunity to nominate and subsequently replace justices. The Fundamental Law, in a further weakening of the guarantees of independence, increased the number of Constitutional Court justices from eleven to fifteen, which makes it possible to select five additional new justices, following the two justices selected in May 2010, with their appointments lasting for a term of twelve years rather than the previous nine, or in other words, for three parliamentary cycles. In future, the president of the Constitutional Court, who, until now, has been elected for a term of three years by the justices, will be selected by parliament for his or her entire judicial term. These changes could not wait until the Fundamental Law entered into force on 1 January 2012. Instead, the president and the new members were selected at the end of July 2011, based on an amendment to the existing Constitution passed on 6 July 2011.[62]

5. Constitutional Entrenchment of Political Preferences

At the time of the Hungarian regime change, the framers of the Constitution preserved the amendment rule of the original 1949 Constitution used to produce a substantively new Constitution. Whatever the original reason for this rule, which requires only two-thirds of the absolute majority of parliament to make any and all changes to the Constitution, it has long been considered insufficient for guaranteeing fundamental-rights protection, adequate constitutional review, and the stability of the basic structure of the Constitution. Observers, including the author of this article, considered this the main deficiency that required framing a new Constitution.[63] The FIDESZ government, in its initial plans, proposed a new amendment rule that would require two-thirds of the votes in two parliamentary sessions, with a vote in between to approve constitutional amendments. Unlike its Spanish prototype, this

---

[62] See http://www.parlament.hu/irom39/03199/03199.pdf (last accessed on 11 April 2022).
[63] See Gábor Halmai, 'Grundstrukturen staatlichen Verfassungsrechts: Ungarn', in Armin von Bogdandy, Pedro Cruz Villalón and Peter M Huber (eds), *IPE vol I* (CF Müller, Heidelberg. 2007) 687–727.

rule did not distinguish between fundamental revision and minor changes. Thus, it promised to entrench ever more deeply a Constitution that was not produced with sufficient consensus. As a result of such legitimation problems, the government abandoned the idea of replacing the purely parliamentary amendment rule. But to compensate for this failure, it entrenched a large number of ordinary policies, thereby removing the power of future parliaments to alter the policy choices of the present one.

The new Fundamental Law mandates that certain issues be decided by the governing majority, while it assigns other issues to laws requiring a two-thirds majority. This makes it possible for the current government, which enjoys a two-thirds majority support, to write in stone its views on economic and social policy. A subsequent government possessing only a simple majority will not be able to alter these choices, even if it receives a clear mandate from the electorate to do so. In addition, the Fundamental Law's prescriptions render fiscal policy especially rigid because significant shares of state revenues and expenditures will be impossible to modify in the absence of statutes adopted by a two-thirds majority. This hinders good governance by making it more difficult for subsequent governments to respond to economic changes. As a result, it may be impossible to manage a crisis efficiently. These risks are present irrespective of whether the governing majority will exercise self-restraint in adopting statutes that require a two-thirds majority (contrary to past experience). The very possibility created by the Fundamental Law to regulate such issues of economic and social policies by means of statutes requiring a two-thirds majority is incompatible with parliamentarism and the principle of the temporal division of powers.[64]

a) As regards pensions, the Fundamental Law itself excludes the possibility that a subsequent governing majority creates a funded pension scheme based on capital investment. Europe and the Western world in general will face serious demographic challenges in the coming decades. One way in which public policy could respond to this challenge is by partially transforming the pay-as-you-go pension system into a funded pension scheme based on capital investment. Comprehensive social debate and assessment of the pros and cons of different public policy solutions must precede such a decision, however. It is not compatible with the functions of the Constitution that the current governing majority excludes the application of one of the available public policy solutions in the Fundamental Law without having been empowered to do so by the electorate. In addition, section 40 of the Fundamental Law assigns the basic rules of the pension system to a cardinal act, which, as mentioned above, requires a two-thirds majority. It is impossible to know today to what extent this statute will regulate the pension system. In any case, the Fundamental Law makes it possible that a two-thirds majority will be required to modify the retirement age and other conditions of eligibility as well as the basis for calculating pensions. This prevents subsequent governments that win popular support in free elections from instituting their own views on pension policy.

b) Section L) of the Fundamental Law specifies that the regulation of family welfare support is also to be subject to two-thirds statutory regulation. Without knowing the text of the planned statute, which has not been enacted yet, it is impossible to decide to what extent the governing majority intends to regulate this issue in the relevant statute requiring a two-thirds majority. It is clear, however, that the relevant prescriptions of the

---

[64] One can argue that the economic crisis created such exceptional measures, like the debt brakes proposed by the German Chancellor, Angela Merkel.

Fundamental Law mean that every detail of family welfare support may subsequently require a two-thirds majority decision to be modified. It must be part of the ruling majority's social policy at any given time to settle questions such as the child's age limit until which maternity benefits are paid, the eligibility conditions and amount of these benefits, or the eligibility of different family types for different kinds of support. Thus, in a parliamentary democracy, there is no justification for writing in stone the views of the current government coalition in this way.

c) Section 40 of the Fundamental Law states that basic rules of taxation are to be determined by a fundamental statute, that is, one requiring a two-thirds majority. This prescription enables the currently ruling government coalition to entrench its own views in a two-thirds statute on tax policies, especially as regards the linear, flat tax and the exceptionally high tax benefits for families. This could easily make it impossible for a subsequent government, having gained power by promising to introduce progressive taxation, to realize its public policies based on the mandate received from voters.

d) In addition to fixing preferences concerning economic and social policies for the long term, the governing parties can also implement their very own personal preferences by appointing and replacing the leaders of independent institutions. Parliament chose former MPs of the larger governing party as president of the State Audit Office for twelve years and as Head of the National Media and Telecommunications Authority for nine years. The chief prosecutor appointed for nine years is a former parliamentary candidate of the larger governing party. Without providing any additional reason, the coming into force of the Fundamental Law empowers the governing parties to nominate only their own candidates for the new positions of Constitutional Court justices, a new president of the Constitutional Court, the head of the ordinary judiciary, as well as new ombudspersons for six, nine, and twelve years, respectively. The adoption of the Fundamental Law includes a statute that prohibits the president of the National Council of Justice, who is also the president of Hungary's Supreme Court, from appointing justices until the Fundamental Law comes into force. Clearly, the objective of this moratorium is that the Head of the Curia, to be chosen for nine years on the basis of the new Fundamental Law, should appoint the heads of the most important courts. This will result in the long-term entrenchment of personal preferences, thus undermining the adequate operation of independent institutions.

e) In a related development, the Fundamental Law gave the Budget Council the right to veto the state budget statute. The ruling government coalition appointed two of the Council's three members until at least 2019. At the same time, the Fundamental Law fails to define unequivocally what is covered by the Council's right to veto. In addition, it does not contain guarantees that would exclude this body's ability to abuse its powers. Such guarantees would be all the more necessary as the governing majority at a given time has the competence and responsibility to draft the budget. This prerogative cannot be limited by a body which seems to be independent but consists of appointees of an earlier government. This raises the possibility that in addition to—or even instead of—considerations regarding the sustainability of budgetary policies, the Budgetary Council may be guided by preferences of public policy when exercising its veto right.

6. A Populist Illiberal Constitutional System

The Hungarian system of governance has become populist, illiberal, and undemocratic.[65] This was Prime Minister Orbán's openly stated intention.[66] The ideological foundation of Orbán's illiberalism can be found in the works of his two court ideologues, the sociologist and former liberal MP Gyula Tellér and the political scientist András Lánczi. It is easy to prove that Orbán, in his 2014 speech on 'illiberal democracy', recited one of Tellér's studies, published earlier that year, which Orbán assigned as compulsory reading for all his ministers.[67] Tellér claims that the 'system of regime-change' failed because the liberal Constitution did not commit the government to protect national interests and that the new 'national system' must therefore strengthen national sovereignty and, with it, allow the government greater freedom. In Tellér's argument, this is a necessary move against the moral command of the liberal rule-of-law regime, according to which 'everything is allowed, what does not harm others' liberty'.

Lánczi's anti-liberal concept can be found in his book *Political Realism and Wisdom,* published in English in 2015, as well as in an article published in 2018, after FIDESZ's third consecutive electoral victory.[68] Lánczi's critique rejects liberalism outright as a utopian ideology, claiming that—like Communism—it is incompatible with democracy.

Illiberal constitutional theorists have attempted to legitimize the new populist constitutional system by referring to political constitutionalism. István Stumpf, a constitutional court justice, whom FIDESZ nominated without consulting with the opposition parties immediately after the new government took over in 2010 and who was then elected exclusively with the governing parties' votes, argued for a strong state in his book and claimed that the changes expanded political constitutionalism.[69] It is remarkable that two other members of the current packed Constitutional Court also argue against legal constitutionalism, denouncing it as 'judicial dictatorship'[70] or 'juristocractic'.[71] In the scholarly literature, Attila

---

[65] As Jan-Werner Müller rightly argues, it is not just liberalism that is under attack in these two countries, but democracy itself. Hence, instead of calling them 'illiberal democracies', we should describe them as illiberal and 'undemocratic' regimes. See Jan-Werner Müller, 'The Problem with 'Illiberal Democracy' (Project Syndicate, 21 January 2016) https://www.project-syndicate.org/commentary/the-problem-with-illiberal-democracy-by-jan-werner-mueller-2016-01?barrier=accessreg (last accessed on 10 April 2022).

[66] In a speech delivered on 26 July 2014 before an ethnic Hungarian audience in neighbouring Romania, Orbán proclaimed his intention to turn Hungary into a state that 'will undertake the odium of expressing that in character it is not of liberal nature'. Citing as models he added: 'We have abandoned liberal methods and principles of organizing society, as well as the liberal way to look at the world. ... Today, the stars of international analyses are Singapore, China, India, Turkey, Russia. ... and if we think back on what we did in the last four years, and what we are going to do in the following four years, then it really can be interpreted from this angle. We are. ... parting ways with Western European dogmas, making ourselves independent from them ... If we look at civil organizations in Hungary, ... we have to deal with paid political activists here. ... [T]hey would like to exercise influence ... on Hungarian public life. It is vital, therefore, that if we would like to reorganize our nation state instead of it being a liberal state, that we should make it clear, that these are not civilians ... opposing us, but political activists attempting to promote foreign interests. ... This is about the ongoing reorganization of the Hungarian state. Contrary to the liberal state organization logic of the past twenty years, this is a state organization originating in national interests.' See the 'Full Text of Viktor Orbán's speech at Băile Tuşnad (Tusnádfürdő) of 26 July 2014' (Budapest Beacon, 29 July 2014) http://budapestbeacon.com/public-policy/full-text-of-viktor-orbans-speech-at-baile-tusnad-tusnadfurdo-of-26-july-2014/ (last accessed on 11 April 2022).

[67] See Gyula Tellér, 'Született-e Orbán-rendszer 2010 és 2014 között?' ['Was an Orbán System Born between 2010 and 2014?'] (March 2014) Nagyvilág.

[68] See András Lánczi, 'The Renewed Social Contract–Hungary's Elections, 2018' (May 2018) IX Hungarian Review at http://www.hungarianreview.com/article/20180525_the_renewed_social_contract_hungary_s_elections_2018 (last accessed on 11 April 2022). For a detailed analysis of Lánczi's arguments, see Kim Lane Scheppele, 'The opportunism of populists and the defense of Constitutional liberalism' (2019) 20 German Law Journal 3.

[69] See István Stumpf, *Erős Állam—Alkotmányos Korlátok* [Strong State—Constitutional Limits] (2014) 244–249.

[70] András Zs. Varga, *From Ideal to Idol? The Concept of the Rule of Law* (Dialóg Campus, Budapest, 2019) 16.

[71] Béla Pokol, *The Juristocratic State: Its Victory and the Possibility of Taming* (Dialóg Campus, Budapest, 2017).

Vincze argued that the Constitutional Court's decision to include the Fourth Amendment in the Fundamental Law—thus, among other things, invalidating the Court's entire case-law preceding the new Constitution—was a sign that political had prevailed over legal constitutionalism.[72] Even those who claim, as do Kálmán Pócza, Gábor Dobos, and Attila Gyulai, that the Court has not acted confrontationally towards the current legislature and the government characterize this behaviour as a special approach within the system of the separation of powers, best described as a partnership in a constitutional dialogue.[73]

The use of 'abusive constitutional' tools, such as constitutional amendments and even replacements, has brought about this backsliding, as both the internal and external democratic defence mechanisms against the abuse of constitutional tools failed.[74] The internal defence mechanisms (Constitutional Courts, judiciary) failed because the new regime managed to abolish all checks on its power, and the international ones, such as the EU toolkits, failed mostly due to the lack of a joint political will to use them.

If we choose, from the many definitions of populism, that of Mudde and Kaltwasser, who describe 'populism' as a 'thin-centered ideology that considers society to be ultimately separated in two homogeneous and antagonistic camps, "the pure people" and the "corrupt elite," and who argue that politics should express the "volonté générale" (general will) of the people',[75] the we can conclude that the Hungarian constitutional system has become populist. This populism rejects the basic principles of constitutional democracy,[76] understood as limited government, the rule of law, and the protection of fundamental rights.[77] In Hungary, the main characteristics of populism as well as its approach to constitutional identity illustrate what Luigi Corrias describes as popular sovereignty.[78] (I discuss the latter in Section D).

For popular sovereignty, as Corrias argues, populism holds the belief that 'the people' are a unit and as such often have a voice in the polity only by means of direct democracy, such as referenda. Particularly while in opposition, for populists such as Orbán, representation merely serves as a tool to give voice to the united people.[79] But as Pinelli rightly points out,

---

[72] Attila Vincze, 'Az Alkotmánybíróság határozata az Alaptörvény negyedik módosításáról: az alkotmánymódosítás alkotmánybírósági kontrollja' ['The Decision of the Constitutional Court on the Fourth Amendment to the Fundamental Law: The Constitutional Review of Constitutional Amendments'] (2013) 3 Jogesetek Magyarázata 12.

[73] See Kálmán Pócza, Gábor Dobos, and Attila Gyulai, 'The Hungarian Constitutional Court: A constructive partner in constitutional dialogue', in Kálmán Pócza (ed), *Constitutional Politics and the Judiciary: Decision-Making in Central and Eastern Europe* (Routledge, London, 2018) Chapter 5.

[74] The category of 'abusive constitutionalism' was introduced by David Landau using the cases of Colombia, Venezuela, and Hungary. See David Landau, 'Abusive Constitutionalism' (2013) 47 UC Davis Law Review 189–260. Abusive constitutional tools have existed from the very beginning of constitutionalism. The recent story of the Polish Constitutional Tribunal is reminiscent of the events in the years after the election of Jefferson, as the first anti-Federalist president of the United States. On 2 March 1801, the second-to-last day of his presidency, President Adams appointed judges, most of whom were Federalists. The Federalist Senate confirmed them the next day. As a response, Jefferson, after taking office, convinced the new anti-Federalist Congress to abolish the terms of the Supreme Court that were to take place in June and December of that year, and Congress repealed the law passed by the previous Congress creating new federal judgeships. In addition, the anti-Federalist Congress had begun impeachment proceedings against some Federalist judges. About the election of 1800 and its aftermath, see Bruce Ackerman, *The Failure of the Founding Fathers: Jefferson, Marshall, and the Rise of Presidential Democracy* (Harvard University Press, Cambridge, MA, 2007).

[75] Cas Mudde and Cristóbal Rovira Kaltwasser, *Populism: A Very Short Introduction* (Oxford University Press, Oxford, 2017) 6.

[76] See Cesare Pinelli, 'The populist challenge to Constitutional democracy' (2016) 7 European Constitutional Law Review 5, 6.

[77] See these 'essential characteristics' of constitutional democracy in Michel Rosenfeld, 'The rule of law and the legitimacy of Constitutional democracy' (2001) 74 Southern California Law Review 1307, 1307.

[78] Luigi Corrias, 'Populism in a Constitutional key: Constituent power, popular power, popular sovereignty and Constitutional identity' (2016) 12 European Constitutional Law Review 6, 12.

[79] Ibid, 18–19.

contemporary populists, especially when in government, do not necessarily reject representation, nor do they necessarily favour the use of referenda.[80] For instance, Orbán's FIDESZ
party tried to undermine the legitimacy of representation after losing the 2002 parliamentary elections. Orbán refused to concede defeat, declaring that 'the nation cannot be
in opposition, only the government can be in opposition against its own people'. After the
2010 electoral victory, he claimed that the majority had delegated its power to the government representing it by staging a 'revolution at the voting booths'. Thus, the populist government tried to interpret the result of the elections as the will of the people, viewed as a
homogenous unit. Also, the Orbán government, after overthrowing its predecessor in 2010
by means of a popular referendum, made it more difficult for its own opposition to initiate
a valid referendum. While the previous law required only 25 per cent of the voters to cast a
vote, the new law requires at least 50 per cent of those eligible to vote to do so; otherwise,
the referendum is invalid.[81] Orbán's ambivalence towards representation and referenda in
the government and in the opposition extends to his attitude regarding established institutions. While he readily attacked the 'establishment' when he was in the opposition, he now
steadfastly protects his own governmental institutions. The situation is different with transnational institutions, such as the EU, which Hungarian populist governments also attack as
threats to their country's sovereignty. A good example is the Hungarian parliament's reaction to the European Parliament's critical report from July 2013 on the constitutional situation in Hungary. The Hungarian parliamentary resolution on equal treatment reads: 'We
Hungarians, do not want a Europe any longer where freedom is limited and not widened. We
do not want a Europe any longer where the Greater abuses his power, where national sovereignty is violated and where the Smaller has to respect the Greater. We have had enough of
dictatorship after forty years behind the iron curtain'. These words directly reflect the Orbán
government's view of 'national freedom' as the liberty of the state (or the nation) to determine its own laws: 'This is why we are writing our own Constitution ... And we don't want
any unconsolidated help from strangers who are keen to guide us ... Hungary must turn on
its own axis.'[82]

Although Hungary became a liberal democracy on an institutional level after 1989, on a
behavioural level, the consolidation of the system has always been very fragile. If one considers liberalism not merely a limit on the public power of the majority but also a concept
that encompasses the constitutive precondition of democracy—the rule of law, checks and
balances, and guaranteed fundamental rights—then Hungary is not a liberal democracy
anymore. Since the 2010 victory of the currently governing FIDESZ party, all of the public
power is in the hands of the representatives of one party. Freedom of the media and religious rights, among others, are seriously curtailed. And before the 2014 parliamentary elections, changes to the electoral system made it unfair, again ensuring a two-thirds majority for
FIDESZ in the Hungarian parliament.

[80] See Cesare Pinelli, 'The Populist Challenge to Constitutional Democracy' (n 76) 5–16, 11.
[81] It is the irony of fate that due to these more stringent conditions, the only referendum that the Orbán government initiated—one against the EU's migration policy—failed. On 2 October 2016, Hungarian voters went to the
polls to answer one referendum question: 'Do you want to allow the European Union to mandate the relocation
of non-Hungarian citizens to Hungary without the approval of the National Assembly?' Although 92 per cent of
those who cast votes and 98 per cent of all the valid votes agreed with the government, answering no (6 per cent
were spoiled ballots), the referendum was invalid because the turnout was only around 40 per cent, instead of the
required 50 per cent.
[82] The English translation of excerpts from Orbán's speech was made available by Hungarian officials, see e.g.,
Financial Times: Brussels Blog, 16 March 2012 http://blogs.ft.com/brusselsblog/2012/03/the-eu-soviet-barroso-
takes-on-hungarys-orban/?catid=147&SID=google#axzz1qDsigFtC (last accessed on 11 April 2022).

The problem with the Hungarian populist and illiberal constitutional system is that the country is currently a member of the European Union, which considers itself a union based on the principles of liberal democratic constitutionalism. Of course, like any other citizens of a democratic nation-state, the citizens of Hungary have the right to oppose joint European measures, for instance on immigration and refugees, or even the development of a liberal political system altogether. However, a democratic process must lead to this conclusion. Many people still hold that they support liberal democracy or at least represent views in line with liberal democracy. But if Hungarians ultimately opt for a non-liberal system, they must accept certain consequences, including leaving the European Union and the wider community of liberal democracies.

D. Constitutional Identity

1. The Abuse of the Concept

As mentioned in Section A, after the Seventh Amendment to the Fundamental Law failed to justify the Hungarian government's non-compliance with the European relocation plan for refugees in 2016, the packed Constitutional Court came to the rescue of Orbán's constitutional identity defence of the government's policies on migration. The Court carved out an abandoned[83] petition of the also loyal Commissioner for Fundamental Rights (hereinafter: Commissioner), filed a year earlier, before the referendum was initiated. In his motion, the Commissioner asked the Court to deliver an abstract interpretation of the Fundamental Law in connection with the Council decision 2015/1601 of 22 September 2015.[84] The Commissioner asked the following four questions:

1. Whether the absolute prohibition of expelling foreigners from Hungary in article XIV para 1 of the Fundamental Law[85] forbids only the Hungarian authorities from engaging in this kind of action or whether it also covers acts performed by the bodies or institutions of the Hungarian State needed to implement an unlawful collective expulsion executed by another State.
2. Whether under article E) para 2, state bodies, agencies, and institutions are entitled or obligated to implement EU legal acts that conflict with fundamental rights stipulated by the Fundamental Law. If they are not entitled or obligated to do so, which state body can establish that fact?
3. Whether under article E) para 2, the exercise of powers bound to the extent necessary, which may restrict the implementation of the *ultra vires* act. If state bodies, agencies, and institutions are not entitled or obligated to implement *ultra vires* EU legislation, which state body can establish that fact?

---

[83] The Constitutional Court has no deadline to decide on petitions.
[84] The petition was based on section 38 para (1) of the Act CLI of 2011 on the Constitutional Court, which reads: 'On the petition of Parliament or its standing committee, the President of the Republic, the Government, or the Commissioner of the Fundamental Rights, the Constitutional Court shall provide an interpretation of the provisions of the Fundamental Law regarding a concrete constitutional issue, provided that the interpretation can be directly deduced from the Fundamental Law.'
[85] Art XIV(1) reads as follows: 'Hungarian citizens shall not be expelled from the territory of Hungary and may return at any time from abroad. Foreigners staying in the territory of Hungary may only be expelled based on a lawful decision. Collective expulsion shall be prohibited.'

4. Whether article XIV para 1 and article E) can be interpreted to either authorize or restrict Hungarian state bodies, agencies, and institutions, within the legal framework of the EU, in relocating a large group of foreigners legally staying in one of the Member States without their expressed or implied consent and without personalized and objective criteria applied during their selection.

The Commissioner's own interpretation was clear from the formulations of the questions. With regard to the first question, the Commissioner argued that 'the rules of international law grant a right for the asylum seekers waiting to be transferred to stay in Italy or in Greece until the end of the asylum procedure'. In the context of the Council decision, the Commissioner concluded that 'the collective expulsion—prima facie—[was] implemented by these two Member States', but he argued that 'the transfer cannot be exercised by a Member State without the reception act of another Member State (according to the petition this Member State would be Hungary if implementing the relocation plan): the latter is an indispensable act of the former one'. The question does not seem to take into account that article XIV para 1 of the Fundamental Law applies explicitly to Hungarian citizens, or to the collective expulsion of foreigners from the territory of Hungary, and that non-Hungarian asylum seekers relocated due to the Council Decision would not be expelled by Italy or Greece. But the petition also passes judgment on EU powers in claiming that 'the European Union has no competence to adopt regulations affecting the staying of certain groups of foreigners in the territory of the Member States'.[86]

By holding the petition admissible, in its decision 22/2016 (XII. 5.) AB,[87] the Court decided to answer the first question related to the interpretation of article XIV of the Fundamental Law in a separate judgment.[88] Imre Juhász, one of the justices, wrote a concurring opinion, in which he disagreed with the majority's decision to separate the part of the petition on interpreting article XIV para 1 of the Fundamental Law. In his view, 'the separation—which is in fact postponing the adoption of the decision for an indefinite period of time—is indeed questionable in the light of the fact that the Council Decision is applicable to the persons who arrive(d) to the territory of Italy or Greece'.

The Court identified question two as a reference to the issue whether a legal act of the European Union can violate fundamental rights, while question three concerned the evaluation of the Union's *ultra vires* acts. The Court argued that it should review these two questions directly at the level of the Fundamental Law, since they are clearly constitutional issues and satisfy the condition of concreteness under article 38 para 1 of the Act on the Constitutional Court.[89] Question four could only be interpreted in the framework of questions two and

---

[86] In my view the legal basis for this is Art 78(3) of the Treaty on the Functioning of the European Union (TFEU) which states that: 'In the event of one or more Member States being confronted by an emergency situation characterised by a sudden inflow of nationals of third countries, the Council, on a proposal from the Commission, may adopt provisional measures for the benefit of the Member State(s) concerned. It shall act after consulting the European Parliament.'

[87] The English translation of the decision is available at the homepage of the Constitutional Court: https://hunconcourt.hu/uploads/sites/3/2017/11/en_22_2016.pdf (last accessed on 11 April 2022). The citations are from this translation.

[88] See Injunction X/3327-31/2015. On the separation: The Constitutional Court has the power to separate parts of a petition and decide them separately from each other. The decision on the interpretation of Art XIV para 1 of the Fundamental Law has not been published yet.

[89] Section 38 para 1 reads: 'On the petition of Parliament or its standing committee, the President of the Republic, the Government, or the Commissioner of the Fundamental Rights, the Constitutional Court shall provide an interpretation of the provisions of the Fundamental Law regarding a *concrete* constitutional issue, provided that the interpretation can be directly deduced from the Fundamental Law' [italics added].

three. Therefore, the Court explained its response to question four in its response to questions two and three. In other words, the Court tried to avoid directly answering the question about the constitutionality of the EU's relocation power.

Answering questions two to four, the Court established that its own jurisdiction was regulated neither by the Fundamental Law nor by the Act on the Constitutional Court concerning fundamental rights review and *ultra vires* review, the latter being composed of a sovereignty review and an identity review. But before the justices created these new powers for themselves, they reviewed the positions taken by the European Court of Justice and the Member States' Constitutional Courts. Referring to *Costa v Enel*,[90] the Hungarian Constitutional Court acknowledged 'the fact that from the point of view of the ECJ, EU law is defined as an independent and autonomous legal order'. But quoting the *Kloppenburg* judgment[91] of the German Federal Constitutional Court, the Hungarian justices stated that it is Member States' 'national enforcement acts that ultimately determine the extent of primacy to be enjoyed by EU law against the relevant Member State's own law in the Member State concerned'.

After reviewing the case law of many of the Member States' Supreme and Constitutional Courts, including the Lisbon judgment of the German Federal Constitutional Court, the Hungarian justices established that 'within its own scope of competences on the basis of a relevant petition, in exceptional cases and as a resort of *ultima ratio,* i.e., while respecting the constitutional dialogue between the Member States, it can examine whether exercising competences on the basis of article E) para 2 of the Fundamental Law results in the violation of human dignity, the essential content of any other fundamental right or the sovereignty (including the extent of the competences transferred by the State) and the constitutional self-identity of Hungary'.[92]

With regard to the fundamental rights review, the Court established that 'any exercise of public authority in the territory of Hungary (including the joint exercise of competences with other Member States) is linked to fundamental right'.[93] The fundamental rights review is based on article E) para 2 and article I para 1 of the Fundamental Law. The latter provision declares that 'The inviolable and inalienable fundamental rights of MAN shall be respected. It shall be the primary obligation of the State to protect these rights.' With these rules in mind, and after referring to the *Solange* decisions of the German Federal Constitutional Court, explicitly to the decision of 15 December 2015 (2 BvR 2735/14), and to the need for cooperation in the EU and the primacy of EU law, the Court stated that it 'cannot set aside the *ultima ratio* protection of human dignity and the essential contents of fundamental rights, and it must grant that the joint exercising of competences under article E) para 2 of the Fundamental Law would not result in a violation of human dignity or the essential content of fundamental rights'.[94]

Regarding the *ultra vires* review, the Court argued that there were two main limits on conferred or jointly exercised powers under article E) para 2: 'the joint exercise of a competence shall not violate Hungary's sovereignty (sovereignty control), and on the other hand it shall not lead to the violation of constitutional identity (identity control)'.[95] But the Court also emphasized that 'the direct subject of sovereignty- and identity control is not the legal act of the

---

[90] *Costa v ENEL* [1964] ECR 585.
[91] BVerfGE 75, 223 [242] (1987).
[92] Decision 22/2016. (XII. 5.) AB. [46].
[93] Ibid, [47].
[94] Ibid, [49].
[95] Ibid, [54].

Union or its interpretation, therefore the Court shall not comment on the validity or invalidity of the application of primacy with respect to such acts of the Union'.[96]

The constitutional foundation of the sovereignty review is article B) para 1 of the Fundamental Law, which states that 'Hungary shall be an independent, democratic rule-of-law State'. Paragraphs 3 and 4 contain the popular sovereignty principle: '(3) The source of public power shall be the people', '(4) The power shall be exercised by the people through elected representatives or, in exceptional cases, directly'. The Court warned that these provisions of the Fundamental Law 'shall not be emptied out by the Union-clause in article E)', and it established that 'the maintenance of Hungary's sovereignty should be presumed when reviewing the joint exercise of competences' that have already been conferred to the EU.[97]

The protection of constitutional identity, the Court argued, is based on article 4 (2) TEU and on 'an informal cooperation with the ECJ based on the principles of equality and collegiality, with mutual respect to each other'.[98] The Court 'interprets the concept of constitutional identity as Hungary's self-identity and it unfolds the content of this concept from case to case, on the basis of the whole Fundamental Law and certain provisions thereof, in accordance with the National Avowal and the achievements of our historical Constitution—as required by article R) para 3 of the Fundamental Law'.[99] The Court held that 'the constitutional self-identity of Hungary is not a list of static and closed values, nevertheless many of its important components—identical with the constitutional values generally accepted today—can be highlighted as examples: freedoms, the division of powers, republic as the form of government, respect of autonomy under public law, freedom of religion, the exercise of lawful authority, parliamentarism, the equality of rights, acknowledging judicial power, the protection of the nationalities living with us'.[100] According to the Court, these are achievements of the Hungarian historical Constitution on which the legal system rests.

The Court held that 'the constitutional self-identity of Hungary is a fundamental value not created by the Fundamental Law, it is merely acknowledged by the Fundamental Law, consequently constitutional identity cannot be waived by way of an international treaty'.[101] Therefore, the Court argued, 'the protection of the constitutional identity shall remain the duty of the Constitutional Court as long as Hungary is a sovereign State'.[102] Because sovereignty and constitutional identity are interrelated in many points, 'their control should be performed with due regard to each other in specific cases'.[103]

Based on the above, the Court returned to the Commissioner's question concerning the transfer of third-country nationals in the context of the EU and answered it in the framework of this abstract constitutional interpretation: 'If human dignity, another fundamental right, the sovereignty of Hungary (including the extent of the transferred competences) or its self-identity based on its historical Constitution can be presumed to be violated due to the exercise of competences based on article E) para 2 of the Fundamental Law, the Constitutional Court may examine, on the basis of a relevant petition, in the course of exercising its competences, the existence of the alleged violation.'[104] This sentence is also the holdings (dictum) of the judgment, which opens the decision.

[96] Ibid, [56].
[97] Ibid, [59]–[60].
[98] Ibid, [63].
[99] Ibid, [64].
[100] Ibid, [65].
[101] Ibid, [67].
[102] Ibid.
[103] Ibid.
[104] Ibid, [69].

In terms of the Constitutional Court's jurisdiction, neither the Fundamental Law nor the Act on the Constitutional Court authorizes the Court to perform this review. In article 24 para 2 of the Fundamental Law, one can find that the listed subjects of review (points a)–c) and e)) are either Hungarian legal norms or judicial decisions. Article T) para 2 of the Fundamental Law lists all the legal regulations of Hungarian authorities but does not mention the legal acts of the European Union, which consequently cannot be subject to any review procedure of the Hungarian Constitutional Court. According to article 23 para 3 of the Act on the Constitutional Court, the Court is authorized to carry out preliminary review of the conformity of an international treaty or of its provisions with the Fundamental Law, but this competence certainly does not apply to EU legal regulations.

Interestingly, three of the justices recognized that the Hungarian Constitutional Court does not have the power to review EU legal acts, but this did not motivate them to write a dissent by rejecting the Commissioner's petition. István Stumpf, in his concurring opinion, claimed that the holdings of the decision are limited to approving the review of 'the joint exercising of competences under article E) para 2 of the Fundamental Law', and although the reasoning deals with the review of EU laws, the holdings 'only reaches a self-evident conclusion'.[105] But he fails to explain how the task could possibly be completed without reviewing the EU legal regulation. In my view, a review of a Hungarian application of an EU decision would not amount to the review of EU law. In his concurring opinion, Béla Pokol takes it for granted that the holdings of the decision declared it possible for the Constitutional Court, in exercising its jurisdiction, to monitor it procedure against the legal acts of the Union. As I have pointed out, however, neither the Fundamental Law nor the Act on the Constitutional Court prescribes as much. Pokol thinks that the Court should have granted only the Government the right to initiate the procedure.[106] In other words, he assumes that the Constitutional Court has no legislative power. László Salamon, the author of the single dissenting opinion, goes even further by stating that 'in addition to establishing its own competence of review, the Constitutional Court should also declare the applicability of this requirement (namely the duty of *ultra vires* review) to the whole of the State's system'.[107] Make no mistake, he did not dissent on the ground that the Constitutional Court exceeded the limits of its own competences but because he thought that the majority decision 'fails to provide a complete answer to the questions aimed at the interpretation of the Constitution, as asked by the Commissioner for Fundamental Rights'.[108]

Viktor Orbán's first jubilant reaction in an interview on Hungarian Public Radio shows how enthusiastic he was that the Court had helped the government's wishes come true by making up for the failed referendum and the Seventh Amendment: 'I threw my hat in the air when the Constitutional Court ruled that the government has the right and obligation to stand up for Hungary's constitutional identity.[109] This means that the cabinet cannot support a decision made in Brussels that violates Hungary's sovereignty.' He added that the Court decision is good news for 'all those who do not want to see the country occupied'.[110] In the same interview, Orbán anticipated the next issue on which Hungary's national constitutional

---

[105] Ibid, [96].
[106] Ibid, [92].
[107] Ibid, [117].
[108] Ibid, [113].
[109] In the context of the Constitutional Court's decision, it is clear that the Prime Minister was referring not merely to the possibility of the government bringing proceedings before the ECJ but to the Court's established power to declare the EU law inapplicable.
[110] 'Orbán: Brüsszel meg akarja szüntetni a rezsicsökkentést' (hvg.hu, 2 December 2016) http://hvg.hu/itthon/20161202_Orban_beszed_pentek_reggel (last accessed on 11 April 2022).

identity can be invoked, referring to the latest EU plan to terminate Hungarian state regulation of public utility prices. He said that the European Commission incorrectly argued that competition in the energy sector leads to lower prices. 'Therefore, Hungary insists on reducing utility rate cuts and we shall defend it in 2017. Although this will be a very tough battle, we have a chance of success'.[111] The battle over asylum seekers resurfaced in another speech, delivered in February 2017, in which Orbán stated, 'I find the preservation of ethnic homogeneity very important'.[112] On 5 March, a newspaper reported on Hungary's shameful treatment of asylum seekers, including severe beatings with batons and the use of attack dogs.[113]

One can ask: what is wrong with Hungary's new constitutional identity? I have to admit that both the failed Seventh Amendment to the Fundamental Law of Hungary and the Constitutional Court's decision on the interpretation of the country's constitutional identity appear to be carefully crafted documents, which seem to fit into the discourse about constitutional identity under several EU Member States' constitutional laws as well as about national identity under EU law. With its seminal judgment in *Internationale Handelsgesellschaft*,[114] the ECJ confirmed that national constitutional norms in conflict with secondary legislation should be inapplicable. On the other hand, Member State constitutions can specify matters of national identity, and Constitutional Courts can use the identity review against EU acts. In other words, national Constitutional Courts must retain the authority for, as the German Federal Constitutional Court puts it, 'safeguarding the inviolable constitutional identity' of their states.

Decisions of the German Federal Constitutional Court and other high courts that claim jurisdiction to protect national identity usually refer to their cooperative relationship with the European Court of Justice, emphasizing their 'Europe-friendliness'[115] with the objective of increasing the level of protection offered by the EU.[116] In the case of the European Central Bank's Outright Monetary Transaction (OMT) programme about the irreversibility of the Euro, the German Court, in its very first preliminary reference, de facto declared the OMT programme illegal and called on the Court of Justice to strike it down.[117] But after the ECJ's ruling delivered on 16 June 2015 reaffirmed the rule that a judgment of the Court of Justice 'is binding on the national courts, as regards the interpretation or the validity of the acts of the EU institutions in question, for the purposes of the decision to be given in the main proceedings',[118] the German Court complied with the ECJ's answer.[119]

---

[111] Ibid.

[112] Speech delivered on 28 February 2017 at the annual gathering of the Hungarian Chamber of Commerce. See Éva S Balogh, 'Viktor Orbán's 'ethnically homogeneous Hungary', Hungarian Spectrum, 3 March 2017. http://hungarianspectrum.org/2017/03/01/viktor-orbans-ethnically-homogeneous-hungary/ (last accessed on 11 April 2022).

[113] The report from Belgrade was published in the Swedish newspaper Aftonblader, available at http://www.aftonbladet.se/nyheter/a/noLbn/flyktingarna-den-ungerska-polisen-misshandlar-och-torterar-oss (last accessed on 11 April 2022).

[114] Case C-11/70, Internationale Handelsgesellschaft mbH [1970] ECR 01125.

[115] See, for instance, the judgment of the GFCC of 24 April 2013 on the Counter-Terrorism Database Act, 1 BvR 1215/07. The Supreme Court of the United Kingdom referred to this judgment in *State v Secretary of State for Transport*, 22 January 2014.

[116] Order of 15 December 2015, 2 BvR 2735/14. Protection of Fundamental Rights in Individual Cases is Ensured as Part of Identity Review. This decision of the German Federal Constitutional Court on the European Arrest Warrant led to the Judgment of the Grand Chamber of the European Court of Justice of 5 April 2016 in the case of *Pál Aranyosi and Robert Căldăraru v Generalstaatsanwaltschaft Bremen* C-404/15.

[117] BVerfG, Case No 2 BvR 2728/13, Order of 7 February 2014.

[118] Case C-62/14 *Gauweiler*, para 16.

[119] BVerfG, 34/2016. Judgment of 21 June 2016.

Similarly to their German colleagues in *Gauweiler*, the justices of the Italian Constitutional Court, in preliminary reference order 24/2017, explain to the ECJ why they think that ECJ Grand Chamber judgment of 8 September 2015 in case C-105/14 in *Taricco* infringes upon the Italian Constitution's principle not to be prosecuted beyond the statute-of-limitations period applicable at the time the criminal offence was committed, and they invite the ECJ to correct or qualify its decision. As Davide Paris rightly observes, even though the ECJ might well be unhappy with this development of 'threatening references of appeal', it is better than seeing national Constitutional Courts invoking constitutional identity to decide whether and to what extent the Member States shall comply with EU law, without the ECJ having the opportunity to express its opinion.[120]

In the framework of a dialogue between national Constitutional Courts and the ECJ, the Spanish Tribunal Constitutional, too, emphasizes the harmony between the European and Spanish basic values and reads the identity clause as confirming that an infringement of the core principles of the Spanish Constitution would also violate the European Treaty.[121] Similarly, in the reading of the *French Conseil d'État*, what is 'inherent' in the constitutional identity of a Member State is what is most crucial and distinctive, namely the 'essential of the Republic'.[122] In the case of Arcelor, the *Conseil d'État* concluded that if there is a protection in the EU legal order equivalent to the principle of rights safeguarded by the Constitution, the review of the legality of EU law should be left to the ECJ.[123] The Czech Constitutional Court, although reserving its power to review the constitutionality of EU law, at the same time reserved this possibility for exceptional cases, such as those 'abandoning the identity of values' or exceeding the scope of conferred powers.[124]

Provided that we ignore the Constitutional Court's lacking jurisdiction to review EU law in the current Hungarian constitutional system, as argued earlier, what is wrong then with the decision of the Hungarian Constitutional Court, which also wants to break with the absolute primacy of EU law?

First, it is important to clarify the legal nature of the decision. It certainly does not aim to review the legality of an EU legislative act. Although, as mentioned above, the parliamentary Commissioner referred to Council decision 2015/1601 of 22 September 2015 on the quota system in his petition to the Constitutional Court, he did not request a review of its legality, and the Court did not provide such review.[125] Hence, the decision cannot be considered an *ultra vires* act nor an identity review of the Council decision itself. Rather, it serves as an announcement of what the Court could do to review such an EU decision, whether it violates

---

[120] Davide Paris, 'Carrot and Stick. The Italian Constitutional Court's Preliminary Reference in the Case Taricco' (2017) QIL Zoom-in 37, 5–20.

[121] Tribunal Constitutional 13 December 2004, Declaration (DTC) 1/2004. Quoted by Monica Claes, 'National Identity: Trump Card or Up for Negotiation?', in Alejandro Saiz Arnaiz and Carina Alcoberro Llivina (eds), *National Constitutional Identity and European Integration* (Intersentia, Cambridge, 2013) 109, 128.

[122] See Conclusions of the Commissaire du Gouvernement: Mattias Guyomar in Societé Arcelor Atlantique et autres, lecture du 8 février 2007. Quoted by Barbara Guastaferro, 'Beyond the exceptionalism of Constitutional conflicts: The ordinary functions of the identity clause' (2012) 31 Yearbook of European Law 263, 270.

[123] Ibid.

[124] Decision 26. 11. 2008, *Lisbon I*, Pl. ÚS 19/08. Quoted by Joel Rideau, 'The Case Law of the Polish, Hungarian and Czech Constitutional Courts on National Identity and the "German Model"', in Alejandro Saiz Arnaiz and Carina Alcoberro Llivina (eds), *National Constitutional Identity and European Integration* (Intersentia, Cambridge, 2013). 243, 255–256.

[125] Independently of this procedure, right after its Slovakian counterpart's submission, the Hungarian government also challenged the quota decision before the European Court of Justice. This procedure is still pending, but the ECJ will not take the text of the Hungarian Constitution or its domestically binding interpretation by the Constitutional Court into account in its decision. Why not? What if Hungary argued that a judgment constituted a violation of Art 4(2) TEU (the EU's obligation to respect Hungary's national identity)?

'human dignity, another fundamental rights, the sovereignty of Hungary or its identity based on the country's historical Constitution.'[126]

As the ECJ has stressed in its standing case law on derogations, EU laws must be interpreted strictly so as to be applicable only when the case at hand entails a 'genuine and sufficiently serious threat to a fundamental interest of society'.[127] There is no strict and exhaustive list of constitutional identity-sensitive matters accepted by the ECJ, but taking into account the ECJ's jurisprudence, there are some more frequently acknowledged issues, such as decisions on family law, the form of State, foreign and military policy, and protection of the national language.[128] The Hungarian Constitutional Court's decision concerned the quota decision of the Council, on the basis of which 1,294 asylum seekers would be relocated from Greece and Italy to Hungary, obligating the Hungarian authorities to process their asylum applications. What 'fundamental interests of the society' can legitimately trump the requirement of sincere cooperation of article 4(3) TEU here? As I pointed out earlier, this could not be the alleged collective expulsion of asylum seekers by Italy and Greece claimed by the Commissioner in his petition because the Hungarian Fundamental Law prohibits the collective expulsion of non-Hungarians from the territory of Hungary and not from a third country. In other words, the human dignity and other fundamental rights of refugees not staying in Hungary cannot be protected under the text of the current Hungarian Constitution.

Another problem with the Constitutional Court's interpretation of the Constitution is that it claims that 'Hungary's constitutional identity is rooted in its historical Constitution'. But the substantive meaning of the text of the Fundamental Law on 'the achievements of our historical Constitution' is extremely vague;[129] there is no legal-scientific consensus in Hungary regarding its precise nature.[130] Presumably, because the case law of the Constitutional Court prior to 2011 has been annulled, it should not include precedents from the Court's accumulated practice of legal interpretation following the regime change. In his concurring opinion, Justice András Zs Varga claims that 'the constitutional governance of the country has been one of the core values the nation has always stuck to, and that has been a living value even at the times when the whole or the majority of the country was occupied by foreign powers'.[131] By contrast, in my view, the thousand years of the Hungarian historical Constitution— with the exception of some brief moments, such as during the failed revolution of 1848 or shortly after 1945, until the communist parties took over, and also after 1989, when liberal

---

[126] See the wording of the holdings of Decision 22/2016. (XII. 5.) AB.

[127] Case C-208/09, *Sayn-Wittgenstein*, para 86.

[128] See these matters mentioned in Pietro Faraguna, 'Taking Constitutional identities away from the Courts' (2016) 41 Brooklyn Journal of International Law 491, 506–508. In addition to the *Sayn-Wittgenstein* case, Faraguna mentions the *Groener* judgment (Case C-379/87) from 1989 and the more recent *Runevi* judgment (Case C-208/09). Barbara Guastaferro discusses also the *Omega and Dynamic Medien* Cases (Case C-391/09), the *Spain v Eurojust* Case (Case 160/03), as well as the *Affatato* Case (Case 3/10), see Barbara Guastaferro, 'Beyond the Exceptionalism of Constitutional Conflicts: The Ordinary Functions of the Identity Clause' (n 122) 263–318. Besides these cases, Monica Claes also mentions, from the pre-Lisbon case law, the *Michaniki* case (Case 213/07) and *Adria Energia AG* (Case 205/08), which referred to the protection of the relevant Member States' national cultural identity rather than to its more political form, see Monica Claes, 'National Identity: Trump Card or Up for Negotiation?' (n 121), 109, 131–132.

[129] Because there is no list of laws officially considered part of the historical Constitution, an extreme interpretation could posit that the Jewish laws adopted in the 1930s, earlier than similar legislation in Nazi Germany, belong to it.

[130] Gábor Schweitzer, 'Fundamental law – Cardinal law – Historical Constitution: The Case of Hungary since 2011' (2013) 4 Journal on European History of Law 124–128.

[131] Decision 22/2016. (XII. 5.) AB. [110].

democracy again seemed to be the 'end of history'[132]—the dominant approach was an authoritarian one.[133]

When the Hungarian Constitutional Court protects Hungary's current constitutional identity under the pretext of protecting asylum seekers' rights against collective expulsion with the real objective of not taking part in the joint European solution to the refugee crisis,[134] it does so in a way that is inconsistent with the requirement of sincere cooperation established by article 4(3) TEU. It promotes national constitutional identity without accepting the constitutional discipline demanded by the European legal order.[135] The reference to national constitutional identity of article 4(2) is legitimate only if the Member State refuses to apply EU law in a situation where a fundamental national constitutional commitment is in play.[136] The Hungarian abuse of constitutional identity is nothing but national constitutional parochialism,[137] which attempts to abandon the common European constitutional whole.

As we saw in Section B, when FIDESZ regained its constitution-making two-third majority after the 2018 parliamentary elections, they successfully adopted the Seventh Amendment, which had failed two years earlier with almost the same content. The Constitutional Court's abusive interpretation of constitutional identity became part of the text of the Fundamental Law.

In its decision 3/2019. (III. 7.) AB, the Constitutional Court also addressed the constitutionality of certain elements of the Stop Soros legislative package and ruled that the criminalization of 'facilitating illegal immigration' does not violate the Fundamental Law. The Court again refers to the constitutional requirement to protect Hungary's sovereignty and constitutional identity hiding behind the alleged obligation to protect Schengen borders against 'masses entering [the EU] uncontrollably and illegitimately', in order to justify this clear violation of the freedom of association and the freedom of expression.[138] Besides infringing the rights of NGOs, the decision deprives all asylum seekers of the protection of all fundamental rights by stating that 'the fundamental rights protection ... clearly does not cover the persons arrived in the territory of Hungary through any country where he or she had not been persecuted or directly threatened with persecution. Therefore, the requirements set forth by article I para 3 of the Fundamental Law regarding the restriction of fundamental rights shall

---

[132] See the results of the research project 'Negotiating Modernity': History of Modern Political Thought in East-Central Europe, led by Balázs Trencsényi and supported by the European Research Council: Balázs Trencsényi and others, *A History of Modern Political Thought in Eastern Europe Volumes I and II* (OUP, Oxford, 2016).

[133] See Ivett Császár and Balázs Majtényi, 'Hungary: The Historic Constitution as the Place of Memory', in Markku Suksi, Kalliope Agapiou-Josephides, Jean-Paul Lehners, and Manfred Nowak (eds), *First Fundamental Rights Documents in Europe* (Intersentia, Cambridge, 2015) 57–69.

[134] In an article, Viktor Orbán warned the 'unionists' of the EU, who call for a United States of Europe and mandatory quotas, that if they refuse to accept that the 'sovereigntists', who reject all quotas, desire a Europe of free and sovereign nations, the mainstream will follow precisely the course that Hungary has set forth to affirm its constitutional values, its Christian roots, its demographic policy and its effort to unify the nation scattered across borders. See Viktor Orbán 'Hungary and the Crisis of Europe: Unelected Elites versus People', National Review, 26 January 2017.

[135] This is what Joseph Weiler calls the principle of constitutional tolerance, which lies at the heart of what makes European integration possible. See Joseph H Weiler, 'In Defence of the Status Quo: Europe's Constitutional Sonderweg', in Joseph H Weiler and M Wind (eds), *European Constitutionalism Beyond the State* (CUP, Cambridge, 2003) 7 ff.

[136] See Mattias Kumm and Victor Ferreres Comella, 'The primacy clause of the Constitutional Treaty and the future of Constitutional Conflict in the European Union' (2008) 3 ICON 473, 491 and 492.

[137] See the term used by Mattias Kumm, 'Rethinking Constitutional Authority: On Structure and Limits of Constitutional Pluralism', in Matej Avbelj and Jan Komárek (eds), *Constitutional Pluralism in the European Union and Beyond* (Hart, Oxford/Portland, 2012) 51.

[138] Para [43] of Decision 3/2019. (III. 7.) AB.

not be applied to the regulation of the above listed cases'.[139] With this statement, the Court denies the core of human dignity: the right to have rights.

2. The Instrumental Role of Religion in National Identity

The Seventh Amendment, adopted on 20 June 2018, also added another element to the constitutional text, to make it part of Hungary's constitutional identity, namely a reference to Christian culture. This new provision reads: 'The protection of Hungary's self-identity and its Christian culture is the duty of all state organizations.'

Members of the opposition parties questioned the purpose of the proposed provision at the preparatory meeting of the judicial committee. The only explanation MPs of the governing FIDESZ party, who had initiated the new text, were able to provide was a paraphrase of a sentence they attributed to Robert Schuman, founding father of the European Union: 'Without Christian culture, there is neither Europe nor Hungary.' The major points of the recent constitutional amendment, namely the criminalization of any civil assistance to refugees and the declaration of homelessness as an unlawful behaviour, are deeply contradictory to the very idea of Christian culture. (It was most probably the same intention of legitimating his anti-European idea that recently led Prime Minister Orbán to reframe his concept of 'illiberal democracy' as a fulfilment of 'Christian democracy'.) But this reasoning does not reveal the compensatory message sent to the European People's Party, FIDESZ's party family in the European Parliament, and to its most powerful member, the German CDU-CSU: 'While we may have strange views on European values, we—like you—are good Christians. Besides the political message of the amendment towards Europe, the new provision will have clear internal consequences for constitutional law, since it can be used as a basis of reference to annul any legal norm allegedly violating Christian culture, a tool that can be useful for the packed Constitutional Court or any court in Hungary.'

This new Constitution, which the parliament passed in April 2011, shows the role religion plays in national legitimation by characterizing the nation referred to as the subject of the Constitution not only as the community of ethnic Hungarians but also as a Christian community, thus narrowing the range of people who can recognize themselves as belonging to it. The preamble to the Fundamental Law, which must be taken into consideration when interpreting the main text, commits itself to a branch of Christianity, the Hungarian Roman Catholic tradition. The preamble affirms that 'We are proud that our king Saint Stephen built the Hungarian state on solid ground and made our country a part of Christian Europe' and that the members of the Hungarian nation recognize Christianity's 'role in preserving nationhood'. It also honours the fact that the Holy Crown 'embodies' the constitutional continuity of Hungary's statehood. Besides the sacral symbols, this choice of ideology is reflected—inter alia—in the Fundamental Law's concept of community and its preferred family model as well as in its provision regarding the protection of embryonic and foetal life from the moment of conception.

While giving preference to the Christian tradition of two millennia, the preamble states that 'we value the various religious traditions of our county'. The choice of words displays its model of tolerance, which does not grant the various worldviews equal status, although following them is neither prohibited nor persecuted. However, it is significant that the tolerance

---

[139] Ibid, para [49].

thus declared only extends to the various 'religious traditions' but does not apply to the more recently established religions, to those that are new to Hungary, or to non-religious convictions of conscience.

The refugee crisis of 2015 demonstrated the intolerance of the Hungarian governmental majority, which styled itself as the defender of Europe's 'Christian civilization' against an Islamic invasion. At the beginning of the crisis, Prime Minister Viktor Orbán claimed that 'Christian culture is the unifying force of the nation ... [and] Hungary will either be Christian or not at all.'[140] In another speech held in early September, Orbán went further by stating that 'The Christian-national idea and mentality will regain its dominance not just in Hungary but in the whole of Europe.' This new era should follow 'the age of liberal blah blah' because 'the crisis of liberal identity' is the origin of mass migration and the consequent refugee crisis: 'For years we have told them that "the world is a global village" ... we have talked about universal human rights to which everybody is entitled. We forced our ideology on them: freedom is the most important thing, we said. We bombed the hell out of those who didn't accept our ideology ... We created the Internet, we declared the freedom of information, and we told them that every human being should have access to it. We sent them our soap operas. They watch what we do ... We sent our TV stars into their homes ... they now think that our virtual space is also their space and that in this virtual space everybody can meet anybody else.... These people, partly because of our culture lent to them or forced upon them, are no longer tied to their own land and to their past.'[141]

But should the alleged defence of Christianity from the 'Muslim hordes' be taken seriously? In a speech on 26 July 2012, Orbán explains why Hungarians must be treated in an authoritarian fashion: *'Joining forces is not a matter of intentions, but of sheer force. With a half-Asian lot such as ours, there is no other way* [than compulsion or force].'[142] This assessment is very similar to that of the late Imre Kertész, the Nobel laureate in literature, who argued that Hungary's misfortune stemmed from its inability to choose between Asia and Western Europe.[143] Historically in Hungary, the bloody conflicts of the Reformation meant that until the Horthy era, no church could fully identify itself with the Hungarian nation. Although the Catholic Church dominated the Protestants, both numerically and politically, it played little historical role in preserving national consciousness, so that Catholicism never became equated with Hungarian patriotism. Under Communism, the Roman Catholic Church served neither as a symbol of national independence nor as a source of protection for the opposition, as was the case in Poland.[144]

Christianity and religion serve as reference points that Orbán's right-wing populism uses opportunistically. FIDESZ, once a liberal party with militantly anti-clerical views, started to become conservative from the mid-1990s, developing an openly positive stance towards religion. Still, religion never constituted a significant part of the party's identity but rather played a purely instrumental, opportunistic role in its political strategy, even after the party joined the European People's Party (EPP), the centre-right party family of the European

---

[140] Orbán's speech in Debrecen on 18 May 2015. http://index.hu/belfold/2015/05/18/orban_magyarorszag_ke reszteny_lesz_vagy_nem_lesz/# (last accessed on 18 January 2021).

[141] Speech in Kötcse on 5 September 2015. https://vastagbor.atlatszo.hu/2015/09/17/a-vagatlan-kotcsei-beszed/ (last accessed on 11 April 2022).

[142] See B Szabó, 'Félázsiai származékoknál, mint mi, csak így megy' ['With a half-Asian lot such as ours, there is no other way'], Népszabadság, 27 July 2012.

[143] 'La Hongrie est une fatalité', Le Monde, 9 February 2012 https://www.lemonde.fr/livres/article/2012/02/09/imre-kertesz-la-hongrie-est-une-fatalite_1640790_3260.html (last accessed on 11 April 2022).

[144] Anna Grzymala-Busse, 'Thy will be done? Religious nationalism and its effects in East Central Europe' (2015) 29 East European Politics and Societies, 228–351.

Parliament.[145] FIDESZ uses religious symbols eclectically, so that Christianity is often mentioned together with the pre-Christian pagan traditions. This refers to the idea of 'two Hungarys': the Western Christian and the Eastern pagan, tribal one.[146] Orbán once voiced his conviction that Hungarians are born in the image of the Turul bird, a symbol of ancient pre-Christian Hungarians, 'the symbol of national identity of living'.[147] FIDESZ interprets this pre-Christianity within the framework of nationalism, and this ethno-nationalism provides a type of surrogate religion that serves as a sufficient basis for political identification. In this respect, FIDESZ follows the authoritarian traditions of the Horthy regime between the two World Wars, in which the nation-religion ('*nemzetvallás*') played a crucial role. We can find another example of Orbán's instrumental use of Christianity in his list of the illiberal regimes he admires, which range from Singapore to China, Turkey, India, and Russia and are all either non-Christian or Orthodox.

In addition to its potential to limit fundamental rights, the state's obligation to protect Christian culture, as included in the Seventh Amendment to the Fundamental Law of Hungary, strengthens the role of religion in order to constitutionally legitimize the concept of an ethnic nation. In this concept, the nation, as subject of the Fundamental Law, is not just the community of ethnic Hungarians but also a Christian community, which means that those who do not identify with Christianity can feel excluded from the nation as well. In this constitutional order, the state is not necessarily obligated to tolerate all religions, and the representatives of Christianity can feel entitled to be intolerant of the representatives of other religions.

---

[145] Only 22 per cent of FIDESZ voters belong to a church, and the same percentage of them consider themselves explicitly non-religious. Political Capital Institute's Research (Budapest, 2011), Research on religion and right-wing politics. Quoted by Andras Bozóki and Zoltán Ádám, 'State and faith: Right-wing populism and nationalized religion in Hungary' (2016) 2(1) East European Journal of Society and Politics 98–122.

[146] See Bozóki and Ádám, 'State and faith' (n 145).

[147] 'Minden magyar a turulba születik' [All Hungarian are born into the Turul bird], Népszabadság, 29 September 2012.

6

The Evolution and *Gestalt* of the
Italian Constitution

*Sabrina Ragone and Giacomo D'Amico**

A. Origins of the Current Constitution	269	a) From the 'conventio ad excludendum' up to 'Tangentopoli'	292
1. Historical Experiences Affecting the Constitution	269	b) The Electoral System as an Element of Change	293
2. Foreign Influence and Use of Comparative Law	274	5. The Development of the Constitution as a Source Subject to Interpretation and Implementation	296
3. Main Critical Points	276	6. Rigidity and Amendability	298
4. Political Equilibria in the Constituent Assembly and their Impact on the Outcome	279	**C. Basic Structures and Concepts**	302
a) Fundamental Choices: Key Figures, Texts, and Theories	280	1. The Value of the Constitution and the Constitutionalization of the Legal System	302
B. The Evolution of the Constitution	283	2. Democracy and Sovereignty	304
1. The Evolution of the Form of Government	283	3. Rule of Law and Protection of Constitutional Rights	307
2. The Evolution of Regionalism	286	4. Separation and Distribution of Powers among Constitutional Bodies and Territorial Entities	309
3. The Evolution of Constitutional Adjudication	289		
4. Critical Features and Junctures	292	**D. Constitutional Identity**	316

A. Origins of the Current Constitution

1. Historical Experiences Affecting the Constitution

The text, scope, and mission of the Italian Constitution—passed by the Constituent Assembly on 22 December 1947, promulgated on 27 December and entered into force on 1 January 1948—were strongly affected by the Second World War and the civil war that broke out in Italy after 8 September 1943, when hostilities between the Italian army and the Anglo-American troops ceased.

From a legal and constitutional perspective, the entry into force of the Constitution led to the final repeal of the former fundamental law, the so-called *Statuto albertino*,[1] which had

---

* The chapter is the result of the joint analysis and elaboration of both authors. More specifically, Sections A.2, A.3, B.1, B.2, B.3, B.6, and C.4 can be attributed to Sabrina Ragone and Sections A.1, A.4, B.4, B.5, C.1, C.2, C.3, and D, to Giacomo D'Amico. The authors would like to thank Ines Ciolli, Pedro Cruz Villalón, and Bogdan Iancu for their insightful comments on a previous version of the chapter.

[1] Giorgio Rebuffa, *Lo Statuto albertino* (il Mulino, Bologna, 2003); Luigi Ciaurro (ed), *Lo Statuto albertino illustrato dai lavori preparatori* (Presidenza del Consiglio dei ministri, Dipartimento per l'informazione e l'editoria, Rome, 1996).

Sabrina Ragone and Giacomo D'Amico, *The Evolution and* Gestalt *of the Italian Constitution* In: *The Max Planck Handbooks in European Public Law*. Edited by: Armin von Bogdandy, Peter M Huber, and Sabrina Ragone, Oxford University Press.
© Sabrina Ragone and Giacomo D'Amico 2023. DOI: 10.1093/oso/9780198726425.003.0006

been passed by the King Carlo Alberto in 1848 and had later become the basic law of the Italian Kingdom after the unification (1861) and the capture of Rome (1870).[2] In fact, the *Statuto* was the Constitution of the Kingdom of Sardinia (which originally included the current Regions of Piedmont, Valle d'Aosta, Liguria, and Sardinia), which was ruled by the Savoy family and of which the first King of a united Italy, Vittorio Emanuele II, was a member.

After the Italian State was established on 17 March 1861, the former historical configuration of the peninsula, divided into numerous little States ended (among these, the largest were the Kingdom of the two Sicilies, the Papal State, the Grand Duchy of Tuscany, and the Kingdom of Lombardy-Venetia, although it was a crown land of the Austrian Empire). The *Statuto* therefore represented an authentic constitutional 'glue', which regulated both the organization of the Kingdom and the rights and duties of the subjects.

Nonetheless, it was still a charter granted by the sovereign. Therefore, it was not based on any democratic process, nor was there a particular procedure for its modification and amendment. Precisely these features meant that it posed little resistance when the institutions of the Kingdom were called to face the birth of the fascist dictatorial regime. Even though it was never formally repealed, the *Statuto* became a void document, totally inadequate to protect the institutions from fascist and squad violence. Probably, with respect to those tragic phenomena, the existence of proper constitutional mechanisms of control and guarantee would have been worth little, but surely, they could have made the rise to power of the Fascist Party more complex.

The ways in which fascism took power clearly demonstrated the weakness of the statutory system. From this point of view, the creation in 1919 of the first *'fascio di combattimento'* (Fasces of Combat) was facilitated by the serious economic and political crisis of the first post-war period, which was accompanied by the rise of the myth of the so-called 'mutilated victory', that is the substantial nullification of the Italian victory in the First World War due to the dispossession of Italian territories assigned to Yugoslavia. The defeat of the fascist movement in the elections held in 1919 (it did not get any seats) only temporarily discouraged its leader, Benito Mussolini. In 1921 it changed its name to the National Fascist Party and started to combine political activities with violence perpetrated by the so-called 'action squads' (hence the expression *'squadrismo'*).

The severe political crisis led to new elections in 1921. On that occasion, from the lists of the so-called National Blocs (which brought together candidates from other political forces as well), thirty-five fascist deputies were elected, including Mussolini. In a climate of continuing crisis, in October 1922 Mussolini organized the so-called March on Rome with the intention of putting pressure on King Vittorio Emanuele III and forcing the current government to resign. The King decided not to declare a state of siege and allotted Mussolini the task to form a new executive, which at first also included members of other parties.

In 1923, in view of the general elections of the following year, the parliament approved a new electoral law (the so-called Acerbo law, named after its first signatory), which modified the proportional system introduced in 1919 and envisaged a significant majority premium (two-thirds of the seats) for the party that obtained at least 25 per cent of the votes.

---

[2] Carlo Ghisalberti, *Storia costituzionale d'Italia 1848–1994* (Laterza, Rome, 2002); Roberto Martucci, *Storia costituzionale italiana. Dallo Statuto albertino alla Repubblica (1848–2001)* (Carocci, Rome, 2002); Denis Mack Smith, *Storia d'Italia* (Laterza, Rome, 2008); Giuseppe Volpe, *Storia costituzionale degli italiani. I. L'Italietta (1861–1915)* (Giappichelli, Turin, 2009); Aurelio Lepre and Claudia Petraccone, *Storia d'Italia dall'Unità a oggi* (il Mulino, Bologna, 2012); Umberto Allegretti, *Storia costituzionale italiana. Popolo e istituzioni* (il Mulino, Bologna, 2014); Massimo L Salvadori, *Storia d'Italia. Il cammino tormentato di una nazione. 1861–2016* (Einaudi, Turin, 2018).

This law, which was passed not only by the deputies of the National Fascist Party, but also by many in the Popular Party, by some liberals, and by the so-called historical right, allowed the National List (composed of candidates from the Fascist Party and the Liberal Party, among others) to obtain—also by virtue of the violent context in which 1924 elections were held—64.9 per cent of the seats, consolidating the government led by Mussolini.

This election constituted a turning point for the constitutional system because the violence and intimidation, which had already characterized the political debate for some years, were publicly denounced by the socialist deputy Giacomo Matteotti. He was kidnapped and killed just a few days after his speech at the Chamber. At that point, even the political forces that had formerly supported Mussolini urged the King to oblige him to leave the office. The King refused to intervene and left any decision on the matter to parliament. Mussolini, with a speech at the Chamber in January 1925, assumed political responsibility for everything that had happened up to that moment, starting the liberticide season of the fascist regime characterized by the so-called 'very fascist laws' (*leggi fascistissime*).

All parties, other than the fascist one, were therefore dissolved, fundamental freedoms were suppressed; the electoral law was amended as to make voters approve or reject a list of deputies proposed by the Grand Council of Fascism in the elections of 1929 (favourable votes prevailed with a very large majority). In 1939, the Chamber of Deputies was abolished and replaced with the Chamber of Fasces and Corporations. Meanwhile, starting in 1938/1939, racial laws were passed, and the regime reached the apex of its authoritarian character.

In essence, the attempt to overcome the political crisis and the party fragmentation determined by the proportional electoral system led, in the short time span of a few years, to the establishment of an authoritarian regime.[3]

As it was previously mentioned, the shift from the system based on the *Statuto* to the republican order was not easy or painless, rather it was characterized, in certain phases, by an authentic civil war. Italy, in fact, was split into two, with the Nazi-fascists in the North and the Centre and the American allies in the South. Decisive in this sense was the entry into the second world conflict, decided in 1940, alongside Germany. Before that, the authoritarian turn of the Mussolini regime with the abovementioned *leggi fascistissime* and, above all, with the racial laws implied a point of no return concerning basic democratic guarantees that had been progressively eliminated or reduced. As a consequence, Italy's participation in the Second World War represented a tragic corollary of the politics pursued during the so-called *ventennio fascista* (1922–1943). Additionally, the economic condition was anything but prosperous and the country struggled, relying almost exclusively on a widespread propaganda system that involved all social groups and all ages.

Not surprisingly, considering the disastrous outcome of Italian participation in the Second World War, tensions broke out within the fascist hierarchy, and they contributed to the decline of Mussolini's political career. During the night between 24 July and 25 July 1943, the 'Grand Council of Fascism' urged the King to again assume his constitutional powers (according to the *Statuto*), such as the command of the Armed Forces, which were still fighting alongside the German *Reich*. The King Vittorio Emanuele III eventually had Mussolini arrested and appointed Pietro Badoglio as the head of the new government, all the while keeping the Italian alliance with Germany. Only on 8 September 1943, the armistice with the American, British, French, Russian, and Canadian Allies was made public. At that point, a new conflict arose between Italy (with the Allies) and the German troops which were

---

[3] Sabino Cassese, *Lo Stato fascista* (il Mulino, Bologna, 2016); Guido Melis, *La macchina imperfetta. Immagine e realtà dello Stato fascista* (il Mulino, Bologna, 2018).

present on Italian soil, as they used to be the main ally of the Italian state. They were joined by the fascists who remained loyal to Mussolini and Germany. In this situation, the King Vittorio Emanuele III escaped to Brindisi and abandoned the army. The so-called *Resistenza* assumed the task of fighting German troops, which had suddenly become invaders.

As a result, the country was split into two: the South was occupied by Americans and British with the King's government; the North became the so-called Italian Social Republic of Salò, a Nazi-fascist puppet state, led by Mussolini. In the central (but not only) regions of Emilia-Romagna and Tuscan, the partisan war was taking place, under the leadership of the National Liberation Committee (CLN in the Italian acronym). The CLN considered it essential, for any change in regime, to decide on the 'institutional question', i.e. whether Italy would become a republic or stay a monarchy.

Therefore, after the fall of Mussolini in 1943, there was first the formation of a military executive, led by General Badoglio, then a government of national unity, again led by him and a series of subsequent executives, including Bonomi, Parri, and De Gasperi, and supported by the six parties of the National Liberation Committee (Italian Communist Party—PCI, Christian Democracy—DC, Action Party—PdA, Italian Liberal Party—PLI, Italian Socialist Party of Proletarian Unity—PSIUP, and Labor Democratic Party—DL). These parties advocated for very different political ideologies, but they were exclusively united by their anti-fascism. In fact, the dramatic experience of the twenty years of fascist regime, of the Second World War, and of the civil war produced the extraordinary effect of unifying those groups that had opposed fascism. The outcomes were, first, the birth of the National Liberation Committee, which was a political and military organization, and, second, the establishment of the first governments led by all these political forces. It was a fairly short but extremely significant experience because, during that period of time, the election of the Constituent Assembly took place,[4] exactly on 2 June 1946. Already in 1947, the territorial branches of the CLN were dissolved and, almost at the same time, in May, Prime Minister Alcide De Gasperi resigned. This meant the end of the De Gasperi III government, which was also supported by leftist parties (namely the socialists and the communists), who did not take part to the following executives.

Meanwhile, in the spring of 1944, the King retired to private life, leaving his son, Umberto II, as the Lieutenant of the Kingdom. The King Vittorio Emanuele III abdicated only in May 1946, with the consequence that his son was King only for less than a month, until the popular referendum on the choice between monarchy and republic took place. The date for both the referendum and the election of the Constituent Assembly was fixed for 2 June 1946. The republican form of State gained higher popular support. Therefore, after the decision was taken to replace the Kingdom, the Constituent Assembly was obliged to respect popular will in the drafting of the Constitution. Not surprisingly, the republican system is the only explicit limit even to the amending power, as article 139 of the Italian Constitution states.

This is the context into which the drafting of the Italian Constitution has to be inserted.[5] The Republican Constitution of 1948 arose from the compromise of the Constituent Assembly, whose task and purpose have to be understood within the historical and political

---

[4] Costantino Mortati, 'La Costituente. La teoria. La storia. Il problema italiano', in Costantino Mortati (ed), *Raccolta di scritti, I, Studi sul potere costituente e sulla riforma costituzionale dello Stato* (Giuffrè, Milan, 1972) 3 ff. A recent analysis of the current importance of the constituent endeavour can be found in Fulvio Cortese, Corrado Caruso, and Stefano Rossi, *Immaginare la Repubblica. Mito e attualità dell'Assemblea Costituente* (FrancoAngeli, Milan, 2018).

[5] AAVV, *Dallo Statuto albertino alla Costituzione repubblicana* (Giuffrè, Milan, 2012); Livio Paladin, *Per una storia costituzionale dell'Italia repubblicana* (il Mulino, Bologna, 2004).

situation as well. In the Constituent Assembly, there was a substantial balance between political parties, to the point that none of them could have supported a government by itself. These were the percentages obtained by the main forces: Catholics (35.21 per cent), Socialists (20.68 per cent), Communists (18.93 per cent), and Liberal forces (6.78 per cent), as it will be detailed. Its task was to draft a Constitution in the sign of discontinuity vis-à-vis both the fascist regime and the previous liberal regime, giving to the Constitution a particular rigidity and strength to resist modifications. At the same time, the Italian Constitution is ideologically plural, because it is not inspired by a single ideology, managing to transfer social developments into 'sensitive legal architectures'.[6]

The drafters of the Constitution had to act within a very uncertain context. Such background was the result of the Second World War, but also the fact that the fascist regime forced political opponents to hide. Above all, the drafters had to improve the political and social unity of the country to avoid the risk of a new civil war. It is not by chance that the Constituent Assembly's debates frequently emphasized the need for social cohesion. Another technical issue was to define the structure of a modern democracy, with the aims of overcoming the nineteenth century model of the *Statuto* and avoiding new authoritarian experiences. According to that source of law, the King, among other privileges, was in charge of appointing and revoking 'his' ministers. This document was particularly flexible, and such a feature virtuously permitted the transformation from the original constitutional monarchy to a parliamentary monarchy. Unfortunately, due to its flexibility, it also failed to prevent the fascist authoritarian drift. It became necessary to draft a Constitution that could not be amended by temporary majorities, containing a system of checks and balances, such as to prevent or (at least) limit the risks of another authoritarian drift.

The undebatable common anti-fascist position provided the main features and determined the spirit of the Assembly, supporting both the Constituent Assembly and the leadership of the ruling parties. Classical liberal ideas influenced the members very little, despite the individual '*auctoritas*' of some pre-fascist great figures. The restoration of the previous system was universally rejected.

Considering the defeat of the monarchy in the referendum and the spread inclination of the electorate towards parties with novel political agendas, the idea of incorporating the values of a social/welfare democratic State was present within the Constituent Assembly (in contrast to liberalism).[7]

As De Siervo pointed out, the will of the 'common promise' was made possible in its most noble sense, thanks to the peculiar political and social conditions at the time (cited as 'constitutional compromise'[8]). Those political forces with the most conspicuous representation within the Constituent Assembly (Christian Democrats, Socialists, Communists, and Liberals) succeeded in a task that would have been impossible if they had not been united by a similar 'anti-fascist' mission. Despite the diversity of ideologies and political strategies, those parties never stepped back from the debates and proposals, engaged in dialogue and

---

[6] Costantino Mortati, 'La Costituente' (n 4); Luigi Vetri, *Dalla Monarchia alla Repubblica: il nuovo Stato italiano. Aspetti storici politici giuridici sulla nuova costituzione italiana* (Corso, 1957).

[7] Gianfranco D'Alessio (ed), *Alle origini della Costituzione italiana. I lavori preparatori della 'Commissione per gli studi attinenti alla riorganizzazione dello Stato' (1945–1946)* (il Mulino, Bologna, 1979). On these issues, see Pietro Scoppola, *Gli anni della Costituente fra politica e storia* (il Mulino, Bologna, 1980) and Gaetano Azzariti, 'Il liberalismo autoritario e la costruzione dello Stato unitario italiano. Vittorio Emanuele Orlando, un liberale al servizio dello Stato' (2011) 1–2 Democrazia e diritto 117–134.

[8] Ugo De Siervo (ed), *Scelte della Costituente e cultura giuridica, Protagonisti e momenti del dibattito costituzionale*, vol 2 (il Mulino, Bologna, 1980). See also the volume by Enzo Cheli, *Nata per unire. La Costituzione italiana tra storia e politica* (il Mulino, Bologna, 2012).

did not adopt obstructionist attitudes that could have led the Constituent Assembly into failure. Interestingly, this attitude continued even after the end of the period of the great coalition governments (1947) which were supported by all these political parties. In terms of concrete constitutional clauses, the anti-fascist common sentiment shaped the formulation of a series of articles in which the opposing ideological positions were present but mediated (such as article 29 on marriage and article 43 on the expropriation of companies for a prevailing general interest).

In addition to the provisions concerning rights and duties of citizens and individuals in general, the reaction to the previous fascist regime is to be identified within the whole complex of constitutional clauses founding a State organization based on an effective and balanced system of powers of initiative, execution, and control (among them, the Constitutional Court), alongside the regulation of political and administrative decentralization, which reached its major target with the establishment of the Regions.

The creation of bodies endowed with supervisory functions of either judicial (like the Constitutional Court) and political nature (like the President of the Republic), the enactment of a system of guarantees for the principle of independence of the judiciary, the recognition of social groups, and territorial autonomous bodies dismembered the monolithic power-block upon which the fascist regime was built, similarly to other authoritarian and totalitarian regimes. In the new constitutional State resulting from the republican Constitution, there no longer exists a sovereign in either the subjective or objective sense. Rather, the traditional concept of sovereignty (which still has its recognition in the Constitution, starting with article 1) is fragmented and perhaps even diluted in the pluralistic construction of the democratic State.

2. Foreign Influence and Use of Comparative Law

Foreign influences in the period preceding the drafting of the Italian Constitution not only depended on cultural reasons, but also, and especially, on political reasons. The ties between some foreign countries (in particular, the USA, the USSR, and the United Kingdom) and the political forces that were part of the CLN Committee had an impact on certain political decisions, such as the exit from the government (in 1947) of the major left parties (Socialists and Communists).

From a strictly legal-constitutional perspective, even before the election of the Constituent Assembly, the activities carried out by the Ministry for the Constituent Assembly, established in July 1945, and (internally) by the Commission for studies concerning the reorganization of the State were particularly significant (so-called Forti Committee).[9] In fact, this Ministry, whose function was precisely to collect and provide data and materials for the study of the new Constitution and its internal Committees (like the Forti Committee) took care of translating into Italian and publishing texts and documents coming from the main foreign legal systems. Thanks to this activity, the main democratic constitutions were made accessible for all members of the Assembly, including those whose cultural background did not cover legal and comparative studies.

During the Constituent Assembly's debates, explicit references to traditional legal and political doctrines were employed for functional purposes. Among other constitutional

---

[9] Gianfranco D'Alessio (ed), *Alle origini della Costituzione italiana* (n 7).

experiences, the founding fathers quite often referred to the French,[10] the German, and the American constitutions. They were considered dialectic models, for instance during the long deliberation on the political system and the dialogue between nationalists and regionalists on the regulation of decentralized and local bodies.

In this respect, the examination that was conducted by the Constituent Assembly on the models of form of government according to which the Italian government could be shaped is significant. The debate on this point took place in the Second Subcommittee (the Constituent Assembly for operational purposes was divided into subcommittees) with a leading role being taken by Costantino Mortati, who was already a well-known jurist, member of the Christian Democrats, and who later became judge of the Constitutional Court. After the in-depth analysis carried out by Mortati, the Second Subcommittee decided to approve an agenda ('*ordine del giorno*'), which was an internal document aiming at advancing and planning the activities of the Assembly. In this document, the Subcommittee voted in favour of 'the adoption of the parliamentary system to be regulated, however, with constitutional mechanisms suitable to protect the needs of governmental stability and avoid its possible degeneration',[11] which reinforced an earlier conclusion that 'neither a presidential system nor a directorial one would meet the conditions of the Italian society'.

This agenda, which took the name of its proponent (Perassi), was repeatedly recalled over the decades, in particular before the transition from the proportional electoral system to the majoritarian system. With this document, the Second Subcommittee, conscious of the mutation of the parliamentary system that had facilitated the rise to power of Mussolini and the fascist regime, concluded that the choice of a different form of government would even increase the risks of an authoritarian drift. It also intended to provide for measures and mechanisms capable of guaranteeing the stability of the upcoming executives. In fact, there were founding fathers who advocated for a stronger executive, such as Egidio Tosato, who referred to comparative models, namely to the French Constitution of 1946.[12] In the application of the Constitution, this intention was frustrated by an excessive political fragmentation which, very frequently until 1994 and then more sporadically, has hindered governmental stability.

The political and contextual inspiration led to some basic choices: participatory democracy with the traits of a welfare state, the combination of the protection of individual rights with collective legal protection, and the balance between politics and societal participation. For these reasons, the historical experience of the Weimar Constitution played an important role, with reference to its structure and principles.[13]

One of the most important experts of the Weimar Constitution was Costantino Mortati. He acutely analysed the constitutional framework and the underlying political and social context in an essay from 1946, which was republished in 2019.[14] Mortati's analysis helped to bring within the Italian constituent debate the unfortunate Weimarian experience, allowing the founding fathers to reflect on the unlikely feasibility of that model, in spite of its extraordinary modernity.[15]

---

[10] Ugo De Siervo, 'Le idee e le vicende costituzionali in Francia nel 1945 e 1946 e la loro influenza sul dibattito in Italia', in Ugo De Siervo (ed), *Scelte della Costituente e cultura giuridica, Costituzione italiana e modelli stranieri*, vol 1 (il Mulino, Bologna, 1980) 298 ff.

[11] Second Subcommittee of the Committee for Constitution, Constituent Assembly, 4 and 5 of September 1946.

[12] Fernanda Bruno, 'Il problema del Governo alla Costituente: il contributo di Egidio Tosato. Suggestione di modelli stranieri e spunti originali' (1981) 46 Il Politico n 1/2 127–155.

[13] Nicola Matteucci, 'La cultura politica nel periodo costituente', in AAVV (ed), *L'Italia negli ultimi trent'anni* (il Mulino, Bologna, 1978) 251 ff.

[14] Costantino Mortati, *La Costituzione di Weimar*, with an essay by Maurizio Fioravanti (Giuffrè, Milan, 2019).

[15] Costantino Mortati, *Problemi di politica costituzionale. Raccolta di Scritti*, vol 9 (Giuffrè, Milan, 1972) 317.

Mortati's reflection on Weimar is, therefore, a significant example of fruitful interaction between doctrinal work and constitutional elaboration. More to the point, the system of checks and balances developed by the Italian drafters has managed to avoid the risks of that authoritarian drift that instead determined the end of the experiment of the Weimar Republic.[16]

Even recently, Italian scholarship has focused on this model, highlighting its merits, and reconsidering its limits;[17] it can therefore be said that, until today, faced with proposals for constitutional amendments, the Weimarian experience and its flaws still represent a relevant reference for our constitutional debates.

The regional structure given to the Italian State was almost completely original. In this regard, although some references were made to foreign models (in particular the republican Constitution passed in Spain in 1931, which had adopted a regional asymmetric system), the choice for a form of decentralization based on Regions responded to the need to curb the separatist pressures of some Regions (Sicily, in particular) and to give recognition to the peculiarities of certain territories (essentially those of the other four special Regions: Friuli-Venezia Giulia, Sardinia, Trentino-Alto Adige, Valle d'Aosta). The remaining Regions (so called 'ordinary') did not have significant historical traditions and were substantially designed without specific ethnic or linguistic parameters, but rather according to previous administrative and statistical partitions. It is no coincidence that these Regions started to be operative only in the early 1970s. Overall, territorial and local government, at the time of the Constituent Assembly, was essentially centred on the Municipalities, which have deep and significant roots in Italian history and were simply acknowledged in the Constitution.

The influence of foreign systems was also relevant with respect to the definition of the basic features of the Constitutional Court,[18] for which there was no domestic model as it represented one of the novelties of the Constitution. As a consequence, during the constituent debates, there were frequent references to the American model[19] and the Austrian Court, which was well-known in Italy thanks to the academic debate between Hans Kelsen and Carl Schmitt. In general, the presence of prestigious legal scholars within the Constituent Assembly contributed to the opening of debates towards foreign experiences and comparative law.

3. Main Critical Points

The 'bargaining nature' of the Italian Constitution is proven by the unprecedented debates among political forces. Several questions were the object of discussion and confrontation, including the form of government and the distribution of powers, the configuration of the

---

[16] Ugo De Siervo, 'Introduzione', in Ugo De Siervo (ed), *Scelte della Costituente e cultura giuridica Costituzione italiana e modelli stranieri*, vol 1 (il Mulino, Bologna, 1980) 13 ff.

[17] Massimo Luciani, 'La "costituzione dei diritti" e la "costituzione dei poteri". Noterelle brevi su un modello interpretativo ricorrente', in AAVV (ed), *Scritti in onore di Vezio Crisafulli*, vol 2 (CEDAM, Padova, 1985) 497 ff. See, more in general, Michele Carducci, *La cultura di Weimar e lo studio del diritto costituzionale comparato* (Pensa, Lecce, 2008).

[18] Vittoria Barsotti and others, *Italian Constitutional Justice in Global Context* (OUP, Oxford, 2016) 12–17; Raffaele Bifulco and Davide Paris, 'The Italian Constitutional Court', in Armin von Bogdandy, Peter M Huber, and Christoph Grabenwarter (eds), *The Max Planck Handbooks in European Public Law*, vol III (OUP, Oxford, 2020) 448–455.

[19] On this point see Peter E Quint, *The Influence of the United States Supreme Court on Judicial Review in Europe*, ibid 862–863.

basis of the Constitution in article 1, the inclusion of principles of welfare state and solidarity, alongside equality, as well as the territorial organization.

The first twelve articles of the constitution contain the values and the 'fundamental principles' that represent the core of the constitutional construction. Article 1 in particular, with a few words, explains the characteristics of the system. Firstly, it starts with the word 'Italy', emphasizing the nature of the Constitution as the basic law of the country as it was formed through history. The definition is that of a 'democratic republic', in order to stress the foundational connection with the will of the people, 'founded on labour'. Labour was placed at the foundation of the Republic, as it is also mentioned in article 4 and then recalled in article 35. Sovereignty belongs to the people and must be exercised by them 'in the forms and within the limits of the Constitution'. The authentic qualitative change of the constitutional State can be found precisely in this last part of article 1, which not only repeats that sovereignty belongs to the people, but also submits its exercise to the respect of the forms and limits established by the Constitution itself. This way, the drafters stressed the mechanisms of control and limitation of power envisaged in the Constitution also with respect to sovereignty.

Specific institutions were subject to concrete debates, such as the number and function of parliamentary chambers, namely whether Italy shall have a bicameral or unicameral system. In these debates the comparative expertise of some members of the Constituent Assembly emerged, such as Calamandrei and Mortati.

The corresponding Subcommittee opted for the (still existing) bicameral system by an overwhelming majority, despite the opposition of a minority in favour of the alternative unicameral system.[20] The prevailing bicameral proposal was constantly accompanied (both in the debates in the Subcommittee and in the plenary sessions) by the need to avoid the danger of a 'duplicate first chamber'. Therefore, the founding fathers agreed that the second Chamber should be built on a different political principle. Nevertheless, the outcome of the debate within the Constituent Assembly was a parliamentary system based on a quasi-symmetric bicameralism, with very limited differentiation between the two branches of parliament (only with respect to active, until 2021, and passive electorate, number of members, national or regional electoral districts, and just until 1963, the duration of the term).

Particularly heated was the debate on the Constitutional Court and, before that, the elaboration of the system of constitutional adjudication. On this point, too, different models were contrasted, from the 'diffuse' to the 'centralized' type, which involved a further step, namely, to choose among the various models of the Constitutional Court.[21]

On these issues, the confrontation between the various political forces was particularly intense. On the one hand, Christian Democrats and 'young' liberals (Martino) were in favour of the establishment of a dedicated tribunal for verifying the constitutionality of ordinary laws, and, on the other hand, Communists, Socialists and 'old' liberals (Vittorio Emanuele Orlando and Nitti) were staunchly opposed.

---

[20] Maurizio Cermel, 'Alle origini dell'opzione bicamerale, tra esigenze di rappresentanza dei territori e di garanzia antitotalitaria', in Gian Candido De Martin, Zbigniew Witkowski, and Piero Gambale (eds), *Parlamenti, politiche pubbliche e forme di governo: esperienze e prospettive in Italia e in Polonia*, Atti del V Colloquio italo-polacco sulle trasformazioni istituzionali, Venezia, Studium Generale Marcianum 19–20 giugno 2014 (CEDAM, Padova, 2016) 135–164. See also Francesca Sgrò, *Il Senato e il principio della divisione dei poteri* (Giuffrè, Milan, 2012).

[21] Enzo Cheli, *Il giudice delle leggi* (il Mulino, Bologna, 1996); Carla Rodotà, *Storia della Corte costituzionale* (Laterza, Rome, 1999); Francesco Paolo Casavola, 'Genesi della Corte costituzionale italiana', in Francesco Paolo Casavola, *Sententia legum tra mondo antico e moderno*, vol 3 (Jovene, Naples, 2005). For an overview of the arguments for the establishment of a court see Mauro Cappelletti, 'Il significato del controllo giudiziario di costituzionalità delle leggi nel mondo contemporaneo' (1968) Rivista di Diritto processuale 483–500.

The risk that with the establishment of the Constitutional Court popular sovereignty could be undermined was at the basis of the position of the latter. They considered this body a 'weird, unusual object' ('*una bizzarria*', according to Togliatti), as well as a real danger for parliamentary institutions.

The decision taken to establish the Constitutional Court did not close the discussions, which then shifted to the definition of how to bring cases before the Court. On this point, however, it was not possible to reach any concrete agreement. Therefore, with the so-called Arata amendment, it was decided not to indicate in the Constitution the mechanisms to access the Court (except those relating to the State/Regions cases), but to postpone this decision until after the entry into force of the Constitution. As it will be explained below, constitutional law n. 1/1948 finally regulated the concrete control.

Another debate within the Constituent Assembly concerned the regulation of economic relations, particularly basic principles of political and social interactions in light of the economic situation of the time (agrarian property, representation, and rights of workers, etc.[22]). These debates demonstrate the common intention to provide the State with instruments of control over the economy.[23] In particular, economic monopolies were targeted in preliminary and plenary debates: Einaudi even described them as 'the deepest evil of contemporary society', a real 'theft'.[24]

The so-called economic constitution (articles 35 to 47) is an excellent example of the compromise among different political forces, in particular those parties that favoured a liberal model for the economy, and those who were supporters of a collectivist economic system or planned economy.[25] On the one hand, in fact, articles 35 to 40 implement article 4, complementing the protection of workers, ensuring their right to a fair salary, weekly rest, vacation, providing for social security and insurance systems, protecting women and children in the workplace, and establishing the right of affiliation to trade unions and the right to strike; on the other hand, article 41 explicitly states that private economic initiative is free. Through this clause, the Constitution excludes any possibility of adopting a socialist economic model; but yet, for the first time, the exercise of enterprises by private individuals cannot take place to the detriment of social cohesion, and the law can establish in this regard 'appropriate programs and controls'. Private property was no longer untouchable, being balanced with its 'social utility',[26] and the law had to provide the means to make it accessible to all. A new perspective on economic issues was introduced through the constitutional amendment of 2012 (constitutional law n. 1/2012) and the introduction of the balanced budget principle.

---

[22] Stefano Rodotà, 'Art. 42', in Giuseppe Branca (ed), *Commentario della Costituzione* (Zanichelli-Foro it., Bologna-Roma, 1982) 85.

[23] Luca Mezzetti (ed), *Costituzione economica e libertà di concorrenza: modelli europei a confronto* (Giappichelli, Turin, 1994).

[24] Luigi Einaudi in Constituent Assembly, 13 May 1947. On this issue, see Luigi Gianniti, 'Note sul dibattito alla Costituente sulla "costituzione economica"' (2000) Astrid-online 1–20.

[25] Fiorentino Sullo, *Il dibattito politico sulla programmazione economica in Italia dal 1945 al 1960* (Giuffrè, Milan, 1960).

[26] Vittorio Foa, 'La ristrutturazione capitalistica e la politica delle sinistre', in AAVV (ed), *Italia 1945–48* (Giappichelli, Turin, 1974) 106.

4. Political Equilibria in the Constituent Assembly and their Impact on the Outcome

To better understand some of the features we have described, a short focus on the historical events immediately preceding the election of the Constituent Assembly becomes necessary. After the end of the fascist regime, in fact, political parties got back to operating, specifically by forming the abovementioned CLN. Nevertheless, Italy was still a monarchy, and its Head of State was—at least formally—Vittorio Emanuele III who, since June 1944, had given his power to his son Umberto II, as we mentioned. This compromise between the Crown and the CLN was made in order to complete the most critical steps of the liberation from the German army. The decision concerning the form of State was then postponed and given over to a popular vote. On the same day, also the election of the Constituent Assembly took place.

The following parties composed the Assembly: Christian Democracy 35.21 per cent, Italian Socialist Party of Proletarian Unity 20.68 per cent, Italian Communist Party 18.93 per cent, Italian Liberal Party 6.78 per cent, Common Man's Front 5.27 per cent, Italian Republican Party 4.36 per cent, National Bloc of Freedom 2.77 per cent, Democratic Labor Party 0.18 per cent, Action Party 1.45 per cent, Movement for the Independence of Sicily 0.74 per cent, Republican Democratic Concentration 0.42 per cent, Sardinian Action Party 0.34 per cent, Peasants' Party of Italy 0.44 per cent, Italian Unionist Movement 0.31 per cent, and Social Christian Party 0.22 per cent.

There is no doubt that these parties had to face severe internal conflicts, which reflected the global split in two blocks which then defined the period of time after the Second World War with the beginning of the Cold War. Therefore, the founding fathers adopted an internal system of checks and balances in order to prevent the risk of one political force enjoying a strong majority.

The groups that composed the Constituent Assembly did not differ exclusively on political grounds, but also cultural, religious, and ideological standpoints. Their only common element was their anti-fascist inspiration. In other words, what united the members of the Assembly during the short period between 1943 and 1947 was the anti-fascist paradigm, alongside the refusal of any authoritarianism. In fact, different cultural impulses (liberal, catholic, socialist, and communist) coexisted, and the religious factor proved determinant for the adoption of several decisions. In particular, while the diverse cultural approach was evident in the drafting of the Third Title of the First Part of the Constitution, devoted to 'Economic Rights and Duties',[27] religion had an impact on various clauses included among abovementioned the fundamental principles (especially articles 7[28] and 8[29] of the Constitution) and to 'Ethical and Social Rights and Duties'[30] (especially articles 29, 30, and 31 of the Constitution).

From this perspective, the relationship between the State and the Catholic Church was particularly delicate when the Constitution was drafted. The capture of Rome in 1870 and the end of the Papal State took place after the so called *non expedit* of 1868, according to

---

[27] This is the official translation, although the Italian text mentions 'economic relations'.

[28] Art 7: 'The State and the Catholic Church are independent and sovereign, each within its own sphere. Their relations are regulated by the Lateran Pacts. Amendments to such Pacts accepted by both parties shall not require the procedure of constitutional amendments'

[29] Art 8: 'All confessions are equally free before the law. Confessions other than Catholicism have the right to self-organization according to their own statutes, provided these do not conflict with Italian law. Their relations with the State are regulated through laws, based on agreements with their respective representatives.'

[30] Again, this is the official translation of 'ethical and social relations'.

which it was considered 'inconvenient' for Catholics to participate in the political activities of the Italian Kingdom. Therefore, a conflict between the State and the Church arose (the so-called *questione romana*), notwithstanding article 1 of the *Statuto* which established that the 'Catholic, Apostolic and Roman Religion' would be the official religion of the State, while any other confession would be tolerated according to the law.

Even if the *non expedit* was formally overruled only in 1919, at the beginning of the twentieth century, Catholics already engaged in political activities, as candidates and then elected members of the parliament. When the Italian Popular Party was founded in 1919, this participation was endorsed and formalized. In 1926, with the consolidation of the fascist regime and the aforesaid 'very fascist laws', this Party was dissolved as well.

During the fascist regime, the State and the Catholic Church signed the so-called Lateran Pacts, according to which the latter acknowledged the existence of the former. In exchange, Catholicism was recognized as the only religion of the State. After the fascist regime and the dissolution of the Popular Party, a new party driven by a strong Catholic inspiration was founded in 1943, namely the Christian Democracy, which existed until 1994 and was the pivotal force of Italian executives for decades.

This party was the most represented within the Constituent Assembly and thanks to its electoral weight and the foresight of its leaders, it managed to achieve a few targets which were crucial for the success of the Assembly, among them, article 7 of the Constitution on the relationship between the State and the Catholic Church. Actually, the performance of the great part of the drafters was inspired by the will to achieve balanced solutions taking into account all distinct positions. More concretely, this search for a compromise between the various ideological approaches led to the drafting of constitutional provisions characterized by statements of principle, which, albeit vague, have prevented the Constitution from becoming outdated, as it was never linked to specific circumstances and ideological vetoes.

In other words, the language of principles that characterizes many constitutional provisions, over time, has triggered a virtuous process of 'mutual semantic interaction and nourishment'[31] between the Constitution and the other legal sources, through mechanisms that are independent of the hierarchical rank of those sources. The protagonists of these hermeneutical processes have so far been the judges and, above all, the Constitutional Court that, after overcoming the discussion on the programmatic or obligatory nature of constitutional provisions, was able to transform a critical feature of the Constitution, namely its vagueness, into a strength allowing for adaptations according to the social, cultural, and economic evolution of the country.

a) Fundamental Choices: Key Figures, Texts, and Theories

Constitutional clauses are broad and elastic in order to provide principles with endurance and flexibility in light of social developments. That is why some scholars observe that they are close to mere 'directive-principles' with a programmatic nature. This indeterminacy could have been a historical necessity: from this perspective, the 'noble compromise' which has been praised for decades would become more comparable to a political strategy than a selfless and free choice.

According to this idea, the Communist Party renounced the idea of a 'Republic of working people', which evoked the Soviet Constitution of 1936, and rather accepted a

---

[31] Antonio Ruggeri, 'Linguaggio della Costituzione e linguaggio delle leggi: notazioni introduttive' (2015) 3 Osservatorio Sulle Fonti 1–23.

drafting of article 1 in which Italy is described as a democratic Republic founded on labour. Symmetrically, Christian Democracy agreed to the expression 'inviolable rights' instead of 'natural rights'.

Article 2 contains the fundamental principle that identifies the social nature of the Italian Constitution as establishing a welfare state. The principle of solidarity gains a double dimension, referring to the 'sovereign people' defending their fundamental rights and to the Republic, actively supervising the enforcement of this principle.[32] It is not a coincidence that this provision immediately follows the democratic principle.

As stated by jurists and historians in the preparatory debates of the Constituent Assembly, the aim of the drafters of the Constitution was to lay the foundations of a welfare state, focusing on the collectivist element for preserving the Republic from new totalitarian experiences.[33] In this provision, labour is the fundamental core and a means for dignity, freedom, and self-determination of people, far from any undemocratic regime.[34]

From this perspective, the evolution of many features of the Italian constitutional system can be considered as a part of an architecture of 'full and empty spaces' that designs the connection between solidarity and responsibility. This methodology essentially led to two questions being left open by the founding fathers: the choice of the electoral system and the mechanisms to trigger constitutional adjudication.

As for the electoral law, the Constituent Assembly discussed the possibility to 'constitutionalize' the proportional system, which was considered to be the system that most closely respects the preferences of the electorate. Nevertheless, the risk of excessive political fragmentation led the drafters to envisage possible changes, and, in the end, they did not constrain future legislative decisions in this respect. Consequently, there is no constitutional provision dealing with electoral matters.

Nevertheless, some constitutional provisions presuppose, to some extent, the existence of a proportional system, excellent examples being the majorities required for the election of the President of the Republic (article 83) or for the approval of a constitutional amendment (article 138), which, in the end, allow the '50 per cent + 1' vote to decide on the matter. It is evident that such majorities, with a majoritarian electoral system, could lose their *ratio*, which is to aggregate most of the political components present in parliament and thus avoid abuse by any party enjoying the majority at some point in time. In fact, the problem arose when, starting from the 1994 general elections, the parliament was elected with a predominantly majoritarian electoral system. It was precisely on this occasion that the idea of raising the majorities required by the Constitution was envisaged (albeit not implemented) as a response to the transformation of the electoral system.

With respect to the mechanisms to trigger constitutional adjudication, which will be specifically discussed in section B.3, it is worth mentioning that the drafters decided to postpone this choice until the approval of a posterior constitutional law (with the so-called 'Arata amendment'), thereby smoothing the operations of the Constitutional Assembly and letting

---

[32] Maurizio Fioravanti, 'Dottrina dello Stato-persona e dottrina della Costituzione. Costantino Mortati e la tradizione giuspubblicistica italiana', in Maurizio Fioravanti, *La scienza del diritto pubblico. Dottrine dello Stato e della Costituzione tra Otto e Novecento* (Giuffrè, Milan, 2001) 657 ff.

[33] Sergio Bartole, *Interpretazioni e trasformazioni della Costituzione repubblicana* (il Mulino, Bologna, 2004); Vezio Crisafulli, *La Costituzione e le sue disposizioni di principio* (Giuffrè, Milan, 1952) 12; Vezio Crisafulli, 'Sull'efficacia normativa delle diposizioni di principio della Costituzione' (1948), in Vezio Crisafulli (ed), *La Costituzione e le sue disposizioni di principio* 51 ff.

[34] Oreste Ranelletti, 'Note sul progetto di Costituzione presentato dalla Commissione dei 75 alla Assemblea Costituente' (1947) IV Foro it 81 ff, now in Oreste Ranelletti, *Scritti giuridici scelti, Lo Stato*, vol 1(Jovene, Naples, 1992) 547 ff.

it conclude within the set deadlines. Furthermore, the decision on such a point would have made the vote on the provisions concerning the Constitutional Court even more complex as there had already been a lively discussion on the very existence of the Court and its composition. Therefore, adding further elements of conflict in an already particularly heated debate could have determined the failure of the entire project to introduce a constitutional body in charge of constitutional adjudication.

The basic choice on the point in question was taken with constitutional law n. 1/1948. It was passed only a few weeks after the Constitution entered into force. In particular, article 1 of this law institutionalized the choice of a concrete model because the possibility to refer a question of constitutionality to the Court was given over, among other options, to ordinary judges deciding concrete cases. During the constituent phase, constitutional lawyers presented the introductory reports on the various subjects addressed to the Constituent Assembly.[35] According to this schedule, Giorgio La Pira and Lelio Basso made the opening presentations on civil liberties in the First Subcommittee; Costantino Mortati opened the debate on legislative power (and, in a broad sense, on the system of government). In the same way, the comparative lawyer Gaspare Ambrosini introduced the Fifth Title on territorial organization, while Giovanni Leone and Piero Calamandrei were in charge of the report on the judiciary and constitutional adjudication.

In spite of the rich political perspectives and evaluations, the importance of the legal culture of the rapporteurs was clear in the introductory reports. This legal approach is more evident in the reports submitted by Costantino Mortati, Luigi Einaudi, and Gaspare Ambrosini. In these documents, the political analysis is strongly intertwined with a public law perspective. The decisive relevance of legal contributions is highlighted in the discussion on the form of government by Tomaso Perassi and Egidio Tosato: first, for the presentation of the agenda voted on 5 September 1946; second, for the definition of formal and substantial powers to be given to the Head of State.

This influence became evident and impacted with different intensities and in different ways during the various stages of the constituent process. The Constituent Assembly opted for a legal approach depending on the subject, the political and professional profiles of the drafters, as well as other factors. As pointed out by Enzo Cheli, although it emerged from liberal traditions and the fascist experience, the lawyers' culture was a non-academic, original one. Overall, it was strongly committed to interpreting the novelties connected to the Italian Resistance. For this reason, lawyers were sensitive to the historical thought on these events, as well as open to the influence of foreign (continental and Anglo-Saxon) experiences linked to other democratic traditions.[36]

The political context therefore decisively conditioned the choices of the founding fathers and, in particular, the jurists who participated in the drafting of the fundamental Charter to the point that 'those constituent jurists most engaged in active roles almost always acted more as jurists-politicians than as jurists-experts, exploiting their political affiliations'.[37]

---

[35] Ugo De Siervo (ed), *Scelte della Costituente e cultura giuridica* (n 9); Barbara Pezzini and Stefano Rossi (eds), *I giuristi e la Resistenza. Una biografia intellettuale del Paese* (FrancoAngeli, Milan, 2016); Sergio Bartole and Roberto Bin (eds), *Vezio Crisafulli. Politica e Costituzione. Scritti 'militanti' (1944–1955)* (FrancoAngeli, Milan, 2018).

[36] Enzo Cheli, *Nata per unire: la Costituzione italiana tra storia e politica* (n 8).

[37] Enzo Cheli, 'I giuristi alla Costituente' (2012) Il contributo italiano alla storia del pensiero: diritto', in www.treccani.it (last accessed on 6 March 2022).

B. The Evolution of the Constitution

1. The Evolution of the Form of Government

One of the most significant evolutionary paths that have characterized the Italian constitutional system certainly affected the form of government.[38] In this regard, although there has not been a total transformation or replacement of the parliamentary system, as it was defined by the drafters of the Constitution, significant changes have occurred, depending on the evolution of the party system and the electoral law.

This is not accidental. In fact, the constitutional regulation of the issue consists exclusively of few provisions (articles 92, 93, 94, and 95), and such a concise set of norms was therefore suited to be 'filled with content' through praxis and constitutional conventions.

In this respect, the Constitution exclusively establishes that the government is composed of the Prime Minister (President of the Council of Ministers, in Italian) and the ministers, who are all appointed by the President of the Republic—the ministers upon the proposal of the selected Prime Minister. The text does not mention the so-called 'consultations', i.e. the meetings arranged by the President before the appointment of the executive. Such consultations with the leaders of parliamentary groups, the speakers of the two Chambers, and former Presidents of the Republic take place before the nominated Prime Minister is formally asked to select and propose a pool of potential ministers.

The core disposition within this short regulation is represented by article 94 of the Constitution, which imposes just one, paramount strict condition: the government has to enjoy, for the entire duration of the administration, from its beginning, the confidence of both Chambers. The 'parliamentary' character of this form of government is a corollary of this clause, which attributes to both Chambers the power to withdraw confidence at any point through a reasoned motion (also vis-à-vis just one minister, as the Constitutional Court allowed individual votes of no confidence in judgment n. 7/1996). The government itself can submit a bill or another proposal to a confidence vote, thus subordinating its permanence to the parliamentary vote.

The brief constitutional description of the executive does not attribute to the Prime Minister a leading role. This explains why he has been traditionally defined as a '*primus inter pares*', underlining his relative primacy among colleagues who are endowed with similar powers and authority. Such primacy depends mainly on the tasks, allotted to the Prime Minister, to, one, direct the government's general policy, two, be responsible for that and, three, take responsibility for ensuring 'the coherence of political and administrative policies, by promoting and coordinating the activity of the Ministers'.[39]

Over the first decades, the interpretation and application of the succinct constitutional regulation on the formation of the government led to the practical elimination of the powers

---

[38] Leopoldo Elia, 'Governo (forme di)', in *Enciclopedia del diritto*, vol XIX (Giuffrè, Milan, 1970) 634–675; Costantino Mortati, *Le forme di governo: Lezioni* (CEDAM, Padova, 1973); Leopoldo Elia and Massimo Luciani, 'Governo (forme di)', in Francesco Calasso (ed), *Enciclopedia del diritto Annali III* (Giuffrè, Milan, 2010).

[39] Art 95. The Constitution is considered as a limitation to political powers, and in particular to the role of the Prime Minister. Nevertheless, the role of the Court with reference to the form of government has not been very incisive. The Court has limited the normative power exercised by the executive through primary sources of law, i.e. law-decrees and legislative decrees. It established, on the one hand, that law-decrees cannot be passed one after the other to provide for stable regulation (judgment n. 360/1996) and that the lack of the prerequisites of the original decree also affect the law converting it into ordinary legislation (judgment n. 171/2007). On the other hand, it has elaborated upon the relationship between the delegation fixed by the legislator and the adoption of legislative decrees by the government (among others, judgments n. 13/1964; n. 111/1972; n. 224/1990 and n. 156/1987).

of proposal of ministers by the Prime Minister, in particular due to the constant presence of coalition governments which gave political parties wider power regarding the selection of the ministers than to the appointed Prime Minister. Something similar happened with reference to the rules put in place to protect governmental stability. The interpretative practice immediately admitted situations of crisis different from the ones envisaged in the Constitution, namely the vote of no confidence by one Chamber, although the Constitution had expressly regulated the parliamentary procedure when the legislature no longer has confidence in the appointed government (article 94). This could have been interpreted as the only constitutionally legitimate instrument to oblige the government to resign, nevertheless the practice of 'extra-parliamentary crises' became the most common. They are triggered by the resignation of Prime Ministers without any previous formal act adopted by the parliament.

The main protagonists of the evolutionary process affecting the parliamentary system have been political parties. Over the decades since the passing of the Constitution, they have never achieved a consensus on any form of legislative regulation of their activity and their internal organization, constantly avoiding the establishment of legal constraints on their activity, organization, and performance. Additionally, the proportional electoral system, which was applied from 1948 to 1993, favoured party fragmentation. This practice increased the 'bargaining' power of those parties which, due to their medium size, on many occasions became the decisive force for the formation of coalition governments (one example being the Socialists—PSI—led by Bettino Craxi).

Actually, as it was mentioned, in the elections of 1948 (the first after the fascist regime and the end of the Second World War), the most representative parties in the Constituent Assembly seemed to stand on two distinct and alternative fronts: on the one hand, the Christian Democrats (DC) and on the other the leftist front (Communists and Socialists). Nevertheless, the potential transformation of the Italian political system into a bipolar system was immediately overcome by the evolution of the system. In the subsequent general elections, in 1953, the majority premium provided for by the new electoral law ('*legge truffa*', law n. 148/1953) in favour of the DC did not work and the corresponding regulation, due to political pressures, was then abrogated.

Thus, after this election, a political-party structure based on this dichotomy started to consolidate political parties with governmental aspirations (first and foremost the DC) and political parties ordinarily destined to the opposition (PCI on the left and MSI—Italian Social Movement—on the right). This phenomenon is what Leopoldo Elia called '*conventio ad excludendum*' against the extremist political forces (on the right and on the left). Such structure remained stable until 1993, even if there were some novelties, such as the participation of the socialist party in the executive and the creation of the so called '*pentapartito*' in the 1980s (meaning, five-party coalition composed by the DC, PSI, PSDI, PRI, and PLI) and finally its transformation into the '*quadripartito*' (with just four) in 1991 as the PRI left it.

In 1993, the parliament, already strongly delegitimized (although elected only in March 1992) by the investigations of the judiciary on corruption and illegal funding of political parties, as well as by a fierce recrudescence of mafia violence (one can recall the massacres of Capaci and Via D'Amelio in which judges Falcone and Borsellino were killed, in May and July 1992), had to react to the electoral referendum which opened the door to the first relevant electoral reform (see section B.4.b).

Meanwhile, the form of government had suffered a strong 'shock' in the late 1980s when the appointment of the leader of the PSI (Bettino Craxi) as Prime Minister had strengthened the reformist mission of the executive, which had emerged already in the early 1980s. The so-called 'Bozzi Committee', a bicameral Committee composed by twenty deputies and twenty senators, in charge of elaborating a list of constitutional and legislative reforms, had been operative between the end of 1983 and the beginning of 1985. Craxi's charismatic personality, combined with the enhancement of his party's role in the Government's stability, contributed to allot particular importance to the role of the Prime Minister, which assumed a new political relevance, albeit within an almost unchanged regulatory framework (with the exception of the approval of law 400/1988 which provided the first comprehensive normative assessment of the executive).

The transition from a purely proportional electoral system to mixed ones with a significant majoritarian component progressively accentuated the leadership aspects[40] of the form of government, especially on the occasion of the administrations led by Silvio Berlusconi (1994–1995, 2001–2006, and 2008–2011). From this point of view, the personalism of the office of Prime Minister was not reduced by the introduction of the new electoral system in 2005. The personalistic turn introduced by Berlusconi into his governments was an attitude followed by Matteo Renzi (2014–2016) although, in some intermediate periods, the prominence of the Prime Minister was more nuanced (Dini 1995–1996, Prodi 1996–1998, 2006–2008, D'Alema 1998–2000, Amato 2000–2001, Monti 2011–2013, Letta 2013–2014, Gentiloni 2016–2018).[41]

The most recent developments in the form of government were influenced also by the return to a mainly proportional electoral law before the 2018 general election. The outcome was a very fragmented parliament which managed to endorse a new executive only a few months after the official start of the term, led by Prime Minister Giuseppe Conte. This government was based on the parliamentary support of two political forces (Five Star Movement and Lega—League), which, after lengthy negotiations, found an agreement through the draft of a so-called 'government contract'. It contained a series of objectives and policies to be pursued through their joint administration. Although many saw novelties in the management of the electoral campaigns, the emergence of new political parties and the signature of the 'contract', the process of forming of the government was consistent with the Italian tradition of the first decades after 1948. A Prime Minister was acting basically as a '*primus inter pares*', as it was previously described, and he was tasked with mediating between the different parties in the government—represented in this case by the two vice Prime Ministers, one from the League and one from the Five Star Movement. The situation changed during the COVID-19 pandemic emergency a few months later, as it gave the Prime Minister a much stronger protagonist role than he had before.

The unexpected withdrawal of confidence to the government 'Conte I' in 2019 by the League led to the formation of a new executive. In this new configuration, the government depended on the support of the Democratic Party, PD, in collaboration with the Five Star Movement. These forces were opposed during the electoral campaign of 2018 and the period during which the former coalition was in place. This new executive was led by Giuseppe Conte as well, who shifted from a centre-right to a centre-left executive. The role of '*primus inter pares*' of the Prime Minister was particularly apparent in these cases considering that the allied parties had divergent ideological, economic and social backgrounds, and aspirations. As it was mentioned, the emergency situation subverted these equilibria. In February

---

[40] Mauro Calise, in several works, among which one shall recall, *La democrazia del leader* (Laterza, Rome, 2016), *Il partito personale. I due corpi del leader* (Laterza, Rome, 2010), *La terza Repubblica. Partiti contro presidenti* (Laterza, Rome, 2006), *Il partito personale* (Laterza, Rome, 2000).

[41] On the evolution of the role of the Prime Minister, see the recent study by Ines Ciolli, *La questione del vertice di Palazzo Chigi. Il Presidente del Consiglio nella Costituzione repubblicana* (Jovene, Naples, 2018).

2021, after one party endorsing the government exited the majority and Conte had to resign, a new executive led by Mario Draghi was supported by a large majority. However, this government was forced to resign as well in July 2022 following the loss of support by the Five Star Movement, Forza Italia, and the League. After the snap general elections held in September 2022, a centre-right government was formed, led by the first female Prime Minister, Giorgia Meloni.

2. The Evolution of Regionalism

The debate between regionalists and anti-regionalists in the Constituent Assembly had involved two groups in particular: the Christian Democracy and the Italian Republican Party on one side and the Communist Party and the conservatives on the other.[42]

On this matter, the historical and political nature of the 'noble compromise', supported by a twofold need, becomes relevant: on the one hand, to avoid the concentration of power in the centre, preventing the risk of a totalitarian shift; on the other hand, to ensure the emergence of a new political class coming from the Regions (Crisafulli[43]). Christian Democracy supported the regionalist perspective with the aim of consolidating its electoral result of 1946. For opposite reasons, the Communist Party resisted the regionalist proposal. This debate is one of the reasons explaining the delay in the implementation of the constitutional provisions related to regional decentralization until the 1970s.

In the Constituent Assembly, two types of Regions were envisaged: ordinary Regions, with modest legislative functions and with a statute (the highest source of law of regional legal systems) that had to be approved by the national parliament through an ordinary law, and special Regions (article 116 of the Constitution), which would be provided with wider legislative matters and with statutes passed as 'constitutional laws' (special pieces of legislation passed with the same procedure as constitutional amendments). The establishment of ordinary Regions took time: only in the 1970s were the first elections of regional parliaments held.[44] Special Regions started to operate right after the entry into force of the Constitution. In particular, in 1946 the Sicilian statute was passed and in 1948 the ones of Sardinia, Valle d'Aosta, and Trentino-Alto Adige. In 1963 the statute of the special Region Friuli-Venezia Giulia was approved.

Concerning ordinary Regions, once political parties reached a certain stability, the issue of implementing the regional system entered in the political debates of the 1960s, during the so-called 'phase of majority filibuster'.[45] In this scenario, Regions were considered as a sort of reorganization of the central system of government. Therefore, the parliament passed the law on the 'implementation of ordinary regions' (n. 281/1970). During the 1980s and the 1990s, a new institutional movement engaged in a political path to innovate the regional institutions 'from below'.[46]

---

[42] Ettore Rotelli, *L'avvento della Regione in Italia. Dalla caduta del regime fascista alla Costituzione repubblicana (1943–1947)* (Giuffrè, Milan, 1967); Giovanni Tarli Barbieri and Ginevra Cerrina Feroni, *Le Regioni dalla Costituente al nuovo Senato della Repubblica* (Edizioni Scientifiche Italiane, Naples, 2016).

[43] Vezio Crisafulli, 'Vicende della "questione regionale"' (1982) 4 le Regioni 495 ff.

[44] Sergio Bartole, 'Supremazia e collaborazione nei rapporti tra Stato e Regioni' (1971) Rivista trimestrale di diritto pubblico 84 ff.

[45] Roberto Bin, 'La struttura del Parlamento e il procedimento legislativo nazionale' (1993) 1–2 Le istituzioni del federalismo 581–592.

[46] Antonio Ruggeri, 'Il regionalismo italiano, dal "modello" costituzionale alle proposte della Bicamerale: innovazione o "razionalizzazione" di vecchie esperienze?' (1998) le Regioni 271–314.

In particular, in the mid-1980s, the need to allot Italian Regions more incisive functions had emerged for several reasons, one of which was to reduce the differences with respect to the five special Regions.[47] The opportunity of enhancing regional autonomy quickly became the main claim of a new political force (the 'Northern League'), which even demanded the secession of Northern Regions from the rest of Italy.

Parallel to the pressures for stronger administrative and legislative decentralization, the need to boost the legitimacy of regional and local governments increased (see B.4.a). It was (partially) satisfied by providing for the direct election of Presidents of the Regions, Presidents of Provinces and Mayors. The first step in this sense was the introduction of direct election of Mayors in Sicily (1992), which was followed immediately afterwards (1993) by a similar regulation for all Italian Municipalities. Only in 1999 (constitutional amendment law n. 1/1999) was the direct election of the Presidents of ordinary Regions introduced and in 2001 (constitutional amendment law n. 2/2001) for special Regions. These reforms also established a peculiar arrangement for the form of government of Regions, which could be derogated in case individual Regions decided otherwise. The new standard form of government for ordinary Regions is based on the so-called '*aut simul stabunt aut simul cadent*' mechanism, according to which the terms of the legislature and the President, although elected separately, must have the same duration. This means that, if a no confidence vote is passed or any other cause of interruption of the President's term occurs, then the legislature also has to be dissolved.

As for the decentralization of legislative and administrative competences, with the first Bassanini law (n. 59/1997), a wide delegation of administrative functions was implemented in favour of the Regions, without affecting the corresponding legislative domains which remained allotted to the State.[48] Through this reform, one of the constitutional principles on which the Italian model of decentralization was originally founded was implicitly amended, namely the principle of 'parallelism' between legislative and administrative functions as laid down in article 118 of the Constitution. This principle implied that Regions enjoyed administrative powers in the same areas in which they were entitled to legislate. This shift represented a sort of anticipation of the constitutional reform which would follow a few years later.

Finally, through constitutional amendment law n. 3/2001, territorial reforms reached their last stage, at least at the constitutional level. With this law, legislative matters allotted to ordinary Regions were strongly (perhaps even excessively) reinforced (article 117 of the Constitution);[49] the limit of national interest, which used to represent a condition for the exercise of legislative power by the Regions,[50] was eliminated; the principle of parallelism was completely overcome, providing for administrative functions to be allocated by virtue of the principles of subsidiarity, adequacy, and proportionality (article 118 of the Constitution);[51] a

---

[47] Augusto Barbera, 'Le Regioni nel sistema politico' (1988) 6 Democrazia e diritto 135–154; Massimo Luciani, 'Un regionalismo senza modello' (1994) 5 le Regioni 1313–1336; Francesca Trimarchi Banfi, 'Il regionalismo e i modelli' (1995) 2 le Regioni 255–263.

[48] Giandomenico Falcon (ed), *Lo Stato autonomista. Funzioni statali, regionali e locali nel decreto legislativo n. 112 del 1998 di attuazione della legge Bassanini n. 59 del 1997* (il Mulino, Bologna, 1998).

[49] Luisa Torchia, 'La potestà legislativa residuale delle Regioni' (2002) 2–3 le Regioni 343–364.

[50] Salvatore Bartholini, *Interesse nazionale e competenza delle Regioni nella giurisprudenza della Corte costituzionale* (CEDAM, Padova, 1967); Augusto Barbera, *Regioni e interesse nazionale* (Giuffrè, Milan, 1973); Augusto Barbera, 'Chi è il custode dell'interesse nazionale?' (2001) 2 Quaderni costituzionali 345–346; Roberto Bin, 'L'interesse nazionale dopo la riforma: continuità dei problemi, discontinuità della giurisprudenza costituzionale' (2001) 6 le Regioni 1213–1222; Rosanna Tosi, 'A proposito dell'interesse nazionale' (2002) 1 Quaderni costituzionali 86–88.

[51] Roberto Bin, 'Le funzioni amministrative nel nuovo Titolo V della Costituzione' (2002) 2–3 le Regioni 65–382; Giandomenico Falcon, 'Funzioni amministrative ed enti locali nei nuovi artt 118 e 117 della Costituzione'

few principles related to 'fiscal federalism' were introduced in the Constitution, through the provision of a stronger financial autonomy (article 119 of the Constitution);[52] and, finally, the preventive control by the State on regional laws was eliminated, turning it into a potential control after their promulgation and publication (article 127 of the Constitution).[53]

There are still several open questions deriving from these reforms. The radical change of the relations between State and Regions was only partially accomplished, as some necessary pieces of legislation are still lacking (for example as it concerns the determination of fundamental principles in those legislative matters in which the State has to fix the basic principles, or the fundamental functions of local authorities, or also as it concerns fiscal federalism, which still remains only partially implemented today). From a different perspective, the constitutional reform of 2001 transferred to ordinary Regions some legislative matters that they can hardly exercise due to their lack of the necessary economic resources. Furthermore, the implementation of the reforms led to an expansion of the cases before the Constitutional Court concerning the attribution of legislative matters and their scope.

At the same time, the constitutional reform of 2001 did not lead to a consistent transformation of the central organization of the State. Consequently, there was no adaptation of national administrations to the renewed structure of the relations between State and Regions, with the result that there are no proper institutional seats for joint decision-making between regional legislatures and the national parliament. The main seat for the encounter of the two territorial levels, which is called 'State-Regions-conference' and involves only the executives, was not included in the Constitution.[54] No transformation of the Senate into a territorially representative Chamber was approved either. The flaws of the original regulation and the posterior amendments explain why there has always been and still is political conflict over territorial decentralization, which reached its peak in the 1990s. The birth and the progressive consolidation in Northern Italy of the so-called Liga Veneta and the Northern League contributed to exacerbate this conflict. These political formations, born as a sort of rebellion against the centralism of traditional parties, entered the governing coalition in 1994 with the first executive led by Silvio Berlusconi. Nevertheless, this administration quickly came to an end precisely because of the exit of the Northern League, which then provided external support to the technocratic government headed by Lamberto Dini. From 1995 to 2000 autonomist, and at times even separatist, demands increased. To thwart such demands, the governments at first led by Romano Prodi and then by Massimo D'Alema and Giuliano Amato supported the approval of the abovementioned constitutional amendment in 2001.

This reform did not appease the claims of the Northern Regions, to the point that, in the subsequent parliamentary term (2001–2006), a new constitutional amendment was drafted (containing the so-called devolution—an improper reference to the British model, which is greatly asymmetrical and provides some territories with exclusively administrative

---

(2002) 2–3 le Regioni 383–398; Cristina Napoli, *Le funzioni amministrative nel titolo V della Costituzione. Contributo allo studio dell'art 118, primo e secondo comma* (Giappichelli, Turin, 2011).

[52] Franco Bassanini and Giorgio Macciotta (eds), *L'attuazione del federalismo fiscale. Una proposta* (il Mulino, Bologna, 2003); Enrico De Mita, *Le basi costituzionali del 'federalismo fiscale'* (Giuffrè, Milan, 2009); Antonio Ferrara and Giulio M Salerno (eds), *Il 'federalismo fiscale'. Commento alla legge n. 42 del 2009* (Jovene, Naples, 2010); Giuseppe Campanelli (ed), *Quali prospettive per il federalismo fiscale? L'attuazione della legge delega tra analisi del procedimento e valutazione dei contenuti* (Giappichelli, Turin, 2011).

[53] Emanuele Rossi, *La legge controllata. Contributo allo studio del procedimento di controllo preventivo delle leggi regionali* (Università di Trento, Trento, 1993).

[54] Guido Carpani, *La Conferenza Stato-regioni. Competenze e modalità di funzionamento dall'istituzione ad oggi* (il Mulino, Bologna, 2006).

functions). This amendment, however, was rejected by the electorate in the constitutional referendum of 2006. The defeat in the 2006 elections of the centre-right coalition, to which the Northern League used to belong, in combination with the economic and financial crisis that affected Italy reaching its apex around 2011/2012, contributed to set aside such projects, while pushing towards a completely opposite process of reduction of territorial autonomy. In fact, in the context of the crisis, the recognition of greater autonomy to territorial bodies was transformed, in public discourse, from a virtuous mechanism into the major cause of unnecessary public spending. It is no coincidence that the constitutional amendment passed by the government led by Matteo Renzi was based on a substantial re-centralization of some regional competences. However, this project also was rejected through a constitutional referendum, specifically on 4 December 2016.

Already at the end of the seventeenth parliamentary term (2013–2018) and even more so during the past parliamentary term (the eighteenth, 2018–2022), with the entry of the League (which, in the meantime, changed its name from the original 'Northern League' into just 'the League') into the Conte I government, new steps were taken towards a novel process of de-centralization involving three ordinary Regions (Lombardy, Veneto, and Emilia-Romagna). These territories requested the central government to activate the mechanism for acquiring additional legislative powers, as provided for by article 116 para 3 of the Constitution (this clause was introduced in 2001). This is what is commonly defined as 'differentiated regionalism'. It consists in a mechanism that, by following a specific agreement between the State and the Region concerned, implemented in a law, can lead to the attribution to the ordinary Region concerned of further legislative powers, and, moreover, to the transfer of those financial resources necessary for the exercise of these new functions. Following the start of this procedure, several other ordinary Regions have expressed the will to follow the same path, while Southern Regions (both ordinary and special) have conveyed strong concerns about the financial effects of such process of 'differentiation'.

The debate on the so-called 'differentiated regionalism' regained momentum with the new government led by Meloni in 2022.

3. The Evolution of Constitutional Adjudication

Constitutional adjudication represented the second biggest novelty of the 1948 Constitution, as well as one of the areas in which a significant evolutionary process can be detected.[55] In particular, unlike what has happened with respect to the evolution of the form of government and the regional organization, the changes affecting the Constitutional Court occurred without any dedicated paramount legislative or constitutional changes.[56]

The Constitution of 1948 provided for the establishment of the Court and its fundamental powers and functions (article 134), its composition (article 135), as well as the effects of the Court's decisions on the legal system (article 136).[57] However, the Constitution

---

[55] Costantino Mortati, 'La Corte costituzionale ed i presupposti per la sua vitalità' (1949) 8–9 Iustitia 69–91.
[56] Piero Calamandrei, *La illegittimità costituzionale delle leggi nel processo civile* (CEDAM, Padova, 1950); Carlo Esposito, 'Il controllo giurisdizionale sulla costituzionalità delle leggi in Italia', in Piero Calamandrei (ed), *La Costituzione italiana. Saggi* (CEDAM, Padova, 1954); Mauro Cappelletti, *La pregiudizialità costituzionale nel processo civile* (Giuffrè, Milan, 1957); Enrico Redenti, *Legittimità delle leggi e Corte costituzionale* (Giuffrè, Milan, 1957); Aldo M Sandulli, *Il giudizio sulle leggi. La cognizione della Corte costituzionale e i suoi limiti* (Giuffrè, Milan, 1967); Virgilio Andrioli, *Studi sulla giustizia costituzionale* (Giuffrè, Milan, 1992).
[57] Raffaele Bifulco and Davide Paris, 'The Italian Constitutional Court' (n 18) 482–488.

postponed the definition of the powers to posterior constitutional laws. In February 1948, the Constituent Assembly (whose powers had been extended for two months) passed constitutional law n. 1/1948. This piece of legislation established the procedures and rules to file a complaint or petition to the Court. Five years later, constitutional law n. 1/1953 and law n. 87/1953 finally completed the regulation and entered into force, thereby actually instituting the Court.[58]

As a matter of fact, the Italian Constitutional Court was established in a context of uncertainty, if not concern, towards constitutional adjudication. Various political forces were very concerned because fifteen men, without any direct popular legitimacy, would nullify the will of the elected representatives in the parliament through their constitutional power to strike down national and regional legislation.[59]

This also partly explains the delay with which the Court began its activity, in 1956, eight years after the Constitution came into force. After the dissolution of the first Chambers and new elections, the Chambers delayed the appointment of their five judges because of the high majority required for the election, which is explained by to the political divisions of the parties.[60] Therefore, the first group of justices of the Constitutional Court was appointed only in 1955.

Despite the initial reservations and mistrust, the Court, over its decades of activity, has proven its ability to play a momentous role within the institutional equilibrium of the State. It has used its powers carefully, but without being excessively deferential vis-à-vis the parliament and the government. This attitude has led the Court to acquire its own legitimacy in the constitutional system, despite the absence of a direct connection with the people.[61] Indeed, its particular composition has been the authentic strength of the Court: the varied background and origin of its judges (law professors, lawyers with at least twenty years of practice, judges belonging to the highest Courts), together with the mixed mechanism of election or appointment (five elected by the Chambers in joint sessions, five appointed by the President of the Republic; five elected by the judiciary), determined a virtuous combination of cultural, social, and political skills, which has always prevented the creation of pre-established and rigid majorities inside the Court.

Over the years, the Court has been able to engage in a fruitful collaboration with the judiciary which has led ordinary judges to become authentic protagonists of constitutional challenges. In fact, as it is the case in other legal systems, the Italian Constitution regulates the concrete control of constitutionality. Through this process, judges can submit a constitutional challenge to the Court and suspend a specific proceeding, if they consider a norm, which they otherwise would have to apply in the case in question, to be unconstitutional. There are at least a few examples of this positive interaction. First, the valuable initial activity of 'cleansing' the Italian legal system of the legal legacies from the former fascist regime; second, the constant push to pursue an interpretation consistent with the Constitution before appealing to the Constitutional Court; third, the recognition of the power of disapplication of norms under certain circumstances (for instance in case of conflict with European

---

[58] Giacinto Bisogni, 'Le leggi istitutive della Corte costituzionale', in Ugo De Siervo, Sandro Guerrieri, and Antonio Varsori (eds), *La prima legislatura repubblicana. Continuità e discontinuità nell'azione delle istituzioni*, vol 1 (Carocci, Rome, 2004).

[59] Carlo Mezzanotte, *Il giudizio sulle leggi*, I, *Le ideologie del Costituente* (Giuffrè, Milan, 1979; Editoriale Scientifica, Naples, 2014); Francesco Bonini, *Storia della Corte costituzionale* (La Nuova Italia Scientifica, Rome, 1996).

[60] Andrea Simoncini, 'L'avvio della Corte costituzionale e gli strumenti per la definizione del suo ruolo: un problema storico aperto' (2004) 4 Giurisprudenza costituzionale 3065–3104.

[61] Carlo Mezzanotte, *Corte costituzionale e legittimazione politica* (Tipografia veneziana, Rome, 1984).

norms, according to the principle of primacy of EU law) and, fourth, more recently, the recurring invitation to submit concrete cases.

This constant channel of communication with ordinary judges did not end even when the Court, in the early 1980s, had to solve the issue of the backlog after the indictment of two ministers in the so-called *Lockheed* case (later, this function of the Court was abolished). During that period, the widespread dismissal of cases on procedural grounds (admissibility usually) was seen as an attitude of 'superficial' rejection of constitutional challenges submitted by other jurisdictions. In reality, it turned out to be a way to allow the Court in the following years to restore this fruitful dialogue because it could decide on concrete cases in a timespan of approximately one year after their submission.

Extremely relevant is the proportionality and reasonableness check that the Court performs on the clauses that are in question.[62] The case law related to such principles spans different phases. At the beginning, the Court referred to article 3 para 1 of the Constitution (on the principle of equality) in order to determine the unconstitutionality of laws or other acts prescribing identical treatments for different situations or distinct treatments for comparable situations. In a second phase, the Court started to consider unreasonable, again on the basis of article 3 para 1, those clauses that were inconsistent with similar situations, adopted as benchmark (i.e. treated as a sort of *tertium comparationis*). Finally, the Court added a third argument to the two abovementioned methodologies, and it aimed at evaluating the reasonableness of the clause itself, without considering potentially analogous situations. Clearly this last line of jurisprudence widens the discretionary assessment of legislature measures by the Court.

Other areas in which the relationship between the Court and ordinary judges has been meaningful are the relations between domestic law and EU law and between domestic law and international law. In this respect, the Court, with some difficulties, has followed the trends of other jurisdictions. This was clear with respect to the value of EU norms. For many years up to 1984, the Court seemed reluctant to recognize that they could be directly applicable. A similar attitude exists today with regard to the Charter of Fundamental Rights of the EU (judgment n. 269 of 2017). So far, the Court has not allowed judges to disapply conflicting Italian norms as it would usually do with directly applicable EU norms.

As for the relationship between domestic law and the European Convention for the Protection of Human Rights (ECHR), the Court, although marking the difference with respect to EU law, has enhanced the innovative scope of a specific constitutional clause included in article 117 para 1 after the constitutional amendment of 2001. This reform also introduced new constraints on State and Regions when exercising their legislative powers: they have to respect 'international obligations', hence obligations deriving from all potential sources, both customary norms and treaties. Through two judgments from 2007 (n. 347 and n. 348), the Court recognized that ECHR norms (and therefore also those of other international treaties) have to be considered when interpreting norms because their infringement would amount to a violation of article 117 para 1. Such violation would determine the constitutional illegitimacy of domestic norms conflicting with it. Subsequent refinements of this jurisprudence

---

[62] Gino Scaccia, *Gli 'strumenti' della ragionevolezza nel giudizio costituzionale* (Giuffrè, Milan, 2000); Andrea Morrone, *Il custode della ragionevolezza* (Giuffrè, Milan, 2001); Luigi D'Andrea, *Ragionevolezza e legittimazione del sistema* (Giuffrè, Milan, 2005); Franco Modugno, *La ragionevolezza nella giustizia costituzionale* (Editoriale Scientifica, Naples, 2007). In general, concerning the systemic effects of the judgments based on reasonableness, Gustavo Zagrebelsky, *Il diritto mite. Legge diritti giustizia* (Einaudi, Turin, 1992).

have clarified the role played by the ECtHR in the interpretation of the ECHR, without radically altering the key points of the former judgments.

On one front (EU law) and on the other (ECHR) the Constitutional Court has been able to become a protagonist in the resolution of disputes, even employing the preliminary reference to the Court of Justice of the European Union concerning both the interpretation and the validity of EU law. In particular, in its most recent decisions, the Constitutional Court has underlined the peculiarity of its role, specifically identifying the most significant issue as the need for balancing among rights (judgments n. 24/2017, n. 269/2017, n. 115/2018, and n. 117/2019).

The period of the increase of State–Regions disputes (which had its peak in the years 2012–2013) seems to have been overcome and concrete control has once again become the main instrument to submit complaints to the Court. The reduction of regional disputes, together with other considerations determined by the peculiarity of the cases submitted, prompted the Court to show some timid signs of opening up to new methods of access. In particular, the decision to admit cases concerning private citizens whose right to vote was supposedly violated by electoral legislation has opened a new possibility to invest the Court with a jurisdiction on electoral laws, albeit with limitations (judgments n. 1/2014 and n. 35/2017). It is clear, however, that the opening of the Court, which is aimed at avoiding the existence of areas of legislation not submitted to constitutional adjudication, is likely to be expanded beyond electoral disputes.

Overall, the Court has managed through its jurisprudence to become the true *viva vox Constitutionis*.

4. Critical Features and Junctures

a) From the '*conventio ad excludendum*' up to '*Tangentopoli*'

During the long phase of the proportional electoral system (1946–1993, called by journalists the 'First Republic'), the Italian parliamentary system could be easily qualified as an example of 'weak' parliamentary rationalization. The parliament counterbalanced the political equilibrium of the government through the relevant mediation of the Head of the State. There was relative freedom for political parties to support coalition governments after the elections. The strong rooting in the society, thanks to long-lasting party structures on the territory, was also a defining feature of the first four decades of constitutional history.

These characters of the Italian political environment also responded to the international context that greatly influenced domestic politics. The consolidation, starting in the 1950s, of two opposing (military and political) blocs, headed respectively by the USA and the Soviet Union, had significant repercussions on national politics, determining the systematic exclusion of the Italian communist party (PCI) from governmental coalitions. This situation, known as the '*conventio ad excludendum*', prevented the replacement and renewal of the Italian establishment inside individual parties.[63] Thus, the PCI, after its exit from the government in 1947, was no longer part of any coalition. Only in 1993 (and just for a few hours) a few members of the Leftist Democratic Party (PDS), heir to the PCI after its dissolution, were appointed as ministers. Finally, in 1996 the executive included ministers designated by

---

[63] Leopoldo Elia, 'Governo (forme di)' (n 38) 634 ff.

the PDS and in 1998 the government was led by a member (Massimo D'Alema) of the left-wing democrats (DS), which had replaced the PDS. On the other side, after the failed attempt in 1960 to form a government with the 'external' endorsement of the far-right party, MSI, for the first time only in 1994 were ministers from a right-wing party appointed. The first Prime Minister from an openly right-wing party (Fratelli d'Italia) was Meloni in 2022.

One can therefore state that the executives from 1948 to 1993 were characterized by a remarkable 'stability' in a sense, but this very often did not coincide with 'governability'. In other words, the stability of executive structures did not favour the development of long-term and far-reaching policies, but often increased the tensions between the majority parties. In addition to that, these parties were also internally divided into groups (an excellent example from this perspective being the DC). The most visible consequence of this phenomenon is the average duration of the governments, eleven months, a period not even sufficient for the sole purpose of completing a budget year.

While the issue of governmental alternation was solved in 1994, as demonstrated by the succession of centre-right and centre-left governments, the same cannot be said for the question of governability, which has often depended on delicate equilibria within multi-party coalitions. Consequently, even if the average duration of governments has become longer, this phenomenon did not always correspond to an increased rate of governability. A decisive factor affecting the transformation in Italian politics and parties at the beginning of the 1990s was the so-called '*Tangentopoli*' scandal (literally city of bribes), a nationwide judicial investigation into political corruption, with the first arrest happening in February 1992, which led to the progressive dissolution of the party system that had been ruling the country for four decades. The scandal also caused major mistrust towards political parties.

This judicial investigation originated from Milan and involved many members of the ruling parties (DC, PSI, PSDI, PRI, and PLI) and marginally those belonging to the opposition (PDS and Northern League). The apex of these investigations was reached with the so-called *Enimont* trial (the name comes from the denomination of two chemical companies: Eni and Montedison), in which the main leaders of the government coalition (especially Craxi and Forlani) were directly involved. This trial represented a point of no return for the leadership of the time, also due to its relevance in the media. Such trial and the subsequent convictions (over a period spanning from 1993 to 2000) had direct repercussions on the political life of the country, sanctioning the definitive failure of some political forces and leading to overcome the party structure of that moment.

b) The Electoral System as an Element of Change

The first Italian electoral system (law n. 6/1948) was essentially proportional, with very low thresholds (corresponding to around 300,000 votes at the national level for each party) and individual preferences, distributed into thirty-two electoral districts with different size and different number of elected MPs. This electoral system, which according to some scholars and political actors, should have been constitutionalized and therefore not amendable through ordinary legislation (Gaspare Ambrosini[64] and Costantino Mortati[65]), was a guarantee of political pluralism. That is mainly why it was the one endorsed by all anti-fascist forces.

---

[64] Gaspare Ambrosini, *Sistemi elettorali* (Sansoni, Florence, 1945).
[65] Costantino Mortati in Second Subcommittee of the Committee for Constitution, Constituent Assembly, 7 November 1946.

Nevertheless, just a few years after the entry into force of the Constitution, in 1953, an attempt was undertaken to ensure the stability of Italian executives through solid parliamentary majorities, with law n. 148/1953 (so-called *legge truffa*, 'fraud-law'), which allotted 65 per cent of the seats to the political party crossing 50 per cent + 1 of the total votes. This piece of legislation was applicable to the elections that took place in 1953, but the Christian Democracy, led by Alcide De Gasperi, did not reach the threshold necessary to obtain the additional seats for just a handful of votes. Therefore, the majority bonus was not assigned. The heated protests following the approval of the law led to its derogation already in 1954, and the original proportional system was again in place until 1993.

After the transformation of the municipal electoral law into a majoritarian system in 1993 (see B.2), a repeal referendum was called for in order to change some norms of the electoral system for the Senate. The re-wording of the law would lead to a transformation of the system into a majoritarian system. The turn-out was very high (around 77 per cent) and the 'yes' reached almost 90 per cent of the votes. The parliament then took the opportunity to amend the electoral system for both Chambers, through laws n. 276/1993 and n. 277/1993. The new mixed system was composed by a majoritarian plurality system to allot 75 per cent of the seats, and the rest was assigned through two different applications of the proportional system.

The preference for a new system, mainly majoritarian, was the result of the political and social situation induced by *Tangentopoli*. All political forces, in particular the ones who had been driving Italian politics for a few decades, were then considered to lack legitimacy in the public eye. And the proportional system was accused of being one of the causes of the degeneration of the party system.

This mainly majoritarian system, applied in 1994, 1996, and 2001 with uninominal electoral districts, led to a shift of the national political framework towards a mainly two-party system, thus creating a radical change in parliamentary mechanisms. Political confrontation, although no explicit indication of the potential Prime Minister was possible under this electoral system, was more and more personalized as electors understood that they were called to choose between two alternative potential governments under the leadership of specific politicians.[66] The basic alternative was between two main blocks formed by different parties—be they traditional or new (like Forza Italia, Silvio Berlusconi's party)—which promised to form stable governments.[67] Consequently, the bipolar construction of domestic politics based on the dichotomy centre-right vs centre-left made it unnecessary to look for inter-party agreements for the formation of coalitions, as it used to happen until the 1990s. Political priorities and directions were discussed and presented during the electoral campaign, which should be contrasted with the former situation where, mainly after the vote, a bargaining process among the political forces for creating the government was undertaken.

This system was changed a few months before the elections to be held in 2006 by the centre-right government. It was concerned with the potential formation of a stable centre-left government, as the opposition was going to win according to the electoral surveys. The new electoral system (law n. 270/2005) led to a transformation of political dynamics, because of the transition from a system based on uninominal constituencies to a proportional system with majority bonus. The model was similar for both Chambers, as the seats were

---

[66] I.e. the leaders of the two opposing coalitions: see Vincenzo Lippolis and Giovanni Pitruzzella, *Il bipolarismo conflittuale. Il regime politico della Seconda Repubblica* (Rubbettino, Rome, 2007).

[67] So-called majoritarian democracy: Roberto Bin, 'Assemblee rappresentative, forma di governo e investitura diretta dell'esecutivo' 215.pdf (www.forumcostituzionale.it) (last accessed on 6 March 2022).

assigned proportionally to closed lists, but the most voted coalition would be given a majority bonus as to reach the absolute majority (regardless of its vote percentage). This system was applied in 2006, 2008 (snap elections), and 2013. The Constitutional Court (judgment n. 1/2014) considered this electoral law unconstitutional in several aspects.[68] Particularly, the Court struck down the majority bonus because it should not be assigned regardless of the votes received by the winning party or coalition. Various constitutional yardsticks were employed in the judgment, including the principles of popular sovereignty (article 1), equality before the law (article 3), and equality of the vote (article 48). The second problem with this electoral law was the mechanism of closed lists, as they would prevent voters from choosing their own parliamentary representatives, thereby only giving them the option of selecting a predetermined list, in which candidates are ranked in order of priority by party leaders. Here, the relevant constitutional norm was freedom of vote (article 48).

Law n. 52/2015 (so-called *Italicum*) was a mixed system, also based on the former model: a proportional system with a majority bonus, but with two (potential) rounds. In the first one, if the winning list gained at least 40 per cent of the votes, it would be allotted the majority bonus obtaining 340 seats out of the 630 seats of the Chamber. If no party achieved 40 per cent, there would have been a run-off second round between the two most voted parties, held two weeks after the first election to determine which party could obtain the bonus. The country was divided into 100 small districts (around six to seven MPs in each list); the threshold was put at 3 per cent at the national level and only the first candidate of each list would have been fixed, while voters could choose up to two candidates within the list (vote of preference).

The Constitutional Court was again brought into the 'electoral' arena and decided upon the constitutionality of this law as well. It struck down the regulation on the run-off procedure. It reasoned that the run-would merely serve to identify the single party that would get more than 50 per cent. The consequence would have been a disproportionate sacrifice of the constitutional principles of representativeness and equality of votes.

The most recent electoral law, n. 165/2017, which was applied in 2018 and 2022, is another mixed system with three-eighths of the seats assigned in single member districts with majoritarian plurality system and the rest with proportional system in multi-member districts (except for the MPs elected by Italians residing abroad). In this last case as well, the change in the electoral system directly impacted political dynamics; in particular, the prevalence of the proportional share in the allocation of seats increased the difficulties of forming a new government. A new phenomenon took place, namely the 'solitary' running of individual parties and movements in the elections, with the potential perspective of joining a coalition in the aftermath of the elections. The result presented considerable difficulties because political parties that had conducted an electoral campaign on very distant positions from each other were pushed to find a common ground in the corresponding programs in order to foster the formation of a new executive. From this perspective, it is significant that, after the 2018 general elections, the relative majority political force (Five Star Movement) tried to form a government both with the PD and, alternatively, with the League and other centre-right parties. At the end of long and exhausting negotiations, the Five Star Movement and the League were able to identify a few common programmatic ideas through a 'government contract', indicating a Prime Minister, Giuseppe Conte, who was then appointed by the President of

---

[68] See Giovanna De Minico, *La forma di governo e legge elettorale. Un dialogo nel tempo* (2018) 9 Astrid; Sara Lieto and Pasquale Pasquino, 'La Corte costituzionale e la legge elettorale: la sentenza n. 1 del 2014' (2014) 1 www.forumcostituzionale.it (last accessed on 6 March 2022).

the Republic, as it was previously recalled. An example of how fragile coalitions are is the end of this first government led by Giuseppe Conte in 2019.

Finally, in January 2020 the Constitutional Court decided against a repeal *referendum* (judgment n. 10/2020) that would have aimed at transforming the current electoral system into a fully majoritarian one, with electoral districts electing one candidate.

5. The Development of the Constitution as a Source Subject to Interpretation and Implementation

In the years immediately following the entry into force of the Constitution, a debate began on the meaning to be attributed to all those constitutional clauses containing principles. In this regard, two conflicting approaches emerged: the first, supported by the Court of Cassation and the most conservative scholarship, considered that these provisions could not be applied directly by judges before legislative implementation; the second, supported by the younger generation of judges and the scholarship educated right after the Second World War, assumed the legal value of the Constitution as a source of law, therefore applying the same categories of validity and applicability of any other norm of the system and concluding that also programmatic norms could be directly applied by the judiciary. A fundamental cultural difference served as the basis for these different positions; it was not accidental, in fact, that the second approach was supported by those first instance judges (called '*pretori*') who were mostly younger and endorsed by scholars educated in the years in which the Constitution was being drafted or immediately afterwards.

The second approach was finally adopted for at least two reasons, the first being the progressive retirement from the judiciary of the most conservative sector and the second being the start of life of the Constitutional Court which, since the abovementioned judgment n. 1/1956, defended the full validity and applicability of constitutional principles. In this context, two scholarly works were extremely relevant: one by Paolo Barile[69] and one by Vezio Crisafulli.[70]

Throughout the 1950s, in an era full of great legal developments, Calamandrei criticized the majoritarian filibuster against the implementation of the constitutional system. In those years, the parliament, starting with laws n. 230/1950 and n. 841/1950, passed the so-called land reform (law n. 379/1967).

During the 1960s, the parliament approved the reform of middle school and the nationalization of the electric companies, while, in 1970, it approved the so-called 'statute of workers' (law n. 300/1970) and law n. 352 which regulated the repeal referendum, and the implementation of the regional system was initiated (see Section B.2). Later, law n. 833/1978 established the National Health Service. This last law in particular was a turning point in the consolidation of the protection of social rights in Italy. It established the creation of a health service for the assistance of all individuals (therefore also for non-citizens illegally present on Italian soil), regardless of their economic condition. In the following decades, this system was further revised and refined (in 1992 and 1999, in particular with legislative decree n. 502/1992 and legislative decree n. 229/1999), also thanks to the introduction of the so-called 'ticket' for some medicines and medical tests or services, i.e. a contribution to be paid as a tax by the users/patients of health services. This mechanism, which obliges patients

---

[69] Paolo Barile, *La Costituzione come norma giuridica* (Barbera, Florence, 1951).
[70] Vezio Crisafulli, *La Costituzione e le sue disposizioni di principio* (n 33).

to pay a part of the cost, introduces into the regulatory framework an element of proportionality with respect to individual income (because higher income groups bear higher costs), but also an element of 'responsibility' for users at least partially affected by health spending. In the same period, with respect to individual freedoms and rights, between the 1970s and the 1980s the law on divorce (n. 898/1970) and the law on transsexualism (n. 164/1982) were approved.

As many of the abovementioned laws show, a relevant phenomenon of constitutionalization of ordinary laws took shape in the sense that a quasi-constitutional value has been allotted to some pieces of legislation, the most relevant cases being the *Bassanini* laws and the electoral laws passed after the 1990s. According to the constitutional period of reference, the importance of specific pieces of legislation assumed a constitutional value in the development of social rights as well, determining their actual content.

As one of the major actors, the Constitutional Court has played a particularly important role, pressing the parliament to regulate several matters.[71] An example of this dialogue concerns the enforcement of the principle of equality between men and women, which was not an effect of the rapid intervention of the parliament, but a result of constitutional judgments. The Court decided on a plurality of sectoral interventions, which later merged into the reform of family law in 1975. Later, also the reform of abortion (regulated by law n. 194/1978) was passed.[72]

Overall, the legislative measures passed between the 1960s and the early 1980s proved the intention of political parties to transform society via constitutional clauses. Later, the issue of institutional organization and administration became more relevant. In 1988, the parliament passed a law regulating the Office of the Prime Minister[73] (as established in article 95 of the Constitution), which also regulated governmental normative powers. Law n. 400/1988 aimed at achieving a twofold purpose: on the one hand, to define the functions and powers of the Prime Minister and the other governing bodies; on the other hand, to regulate the structure of the Office of the Prime Minister. According to Livio Paladin, this was 'not a real legal reform, but rather a proper implementation of the Constitution'.[74]

Furthermore, law n. 241/1990 regulated the administrative procedure and the access to the documents of the public administration, while law n. 146/1990 concerned strikes in public services. In the same decade, law n. 142/1990 regulated local entities as per article 5 of the Constitution. The 1990s were characterized by the adoption of several legislative pieces pursuing further territorial decentralization, especially through the so-called *Bassanini* laws (see B.2) which, as explained above, achieved the highest level of decentralization possible without a constitutional amendment. Bassanini was a constitutional law professor and member of the PDS and then DS, appointed as minister for public sector and regional affairs between 1996 and 1998. The following reforms were mainly passed through constitutional amendments.

Through the decades, in fact, the very idea of the Constitution has suffered serious political attacks. To grasp this phenomenon, a subjective element has to be taken into account.

---

[71] Sergio Bartole, *Interpretazioni e trasformazioni della costituzione repubblicana* (n 34).

[72] Sergio Paolo Panunzio, 'Le vie e le forme per l'innovazione costituzionale in Italia: procedura ordinaria di revisione, procedure speciali per le riforme costituzionali, percorsi alternativi', in Angelo Antonio Cervati, Sergio Paolo Panunzio, and Paolo Ridola (eds), *Studi sulla riforma costituzionale. Itinerari e temi per l'innovazione costituzionale in Italia* (Giappichelli, Turin, 2001) 73–191.

[73] Eugenio De Marco, *Le funzioni amministrative del Presidente del Consiglio dei Ministri* (CEDAM, Padova, 1990) 61 ff.

[74] Livio Paladin, 'Verso una nuova legge generale sul Governo' (1987) 3 le Regioni 301–309.

Until the 1990s, political leaders used to belong to those parties which were represented in the Constituent Assembly, whereas this changed in the following period. All the political and judicial events of the years 1993–1994 led to a dramatic change of the political class. Contrary to the previous eleven parliamentary terms, those following the 1994 general election were characterized by the alternation of parliamentary majorities and mainly by the disappearance of traditional parties. This was particularly true for the right-wing parties at the beginning, due to the establishment of a new political elite which was composed of new leaders who did not feel so attached to the Constitution, although the rhetoric of the *homo novus* is now spread throughout the entire political spectrum. These changes explain why political conflicts have moved from the legislative level to the constitutional level over the past two decades. The interpretation of the amending power itself, which had been extremely moderate until the 1990s, was radically changed.

6. Rigidity and Amendability

Title VI, Part Two of the Italian Constitution details the complex amending procedure, which requires at least the 50 per cent plus one majority. This clause is a result of the 'noble compromise', capable of tempering constitutional rigidity, and allocating decisive power and skills within the whole system.[75]

The choice for the 'rigidity' of the Italian Constitution, as Costantino Mortati affirmed, is clear in the amending procedure enshrined in article 138. Two consecutive votes are needed on the same text by each Chamber, with an interval of at least three months between them. If the two-thirds majority is achieved in both Chambers in the second vote, the amendment enters into force automatically. If only the 50 per cent plus one majority is achieved in the second vote, then a referendum can be requested (referenda on constitutional amendments were in fact held in 2001, 2006, 2016, and 2020).[76]

The only explicit limit to the amending power is enshrined in article 139. It establishes that the 'republican form' cannot be subject to change.[77] Different and contrasting opinions about the establishment of absolute limits to the amending power were voiced in the Constituent Assembly.[78] Prestigious scholars pointed out that the republican form must be assumed as a 'constant element of the regime or of the material Constitution, in which a composite core of legal principles and elements have to be considered essential of the republican form; all of them are qualified by their degree of immutability'.[79] Over time, the Constitutional Court has elaborated a hierarchical division of constitutional norms among themselves in relation to canon law and European law. When establishing the limits of these two sets of norms, the Constitutional Court held that they could not infringe upon certain constitutional principles

---

[75] Alessandro Pace, *Costituzioni rigide e costituzioni flessibili* (CEDAM, Padova, 2000); for a comparative approach, Maria Paola Viviani Schlein, *Rigidità costituzionale. Limiti e variazioni* (Giappichelli, Turin, 1997).

[76] The Italian Constitution provides for several sources with the same rank of the Constitution, namely constitutional amendment laws and other constitutional laws listed in the Constitution (Art 138, e.g. laws concerning the Constitutional Court as per Art 137 or the statutes of autonomy of 'special' Regions as per Art 116). As it was recalled above, constitutional amendments have been pursued, successfully or not, throughout the history of the Republic, while constitutional laws have been adopted when required by the Constitution.

[77] Ugo De Siervo, 'Origine e significato della rigidità della nostra costituzione', in Eugenio Ripepe and Roberto Romboli (eds), Cambiare Costituzione o modificare la Costituzione? (Giappichelli, Turin, 1995); Paolo Barile and Ugo De Siervo, *Revisione della Costituzione*, vol 15 (Novissimo Digesto italiano, UTET, Turin, 1968).

[78] Mario Dogliani, 'Origine e sviluppo dell'ordinamento costituzionale italiano', in Mario Dogliani, *La ricerca dell'ordine perduto. Scritti scelti* (il Mulino, Bologna, 2015).

[79] Alessandro Pizzorusso, 'Art. 139 Cost.', in Giuseppe Branca (ed), *Commentario della Costituzione* (n 23) 736.

(although they generally prevail over other provisions). Later, also recalling these previous judgments, the Court identified an unchangeable fundamental core, which is composed of both the explicit eternity clause of the Constitution and other supreme principles that define its identity. Judgment n. 1146/1988 is the leading case on this doctrine, although, in that case, the object of the complaint were articles of a statute of autonomy (statutes of autonomy of special Regions are in fact constitutional laws).

Replying to the question raised by the judge of the specific case, the Court stated that 'the Italian Constitution contains some supreme principles that cannot be subverted or modified in their essential content, not even through constitutional amendments or other constitutional laws'.[80] According to the justices, these include the principles that the Constitution itself explicitly fixes as absolute limits to the amending power, such as the republican form (article 139 Constitution), but also the principles that, despite not being expressly mentioned among those exempted from constitutional amendments, belong to the essence of the supreme values on which the Italian Constitution is based. Once it clarified that certain elements cannot be eliminated, the Constitutional Court added that the institution that has the power to verify the constitutionality of all sources of constitutional rank is the Court itself, because 'if it were not so, the absurd result would be that the system of judicial guarantees of the Constitution is defective and ineffective, precisely in relation to those norms with the higher value'[81] (which means, constitutional norms contained either in amendments or constitutional laws as such). The conclusion of the argument is clear: if there were no supervisor of the amendments, then the set of guarantees of the Constitution would be insufficient precisely with respect to those sources of law that, due to their rank, may truly affect the fundamental values of the system. The first key element of this case law is that the express limit to the amendments (the Republic) is not the only limitation. There are other non-reformable principles, which are those that embody the supreme values of the system, and fundamental rights, at least with reference to their essential content, and they cannot be amended.

So far, the Constitution has been amended nineteen times.[82] The last amendments were passed in 2012, 2020, 2021, and 2022. Particularly, in 2021 the age to be able to elect the members of the Senate was lowered to eighteen. In 2022, articles 9 and 41 of the Constitution were modified introducing an explicit reference to environmental protection as a fundamental principle, as well as to the interest of future generations and the protection of animals.

The amendment adopted in 2020 aimed to cut the number of deputies and senators, while the previous one dates back to 2012, during the Monti government, for the introduction of the 'balanced budget rule' in the Constitution, modifying article 81 of the Constitution (plus articles 97, 117, and 119). This reform can only be understood in the political and economic context in which it was passed, i.e. during the financial crisis and after the appointment of the technocrat Mario Monti as Prime Minister by the President

---

[80] Constitutional Court, Sentenza n. 1146/1988 point 2.1.

[81] Ibid.

[82] Costantino Mortati, 'Concetto, limiti, procedimento della revisione costituzionale' (1952), in Costantino Mortati (ed), *Raccolta di scritti, II, Scritti sulle fonti del diritto e sull'interpretazione* (Giuffrè, Milan, 1972); Stefano M Cicconetti, *La revisione della Costituzione* (CEDAM, Padova, 1972); Gaetano Silvestri, 'Spunti di riflessione sulla tipologia e sui limiti della revisione costituzionale', in AAVV, *Studi in onore di P. Biscaretti di Ruffia*, vol 2 (Giuffrè, Milan, 1987); Mario Dogliani, 'Potere costituente e revisione costituzionale' (1995) 1 Quaderni costituzionali 7–32; Alessandro Pizzorusso and others, 'Leggi costituzionali e di revisione costituzionale (1994–2005)', in Giuseppe Branca and Alessandro Pizzorusso (eds), *Commentario della Costituzione* (Zanichelli-Foro it., Bologna-Roma, 2006); Vincenzo Baldini (ed), *La Costituzione e la sua revisione* (Pisa University Press, Pisa, 2014); Ugo Adamo and others, *Alla prova della revisione. Settanta anni di rigidità costituzionale* (Editoriale Scientifica, Naples, 2019).

of the Republic. The amendment was considered to be a sign towards financial markets and EU institutions, in order to prove Italian institutions and administration were still to be trusted and relied upon.

In 1963, the legislature amended articles 56, 57, and 60, concerning the election, composition and duration of the Chambers. The amended text stated the number of Deputies (630) and of the Senators (315), which was then reduced in 2020 to 400 and 200. Furthermore, the same amendment established that every Region had a minimum of seven senators (six in the text of 1948), except for Valle d'Aosta (only one senator); this number was lowered to three in 2020. The amendment in 1963 also concerned the identical duration of the legislature: five years for both Chambers, while the original text fixed a different duration for the Senate (six years). After the praxis emerged to call for snap elections for the Senate in 1953 and 1958, the parliament decided to amend the Constitution in that sense. The same year, the Constitution was amended for the establishment of a new Region called Molise (represented by two senators).

Another amendment, in 1967, reduced the term of the Constitutional Court judges from twelve years to nine. It also regulated, in case of presidential impeachment, the institution of a special bench, which would complement the composition of the Court, consisting of sixteen citizens chosen from a list of individuals having the same qualification needed to become a senator.

In 1989, article 96 was changed: deputies, senators, and ministers, even if they have left office, are subject to ordinary jurisdiction for the offences committed in the exercise of their duties. In this case as well, the Chamber of Deputies or the Senate have to authorize the proceeding in accordance with the corresponding constitutional provisions. In the previous formulation, a joint session of the parliament was necessary to start the proceeding for any criminal offence committed in the exercise of the Prime Minister's or the ministers' duties. After the amendment a new Tribunal, called Ministers' Tribunal, was established in the seat of each Court of Appeal's district and was composed by three judges. The authorization to pursue the investigation must be given by the chamber to which the minister belongs or, otherwise, by the Senate.

The amendment of 1991 established the so-called 'white semester' of the President of the Republic, an amendment which involved changing article 88. During this period, i.e. the last six months of his term, he cannot dissolve the Chambers, unless it happens to correspond to the last six months of the legislative term. Another amendment, passed in 1992, involved article 79. It concerned the amnesty and the pardon. The series of amendments and their *ratio* prove that the relationship between the Constitution and politics has changed over time. If the Constitution was considered by those political forces that contributed to its drafting as a program to be implemented until the 1990s, this spirit vanished afterwards. The 'sacred' value of the compromise achieved in the Constituent Assembly has diminished through the decades. This phenomenon occurred because political discourse started to attribute political instability to the flaws of constitutional design, which in turn explain the two attempts to amend the regulation of the form of government in 2006 and 2016, and why this feature was the main object of the potential changes to be passed by the bicameral committees created in the 1990s. In 1993, during the abovementioned political scandal of *Tangentopoli*, article 68 on parliamentary immunity was amended. In fact, constitutional amendment law n. 3/1993, while confirming the immunity for opinions expressed and the votes given in the exercise of their functions, eliminated the requirement for a prior authorization by the corresponding Chamber to start criminal proceedings. An authorization is therefore only needed in the cases of personal or domiciliary search, arrest or other measures affecting personal freedom, wiretapping of telephones, check of communications, and seizure of correspondence (with few exceptions).

As further evidence of the changing equilibrium between political forces and constitutional sources in the 1990s, we can point to the most significant amendment ever passed in 2001, when the territorial organization of the State was changed, as it was already mentioned (see Section B.2). In the final votes, the amendment was not endorsed through a two-thirds majority, therefore a constitutional referendum took place, which was the first successful one before 2020 (as in 2006 and 2016 the amendments were rejected by popular vote). The overall idea of this amendment was coherent with the political trends recalled before, that is, to increase decentralization and the devolution of powers to territorial entities.[83]

Finally, two overarching reforms were rejected through constitutional referenda in 2006 and 2016. Both concerned the form of government, which has traditionally represented the most criticized aspect of the constitutional design of 1948.

The former, which took place during Silvio Berlusconi's government, aimed to amend the political system. In particular, while reducing the number of MPs, it would have changed the bicameral model transforming it into an asymmetrical system, with a federal Senate outside the confidence relationship circuit. The most criticized aspect was the modification of the powers of the Prime Minister (the model was called '*premierato*'). With these powers, the Prime Minister would have been in charge of appointing and dismissing individual ministers and determining national politics (not just coordinating). The reform would have introduced a constructive vote of no confidence as well, along the lines of the German *konstruktives Misstrauensvotum*, or the Spanish *moción de censura constructiva*. It would have partially affected the division of powers between State and Regions, giving back to the State some of the legislative matters devolved to the regional level in 2001, reestablishing a clause on 'national interest' (also eliminated in 2001) and introducing a supremacy clause.

The latter, which took place in 2016 during Matteo Renzi's government, would have also affected the form of government and the bicameral system. In particular, the reform would have ended the so-called 'perfect bicameralism', changing the composition and functions of the Senate, the legislative procedure and also the election of the President of the Republic. Other clauses would have amended the regulation of repeal referendum and popular initiative laws. Also, a new division of legislative powers between State and Regions was envisaged. Concerning the parliament, only the Chamber of Deputies would have represented the entire nation and have been in charge of the confidence relationship with the government, all the while it would have still enjoyed full law-making power. The Senate would have been reduced to 100 indirectly elected members, with ninety-five members elected by regional parliaments in lists composed of regional MPs and Mayors and five members appointed by the President of the Republic. Media and political debates on this reform have involved major institutional and academic figures, such as Sabino Cassese (in favour) and Gustavo Zagrebelsky (against). The main arguments in favour of the amendment were that it would increase the stability of the government and it would rationalize the form of government in a new political context in which the fear of authoritarian drifts was certainly

---

[83] Several other minor amendments can be recalled. In 2000, Art 48 had been amended for the establishment of the electoral districts for Italian residents abroad. The Amendment of 2002 abolished the transitional provision of the Constitution which stated that the members of the Savoy family and their descendants were not entitled to vote and could not hold any public or elective office. Furthermore, this provision prohibited the former Savoy kings, their spouses, and their male descendants to enter and stay in the national territory. In 2003, Art 51 was modified as to state that, 'The Republic shall adopt specific measures to promote equal opportunities between women and men.' In 2007, death penalty was abolished even from martial law in case of war (Art 27).

reduced if compared to 1948. Additionally, the length of the legislative procedure would have been shortened and there would have been spending cuts. Finally, there would have been a clear guarantee of the representation to the territorial entities through a regional Senate. The main arguments against were based on the risk of concentration of power, reinforced by the electoral system regulated in 2015 (the abovementioned *Italicum*) and the reduction of representation due to the indirect election of senators. As a general critique, as the amendment affected several clauses, the opponents claimed that comprehensive reforms should be passed with the approval of all main political forces (although the endorsement of the reform was much more bipartisan until the election of Sergio Mattarella as President of the Republic). Nevertheless, the majority of the discussions focused on the political value of the referendum, since the Prime Minister had announced he would resign in case the amendment did not pass—and this was the case.

C. Basic Structures and Concepts

1. The Value of the Constitution and the Constitutionalization of the Legal System

Grasping the position of the Constitution within the Italian legal and political system requires a few clarifications. First, it is necessary to recall the major missions of the Constitution according to domestic constitutional scholarship:[84] a) frame the basic values of the system, through principles; and b) establish the 'rules of the game', namely the limitations of political power through the separation of powers and mechanisms for checks and balances. Second, this leads to: a) the recognition and protection of fundamental rights and corresponding duties, which embody those basic values; and b) the enactment of a set of norms implementing, through dedicated means, the principle of the separation of powers.

From a strictly legal perspective, and particularly the viewpoint of the interconnections of the sources of law, the Constitution was considered the 'super-primary' source,[85] binding upon any subordinate source. As it was mentioned, the core identity of the Constitution, according to judgment n. 1146/1988, applies to constitutional laws and amendments, and not only on the other para-constitutional sources, like the Lateran Pacts or the norms of the EU (which cannot violate the supreme principles, so-called *controlimiti*).

More than its formal value, the debates assessing the role of the Constitution during the first years after it entered into force focused on how and through which tools to achieve and substantiate its 'primacy'. In fact, the text of the Constitution, due to the plethora of principles, led some constitutional scholars, as well as the most conservative section of the judiciary (mainly members of the Court of Cassation educated during the fascist regime) to oppose the direct applicability of constitutional clauses. They labelled them as 'merely programmatic' norms for the implementation of which legislative intervention would be

---

[84] On the diverse opinions of constitutional experts, see Costantino Mortati, 'Costituzione dello Stato (Dottrine generali e Costituzione della Repubblica italiana)', in *Enciclopedia del diritto*, vol XI (Giuffrè, Milan, 1962) 139 ff; Franco Modugno, 'Costituzione (teoria generale), in *Enciclopedia giuridica Treccani*, vol X (UTET, Turin, 1988); Augusto Antonio Barbera, 'Costituzione della Repubblica italiana', in *Enciclopedia del diritto Annali VIII* (Giuffrè, Milan, 2015) 263 ff.

[85] This definition derives from the fact that, when the Constitution entered into force, the hierarchy of norms was fixed within the Civil Code's preliminary norms (from 1942), in which the primary source was the law, consistently with the liberal model of the nineteenth century.

required. In other words, this thesis attributed to politics the task of implementing constitutional provisions, excluding their application until the corresponding laws would be enacted. This interpretative solution—in addition to the fact that the Constitutional Court (which was then in charge of checking the consistency of ordinary pieces of legislation with the Constitution, according to article 134 of the Constitution) was established only in 1955 and started its activity in 1956—would have nullified the very existence of the Constitution and postponed *ad libitum* the true application of its clauses.

This attitude can be contrasted with the position, already mentioned (see B.5), of those who underlined the value of the Constitution as a 'norm', therefore arguing that its provisions contained 'immediately obligatory rules'. These rules bind any legal practitioner (judge, lawyer, administrative body, etc.). The second reading of the Constitution soon became widespread, and it gave full effect to constitutional clauses both within the hierarchy of the sources of law and in the political sphere.

From what has just been said, it can be deduced that the Constitution contains a set of obligatory norms for all political actors, and they must act exclusively within its limits. On this basis, for example, various Presidents of the Republic have refused to dissolve the Chambers when the government had lost the parliamentary confidence, but it was still possible to form an alternative government (e.g. in 1994 after the Berlusconi I government, in 2011 after the Berlusconi IV government, in 2019 after the Conte I government, and in 2021 after the Conte II government). In such cases, in response to the request for dissolution of the Chambers, which came from the political party who had left the executive, the President of the Republic refused to invoke article 94 of the Constitution. This provision allows him to appoint a new government enjoying the confidence of the parliament.

At the same time, the Constitution defines, in the part devoted to fundamental principles, the mission of the political action of any future government. Two of the provisions containing the fundamental principles are significant in this regard. First of all, the abovementioned article 1, which traces a precise path aimed at ensuring the protection and enhancement of work as the founding principle of public policy action.[86] It is no coincidence that article 4 qualifies work as a right but also as a duty.

The same can be said with respect to the principle of equality according to article 3 of the Constitution. It also determines, especially in its second paragraph dedicated to the so-called substantial equality, an extremely ambitious goal to pursue. Having established that, 'It is an obligation for the Republic to remove those obstacles of economic or social nature which constrain freedom and equality of citizens, thereby impeding the full development of the human person and the effective participation of all workers to the political, economic and social organization of the country' implies the involvement of all public authorities in such responsibility.

How are these constitutional provisions practically enforced? In other words, how can one assert their binding nature with respect to political actions?

Of course, the role played by the legislator (the parliament with the government, which enjoys legislative initiative and participates in law-making), is to 'remove the obstacles' mentioned in article 3 para 2 of the Constitution giving effect to the principle of equality. This postulates the allocation of all necessary resources to guarantee the exercise of the so-called social rights, for which the intervention of the State is unavoidable (the right to work, health, study, social assistance and security, etc.). In addition to the significant example of the right to health

---

[86] Costantino Mortati, 'Art 1', in Costantino Mortati and others (eds), *Art. 1-12. Principi fondamentali*, in *Commentario della Costituzione, a cura di G Branca* (Zanichelli-Foro it., Bologna-Roma, 1975).

and the establishment of the National Health Service in 1978, all mechanisms related to social assistance and social security are relevant in this respect, as they provide mechanisms, which ensure economic support, respectively, in times of need (in case of an accident or other reasons that prevent somebody from working) or at the end of somebody's working age.

The role of the Constitutional Court is essential as well because it is called to check that laws and equivalent sources of law passed at both the national and the regional level fulfil constitutional provisions. In the case of the aforementioned principles, constitutional adjudication takes on an even more penetrating function insofar as it becomes a check on the consistency and congruity of the contested norms with respect to the pursuit of the objectives indicated by the constitutional provisions in question.

Several fundamental principles were always going to remain relevant even many years after the entry into force of the Constitution. By contrast, there are other constitutional provisions that became obsolete much sooner. In some cases, this phenomenon occurred so quickly as to prevent certain provisions from being implemented; consider the failure to implement articles 39 and 49 of the Constitution, which concerned the regulation and registration of unions and political parties. In other cases, constitutional clauses have become anachronistic, such as the norms on the nationalization of companies.

However, none of these issues can reduce the extraordinary effect produced by the entry into force of the Republican Constitution, which determined the progressive constitutionalization of the system. This phenomenon brought about the penetration of constitutional principles into the cultural and social, even before they entered the legal, fabric of the country. It happened in various ways: certainly through the progressive spread of the so-called constitutional culture, both through institutional channels (university courses but also the study of so-called civic education in high schools), and through spontaneous actions of individuals, associations and groups who engaged in projects and fights claiming they were implementing constitutional principles (one explanatory example of that is the battle against the mafias and generally against corruption and illegality).

The constitutionalization of the system also relied upon institutional actors. With few exceptions represented by extremist forces, political parties have always defended a commonality of constitutional principles. At the same time, the so-called 'guarantee bodies' (i.e. those public institutions primarily in charge of protecting the constitutional order), namely the President of the Republic and the Constitutional Court, have often blocked attempts to depart from fundamental principles.

Finally, the constitutionalization of the system has been pursued by ordinary judges, who, exercising their jurisdiction, have not pursued exclusively a strictly formal and positivistic application of the existing norms to the cases. In fact, they have become crucial actors of the eradication of fascist legislation from the legal system and, especially in recent years, they have engaged in the opening of the legal system towards new perspectives for the protection of fundamental rights deriving from supranational jurisdictions.

2. Democracy and Sovereignty

In the history of Western and Italian political thought, the concept of 'democracy' has been infused with the most various contents.[87] In particular, the most problematic issue at stake

---

[87] Luigi Bobbio, 'Dilemmi della democrazia partecipativa' (2006) 4 Democrazia e diritto 11–26; Gaetano Azzariti, *Critica della democrazia identitaria* (Laterza, Rome, 2005).

when debating democracy is connected to the function of limitation to political power. As scholarship has pointed out, many authors have dealt conjunctly with the ideas of 'authority' and 'freedom'.[88]

The constitutional concept of democracy cannot be understood exclusively as the exercise of the right to vote in periodical general elections, as it is phrased in article 1, according to which the people are not just entitled to sovereignty for the constituent process, but they are allowed as well to exercise it (also and mainly) throughout the instruments provided by the Constitution itself. The 'forms' and 'limits' of such exercise are established by the Constitution as well. The instruments of popular sovereignty correspond to the classic dichotomy of democracy (representative and direct), which is accepted by the Constitution. The former can be found in article 48, which fixes the right to vote as a prerogative of all citizens and adopts a procedural view of democracy. The corresponding limitation is included in article 67, which prohibits binding mandates for MPs. In fact, there is no possibility to recall MPs during their mandate as representatives of the nation, therefore disrupting the link between the electorate and their representatives during the parliamentary term. Representative democracy is also applied at the regional and local levels, with the changes and modifications highlighted before, providing the Italian system with a multilayered democratic process.

This meaning of democracy is strictly connected, in the constitutional system, to the functions of political parties as the channels for the representation of social and political requests. Article 49 of the Constitution recognizes the right of citizens to freely associate in parties in order 'to contribute to the determination of national politics through a democratic method', thereby forming an inclusive environment within a framework of political pluralism. Political parties, in fact, are not the only subjects entitled to participate in domestic politics, but they are called to 'contribute' to that aim by being freely operating associations. The condition of the 'democratic method' has been understood by scholars as to impose on the parties the principle of respect for democratic procedures, and not as the need of pursuing specific targets.

With respect to direct democracy, several mechanisms are provided for by the Constitution: petition (article 50), legislative initiative (article 71) and referendum, both at the national (articles 75 and 138), and the regional level (articles 123 and 132). Referenda, both repeal and constitutional ones, have played a major role in the democratic development of the State.

The initiative of repeal referenda by political parties, especially by the Radical Party, has been very important to submit to popular vote several sensitive issues. A quota of electors (500,000) or five regional parliaments can propose a referendum in order to derogate, totally or partially, a piece of legislation. The turnout must be at least half of the electorate for the vote to be valid (and this explains why several campaigns against referenda in the past were based on urging people not to vote). Not all laws can be amended through this mechanism, as tax laws, budgets, amnesties, and ratification of international treaties are explicitly excluded. Envisaged by article 75 of the Constitution, the repeal referendum was concretely regulated only in 1970, with a delay of more than twenty years. After that, several historical reforms, including the legalization of divorce and abortion, the introduction of conscientious objection, the prohibition on constructing nuclear power plants, the reforms of the

---

[88] Gaetano Azzariti, 'Concezioni della democrazia e opinione pubblica: la Corte costituzionale tra conflitti plurali e unità costituzionale', in Vincenzo Tondi della Mura, Michele Carducci, and Raffaele Guido Rodio (eds), *Corte costituzionale e processi di decisione politica*, Atti del seminario di Otranto-Lecce svoltosi il 4–5 giugno 2004 (Giappichelli, Turin, 2005) 879–903.

electoral system, among others, have been promoted and achieved through repeal referenda. Constitutional referenda have taken place so far only four times, in 2001, 2006, 2016, and 2020, and were also dramatically politicized as it was pointed out before.

Finally, with respect to the protection of democracy, Italy does not have any specific clause on the issue, differently of Germany or Spain. The only exception is the prohibition of the 'reorganization, in any form, of the dissolved fascist party' sanctioned by the twelfth transitory provision of the Constitution, to be interpreted as the ban of a specific, historically determined party.

If the application of the democratic principle in a particularly uneven society was the main issue[89] over the past years, this gap has been filled in the public sphere through the strengthening of the traditional instruments of popular participation in combination with the application of technological tools. The peculiar situation of the media and the control of the majorities has led to a political dysfunction that still characterizes the Italian political landscape.[90] In particular, the management of mass media (televisions and newspapers, above all) has marked the political agenda of Italian governments for a long period of time. The original public monopolistic management that characterized television communications for some decades, by virtue of the few frequencies available on a national scale, was replaced by a public–private oligopoly (criticized by the Constitutional Court in numerous pronouncements but never annulled) composed of one public entity (RAI-TV) and one private entity (Fininvest) on the market.

This situation, also legitimized by certain measures passed *ad hoc* by governmental interventions, such as the decree-laws adopted between 1984 and 1985,[91] had serious repercussions on cultural and social pluralism. Additionally, the beginning of Berlusconi's political career in 1993 impacted upon political pluralism. Useless, if not counterproductive, legislative interventions were carried out with the so-called Mammì law (n. 223/1990)[92] and, later, the so-called Gasparri law (n. 112/2004).[93] They have not solved the problem of pluralism in the media. On the contrary, they ended up legitimizing the *status quo* (for instance, the so-called SIC, 'integrated communications system', regulated in 2004, which led to the expansion of the relevant basis for the calculation of incomes and revenues used to assess the concentration of ownership of the media).

The issue of pluralism in the media was overcome in practice by the advent of digital technology which has led to a significant expansion of the number of operators who can access the broadcasting market. However, serious problems related to the management of the public radio and television service remain, especially during electoral campaigns. These

---

[89] Gustavo Zagrebelsky, *Il 'crucifige!' e la democrazia* (Einaudi, Turin, 1995).

[90] Giuseppe De Vergottini, 'La persistente sovranità' (2014) Consulta OnLine.

[91] Decree-law n. 694/1984; decree-law n. 807/1984; decree-law n. 223/1985.

[92] This law effectively remedied the public (*Rai*)/private (*Fininvest*) duopoly existing at that time in television broadcasting, which was determined following the violation of the previous regulation by the private broadcaster. Fininvest, in fact, through technical tricks and enjoying political endorsement, had opened a breach in the public monopoly provided for by the previous law. In particular, this law allowed the ownership of three out of nine national network concessions that could be granted to private individuals (or twelve in total), or ownership of 25 per cent of the total number of networks. This provision was then struck down by the Constitutional Court with judgment n. 420/1994, which, however, left the task of dictating the new rules to the legislator, who intervened fourteen years later with the Gasparri law.

[93] This law was passed after several judgments by the Constitutional Court and messages from the President of the Republic defending the value of pluralism. In particular, it reformed the reference package for calculating revenues and determining the maximum limit of available radio and television frequencies by an operator. It is the so-called SIC (Integrated Communications System, which includes daily and periodical press, published also via internet, radio and television, cinema and advertising). No one can achieve, either directly or through controlled entities, revenues exceeding 20 per cent of the total revenues of the integrated communications system.

issues were only partially tackled by the legislative provisions on the so-called *par condicio*,[94] which tries to ensure equal conditions for political parties and candidates with respect to elections. The question of the so-called 'conflict of interest' between ownership/management of mass media and the assumption of political offices is still unsolved, although it was on the political agenda of different parties over a period of decades.

The most recent challenge to the constitutional concept of democracy is today the emergence of new democratic decision-making processes online. In this respect, we refer especially to the Five Star Movement and their blog which is used as a platform to express political preferences and even to expel members of the party (until 2021, the so-called Rousseau platform[95]).

Necessarily linked to the concept of democracy is that of sovereignty. Article 1 of the Constitution specifies that sovereignty belongs to the people, although the exercise of sovereignty must respect the forms and limits established in the Constitution itself. From this point of view, the qualitative shift of post-Second World War liberal democracies lies in replacing the conception of sovereignty as some absolute (or partially limited) power but attributed to one subject (the Monarch or the abstract entity of the State), with a new conception in which the people (the electorate) exercise sovereignty either directly or indirectly through the action of democratic representative institutions.

With respect to this constitutional provision, some scholars consider it a merely formal attribution of sovereignty to the people, while substantive sovereign power lies elsewhere. In particular, according to various authors,[96] post-war liberal-democratic Constitutions produced a sort of 'objectification' of sovereignty, therefore making the question on 'who owned it' irrelevant.

From this perspective, the sovereign would no longer be a natural person or, least of all, a legal person or an abstract entity. Rather, sovereignty would become the constitutional value founding the State, and primarily, those of freedom and equality, values from which justice could be derived. Such conception of sovereignty would find its foundation in the Kelsenian *Grundnorm*, which, at its highest level, was constituted by the radical choice between pacifism and imperialism. This reconstruction of sovereignty, which does not prescribe the identification of a subject of sovereignty, however, presupposes that there are custodians or, more correctly, interpreters of sovereign values. Such are all the institutional actors and, ultimately, the judges of the Constitutional Courts.

3. Rule of Law and Protection of Constitutional Rights

The scope and type of protection afforded to individual rights have had strong implications for the configuration of the constitutional concept of the rule of law. The Constitution kept the traditional connection with the application of the principle of legality by public authorities. It specifically established forms of control of legislation and normative acts adopted by the executive, while providing for different checks on the exercise of power by public administrations (as the separate administrative judicial system proves).[97]

---

[94] Franco Modugno (ed), *Par condicio e Costituzione* (Giuffrè, Milan, 1997).

[95] Salvatore Cannavò, *Da Rousseau alla piattaforma Rousseau* (PaperFirst, Rome, 2019).

[96] Gaetano Silvestri, 'La parabola della sovranità. Ascesa declino e trasfigurazione di un concetto' (1996) 1 Rivista di Diritto costituzionale 3 ff.

[97] On the evolution of the administrative model in Italy, see 'the liberal period' analysed by Bernardo Giorgio Mattarella, 'Evolution and Gestalt of the Italian State', in Sabino Cassese, Armin von Bogdandy, and Peter M Huber (eds), *The Max Planck Handbooks in European Public Law, vol I* (OUP, Oxford, 2018) 344–356.

Within this model, a paramount role is allotted to the judiciary as the main actor in the protection of rights and to the Constitutional Court, which is entitled to interpret and apply the Constitution. In this respect, constitutional provisions related to rights are often principles, thus imposing a particular interpretative exegesis from the methodological perspective. The 'balancing technique' involves managing the conflicting principles to the constitutional framework of a pluralistic State in order to rationalize the application of the principle to the concrete case.[98] This fundamental theory is based on an implicit meta-principle which leads to the combination of conflicting principles: there is no prevalence of constitutional principles over the others (see for instance the so-called *Ilva* case n. 85/2013, in which the Court stated that, like other contemporary democratic and pluralistic Constitutions, the Italian Constitution requires a continuous and reciprocal balance between fundamental principles and rights, although there cannot be a claim of absolute supremacy for any of them). This principle has been considered as one of the techniques of resolution in constitutional cases par excellence.[99] In several cases, the Constitutional Court has justified the use of such a technique; for instance, when the declaration of unconstitutionality of a provision paradoxically determines even worse effects in terms of infringement upon the Constitution (judgment n. 13/2004 point 4). Also, it said that 'The institutional task entrusted to this Court requires that the Constitution must be guaranteed as a unitary system, to ensure systematic and undivided protection of all the rights and principles, involved in the decision' (judgment n. 264/2012, point 4.1). Without a principle of balance, 'there would be an unlimited expansion of a single right, which would become a tyrant for other legal situations recognized and protected by the Constitution' (judgment n. 85/2013). The second technique often used by the Constitutional Court in order to verify the compatibility of pieces of legislation with the Constitution is the application of the proportionality check. This way, the Court evaluates whether the legislative measures are consistent and proportionate with the targets being pursued.

The application of the rule of law has been expanded by the Court so as to create a sort of hierarchical division of constitutional norms among themselves, as it was explained above. There is a sort of inner 'constitutional rule of law' which is, first, composed by the clauses that contribute to define the fundamental core of the constitution and, second, based on an extensive interpretation of the 'republican form'. This is the only explicit limit to constitutional amendments. It has been interpreted by the Court so as to include the protection of inviolable rights and other supreme principles.

Regarding this last consideration, it is necessary to add a peculiar interpretative approach followed by the Constitutional Court concerning the protection of fundamental rights in relation to the provisions of supranational treaties and, in particular, the European Convention on Human Rights. In this regard, judgment n. 264/2012 states that:

> In the constitutional jurisprudence it has been repeatedly affirmed that, with reference to a fundamental right, compliance with international obligations can never be the cause of a decrease in protection if compared to domestic law; it can and must, *vice versa*, constitute

---

[98] Riccardo Guastini, 'La "costituzionalizzazione" dell'ordinamento italiano' (1998) 11 Ragion pratica 185–206; Giuseppe Limone, 'Lo statuto teorico dei principi fra norme e valori', in Domenico Amirante (ed), *La 'forza' normativa dei principi giuridici e il diritto ambientale. Profili di teoria generale e di diritto positivo* (CEDAM, Padova, 2006).

[99] Omar Chessa, 'Bilanciamento ben temperato o sindacato esterno di ragionevolezza? Note sui diritti inviolabili come parametro del giudizio di costituzionalità' (1998) Giurisprudenza costituzionale 3925–3952; Roberto Bin, *Diritti e argomenti. Il bilanciamento degli interessi nella giurisprudenza costituzionale* (Giuffrè, Milan, 1992).

an effective tool for expanding its protection. After all, Article 53 of the Convention establishes that the interpretation of the ECHR cannot lead to levels of protection which would be lower than those ensured by national legal sources. Consequently, the comparison between the protection provided by the Convention and the constitutional protection of fundamental rights must be carried out with the aim of maximizing the expansion of guarantees, a concept in which we have to include, as it was already clarified in judgments n. 348/2007 and 349/2007, the necessary balance with other constitutionally protected interests, that is, with other constitutional norms, which guarantee fundamental rights potentially affected by the expansion of the protection of another. The reference to the national 'margin of appreciation'—elaborated by the Strasbourg Court, and relevant as long as it represents an element of flexibility within the rigidity of the principles formulated at the European level—must always be present in the evaluations of this Court, conscious of the fact that the protection of fundamental rights must be systemic and not divided into a series of uncoordinated and potentially conflicting norms (point 4.1)

This judgment and others containing similar statements[100] show the concern of the Italian Constitutional Court with respect to how the multi-level protection may lead to a reduction in the standard of protection of fundamental rights. From this perspective, the Court identifies and claims a peculiar role compared to that of the ECHR. Rather than taking a more compartmentalized approach where every single right is taken into consideration separately, it has the task of ensuring systemic protection of fundamental rights, in some cases through balancing operations.[101]

The criterion or principle of the maximum expansion of the protection has a specific legal basis in article 53 of the ECHR (as well as in article 53 of the Charter of Fundamental Rights of the EU). It basically aims to guarantee that the system of multilevel protection of rights ensures only a level of protection equal to or higher than that guaranteed within the single State.

4. Separation and Distribution of Powers among Constitutional Bodies and Territorial Entities

As it was recalled, one of the main conflicts to be solved within the Constituent Assembly was the choice of the form of government. Once it was decided that it would be a parliamentary system, political debates focused on the structure and role of the parliament. It is a peculiar institution in the Italian system. In fact, the executive must enjoy the confidence of

---

[100] See judgments n. 317/2009; n. 80/2011; n. 85/2013; n. 170/2013; n. 202/2013; n. 191/2014; n. 223/2014; n. 49/2015; n. 67/2017 and n. 254/2019.

[101] *Ex plurimis*, on this case law, Massimo Luciani, 'Alcuni interrogatovi sul nuovo corso della giurisprudenza costituzionale in ordine ai rapporti fra diritto italiano e diritto internazionale' (2008) 2 Corriere giuridico 201–205; Roberto Conti, 'La Corte costituzionale viaggia verso i diritti Cedu: prima fermata verso Strasburgo' (2008) 2 Corriere giuridico 205–222; Antonio Ruggeri, 'La CEDU alla ricerca di una nuova identità, tra prospettiva formale-astratta e prospettiva assiologico-sostanziale d'inquadramento sistematico (a prima lettura di Corte cost. nn. 348 e 349 del 2007)' (2007) Forum di Quaderni costituzionali 1–8; Vincenzo Sciarabba, *Tra fonti e Corti. Diritti e principi fondamentali in Europa: profili costituzionali e comparati degli sviluppi sovranazionali* (CEDAM, Padova, 2008); Federico Sorrentino, 'Apologia delle "sentenze gemelle" (brevi note a margine delle sentenze nn. 348 e 349/2007 della Corte costituzionale)' (2009) 2 Diritto e Società 213–224; Carmela Salazar and Antonino Spadaro (eds), *Riflessioni sulle sentenze 348-349/2007 della Corte costituzionale* (Giuffrè, Milan, 2009); Roberto Conti, *La Convenzione europea dei diritti dell'uomo. Il ruolo del giudice* (Aracne, Rome, 2010); Giorgio Repetto, *Argomenti comparativi e diritti fondamentali in Europa. Teorie dell'interpretazione e giurisprudenza sovranazionale* (Jovene, Naples, 2011); Diletta Tega, *I diritti in crisi. Tra Corti nazionali e Corte europea di Strasburgo* (Giuffrè, Milan, 2012).

both Chambers (meaning that just one of the Chambers can withdraw confidence in the executive, thereby obliging the government to resign), which are given almost completely the same tasks. This arrangement was intended to ensure greater reflection on legislation and the avoidance of concentration of power in just one body. In practice, it led also to elements of malfunctioning, especially during those legislative terms in which there was a difference in majorities between the two Chambers, as well as in terms of the excessive length of the legislative procedure.

Over the years, the interaction between parliament and government has been a central theme for constitutional scholars because it is considered to be a major element to grasp the separation of powers. Academics have focused particularly on the dialectics between majority and opposition, as well as the issues of the confidence relationship.[102] The system of government established by the Constitution, as it was conceived by the founding fathers, was based on the principle of the 'centrality of party intermediation in the formation of political choices', and the stability of the executive power had to depend on the existence and maintenance of the corresponding parliamentary majority.[103] The relationship between legislative and executive has changed over time, while a degree of instability and party fragmentation have characterized the evolution of the system so far.

Both the role of the Prime Minister and the President of the Republic have undergone several phases. The former's leadership has been progressively emphasized by the increasing personalization of politics. That process started in the 1990s with the entry into politics of Berlusconi, although an alternation between strong leaders, technocrats, and less known leaders has been the *leitmotiv* of the past decade (with Silvio Berlusconi himself, Mario Monti, Enrico Letta, Matteo Renzi, Paolo Gentiloni, Giuseppe Conte, and Mario Draghi). The latter's role, which was mainly meant to be the guarantee of the proper functioning of democratic institutions, has been interpreted differently by the Presidents and also adapted to political changes. The power of appointment of the Prime Minister, for instance, was significantly and strategically used by President Giorgio Napolitano when managing the political crisis of 2011 after Berlusconi's resignation. Napolitano was 'induced' to appoint Mario Monti, whom he had previously appointed senator for life. Also, in the formation of the Letta government, the preferences of the President were evident. Until 2018, the role played by the Presidents in the selection of ministers had been less known. In spite of the veto having been exercised by other Presidents in the past, President Mattarella was caught in a political crisis when he refused to appoint the first minister for finance (Paolo Savona) proposed by the Five Star Movement and the League.[104]

The Constitutional Court has rarely been involved in the solution of very political conflicts among branches of power, with the exception, for instance, of the decision on the power of grace, stating that it is a presidential prerogative and not a ministerial function (judgment n. 200/2006). More recently, the opposition brought before the Court a violation of the legislative procedure in the approval of 2018 budgetary law. This case triggered a decision by the Court in which it opened the door to parliamentary opposition and minority, while not

---

[102] Renzo Dickmann and Sandro Staiano, *Funzioni parlamentari non legislative e forma di governo: l'esperienza dell'Italia* (Giuffrè, Milan, 2008).

[103] Paolo Ridola, 'Le regole costituzionali del pluralismo politico e le prospettive del diritto dei partiti' (1993) Giurisprudenza costituzionale 2960.

[104] *Ex plurimis*, Enzo Cheli, 'Natura giuridica del potere di nomina dei Ministri' (2018) 3 Quaderni costituzionali 671–673; Valerio Onida, 'In regime parlamentare la scelta dei Ministri fa parte dell'indirizzo politico del nuovo Governo' (2018) 3 Quaderni costituzionali 674–676; Luigi Ferraro, 'La nomina del Ministro Savona e le "accuse" al Presidente Mattarella' (2018) Forum di Quaderni costituzionali 1–10.

providing protection in the concrete case and leaving the issue open for future cases (judgment n. 17/2019).[105]

Even if no extremely significant attacks on the Constitutional Court have occurred, a clear and recurrent conflict between political parties and the judiciary has been a part of Italian public debates, starting with the investigations that revealed the role of the P2 Masonic lodge (1981), the political collusion of mafia after the killing of General Dalla Chiesa (1982), or uncovered the clandestine armed network, with anti-revolutionary functions, called 'Gladio' and linked to the secret services (1990). These cases led to campaigns against the autonomy of the judiciary as it was accused of attacking legitimately elected leaders. Such a discourse was initiated by Silvio Berlusconi and was followed by other leaders and recently by the former Minister of Interior Matteo Salvini after he received the notification that an investigation had been initiated.

With respect to the principle of the separation of powers, being a parliamentary system there is no pure separation of functions. The law-making function is partially shared by parliament and government, as the latter enjoys legislative initiative and can pass primary sources of law.[106] The executive function is held by the government and the administration. The protection of the supremacy of the Constitution is allotted to the Constitutional Court, but also to the President of the Republic. Actually, the judiciary is the only power whose function is strictly separated from the others as the dedicated constitutional clauses prove. Article 104 defines it as autonomous and independent from all other powers, while article 101 states that judges are only subject to the law. There is also a specific body, the Superior Council of the Judiciary (*Consiglio superiore della magistratura*—CSM), which is in charge of hiring, assignments, transfers, promotions, and disciplinary measures vis-à-vis individual members of the judiciary. Two-thirds of this body are composed of members elected by and among ordinary judges belonging to the various jurisdictions and one-third by the two Chambers of the parliament in joint session. Their membership is drawn from full professors of law and lawyers who have practiced for at least fifteen years. There are three members *ex lege*, regardless of their appointment or election, who remain in office in the CSM as long as their own office lasts: The President of the Republic, who chairs the CSM, the First President of the Court of Cassation, and the Attorney General of the Court of Cassation.

The CSM was established in order to guarantee autonomy and independence of the judiciary with respect to other powers. To this end, all acts concerning the status of any ordinary judge fall within its competence and therefore are decided upon by a body in which there is a majoritarian component (two-thirds) of ordinary judges. In fact, the founding fathers believed that the ultimate goal of the judiciary, namely impartial adjudication, could be better achieved by ensuring the autonomy and independence of the judiciary.

---

[105] *Ex plurimis*, Nicola Lupo, 'Un'ordinanza compromissoria, ma che pone le basi per un procedimento legislativo più rispettoso della Costituzione' (2019) 4 federalismi.it 1–15; Andrea Morrone, '*Lucciole per lanterne*. La n. 17/2019 e la terra promessa di quote di potere per il singolo parlamentare' (2019) 4 federalismi.it 1–9; Valerio Onida, 'La Corte e i conflitti interni al Parlamento: l'ordinanza n. 17 del 2019' (2019) 3 federalismi.it 1–9. For further comments see the dedicated page on this judgment of Consulta OnLine: https://www.giurcost.org/ (last accessed on 6 March 2022).

[106] In particular, the executive is entitled to pass legislative decrees upon delegation by parliament, as stated by Art 76 ('The exercise of the legislative function may not be delegated to the government unless principles and criteria have been established and then only for a limited time and for specified purposes'). Additionally, the government can adopt, in case of necessity and urgency, under its own responsibility, a temporary measure (law-decree). It is obligatory to submit such decree to parliament for the corresponding transposition into law, within sixty days of its publication (Art 77).

The peculiar composition of the CSM and the nature of its attributions have been, over the years, the causes of critiques and accusations of self-referentiality.[107] This phenomenon has affected various of the tasks assigned to this body; for example, disciplinary proceedings against judges have often been characterized by partial attitudes leading to the acquittal of the indicted judges.[108] In this respect, one might also recall the issue of the conferral of managerial positions.[109] Very often, the CSM has proceeded according to the logic of belonging to specific internal groups (so-called *correnti*), rather than on the basis of competence and specialization. In this context, the so-called *correnti*,[110] which used to be an expression of ideological and cultural pluralism among judges, have often become real factions or '*correnti di persone*' (Spangher). They usually act to place their members in leading positions. This phenomenon has put at the centre of the political debate the possible amendment of the system for the election of two-thirds of the members of the CSM coming from the (ordinary) judiciary, as well as the establishment of more objective criteria for the conferral of managerial positions. These considerations do not reduce the validity of the constitutional framework, which still remains a model for other legal systems,[111] but lead to reflect on new mechanisms for selecting the members of the CSM and limiting the role of the *correnti*.

In addition to the CSM, other legal institutions are provided to guarantee the independence of judges: for example, the so-called 'immovability' (*inamovibilità*), in the sense that the judges cannot be transferred from their assigned office, unless they give their consent and there is a formal act adopted by the CSM (except in cases of so-called 'contextual incompatibility', i.e. when a judge, independently of any personal responsibility, cannot exercise his functions in a specific place with independence and impartiality); the selection process through public examinations; several limitations to being involved in politics and joining political parties; the ban on entering into secret associations (article 18 of the Constitution); legal regulation of a remuneration that shall be adequate to ensure their independence; some limitations to carrying out extrajudicial assignments; a career progression mechanism based essentially on seniority.

The Italian Constitution, in addition to providing for the presence of ordinary judges that are established and regulated by the norms on the judiciary, states that it is forbidden to establish extraordinary and special judges. These are two distinct prohibitions. The first (the ban on setting up extraordinary judges) is connected to article 25 of the Constitution and therefore to the principle that 'no case may be removed from the natural judge which is competent for the case according to the law'. By 'extraordinary judges', we mean in fact those judges established *ad hoc* to adjudicate upon a certain situation or person after the facts have happened. If the appointment of this type of judges were allowed, the impartiality of the jurisdiction would be seriously compromised. The expression 'natural judge' must therefore be understood as the judge who, previously designated based on substantive and territorial criteria and the so-called 'tables of judicial offices', is called to exercise jurisdiction at a certain time, in a given place and on a specific fact scenario.

---

[107] Edmondo Bruti Liberati and Livio Pepino (eds), *Autogoverno o controllo dei magistrati? Il modello italiano di Consiglio Superiore* (Feltrinelli, Milan, 1998).

[108] On the responsibility of judges, see Mauro Cappelletti, *Giudici irresponsabili?* (Giuffrè, Milan, 1988).

[109] Carlo Guarnieri, 'Appointment and career of judges in continental Europe: the rise of judicial self-government' (2004) 9 Swiss Political Science Review 169–187.

[110] Carlo Guarnieri, 'Elites, correnti e conflitti fra i magistrati italiani: 1964–1976' (1976) Politica del diritto 653–682; Carlo Guarnieri, 'Origini, sviluppo e problemi delle «correnti giudiziarie», in Antonio Bevere (ed), *I magistrati e le correnti. Alla ricerca dell'indipendenza da se stessi* (Edizioni Scientifiche Italiane, Naples, 2008).

[111] Simone Benvenuti and Davide Paris, 'Judicial self-government in Italy: Merits, limits and the reality of an export model' (2018) 19, n 7 German Law Journal 1641–1669.

The prohibition to establish special judges aims at guaranteeing the unity of the jurisdiction and must be understood as a relative and not absolute principle. The Constituent Assembly, in fact, after having banned the establishment of special judges, still envisaged a few, for example, the Council of State, the Court of Audit, military judges, etc. Accordingly, the prohibition concerns the establishment of new additional judges which are different from those already regulated in the Constitution. The same problems of autonomy and independence also arise for these judges. The Constitution provides in this regard that 'the law ensures the independence of judges of special courts, of state prosecutors of those courts, and of other individuals participating in the administration of justice' (article 108 para 2 of the Constitution). Implementing this constitutional provision, the legislator has provided for a series of institutes and tools aimed at this purpose, including the establishment of self-government bodies which are similar to the CSM.

From the vertical perspective, the separation of powers between State and Regions does not affect all branches. While there are executive and legislative powers at the regional level, the judiciary has not been built according to territorial decentralization. The principle of separation has been mainly referred to the evolution of the attribution of legislative matters, which, as it was already highlighted, was initially based on a typically regional method (where Regions could only pass legislation on a fixed list of matters, respecting the principle of national interest) to a typically federal method in 2001 (where Regions hold the general competence, while there is a list of fixed matters for the State). In terms of administrative powers, the initial principle of 'parallelism' between the entitlement of legislative functions and the corresponding administrative ones was also amended in a manner that favoured the Regions.

The main constitutional reference with respect to the territorial form of the State is article 5. It contains the principle of unity and indivisibility and thereby recognizes at the same time territorial autonomy as a core element. The dichotomy between unity and decentralization is the key to grasp the Italian model. The joint recognition of the unity of the State and territorial bodies should not seem contradictory; in fact, the drafters of the Constitution deliberately combined these two principles in order to underline their complementarity, as there can be no autonomy outside and without the recognition of a unitary framework and, at the same time, there can be no unity without the guarantee of forms of territorial autonomy.

The Italian founding fathers opted for a regional organization of powers based on two kinds of Regions: the special ones and the ordinary ones. They were only established in the 1970s, as it was mentioned above. Beside these regional entities, there are two Autonomous Provinces, Trento and Bolzano (due to the special status of the Region Trentino-Alto Adige). They have special legislative and administrative functions as well as financial autonomy.

The system underwent major reforms between the end of the 1990s and the early 2000s,[112] while posterior major reforms which could have affected Regions ultimately failed (2006 and 2016). Overall, Regions remain situated within the unity of the State, which is the exclusive holder of sovereignty as the exponential body of the entire national community interests. As far as this principle of sovereignty is concerned, we can look to the Constitutional Court's decision in judgment n. 274/2003. There, it clarified the unique position of the State with respect to the general structure of the Republic. This setting can be 'inferred not only from article 5 of the Constitution, but also from the recurring idea of a unitary need, vested for

---

[112] Stelio Mangiameli, *La riforma del regionalismo italiano* (Giappichelli, Turin, 2002).

instance by the need for the respect of the Constitution, as well as by the constraints arising from EU law and international obligations' (point 2.1).

The evolutionary process until the financial crisis was consistently aimed at increasing powers and functions of territorial entities, while providing them with improved democratic value through the direct election of political leaders. This process was stopped and reversed over the past ten years (in both respects) as more checks were introduced on the functioning of territorial bodies and Provinces were transformed into indirectly elected bodies (law n. 56/2014). Nevertheless, the negative financial effects of the crisis did not affect all Regions equally and some of them now claim wider powers. This explains why the current challenge of the territorial model is the so-called 'differentiated regionalism', which was included in the Constitution in 2001 but exploited only after 2017[113] (see Section B.2).

With respect to the relationship between the territory and the Republic, the Constitutional Court, when deciding upon the call for a referendum on the independence of Veneto, stated that the principle of unity cannot be the object of any referendum nor of a constitutional amendment (judgment n. 118/2015). This shows that the territorial organization constitutes a characterizing feature of the State, albeit within the unitary framework established, in principle, by article 5, and, in detail, by constraints on the exercise of legislative, administrative, and financial tasks by the Regions. Such constraints aim at guaranteeing basic uniformity among the Regions and, consequently, an equal minimum level of protection of citizens residing in the various parts of the Italian territory.

Other constitutional provisions recall the conception of the entirety of the country and the political unity. The term 'Constitution' itself plays a role, from the perspective of the hierarchy of norms, as in article 1 it is portrayed as the regulatory framework for the exercise of sovereignty, and in article 117 it is included as an explicit yardstick for the validity of national and regional legislation.

Again, in article 1 we can find a reference to the concept of 'people' as the subject holding sovereignty. The people are also mentioned in article 71 with reference to popular legislative initiative and then when the Constitution states that justice is administered in the name of the people (article 101). In this respect, 'citizenship' is also mentioned in the text. Part I of the Constitution is entitled 'Rights and duties of citizens' and both article 3 and article 4 refer to citizens. Article 22 establishes that no one can be deprived of his legal capacity, citizenship, or name for political reasons. Nevertheless, the true content of this concept can only be grasped in its legislative implementation as all forms of acquisition of Italian citizenship are regulated through law. Such forms have been discussed in public fora over the past few years. Several reforms have been proposed to grant citizenship according to the principle of the so-called *ius soli*. The first bill was presented (but never approved) by the Minister of Social Affairs Livia Turco in 1999 and it aimed at granting citizenship to children born in Italy from foreigners who had lived legally on Italian soil for at least five years, thereby ensuring equal treatment to those children when starting schooling. A new bill was proposed by Giuliano Amato, who was the Minister of Interior at the time, but the electoral victory in 2008 of the centre-right coalition froze the debate concerning this piece of legislation. Nevertheless, a bipartisan bill was proposed in 2009 (which also did not pass). It would have granted Italian nationality, among others, to eighteen-year-olds born in Italy to foreigners who had lived

---

[113] *Ex plurimis*, Roberto Bin, ''Regionalismo differenziato'' e utilizzazione dell' art 116, terzo comma, Cost. Alcune tesi per aprire il dibattito' (2008) 1 Le istituzioni del federalismo 7–20; Lorenza Violini, 'L'autonomia delle Regioni italiane dopo i referendum e le richieste di maggiori poteri ex art 116, comma 3, Cost.' (2018) 4 Rivista AIC 319-65.

legally in the country for more than five years, although such grant was subject to passing a test on culture and language. In 2011, a movement in favour of opening citizenship was formed and supported by a leading representative of the Democratic Party (Graziano Delrio) and it led to two popular initiative bills submitted to the parliament in 2012. After a first approval of a joint bill combining these initiatives with others, this law was not approved before the end of the legislative term, although it was constantly present in public debates on *ius soli* and *ius culturae*.

With reference to Italy as a political entity, the main terms employed in the Constitution are Republic, State, and Nation. As it was previously explained, the republican form is the only explicit limit to constitutional amendments as it was decided upon through the referendum of 1946 and the term 'Republic' is present in several of the basic principles of the Constitution, which span from article 1 to article 12 (specifically articles 1, 2, 3, 4, 5, 6, 9, and 12). In particular, in the first part of the Constitution, this term is used to identify the relationship between the state and the society, as well as the one providing services and protecting individual and collective rights. The term 'State' is used to identify the international subjectivity of Italy (articles 7, 8, 11) or to refer to the State in contrast with territorial entities (article 5). In article 114, from the perspective of the vertical separation of powers, the Republic is identified as the global entity which also includes the State, alongside Municipalities, Provinces, Metropolitan Cities, and the Regions. Altogether, they 'compose' the Republic. In Italian scholarship, often, the 'State as a community' has been distinguished from the 'State as a machinery', which would be represented by the bureaucracy of the State with the highest structures representing the authority (Costantino Mortati[114]). The element which could bring together both concepts would be the principle of solidarity as the essential foundation of the democratic relationship between the State components—as stated by abundant constitutional jurisprudence.[115]

Finally, some clauses use the term 'Nation'. Among basic principles, article 9 stated that the Republic protects the natural landscape and the historical and artistic heritage of the Nation. With respect to politics, article 67 established that each MP represents the Nation; article 59 that five senators can be appointed who have honoured the Nation; article 49 that political parties contribute to determine national politics; article 87 that the President of the Republic is the Head of the State and represents national unity; article 98 that civil servants are exclusively at the service of the Nation.

The flag, described in article 12, is attributed to the Republic and not to the Nation or the State, underlying its connection with citizenship. Recently, the Constitutional Court, dealing with the symbolism of the national flag, issued judgment n. 183/2018, stating that the Italian flag is a constitutional symbol of the Republic, a reminder of its independence and national unity founded since 1948 on a rigid, democratic and pluralistic Constitution, and embodied in the fundamental principles of the Constitution.[116] The Court had already highlighted the ideological neutrality of the national flag in the past.[117] In judgment n. 189/1987, the Court stroke down some provisions of law n. 1085/1929, in order to derogate from the prohibition to expose foreign flags in public (subsequent to a previous authorization).

---

[114] Costantino Mortati, *Istituzioni di diritto pubblico*, vol 1 (CEDAM, Padova, 1991) 46.

[115] Gaetano Silvestri, 'La parabola della sovranità. Ascesa declino e trasfigurazione di un concetto' (n 97) 3 ff; Gaetano Silvestri, 'Verso uno ius commune europeo dei diritti fondamentali' (2006) 1 Quaderni costituzionali 7 ff.

[116] See Giuseppe Renato, 'Bandiera (dir. pubbl.)', in Francesco Calasso (ed), *Enciclopedia del diritto*, vol 5 (Giuffrè, Milan, 1959) 38.

[117] Giovanni Luchena and Raffaele Manfrellotti, 'Profili giuridici della bandiera tra modello costituzionale e ordinamento comunitario' (2017) Diritto pubblico europeo – Rassegna online (last accessed on 6 March 2022).

D. Constitutional Identity

The concept of constitutional identity as such has not been present in the Italian debate, although, in recent years, it has acquired more relevance under the influence of European integration.

The first elaboration of the fundamental core of the Constitution, as previously recalled, was undertaken by the Constitutional Court with respect to potential constitutional amendments, which cannot violate specific constitutional principles. During the 1970s, the Constitutional Court stated that the supreme principles of the constitutional system should not be compromised by the Lateran Pacts of 1929 (or the amendments thereto), which, as it was previously mentioned, have constitutional status. Later, in judgment n. 1146/1988, the Court decided that the supreme principles in the constitutional order cannot be changed in their 'essential content' and include both the republican form ex article 139 of the Constitution and those principles that belong to the essence of the supreme values on which the Italian Constitution is based. While the Constitutional Court has given itself the power to check the compliance of constitutional amendments with such principles, the Court did not define what those they are and what scope they shall have. Elaboration of this concept through constitutional case law is the only possible outcome. As a matter of fact, in subsequent judgments, the Court affirmed that the parliamentary form of government does not belong to this hard core of the constitution (judgment n. 2/2004), while the unity of the Republic does (judgment n. 118/2015, see C.4).

The role of the Court has also been paramount in defining which aspects of the Constitution cannot be violated by EU norms. The first line of jurisprudence is the one related to the concept of 'controlimiti',[118] such as those fundamental aspects that cannot be affected by European sources, but that otherwise prevail over domestic norms. Judgment n. 183/1973 elaborated upon them as the last resort to safeguard supreme principles and fundamental rights from any possible risk of internal or external attack, with reference to European integration. In this regard, the Court stated that precise provisions of European Treaties provide guarantees, and it was difficult to imagine even abstractly the hypothesis of common norms conflicting with the Italian Constitution. It added that, under article 11 of the Constitution, limitations of sovereignty were permitted exclusively for the achievement of the purposes indicated therein and never for the infringement upon constitutional principles. If such a case ever arose, the Court would be in charge of protecting the basic principles.

From that moment on, the reference to the concept of *controlimiti* has become a constant element in the subsequent constitutional jurisprudence, especially when in 1984 the Court (decision—*ordinanza*—n. 170/1984) considered that the antinomy between a European norm and domestic norm should be solved with the non-application of the latter and not with a challenge before the Court itself. Only in that situation when the regulation is in conflict with the aforementioned fundamental principles, the judge should raise the question of constitutionality, and the judgment would then concern the law implementing the Treaties of the EU (with respect to the clause establishing the obligatory value of that regulation).

For a long time, the use of such weapon remained a mere 'threat' as the counter-limits had never been applied. In 2017 (decision—*ordinanza*—n. 24/2017), with the third reference that the Italian Court submitted to the Court of Justice for a preliminary ruling in the context

---

[118] Simona Polimeni, *Controlimiti e identità costituzionale nazionale. Contributo per una ricostruzione del 'dialogo' tra le Corti* (Editoriale Scientifica, Naples, 2018).

of the well-known *Taricco* case (the first time was in 2008 and the second in 2013), the issue became relevant again. The Court, in fact, affirmed that the principle of the statute of limitations is a substantive criminal norm. It is connected to the principle of legality in criminal matters and is consequently a 'supreme principle' within the Italian legal system. It entered into a dialogue with the Court of Justice, which had allowed the non-application of the domestic rule, letting the domestic judiciary decide on the matter. This scrutiny was attributed to the Constitutional Court at the internal level, which pursued collaboration and dialogue with European judges, allotting supreme value to the statute of limitation. As this last case shows, it is not possible to reconstruct a priori what the fundamental or basic principles of the Constitution are because they are identified on a case-by-case basis depending on the threat and the value at stake. The Court of Justice replied to the preliminary reference of the Court with a judgment issued on 5 December 2017 (Case C-42/17), which, concurring with the reasoning of the Italian Constitutional Court, affirmed that there is no obligation for the domestic judge to disapply internal legislation that is in conflict with EU law when any such application would entail the violation of a supreme principle (in the present case, the rule of law and in particular the 'principle that offences and penalties must be defined by law'). After that, the Constitutional Court decided upon the case based on the European ruling (judgment n. 115/2018).[119]

In a similar case (decision—*ordinanza*—n. 117/2019) concerning a preliminary reference (submitted for both the interpretation and the validity of EU norms), the Italian Constitutional Court asked the Court of Justice of the EU to rule on the compatibility of EU legislation with some articles of the Charter of Fundamental Rights, particularly in light of the jurisprudence of the ECtHR and the constitutional traditions common to the Member States. These constitutional traditions are elaborated upon by the Court as deriving from the supreme principles of the Italian constitutional system and they represent a limit to the application of the rules of EU law into the national system.[120]

---

[119] Caterina Paonessa and Lorenzo Zilletti, *Dal giudice garante al giudice disapplicatore delle garanzie. I nuovi scenari della soggezione al diritto dell'Unione europea: a proposito della sentenza della Corte di giustizia Taricco* (Pacini Giuridica, Pisa, 2016); Alessandro Bernardi and Cristiano Cupelli, *Il caso Taricco e il dialogo tra le Corti. L'ordinanza 24/2017 della Corte costituzionale* (Jovene, Naples, 2017); Chiara Amalfitano, *Primato del diritto dell'Unione europea e controlimiti alla prova della 'saga Taricco'* (Giuffrè, Milan, 2018).

[120] In a different case from the previous ones, the Constitutional Court referred to the basic principles of the constitutional system and to fundamental rights in order to pursue their protection also with respect to norms of customary international law (in particular, States' immunity from civil jurisdiction of other States—decision—ordinanza—n. 238/2014). See *ex plurimis*, Antonio Ruggeri, 'La Corte aziona l'arma dei "controlimiti" e, facendo un uso alquanto singolare delle categorie processuali, sbarra le porte all'ingresso in ambito interno di norma internazionale consuetudinaria (a margine di Corte cost. n. 238 del 2014)' (2014) Consulta Online; Tania Groppi, 'La Corte costituzionale e la storia profetica. Considerazioni a margine della sentenza n. 238/2014 della Corte costituzionale italiana' (2015) Consulta Online.

7

The Evolution and *Gestalt* of the Lithuanian Constitution

Irmantas Jarukaitis

A. Origins of the 1992 Constitution of Lithuania	319	2. Lithuania's Integration into Trans-Atlantic Structures and its Impact on the Constitution	340
1. The Early Origins of the Lithuanian Constitutionalism	319	a) Ratification of the ECHR and Its Impact on the Constitution	341
2. Evolution of the Lithuanian Constitutionalism during the Interwar Period	324	b) The EU Membership and Its Impact on the Lithuanian Constitutional Order	344
3. Re-establishment of the Independence and Adoption of the 1992 Constitution	327	**C. Basic Principles and Structures of the 1992 Constitution**	352
a) Events of 1987–1990 and Adoption of the Act on the Re-establishment of the State of Lithuania of 11 March 1990	327	1. Main Features of the 1992 Constitution and Its Role in the National Legal Order	353
b) Drafting and Adoption of the Constitution of 1992	330	2. Basic Constitutional Principles Describing the Republic of Lithuania	356
B. The Evolution of the 1992 Constitution: Between the Rigidity and the Flexibility	333	3. Rule of Law and Fundamental Rights	361
		4. Constitutional Organs and Separation of Powers	365
1. Central Role of the CC in Developing the Constitution	333	a) Central Role of the *Seimas* in the Constitutional Setup of Lithuania	366
a) Establishment of the CC and Its Powers	334	b) The President of the Republic	369
		c) The Government	373
b) Jurisprudence of the CC: From the Constitution as a Higher Law to an Inspirator of Legislative Choices	335	d) The Judicial Branch	374
		D. The Lithuanian Constitutional Tradition and the Constitutional Identity	376

A. Origins of the 1992 Constitution of Lithuania

1. The Early Origins of the Lithuanian Constitutionalism

The current Constitution of the Republic of Lithuania was adopted by way of a referendum on 25 October 1992, once Lithuania had its independence restored in 1990 after fifty years of Soviet occupation. It was an unprecedented event—the Baltic States, including Lithuania, were able to regain their independence after a long period of Soviet rule, accompanied by terror and constant attempts to eradicate the national identity.[1] As one author put it, the long

---

[1] On the continuity of the Lithuanian state see Dainius Žalimas, 'Legal issues on the continuity of the Republic of Lithuania' (2001) 1 Baltic Yearbook of International Law 1–22.

Irmantas Jarukaitis, *The Evolution and* Gestalt *of the Lithuanian Constitution* In: *The Max Planck Handbooks in European Public Law*. Edited by: Armin von Bogdandy, Peter M Huber, and Sabrina Ragone, Oxford University Press. © Irmantas Jarukaitis 2023.
DOI: 10.1093/oso/9780198726425.003.0007

320 IRMANTAS JARUKAITIS

moral, political and legal challenge that lasted for more than fifty years ended in a great victory of international law.[2]

However, this restoration of Lithuanian independence, which led to the adoption of the current Constitution, was only one, albeit a very important moment of the modern Lithuanian constitutionalism. Historic circumstances were not very generous in terms of consistent and uninterrupted development of Lithuanian constitutionalism. One may identify two deep ruptures dividing its development: the old (noblemen) constitutional tradition (sixteenth century–1792); modern (interwar) (1918–1940) and contemporary (1990–to date) periods. These periods, to different extents, informed the ideas and the content of the 1992 Constitution. Different from many European states, the Grand Duchy of Lithuania and, after the Lublin Union of 1569, the Polish–Lithuanian Commonwealth did not know the idea of absolute power because they never were absolute monarchies during the Middle Ages.[3] The early origins of Lithuanian constitutionalism may be related to the adoption of the Lithuanian Statutes and some other acts of constitutional nature. The First Statute was adopted in 1529, which was superseded by the Second Statute of 1566 and then by the Third Statute, which was adopted in 1588.[4] The Statutes were the supreme law of the land. Despite being adopted by the king (the First Statute after consulting the Noblemen Council; the Second and the Third Statute after consulting the Sejm), they are treated by the academic doctrine as the Constitutions of the noblemen state[5] because of their aim[6] and content. The nation—the noblemen—played an important role in the governance of the state.[7] The noblemen democracy rested on three main pillars: *liberum veto*,[8] the right to elect a king and the right to confederation.

Alongside the Statutes, the 1569 Lublin Union Act, *pacta conventa* (agreements concluded between the noblemen and newly elected king concerning conditions of governance of the state),[9] 1697 *Coaequetio jurium* Act and the Cardinal Laws of 1768 and 1775 were part of the constitutional order once the Lublin Union Act established the Commonwealth of Two Nations.[10] They have enshrined basic legal principles and rules, which later became inherent features of modern constitutionalism: the supremacy and direct application of the Statutes; origins of noblemen sovereignty and parliamentarism (including direct elections of the Sejm, the performance of legislative function, introduction of taxes, declaration of war,

---

[2] Romain Yakemtchouk, 'Les Républiques Baltes en droit International: Echec d'une annexation opéreé en violation du droit des Gens' (1991) 37 Annuaire Français De Droit International 259–281.

[3] See the recent study by Zenonas Norkus, *An Unproclaimed Empire: The Grand Duchy of Lithuania: From the Viewpoint of Comparative Historical Sociology of Empires* (Routledge, London, 2017).

[4] Although in Poland the Third Statute was treated as 'unconstitutional' (contrary to the 1569 Lublin Union), it was applicable in the territory of Lithuania until 1840.

[5] Vaidotas A Vaičaitis, 'Lietuvos statutai kaip Lietuvos konstitutionalizmo šaltinis' (2013) 89 Teisė/Mokslo darbai, 55–68; Jevgenij Machovenko, 'Piliečio ir valstybės santykiai 1791 m. gegužės 3 d. Konstitucijoje: paveldas ir pamoka', in Egidijus Kūris and Elena Masnevaitė (eds), *Lietuvos Respublikos Konstitucijos dvidešimtmetis: patirtis ir iššūkiai* (Lietuvos notarų rūmai, Vilnius, 2012) 8–9.

[6] Alongside other aims (consolidation of the legal system; strengthening of the legal status of the noblemen vis-á-vis the king), the Statutes sought the establishment of the sovereignty of law, especially given the fact that at that time kings haven't resided in the territory of Lithuania for more than 100 years, see Vaidotas Vaičaitis, 'Lietuvos statutai kaip Lietuvos konstitutionalizmo šaltinis' (n 5) 58.

[7] Noblemen accounted for approximately ten per cent of the population. Davies called such state organization a 'noblemen democracy', see Norman Davies, *Goa's Playground: A History of Poland in two volumes. Volume I. The origins to 1795* (Columbia University Press, New York, 1981).

[8] The right of *liberum veto* of noblemen meant that every act of the Sejm had to be passed unanimously. Later it proved particularly detrimental to the effective governance of the state: Alfonsas Eidintas and others, *The History of Lithuania* (Eugrimas, Vilnius, 2015) 84.

[9] The first *pacta conventa* was concluded with the elected king Henrik Valua.

[10] Jevgenij Machovenko, '1791 metų Abiejų Tautų Respublikos Konstitucija', in Dainius Žalimas (ed), *Lietuvos Konstitucionalizmas. Ištakos, Raida ir Dabartis* (Lietuvos Respublikos Konstitucinis Teismas, Vilnius, 2018) 47.

nomination of certain state officials by the parliament); the rule of law; a court as an institution of justice, including the principles of independence of judges and requirements for their impeccable reputation; the principle *nemo debet esse iudex in propria causa*; and *status libertatis* guaranties.

Lithuanian authors analysed these acts mostly from the perspective of legal history. Still, they are mentioned as the 'legal foundations' in the Preamble of the 1992 Constitution and some studies treat them as early origins of Lithuanian constitutionalism.[11] The Statutes did not have direct impact on the contents of the 1992 Constitution but are viewed as reflections of the continuous development of the statehood and the legal tradition of Lithuania.

Another important milestone is the Polish–Lithuanian Commonwealth assuming a position at the forefront of modern European constitutionalism. The Polish–Lithuanian Commonwealth adopted the first modern European Constitution—the Constitution of 3 May 1791,[12] later supplemented by the Mutual Pledge of Two Nations of 20 October 1791.[13] Its drafting and adoption was predetermined by the necessity to address the inefficiencies of the governance of the state[14] that led to its demise and inability to compete with neighbouring powers.[15] No doubt, the 1791 Constitution was influenced by the external constitutional thought of those times,[16] however, first and foremost, it was the product of an internal constitutional tradition that developed over 200 years.

Adopted four months earlier than the Constitution of France of 1791, it was, however, not as radical as the US or the French Constitutions. It did not abolish the serfdom of peasants and it granted civic rights only to certain categories of townspeople, thus, the system of estates was not completely abandoned. The 1791 Constitution was based on the idea of sovereignty of the nation (consisting of noblemen[17] and townspeople[18]). Further, the principle of election of a king was abandoned in favour of hereditary monarchy. Thus, it may not be labelled as a revolutionary constitution and, to some extent, it followed the evolutionary path as laid down by the earlier constitutional tradition.

On the other hand, the main ingredients of the modern constitutionalism were part of it and, therefore, it may be considered the turning point marking the transition from the old system of noblemen governance to the modern period of Enlightenment. The Constitution established the classic principle of division of public power. The legislative function and adoption of the most important decisions (budget, taxation, declaration of war, etc.) was

---

[11] Vaidotas Vaičaitis, 'Lietuvos statutai kaip Lietuvos konstitutionalizmo šaltinis' (n 5) 55–68. However, the idea, that the Constitution of 1992 is not only the outcome of the current political processes, but the reflection of the longstanding Lithuanian legal tradition, is not new: Stasys Stačiokas, 'Mykolas Römeris ir mūsų dienų Lietuva', in Mykolas Römeris, *Konstitucinės ir teismo teisės pasieniuose* (ALF 1994) IV.

[12] Academic community points to the composite nature of the Constitution. The Constitution of 3 May 1791 itself (the Law on Government ('*Valdymo įstatymas*', '*Ustawa Rządowa*'), the Law on Cardinal Rights of 8 January 1791, the Law on the Dietines of 24 March 1791, the Law of the Towns of 18 April 1791, and the Mutual Pledge of Two Nations of 20 October 1791). See the text of the Constitution with related acts and comments in Polish, Lithuanian, and English: Juliusz Bardach, *Konstytucja 3 Maja 1791. 1791 gegužės 3-osios Konstitucija. The Constitution of 3 May 1791* (Wydawn. Sejmowe, Warszawa, 2001).

[13] In some texts, the name of the Pledge ('*Zaręczenie wzajemne obojga narodów*'; '*Abiejų Tautų tarpusavio įžadas*') is translated as 'The Mutual Guarantee of Two Nations'.

[14] Drafters of the Constitution, Hugo Kolontaj, Józef Vybickis, Stanislaw Stašic, and Ignacy Potackis were active supporters of ideas of the Enlightenment.

[15] Alfonsas Eidintas and others, *The History of Lithuania* (n 8) 108–116. The 1791 Constitution was adopted already after the First Partition of the Commonwealth, undertaken by Austria, Prussia, and Russia in 1772.

[16] Jevgenij Machovenko, '1791 metų Abiejų Tautų Respublikos Konstitucija' (n 10) 152–158.

[17] The 1791 Constitution abolished the most important rights of the noblemen: the right to elect the king, *liberum veto* and the right to form confederations.

[18] Some argue that the term 'nation' in the Constitution of 1791 refers not only to noblemen and townsmen, but to peasants as well: Alfonsas Eidintas and others, *The History of Lithuania* (n 8) 108.

entrusted to the two-chamber parliament, chaired by the king, although his legislative powers were limited. By establishment of the principles of majority and equality, the nation was transformed into the main engine of modernization and the source of legitimacy of public power. The executive power was vested with the king and the government. They were called the Guardians of Laws. Importantly enough, the Law on Government established the elements of control of the executive by the parliament—ministers had the obligation to submit information on their activities to it and could be removed from the office by a two-thirds majority. The Law on Government explicitly provided that the judicial power may not be performed by the legislative or the executive, therefore, the separate court system was established.

Thus, the Constitution managed to lay the basis for a strong (but by no means absolute) and efficient system of public authority that focused on the parliament and the king. From a geopolitical perspective, the 1791 Constitution should be seen not only as a step of transformation of the internal structure of public power, but as a necessary move in order to ensure de facto independence vis-á-vis neighbours of the Commonwealth.

Speaking of the constitutional values enshrined in the Constitution, the sole fact of its adoption may be treated as a reflection of the rule of law. It established its own supremacy over ordinary laws, the principle of limited public powers and the principle of justice. It was based on the principle of the sovereignty of the nation, the Sejm was elected, and, although the term 'republic' (*rzeczpospolita*) was mainly used as a synonymous of the term 'state', one may find some origins where this term is used as referring to the true republican, democratic ideals.

Due to historical circumstances (the Third Partition of the Commonwealth led to the loss of the statehood, wiping out one of the biggest European states of those times), the Constitution was renounced fourteen months later. Thus, its impact on later development of constitutionalism was limited.[19] However, it was vividly discussed in other European countries, translated into both French and English the year of its adoption, and, in 1821, the Italian translation followed. Positive comments stressed the modern content of the Constitution and the peaceful nature of the 'gentle revolution'. However, given the danger for neighbours stemming from the modern reforms, the adoption of the Constitution was, without any doubt, one of the reasons for the further partition of the Commonwealth. The price for being at the epicentre of the first wave constitutionalism was especially high.[20]

For a long time, the attitude of Lithuanian historians, lawyers and politicians to the 1791 Constitution was at best cautious, but mainly negative. It was not a coincidence that, different from the Lithuanian Statutes, the 1791 Constitution is not mentioned in the Preamble of the 1992 Constitution. Whereas in Poland it had always been treated as a genuine part of the Polish legal heritage, the predominant view in Lithuania persisted that it symbolized the end of Lithuanian statehood, because the Law on Government turned the federal Commonwealth, established by the Lublin Union, into the unitary state of Poland.

Such an approach was contested by stressing several aspects of the 1791 Constitution and its adoption circumstances.[21] *Travaux préparatoires* of the Constitution reveal that initially

---

[19] Egidijus Jarašiūnas, 'Apie pirmąsias konstitucijas ir jų reikšmę' (2010) 120 (2) Jurisprudencija 23–51. Nevertheless, later Polish and Lithuanian uprisings against Russia in the nineteenth century took their inspiration from the 1791 Constitution and the Statutes.

[20] As Catherine II of Russia has put it, 'the Poles have surpassed the frenzy of the French National Assembly' and has formulated the task of Targovica confederation as 'stamping out the revolutionary plague in Warsaw'.

[21] Stasys Stačiokas, 'Europos konstitucijų eros pradžia Lietuvoje' (2013) 3 (31) Konstitucinė jurisprudencija 216–223.

the Four-Year Sejm favoured the continuation of the Lublin Union tradition, but the text that was finally adopted avoids mentioning the Commonwealth, the Grand Duchy and mainly speaks of homeland, native land and Poland. Still, those who treat the 1791 Constitution as part of the Lithuanian constitutional tradition point to the fact that a majority of the delegates of the Four-Year Sejm from the Grand Duchy voted in favour of the adoption of the Law of the Government. The majority (thirty-three) of *dietines* (local parliaments) of the Grand Duchy swore an oath to or approved the new Constitution in 1792. The Constitution was translated into the Lithuanian language; actually, it was the first political and legal document ever published in Lithuanian. The most powerful arguments come from the contents of the Mutual Pledge of the Two Nations. It was passed unanimously by the Sejm[22] and explicitly restored the dualism of Lithuanian and Polish Commonwealth, that is, the idea of the union of two nations.[23]

Of course, both the process and the result the 1791 Constitution should be viewed as part of a bigger picture. That bigger picture is the trajectory of transformations in Europe during those times. Regretfully, Lithuania could not continue on this trajectory and its further evolution was interrupted for more than hundred years, when the state of Lithuania was reborn with its new identity (as a national state) based on ethnicity.

Recently, one may detect some gradual changes of attitude towards the 1791 Constitution in Lithuania. Paradoxically, there were Polish historians, especially Juliusz Bardach, who 'discovered' the 1791 Constitution for Lithuania. The academic community completed several studies of the 1791 Constitution as part of Lithuanian constitutional tradition, while the parliament of Lithuania adopted two resolutions (in 2007 and 2011) which recognized the 1791 Constitution as part of the common historical legacy of Lithuania and Poland.

Certain parallels may be drawn between the constitutional heritage of the Commonwealth and the ongoing discussions concerning the nature of EU integration and its further direction. After the Lublin Union, the single Parliament of the Commonwealth of the two nations functioned for more than 200 years and ceased to exist only after the interference of foreign forces, although its success was mixed. The Pledge reconfirmed the existence of two nations under the roof of the single Constitution. Thus, the constitutional tolerance that was part of the Commonwealth could be seen as distant forerunners of *sui generis* EU constitutionalism, which is also not based on the idea of the single European *demos*, but the principle of tolerance to other identities—the respect of national identity being at the core of EU constitutional architecture. In those times, geopolitical challenges could not be overcome only at the national level, they also stimulated the regional integration. The same pressure on Europe is felt nowadays by geopolitical tensions and the forces of globalization. This pressure and unique nature of European integration process, as a peace plan, begs for convincing concepts of legitimacy for the exercise of public power at the EU level. On a more technical level, the unanimity requirement, still applicable in some areas of decision making within the Council, distantly echoes *liberum veto* as the expression of sovereign power and does not foster the atmosphere for compromise seeking on important issues.

---

[22] The draft of the Pledge was introduced before the Sejm by K N Sapiega.

[23] It explicitly recognized 'the laudable and desirable relationship between our Two Nations, which was by the Act of Union created forever by our ancestors, and many times confirmed by the common agreement of the Polish Crown and the Grand Duchy of Lithuania'. Thus, it reflected the federal nature of the state and, what is equally important, asserted the equal representation within the bodies of state governance of its two constituents.

2. Evolution of the Lithuanian Constitutionalism during the Interwar Period

The Third Partition took away Lithuanian statehood for more than hundred years, but it was not able to eradicate the national self-awareness. Two unsuccessful uprisings (1830–1831 and 1863–1864) took place against the Russian rule and led, among other things, to the closure of Vilnius University, the abolishment of the Third Statute, the prohibition of Lithuanian press and Lithuanian language in schools. However, the direction of development of the European intellectual thinking, predetermined by the Spring of Nations, was already too strong to resist.[24] The First World War (the territory of Lithuania was occupied by Germany) created a favourable geopolitical and international context for pursuing the cause of independence of Lithuania.

Through long-running efforts of Lithuanian intelligentsia, the Act of Independence of Lithuania of 16 February 1918 was unanimously adopted and proclaimed[25] by the Council of Lithuania.[26] The Act[27] marked the reestablishment of the independent state[28] and laid down the basis of the modern legal system. It not only proclaimed the independence of Lithuania, but it also included the elements that marked the continuity between the re-established Lithuania and the Grand Duchy of Lithuania.[29]

The Act of Independence is of special importance to the Lithuanian constitutional thinking. It later served as the constitutional basis for adoption of the acts of an equally fundamental nature (first of all, the Act on the re-establishment of the Independent State of Lithuania of 11 March 1990 and the Constitutional Act on the Non-Alignment of the Republic of Lithuania to Post-Soviet Eastern Unions of 8 June 1992). Because of its founding nature, it is treated by Lithuanian academic doctrine as a metaconstitutional document that established the core constitutional values of Lithuanian constitutional system.

Once independence was proclaimed, the Republic of Lithuania experienced a short interwar period of its further constitutional tradition, which was rich and diverse. In terms

[24] The end of the nineteenth to the beginning of the twentieth century marks the emergence of the national ideology, with Lithuanian press being at the heart of it.

[25] The Council of Lithuania, as the sole representative of the Lithuanian nation, based on the right to national self-determination, proclaimed the restoration of the independent state of Lithuania, founded on democratic principles, with Vilnius as its capital, and declared the termination of all state ties which had formerly bound it to other nations. The Council authorized a democratically elected Constituent Assembly to finalize the process of defining the foundations of the Lithuanian state and its international relations with other states. See the English translation of the Act.

[26] The Council of Lithuania was elected by the Congress of Lithuania, which took place in 1917 and consisted of twenty members, seven of them were lawyers. The Council was chaired by Jonas Basanavičius, prominent intellectual, and active promoter of the cause of Lithuanian independence.

[27] The Act refers to 'the Lithuanian nation' and its right of self-determination, but this notion of the nation should be understood as historic Lithuanian nation, not the civic nation (there was no state) or the noblemen nation of the eighteenth century, which mainly spoke Polish. All members of the Council were Lithuanian speaking intellectuals, coming from the ethnic Lithuanian lands.

[28] In Poland, the idea of reestablishment of the Polish–Lithuanian Commonwealth, that existed before the Third Partition, had a wide support. In Lithuania the perception was already different, the new generation of Lithuanian intellectuals of the end of the nineteenth/ beginning of the twentieth century promoting the idea of the independent state of Lithuania. The proclamation of the Act of Independence and inability to find a compromise resulted in military conflict with Poland and the loss of Vilnius in 1919, the issue that dominated the interwar Lithuanian–Polish tense relations. Unfortunately, the longstanding political and cultural cooperation between two nations was replaced by confrontation.

[29] The act speaks about the restoration (liet. *atstatanti*) of the statehood with Vilnius as the capital (such provision was included in the Third Statute). Thus, the Act sought to reconcile the continuity of the state tradition with the new identity of the re-established state.

of the evolution of the constitutional thinking, it basically coincided with the second wave of European constitutionalism, and, as in the rest of Europe, it was a twisted one.

The Act of Independence was followed by two temporary constitutions. When the Constituent *Seimas* was elected in 1920,[30] it passed the Resolution on 15 May 1920, according to which the *Seimas* 'expressing the will of the Lithuanian people, hereby proclaims that the independent state of Lithuania shall be restored as a democratic republic within its ethnological borders and free from any bonds that have ever existed with other states'. Through this document, the Constituent *Seimas* not only reaffirmed the re-establishment of the statehood, but proclaimed the republican form of the governance, thus finalizing the establishment of the First Republic of Lithuania.[31]

The first permanent Constitution was adopted by the Constituent *Seimas* on 1 August 1922. It was a modern constitution based on the principles of the rule of law and the separation of powers, thereby reflecting the democratic principles of the Third French Republic. The 1922 Constitution rested on the principle of people's sovereignty.[32] It established the parliamentary republic, and for the first time, Lithuanian language gained constitutional status. The principle of separation of public powers was expressly enshrined in the Constitution. The governance was dominated by the *Seimas*, which was elected by citizens[33] for a three-year term. It performed the classic functions of the parliament. The executive power was vested with the President and the Cabinet of Ministers.[34] The law of the *Seimas* established the court system.[35]

The Constitution explicitly established its own supremacy over other sources of law.[36] Chapter II of the Constitution was devoted to fundamental rights and freedoms. It established the principle of equality and prohibition of discrimination based on origin, religion, and ethnicity, thus including the classic personal and political rights and freedoms, although they were guaranteed only to citizens. Additionally, for the first time, it included provisions concerning the social protection of citizens in case of illness, old age, unemployment, and accidents, protection of maternity. Furthermore, article 81 prescribed the establishment of the obligatory elementary education in Lithuania. Finally, Chapter VII provided for broad autonomy of ethnic minorities who lived in Lithuania.

To sum up, the 1922 Constitution marks one of the most important milestones in the modern history of Lithuanian constitutionalism and it made the huge impact on the later constitutional culture and the 1992 Constitution. It is treated as the Act of the Nation, the most important constitution of the interwar Lithuania. The academic doctrine supports the thesis that it was a successful reflection of the needs of society of those times, a true

---

[30] It was the first parliament, elected by direct, democratic, universal, equal, and secret suffrage.

[31] Besides, the Constituent *Seimas* adopted the temporary Constitution of 2 June 1920, because after its election, the powers of the State Council and other state institutions, conferred to them by the earlier mentioned Constitutional Acts, have expired.

[32] Here the nation is already understood as a civic nation, since the Preamble of the Constitution refers to the nation, in the name of which the earlier mentioned temporary constitutions were adopted.

[33] The active right of elections was granted to all Lithuanian citizens (men and women) from the age of twenty-one, the passive right of elections from the age of twenty-four.

[34] The President was elected by the *Seimas* for a three-year term and could be removed from the office by a two-thirds majority of the *Seimas*. He formed the government and was the Chief Commander of the Army.

[35] According to art 68, courts had the power to decide on the legality of administrative acts, but this provision was a dead letter, since courts did not dare to directly apply this provision, because there was no law, laying down detailed provisions implementing this constitutional provision.

[36] A three-fifths majority of the *Seimas* was required in order to pass the constitutional amendment.

326 IRMANTAS JARUKAITIS

compromise between different social groups of Lithuania.[37] As will be seen, some aspects of the 1992 Constitution are clear reflections of the constitutional heritage of 1922.

The later constitutional path of interwar Lithuania was less bright. Although the 1922 Constitution laid down the guidelines and provisions as regards the future evolution of Lithuanian constitutional tradition, this development was interrupted by a *coup d'état* in 1926.[38] The coup caused a series of constitutional problems, which then negatively impacted the coherent and meaningful course of constitutionalism. The 1928 Constitution was proclaimed without following the procedure that was prescribed by the 1922 Constitution[39] and it paved the way to authoritarian tendencies.[40] It strengthened the powers of the President and ensured his dominance over the *Seimas*. De facto elections of the *Seimas* took place only in 1936 and they were not democratic. The President could dissolve the *Seimas* at will and decide when to hold elections. When the *Seimas* was not in session, the State Council was empowered to draft and debate legislation, but only the President had the power to enact laws. The President was to be elected for seven years by a select group of national representatives, and he was to personally oversee all appointments and dismissals. In effect, the constitution formalized the existing situation because it legalized the authoritarian regime of the President.

Finally, the last interwar Constitution of 12 May 1938 cemented the authoritarian rule by wiping out the remaining elements of democratic rule and establishing the cult of the President of the State. It was based on the idea of the state as the perfect form of the nations' freedom and subordinated the citizens to the state. This trajectory of the interwar constitutionalism, although interrupted again by the events of 1939–1940, later made a substantial impact on the drafting of the current 1992 Constitution, especially on the question concerning the role of the Parliament, the President and the Government and the balance of powers of those institutions being at the core of discussions.

With the Molotov-Ribbentrop Pact signed in 1939, Lithuania was brought into the sphere of interests of the USSR. The invasion of the Soviet Union in 1940 resulted again in the loss of the independence of Lithuania for the next fifty years. However, the armed resistance for the independence, still being largely unknown to the Western societies,[41] was far from over and it continued both during the Second World War and long after the end of it.[42] From the point

[37] Mindaugas Maksimaitis, 'Konstitucijų legitimumo problemos tarpukario Lietuvoje' (2013) 1 Konstitucinė jurisprudencija 339, 344.

[38] After three years of rule by the Christian Democratic bloc, it lost the parliamentary elections in 1926. A new coalition was formed for the first time by the left. From autumn of 1926 onward, the opposition began to speak more frequently about the threat communism posed to Lithuania's independence. The government was blamed for not controlling the communists because the number of security police and intelligence personnel had been reduced. The army stepped into the political arena. On the morning of 17 December 1926, a group of army officers led their troops into the city and posted guards at key government buildings. They dismissed the *Seimas* and arrested the President, all ministers, and several *Seimas* members. The same day Antanas Smetona, the first President of the Republic and leader of the National Unionists (he was the member of the Council of Lithuania adopting the Act of Independence of 16 February 1918), was asked to be the new President and he agreed. President Kazys Grinius agreed to step down, believing that a new government would yet abide by the Constitution.

[39] The Constitution was announced by the President 'with the unanimous support of all cabinet ministers' on 15 May 1928. As a mitigation of its lack of a constitutional legitimacy, art 106 of the Constitution, stating that the nation should be consulted as regards the Constitution, not later than ten years after its adoption, was inserted, although not followed in practice.

[40] Given its form of adoption the proclamation of the Constitution of 1928 was treated as another coup by the academic doctrine: Mindaugas Maksimaitis, 'Konstitucijų legitimumo problemos tarpukario Lietuvoje' (n 37) 346.

[41] For main facts and figures: Dainius Žalimas, 'Legal status of Lithuania's armed resistance to the Soviet occupation in the context of state continuity' (2011) 11 (1) Baltic Yearbook of International Law 67–112.

[42] The organized military resistance lasted until 1953; the last active resistance fighter fell in 1965, while the last hiding partisan managed to escape arrest and came from his hideout at the very end of his life in 1986, only a year before the first large anti-Soviet demonstration of 23 August 1987 took place in Vilnius. Historians count that

of view of constitutional tradition and its continuity, the Declaration of the Council of the Lithuanian Freedom Fight Movement[43] of 16 February 1949 is of particular importance.[44] It subscribed to the ideas of the 1922 Constitution and reflected the principles of modern constitutionalism. Although the contents of the Declaration remained only a vision until 1990, it is of particular significance both from the point of view of public international law as one of reflections of continuity of the statehood of Lithuania[45] and, at the same time, forms the part of the heritage of Lithuanian constitutional tradition, being the organic element in the system of the founding constitutional documents of Lithuania alongside the Acts of Independence of 16 February 1918 and 11 March 1990.[46]

3. Re-establishment of the Independence and Adoption of the 1992 Constitution

During the Soviet rule, the Soviet Republic of Lithuania had its 'own' 'constitutions', however, one may not seriously consider that period as being part of a common constitutional heritage of nowadays Lithuania both because of the fact of the annexation and because the content of those documents was alien to the constitutional ideals of the Western civilization.

a) Events of 1987–1990 and Adoption of the Act on the Re-establishment of the State of Lithuania of 11 March 1990

The main events setting the scene for the restoration of the independence of Lithuania and paving the way to the adoption of the 1992 Constitution started in 1987, although the resistance to the Soviet rule continued in different forms during all periods of occupation.[47] One of the most important developments triggering the restoration of the independence was the establishment of an 'initiative group' of the Lithuanian Reform Movement (*Sąjūdis*) by a group of Lithuanian intellectuals in the hall of the Lithuanian Academy of Science on 3 June 1988. With deep roots in Lithuanian society,[48] *Sąjūdis* instantly became the main driving force in the process of the re-establishing of independence.[49] Even before elections of 1990,

---

every third adult Lithuanian was victimized by the Soviet genocide: Alfonsas Eidintas and others, *The History of Lithuania* (n 8) 249–256.

[43] It took several years to consolidate different territorial formations of partisan resistance. The aim was achieved in 1949, when the meeting of all chiefs of military formations was convened. These chiefs elected the Council of the Lithuanian Freedom Fight Movement.

[44] English translation of the Declaration available at http://www.lrkt.lt/en/legal-information/lithuanias-indep endence-acts/declaration-of-the-council-of-the-lithuanian-freedom-fight-movement/364 (last accessed on 22 March 2022).

[45] Dainius Žalimas, 'Legal Status of Lithuania's Armed Resistance to the Soviet Occupation in the Context of State Continuity' (n 41) 92.

[46] Lina Griškevič and others, *Lietuvos konstitucionalizmo istorija: Istorinė Lietuvos konstitucija: 1387 m. —1566 m. —1791 m. —1990 m* (Vilniaus universiteto leidykla, Vilnius, 2016) 244–245.

[47] For a chronology of main events of 1985–1992 in the Baltic states: Anatol Lieven, *The Baltic Revolution. Estonia, Latvia, Lithuania and the Path to Independence* (Yale University Press, New Haven, 1994) 426–431.

[48] There were already 1,200 *Sąjūdis* groups with 300,000 members by the end of September 1988.

[49] Initial demands were more distant from 'pure' politics (to recognize Lithuanian as official language, to teach Lithuanian history as the main subject of history, etc.), but it rapidly turned to questions of restoration of national symbols, demands for broad reforms of society based on the humanist ideals, and public denouncement of the Molotov–Ribbentrop pact. 23 August 1989 witnessed a protest campaign—the Baltic Way—to mark the fiftieth anniversary of the signing of the Molotov–Ribbentrop pact. Two million people formed a chain stretching 670km from Vilnius to Tallinn. The next day *Sąjūdis* announced that it would seek total independence of Lithuania through parliamentary processes.

during which time the majority at the Supreme Council of the Lithuanian SSR was held by the communist party, amendments were made to the Constitution of the Lithuanian SSR from 1988 to 1990 that designated Lithuanian as national language, legalized the pre-Soviet Lithuanian national anthem and national tri-colour flag, abolished the 'leading role of the communist party', and declared supremacy of Lithuanian laws over those of the USSR.[50]

The new elections to the Supreme Council, which were the first truly free and democratic elections in Lithuania during the last fifty years, took place in February–March 1990 and two main political forces—*Sąjūdis* and the Communist Party of Lithuania confronted each other.[51] The main slogan of *Sąjūdis* was '*vote for candidates of Sąjūdis, vote for Independence*' and aggressive agitation secured its absolute majority (ninety-six out of 133 MPs elected) in the new Supreme Council.[52] A group of *Sąjūdis* deputies had prepared the set of documents for the immediate restoration of the independence of Lithuania.

On 11 March 1990, the Supreme Council of the Lithuanian SSR was renamed to the Supreme Council of the Republic of Lithuania changing both the name of the institution and reinstating Lithuania's old state name. The same evening the Supreme Council adopted the Act on the Re-establishment of the State of Lithuania by absolute majority of votes (124 votes 'for', no votes 'against' and six abstentions).[53]

The main source of inspiration for the drafters of the Act of the Re-establishment of the State was without any doubt the 1918 Act of Independence. The text of the Act of 11 March 1990 also reflects the aspiration to emphasize the continuity of the Lithuanian state despite the Soviet occupation. It speaks about the fact that 'the execution of the sovereign powers of the State of Lithuania abolished by foreign forces in 1940 is re-established' and asserts that 'henceforth Lithuania is again an independent state'.[54] The Act reflects the idea of the continuity of the statehood. According to the Act, it is not the State that is re-established, but only the execution of the sovereign powers. Further, alongside the adoption of the Act of 11 March, the next immediate step was the adoption of the Law on the Reinstatement of the Validity of the Last Pre-war Constitution of the Then Independent Republic of Lithuania— the Constitution of 12 May 1938.[55] The Law complemented the formal logic in order to emphasize the continuity of the state. However, it was obvious that the social, political and legal environment was profoundly different than before the Second World War and the 1938 Constitution was not able to perform its functions. Therefore, on the same day, the Supreme Council adopted a law suspending the validity of the Constitution of 12 May 1938 and approving the Provisional Basic Law, which was applicable until the entry into force of the 1992 Constitution.[56] As its name suggests, the Provisional Basic Law was seen as a temporary

---

[50] Algirdas Jakubčionis, 'Sąjūdis. Siekis Atkurti Nepriklausomą Lietuvą' in Lietuvos Respublikos Konstitucinis Teismas (ed), *Lietuvos Konstitucionalizmas. Ištakos, Raida ir Dabartis* (Vilnius, 2018) 124–129.

[51] In fact, more political parties and organisations participated in the elections.

[52] Seventy-two per cent of those, having the right to vote, participated in the elections.

[53] See the English translation of the Act at http://www.lrkt.lt/en/legal-information/lithuanias-independence-acts/act-of-11-march/366 (last accessed on 22 March 2022).

[54] Most Western countries had followed a consistent practice of non-recognition of the annexation of the Baltic countries. Such non-recognition has played an important role in treating the Act of 11 March 1990 as the act of re-establishment of Lithuania.

[55] The Act mentions namely the 1922 Constitution as a source of inspiration, because of the authoritarian nature of the 1938 Constitution. However, when Lithuania was annexed in 1940, the 1922 Constitution was already abolished, thus, the 1938 Constitution was the last pre-war Constitution of Lithuania. The Law terminated the validity of constitutional acts of the Lithuanian SSR and validity of Soviet Union acts in the territory of Lithuania and reinstated the validity of the 1938 Constitution. The Law stated as well that the restatement of the 1938 Constitution does not automatically reinstate the validity of laws, which were in force before 15 June 1940.

[56] It was impossible to evaluate the compatibility of all applicable legislation vis-à-vis the Provisional Basic Law during the short period, thus, it established a general rule that all legal acts of Lithuania were valid to the extent they were compatible with the Provisional Basic Law.

THE EVOLUTION AND *GESTALT* OF THE LITHUANIAN CONSTITUTION   329

solution. Although it established many features of typical Western constitutions such as basic human rights, respect for private property, multiparty system, etc., and was therefore profoundly different from the constitutions of the Lithuanian SSR, its structure, concepts and formulations echoed the long-lasting Soviet heritage.[57] One of the reasons of such content was the need to ensure its operability given the huge body of legislation adopted during the Soviet rule.

Adoption of the Act of 11 March 1990 opened the new chapter, the chapter of contemporary Lithuanian constitutionalism. However, de facto consolidation of the independence was far from being over. Various attempts to disrupt Lithuania's statehood were made by the Soviet Union[58] after 11 March reaching the most brutal and outrageous form on 13 January 1991 when the Soviet forces opened fire to civilians leaving fourteen dead and more than 1000 wounded.[59] These events made the imprint on the development of the constitutional law of Lithuania and had the impact on the content of 1992 Constitution. Faced with this course of events, the Supreme Council adopted two further acts, which later became the cornerstones of the 1992 Constitution: the Constitutional Law of the Republic of Lithuania on the State of Lithuania of 11 February 1991[60] and the Constitutional Act of the Republic of Lithuania on the Non-Alignment of the Republic of Lithuania to Post-Soviet Eastern Unions of 8 June 1992.[61]

---

[57] Egidijus Kūris, 'Konstitucija, teisėkūra ir konstitucinė kontrolė: retrospekciniai ir metodologiniai svarstymai', in Egidijus Kūris and Elena Masnevaitė (eds), *Lietuvos Respublikos Konstitucijos dvidešimtmetis: patirtis ir iššūkiai* (Lietuvos notarų rūmai, Vilnius, 2012) 61.

[58] Formally, it ceased to exist on 31 December 1991.

[59] After the proclamation of the independence, the Soviet Union deployed additional armed forces to Lithuania and started its economic blockade. When these actions did not persuade the Supreme Council to renounce the Act of 11 March 1990, Michail Gorbachev adopted a decree allowing the Soviet army to use the force in order to ensure forced conscriptions of Lithuanians to the Soviet army on 1 December 1991. Finally, he sent the ultimatum to the 'Supreme Council of the Lithuanian SSR' demanding the renouncement of the Act of 11 March and the restoration of application of the Constitution of USSR in Lithuania. The Supreme Council responded it had neither the right nor mandate of the peoples to do that. After that, the Soviet army attacked various objects in Vilnius that were surrounded by civilians. Because of negative reactions to those events by democratic states, there were no attempts to attack the building of the Supreme Council, which was surrounded by civilians as well.

[60] The massacre of 13 January prompted the Supreme Council to adopt a decision of 16 January 1991 organizing a plebiscite. It took place on 9 February 1991 and people were asked a question, whether they support the drafting of a new constitution, based on the fundamental thesis, that Lithuania is an independent democratic republic. Of more than 2.2 million of those who took part (84.43 per cent of all voters), more than three-quarters (90.47 per cent) supported this thesis. This result inspired the Supreme Council to adopt the above-mentioned Constitutional Law consisting of two articles proclaiming that 'the statement 'The State of Lithuania shall be an independent democratic republic' is a constitutional norm of the Republic of Lithuania and a fundamental principle of the State' and that 'the constitutional norm and the fundamental principle of the State as formulated in the first article of this Law may be altered only by a general poll (plebiscite) of the Nation of Lithuania provided that not less than three-quarters of the citizens of Lithuania with the active electoral right vote in favour thereof'. Adoption of the Constitutional Law coincided with the first international recognition of the reestablishment of independence, which was done by Iceland's Alþing. It took another seven months for other states to follow suit: after the failure of the Moscow putsch, all the world's major countries recognized Lithuania as part of the international community during August 1991.

[61] Although Belavezha Accords of 8 December 1991 declared the dismantlement of the Soviet Union, it established the Commonwealth of the Independent States in which some of the former Soviet Union republics decided to participate. Faced with various efforts and suggestions to become the member of the CIS and wishing to dispel all doubts about that the Supreme Council adopted the Constitutional Act on 8 June 1992, proclaiming that Lithuania resolves to 'develop mutually advantageous relations with each state that was formerly a component of the USSR, but never join, in any form, any new political, military, economic, or other unions or commonwealths of states formed on the basis of the former USSR'. Further, art 3 of the Act states that 'there may be no military bases or army units of Russia, or the Commonwealth of Independent States or its constituent states, on the territory of the Republic of Lithuania'. At the time of adoption of the Act (and the 1992 Constitution) the Russian army was still in the territory of Lithuania and its withdrawal was subjected to heated negotiations. The last Russian troops left Lithuania on 31 August 1993, already after the adoption of the 1992 Constitution. The Constitutional Act had the impact on the content of art 137 ('there may not be any weapons of mass destruction and foreign military bases on the territory of the Republic of Lithuania') of the Constitution and later served the CC as one of the cornerstones of

b) Drafting and Adoption of the Constitution of 1992

Although the Provisional Basic Law functioned for more than two years, its halfway nature and rapid changes within a society quickly revealed deficiencies and predetermined the necessity for its numerous amendments.[62]

The idea to draft an entirely new constitution, based on the liberal values, emerged already before the reestablishment of Lithuanian independence. The Plenum of the Supreme Council of the Lithuanian SSR formed a working group with the task to improve the constitutional legislation on 22 June 1988. The working group prepared the qualitatively new draft of a constitution, which was supported by *Sąjūdis*. It was presented for deliberation to the Supreme Council, but the Council never discussed it because of its apparently radical nature. This prompted *Sąjūdis* to declare it would further refine the draft on its own.[63] Thus, the idea of a new constitution was clearly linked with the quest for the restoration of the statehood.

Once Lithuania regained its independence, it took two years to draft a text, which was meant to become a new constitution.[64] First, the Supreme Council formed a working group on 7 November 1990. The Group produced the outline of a constitution that reflected the main principles of a democratic republic.[65] Although the Supreme Council did not formally discuss the outline, it was submitted to public discussions in the media and made an impact on further discussions on direction of constitutional developments and contents of the 1992 Constitution.[66] Further, the Supreme Council decree paved the way for the establishment of a temporary commission for drafting of a constitution (further, the Temporary Commission)[67] and a working group (composed of lawyers[68]) which was given the task of drafting a new constitution, which should be based on the results of discussions on the earlier mentioned outline. The first draft of a constitution was produced on 26 February 1992. It was translated into English and intensively discussed in the US in different formats and institutions.[69] The Temporary Commission approved the draft prepared by the working group and it was submitted to the Supreme Council for discussions. However, three members

---

jurisprudence concerning Lithuania's membership in the NATO and for development of the constitutional principle of geo-politic orientation.

[62] Egidijus Kūris, 'Konstitucija, teisėkūra ir konstitucinė kontrolė: retrospekciniai ir metodologiniai svarstymai' (n 57) 59–68.

[63] The draft was based on the principle of sovereignty of Lithuania. It contained provisions concerning the establishment of the CC, these provisions were to a major extent carried over to the 1992 Constitution.

[64] The synthesis of historic events and the process of drafting of the 1992 Constitution is made on the basis of the following articles: Juozas Žilys, 'Kelias į Lietuvos Respublikos Konstituciją: pagrindiniai teisiniai politiniai ženklai' (2012) 2 Nepriklausomybės sąsiuviniai 6–25; Vytautas Sinkevičius, '1992 m. Konstitucijos rengimas: to laikotarpio užrašų fragmentai', in Egidijus Kūris and Elena Masnevaitė (eds), *Lietuvos Respublikos Konstitucijos dvidešimtmetis: patirtis ir iššūkiai* (Druka, Klaipėda, 2012) 19–29; Jonas Prapiestis, 'Valstybingumo atkūrimo ir konstitucinio įtvirtinimo ištakose' (2012) 19 (3) Jurisprudencija 859–888.

[65] The group was composed of Vytautas Landsbergis (the Chairman, later became the Chairman of the Supreme Council of 1990–1992 and 1996–2000), Juozas Bulavas, Algimantas Dziegoraitis, Juozas Galginaitis, Valdemaras Katkus, Pranas Kūris, Kęstutis Lapinskas, Zenonas Namavičius, Vytautas Pakalniškis, Artūras Paulauskas, Jonas Prapiestis, Stasys Stačiokas, Vytautas Stankevičius, Gediminas Šerkšnys, Aurimas Taurantas, and Juozas Žilys. The majority of members were lawyers, professors of the Vilnius University Faculty of Law, holding as well various posts at public institutions. Some of them (Kęstutis Lapinskas, Zenonas Namavičius, Jonas Prapiestis, Stasys Stačiokas, Juozas Žilys) later became judges of the CC; Pranas Kūris became judge of the ECtHR, later judge of the ECJ.

[66] Independently, various individually drafted texts were published in the media as well.

[67] All parliamentary fractions were proportionally represented by the members of the Supreme Council.

[68] The group was composed of Juozas Žilys, Vytautas Sinkevičius, Gediminas Bulotas, Egidijus Kūris, Šarūnas Vilčinskas, Jonas Prapiestis, Remigijus Mockevičius, and Jūratė Ladauskaitė. Later Juozas Žilys and Egidijus Kūris became presidents of the CC, currently Egidijus Kūris is judge of the ECtHR.

[69] At that time, the biggest Lithuanian community abroad was in the US.

of the Temporary Commission submitted alternative versions of the whole range of draft articles. The main disagreement concerned the role of the President in the future constitutional setup.[70] The Supreme Council approved the draft of the Temporary Commission and ordered its communication to the public for discussions. However, the coalition, formed around *Sąjūdis*, proclaimed a declaration that called for the preparation of the alternative draft of a constitution on 6 May 1992, which was later published in media. Given the fact there were two parallel drafts, supported by two major forces of the Supreme Council, an informal group, aimed at finding the compromise and drafting a single text was formed. Members of the Supreme Council Kęstutis Lapinskas and Egidijus Jarašiūnas[71] were entrusted with the task to draft this single text and to discuss it at the Temporary Commission. It was also decided that the draft should get the approval of the absolute majority of all members of the Supreme Council and, only after that, it should be submitted to a referendum. Given the persisting differences between members at the Temporary Commission, Juozas Žilys and Vytautas Sinkevičius (then the Head and Deputy Head of the Legal Section of the Supreme Council) were asked to draft a final compromise text. This document was presented to the Supreme Council on 12 October 1992.[72] The referendum on the approval of the draft constitution was organized for 25 October 1992 and 56.75 per cent of those who had the right to vote approved it.[73] The 1992 Constitution entered into force on 2 November 1992.

The rather quick pace of drafting and adoption of the 1992 Constitution could suggest it was a fluid and harmonious process; however, this was far from being so. In fact, the whole process of adoption of the Constitution took place in conditions of a very heated and divided political environment and could be seen as a three-act drama (the initial proposal in favour of the parliamentary republic; the counteroffer in favour of a strong president and the final compromise). One of the reasons for that was the fact that soon after the elections of the Supreme Council of 1990, the fragmentation of *Sąjūdis* had begun and it led to the establishment of several fractions at the Supreme Council.[74] For various reasons, *Sąjūdis* proposed to establish the institution of the President under the basis of the Provisional Basic Law without waiting for the adoption of a new constitution. This caused heated polemics within the Supreme Council. Its majority had not supported such an idea; however, it conceded that the question should be decided by a referendum. The referendum took place on 23 May 1992 and failed because of the absence of the required majority for approval of the proposal.[75] Such an outcome led to yet another political crisis.[76] Fortunately, the Supreme Council was wise to agree to hold early elections and submission of a draft constitution for a referendum at the same date. This step stimulated the search of a compromise, and the compromise was

[70] The majority of the Temporary Commission supported ideas of parliamentary republic, whereas alternative draft envisaged the President with extensive public powers of the Head of State.

[71] Both became judges of the CC, Egidijus Jarašiūnas later was nominated judge at the CJEU.

[72] Despite heated debates, ninety-two deputies voted for, two against, and six abstained. Still, it is clear that different political groups hoped to amend the adopted Constitution after the elections of the Supreme Council, because art 153 of the Constitution, providing for a possibility to amend the whole range of articles of the Constitution by a three-fifths majority vote of all MPs of the *Seimas* by 25 October 1993 was inserted during the last stage of drafting as some sort of compromise. This option significantly changing the balance struck was not used, because no political power had received such a majority at the 1992 elections.

[73] 75.42 per cent of those, participating in the referendum, voted in favour, 15.78 per cent were against.

[74] Members of *Sąjūdis* were committed to the cause of independence, however, once this aim was achieved, the process of polarization of views on different issues emerged leading to formation of various fractions.

[75] The results of the referendum had certain impact on the content of later draft constitution because it weakened positions of those supporting a strong role of the President.

[76] After the referendum, the new majority was formed at the Supreme Council, leaving the government without parliamentary support. The confrontation within the Supreme Council reached such a level, that its different fractions started holding separate sessions.

reached by entrusting the finalization of the draft to lawyers who were not the members of the Supreme Council.

As mentioned, the main object of disagreement during the drafting process of a constitution was the overall setup of the exercise of the public power, especially the role of the President in it. The majority of the Temporary Commission supported the idea of parliamentary republic, the 1922 Constitution being the main source of inspiration.[77] For others, the 1922 Constitution was only an 'ideal form', whereas its 'real substance' was more debatable, not prone to adaptation to the situation of our times, where the necessity of stability required efficient exercise of power. Needless to say, the constitutional experience of other European states was analysed and used as a source of reference as well.[78] The fact that the 1992 Constitution was adopted by way of a referendum, which was a first time in the history of Lithuanian constitutionalism, allows us to perceive it as a real social contract. Still, very practically speaking, the 1992 Constitution was a fragile compromise between political forces in a much-polarized political landscape. There are certain symbolic elements of an evolutionary character in the Constitution. However, in reality, it is a typical revolutionary constitution, similar to the constitutions of other Central and Eastern European states adopted after the fall of the Berlin Wall. Both its structure and content support such a thesis. Chapter I and the whole text of the Constitution,[79] especially its sovereigntist language,[80] is a reflection of fears that were feeding the drafters of the Constitution. These fears were the permanent struggle for the statehood, especially after fifty years of the Soviet occupation with the persistent threat to remain in the sphere of the former USSR structures, the interwar conflict with Poland over the Vilnius region,[81] and the authoritarian interwar experience of Lithuania. Some of those broader fears found very specific expressions in the Constitution.[82] The compromise reached meant that certain delicate questions were left open and later found the answers in the jurisprudence of the Constitutional Court of the Republic of Lithuania (hereinafter the CC).

---

[77] Academic works of the interwar Lithuanian constitutionalist Mykolas Römeris has played its part as well: Egidijus Jarašiūnas, '1992 metų Lietuvos Respublikos Konstitucija: vizija, teisės aktas, teisinė tikrovė' (2006) 1 Konstitucinė jurisprudencija 330, 333.

[78] The constitutional experience of France, Spain, Germany, and the US was analysed during the drafting process: Egidijus Jarašiūnas, '1992 metų Lietuvos Respublikos Konstitucija: vizija, teisės aktas, teisinė tikrovė' (n 77).

[79] Chapter I establishes provisions related to state organization, whereas basic rights are established in Chapter II. This is the reflection of the course of discussions, content of Chapter I consuming the majority of time, whereas Chapter II was influenced by the ECHR, reducing the room for disputes. Further, art 1 speaks of Lithuania as first, '*independent*' and only then '*democratic*' republic; art 3 para 2 provides that 'the Nation and each citizen shall have the right to resist anyone who encroaches on the independence, territorial integrity, and constitutional order of the State of Lithuania by force'; art 137 prohibits weapons of mass destruction and foreign military bases on the territory of Lithuania.

[80] 'Sovereignty/sovereign' is mentioned seven times, 'independent/independence'—six times in the Constitution.

[81] Art 17: 'the capital of the State of Lithuania shall be the city of Vilnius, the long-standing historical capital of Lithuania' is taken over from the 1918 Act of Independence.

[82] Art 12 para 2 provides, that 'with the exception of individual cases provided for by law, no one may be a citizen of both the Republic of Lithuania and another state at the same time'. This provision is yet another reflection of the fear of possible manipulations with the citizenship by 'external' actors (see further below section C.2). Another reflection of a similar fear—art 47 of the Constitution. Its initial version completely precluded the selling of land to foreigners. Later this provision was subject to two gradual amendments (first, as regards non-agricultural land in the course of the implementation of the Europe Agreement and second as regards agricultural land in the course of accession to the EU). Lithuania was not alone among other Central Eastern European countries having such fears: Irmantas Jarukaitis, 'Lithuania', in Alfred E Kellermann and others (eds), *The Impact of EU Accession on the Legal Orders of New EU Member States and (Pre-) Candidate Countries. Hopes and Fears* (TMC Asser Institute, The Hague, 2006) 396–7.

B. The Evolution of the 1992 Constitution: Between the Rigidity and the Flexibility

The transition from the Soviet regime to the 1992 Constitution was, without any doubt, the biggest (revolutionary) constitutional transformation in the contemporary history of Lithuania. Still, the adopted Constitution was only the initial point of departure, almost like a constitutional vision chosen by the Lithuanian nation for its future development. In order to follow its evolution, one has to take into account its basic features and other (external) factors that predetermined the possible modes and pace of its development.

First, the 1992 Constitution has a rigid, detailed character. It sets the binding legal framework around which the whole national legal system revolves. Such character means that it occupies a central place in the national legal system, secures its viability through the practice of ordinary courts and discourse of political actors. Further, it establishes a high threshold for the adoption of constitutional amendments, which so far proved difficult to pass. On the one hand, this ensures the stability of the Constitution. On the other hand, it means that its transformative potential is mainly in the hands of the CC. As will be seen, the CC has fully exploited this role and secured its central place as the interpreter of the Constitution. This formed the basis for the second transformation from the Constitution as an imperative vision to the living Constitution, which is continuously developed through the Court's practice. For its part, the second transformation is heavily influenced by two 'external' factors, the ratification of the European Convention of Human Rights (the 'ECHR') and Lithuania's accession to the EU. These factors merit special attention because of the emphasis of the present research on the European dimension of national constitutions, but even more so because of their profound horizontal impact on national constitutional law.

1. Central Role of the CC in Developing the Constitution

The textual rigidity of the Constitution is counter-balanced by the fact that, for the first time in the Lithuanian constitutional tradition, the 1992 Constitution envisages the establishment of a constitutional court. It can be seen as one of the biggest developments in the Lithuanian constitutional tradition. It is destined to protect the Constitution and to assure its harmonious development. De facto established in 1993, the CC became a very strong player both in terms of the protection of fundamental rights and as an adjudicator in disputes between different branches of public power.[83] The Constitution is also a very important legal tool for performing judicial functions of general competence courts and administrative courts of Lithuania. These courts are very active in questioning the legality of acts of the parliament, the President and the government and referring cases to the CC. Thus, although de jure the CC has the sole responsibility for scrutinizing the constitutionality of acts of those institutions, other national courts contribute to the establishment of de facto decentralized system of constitutional review.

---

[83] Under art 103, the CC is composed of nine judges, each appointed by the *Seimas* for a single nine-year term. It is reconstituted every three years by one-third, the candidates are proposed by the President of the Republic, the Speaker of the *Seimas* and the President of the Supreme Court. In order to become a judge of the CC, a candidate must be the Lithuanian citizen, have an impeccable reputation, a higher education in law, and not less than a ten-year length of service in the field of law or in a branch of science and education as a lawyer. In practice, professors of law or judges from the highest judicial positions are nominated as judges of the CC. Separate opinions were allowed at the CC only from 2008.

a) Establishment of the CC and Its Powers

The interwar period witnessed some discussions on the necessity and possible ways of securing the paramount role of a constitution and a review of constitutionality of ordinary legislation.[84] Historical circumstances, however, were not favourable for bringing to life certain jurisdictional tools aimed at control of constitutionality of statutory law.

In the wake of the adoption of the 1992 Constitution, the idea of the establishment of a constitutional court was brought up for the first time in 1988. Different *travaux préparatoires* show there were no conceptual differences of opinion on the necessity of having certain judicial mechanisms for constitutional review. Indeed, all drafts that were prepared by working groups and established by the Supreme Council envisaged its establishment.[85] Thus, although new to the Lithuanian constitutional tradition, it was one of the least challenged parts of the institutional design.[86] Public discourse reveals the CC was seen as an institution that had the mission to, one, restore the reputation of law in general, two, secure the rule of law and three, protect the fundamental rights and the values that were negated during the Soviet times.

The potential and actual ability of the CC to develop the Constitution through its jurisprudence depend on several factors. First, there is the powers it has and the self-perception of its (passive/active) role vis-à-vis, first, the legislator. Second, the subjects, having the right to address the CC and, finally, the actual willingness/consciousness of those subjects to use the right to seize the Court with relevant constitutional issues.

Comparing the powers the CC has and the object of its control[87] with other similar European counterparts, one may note that the CC was entrusted only with *ex post* abstract review powers vis-à-vis the binding acts (both of general or individual nature) of the *Seimas*, the President, and the government.[88] This power is complemented by its jurisdiction to rule on some other specific questions.[89] These acts (or their parts) may be the object of abstract constitutional control in terms of the contents of norms, the extent of regulation, the form of an act, as well as the procedure of their adoption.[90]

---

[84] All three permanent interwar Constitutions provided that no law contradicting the Constitution was valid.

[85] Still, some drafts favoured the conferral of a constitutional review to the Supreme Court of Lithuania. Of course, there were different points of view regarding the mode of functioning and powers of such an institution. For example, the initial draft of 1998 envisaged not only *ex post*, but *ex ante* constitutional review powers.

[86] This stands in contrast with later reflections over activities of the CC once it started developing its jurisprudence.

[87] Art 105.

[88] Thus, in general, the inaction of those institutions may not be subjected to the constitutionality review. However, indirectly such a question could arise in the course of evaluation, whether there is a legal basis to ascertain the existence of a legislative omission in a particular case, or in the course of impeachment procedures.

[89] Only one of these is de facto equal to the primary function of the abstract constitutional review: under art 105 para 3 the CC is vested with the function of delivery of *conclusions*, whether international treaties are in conflict with the Constitution. So far, the CC was called upon to perform this function only once, to provide *ex ante* opinion on the compatibility of the ECHR vis-à-vis the Constitution (see below section B.2.a). Three other functions (art 105 para 3: the provision of *conclusions* 1) whether there were violations of election laws during the elections of the President of the Republic or the elections of the members of the *Seimas*; 2) whether the state of health of the President of the Republic allows him to continue to hold office; 3) whether the concrete actions of the members of the *Seimas* and state officials against whom an impeachment case has been instituted are in conflict with the Constitution) are more related to evaluation of the factual circumstances of a particular case, but of course, in the light of requirements of the Constitution. When the CC delivers an *opinion*, art 107 para 3 stipulates that on the basis of such conclusion of the CC, it is up to the *Seimas* to take a final decision. In its later jurisprudence the CC balanced its powers vis-à-vis the legislator by stating that the *Seimas* may not decide on *legal issues*, i.e. may not overrule legal findings established by the CC, but can only adopt a certain *political* decision drawing conclusions from those legal findings (e.g. if the CC finds incompatibility of international treaty with the Constitution, the *Seimas* has two options: to amend the Constitution or to refuse to ratify a treaty). The same is in the course of the impeachment procedure where the CC may establish a violation of the Constitution by MP or other state official, but it is up to the *Seimas* to vote, whether he/she should be removed from the office.

[90] Art 64 para 1 of the Law on the Constitutional Court.

The Constitution limits the circle of subjects having the right to address the CC.[91] At the time of its adoption, the 1992 Constitution did not envisage the right to address the CC via an individual constitutional complaint.[92] This situation persisted until 2019, thereby leaving the CC in absolute minority in comparison to other European constitutional judicial review bodies.[93]

Given the fact that the CC was new to the Lithuanian constitutional tradition, it took some time to define its role in the institutional system. Still, a retrospective glance reveals that, over a short period of time, the CC was able to establish itself as a credible, independent and powerful adjudicator, thereby contributing a lot by efficiently ensuring the rationalizing, stabilizing, and protective functions of the Constitution.[94] Obviously, the ability of the CC to develop its practice depends on the activeness of the litigants that have the right to address it. The experience gained so far allows for drawing conclusions about the main players and contexts feeding the jurisprudence of the CC. First, it is evident that the most active 'employers' of the CC are the courts of Lithuania. This trend is natural given the fact that courts face the everyday application of the legislation, which includes various limitations of basic rights.[95] The second most active group of litigants are groups of MPs of the *Seimas*. These referrals to the CC deal, as a rule, with the struggle for political power; specifically, the opposition will challenge various measures that have been adopted by the majority of the parliament.[96] Two economic crises contributed to the enrichment of the constitutional jurisprudence as well.[97] Finally, Lithuania's integration into transatlantic organizations left a deep horizontal imprint both on the text of the Constitution and the jurisprudence of the CC.

b) Jurisprudence of the CC: From the Constitution as a Higher Law to an Inspirator of Legislative Choices

The diversity of issues faced by the CC have allowed it to build a vast jurisprudence that reveals the potential of the Constitution. The CC jurisprudence may be split up into several stages and directions that contribute to both the stability and the flexibility of the Constitution.

Once established, the CC faced the necessity to define the status of the Constitution and, naturally, its own place in the institutional system. Different provisions and principles of the Constitution had to be interpreted for the first time; the CC was, of course, in search of an optimal methodology of interpretation of the Constitution. Because of that, initially one

---

[91] Under art 106, the government, not less than one-fifth of all MPs of the *Seimas* (at least twenty-nine), and courts have the right to seize the CC concerning constitutionality of acts of the *Seimas*. The conformity of the acts of the President with the Constitution and laws may be questioned by not less than one-fifth of all MPs of the *Seimas* and courts. The conformity of the acts of the government with the Constitution and laws may be questioned by not less than one-fifth of all MPs of the *Seimas*, courts, and the President.

[92] *Travaux préparatoires* of the Constitution are silent to what extent this question was discussed and why it was decided not to establish such a right of individuals.

[93] Currently only Bulgaria, Italy, and Moldova do not have such an institution. For further developments in Lithuania see below section C.3.

[94] Egidijus Šileikis, *Alternatyvi konstitucinė teisė* (Teisinės informacijos centras, Vilnius, 2005) 493–495.

[95] For example, in 2014–2017 references from courts accounted to sixty to 85 per cent of all case load of the CC: http://www.lrkt.lt/en/about-the-court/activity/annual-reports/183 (last accessed on 22 March 2022).

[96] This trend of abstract constitutional review of legislation is supplemented by a comparatively high number of impeachment procedures including the first impeached Head of State in Europe in 2004 (see below section B.2.a), followed by several procedures against MPs.

[97] The economic crisis of 1998–1999 was predetermined by the (then existing) dependence of Lithuania's economy on the Russian market and its crisis, whereas the last world economic crisis hit Lithuania particularly badly, although the sharp decline in 2009–2011 was followed by a very brisk economic recovery. Both crises contributed to the development of the CC jurisprudence in terms of development of social rights and their limits, the principles of legitimate expectations, proportionality, and the right to judicial protection.

may detect a tendency to rely on the literal method of interpretation, an incomplete separation of interpretation of the Constitution from that of the ordinary law,[98] and a certain self-restraint in the exercise of powers. The CC was more willing to indicate what the legislator was not allowed to do, rather than specifying what it might do. Generally speaking, it had not expanded the object of its control and it had avoided dealing with lack of a regulation that was necessary in order to implement the Constitution.[99]

Still, the Court gradually developed the jurisprudence that reflected the understanding that the constitutional law is a higher and autonomous law of the land which was separate from and above the ordinary legislation.[100] Activities of all state institutions are subordinated to the requirements of the Constitution as well. Over time, the CC clarified its own status by stating that it alone had the prerogative of an official interpretation of the Constitution.[101] It started developing the idea of jurisprudential constitution, that is, the idea that the jurisprudence of the CC is an integral part of positive constitutional law and has the same value as the text of the Constitution. The ideas of 'the living Constitution', 'the soul of the Constitution', and the Constitution as an autonomous, complete, and self-sufficient source of law without any gaps entered the vocabulary of the CC. Interestingly enough, this line of case law coincided with the development of the jurisprudence concerning guaranties of independence of ordinary judiciary.[102] The end of the first decade of activities of the CC witnessed the consolidation of its jurisprudence, according to which the Constitution is an integral act and all provisions of the Constitution are interrelated to the degree that the content of some provisions of the Constitution determines the content of other provisions. For the CC, the provisions and principles of the Constitution constitute a harmonious system and no provision of the Constitution can prevail over other provisions because the nature of the Constitution as an act of supreme legal power and the idea of constitutionality implied that there are not, nor can there be, any gaps or internal contradictions in the Constitution.[103] The CC was also able to develop the normative-systemic body of the constitutional principles, among which the principle of the rule of law was seen as the systemic, 'backbone' principle around which the whole national legal system revolved.[104] Later on, this body of the constitutional principles allowed the CC to further develop its jurisprudence in different directions, including the protection of human rights, various constitutional imperatives addressed to state institutions

---

[98] For example, in the Conclusion of 24 January 1995 on compatibility of certain provisions of the ECHR with the Constitution, the CC noted in the *obiter dictum*, that it flows from provisions of the Civil Code that in case of conflict between national civil legislation and Lithuania's ratified international treaties, later have primacy of application, whereas such a 'way of deciding the competition of norms shall not be applied in criminal proceedings. In such cases criminal laws and laws of criminal procedure of the Republic of Lithuania shall be directly applied, whereas international treaties shall be applicable only in special cases prescribed by law (art 71 of the Criminal Code, and arts 20 ... 222 of the Code of Criminal Procedure)'. However, several years later, in the Ruling of 12 July 2001 the CC stressed that 'the Constitution shall be an integral and directly applicable statute (para 1 of art 6 of the Constitution), therefore, the principles and norms of the Constitution pointed out in the petitions of the petitioners will be interpreted by linking them with other principles and norms of the Constitution'. Later, Lithuanian courts ignored the above-mentioned *obiter dictum* of the CC, the ECHR being routinely applied in all types of cases, be it civil, criminal or administrative.

[99] Egidijus Šileikis, 'Aktyvistinė konstitucinė justicija kaip subtili diskrecija inspiruoti teisinius modelius' (2006) 12 Jurisprudencija 54.

[100] Egidijus Kūris, 'Konstitucijos dvasia' (2002) 30 (22) Jurisprudencija 16–31; Egidijus Jarašiūnas, 'Aukščiausioji ir ordinarinė teisė: požiūrio į konstituciją pokyčiai' (2002) 33 (25) Jurisprudencija 30–40.

[101] Ruling of 30 May 2003.

[102] See Section C.4.d.

[103] Rulings of 24 December 2002, 30 May 2003, 25 May 2004; 13 December 2004; 28 March 2006.

[104] Egidijus Kūris, 'Koordinaciniai ir determinaciniai konstituciniai principai (1)' (2002) 26 (18) Jurisprudencija 30–55; Egidijus Kūris, 'Koordinaciniai ir determinaciniai konstituciniai principai (2)' (2002) 27 (19) Jurisprudencija 59–74.

THE EVOLUTION AND *GESTALT* OF THE LITHUANIAN CONSTITUTION   337

in the course of legislative process and other activities. Needless to say, some of the above-mentioned ideas may seem to be the very basic truths of constitutional law, but, in times of infancy of political and legal culture, they were by no means obvious 'discoveries'.[105]

Alongside such developments, the CC started forming its jurisprudence in the field of protection of basic rights,[106] the relationship between international law and the national legal system,[107] the citizenship, answering certain questions, left by the drafters of the Constitution concerning the balance of powers between the *Seimas*, the President, and the government, etc.[108]

The consolidation of the concentrated constitutional review model and the formation of the 'initial' base (the network of already interpreted principles and provisions) secured the transition from the Constitution as a 'potential' to the actual, living Constitution. Such consolidation laid down the basis for a qualitatively new stage of its interpretation.[109]

The second decade of the existence of the CC witnessed the search for deeper systemic interrelations between various principles and provisions of the Constitution and the emphasis on the teleological method of interpretation.[110] The consolidation of its central role as the official interpreter of the Constitution prompted the Court to gradually change its stance, the intensity and scope of control vis-à-vis the legislator by reconsidering its role as a 'mere' or negative compliance checker by adding the amplitude of a pro(active) inspirator of various (conceptual) legislative choices that the legislator had from the point of view of the Constitution,[111] as well as developing the principle of consistent interpretation of the ordinary legislation in the light of the Constitution.[112] At the same time, the Court further increased its powers by discovering the idea of constitutionally prohibited legislative omissions.[113] It also insisted on the fact that no legal act producing legal effects may escape the constitutional control.[114]

Further, treating the stability of the text of the Constitution as one of the preconditions for stability of the Constitution as a 'legal reality', the CC underlined that the development of the constitutional jurisprudence is a permanent process which involved adding new elements in order to preserve its stability, as well as its smooth continuous expansion. Besides, in this

---

[105] In the spirit of textual approach to the Constitution, some lawyers and politicians suggested that rulings of the CC had the power of an implementing act at most, were unhappy in general about the fact that the CC finds 'something between the lines of the Constitution', speaks about the 'spirit of the Constitution', etc.

[106] One of the most important rulings—the Ruling of 9 December 1998 by which the CC found provisions of the Criminal Code establishing the death sentence contrary to arts 18, 19, and 21 para 3 of the Constitution. Although the Constitution did not establish an explicit prohibition of the death penalty, the CC based its decision on the innate nature of fundamental rights. Further, in its Ruling of 29 December 2004 the CC consolidated its jurisprudence by explaining the conditions, under which limitations of fundamental rights are permitted. In its Ruling of 19 August 2006, the CC stressed that the Constitution is an anti-majoritarian act, which establishes not only negative, but positive obligations on state institutions to ensure effective protection of basic rights.

[107] In its Conclusion of 24 January 1995 and the Ruling of 17 October 1995 the CC decided that art 138 para 3 of the Constitution establishes the monist approach of the Constitution vis-à-vis international treaties ratified by the *Seimas*. The monist approach does not mean that international treaties have a primacy over the Constitution, which remains the supreme law of the land.

[108] Egidijus Kūris, *Konstitucinė justicija Lietuvoje: pirmasis dešimtmetis. Konstitucinis teisingumas ir teisės viešpatavimas* (Lietuvos Respublikos Konstitucinis Teismas, Vilnius, 2002) 1.

[109] Egidijus Jarašiūnas, 'Jurisprudencinė konstitucija' (2006) 90 (12) Jurisprudencija 26.

[110] That by itself entailed a systemic interpretation of provisions of the Constitution and control of provisions of ordinary law, which were not indicated by applicants.

[111] Rulings of 14 March 2002 (ownership of pharmacies), 1 July 2004 (annual vacation of MPs of the *Seimas*), and 16 January 2006 (the completion of motives after the pronouncement of an operative part of a judgment).

[112] For example, the Rulings of 11 July 2014; 11 January 2019.

[113] In its Ruling of 8 August 2006, the CC established the notion of a legislative omission describing it as 'a legal gap at the level of ordinary legislation, which is prohibited by the Constitution (or other act of a higher legal force)'.

[114] Rulings of 8 August 2006; 24 September 2009; 28 September 2011.

context the CC accepted that a reinterpretation of the Constitution (including the jurisprudence of the CC) may be needed.[115]

The confirmation of the supremacy of the Constitution had a stabilizing effect and prompted the CC to think about the openness of the Constitution and its limits. The initial definition of the 'algorithm' used to describe the impact of the ECHR and EU law on the Constitution later translated into quantitative and qualitative increase of the case law of the CC, in which the impact of the ECHR and the EU law of various intensity may be detected.[116] Because of this, some authors started speaking about the conceptual impact of the Constitutional Act and EU law on the methodology of interpretation of the Constitution.[117]

The last decade of activities of the CC reveals further development of the elements both entrenching the stability of the Constitution as well as its flexibility. The CC continues to develop ideas for securing the stability of the Constitution. Two rulings of the CC adopted in the context of the introduction of the Euro in Lithuania merit particular attention.[118] Interestingly enough, the strengthening of the stability of the Constitution coincided with and was finally defined in the context of Lithuania's membership in transatlantic organizations leading to the formulation of the constitutional principle of geopolitical orientation.[119] Meanwhile, the earlier emphasis on the supremacy of the Constitution was counterbalanced by the idea of openness of the Lithuanian constitutional law vis-à-vis international and EU law.[120]

---

[115] Ruling of 28 March 2006. The CC noted that the most obvious circumstance, which could trigger the necessity of the reinterpretation is an amendment of the Constitution. Obviously, it depends on the precise nature and content of that amendment. Recently the CC rejected the possibility of reinterpretation of art 12 of the Constitution (to be more precise, its earlier jurisprudence concerning double citizenship) by stating that the adoption of the Constitutional Act on Lithuania's membership in the EU may not be treated as a basis for such reinterpretation, because EU law does not regulate issues of Lithuanian or double citizenship (see Decision of 20 October 2017). Further, the CC accepted the possibility of reinterpretation without such amendments as well. For the CC, it might be possible to deviate from the earlier precedents, but only when it is unavoidably and objectively necessary, constitutionally grounded and reasoned. It stressed, that the said necessity of reinterpretation might be determined only by certain circumstances, such as the necessity to increase possibilities for implementing the innate and acquired rights of persons and their legitimate interests, the necessity to better defend and protect the values enshrined in the Constitution, the need to create better conditions in order to reach the aims of the Nation declared in the Constitution, the necessity to expand the possibilities of the constitutional control in order to guarantee constitutional justice and to ensure that no legal act would have the immunity.

[116] See below sections B.2.a and B.2.b.

[117] Irmantas Jarukaitis, *Lietuvos Respublikos narystės Europos Sąjungoje konstituciniai pagrindai* (Justitia, Vilnius, 2011) 260–305; Egidijus Šileikis, 'The Influence of Lithuania's Membership in the European Union on the Interpretation of the Lithuanian Constitution', in Gintaras Švedas and others (eds), *Lithuanian Legal System under the Influence of European Union Law* (Vilnius University, Vilnius, 2014) 61–88.

[118] Rulings of 24 January 2014 and 11 July 2014. In both rulings, the CC developed the idea that amendments of the Constitution (i.e. the laws amending the Constitution) may be subjected to the constitutional control both from procedural and material points of view. One of such material limitations—the prohibition of 'amendments to the Constitution that would deny the international obligations of the Republic of Lithuania ... and at the same time—the constitutional principle of *pacta sunt servanda*, as long as the said international obligations have not been renounced in accordance with the norms of international law'. Further, the Ruling of 11 July 2014 may be called a revolutionary one both because the CC departed from its earlier practice (see the Ruling of 22 July 1994) without mentioning that fact and because it restricted the right to call a referendum (which is one of the most obvious emanations of people's sovereignty) if draft amendments of the Constitution proposed for a vote in popular referendum are not in line with Lithuania's existing international/EU obligations. The effect of such ruling is that the Central Electoral Commission (an administrative body!) has the obligation to refuse the registration of referenda initiatives aimed at such amendments.

[119] See below section B.2.b.

[120] Two recent rulings of the CC merit attention. In its Ruling of 14 December 2018, the CC decided that provisions of the Civil Code restricting the powers of Lithuanian courts to distribute litigation costs incurred in the course of preliminary rulings procedure before the CJEU are contrary to art 30 of the Constitution and the principle of the rule of law. Meanwhile, in its Ruling of 11 January 2019 the CC held that the relevant provisions of the Law on the Status of Foreigners are not contrary to the Constitution and should be interpreted as not precluding the granting of a temporary residence permit on the basis of a family reunion to a foreigner who had married a

Looking at those twenty-six years of activities, it is hard to overestimate the CC's contribution in securing respect for the rule of law in general, the effective protection of basic rights, as well as settling of disputes between different branches of public power. The CC was able to establish its prominent place, to secure the stability of the Constitution and its gradual development. Statistics reveal that, as a rule, decisions of the CC are respected.[121]

However, these achievements came with a price. Plain statistics do not reflect the tensions that various pieces of the CC jurisprudence have generated. Its activist stance prompted a critique regarding both its powers in general as well as particular decisions.[122] Although, to date, this critique has not materialized in any formal actions by politicians, sometimes the public discourse became especially heated with suggestions ranging from limitation of the CC powers (for example, in the field of economic relations[123]) to its total dismantling. The CC is probably the only court in Europe which had to deal with the suggestion, to use the metaphor of Egidijus Kūris,[124] of self-destruction.[125] Over time, there were attempts to overrule some parts of its jurisprudence.[126] Finally, the most telling example revealing the fears of conferring more powers to the CC was the long lasting failure to introduce the individual constitutional complaint.[127] These examples are good indicators that show the real

---

Lithuanian citizen of the same sex in another EU Member State despite of art 38 para 3 providing that a 'marriage shall be concluded upon the free mutual consent of man and woman'. In its reasoning, the CC heavily relied on judgments of the CJEU of 5 June 2018, *Coman* [2018] (ECLI:EU:C:2018:385) and the Constitutional Court of Romania of 18 July 2018.

[121] According to the Annual Report of the CC of 2017, it produced 186 rulings, in which the contradiction with the Constitution was found during the period of 1993–2017. Of those, twelve rulings (6 per cent) were not implemented: http://www.lrkt.lt/data/public/uploads/2018/03/metinis-pranesimas-2017-internet.pdf (last accessed on 22 March 2022).

[122] Several sensitive issues may be highlighted: the consequences of impeachment procedures, the jurisprudence related to double citizenship; the jurisprudence finding certain austerity measures unconstitutional.

[123] These suggestions were inspired by the CC judgments striking down certain austerity measures and are not justified given the fact that the CC accords wide margin of appreciation for political institutions as regards the adoption of (macro) economic decisions. Obviously, the CC verifies these decisions from the point of view of their compatibility with constitutional principles. So far, the CC stroke down various pieces of legislation (not only austerity measures) infringing the principles of non-discrimination and the grant of unlawful privileges (Rulings of 20 April 1995; 17 March 2003; 26 January 2004), non-respect of legitimate expectations and excessive restrictions on economic activities (Ruling of 23 February 2000), breach of proportionality (Ruling of 14 March 2002), and the rights of consumers (Rulings of 17 March 2003; 20 September 2010).

[124] Egidijus Kūris, 'Konstitucija kaip teisė be spragų' (2006) 90 (12) Jurisprudencija 8.

[125] The Ruling of 6 June 2006. The group of MPs of the *Seimas*, unhappy about the Opinion of the CC of 31 March 2004 concerning the impeachment of (then President) Rolandas Paksas, challenged the constitutionality of title 'the Constitutional Court—a Judicial Institution' and art 1 para 3 of the Law on the Constitutional Court, under which the CC was described as a free and independent court which implements judicial power *vis-á-vis* para 1 and 2 of art 5 and para 1 of art 111 of the Constitution. The logic of the applicants was simple: constitutional provisions concerning the status of the CC were not in Chapter IX 'Courts', but in separate Chapter VIII 'The Constitutional Court'. Thus, the applicants maintained that the CC was not a court from the point of the Constitution and, consequently, it had not performed the public powers in Lithuania, therefore, its decisions were not binding. The CC obviously disagreed. Interestingly enough, while providing for various ('more legal') arguments, supporting its findings, the CC noted that the applicants chose to address namely the CC and this act by itself indicated the acceptance of the CC as judicial authority.

[126] Overtime, various initiatives were taken (mainly by MPs of the *Seimas*) by adopting new laws with the aim to circumvent some parts of jurisprudence of the CC or new references to the CC asking to reinterpret its earlier practice.

[127] The *Seimas* adopted the Conception on the individual constitutional complaint back in 2007 and envisaged the adoption of relevant constitutional amendments in 2008. The Conception was amended in 2009 by changing the above-mentioned dates to 2009–2010, justification being the economic crisis. However, the end of the economic crisis did not witness any further action. It was public secret that the reluctance to proceed with amendments was predetermined by dissatisfaction with certain pieces of the CC jurisprudence. At last, the relevant constitutional amendments were tabled before the *Seimas* in 2017 but were not adopted because of a lack of support. Finally, they were adopted on 21 March 2019 and entered into force on 1 September 2019.

impact of the CC jurisprudence on the everyday functioning of the state and society. On the other hand, they confirm the thesis that various constitutional ideals and principles may never be taken for granted.

2. Lithuania's Integration into Trans-Atlantic Structures and Its Impact on the Constitution

Once Lithuania re-established its independence, it immediately took steps to restore its international relations and started participating in various fora of international cooperation.[128] The 1992 Constitution, although not specifically mentioning the European integration, was very explicit vis-à-vis an international cooperation and international law from the beginning. Most specifically, it contained a clause concerning Lithuania's membership in international organizations[129] and also included provisions that accepted general principles of international law[130] and incorporated ratified treaties into the national legal order.[131]

The ECHR and EU law are treated as the most prominent examples of extra-national legal orders having far reaching impacts on national constitutionalism. When it comes to Lithuania, constitutional reforms and developments of the CC jurisprudence described below fully confirm this thesis. The ECHR, at least theoretically, poses fewer challenges to national constitutions because, one, it does not claim to define its place within national legal systems or the mechanisms of its implementation and enforcement at national level. Secondly, it sets only minimal protection standards and thirdly, it has a subsidiary character.[132] Besides, the ECHR does not challenge the status of national constitutional or highest courts in their national legal systems. Still, looking from the functional point of view, the ECHR coincides with one dimension of national constitutionalism, namely, constitutionalism as a limit to public power. From that perspective, a national constitution (and the ECHR) is first of all anti-majoritarian acts drawing a line between autonomy of an individual and needs of a community to which he or she belongs. Thus, the standard of protection ensured by a national constitution may not be lower than that established by the ECHR. Paradox or not, in case of Lithuania, the practice of the ECtHR has caused so far bigger tensions with the Constitution than the EU law.

The impact of EU law on national constitutionalism is more conceptual in nature. Obviously, EU law unequivocally claims a constitutional nature (although of lesser intensity compared to state constitutionalism) for itself. As Joseph HH Weiler has put it, 'the constitutional thesis claims that in critical aspects the Community has evolved and behaves as if its founding instrument were not a Treaty governed by international law but, to use the language of the European Court of Justice, a constitutional charter governed by a form of

---

[128] Lithuania joined the European Security and Co-operation Conference on 10 September 1991; became the member of the UN on 17 September 1991; the member of the Council of Europe on 14 May 1993, etc.

[129] Art 136: 'The Republic of Lithuania shall participate in international organisations provided that this is not in conflict with the interests and independence of the State'.

[130] Art 135: 'In implementing its foreign policy, the Republic of Lithuania shall follow the universally recognised principles and norms of international law ... and shall contribute to the creation of the international order based on law and justice'.

[131] Art 138 para 3: 'International treaties ratified by the *Seimas* of the Republic of Lithuania shall be a constituent part of the legal system of the Republic of Lithuania'. Further comments concerning the above-mentioned constitutional provisions see, for example: Irmantas Jarukaitis, 'Lithuania' (n 82) 385–390.

[132] Danutė Jočienė, 'Lithuania: The European Convention on Human Rights in the Lithuanian Legal System: The Lessons Learned and Perspectives for the Future' in Iulia Motoc and Ineta Ziemele (eds), *The Impact of the ECHR on Democratic Change in Central and Eastern Europe* (CUP, Cambridge, 2016) 234–265.

constitutional law'.[133] Despite the failure of the EU Constitutional Treaty, the Lisbon Treaty reflects the stronger constitutional claims and as of 1 December 2009, the EU became, to borrow terminology put forward by Neil Walker, a 'more serious constitutional entity'.[134] These constitutional ambitions challenge, among other things, the traditional understanding of constitutional law because they 'assume a constitution, without a traditional political community defined and presupposed by that constitution'. Additionally, they 'challenge the legal monopoly of States and the hierarchical organisation of the law (in which constitutional law is conceived as the "higher law")'.[135] Thus, the main question is how Lithuania and the CC (in particular) have responded to those claims both before and after accession to the ECHR and the EU. On the one hand, the CC has given ratified international treaties a status equal to ordinary laws. According to the CC jurisprudence, in case of conflict between national law and a ratified international treaty, the latter prevails. Nevertheless, the primacy of ratified international treaties does not extend over the Constitution, which is supreme in the Lithuanian legal system.[136] As will be demonstrated, although the response to those claims was different in terms of textual amendments of the Constitution, the jurisprudence of the CC clearly distinguishes the ECHR from other 'ordinary' sources of international law and, over time, it was accorded a special place in its jurisprudence similar to that of EU law.

a) Ratification of the ECHR and Its Impact on the Constitution

Once Lithuania acceded to the Council of Europe and decided to ratify the ECHR, the abovementioned constitutional provisions were seen as a sufficient basis for its ratification. Prior to the ratification of the ECHR the Lithuanian legal system was screened in order to ensure the latter's compatibility with the former.[137] Such screening led to numerous modifications of national ordinary law, particularly in the field of criminal law. However, these modifications were made with the aim to ensure harmony between the Convention and national law, not because of the specific nature of the Convention.[138] Besides, prior to the ratification of the ECHR, the President of the Republic asked the CC whether certain provisions of the ECHR were in line with the Constitution.[139] The Court found no contradictions and paved the way for its ratification.[140]

Despite the status of ordinary law and the above-mentioned refusal to base the interpretation of the Constitution on ordinary legislation, the CC started using the ECHR and the practice of the ECtHR as a 'source of inspiration' immediately after its establishment

---

[133] Joseph H H Weiler, *The Constitution for Europe: Do the New Clothes Have an Emperor? And other Essays on European Integration* (CUP, Cambridge, 1999) 221.

[134] Neil Walker, 'After the Constitutional Moment', in Ingolf Pernice and Miguel P Maduro (eds), *A Constitution for the European Union: First Comments on the 2003-Draft of the European Convention* (Nomos, Baden-Baden, 2004) 25.

[135] Miguel P Maduro, *We, the Court: The European Court of Justice & the European Economic Constitution. A Critical Reading of Article 30 of the EC Treaty* (1st published 1998, Hart Publishing, Oxford, 2002) 175.

[136] Irmantas Jarukaitis, 'Lithuania' (n 82) 385–390.

[137] Regarding the screening and the impact of the ECHR on Lithuanian law: Danutė Jočienė, *Europos žmogaus teisių konvencijos taikymas užsienio valstybių ir Lietuvos Respublikos teisėje* (Eugrimas, Vilnius, 2000) 129–132.

[138] Some authors suggested to reflect explicitly the specific nature of the ECHR in the Constitution and to accord it the status equal to the Constitution, but these proposals were never discussed at the political level: Danutė Jočienė, *Europos žmogaus teisių konvencijos taikymas užsienio valstybių ir Lietuvos Respublikos teisėje* (Eugrimas, Vilnius, 2000) 143.

[139] To date this *ex ante* review procedure was used only once.

[140] The CC ruled not only on the compatibility of the content of the ECHR with the Constitution but expressed its views concerning the effect of the Convention at national level by pointing out, that the 1992 Constitution adopted a monist approach towards ratified international treaties in its Conclusion of 24 January 1995. The ECHR took effect in Lithuania on 20 June 1995.

and before the ECHR was ratified.[141] Once Lithuania ratified the ECHR references to the Convention and jurisprudence of the ECtHR became a common practice of the CC.[142] Additionally, the absence of references to the ECHR in some of its rulings does not mean that it did not consider them once rendering particular decisions. Further, the CC explicitly recognized the specific nature of the ECHR and its impact on the national constitutional law. In the abovementioned conclusion concerning the compatibility of the ECHR with the Constitution, the CC highlighted its specific features and emphasized that the Convention (to some extent) performs the same functions as the Constitution.[143] Several years later, the CC made a step forward and noted that 'the jurisprudence of the European Court of Human Rights as a source of interpretation of law is also important to the interpretation and application of Lithuanian law'.[144] Thus, while it avoided a statement that the jurisprudence of the ECtHR is a source of Lithuanian constitutional law, the CC recognized that, in fact, it is a source of interpretation of Lithuanian constitutional law. As the former president of the CC Egidijus Kūris noted, such an approach meant a 'silent' commitment of the Court to take into account the jurisprudence of the ECtHR in every relevant case, although that fact does not need to be highlighted in every single ruling.[145] So far, no other source of international law received such a specific treatment, with the exception of EU law, which is a special case.

The CC resorts to the ECtHR jurisprudence in a different manner and intensity depending on a particular case.[146] Its technique is to use the jurisprudence of the ECtHR as a source of interpretation of the Constitution and, different from some other countries, the CC does not use the Convention as a legal yardstick to evaluate the legality of ordinary legislation, at least theoretically.[147] Nevertheless, it seems that recently the CC has decided to accept a deeper horizontal penetration of the ECHR at the level of ordinary law in cases of conflict between national legislation and the ECHR.[148] The practice of ordinary courts of Lithuania confirms the thesis that the ECHR is firmly entrenched at the national level, since it is routinely applied

[141] Rulings of 27 May 1994, 18 November 1994, 20 April 1995.

[142] See, for example, the Ruling of 28 May 2008; the Ruling of 7 January 2008; the Ruling of 29 December 2004. To date, the CC has resorted to the ECtHR practice in more than forty cases.

[143] 'The ... Convention ... is a peculiar source of international law, the purpose of which is different from that of many other acts of international law. This purpose is universal, i.e., to strive for universal and effective recognition of the rights ... and to achieve that they were observed while protecting and further implementing human rights and fundamental freedoms. With respect to its purpose, the Convention performs the same function as the constitutional guarantees for human rights, because the Constitution establishes the guarantees in a state and the Convention — on the international scale.'

[144] Ruling of 8 May 2000.

[145] Egidijus Kūris, 'Lietuvos Respublikos Konstitucija ir Europos teisės iššūkiai' (2004) 6 Justitia 33–38.

[146] Such references may range from complementary and supporting, when the arguments of the ECtHR are used to strengthen the line of argumentation, chosen by the CC, to the harmonizing, where provisions of the Constitution are given exactly the same content as those of the Convention, as interpreted by the ECtHR. For more details see Karolina Bubnytė, 'Žmogaus teisių ir pagrindinių laisvių apsaugos konvencijos poveikis Lietuvos konstitucinei justicijai—poveikis ir būdai' (2013) 39 Teisė/Mokslo darbai 136–158.

[147] For example, the practice of Constitutional Courts of Austria, Italy, Latvia.

[148] In its Decision of 9 May 2016, the CC refused to rule on the substance of the reference from the SACL in a case, where the later posed a question of compatibility of the Detention Law, which at that time had not provided for long-term visits for family members of detained persons vis-à-vis the Constitution. The CC, relying on jurisprudence of the ECtHR, pointed out that there is a clear conflict between the Law and the *ECHR* and insisted that at stake is only an issue of the proper application of relevant rules in case of their conflict—given the fact that the ECHR has primacy over a law passed by the parliament, it's up to an ordinary court to apply relevant rules. Such decision is a sharp turn of approach, since it means that in similar situations of conflict (presumably, where the ECtHR practice is formed) there is no necessity to apply to the CC in order to strike down various provisions of national law from the point of view of the Constitution, if they are contrary to the ECHR. In fact, such approach mirrors that of the CJEU in *Simmenthal II* judgment as regards the powers of ordinary national courts to disapply national provisions that are in conflict with EU law without addressing national constitutional courts.

in different categories of cases.[149] The approach of the CC, which attaches a great importance to the ECHR, is not a coincidence. Given the fact that, after its establishment, the CC had to develop its jurisprudence concerning protection of fundamental rights and to build a certain experience, the practice of the ECtHR was a natural point of departure. Besides, such references could be seen in the context of the search for a deeper legitimacy, especially taking into account the above-mentioned clashes with other branches of political power.

Nevertheless, the readiness of the CC to accord the ECHR a quasi-constitutional status in the Lithuanian legal system has its limits, particularly when it comes to the supremacy of the Constitution. A high-profile clash between the jurisprudence of the CC and the ECtHR demonstrates this. The conflict had its roots in the impeachment procedure of 2004 leading to the removal of the (then) President from the office.[150] As a follow-up to the impeachment procedure, the CC had to rule on the consequences of the removal of such persons from the office and declared that the Constitution had established a prohibition to hold a public office requiring taking the oath for life.[151] The Grand Chamber of the ECtHR disagreed with this position and found a violation of article 3 of Protocol I of the ECHR in 2011.[152] The CC refused to reinterpret its earlier practice following the ECtHR judgment. However, it clearly specified that the *pacta sunt servanda* principle entails the obligation of Lithuania to implement the ECtHR judgment and indicated a particular way to do that, specifically via a constitutional amendment.[153] Obviously the CC wanted to balance both the supremacy and the stability of the Constitution and its overall integrity against the necessity to implement international obligations.[154]

[149] Irmantas Jarukaitis, 'Report on Estonia, Latvia and Lithuania', in Giuseppe Martinico and Orreste Pollicino (eds), *National Judges and Supranational Laws: On the Effective Application of the EC Law and the ECHR* (Europa Law Publishing, Amsterdam, 2010) 194–195. This is especially evident when it comes to the application of the ECHR by administrative courts, notably, in cases related to prison conditions, legal status of foreigners, restitution of property, etc. Good illustration from that perspective—*Borisov v Lithuania*, App no 9958/04, 14 June 2011, in which pointing to the relevant decision of the SACL the ECtHR decided to strike the application out of list of cases.

[150] Rolandas Paksas was elected the President in 2003 and later was accused, among the other things, of having accepted the funding for the presidential campaign from a Russian businessperson who was granted in return the Lithuanian citizenship. By its Conclusion of 31 March 2004 , the CC found that Rolandas Paksas breached his oath and grossly violated the Constitution. Following that, the *Seimas* impeached Rolandas Paksas in April 2004.

[151] Immediately after his removal, Rolandas Paksas registered as a candidate for the new presidential elections. As a response, the *Seimas* adopted amendments of the Law on Presidential Elections disqualifying an impeached person from participation in such elections for a five-year term. The group of MPs challenged those amendments as unconstitutional. In its Ruling of 25 May 2004, the CC found those amendments unconstitutional, but ruled that the breach of oath and gross breach of the Constitution meant that an impeached person may *never* hold the office, for which the Constitution requires to take oath. Following that ruling relevant electoral laws were amended in order to ensure their compatibility with the Constitution.

[152] *Paksas v Lithuania*, App no 34932/04, 6 January 2011. The ECtHR was not satisfied with the proportionality of such limitation of the passive right to vote in the light of the principle of democracy. Nevertheless, given the fact that it's quite common in the European constitutional tradition to limit a number of terms for politicians who didn't breach a constitution for the sake of democracy, one may ask, to what extent such evaluation of national measure is convincing, especially given the particular (geo)political context.

[153] In its Ruling of 5 September 2012 the CC ruled that by itself the judgment of the ECtHR might not serve as the constitutional basis for reinterpretation of the official constitutional jurisprudence if such reinterpretation, in the absence of amendments of the Constitution, had changed the integrity of overall constitutional regulations and if it had disturbed the system of the values entrenched in the Constitution and had diminished the guarantees of protection of the supremacy of the Constitution. One dissenting opinion favoured a reinterpretation of the Constitution without the necessity of constitutional amendments.

[154] Such an approach makes sense given the fact that the restriction itself stems from the Constitution, but it does not establish a particular (proportionate) period of restriction. Thus, the *Seimas* having the right (and, in this case, the obligation) to amend the Constitution, has a certain discretion in deciding what period of restriction would be proportionate. Finally the *Seimas* implemented the judgment of the ECtHR and the ruling of the CC in 21 April 2022 by supplementing art 74 of the Constitution with para 2, which stipulates that a person who has been removed from office or whose mandate of a member of the *Seimas* has been revoked by the *Seimas* in accordance with the impeachment proceedings for a gross violation of the Constitution or for breach of his oath may take up an office specified in the Constitution, the commencement of which, in accordance with the Constitution, is

b) The EU Membership and Its Impact on the Lithuanian Constitutional Order

Initially, the 1992 Constitution did not contain any explicit references to the European integration. Obviously, at the time it was drafted and adopted, Europe experienced a period of Euro-enthusiasm, which was marked by the fall of the Berlin wall, the entry into force of the Maastricht Treaty and the birth of the EU and the 1993 Copenhagen Summit that opened the way for future EU enlargements. However, *travaux préparatoires* of the Constitution reveal the absence of discussions on the future probability of Lithuania's participation in the European integration process and the necessary constitutional arrangements. This is not surprising given the fact that political and social reality was characterised by other priorities.[155] Still, the 1992 Constitution contained some (value) references for the future direction of the development of the state, first of all, the Constitutional Act on the Non-Alignment to Post-Soviet Eastern Unions of 1992, as well as articles 135–136 of the Constitution.

When the 1993 Copenhagen Summit opened the way for future enlargements, Lithuania quickly took decisions in order to be part of the European integration process.[156] Once the Europe agreement came into force, Lithuania, as was the case with other acceding states, started wider deliberations on what would be the impact of the EU membership on national constitutions and should (and if so, how) national constitutions be amended in order to reflect the fact that such membership has a profound, horizontal impact on some core national constitutional principles, remembering that basically all dimensions of national constitutionalism are affected by EU membership.[157] Views of academic community and politicians on the issue were very diverse and discussions concerning the necessity, content, and form of constitutional amendments related to the membership in the EU lasted for several years.[158] Finally, a consensus was reached among major political parties represented in the *Seimas*

---

subject to the taking of the oath provided for in the Constitution, when at least ten years have elapsed from the decision of the *Seimas* by which he was removed from office or his mandate of a member of the *Seimas* was revoked. The amendment came into force 22 May 2022.

Of course, it doesn't mean that there were no other tensions between the ECHR and Lithuanian law. One of the latest examples relates to particular circumstances of the Soviet aggression against Lithuania as reflected in the judgment of the ECtHR (*Vasiliauskas v Lithuania*, App no 35343/0, 20 October 2015), concerning a definition of the genocide, the Grand Chamber pronouncing its judgment by nine votes against eight. One of the issues before the ECtHR was the question to what extent Lithuanian courts had duly justified their conclusions that the Lithuanian partisans had constituted a significant part of a 'national' and 'ethnic' group protected under international law. The CC, for its part, adopted the Ruling of 18 March 2014 in which, relying on jurisprudence of the ECtHR, found the relevant provisions of the Criminal Code contrary to the constitutional principle of *nullum crimen, nulla poena sine lege* to the extent they had established a retrospective responsibility for the crime of genocide that was given a wider definition than that established by international law (i.e. encompassing acts against social and political groups). Still, the CC noted that as genocide may be qualified various acts against certain political and social groups (including partisans) if these acts were part of a wider plan to eliminate those groups as significant part of the Lithuanian nation, the extermination of which had the impact on its survival. In its recent judgment (*Drelingas v Lithuania*, App no 28859/16, 12 March 2019) the ECtHR (the Chamber of seven judges) was satisfied with the analysis undertaken by Lithuanian courts concerning the qualification of partisans as significant national group and found no violation of art 7.

[155] The major concern was securing the real functioning of the state, its viability. During drafting of the Constitution such discussions would have been a bit premature, it was not clear, if the EU would be willing to accept new members. Finally, given the context of the re-establishment of the independence, a discourse about the membership 'in a new union' could have been treated as provocative to some extent given the recent experience of break out from the Soviet Union notwithstanding the fact that those two are hard to compare.

[156] Lithuania signed the Europe agreement on 12 June 1995, ratified it on 20 July 1996. It entered into force on 1 February 1998. The application for the EU membership was submitted on 8 December 1995.

[157] Given that it's not surprising that the big part of constitutional amendments, adopted until now, are related to Lithuania's membership in the EU.

[158] More about the process of drafting of constitutional amendments see: Irmantas Jarukaitis, 'Lithuania' (n 82) 385–390.

that constitutional amendments were necessary. The Constitutional Act on Membership of the Republic of Lithuania in the European Union (hereinafter the Constitutional Act, CA) was adopted on 13 July 2004 by the *Seimas* and came into force one month later.[159] If the content of the CA with EU-related constitutional provisions adopted in other EU Member States is compared, it can be seen that it is one of the most complex solutions of such kind and covers a broad range of issues. First of all, the Preamble indicates some deeper values/assumptions on which Lithuania's membership in the EU is based. Further, it provides the constitutional basis for a vertical transfer of public powers exercised at the national level (before EU membership) to a supranational level. It defines the relationship between EU and national legal system. Finally, it establishes the constitutional basis for a special cooperation mechanism between the *Seimas* and the government when dealing with EU matters and envisages a specific procedure of adoption of EU-related decisions within the government.

Several general remarks could be made about the content of the CA. First, by adoption of the Act, the *Seimas* recognized the *sui generis* nature of the EU and its legal system. Several facts confirm such conclusion. As mentioned, article 136 of the Constitution establishes a basis for Lithuania's membership in 'international organizations'. However, that provision was considered inadequate and not voluminous enough for a membership in the EU, which could not be seen as just another international organization given its peculiar features. Besides, this conclusion is supported by positions of the *Seimas* and the Government at the European Convention,[160] proceedings for which coincided with the drafting of EU-related national constitutional amendments and the explanatory memorandum of the draft CA stating, among the other things, that, when acceding to the EU, Lithuania becomes a member of a broader political community, the members of which are not only states, but EU citizens as well.[161] Further, the Preamble of the CA recognizes that the EU is built on the same core values that are enshrined in the Constitution. It also spells out a clear willingness on the part of Lithuania to participate in the process of integration and, by doing this, to develop and promote these constitutional ideals and ensure they are materialized throughout the whole of Europe.[162] On the other hand, it recognizes that Lithuania's membership in the EU creates preconditions for the better attainment of some national constitutional ideals in Lithuania, especially security and high-level living standards.[163]

Given a wide scope and the nature of public powers that the EU possesses and the particularities of their exercise, it could be stated that one of the aims of EU-related constitutional amendments is the reconstruction of a system of the public powers, as defined by the Constitution. In that sense, the whole CA and its article 1 (in particular) are related to the rationalizing and organizational function performed by the Constitution. It reflects the fact that while retaining a status of a state political community, Lithuania became a part of a

---

[159] See the English translation of the Constitutional Act at http://www3.lrs.lt/cgi-bin/preps2?Condition1=237876&Condition2= (last accessed on 22 March 2022).

[160] The Resolution of 19 December 2001 of the *Seimas* On negotiations of Lithuania's membership in the European Union: http://www3.lrs.lt/owa-bin/owarepl/inter/owa/U0113594.doc (last accessed on 22 March 2022); the Resolution of 29 May 2003 of the *Seimas* On discussion concerning the future of Europe: http://www3.lrs.lt/owa-bin/owarepl/inter/owa/U0113597.doc (last accessed on 22 March 2022) as well as Decree of the Government of 25 September 2003 On the Governments' position with regard to the draft EU Constitutional Treaty (*Valstybės žinios* 2003 No 42-9159).

[161] The explanatory memorandum of the draft CA: http://www3.lrs.lt/pls/inter3/dokpaieska.showdoc_l?p_id=223996 (last accessed on 22 March 2022).

[162] '[E]xpressing its conviction that the European Union respects human rights and fundamental freedoms and that membership in the European Union will contribute to a more effective safeguarding of human rights and freedoms' and 'seeking to ensure full participation of the Republic of Lithuania in European integration'.

[163] '[S]eeking to ensure ... the security of the Republic of Lithuania and welfare of its citizens.'

broader European political community. Such participation in a wider political community triggers different changes with regard to the exercise of public powers. Among the other things, it modifies the principle of democracy,[164] which is at the heart of the Constitution. From that point of view, the modification is twofold. First, article 1 of the CA recognized that, alongside a horizontal division of public powers among state institutions, there also emerged a vertical division after accession to the EU, which was not envisaged before the adoption of the CA. Thus, the EU membership triggered a re-drawing of political boundaries and Lithuania became a part of a broader European political community, which is, among other things, based on the principle of majoritarian decision-making, whereas the legitimacy of the exercise of public powers is secured through national and supranational 'channels'.

Further, the EU accession and the CA modified the principle of (horizontal) separation of powers. A new balance was established between the *Seimas* and the government. Although the *Seimas* actively participates in EU decision making, the governments' powers, given its legislative role in the EU Council, were substantially enhanced.[165] Moreover, a balance of powers between national courts was redefined as well. Taking into account the principles the CJEU pronounced in the *Simmenthal II* decision,[166] powers of review of some national legal acts concerning their compatibility with Lithuania's ratified international agreements shifted from the CC[167] to ordinary courts as far as primary and secondary EU law was concerned. The ordinary courts acquired more powers, since after accession they have the power to set aside national legal acts which are not in conformity with EU law.

Article 2 of the CA merits attention as well. Basically, it describes the way in which the consequences of transferred public powers (adopted EU legal acts) 'flow' back to national level and become the part of national legal system. Again, given its *sui generis* nature, the relative autonomy of EU law was recognized because the Constitution makes a clear distinction between public international law and EU law. However, the mere adoption of article 2 of the CA means that one of the core tenets of the CJEU practice (the absolute autonomy of EU law and its self-referentiality) was rejected because, from the point of view of the 1992 Constitution, the basis of validity of EU law in Lithuania and its primacy over national law emanate from the Constitution, not EU law. Using the terminology of HLA Hart,[168] the rule of recognition remains at the national level: article 2 of the CA simply adjusted the criteria of validity in order to embrace EU law and to ensure its validity and effectiveness at the national level. Thus, the Constitution demonstrates its normative insularity, but, on the other hand, shows its cognitive openness[169] taking into account the changed social reality, namely Lithuania's membership in the EU. Accordingly, both article 2 of the CA[170] and the CC are entirely explicit that article 2 of the Act established 'only' a collision rule in case of difference between two legal rules, belonging to different legal systems, but there was no intention on

---

[164] Here the principle of democracy is understood in its narrow sense—as participation and representation in decision making.

[165] See sections C.2 and C.4.

[166] *Amministrazione delle Finanze dello Stato v Simmenthal Spa* [1978] (ECLI:EU:C:1978:49).

[167] In the Ruling of 25 April 2002, the CC just hinted that it has powers to review the compatibility of decrees of the government with Lithuania's ratified international agreements, whereas in the Ruling of 16 January 2007 the Court has actually performed such kind of review and ruled that a particular decree of the President of the Republic did not contradict only the Constitution of Lithuania, but art 6 para 2 of the ECHR as well.

[168] HLA Hart, *Teisės samprata* (Pradai, Vilnius, 1997).

[169] Gunther Teubner, *Law as an Autopoietic System* (Blackwell, Oxford, 1993).

[170] Art 2 of the CA provides for priority '*in case of conflict*'.

the part of the *Seimas* to shift the rule of recognition from article 7 para 1 of the Constitution to article 2 of the CA. This opinion is shared by the academic community[171] and the CC.[172]

Nevertheless, the consequences of this provision clearly go beyond being a mere rule of conflict. Without going too deep into article 2 of the CA, its substance could be summarized as follows. First, it provides *expressis verbis* that EU law becomes 'law of the land' in Lithuania. That means that Lithuanian courts and other state institutions have a constitutional duty to properly implement and apply EU law, to interpret national law in conformity with EU law, to ensure its effectiveness and safeguard its primacy in case of conflict. Accordingly, private persons have the constitutional right to rely on the provisions of EU law and to require a reference of the issue to the CJEU where EU law is involved, whereas national courts have the constitutional right and duty to refer questions concerning validity and interpretation of EU law[173] before the CJEU. Thus, Lithuanian courts became the European courts, whereas the CJEU became 'a court' within the meaning of the 1992 Constitution as well.[174] Further, national legislative and other institutions have the constitutional obligation to ensure timely and effective implementation of EU law and to set necessary preconditions for its effective functioning at the national level.

Several other issues related to the constitutional basis of Lithuania's accession to the EU should be noted. As has already been mentioned, the CA was adopted after Lithuania's accession to the EU and came into force on 14 August 2004. The reason of such lateness is not clear since, as the voting results in the *Seimas* show, political support for the CA was high.[175] Realizing the risk of uncertainty and understatement of the value of the CA, the CC preempted the probable doubts about the constitutionality of, say, the application of EU regulations between 1 May 2004 and 14 August 2004 and decided to correct the faults of political process by stating that Lithuania's membership in the EU 'is constitutionally confirmed by the Constitutional Act'.[176] Thus, the CC clearly indicated to likely applicants that it would reject any complaints about unconstitutionality of (application of) EU legislation based on the arguments about the belated adoption of the CA.

Further, it is highly probable, that the adoption of the CA and its extensive impact on the Constitution prompted the CC to start developing jurisprudence on reinterpretation of the Constitution. Some examples of 'pre-accession' jurisprudence of the CC reveal that such

---

[171] Egidijus Kūris, 'Lietuvos Respublikos Konstitucija ir Europos teisės iššūkiai' (n 145) 36; Irmantas Jarukaitis, 'Adoption of the Third Constitutional Act and its impact on the National Constitutional System' (2006) Teisė/ Mokslo darbai 29–30.

[172] See n 173.

[173] Such an approach advanced in academic doctrine for some time for example, Irmantas Jarukaitis, 'Adoption of the Third Constitutional Act and its Impact on the National Constitutional System' (n 171) recently found the support the in jurisprudence of the CC: see the Ruling of 14 December 2018.

[174] For example, under art 12 para 2 of the Law on the Bank of Lithuania 'a decision regarding the dismissal of the Chairperson of the Board of the Bank of Lithuania on the grounds provided for in paragraph 1 of this article shall be made by the Seimas of the Republic of Lithuania on the recommendation of the President of the Republic'. Under art 105 para 1 of the Constitution a constitutionality of decisions of the Seimas may be questioned before the CC. At the same time, art 12 para 4 of the Law on the Bank of Lithuania provides, that '[t]he Chairperson of the Board of the Bank of Lithuania shall have the right to refer to the European Court of Justice a decision regarding his dismissal prior to the expiration of his term of office within two months from the announcement of the decision or from the receipt of the notification thereof or, if the above has not occurred, from the date when the decision became known to the plaintiff on the grounds that the decision was in breach of the Treaty Establishing the European Community or any other legal provision related to the application of the above Treaty'. See the recent judgment of the CJEU of 26 February 2019 as well: *Rimsevics* [2019] (ECLI:EU:C:2019:139).

[175] During the first voting concerning the adoption of the CA on 30 March 2004 out of 141 MPs 117 voted 'for', four— 'against', zero— 'abstained'. During the second voting on 13 July 2004 115 voted 'for', five— 'against', zero— 'abstained'.

[176] For example, the Ruling of 13 December 2004.

re-interpretation of the Constitution may be necessary.[177] Finally, the accession to the EU prompted not only adoption of the CA. Provisions of the Constitution, which were considered to be not in line with requirements of EU law, were amended both before and after Lithuania's accession to the EU.[178] Given the overall impact of the CA on the Constitution, it could be treated as a systemic amendment of the whole Constitution.[179]

Obviously, Lithuania's EU membership left an imprint not only on the text of the Constitution but had a deep impact on the CC jurisprudence as well. Although, different from some other EU Member States, there were no direct constitutional challenges to Lithuania's membership in the EU or requirements stemming from EU law, the CC had plenty of opportunities to dwell on the subject. Similarly, as with the ECHR, the CC started referring to EU law already in its early years of existence long before the accession took place. One of the first such rulings was the abovementioned judgment concerning constitutionality of the death penalty.[180] Some 'pre-accession' rulings of the CC reveal not only the positive, but also the negative reference to EU law, in the sense that the absence of EU law was used as a doctrinal argument for taking a certain direction of interpretation of the Constitution.[181] Needless to say, before Lithuania's accession to the EU, the CC used EU law simply as one among many (doctrinal) sources of inspiration for interpretation of the Constitution. Decisions of the CJEU were never cited, however, some of rulings heavily relied on EU law.

Lithuania's accession to the EU completely changed the status of EU law at national level and it became an integral part of national law. The approach of the CC to EU law as a doctrinal source of interpretation of the Constitution remained unchanged for some time.

Nevertheless, later CC jurisprudence reveals a gradual change of attitude. First, the Ruling of 14 March 2006 is of particular importance.[182] Here, the CC pointed out that 'the Constitution consolidates not only the principle that in cases when national legal acts

---

[177] Irmantas Jarukaitis, 'Lithuania's Membership in the European Union and Application of EU Law at National Level', in Adam Lazowski (ed), *The Application of EU Law in the New Member States: Brave New World* (CUP, Cambridge, 2010) 232–234.

[178] In order to secure the right of foreign nationals to acquire land in Lithuania art 47 was amended twice before the accession. The first amendment (regarding non-agricultural land) was adopted in 1996 in order to secure the entry into force of the Europe Agreement. The second one (concerning agricultural land)—in 2003 to secure the accession to the EU. The same was done with regard to the right of EU citizens to participate in municipal elections—art 119 was amended: Irmantas Jarukaitis, 'Lithuania' (n 82) 396–397. Besides, taking into account Lithuania's prospective accession to the Eurozone art 125 para 2 (which before amendments provided that 'the right of issue of currency shall belong exclusively to the Bank of Lithuania') was amended by simply abrogating above-mentioned provision on 25 April 2006.

[179] Discussions concerning the necessity of the CA as the constitutional basis for Lithuania's accession to the EU revealed different views. Majority treated the adoption of the CA (or similar amendments) as a necessary precondition of the accession. About these discussions: Irmantas Jarukaitis and Gintaras Švedas, 'The Constitutional Experience of Lithuania in the Context of European and Global Governance Challenges', in Anneli Albi and Samo Barducki (eds), *National Constitutions in European and Global Governance: Democracy, Rights, the Rule of Law* (Springer, Heidelberg, 2019) 997–1046. Nevertheless, some argued that the European orientation of the Constitution could have been deduced from the overall content and the spirit of the Constitution, thus, the CA was not necessary. Egidijus Šileikis, 'Konstitucijos 25-mečio fenomenas: subrandinimo veiksniai ir iššūkiai' (2018) Teisė/Mokslo darbai 17. The CC sided with the majority, pointing out in its Ruling of 24 December 2014 that the CA established the constitutional basis of Lithuania's membership in the EU and that 'in case such constitutional grounds were not consolidated in the Constitution, the Republic of Lithuania would not be able to be a full member of the European Union'.

[180] The ruling of 9 December 1998. The CC took note of the EP resolution of 13 June 1997 and of the Declaration on the Abolition of the Death Penalty of 10 November 1997 of the Conference of the Representatives of the Governments of the EU Member States. In the Ruling of 6 October 1999 concerning constitutionality of temporary exclusive rights granted by the law to particular telecommunications operator the CC extensively relied on EU law.

[181] For example, the Ruling of 14 March 2002.

[182] Ruling of 14 March 2006.

establish the legal regulation which competes with that established in an international treaty, then the international treaty is to be applied, but also, in regard of European Union law, establishes *expressis verbis* the collision rule, which consolidates the priority of application of European Union legal acts in the cases where the provisions of the European Union arising from the founding Treaties of the European Union compete with the legal regulation established in Lithuanian national legal acts (regardless of what their legal power is), save the Constitution itself'. Such *obiter dictum* stimulates some thoughts. Apparently, it reflected the Court's desire to re-assess the constitutional reality once Lithuania acceded to the EU and the CA was adopted. The CC felt it necessary to re-affirm that the ultimate source of authority rested within the Constitution, despite the existence of the CA. Such point of view is supported by the fact that the cited part of the ruling was not, strictly speaking, necessary to reach its *ratio decidendi*. Thus, the CC indicated that it saw article 2 of the CA as a conflict rule, not an amendment to article 7 of the Constitution. Further, the Court made it clear that, even as a conflict rule, it did not automatically extend over the Constitution. Although it could be read as a declaration of the unconditional supremacy of the Constitution over EU law, such a conclusion would be too far-reaching considering that the CC did not explicitly rule on what the relationship between EU law and the Constitution was. While earlier jurisprudence shows the Court's willingness to take the European dimension into account, this ruling is an implicit hint that if an express conflict between EU law and national constitution arises, the resolution of which is impossible through the use of the principle of consistent interpretation, the Constitution would prevail.

Later jurisprudence of the CC demonstrates that such scenario is unlikely. In its Ruling of 21 December 2006, the CC made a step forward and adapted to EU law the algorithm that had earlier coined for the ECHR.[183] Without any doubt, such statement may be treated as an explicit recognition of the impact of EU law on the Constitution. It does not eliminate all grounds for conflict, but rather indicates the Court's willingness to do its best to avoid it. A further step in developing a coherent approach to EU law was taken on 8 May 2007 when the CC made its first reference to the CJEU. Such decision is extraordinary from various perspectives,[184] especially from the perspective of national (constitutional) law. First, the fact that, different from other pieces of national legislation governing procedural issues of courts' proceedings, the Law on the Constitutional Court was not supplemented with provisions concerning references to the CJEU after Lithuania acceded to the EU, merits attention. One may think the *Seimas* did not project that the CC would be willing to use the preliminary rulings procedure. Therefore, the formal normative basis, which served as a background to the CC's decision to refer the issue to the CJEU[185] and its arguments explaining the necessity of reference,[186] need further examination. Given the fact that the CC expressly recognized

---

[183] Citing for the first-time numerous decisions of the Court of First Instance and the CJEU the CC noted that '[t]he Constitutional Court has stated several times that the jurisprudence of the European Court of Human Rights, as source of legal interpretation, is important for interpretation and application of Lithuanian law. The same should be said about the jurisprudence of the Court of First Instance and the European Court of Justice'.

[184] Although later the attitude of some constitutional courts of the EU Member States vis-à-vis the use of the preliminary ruling procedure has changed, in 2008 the CC was among few constitutional courts that ever did that.

[185] The CC based its decision on art 102 of the Constitution, art 234 of the EC Treaty and arts 1 and 28 of the Law on the Constitutional Court. These national rules simply describe the nature and powers of the CC, but do not establish a specific ground for suspension of procedures in cases of the use of preliminary rulings procedure. Thus, the only *express* legal basis of the reference mentioned by the CC was art 234 of the EC Treaty. Besides, whereas in its earlier practice the CC stressed its paramount place in ensuring and developing the principle of rule of law in national legal system, here the CC referred to art 220 of the EC Treaty and recognized the role of the CJEU in ensuring the principle of rule of law.

[186] The CC reiterated its exclusive role in the national constitutional system in guaranteeing the supremacy of the Constitution and constitutional legality. Further, it noted that the Law on Electricity was adopted *inter alia*

the CJEU's role in ensuring the principle of rule of law and its statement that 'it is necessary to construe the disputed provision ... in the context of the legal regulation established in the said directive', one may argue that the Court derived the constitutional right (or even a duty) to refer questions on EU law to the CJEU from article 2 of the CA, which is applicable both to the CC and other national courts as well. Such statement is related to another striking fact: the CC referred to the CJEU even earlier than Lithuanian courts of general competence did.[187] Still, one may not overlook the fact that the text of the reference was permeated with the aureole of supremacy of the Constitution, which then prompted some to criticize the CC for the failure to articulate its position on the effects of the CJEU judgment and to take it into account in this particular case.[188]

Although the CC did not explain to what extent it felt bound to resort again to the preliminary rulings procedure in the abovementioned case, one could have expected it to do so in other cases as well, especially when references to EU law are quite frequent in its practice.[189] However, it took some time to articulate a clear position on the issue, specifically because the CC ignored several requests to refer the matter to the CJEU and did not explain such a stance.[190] However, in its Ruling of 3 April 2015, which rejected the request of the representative of the applicant to refer the matter to the CJEU, the CC pointed out that under article 267(3) TFEU a reference to the CJEU is made if the content of EU law is not clear, whereas, in this case, the CC found no problems of interpretation of EU law.[191] Finally, the CC, in its Decision of 20 December 2017, in which it referred to the CJEU questions of interpretation of EU law for the second time, explicitly mentioned article 267 TFEU. It noted that its decisions are binding and final and pointed out that, in those circumstances, it had the obligation to resort to the preliminary rulings procedure. The content of the Decision is visibly different in comparison to the first one, which was adopted in 2007, in which a question was referred to the CJEU. This difference reflects developments of the attitude of the CC vis-à-vis the EU membership.[192] Such a state of affairs leads to the conclusion that the CC and the CJEU cooperation will intensify in the future.

The impact of EU law on the CC jurisprudence is not only prospective in a sense that, as mentioned above, it recognized the possibility of reinterpretation, a possibility which is

---

with the aim to implement Directive 2003/54/EC. Then it referred to art 2 of the CA, repeated the *obiter dictum* of above-mentioned ruling ('save the Constitution itself') and added that 'it is necessary to construe the disputed provision of the Law which, as mentioned, was passed while implementing inter alia Directive 2003/54/EC, in the context of the legal regulation established in the said directive'.

[187] This was the second reference made by Lithuanian courts to the CJEU. The first was made by the SACL, whereas courts of general competence made their references later.

[188] The first dissenting opinion ever in the history of the CC was delivered namely in this case by judge rapporteur.

[189] The CC resorted to EU law in eighteen rulings during 2004–2019. The method of using the EU law as part of argumentation provided by the CC is virtually the same as with the ECHR: in in some rulings EU law argument has only supportive function, whereas in others (for example, the Ruling of 3 April 2015) EU law arguments form the essential part of the reasoning.

[190] Rulings of 5 September 2012, 13 March 2014.

[191] This ruling concerned the mode of establishment and financing of the liquefied gas terminal, the project, which is treated as one of the cornerstones of Lithuania's energy security. It is extraordinary in terms of extensive analysis and reliance on EU law.

[192] The general mood is quite different, the CC not mentioning the supremacy of the Constitution, the formula 'save the Constitution itself'. Instead, it points to the earlier jurisprudence (see further), treating Lithuania's membership in the EU as the constitutional value, underlined the constitutional obligation to properly implement EU obligations and even went as far as stating that as 'the areas of agriculture and internal market fall under shared competence between the European Union and the Member States, *there are no grounds for interpreting the provisions of the Constitution linked to these areas, inter alia, article 46 thereof, in a different manner than the specified areas are regulated by European Union law*'.

especially triggered by amendments of the Constitution. If the CA is treated as a horizontal amendment of the whole Constitution, it is not surprising that the CC has started to re-evaluate its practice that had been formed before EU accession and identified areas in which reinterpretation of the Constitution was needed.[193]

These developments of the CC jurisprudence cover different substantive and procedural aspects stemming from the EU membership. Still, one case in which EU integration was at the heart allowed the CC to consolidate its overall methodological approach to Lithuania's EU membership and various constitutional implications stemming from the CA.[194] The CC underlined in its Ruling of 24 January 2014 that Lithuania's membership in the EU is a constitutional imperative based on the sovereign choice of the nation. For the CC, Lithuania's fully-fledged EU membership[195] is a constitutional value and it treated the CA as the expression of a positive geopolitical orientation of Lithuania,[196] thus strengthening the stability and protection of the Constitution. Such positive geopolitical orientation is based on the structural compatibility of universal values, on which the Western civilization is based, as well as on belief that EU membership is closely related to the core constitutional values.[197] This categorization of the EU membership led the CC to the conclusion that no constitutional amendments negating Lithuania's commitments stemming from the EU membership can be made, unless the constitutional basis of Lithuania's EU membership is renounced by way of referendum.[198]

Such attitude of the CC to the EU membership is not accidental. It reflects the historical experience (that is why both the positive and the negative aspects of geopolitical orientation are mentioned) and a general mood in Lithuanian society, which is constantly one that

[193] In its Ruling of 26 September 2006 the CC stated that '[i]t needs to be noted that the Constitutional Court has formed the official constitutional doctrine of taxes and other obligatory payments in inter alia the constitutional justice cases in which one investigated the constitutionality of legal acts (parts thereof) *which had been passed before 14 August 2004*, when the Constitutional Act of the Republic of Lithuania 'On Membership of the Republic of Lithuania in the European Union', which, under article 150 of the Constitution, is a constituent part of the Constitution, came into force .... *Upon entry into force of the Constitutional Act of the Republic of Lithuania "On Membership of the Republic of Lithuania in the European Union"*, the official constitutional doctrine of taxes and other obligatory payments, which had been formed until then, *is developed by taking account of the said amendment to the Constitution'.*

[194] In order to pave the way to the future entry in the Eurozone (this happened 1 January 2015), art 125 of the Constitution was amended in 2006 by the *Seimas*. The group of MPs challenged the amendment on procedural grounds. The CC accepted those arguments and found the amendment unconstitutional. However, the CC insisted that the imperative of Lithuania's participation in the EU (including the Eurozone) stem from the CA, thus, the annulment of the amendment had no impact on Lithuania's membership in the Eurozone.

[195] The Preamble of the CA expressly speaks about the *'fully-fledged* participation of the Republic of Lithuania in the European integration'. This fact and the structural compatibility of the fundamental values allowed the CC deduction of the constitutional obligation of Lithuania to participate as a fully-fledged EU Member State in the EU integration by adopting the common currency and conferring exclusive competence in the area of monetary policy to the EU.

[196] The principle of positive geopolitical orientation embraces Lithuania's membership in the NATO as well. The CC hinted to the existence of the principle of geopolitical orientation already in its Ruling of 7 July 2011, where it had to deal with a question of constitutionality of provisions, implementing the basic principles of the NATO. One of the arguments of opponents was that the Constitution did not allow for the stationing of foreign troops in Lithuania, they claimed that the Constitution provided no basis for acceptance of art 5 of the NATO Treaty, establishing the principle of collective self-defence. The CC interpreted the Constitution in the context of geopolitical situation and other factors having the impact on state security. Using teleologic and systemic interpretation of the Constitution the CC concluded that it has established the principle of geopolitical orientation, predetermining Lithuania's membership in the EU and the NATO, whereas the Constitution had not prohibited the establishment of military bases, which were jointly operated with allied forces from other NATO countries.

[197] The CC indicated the fundamental values of the Constitution: the independence, democracy, the republic, and the innate nature of fundamental rights and then pointed out these are universal values of the European and North American States.

[198] Rulings of 24 January 2014 and of 12 November 2015: the CC omitted references to the supremacy of the Constitution, emphasized in the Ruling of 14 March 2006.

is most favourable to the European integration. Here, one may note a certain paradox. The EU membership entailed the unprecedented transfer of public powers to the supranational level, however, given bitter historic experience of Lithuania, such membership creates better preconditions for development of its statehood and constitutional ideals compared to what it had for more than last two hundred years. Rhetoric about the imperative of fully fledged EU membership, from which the constitutional obligation to participate in the Eurozone was derived, echoes to some extent the idea of 'an ever-closer union among the peoples of Europe'. Still, one may pose a question, what are the limits of such a constitutional obligation.[199] The CC gives some general clues on that question since it started speaking about the core constitutional principles which may not be negated.[200]

To sum up, the CC's approach to EU integration is truly positive. It does not mean there will be no conflicts on particular issue, but it is rather unlikely. Such conclusion is predetermined by the fact that the CC gradually internalizes different EU law imperatives and makes them part of national constitutional law.

Finally, one may note a visible impact of EU law on the practice of ordinary courts as well. The jurisprudence of administrative courts and courts of general competence shows that, after seventeen years of membership, EU law is firmly entrenched in domestic court practice. The principles of primacy and direct effect of EU law are well recognized and the preliminary rulings procedure is regularly used by Lithuanian courts.[201]

To conclude, Lithuania's EU membership had the most far-reaching explicit and implicit impact on the 1992 Constitution. It triggered various systemic and horizontal modifications of the core constitutional principles and particular provisions as well. This impact is reflected in the CC jurisprudence, which has an integrative influence and, at the same time, stabilizes both the EU and national legal systems. Arguably, the CC jurisprudence confirms the pluralistic understanding of the relationship between EU and national legal systems where there is relative autonomy but also the influence of the 'other' legal system is recognized, without renouncing the identity of national legal system. So far, the CC has been successful in establishing a delicate balance between, on the one hand, the supremacy of the Constitution (based on the idea of national constitutional law as a 'higher law'), the exclusive role it plays in national constitutional system, and the mechanism of national constitutional review, and, on the other hand, the needs of European integration.

C. Basic Principles and Structures of the 1992 Constitution

The content of the 1992 Constitution may be analysed in the general historic context in which it was born, namely the fall of totalitarian regimes in the Central and Eastern European states and the collapse of the Soviet Union. Thus, the aspiration was to establish a constitution which would reflect the universal values of the Western civilization: the rule of law, democracy, protection of fundamental rights, all of which would lay the basis for the harmonious development of the state community. Of course, the historic constitutional heritage was seen also as an important guideline for the future.

---

[199] For example, does it mean that Lithuania has a constitutional obligation to participate in all areas of reinforced cooperation, may not negotiate various opt-outs, etc?

[200] See Section D.

[201] For more details see Irmantas Jarukaitis, 'Report on Estonia, Latvia and Lithuania' (n 149) 195–201.

1. Main Features of the 1992 Constitution and its Role in the National Legal Order

The 1992 Constitution is characterized by a rigid, detailed form. Different from the interwar constitutions, it has a more normative nature, rather than only a political nature. The CC jurisprudence and academic writings reflect the classic understanding of the Constitution: the Lithuanian people (the nation) are the source of the Constitution, which is supreme law of the land. The Constitution reflects the social contract, an imperative vision, a democratically accepted obligation by all of the citizens of Lithuania for the current and future generations to live according to the fundamental rules entrenched in the Constitution and to obey them in order to ensure the legitimacy of the governing power, the legitimacy of its decisions, as well as to ensure human rights and freedoms, so that harmony exists in society. The CC makes it clear that the Constitution is based on universal, unquestionable values which are sovereignty belonging to the Nation, democracy, the recognition of and respect for human rights and freedoms, respect for the law and the rule of law, limitation of the scope of powers, the duty of state institutions to serve the people and their responsibility to society, public spirit, justice, and striving for an open, just and harmonious civil society and state under the rule of law.[202] According to the CC, the Constitution is characterized by its supremacy and direct application, integrity, the lack of any gaps or internal inconsistencies, stability and its vitality.

Given the historic experience and circumstances of its drafting, the Constitution pays the utmost attention to its stabilizing function by establishing very rigid procedures for its amendment. It provides for different procedures and requirements in this regard, thus establishing a certain *de facto* internal hierarchy of its provisions. In any case, these procedures require a wide support both among the public in general and among the political parties represented in parliament, thereby ensuring that the constitutional amendment procedure is above the ordinary political process.[203] This is especially true for Chapter I of the Constitution.[204] These constitutional provisions are interpreted strictly by the CC.[205]

---

[202] Rulings of 25 May 2004; 19 August 2006; 24 September 2009; 24 January 2014; Decisions of 20 April 2010; 19 December 2012.

[203] Art 148 para 1: 'the provision of article 1 of the Constitution "the State of Lithuania shall be an independent democratic republic" may only be altered by referendum if not less than three-quarters of the citizens of Lithuania with the electoral right vote in favour thereof'. Other provisions of Chapter I and of the Fourteenth Chapter ('The Alteration of the Constitution') may be amended only by a referendum. Provisions of other chapters of the Constitution may be adopted by the *Seimas*: these must be considered and voted at the parliament twice with a break of not less than three months between the votes. A draft law amending the Constitution is deemed to be adopted if, during each of the votes, not less than two-thirds of all the MPs of the *Seimas* (94 out of 141) vote in favour. A failed amendment of the Constitution may be submitted to the *Seimas* not earlier than after one year.

[204] The experience shows that the threshold of art 8 para 1 of the Law on Referendum (in order for a mandatory referendum to be deemed having taken place, over one half of the citizens, having the right to vote and having been registered in electoral rolls, have to take part in it) is the most difficult to pass. Furthermore, in order to amend art 1 of the Constitution, the Constitutional Act of 8 June 1992, 'On Non-Alignment of the Republic of Lithuania To Post-Soviet Eastern Alliances', at least votes of three-fourths of the citizens having the right to vote and having been registered in electoral rolls, are required; amendments of Chapters I and XIV require votes of more than half of the citizens, having the right to vote and having been registered in electoral rolls.

[205] Recently the CC ruled that art 1 of the Constitution consolidates the fundamental constitutional values—the independence of the state, democracy and the republic—which are inseparably interrelated and form the foundation of the State of Lithuania, as the common good of the entire society consolidated in the Constitution; they must not be negated under any circumstances. Further, it pointed out that the principle of recognition of the innate nature of human rights and freedoms should also be regarded as a fundamental constitutional value that is inseparably related to the constitutional values—independence, democracy, and the republic—which constitute the foundation of the State of Lithuania as the common good of the entire society consolidated in the Constitution; the innate nature of human rights and freedoms may not be negated either. Given the constitutional imperative to ensure that no amendments of the Constitution violate the harmony of the provisions of the Constitution or the harmony of the values consolidated by them, the Constitution does not permit any such amendment that would

The limitation of the number of subjects that have the right to formally initiate the amendment procedure also serves the same stabilization function.[206] The rigidity of the Constitution is furthermore reinforced by the recent CC jurisprudence concerning the constitutionality of constitutional amendments.[207] Given all those features, it is not surprising that, to date, the number of amendments of the Constitution is relatively low, especially taking into account dynamic changes within a society that has been trying to get rid of its Soviet past and to return to the Western values,[208] although there have been many attempts to modify different parts of the Constitution. Such rigidity of the Constitution and the necessity to ensure its viability predetermines the central place of the CC in the process of development of the Constitution.

Speaking of legal nature, article 7 para 1 of the Constitution explicitly proclaims its supremacy over other sources of law, whereas article 6 provides for its direct applicability.[209] Nevertheless, attention should be paid to a certain tension between its provisions (or rather the necessity to establish a proper algorithm of their systemic interpretation). This tension could probably be attributed to the fact that the Constitution partially establishes a *Kelsenian* model of the constitutional review, but then it goes further by establishing principles and provisions related to human rights and submits them to adjudication by the CC. On the one hand, article 6 proclaims the direct applicability of the Constitution, which is further reinforced by article 30 para 1 and article 110 para 1 of the Constitution.[210] On the other hand, article 107 para 1 of the Constitution stipulates the consequences of the CC rulings.[211] The CC rulings are final and have *erga omnes* effects. Besides, via its interpretation of article 107 para 1, the CC has held that until the Constitutional Court has adopted a decision that the act in question is in conflict with the Constitution, it is presumed that such a legal act is in compliance with the Constitution and that the legal effects that have appeared on the basis of the act in question are legitimate.[212] Obviously, considerations related to stability

---

deny at least one of the above-mentioned constitutional values underlying the foundations of the State of Lithuania as the common good of the entire society, with the exception of the cases where art 1 of the Constitution would be altered (by a referendum with a three-quarters majority) (the Ruling of 24 January 2014).

[206] Under art 147, only a group of not less than one-fourth of all the MPs of the *Seimas* or not less than 300,000 voters may submit amendments to the Constitution before the *Seimas*. The Constitution may not be amended during a state of emergency or martial law. Retrospectively looking, different political powers were not able to sustain the lasting constitutional majority during 1992–2021.

[207] Rulings of 24 January 2014 and 11 July 2014. The CC pointed out that when adopting amendments of the Constitution, both procedural and material safeguards, stemming from the nature and purpose of the Constitution, must be respected. Failure to respect those safeguards may result in the declaration of unconstitutionality of relevant constitutional amendments. The procedural safeguards are established in Chapter XIV of the Constitution. The material safeguards, at least the values, established by art 1 of the Constitution (the independence of the state, democracy, and innate nature of human rights) are treated as 'eternal' and may not be annulled by the constitutional amendments. According to the CC, the Constitution does not establish preconditions for a 'democratic suicide'.

[208] It's not surprising that a big part of constitutional amendments adopted up to date were predetermined by the EU membership.

[209] 'The Constitution shall be an integral and directly applicable act. Everyone may defend his rights by invoking the Constitution'. This provision is reinforced by art 30 para 1 stating that 'a person whose constitutional rights or freedoms are violated shall have the right to apply to a court'. The earlier jurisprudence of the CC treated this right as absolute: see the Ruling of 30 June 2005. Still, the more recent practice of the CC recognizes that guaranties protected by these provisions may be balanced vis-à-vis other constitutional imperatives.

[210] Art 110 para 1: 'judges may not apply any laws that are in conflict with the Constitution'.

[211] Art 107 para 1: 'a law (or part thereof) of the Republic of Lithuania or another act (or part thereof) of the Seimas, an act (or part thereof) of the President of the Republic, or an act (or part thereof) of the Government may not be applied from the day of the official publication of the decision of the Constitutional Court that the act in question (or part thereof) is in conflict with the Constitution of the Republic of Lithuania'.

[212] Rulings of the CC 30 December 2003, 22 December 2010, 25 October 2011.

of already formed relations and the necessity to ensure the effectiveness of the Constitution have to be reconciled. Apparently, for the CC, the Constitution establishes *ex nunc* effects of the CC rulings. Still, the CC has admitted that this rule is not absolute and has indicated that, at least in three situations, its rulings would have *ex tunc* effect: a) if a legal act under review would negate the essential constitutional values (independence, democracy, republic and the innate nature of fundamental rights and freedoms); b) if a legal act would be adopted to simply overrule a previous ruling of the CC that found that a certain piece of legislation was incompatible with the Constitution; c) when a court of general competence or an administrative court deals with a particular case and has to refuse to apply a provision which was declared unconstitutional.[213] The last situation generates the biggest disputes so far because the CC is reluctant to provide a generalized solution to the question, specifically, to what extent ordinary courts may refuse to apply unconstitutional provisions. Does it relate only to a case, referred before the CC, or to all similar cases, pending before ordinary courts and waiting for a ruling of the CC, or maybe even to cases which were initiated after a ruling of the CC (provided that time limits to address the court have not expired or were properly renewed)? There is no unanimous answer to this question neither in the court practice, nor in Lithuanian academic doctrine.[214] As a rule, the CC does not specify the retroactive effects of its rulings. Additionally, sometimes, if there is a necessity for it, the CC will delay the publication of its rulings, thereby allowing the legislator to remove *lacunae legis*. However, recent CC practice shows that, in some situations, it favours systemic solutions adopted by the legislator, instead of allowing litigation in numerous cases.[215]

[213] Dainius Žalimas, 'Lietuvos Respublikos Konstitucija—jurisprudencinė Konstitucija', in Lietuvos Respublikos Konstitucinis Teismas (ed), *Lietuvos konstitucionalizmas. Ištakos, raida ir dabartis* (n 10) 274–288.

[214] A good reflection of ongoing discourse is the Judgment of the SACL of 21 March 2019 (Case No. A-3322-1062/2019). The judgment was adopted by a chamber of five judges with two separate opinions. The main source of disagreement was the question whether there was a legal basis to award moral damages to an applicant claimed by him for restrictions of a freedom of communication during the period of 5 May 2014 until 1 September 2015. The restriction was declared unconstitutional by the Ruling of the CC published on 27 February 2015. Thus, the main issue of a disagreement was the retroactive effects of the CC ruling. The majority of the SACL found that despite of the fact that relevant provisions were declared unconstitutional only later, there was a basis for evaluation, whether during the relevant period the rights of the applicant were violated.

[215] The last economic crisis forced the *Seimas* to adopt austerity measures, reducing various social guaranties and salaries in the public sector. Some of those measures were found to be unconstitutional by the CC. One of those rulings—the Ruling of 1 July 2013. The constitutional case was initiated by references of several administrative and general competence courts, which were flooded with thousands of claims to award diminished part of salary from an employer claiming at the same time that the reduction of a salary was unconstitutional. The CC found the reduction of salaries of state officials contrary to various constitutional principles (the ruling itself was subjected to heavy criticism from the part of politicians, media, and some scholars). Further, it specified that the legislator has the obligation to adopt a legislation compensating disproportionate losses of affected persons without undue delay and decided that the Ruling would be published 1 October 2013. The *Seimas* ordered the government to submit a draft law implementing the CC ruling before 1 May 2014. The government failed to do that within the prescribed term and asked for a prolongation. The *Seimas* adopted the law of 11 September 2014 ordering the government to submit a new draft law until 1 May 2015. Because of that, administrative courts were left in uncertainty, it was not clear, how to deal with all cases, pending before them. Therefore, the SACL referred again to the CC challenging the constitutionality of the Law of 11 September 2014 as contrary to the rule of law, the principle of good governance, legitimate expectations of affected persons, and their right to judicial protection by unreasonably delaying the term of adoption of the compensation mechanism. In the Ruling of 19 November 2015, the CC found the Law not contrary to the Constitution. It ruled that due to the various external factors (EU obligations, uncertain geopolitical situation, etc.) the government had difficulties in deciding how the compensation mechanism should look like. In reality, the impact of the constitutional challenge of the above-mentioned Law was such that the *Seimas* finally adopted the law on the compensation mechanism just before the adoption of the CC Ruling of 15 November 2015, a circumstance that most probably played its part on the outcome of the case. After such ruling of the CC, the SACL formed a practice, rejecting litigants claims by stating that their rights are remedied by the Law establishing the compensation mechanism, thus, it was not necessary to award diminished part of a salary in individual cases.

Of course, not all constitutional provisions are directly enforceable before courts, mainly those related to constitutional rights and freedoms. Overall, given its structure and content, one may say the 1992 Constitution performs traditional functions accorded to it by the classic constitutional doctrine.[216] First, it is treated as a fundamental legal document that establishes the state of Lithuania. Chapter I of the Constitution ('the State of Lithuania') revolves around the notions of people's (national) sovereignty and state sovereignty, democratic rule, the limitation and separation of powers, the supremacy of the Constitution and its direct applicability, the official state language (Lithuanian) and the symbols of the state. Chapter II ('The Human Being and the State') establishes the fundamental rights and freedoms of individuals, whereas Chapters III ('Society and the State') and IV ('National Economy and Labour') are reflections of the communal and societal aspects of the Constitution. The remainder (Chapters V–XIII) deals primarily with the organization and functioning of public power. Thus, the Constitution may be treated as a material reflection of the usual dimensions of constitutionalism:[217] constitutionalism as a limit to public power, constitutionalism as a polity expression and constitutionalism as deliberation or, using the notion proposed by Joseph Raz, a 'thick' constitution.[218] As regards the centre of gravity among these constitutional dimensions, article 1 speaks of Lithuania as an 'independent democratic republic'. Thus, the independence of the state is placed before its democratic nature. Moreover, different compared to some other EU Member States, Chapter I of the Constitution is devoted not to constitutional rights, but to the state as a common good of the Lithuanian people. This sequence is not accidental given the historical experience and the fact that the Constitution was adopted at the time when the Soviet army was still in the country. Bearing in mind this, sovereigntist language of the Constitution,[219] the CC jurisprudence, the political culture and the general mood among the public, we can draw the conclusion that the Constitution first of all gravitates to the reflection of the continued statehood of Lithuania, although this does not mean that other dimensions of the Constitution are less important.

2. Basic Constitutional Principles Describing the Republic of Lithuania

The 1992 Constitution reflects the classic continental approach based on the idea that all public power stems from the people who act as *pouvoir constituant*. The whole content of Chapter I of the Constitution is permeated with this idea and reflects the inseparable link between the sovereignty of the people,[220] who confer the legitimacy to all public power, which in turn is realized directly[221] or through state institutions, and democracy.[222] Thus, one may

---

[216] Egidijus Šileikis, *Alternatyvi konstitucinė teisė* (n 94) 52–71.

[217] For example, Miguel P Maduro, 'How Constitutional Can the European Union Be? The Tension Between Intergovernmentalism and Constitutionalism in the European Union' (2004) 5 New York University Jean Monnet Working Paper, available at SSRN https://ssrn.com/abstract=1576145 (last accessed on 22 March 2022).

[218] For the notion of a 'thick' constitution see, in particular, Joseph Raz, 'On the Authority and Interpretation of Constitutions: some Preliminaries', in Larry Alexander, *Constitutionalism* (CUP, Cambridge 1998) 152–193.

[219] Irmantas Jarukaitis, *Lietuvos Respublikos narystė Europos Sąjungoje konstituciniai pagrindai* (n 117) 261–266.

[220] Art 2: 'the State of Lithuania shall be created by the Nation. Sovereignty shall belong to the Nation'. Art 3: 'No one may restrict or limit the sovereignty of the Nation or arrogate to himself the sovereign powers belonging to the entire Nation. The Nation and each citizen shall have the right to resist anyone who encroaches on the independence, territorial integrity, and constitutional order of the State of Lithuania by force'.

[221] As regards the close link between people's sovereignty and direct democracy, see the Ruling of 22 July 1994.

[222] Art 4: 'the Nation shall execute its supreme sovereign power either directly or through *its* democratically elected representatives'. This emphasis is especially relevant when it comes to the exercise of public power by the EU institutions.

THE EVOLUTION AND *GESTALT* OF THE LITHUANIAN CONSTITUTION   357

sum up those provisions as follows: the Republic of Lithuania is a sovereign state, its powers stem from the people, and the people's democratic representation is mainly ensured by the *Seimas*.[223]

Of course, given the prominent place the concept of sovereignty plays in the text of the 1992 Constitution, one may ask how it is conceptualized in both academic works and the CC jurisprudence, especially given the fact of EU membership. Two preliminary remarks should be made regarding sovereignty as a theoretical concept and legal principle. First, it is clear that, in general, legal commentators do not agree on the content of the concept of sovereignty. The statement that disagreement and conflict are constitutive elements of the concept of sovereignty, thereby leading to its description as an essentially contestable concept, seems to be accurate.[224] Secondly, considering its historic origins and later developments, there is no basis to equate sovereignty and the actual powers performed by a political community. Thus, a definition of sovereignty as a sufficiently effective claim to ultimate (constitutional) power in the context of the sovereignty discourse, but nothing more, is fitting.[225] Accordingly, the claim that EU Member States are sovereign is not under challenge, whereas the EU itself has never made such a claim,[226] although one may agree with a proposition that a claim to autonomy of EU law may be viewed as a claim in that direction, but of much less intensity.

Lithuanian authors tend to recognize the relative character of the concept of sovereignty. Even before the Second World War, one of the most prominent professors argued that neither the external nor the internal aspects of state sovereignty may be treated as absolute since (externally) a state is subject to international law, whereas internally state powers are subject to peoples' needs.[227] Contemporary writings associate the concept of sovereignty with the following dimensions: the self-determination of the people of how to live and the right to establish their own state;[228] the right to make political constitutional decisions independently; and the principal existence of the state as a member of the international community alongside other states.[229] They also see it as the discursive form through which a political community permanently expresses claims to the supreme public powers, thereby ensuring the continuous identity and independent status of that political community.[230] The CC has so far been laconic on the content of the principle of sovereignty, however, its practice confirms a close link between the principles of people's sovereignty, state sovereignty and democracy.[231]

---

[223] Such order follows the tradition of the Constitutions of 1922 and 1938, with Chapter I devoted to the structural description of the state.

[224] Samantha Besson, 'Sovereignty in Conflict' (2004) 8 European Integration Online Papers 15–16.

[225] For example, Wouter G Werner and Jaap H De Wilde, 'The endurance of sovereignty' (2001) 7 European Journal of International Relations 283–313; Neil Walker, 'Late Sovereignty in the European Union', in Neil Walker (ed), *Sovereignty in Transition* (Hart Publishing, Oxford, 2003) 19–32.

[226] Such a point of view concerning the adoption of constitutional decisions related to the self-determination or future direction of development of a state community is reinforced by the judgment of the CJEU of 10 December 2018 C-621/18 *Wightman* (ECLI:EU:C:2018:999) paras 56–59, 65.

[227] Mykolas Römeris, *Valstybė ir jos konstitucinė teisė. II dalis. Konstitucinės institucijos. I tomas. Suverenitetas* (Pradai, Vilnius, 1995) 245.

[228] Egidijus Jarašiūnas, 'Konstitucijos teorijos pagrindai', in Egidijus Jarašiūnas and others, *Lietuvos konstitucinė teisė* (Vilnius 2001) 496.

[229] Vilenas Vadapalas, 'Delimitation of Competences Between the European Union and the Member States: the Look from the Candidate Country', in Dimitris Melissas and Ingolf Pernice (eds), *Perspectives of the Nice Treaty and the Intergovernmental Conference in 2004* (Nomos, Baden-Baden, 2004) 14–15.

[230] Irmantas Jarukaitis, *Lietuvos Respublikos narystės Europos Sąjungoje konstituciniai pagrindai* (n 117) 163–188.

[231] In its Ruling of 19 September 2002, the CC noted, that '[i]n article 1 of the Constitution the fundamental principles of the Lithuanian State are established: the Lithuanian State is free and independent; the republic is the form of governance of the Lithuanian State; state power must be organized in a democratic way, and there must be a democratic political regime in this country'.

As regards the 'holder' of sovereignty as the ultimate power, the Constitution uses two different terms: 'the Lithuanian Nation' (*liet. 'lietuvių tauta'*) and 'the Nation of Lithuania' (*liet. 'Lietuvos tauta'*) or simply 'the Nation'. The first is used in the Preamble of the Constitution (and, implicitly, in other articles of the Constitution) in order to reflect the ethnic origins of the nation in the historic context. It also emphasizes the fact that the Lithuanian Nation (i.e. the ethnic nation) created the State of Lithuania a long time ago, defended its independence and preserved its spirit, native language, and writing. Still, the Preamble of the Constitution explicitly provides that the Lithuanian Nation shall foster national concord in the land of Lithuania. Thus, it expressly recognizes that also non-Lithuanians (people of other ethnical nations) have resided in the lands of Lithuania over centuries and, together with the Lithuanians, created and defended the State of Lithuania.

For the definition of the holder of the sovereignty, the Constitution uses the second term and refers to the whole of the citizens of the State of Lithuania as the civil Nation (state community). This idea is reflected in different parts of the Constitution.[232] Obviously, the citizenship expresses legal membership of a person in the State of Lithuania and reflects legal belongingness of the person to the Nation as a state community. According to the CC, the Lithuanian civil Nation is a state community which unites the citizens of the corresponding state (irrespective of their ethnical origin) and the whole of citizens that make up the Lithuanian civic Nation. The Nation includes all citizens, regardless of whether they belong to the nominal nation (they are Lithuanians) or to national minorities.[233] All citizens are equal, meaning that they may not be discriminated or granted any privileges on the grounds of their ethnical origin and nationality. Still, the CC has held that the integration into the society of Lithuania, that is, becoming a fully fledged member of the state community, involves some efforts, including learning the state language. For the CC, namely only the citizens of the reborn State of Lithuania adopted and proclaimed the 1992 Constitution, have the right to create the State of Lithuania, to decide as to what State of Lithuania must be and to establish its constitutional order, the organization of institutions exercising state power, and the basics of relations between the person and the state, etc.[234]

Article 12 of the Constitution establishes provisions related to the citizenship of the Republic of Lithuania.[235] One of the most sensitive issues that feeds both political and public discourse until today, given the high rate of emigration from Lithuania, is the question to what extent the Constitution 'tolerates' double citizenship. The CC interpreted article 12 para 2 of the Constitution to the effect that 'the law may and must provide individual cases, when a person may be a citizen of both the Republic of Lithuania and another state', but 'such cases established by law can be very rare (individual), that cases of dual citizenship must be extraordinarily rare, exceptional, that under the Constitution it is not permitted to establish any such legal regulation under which cases of dual citizenship would be not extraordinarily rare exceptions, but a widespread phenomenon'.[236] Later on, called upon to reinterpret its

---

[232] Art 2 provides that the State of Lithuania shall be created by the Nation and sovereignty shall belong to the Nation; art 4 provides that the Nation shall execute its supreme sovereign power either directly or through its democratically elected representatives, the notion 'Nation' is used precisely in this sense.

[233] Under art 37 of the Constitution, citizens belonging to ethnic communities have the right to foster their language, culture, and customs.

[234] Rulings of 30 December 2003, 25 May 2004, 10 May 2006, 13 November 2006.

[235] Art 12: 'Citizenship of the Republic of Lithuania shall be acquired by birth or on other grounds established by law. With the exception of individual cases provided for by law, no one may be a citizen of both the Republic of Lithuania and another state at the same time. The procedure for the acquisition and loss of citizenship shall be established by law.'

[236] Rulings of 30 December 2003, 13 November 2006.

THE EVOLUTION AND *GESTALT* OF THE LITHUANIAN CONSTITUTION   359

jurisprudence,[237] the CC refused to do that and specified that only amendments of article 12 para 2 of the Constitution may secure the desired result.[238]

Speaking of the exercise of the sovereign power, it may not be separated from the principle of democracy. The CC and academic works confirm that the notion of democracy may be conceived in a narrow sense (as the principle of majority of decision making),[239] although, in general, article 1 and the whole of the Constitution reflect the ideals of liberal democracy.[240] The content of the Constitution instructs that the principle of democracy may be associated with at least the following elements: the sovereignty of the state community, political rights of citizens of that community, a multiparty system, media freedom, the majoritarian decision making itself,[241] a free mandate, the government's accountability to the *Seimas*, and the general principle of good governance.[242]

The 1992 Constitution reflects both the notions of direct and representative democracy. According to Article 4 of the Constitution, the Nation executes its supreme sovereign power either directly or through its democratically elected representatives. article 9 specifies that the most significant issues concerning the life of the State and the Nation shall be decided by referendum.[243] Obviously, the representative democracy is primarily related to the central role played by the directly elected *Seimas*.

---

[237] The main question is to what extent persons who left Lithuania and reside in other states after the restoration of independence of Lithuania in 1990 and acquired citizenship of those states, may at the same time be citizens of Lithuania and another state irrespective of the fact that such legal regulation would create preconditions for a large part of citizens of Lithuania to be also citizens of other states at the same time.

[238] Decisions of 13 March 2013 and 20 October 2017. In the later constitutional case the petitioner, the *Seimas*, argued for the necessity of the reinterpretation of the CC jurisprudence given Lithuania's accession to the EU, the adoption of the CA, as well as the later CC jurisprudence concerning the positive geopolitical orientation. The CC, relying on its earlier jurisprudence, noted that Lithuania's membership in the EU doesn't have an influence on Lithuanian citizenship, since the EU does not have competence in matters of national citizenship. The referendum took place 12 May 2019 but majority, necessary to amend art 12, was not reached.

[239] Ruling of 22 July 1992: 'one of the democratic principles in the adoption of decisions is the majority principle. This principle is also determined in the Constitution establishing the procedures for the activity and law enactment carried out by the *Seimas* and other authorized institutions, also regulating other questions'.

[240] Ruling of 19 September 2002: 'Article 1 of the Constitution provides that the State of Lithuania shall be an independent and democratic republic. The provision . . . means that in the state one must ensure the supremacy of the Constitution, the protection of human rights and freedoms, the equality of all persons before the law and the court, the right to judicial defence, free and periodical elections, the separation and balance of powers, the responsibility of authority before the citizens, the democratic process of decision-making, political pluralism, opportunities for development of a civil society, etc'.

[241] Still, the CC insists on the necessity to establish guaranties of activities for the opposition in the *Seimas*: see the Ruling of 25 January 2001.

[242] Egidijus Šileikis, *Alternatyvi konstitucinė teisė* (n 94) 251–254.

[243] Speaking of Lithuania's membership in the EU, art 4 para 5 of the Law on Referendums provides for a mandatory referendum concerning the participation of the Republic of Lithuania in international organizations 'should this participation be linked with the partial transfer of the scope of competence of Government bodies to the institutions of international organizations or the jurisdiction thereof'. The referendum took place on 10-11 May 2003. A simple statement 'I am for Lithuania's membership in the European Union' was submitted to a vote: 63.37 per cent of the citizens participated in the referendum, of whom a notably high 90 per cent voted in favour of Lithuania's accession to the EU. From the point of view of democratic legitimacy, the referendum was of utmost importance, especially because of the far-reaching consequences of EU membership. There were calls to hold a referendum concerning the ratification of the EU Constitutional Treaty, but it was decided to ratify it at the parliament. Two unsuccessful referenda initiatives related to EU were promoted in 2013–2014. One concerned a proposed amendment of art 47 of the Constitution, aimed at restricting the right of foreigners to buy land in Lithuania. It failed, as only 14.98 per cent of eligible voters participated. The second concerned the proposed amendment of art 125 of the Constitution and art 1 of the CA. The initiators proposed amending the Constitution in order to re-establish the right of the Bank of Lithuania to emit bank notes. The Central Electoral Commission refused to register the initiative, arguing that such amendments would not be compatible with the Constitution. The SACL, after verifying with the CC whether the Central Electoral Commission had such authority under the Constitution, supported the findings of the Central Electoral Commission on 18 July 2014 (Ruling of the SACL of 18 July 2014 in Case No. R-858-11-14).

Article 1 of the Constitution refers to the republican form of governance. Interestingly enough, the Act of Independence of 16 February 1918 does not mention republic and it only entered into official constitutional vocabulary with the adoption of the Constitution of 1920.[244]

As mentioned, the question of balance of powers was the main object of heated discussions during the drafting of the 1992 Constitution. The main source of disagreement was the role and powers of the President in the overall institutional setup.[245] This issue surfaced later and had to be dealt with by the CC. Taking into account the powers of the President, going beyond those, usually accorded by the parliamentary model, the CC described the Lithuanian governance model as the parliamentary republic, with certain features of mixed (half-presidential) form of governance. For the CC, this has been reflected in the powers of the *Seimas*, those of the President of the Republic and the government, as well as in the legal arrangement of their reciprocal interaction. The CC confirmed that the Lithuanian constitutional system establishes the principle of the responsibility of the Government to the *Seimas* and thus determines a respective way of Government formation.[246]

Speaking of territorial organization, Article 10 para 1 of the Constitution establishes the unitary state organization expressing the idea of a united and indivisible state.[247] The text of article 10 para 1 of the Constitution, which prohibits division of the territory into 'state-like formations', is yet another reflection of the historic experience given the fact that, during the process of re-establishment of the independence, there were some attempts to create 'autonomous' formations that would have had specific status in the territory of Lithuania.

There is no doubt that Lithuania's membership in the EU had a profound impact on the principle of democracy. By becoming a part of the European political community, Lithuanian citizens acquired the right to participate directly or indirectly in adoption of decisions that directly impact their lives, thus meaning that they could secure their interests more effectively. Their participation and representation in decision making is secured both through national and supranational institutions, including the European Parliament (the EP). On the other hand, decisions, which have been adopted within this wider political community, are taken not only by the members of Lithuanian political community ('national majority'), but also by members of other national political communities (or the 'European majority'). Accordingly, in areas of EU competence, Lithuanian citizens and other European citizens or nationals of other EU Member States form the common European community. Within this community, political decisions are being made, but, at the same time, it means that, in certain cases, the whole national community may become 'a minority' (e.g. in cases it is outvoted in the EU Council). Of course, this political community is partially based on different principles than state community considering that the creation of the wider European community does not mean the end of national/state political community or its identity.[248] However, one

---

[244] In order to foster the recognition of Lithuanian statehood there were some (unrealized) attempts to crown the count of Württemberg as the king of Lithuania.

[245] For description of those powers, see Section C.4.

[246] One of the most important decisions of the CC, the Ruling of 10 January 1998. Before it, there was no agreement, whether the government must resign once a new President is elected, or may it continue to work under its programme, approved by the *Seimas* for the rest of its term. The CC pointed out that the government is accountable to the *Seimas*, thus, differently from elections of the *Seimas*, elections of the President do not automatically trigger the resignation of the government.

[247] Art 10 para 1: 'the territory of the State of Lithuania shall be integral and shall not be divided into any state-like formations'.

[248] Attention should be drawn to the careful language of the CA, since the Preamble expressly refers to the duty of the EU to respect the national identity and constitutional traditions of its Member States, while art 1 of the CA speaks of 'trust of competences', but not their ultimate surrender/renouncement.

may argue, that there is a common minimum value affinity among the members of such community, thereby ensuring its (relative) stability and development. Thus, Article 1 of the CA opens up the national constitutional order and 'stretches' the limits of public powers, which were previously sanctioned and limited by Article 4 of the Constitution (and thus, the limits of the Constitution itself), since, after adoption of the CA, the Constitution embraces not only public powers exercised by the state institutions, but by supranational institutions as well.[249] The CC jurisprudence shows explicit recognition of the expansion of the boundaries of political community prompted by the EU membership.[250] Still, similar to some other constitutional courts, the CC tends to distinguish the role of the *Seimas* and that of the EP in the context of democratic discourse.[251]

3. Rule of Law and Fundamental Rights

The principle of the rule of law is the cornerstone principle of the entire national constitutional system. Although the principle (in Lithuanian '*teisinės valstybės principas*': '*a state governed by the rule of law*') and its various manifestations (like legal certainty, legitimate expectations, etc.) are not explicitly enshrined in the Constitution (apart from the Preamble, which speaks of the Lithuanian nation as 'striving for an open, just, and harmonious civil society and State under the rule of law'), it is infused in many of its core provisions.

Lithuanian authors are unanimous in treating the rule of law as an independent horizontal (constitutional) legal principle which co-ordinates and determines the whole (constitutional) legal system. Various elements of the principle are among the most important factors ensuring the proper functioning of the Constitution.[252]

The CC started invoking the principle of rule of law in the very early years of its existence.[253] It has consistently pointed out that the principle is a universal legal principle upon

---

[249] Egidijus Šileikis, *Alternatyvi konstitucinė teisė* (n 94) 149.

[250] In the Ruling of 21 December 2006 when defining duties of the public broadcaster the CC noted that '*[t]he principle of democracy* entrenched in the Constitution inter alia implies that the law must establish the legal regulation where, at the time of election campaigns, the public broadcaster gives air-time to the political parties and political organisations, *the candidates to the Seimas, to the European Parliament*, to the post of the President of the Republic and to municipal councils who participate in the election'. Thus, the EP is mentioned on equal footing with the *Seimas* in the context of the principle of democracy, thus, democratic legitimacy. In the Ruling of 9 February 2007 the CC stated that 'the right to self-government is implemented through *democratic* representation; municipal councils, through which the right to self-government is implemented, may not be formed in a way so that there might arise doubts as to their *legitimacy and legality*, inter alia, as to the fact whether the principles of a democratic state under the rule of law were not violated in the course of election of *persons* to political representative institutions'. Here, the CC doesn't use the term 'citizens' but 'persons' instead, since after amendments of art 119 of the Constitution the right to participate in municipal elections is conferred not only to Lithuanian citizens, but to all persons, permanently living in Lithuania. Again, for the CC democratic participation and legitimacy of adopted decisions are not confined solely to community, based on national citizenship.

[251] The CC resorts to different rhetoric when it comes to description of the *Seimas* and the EP. It emphasizes that under the Constitution only the *Seimas* is the representation of the Nation (liet. *Tautos atstovybė*), through which the Nation executes its supreme sovereign power. For the CC, the constitutional nature of the *Seimas* as the representative of the Nation determines its special place within the system of institutions of state power, as well as its functions and powers. When exercising its constitutional powers, the *Seimas* performs classical functions of a parliament of a democratic state under the rule of law: see the Rulings of 25 May 2004 and 1 July 2004. Although not expressing any doubts about the democratic legitimacy of the EP the CC describes it in rather neutral technocratic language, laconically pointing out that the EP 'represents citizens of the European Union and is to be regarded as a representative political institution' and making clear that the EP 'is not the representation of the Nation'. Still such perception does not preclude the application of the electoral rights, established in art 34 para 2 of the Constitution, to elections of the EP: see the Ruling of 9 November 2010.

[252] Egidijus Kūris, 'Koordinaciniai ir determinaciniai konstituciniai principai (1)' (n 104) 241–254; Egidijus Šileikis, *Alternatyvi konstitucinė teisė* (n 94) 198–210.

[253] Ruling of 13 December 1993.

which the whole Lithuanian legal system, as well as the Constitution itself, are based and that the content of the principle is revealed in various provisions of the Constitution. It is construed as inseparable from striving for an open, just, and harmonious civil society and law-governed state, as promulgated in the Preamble of the Constitution. The CC underlined that freedom of state power is limited by law: all legal subjects, including the law-making subjects, must obey the law and the discretion of all the law-making subjects is limited by the supreme law (the Constitution). All the legal acts and decisions of all the state and municipal institutions and officials must be in compliance with the Constitution. For the CC, this is a very voluminous constitutional principle which comprises various interrelated imperatives.[254] The Court develops the content of this principle taking account of various provisions of the Constitution, the content of other constitutional principles, such as the supremacy of the Constitution, its integrity and direct applicability, sovereignty of the Nation, democracy, good governance, the restriction of state power and service of state institutions to the people, publicity of law, justice (comprising, *inter alia*, natural justice), separation of powers, public spirit, equality of persons before the law, court, state institutions and officials, respect to and protection of the human rights and freedoms (including the recognition that the human rights and freedoms are of innate nature), coordination of interests of the person and society, secularity of the state and its neutrality in world-view matters, social orientation of the state, and social solidarity.[255] These imperatives are valid both in the course of adoption of a statutory legislation as well as when adopted legislation is implemented and applied.

Different elements directly related to the rule of law may be identified in the CC practice. They include at least the following: the innate nature of fundamental rights and freedoms; rules of general application must be established by laws passed by the *Seimas*; the supremacy of laws and hierarchy of different legal acts, which are all subordinated to the Constitution; the accessibility of legal provisions; legal certainty and the integrity of law; *nullum crimen, nulla poena sine lege*; the right to judicial protection; natural justice; due process of law; the independence and impartiality of judges and courts; continuity of court practice;[256] legitimate expectations;[257] proportionality;[258] and the constitutional imperative to observe the public international law principle *pacta sunt servanda*. Recently, the CC added the EU law dimension by ruling on the constitutionality of the statutory limitation to distribute litigation costs incurred in the course of a preliminary rulings procedure at the CJEU.[259]

As one may see, the principle has extensive content. The CC treats the principle as one of utmost importance for the systemic interpretation of various constitutional provisions, even if it has not been singled out as one of the core constitutional principles that can only be renounced under the Article 148 para 1 procedure. Because of that, when making the finding that certain contested provision of statutory regulation is contrary to the principle of rule of law, the CC does not indicate a particular provision of the Constitution. Furthermore,

---

[254] Such thesis that the rule of law is inseparable from other core constitutional principles is confirmed in academic writings as well: Egidijus Šileikis, *Alternatyvi konstitucinė teisė* (n 94) 199.

[255] Rulings of 23 February 2000, 11 January 2001; 13 December 2004.

[256] Rulings of 28 March 2006, 8 August 2006, 22 October 2007.

[257] Ruling of 23 February 2000. The principle of legitimate expectations entered the CC vocabulary rather late, mainly as a response to various austerity measures: Egidijus Šileikis, *Alternatyvi konstitucinė teisė* (n 94) 254.

[258] Ruling of 5 March 2013.

[259] Ruling of 14 December 2018. The CC found a violation of the principle of rule of law and art 30 of the Constitution. According to the CC, Lithuanian courts have a constitutional obligation to refer to the CJEU in cases where EU law is applicable, such referral is a precondition for delivery of just and reasoned judgment, whereas inability of a court to distribute costs would unreasonably limit person's right to judicial protection. The CC extensively analysed the CJEU jurisprudence as regards preliminary rulings procedure and procedural rights of parties in the main proceedings.

the principle itself is justiciable and applicants may challenge different legal provisions as regards to their compatibility with the principle. Recently, the CC went so far as to say that the rule of law binds the sovereign (that is, the people) itself in that it does not allow for the introduction of constitutional amendments that would contravene Lithuania's international obligations or obligations stemming from EU law. In order to introduce such constitutional provisions, international or EU obligations would have to be renounced or modified in a way that would not contradict the proposed amendments.[260] Overall, given the fact that the rule of law is inseparable from protection of fundamental rights and freedoms, one may argue that, although it is not explicitly included in the constitutional nucleus by the CC, it merits such qualification because of its fundamental nature.

Needless to say, one of the core functions of the Constitution is the protection of fundamental rights and freedoms. According to Article 18 of the Constitution, human rights and freedoms are innate. The CC emphasizes that Lithuania's constitutional system is based on the idea of priority of fundamental rights and freedoms as the highest value.[261] Although, technically speaking, Article 18 is not included in Chapter I of the Constitution, which may be amended only by way of a referendum, the CC has ruled that the innate nature of fundamental rights and freedoms is inseparable from the other fundamental provisions of the Constitution established in Article 1. Therefore, Article 18 may be amended only by a referendum in which the supermajority envisaged for amendments to Article 1 is required.[262] For the Court, the innate nature of those rights and freedoms predetermines one of the main tasks for the state: to ensure their protection.[263] This leads to various negative and positive obligations on the part of the state institutions in order to ensure their effective protection.[264]

The structure of the 1992 Constitution reflects the classical classification of right and freedoms: Chapter II of the Constitution ('the Human Being and the State') establishes traditional civil and political rights, whereas Chapter III ('Society and the State') and Chapter IV ('the National Economy and Labour') provide for economic, social, and cultural rights.

It is important to mention that, different from some constitutions of other European states, the 1992 Constitution explicitly bestows Lithuania with a market economy and freedom of individual economic activity.[265] The CC jurisprudence confirms that, as an individual freedom, this freedom is enforceable before courts.[266] Further, although the 1992 Constitution does not explicitly establish the principle of a social state, both the CC[267] and Lithuanian commentators[268] tend to speak about the principle of social solidarity and the

---

[260] Rulings of 24 January 2014 and 11 July 2014.

[261] Ruling of 23 November 1999.

[262] Ruling of 24 January 2014.

[263] Ruling of 29 December 2004.

[264] Ruling of 19 August 2006.

[265] Art 46 of the Constitution. The CC treats it both as systemic constitutional principle and as subjective or individual constitutional freedom: see the Ruling of 26 January 2004.

[266] Rulings of 23 February 2000, 29 November 2001, 14 March 2002, 13 May 2005, 31 May 2006, 5 July 2007. Still, when annulling market regulation measures the CC reinforces its argumentation with elements of the rule of law (proportionality, legal certainty, legitimate expectations, etc.). The issue of freedom of economic activity (a freedom of contract) is an essential element in the second referral of the CC to the CJEU, although the CC formulated only questions related to interpretation of secondary EU law. See as well the Opinion of the Advocate General M Bobek of 7 March 2019 in Case C-2/18.

[267] Ruling of 1 July 2013.

[268] Kūris notes that the principle of social state is first and foremost, 'the principle of a rich state': Egidijus Kūris, 'Koordinaciniai ir determinaciniai konstituciniai principai (1)' (n 104) 266–270. Similarly: Egidijus Šileikis, *Alternatyvi konstitucinė teisė* (n 94) 210–214.

social orientation of the Constitution. CC practice has confirmed that some of those social rights are justiciable.[269]

The 1992 Constitution does not contain any specific provisions establishing general conditions under which restrictions of fundamental rights and freedoms may be imposed. However, different provisions of the Constitution establish various grounds for derogation, for example, Article 20 ('no one may be deprived of his freedom otherwise than on the grounds and according to the procedures which have been established by law'); Article 22 ('information concerning the private life of a person may be collected only upon a justified court decision and only according to the law'); Article 25 ('freedom to express convictions, to receive and impart information may not be limited otherwise than by law, if this is necessary to protect the health, honour and dignity, private life, and morals of a human being, or to defend the constitutional order'), etc. Over time, the CC developed a general standard for limitations of fundamental rights and freedoms. Putting aside the absolute rights,[270] a restriction of fundamental rights and freedoms is permitted if all the following conditions are met: the limitation is imposed by a law adopted by the *Seimas*; these restrictions are necessary in a democratic society in order to protect the rights and freedoms of other persons as well as the values established in the Constitution together with constitutionally important objectives; the restrictions must not deny the nature and essence of the rights and freedoms; and the constitutional principle of proportionality is observed.[271] Speaking of proportionality, the CC underlines that measures provided for in the law must be in line with the legitimate objectives which are important to society. They must also not restrain the rights and freedoms of a person to any degree more than what is necessary in order to reach these objectives.[272] Additionally, this requirement implies *inter alia* an obligation for the legislator to establish such a regulation that would create preconditions to sufficiently individualize the limitations of the rights and freedoms: the regulation limiting the rights and freedoms must allow to assess as much as possible an individual position of each person and, by taking account of all the important circumstances, to individualize respectively the concrete measures that limit the rights of a concrete person.[273]

Pursuant to Article 6 para 2 and Article 30 para 1 of the Constitution, the fundamental rights and freedoms are directly enforced by the Lithuanian courts, which, if necessary, can act as intermediaries between a litigant who claims a violation of his constitutional rights and the CC. From that perspective, the establishment of the system of administrative courts in 1999 was of particular importance: statistics reveal that administrative courts are the main 'employers' of the CC.[274] Speaking of the European dimension, both jurisprudence of the CC and the SACL reveal that the impact of the ECHR is much more visible in comparison with

---

[269] In the Ruling of 6 February 2012 the CC ruled that the reduction of social pensions for working persons contravenes art 48 para 1 of the Constitution, as '[e]ach human being may freely choose a job or business'; in the Ruling of March 5, 2013, the CC ruled that certain aspects of the reduction of maternity allowances were not in line with the principle of the rule of law (were not proportionate); in the Ruling of 1 July 2013 the CC ruled that the uneven reduction of the salaries of state officials, where the salary reductions of highly paid state officials were greater in comparison to those of persons who earned less, was not in line with art 29 para 1: 'All persons shall be equal before the law', art 48 para 1 'Each human being ... shall have the right ... to receive fair pay for work' and the principle of the rule of law' (proportionality principle).

[270] Art 19 (the right to life); art 21 (human dignity, prohibition of torture, inhumane and degrading treatment); art 31 para 4 (*nullum crimen nulla poena sine lege*).

[271] Rulings of 14 March 2002, 29 December 2004.

[272] Ruling of 11 December 2009.

[273] Ruling of 7 July 2011.

[274] See Section C.4.d.

the EU Charter of Fundamental Rights, although some references to the Charter may be found in the practice of the SACL.[275]

Further, speaking of non-judicial tools of protection, Article 73 of the Constitution lays down the basis for the establishment of the *Seimas* Ombudsmen, which is an extrajudicial institution. It de facto started functioning in December 1994 and plays an important role in dealing with both systemic and individual cases of violation of fundamental rights.[276]

Finally, as mentioned above, amendments of Articles 106 and 107 of the Constitution, which introduce the individual constitutional complaint before the CC, were adopted on 21 March 2019. These amendments establish the right of an individual to directly address the CC with a constitutional complaint that attacks a legal act of the *Seimas*, the government, or the President, although all other national legal remedies must have been exhausted first. The finding of the CC that such an act violates the Constitution would serve as a basis to renew a judicial proceeding in order to reconsider a case, which was decided on the basis of an unconstitutional act.[277]

4. Constitutional Organs and Separation of Powers

The 1992 Constitution is based on the principle of division of public powers. Article 5 reflects this basic idea by stipulating that, in Lithuania, state power shall be executed by the *Seimas*, the President of the Republic and the Government, and the Judiciary, with the Constitution as the limit of the scope of their powers. Accordingly, Chapter V ('the *Seimas*') is devoted to the establishment of constitutional provisions related to the parliament, Chapter VI ('the President of the Republic') and Chapter VII ('the Government of the Republic of Lithuania') deals with the executive arm of the governance, whereas Chapter VIII ('the Constitutional Court') and Chapter IX ('Courts') establish constitutional basis of organization of judicial branch. Over time, the CC had plenty of opportunities to dwell both on the principle of separation of powers as well as on different practical consequences stemming from it. According to the CC, the principle means that the legislative, executive and judicial powers must be separated, sufficiently independent, and that there must be a balance between them. Every power is exercised through its institutions which are granted the competence corresponding to their purpose.[278] Thus, one may trace all classic elements of the principle of separation of powers: the separation *stricto sensu*, the balance of powers between different branches of governance and, finally, their interdependence, or, as the CC calls it, the principle of interfunctional partnership. It means that the separation of powers does not lead to an isolation of institutions, quite to the contrary, in order to accomplish tasks and functions of the state, the activities of state institutions have to be based on their cooperation.[279]

---

[275] In most cases, these are references to the principle of good administration and the CJEU practice developing this principle. See, for example, the Judgment of the extended chamber of the SACL in administrative Case No A858-2332/2011 of 17 October 2011; the Judgment of the SACL in administrative Case No eA4702-858/2017 of 16 October 2017.

[276] In line with the Paris Principles of the United Nations Resolution, the *Seimas* Ombudsmen were accredited as a National Human Rights Institution and got an A status in 2017, see http://www.lrski.lt/en/national-human-rig hts-institution-nhri.html (last accessed 22 March 2022).

[277] The Law, amending the Constitution, entered into force on 1 September 2019. Amendments of the Law on the Constitutional Court were adopted and necessary internal structural changes within the CC were undertaken.

[278] For example, the Ruling of 18 October 2000.

[279] Ruling of 10 January 1998.

a) Central Role of the *Seimas* in the Constitutional Setup of Lithuania

The Constitution emphasizes the central role played by the *Seimas* in the system of national political institutions. It is composed of representatives of the Nation—141 members elected for a four-year period on the basis of universal, equal, direct suffrage and secret ballot (Article 55 para 1 of the Constitution). In view of this constitutional provision, only the *Seimas* is a representation of the Nation.[280]

The *Seimas* is elected using a mixed electoral system. The territory of Lithuania is divided into seventy-one single-member constituencies from which seventy-one MPs are individually elected. Additionally, one multi-member constituency is formed where citizens may cast their votes and elect seventy MPs according to the proportional system. Citizens from the age of eighteen may vote, while those who are at least twenty-one and permanently reside in Lithuania may stand as candidates. The list of candidates of the party takes part in the distribution of mandates only if not less than five per cent of the voters participating in the election voted for it. For joint lists of different parties, the threshold is seven per cent.

The constitutional nature of the *Seimas* as the representation of the Nation predetermines its unique place in the overall institutional system and its functions and powers. The *Seimas* is the centre of representative democracy and the political system, consolidating links of a political system and ensuring the functioning of the state. The *Seimas* exercises the sovereignty of the Nation, the latter being the only source of its constitutional powers. Following such a logic, the essential duty of the *Seimas* is to express the will of the Nation by adopted laws, i.e. to transform the will and expectations of the Nation into the will of the state.[281]

When exercising public powers as a legislator, the *Seimas* is independent as far as these powers are not restricted by the Constitution, but it must always ensure the continuous implementation of its powers provided for in the Constitution.[282] The powers of the *Seimas* are stipulated by Article 67 of the Constitution, but the list is not exhaustive. Other competencies may be provided for by law, but the status of the *Seimas* and the constitutional principle of separation of powers enshrined in the Constitution may not be violated. Like other institutions, the *Seimas* cannot refuse or delegate to other institutions the powers or functions provided for in the Constitution.

The Constitution identifies the main functions and powers of the *Seimas*: to legislate (legislative function); to exercise parliamentary control over the executive and other public authorities (except courts) (control function); to establish state institutions, to appoint and dismiss their heads and other state officials (founding function);[283] to approve the state budget and supervise its implementation (budgetary function).[284]

The parameters of the activities of the *Seimas* are defined by the Constitution, whereas the structure and procedures of work are determined by the Statute of the *Seimas*. This presupposes that the Statute of the *Seimas*, although not having the form of a law, has the force of law.[285]

---

[280] Ruling of 30 December 2003.

[281] Vytautas Sinkevičius, 'Seimas—Tautos atstovybė (konstituciniai pagrindai)' (2006) 87 (9) Jurisprudencija 52–60.

[282] Ruling of 24 February 1994.

[283] Including judges of the CC, the Supreme Court and their Presidents, as well as the Auditor General, the Chairperson of the Central Bank upon the proposal of the President.

[284] Ruling of 1 July 2004.

[285] The Statute of the *Seimas* is adopted, amended and supplemented by a statute, not the law, not all the rules of legislation are applied to these procedures, because the adopted statute is signed not by the President of the Republic but by the Speaker of the *Seimas*. It means that the President has no power to veto the Statute or its amendments. This ensures the independence of the *Seimas* to determine its own structure and working procedures. The

When it comes to the status of MPs of the *Seimas*, the most significant feature is the principle of a free mandate. It is described by the Constitution as follows: 'While in office, the Members of the *Seimas* shall follow the Constitution ... the interests of the State, as well as their own consciences, and may not be restricted by any mandates.'[286] The CC describes the essence of free mandate as lying in the freedom of a representative of the Nation to implement the rights and duties vested in him/her without being encumbered by any mandates, political requirements of parties and organisations that nominated him/her. It means as well that the Constitution does not recognize the right to revoke a MP of the *Seimas*. The basic function of this free mandate is to ensure independence and equality of rights of MPs of the *Seimas*.[287] However, a free mandate does not imply an absolute freedom of action of a MP of the *Seimas*. He should, at a minimum, be able to fulfil the requirements arising from the Constitution and must not take decisions that would be incompatible with the Constitution. This free mandate must not be used in a manner contrary to the interests of the nation and the state.

The main rights and duties of MPs are defined in the Constitution and are specifically regulated by the Statute. It stipulates in detail the privileges that they enjoy. The essential privileges are the prohibitions on initiating criminal proceedings against a MP without the consent of the *Seimas*, arresting him or otherwise restricting his freedom, and persecuting him for his speeches and votes in the *Seimas*.[288]

Still, immunities and indemnities of a MP may not result in unjustified privileges. The immunity may be waived by the *Seimas* when there are grounds to believe that a MP has committed a crime. In this case, the Prosecutor General approaches the *Seimas* with the request and the latter has to decide whether to establish a commission for the consent of the *Seimas* concerning the initiation of criminal proceedings, arrest or other restrictions of his freedom or to initiate preparatory steps leading to the impeachment proceedings. The *Seimas* will then adopt a resolution granting or refusing a request of the Prosecutor General on the basis of the conclusion drawn by the commission. The Constitution establishes a special procedure for the loss of the mandate of a MP. Under Article 74 of the Constitution, the mandate of a MP may be revoked by a three-fifths majority vote of all MPs of the *Seimas*. When deciding on the revocation of the mandate of a MP, the *Seimas* must proceed on the basis of an opinion, delivered by the CC, in which the Court has to establish whether there was a gross violation of the Constitution or the oath.[289]

Lithuania's accession to the EU had a very significant impact on the role of the *Seimas* in the national institutional setup. Article 5 of the Constitution, as interpreted by the CC before the accession, established a strict separation of powers as regards the legislative and executive functions, with the consequence that no delegated legislation by the government was allowed.[290] Thus, the government's powers in the EU Council completely modified the principles of democracy and the separation of powers from the point of view of Lithuanian

---

CC stated that by that the discretion of the *Seimas* is established, still this discretion is not absolute and may not violate the Constitution, it is subjected to the constitutional review of the CC: the Ruling of 25 January 2001.

[286] Art 59 para 4 of the Constitution.
[287] Ruling of 9 November 1999.
[288] Art 62 of the Constitution.
[289] Juozas Žilys, '1992 metų Lietuvos Respublikos Konstitucijos esmė ir pagrindiniai bruožai', in Lietuvos Respublikos Konstitucinis Teismas (ed), *Lietuvos konstitucionalizmas. Ištakos, raida ir dabartis* (n 10) 209–212.
[290] Rulings of 14 January 2002; 13 December 2004. Because of that, Lithuania's accession to the EU had the profound impact on the principle of separation of powers (and the principle of democracy as well), since the government acquired legislative rights through participation in the Council.

constitutional law. In order to counterbalance these changes, Article 3 of the CA established provisions regulating the involvement of the *Seimas* in the EU decision-making process and providing for a parliamentary control of the Government when it acts at the EU level.[291] These provisions of the CA aim at reconciling the necessity of having a close involvement of the *Seimas* when the Government participates in the EU Council with the need to leave enough bargaining flexibility for the latter. Detailed implementing provisions are established in Chapter 27[1] of the Statute of the *Seimas*.[292] The Statute accords the main powers of parliamentary control to the European Affairs Committee (further—EAC) and, in the field of the Common Foreign and Security Policy and other external issues, to the Foreign Affairs Committee (FAC), which is given the right to issue opinions on behalf of the *Seimas*. In some cases, the Statute requires discussions to be held (for example, deliberations on the compliance of draft EU legal initiatives with the principle of subsidiarity) not in the EAC but in the plenary session. The Government has a duty to inform the *Seimas* in writing of proposals to adopt EU legal acts and other relevant EU documents. Once the European Commission communicates its annual work programme, the specialized committees of the *Seimas* identify the priorities for the upcoming year in order to focus on the issues that are most relevant for Lithuania, and the finalized version of these priorities is submitted to the government. The institution responsible for the preparation of the Lithuanian position concerning a proposal to adopt an EU legal act or other EU document has the obligation to submit this position to the *Seimas* immediately after its preparation. This submission cannot be made any later than three days prior to the debate on this position in the EU institutions. At the executive level, the formation of the Lithuanian position is initiated and conducted through the LINESIS electronic platform, which records all the changes made in the Lithuanian position throughout its preparation. Once received in the *Seimas*, the position is forwarded to the specialized committees and to the EAC or the FAC. Having deliberated on a position, a specialized committee may either approve the position or propose amendments and review of the position. Its position is communicated either to the EAC or the FAC. The position is deliberated on at a meeting of the EAC or the FAC where the Prime Minister or the appropriate minister presents the position and answers questions. Then, the conclusions of the specialized committees are presented and discussions on the position are held. The committee decides by consensus or by a vote whether it should, on behalf of the *Seimas*, state its opinion about the position. If so, the chair of the meeting proposes the wording of the opinion and the opinion is adopted in a vote. Both committees may require a minister to maintain a parliamentary reservation during the deliberation of issues that are considered as highly relevant or relevant in the EU institutions. Article 180 establishes the obligation of the Prime Minister and ministers to submit an oral or written report on the fate of the Lithuanian position after the relevant meeting of the European Council or the EU Council.

---

[291] Art 3 of the CA: 'The Government shall inform the Seimas about the proposals to adopt the acts of European Union law. As regards the proposals to adopt the acts of European Union law regulating the areas that, under the Constitution of the Republic of Lithuania, are related to the competences of the Seimas, the Government shall consult the Seimas. The Seimas may recommend to the Government a position of the Republic of Lithuania in respect of these proposals. The Seimas Committee on European Affairs and the Seimas Committee on Foreign Affairs may, according to the procedure established by the Statute of the Seimas, submit to the Government the opinion of the Seimas concerning the proposals to adopt the acts of European Union law. The Government shall assess the recommendations or opinions submitted by the Seimas or its Committees and shall inform the Seimas about their execution following the procedure established by legal acts.'

[292] The English translation of the Statute is available at http://www3.lrs.lt/pls/inter3/dokpaieska.showdoc_l?p_id=473761 (last accessed on 22 March 2022).

Additionally, Article 180[6] of the Statute establishes a subsidiarity control procedure under which draft EU legislation is scrutinized by the specialized committees and their positions are submitted to the EAC or the FAC. If one of these committees decides that a draft EU law does not respect the principle of subsidiarity, it prepares a draft *Seimas* resolution with a reasoned opinion. The resolution is debated by the *Seimas* sitting in accordance with the special urgency procedure. If adopted, the *Seimas* resolution regarding the reasoned opinion is forwarded to the government. To sum up, the system functions rather effectively, there is quite a high degree of information exchange and harmonization of positions between the Government and the *Seimas*. In practice, the role of the *Seimas* in the EU decision-making is quite important.[293]

Further, as mentioned, the Constitution places the emphasis on the central role of the *Seimas* in budgetary matters. Additionally, under Article 128 para 1 of the Constitution '[d]ecisions concerning the State loan and other basic property liabilities of the State shall be adopted by the *Seimas* on the proposal of the Government'. Later on, the CC expanded the principle of democracy to the extent that all decisions related to 'basic property liabilities', i.e. having significant financial implications on the state budget, have to be approved by the *Seimas*.[294] This predetermined, for example, the role of the *Seimas* in the context of the ESM Treaty.[295]

Finally, in the context of the ongoing discussions concerning further steps of economic and political integration, any veto powers on the part of EU institutions in the course of adoption of the national budget, given the budgetary powers of the *Seimas*, would be hardly in line with article 67 para 14 of the Constitution.[296] Similarly, the question could be posed whether the loss of such powers at the national level could be counterbalanced by the increase of EP powers without the amendments of the Constitution should the scenario, involving the establishment of EU revenue rising and spending powers, be chosen. Needless to say, the budgetary function of the *Seimas* is at the heart of the principle of democracy, it is an expression of solidarity of the national polity. The transfer of such powers to the supranational level would have a significant impact on this constitutional function that national budget performs, thus, the position of some national courts, which stresses that national parliaments must retain control of fundamental budgetary decisions, is understandable.

b) The President of the Republic

According to Article 77 of the Constitution, the President of the Republic (hereinafter the President) is the Head of State. The President represents the state of Lithuania and does everything what he/she is entrusted to do by the Constitution and the laws. These general provisions define in laconic manner the legal status of the President, all other powers and functions that are entrenched in the Constitution and other laws.

---

[293] Egidijus Jarašiūnas, 'Lietuvos Respublikos narystės Europos Sąjungoje konstituciniai pagrindai', in Lietuvos Respublikos Konstitucinis Teismas (ed), *Lietuvos konstitucionalizmas. Ištakos, raida ir dabartis* (n 10) 247–248.

[294] Ruling of the CC of 18 October 2000.

[295] The Law on ratification of the ESM Treaty (art 2) established the obligation of the government to obtain *ex ante* approval of the *Seimas* concerning (a) the maximum lending volume and the adequacy of the authorized capital stock of the ESM under art 10 (para 1) of the ESM Treaty; (b) possible amendments to the contribution key for subscribing to ESM authorised capital stock under art 11 of the ESM Treaty, if it increases financial obligations of Lithuania. Besides, the government adopted a decree concerning the representation of Lithuania in the ESM, according to which, if necessary approval of the *Seimas* was not received, the representative of Lithuania must abstain during the vote.

[296] 'The Seimas . . . shall approve the State Budget and supervise its execution.'

The Constitution and the Law of the President establish detailed rules on the status of the President. Article 5 of the Constitution provides that, in Lithuania, state power shall be vested in the *Seimas*, the President of the Republic and the Government, and the Judiciary, thereby confirming that the President is a part of the executive branch of governance. Thus, a dualistic model of the executive power characterizes the Lithuanian constitutional system: the President exercises some of those powers independently, while others are shared with the government.[297]

The status of the President as the Head of State is exceptional. It differs from other state officials because, first of all, he/she is elected (for a five-year term) directly by universal suffrage.[298] According to the CC, this mandate means that the President symbolizes the State of Lithuania, the values of the nation, and personalizes the Republic of Lithuania in international relations.[299] The constitutional powers of the President and his privileges presuppose a special responsibility for the state and the nation. In this context, the political, legal significance of the oath of the President is emphasized by the CC. The elected President begins his duties when, with the participation of MPs of the *Seimas*, he/she swears to the people to be faithful to the Republic of Lithuania and the Constitution, to honestly perform his duties and to be just and fair to everybody. A person elected the President must suspend his activities in political parties and political organizations until the beginning of a new campaign for the presidential elections.[300]

As the Head of State, the President enjoys general immunity. According to Article 86 para 1 of the Constitution, the person of the President is inviolable: while in office, he/she may be neither detained nor held criminally or administratively liable. Article 86 para 2 stipulates that the President may be removed from office only for a gross violation of the Constitution or a breach of the oath, or when he/she is found to have committed a crime. The removal of the President from office is decided by the *Seimas* after the pronouncement of an opinion of the CC. As mentioned, such impeachment procedure was applied once against the President and it led to his removal from the office in 2004.

The President is entrusted with rather extensive powers in terms of formation of other branches of governance and the exercise of public powers. These are described in Article 84 of the Constitution and cover broad range of issues related to foreign, security, and internal issues.

Speaking of the *Seimas*, the interaction of these two institutions is based not only on the independence, but also on cooperation in the exercise of powers. The President calls the regular elections of the *Seimas*. They are held on the second Sunday of October at the end of the term of office of the *Seimas*.[301] Under Article 58 para 2 of the Constitution, the early elections of the *Seimas* may be called not only by the *Seimas* itself, but also by the President in specific cases that are provided for in the Constitution.[302] However, when the President calls

---

[297] Ruling of the CC of 13 December 2004.

[298] Under art 78 para 1 of the Constitution, a Lithuanian citizen by descent who has lived in Lithuania for not less than the last three years, if he has reached the age of forty prior to the election day and may stand for election as a Member of the *Seimas*, may stand for election as the President.

[299] Ruling of 25 May 2004.

[300] Art 83 para 2 of the Constitution.

[301] Art 143 of the Constitution establishes one exception: if regular elections must be held during martial law, the President has to adopt the decision to extend the term of powers of the *Seimas*. In such case, elections must be called not later than three months after the end of martial law.

[302] 1) if the *Seimas* fails to adopt a decision or the new programme of the government within thirty days of its presentation, or if the *Seimas* twice in a row gives no assent to the programme of the government within sixty days of its first presentation; 2) upon the proposal of the government, if the *Seimas* expresses the vote of no confidence for the government.

early elections, the newly elected *Seimas*, by a majority of three-fifths of all MPs, may, within thirty days after the first meeting, call the early elections of the President. The President may convene extraordinary sessions of the *Seimas* in the event of an armed attack, as well as when the constitutional order of the state is in threat.

When it comes to the legislative function, under Article 68 para 1 of the Constitution, the President has the right to initiate legislation. This power is implemented by submitting draft laws before the *Seimas* that seek to implement his political programme or to respond to the needs of society. Further, in the course of promulgation of laws adopted by the *Seimas*, the President has the right to return the law passed for re-examination to the *Seimas* (with reasons provided).[303] In practice, the President is quite active using both of these rights (initiating legislation and referral of laws back for re-examination). Depending on the situation with the majority in the *Seimas*, the use of those powers may prove rather effective.

Speaking of the President's relationship with the government, it should be noted that they are close given the fact that the President directly participates in the formation of the government after the elections of the *Seimas* or, later, when the composition of the government changes because of various reasons. The powers of the President are quite far reaching as well: to nominate the Prime Minister with the assent of the *Seimas* or to dismiss him; to task the Prime Minister with the formation of the government and to approve its composition; to accept the resignation of the Government and, if necessary, task it with continuing to exercise its duties, or task one of the ministers with exercising the duties of the Prime Minister until a new government is formed; to accept the resignations of ministers and to task (or not) them with exercising their duties until a new respective minister is appointed; to propose, within fifteen days, the candidate of the Prime Minister for consideration by the *Seimas* upon the resignation of the government or after it returns its powers; and to appoint and dismiss ministers upon submission by the Prime Minister. Still, in the course of formation of the government, the actions of the President must ensure the interaction of the authorities in order to create an effective government, i.e. the government which would have the confidence of the *Seimas*. Thus, the President, in principle, is not free to choose the Prime Minister or ministers because, in all cases, their appointment depends on the confidence of the *Seimas*. On the other hand, when the President approves the composition of the government, it acquires the power to act only when the *Seimas* approves its programme.[304] The practice shows that, de facto, the political influence of the President on the formation of the government's personal composition is substantial.

After elections of the President, the government must return the mandate to the newly elected President. However, as mentioned above, the CC has ruled that the government must not resign because, after the change of the Head of State, the Government still has the political confidence of the *Seimas*. Still, the return procedure may not be treated as only an expression of inter-institutional courtesy because it gives the President the opportunity to check whether the *Seimas* still has confidence in the government. Once the President has submitted the candidacy of the Prime Minister who had returned the mandate to the *Seimas* for consideration and the *Seimas* approved it, the President must appoint the Prime Minister to confirm the composition of the government and, if more than half of the ministers have not changed, it means that the government has been re-authorized to act. In this way, a new period of the government's mandate begins and therefore changes of ministers of the

---

[303] The law reconsidered by the *Seimas* is deemed to have been adopted if the amendments submitted by the President are adopted, or if more than half of all the MPs of the *Seimas* vote for the law.
[304] Ruling of the CC of 10 January 1998.

372 IRMANTAS JARUKAITIS

government are counted from the beginning of these mandates.[305] If the *Seimas* rejects the Prime Minister's candidacy, the government has to resign and this resignation serves as a constitutional basis for the initiation of the formation of the new government.[306]

Under Article 96 of the Constitution, ministers of the government are responsible not only to the *Seimas*, but also to the President. Although this responsibility is not specified in the legal acts, it presupposes that ministers, if required, must provide information to the President and report on important issues of governance. Further, given the important role of the President in the field of foreign policy, the Minister of Foreign Affairs has to coordinate the implementation of the foreign policy of the state with the President.[307] The President has an additional tool to control the activities of the government since, according to Article 106 para 3 of the Constitution, the President may challenge the legality of acts of the government before the CC. Such referral suspends the validity of these acts.

Decrees are the main legal expression of activities of the President. A specific category of decrees referred to in Article 84 of the Constitution must be countersigned by the Prime Minister or the appropriate minister.[308] In these cases, the responsibility for such decree's rests with the Prime Minister or a minister who signed it.

Finally, when it comes to judicial branch and the prosecution, the powers of the President are essentially related to formation of these authorities. According to Article 84 para 11, the President appoints judges and presidents of regional and district courts and changes their places of work, appoints and dismisses, upon the assent of the *Seimas*, judges and the president of the Court of Appeal and the Prosecutor General of the Republic of Lithuania. Additionally, the President appoints judges and presidents of regional administrative courts and the SACL as well. The Supreme Court is formed in cooperation of both the *Seimas* and the President because judges and the president of the Supreme Court are appointed and dismissed by the *Seimas* upon proposal of the President. The same applies to the formation of the CC. The President participates in its formation by submitting to the *Seimas* one candidate out of three, and when all judges of the CC are appointed, he submits to the *Seimas* the candidate for the President of the CC. Both judges and the President of the CC are appointed by the *Seimas*.

Under Article 112 of the Constitution, the Judicial Council advises the President on the appointment, promotion, and transfer of judges, or their release from duties (except for judges of the Supreme Court and the CC). Such advice of the Judicial Council has legal consequences because, without it, the President may not adopt a decision. Thus, the Judicial Council not only provides support in forming the judicial branch, but also counterbalances the powers of the President and thus ensures independence of judiciary.[309]

One may say that the actual weight of the President depends mainly on two factors. First, he/she is elected through direct elections. To date, there was a tendency to elect the President not from the parties which have the majority in the *Seimas*. Because of that, the real impact

---

[305] Ruling of the CC of 17 December 1998.

[306] Ruling of the CC of 10 January 1998.

[307] Under art 84 para 1 the President decides the basic issues of foreign policy and, together with the government, conduct foreign policy. Besides, the President has wide ranging powers in the field of state security and defence matters. The main issues of national defence are considered and co-ordinated by the State Defence Council, which consists of the President (the Head of the Council), the Prime Minister, the Speaker of the *Seimas*, the Minister of National Defence, and the Commander of the Armed Forces. The President is the Commander-in-Chief of the Armed Forces.

[308] These relate to appointment of diplomatic representatives; conferral of the highest diplomatic ranks and special titles; conferral of the highest military ranks; granting of the citizenship.

[309] Ruling of the CC of 21 December 1999.

the President has in politics depends very much on his personality, activeness, and the ability to mobilize the public and political partners or opponents. Opinion polls in Lithuania reveal that the President constantly enjoys a higher confidence of voters than the *Seimas* or the government, which gives his actions more legitimacy. The President *de jure* and *de facto* plays an important role in the formation and implementation of the foreign and the European policy. For example, national legal acts do not specify who, the President or the Prime Minister, should represent Lithuania in the European Council. Over time, the practice differed, but, over the last decade, it is the President who participates in the European Council meetings. The importance of this foreign and European affairs-related activity is reflected, among the other things, by the facts that the President Valdas Adamkus was named the European of the Year in 2007, while the President Dalia Grybauskaitė received the International Charlemagne Prize in 2013. The intertwining of competences in various fields of activities with other branches of governance sometimes might lead to different clashes. For example, some candidates to the Supreme Court or the Prosecutor General might be rejected by the *Seimas*, candidates to other judicial positions might be refused by the Judicial Council, or different positions might be taken on various issues of foreign and European policy by the President and the Prime Minister. Still, these clashes never reached the most extreme forms, for example, the call of early elections of the *Seimas*, etc.

c) The Government

In the Lithuanian system of executive power, the government, as a collegial body of general competence, consists of the Prime Minister and ministers. Article 94 of the Constitution defines the main powers of the government,[310] whereas the law on the government specifies how these powers are exercised and what legal and organizational measures are used in the activities of the government in solving the tasks related to the state administration.

The status of the government in the political system is characterized by the fact that, under article 96 of the Constitution, it is jointly and severally responsible to the *Seimas*. This constitutional provision is fundamental and predetermines the ability of the government to function only when it has the confidence of the *Seimas*. The expression of such confidence is the approval by the *Seimas* of the candidate for the Prime Minister, and, once the President approves the composition of the government, approval of the programme of the government. The programme of the government is based on the programme of the political forces that won elections of the *Seimas*; however, their content acquires legal significance through the government programme and it obliges both the government and the majority of the *Seimas* supporting it to act accordingly. Therefore, the government's programme is a legal document establishing guidelines for state action over a certain period. By expressing its confidence to the government programme, the *Seimas* undertakes to oversee its implementation. Thus, the government's programme is the basis of the government's political and legal responsibility to the *Seimas*, which is, as mentioned, joint and several in nature. Failure to implement the programme may provoke a loss of confidence of the *Seimas*.

Article 101 para 2 of the Constitution provides that the government must resign when more than half of the ministers have been replaced and the government has not again

---

[310] 1) management of national affairs, protection of the territorial inviolability, guaranteeing state security and public order; 2) execution of laws, the resolutions of the *Seimas*, as well as the decrees of the President; 3) coordination of the activities of ministries and other institutions of the government; 4) preparation of a draft state budget and its submission to the *Seimas*; execution of the state budget and submission to the *Seimas* of a report on the execution of the budget; 5) preparation of draft laws and their presentation to the *Seimas* for consideration; 6) establishment of diplomatic ties and maintenance of relations with foreign states and international organizations.

received the support of the *Seimas*. Under article 101 para 3 of the Constitution, the government must also resign when the *Seimas* twice in succession does not give its assent to the programme of the newly formed government; when the *Seimas*, by a majority vote of all the MPs of the *Seimas* and by secret ballot, expressed no confidence in the government or in the Prime Minister; when the Prime Minister resigns or dies; and when, after the elections to the *Seimas*, a new Government was formed. A vote of no confidence may be expressed against an individual minister. In such case, he must resign when more than half of all the MPs of the *Seimas* support such no confidence by secret ballot. Obviously, one of the most important reasons for the resignation of a government is the failure to acquire or loss of confidence of the *Seimas*. However, the Constitution provides for various forms of expression of distrust. In any case, the resignation of the government means that its term is over, and the new government formation procedure has to begin.

The 1992 Constitution envisages not only resignation of the government, but also the return of its powers. The need for this procedure arises after the elections of the *Seimas* or the President. The government's powers are returned because there is no longer the *Seimas* which has approved the government's programme or the President who has approved the composition of the government. In the first case, after the elections of the *Seimas*, the government's powers are returned to the President who instructs to hold an office until a new government is formed.

In the second case, after the elections of the President, the government also returns its powers to the newly elected President. However, in this case, the Constitution does not require the government to resign. This is because after the change of the head of state, the *Seimas*'s confidence in the government remains. Thus, as a rule, the assignment of the President to perform duties should be given to the same government, unless the government decides to resign, although this is usually not the case.

d) The Judicial Branch

According to article 109 of the Constitution, justice in Lithuania is administered only by courts. They have to be independent. The Constitution envisages the establishment of the CC (articles 102–108), the general competence court system (articles 109–117), as well as the possibility of establishment of specialized courts (article 111 para 2). Currently, the court system of Lithuania is composed of the CC, which exercises the concentrated constitutional review function, general competence courts, and administrative courts.

The general competence court system is the oldest one and is composed of the Supreme Court of Lithuania, the Court of Appeal, five regional courts and twelve district courts. These are courts of general jurisdiction dealing with civil and criminal cases. Additionally, district courts hear cases of administrative offences. The regional courts, the Court of Appeal, and the Supreme Court of Lithuania have separate civil and criminal divisions.

District courts are first instance courts for criminal cases, civil cases, and cases of administrative offences. They deal as well with questions related to the enforcement of judgments. Judges of district courts also perform the functions of a pre-trial judge in criminal cases and decide on detention of foreigners. Regional courts act as first instance courts in more complicated criminal and civil cases and as appeal instance for judgments of district courts. The Court of Appeal is appeal instance for judgments delivered by regional courts as courts of first instance. It also has the competence to deal with requests for the recognition of decisions of foreign or international courts and foreign or international arbitration awards and their enforcement in Lithuania. Finally, the Supreme Court of Lithuania is the only court of cassation for reviewing effective judgments of the general competence courts. Its primary function is to develop a uniform court practice in the interpretation and application of law.

The system of administrative courts is rather new to the Lithuanian legal system as it was created in 1999 with an idea to create better preconditions for protection of fundamental rights, although one may find certain beginnings of an administrative adjudication system already in the interwar period. It consists of two regional administrative courts and the SACL. The jurisdiction of these courts is specified in the Law on Administrative Proceedings. Regional administrative courts act as courts of first instance dealing mainly with legality of individual administrative acts or inaction of state or municipality institutions. Judgments of regional administrative courts may be appealed to the SACL, which deals with both questions of law and fact. The SACL does not act as the court of cassation—currently the right of appeal before the SACL is not limited. However, given the ever-increasing number of cases and the overload of the SACL, discussions have recently started concerning the necessity of introduction of a limited appeal system. Alongside dealing with questions of legality of individual administrative acts, the SACL acts as the first and last instance court providing the abstract legality review of normative acts adopted by ministers and other state institutions. Besides, it hears election cases as well.

Finally, given the possibility of overlap of jurisdiction between general competence courts and administrative courts, a jurisdiction conflict panel deals with such jurisdiction disputes. It consists of the President of the Civil Cases Division of the Supreme Court, the vice-president of the SACL, and one judge appointed by the presidents of these courts.

Given the Soviet-time experience, it is not surprising that the issue of effective safeguarding of the independence of judicial branch features prominently in the legal discourse. Over time, the CC had plenty of opportunities to dwell on this issue and developed wide and consistent jurisprudence as regards material, procedural guaranties of the judiciary, their self-governance, the status of judges, as well as constitutional requirements, related to the *quality* of justice.[311] The CC practice stresses the importance of the self-governance of the judiciary branch, treats it as a precondition for a strict separation of the judicial branch from the legislator and especially the executive.

The system of self-governance of the judiciary is organized with the aim to establish an equilibrium between the independence imperative with the necessity to assure the transparency and involvement of society. In practice, this means that the General Meeting of Judges and the Judicial Council, which are composed only of judges, decides the main issues related to the judiciary. On the contrary, the self-governance bodies dealing with recruitment and promotion of judges (the Examination Commission of Candidates to Judicial Office; the Selection Commission of Candidates to Judicial Office and the Permanent Commission for the Assessment of Activities of Judges) or their disciplinary responsibility (the Judicial Ethics and Discipline Commission and the Judicial Court of Honour) are composed not only of judges, but of representatives from society as well.

---

[311] Rulings of 6 December 1995; 21 December 1999; 8 August 2000; 12 January 2001; 16 January 2006; 28 March 2006; 21 September 2006.

D. The Lithuanian Constitutional Tradition and the Constitutional Identity

The concept of constitutional identity is multifaceted. It may be analysed from different angles. Some authors treat it as an 'essentially contested concept'.[312]

However, in the context of the European integration, the idea of constitutional identity has a much more focused meaning and may be related, among the other things, to the conceptual questions concerning the nature and finality of the European integration process and, accordingly, the place of EU Member States in it. In this social and political context, within which this concept is relevant, one must recall different visions of the finality of the European integration. While many founding fathers of the European Communities were determined federalists,[313] Maduro, for example, notes that the obligation to respect national identities of the Member States has existed from the outset and it forms 'the very essence of the European project initiated at the beginning of the 1950s, which consists of following the path of integration whilst maintaining the political existence of the States'.[314] The question of finality of the integration process was not settled at the beginning.[315] Given the functional (economic) side of the European Communities, the question of the nature and legal qualification of the integration process was less pressing in the 1950s. With the Maastricht Treaty, it became obvious that the European integration could not be described as 'economic' anymore, claims of the EU to the status of *sui generis political community* became self-evident, although there is no doubt that initial economic integration has served deeper *political* goals from the outset. So, as a matter of legal and political reality, article F(1) of the TEU, which obliged the EU to respect the national identities of its Member States, was of paramount importance for a discourse on the nature and finality of the European integration.

Discussions on the subject became even more heated after the Maastricht Treaty culminating in the Laeken Declaration, the European Convention, the Treaty establishing a Constitution for Europe, and, finally, the Lisbon Treaty. Participants of that discourse had (and still to large extent have) totally different ideas even about the question what the EU currently is, let alone about the question, what it should be or become in the future. Some simply point to the empirical fact that the Member States are not ready to surrender their statehood,[316] whereas others are sure that they are not only ready, but have to transform the EU into a state.[317] Yet, for others, the transformation of the EU into a state would mean a total negation of the basic underlying ideas about the causes and aims of the integration process, specifically it would involve turning away from the constitutional principle of tolerance to a different identity, meaning that the continuous existence of the Member States and respect for their national identities is one of the core features of *sui generis* EU constitutionalism.[318]

---

[312] Michel Rosenfeld, 'Constitutional Identity', in Michel Rosenfeld and András Sajó (eds), *Oxford Handbook on Comparative Constitutional Law* (OUP, Oxford, 2012) 756.

[313] Stefan Oeter, 'Federalism and Democracy', in Armin von Bogdandy and Jürgen Bast (eds), *Principles of European Constitutional Law* (Hart Publishing, Oxford, 2011) 57.

[314] Opinion of Miguel P Maduro in CJEU Case C-213/07 *Michaniki AE* [2008] (ECLI:EU:C:2008:544) para 31.

[315] The Schuman declaration is silent on that point and neither explicitly, not implicitly speaks about the final 'state' or result of the integration.

[316] Jeffrey Goldsworthy, 'The Debate about Sovereignty in the United States: A Historical and Comparative Perspective', in Neil Walker (ed), *Sovereignty in Transition* (Hart Publishing, Oxford, 2003) 444.

[317] G Federico Mancini, 'Europe: The case for statehood' (1998) 4 European Law Journal 29–38.

[318] Joseph HH Weiler, 'In Defence of the Status Quo: Europe's Constitutional *Sonderweg*', in Joseph HH Weiler and Marlene Wind (eds), *European Constitutionalism Beyond the State* (CUP, Cambridge, 2003) 7–23; Miguel P Maduro, 'Europe and the Constitution: What if this is as Good as it Gets?', in Joseph HH Weiler and Marlene Wind (eds), *European Constitutionalism Beyond the State* (CUP, Cambridge, 2003) 74–102.

Still, the participants of such discourse may not neglect the legal reality: the current basic structure of the EU reflected in the Founding Treaties, including article 4(2) of the TEU, as well as a legal discourse of national courts and the CJEU. Briefly, this judicial discourse predates the Maastricht Treaty[319] and has intensified over time, especially with the Lisbon Treaty.[320] The content of this discourse reveals close links between the notion of national identity, which is reflected in article 4(2) TEU, and the notion of the constitutional identity, which is employed by national courts. When it comes to the CJEU, the national identity clause may be an implicit or explicit legal argument making the impact on definition of the reach and scope of application of the EU primary law or its content (especially fundamental economic freedoms (*Schmidberger, Omega Spielhallen, Anton Las* case law) and provisions on EU citizenship (*Sayn Wittgenstein, Runevič-Vardyn* case law), as well as the scope of application, its content, and legality of secondary EU law (*Tanja Kreil, Alexander Dory, Michaniki, Melloni, BK v Republika Slovenija (Ministrstvo za obrambo)* case law). Apparently, national courts develop the notion of the constitutional identity as embracing two intertwined aspects. The first relates to preservation of the statehood per se, whereas the other concerns the question on what the quality of the statehood is (extent of retained powers and the mode of their exercise). Both aspects are seen as reflections of national constitutions, thus, at least implicitly, one may say that national courts treat concepts of national identity and constitutional identity as synonyms.

To sum up, the obligation to respect national identity, established by article 4(2) of the TEU, performs two related functions. First, is serves as a symbolic, basic recognition of a statehood as the necessary component of the European integration.[321] Further, although it competes with principles promoting unity within the EU, the respect for national identity acts as a general principle of EU law, specifically protecting diversity. From that perspective, it is one of the legal arguments that plays a part in establishing the equilibrium between the springs of unity (integration) and diversity (national identity) at the EU level. In this role, the principle is of importance for EU legislative process as well as for the interpretation of primary and secondary EU law in defining its content and scope of application. While its initial appearance in the Maastricht Treaty may be more attached to the first function, intentions of drafters of expanded version of the identity clause of the Lisbon Treaty reveal aspirations to place more emphasis on the clause as a limit to the exercise of EU powers. The CJEU practice confirms that the respect for national identity is one of the legal imperatives, although it is by no means absolute. However, the CJEU denies the proposition that the obligation to respect national identity may be regarded as a qualification of the principle of primacy of EU law and post-Lisbon article 4(2) brings nothing new from that perspective.

---

[319] As regards a 'national' point of view, see, for example, Decision of 22 October 1986 of the German Constitutional Court, BVerfGE 73, 339 2 BvR 197/83: 'The provision does not confer a power to surrender by way of ceding sovereign rights to international institutions the identity of the prevailing constitutional order of the Federal Republic by breaking into its basic framework, that is, into its very structure. That applies in particular to legislative instruments of the international institution, which, perhaps as a result of a corresponding interpretation or development of the underlying treaty law, would undermine essential, structural parts of the Basic Law. An essential part which cannot be dispensed with and belongs to the basic framework of the constitutional order in force is constituted in any event by the legal principles underlying the provisions of the Basic Law on fundamental rights.' For its part, the ECJ started developing its practice as well before the Maastricht Treaty: see the Judgment of 28 November 1989, Case C-379/87 *Anita Groener* (ECLI:EU:C:1989:599).

[320] Namely the Lisbon Treaty sparked the biggest reactions, constitutional (supreme) courts of eight Member States so far produced ten decisions.

[321] From that perspective Weiler's statement that 'to protect national sovereignty is *passé*; to protect national identity by insisting on constitutional specificity is *à la mode*' is a relevant one: Joseph HH Weiler, 'In Defence of the Status Quo: Europe's Constitutional *Sonderweg*' (n 318) 16.

The interface between the concept of national identity under EU law and concepts of constitutional identity developed by some national constitutional courts reflects close links between EU and national legal systems, although it is not possible to conclude that content of these concepts is identical. Both EU and national legal systems search for optimal equilibrium between the imperatives of integration and national identity, however, at least theoretically, the results of such search may be different. Looking at the first aspect of the identity clause (as the reflection of political self-determination), these concepts coincide because they both reflect the lasting statehood of the Member States. When it comes to the second aspect (the obligation to respect the national identity in the exercise of EU competencies), the picture is more complex. On the one hand, both concepts are based on the same idea that certain core matters should be left for the Member States. However, the content of these concepts may differ from one Member State to the other (for example, the Constitutional Court of Poland singles out the principle of social justice as belonging to the core of constitutional identity,[322] whereas this principle is not mentioned in the practice of the CC). The degree of respect, which may be required under national constitution and the EU law, may differ as well.

Speaking specifically of Lithuania, the discourse on the constitutional identity, both academic and judicial, so far is limited.[323] To some extent this might be explained by the fact that, before Lithuania's accession to the EU, the main preoccupation was the integration into EU structures. Still, given the above-described bitter experience of the Lithuanian nation with forced attempts to obliterate national identity, the question on what kind of union Lithuania accedes was of utmost importance. Public debates before the referendum concerning the future membership in the EU and discussions within the *Seimas* concerning the constitutional amendments, which established a basis for Lithuania's membership within the EU, attached a great deal to the fact that the EU is based on respect for national identities of the Member States, as explicitly reflected in the Preamble of the CA.[324]

The CC only recently started dealing with this issue. In its Decision of 19 December 2012 and the Ruling of 24 January 2014 the CC treats the membership within the EU as a fundamental constitutional value, particularly emphasizing a constitutional imperative on the part of Lithuania to participate in the European integration process, seeing it as a source of peace, stability, tolerance, and prosperity in Europe. At the same time, the CC is very explicit about the fact that the independence of the state, democracy, and republic, respect for fundamental rights and freedoms are the core constitutional principles and they may not be negated.[325]

Given the above-mentioned proviso '*save the Constitution itself*' in the ruling of 14 March 2006, along with the core principles enunciated in the ruling of 24 January 2014, one may speculate that, similar to other constitutional courts, the CC has accepted the existence of

---

[322] Decision of 24 November 2010 concerning the constitutionality of the Lisbon Treaty.

[323] Egidijus Jarašiūnas, 'Pagarba nacionaliniam tapatumui pagal Europos Sąjungos teisę: aiškinimo potencialas ir Europos Sąjungos Teisingumo Teismo Jurisprudencija' (2014) 93 Teisė 7–28; Irmantas Jarukaitis, 'Respect for the National Identities of the Member States as a General Principle of European Union Law', in Juozas Bernatonis and others (eds), *Lithuanian Legal System under the Influence of European Union Law* (Vilnius University, Vilnius, 2014) 575–620.

[324] The Preamble of the CA states that the *Seimas* adopted this Act by, *inter alia*, 'noting that the European Union respects the national identity and constitutional traditions of its Member States'.

[325] 'Article 1 of the Constitution consolidates the fundamental constitutional values: the independence of the state, democracy and the republic; they are inseparably interrelated and form the foundation of the State of Lithuania, as the common good of the entire society consolidated in the Constitution, therefore, they must not be negated under any circumstances ... the principle of recognition of the innate nature of human rights and freedoms should also be regarded as a fundamental constitutional value that is inseparably related to the constitutional values: the independence, democracy and the republic.'

'ordinary' constitutional rules, which are more prone to impact by EU law, and the constitutional nucleus, which is more resistant to the influence of EU law. It should be noted that the CC did not mention some of the principles referred to by other constitutional courts, for example, the rule of law, social orientation of the state or the principle of subsidiarity.[326]

It seems that for the CC, this is the 'constitutional nucleus', the expression of the constitutional identity, which may not be transgressed. Still, one may speculate that the crucial word in the above construction is the word 'negated', which indicates that the Court is ready to some extent to accept modifications. Speaking of the principle of democracy, the membership in the EU already modified it in a profound way, although such modification was preceded by the constitutional reform. The practice of the CC, placing Lithuania's membership in terms of geopolitical choice, seems to support the premise that the Constitution is flexible enough to embrace future steps of deeper integration as regards, for example, national budgetary policy control or crisis measures. From that perspective the attitude of the Supreme Court of Estonia treating the ratification of the ESM Treaty as (acceptable and proportionate) limitation (or rather, transformation) of the principle of democracy seems compelling for Lithuania as well.[327] Given the current ongoing discussions about the further directions and depth of the political and economic integration, it seems that both national constitutional courts and the CJEU will have plenty of opportunities to dwell on the subject.

[326] Regarding the rule of law, one could attach it to the innate nature of human rights. On the other hand, a question may be asked, whether the constitutional status of Lithuanian language merits to be included in this list?

[327] Judgment of the Estonian Supreme Court of 12 July 2012 in Case 3-4-16-12.

8

The Evolution and *Gestalt* of the Dutch Constitution

Leonard F M Besselink

A. Introduction	382	International Relations, and the Fall of the Wall	397
B. Origins of the Current Constitution	384	5. The Minor Amendments	399
1. What is the Constitution?	384	6. Perennial Controversies	400
2. National Constitutional Development: International Parameters and National Causes	384	**C. The Evolution of the Constitution: The Institutional Parameters of Constitutional Development**	401
a) The Historical Experiences	384	1. Constitution-Making Power: The Rigidity of the Constitution	401
b) The Years	385	2. The Role of the Government in Constitution Making	403
3. The Great Transformations	385	3. The Role Played by Parliament	404
a) The Original Constitution: 1814 or 1815?	385	4. The Role of Courts: The Unwritten Rules and Principles of Constitutional Law	405
b) The Republican Pre-History of the Kingdom (1579–1795): Republic without Sovereign	387	5. The Role of Foreign Constitutional Law	408
c) Post-Revolutionary Constitutional Instability: The Batavian Republic, the Kingdom Holland, and Formal Part of France (1795–1813)	388	**D. Basic Structures and Concepts**	409
		1. The Relation of the Constitution to Other Parts of the Legal Order	410
		a) Supra-Constitutional Norms	410
d) Regained Independence and the Constitution of 1814	389	b) The Constitutional Rank of International Law	411
e) The 1840s and the Liberal Reform of 1848	389	c) The Constitutional Position of EU Law	412
f) Settling for a Parliamentary System of Government: The 1860s	391	d) Infra-Constitutional Norms	412
g) Towards Democracy: 1917	393	e) Constitutionalization and Private Law	413
4. The Adaptations	394	2. The Relation of the Constitution to Politics and Democracy	415
a) 1922 and Beyond: Consolidating Parliamentary Democracy and 'Pillarization'	394	3. *Rechtsstaat*: Fundamental Rights and Legality	420
b) After the Second World War: The Failed Constitutional Reform (1954–1983)	395	4. Horizontal and Vertical Division of Powers	424
c) Adapting to the International Environment: Decolonization,		5. The Absence of an Overarching Concept of Political Unity	427
		E. Constitutional Identity	428

Abbreviations

AB   Administratiefrechtelijke beslissingen
ABRvS   Afdeling bestuursrechtspraak Raad van State
CDA   Christen Democratisch Appèl [Christian Democrat Party]

CMLRev	Common Market Law Review
D66	Democraten '66 [social liberal party]
ECHR	European Convention for the Protection of Human Rights and Fundamental Freedoms
EK	Eerste Kamer [Upper House]
HR	Hoge Raad
ICCPR	International Covenant on Civil and Political Rights
LJN	Landelijk Jurisprudentie Nummer
NJ	Nederlandse Jurisprudentie
NJB	Nederlands Juristenblad
PCIJ	Permanent Court of International Justice
PvdA	Partij van de Arbeid [Labour Party]
Rb	Rechtbank
RM Themis	Rechterlijk Magazijn Themis
Stb	Staatsblad
TK	Tweede Kamer
W	Weekblad voor het Recht

A. Introduction

One way of distinguishing constitutions in historical terms is between, on the one hand, modern revolutionary, blue-print, single document constitutions, which have their origin in an identifiably more or less revolutionary constitutional moment—usually connected with some form of political cataclysm (a war or revolution causing political, social, and economic collapse)—and, on the other hand, constitutions which are the product of an incremental historical process and in which socio-political developments and evolutions become codified. The constitutional system of the Netherlands[1] is definitely to be grouped in the latter category of what one may call 'evolutionary' constitutions. It is, in other words, more like the British Constitution and those of the Nordic countries (at least as they were until a few decades ago), and indeed more like that of the European Union[2] than the continental European constitutions of Germany, Italy, or France.

Among distinctive features that places it in the group of 'evolutionary' constitutions is the multi-source nature of which the Constitution (*Grondwet*, literally Basic Law, but this is never used in translations into English) is but one source, though an important one, between

---

[1] Legislation: The texts of all Acts of Parliament are published officially in the *Staatsblad*, each Act being published in a separate *Staatsblad*, carrying a year and a separate number, every year starting with 1. It is published only electronically since can be consulted at https://www.officielebekendmakingen.nl/staatsblad. It contains every *Staatsblad* published after 31 December 1994.

With few exceptions, after amendment of ordinary legislation, only the respective amendments are published in the *Staatsblad*. There are various consolidated versions published in commercial editions, of which *Schuurmans en Jordens* used to be most complete, but this publication has been discontinued in February 2012. All consolidated legislation in force at any moment since 1 May 2002 or lapsed since, however, can be consulted at http://wetten.overheid.nl/.

Most case law, particularly of courts of the highest instance, but also much of the case law of lower courts, can be found via https://uitspraken.rechtspraak.nl/.

This chapter was completed in autumn 2019; later developments have not been incorporated.

[2] See Leonard F M Besselink, 'The Notion and Nature of the European Constitution after the Lisbon Treaty', in Jan Wouters, Luc Verhey, and Philipp Kiiver (eds), *European Constitutionalism beyond Lisbon* (Uitgeverij Intersentia, Cambridge, 2009) 261–281.

various sources of constitutional law. Another constitutional document, which is of superior rank to the *Grondwet*, is the Charter for the Kingdom (*Statuut voor het Koninkrijk*). It regulates the constitutional relations between the European and Caribbean countries that form part of the Kingdom, in a quasi-federal manner. However, as we will explain below, also directly effective provisions of international treaties, particularly human rights treaties, are considered to be a source of national constitutional law, with overriding effect towards conflicting norms. Also, there are important rules of customary constitutional law, particularly regarding the parliamentary system, the principle of monism in the relation between international and national law, as well as certain aspects of the principle of judicial deference towards the legislature.

In this chapter, the term 'Constitution' (with a capital C) is used when we refer to the *Grondwet van het Koninkrijk der Nederlanden*. When we refer to the broader complex of constitutional norms, we refer to 'the constitution' (in lower case), or as the 'constitutional order' or 'constitutional system'.

Other distinctive features are the absence of constitutional review of acts of parliament by courts without sovereignty of parliament, an openness to international law and international society, the lack of an explicit constitutionally relevant concept of sovereignty, and an overall low degree of ideology in the text of the Constitution: it lacks a preamble with its attendant rhetoric. Terms like 'democracy', 'the people', or 'nation', are absent so far.[3] We will describe these features below. They can only be properly understood when viewed in historical perspective.

Given the evolutionary nature of the Netherlands' Constitution, the 'origin' of the constitution and its evolution cannot be strictly separated. Which of the texts bearing the name Constitution (*Grondwet*) should be considered to be the original of the present one is hard to say for reasons that we presently explain, but is not much of an issue. Also, any attempt at identifying original constituent power is meaningless; there has never been a body that could claim to have been a constituent assembly that coined the original, 'first' constitution. Most constitutional reforms were the product of political circumstances, often international political circumstances, prepared textually by a committee appointed by the government, only in recent times after consultation and with the approval of the Lower House (*Tweede Kamer*): the so-called *Staatscommissies* (Royal Committees). They were not quite like a constituent assembly, though, as we shall see, formally that was called for at the end of the Republic in 1795, by the States-General at its own abolition.

The historical evolutionary nature of the constitution necessitates a format that is slightly different from other chapters in this book in the first two parts. In Part B we sketch the outlines of the historical development of the constitution, which is marked by continuity and incrementalism. In Part C, we describe the institutional parameters of constitutional development. Part D looks at the fundamental concepts and structures of the constitutional system, while Part E concludes this contribution with a discussion of the constitutional identity which inheres in these.

---

[3] A constitutional amendment is awaiting a second reading, which proposes to open the Constitution with an unnumbered provision which reads: 'The Constitution guarantees fundamental rights and the democratic state under the rule of law [*democratische rechtsstaat*]', Act of 9 March 2018, *Staatsblad* 2018, 86. It was adopted with slightly over two-thirds of the vote in the Lower House, but with majority of three votes only in the Upper House, which makes its fate at second reading (when two-thirds of the vote is required) quite uncertain. The provision is mainly criticized for being only aimed at interpreting the provisions of the Constitution, while the government made clear this interpretation should be restricted to interpretation by the legislature and not the judiciary.

B. Origins of the Current Constitution

1. What is the Constitution?

Usually, the original of the present Constitution is taken to be either that of 1814, which is the first one promulgated after the Netherlands regained independence after its incorporation into the Napoleonic Empire (1810–1813), or that of 1815, which is the one which incorporated Belgium as determined by the Congress of Vienna and formally declared the Netherlands a Kingdom (it had previously been a Principality). Neither of these original texts (1814/1815) constitutes anything like present constitutional reality. The text of the present Constitution was adopted in its present form after a general revision in 1983, but substantively, this text was not the product of major constitutional innovation either, rather a consolidation and modernization of the previous Constitution, which was the 12th amendment since 1815 (which has itself been amended ten times between 1983 and 2018).

Whichever Constitution one would begin with, the present one can only be understood as a product of both long-term and short-term developments. Indeed, as we argue below, even the experience of two centuries of the Republic of the United Provinces has had a long-lasting influence in some constitutionally relevant respects, but many elements are dependent on shorter term contingencies.

Here we take 1814/1815 as the origin of the present Constitution in order to discuss the constitutional moments which have led to the amendments and revisions which have been the most decisive in shaping the present Constitution.

2. National Constitutional Development: International Parameters and National Causes

a) The Historical Experiences

At the basis of the constitutional transformations and adaptations are historical experiences, many of which coincide with international political developments. Many of these are also shared by other European countries, though such international events are translated into and channelled through one's own traditions, institutions, and particularities to arrive at solutions which turn out to be peculiar to each country. In other words, the same international events may not have had quite the same constitutional impact abroad which they had in the Netherlands.

The great influence of international events on constitutional development reflects two fundamental external facts of the Netherlands political history: its geographic size and geographic location. Both have entailed an openness towards the outside world.

The Netherlands is a relatively small European country, although, from the early seventeenth century until the end of the Second World War, it possessed important overseas colonies, in particular in the Malay Archipelago. These made the Kingdom an economic world power. Within Europe, the geographic size of the Netherlands has basically been as small as it is now, but to an extent this has been compensated for by its location in the delta of two main continental rivers, the Rhine and Meuse, which made large parts of the European continent its hinterland, while the North Sea coast opened up the country to other parts of the world. Its economic potential, and its colonial empire in particular, was based on its sea power as well as its favourable location for international trade.

This openness to the outside world was continued after the Netherlands' major colony, Indonesia, gained independence after the Second World War. Politically, its international orientation was to a large extent westward (North Atlantic), but at the same time in favour of supranational integration of Western Europe. In this respect, the economic and trade interest was again dominant, although throughout, the twentieth century, international policies have had certain moralistic overtones. The 'Merchant and the Vicar' (*koopman en dominee*) have gone hand in hand in Holland.

Apart from the international context as explanatory background factor to constitutional change, there have been purely endogenous reasons for a number of constitutional amendments which have occurred. One may submit that in constitutional affairs a certain primacy of national socio-political relations has dominated since the 1990s: while the world globalized, the constitutional debate in the Netherlands gradually became reduced to national concerns.

b) The Years

Within the process of constitutional development and change through constitutional amendment one can distinguish between moments of transformation, moments of constitutional adaptation, and the more minor changes as reflected in the Constitution.

Overall, we can say that, in the Netherlands, the transformations mainly took place in the 'long nineteenth century',[4] the first one being the political transformation which brought about the 1814/1815 Constitutions, the last one that of 1917. The amendments of roughly the first half of the twentieth century (except for the one of 1917, which we mentioned) are forms of constitutional change which can rather be characterized as adaptations to the political environment. The second half of the twentieth century has seen an ever-increasing number of constitutional amendments, but paradoxically few of these—if any—transformed the constitution, even though in 1983 a fully revised of the text of the Constitution entered into force.

The various amendments are represented in Figure 8.1. We briefly elucidate them in the next sections.

3. The Great Transformations

a) The Original Constitution: 1814 or 1815?

The present Constitution of the Kingdom of the Netherlands[5] dates back to the beginning of the nineteenth century. There is no agreement on whether it is the Constitution of 1814 or that of 1815 which is legally the original of the present Constitution. The reason for this is partly legal, and concerns the issue whether procedures for revision were followed or not; and partly it is a matter of what is meant with 'original'.[6]

---

[4] I.e. from the French Revolution until the end of the First World War.

[5] As per January 2019, the last amendment dates from 26 November 2018 (Stb. 2018, 493); the last consolidated version was published in Stb. 2019, 33 of 16 January 2019.

[6] Roelof Kranenburg, *Het Nederlands staatsrecht* (8th edn, Tjeenk Willink & zoon, Haarlem, 1958) 46, had serious doubts on whether the 1815 Constitution was a new Constitution; Alexander F De Savornin Lohman, *Onze Constitutie* (4th edn, Kemink, Utrecht, 1926) 59, denied it was; whereas Antonius Struycken, *Het staatsrecht van het Koninkrijk der Nederlanden* (Gouda Quint, Arnhem, 1928) 54; Combertus W van der Pot, *Handboek*

386 LEONARD F M BESSELINK

The great transformations

1579	Union of Utrecht
1798	post-revolutionary instability until the end of 1813
1814/1815	the Post-Napoleonic settlement
(1840) 1848	the liberal revolution
1917	the democratic break-through

The adaptations

1887	parliamentary consolidation
1922	after the War
1948	Post-Colonial Constitution
[1949]1953/1956[1963]	Post-Colonial Internationalism
[1972] 1983	*Zeitgeist* of the 1960s
2000	after the fall of the Wall

The minor amendments
1884, 1938, 1972, 1987, 1995, 1999, 2000, 2002, 2005, 2008…

Figure 8.1 Constitutional transformations, adaptations, and minor amendments

The formal continuity of the 1814 and 1815 Constitutions is problematic in as much as the terms of the procedures for constitutional amendment could not be followed at the time. The amendment of the 1814 Constitution, in order to reflect the unification with Belgium, could not legitimately be passed by complying to the formal procedures, as that would only involve the institutions of the Northern Netherlands without any representation of the Belgians. This would amount to imposing a constitution on the Southern Netherlands. Instead a Constitution was negotiated in a royal committee composed of equal numbers of Dutch and Belgian representatives, which, in accordance with Belgian desires,[7] introduced such features as bicameralism (a nobility of the blood was politically prominent in the Southern Netherlands, and these wished not to assemble with the commons) and entrenchment of the prohibition of censorship (which in the Netherlands had already been abolished by royal decree in 1814, but had no further constitutional basis).

The text negotiated in the royal committee was adopted by the institutions of the Northern Netherlands with near unanimity. It was then presented to Belgian noblemen and outstanding citizens who, only by applying 'Dutch arithmetic', were considered to have voted in favour.[8] This referendum was not provided for in the provisions on constitutional amendment of 1814 and, to that extent, implied discontinuity with the Constitution of 1814.[9] Also

---

van het Nederlandse staatsrecht (16th edn, Kluwer Juridische Uitgevers, Deventer, 2014) 138, hold that the 1815 Constitution was not an amendment of that of 1814, but a new Constitution.

[7] Herman T Colenbrander, *Ontstaan der Grondwet*, vol II (first published 1908, Nijhoff, s'Gravenhage, 1909).

[8] Of these 1323 cast a vote, 796 negative and 527 a positive vote. Of the noes, 126 voters declared on their ballot paper that they had voted against only because they were opposed to the clauses on freedom of religion which implied the equality of the Protestant and Catholic religion. These clauses had been imposed by the Vienna Congress and were therefore not liable to amendment. William I assumed therefore that those 126 votes were otherwise in favour of the Constitution and had therefore to be considered such, shifting the balance of 670 noes to 653 yes. On top of that, he assumed that those who did not show up at the ballot box acquiesced in the proposal, which added a further 281 to those in favour—a trick that William learnt from Napoléon. Thus, a majority was reached.

[9] Pieter J Oud, *Het constitutionele recht van het Koninkrijk der Nederlanden*, vol 1 (2nd edn, WEJ Tjeenk Willink, Zwolle, 1967) 4–10.

the text of the 1815 Constitution contained several novelties, was both in Dutch and French, and was established and promulgated *in toto*.[10]

Are these formal and legalistic reasons conclusive evidence for considering the Constitution of 1815 the original one? Not if one is aware that the union with Belgium soon proved to be a brief, temporary and constitutionally unsuccessful addition to the political formation of the Northern Netherlands as it had existed as a polity since the sixteenth century; it was ended in formally and legally the same 'unconstitutional' manner in which it had begun, but this time the other way round: without the Belgians participating in the institutions involved in constitutional amendment. Politically, the real constitution was the Constitution of 1814, which established the political entity as we still know it, not the Constitution of 1815. Apart from the failed union with Belgium, the latter's lasting importance is the fact that it made William I to what he already was—a king—and the country to what it in reality had been: a kingdom. Moreover, it left bicameralism as a heritage.

The somewhat debatable origin of the Constitution is symptomatic for the historical–evolutionary nature of the constitution of the Netherlands. The events of 1815 are evidence of the codifying nature of the Constitution: even when it comes to the nature of the state itself, it does not aim to modify future reality, but codifies a reality that historically and politically precedes it. The 1814 Constitution, then, was 'original' only in a sense, and incorporated some of the accumulated experience of its precursors, to which we devote some attention, as it both highlights some aspects of the constitutional culture to this day.

b) The Republican Pre-History of the Kingdom (1579–1795): Republic without Sovereign

The Constitution of 1814 had come about at the end of a period of more than eighteen years of political instability in the aftermath of the French Revolution. This period of instability began with the ending of the Republic of the United Provinces, a Republic which had its constitutional foundation in the *Unie van Utrecht* of 1579, a Treaty of alliance between the Provinces, and which lasted until 1795, when, formally in full accordance with the constitutional principles and procedures of the Republic, the State's General and the Provinces decided to end the Republic by calling for a constitutional assembly to convene on the principles of a new Republic. Even the Revolution which had started in France did not interrupt formal constitutional continuity with this Republic.

By 1795, this confederal Republic had developed into an inefficient polity run by a quasi-hereditary or otherwise co-opting ruling elite known as the '*Regenten*'. They were mostly patricians, that is to say aristocrats of merit as opposed to nobility by blood, whose merit originally was a contribution to the wealth and wellbeing of the country, but which was sometimes only remotely related to the actual successors in office. Also, the highest office in the Republic, that of *stadtholder* (literally *locum tenens*), shared some of this fate. This office—each province had its own *stadtholder*—found its origin in the impossibility to find a permanent successor to the last sovereign, King Philip II of Spain, who had been abjured in 1581, nine years after William the Silent called for a revolt. A succession of foreign dignitaries had been approached to be the personification of the polity in each of the Provinces, ranging from the Duke of Anjou to Elizabeth I of England. But in the end, none of them proved acceptable to the Provinces, also because they claimed a kind of sovereign lordship or

---

[10] Also, the revision resulting in the 1983 *Grondwet* was through article-by-article amendment. After the promulgation of a constitutional amendment a consolidated version is usually published in the *Staatsblad*, but this was not done after the amendments of 1884, 1917, 1999, 2000, and 2005.

kingship which had been a cause of the revolt that led to Philip's abjuration. So, in the meantime, each Province itself appointed a *stadtholder* as substitute for the absent sovereign.

Sovereignty for the Provinces resided in each Province itself and in the traditional constitutional arrangement which was deemed best to secure political liberty. This was of lasting importance: the Republic did without a personified sovereign for more than two centuries, while during these centuries it even functioned without its surrogate—the *stadtholder*—for nearly seventy-five years during the so-called *stadhouderloze tijdperken* (the two *stadtholder*-less eras from 1650 to 1672, and from 1702 to 1747).

For an office that was not meant to be the embodiment of sovereignty, it is somewhat curious that it turned from a quasi-elective office into a hereditary one, eventually concentrated in one and the same person for all provinces. It was occupied by members of the family of Orange in most provinces. Holland and Zeeland had introduced the hereditary *stadtholder* already in 1674, while Frisia had introduced it in 1675. Until 1647, Frisia had usually chosen a *stadtholder* from the House of Nassau-Dietz, and the other provinces from the House of Orange; the two Houses merged in 1747, William of Orange-Nassau becoming hereditary *stadtholder* in all provinces, as remained the case for all his successors.

For more than two centuries, the Netherlands experienced a state in which the component provinces each claimed sovereignty without there being a single office to personify this sovereignty, nor would the confederate state itself be sovereign over the provinces or, for that matter, have a sovereign. Against this historical background, it is not so unnatural that to this day, neither in constitutional practice, nor in constitutional theory, nor in the Constitution of the Netherlands itself is there any strong concept of sovereignty to be found. Only in recent years, concomitantly with the recurrence of the topos of 'sovereignty' in mainly populist political rhetoric, has the study of the concept of sovereignty regained interest among younger academics.[11]

c) Post-Revolutionary Constitutional Instability: The Batavian Republic, the Kingdom Holland, and Formal Part of France (1795–1813)

During the eighteenth century, republican traditions, and virtues at the basis of the Republic eroded. Thus, by the end of the century, the 'patriots', ignited by the French Revolution, could understandably conceive of the governing class in the last phase of the Republic as an *ancien régime*. Initially, the Batavian Republic, as successor to this *ancien régime*, was modelled on the ideas of the French Revolution. It proved to be a constitutionally highly unstable state, with a succession of largely abortive 'Batavian' constitutions; those of 1798, 1801, and 1805, which reflected increasingly French influence and interference even at the textual level, issuing in the Kingdom of Holland under the French puppet King Louis Napoléon in 1806, under a constitution more or less dictated by the French. A few years later the situation became more straightforward as the Netherlands came under direct French rule that lasted from 1810 until the end of 1813.

---

[11] Thierry Baudet, *The Significance of Borders: Why Representative Government and the Rule of Law Require Nation States* (2012) PhD dissertation Leiden University, open access at https://openaccess.leidenuniv.nl/handle/1887/19141 (last accessed on 24 March 2022) (Baudet entered into politics on a populist right wing ticket with his *Forum voor Democratie*, established in 2015, and became member of the *Tweede Kamer* that year); Michiel Duchateau, *Het Europees Parlement als transnationale volksvertegenwoordiging: Over volkssoevereiniteit, (con) federalisme en Europese volksvertegenwoordiging* (Kluwer, Deventer, 2014), PhD dissertation RU Groningen; Jan Willem Casper van Rossem, *Soevereiniteit en pluralisme: een conceptuele zoektocht naar de constitutionele grondslagen van de Europese rechtsorde* (Kluwer, Deventer, 2014) PhD dissertation Utrecht University.

d) Regained Independence and the Constitution of 1814

The unstable Batavian/French period formally ended with the proclamation of 21 November 1813 by which two prominent statesmen, Van der Duyn van Maasdam[12] and Hogendorp,[13] took upon themselves the provisional 'general government' (*Algemeen Bestuur*) of the country at national level, thus constituting the new state of the Netherlands.[14]

Hogendorp was the architect of the proclamation of 1813, but, more importantly, also of the Constitution of 1814. He had been working on a revision of the *Unie van Utrecht* ever since the end of the old Republic, proposing to reinforce central government in the person of the Prince together with a first minister, *raadspensionaris*, as a kind of chancellor, next to (not under) him. Hogendorp's idea was to 'restore the old Republic', but with stronger central government under the Prince of Orange and a chancellor, with the States-General in a central role. Additionally, the provinces would be regions within a unitary state and no longer the old 'sovereign' powers. This was elaborated in his *Schets eener Constitutie* (Sketch of a Constitution),[15] which William I gave as the starting point for the deliberations of the Royal Constitutional Committee which he commissioned to design the Constitution of 1814.

One lasting contribution of the instability of the Batavian/French period to the settlement of 1814/1815 is the option for a decentralized unitary state. It resulted from the compiled experience of over-emphasis on decentralized units during the highly confederal Republic and of over-centralization during the 'French' period, both being at best inefficient and at worst ineffective. The option for a decentralized unitary state was evident on the one hand in the centralized government in the King (particularly under William I), but also the retention of a good amount of decentralization in provinces and municipalities as constitutionally recognized original communities with autonomous powers of their own, as it exists to this day. In terms of regulating the exercise of political power at the national level, however, the Constitution of 1814/1815 was far from anything like a democratic state. To become so, the Constitution and constitutional practice had to undergo a radical transformation which began in the 1840s and was carried to its full constitutional conclusion only in 1922.

e) The 1840s and the Liberal Reform of 1848

The Constitution of 1814 (as well as that of 1815) was not a *constitution octroyée*. To the contrary, William I had asked for a constitution as a condition for accepting power as sovereign prince, *soeverein vorst*, in one of his first proclamations.[16] This constitutionalist stance did not transpire in the way he exercised his powers. William I governed in an autocratic manner and to a large extent by royal decree. This was based on an interpretation of the Constitution to the effect that it did not forbid this practice, and therefore gave the King the freedom

---

[12] *Adam FJA Graaf [Count] van der Duyn van Maasdam*, 1771–1848, a moderate liberal who had been a member of the court of the Prince of Orange-Nassau that was to be the later King William I. William II appointed him in 1848 as a member of the *Eerste Kamer* in order to help the liberal revision of the Constitution to a majority.

[13] *Gijsbert Karel van Hogendorp*, 1762–1834, from the old *regenten* party, but a liberal mind; was later made a count, *graaf*, by William I.

[14] On the chaotic events of 1813, see Wilfried Uitterhoeve, *1813, Haagse Bluf: De Korte Chaos van de Vrijwording* (Vantilt, Nijmegen, 2013).

[15] Written in three different versions in 1812–1813 and circulated at limited scale around November and December 1813, but not published until Johan Rudolf Thorbecke included it in his *Aanteekening op de Grondwet*, 1839.

[16] Proclamation of 2 December 1813, Staatscourant 1813, no. 2: 'Your trust, your love places sovereignty in my hands, as all sides are calling for me to accept it, and as the fatherland's distress and the state of Europe is demanding it. Well then, I will sacrifice my reservations to your wishes; I will accept what the Netherlands offers me, but I will also accept it only under guarantee of a wise constitution, which will guarantee your freedom against future abuses.' Translation by the author.

to regulate by royal decree all matters that had not been covered by an Act of Parliament. Parliament's own approach contributed to that view. In 1818 it adopted an Act (the so-called *Blanket Act*) which made infringement of royal decrees a criminal offence. This legitimated the King's power. Only in 1887, that is to say after the parliamentary system of government had taken shape, the *Hoge Raad* (Supreme Court) ruled in the *Meerenberg* case of 1879[17] that many decrees were unconstitutional. It derived from the system of the Constitution that the power to regulate a matter by royal decree must explicitly be based on an Act of Parliament or a provision of the Constitution itself.

The personal regime of William I made him the object of broader political dissatisfaction and exposed him to fierce political criticism in the course of his government. Thus, the Belgians, who had never been very happy with the union with the Northern Netherlands imposed by the Vienna Congress, revolted in 1830. Notwithstanding the fact that their wish for independence was thus realized and was even sanctioned by the great powers, William I was not willing to give in easily to the facts of life. He not only kept the country in a state of military alert at great financial expense, but also would only agree to adapt the constitutional revision to reflect the new situation ten years later, when he gave in to international reality.

This revision was accompanied by a debate about a broader modernization of the Constitution than the government was prepared to propose, a debate which had already begun in the 1830s and was caused by the Constitution's obvious condonement of autocratic government. It not only adapted to the reality of Belgium's independence, but also introduced criminal ministerial responsibility and increased powers of the Lower House over the biennial budget.

In hindsight, the introduction of this very limited form of ministerial responsibility urged by the Lower House against the initial views of the government in 1840 was indeed a systemic change in the form of government. The new provision required a countersignature of a minister for every royal decree and royal ratification of Acts of Parliament and created criminal responsibility for the co-signing ministers should the relevant royal decrees and Acts of Parliament contravene the law. The systemic nature of the change is on account of the fact that the King could no longer take decisions without involving a minister, as William I had usually done—the Constitutions of 1814 and 1815 only required him to hear the *Raad van State* (Council of State[18]) and made no mention of a council of ministers, nor of the powers of ministers in relation to the King, thus legitimating the circumvention of the political influence of ministers.

The 1840 reform was to the distaste of William I. He abdicated in favour of his son William II, who initially seemed more liberal, but soon tried his best to avoid the council of ministers from developing into a politically homogenous governmental actor.

Economic and financial crisis was around by the 1840s, with occasional rioting consequently adding to the sense of crisis in politics. There was an ever-increasing constitutional debate, kept alive by a fairly small minority of liberals. Thorbecke, a law professor in Leiden, was pivotal in this. He had already been a member of the doubled Lower House, which was elected for the purpose of voting on the Constitution of 1840, and he was briefly a member in 1844–1845. In the Autumn of 1844, he launched a proposal for constitutional reform, which was supported by eight other members of parliament (hence its nickname of the proposal of the 'nine men', *negenmannen*). The Lower House answered the question whether

---

[17] HR 13-01-1879, W 4330 (*Meerenberg*), ECLI NL:HR:1879:1.
[18] Art 32 of the Constitution of 1814; art 73 of the Constitution of 1815.

to introduce a bill to amend the Constitution negatively by thirty-four against twenty-one votes. The quest for constitutional modernization, however, remained a nagging matter.

When revolution broke out in February 1848 in France, the response in political circles was reactionary, but this mood changed when in March revolutionary events took place in Germany and some governments there gave in to liberal demands. Revolutionary outbreaks abroad would turn out to be decisive for constitutional reform in the Netherlands.

The pressure of events on the hesitating and undetermined King mounted. In January, the King had already introduced a series of minor amendments in the Lower House, which could hardly be termed liberal. And on 13 March he suddenly decided to take action. Without consulting his ministers, he called for the speaker of the Lower House and informed him that the King would appreciate to receive the opinion of the House concerning a more far-reaching reform of the Constitution. The conservative ministers took this manoeuvre behind their backs as an affront and resigned. Four days later, the King next decided to appoint a committee of five men to tender their advice on a new cabinet and to develop a proposal for constitutional reform. (The royal decree was not countersigned by a minister, but merely by his own secretary, which was no doubt unconstitutional.) Though—to his horror—bypassed for membership of a new cabinet, Thorbecke chaired the committee's work on the Constitution, drafted its provisions in line with his well-known liberal views, and was able to present them to the King in less than a month. It proposed, amongst other things, direct elections for both Houses of Parliament and full political ministerial responsibility, counterbalanced by a governmental right to dissolve the Houses of Parliament by royal decree.

The bills did not easily pass the predominantly conservative parliament. But with all kinds of royal interventions, including the appointment to the Upper House of five new members to the liberal cause in order to acquire a majority for the bills, they were eventually adopted. Shortly after, William II died of a heart attack.

The 1848 Constitution was the product of the pressures of international developments in Europe.[19] What converted William II and the conservative majority to agree to the liberal amendments to the Constitution was fear, which was fed by what was happening abroad. Another factor for the King also his dynastic interest. As he put it, on 16 March 1848, right in the middle of the crisis, in a meeting with the ambassadors of Austria, England, Russia, and Prussia (!), he managed to convert from very conservative to very liberal within twenty-four hours.[20] Once again, the European international context proved decisive; it provided a constitutional moment in which an amendment, which aimed at true reform, was achieved.

f) Settling for a Parliamentary System of Government: The 1860s

Transformations are not a matter of textual amendment only, in particular when it concerns major reforms. The greater the intended transformation, the more important (and often difficult) is its achievement in practice. Notwithstanding its huge importance, the 1848 amendment of the Constitution was not the final and definitive settlement for a parliamentary system of government in practice. It was the parliamentary events in the 1860s which settled for a parliamentary system of government. Two successive events in parliamentary history established the relevant customary law definitively.

Firstly, there was the conflict over the sudden resignation of the Minister of Colonial Affairs, P Mijer, and his appointment as governor-general of the East Indies in 1866. Being considered the most important man in a newly appointed cabinet, his unexpected and

---

[19] See Johann C Boogman, *Rondom 1848* (Fibula-Van Dishoeck, Haarlem/Unieboek, Bussum, 1978) 51.
[20] Jeroen van Zanten, *Koning Willem II, 1792–1849* (Boom, Amsterdam, 2013) 541

unannounced resignation led to dismay in the Lower House. The government defended his resignation as minister and appointment as governor-general by referring to the King's decision to do so as a personal prerogative. This caused a resolution, passed on 27 September 1886, which, in so many words, 'disapproved of the line of conduct with regard to the stepping down of the minister of Colonial Affairs'. The next day the Lower House was dissolved by royal decree. Although the majority after elections remained liberal, the new Lower House only debated the matter, generally reminding of the rule of ministerial responsibility, however without passing a new resolution against the cabinet, which had stayed in power.

A second affair concerned Luxembourg in the aftermath of the French–Prussian war of 1866. King William III, through a personal union, was also head of state (Grand Duke) of Luxembourg. In the aftermath of the French–Prussian war, Napoléon III approached William III to sell Luxembourg to France by treaty. Initially, such a transfer seemed to be tolerated by Bismarck, but when the Chancellor was called to account in the *Reichstag* (1 April 1867), the matter was declared a *casus belli*. Internationally, the matter was resolved at an international conference in London at which the independence and neutrality of Luxembourg was guaranteed by the great powers and the Netherlands. At the national level, the Lower House thought the whole affair had not been handled properly by the government as it had no responsibility for Luxembourg, nor was there any national interest in guaranteeing its neutrality. The conflict expressed itself in the rejection of the budget for Foreign Affairs by the Lower House. The cabinet tendered its resignation, but the King refused it and instead dissolved the Lower House (January 1868). The subsequent elections did not change the political composition of the Lower House and, this time, the new Lower House passed a resolution expressing its opinion, 'that no interest of the country required the most recent dissolution of the House'. Because after this motion of censure the ministers did not immediately resign, the pressure was further stepped up by again rejecting the budget for Foreign Affairs. Subsequent to this rejection, the ministers tendered their resignation, and this time the King called for a new cabinet to be formed, so that they could be replaced in accordance with the political preferences of the Lower House.

Three essential features of the parliamentary system were distilled from these events:

1) the scope of political ministerial responsibility as extending to all and every exercise of royal power was confirmed in practice, thus extending parliament's power to approve and disapprove of all exercise of governmental power;
2) the rule that when parliament expresses a motion of censure the cabinet is forced to resign; and
3) that if instead of resignation of the members of the cabinet the course is taken of a dissolution of parliament, the subsequent elections are decisive, and no further possibility of dissolution exists for the government.[21]

These constitutional rules remain customary constitutional law to this day. If the 1868 events did not establish it, they at least confirmed the parliamentary system of government.[22] The establishment of the rules in practice brought the reform of 1848 to its logical conclusion.

---

[21] See Section C.3.

[22] Pieter J Oud, *Honderd Jaren: een eeuw van staatkundige vormgeving in Nederland 1840–1940* (Van Gorcum, Assen, 1971) 89.

g) Towards Democracy: 1917

The parliamentary system developed further in the decades after 1868. Thus, until 1887, only when a political conflict occurred within the cabinet, or alternatively between the cabinet and the Lower House, a cabinet would resign. Since the elections of 1887, a cabinet would also resign because of the result of regular periodic elections the Lower House. Since 1917, a convention has taken root for the cabinet to resign on the day (or eve) of the elections, in other words, before electoral results are certain. This then opens the way for the forming of whatever cabinet may prove to have a sufficient political basis in the Lower House. This convention is related to the replacement in that year of the majoritarian electoral system of a single constituency first-past-the-post system, by a system of strict proportional representation. In this system, elections no longer resulted in clear political majorities, thereby creating the necessity of forming coalitions between the minority groups in parliament.

The parliamentary system of government established in the 1860s did not achieve democracy in its modern sense. Electoral rights were held only by a few wealthy men. The general franchise was not achieved until 1917 in practice and was constitutionally entrenched only in 1922. The reason why it took so long is because of the political linkage which was made with the other issue which dominated politics throughout the second half of the nineteenth century: the issue of state subsidies for protestant and catholic schools: the so-called 'school struggle'. In 1848, the Constitution had introduced liberty of education, which was initially interpreted to prohibit state subsidies for schools which were not run by public authorities. Later on, such subsidies were a matter of political undesirability rather than of constitutionality. Protestants and Catholics came to stand in opposition to the liberals (and later also to the socialists). As long as the issue of state subsidies for denominational education as a corollary of the equal liberty of education was not solved, the Protestant and Catholic groups in the Lower House would not cooperate on introducing the general franchise (the so-called *non possumus* policy).[23] In 1887 the main political groups agreed to a constitutional amendment which extended the right to vote to male residents of Dutch nationality who fulfilled certain criteria of suitability and social welfare which were to be determined by an Act of Parliament. This '*caoutchouc* provision' shifted the emphasis from constitutional amendment to electoral reform by an Act of Parliament. Although this made it possible to extend the franchise, it did not silence the call for a truly universal suffrage—an issue on which political parties remained internally split until the beginning of the twentieth century. To be precise, even the socialists were at best lukewarm about the right to vote for women. It was only after the First World War had begun—where the Netherlands remained neutral—that a breakthrough was made: an agreement was found on a constitutional amendment which grants denominational primary schools' financial equality to public schools (those established and operated under responsibility of local government), in return for consent to general suffrage.

The constitutional amendment which entered into force in 1917 stipulated general suffrage for men, opened the possibility of extending the franchise also to women by Act of Parliament,[24] abolished the constituencies and introduced proportional representation.[25] In

---

[23] In certain catholic circles there was an awareness that the franchise would increase their presence and profile in politics, a reason why Dutch Catholics earlier in that century had not rejected the idea of popular sovereignty as Calvinist Protestants had done. As the nineteenth century progressed, Catholics were in the process of social, cultural, and political emancipation from earlier open discrimination, which explains their more pragmatic approach to the franchise than that of the Protestants, with whom they allied for reasons of support of their denominational schools.

[24] Art 80 of the Constitution 1917.

[25] Transitory Art VII of the Constitution, amending the *Kieswet* (Electoral Act).

1919, women were granted the right to vote (and by implication to stand for election also, although this did not seem to be contemplated as a probable eventuality), and this was entrenched in the amendment of 1922.

The 1917 breakthrough after decades of deadlock was related to the war surrounding the country. This is not a one-to-one relationship, but it certainly provided a push to come to a constitutional settlement which could satisfy both sides to the conflict. Thus, again the international context played a role at the background of this constitutional reform.

4. The Adaptations

a) 1922 and Beyond: Consolidating Parliamentary Democracy and 'Pillarization'

Also, the constitutional amendment of 1922 can be viewed against the background of the international situation, particularly the devastation which the war had brought on Europe and the revolutionary movements of 1918 in Russia and elsewhere. Democratization was a major element in the reform. Apart from the entrenchment of the universal suffrage, which we mentioned above, and an amendment to restrict the succession to the throne to the descendants of Queen Wilhelmina,[26] the main amendments were the increased role of parliament in international affairs: declaring war and concluding treaties was made dependent on prior approval of the State's General. A provision was introduced to the effect that before resorting to war, the government shall attempt to resolve conflicts with foreign powers through judicial and other peaceful means.[27] The amendment on prior approval of treaties, though intended as a major tool of democratization, was technically not successful, in as much as in the course of the parliamentary treatment the government began shifting its position and distinguishing 'treaties' from 'other international agreements', the former requiring prior approval, the latter (whose definition varied, but extended particularly to international engagements in less solemn form) only needing notification to parliament. This failure was to be corrected with the constitutional amendment of 1953, when the principle of prior parliamentary approval was extended to all international treaties, whatever their name or form; also, treaties that diverge from the constitution can only be approved with a majority of two-thirds in both Houses. This requirement is now article 91 of the Constitution.

There had been discussion of the introduction of referenda, but all relevant proposals were rejected in the Lower House. The democracy, to which the Constitution referred, remained representative democracy.

It would be a serious mistake, however, to think that, in the Dutch context, representative democracy is the same as parliamentary democracy. Quite to the contrary, parliamentary representation was only one aspect of a much broader concept of democracy, which was a consequence of the permanent minorities of which civil society was composed. As of approximately the 1870s, society began articulating itself into four religious and ideological streams: Protestant, Catholic, Socialist, and Neutral. These developed into four 'pillars',

---

[26] Wilhelmina was Queen since the death of her father in 1890, but during her minority until 1898, when she reached the age of eighteen, the royal authority was exercised by the Queen-Widow, Princess Emma of Waldeck and Piermont. Wilhelmina reigned until 1948. Wilhelmina had been fairly seriously ill several times and had several miscarriages. The constitutional amendment restricting the royal succession was intended to keep from the throne far removed German cousins and nephews, who tended to assemble in The Hague during such periods of ill health. It became feasible only after she had given birth to her daughter, Juliana, her only child.

[27] Art 57 of the Constitution of 1922.

each of them closed onto themselves, each having their own sports clubs, trade unions, employers' organizations, newspapers, broadcasting associations, social clubs, and political parties, through which their political elites brokered the political compromises to keep society together—the ending of the struggle over financial equality of schools and electoral rights was one of its feats.

It was during the period stretching from secularization of the 1960s to the de-ideologized 1990s that the pillarized society was gradually dismantled.

Pillarized society also had a constitutional aspect. In 1922, the Constitution provided that, by Act of Parliament, public bodies with powers of regulation, other than those expressly mentioned in the Constitution, could be established.[28] In 1938, this provision was elaborated to provide for the possibility of supervision over these public bodies, including the right to quash their decisions in case they conflicted with the law or the general interest. Also, there was added a set of provisions on public regulatory bodies for professions and industries.[29] These provisions still occur in the present-day Constitution[30] and are the basis for the consociational organization of the economy in which representatives of government, trade unions and employers' organizations, consult, discuss, and agree on main aspects of the economy and economic policies.

b) After the Second World War: The Failed Constitutional Reform (1954–1983)

During the German occupation of the country in the Second World War and immediately after, much time was spent on a reconsideration of the constitutional order—usually in vague and undefined terms of 'renewal'.[31] In the Speech from the Throne of 1946, the government announced a general revision of the Constitution, but in practice this turned out not to be a very pressing concern. After the liberation, wartime ideas about a new constitutional system were soon frustrated. They had been mostly too vague and undefined. The traditional political parties regained the position they had before the war, thus effectively returning to previous constitutional relations.

In 1950, a *Staatscommissie* (Royal Committee), established by royal decree and composed of both constitutionalists and politicians from the main political parties and chaired by Minister van Schaik, was given the task to tender its advice on a general revision of the Constitution. Its 1954 final report did not propose systemic changes, did not receive much acclaim, and was shelved,[32] with the exception of some amendments on international treaty-making, as suggested in an interim report of 1952 which we briefly discuss below in Section 4.c.

The second half of the 1960s seemed at first to be a turning-point. Social and cultural movements and social contestation of the 'establishment' evidenced by the Dutch version of the beatniks, *Provos*, also affected the political environment. The announced marriage of the probable heir to the throne, Beatrix, with a German, was a focal point of socio-political and cultural contestation, with smoke bombs and alternative 'happenings' marking the wedding in Amsterdam in March 1966.

1966 was also the year that a committee calling itself *Democraten '66* (D66) issued a pamphlet in which serious concern was expressed about the state of the political system, the

---

[28] Art 194 of the Constitution of 1922.
[29] Art 152 to 4 of the Constitution of 1938.
[30] Art 134 of the Constitution.
[31] Simons, *Twintig jaar later* (Samson 1966).
[32] For an overview, see Henc van Maarseveen and Monique Koopman, *De parlementaire geschiedenis van de Proeve van een nieuwe Grondwet (1950-begin 1967)*, (Staatsuitgeverij, 's-Gravenhage, 1968) 1–18, and *passim*.

political parties and the parliamentary system of government. Direct election of the Prime Minister and abolition of proportional representation as the very cause of the prevalent culture of permanent compromise and unclear decision-making were the centre pieces of the proposed overhaul of the constitutional system. For the Minister for the Interior, who was responsible for constitutional affairs, it was a reason to commission a Draft for a New Constitution, *Proeve van een nieuwe Grondwet*, written by civil servants in consultation with a number of professors of constitutional law.

In 1967, the government installed another *Staatscommissie*, chaired by former Prime Minister Cals,[33] and co-chaired by Andreas M Donner, professor of constitutional law and later president of the European Court of Justice and member of the European Court of Human Rights.[34] This *Cals-Donner* committee proposed to retain the principle of proportional representation, but proposed electoral districts in each of which at least ten members of the Lower House would be elected, thus enhancing the relation between voters and elected.[35] In elections for the Lower House, the committee proposed voters would cast a vote for the person who they deemed should lead a cabinet; but only in case a person would obtain an absolute majority of the votes cast, the King would have to appoint this person as the one to form a cabinet that he was to lead.[36] Under this proposal, the necessity for a cabinet to have sufficient confidence of a majority of the Lower House would remain unaltered. This proposal was in effect intended to mean that the elections gave an indication of who was to be charged with forming a cabinet, rather than being a direct election of the Prime Minister. The exceptional case in which a candidate would receive an absolute majority of the vote would, according to the committee, in practice, always be a candidate who would have the support of a majority in parliament.[37]

These proposals were hotly debated in parliament. Two members of the Lower House introduced a bill which proposed a directly elected Prime Minister *tout court*—an option which had been rejected by the *Staatscommissie*.[38] But neither this nor the proposals of the committee were accepted by parliament.

Nevertheless, the proposals of the *Cals-Donner* committee were the starting-point for a series of bills introduced by the government, aiming to revise the whole of the Constitution.

This general revision of the Constitution was finally achieved in 1983, after a relatively minor adaptation in 1972, lowering the ages for right to vote and to stand for election. The

---

[33] Jozef MLTh Cals (1914–1971), a catholic politician who had been Prime Minister from 1965 until 1966.

[34] Andreas M Donner (1918–1992), at that point in time Judge at the European Court of Justice; member of the Calvinist *Anti-Revolutionaire Partij*, later Christian Democrat Party (CDA); law professor at the Protestant Free University of Amsterdam from 1945–1958; he was member of the European Court of Justice from 1958 until 1979; professor of constitutional law in Groningen (1979–1984); member of the European Court of Human Rights (1984–1987); previously member of the *Van Eysinga*-commission which prepared the constitutional amendments of 1953 and of the *Kranenburg*-commission which prepared the amendments of 1956, concerning international relations and the effect of treaties in the national legal order.

[35] The proposed art 42 para 1 read: 'Elections are based on proportional representation within the boundaries established by an Act of Parliament. An Act of Parliament can provide that with a view to elections of each of the Houses of Parliament the country shall be divided into separate electoral districts in each of which at least ten members shall be elected'; see *Eindrapport van de Staatscommissie van advies inzake de Grondwet en de Kieswet*, 1971, vol II.

[36] The proposed art 32 read: 'Simultaneously to elections for the *Tweede* Kamer (Lower House), and in accordance with rules to be established by an Act of Parliament, a vote shall be cast on the question who shall be charged with leading a cabinet which is to be formed. In case a candidate receives the absolute majority of the votes cast in this election, the King shall charge him with the forming of a cabinet which he shall lead', *Eindrapport van de Staatscommissie van advies inzake de Grondwet en de Kieswet*, 1971, vol II.

[37] See *Tweede Rapport van de Staatscommissie van advies inzake de Grondwet en de Kieswet*, 1969.

[38] Bill by the members Van Thijn (of the social democrat *Partij van de Arbeid*) and Goudsmit (D66), which was defeated in the Lower House in 1971.

1983 revision was in the end largely cosmetic and confirmed the historically incremental and very unrevolutionary nature of the Constitution. Alternatives were considered, but no major systemic changes were made. The language of the text was modernized, and many matters of detail were removed from the Constitution or delegated to the legislature ('deconstitutionalization'). Some called it 'a face-lift for an old lady'.[39]

The system of government remained untouched. Measured by its initial ambition, the revision could be considered a failure. On the other hand, it proved that the system of government was so deeply entrenched in practice and in law that it was found not to be easily changeable.

The greatest novelty was the regrouping of previously incorporated fundamental rights and the formulation of new ones in the opening chapter of the Constitution. This was a sign of the times in which constitutional matters began to concern less the system of government than the assertion of individual rights.

Notwithstanding its modesty, the Constitution found its present shape in 1983 and can be expected to last for some time to come. This is further confirmed by a whole series of amendments that were adopted since. Most of these amendments are unimportant, sometimes to the point of triviality. Before we say something about these, we first have to discuss the adaptations to the international environment which were translated into constitutional amendments both before and after 1983.

c) Adapting to the International Environment: Decolonization, International Relations, and the Fall of the Wall

Practically the only circumstance necessitating constitutional amendment after the Second World War was in the context of international relations, which had undergone drastic changes. Again, this was a matter of adaptation to a changing environment, rather than an amendment causing changes in the political environment. The international situation had changed in three constitutionally relevant respects: the process of decolonization, the outbreak of the Cold War and its ending in 1989, and increased international cooperation, especially in transatlantic and European context.

Of these, the most pressing was the process of decolonization. Indonesian nationalists headed by Sukarno had declared Indonesian independence on 17 August 1945. After what was in effect a colonial war during two so-called *politionele acties* (July 1947–January 1948 and December 1948–January 1949), sovereignty was finally officially transferred on 27 December 1949. Looking at the East Indies, only Dutch New Guinea was initially left. The relation with the Dutch West Indies was renegotiated in terms that granted these countries autonomy within the Kingdom at the end of the 1940s and beginning of the 1950s. The Dutch West Indies comprised Surinam (in South America) and six Caribbean islands, which before 1948 were known by the name of the largest, Curaçao, and were subsequently called the Netherlands Antilles. In 2010, the Netherlands Antilles was broken up into three different islands acquiring the status of autonomous 'countries', and the three remaining small islands were added to the European Netherlands. The process of decolonization was well beyond the control of the constitutional provisions on the colonies.

Decolonization led initially to adaptations of the Constitution through a number of amendments passed in 1948. These changed the names of the territories mentioned in various constitutional provisions and made it possible to enter into a federation with Indonesia and

---

[39] Aalt W Heringa and Tom Zwart, *Grondwet 1983* (3rd edn, WEJ Tjeenk Willink, Zwolle, 1991).

to come to an arrangement granting autonomy to other parts of the Kingdom. As the federation with Indonesia soon proved stillborn, later amendments of the Constitution could only adapt to post-colonial reality. This happened in 1956 and 1963. The first, among other things, removed all mention of Indonesia and the envisaged federation with Indonesia. Relations with the Western parts of the Kingdom were reorganized in a Charter for the Kingdom of the Netherlands, *Statuut voor het Koninkrijk der Nederlanden* of 1954, with supra-constitutional status. The amendment of 1963 removed the mention of the Netherlands New Guinea, sovereignty over which had been transferred to Indonesia under strong international pressure a year earlier.

The Cold War led to several bills on excluding members from representative assemblies (including the Houses of Parliament) who had demonstrated a sympathy towards revolutionary aims. A somewhat similar proposal had been rejected in 1938, but the *staatscommissie-Van Schaik* had included it in an interim-report of 1952. In 1948, in response to the communist putsch in Prague, a successful initiative to amend the Constitution with a view to introduce the possibility of a civilian state of siege had been adopted. The committee's proposal of 1952, however, was rejected by the government and was not included in the bills it introduced on a number of other issues.

More successful were the proposals this same *Van Schaik* committee had made in its interim report, which built on the work of a parallel *Van Eysinga* committee. A new provision was adopted to the effect that the government 'shall promote the development of the international legal order'[40]—one of the few 'ideological' provisions one can still find in the Constitution.[41] Also, the failure of 1922 to submit in principle all treaties, irrespective of the form they take, to prior parliamentary approval was rectified. All this was accomplished in 1953.

On the status of treaties and of decisions of international organizations in the national legal order, the committee proposed to grant them *direct effect* in the domestic legal order, which was taken over in the amendment bill by the government and adopted by parliament. An amendment initiated by Serrarens—a member of the Lower House, later the first Dutch judge of the European Court of Justice[42]—stipulating expressly also their *priority* over any contrary national legislation, was adopted against the wishes of the government.[43]

In 1956, the provisions on the status of treaties and decisions of international organizations were amended in order to specify that this priority concerned only 'provisions which are binding on everyone', *een ieder verbindende bepalingen*. This was done upon the proposal of an advisory commission which was established by the government. Again, Andreas M Donner, the later president of the ECJ, was a member of this commission.[44] Thus the concept

---

[40] Art 58 of the Constitution of 1953.

[41] Art 90 of the Constitution in the edition of 2019.

[42] *Petrus Joannes Servatius Serrarens* (1888–1963), was a prominent catholic trade union leader; his appointment to the delegation to the ILO in 1921 instead of the socialist trade unionist Oudegeest, led to the very first Advisory Opinion of the Permanent Court of International Justice of 31 July 1922, *Nomination of the Workers' Delegate to the International Labour Conference*, PCIJ, Series B, n 1 (1922); Serrarens had been, amongst others, member of the Governing Body of the ILO and member of the Parliamentary Assembly of the Council of Europe; he was the only non-lawyer as judge of the Court of Justice, which was from 1952 to 1958.

[43] Arts 65, 66, and 67 of the Constitution 1953.

[44] Interestingly, Donner voted in all committees against proposals of granting direct effect and priority of international law over conflicting law; so it was not a surprise that as a judge in the ECJ he voted against *Van Gend & Loos*, see Pierre Pescatore at https://www.cvce.eu/en/obj/interview_with_pierre_pescatore_the_early_judgments_of_the_court_of_justice_1962_1966-en-1238d611-2883-43fa-921f-ac5861229ffa.html (last accessed on 24 March).

behind what was later developed by the ECJ as the doctrine of 'direct effect' was introduced in the Netherlands Constitution in the 1950s. Its consequences are discussed below (D.1.d.ff).

The radical change in the European, and indeed the global context which came with the fall of the Wall, was reflected in the constitutional amendment of the year 2000 which concerned defence. It changed the description of the tasks of the armed forces. These no longer only concerned the 'protection of the State's interests' but also 'maintaining and promoting of the international legal order' (article 97 para 1 of the Constitution), thus adapting to the tasks which the armed forces—with a problematic constitutional basis—had already assumed in the 1990s.[45] Also, a provision was inserted which imposed the obligation on the government to inform the States General prior to the deployment or making available of the armed forces for the purpose of maintaining and promoting the international legal order, including humanitarian assistance in armed conflict, unless compelling reasons prevent the government from giving such information in advance, in which case the information is to be provided as soon as possible (article 100 of the Constitution). This duty to give information is to enable parliament to debate such use of the armed forces and, within the normal rules of the parliamentary system, to influence the relevant decisions.[46]

This was to date the last amendment of Constitution which can be considered an adaptation to a new reality in the outside world.

5. The Minor Amendments

The list of amendments made to the Netherlands Constitution which are of minor importance is long even when it is acknowledged that it is debatable what is 'minor' and what 'important':

1884 amendment to abolish the prohibition of constitutional amendments during a regency[47]

1938 increase in the income of the Crown and that of members of the Lower House; introduction of ministers without portfolio (not heading a ministerial department); extension of the provisions on public bodies for industry and the professions

1972 lowering of the age to vote and stand for elections, abolition of state subsidies for protestant ministers and catholic clergy, adaptation of income of members of parliament and of the members of the Royal House

1987 a technical redrafting of article 12, concerning entering the home against the will of an occupant by public officials[48]

1995 amendment to clarify beyond doubt that the armed forces do not need to have conscripts in active service

1999 lapse of a large number of transitory provisions, which had extinguished; amendment of the provision on ombudsman institutions in order to make explicit mention

---

[45] See Leonard FM Besselink, 'Military Law in the Netherlands', in Georg Nolte (ed) *European Military Law Systems* (Gruyter, Berlin, 2003) 547–556.

[46] A large number of members of parliament believe that this article may not give parliament a formal right of approval, but at least a 'substantive' one. This argument is difficult to sustain, as the government denies that there is a true right of approval.

[47] Wilhelmina, born in 1880, was the only foreseeable successor to the throne, which might mean a long period of a regency—as indeed it turned out to be (from 1890 to 1898).

[48] The obligation of prior identification and notice can be restricted by an Act of Parliament.

of the National Ombudsman (established in 1981) without making any change to his position; amendment on guardianship and parental authority over the King who has not attained majority

2002 further amendment of article 12, in order to make exceptions for the necessity to provide a written report of the entry of a home against the will of the occupant in case when national security is involved

2005 provision enabling to provide for replacement of pregnant or ill members of representative bodies (parliament. provincial and municipal councils) by Act of Parliament

2006 amendment of article 23 on education in order to make it possible for primary schools to be housed in a building together with denominational schools

2008 rescinding of the mayor being chair of the municipal council, and of the royal commissioner being chair of provincial council; rescinding of being excluded from the right to vote if a person has been declared legally incompetent by judicial decision for reason of mental disorder

2017 providing a constitutional basis for 'public bodies' for the Caribbean parts of the Netherlands that were joined to the country of the Netherlands in 2010

2018 scrapping appointment of mayors of municipalities and King's commissioners in the provinces by royal decree[.]

This very list conveys the great variety of mostly not very pressing or very important constitutional matters. The withdrawal of transitory provisions which as a consequence of the lapse of time have lost their meaning is trivial but amending the provision on the King's guardianship in order to bring it in conformity with the Civil Code (!), as one did in 1999, does say something about the place of the Constitution within the legal order in relation to 'ordinary' legislation.

6. Perennial Controversies

The previous section may suggest that one is constitutionally lost in trivialities. This may be true as far as the actually promulgated amendments are concerned. It is not true about the attempts at constitutional amendment which have so far failed.

Thus, the issue of reforming the system of government has remained controversial. The matter of bridging the gap between voters and the elected has been the object of various official committees, first the Royal Committee (*Staatscommissie*) *Biesheuvel/Prakke*.[49] Next, a series of studies were commissioned by a committee of the Lower House between 1988 and 1993 (*Deetman* Committee). It produced many valuable analyses, although the whole exercise and its proposals constituted something like a *déja-vu* after the mainly abortive discussions on this point prior to the revision of the 1983 Constitution. Among the issues discussed and proposals put forward were the introduction of binding referenda, the direct elections of mayors of municipalities and of the King's commissioners in the provincial administrations. It received no actual follow-up at the time, although the amendment of 2018 to remove the constitutional provision on the appointment of mayors and King's commissioners by royal decree might make these into elective offices if the legislature would decide so.

---

[49] *Eindrapport van de staatscommissie van advies inzake de relatie kiezers–beleidsvorming*, 's-Gravenhage, 1985.

Unsuccessful bills were introduced to reform the electoral system towards a German system, which, apart from purportedly bridging the gap between voters and those elected, might possibly lead to an easier articulation of majorities, but remaining within the boundaries of the constitutionally required principle of proportional representation. In 2017, a new Royal Committee on the Parliamentary System was yet again appointed by the government. It came up with a large number of proposals, amongst others to adapt elements of the electoral system, and reduce the powers of the Upper House (*Eerste Kamer*) to reject bills and introduce binding referenda and constitutional adjudication by a special constitutional court.[50]

The study of pending amendments is fraught with difficulties as few of them eventually pass. Suffice it is to mention the most far-reaching amongst the proposals over recent decades. That is the proposal to limit the constitutional prohibition for courts to review the constitutionality of Acts of Parliament—a prohibition on which we have to say more below. The bill, initiated by members of the Lower House in 2002,[51] excepts judicial review against classical constitutional fundamental rights from the prohibition.[52] It was passed at the first reading in both houses, but got bogged down in second reading after stalling for many years in a succession of Lower Houses. It was eventually declared to have lapsed in 2018.[53]

C. The Evolution of the Constitution: The Institutional Parameters of Constitutional Development

Having described in broad outline the historical development of the Constitution, we turn to a discussion of the parameters of constitutional development and change. We do so by looking at the various sources of constitutional law.

1. Constitution-Making Power: The Rigidity of the Constitution

The Constitution is a rigid constitution. Its amendment proceeds as follows. First an Act of Parliament adopted by both Houses must formulate the proposed amendment to the Constitution. After this, the Lower House elections are held. After the new Lower House has convened, the amendment is considered by each of the Houses in the so-called 'second reading'. In second reading, each House can only adopt an amending bill with at least two-thirds of the votes.[54] This is basically the procedure which has existed since 1848,[55] but, also before that, the Constitution was rigid. The Lower House elections prior to consideration at second reading has required a dissolution by royal decree, but this formal requirement is expected to be dropped in 2021 as a consequence of a constitutional amendment bill which,

---

[50] *Lage Drempels, Hoge Dijken: Democratie en rechtsstaat in balans*, Final Report of the *Staatscommissie parlementair stelsel* (Boom, Amsterdam, 2018) English translation at https://archief06.archiefweb.eu/archives/archiefweb/20210508020000/https://www.staatscommissieparlementairstelsel.nl/documenten/rapporten/samenvattingen/072019/18/download-the-english-translation-of-the-final-report-of-the-state-commission (last accessed on 7 April 2022).

[51] Kamerstukken TK, 2001–2002, 28 331, nn 1–3.

[52] Kamerstukken EK, 2004–2005, A, is the definitive version of the bill.

[53] Kamerstukken TK, 2018–2019, 32334, n 13.

[54] Art 137 of the Constitution.

[55] Before 1995 not only the Lower House, but also the Upper House was dissolved before the second reading. Because the Upper House is elected by the *Provinciale Staten* (provincial councils) which themselves are not dissolved, the Upper House was usually re-elected with the same results as the previous House. This was considered being a meaningless ritualistic way of proceeding and was therefore abolished.

however, retains the existing requirement of a second reading in both Houses after Lower House elections (with adoption by qualified majority of at least two-thirds of the vote in both Houses).[56]

The precise meaning of the dissolution within this procedure can be easily misunderstood. For various reasons it cannot be considered a plebiscitarian element. Firstly, dissolution traditionally coincides with regular elections of the Lower House (which was one reason behind the proposal to abolish it). This means that proposed constitutional amendments that were adopted by an Act of Parliament at the first reading have hardly ever played a role in those elections and electoral campaigns; the general political programmes and political issues of the day, not the proposed constitutional amendment, dominate the campaigns of political parties at general elections. Moreover, the dissolution of the Lower House was never been meant to give the electorate the opportunity to vote on the text of the constitutional amendment as in a referendum. The election is merely the election of a House with constitution-making power, a power it exerts together with the Upper House and government.

In recent practice, the matter of which Lower House that has been elected after dissolution for reason of a constitutional amendment that was adopted at first reading, should adopt the bill at second reading, has become confounded. The reason for this was the sometimes rapid succession of general elections due to political instability, in combination with a late introduction of the bill in parliament, which prevented the second reading by the Lower House elected for the purpose. After 2003 this led to the practice of waiting with the actual second reading until the chances for adoption with the requisite majority of at least two-thirds of the vote were more auspicious. A solid body of opinion held this practice unconstitutional, but was initially condoned by an opinion of the Council of State, although it later retracted its initial view.[57] The amendment of the constitutional amendment procedure, envisaged for 2021 as just mentioned, will resolve the matter, as it determines unequivocally that only the Lower House elected after adoption of an amendment proposal at first reading, can deal with the proposal at second reading—not a subsequently elected Lower House.

The rigidity of the Constitution has been lamented by a long succession of constitutional lawyers from Thorbecke onwards.[58] No doubt the procedure for constitutional revision has made the adoption of some more far-reaching proposals difficult. This contributes to explaining why there have been some constitutional revisions on rather unimportant and uncontroversial issues, and which were often left over after the more substantial proposals were rejected.

This state of affairs is inherent in the kind of entrenchment which is intended by the provisions on constitutional revision: only those rules which can count on the support of a large majority of at least two thirds in both Lower House and in the Upper House can be raised to constitutional status.

---

[56] Act of 14 October 2020, *Staatsblad* 2020, 430. This act was at first reading adopted with overwhelming majorities in both Houses and is therefore expected to be adopted with the required two-thirds majorities at second reading in 2021.

[57] Advisory Opinion of the *Raad van State*, 17 October 2003, *Kamerstukken II* 2003/04, 29200 VII, nr 36, p 4, argued that it has never been the intention of the makers of the Constitution to let a later House than the one elected after the appropriate dissolution decide on the amendment in second reading; although previous language of the relevant provision excluded such a practice, an unintended rephrasing of 1995 did not literally exclude it; this the *Raad van State* considered decisive. Probably for purely political reasons, this view was embraced by government and parliament. Advisory Opinion *Raad van State*, 29 September 2017, *Kamerstukken II* 2017/18, 32334, nr 11, p 8, retracted on the unconditional view of 2003, and considered a second reading by a subsequently elected Lower House only acceptable in circumstances which make it practically impossible for the Lower House elected after a dissolution to consider and deal with the bill itself.

[58] E.g. Jit A Peters, *Wie beschermt onze Grondwet?* (Vossius Press, Amsterdam, 2003).

Unlike the constitutions of other European countries, the Constitution does not provide for certain unchangeable provisions. Usually, it is assumed that there are no such unchangeable provisions. Nevertheless, one author has argued that certain fundamental rights as found in the Constitution and in the European Convention of Human Rights are unchangeable even for the constitution-making power.[59]

In an advisory opinion on the possibility of implicitly changing the Constitution in a treaty, the *Raad van State* took a similar position. It suggested that it was impermissible to diverge from the ECHR and the 'Treaties establishing the European Union [*sic*]' and from certain fundamental rights provisions in Chapter 1 of the Constitution if these were substantially infringed by the conclusion of a treaty.[60] This opinion referred to the power of the treaty-making power, not to the constitution-making power. However, the treaty-making power in the case of treaties which diverge from the Constitution is vested in the legislature by a majority of at least two thirds of the vote in both Houses of Parliament together with the government (article 91 para3 of the Constitution); just as the constitution-making power resides essentially in the 'second reading' of constitutional amendment, which is a majority of at least two-thirds of the vote in both Houses of Parliament. Thus, the opinion of the *Raad van State* may logically extend also to the limits which the constitution-making power has to observe.

2. The Role of the Government in Constitution Making

The overwhelming majority of constitutional amendments were passed at the initiative of the government, as agreed with the state of affairs in legislative matters generally. The Lower House (contrary to the Upper House) has the right of initiation, and this extends also to bills proposing a revision of the Constitution, but the Lower House has made relatively little use of its right of initiation. An exception to this is the (by Dutch standards) extremely rapid adoption of the initiative to introduce a civilian state of siege in 1948: it took only months to have it passed in two readings, which was helped by the fact that elections were due anyway.

In the 1960s, the Ministry of the Interior set up a department for constitutional affairs. It played a significant role in preparing the revised Constitution of 1983.

As we noticed above, the government makes regular use of official advisory commissions especially established to investigate the desirability of major constitutional amendments, in recent decades after consultation and with the approval of parliament. These committees were initially chaired by a minister while also active politicians took part as well as constitutionalists, but on later occasions it was mainly an experienced elderly statesman who would chair such a committee together with a prominent constitutional lawyer (e.g. the *Cals-Donner* and *Biesheuvel-Prakke* committees mentioned above).[61]

This way of proceeding highlights the effort to seek broad consensus and expert input in the process of constitution-making and takes the issue of constitutional reform at arm's

---

[59] GFM van der Tang, 'Artikel 137', in Piet Akkermans and Adriaan Koekkoek (eds), *De Grondwet* (WEJ Tjeenk Willink, Zwolle, 1992) 1188.

[60] Advisory Opinion of the *Raad van State*, 19 November 1999 on foreign jurisdiction in the Netherlands (the Scottish court which had to adjudicate the *Lockerbie* case in the Netherlands pursuant to a Security Council Resolution), *Kamerstukken TK* (Parliamentary Documents of the Lower House) 1999–2000, 26 800 VI A, p 6.

[61] The elderly statesman approach was recently adopted by the royal committee on the parliamentary system of 2017–2018, which was chaired by Johan Remkes, who had been minister in three cabinets, member of parliament and King's Commissioner in the province of North-Holland.

length of day-to-day politics. Thus, it does justice to the nature of constitutional norms as requiring a large degree of consensus. On the other hand, this less ideological nature makes it duller and risks making the Constitution a matter for experts only.

3. The Role Played by Parliament

Apart from its role in the procedure of amending the Constitution, the constitutional activity in parliament is fairly low and constitutional culture is not very strong, particularly in the Lower House. Parliament has rarely initiated successful bills amending the Constitution. It does not have separate committee on constitutional affairs as this is considered to be part of the work of the standing committee for the Interior of the Lower House and that of the Upper House.

Unlike the British Lower House, which has a committee for scrutinizing the compatibility of bills with the Human Rights Act as well as a committee to scrutinize delegated legislation, or the Finnish parliament, which has a constitutional committee to review the constitutionality of bills (the famous *Perustuslakivaliokunta*, which has been retained after the prohibition of judicial review of Acts of Parliament was lifted in 2000), there is no parliamentary committee, nor any other parliamentary mechanism to guard the constitutionality of parliament's or the government's products.

Hence, the government is not very eager to raise constitutional issues concerning its own acts and proposals. In most cases, if an objection of a constitutional nature is put forward, it merely tends to seek arguments in favour of its own view of the constitutionality of its action without seriously, if at all, explaining and considering arguments which might lead to a different conclusion.

This state of affairs is, to some extent, compensated for by the advisory opinions of the *Raad van State* which is always consulted on bills. On occasion, the *Raad van State* has shown an unwarranted degree of literalness in its interpretation of constitutional provisions, making the letter of the law more decisive than either the intention of the provision or the system of the Constitution,[62] which removes it far from judicial canons of interpretation as used by most constitutional tribunals in Europe.

Together with the government, parliament has a role to play in the development of certain norms of customary constitutional law. In Dutch doctrine, there is consensus on the principle that the forming of a customary norm of constitutional law requires an *opinio iuris sive necessitates* and a practice expressing it. The *opinio iuris* must exist among the relevant actors which are to be bound by the rule or to whom it applies. Thus, for customary norms concerning the parliamentary system to exist, *opinio iuris* must exist both with parliament and the government. There is some academic controversy on the element of *necessitas*: some argue that the continuity of state government or the coherence of the constitutional system must be at risk should the rule not exist; if the coherence of the system or the continuity of state government is not affected by the absence of the rule, then the relevant practice, even if desirable, is not a rule of customary law, but merely a practice or non-legal convention of the constitution. On the whole, there is a reticence to accept too easily the existence of a customary or unwritten rule of constitutional law,[63] but a number have been recognized in constitutional practice and in the case law.

---

[62] See Tang, 'Artikel 137' (n 59).
[63] See Constantijn AJM Kortmann, *Constitutioneel recht* (7th edn, Kluwer, Deventer, 2016) 132–133.

The main norm accepted in parliamentary practice is the rule of confidence which holds that if the Lower House passes a motion of censure addressed to the cabinet or a minister, the cabinet or minister will have to offer its resignation to the King, who is under the obligation to grant the dismissal, unless the government decides to dissolve the Lower House.

This alternative of dissolving the Lower House instead of offering the resignation of the cabinet has not been practiced since the 1930s for two reasons. Firstly, cabinets are coalition cabinets of which the members entertain close relations with their respective political groups in parliament. Consequently, when conflict occurs between coalition partners *in* parliament, this split will spill over into the cabinet, whilst a split between coalition partners within the cabinet will spill over to parliament. If the conflict is 'put to the country' by dissolution and elections, the cabinet-split will be a fact and independent from the outcome of the elections. In other words, dissolutions are used to solve the political crisis by the formation of a new cabinet after elections; the elections are not a test for a cabinet to see if it could stay on if the results of the elections are favourable. Secondly, since 1922 cabinets offer their resignation on the eve of elections for the Lower House, thus clearing the way for forming of a new cabinet after the elections. In practice, the dissolution of the Lower House when a political crisis exists is a matter on which the leaders of all groups in the Lower House are consulted by the King (who upon the fact that the cabinet has offered its resignation always consulted the leaders of the political groups in the Lower House on how to proceed).[64] Thus, although informally, consent of the majority of the House on a dissolution is sought. All this makes the customary constitutional norm that, in case of a motion of censure, the government can resort to the Lower House's dissolution at best theoretical.

This practical state of affairs also affects the relevance of another late nineteenth century unwritten norm that in case of a crisis of confidence between parliament and the cabinet, the cabinet cannot dissolve the Lower House more than once: if a crisis leads to a dissolution of the Lower House, and elections do not lead to support for the cabinet in that crisis, the cabinet will have no alternative but to resign. A situation of conflict in which the cabinet could even contemplate dissolving parliament twice over the same issue can hardly be conceived in practice considering that coalitions with narrow political relations between the individual ministers and their political constituency in parliament are necessary. This renders the rule theoretical.

4. The Role of Courts: The Unwritten Rules and Principles of Constitutional Law

Since 1848, the Constitution prohibits courts from reviewing the constitutionality of Acts of Parliament (since 1953 also of treaties) as is now provided for in article 120.[65] Yet, courts, particularly those of highest instance, play an important role in constitutional development and constitute sources of constitutional law. After all, courts can establish the constitutionality of all acts other than Acts of Parliament (and treaties), unless in case judging such other

---

[64] Until 2012 the King retained a role in the forming of a cabinet, by consulting the political forces, most prominently the political groups in the Lower House on who to appoint with what mandate to form a cabinet. Clearly, the King could never take a personal view, but had to go by majority opinion in the Lower House, given the parliamentary system of government. The King's role was taken over by the Lower House itself, personified by the Speaker of the House.

[65] Presently art 120 of the Constitution: 'The compatibility of Acts of Parliament and treaties with the Constitution [*Grondwet*] shall not be reviewed by the courts.'

acts unconstitutional necessarily implies the unconstitutionality of the Act of Parliament which is at the basis of that act—this will be the case if the content of the delegated legislation is actually determined by the Act of Parliament on which it rests.

The power to interpret the Constitution and adjudicate constitutional issues is not concentrated: the system of constitutional adjudication is diffuse.

Many courts have interpreted the scope and meaning of constitutional rights. Case law on other provisions of the Constitution, however, is relatively scarce, but not absent. This case law developed certain principles of the Constitution, as well as unwritten principles of constitutional law.

Of the more important constitutional principles, the case law of courts was crucial with regard to:

- the status of international law in the national legal order,
- the division of powers between the executive and legislature (the principle of legality), and
- the division of powers between the legislature and the judiciary and the distinction of political from legal questions.

We will say a few words about each.

The rule of unwritten constitutional law that treaties can be invoked as treaties before courts, and do not need specific transformation into national law, is derived from the case law of the *Hoge Raad* in a standard case which dates back to 1919.[66] The case law has, since this judgment, assumed that international law, which has become binding on the Kingdom under public international law, is binding in the national legal order.

This monist view is reinforced by the constitutional provision that self-executing, or directly effective, international provisions have priority over conflicting national law (see below D.1.d).[67] The *Hoge Raad* interpreted this provision to mean *a contrario* that courts cannot review Acts of Parliament against international provisions that are not directly effective.[68]

A further example of an unwritten principle of constitutional law established by case law is the principle of legality which the *Hoge Raad* derived from the general system of the Constitution in the *Meerenberg* case of 1879.[69] The case concerned a royal decree containing a general rule that mental hospitals were to hold a register of its patients, on pain of a penal fine determined by an Act of Parliament. The *Meerenberg* institution had failed to comply and was prosecuted. In the highest instance the matter turned on whether the government had the power to issue the said royal decree, although there was no basis for that decree in an Act of Parliament, other than the Act of Parliament which imposed a fine on the transgression of royal decrees in general (the *Blanketwet* of 1818). In its judgment concerning the powers of the executive versus those of the legislature, and hence the powers between government and parliament, the *Hoge Raad* found that the Constitution did not grant a general legislative or regulative power to the government, and that it followed from the scheme and structure of the Constitution that legislative power can only be derived either from the Constitution itself or from an Act of Parliament delegating such power to the government. In

---

[66] HR 3 April 1919, NJ 1919, 371.
[67] At present art 94 of the Constitution.
[68] HR 6 March 1959, ECLI:NL:HR:1959:131 (*Nyugat II*); reiterated in HR 14 April 1989 ECLI:NL:HR:1989:AD5725 (*Harmonisatiewet*), paragraph 3.2, and HR 18 September 2001, ECLI:NL:HR:2001:AB1471 (*Desi Bouterse*).
[69] See n 15.

this case it found such an act or direct basis in the Constitution itself was absent, while also the Blanket Act did not provide a basis for the said royal decree.

From this judgment, which was phrased in broad and general language, the unwritten constitutional principle of legality was derived according to which legislative power can only be exercised by the executive if it has a specific basis in an Act of Parliament. This found partial expression in a constitutional amendment of 1887 according to which royal decrees containing general administrative regulations can only be enforced with criminal sanctions if it has a basis in an Act of Parliament.[70]

The principle was further elaborated in a judgment of the *Hoge Raad* of 22 June 1973 on fluoridizing drinking water in which it held that not only measures enforced with penal sanctions, but any measure which imposes a burden on citizens or are otherwise burdensome, must have a basis in an Act of Parliament.[71] This is the unwritten part of the principle of legality.

Also, regarding the interpretation of the division of powers between the legislature and courts, the case law developed relevant constitutional rules and principles.

As already mentioned, the Constitution prohibits courts from reviewing the constitutionality of Acts of Parliament (article 120 of the Constitution). The text of the provision does not cover review of the legality of bills, nor the question whether a failure to legislate can be adjudicated. Nevertheless, the case law of the *Hoge Raad* has made clear that courts are not allowed to intervene in the legislative process, nor can courts order parliament (or directly elected decentralized representative bodies) to legislate in a particular manner. This not only applies to purely national cases. Courts may not order parliament to legislate in case it has failed to adopt an Act of Parliament in order to implement an EU Directive (Directive 91/676, the Nitrate Directive).[72] This broad prohibition of court orders to legislate, inspired as it was by considerations of not entering too far into the political domain, was narrowed down recently. In a case concerning an old and small orthodox-protestant political party which has traditionally held about two out of 150 seats in the Lower House (and one in the Upper House), SGP (*Staatkundig Gereformeerde Partij*), which has always had a prohibition for women to be part of representative or executive bodies as this would contravene the biblical order of creation, the civil chamber of the *Hoge Raad*, having established a contravention of the non-discrimination clauses in the Constitution (article 4), the ICCPR (articles 25 and 2), and in particular the Convention on the Elimination of All Forms of Discrimination against Women (article 7), narrowed down the prohibition to a judicial order to take judicially specified legislative measures. It, however, upheld the view of the Court of Appeal that the State has to take measures with the effect of the SGP to grant the right to stand for election to women. These had to be measures that are both effective and make the least possible infringement of the fundamental rights of the political party and its members, without further specifying the nature or substance of such measures would need to be.[73] In the recent *Urgenda* judgment of the *Hoge Raad* on the emission reduction targets for greenhouse gases

---

[70] The present art 89 para 1 and 2 of the Constitution.

[71] HR 22 June 1973, ECLI:NL:HR:1973:AD2208 (*Fluoridering*).

[72] HR 19 November 1999, ECLI:NL:HR:1999:AA1056 (*municipality of Tegelen*) on an alleged infringement of a procedural rule contained in an Act of Parliament, which affects the merger by Act of Parliament of two municipalities; HR 21 March 2003, ECLI:NL:HR:2003:AE8462 (*Waterpakt*), see (2004) 41 CMLRev 1429–55; this approach was confirmed as regards an injunction to a provincial council to pass a provincial bye-law in order to comply with an EU Directive, HR 1 October 2003, ECLI:NL:HR:2003: AO8913 (*Frisian Fauna Protection*).

[73] HR 9 April 2010, ECLI:NL:HR:2010:BK4549.

for 2020, it confirmed that the prohibition of court orders to legislate only concerns the particular content of the legislation.[74]

This case law must be understood from the perspective of the separation of powers between the legislature and the judiciary. The considerations in these cases refer to the inherently political nature of legislating, and—in case of failure to comply with an EU Directive—of the political nature of the choice either to legislate or to let it come to infringement proceedings under article 258 TFEU.

The case law just mentioned suggests a doctrine of separation of powers which seems to hinge on the dividing line between discretionary decisions to be left to the legislature and legal issues which are the domain of courts of law. There is a tendency in the case law of the *Hoge Raad* of the 1990s towards a restrictive interpretation of the competence of courts in cases in which political issues are prominent in the area of foreign affairs.

This tendency is similar to a *political question doctrine* that mainly concerns issues of foreign policy. It was developed in cases concerning the use of nuclear weapons (in a case concerning the threat or use of nuclear weapons)[75] and the use of armed force in international interventions (in the case on *NATO bombardments in Kosovo*).[76] Such use of Dutch armed forces hinged on the question of their lawfulness under public international law, but another dimension to this question involved an interpretation of article 90 of the Constitution, which imposes on the government the obligation to promote the development of the international legal order, in the case of the Netherlands' participation in international operations in Afghanistan.[77]

The reasoning in these cases followed a common pattern. First the *Hoge Raad* stated that foreign policy decisions highly depend on political considerations related to the circumstances of the moment; next it held that courts must show a large measure of restraint in adjudicating claims which aim at declaring unlawful and forbidden certain acts implementing political decisions in the field of foreign policy and defence; and finally, a conclusion that 'it is not up to civil courts to come to such political decisions'. Extending this to the interpretation of article 90 of the Constitution, it stated that this provision does not give any clues as to how it should be implemented by the government and leaves considerable political discretion with which courts cannot interfere.

This political question doctrine has also been extended to later case law of lower courts.[78]

5. The Role of Foreign Constitutional Law

In the context of constitutional development, foreign constitutional law has been used heuristically, though altogether the role of foreign examples has been limited throughout Dutch constitutional history. In its design, the Republic of the United Provinces followed no clear contemporary or ancient example consciously, although ancient examples were idealized to legitimate the Republic.[79] The French influence at the end of the eighteenth century was

---

[74] HR 20 December 2019, ECLI:NL:HR:2019:2006; unofficial English version ECLI:NL:HR:2019:2007.

[75] HR 21 December 2001 (*Nuclear Weapons*) ECLI:NL:HR:2001:ZC3693.

[76] HR 29 November 2002 (*Nato bombardments Kosovo*) ECLI:NL:HR:2002:AE5164.

[77] HR 6 February 2004, ECLI:NL:HR:2004: AN8071.

[78] E.g. Rb Den Haag 4 May 2005, ECLI:NL:RBSGR:2005:AT5152, refusing a request to arrest President Bush upon his entry into the Netherlands; Gerechtshof Den Haag 22 November 2019 (*Repatriation of ISIS Women and Children*), ECLI:NL:GHDHA:2019:3208.

[79] In the seventeenth century, literature references were made to Ancient Israel, Greece, and Rome, for instance in the early work of Grotius; later on, references to the Venetian republic and the Helvetian confederation abound.

evident in the Constitution of the Batavian Republic of 1798, but this lasted only briefly, and its successors were basically dictated by Paris. Throughout the nineteenth century, the French Revolution and its aftermath formed a dreaded example, rather than a constitutional model. In practice the constitution developed in many ways in the manner of the British parliamentary model, ending up in a kind of Westminster model of parliamentarism though with its own distinct traits in terms of political representation. Even during the general revision leading to the Constitution of 1983, no direct comparative exercises of any substantive scope were undertaken. The codification of a catalogue of fundamental rights as a first chapter to the Constitution of 1983 was obviously inspired by the German example. Traces thereof, without explicit reference to German constitutional law, can be found in the parliamentary documents from the government.[80]

Since 1983, comparative constitutional law has become more important. Discussions on constitutional change are now often accompanied by explicit comparisons with other countries, mainly for informing the discussion, but also heuristically. This has been the case for instance in the report by the *staatscommissie Biesheuvel/Prakke* on introducing a corrective referendum. Also, more recent discussions on reforming the electoral system are partly based on and informed by explicit discussions of foreign examples.[81]

In 1992, a new assembly hall for the Lower House was built, and its interior was changed from the British oppositional to the German *Bundestag* hemisphere model. This change to a continental orientation may be symbolic.

D. Basic Structures and Concepts

The Constitution provides the political system with little more than a framework which is largely dominated by the political system itself. Courts have no role to play in this regard. The Constitution is an epiphenomenon: it is more the reflection of the political system as opposed to the political system being the reflection of it, notwithstanding attempts at political reform through constitutional amendment.

The shift in European constitutionalism from focusing on the political system (and electoral rights) in the long nineteenth century, towards individual, judicially enforceable fundamental rights beyond political rights in a strict sense (in the twentieth century) had a different character in the Netherlands from most other European countries: rights are to a considerable extent located outside the Constitution itself.

To understand this, we first describe the place of the Constitution in the broader context of the Netherlands constitutional order by looking at its place in the hierarchy of norms and its relation to the national and international/European legal order, and the political system, respectively.

In further sections we briefly discuss the idea of the *Rechtsstaat* and its manifestation in the Netherlands.

Finally, we discuss the basic features of the horizontal and vertical division of powers and the absence of the notion of the nation or another encompassing equivalent.

---

[80] On the history of the chapter on fundamental rights of the 1983 Constitution, see Jan J Pelle, *In de staatsrechtsgeleerde wereld: de politieke geschiedenis van hoofdstuk 1 van de Grondwet van 1983* (Gouda Quint, Deventer, 1998) (hereafter Pelle, *politieke geschiedenis*).

[81] Jan A Van Schagen and Henk R B M Kummeling, *Proeve van een nieuw kiesstelsel* (WEJ Tjeenk Willink, Deventer, 1998), which looked at Germany in particular; also, the report of the Royal committee looks consciously at foreign examples, see n 48.

1. The Relation of the Constitution to Other Parts of the Legal Order

The Constitution, *Grondwet*, is a nucleus of the broader constitution. But the totality of legal norms making up the constitution (the substantive *bloc de constitutionnalité*) is larger than the total of the provisions of the Constitution alone. It extends figuratively speaking both 'upwards' and 'downwards'.

This state of affairs is intimately connected with the nature of the formal constitution as a textual instrument which registers and articulates a state of affairs in a legally binding manner as it normatively operates in a wider political reality. As already mentioned, the unwritten constitutional law also plays its part in this. This is another expression of the particular character of the Netherlands' Constitution which does not even contain some of the most important constitutional norms.

To the extent that there is a certain 'constitutionalization' of private law in the Netherlands, this may be explained from the place of international human rights treaties, rather than from the position of the Constitution.

a) Supra-Constitutional Norms

In order to determine the relation of the Constitution to the legal order, it is necessary to establish its hierarchical position.

It is beyond doubt that the Constitution. *Grondwet*, has a superior rank vis-à-vis ordinary legislation, that is to say, Acts of Parliament and delegated legislation. The fact that courts cannot review the constitutionality of Acts of Parliament does not change the hierarchical order between Constitution and Acts of Parliament. There can be no doubt that parliament and government, together acting as the legislature,[82] are bound by and subjected to the Constitution; parliament is not sovereign.

Although the Constitution has a higher rank than Acts of Parliament, it does not have highest rank in the hierarchy of norms. Two sets of norms have higher rank than the *Grondwet*, and at least some of these must substantively be considered constitutional norms—this is the 'upward' extension of the constitution.

The first is the Charter for the Kingdom, *Statuut voor het Koninkrijk* of 1954, which governs the relations between the four countries which make up the Kingdom: the Netherlands (which since 2010 includes three very small islands in the Caribbean[83]), and the three autonomous Caribbean islands of Aruba, Curaçao, and St Maarten respectively. The former has some seventeen million inhabitants, the latter a total of 350,000 inhabitants.

The *Statuut* basically reserves a series of powers to the Kingdom as matters for the whole realm, of which the most important are foreign affairs, defence, and nationality. Legislation on such matters which is to be applied in more than one country is adopted by a special procedure which grants a consultative role to the parliaments of the overseas countries and their plenipotentiary ministers representing their government at The Hague. All matters which the *Statuut* does not declare matters for the whole realm are left to the autonomy of each country.

The *Statuut* provides that it is of higher rank than the Constitution: 'The Constitution shall have regard to the provisions of the Charter.'[84] As a consequence, the Constitution

---

[82] Art 81 of the Constitution.
[83] Bonaire with approximately 19,000 inhabitants, St Eustatius with nearly 3,000 inhabitants, and Saba with approximately 2,000 inhabitants.
[84] Art 5 para 2 of the Charter.

provides for a simplified amendment procedure to adapt it to changes in the Charter (article 142 Constitution). In as far as matters concerning legislative and executive powers, the organs of the Kingdom, Kingship and the succession to the Throne, have not been provided for in the Charter, the relevant provisions of the Constitution apply in affairs for the realm.[85]

b) The Constitutional Rank of International Law

The second, more significant exception to the superior rank of the Constitution is a consequence of article 94 of the Constitution: 'legislative provisions', *wettelijke voorschriften*, in force within the Kingdom shall not be applicable if such application is in conflict with provisions of treaties and of decisions of international organizations which 'are binding on everyone', i.e. directly effective self-executing provisions.

It is generally assumed that the expression 'legislative provisions' includes the provisions of the Constitution itself, and this was also the opinion of the government in the lead up to the Constitution of 1983.[86]

There is a more nuanced opinion in the literature. It places the issue whether constitutional provisions can be trumped by directly effective international provisions in the context of the requirement that a treaty, which diverges from the Constitution, be approved with a majority of two-thirds of the vote in both Houses of Parliament (article 91 para 3 of the Constitution). Whether there is such divergence from the Constitution is exclusively for the legislature to decide, and not for courts; courts cannot review the constitutionality of treaties as article 120 of the Constitution provides since 1953 (the moment of the introduction of article 91 para 3 of the Constitution) and therefore must assume that an incompatibility between a constitutional provision and a treaty provision can only exist for treaties approved under article 91 para 3 of the Constitution.[87] Although this view is better compatible with the system and structure of the Constitution, it has so far not been followed by courts.

The consequence of articles 93 and 94 of the Constitution is that directly effective self-executing provisions of treaties prevail over contrary legislative provisions. To the extent that directly effective international provisions are substantively of a constitutional nature, they are mostly considered to have superior status. Such provisions are typically the provisions on classic human rights provisions. As these primarily aim to regulate the relations between the state organs and individuals, they are sources of constitutional law of the Netherlands. This is true of e.g. the provisions of the European Convention for Protection of Human Rights and Fundamental Freedoms and of its Protocols to which the Kingdom is a party, and the provisions of the International Covenant on Civil and Political Rights.

Precisely because courts have to give priority to these provisions over conflicting norms, the constitutional importance of human treaties is very great, all the more because courts cannot review Acts of Parliament for their compatibility with the fundamental rights contained in the Constitution itself; they can, and do, review Acts of Parliament against directly effective human rights treaties.

The superior status of directly effective provisions of treaties and of decisions of international organizations is usually taken in a hierarchical sense. Also, at the time of the constitutional amendments of 1953 and 1956, public international law, either in general or the

---

[85] Art 5 para 1 of the Charter.

[86] TK 1977–1978, n 15 049, n 3, 13.

[87] Camilo B Schutte, *'De stille kracht van de Nederlandse Grondwet. Beschouwingen rond het verbod aan de rechter om verdragen aan de Grondwet te toetsen'* (2003) 2003-1 RM Themis 26–40; Leonard F M Besselink and Ramses A Wessel, *De invloed van ontwikkelingen in de internationale rechtsorde op de doorwerking naar Nederlands constitutioneel recht* (Kluwer, Alphen aan den Rijn, 2009) 52–55.

specific provisions intended here, was taken to be 'higher' law. The alternative view, in which article 94 of the Constitution is understood as a conflict rule designed to solve a collision between non-hierarchically ranked norms (*Anwendungsvorrang*), not often considered. In the literature, there is only one authoritative writer who seems to take this view, and even here this has gone largely unnoticed.[88]

c) The Constitutional Position of EU Law

Articles 93 and 94 were introduced in the early 1950s into the Constitution with a view to guarantee the effect of international treaties and of decisions of international organizations that were established after the Second World War, especially the European Coal and Steel Community. These provisions are a matter of constitutional principle, but also in judicial practice since the 1980s, have facilitated the primacy of EU law in the Netherlands. *Van Gend & Loos* and *Costa/ENEL* were in a sense an analogical application of the constitutional ideas of the Netherlands' Constitution to the European Communities. *Simmenthal II* did not cause a stir since the dominant interpretation of our constitutional provisions on the rank and effect of international law in the national legal order already took on board the primacy also over constitutional provisions. That this would in foreign eyes be something of a paradox— the Constitution contained a principle concerning its own disapplication—did not occur to predominant constitutional doctrine in the Netherlands. In a sense, it only brought to light again the relative meaning of the Constitution within the broader constitution, which encompasses also international norms of a constitutional nature (like human rights treaties).

It was only in the 1980s, though, that the more extreme view entered into constitutional doctrine, and later in some of the case law, that, given the autonomy of the EC/EU legal order propounded in the case law of the European Court of Justice, article 93 and 94 of the Constitution were irrelevant to the operation of European law in the national legal order. This was also translated into some of the case law of the Council of State[89] and of the penal chamber of the *Hoge Raad*.[90] Although not all courts seem to accept this view—which is predominant in the Dutch doctrine—it is an extraordinary overturning of the explicit intention of the makers of the Constitution.[91]

d) Infra-Constitutional Norms

The totality of constitutional norms (*bloc de constitutionnalité* in a substantive sense) also extends, figuratively speaking, downwards to norms which are established in instruments which take the form of an act, which is usually of 'lower' rank than the Constitution. In the general revision of 1983, many matters which were previously regulated in detail in the Constitution have then been delegated to the legislature. For instance, the manner of approval of treaties and the exceptions to the principle that the Kingdom cannot become a party unless parliament has approved the treaty, was regulated in detail from 1953 until 1983.[92] Since 1983, the Constitution provides in article 91 that the manner of and the exceptions to the requirement of prior approval shall be laid down by an Act of Parliament.

---

[88] Constantijn AJM Kortmann, *Constitutioneel Recht* (5th edn, Kluwer, Deventer, 2005) 364.

[89] Afdeling bestuursrechtspraak Raad van State 7 July 1995, AB 1997/117 translation in (1995) 2 Maastricht Journal 15–9; reprint in Andrew Oppenheim (ed), *The Relationship between European Community law and National Law: The Cases.* Volume 2 (CUP, Cambridge, 2003) 401–406.

[90] HR 2 November 2004, ECLI:NL:HR:2004:AR1797.

[91] Although approved with at least two thirds of the vote, the legislature is assumed to have held that the Treaties do not diverge from the Constitution at least when the issue was discussed at the time of the approval of the Treaty of Maastricht.

[92] Arts 60–64 Constitutions 1953–1972.

The subsequent Act regulating this matter must be considered 'organic' law. Several other examples could be given.

There is in the Netherlands no hierarchical consequence attached to the acts of parliament which are organic law, i.e. acts which elaborate or implement norms provided for in the Constitution. Their rank remains that of an Act of Parliament like any other Act of Parliament.

More complicated is the status of organic law created by other instruments than Acts of Parliament. These are usually considered to be of lower rank than Acts of Parliament, like royal decrees and ministerial decrees. The assumption used to be that their rank was not changed due to their material status of organic law. However, the fact that these instruments have a direct basis in the Constitution may put them on par with Acts of Parliament or even at a higher level than normal Acts of Parliament. Recent case law suggests that this view is correct.

The relevant judgment concerned an Act of Parliament which named the Minister of one ministerial department (Welfare, Public Health and Culture) as the competent minister under whose responsibility asylum seekers were to be provided with certain facilities. After a reshuffle of tasks among ministries, this matter was brought under the competence of another Minister (Justice) by royal decree based on article 44 of the Constitution.[93] The *Afdeling bestuursrechtspraak Raad van State* (Administrative Law (Judicial) Division of the Council of State) decided in the highest instance that the royal decree could change the internal division of tasks between ministers because, if this were to require an amendment of all relevant legislation, this would obviate the purpose of article 44 of the Constitution. It held that an Act of Parliament cannot detract from the power of the government under the Constitution, although the exercise of such power remains subject to the normal principles of the parliamentary system—and thus a royal decree based directly on a constitutional provision has priority over a normal Act of Parliament.[94]

e) Constitutionalization and Private Law

The relation of the Constitution to the legal order can also be viewed from the perspective of the manner in which constitutional norms permeate the rest of the legal order which itself is not of a constitutional nature—it concerns 'constitutionalization' of areas that are not primarily constitutional law, both those that concern the relations between public authorities and citizens but between private persons (legal and natural).

The phenomenon mainly focuses especially on the role of fundamental rights in the relevant field of the law, such as the role of fundamental rights and principles in criminal procedure and in administrative proceedings, but also particularly in private law.

The modern literature on the constitutionalization of private law extends further than the nineteenth century view of fundamental rights as establishing civil society, a sphere of freedom as against the State, which the civil code regulates in terms of that freedom among citizens, i.e. fundamental rights and freedoms enabling civil law. It is about the penetration of constitutional rights and freedoms as goods that must be upheld also *within* the civil relations regulated by private law. As a consequence, much of the relevant literature still concentrates on the direct or indirect 'horizontal' effect which can be attributed to constitutional fundamental rights in relations between citizens *inter se*.

---

[93] Art 44 of the Constitution, which provides that ministries are established by royal decree.
[94] ABRvS, 10 October 2004, ECLI:NL:RBAMS:2001:AB0942.

The case law of the *Hoge Raad* suggests that it is possible to rely on rights such as the right to privacy, freedom of religion, or freedom of expression also in relations between citizens; at any rate one can invoke them in cases between citizens before a court of law. It is hard to distil from the language of the relevant judgments whether the effect of fundamental rights—in the Netherlands context, both those found in the Constitution and those found in for instance the ECHR and ICCPR—is direct, i.e. the relevant fundamental rights work per se in relations between citizens *inter se*, or whether these fundamental rights have only indirect effect, i.e. are mediated through the proper terms, concepts, and norms of private law. Some horizontal effect seems to be accepted both in the case law of lower courts, particularly courts of first instance hearing cases on interim injunctions, and of the *Hoge Raad*.

A standard judgment[95] of the *Hoge Raad* is the *Aidstest* case,[96] concerned a civil case between a victim who asked for a court order to submit her rapist, X, to an HIV test, both in order to limit the damage she suffers as a consequence of the rape and to spare her a further traumatic experience. The legal basis adduced for this is reparation in kind. The *Hoge Raad* held that:

> On the basis of the rules [on tort] under article 1401 [now: 6:162] *Burgerlijk Wetboek* [Civil Code] [the victim] has a right to the consequences being limited as much as possible by the offender, and that these are relieved as much as possible by a suitable form of compensation. … [She] has a right to cooperation by X in the form of him taking a blood test. In this respect, X cannot successfully rely on his right to physical integrity derived from article 11 of the Constitution, as this right has its limits in restrictions by or pursuant to an act of Parliament. At any rate between citizens *inter se*, such a restriction can in principle be founded on article 1401 [of the Civil Code], this also in connection with the norms of propriety which must be respected in social intercourse which inhere in this article.
>
> In the light of the [established facts], such a restriction must here be assumed. The interest of plaintiff in X having to take a blood test is of sufficient weight in relation to X's interest protected by his fundamental right, to justify this restriction. Moreover, this restriction, which is obvious in the framework of the relevant norms, can be deduced with sufficient clarity form these norms.

How can we understand this 'constitutionalization' of private law?

First of all, it is true that the *Hoge Raad* refers in both cases to constitutional fundamental-rights provisions which restrict the exercise of such fundamental rights and seems to be applying them directly in the private law context of the case. This suggests that those provisions have a direct effect and applicability in private relations of citizens *inter se*, thereby granting them direct horizontal effect. This would imply that the constitutional provisions actually govern private law and suggests that the Constitution is an overarching superior legal instrument of such fundamental importance that it governs the whole of the legal order.

The context of at least the *Aidstest* judgment, however, is the civil law duty to limiting the damage caused by an unlawful act. Also, the interpretation of the restriction clause is entirely

---

[95] In an earlier case about a judicial order restraining religiously inspired discriminatory speech HR 2 February 1990, ECLI:NL:HR:1990:AB7894 the HR held 'that art 6 para 1 Constitution, art 9 para2 European Convention on Human Rights and art 18 para 3 of the International Convention on Civil and Political Rights permit certain restrictions imposed on the exercise of the freedom of religion, and that art 1401 Burgerlijk Wetboek [Civil Code], which protects against utterances which are offensive, unnecessarily aggrieving or which invite discrimination, must be considered to provide such a justified restriction.' This suggests direct horizontal effect.

[96] Hoge Raad 18 June 1993, ECLI:NL:HR:1993:ZC1002, *Y v. X* [*Aidstest*] (interim injunction proceedings).

specific to the private law context. It is one element in the balancing of a number of interests in a private law context of tort law which works with 'open' norms. This may lead one to conclude that the fundamental right is given indirect effect only, in as much as the effect is mediated by principles of private law.[97]

Although the case cited article 11 of the Constitution only, this is rather exceptional, and should not lead one into thinking that this 'constitutionalization' is mainly steered by the Constitution. The case law on horizontal effect shows it is at least as much dominated by the ECHR and similar human rights treaties, which are predominantly understood to have supra-constitutional rank.

2. The Relation of the Constitution to Politics and Democracy

The relation of the Constitution to politics is mainly considered to be one of providing the framework for the political system. Substantive notions of democracy are implicit in the provisions of the Constitution. The term 'democracy' does not appear in the text of the Constitution. In the Dutch context, democracy has been taken to refer not only to the political institutions, but also to the manifold varieties of citizens' participation in the public domain through the institutions of civil society and direct participation. We make a few remarks first about the Constitution as a political constitution,[98] second about the representational nature of the political institutions and finally about the broader concept of democracy of civil society's and citizens' participation within public law.

The Constitution is still very much a political constitution like it was in the nineteenth century. It provides primarily a framework for politics to function.

This 'framework' nature of the Constitution, according to which the Constitution provides guidelines only for the political system, is confirmed by the fact that courts have no role to play in the political process. It is practically inconceivable that a member of parliament would go to court to complain of an alleged infringement of the Constitution by another actor in the political or decision-making process.

The framework in the Constitution itself is quite sketchy for that matter, which deliberately has not codified the fundamental rule of the parliamentary system, the rule of no confidence, which exists only as a rule of customary constitutional law. It is kept that way to retain some flexibility in the system. Should there arise new political relations, the system can adapt to that and does not require constitutional amendment, so the reasoning goes.

Although certain elements of the political system related to the parliamentary system have been codified in the Constitution, such as accountability through ministerial responsibility,[99] and the system of proportional representation within the limits set by Act of Parliament,[100] there are some examples of political conventions which are so closely involved with the functioning of the system of government that they may have constitutional status. Moreover, they exhibit potentialities of change and development which confirm the relative flexibility of the system.

---

[97] This was the conclusion of Advocate General Koopmans in his opinion to the *Hoge Raad* in the *Aidstest* case (ibid).
[98] John A G Griffith, 'The political constitution' (1979) 42 Modern Law Review 1, 21.
[99] Art 42 para 2.
[100] Art 129 para 2.

There are several examples of this flexibility. One of them was sketched above, where the development of the governmental right to dissolution of the Lower House in the direction of a right of 'self-dissolution' was sketched (section C.3).

Another example is the increased profile of the Prime Minister. His position has in practice gradually developed from one among equals towards one above equals (though not unambiguously). This has also left traces in the *Reglement van Orde van de ministerraad* (Rules of Procedure of the Council of Ministers). The Prime Minister is not merely chairing a meeting of equals but has—usually in coordination with ministers concerned but sometimes without his cooperation—agenda-setting powers.[101] Thus, he can push decision-making in the council of ministers against the wishes of individual ministers.

Perhaps more significant is a recent development in the practice of large political parties during elections. The Prime Minister is not directly elected because the elections are elections for the members of the Lower House only. Since the convention of 1922, according to which cabinets offer their resignation on the eve of elections for the Lower House, elections for the Lower House imply the forming of a new cabinet, based on the results of the elections. Nowadays, in electoral campaigns of political parties, the name of their candidate for the post of Prime Minister, should the party win in the elections, is put forward. The *Partij van de Arbeid* (Labour Party) failed to do so in the elections of 2003. Under huge pressure from other parties, who ridiculed the unclarity and unforthcoming position as to their candidate Prime Minister, it was forced to reveal to the electorate their candidate. If one persists with this practice, as has been the case, the Lower House elections informally also become elections on Prime Ministerial candidates, without any formal rule on elections for the Prime Minister being included in the text of the Constitution.[102]

Within the general political institutions, democracy has been taken in a strictly representative manner; democracy is representative democracy. Until a few decades ago, referenda were considered undesirable and not fitting in a constitutional system based on representative democracy.

At the national level, the Constitution gives legislative power to parliament and government acting together. A binding referendum is by many considered to be an interference with this clear attribution of legislative power. Hence, it is argued, the introduction of a binding referendum on legislative acts requires constitutional amendment. The same applies *mutatis mutandis* for provincial and municipal referenda because the Constitution locates the legislative power at provincial and municipal level in the provincial and municipal councils.[103] As mentioned above, the *staatscommissie Biesheuvel/Prakke* proposed the introduction of a corrective and binding legislative referendum at the national level in 1985,[104] but this was not taken up at the time. Two attempts to follow up on this, one in 1999 and one in 2004, were aborted. In both proposals the thresholds for holding a referendum were high.

Without constitutional amendment, only *consultative*, legally non-binding, referenda are constitutional. In 2001 a Temporary Referendum Act, *Tijdelijke referendumwet*, made the organization of a consultative referendum possible, but never led to a referendum, and expired

---

[101] Arts 6, 7, and 16 of the Rules of Procedure of the Council of Ministers.

[102] Griffith as the proposal of the *Cals-Donner* committee, above section B.4.b.

[103] Art 127 of the Constitution. Some municipalities have byelaws which make the calling of a consultative, non-binding referendum possible.

[104] *Eindrapport van de staatscommissie van advies inzake de relatie kiezers–beleidsvorming: Referendum en volksinitiatief*, 1985; a later committee established by the Lower House endorsed the earlier commission's referendum proposals: Rapport Tweede Kamer externe commissie vraagpunten staatkundige, bestuurlijke en staatsrechtelijke vernieuwing «Het bestel bijgesteld», Kamerstukken TK 1992/1993, 21 427, nn 36–7 and TK 1993/1994, 21 427, nn 64–5.

on 1 January 2005. The infamous national referendum on the EU Constitutional Treaty of 1 June 2005, was made possible by the adoption of a special act at the initiative of the Lower House. It was consultative and preceded final political decision-making. The high turn-out (63 per cent) and the clear negative of some 62 per cent of the voters made any further consideration of ratification impossible. Thus, merely consultative referenda turned out to be politically binding.

This was confirmed in two later consultative referenda that were based on an Act on the Consultative Referendum of 2014. In order to organize a referendum, an introductory request of 10,000 people had to be supported by at least 300,000 people with the right to vote. A referendum had to concern an Act of Parliament and would have to be called within eight weeks after an act received royal consent, for which purpose the entry into force would have to be postponed until after the referendum. Two referenda were held, one concerning the Act of Approval of the Association Agreement of the EU with Ukraine in 2016 and on the Act on the Intelligence and Security Services in 2018. In both cases a majority rejected the Act in question. In both cases the government and parliament followed the outcome, in the sense that the government negotiated an interpretative declaration to the Association Agreement and changed the Act on the Intelligence and Security Services on points on which most concern was expressed in the referendum campaigns.

In 2018, based on the coalition agreement between the Christian Democrat party, CDA (against referenda), the Liberal Party, VVD (also against referenda), the orthodox Christian party CU (against referenda), and the centre-left liberals D66 (in favour of referenda), the Act on the Consultative Referenda was rescinded, and a pending amendment of the Constitution to enable the introduction of a legally binding referendum, which had passed on first reading, was withdrawn in 2018. Far from ending the debate on binding referenda, a member of the Lower House introduced a bill to introduce binding legislative referenda at national and decentral level in 2019, which acquired a majority in both Houses at first reading (in the Lower House with a nearly two-thirds majority, but in the Upper House with only a very small majority of three votes).[105] This constitutional amendment sets the majority required for rejecting an adopted piece of legislation by referendum in such a manner that it does not undermine the representative nature of parliament, but acts as an at least equally representative popular correction: the number of votes required to reject legislation must comprise at least a majority of the number of validly cast votes by citizens in the last elections for the Lower House. Thus, the majority of citizens required to correct a bill adopted by parliament is aligned to the number of citizens having cast a vote for the Lower House. This is a numerical alignment of direct democracy to representative democracy that may be understood as a guarantee of the representative nature of democracy in the Netherlands. It reinforces instead of weakens representative democracy.

As we discussed above (section C.1), the dissolution of the Lower House with a view to amendment of the Constitution is not a referendum in disguise, nor does it introduce a plebiscitarian element in the constitutional system. Quite to the contrary, the election of a new Lower House guarantees the *representative* nature of the constitution-making power which is to decide on the amendment proposed by the legislature in 'first reading'.

The explanation for this emphasis on the representative nature of democracy in the political institutions is historical. Before secularization struck, Dutch society was composed

---

[105] The act containing the proposal adopted at first reading is, the Act of 1 February 2021, *Staatsblad* 2021, 58.

of minorities of political and religious denominations which acted in the political system through their political elites in a strictly representative manner.

It should be emphasized that the 'pillarized' society almost by definition had to be representative in nature as their structure each represented their own denominational constituency.

Precisely this representative nature enhanced the respect for minority positions in an electoral system based on proportional representation in which no particular political group could claim a majority position. Since denominational politics waned, the floating vote has increased and so has the request for introducing features of direct democracy within the political system at national level.

The historic background of the social composition of the Netherlands also explains the constitutional status granted to what are essentially institutions of civil society, like the public bodies of professions, trade, and industry under article 134 of the Constitution.[106] These have been given powers to legislate and carry out executive tasks; for instance, those public industrial bodies involved in agriculture have an important role to play in implementing EU legislation.[107]

So, as already pointed out,[108] in the Dutch context, representative democracy is not the same as parliamentary democracy. It is consociationalism, and was expressed by reference to the public bodies we just mentioned in 1938, not because of quasi-fascist corporatist thought (which had little support in those days in the Netherlands), but because of the historical situation in which denominational and political minorities were not only organized in political parties, but organized the whole of their social and religious life in 'pillars' of own organizations, some of which in relation to the economy were given a status under public law for which a constitutional basis was created.

One important symptom of the nature and form of public society in the Netherlands is the system of public broadcasting. From the very beginnings of radio broadcasting, this has always been based on associations of citizens. They are private law associations; citizens are members from one (or nowadays sometimes more or increasingly none) of these; they function internally as any private association might. To put it in a somewhat more simplified manner, they have a licence to broadcast on the four public radio stations and three public television channels. These associations were—and to a very large extent still are—denominational (that is, protestant, catholic, socialist, liberal, neutral, and, for some decades now, also popular and youth oriented), but, under the pressure of secularization, there is a drift towards a stronger state-controlled form of broadcasting. This is politically controversial, and it is uncertain in which direction the broadcasting system is developing.

In the late 1960s the idea of participation of social groups evolved towards citizens' participation. The idea of *medezeggenschap* in companies and universities took shape as of those years.

At the central level, there had developed over the years an enormous culture of consultation. Usually (but not exclusively) this consultation was through a very large number of official advisory bodies in nearly every field of government activity in relation to any topic; some say over a hundred of such bodies existed. In those advisory commissions and committees,

---

[106] Art 134 para 1.
[107] Art 134 para2:3. Supervision of the administrative organs shall be regulated by an Act of Parliament. Decisions by the administrative organs may be quashed only if they conflict with the law or the public interest.
[108] See Section B.4.a.

most social interests and experts were represented, thus creating a firm basis of social consensus and support for government measures in the field.

In 1996, an act was passed by which most of the consultative commissions of experts and social actors at national level were abolished and channelled into a limited set of advisory commissions, in principle one per ministerial department. This Act was referred to in popular parlance as the 'Desert Act' (*woestijnwet*).[109] Simultaneously, an Act was passed streamlining whatever advisory committee was left and determining that their members could only be experts and not civil society's representation.[110] Arguably, this reduces social input in the early stages of the decision-making process. Studies have suggested that there are still many ad hoc commissions and committees, but now mostly manned with politically selected persons.[111]

Also, individual citizens were consulted in decision-making at decentralized levels. This was often based on municipal and provincial byelaws, later codified in the *Algemene wet bestuursrecht* (General Administrative Law Act), which entered into force in 1994. In its chapter on dealings between citizens and administrative authorities, it originally included two procedures of citizen participation in decision-making, a simplified one and a (very) extensive one. In July 2005, these two procedures were simplified into one uniform procedure for the preparation of decisions.[112]

The norms regulate the way citizens are informed of applications for decisions, the publication of draft decisions and the moments and manners in which citizens can state their views on these to the relevant public authorities, and how public authorities must take these into account. A public authority can decide if these norms apply, unless its application has been prescribed by statutory regulation, as was done e.g. in legislation on decision-making in the fields of urban and rural planning and concerning the environment.

In the Netherlands, democracy is a broad concept which is not restricted to the political system in the narrower sense of the term. This might one lead to expect there to be theories of popular sovereignty. But this proves not to be the case.

In the literature, several traces of early ideas of popular sovereignty have been identified.[113] After the definitive demise of French revolutionary ideas after the ousting of the French in 1813, however, a theory of sovereignty of the people was impossible to sustain, if only because protestant political thought in a principled manner rejected the French Revolution for its alleged denial of God's sovereignty. This was so for the two major protestant Christian-democrat parties, the *Christelijk-Historische Unie* and the oldest political party in the Netherlands the *Anti-Revolutionaire Partij*, both of which merged with the catholic party into the Christian-Democrat Party, *CDA*, in the early 1970s.

In other words, neither sovereignty nor popular sovereignty were clearly articulated in constitutional theory, beyond the notion of influence of the people or democracy, and this concept taken in a much broader sense than in, for instance, German constitutional theory (and practice).

---

[109] Act of 3 July 1996, *Stb.* 377.

[110] Act of 3 July 1996, *Stb.* 378.

[111] Wijnand Duyvendak and Rinus van Schendelen, *Schaduwmacht in de schijnwerpers* (Sdu Uitgevers, Den Haag, 2005).

[112] Art 3:10–3:17 of the *Algemene wet bestuursrecht*.

[113] See for instance Martin van Gelderen, *The Political Thought of the Dutch Revolt 1555-1590* (CUP, Cambridge, 1992). Some of the sources are published in Martin van Gelderen (ed and transl), *The Dutch Revolt* [Cambridge Texts in the History of Political Thought] 1993.

3. *Rechtsstaat*: Fundamental Rights and Legality

The idea of the *rechtsstaat*—the Dutch is borrowed from the German—is part of the vocabulary of political and sometimes popular discourse. Its content and meaning within this discourse are very diverse, as we shall presently see.

A legally clearer notion associated with the *rechtsstaat* is that of the protection of fundamental rights. This has become in many ways the main core of the constitutional system. It is so, however, in an entirely different manner from other European countries: as we already remarked in passing, its substance is to a considerable extent located outside the Constitution itself. We deal with this after discussing the uses made of the concept of the *rechtsstaat*.

The concept of the *rechtsstaat* has various connotations in the Dutch context. In the constitutionalist sense the term refers to the public legal order being governed by the rule of law. In the literature it is taken to comprise legality, division of powers and, last but not least, the protection of fundamental rights.[114] When it is also taken to comprise democracy, it becomes a quite broad concept.

In popular and political discourse, the concept becomes even more stretched, as shorthand for a desired material content of legal norms or the political order, a normative concept which does not refer to a present state of law, but to a desired state of law. Also, the concept of *rechtsstaat* is frequently not used for indicating the limits to the exercise of public authority, but, to the contrary, as the principle that citizens are bound to observe the law.[115] This suggests that the notion is not merely relevant to the behaviour of public authorities, but as much to citizens' behaviour. The conclusion must be that the notion of the *rechtsstaat* is much broader than the notion of the rule of law which binds public authorities. From a liberal concept which aims to protect citizens against infringement of his liberty by the state, it has become a (neo-)republican concept in which it is assumed to bind the citizen as much as state organs to the major principles and norms of political society. A less optimistic view would be that this approach risks turning the concept upside down.

There is very little case law which uses the notion in any significant manner. When they do, it is sometimes used to indicate the particular position which an independent court of law or a judge takes within the legal order, sometimes to restrict his competence,[116] but sometimes also to enhance his jurisdiction.[117]

---

[114] Thus, for instance MC Burkens, Henk RBM Kummeling, Ben P Vermeulen, and Rob Widdershoven, *Beginselen van de democratische rechtsstaat* (8th edn, Wolters Kluwer, Deventer, 2017) is a textbook which is used in several law faculties as a first-year textbook introduction to constitutional law.

[115] For instance in Rb Alkmaar, 15 June 2005 ECLI:NL:RBALK:2005:AT7611, to qualify the seriousness of a punishable delict of stalking and threatening of a judge; Rb Alkmaar (interim injunctions), 19 May 2005, LJN: AT5806, holding that 'it is not in accordance with modern ideas of the *rechtsstaat* to publicly put to shame a person in an *ad hominem* manner' by publishing a person's photograph on a public website, accompanied by derogatory text; Rb Arnhem, 26 April 2005, ECLI:NL:RBARN:2005:AT4651: 'To try to escape from detention by taking a public prosecutor and an interpreter hostage, is a flagrant infringement of the principles of the *rechtsstaat*'; Gerechtshof Arnhem 7 June 2002, LJN: AN8937 and LJN: AN 8932, political motives 'cannot within the *rechtsstaat* be a justification of proven cases of arson'. Rb Amsterdam, 15 July 2005, ECLI:NL:RBAMS:2005:AT9532. The case concerned an immediate expulsion of an imam for reasons of national security, which did not allow the person involved to await the outcome of a complaint's procedure, and which was based on an intelligence report concerning this person which had not been verified by the Minister of Justice. The court noticed that each of the parties to the conflict accused the other of acting in a manner which fundamentally infringes the *rechtsstaat*.

[116] For instance Gerechtshof 's-Hertogenbosch, 5 August 2003, ECLI:NL:GHSHE:2003:AI0847: the fact that courts are bound to Acts of Parliament and cannot adjudicate their inherent merits or their fairness is 'one of the pillars of the democratic *rechtsstaat*, in which the judicial and legislative power are separate'.

[117] For instance the fiscal chamber of the Hoge Raad, as well as the judicial branch of the Raad van State, decided that on the basis of the position and role of courts in the *rechtsstaat*, the impossibility to pay a court fee cannot deprive access to an appeal court, and is not to be regarded as a default on the part of the person involved, see HR 28 March 2014, ECLI:NL:HR:2014:699; RvSt 21 August 2019, ECLI:NL:RVS:2019:2810.

A more precise notion associated with the *rechtsstaat* is the protection of fundamental rights. This has become in many ways the main core of the constitutional system. Fundamental rights protection has two different sources: rights formulated in the Constitution, and rights formulated in human rights treaties to which the Netherlands is a party and which, on the basis of the rule of monism, form an inherent part of the national legal order, or, more precisely, of the constitutional order.

Fundamental rights that are part of the Constitution are enshrined mainly in its first chapter, but some, like the right to vote and stand for parliamentary elections and the prohibition of the death penalty, are found elsewhere. They include as classic rights:

- the prohibition of discrimination and the right to equal treatment,
- the right to leave the country,
- the equal right of Dutch nationals to appointment in the public service,
- the right to vote and stand for election,
- the right to petition,
- freedom of religion,
- freedom of expression,
- right of association, assembly and demonstration,
- the right to privacy,
- the right to physical integrity,
- protection of the home,
- privacy of correspondence, telephone and telegraph,
- the right to compensation for expropriation in the public interest,
- personal liberty and *habeas corpus*,
- *nulla poena sine lege praevia*,
- access to courts according to the law,
- legal representation,
- the right to free choice of work,
- the right to provide education,
- the right to equal public financial support of public and private education,
- prohibition of imposing capital punishment.

Also, a number of social, economic, and cultural rights are included, to wit:

- the promoting 'sufficient' employment,
- minimum subsistence and division of wealth,
- protection of the environment,
- public health,
- sufficient living accommodation,
- social and cultural development and leisure activities,
- education and the right to sufficient primary education.

Many, but not all, fundamental rights provisions in the Constitution contain a clause regulating the restriction of their exercise, particularly regarding the classic fundamental rights.[118] In most cases, they define the public authority which can legitimately restrict the

---

[118] The prohibition of discrimination and the right to equal treatment of art 1 of the Constitution. Other examples are the right to petition (art 5 of the Constitution) and the prohibition to impose the death penalty (art 114 of the Constitution).

exercise of a right. This body is invariably the legislature. By an Act of Parliament, it can restrict the exercise of a right. Often this power can also be delegated to other legislatures by an Act of Parliament. Sometimes it is reserved to the legislature itself, as is the case with:

- the right to leave the country (article 2 para 4 of the Constitution),
- electoral rights (article 4 of the Constitution),
- the right to profess one's religion of belief (except the right to do so outside buildings or delimited spaces, which refers in particular to religious processions) (article 6 of the Constitution),
- freedom of expression with regard to the content of the thought expressed (article 7 of the Constitution),
- the right to associate (article 8 of the Constitution), the right to assemble and demonstrate except with regard to restrictions aiming at the protection at health, or in the interest of the combat or prevention of disorder which may be delegated by an Act of Parliament (article 9 of the Constitution),
- the privacy of correspondence (article 13 of the Constitution).

Only occasionally do limitations have to be in the interest of certain specified objectives (this is the case with the freedom of religion professed outside buildings and delimited premises, the right of association, and the right to assemble and demonstrate). Otherwise, there are no substantive criteria.

No proportionality principle comparable to those in articles 8–11 ECHR can be found in the Netherlands Constitution. Worse, the *Hoge Raad* has confirmed the view that a restriction imposed is not subject to the principle of necessity as in the ECHR, and therefore neither to the proportionality principle.[119] This is controversial because it implies that the makers of the Constitution are supposed to have allowed unnecessary and therefore disproportional restrictions to be imposed.

In principle the classic rights are justiciable, while many of the social, economic, and cultural rights are framed as policy objectives that cannot easily be invoked in court.[120] This is not to say that they have no legal value. The literature submits that under certain circumstances these can be considered as standstill-provisions, i.e. that they would prohibit acts of public authorities which aim to reach objectives which are the contrary to the objectives formulated in these provisions.[121] And, in some cases,

---

[119] HR 2 May 2003, ECLI:NL:HR:2003:AF3416, paragraph 4.3.4, where it states that art 7 of the Constitution 'does not require a restriction of the freedom of expression to be necessary in a democratic society'.

[120] For instance, art 19 para 1: it shall be the concern of the authorities to promote the provision of sufficient employment; art 20 para 1: it shall be the concern of the authorities to secure the means of subsistence of the population and to achieve the distribution of wealth; art 21: it shall be the concern of the authorities to keep the country habitable and to protect and improve the environment; art 22: 1. The authorities shall take steps to promote the health of the population. 2. It shall be the concern of the authorities to provide sufficient living accommodation. 3. The authorities shall promote social and cultural development and leisure activities; art 23 para 1: Education shall be the constant concern of the Government.

[121] Aalt W Heringa, *Sociale grondrechten – hun plaats in de gereedschapskist van de rechter* (dissertation RULeiden, 1989); Henk RBM Kummeling, 'Grondrechten en de taak van de overheid in het licht van zelfregulering', in Henk RBM Kummeling and Sophie C Van Bijsterveld (eds), *Grondrechten en zelfregulering* (WEJ Tjeenk Willink, Deventer, 1997) 31–50; Frank MC Vlemminx, 'Het juridisch tekort van de sociale grondrechten in de Grondwet' (1996) NJB, 1201; Frank MC Vlemminx and Henk RBM Kummeling, 'Algemene situering van sociale grondrechten in de Nederlandse rechtsorde', in Bernard Hubeau and Roel De Lange (eds), *Het grondrecht op wonen* (MAKLU, Antwerp, 1995); As to the equivalent provisions in international treaties, Godefridus JH van Hoof, 'The Legal Nature of Economic, Social and Cultural Rights: a Rebuttal of some Traditional Views', in Philip Alston and Katarina Tomasevski (eds), *The Right to Food* (Nijhoff, The Hague, 1984) 97–111.

courts have referred to them as an additional element in construction of other legal norms.[122]

One barrier to review against constitutional fundamental rights is the prohibition for courts to review the constitutionality of Acts of Parliament (article 120 of the Constitution). This has two important consequences.

Firstly, a large number of constitutional-rights provisions allow restrictions by or pursuant to Acts of Parliament. The constitutionality of such acts cannot be reviewed. Also, the constitutionality of delegated measures which restrict the exercise of a fundamental right cannot be reviewed to the extent that the restriction by delegated instrument is determined by the Act of Parliament; in this case, reviewing the constitutionality of the delegated instrument implies the review of the Act of Parliament on which it depends. Just to avoid misunderstanding: if the actual restriction is imposed by a delegated act and does not substantively derive from the Act of Parliament, courts can indeed review their constitutionality, which is why courts have reviewed municipal byelaws, e.g. against the constitutional right of freedom of expression.

Secondly, the prohibition for courts to review the constitutionality of Acts of Parliament under article 120 of the Constitution shifts judicial review towards review against human rights contained in treaties under article 94 of the Constitution. This is the only possibility as regards an alleged infringement by an Act of Parliament.

As article 94 of the Constitution implies the priority of directly effective provisions of human rights treaties, human rights treaties are of enormous constitutional importance in the Netherlands legal order.

The human rights treaties to which the Netherlands is a party comprise among others the European Convention for the protection of Human Rights and Fundamental Freedoms and its Protocols except Protocol nr 7, European Social Charter (the Netherlands is not a party to the Revised European Social Charter), ICCPR and its two Protocols, ICESCR, International Convention on the Elimination of all Forms of Racial Discrimination (CERD), Convention Against Torture and Other Cruel, Inhuman or Degrading Treatment or Punishment, Convention on the Elimination of All Forms of Discrimination Against Women (CEDAW) and its optional protocol, the Convention on the Rights of the Child and its two protocols, and the Convention on the Political Rights of Women, a number of ILO treaties, and several treaties in the framework of the Council of Europe which have a fundamental rights dimension, such as the European Convention on the Prevention of Torture and its Protocols, the Framework Convention for the Protection of National Minorities.

As a general guideline, the provisions on classic human rights tend to be 'binding on all persons' in the sense of article 94 of the Constitution, that is to say, they are directly effective, self-executing provisions against which courts can review all public acts under, whereas provisions on social and cultural rights tend not to have that character and complaints of their infringement are therefore not justiciable.

---

[122] Thus, in one case concerning a seriously ill mother and her three children, of which one had psychiatric problems, who had no housing and which the municipality of Utrecht had refused to provide a dwelling, the concern of public authorities to provide sufficient living accommodation under art 22 para 2 of the Constitution was taken as the key starting point for interpreting other legal instruments and the duty of the municipality to act lawfully; Pres. Rb Utrecht 18 June 1991, NJ 1992, 370. Another case concerned the access to a special primary school for handicapped persons, which had been refused due to lack of sufficient staffing, in which the President of the *Afdeling Rechtspraak Raad van State* found an additional argument to nullify this refusal in the principle behind the duty of public authorities to provide sufficient primary education in all municipalities (art 22 para 4 of the Constitution), President Afdeling Rechtspraak Raad van State, 10 May 1989, AB 1989, 481.

4. Horizontal and Vertical Division of Powers

The horizontal division of powers is no longer apparent from the text of the Constitution. Until 1983 the Constitution used the language of the *trias politica*. The fifth part of chapter V of the Constitution was entitled 'On the legislative power', '*Van de wetgevende macht*', and its first article read: 'The legislative power is exercised jointly by King and States General.'[123]

The executive power was also mentioned: 'The executive power is vested in the King.'[124] The matter with the judiciary was more subtle. One provision stated that 'the judicial power is to be exercised by the judges that an Act of Parliament indicates',[125] while another provision attributed the settlement of disputes over property and related issues to 'the judicial power'.[126]

We notice that the substantive power was distinguished and attributed to three different institutions, although as regards the judicial power, it is hard to say whether the institution preceded the substantive power or the other way around.

Be that as it may, the Constitution of 1983 brought change in as much as the most omnipresent of modern governmental power (the executive power) was no longer mentioned in the Constitution, while the legislative power was no longer called legislative power:

'Acts of Parliament shall be enacted jointly by the Government and the States General.'

So, in 1983, the executive power was hidden both institutionally and substantively, while the legislative power was robbed of its substance, reduced to an institution whose competence was turned into a circular formality. The provisions on the judicial power were not changed radically, and retained its institutional, formal character.

One can say that even though in the Constitution the chapters on the King and the government come before that on the parliament, the legislative power has dominated the executive power. This was affirmed in the nineteenth century process of the liberal constitutional reforms and the development of a parliamentary system of government, culminating in the *Meerenberg* case of the *Hoge Raad* (see Section C.4). The executive is thus subjected to the laws enacted by the legislative power, that is the power whose exercise requires the cooperation of parliament.

However, as is the case everywhere else in Europe, legislative power has become delegated to a large extent to the executive. The executive dominates the legislature in the sense that in practice it is the one who, in nearly all cases, takes the legislative initiative. In the parliamentary system of the Netherlands there is, of course, a great sense of not imperilling coalition relations, which mediates and dampens this executive predominance. In turn, the deliberative moderation of executive dominance is limited by the practice of settling the more divisive issues between coalition partners outside the assembly hall, in informal meetings between the leaders and the spokesmen on relevant affairs of political groups, and in meetings of leaders with the Prime Minister and other relevant members of the cabinet.

The growth of executive dominance in government has been compensated by forms of judicial control beyond what was usual before the 1960s. In the Netherlands, this has taken two forms.

---

[123] Art 119 of the Constitution of 1972: 'Legislative power is exercised by the King and States General jointly.'

[124] Art 56 of the Constitution of 1972: 'Executive powers shall lie with the King.'

[125] Art 169 of the Constitution of 1972: 'Judicial power shall be exercised only by the judges indicated by act of Parliament.'

[126] Art 167 of the Constitution of 1972.

First of all, judicial review of administrative action was introduced and took full shape with the *Algemene wet bestuursrecht*, which opens an appeal to judgments of the administrative section of the district courts (*rechtbank*) on individual decisions of administrative organs after a reconsideration by the administrative organ on complaint. The administrative courts review the disputed decision against the law and general principles of proper administration. Usually, appeal in the higher instance lies with the *Afdeling Bestuursrechtspraak* of the *Raad van State* (Administrative Law (Judicial) Division of the Council of State). But in social security affairs and civil servants' matters appeal lies with the *Centrale Raad van Beroep* (Central Appeals Council), whereas in accordance with specific legislation certain economic law cases are appealed to the *College van Beroep voor het Bedrijfsleven* (Regulatory Industrial Organization Appeals Court).

Parallel to the expansion of administrative litigation, the civil courts have become quite active in reviewing cases against public bodies, which they are competent to do whenever administrative courts had no competence to hear the case. Thus, the review of regulations issued by the executive has become a full review not only on points of *vires* and legality, but also substantively against principles such as reasonableness and proportionality, which are sometimes applied with less reservations than in administrative courts.

While the relation between judiciary and executive has seen a steady increase of the role of the judiciary and administrative courts,[127] no very fundamental change has occurred in the relation between the legislative power and the judiciary since 1848, or at least since the power to review the compatibility with self-executing treaty provisions was introduced.

We briefly indicated above (Section C.4) that the prohibition under Article 120 of the Constitution concerns primarily the division of powers between legislative and judicial power.

It is standing case law that regulatory acts can be reviewed for their compatibility with higher law,[128] including both the Constitution and unwritten general principles of law; but such review does not extend to Acts of Parliament.

This was confirmed in the important *Harmonisatiewet* judgment of the *Hoge Raad* in which the scope of the prohibition of article 120 of the Constitution regarding acts of parliament was reassessed.[129] The case concerned the allegation that an Act of Parliament, which aimed at reducing the number of years during which students could receive a grant, was in conflict with the principle of legal certainty because it also affected students who had already begun their studies under the assumption that they would profit from such grants for the full duration of their studies. One of the central questions was whether article 120 of the Constitution, which in its 1983 reading speaks only of review of the 'constitutionality' of acts of parliament, should be understood as also prohibiting review against unwritten fundamental legal principles. This question arose all the more because, *before* 1983, the provision spoke of the 'inviolability' of acts of parliament, which was taken to cover any form of judicial review.

---

[127] In the Netherlands, except for the administrative law sections in district courts, and the tax chamber at the *Hoge Raad*, the members of other administrative courts are not constitutionally members of the judiciary in the sense of art 116 para 1 and 112 para 2 of the Constitution; art 116: '1. The courts which form part of the judiciary shall be specified by act of Parliament'; art 112: '2. Responsibility for the adjudication of disputes which do not arise from matters of civil law may be granted by act of Parliament either to the judiciary or to courts that do not form part of the judiciary. The method of dealing with such cases and the consequences of decisions shall be regulated by act of Parliament'. Judges and the procedure in administrative courts live up to all requirements for judges who formally are part of the judiciary.

[128] HR 16 May 1986, ECLI:NL:HR:1986:AC9354.

[129] HR 14 April 1989, ECLI:NL:PHR:1989:AD5725.

The question was answered in the negative: it was held that 'however much the act infringed the principle of legal certainty, and although there are many reasons why the prohibition of article 120 of the Constitution might have to be read as narrowly as possible, the *Hoge Raad* deduced from the history of the provision of 1983 that it had not been the intention to narrow the prohibition's scope, so that review against unwritten legal principles would be allowed.

In using this language, the *Hoge Raad* indicated that the relevant Act was indeed considered to infringe the principle of legal certainty.[130] It may be inferred from this that courts are only unable to attach to a judgment on the infringement of such a principle the legal consequence of the inapplicability or invalidity of an Act of Parliament, but that they can indeed pass judgment on the compatibility with unwritten fundamental principles. As such unwritten principles are covered by the prohibition of article 120 of the Constitution, one may also assume that a judgment of incompatibility with a provision of the Constitution could be made by a court, as long as the court does not disapply the relevant Act of Parliament. This would bring the situation very close to the situation in the UK under the Human Rights Act 1998, where such declarations of incompatibility have been formalized. It should be emphasized, however, that the *Hoge Raad* has never ever since this one judgment repeated a similar declaration of incompatibility.

When we look at the case law on injunctions against legislative acts, the separating line between the judicial and legislative power is thin, but quite clear.

As we pointed out in Section C.4, the *Hoge Raad* has confirmed that orders to legislate in a specified manner are impossible, even when it regards legislative acts of territorially decentralized legislatures.[131] That would infringe the separation between the legislative and the judicial powers.

The *Hoge Raad* does allow court orders *not* to apply executive legislation (so any regulations issued by any instrument other than an Act of Parliament) and legislation by territorially decentralized bodies when this legislation conflicts with higher norms. Such an order cannot, of course, apply to Acts of Parliament if it concerns an alleged infringement of provisions of the Constitution or unwritten general legal principles, since this is the very essence of the prohibition of article 120 Constitution, as explained in the *Harmonisatiewet* judgment. The exception remains article 94: a conflict with provisions of treaties and of decisions of international organizations which are 'binding on all persons'. In this case, also Acts of Parliament can be reviewed, and an order not to apply them is indeed possible.

Also, there is the possibility of damages for legislative executive decisions which infringe on unwritten principles of law or other higher norms including constitutional norms.[132] *Francovich* damages can no doubt be awarded under the law of the Netherlands without infringement of the separation of powers, and this extends to Acts of Parliament (*Factortame* liability), although no case has yet occurred in practice, as fits with the separation of powers and the intention of Article 94 of the Constitution.

---

[130] Ibid: '3.1. The first part of the grounds adduced in this appeal, raises the question whether art 120 of the Constitution leaves courts the freedom to review the conformity of acts of Parliament with fundamental principles of law. In the judgment of 16 May 1986, NJ 1987, 251, it has been implied that according to the Supreme Court this question ought to be answered in the negative. In that judgment the Supreme Court wishes to persist B however strongly it considers the provisions of the so-called Harmonization Act (Act of 7 July 1987, *Stb*. 334) to be in conflict with the justified expectations of the students involved and hence with the principle of legal certainty.'

[131] See Section C.4.

[132] HR 24 January 1969, ECLI:NL:HR:1969:AC4903 (*Pocketbooks II*).

As far as the country of the Netherlands within the Kingdom is concerned, the vertical division of powers is based on a model of decentralization within a unitary state. The Kingdom itself, comprising the country of the Netherlands, the three countries of Aruba, Curaçao, and St Maarten in the Caribbean, is better characterized as federal in nature.

The federal character resides in the fact that the *Statuut voor het Koninkrijk* (Charter for the Kingdom) reserves certain matters concerning the whole realm to the Kingdom, while leaving the rest to the autonomy of each of the countries. It does, however, also exhibit a confederal trait inasmuch as it grants the right of unilateral withdrawal from the Kingdom to Aruba (articles 58–60 *Statuut*). On the other hand, it provides for supervisory mechanisms, which suggests more unitary elements, although these have hardly been used (articles 49–53 *Statuut*).

As regards territorial decentralization within the Netherlands (in Europe), the Constitution speaks of the powers of provinces and municipalities to regulate and administer their domestic affairs, which 'shall be left' to their administrative organs.[133] This constitutionally guaranteed 'autonomy' has the flavour of federalism. But this is misleading. In fact, the tasks which municipalities and provinces carry out in practice are mainly tasks which have been required by higher legislation.[134] Also, the constitutionally founded mechanisms of supervision, which may extend also over autonomous decision-making, highlight the unitary guarantee of the exercise of decentralized powers. Thus, not only may the government quash provincial and municipal decisions for conflicting with law, but also with the general interest. Obviously, the government determines what is in the general interest.[135]

Most effectively, the unitary element is retained through controlling the financial position of municipalities (which is the more important of the two territorially decentralized bodies, the other being provinces). Although municipalities have autonomous taxation powers, regulated by an Act of Parliament, and the most important of autonomous taxes (the tax on immovable property) accounts for over eighty per cent of the municipal taxes and levies, these in turn form less than nine per cent of the total municipal income.[136]

5. The Absence of an Overarching Concept of Political Unity

Neither the Netherlands Constitution nor the constitutional system of which it forms part is based on an explicit overarching foundational concept. Neither sovereignty, the people, the nation, the Constitution, nor citizenship play that role. About sovereignty, we have said enough. The history of provincialism during the Republic also made a unified concept of 'the people' difficult, while, in the nineteenth century, protestant circles rejected the concept of popular sovereignty of the French Revolution—though rooted in proto-Calvinist ideas of the Dutch revolt as popular revolt against a tyrant. The nation was for similar reasons never a strong unifying concept, although patriotism was triggered during the German occupation (1940–1945), but obviously not in pseudo-mythical foundational sense.

The Constitution is in character not foundational, as we pointed out above at several places, although recently, politicians have suggested that immigrants should be taught 'the

[133] Art 124 para 1 of the Constitution.
[134] Art 124 para 2 of the Constitution.
[135] Art 132 para 4 of the Constitution.
[136] For a critical analysis of recent tendencies, see the Council of Europe Report: Local and regional democracy in Netherlands, Kathryn Smith, Odd Arild Kvaloy and Dian Schefold (rapp), CG(12)16 PART2 Conseil de l'Europe. Congrès des Pouvoirs locaux et régionaux de l'Europe. Strasbourg.

principles and values of the Constitution'. But this suggestion is conspicuous for its strangeness to the constitutional culture.

Citizenship in the past did not have a strong connotation either. The notion was virtually absent. Thus, one may notice that the EU Treaties, which introduced the notion of EU citizens in the Treaty of Maastricht, in the Dutch translation quickly shift the concept of 'citizens', *burgers*, to 'subjects', *onderdanen*. Consequently, the Dutch legislation consistently speaks not of 'citizens', *burgers*, or 'nationals' of Member States, but of 'subjects', *onderdanen*, of Member States also those who are nationals of countries without a King (or Grand duke).

Some inklings of a stronger concept of citizenship have become discernible though. Since the debate on the 'multicultural society' and the 'failed integration' of minorities took shape, nearly synchronous with the successful campaign of the unfortunate Pim Fortuyn,[137] official government policy has shifted the meaning of citizenship. Whereas previously the principle seemed to be that citizenship was a consequence of or at least attendant to long-term residence and nationality, now this relation has reversed: first one must show that one can be a citizen, who must be shown through the passing of 'integration' tests, *inburgeringsexamens*, which guarantee a certain knowledge of the language and society of the Netherlands, as a condition for long term residence, citizenship rights, and nationality. This may suggest a tendential inversion towards a (neo-)republican view, this time of citizenship.

It is hard to predict whether this new tendency diminishes the pragmatic approach the Netherlands has shown over the past centuries towards the constitutional concept of citizenship.

E. Constitutional Identity

In comparison with other European constitutions, the most distinctive features of the Netherlands Constitution are an openness to international law and international society, the absence of constitutional review of Acts of Parliaments by courts without sovereignty of parliament, the lack of an explicit constitutionally relevant concept of sovereignty, and an overall low degree of ideology in the text of the Constitution: it lacks a preamble with its attendant rhetoric, while terms like 'democracy', 'people', or 'nation' are absent so far.

These characteristics can be explained on the one hand from the geographic and geopolitical position of the Netherlands within Europe, and from historical developments on the other. The geographic and geopolitical position of a relatively small country in the delta of great rivers, its location at crossroads between the United Kingdom to the West, Germany to the East, and (with Belgium as a buffer in between) France to the South, explains to a large extent the political and economic orientation, and the openness towards the outside world. Historically, the country had its *floruit* in the seventeenth century, when it was a confederation of provinces which claimed sovereignty—a confederation which functioned for over two centuries. The period immediately after the French Revolution was in a sense an interim period of centralism, initially national centralism with strong French influence, via indirect French rule to incorporation of the country into the Napoleonic Empire in 1810. This

---

[137] This was not merely Pim Fortuyn's work; in the conservative liberal party it was Frits Bolkestein, the later EU Commissioner, who had already repeatedly insisted on more active integration policies, while from Labour circles, it was Paul Scheffer who in January 2000 published an influential essay on the new 'social question' which was posed by lax and failed integration policies.

centralism was abandoned in the nineteenth century when the Prince of Orange was made the monarch three years later, in favour of a decentralized unitary state.

The great constitutional transformations which have stamped the development of the present Constitution are the liberal revolution of 1848, which led to the introduction of a full-fledged parliamentary system. It survives to this day. It was perfected into a more truly democratic system with the introduction of the general franchise at the beginning of the twentieth century. The social makeup of the country at the time, consisting as it did of denominational and social minorities, led to a system of proportional representation which was introduced simultaneously with the democratic reforms.

With secularization since the end of the 1960s, the tenability of this system of government became more controversial, when reforms towards a majoritarian system with more quasi-presidential features were proposed. None of these proposals proved successful, but the constitutional debates did lead to an overall revision, leading to a modernized Constitution in 1983—a Constitution which was novel mainly in placing a fuller catalogue of fundamental rights at the opening of its text (Chapter I of the Constitution).

The quest for reform has, however, not stopped. All the proposals for electoral reform, strengthening the position of the Prime Minister or the government, and introduction of the referendum in an effort at breaking through the politics of compromise towards a system which is perceived as more efficient and effective, have returned again and again. Partly, this was because of the presence in a number of coalitions of a party for constitutional reform D66. As most of the time a small, but needed, coalition partner, it had a leverage on the agenda which was greater than its size. Partly, the discussions have recurred because of secularization's effect on homogenizing society and politics. What was a 'pillarized' society of denominational minorities in the second half of the nineteenth and first half of the twentieth century is no more. This has also meant that the conditions for exercising political power have changed, which, on the one hand, has resulted in the opening of the way to reforms which no longer require mediation and moderation towards all major minorities. On the other hand, the perception is that it has led to a relative estrangement of the public from politics and the political system, which in turn has led into a call of effective, output oriented government.

The introduction of 'new' migrant minorities in the 1970s has created problems of accommodation. These minorities, though quite small, find themselves in different circumstances than the denominational minorities of the nineteenth and twentieth centuries. They are, on the whole, socially more disadvantaged and adhere to a 'stranger' religion which organizes itself differently from the 'old' religious and secular denominations. They also are characterized by weak structures of social and political representation and are confronted with a new largely homogeneously agnostic or secularized majority. This has fed both into mutually opposed forms of fanaticism in the fringes of both sides, which an increasingly fragmented mainstream politics has had difficulty to accommodate in terms of constitutional values or principles.

An important feature of the Netherlands' Constitution is its very relative meaning in political and legal practice. In this respect it can be characterized as an incremental constitution which reflects, rather than steers, developments in public society. It is accompanied by such features as the prohibition on courts reviewing the constitutionality of Acts of Parliament and of treaties, and a relatively weak constitutional culture. It is 'not done' to win an argument in parliament based on considerations of (un-)constitutionality, which are considered to be 'unpolitical' considerations.

Another basic and distinct feature of the Netherlands constitutional system is its openness towards international legal developments. The priority of directly effective provisions of international origin is pivotal in this. This provides compensation for prohibition for courts to review constitutionality of Acts of Parliament. Also, it confirms the 'relative' status of the Constitution within the broader notion of constitutional law.

This place of international provisions has reinforced the role of the human rights treaties, particularly the ECHR, which have not merely constitutional status, but have thus acquired supra-constitutional status.

All these features together provide the constitutional system with a great flexibility in view of national, European, and international developments as they occur. The question may arise whether the identity which thus transpires, can ever set a substantive limit to European integration in the framework of the European Union.

Formal limits seem not to fit in well with the priority which (self-executing) international law enjoys in the national constitutional order. Yet, there are two substantive points of constitutional law which can play a role.

The first is the role of the ECHR. Precisely because of its supra-constitutional importance in the Netherlands, the fact that the European Union is not formally a party to this human rights instrument is viewed as a disadvantage.[138] This view found broad support in the Lower House.

Secondly, the *Hoge Raad* did draw a line on the role of the national judiciary in enforcing EU law by prohibiting courts from giving court orders that enjoin the legislature to pass specific legislation, even when it concerns the implementation of EU law. Thus, looking at the 'deep structure' of the relevant issues, the separation of powers between the judiciary and the legislature might be a battleground for a principle of democracy to be enforced in the face of EU law—even though such a principle of democracy is not made explicit in the relevant case law, and even though we do not see much battle on the frontiers of the national and EU legal orders in the Netherlands.

These are the specificities of the constitutional law of the Netherlands. There are also many things it holds in common with other European countries. The historical background to the great transformations of the nineteenth and early twentieth century are largely shared between these countries and the Netherlands. Also, we can notice that the Constitution has shifted in emphasis on the 'political' constitution in the nineteenth century, relating as it did to the governmental system, towards a 'rights' constitution by the end of the twentieth century, with full emphasis on the protection of individual fundamental rights beyond political rights in the strict sense. While in respect of governmental and executive structures there is no great common law of Europe emerging, this may be different regarding the protection of individual fundamental rights. It is here that both the commonality and specificity of constitutional systems in Europe will emerge.

---

[138] For that very reason, in an advisory opinion to the government the *Raad van State* was exceedingly critical of the (then: draft-) EU Charter of Fundamental Rights. It 'strongly advised' not to make it a binding text because of possible divergences with the ECHR; Kamerstukken TK, 2000–2001, 21 501-20, A, p 8.

9

The Evolution and *Gestalt* of the Polish Constitution

Michal Szwast, Marcin Szwed, and Paulina Starski

A. The Origins of the Constitution	433	**D. The Axiology of the Constitution**	
1. Poland's Constitutional Past: Polish		**of 1997: Basic Structures and Concepts**	463
Constitutionalism throughout the		1. The Constitution and its Supremacy	464
Centuries	433	2. The Constitutional Concept of Sovereignty,	
2. 'Constitutional Moment' in Times of		the 'Nation', and the 'Common Good'	469
Transition: The Path to the 1997		3. The Constitution and the 'Democratic	
Constitution and its Substance	438	State Ruled by Law'	471
a) The Process	438	a) The Constitution and Democracy	471
b) The Substance	441	b) The Constitutional Concept of the	
B. The Constitution, its Rigidity,		Rule of Law	474
and Evolution	444	4. The Constitutional Protection of	
1. Constitutional Rigidity	444	Human Rights: Dignity of the Person,	
2. The Constitutional Tribunal as a Catalyst		Equality, and Freedom	476
of Constitutional Evolution and a Forum		5. The Constitution and the Separation	
for the Resolution of Constitutional		of Powers	481
Conflicts	449	a) The Legislative	482
a) The Constitutional Tribunal as a		b) The Executive	483
Catalyst of Constitutional Evolution	450	c) The Judiciary	485
i. Dynamic Composition	450	6. The Constitution and the Form of	
ii. Dynamic Jurisprudence and		the State	486
Triggers of 'Normative Movement'	451	7. The Constitution and its Identity	488
b) Resolution of Conflicts before the		**E. Conclusion and Outlook**	490
Constitutional Tribunal	453	**Epilogue**	490
C. The Caesura: The Dismantlement			
of the Constitutional Order	457		

We, the Polish Nation—all citizens of the Republic,
[…] Aware of the need for cooperation with all countries for the good of the Human Family, Mindful of the bitter experiences of the times when fundamental freedoms and human rights were violated in our Homeland, Desiring to guarantee the rights of the citizens for all time, and to ensure diligence and efficiency in the work of public bodies[…].[1]

'Mamy zatem niezmienioną konstytucję, pomyślaną jako konstytucja społeczeństwa otwartego, inkluzywnego, demokratycznego (parlament odgrywający swoją rolę, podział władz rozumiany i praktykowany na serio) i najnowsze ustawodawstwo, hołdujące de facto innej koncepcji aksjologicznej i w wielu wypadkach wypaczające zasady konstytucyjne.[2]

---

[1] Excerpt from the Preamble of the Polish Constitution of 1997.
[2] Ewa Łętowska, 'Sprawiedliwość konstytucyjna po (?) kryzysie konstytucyjnym', presentation during the II Congress of Civil Rights (II Kongres Praw Obywatelskich) (16 December 2018) https://archiwumosiatynskiego.pl/wpis-w-deba cie/prof-letowska-kryzys-postepuje-przez-obnizanie-standardow-dzialania-wladzy/ (last accessed on 23 April 2022).

Michal Szwast, Marcin Szwed, and Paulina Starski, *The Evolution and* Gestalt *of the Polish Constitution* In: *The Max Planck Handbooks in European Public Law*. Edited by: Armin von Bogdandy, Peter M Huber, and Sabrina Ragone, Oxford University Press.
© Michal Szwast, Marcin Szwed, and Paulina Starski 2023. DOI: 10.1093/oso/9780198726425.003.0009

['We have our Constitution, understood as a constitution of an open, inclusive and democratic society (with the parliament playing its role, separation of powers taken and implemented seriously), still unchanged and the newest legislation *de facto* favouring a different axiological conception and in many cases perverting constitutional principles.][3]

Writing about the *Gestalt* of the Polish Constitution in current times in which we have become witnesses to the dismantlement of Poland's constitutional order poses an enormous challenge. The pressing questions seem to be whether the text of Poland's 1997 Constitution is worth more than the paper it is written on and whether constitutional doctrine, as particularly shaped by the Polish Constitutional Tribunal (*Trybunal Konstytucyjny*) (CT) before its unconstitutional capture that this chapter is in the end designed to elucidate, is of any relevance at all.

Considering these constitutionally existential questions some general remarks are needed at the outset.

First, the capture of institutions, which has occurred since 2015 and has been incrementally deepening, has unhinged the system of coordinates that give the Polish constitutional state its shape. Yet, it is a commonly accepted legal truth that violations of legal norms do not invalidate the 'ought' that forms their core.[4] It is our submission and (theoretical) premise that the 'ought' of the Polish Constitution is still 'there'.

Second, the Polish Constitution and Polish constitutional law, as shaped by the jurisprudence of the CT before its capture, have not become irrelevant in practice. Discussions on the illiberal reconfiguration of the Polish state orchestrated by the 'United Right' government led by *Prawo i Sprawiedliwość* (Law and Justice)[5] take place against the background of the Polish Constitution and the 'language' it provides. Different political and social forces within Poland fight about what is 'constitutional' and what is 'unconstitutional'.[6] Since the Constitution has remained the major point of reference shaping political discourses and power struggles, it is not only timely, but of particular urgency, to remind ourselves of the major pillars of Polish constitutionalism, its heritage as well as the axiology of the Constitution of 1997.[7] This is the prerequisite for making determinations on the '(un)constitutionality' of certain governmental actions and to expose the distorted employment and interpretation of constitutional provisions and concepts by the current government.

Third, the 'resurrection' of Poland as a state governed by the rule of law will only be possible on the basis of its, yet not invalidated, constitutional foundations. It is our goal to sketch them within this chapter.

---

[3] Translation by the authors.

[4] Cf. Hans Kelsen, *Pure Theory of Law* (first published 1934, Max Knight (tr), 2nd edn 1960, University of California Press, Berkeley, 1967) 6 f.

[5] 'United Right' (*Zjednoczona Prawica*) is the term for an informal coalition between different political parties whose composition has changed repeatedly: It included 'Law and Justice' (*Prawo i Sprawiedliwość*), 'Solidary Poland' or 'United Poland' (*Solidarna Polska*), and 'Agreement' (*Porozumienie*). In the parliamentary elections, candidates of all those parties run from the lists of the 'Law and Justice' electoral committee and in the *Sejm* all their deputies belong to the 'Law and Justice' parliamentary club. However, all political parties forming the 'United Right' remain separate entities, with their own leaders and programmes and, according to the media relations, there are regular tensions between them.

[6] Wojciech Sadurski, *Poland's Constitutional Breakdown* (OUP, Oxford, 2019) 186.

[7] Adopted on 2 April 1997 and accepted within a national referendum held on 25 of May 1997 finally entering into force on 17 October 1997. See 'The Constitution of the Republic of Poland of 2 April 1997' (Dziennik Ustaw, No 78, item 483 (1997)). For the English translation see https://www.sejm.gov.pl/prawo/konst/angielski/kon1.htm (last accessed on 23 April 2022).

Yet, when we write here about legal norms, principles, and doctrines permeating Polish constitutional law three crucial points are to be kept in mind.

First, the constitutional reality before 2015 is much different from the reality that we have been witnessing since 2015. Second, as things stand now, nothing about the state of Polish constitutional law is ordinary. The ordinary has been unhinged. Hence, this chapter is an exercise in writing about the ordinary in times in which it is contested. We are writing in times of the 'extraordinary'. Third, for around seventeen years the constitutional order established by the 1997 Constitution appeared in substance—despite some deficits—more or less intact. The reinstatement of the authority of the 1997 Constitution is not impossible,[8] since the necessary conceptual 'material' endowed with normative force is still existent. A reinstatement requires, however, major shifts in a divided society.

In light of these considerations this chapter will illustrate the origins of the 1997 Constitution (Section A), its formal rigidity yet dynamic evolution (Section B), sketch the dismantlement of the Polish constitutional order since 2015 as a crucial caesura in contemporary Polish constitutionalism (Section C), and contrast it with the axiology of the 1997 Constitution (Section D), before closing with a conclusion (Section E).

A. The Origins of the Constitution

Constitutions are more than mere legal documents: they are expressions of culture, a measure of cultural identity, and also normative heritage impacting on future development.[9] The *Gestalt* of the Polish Constitution of 1997 (henceforth, 'Constitution') which is in force today is in that sense a product of Polish (constitutional) history and essentially shaped by it.[10] The Constitution itself acknowledges the significance of the 'constitutional past': in its Preamble it explicitly '[r]ecall[s] the best traditions of the First and the Second Republic',[11] stressing 'the bitter experiences of the times when fundamental freedoms and human rights were violated in [the] Homeland'[12] thereby attributing to a part of Poland's history constitutional normativity. Hence, already the constitutional text itself and its *invocatio historiae* advises us to take a look at its predecessors. Polish constitutional history throughout the centuries is characterized by two opposing moments—continuities on the one hand, and ruptures on the other hand.

1. Poland's Constitutional Past: Polish Constitutionalism throughout the Centuries

Roots of Polish constitutionalism go far back in time.[13] In the thirteenth century, Poland was formed by several duchies organized to some extent along the idea of government by representation—delegates speaking for and representing the nobility convened in provincial

---

[8] This aspect raises – as a matter of course – various questions of constitutional theory.

[9] For more on this Ryszard M Małajny, 'Pojęcie konstytucji' (2018) 2 Państwo i Prawo 3, 21.

[10] See only Konrad Jajecznik, 'Konstytucja RP z 1997 roku na tle polskiego dziedzictwa konstytucyjnego XX wieku' (2007) 1 (10) Społeczeństwo i Polityka 13 f.

[11] See Preamble para 8.

[12] See Preamble para 12.

[13] See Arkady Rzegocki, '8 Polish Constitutional Traditions', in Arkadiusz Górnisiewicz and Bogdan Szlachta (eds), *The Concept of Constitution in the History of Political Thought* (De Gruyter, Berlin, 2019) 113 f.

assemblies called '*sejms*'.[14] Democratic structures formed, however, a privilege of the nobility.[15] The ideas of parliamentarism, the rule of law, and the separation of powers began to flourish by the end of the seventeenth century[16] and an elective monarchy system evolved. Some consider Poland a constitutional monarchy from the sixteenth century on.[17] One important document representing core ideas of early Polish constitutionalism is *De Optimo Senatore* written by Wawrzyniec Grzymała Goślicki in 1568. At its centre stands the thesis that the law binds the ruler (*lex et rex*)—an early and rudimentary expression of the rule of law idea.[18]

Polish 'constitutionalism' evolved around constitutional texts which still exert influence on the Polish Constitution of 1997. Various past constitutions and constitutional projects served as points of reference, sources of inspiration but also negative blueprints in terms of its design and the 1997 Constitution's 'coming into being'.[19]

First, the constitution of 3 May 1791[20]—which has remained the subject of national pride being the first European (the French Constitution was adopted on 3 September 1791) and the second constitution in the world of that kind (after the Constitution of the United States adopted in 1787)—and the First Polish Republic have put their mark on the constitutional design of the 1997 Constitution as did the experience of the Polish state's non-existence for over 123 years.[21] The 1791 Constitution was adopted for the Polish–Lithuanian Commonwealth by the Great Sejm, so-called *Four-Year Sejm* which met in 1788–1792. It was designed to reform the elective monarchy system existing so far, which struggled with inefficiency. Edmund Burke was in awe of the 1791 Constitution.[22] It introduced a constitutional monarchy following the concept of the social contract and the idea of the separation of powers in the sense of *Rousseau* and *Montesquieu*.[23] While serfdom was not abolished entirely, its effects were alleviated.[24] The guarantees of *habeas corpus*, previously restricted only to nobility ('*szlachta*'), were extended to '(towns)people'. The 1791 Constitution banned the *liberum veto*, a privilege previously attributed to *Sejm* deputies, which allowed them to veto and consequently to undo all the laws adopted during *Sejm* sessions. The parliament created under the 1791 Constitution displayed a bicameral structure. It consisted of a *Sejm*, whose deputies were elected, and a Senate comprised of appointed senators. The 1791 Constitution installed a hereditary monarchy. This reconfiguration served one important goal: It was intended to diminish foreign influence on the election of the Polish king. Furthermore, the 1791 Constitution established an independent judiciary (with elected judges), separate

---

[14] Mark Brzezinski, *The Struggle for Constitutionalism in Poland* (Macmillan, New York, 1998) 32.

[15] Ibid, 33.

[16] Ibid, 37.

[17] Arkady Rzegocki, '8 Polish Constitutional Traditions' (n 13) 113.

[18] Hermann Vahle, 'Wawrzyniec Goślickis Werk „De optimo Senatore"' (1972) 20 Jahrbücher für Geschichte Osteuropas 161 f.

[19] See generally Lech Garlicki and Zofia A Garlicka, 'Constitution Making, Peace Building, and National Reconciliation—The experience of Poland', in Laurel E Miller (ed), *Framing the State in Times of Transition: Case Studies in Constitution Making* (United States Institute of Peace, Washington, 2010) 391 f.

[20] See on this Jerzy Lukowski, 'Recasting Utopia: Montesquieu, Rousseau and the Polish Constitution of 3 May 1791' (1994) 1 The Historical Journal 37, 65.

[21] See also William W Hagen, 'The Partitions of Poland and the Crisis of the Old Regime in Prussia 1772–1806' (1976) 9 Central European History 115.

[22] On Burke and the 'Polish question': Anna Plassart, 'Edmund Burke, Poland, and the Commonwealth of Europe' (2020) 64 The Historical Journal 885.

[23] Jean-Jacques Rousseau, 'Social Contract', in Susan Dunn (ed), *The Social Contract and The First and Second Discourses* (Yale University Press, New Haven, 2002) Book I, Chapter II (page 171f); Charles de Montesquieu, 'Spirit of Laws', in *The Complete Works of M de Mortesquieu* (T Evans, London, 1777) Vol. I, Book II, Chapter II.

[24] Cp. Marian Hillar, 'The Polish Constitution of May 3, 1791' (1992) 37 The Polish Review 185, 204.

from the king and the parliament. Despite being in force for less than nineteen months, its legacy permeated the evolution of the Polish constitutional state. Undoubtedly, the 1791 Constitution and its normative axiology nurtured Polish aspirations to regain independence and sovereignty. These aspirations manifested themselves in many citizen uprisings against states occupying Poland in the nineteenth century.[25] In that sense, it was also interpreted as a programmatic manifestum for the (re)acquisition and preservation of the independence of the Polish state.

Second, the interwar period (the phase of the Second Polish Republic, 1918–1939) did serve in many respects as a model for the drafters of the 1997 Constitution, of which its Preamble— referencing to 'the best traditions of the First and the Second [Polish] Republic'—is reflective. Yet, assessing this period can only engender ambivalent results if seen through the prism of modern constitutionalism. Various statutes and practices shaping the Second Polish Republic appear incompatible with the rule of law in its contemporary guise, some of them rather corresponding to 'bitter experiences of the times when fundamental freedoms and human rights were violated in our Homeland', which the Preamble to the 1997 Constitution links—to a certain extent falsely—only to the period of the communist regime (1944–1989).

The leadership of Piłsudski altered the constitutional *Gestalt* of the Second Polish Republic. The 1921 Constitution—the first constitution[26] following the recovery of the sovereignty of the Polish state—implemented the idea of parliamentary democracy being largely influenced by the French Constitution of the Third Republic, which enshrined modern principles and values.[27] It drew on the achievements of the 1791 Constitution and established, on the one hand, a line of 'constitutional continuity', while simultaneously adopting constitutional features common to modern European constitutions from the nineteenth and early twentieth century on the other hand. Article 2 of the 1921 Constitution proclaimed that 'Sovereignty in the Republic of Poland belongs to the nation. The legislative organs of the nation are: in the domain of legislation, the Sejm and the Senate; in the domain of executive power, the President of the republic; jointly with the responsible ministers; in the domain of the administration of justice, independent courts'.[28] As Piotrowski points out, this particular combination of popular sovereignty with the idea of separation of powers within one single provision appears 'progressive', yet, at the same time, it is in accordance with the foundations of the 1791 Constitution.[29] The fact that the 1921 Constitution installed broad substantive and procedural guarantees for the protection of fundamental rights is a further moment evidencing its 'modern' *Gestalt*: article 95 stated, for example, that '[t]he Republic of Poland guarantees on its territory, to all, without distinction of extraction, nationality, language, race or religion, full protection of life, liberty and property'.[30] Unfortunately, in its original liberal and 'enlightened' form, it was in force only for five years.

The 1926 Novella to the 1921 Constitution as well as the Constitution of 23 April 1935 following Piłsudski's *coup d'état* on 11 May 1926 were designed to concentrate powers

---

[25] See more about the 1791 Constitution in Chapter 7 on Lithuania by Irmantas Jarukaitis.
[26] It was preceded by the 'Small Constitution' of 1919 (Dziennik Ustaw , No 19, item 226 (1919)).
[27] Maria Kruk, 'The Systematic Order of the Constitution of the Republic of Poland of 2nd April 1997', in Paweł Sarnecki and others (eds), *The Principles and Basic Institutions of the System of Government in Poland* (Albert Pol tr, Sejm Pub Office, Warsaw, 1999) 29, 35.
[28] Translation taken from 'Constitution of the Republic of Poland', 14 Current History (1916–1950) 358.
[29] Ryszard Piotrowski, 'Tradycja i nowoczesność w polskich konstytucjach', in Łukasz Pisarczyk (ed), *Między tradycją a nowoczesnością. Prawo polskie w 100-lecie odzyskania niepodległości* (Wolters Kluwer, Warsaw, 2019) 34.
[30] For translation see (n 28).

around the President.[31] This culminated in the stipulation that the President would be responsible towards 'God and history for the destinies of the State' (article 2 para 2).[32] The 1935 Constitution and the process of its adoption—being in that sense 'revolutionary' in nature—did not comply with the procedural and material prerequisites that the 1921 Constitution provided for constitutional amendments. It consolidated the—factually already established—presidential system of an authoritarian nature that had evolved since 1926. Struggles surrounding the strong position of the President within the Polish political system are perceivable to this date. The 1935 Constitution is to be seen as a rupture in Poland's constitutional history and traditions[33] since it eradicated the idea of democracy from the Polish legal system. The era of the 1935 Constitution was overshadowed by the aggression against Poland and the abhorrent atrocities during the Second World War on the part of the German *Reich*. These experiences of victimhood, injustice, abandonment by other European powers and the negation of the right of the Polish state to exist shape, to this day, Polish self-awareness and also exert an influence on the substance of subsequent constitutions, including the current one as well as the general constitutional discourse.

Third, the Polish People's Republic (1945–1989) and its 'order'—especially the Constitution of 22 July 1952[34]—served as a negative blueprint for the current Constitution, albeit the rupture has not been clear-cut and continuities remained also within the transitional phase, which was shaped by opposing political forces. The 1952 Constitution—whose provisions were partly amended by Stalin himself[35]—'lacked sufficient guarantees and procedures to be judicially enforceable'[36] and was perceived rather as a mere political declaration and ideological pamphlet than a binding, genuinely legal framework which would constrain the exercise of state authority. This perception started to change incrementally with the first judgment of the then already established Polish CT,[37] which was rendered on 28 May 1986.[38] In essence, the Tribunal stipulated within this foundational judgment that encroachments upon individual rights on the part of the executive have to find their basis in parliamentary statutes,[39] thereby setting the basis for the idea of a rule of law. Already at this point a process of legal transition started which finally culminated in a radical transformation of the Polish

---

[31] See Ryszard Balicki, 'Head of State', in Bogusław Banaszak and others (eds), *Constitutional Law in Poland* (Kluwer, Alphen aan den Rijn, 2012) 113, 113, para 105.

[32] See for an English translation http://libr.sejm.gov.pl/tek01/txt/kpol/e1935-spis.html (last accessed on 23 April 2022).

[33] Ryszard Piotrowski, 'Tradycja i nowoczesność' (n 29) 34.

[34] Before that the 'Small Constitution' of 1947 came into force (Dziennik Ustaw, No 18, item 71) which provided for the enactment of a new constitution.

[35] See Wojciech Sadurski, *Poland's Constitutional Breakdown* (n 6) 35 referring to Jerzy Eisler, *Czterdzieści pięć lat, które wstrząsnęły Polską* (Warsaw 2018) 148.

[36] Lech Garlicki and Zofia Garlicka, 'Constitution Making' (n 19) 391, 393.

[37] The CT was formally established already in 1982 (see article 33a of the amended 1952 Constitution). Yet the relevant parliamentary statute which made it operational was not passed until 1985 (Ustawa z dnia 29 kwietnia 1985 o Trybunale Konstytucyjnym [Constitutional Tribunal Act of 29 April 1985], Dziennik Ustaw,No 22, Item 98 (1985) 245). It was granted the power of judicial review in 1986. Obviously, the CT operated under communist rule which limited its capacity to function as an effective counterweight to the ruling authorities. See on the history of the Tribunal Mark F Brzezinski and Leszek Garlicki, 'Judicial Review in Post-Communist Poland: The Emergence of a Rechtsstaat' (1995) 31 Stan J Int'l L 13, 21 f.

[38] See CT, Judgment of 28 May 1986, Ref. No. U 1/86, OTK 1986; Marcin Wiącek, 'Komentarz – wyrok TK U 1/86', in Leszek Garlicki, Marta Derlatka, and Marcin Wiącek (eds), *Na straży państwa prawa, Trzydzieści lat orzecznictwa Trybunału Konstytucyjnego* (Wolters Kluwer, Warsaw, 2016) 33 f.

[39] See also Leszek Garlicki, 'Pierwsze orzeczenie Trybunału Konstytucyjnego (refleksje w 15 lat później)', in Ferdynand Rymarz and Adam Jankiewicz (eds), *Trybunał Konstytucyjny. Księga XV-lecia*, vol XV (Biuro Trybunału Konstytucyjnego, Warsaw, 2001) 40 f.; Lech Garlicki, 'Constitutional Court of Poland 1982 – 2009', in Pasquale Pasquino and Francesca Billi (eds), *The Political Origins of Constitutional Courts – Italy, Germany, France, Poland, Canada, United Kingdom* (Olivetti Foundation, Rome, 2009) 13, 20.

state structure and its basic rationale in 1989.[40] And indeed, the basic reasoning of some judgments rendered by the CT, particularly in the final phase of the Polish People's Republic, found their way into the first chapter of the 1997 Constitution.

Poland's transition from communist autocracy to democratic rule has been facilitated by one key moment of history: the conclusion of the Round Table Agreement of 5 April 1989.[41] This compact might even be seen as the truly 'constitutional moment' in the process of the democratization of Poland.[42] The Round Table Agreement was concluded by the *Solidarność* trade union on the one hand and the governing entities—most importantly both the communist party as well as the government—on the other hand. It presented a compromise between different political forces and positions paving the way to a new system of elections.[43] Interestingly, both the communists as well as the opposition assumed that the Round Table Agreement installed an arrangement which allowed the communists to stay in power, while granting the opposition the option to block certain governmental initiatives.[44] Yet, the outcome of the elections held in June 1994 was nothing less than a landslide defeat of the communists which reconfigured the political system of coordinates.[45]

The transformation of the Polish state from communist rule to a 'democracy' whose fate had been sealed at the Round Table was formalized by some amendments to the 1952 Constitution which were already adopted in 1989. The first amendment of 7 April 1989 set the frame for democratic elections, restituted the office of the President, reintroduced the Senate and strengthened the judiciary.[46] Yet it left the provision stipulating the supremacy of the *Sejm* intact. The second amendment of 29 December 1989[47] injected *inter alia* a new article 1 into the constitutional text which declared Poland to be a 'democratic state of ruled by law implementing the principles of social justice'.[48] It served the reconfiguration of the axiology of the Constitution.[49] Difficulties in adopting a new constitution brought about a rather long phase of interim solutions which is a typical phenomenon of Polish constitutionalism ('Small Constitutions' were also adopted in 1919 and 1947). The transitional phase between the end of the Polish People's Republic and the current Polish constitutional state was from 1992 on governed by the Constitutional Act on the Procedures of Preparation and

[40] While the CT was an institution which was superimposed on the socialist state structure with limited options to manoeuvre effectively, it had the potential 'to take on a democratic life of [its] own' (see Ryszard Cholewinski, 'The Protection of Human Rights in the New Polish Constitution' (1998) 22 Fordham Int'l LJ 236, 246) and it did so.

[41] See an English translation of the Round Table Agreement of 5 April 1989 at https://polishfreedom.pl/en/document/round-table-agreement (last accessed on 23 April 2022). See Andrzej Garlicki, *Rycerze Okrągłego Stołu* (Czytelnik, Warsaw 2004).

[42] Wojciech Sadurski, *Poland's Constitutional Breakdown* (n 6) 36 ff; Bruce Ackerman, *Revolutionary Constitutions* (Harvard University Press, Cambridge, 2019) 227 f.

[43] Wojciech Sadurski, *Poland's Constitutional Breakdown* (n 6) 37.

[44] Ibid.

[45] Andrzej Rapaczyński, 'Constitutional Politics in Poland: A Report on the Constitutional Committee of the Polish Parliament' (1991) 58 University of Chicago Law Review 595, 600; Wojciech Sadurski, *Poland's Constitutional Breakdown* (n 6) 37.

[46] Ustawa z dnia 7 kwietnia 1989 r. o zmianie Konstytucji Polskiej Rzeczypospolitej Ludowej [Law of 7 April 1989 Amending the Constitution of the Polish People's Republic], Dziennik Ustaw, No 19, item 101 (1989).

[47] Ustawa z dnia 29 grudnia 1989 r. o zmianie Konstytucji Polskiej Rzeczypospolitej Ludowej [Law of 29 December 1989 Amending the Constitution of the Polish People's Republic], Dziennik Ustaw, No 74, item 444 (1989) ('Rzeczpospolita Polska jest demokratycznym państwem prawnym, urzeczywistniającym zasady sprawiedliwości społecznej.').

[48] Translation by the authors following the translation of Article 2 of the 1997 Constitution to be found at https://www.sejm.gov.pl/prawo/konst/angielski/kon1.htm (last accessed on 23 April 2022).

[49] Lech Garlicki and Zofia Garlicka, 'Constitution Making' (n 19) 393 f.

Passing of the New Constitution of 23 April 1992[50] (henceforth: 'Constitutional Act') as well as the 'Small Constitution' of 1992.[51] The Constitutional Act set the basis for the constitution-making process and the 'Small Constitution' amended major aspects of the Constitution of the People's Republic radically. It broke with the idea of the *Sejm* as the supreme body of the state and rather installed a model of separation of powers and strengthened the position of deputies and senators.[52] While its article 77 declared that the 1952 Constitution lost its validity in its entirety,[53] various provisions of the latter remained, however, in force until 1997 via this very provision.[54]

Before the adoption of the 1997 Constitution, a phase of advanced 'judicial activism' aimed at giving shape to the new system and creating the basis for the constitutional future of the Polish state could be witnessed. This activism is echoed in various stipulations of the 1997 Constitution and influences its interpretation to this date. Overall, the interim phase in which various 'constitutional' ad hoc solutions were sought and implemented not only foreshadowed but also laid the grounds for what would then ultimately become the final Constitution of 1997.[55]

2. 'Constitutional Moment' in Times of Transition: The Path to the 1997 Constitution and its Substance

Overall, it took eight years to design the 1997 Constitution and Poland was one of the last states in transition within the Eastern and East-Southern sphere to adopt a constitution.

a) The Process

In terms of the 1997 Constitution, the drafting and deliberation process took place against the background of considerable ideological struggles occurring after 1989. The 'constitutional debate had the character of a fundamental dispute, and not of a dispute over concrete articles and concrete provisions only'.[56] Conflicts were fought out not only in terms of the substance of the Constitution but also the legitimacy of its adoption process and the institutions participating within it. The constitution-making process mingled with 'ordinary politics' and the drafting process as such 'took place in the lion's den of daily politics' leading to continuous claims about its illegitimacy.[57] The process witnessed and was influenced by

---

[50] Ustawa Konstytucyjna z dnia 23 kwietnia 1992 r. o trybie przygotowania i uchwalenia Konstytucji Rzeczypospolitej Polskiej [The Constitutional Act of 23 April 1992 on the procedure for the drafting and passing of the Constitution of the Republic of Poland], Dziennik Ustaw, No 67, item 336 (1992).

[51] Ustawa konstytucyjna z dnia 17 października 1992 r. o wzajemnych stosunkach między władzą ustawodawczą i wykonawczą Rzeczypospolitej Polskiej oraz o samorządzie terytorialnym [The Constitutional Act of 17 October 1992, on the Mutual Relations between the Legislative and Executive Institutions of the Republic of Poland and on Local Self-government], Dziennik Ustaw, No 84, item 426 (1992).

[52] Lech Garlicki and Zofia Garlicka, 'Constitution Making' (n 19) 394; Mark Brzeziński and Leszek Garlicki, 'Judicial Review' (n 37) 13 f.

[53] A similar technique was employed in the case of the 1935 Constitution.

[54] See article 77: 'The Constitution of the Republic of Poland of 22 July 1952 shall cease to have effect except that the provisions of Chapters 1, 4, 7 (with the exception of Article 60 (1)), 8, 9 (with the exception of Article 94), 10 and 11 shall continue in force.' See http://www.servat.unibe.ch/icl/pl02000_.html (last accessed on 23 April 2022).

[55] Hanna Suchocka, 'Checks and Balances under the New Constitution of Poland' (1998) St. Louis-Warsaw Transatlantic LJ 45, 50.

[56] Paweł Spiewak, 'The Battle for a Constitution' (1997) 6 E Eur Const Rev 89, 90. Generally on the process described within the following passages Mirosław Wyrzykowski, 'Introductory Note to the 1997 Constitution of the Republic of Poland' (1997) St. Louis-Warsaw Transatlantic LJ 1.

[57] Cf. Wiktor Osiatynski, 'A Brief History of the Constitution' (1997) 6 EECR 66, 66 f.

three elections (1989, 1991, and 1993—in the latter case following a dissolution of the *Sejm*), a vastly fragmented *Sejm* in its first term of 1991 and also unexpected changes in government[58] which delayed deliberations.

From 23 April 1992 on, the constitution-making process was governed by the Constitutional Act: since then the 'epicentre' of deliberations was the Constitutional Commission (*Komisja Konstytucyjna*) of the National Assembly, while two separate Constitutional Commissions—one of the Senate and one of the *Sejm*—were active before that.[59] In fact, the initial duality of Commissions proved to be a central strategic mistake of the first years of 'formalized' constitution-making from 1990 to 1993.[60]

The Constitutional Commission comprised forty-six deputies and ten senators (article 4 para 1 Constitutional Act). Representatives of the Council of Ministers, the President, as well as the CT, were given the right to participate and to submit motions (article 4 para 3 Constitutional Act). The right of constitutional initiative and hence the prerogative to submit constitutional drafts to the National Assembly was initially granted—besides to the Constitutional Commission—to fifty-six members of the National Assembly and also the President (article 2 Constitutional Act).

Only a few lawyers were members of the Constitutional Commission of 1992.[61] Yet the Constitutional Commission took opinions of law professors, churches, trade unions, the government, as well as non-parliamentary actors into account. The key scholarly heads dominating the constituent phase were members of the Institute of Public Affairs (IPA, *Instytut Spraw Publicznych*—Mirosław Wyrzykowski, Ewa Łętowska, Wiktor Osiatyński, Ryszard Chruściak)—as well as academics mostly from the University of Warsaw (Lech Garlicki, Piotr Winczorek, Maria Kruk-Jarosz) but also the Jagellonian University (Paweł Sarnecki) and the Polish Academy of Sciences. Other relevant names were Kazimierz Działocha, Stanisław Gebethner, Henryk Groszyk, Michał Pietrzak, Andrzej Rzepliński, Janusz Trzciński, Władysław Kulesza, Leszek Wiśniewski, and Krzysztof Kolasiński, who all participated as experts in the hearings of the Constitutional Commission.

The 1997 Constitution's entry into force was dependent on a supporting two-thirds majority in the National Assembly plus the positive outcome of a national referendum in which every citizen entitled to vote in the general elections had the right to participate (article 10 para 1 Constitutional Act), thereby giving the 'will of the people' significance within the constitution-making process in an unmediated way. The Constitutional Act did not establish any total turn-out requirement in terms of the number of voters that would have to participate in order for the referendum to be binding. The draft was to be considered within the National Assembly within two readings. The President was given the right to submit amendments to the adopted texts which would be considered by the Assembly within a third reading (article 8 para 2 Constitutional Act). The National Assembly could adopt proposed amendments by absolute majority of votes or reject them by a two-thirds majority in the presence of at least half of the statutory members of the National Assembly (article 8 para 3 Constitutional Act).

---

[58] The resignation of Prime Minister Józef Oleksy in 1995.

[59] See Piotr Winczorek, 'The Political Circumstances of the Drafting of the Republic of Poland's Constitution of 2 April 1997', in Mirosław Wyrzykowski (ed), *Constitutional Essays* (Institute of Public Affairs, Warsaw, 1999) 15, 18 f.

[60] See Marian Grzybowski, 'Wpływ Europejskich rozwiązań konstytucyjnych na unormowania Konstytucji RP z 1997 roku – zagadnienia wybrane' (2017) 6 Przegląd Sejmowy 43, 44.

[61] Wiktor Osiatynski, 'Poland's Constitutional Ordeal' (1994) 3 E Eur Const Rev 29, 31.

It was the basic task of the Constitutional Commission to discuss and unify proposals that were referred to it by the National Assembly (after their first reading in the National Assembly—see article 6 Constitutional Act) or drafted on its own initiative (article 5 para 2 Constitutional Act).

The work of the Commission was overshadowed by a considerable power shift. Shortly after the Constitutional Commission was established and commenced with its work, the *Sejm* was dissolved (in May 1993) upon a vote of no-confidence. Not only led this to a discontinuation of the deliberations on a future constitution within the Constitutional Commission (it had to be reconstituted during the new term), the elections also resulted in a change in the political landscape within the *Sejm* and Senate: SLD (*Sojusz Lewicy Demokratycznej* or the 'Democratic Left Alliance'—the main successor of the former communist party) held together with the Peasant Party the majority, parties that aligned with the *Solidarność* movement constituted the minority, various right-wing parties—after the implementation of a five per cent limitation-clause and the adoption of the *d'Hondt* method of calculating votes and seats—were not represented within the parliament. In total, thirty-five per cent of voters were not represented in the *Sejm*[62] and the major initiators of the political transformation process operated as an extra-parliamentary opposition. In reaction to this special constellation within and outside the *Sejm* as a result of the 1993 election, the Constitutional Act was amended in 1994 to make room for a submission of constitutional proposals by a group of citizens (at least 500,000).[63] And indeed one 'popular draft' collected by *Solidarność* and centre-right parties was submitted.

The first reading of, in total, seven constitutional projects began in September 1994 within the National Assembly. All of them were referred to the Commission for further deliberations.[64]

The governmental coalition that formed after the parliamentary election in 1993 was incapable of carrying one constitutional project successfully on the basis of its simple majority. Hence, the necessity arose to form a coalition extending beyond the governmental parties. The Constitutional Commission was then dominated by four groupings—SLD, PSL (*Polskie Stronnictwo Ludowe* or the Polish Peasants' Party)—both members of the ruling coalition—UW (*Unia Wolności* or 'Union of Freedom') and UP (*Unia Pracy* or 'Union of Labour')—the latter two being the major opposition parties. These four groupings managed to form a 'constitutional coalition' within the National Assembly at the end of 1996 and beginning of 1997.[65]

In its works leading to its own final constitutional draft,[66] the Constitutional Commission employed a strategy of compromise and appeasement also with regard to political forces outside the 'constitutional coalition'. Being met with heavy criticism by right-wing parties within and outside the *Sejm*, by the Roman Catholic Church as well as *Solidarność*, the

---

[62] Bogusław Banaszak, 'Introduction', in Bogusław Banaszak and others (eds), *Constitutional Law* (n 31) para 24.

[63] Ustawa konstytucyjna z dnia 22 kwietnia 1994 r. o zmianie ustawy konstytucyjnej o trybie przygotowania i uchwalenia Konstytucji Rzeczypospolitej Polskiej [Constitutional Act of 22 April 1994 amending the Constitutional Act on the procedure for the preparation and adoption of the Constitution of the Republic of Poland], Dziennik Ustaw, No 61, item 251 (1994). The key condition was that these groups of citizens 'can muster for their draft the support of at least five hundred thousand persons eligible to vote in Sejm elections', see Piotr Winczorek, 'The Political Circumstances' (n 59) 15, 24.

[64] For an analysis of the different drafts Maria Kruk (ed), *Jaka konstytucja? Analiza projektów Konstytucji RP zgłoszonych Komisji Konstytucyjnej Zgromadzenia Narodowego w 1993 r.* (Wydawnictwo Sejmowe, Warsaw, 1994).

[65] See here and before Mirosław Wyrzykowski, 'Introductory Note' (n 56) 2.

[66] See Marian Grzybowski, 'Wpływ Europejskich rozwiązań' (n 60) 45.

Constitutional Commission incorporated various of their ideas into the final constitutional draft. In most cases this 'appeasement strategy' failed to silence these critical voices entirely. The drafting process progressed under the impression of the presidency of Lech Wałęsa from 1990 to 1995, who made use of his presidential powers under the 1992 Constitution in an extensive manner, as well as the intense campaign before the presidential elections in 1995. The short experiences made during the transitional phase in terms of the operation of the legislative and executive organs under the 'Small Constitution' were taken into consideration.[67]

The final constitutional text—which was then to be approved via a constitutional referendum—was adopted with an overwhelming majority of votes both in the Constitutional Commission[68] as well as in the National Assembly in its third reading.[69] Nevertheless, voices of the extra-parliamentary opposition found that 'the revolution of 1989 was betrayed',[70] stressing that one-third of voters were not represented within the legislative organs which rendered the whole process illegitimate.[71] Consequently, the referendum itself was accompanied by an intense 'anti-campaign' led by right-wing parties—joining forces within the *Akcja Wyborcza Solidarność*—as well as the Catholic Church.[72] Nevertheless, the bill was finally approved by a majority of 52.7 per cent of supporting votes and 45.9 per cent rejecting votes—a rather narrow margin—with a turn-out of 42.86 per cent of eligible voters (22.6 per cent of the electorate voted in favour and 17.2 per cent against the constitutional draft).[73]

This concert of diverse political powers and ideological struggles which were fought in and outside the parliament continues to put its mark on the current Constitution.

b) The Substance

In its substance the 1997 Constitution can fairly be characterized as a 'constitution of compromise'.[74] It was the outcome of various ideological battles which continue to be fought out even nowadays.[75] The relationship between the state and the church and its position within the state was heavily debated. This debate provoked controversies over the specific wording of the Preamble.[76] Disputes arose in terms of the system of values forming the basis of the state organization, the general role of the Constitution, as well as the position of international law within the Polish legal order. The question of bicameralism versus unicameralism, the options of presidential versus parliamentary/chancellor system as well as the overall position of the President within the constitutional architecture, were likewise intensely discussed. The same applies to the specific shape of territorial self-government that was to be opted for. Beyond that, the installation of an effective system of protecting fundamental rights and freedoms[77] was of central importance in light of the abuses of state authority that characterized the era of communism. It was controversial whether to include economic and social

---

[67] Cf. here and before Marian Grzybowski, 'Wpływ Europejskich rozwiązań' (n 60) 55.

[68] Majority of forty-two votes with one abstention and two votes against (decision of 16 January 1997).

[69] With the support of 461 deputies and senators. 497 voted.

[70] Paweł Spiewak, 'The Battle' (n 56) 90.

[71] See Wiktor Osiatynski, 'Poland's Constitutional Ordeal' (n 61) 32.

[72] See Wiktor Osiatynski, 'A Brief History' (n 57) 66.

[73] Jan Wawrzyniak, *Zarys polskiego ustroju konstytucyjnego* (Branta, Bydgoszcz, 1999) 87; Jan Skórzyński, 'Historia polskich referendów' *Polityka* (25 August 2015) https://www.polityka.pl/tygodnikpolityka/historia/1630 593,2,historia-polskich-referendow.read (last acessed on 23 April 2022).

[74] See here and in terms of the considerations concerning the substance of the Constitution depicted below Mirosław Wyrzykowski, 'Introductory Note' (n 56) 3.

[75] See on this Marek Mazurkiewicz, 'The Draft of the Constitution of the Republic of Poland', in Mirosław Wyrzykowski (ed), *Constitution-Making Process* (Institute of Public Affairs, Warsaw, 1998) 115, 116.

[76] Cf. Stanisław Janczura, 'Wpływ polskich tradycji ustrojowych, warunków politycznych i zewnętrznych na ustrój polityczny określony w Konstytucji z 1997 roku' (2004) 4 Studia Iuridica Lublinensia 113, 117.

[77] See generally Ryszard Cholewinski, 'The Protection of Human Rights' (n 40) 236.

rights into the constitutional text and, if that was to be done, what their nature and scope would be. The protection of life (and consequently—the constitutional permissibility of abortion and death penalty) was a further key issue together with the inclusion of the right to property as well as a possible constitutional framework specifying the economic order. With regard to the latter matter, both propagators of a neoliberal model as well as voices favouring an interventionist model were represented within the Constitutional Commission as well as the National Assembly.[78]

Yet, the key determinants for the drafters—at the least for the majority—were first, to establish a constitutional order that marked a clear break with the authoritarian rule which governed the Polish People's Republic and, second, to make Poland 'fit' for a speedy integration in international and supranational organizational structures.

These major objectives—which form the basis of the 'axiology' of the Constitution—can be broken down into certain key aspects that were regarded as essential. First, the drafters deemed a closed list of sources of law and the subjection of state authorities to these as crucial. Second, the effective protection of fundamental rights, which conformed with European and international standards, became a central issue. Yet fundamental rights were defined in a general manner, thereby leaving their exact scope and possible limitations to further constitutional discourse and jurisprudence. Third, an effective system of checks and balances seemed critical to mark the departure from the 'unity of state power'-doctrine that was characteristic for communist times. Considerable ambiguity remained, however, in terms of the character of the established political system as 'parliamentary' or rather 'presidential'. Beyond that, the position of the Roman Catholic Church within the constitutional order was not clearly delineated and left to be decided by a concordat.[79] In the end, this is also reflected in the Preamble of the 1997 Constitution which appears ambiguous in terms of the status of the Christian foundations: it describes the Polish culture as 'rooted in the Christian heritage of the Nation and in universal human values' and refers both to 'those who believe in God as the source of truth, justice, good and beauty [a]s well as those not sharing such faith but respecting those universal values as arising from other sources . . .'.

In its substance, the 1997 Constitution is permeated by various normative features of constitutional design that align with the liberal 1921 Constitution, whilst dissociating from the axiology of the Constitution of the Polish People's Republic of 1952 (as well as the authoritarian 1935 Constitution). Amongst these are the Preamble including its reference to God (however not in the form of the classic *invocatio dei*), the definition of the state as 'the common good of all its citizens'[80] (which can, however, also be found in the 1935 Constitution), the unitary nature of state, the principle of the supremacy of the Constitution, the bicameral parliament whose chambers exert different political power (the leading role of the *Sejm* and the limited powers of the Senate), the parliamentary system of government, the office of the President endowed with substantial competences, the constitutional accountability of chief public officials, the principle of equality of citizens before the law, the key role attributed to family farms for the agricultural system of the state and work for the development of the state and society, the equality of churches along with strong guarantees of freedom of conscience and religion as well as the civic duty of military service and defence of Poland.

---

[78] Marian Grzybowski, 'Wpływ Europejskich rozwiązań' (n 60) 54.
[79] See article 25 para 4.
[80] See article 1.

Besides the formative and determining effect of Poland's constitutional past, there was a perceivable comparative influence—foreign constitutions, constitutional jurisprudence, as well as constitutional scholarship—on the design of the 1997 Constitution. It is shaped by the 'principal ideas of both European and American constitutionalism',[81] the latter serving already as an inspiration for the Constitution of 1791.[82] The overall 'Western' character of the *Gestalt* of the 1997 Constitution is not least the effect of conditionality shaping the pre-accession and accession process to the EU[83] as well as a consequence of Poland's objective to become a member of the North Atlantic Treaty Organization (NATO). One of the general purposes of the Constitution was an 'institutional and ideological integration with the West',[84] from which a detachment occurred during the years of communist, authoritarian rule. In terms of the fundamental rights enshrined in the 1997 Constitution, their basis is to be seen in line with Western traditions whose starting point would be Jewish-Christian philosophy.[85] Furthermore the European Convention on Human Rights (ECHR),[86] the International Covenant on Civil and Political Rights (ICCPR),[87] the International Covenant on Economic, Social and Cultural Rights (ICESCR),[88] as well as other international human rights instruments, were considered. Likewise, the American Bill of Rights served as a source of inspiration.

The German *Grundgesetz* (Basic Law) in the shape given by the jurisprudence of the Federal Constitutional Court (FCC) has been particularly influential, especially concepts like the principle of proportionality (to be found in article 31 para 3 of the Polish Constitution), *Rechtsstaat* (article 2 of the Constitution), human dignity (article 30 of the Constitution) (serving as the foundation of the constitutional order), as well as the concept of *Wesensgehalt*—the essence of a right (second clause of article 31 para 3 of the Constitution). Specific institutional arrangements like the constructive vote of no-confidence as operating in the Basic Law found their way into the Polish model of checks and balances. Most influential Polish constitutionalists—*inter alia* Lech Garlicki and Kazimierz Działocha—knew German and had a thorough knowledge of German scholarship, jurisprudence and discourse. Garlicki linked the inspiring effect of the German constitutional order to 'geographical proximity and traditional influence on Polish scholars'.[89] The presidential model of the Fifth French Republic influenced the framework of the Polish presidency.[90] In spite of these mainly 'Western' sources of inspiration, a few remnants of Soviet concepts are still identifiable within the current constitutional framework. In terms of the 'modes of inspiration', it occurred occasionally in a rather 'semiconscious' manner. While specific foreign constitutional concepts were widely considered during the deliberations on the Constitution's design,[91] their import was frequently seen critically[92] and genuinely 'Polish' solutions were

---

[81] Paweł Sarnecki, 'The Origin and Scope of the Polish Constitution', in Paweł Sarnecki and others (eds), *The Principles and Institutions of the System of Government in Poland* (Albert Pol tr, Sejm Publication Office, Warsaw 1999) 13, 17.

[82] Albert P Blaustein, 'Our Most Important Export: The Influence of the United States Constitution Abroad' (1987) 3 Conn J Int'l L 15, 16.

[83] Anna Śledzińska-Simon, 'Constitutional identity in 3D: A model of individual, relational, and collective self and its application in Poland' (2015) 13 ICON 124, 141.

[84] Lech Garlicki, 'Constitutional Court of Poland' (n 39) 30.

[85] Lech Garlicki, *Polskie prawo konstytucyjne. Zarys wykładu* (Wolters Kluwer, Warsaw, 2019) 99.

[86] ETS 5; 213 UNTS 221.

[87] 999 UNTS 171.

[88] 993 UNTS 3.

[89] Lech Garlicki, 'Constitutional Court of Poland' (n 39) 23.

[90] Marian Grzybowski, 'Wpływ Europejskich rozwiązań' (n 60) 56.

[91] See Ada Paprocka, 'An Argument from Comparative Law in the Jurisprudence of the Polish Constitutional Tribunal' (2018) 8 Adam Mickiewicz University Law Review 237, 241.

[92] See Wiktor Osiatynski, 'Paradoxes of Constitutional Borrowing' (2003) 1 Int'l J Const L 244, 255 (n 39).

sought. The comparative approach worked hence both in a positive as well as in a negative way, but it always remained inspirational. The decision which 'design' of constitutional provisions to opt for was in the end not based on an in-depth assessment of the experiences of other states with their constitutional models. Rather, it was the consequence of political necessities to find a compromise in light of the challenging power constellations[93] within the National Assembly as well as the Constitutional Commission.

B. The Constitution, its Rigidity, and Evolution

The role of formal amendments[94] to the 1997 Constitution is marginal; it can be characterized as 'rigid' (1). However, a change in constitutional substance is not only the result of changes to its text, but is also an effect of its (dynamic) interpretation[95] and of informal activities.[96] The frequency of 'informal amendments'[97] and a constitution's evolutionary dynamic typically increase along with the degree of a constitution's 'stiffness' and 'rigidity' in the sense of its resistance towards formal amendments.[98] Various instances of a dynamic evolution of the 1997 Constitution in that sense have surfaced in the course of its history.[99] The Constitution has evolved in the course of the application of its norms by the CT and the adjudication over constitutional conflicts (2).

1. Constitutional Rigidity

Twenty bills to amend the Constitution have been submitted to the *Sejm* between the entry into force of the Polish Constitution in October 1997 and 2019. The initiators of sixteen of them were Members of the *Sejm* and four were submitted by Presidents of Poland. In the parliamentary term of 1997–2001 two bills were submitted, 2001–2005 none, 2005–2007 seven,

---

[93] Marian Grzybowski, 'Wpływ Europejskich rozwiązań' (n 60) 55.
[94] Scholarship distinguishes formal and informal constitutional amendments. This distinction was reflected in one of the leading topics during the twentieth International Congress of Comparative Law which took place in July 2018 in Fukuoka – 'Formal and informal constitutional amendment'. The general report was drafted by Mortimer Sellers (University of Baltimore), whereas the Polish national report was drafted by Janusz Trzciński and Michał Szwast. Formal amendments are modifications (deletion, addition or change of wording) of the text of the Constitution (partial formal amendment). The most invasive form of changing the constitutional order is obviously a replacement of the constitution by a completely new one (revision of the constitution).
[95] Jarosław Szymanek, 'Determinanty procesu zmiany konstytucji' ['Determinants of amendments to the Constitution'], (2015) 3 Przegląd Legislacyjny 9, 22 See also Kenneth C Wheare, *Modern Constitutions* (OUP, Oxford, 1966).
[96] Janusz Trzciński and Michał Szwast, 'Formal and informal amendments to the constitution', in Biruta Lewaszkiewicz-Petrykowska (ed), *Rapports Polonais. XXe Congrès International de Droit Comparé. XXth International Congress of Comparative Law. Fukuoka, 22–28 VII 2018* (Łódź, 2018) 227. See generally Peter Badura, 'Verfassungsänderung, Verfassungswandel, Verfassungsgewohnheitsrecht', in Josef Isensee and Paul Kirchhof (eds), *Handbuch des Staatsrechts der Bundesrepublik Deutschland* (CF Müller, Heidelberg, 1992), § 160, para. 1 f.
[97] See in particular Leszek Garlicki, 'Niekonstytucyjność: formy, skutki, procedury' ['The unconstitutionality: forms, effects, procedures'] (2016) 9 Państwo i Prawo 3, 11; Toma Birmontienė, 'Interpretation v. amendment of the Constitution: The role of the Constitutional Tribunal', in Andrzej Szmyt and Bogusław Banaszak (eds), *Transformation of law systems in Central, Eastern and Southeastern Europe in 1989-2015: liber amicorum in honorem prof. dr. dres. H. C. Rainer Arnold* (Gdańsk University Press, Gdańsk, 2016) 331; Janusz Trzciński and Michał Szwast, 'Formal and informal amendments' (n 96) 227 f. Report on Constitutional Amendment adopted by the Venice Commission at its 81st Plenary Session (Venice, 11–12 December 2009), CDL-AD(2010)001-e para 111, available at http://www.venice.coe.int/webforms/documents/?pdf=cdl-ad(2010)001-e (last accessed on 23 April 2022).
[98] Cf. Janusz Trzciński and Michał Szwast, 'Formal and informal amendments' (n 96) 227 f.
[99] Ibid.

THE EVOLUTION AND *GESTALT* OF THE POLISH CONSTITUTION   445

2007–2011 seven, 2011–2015 three, and in 2015–2019, only one.[100] On average less than one amendment initiative per year can be identified. The political will to amend the Constitution formally has been relatively small. From among the aforementioned twenty bills to amend the Constitution, only two were adopted (in 2006 and 2009). The necessary majority of two-thirds of the votes of the deputies of the *Sejm* has proven to be a major hurdle. History has shown that it is difficult to obtain political agreement on constitutional amendments in a strongly polarized Polish parliament, even if they concern issues which are in axiological terms relatively neutral.[101] Overall the Polish Constitution is among the most 'rigid' constitutions in Europe.[102] The drafters of the Constitution assumed that the 'supreme law of the Republic of Poland' (article 8 para 1) should be protected against temptations to amend it by changing parliamentary majorities that may want to adapt it to short-term political interests—which is not untypical for continental European states.

A formal amendment of the Constitution requires the enactment of a bill to amend the Constitution (article 235). The adoption procedure itself differs from the procedure governing the enactment of ordinary statutes. The initiative to submit a bill to amend the Constitution to the *Sejm* lies exclusively with 'at least one-fifth of the statutory number of Deputies [Members of *Sejm*]; the Senate; or the President' (article 235 para 1).[103] A popular initiative by a group of citizens is not enshrined evidencing a 'constitutional reluctance' towards elements of direct democracy at the initial stage of the amendment procedure.

Constitutional amendments are enacted by way of 'a statute adopted by the Sejm and, thereafter, adopted in the same wording by the Senate within a period of 60 days' (article 235 para 2) limiting the former to a mere 'yes/no' decision. In order to prevent precipitate constitutional amendments, the first reading of a bill 'may take place no sooner than 30 days after the submission of the bill to the Sejm' (article 235 para 3). A bill to amend the Constitution is adopted by the *Sejm*—in contrast to the ordinary legislative procedure[104]—'by a majority of at least two-thirds of votes in the presence of at least half of the statutory number of Deputies, and by the Senate by an absolute majority of votes in the presence of at least half of the statutory number of Senators' (article 235 para 4) which is the key moment manifesting the Constitution's rigidity. Particular parts of the Constitution are subject to even stricter safeguards indicating a normative hierarchy within the substance of the Constitution: 'The adoption ... of a bill amending the provisions of Chapters I, II or XII of the Constitution [by the *Sejm*] shall take place no sooner than 60 days after the first reading of the bill' (article 235 para 5). This concerns basic state policies and principles, freedoms, rights, and obligations

---

[100] Information available at the website of the *Sejm* www.sejm.gov.pl (last accessed on 23 April 2022).

[101] The controversial issue of 'trainee judges' ('*asesorzy sądowi*') is instructive in this context. In the Judgment of 24 October 2007, Ref. No. SK 7/06, the CT recognized that 'trainee judges' (appointed by the Minister of Justice for a definite period of time) must not adjudicate on court cases, since this would be incompatible with the right to an independent court guaranteed in article 45 para 1 of the Constitution. Subsequently the President attempted—in the end unsuccessfully due to the end of the parliamentary term—to initiate an amendment to the Constitution aimed at enshrining 'trainee judges' as an institution within the Constitution. Later, the legislator preferred to regulate 'trainee judges' once again within a statute (2015) even at the expense of violating the right to a fair trial and risking potential challenges before the CT as well as the ECtHR. This evidences once more how reluctant the political forces within the parliament are towards amending the Constitution.

[102] Bartosz Szczurowski and Piotr Tuleja, 'Komentarz do Art. 235 Konstytucji' ['Commentary on article 235 of the Constitution'] in Marek Safjan and Leszek Bosek (eds), *Konstytucja RP (Constitution of the Republic of Poland)*, Vol II (CH Beck, Warsaw, 2016) para VI.3.

[103] The right to submit a bill concerning an ordinary statute belongs to the Deputies (Members of *Sejm*), to the Senate, to the President of the Republic, to the Council of Ministers or to a group of at least 100,000 citizens having the right to vote in elections to the *Sejm*.

[104] According to article 120 of the Constitution, the *Sejm* shall pass bills by a simple majority, in the presence of at least half of the statutory number of Deputies, unless the Constitution provides for a different majority.

of individuals and procedure for amending the Constitution itself. If a bill to amend the Constitution concerns the provisions of Chapters I, II, or XII, at least one-fifth of the statutory number of Deputies, the Senate, or the President 'may require, within 45 days of the adoption of the bill by the Senate, the holding of a confirmatory referendum' (article 235 para 6). These entities may submit applications to that respect to the Marshal of the *Sejm*, who orders the holding of a referendum within sixty days. Amendments to the Constitution are deemed accepted in this case if the majority of voters expresses support for them (article 235 para 6), without a special turnout requirement. Subsequent to the procedural steps specified in paras 4 and 6, the Marshal of the *Sejm* submits the adopted statute to the President for signature. The President 'sign[s] the statute within 21 days of its submission and orders its promulgation in the Journal of Laws of the Republic of Poland' (article 235 para 7).

There are some peculiarities of Polish constitutional law in terms of constitutional amendments if compared to other European constitutional orders. Four shall be mentioned here:

First, the prevailing view among legal scholars is that the Constitution of 1997 does not contain unalterable constitutional substance.[105] Safeguard clauses that identify constitutional provisions that are not subject to amendment are to be found in the constitutions of several European countries, for example of Italy,[106] Germany ('eternity clause'),[107] France[108] or the Czech Republic.[109] Some voices reject the possibility of deriving 'amendment prohibitions' via the interpretation of the Constitution[110] since its drafters were aware of the existence of safeguard clauses in other countries and consciously refrained from incorporating them into the constitutional text.[111] On the contrary, Piotrowski, however, claims—arguing teleologically—that unamendable constitutional substance would include the Preamble, article 2 (rule of law) and article 30 (human dignity). In his opinion the constitutional legislator may amend the constitution or even adopt a new constitution, but is prohibited from rejecting the concept of a constitution conforming with standards of constitutional democracy.[112] Trzciński and Szwast argue that 'the substantive conditions deciding on the

---

[105] Such view is purported, *inter alia*, by Bartosz Szczurowski and Piotr Tuleja, 'Komentarz do Art. 235 Konstytucji' (n 102) para V.A.6.; Mariusz Jabłoński, 'Artykuł 235 jako podstawa zmiany i uchwalenia nowej Konstytucji RP' ['Art 235 as a basis for amending and adopting a new Constitution of the Republic of Poland'], in Bogusław Banaszak (ed), *Konieczne i pożądane zmiany Konstytucji RP* [*Necessary and desirable amendments of the Constitution of the Republic of Poland*] (Acta Universitatis Wratislaviensis, Wrocław, 2010) 33; Wojciech Sokolewicz, 'Komentarz do Art. 235 Konstytucji', ['Commentary on article 235 of the Constitution'] in Leszek Garlicki (ed), *Konstytucja Rzeczypospolitej Polskiej. Komentarz* [*Constitution of the Republic of Poland. A Commentary*], vol 2 (Sejmowe,Warsaw, 2001) 7–8; Leszek Garlicki, 'Aksjologiczne podstawy reinterpretacji Konstytucji', ['Axiological foundations of the reinterpretation of the Constitution'] in Marek Zubik (ed), *Dwadzieścia lat transformacji ustrojowej w Polsce. 51. Ogólnopolski Zjazd Katedr i Zakładów Prawa Konstytucyjnego, Warszawa, 19-21 czerwca 2009 r.* [*Twenty years of political transformation in Poland. 51. National Congress of Divisions and Departments of Constitutional Law, Warsaw, June 19-21, 2009*] (Warsaw, 2010) 99. See generally Yaniv Roznai, *Unconstitutional Constitutional Amendments* (OUP, Oxford, 2017).

[106] According to article 139 of the Constitution of Italy (*Costituzione della Repubblica Italiana*, GU Serie Generale n. 298 of 27 December 1947), the form of Republic shall not be subject to constitutional amendment.

[107] See article79 para 3 of the Basic Law for the Federal Republic of Germany (Grundgesetz für die Bundesrepublik Deutschland of 23 May 1949 – BGBl. S. 1).

[108] Article 89 of the Constitution of France (Constitution du 4 octobre 1958 instituant la Ve République) provides that 'The republican form of government shall not be the object of any amendment.'

[109] According to article 9 para 2 of the Constitution of the Czech Republic (*Ústava České republiky* of 16 December 1992), 'the substantive requisites of the democratic, law-abiding State may not be amended.'

[110] Bartosz Szczurowski and Piotr Tuleja, 'Komentarz do Art. 235 Konstytucji' (n 102) para V.A.6; Wojciech Sokolewicz, 'Komentarz do Art. 235 Konstytucji' (n 105) 7–8; Leszek Garlicki, 'Aksjologiczne podstawy' (n 105) 99.

[111] Wojciech Sokolewicz, 'Komentarz do Art. 235 Konstytucji' (n 105) 6–7.

[112] Ryszard Piotrowski, 'Zagadnienie granic zmiany konstytucji w państwie demokratycznym', ['The issue of the limits to amendments of the Constitution in a democratic state'] in Jacek Czajowski (ed), *Ustroje, doktryny, instytucje polityczne: księga jubileuszowa profesora zw. dra hab. Mariana Grzybowskiego* [*Regimes, doctrines, political institutions: Jubilee Book dedicated to Prof. Marian Grzybowski*] (Jagiellonski University, Kraków, 2007) 282.

permissibility of the amendment to the Constitution ... may be deduced from the 'identity of the constitution'—i.e., from provisions whose amendment will result in a different constitution than the one that was accepted by the legislator and by the people in the referendum (as in Poland)'.[113] These authors suggest classifying the principle of common good, the rule of law, the principle of supremacy of the Nation, the principle of direct application of the Constitution, the separation of powers, human dignity and the principle of proportionality as the pillars on which the Constitution of 1997 is based.[114] Admittedly, these views have remained rather isolated and the legislator's power to amend the Constitution is regarded as unlimited, although amendments resulting in a lower level of human rights protection or a curtailment of the guarantee of a democratic state ruled by law could form the basis for intervention on the part of the EU bodies (Articles 2, 7 TEU).[115]

Second, according to the prevailing—whilst not uncontroversial—position in Polish legal scholarship, the Constitution of 1997 does not distinguish between partial formal amendments and the replacement of the Constitution with a completely new one. A revision of the 1997 Constitution could hence be based on the amendment procedure delineated in article 235.[116]

Third, 'constitutional acts' or 'constitutional statutes' existing parallel to the Constitution and endowed with the same legal force and rank in the hierarchy of sources of law as the Constitution are alien to the Polish constitutional system. The Polish Constitution falls therefore into the category of uniform constitutions. This is supported by article 87 which enlists sources of law exhaustively without mentioning constitutional acts.[117]

Fourth, the predominant view is that it is not permissible to hold a nationwide referendum—article 125[118]—which would result in the necessity to amend the Constitution since this would constitute an evasion of article 235.[119] This point has been, however,

---

[113] Janusz Trzciński and Michał Szwast, 'Formal and informal amendments' (n 96) 218.

[114] Ibid.

[115] See also Bartosz Szczurowski and Piotr Tuleja, 'Komentarz do Art. 235 Konstytucji' (n 102) para II.1.

[116] This view is supported by, amongst others, Bartosz Szczurowski and Piotr Tuleja, 'Komentarz do Art. 235 Konstytucji' (n 102) para V.A.8; Mariusz Jabłoński, 'Artykuł 235' (n 105); Marzena Laskowska, 'Pojęcie zmiany konstytucji' ['The concept of constitutional amendment'] (2018) 12 Państwo i Prawo 19, 28 ff; Wojciech Sokolewicz, 'O gradacji zmian konstytucji', ['On different degrees of constitutional amendments'] in Leszek Garlicki (ed), *Konstytucja, wybory, parlament. Studia ofiarowane Zdzisławowi Jaroszowi* [*Constitution, elections, parliament. Studies dedicated to Zdzisław Jarosz*] (Liber, Warsaw, 2000) 192. For the opposing view see Trzciński and Szwast. They point out that the adoption of a new constitution has always been—in the Polish constitutional tradition—subject to separate rules which were not regulated by the constitution then in force. The adoption of the current Constitution was governed by the 'Constitutional Act of 23 April 1992 on the procedure of preparation and adoption of the Constitution of the Republic of Poland' (see n 50) as already mentioned. According to Trzciński and Szwast the provisions governing the amendment of the Constitution form the basis for adopting a new constitution. The Constitution would have to expressly permit it, Janusz Trzciński and Michał Szwast, 'Formal and informal amendments' (n 96) 218. The distinction between the legislator who amends (pouvoir constitué) the constitution and the entity that legitimizes a new constitution (pouvoir constituent) is common to constitutional legal doctrine. It can be likewise – for example – identified in German constitutional discourse.

[117] Bartosz Szczurowski and Piotr Tuleja, 'Komentarz do Art. 235 Konstytucji' (n 102) para V.A.7; Andrzej Szmyt, 'Zagadnienie dopuszczalności ustawy konstytucyjnej w praktyce ustrojowej pod rządami konstytucji z 1997 r.' ['The admissibility of a constitutional act in systemic practice under the constitution of 1997'], in Andrzej Szmyt (ed), *Konstytucyjny system źródeł prawa w praktyce* [*The Constitutional System of Sources of Law in Practice*] (Sejmowe, Warsaw, 2005) 43–44. For the opposite view see: Marek Zubik, *Prawo konstytucyjne współczesnej Polski* [*Constitutional law of contemporary Poland*] (CH Beck, Warsaw, 2020) 31.

[118] According to article 125 para 1 a nationwide referendum may be held in respect to matters of particular importance to the State. Article 125 para 3 provides that the result of a nationwide referendum is binding on state authorities (which then are obliged to enact appropriate legislation), if more than half of the number of those having the right to vote have participated in it.

[119] Bartosz Szczurowski and Piotr Tuleja, 'Komentarz do Art. 235 Konstytucji' (n 102); Bogumił Naleziński, 'Komentarz do Art. 125 Konstytucji' ['Commentary on art 125 of the Constitution']. in Marek Safjan and Leszek Bosek (eds), *Konstytucja RP* (n 102) para V.B.c.9; Piotr Uziębło, 'O dopuszczalności konstytucyjnego referendum

contested in political practice and discourse. On 6 September 2015 a nationwide referendum was ordered by the President with the consent of the Senate. One of the referendum questions was: 'Are you in favour of introducing single-member electoral districts in the elections to the Sejm?' In accordance with article 96 para 2 multi-mandate electoral districts operate within elections to the *Sejm*, which is commanded by the proportional electoral system specified in the Constitution. Therefore, in the event of the validity of this referendum and the Nation's support for the solution proposed by it, it would have been necessary to amend article 96 para 2. Despite a wide rejection of constitutionalists,[120] the referendum was upheld in the end, but already due to the low turnout rate of 7.8 per cent, it was clear that it was not binding.

Similar doubts can be raised in terms of the unrealized initiative of President Andrzej Duda from 2018 to hold a referendum on various constitutional aspects. These concerned, *inter alia*, amendments to the Constitution in terms of the model of executive power that it establishes, the electoral system with respect to elections to the *Sejm*, giving Christian pillars of the state a more prominent role in the Constitution and the determination of the retirement age. The Senate, however, did not agree to hold that referendum.

Constitutional rigidity gave way in two instances: one of the two successful constitutional amendments is the result of supranational obligations on the part of Poland and a respective CT ruling (amendment of 8 September 2006), the second (amendment of 7 May 2009) concerned necessary qualifications of members of the *Sejm* and Senate.

On 27 April 2005[121] the CT ruled that article 607t para 1 of the Act of 6 June 1997—Code of Criminal Procedure—was incompatible with article 55 para 1 of the Constitution to the extent that it permitted the transfer of a Polish citizen to a Member State of the EU on the basis of the European Arrest Warrant (EAW).[122] In its reasoning the CT pointed out that ensuring the conformity of the Polish legal order with stipulations of EU law required the intervention of the legislator. Considering article 9 of the Constitution, which states that '[t]he Republic of Poland shall respect international law binding upon it', and the obligations resulting from Poland's EU membership, it was, the CT held, necessary to amend the existing law, possibly including the Constitution, which could not be reinterpreted as allowing the extradition of Polish citizens (irrespective of the decreasing importance of citizenship in the determination of the legal status of an individual internationally and nationally).[123]

In the aftermath of the CT judgment the President submitted a bill to amend article 55 of the Constitution to the *Sejm* which was adopted with an overwhelming majority,[124] thereby rendering compliance under the system of the EAW possible. In this case, constitutional

---

konsultacyjnego' ['On the permissibility of a consultative constitutional referendum'] (2018) 1 'Krajowa Rada Sądownictwa' 5.

[120] See on the specific facts and the legal questions the expert opinions by Bogusław Banaszak, Ryszard Piotrowski, and Marcin Wiszowaty, available at the website of the Senate https://www.senat.gov.pl/gfx/senat/pl/senatekspertyzy/2965/plik/oe_234__2.pdf (last accessed on 23 April 2022). See on the result National Electoral Commission, Announcement of 7 September 2015 at https://referendum2015.pkw.gov.pl/pliki/1441637773_Ob wieszczenie.pdf (last accessed on 8 December 2022). On President Duda's initiatives mentioned below Marcin Matczak, 'A Constitutional Referendum to Delegitimize the Constitution' VerfBlog, 7 May 2018, https://verfassu ngsblog.de/a-constitutional-referendum-to-delegitimize-the-constitution/ (last accessed on 7 December 2022).
[121] CT, Judgment of 27 April 2005, Ref. No. P 1/05.
[122] Council Framework Decision 2002/584/JHA of 13 June 2002.
[123] See Janusz Trzciński and Michał Szwast, 'Formal and informal amendments' (n 96) 240–241.
[124] The constitutional amendment was adopted with a large majority of votes of deputies: 344 for, forty-eight against, twenty-nine abstained, see at http://orka.sejm.gov.pl/proc5.nsf/opisy/580.htm (last accessed on 7 December 2022). The final act is to be found in Dziennik Ustaw, No 200, item 1471 (2006).

rigidity did not stand in the way of fulfilling supranational obligations and parliamentary forces aligned to that respect.

The second almost unanimously adopted[125] amendment introduced article 99 para 3 into the constitutional text according to which '[n]o person sentenced to imprisonment by a final judgment for an intentional indictable offence may be elected to the Sejm or the Senate'. The initiators of the amendment pointed out that the bill met the expectations of the public, according to which 'the law in the parliament should not be passed by criminals'.[126]

2. The Constitutional Tribunal as a Catalyst of Constitutional Evolution and a Forum for the Resolution of Constitutional Conflicts

The Polish Constitution becomes alive and evolves when it is interpreted and applied.[127] In that regard the CT has played a major role determining the Constitution 'in practice'. It is entrusted with the supervision of the constitutionality of statutes, other legal provisions and international agreements, adjudicates on the constitutional conformity of party activities, on disputes over authority between constitutional organs as well as on constitutional complaints (article 188). Hence, the CT is a co-bearer of constitutional authority, concretizing the Constitution in its case law and formulating detailed legal principles which complement general constitutional provisions.[128] Furthermore, it has served as a central forum for the resolution of constitutional conflicts in Poland. It has both the competence to, first, adjudicate on the validity of rules within the normative hierarchy (including the sole competence to adjudicate on the conformity of statutory provisions with the Constitution) and, second, settle disputes between constitutional organs of the state.[129] Its adjudicative activity in all of these dimensions is a potential trigger of a constitutional evolution. 'Evolution by adjudication' and the perception of constitutions as living instruments'[130] is typical for Central and Eastern European countries. In various cases beyond Poland, constitutional control instruments centralized at constitutional courts were implemented during the period of political transformation.[131]

At this stage a caveat must be stated. When analysing the role and function of the jurisprudence of the CT, it has to be kept in mind that it became victim of the dismantlement of the constitutional order starting in 2015 (see Section C). It has been reduced to merely a formal

---

[125] 404 Members of the *Sejm* voted for it, nine members abstained, no member voted against it.

[126] See Explanatory memorandum of the bill to amend the Constitution at http://orka.sejm.gov.pl/Druki6ka.nsf/0/1B1E234455AAA424C1257434002C004C/$file/432.pdf (last accessed on 23 April 2022). See also Dziennik Ustaw., No 114, item 946 (2009).

[127] Krzysztof Wojtyczek, *Sądownictwo konstytucyjne w Polsce. Wybrane zagadnienia* [*Constitutional judiciary in Poland. Selected issues*] (Biuro Trybunału Konstytucyjnego, Warsaw, 2013) 247.

[128] Krzysztof Wojtyczek, *Sądownictwo konstytucyjne* (n 127) 244. See also Leszek Garlicki, 'Standardy demokratyczne Rady Europy a Konstytucja RP (doświadczenia praktyki ustrojowej)' ['Democratic standards of the Council of Europe and the Constitution of the Republic of Poland (experiences of systemic practice)'], in Jerzy Jaskiernia and Kamil Spryszak (eds), *Dwadzieścia lat obowiązywania Konstytucji RP. Polska myśl konstytucyjna a międzynarodowe standardy demokratyczne* [*Twenty Years of the Constitution of the Republic of Poland's Binding Nature. Polish Constitutional Thought and International Democratic Standards*] (Adam Marszalek, Toruń, 2017) 434.

[129] The courts, in particular, the highest courts, namely the Supreme Court and the Supreme Administrative Court, play also a role in this respect which cannot, however, be covered here in-depth.

[130] Janusz Trzciński and Michał Szwast, 'Formal and informal amendments' (n 96) 230.

[131] Report on Constitutional Amendment adopted by the Venice Commission at its 81st Plenary Session (Venice, 11–12 December 2009), CDL-AD (2010) 001-e, para 110, available at http://www.venice.coe.int/webforms/documents/?pdf=cdl-ad(2010)001-e (last accessed on 23 April 2022).

existence devoid of constitutional legitimacy. Yet, before its capture the CT breathed life into the Polish constitutional order. It stood at its centre. In recent years a reconfigured CT has departed from previous well-established jurisprudence to a large extent. What we describe here is what the CT was, what role it played, what substance it gave to the Constitution before its capture. This section is hence designed as a reminder of what the CT could potentially become again in the future.

a) The Constitutional Tribunal as a Catalyst of Constitutional Evolution

Until 2015 the CT produced rich jurisprudence which has given the Constitution actual shape. In that regard the 1997 Constitution can be seen as a 'court constitution'[132] which renders the question who is appointed to the CT of major significance.

i. Dynamic Composition

Judges of the CT are chosen by the *Sejm* for an individual term of nine years (article 194 para 1). Therefore, the composition of the CT is subject to variations. The interpretation of the Constitution and the way in which the CT adjudicates constitutional cases depends largely on legal views, axiological attitudes, and sometimes, unfortunately, also political preferences of respective judges. Wojtyczek accurately asserts that judges of constitutional courts are constantly tempted to use the judicial control of statutes to interfere in the current political affairs on the basis of equity considerations, according to their private vision of what is better for the state. Therefore, they put themselves at risk of being accused of arbitrariness in their judgments and the substitution of the legislator's decisions with their own subjective assessments.[133] Judges' political and moral views influence how they interpret and apply the law in different and often unconscious ways,[134] in spite of the disciplining effect of legal methodology. In the past the CT had issued many rulings concerning 'morally sensitive issues' such as the permissibility of abortion,[135] the 'conscience clause' of medical professions[136] or the presence of religious education in public schools,[137] and sometimes it was even accused of being dominated by the conservative and catholic point of view.[138] Therefore, the appointment procedure of judges to the CT, with regard to their qualifications as well as the bodies responsible for their appointment, must ensure that only persons of unquestionable independence and impartiality will be appointed. In practice, the composition of the CT has always been dominated by law professors, although there have also been instances of the election of active politicians.[139] The importance of the selection of judges became particularly apparent in the course of the last years in which the CT departed significantly from previous case law.

While the CT is the entity endowed with constitutional authority to give shape to the 1997 Constitution, the influence of academia on the evolution of Polish constitutional law

---

[132] Wojciech Brzozowski, 'Obejście konstytucji' ['Evasion of the constitution'] (2014) 9 Państwo i Prawo 3, 8; Janusz Trzciński and Michał Szwast, 'Formal and informal amendments' (n 96) 230.

[133] Krzysztof Wojtyczek, *Sądownictwo konstytucyjne* (n 127) 267.

[134] Ibid, 94.

[135] CT, Judgment of 28 May 1997, Ref. No. K 26/96.

[136] CT, Judgment of 7 October 2015, Ref. No. K 12/14.

[137] CT, Judgment of 30 January 1991, Ref. No. K 11/90; CT, Judgment of 2 December 2009, Ref. No. U 10/07.

[138] See e.g. Karolina Kocemba and Michał Stambulski, 'Gotowanie żaby. Historia prawicowego konstytucjonalizmu w Polsce', *Kultura Liberalna* (30 October 2020) https://kulturaliberalna.pl/2020/10/30/koce mba-stambulski-historia-prawicowego-konstytucjonalizmu-w-polsce/ (last accessed on 23 April 2022).

[139] See, for example, the election of Marek Kotlinowski in 2006, the then MP of right-wing League of Polish Families and Deputy Marshal of the *Sejm*.

should not be neglected. First, mostly law professors served as judges at the Tribunal (at least until 2015, mostly scholars and acknowledged legal specialists were sitting on the bench of the CT representing different academic factions; this has changed). The CT bench not only comprises professors of constitutional law, but also various branches of substantive and procedural law: civil, criminal, and administrative law. This has significantly affected the way that the CT has adjudicated: the reasoning presented in the CT's judgments usually includes much more extensive legal argumentation than usual within the judgments of the Polish Supreme Court or the Supreme Administrative Court. The number of judges with academic backgrounds is definitely smaller within these courts. Secondly, the views of legal scholarship have had a significant influence on the jurisprudence of the Polish CT. In nearly every judgment, the CT has referred to the views of legal scholarship—mainly of constitutional law, but also often to the views of authors representing more specialized areas of legal scholarship, which are relevant to specific cases handled by the CT. Usually the CT cites legal texts of Polish authors, but there are also judgments referring to foreign legal scholarship. The Tribunal has referred to scholarship to strengthen its own argumentation. However, there are cases in which scholarly views have become de facto the main basis for the settlement of disputes.

ii. Dynamic Jurisprudence and Triggers of 'Normative Movement'

The jurisprudence of the CT has lived through a process of change itself continuously. Some trends which seem to have manifested in its jurisprudence have been reinforced and others have been weakened by subsequent judgments. This is to a large extent the result of three circumstances; namely, first, the variability of the composition of the CT—new judges may have different views on pre-determined issues and the way of interpreting the text of the Constitution. Second, there is the variability of the social context—the CT has adapted the Constitution's meaning to the current social variations. Third, there is the rigidity of the Constitution as delineated above which has been conducive to evolutive interpretation.[140]

Obviously, fundamental rights are a major normative area which has evolved throughout the CT's case law: the Tribunal derived from the right to a fair trial a new element—a right to the proper structure of the system of judicial authorities. The CT ruled on a constitutional complaint finding that judicial assessors (trainee judges) did not enjoy sufficient guarantees of judicial independence.[141] The broader effect of this judgment was that not only procedural and substantive provisions but also statutory provisions determining the organization of the judicial system as well as the status of judges—hence provisions of organizational character—may be invoked within and form the basis for a constitutional complaint and constitute violations of the right to a fair trial.

One major facilitator of the evolution of the Polish Constitution has been Poland's embeddedness within the international and European legal order and its linkages to other constitutional orders: among the legal texts that have had the greatest impact on the development of the Polish Constitution and the jurisprudence of the CT are international agreements binding Poland, the jurisprudence of international tribunals, which further specifies the content of these agreements, as well as the jurisprudence of constitutional courts of other states.

International agreements which Poland ratifies subsequent to the adoption of a statue which authorizes the ratification form part of the domestic legal order (see article 91 para

---

[140] Krzysztof Wojtyczek, *Sądownictwo konstytucyjne* (n 127) 245.
[141] CT, Judgment of 24 October 2007, Ref. No. SK 7/06.

1)[142] and take precedence over ordinary statutes.[143] If they cannot be reconciled with the provisions of ordinary statutes, the CT may adjudicate on the conformity of these legal provisions with such international agreements.[144] International agreements in the field of human rights protection, in particular the ECHR, have had a significant impact on the development of the Polish Constitution. Even in cases in which the competent entity initiating proceedings before the CT has not alleged that Polish law violates the provisions of an international agreement, the latter nevertheless constitutes a legal benchmark for the CT when assessing the conformity of Polish law with constitutional provisions that correspond to provisions of international agreements. The CT has also resorted to the jurisprudence of international (especially ECtHR) and supranational courts (CJEU) widely. In several judgments the CT expressed the view that article 45 para 1 of the Constitution (right to fair trial) is to be read in light of article 6 para 1 ECHR, and standards set by the ECHR and identified by the ECtHR should be used for constructing a constitutional standard.[145]

The CT has not only referred to international and supranational jurisprudence but has also sought to develop a common and uniform standard of application of the concurrent regulations.[146] Furthermore the CT has interpreted the Constitution in a way favourable or 'cordial' to international law (therein being quite similar to the FCC).[147] This interpretation technique allows for giving domestic provisions the meaning closest to applicable international rules. Acts of international law have been invoked by the CT widely—either for 'ornamental' purposes only (to strengthen argumentation) or as a basis for creating a common constitutional and international law standard which could serve as a normative benchmark for solving a particular constitutional case: after the Constitution entered into force, the ECHR was referred to within the *rationes decidendi* of its judgments about 450 times, the ICCPR nearly 150 times, the Charter of Fundamental Rights of the European Union[148] fifty times, the European Charter of Local Self-Government[149] fifty times, and the Convention on the Rights of the Child[150] twenty times.[151] The CT has emphasized that 'the respect of Poland's international obligations and care for the cohesion of the legal order (shaped as much by the domestic law as—in the degree which is constitutionally accepted—by international agreements and by supranational law), requires that there be no discrepancy between law (contents of the regulations, legal principles, legal standards) shaped by different centres of judgement on the binding force of the law, and organs applying and interpreting

---

[142] See Władysław Czapliński, 'International Law and Polish Municipal Law: Recent Jurisprudence of the Polish Supreme Judicial Organs' 53 ZaöRV (1993) 871, 873.

[143] Cf. Stanisław Biernat and Monika Kawczyńska, 'The Role of the Polish Constitution (Pre-2016): Development of a Liberal Democracy in the European and International Context' in Anneli Albi and Samo Bardutzky (eds), *National Constitutions in European and Global Governance: Democracy, Rights, the Rule of Law* (TMC Asser Press, The Hague 2019) 745, 784; Władysław Czapliński, 'Relationship between International Law and Polish Municipal Law in Light of the 1997 Constitution and of Jurisprudence' 31 Revue Belge de Droit International (1998) 259, 267.

[144] See Władysław Czapliński, 'International Law' (n 142) 873.

[145] Judgments of the CT of 4 March 2008, Ref. No. SK 3/07; of 27 May 2008, Ref. No. P 59/07; of 10 July 2008, Ref. No. P 15/08; of 17 December 2008, Ref. No. P 16/08; of 30 July 2014, Ref. No. K 23/11.

[146] Piotr Kapusta, 'Wykładnia Konstytucji RP przychylna prawu międzynarodowemu i prawu UE' ['The Interpretation of the Constitution of the Republic of Poland in a way favorable to international law and EU law'], in Jerzy Jaskiernia and Kamil Spryszak (eds), *Dwadzieścia lat obowiązywania Konstytucji* (n 128) 487–488.

[147] On the concept of '*Völkerrechtsfreundlichkeit*' see e.g. Christian Tomuschat, 'Die staatsrechtliche Entscheidung für die internationale Offenheit', in Handbuch des deutschen Staatsrechts XI (3rd edn, CF Müller, Heidelberg, 2013) § 226 para 9.

[148] 2010 OJ (C83) 389.

[149] ETS 122 – Local Self-Government, 15.X.1985.

[150] 1577 UNTS 3 (1989).

[151] Information provided in the judgments database of the CT, available at https://ipo.trybunal.gov.pl/ipo (last accessed on 23 April 2022).

law'.[152] Accordingly, a judgment of the ECtHR, referring to an individual case and prejudging the violation of a standard resulting from the ECHR by Poland, 'must thus have an effect on the assessment of regulations carried out by the Constitutional Tribunal'.[153]

Foreign constitutions and the jurisprudence of foreign constitutional courts have had a significant impact on the development of the Polish Constitution and its interpretation by the CT as well. The CT has relatively often employed the comparative method when interpreting the Constitution, referring, in particular, to the legal systems of European countries. The CT has referred to the case law of the FCC frequently, especially when constitutional issues similar to those before the CT have been previously resolved by the FCC. To mention some examples: the CT has interpreted the principle of the separation of powers in line with the jurisprudence of the German FCC (see further below). Beyond that, the CT has broadly referred to FCC jurisprudence in a judgment ruling on the constitutionality of the Polish Act of 22 November 2013 on proceedings against persons with mental disorders posing a threat to life, health, or sexual freedom of other persons which allowed for further isolation of persons sentenced to imprisonment after termination of their sentences.[154] In its reasoning the CT made reference to the position of the FCC in several judgments regarding the institution of preventive isolation of dangerous persons.[155] The CT furthermore took the judgment of the FCC of 15 February 2006[156] into consideration, in which it declared that a statute that allowed for the destruction of a civil aircraft 'when state security reasons require it, and the aircraft has been used for illegal purposes, in particular as a means of a terrorist attack' violated the constitutional principle of human dignity.[157] Furthermore, the jurisprudence of the CT on the status of EU law and its competence to adjudicate on issues of EU law is inspired by the *Solange* judgments of the FCC.[158] Its ruling on the Lisbon Treaty resonates with the rationale of the FCC (see more further below).

Not only is the Polish Constitution, therefore, characterized by an openness to international law, it is also the CT that—until the dismantlement of the constitutional order—has been open and responsive to the jurisprudence of international, European (see also below), and foreign national courts and tribunals. These have been major triggers for developing legal doctrine and an evolution of the 'normative marrow' of the 1997 Constitution.

b) Resolution of Conflicts before the Constitutional Tribunal

The function of the CT as a forum for the resolution of conflicts became frequently visible. Relevant conflicts concerned normative collisions within the multi-level structures of normativity that the Polish State is embedded in as well as horizontal inter-organ tensions.

---

[152] CT, Judgment of 18 October 2004, Ref. No. P 8/04, para 92. Translation taken from Ewa Łętowska, 'Human Rights – Universal and Normative? (A few remarks from the Polish Perspective)' in *Rapports Polonaise, XVIIIth International Congress of Comparative Law*, 2010, 267, 279 (footnote 19).

[153] Ibid.

[154] CT, Judgment of 23 November 2016, Ref. No. K 6/14. See on the Act Dziennik Ustaw, item 24 (2014).

[155] The Polish CT referred to German Federal Constitutional Court's judgments in cases 2 BvR 2302/11, 2 BvR 2365/09, 2 BvR 1048/11, 2 BvR 2365/09, 2 BvR 740/10, 2 BvR 2333/08, 2 BvR 1152/10, 2 BvR 571/10.

[156] Federal Constitutional Court, Judgment of 15 February 2006, BvR 357/05.

[157] CT, Judgment of 30 September 2008, Ref. No. K 44/07. The judgment concerned article 122a of the Aviation Act (2002) (translation by the authors). The CT pointed out in its reasoning—referring to the German Federal Constitutional Court's judgment of 15 February 2006—that the effect of the provision under review is "the 'depersonification' and 'reification' of those persons on board the renegade aircraft who are not aggressors ...", see for this translation Wojciech Sadurski. Rights Before Courts (Springer, Dordrecht, 2nd edn. 2014) 181 et seq. These people only become the object of the rescue operation, aimed at preventing hypothetical, further and probably larger losses than the targeted terrorist attack could cause.

[158] CT, Judgment of 11 May 2005, Ref. No. K 18/04.

An example of a serious conflict that was to be resolved before the CT and led to a 'constitutional recalibration' concerned Poland's accession to the EU. Three Eurosceptic groups amongst the *Sejm* Members questioned the conformity of the Treaty on Poland's accession to the European Union (EU), signed on 16 April 2003 in Athens (hereinafter: Treaty) with the Constitution and initiated a review proceeding before the CT. The ruling in this case was fundamental not only for the membership of Poland in the EU, but also for determining the relationship between national law (including the Constitution) and EU law, as well as the scope of the CT's competence to adjudicate on EU law.[159] In its judgment of 11 May 2005 the CT ruled that the provisions of the Treaty were consistent with the Constitution.[160]

First, the CT analysed the conformity of the delegation of certain competences to EU institutions with the constitutional principle of sovereignty (article 4). According to article 90 para 1, '[t]he Republic of Poland may, by virtue of international agreements, delegate to an international organization or international institution the competence of organs of State authority in relation to certain matters'. The CT explained that the delegation of competences 'in relation to certain matters' must be understood as prohibiting the conferral 'of all the competences of a given organ of the state', the conferral of 'competences in relation to all matters in a given field' and the conferral of 'competences in relation to the essence of the matters determining the remit of a given state organ'.[161] In light of this, the competences which are delegated are to be defined exactly. By accepting the Constitution in the referendum, the 'Nation' itself decided that it would also accept the possibility of subjecting Polish authorities and citizens to the law established by an international organization or an international body (secondary law). Beyond that, the Nation consented—within the referendum—that such law would apply directly and have precedence in the event of a conflict of laws. However, the CT stressed that the provisions of the Constitution do not constitute grounds for authorizing an international organization (or its bodies) to enact law or make decisions that would contradict the Constitution. In particular, the Constitution cannot be used to delegate competences to the extent that 'would prevent the Republic of Poland from functioning as a sovereign and democratic state'.[162]

The CT also focused on the relationship between the Constitution and EU law. Considering the principle of the primacy of EU law over domestic law developed by the CJEU, the CT ruled that collisions in a multi-level legal system should be resolved by ways of a reciprocal, harmonious interpretation.[163] However, in the case of a contradiction between constitutional rules and principles and EU law (having direct effect) which are unresolvable by mere interpretation ('irreconcilable collision') the supremacy of the EU norm in relation to the constitutional norm cannot be accepted. In such circumstance, it would fall within the sphere of competence of the Polish legislative to decide upon the amendment of the Constitution, the initiation of a change of EU law or, ultimately, upon opting for a withdrawal from the EU.[164] This decision should be taken by the sovereign, which is the Polish

---

[159] See Krzysztof Wójtowicz, 'Komentarz do wyroku Trybunału Konstytucyjnego z dnia 11 maja 2005 r. sygn. akt K 18/04' [Commentary on the judgment of the Constitutional Tribunal of May 11, 2005, Ref. No. K 18/04], in Leszek Garlicki, Marta Derlatka and Marcin Wiącek (eds), *Na straży państwa prawa* (n 38) 502; Krzysztof Wójtowicz, *Sądy konstytucyjne wobec prawa Unii Europejskiej* [*Constitutional Courts with regard to the Law of the European Union*] (Biuro Trybunału Konstytucyjnego, Warsaw, 2012).

[160] CT, Judgment of 11 May 2005, Ref. No. K 18/04. For the Treaty cf. OJ 2003 L 236, 17 f.

[161] See also CT, Judgment of 24 November 2010, Ref. No. K 32/09, para 2.1.

[162] Ibid, para 2.5.

[163] Cp. Krzysztof Wójtowicz, 'Komentarz' (n 159) 517.

[164] See generally Aleksandra Kustra, 'The Polish Constitutional Tribunal and the judicial Europeanization of the Constitution' (2015) XXXV Polish Yearbook of International Law 193.

Nation, or the state organ, which according to the Constitution is entitled to represent the 'Nation'.[165]

In its 'accession judgment', the CT also confirmed the conformity of the mechanism of the preliminary ruling procedure with the Constitution. According to the CT the application of EU law (in accordance with case law of the CJEU) in the settlement of a specific case in line with a preliminary ruling by the CJEU is a consequence of the previously made sovereign decision of Poland to join the EU. By ratifying the Treaty, Poland approved the division of functions within the institutional system of the EU. It would be the CJEU that is competent to interpret EU law and safeguard its uniform application. Yet, the interpretation of the EU law, carried out by the CJEU, shall not go beyond the powers that have been conferred upon the EU by Member States. Furthermore, it should stand in line with the principle of subsidiarity that determines the activities of EU institutions as well as correspond with the idea of a mutual loyalty between EU institutions and Member States.[166]

Obviously, EU law has become a major force in the evolution of the substance of the Polish Constitution. One example is particularly illustrative in that regard (and here we come back again to the CT's accession judgment): the CT—under the influence of EU provisions—reviewed the meaning of article 62 para 1 of the Constitution, which explicitly restricts the right to vote for organs of local government only to Polish citizens.[167] This became particularly relevant considering article 22(1) TFEU (formerly article 19 TEC) which establishes that '[e]very citizen of the Union residing in a Member State of which he is not a national shall have the right to vote and to stand as a candidate at municipal elections in the Member State in which he resides, under the same conditions as nationals of that State'. In light of this, under EU primary law, the right to vote in municipal elections which was under the constitutional provisions granted exclusively to Polish citizens has been extended to EU citizens.[168] The CT ruled that article 22 para 1 TFEU (formerly article 19 para 1 TEC) is not inconsistent with articles 1 and 62 para 1 of the Constitution.[169] The unequivocal linguistic layer of the text of the Constitution has thus been adapted in light of the EU integration. However, some authors have assessed that such a far-reaching reinterpretation contrary to the express wording of the Constitution was unacceptable and that it was advisable to pass an appropriate formal amendment to the Constitution.[170]

Not always did an interference on the part of the CT resolve constitutional conflicts and, in some cases, the CT stands at the centre of constitutional conflicts.

One of these 'spheres of conflict' concerns the competence of the CT to issue so-called 'interpretative judgments'. The latter rule on the conformity or non-conformity of a given provision with higher-ranking provisions and also on the specific interpretation of lower-ranking provisions.[171] The CT issues interpretative judgments regularly. They only decide on the conformity or non-conformity of a given provision in the shape of a specific

---

[165] CT, Judgment of 16 November 2011, Ref. No. SK 45/09 para. 2.7; CT, Judgment of 11 May 2005, Ref. No. K 18/04.

[166] Ibid.

[167] See CT, Judgment of 11 May 2005, Ref. No. K 18/04; Krzysztof Kozłowski, 'Ewolucja pojęcia obywatelstwa w okresie obowiązywania Konstytucji RP z 1997 r.—zagadnienia wybrane' ['The evolution of the concept of citizenship under the Constitution of the Republic of Poland of 1997—selected issues'], in Jerzy Jaskiernia and Kamil Spryszak (eds), *Dwadzieścia lat obowiązywania Konstytucji* (n 128) 195 f.

[168] Kozłowski, ibid, 196.

[169] CT, Judgment of 11 May 2005, Ref. No. K 18/04, ruling 9.

[170] Krzysztof Kozłowski, 'Ewolucja pojęcia obywatelstwa' (n 167) 196.

[171] See Monika Florczak-Wątor, *Orzeczenia Trybunału Konstytucyjnego i ich skutki prawne* [*Decisions of the Constitutional Tribunal and their Legal Consequences*] (Ars boni et aequi, Poznań, 2006) 93–103; Krzysztof Wojtyczek, *Sądownictwo konstytucyjne* (n 127) 227–228.

interpretation that surfaced in the jurisprudence of ordinary courts. Thus, the CT indicates which interpretation is constitutionally incompatible, thereby 'saving' the provision. The Supreme Court has denied the CT's competence to issue such interpretative judgments in several findings.[172] It has contested in particular negative interpretative judgments which indicate how a provision must not be understood by the courts[173] and has assumed that negative interpretative judgments of the CT cannot form the basis for reopening court proceedings after the CT's judgment.[174] The interpretation of legal provisions would lie within the competences of courts which decide on specific cases and no other body would be competent to impose its interpretation on them as solely binding. According to the position of the Supreme Court, the courts are bound only by such rulings of the CT which declare a provision to be void due to its unconstitutionality (article 190 para 1).[175] This long-lasting conflict between the two most important judicial bodies within the Polish constitutional order is obviously largely detrimental to legal certainty and has affected the level of public trust in the courts negatively.

A further example[176] of a central conflict that raised questions in terms of an evolutive interpretation of the Constitution—and is not yet resolved—concerns the admissibility of judicial proceedings to challenge the refusal of the President to appoint judges, contrary to a motion to appoint filed by the National Council of the Judiciary. According to article 179 of the Constitution, judges are 'appointed for an indefinite period by the President of the Republic on the motion of the National Council of the Judiciary'. The presidential act of appointing a judge is her/his prerogative (article 144 para 3 pt 17) and does not require the countersignature of the Prime Minister for its validity. In practice, two different Presidents refused to appoint around a dozen of judges despite the motion of the National Council of the Judiciary.[177] Persons who were not appointed filed complaints to administrative courts demanding the judicial review of the legality of the relevant presidential omissions. In the case law of administrative courts, such complaints were consistently rejected, because the courts assumed that they did not have the competence to control the exercise of presidential prerogatives.[178] In Poland, therefore, no judicial proceeding exists in which it would be possible to review and challenge presidential refuses to appoint judges. Such arbitrariness is detrimental not only to the formation of an independent judiciary, but also to the constitutional right of equal access to the public service of candidates for the office of a judge (article 60).

---

[172] See *inter alia*: Supreme Court of Poland, Decision of 6 May 2003, Ref. No. I CO 7/03 and resolution of seven judges of the Supreme Court of 17 December 2009, Ref. No. III PZP 2/09.

[173] Krzysztof Wojtyczek, *Sądownictwo konstytucyjne* (n 127) 228.

[174] Resolution of seven judges of the Supreme Court of 17 December 2009, Ref. No. III PZP 2/09. According to article 190 para 4 of the Constitution, 'a judgment of the Constitutional Tribunal on the non-conformity to the Constitution, an international agreement or statute, of a normative act on the basis of which a legally effective judgment of a court, a final administrative decision or settlement of other matters was issued, shall be a basis for reopening proceedings, or for quashing the decision or other settlement in a manner and on principles specified in provisions applicable to the given proceedings'.

[175] Resolution of seven judges of the Supreme Court of 17 December 2009, Ref. No. III PZP 2/09.

[176] Another significant conflict concerned the competence of the President and Prime Minister in terms of the representation of Poland within the European Council which we will discuss further below when reflecting on the separation of powers (see D. 5.).

[177] In 2008, the President of the Republic of Poland refused to appoint five persons to hold office as judges of regional courts and five persons to hold office as judges of district courts. In 2016, the President refused to appoint one person as a judge of a voivodship administrative court, one person as a judge of the Court of Appeals, seven persons as judges of regional courts, one person as a judge of district court. These decisions were not substantiated.

[178] See, for instance Decision of the Supreme Administrative Court of Poland of 9 October 2012, Ref. No. I OSK 1874/12 and Decision of the Supreme Administrative Court of Poland of 9 December 2017, Ref. No. I OSK 857/17.

This leaves us with following preliminary observations. While the Constitution can be characterized as rigid, the jurisprudence of the CT has kept the Constitution very much alive. The Constitution of 1997, as it has been interpreted by the CT (until its illiberal capture), allows for and safeguards the fulfilment of obligations stemming from international and European Law on the part of Poland. Consequently, as intended by the drafters, the 1997 Constitution, in the guise of the jurisprudence of the CT (until its political instrumentalization), created the basis for Poland's 'Western' and European integration. The CT became a vibrant part of the multi-level cooperation of and discourse between courts in Europe. This development has come to a halt since 2015.

C. The Caesura: The Dismantlement of the Constitutional Order

The year 2015 marked a major challenge for the Polish constitutional order. The 2015 elections led to a change of the power equilibrium in the Polish parliament, resulting in the formation of the 'United Right' government. In the same year Andrzej Duda, a key figure of the 'United Right', was elected to become the President of Poland. This very year and these changes in the political landscape marked the beginning of the so-called 'constitutional crisis' in Poland.[179]

The most vivid manifestations of the 'constitutional crisis' which is not yet settled are, somewhat euphemistically put, 'extra-constitutional changes of the constitutional order' by the 'United Right' not having the appropriate majority within the legislative bodies to adopt formal amendments to the Constitution.[180] Between 2015 and 2019, various unconstitutional activities of the most important executive bodies (including the President and the Prime Minister) took place in Poland. Beyond that, unconstitutional bills were passed. The Constitution has been disregarded or interpreted in bad faith by public authorities in order to achieve ad hoc political goals. These encroachments upon Poland as a state ruled by law have been justified by politicians in media statements frequently with the democratic mandate given by the Polish people within elections—echoing a distorted majoritarian concept of democratic rule which eradicates minority protection—or the necessity of a fundamental change within the Polish state which would be expected by the Polish people.[181]

At this point only some moments indicative of the dismantlement of the constitutional order shall be mentioned. A major moment of this crisis was the paralysis and political instrumentalization of the CT which has had severe implications for the way constitutional

---

[179] See here and for the depiction of the various moments of the 'constitutional crisis' in the text further below for example Małgorzata Szuleka, Marcin Wolny and Marcin Szwed, *The Constitutional Crisis in Poland 2015–2016*, Helsinki Foundation for Human Rights 2016, at https://www.hfhr.pl/wp-content/uploads/2016/09/HFHR_The-constitutional-crisis-in-Poland-2015-2016.pdf (last accessed 23 April 2022). See also Paulina Starski, 'The Power of the Rule of Law: The Polish Constitutional Tribunal's Forceful Reaction', VerfBlog, 17 March 2016, https://verfassu ngsblog.de/the-power-of-the-rule-of-law-the-polish-constitutional-tribunals-forceful-reaction/ (last accessed on 23 April 2022); Paulina Starski, 'Constitutionalism in times of extraordinary developments: Resolving the Polish constitutional crisis', *constitutionnet.org* (13 April 2016), at http://constitutionnet.org/news/constitutionalism-times-extraordinary-developments-resolving-polish-constitutional-crisis (last accessed on 23 April 2022).

[180] See Janusz Trzciński and Michał Szwast, 'Formal and informal amendments' (n 96) 237 and scholarship cited therein, in particular: Mirosław Wyrzykowski, 'Bypassing the Constitution or changing the constitutional order outside the constitution' in Andrzej Szmyt and Bogusław Banaszak (eds), *Transformation of Law Systems* (n 97) 159 f.

[181] See e.g. 'Kaczyński: Państwo prawa nie musi być państwem demokratycznym' Dziennik Gazeta Prawna (4 June 2016) https://www.gazetaprawna.pl/wiadomosci/artykuly/949242,kaczynski-panstwo-prawa-nie-musi-byc-panstwem-demokratycznym.html (last accessed on 23 April 2022).

conflicts are and can be resolved in Poland. Examples of the President's unconstitutional actions include the refusal to take the oath from three judges of the CT chosen by the *Sejm* in accordance with law, taking the oath from three judges chosen to the CT unlawfully, pardoning one politician of the ruling party who was not convicted by a final court judgment[182] (the criminal proceedings concerning his *ultra vires* acts were still pending), appointing judges to the Supreme Court despite an ongoing appeal procedure against the resolutions of the National Council of the Judiciary to that respect, retiring the judges of the Supreme Court and the Supreme Administrative Court without any justification on the basis of an obviously unconstitutional statute.[183] The refusal of the Prime Minister to order the publication of the judgments of the CT in the Journal of Laws—despite the explicit wording of article 190 para 2[184]—manifested her disregard for the Constitution.

Between 2015 and 2019 the *Sejm* passed bills that deprived some constitutional bodies (e.g. the National Council of Radio Broadcasting and Television) of their key competences or allowed arbitrary staff changes in public bodies and courts, leaving the determination of their composition to the sole discretion of executive authorities. Examples of the latter include the already mentioned lowering of the retirement age of the judges of the Supreme Court and the Supreme Administrative Court and rendering them dependent on arbitrary decisions of the President in that matter, replacing the presidents of the common courts, 'staff cleansing' in the civil service and tax administration, resulting in the dismissal of thousands of employees and officers, shortening the term of office of the First President of the Supreme Court and the National Council of the Judiciary which were constitutionally determined, as well as allowing the election of judges to the National Council for the Judiciary by the *Sejm*.[185] These changes were mainly directed at the personal composition of the relevant bodies. They were intended to completely subordinate the latter. This is particularly severe in light of the fact that these bodies enjoy constitutionally determined independence and serve as protective shields against the arbitrariness of decisions made by public authorities and violations of human rights of individuals by the acts (and omissions) of the executive and legislative.

Obviously, these acts will not be determined as unconstitutional in the near future by the CT (albeit the CJEU asserted that Poland violated, with its attack against the independence of the judiciary, EU law in various respects as we shall see in a moment).[186] The personal changes and modifications regarding the organization and procedure of the CT introduced at the turn of 2015 and 2016 resulted not only in the Tribunal's blockade but also in its politization up to the point of severe doubts as to its impartiality and independence. The CT currently legitimizes in its jurisprudence the unconstitutional changes implemented since 2015. As a result, a significant decrease in the number of cases submitted to the CT can be observed, showing that authorized entities (e.g. the Commissioner for Citizen's Rights, courts or individuals) do not perceive the CT as an independent body that effectively

---

[182] In the resolution of 31 May 2017, Ref. No. I KZP 4/17, the Supreme Court held that the presidential right of pardon may be applied only with regard to persons who have been convicted by final court judgment. The Constitutional Tribunal, in its Judgment of 17 July 2018, Ref. No. K 9/17, purported a different view and held that the President has a competence to pardon even before a final conviction (so-called 'individual abolition').

[183] Ustawa z dnia 12 lipca 2017 r. o zmianie ustawy – Prawo o ustroju sądów powszechnych oraz niektórych innych ustaw, Dziennik Ustaw, item 1452 (2017).

[184] According to article 190 para 2 of the Constitution, 'judgments of the Constitutional Tribunal regarding matters specified in Article 188, shall be required to be immediately published in the official publication in which the original normative act was promulgated. If a normative act has not been promulgated, then the judgment shall be published in the Official Gazette of the Republic of Poland, *Monitor Polski*.'

[185] They were elected by judges before.

[186] See e.g. CJEU, Judgment of 5 November 2019, Case C-192/18 (ECLI:EU:C:2019:924).

protects human rights in Poland.[187] This view is shared by various international bodies.[188] All activities of the legislative or executive authorities, *praeter* or *contra* the applicable constitutional rules, have resulted in the emergence of the phenomenon of a 'real constitution'—a term that describes the 'real' and not politically disformed content of the Constitution. These activities degenerate the content and previous understanding of the text of the Constitution which formed in judicial decisions based on appropriate procedures[189] and bodies whose composition conformed with constitutional and statutory demands.

When analysing the constitutional foundations of the system of Poland—as shall be done in a moment—one should bear in mind the significant discrepancy between, on the one hand, the letter of the Constitution and the established understanding of its founding principles, and the political realities during the so-called 'rule of law-crisis' on the other. In theory, the 1997 Constitution, establishing a system of liberal democracy based on respect for the independence of the judiciary, the rule of law and the protection of human rights, remains binding and has not even been amended. In practice, however, under the rule of the 'United Right', some of these principles and concepts were called into question. This unconstitutional practice is not able to change the Constitution and so it would not be justified—as this chapter suggests—to discuss the constitutional foundations of the Republic of Poland solely through the prism of the 'rule of law-crisis'. Nevertheless, it is also impossible to completely ignore the political transformations that have taken place in recent years.

Before the 'United Right' came to power, basic constitutional principles, such as the independence of the judiciary or the separation of powers were not fundamentally questioned. Regrettably, this does not mean that the political practice has always fully complied with the letter and spirit of the Constitution. Particularly controversial in this regard was the election of judges of the CT by the parliament in 2015,[190] which was subsequently recognized as partly[191] unconstitutional by the CT[192] and served the 'United Right' as a useful pretext for the adoption of unconstitutional changes. Of course, it can be argued that such practices were only an excuse for an attack on the Constitution by the current government which would have happened regardless of the circumstances, but it would be ill-guided to ignore that they created an atmosphere of disrespect for the Constitution.

An important factor facilitating the attack on the Constitution was the low public trust in the judiciary. Research by the Public Opinion Research Center (CBOS)[193] shows that in March 2015, i.e. half a year before the 'United Right' took power, only 25 per cent of

---

[187] Sixty-two applications, seventy-four questions of law, and seventy-one constitutional complaints have been submitted to the CT in 2013. However, in 2017, only eighteen applications, twenty-one court's questions of law and thirty-two constitutional complaints were submitted.

[188] See Report of UN the Special Rapporteur on the independence of judges and lawyers on his mission to Poland, point 73, where it is pointed out that '[t]he first victim of this unilateral approach has been the Constitutional Tribunal. Today, the Tribunal is still in place and its functions—as set out in the Constitution—have not been formally changed. Its legitimacy and independence, however, have been seriously undermined and the Tribunal cannot ensure, at present, an independent and effective review of the constitutionality of legislative acts adopted by the legislator. This situation casts serious doubts over its capacity to protect constitutional principles and to uphold human rights and fundamental freedoms', see http://doc.rmf.pl/rmf_fm/store/UN_REPORT.pdf (last accessed on 23 April 2022).

[189] Leszek Garlicki, 'Standardy demokratyczne' (n 128) 434.

[190] See e.g. Wojciech Sadurski, *Poland's Constitutional Breakdown* (n 6) 62.

[191] The election of two judges whose terms of office ended on 2 December 2015 or would end on 8 December 2015 was found to be inconsistent with article 194 para 1 of the Constitution.

[192] CT, Judgment of 3 December 2015, Ref. No. K 34/15.

[193] Public Opinion Research Center (CBOS), Report concerning the Assessment of pPublic Institutions, Warsaw, March 2015, 13 at https://www.cbos.pl/SPISKOM.POL/2015/K_042_15.PDF (last accessed on 23 April 2022).

respondents assessed the courts and the judiciary positively. The negative assessment was even greater: it amounted to as much as 52 per cent. The ratings of the CT were a little bit more favourable—only 12 per cent of respondents assessed it negatively, and 42 per cent positively. However, the largest group of respondents, as much as 46 per cent, gave the answer 'It's hard to say', which may suggest that a large part of society was not even aware of the functions of the CT.[194] This leads us to another problem, which would be the relatively low awareness of the constitutional standards amongst Polish citizens. According to the survey conducted in 2017, although 68 per cent of the respondents answered that the provisions and principles of the Constitution have an important or very important influence on the lives of ordinary citizens, 45 per cent admitted to not having read the Constitution even partly.[195] Symptomatically, the highest rate of those who admitted that they had not read the Constitution was the potential electorate of 'Law and Justice'.[196]

Overall, the rule of law crisis has revealed several flaws of the Polish Constitution (see further below). In particular, the election of CT judges solely by the *Sejm* (see above) without the participation of other organs of power or non-political circles led to an excessively politicized election process.

Finally, when discussing the reasons of why the support for the 'United Right'—despite all its unconstitutional moves—remains at a constant, high level (about 40–45 per cent[197]), social issues must not be ignored. Apparently, the expansion of the welfare state through an increase in spending on social benefits (in particular the so-called '500+' programme[198]) and the lowering of the retirement age[199] has been for many citizens far more important than the negative effects of attacks on the rule of law. This might be short-sighted, but, at the same time, it shows that social and economic inequalities may threaten the 'democratic state ruled by law' and can be used by various populist groups to undermine the constitutional order.

These political and social circumstances are to be considered when contextualizing the legal changes introduced by the 'United Right' and when making an effort to understand the 'constitutional crisis'. The latter endeavours require also to pay due attention to the justifications put forward by the 'United Right' for its actions.

The activists of the 'United Right' perceived the CT as an undemocratic 'third chamber of parliament'.[200] If the Tribunal was not reformed, 'United Right' representatives argued, it would block all laws that were necessary to implement the 'repair of the Republic' programme.[201] 'United Right' politicians and media sympathetic to them also pointed out, *inter alia*, that the system of constitutional adjudication is not necessary at all, which could be

---

[194] Ibid, 15.

[195] CBOS, Report for the Twentieth Anniversary of the Adoption of the Polish Constitution, Warsaw, March 2017, 3–5 at https://www.cbos.pl/SPISKOM.POL/2017/K_037_17.PDF (last accessed on 23 April 2022).

[196] Ibid, 5.

[197] In the last election to the *Sejm* (13 October 2019) the 'Law and Justice' received approximately 43.6 per cent of votes see at https://sejmsenat2019.pkw.gov.pl/sejmsenat2019/pl/wyniki/sejm/pl (accessed on 7 December 2022).

[198] 500 + is a welfare benefit for parents of a value of PLN 500 (about EUR 120) monthly per each child.

[199] In 2012 the parliament, dominated by the Civic Platform and its coalition partner (the Polish People's Party (*Polskie Stronnictwo Ludowe*)), adopted a law which raised a retirement age from sixty (for women) and sixty-five (for men) to sixty-seven for both sexes. In 2017 Law and Justice reversed these changes.

[200] Janusz Wojciechowski, 'Trybunał Konstytucyjny to trzecia izba parlamentu' [The Constitutional Tribunal is the Third Chamber of the Parliament] *NaszDziennik.pl* (24 November 2015) https://naszdziennik.pl/polska-kraj/147695,trybunal-konstytucyjny-to-trzecia-izba-parlamentu.html (last accessed on 23 April 2022).

[201] Andrzej Gajcy and Michał Szułdrzyński, 'Kaczyński: Nie chcę większości w TK' [Kaczyński: I don't want the majority in CT], interview with Jarosław Kaczyński, chairman of the 'Law and Justice', *Rzeczpospolita* (17 January 2016) https://www.rp.pl/tk_kaczynski#ap-5 (last accessed on 23 April 2022), where Kaczyński explains that: '[the Constitutional Tribunal] was supposed to be a kind of third chamber of the parliament that would not allow a new, legally elected authority for what we call the repair of the Republic'.

evidenced by the fact that, in many Western democracies, there were no similar bodies.[202] Eventually, however, the 'United Right' refrained from abolishing the CT or even from weakening its formal powers. This was not necessary, because the personal changes in the CT were sufficient to achieve its political neutralization. The Tribunal is no longer an obstacle to the implementation of the ruling majority's policies, as it issues fewer judgments than in the past (for instance, in 2014 there were seventy-three judgments on merits of the case, sixty-three judgments in 2015, thirty-six judgments in 2016, 2017, and 2018 respectively, and thirty-one judgments in 2019)[203] and even when it examines some controversial laws passed by the PiS-dominated parliament, it usually rules that they are in accordance with the Constitution.[204] What is more, the ruling majority sometimes treats the CT as a useful tool to achieve its own political purposes.[205] In this way, the activities of the CT may be considered as an illustration of a broader phenomenon described in the literature as an 'abusive judicial review'[206] or the emergence of 'inverted constitutional courts'.[207]

With regard to the attacks on the independence of the Supreme Court and common courts, two arguments were often raised. First, although 'United Right' activists did not deny the very significance of the independence of the judiciary, they argued that in the Polish reality this independence led to the judges being granted the status of an 'extraordinary caste' with undeserved privileges.[208] The fight against this phenomenon was to be fought by introducing new rules for the selection of judges sitting on the National Council of the Judiciary and creating a special Disciplinary Chamber at the Supreme Court. Eventually, however, these reforms did not lead to any noticeable 'moral renewal' of the judiciary. Furthermore, despite the frequent use of rhetoric referring to democracy and the will of the sovereign on the part of the 'United Right' the majority of the introduced legislative reforms did not lead to an actual increase in the direct influence of citizens on the administration of justice. The only exception has been the introduction of lay judges (pol. *ławnicy*) to certain types of proceedings before the Supreme Court.[209]

---

[202] See e.g. 'Min. Waszczykowski do Timmermansa: To kiedy w Holandii powstanie Trybunał Konstytucyjny?' [Minister Waszczykowski to Timmermans: So when will the Constitutional Tribunal be established in the Netherlands?] *Telewizjarepublika.pl* (17 February 2017), https://telewizjarepublika.pl/min-waszczykowski-do-timmermansa-to-kiedy-w-holandii-powstanie-trybunal-konstytucyjny,44738.html (last accessed on 23 April 2022).

[203] Information provided in the judgment database of the CT https://ipo.trybunal.gov.pl/ipo (last accessed on 23 April 2022). See also e.g. Beata Szepietowska, 'Działalność orzecznicza Trybunału Konstytucyjnego w latach 2014–2017' [Judicial activity of the Constitutional Tribunal in the years 2014–2017], in Katarzyna Łakomiec (ed), *Funkcjonowanie Trybunału Konstytucyjnego w latach 2014–2017* [*The functioning of the Constitutional Tribunal in the years 2014–2017*] (Fundacja Batorego, Warsaw 2018) 23–32, http://www.batory.org.pl/upload/files/Progr amy%20operacyjne/Forum%20Idei/Funkcjonowanie%20Trybunalu%20Konstytucyjnego.pdf (last accessed on 23 April 2022).

[204] See in particular, CT, Judgment of 16 March 2017, Ref. No. Kp 1/17 (concerning amendment to the Law on assemblies); CT, Judgment of 25 March 2019, Ref. No. K 12/18 (concerning amendment to the Act on the National Judiciary Council).

[205] Wojciech Sadurski, *Poland's Constitutional Breakdown* (n 6) 79–84.

[206] David Landau and Rosalind Dixon, 'Abusive Judicial Review: Courts Against Democracy' (2020) 53 UC Davis Law Review 1313.

[207] Pablo Castillo-Ortiz, 'The Illiberal Abuse of Constitutional Courts in Europe' (2019) 15 European Constitutional Law Review 48, 67–71.

[208] See e.g. 'Ziobro: Zmiany w KRS są konstytucyjne. Chcemy, aby odeszła do historii nadzwyczajna kasta', *Dziennik.pl* (30 January 2017) https://wiadomosci.dziennik.pl/polityka/artykuly/541435,zbigniew-ziobro-krs-krajowa-rada-sadownictwa-konstytucja-sedziowie-pis.html (last accessed on 23 April 2022); 'Zbigniew Ziobro: prawo w Polsce jest i będzie równe wobec wszystkich', *Fakt* (5 February 2020) https://www.fakt.pl/wydarze nia/polityka/zbigniew-ziobro-komentuje-podpisanie-ustawy-dyscyplinujacej-sedziow/82f05v7 (last accessed on 23 April 2022); 'Ziobro: dzisiejszy dzień to koniec „nadzwyczajnej kasty"' *TVP Info* (20 July 2017) https://www.tvp. info/33294822/ziobro-dzisiejszy-dzien-to-koniec-nadzwyczajnej-kasty (last accessed on 23 April 2022).

[209] Namely in the proceedings before the Disciplinary Chamber and in the proceedings concerning the so-called extraordinary complaint.

The second argument that the 'United Right' employed to justify changes in the judiciary is based on the idea of 'de-communization'. The almost paranoid and at times merely ostensible fight against the 'communist baggage of the past' has always played an important role in the 'United Right' programme. In the sphere of the judiciary, 'de-communization' was particularly referred to in the context of the mandatory age reform of the Supreme Court. Lowering the age and giving the President the power to decide whether a judge can still perform active judicial service was allegedly aimed at those who, in the past, convicted activists of the anti-communist opposition, thereby taking them off the Supreme Court.[210] However, this rhetoric is far from convincing: first, the lowering of the retirement age affected also judges who were in no way involved in human rights violations during the era of communism.[211] In this context it is worth noting that even the former undersecretary of state in the Ministry of Justice, judge Łukasz Piebiak, stated in 2016 that the number of judges who started their professional careers already in times of communism, was relatively low: 'out of the total number of 9,958 common judges—district, circuit and appellate courts (as of 31 March 2016), almost 44 per cent (4,376) were born after 1972, and only 25 per cent of the total number of judges (2,578) are those born before 1964, that is, those who turned twenty-five in 1989 and could work professionally'.[212] Second, media reports showed that one of the most prominent 'United Right' politicians who took an active part in legislative activities leading to the statutes 'reforming' the judiciary, and in 2019 became a judge of the CT, served as a prosecutor in the 1980s, allegedly signed the act of indictment against an anti-communist activist.[213]

As a result of the dismantling of the constitutional order and the capture of its institutional safeguards, it became necessary to look for alternative mechanisms to protect the rule of law and individual rights and freedoms within the Polish constitutional order. Proposed alternative solutions involved a more frequent direct application of the Constitution by ordinary courts and activating the so-called 'dispersed constitutional review' of statutes. In practice, however, courts have rarely used this option (see below). Hope then focussed on international instruments, in particular proceedings before the CJEU. Polish courts, having lost their confidence in the CT, began to submit, more and more frequently, preliminary references to the CJEU.[214] Many of these references concerned various aspects of the protection of the rule of law, especially the preservation of an independent judiciary.[215] Importantly,

---

[210] See e.g. 'Morawiecki: Widzę w SN tych samych sędziów, którzy skazywali moich kolegów na więzienie' [Morawiecki: I see in the Supreme Court the same judges who sentenced my colleagues to prison], *Dziennik.pl* (7 October 2017), https://wiadomosci.dziennik.pl/polityka/artykuly/559846,mateusz-morawiecki-system-sadowniczy-kula-u-nogi-rozwoju-gospodarczego.html (last accessed on 23 April 2022).

[211] Most notably, it affected judge Stanisław Zabłocki, who worked as a lawyer during communism and in 1990 represented Polish war hero, Witold Pilecki, sentenced to death by communists, in his posthumous legal rehabilitation trial.

[212] Łukasz Piebiak, undersecretary of state in the Ministry of Justice, response to the interpellation no 3813, 29 June 2016, https://www.sejm.gov.pl/sejm8.nsf/interpelacjaTresc.xsp?documentId=3636196D666C5562C1257FE20048F4C9&view=S (last accessed on 23 April 2022). Translation by the authors.

[213] 'The inside story of prosecutor Piotrowicz's career. How can you lie like that to people?', *TVN24* (15 November 2017) https://www.tvn.pl/tvn24-news-in-english,157,m/the-inside-story-of-prosecutor-piotrowicz-s-career-how-can-you-lie-like-that-to-people,790403.html (last accessed on 23 April 2022).

[214] In 2015 Polish courts submitted fifteen references for preliminary rulings, nineteen in 2016, nineteen in 2017, thirty-one in 2018, and thirty-nine in 2019 (Court of Justice of the European Union, *Annual Report 2019. Judicial Activity*, Luxembourg 2020, 163, https://curia.europa.eu/jcms/upload/docs/application/pdf/2020-05/qd-ap-20-001-en-n.pdf (last accessed on 23 April 2022).

[215] See e.g. Request for a preliminary ruling from the Supreme Court lodged on 3 October 2018, Case C-625/18; Request for a preliminary ruling from the Supreme Administrative Court lodged on 28 December 2018, Case C-824/18; Request for a preliminary ruling from the Supreme Court lodged on 26 June 2019, Case C-487/19; Request for a preliminary ruling from the Circuit Court in Warsaw lodged on 15 October 2019, Case C-749/19; Request for a preliminary ruling from the Circuit Court in Łódź lodged on 3 September 2018, Case C-558/18.

the European Commission became aware of the threat to the European integration resulting from the 'rule of law crisis' in Poland and brought several actions against Poland under Article 258 TFEU to the CJEU.[216] As a result, the CJEU has, in recent years, issued several highly significant judgments in cases relating to the 'rule of law crisis' in Poland. These concerned the lowering of the compulsory retirement age of judges of the Supreme Court[217] and the independence of the judges of the newly set up Disciplinary Chamber of the Supreme Court.[218] The former de facto forced the Polish authorities to withdraw from the extremely controversial reform, while the latter paved the way for the questioning of judgments issued by judges whose independence was in doubt and whose appointment had been illegal.[219]

To sum up: the 'United Right' and its legislative projects have significantly weakened many constitutional guarantees forming part of the rule of law, including, in particular, the independence of the judiciary and the CT. These 'reforms' have not yet pursued the implementation of some coherent vision of the state and its architecture but were rather aimed at the elimination of systemic safeguards that the 'United Right' treated as useless obstacles to its endeavours. The constitution has been violated severely in various respects and institutions have been captured in an illiberal turn. This 'constitutional crisis' marks a rupture in the evolution of the Polish legal order as a 'liberal democracy' and a deviation from the axiology of the 1997 Constitution which we shall turn to now.

D. The Axiology of the Constitution of 1997: Basic Structures and Concepts

Considering the 'constitutional crisis' delineated above, it is crucial to remind ourselves of the axiology of the 1997 Constitution. We submit that it continues to enjoy legal validity. This section shall evidence two points. First, the Polish constitutional system has been intact for a considerable time and second, the constitutional edifice particularly created by jurisprudence of the CT before its unconstitutional capture resembles all the characteristics of a modern constitutional democracy while not being without flaws. This exercise shall—contrasted with the previous section—serve four further goals. First, it shall remind us of the significance of socio-political conditions and the societal will for a constitutional system to persevere in reality. Second, it shall mark a silver lining on the horizon in terms of the 'resurrection' of the Polish state as a democracy ruled by law. Third, it shall highlight relevant flaws in the constitutional system which might guide constitutional reforms in the future. Fourth, it shall contextualize and highlight some of the distorted lines of argument put forward by the 'United Right' government justifying its actions. Thematically seven normative complexes shall be addressed here which mark the foundation of the 1997 Constitution: (1) the supremacy of the Constitution; (2) sovereignty, the 'Nation', and the 'common good'; (3) the concept of the 'democratic state ruled by law'; (4) human rights; (5) the separation of powers; (6) the form of the state; as well as (7) constitutional identity.

---

[216] Action brought on 15 March 2018, Case C-192/18; Action brought on 2 October 2018, Case C-619/18; Action brought on 25 October 2019, Case C-791/19.

[217] CJEU, Judgment of 24 June 2019, Case C-619/18 *Commission v Poland* (ECLI:EU:C:2019:531).

[218] CJEU, Judgment of 18 November 2019, Joined Cases C-585/18, C-624/18 and C-625/18 *A.K. and Others* (ECLI:EU:C:2019:982).

[219] See e.g. resolution of the formation of the combined three chambers of the Supreme Court of 23 January 2020, Ref. No. BSA I-4110-1/20; Michał Krajewski and Michał Ziółkowski, 'EU judicial independence decentralized: A.K.' (2020) 57 Common Market Law Review 1107, 1116.

1. The Constitution and its Supremacy

The Polish Constitution—which is sometimes also called 'basic statute'[220] corresponding to the German term *Grundgesetz*—is a normative act. It is not merely a political declaration but a source of law. It contains legal norms of an abstract and general character, which are universally binding. All provisions of the Constitution have normative content and are not only programmatic or 'symbolic' in nature.[221] This applies even to the Preamble[222] from which the CT derived important legal norms, including the principle of subsidiarity.[223] The consequence of the normative character of the Constitution is that it forms the legal benchmark for actions of public authorities[224] binding state bodies in all their official conduct.[225] Therefore, the most important constitutional public officials may be held constitutionally accountable before the Tribunal of State (article 198).

The Constitution, as the source of law, enjoys supreme legal force (article 8 para 2). Its normative supremacy requires all sub-constitutional norms to be consistent with it—both in terms of their substance as well as in terms of the procedure of their adoption.[226] Lawmakers are obliged to adopt statutes which realize constitutional norms[227] and to refrain from the adoption of unconstitutional statutes. Should ordinary statutes contradict the Constitution, they may be declared void by the CT (see below) or—according to the majority view at least in the context of sub-statutory norms—disapplied by the courts. The Constitution's supremacy has facilitated a constitutionalization of ordinary statutes which took various forms. It is also to be understood considering article 8 para 2 which provides that, unless the Constitution stipulates otherwise, it may be applied 'directly'.[228]

In detail: First, ordinary statutes are to be interpreted in conformity with the Constitution.[229] Second, the CT provides 'legislative guidelines' to the parliament by interpreting the constitutional text. Third, the Constitution requires public authorities to take positive action which manifests in different respects. Some transitional provisions of the Constitution required the adoption of statutes in order to implement certain

---

[220] Lech Garlicki, *Polskie prawo* (n 85) 44–45.

[221] Kazimierz Działocha, 'Komentarz do Art. 8 Konstytucji' ['Commentary on art 8 of the Constitution'], in Leszek Garlicki and Marek Zubik (eds), *Konstytucja Rzeczypospolitej Polskiej. Komentarz* [*Constitution of the Republic of Poland. A Commentary*], vol I (Wyd. Sejmowe, Warsaw, 2016) 258; Piotr Tuleja, 'Komentarz do Art. 8 Konstytucji' ['Commentary on art 8 of the Constitution'], in Marek Safjan and Leszek Bosek (eds), *Konstytucja RP* [*Constitution of the Republic of Poland*], vol I (CH Beck, Warsaw, 2016) 326.

[222] See e.g. Małgorzata E Stefaniuk, *Preambuła aktu normatywnego w doktrynie oraz w procesie stanowienia i stosowania polskiego prawa w latach 1989–2007* [*Preamble to a normative act in legal doctrine and in processes of adopting and applying Polish law in the period 1989–2007*] (Lublin, 2009) 330–354, 443–450.

[223] CT, Judgment of 14 December 2010, Ref. No. K 20/08; CT, Judgment of 21 October 2014, Ref. No. K 38/13.

[224] Kazimierz Działocha, 'Komentarz do Art. 8 Konstytucji' (n 221) 258; Andrzej Mączyński and Agnieszka Łyszkowska, 'Bezpośrednie stosowanie Konstytucji RP przez Trybunał Konstytucyjny' ['Direct application of the Constitution of the Republic of Poland by the Constitutional Tribunal'], in Kazimierz Działocha (ed), *Bezpośrednie stosowanie Konstytucji Rzeczypospolitej Polskiej* [*Direct application of the Constitution of the Republic of Poland*] (Wydawnictwo Sejmowe, Warsaw, 2005) 28.

[225] Piotr Tuleja, 'Komentarz do Art. 8' (n 221) 316.

[226] Kazimierz Działocha, 'Komentarz do Art. 8' (n 221) 267–8; Lech Garlicki, *Polskie prawo* (n 85) 51.

[227] Kazimierz Działocha, 'Komentarz do Art. 8' (n 221) 264; Bogusław Banaszak, *Konstytucja Rzeczypospolitej Polskiej. Komentarz* [*Constitution of the Republic of Poland. A Commentary*] (CH Beck, Warsaw, 2012) 82–83.

[228] Kazimierz Działocha, 'Komentarz do Art. 8' (n 221) 300.

[229] See e.g. Supreme Court, Resolution of 7 judges of 27 March 2018, Ref. No. III CZP 69/17 (necessity of interpreting the provisions of the Civil Code related to the protection of personal rights in the light of the Constitution); Supreme Court, Decision of 27 October 2005, Ref. No. III CK 155/05 (Constitution as the legal basis of the principle of a patient's autonomy); Supreme Administrative Court, Judgment of 30 October 2018, Ref. No. II OSK 1869/16 (concerning legal status of children born by surrogate mothers). See e.g. Maciej Gutowski, 'Bezpośrednie stosowanie Konstytucji w orzecznictwie sądowym' ['Direct application of the Constitution in judicial practice'] (2018) 1 Ruch Prawniczy, Ekonomiczny i Socjologiczny 95–100.

standards.[230] Beyond the transitional context, the Constitution explicitly imposes certain positive obligations on state authorities, including the parliament, requiring them to pursue specific objectives or to regulate particular matters via statute (for instance article 15 para 2:'The basic territorial division of the State shall be determined by statute ...'; article 70 para 1:'The manner of fulfilment of schooling obligations shall be specified by statute.'; article 182: 'A statute shall specify the scope of participation by the citizenry in the administration of justice.'). Some provisions entail programmatic elements and enshrine objectives which are binding on public authorities, without indicating specific, concrete steps to be taken in order to realize them.[231] According to the CT public authorities enjoy a wide, albeit not unlimited,[232] discretion as to how and with which means to pursue objectives defined in programmatic norms.[233] However, and additionally, constitutional provisions which do not explicitly impose obligations on authorities to adopt certain statutes or pursue some objectives may serve as guidelines for politics.[234] This applies particularly to fundamental rights (see below) which usually entail both a negative as well as a positive dimension. Therefore, the political discretion of authorities, also in the socio-economic sphere, is limited by their constitutional positive obligations and the axiology of the Constitution.[235] Fourth, many important legal reforms, in some cases many years after the Constitution entered into force, were adopted as a result of the judgments of the CT. Some of them concerned provisions which were crucial for the protection of fundamental rights. Various judgments required changes in the organization of state bodies. For instance, the already mentioned CT ruling concerning court assessors[236] led to the implementation of a new model of education of candidates for judges.

The most controversial dimension of the concept of direct application of the Constitution concerns the competence of courts to review the constitutionality of legal norms and to refuse to apply those which they deem to be unconstitutional without referring the matter to the CT. Views have remained divided on such a 'dispersed judicial review': according to some legal scholars, courts may autonomously refuse to apply unconstitutional sub-statutory norms, but must not refuse to apply statutes.[237] That is because judges are subject not only to the Constitution, but also to statutes pursuant to article 178 para 1.[238] Furthermore, a 'dispersed judicial review' could be inconsistent with the powers of the CT, which is the sole body competent to examine the constitutionality of statutory norms. While the contrary

---

[230] See article 236 of the Constitution.

[231] See e.g. Paweł Sarnecki, 'Normy programowe w Konstytucji i odpowiadające im wolności obywatelskie' ['Programmatic norms in the Constitution and corresponding civil liberties'], in Leszek Garlicki and Andrzej Szmyt (eds), *Sześć lat Konstytucji Rzeczypospolitej Polskiej. Doświadczenia i inspiracje* [*Six Years of the Constitution of the Republic of Poland: Experiences and Inspirations*] (Warszawa 2003) 253.

[232] See e.g. Janusz Trzciński, 'Konstytucyjne prawo do ochrony zdrowia na tle Art. 35 Karty Podstawowych Praw Unii Europejskiej', in Leszek Garlicki and Andrzej Szmyt (eds), *Sześć lat Konstytucji* (n 231) 304.

[233] See e.g. CT, Judgment of 21 October 2014, Ref. No. K 38/13—with regard to article 69 of the Constitution; CT, Judgment of 21 March 2005, Ref. No. P 5/04—with regard to article 65 para 5 of the Constitution; CT, Judgment of 9 September 2003, Ref. No. SK 28/04—with regard to article 75 para 1 of the Constitution.

[234] Cp. Kazimierz Działocha, 'Komentarz do Art. 8' (n 221) 264; Bogusław Banaszak, *Konstytucja* (n 227) 82–83.

[235] However, the extent of this limitation varies depending on the issue area which is at stake. For example, according to the CT the lawmaker enjoys a wider discretion in terms of regulating socio-economic life (see e.g. CT, Judgment of 26 April 2005, Ref. No. P 3/04).

[236] CT, Judgment of 24 October 2007, Ref. No. SK 7/06 (see above).

[237] Kazimierz Działocha, 'Komentarz do Art. 8' (n 221) 316–318; Leszek Garlicki, 'Bezpośrednie stosowanie Konstytucji' ['Direct application of the Constitution'], in *Konferencja naukowa: Konstytucja RP w praktyce* [*Academic Conference: Constitution of the Republic of Poland in Practice*] (Warsaw 1999) 29–32; Piotr Tuleja, *Stosowanie Konstytucji RP w świetle zasady jej nadrzędności (wybrane problemy)* [*Application of the Constitution of the Republic of Poland in the Light of the Principle of its Supremacy: Selected Problems*] (Kraków 2003) 373.

[238] Kazimierz Działocha, 'Komentarz do Art. 8' (n 221) 317; Leszek Garlicki, 'Bezpośrednie stosowanie' (n 237) 31.

position is also identifiable in scholarship,[239] the jurisprudence of courts has been, with exceptions,[240] indeed very restrained in this regard.[241] The dynamics of this controversy have changed in the course of the 'constitutional crisis': the paralysis of the CT raised the question whether and to what extent ordinary courts may substitute its role. The terms 'constitutional self-defence'[242] and 'doctrine of necessity'[243] surfaced. One can generally observe a wider support for constitutional review by ordinary courts, even among those who in the past defended the monopoly of the CT to carry out judicial review with regard to statutes.[244] Nevertheless, even now courts prefer to resolve compatibility conflicts between statutes and the Constitution via pro-constitutional interpretation[245] or the application of international and EU law[246] to explicit declarations of the unconstitutionality of statutory norms.

The CT has not accepted any exceptions to the principle of the supremacy of the Constitution. Ratified international treaties may be sources of universally binding norms, and, if they are 'ratified upon prior consent granted by statute' (article 91 para 2), they have legal force superior to statutes but, still, inferior to the Constitution.[247] The status of EU law is relatively similar—both primary law as well as secondary law is superior to statutes while ranking below the Constitution.[248] While this view potentially collides with the principle of the primacy of EU law as understood by the CJEU,[249] and for this very reason has been criticized by some legal scholars,[250] it has formed—as seen above—an

[239] See e.g. Bogusław Banaszak, *Konstytucja* (n 227) 89–96; Andrzej Bator, 'Bezpośrednie stosowanie Konstytucji Rzeczypospolitej Polskiej' ['Direct application of the Constitution of the Republic of Poland'] (2006) 10 Państwo i Prawo 96, 101–03; Walerian Sanetra, 'Bezpośrednie stosowanie Konstytucji w orzecznictwie Sądu Najwyższego' ['Direct application of the Constitution in the case law of the Supreme Court'], in Kazimierz Działocha (ed), *Bezpośrednie stosowanie Konstytucji Rzeczypospolitej Polskiej [Direct Application of the Constitution of the Republic of Poland]* (Wydanictwo Sejmowe, Warsaw, 2005) 58.

[240] See e.g. Roman Hauser and Janusz Trzciński, *Prawotwórcze znaczenie orzeczeń Trybunału Konstytucyjnego w orzecznictwie Naczelnego Sądu Administracyjnego [Lawmaking Effects of the Judgments of the Constitutional Tribunal in the Case Law of the Supreme Administrctive Court]* (Wolters Kluwer, Warsaw, 2010) 20–45.

[241] See e.g. Krzysztof Pietrzykowski, 'Kontrola konstytucyjności prawa a stosowanie prawa w świetle orzecznictwa Sądu Najwyższego (zagadnienia wybrane)' ['Judicial review of the constitutionality of law and application of law in the light of the case law of the Supreme Court (selected issues)'], in Jakub Królikowski, Jan Podkowik, and Jarosław Sułkowski (eds), *Kontrola konstytucyjności prawa a stosowanie prawa w orzecznictwie Trybunału Konstytucyjnego, Sądu Najwyższego i Naczelnego Sądu Administracyjnego [Constitutional review of law and the application of law in the case law of the Constitutional Tribunal, the Supreme Court and the Supreme Administrative Court]* (Wolters Kluwer, Warsaw, 2017) 38.

[242] Tomasz Koncewicz, 'The "emergency constitutional review" and Polish constitutional crisis. Of constitutional self-defense and judicial empowerment' (20_6) 2 Polish Law Review 73.

[243] Piotr Mikuli, 'Doktryna konieczności jako uzasadnienie dla rozproszonej kontroli konstytucyjności ustaw w Polsce' ['Doctrine of necessity as the justificaticn for decentralized constitutional review in Poland'] (2018) 2 Gdańskie Studia Prawnicze 635.

[244] See e.g. Leszek Garlicki, 'Sądy a Konstytucja Rzeczypospolitej Polskiej' ['The courts and the Constitution'] (2016) 7 Przegląd Sejmowy 7, 20–23; Ryszard Balicki, 'Bezpośrednie stosowanie Konstytucji' ['Direct application of the Constitution'] (2016) 4 Krajowa Rada Sądownictwa 13, 18–19.

[245] See e.g. Court of Appeals in Wrocław, Judgment of 27 April 2017, Ref. No. II AKa 213/16 (concerning the pro-constitutional interpretation of the provision regulating the admissibility of evidence obtained unlawfully in criminal proceedings).

[246] See e.g. Circuit Court in Suwałki, Judgment of 29 October 2019, Ref. No. III U 819/19 (concerning a statute which decreased pensions of former officers of communist state security authorities).

[247] Małgorzata Masternak-Kubiak, *Przestrzeganie prawa międzynarodowego w świetle Konstytucji Rzeczypospolitej Polskiej [Compliance with international law in the light of the Constitution of the Republic of Poland]* (Kantor Wydawniczy Zakamycze, Kraków, 2003) 206–228.

[248] Cf. Stanisław Biernat and Monika Kawczyńska, 'The Role of the Polish Constitution (Pre-2016)' (n 143) 755.

[249] See e.g. ECJ, Judgment of 17 December 1970, C-11/70, *Internationale Handelsgesellschaft mbH v Einfuhrund Vorratsstelle für Getreide und Futtermittel* (EC_I:EU:C:1970:114).

[250] Eugeniusz Piontek, 'Zasada pierwszeństwa prawa wspólnotowego w orzecznictwie państw członkowskich' ['The principle of primacy of EU law in the case law of Member States'] (2009) 5 Państwo i Prawo 19, 28–30;

integral element of the case law of the CT from the moment of Poland's accession to the EU.[251]

While the supremacy of the Constitution is well established in legal doctrine, the mechanisms that the Polish constitutional order provides for its enforcement are deficient—which did particularly become apparent during the 'constitutional crisis'.

First, certain legal acts of state bodies cannot be the subject of constitutional review by an independent body. The competences of the CT set up in the Constitution[252] are limited to the review of normative acts as opposed to individual-concrete acts. That is why in 2016 the CT refused to review the constitutionality of the resolution of the *Sejm*—dominated by the 'Law and Justice' majority—declaring the resolutions on the election of judges to the CT which were adopted by the *Sejm* during the previous term of its office invalid.[253] These resolutions were adopted to elect three judges to replace correctly elected judges who were not sworn into office by the President. The legal status of the new judges has been often questioned, not only by legal scholars, but also the Commissioner for Human Rights (Ombudsman)[254] and some courts.[255] Another example of an individual act which could not be subjected to any form of legal review were the President's refusals to appoint judges.[256]

Second, the Constitution lacks effective mechanisms for reviewing the constitutionality of legal omissions: The CT may review the constitutionality of partial legislative omissions, that is provisions 'which from the point of view of the principles (and obligations) formulated in the text of the Constitution are characterised by a too narrow scope of application, or such, which due to the object and purpose of regulation, omit substantial content'.[257] When the CT rules that a provision constitutes an unconstitutional partial legislative omission, the parliament is constitutionally obliged to adopt the relevant necessary amendments.[258] Yet, the CT does not have the competence to review the constitutionality of complete legislative omissions, that is matters which were 'consciously left outside the scope of legal regulation by the legislator'.[259] In these situations, the CT may make use of its statutory[260] competence to issue a 'signalling resolution' (see also below) in which it appeals to the parliament to change the law in order to fill unconstitutional legislative gaps. So far, the CT has issued seventy-eight signalling resolutions (fifty-eight after the current Constitution entered

Krzysztof Wojtyczek, 'Trybunał Konstytucyjny w europejskim systemie konstytucyjnym' ('The Constitutional Tribunal in the European Constitutional System') (2009) 4 Przegląd Sejmowy 177, 179–182.

[251] See e.g. CT, Judgment of 27 April 2005, Ref. No. P 1/05; CT, Judgment of 22 June 2005, Ref. No. K 18/04; CT, Judgment of 16 November 2011, Ref. No. SK 45/09.

[252] See article 188 of the Constitution.

[253] CT, Decision of 7 January 2016, Ref. No. U 8/15.

[254] The Ombudsman has regularly submitted motions for the exclusion of one of those three judges from the CT in proceedings initiated by his motions (list of the motions is available on the website of the Ombudsman: https://www.rpo.gov.pl/pl/content/sprawy-przed-TK-w-ktorych-RPO-zlozyl-wniosek-o-wylaczenie (last accessed on 23 April 2022)).

[255] See Regional Administrative Court in Warsaw, Judgment of 20 June 2018, Ref. No. V SA/Wa 459/18 (judgment is not final yet).

[256] Supreme Administrative Court, Decision of 7 December 2017, Ref. No. I OSK 857/17.

[257] Marian Grzybowski, *Legislative Omission in Practical Jurisprudence of the Polish Constitutional Tribunal*, http://www.confeuconstco.org/reports/rep-xiv/report_Poland_en.pdf (last accessed on 23 April 2022). See also CT, Judgment of 10 March 2009, Ref. No. P 80/08.

[258] See e.g. CT, Judgment of 27 June 2013, Ref. No. K 36/12; CT, Judgment of 20 November 2012, Ref. No. SK 3/12; CT, Judgment of 23 October 2007, Ref. No. P 10/07.

[259] Marian Grzybowski, *Legislative Omission* (n 257); CT, Decision of 30 May 2006, SK 3/06.

[260] See article 35 para 1 of the ustawa z dnia 30 listopada 2016 r. o organizacji i trybie postępowania przed Trybunałem Konstytucyjnym (*Act of 30 November 2016 on the Organization and the Mode of Proceedings before the Constitutional Tribunal*), Dziennik Ustaw, item 2017 (2016) with further amendments.

into force).[261] However, there is no mechanism which would secure the implementation of signalling resolutions, and, hence, some of them have been completely ignored by the legislative bodies.[262] The competence of the CT with respect to the non-fulfilment of positive obligations is limited, thereby rendering the enforcement of the latter more difficult.

Third, the execution of the judgments of the CT is not sufficiently effective.[263] This concerns in particular judgments which require the adoption of certain legislative measures by the parliament. Although theoretically there are special provisions in the Senate's Rules of Procedure dedicated solely to the implementation of CT rulings, in practice one can find examples of judgments which have not yet been implemented despite the lapse of many years.[264]

Fourth, the system of constitutional accountability before the Tribunal of State does not function properly in practice.[265] This is particularly due to the high requirements as to the majority in parliament needed to trigger relevant proceedings. As a result, after 1997, only one person was held accountable before the Tribunal of State, but even then, the proceedings were eventually discontinued due to the statute of limitations.[266]

Irrespective of the Constitution's supremacy the CT does also acknowledge—reminiscent of the 'political question doctrine'[267]—that there are spheres which are strictly political in nature. This makes them inept to be subjected to constitutional review. These include, for example, policies designed to combat unemployment[268] or fiscal policy.[269] This does not mean, however, that the realm of politics is not permeated by constitutional law. The Constitution sets the frame for politics to unfold and regulates political life. To mention just a few examples: the Constitution governs both elections as well as the legislative process, it defines the purposes of political parties (article 11), sets requirements as to their internal structure (article 11), and imposes limits on the freedom of their creation and functioning (article 13). It also empowers the CT to assess the constitutional conformity 'of the purposes and activities of political parties' (article 188 pt 4).

---

[261] Information provided in the judgments database of the CT (as of 31 December 2019), available at https://ipo.trybunal.gov.pl/ipo (last accessed on 23 April 2022).

[262] See e.g. Adam Sulikowski, 'Postanowienia sygnalizacyjne TK. Założenia instytucjonalne, praktyka, wykonywanie' ['Signalling resolutions of the Constitutional Tribunal. Institutional assumptions, practice, implementation'], in Kazimierz Działocha and Sylwia Jarosz-Żukowska (eds), *Wykonywanie orzeczeń TK w praktyce konstytucyjnej organów państwa* [*Implementation of the Constitutional Tribunal's Judgments in the Constitutional Practice of State Bodies*] (Wydawnictwo Sejmowe, Warsaw, 2013) 278.

[263] See e.g. Zbigniew Maciąg, 'Stosowanie Konstytucji RP a problem niewykonywania wyroków Trybunału Konstytucyjnego' ['Application of the Constitution of the Republic of Poland and the problem of the non-exexution of judgments of the Constitutional Tribunal'], in Zbigniew Maciąg (ed), *Stosowanie Konstytucji RP z 1997 roku—doświadczenia i perspektywy. Międzynarodowa konferencja naukowa* [*Application of the Constitution of the Republic of Poland of 1997—Experiences and Perspectives. International Academic Conference*] (Kraków 2006) 273–281.

[264] For example, the judgment concerning welfare benefits for persons caring disabled family members (CT, Judgment of 21 October 2014, Ref. No. K 38/13).

[265] In a survey conducted in 2017, 82 per cent of Polish scholars specialising in constitutional law responded that the constitutional model of responsibility for violations of the Constitution is insufficient (see Monika Florczak-Wątor, Piotr Radziewicz, and Marcin Wiszowaty, 'Ankieta o Konstytucji Rzeczypospolitej Polskiej. Wyniki badań przeprowadzonych wśród przedstawicieli nauki prawa konstytucyjnego w 2017 r.' ['Survey on the Constitution of the Republic of Poland. Results of research carried out among representatives of constitutional law scholarship in 2017'] (2018) 9 Państwo i Prawo 3, 10.

[266] CT, Decision of 3 July 2019, Ref. No. TS 2/07.

[267] See e.g *Marbury v Madison*, 1803, 5 US (1 Cranch) 137 (177).

[268] CT, Judgment of 21 March 2005, Ref. No. P 5/04.

[269] CT, Judgment of 18 November 2014, Ref. No. K 23/12 (Pol.). This does not mean, however, that tax law is completely immune to constitutional review. The CT issued various judgments in which it ruled that certain provisions of tax statutes violated the Constitution (see e.g. CT, Judgment of 28 October 2015, Ref. No. K 21/14; CT, Judgment of 29 July 2014, Ref. No. P 49/13; CT, Judgment of 17 July 2012, Ref. No. P 30/11).

The supremacy of the Constitution is obviously undermined by the current political atmosphere in Poland. Actions of the 'United Right' aimed at weakening the system of guarantees of independence of the judiciary and the de facto paralysis and politicization of the CT[270] resulted in a situation in which the legal force of the Constitution and its practical significance is severely challenged. Some members of parliament have even claimed that the 'good of the Nation' should take precedence over the law, which would include the Constitution.[271] In the same tone, the leader of the ruling party, Jarosław Kaczyński, commented that the Constitution was 'just a little book. How can it be a sovereign? Those who apply it may be a sovereign'.[272] At the same time, however, many people opposing the ruling party's politics started to perceive the Constitution as a symbol of the ideals of democracy and the rule of law. The Constitution itself offers—as already stressed at the outset—powerful concepts that shape political discourses and might foster the re-installation of Poland as a 'state ruled by law'.

2. The Constitutional Concept of Sovereignty, the 'Nation', and the 'Common Good'

Sovereignty as a concept entails an inward (the ultimate power within a state) and outward face (referring to the ultimate power outside of the state in the 'international realm'). Within the Polish constitutional order both manifestations are interconnected by the concept of the 'Nation'.[273]

The concept of 'sovereignty' in its external dimension is to be seen particularly in light of the Polish past and the inexistence of Poland as a (sovereign) state for over 123 years which is still perceived in a traumatic manner. This 'trauma' continues to shape current political discourses. The Constitution oscillates between the poles 'preservation of independence' on the one hand and 'integration' of the Polish state into the international and supranational legal order on the other hand: the Preamble stresses that the 'Homeland ... recovered, in 1989, the possibility of a sovereign and democratic determination of its fate'. Article 104 para 2, determining the oath of deputies, mentions the obligation 'to safeguard the sovereignty and interests of the State'—an obligation that article 126 para 2 conveys to the President in a similar manner ('safeguard the sovereignty and security of the State'). In its judgment on the conformity of the Lisbon Treaty with the Constitution[274] (see above) the CT held that the principle of preserving Poland's external sovereignty should guide the process of Poland's integration in the EU. This principle sets limits to the transfer of competences to the EU by requiring that in the fields which constitute the essence of Polish statehood and

---

[270] See e.g. Małgorzata Szuleka, Marcin Wolny and Marcin Szwed, *The Constitutional Crisis* (n 179); Marcin Wolny, '"Pracuje Tak, Jak Powinien"? Trybunał Konstytucyjny w 2017 roku' ['"Works as it should"? – Constitutional Tribunal in 2017'] Helsinki Foundation for Human Rights 2018 https://www.hfhr.pl/wp-content/uploads/2018/03/HFPC-Pracuje-tak-jak-powinien-raport-TK-2017.pdf) (last accessed on 23 April 2022).

[271] Kornel Morawiecki, Speech on the second sitting of the parliament of the eighth term of office, 25 November 2015.

[272] 'Kaczyński: nie miałem innego wyjścia. To był imperatyw moralny' [Kaczyński: I had no other choice. It was a moral imperative] *TVP Info* (29 July 2017) https://www.tvp.info/33279000/kaczynski-nie-mialem-innego-wyjscia-to-byl-imperatyw-moralny (last accessed on 23 April 2022). Translation by the authors.

[273] See e.g. Bogusław Banaszak, *Konstytucja* (n 227) 64; Ryszard M Małajny, *Polskie prawo konstytucyjne na tle porównawczym* [*Polish constitutional law—comparative aspects*] (CH Beck, Warsaw, 2013) 150; Kazimierz Działocha, 'Komentarz do Art. 4 Konstytucji' ['Commentary on Article 4 of the Constitution'], in Leszek Garlicki and Marek Zubik (eds), *Konstytucja Rzeczypospolitej Polskiej* (n 221) 194–204.

[274] CT, Judgment of 24 November 2010, Ref. No. K 32/09.

sovereignty decisive competences should remain with Poland's authorities—a point that we shall return to.

In terms to the internal dimension of sovereignty the Constitution itself refrains from employing this concept explicitly in order to denote the ultimate power within the Polish state.[275] Yet, the principle of the 'sovereignty of the nation' can be extracted from article 4 para 1, which vests the 'Supreme power in the Republic of Poland ... in the Nation', and the Preamble to the Constitution, which is written in the name of 'the Polish Nation—all citizens of the Republic' implying that it is this 'Nation' which has the ultimate and constituent power in the state.[276] The term 'Nation' is also employed in article 5 which requires the Republic of Poland to 'safeguard the national heritage', and in article 6 which obliges the state to ensure 'people's equal access to the products of culture which are the source of the Nation's identity, continuity and development'. Furthermore, the Constitution makes clear that Members of the *Sejm* are representatives of the 'Nation' (article 104) and the President is elected by the 'Nation' (article 127 para 1). While the concept of 'Nation' reflects—together with the principle of the 'common good' (article 1)—the 'entirety' of the 'political unity' that the Polish state represents, it is obviously overladen with preunderstandings frequently serving as a political battle word, particularly being invoked by the 'United Right'.

The Preamble suggests that the Nation includes 'all citizens of the Republic',[277] thereby conceptualizing the 'Nation' in a legal and political and not ethnic manner.[278] It includes all citizens, regardless of their ethnicity or voting rights,[279] which has found confirmation in the jurisprudence of the CT:[280] no factors other than citizenship, such as nationality, race, or religion, are relevant for establishing that an individual belongs to the 'Polish Nation'.[281] The term 'Nation' encompasses the citizenry which stands for itself and is not to be equated with the parliament[282] or the ruling majority and its supporters[283]—the latter being currently repeatedly and distortedly connoted by the 'United Right'.

The 'Nation' is the entity to which the Republic of Poland (*Rzeczpospolita*) as the 'common good' is allocated (article 1). The 'common good' refers to the entire human community organized in a political form of the state—it is the sum of 'the conditions of social life that enable and facilitate the integral development of ... members of the political community'.[284] This concept circulates around public interest[285] as opposed to an individual's good or a

---

[275] Monika Florczak-Wątor, 'Komentarz do Art. 4 Konstytucji', [Commentary on article 4 of the Constitution]) in Marek Safjan and Leszek Bosek (eds), *Konstytucja RP* (n 221) para VIII.2.

[276] See e.g. Małgorzata Stefaniuk, *Preambuła aktu* (n 222) 262–264; Ryszard Piotrowski, 'Konstytucja i granice władzy suwerena w państwie demokratycznym' ['Constitution and the limits of the sovereign's power in a democratic state'], in Jerzy Jaskiernia and Kamil Spryszak (eds), *Dwadzieścia lat obowiązywania Konstytucji* (n 128) 702.

[277] See e.g. Marek Piechowiak, 'Komentarz do Preambuły do Konstytucji RP' ['Commentary on the Preamble of the Constitution of the Republic of Poland'], in Marek Safjan and Leszek Bosek (eds), *Konstytucja RP* (n 221) 132–133.

[278] See e.g. Marek Dobrowolski, *Zasada suwerenności narodu w warunkach integracji Polski z Unią Europejską* [*The principle of the sovereignty of the nation under the conditions of Poland's integration into the European Union*] (Wydawnictwo KUL, Lublin, 2014) 67; Bogusław Banaszak, *Konstytucja* (n 227) 63–64; Piotr Winczorek, *Komentarz do Konstytucji Rzeczypospolitej Polskiej z dnia 2 kwietnia 1997 r.* [*Commentary on the Constitution of the Republic of Poland of 2 April 1997*] (Liber, Warsaw, 2000) 23; Monika Florczak-Wątor, 'Komentarz do Art. 4 Konstytucji' (n 275) 272; Kazimierz Działocha, 'Komentarz do Art. 4' (n 273) 198.

[279] Monika Florczak-Wątor, 'Komentarz do Art. 4' (n 275) 272–273.

[280] CT, Judgment of 31 May 2004, Ref. No. K 15/04.

[281] CT, Judgment of 21 September 2015, Ref. No. K 28/13.

[282] Kazimierz Działocha, 'Komentarz do Art. 4' (n 273) 224.

[283] Ryszard Piotrowski, 'Konstytucja i granice' (n 276) 719.

[284] CT, Judgment of 21 September 2015, Ref. No. K 28/13.

[285] Marek Piechowiak, 'Komentarz do Art. 1 Konstytucji', ['Commentary on article 1 of the Constitution'] in Marek Safjan and Leszek Bosek (eds), *Konstytucja RP* (n 221) para III.J.b.15.

particular group interest.[286] The CT identified within its rich jurisprudence on this matter various normative aspects that form elements of the 'common good' including the state[287] and its security,[288] universal access to culture, arts and science,[289] the protection of the natural environment,[290] the impartiality of courts and judges,[291] labour,[292] public property,[293] and civil service.[294]

The ideas of 'Nation' and 'common good' collide with a highly divided and polarized society in contemporary Poland which becomes particularly visible within elections. Division lines run between cities and rural areas, the young and the old, the wealthy and the poor. Despite this reality, the 'United Right' makes frequently use of symbolisms surrounding the ideas of 'Nation' and the 'common good' reducing it to 'kitsch' serving populist goals whilst deepening societal divisions with its political agendas.

3. The Constitution and the 'Democratic State Ruled by Law'

Article 2 stipulates that '[t]he Republic of Poland shall be a democratic state ruled by law and implementing the principles of social justice'. Both the CT and scholarship have derived from this provision the constitutional principle of a 'democratic state ruled by law'.[295] Therefore, (a) democracy and (b) the rule of law constitute parts of the same principle and must be interpreted in their interrelatedness.[296]

a) The Constitution and Democracy

The epicentre of Poland's transitional process has been the turn to democracy. The CT has underlined that the concept of democracy to be found in article 2 must be interpreted also in light of other constitutional principles, in particular the sovereignty of the 'Nation' (article 4), the principle of the separation of powers (article 10), and different forms of associations designed to organize political will in the widest sense (article 12).[297]

The Constitution refrains from defining the notion of 'democracy', however, in article 4 para 2, it distinguishes two forms of democratic governance: indirect (representative) and direct democracy. The CT has held repeatedly that under the current Constitution direct forms of democratic decision-making have only a supplementary function.[298]

---

[286] CT, Judgment of 30 January 2001, Ref. No. K 17/00.
[287] CT, Judgment of 25 February 2014, Ref. No. SK 18/13.
[288] CT, Judgment of 3 July 2001, Ref. No. K 3/01 and CT, Judgment of 10 April 2002, Ref. No. K 26/00.
[289] CT, Judgment of 24 January 2006, Ref. No. SK 40/04.
[290] CT, Judgment of 2 February 1999, Ref. No. U 4/98 and CT, Judgment of 28 September 2015, Ref. No. 20/14.
[291] CT, Judgment of 27 January 1999, Ref. No. K 1/98.
[292] CT, Judgment of 14 June 2011, Ref. No. Kp 1/11.
[293] CT, Judgment of 18 October 2016, Ref. No. P 123/15.
[294] CT, Judgment of 14 June 2011, Ref. No. Kp 1/11.
[295] See e.g. Leszek Garlicki, 'Principles of the system', in Piotr Korzec, Jakub Urbanik, and Mirosław Wyrzykowski (eds), *Polish constitutionalism: a reader* (Faculty of Law and Administration of the University of Warsaw, Warsaw, 2011) 59–65; Bogusław Banaszak, *Prawo konstytucyjne* [*Constitutional Law*] (CH Beck, Warsaw, 2017) 181–195; CT, Judgment of 12 May 2016, Ref. No. P 46/13.
[296] Iwona Małajny and Ryszard M Małajny, 'Zasada demokratycznego i sprawiedliwego państwa prawa (uwagi porządkujące na tle Art. 2 Konstytucji III RP)' ['The Principle of the Democratic and Just State Based on the Rule of Law (Remarks on the Background of art 2 of the Constitution of the Third Republic of Poland)]' (2012) 27 Gdańskie Studia Prawnicze 255, 265–266.
[297] CT, Judgment of 11 July 2012, Ref. No. K 8/10.
[298] See e.g. CT, Judgment of 3 November 2006, Ref. No. K 31/06.

The Constitution mentions only two mechanisms of direct democracy explicitly: the referendum and legislative initiatives initiated by citizens (citizens' legislative initiative). Four types of referenda are identifiable within the constitutional text: 'nationwide referend[a] ... in respect of matters of particular importance to the State' (article 125), nationwide referenda on the consent for the ratification of international agreements on the basis of which Poland transfers certain sovereign powers to an international organization or international institution (article 90 para 3 and para 1), referenda on the acceptance of constitutional amendments (article 235 para 6) as well as local referenda (article 170). Referenda are not merely consultative—they are binding on authorities provided that the requirement of a minimum turnout is met.[299] Still, as tools for law-making, referenda are limited: They cannot be held to adopt statutes, to circumvent the constitutional procedure for amending the constitution, dismiss the government or substitute other decisions which are constitutionally reserved for particular organs, meaning that they cannot reshape the architecture of competences.[300]

The second form of direct democracy is the citizens' legislative initiative. This instrument allows a group of 100,000 citizens to introduce bills to the *Sejm* without imposing any obligation on the parliament to adopt them. Whilst this constitutional 'reluctance' towards mechanisms of direct democracy is criticized in legal discourse,[301] it is not atypical for modern constitutional states. Quite to the contrary, in comparison to other (European) constitutional orders the Polish Constitution appears rather progressive.

Not only does the 1997 Constitution install a system of representative democracy,[302] it also regulates elections in a relatively detailed way.[303] It requires that elections provided for by the Constitution (i.e. parliamentarian, presidential, and elections regarding constitutive organs of the units of local self-government) are universal, direct and conducted by secret ballot.[304] These general principles have been filled with detailed normative substance by the CT.[305] Within the architecture of representative democracy set up by the 1997 Constitution political parties play a major role. Article 11 enshrines the freedom to create political parties and obliges the state to protect their functioning. This freedom is yet limited. First, the Constitution requires political parties to 'be founded on the principle of voluntariness and upon the equality of Polish citizens' (article 11 para 1), their financing 'shall be open to public inspection' (article 11 para 2) and they cannot 'provide for the secrecy of their own structure or membership' (article 13). Furthermore, the Constitution prohibits parties 'whose programmes are based upon totalitarian methods and the modes of activity of nazism, fascism and communism, as well as those whose programmes or activities sanction racial or national hatred, the application of violence for the purpose of obtaining power or to influence the State policy' (article 13). In case of a party's non-compliance with this prohibition it may be banned by virtue of a judgment of the CT. Therefore, the Constitution endorses, to some

---

[299] The requirement of a minimum turnout does not apply to the referendum for the acceptance of a constitutional amendment.

[300] Lech Garlicki, *Polskie prawo* (n 85) 201–202; Piotr Winczorek, *Komentarz do Konstytucji* (n 278) 24.

[301] See e.g. Jerzy Kuciński and Waldemar J, Wołpiuk, *Zasady ustroju politycznego państwa w Konstytucji Rzeczypospolitej Polskiej z 1997 roku* (*The Principles of Political Organization of the State in the Constitution of the Republic of Poland of 1997*) (Wolters Kluwer, Warsaw, 2012) 279; Bogusław Banaszak, *Konstytucja* (n 227) 68–69.

[302] CT, Judgment of 3 November 1999, Ref. No. K 13/99.

[303] See e.g. articles 96 para 2, 97 para 2, 98 para 2 and para 5, 99–101, 127 of the Constitution.

[304] Additionally, elections to the *Sejm*, to constitutive organs of units of local self-government and presidential elections must be equal. Elections to the *Sejm* must also be proportionate.

[305] On the basis of CT, Judgment of 20 July 2011, Ref. No. K 9/11.

extent, the concept of 'militant democracy',[306] although in practice the CT is very reluctant to declare that a programme or activities of a political party are unconstitutional (so far, it has never happened).[307]

The Constitution also acknowledges civil society as a key element of a vital democracy (article 12). In that regard, fundamental freedoms play a pivotal role, which the CT has also stressed in its jurisprudence: democracy would not only require regular elections of the sovereign's representatives and safeguarding political pluralism, but also the protection of the freedom of association,[308] the freedom of assembly,[309] freedom of expression,[310] and right of access to public information.[311]

Whilst democracy is a foundational pillar of the Polish constitutional order it is embedded in a system of other constitutional principles which counterbalance it. First, Poland is not merely a 'democratic state' but a 'democratic state ruled by law'. Therefore, the majoritarian principle of democracy have to be reconciled with the standards of the rule of law.[312] Unlike the Constitution of 1952, the contemporary constitutional framework does not endorse the principle of the supremacy of the parliament. Supremacy is attributed to the Constitution. The idea of an omnipotent parliamentarian majority is incompatible with the Constitution's axiology which requires parliamentary activities and legislation in particular to conform to its stipulations.[313] A democratically elected parliament must not violate the Constitution even in the name of 'the good of the Nation'.[314] This simple, yet foundational, normative truth forming the basis of the rule of law has been questioned by the current Polish government frequently and this contestation finds no justification in the pattern of the Constitution as such. It is purely *contra constitutione*.

Second, democracy and social justice are interlinked. Article 2 provides that the Republic of Poland, as a democratic state ruled by law, must implement 'the principles of social justice'. The 'constitutional crisis' and its socio-political context have evidenced one crucial aspect: social inequalities endanger the success of the Polish constitutional project. As it has been put rightly in scholarship, 'the excessive social inequalities may cause constitutional democracy to be reduced to an ambiguous project enjoying limited understanding and social support'.[315]

The challenge that the 'constitutional crisis' and the contemporary governmental reforms[316] pose for Poland as a liberal[317] and constitutional democracy[318] can only be addressed successfully if the 'social question' is taken into account seriously.

---

[306] On this concept see Karl Loewenstein, 'Militant Democracy and Fundamental Rights, I' (1937) 31 American Political Science Review 417. See generally Jan-Werner Müller, 'Militant Democracy', in Michel Rosenfeld and András Sajó (eds), *The Oxford Handbook of Comparative Constitutional Law* (OUP, Oxford, 2012) 1253.

[307] See e.g. Agnieszka Bień-Kacała and Andrzej Jackiewicz, 'Militant democracy—demokracja, która sama się broni (?)' ('Militant democracy—democracy that defends itself (?)') (2017) 8 Państwo i Prawo 25, 34–37.

[308] CT, Judgment of 11 July 2012, Ref. No. K 8/10.

[309] CT, Judgment of 18 January 2006, Ref. No. K 21/05.

[310] See e.g. CT, Judgment of 20 July 2011, Ref. No. K 9/11.

[311] CT, Decision of 2 December 2015, Ref. No. SK 36/14.

[312] See e.g. Wojciech Sokolewicz and Marek Zubik, 'Komentarz do Art. 2 Konstytucji' ('Commentary on article 2 of the Constitution'), in Leszek Garlicki and Marek Zubik (eds), *Konstytucja Rzeczypospolitej Polskiej* (n 221) 108.

[313] CT, Judgment of 22 September 2006, Ref. No. U 4/06.

[314] CT, Judgment of 3 December 2015, Ref. No. K 34/15.

[315] Ryszard Piotrowski, 'Demokratyczna tożsamość Konstytucji RP' ('The democratic identity of the Constitution of the Polish Republic'), in Konstanty A Wojtaszczyk, Paweł Stawarz, and Justyna Wiśniewska-Grzelak (eds), *Zmierzch demokracji liberalnej?* (*The Demise of Liberal Democracy?*) (Aspra JR, Warsaw, 2018) 453. See also Piotr Tuleja, 'Komentarz do Art. 2 Konstytucji' ('Commentary on article 2 of the Constitution') in Marek Safjan and Leszek Bosek (eds), *Konstytucja RP* (n 221) 243.

[316] See e.g. Ryszard Balicki, *Demokracja—uniwersalna ewolucja* (*Democracy—Universal Evolution*), in Jerzy Jaskiernia and Kamil Spryszak (eds), *Dwadzieścia lat obowiązywania Konstytucji* (n 128) 746–749.

[317] Ryszard Piotrowski, 'Demokratyczna tożsamość' (n 315) 452.

[318] CT, Judgment of 22 September 2006, Ref. No. U 4/06.

b) The Constitutional Concept of the Rule of Law

The principle of the 'democratic state ruled by law' became an element of the Polish constitutional order in December 1989[319] when article 1 of the communist Constitution, according to which 'The People's Republic of Poland is people's democracy', was given a new wording—identical to article 2 of the current Constitution. It soon turned out that the amendment would not merely play a symbolic role but would also entail an important normative principle.

In the period before the 1997 Constitution entered into force, the CT interpreted the clause of 'democratic state ruled by law' progressively, deriving from it many important legal norms which were not explicitly entailed in the constitutional provisions then in force[320] (e.g. the protection of fundamental rights,[321] the principle *nullum crimen sine lege*,[322] the principle of proportionality,[323] and the separation of powers[324]). After 1997 the CT displayed a more restrained approach towards the 'state ruled by law' clause.[325] The reason for this has not been ignorance but rather the detailedness of the text of the 1997 Constitution. Many important principles, which in the past had to be derived from the 'rule of law' clause (as separation of powers, independence of the judiciary, etc.), now find their explicit constitutional basis in self-standing provisions.

Article 2 continues to serve, however, in the case law of the CT as the basis for not explicitly enshrined standards concerning the law-making process and the necessary qualities of law. One important standard derived from article 2 is the principle of the protection of the citizen's trust in the state or, as it is sometimes called in an inverted form, the principle of loyalty of the state towards its citizens. This principle imposes certain minimum standards of integrity on state organs prohibiting the treatment of individuals in a disloyal, dishonest or deceptive manner. Therefore, law must be foreseeable, it must not deceive individuals, make empty promises or allow state authorities to abuse their powers.[326]

Another principle derived from article 2 is the prohibition of a retroactive application of law.[327] Only in the context of criminal law (and of course, only with regard to legal

---

[319] Ustawa z dnia 29 grudnia 1989 r. o zmianie Konstytucji Polskiej Rzeczypospolitej Ludowej [Act of 29 December 1989 amending the Constitution of the People's Republic of Poland], Dziennik Ustaw, No 75, item 444 (1989).

[320] See e.g. Piotr Tuleja, 'Komentarz do Art. 2 Konstytucji' (n 315) 221; Tatiana Chauvin, J Winczorek and Piotr Winczorek, 'Wprowadzanie klauzuli państwa prawnego do porządku konstytucyjnego Rzeczypospoliej Polskiej' ('The Introduction of the rule of law clause into the constitutional order of the Republic of Poland'), in Sławomira Wronkowska-Jaśkiewicz (ed), *Zasada demokratycznego państwa prawnego w Konstytucji RP* (*The Principle of the Democratic State Ruled by Law in the Constitution of the Republic of Poland*) (Wydawn Sejmowe, Warsaw, 2006) 44–45.

[321] See e.g. Leszek Garlicki, 'Materialna interpretacja klauzuli demokratycznego państwa prawnego w orzecznictwie Trybunału Konstytucyjnego' ['Substantive interpretation of the democratic state ruled by law clause in the case law of the Constitutional Tribunal'], in Sławomira Wronkowska-Jaśkiewicz (ed), *Zasada demokratycznego państwa* (n 320) 130–133.

[322] See e.g. CT, Ruling of 26 April 1995, Ref. No. K 11/94.

[323] See e.g. CT, Ruling of 26 April 1995, Ref. No. K 11/94; CT, Ruling of 17 October 1995, Ref. No. K 10/95.

[324] CT, Ruling of 19 June 1992, Ref. No. U 6/92.

[325] Piotr Tuleja, 'Komentarz do Art. 2 Konstytucji' (n 315) 230.

[326] Lech Garlicki, *Polskie prawo* (n 85) 77; CT, Judgment of 17 July 2011, Ref. No. P 30/11; CT, Judgment of 28 February 2012, Ref. No. K 5/11.

[327] Mirosław Wyrzykowski, 'Zasada państwa prawnego—kilka uwag' ('A few remarks on the principle of the democratic state ruled by law'), in Marek Zubik (ed), *Księga XX-lecia orzecznictwa Trybunału Konstytucyjnego* (*Book commemorating Twenty Years of the Jurisprudence of the Constitutional Tribunal*) (Biuro Trybunału Konstytucyjnego Warsaw, 2006) 251–255; Wojciech Sokolewicz and Marek Zubik, 'Komentarz do Art. 2' (n 312) 136–40; Piotr Tuleja, 'Komentarz do Art. 2 Konstytucji' (n 315) 226.

provisions which are less favourable for the defendant) the principle of *lex retro non agit* finds an explicit constitutional basis (article 42 para 1) being here absolute in nature).[328] In other spheres of law, it is inferred from the principle of the democratic state ruled by law.

A further important standard emanating from the principle of the 'democratic state ruled by law' is the requirement of a proper *vacatio legis*.[329] According to the CT, in general, the entry into force of a newly adopted statute should be preceded by an adequate adjustment period which allows citizens and state authorities to prepare for the consequences of reforms.[330] The length of this period depends on the subject of the relevant reform and its scale.

The CT identified also certain important standards with regard to the protection of vested rights and legitimate expectations as elements of the principle of democratic state ruled by law.[331] According to the CT, the protection of vested rights is not absolute and new statutes may in some justified (also economically) circumstances interfere with vested rights.[332] Moreover, only those rights which were acquired fairly are protected—that is why in a judgment from 2010 the CT ruled that the regulations which deprived former officers of communist state security authorities of their privileges in the sphere of the old-age pension system did not violate the Constitution.[333] In this context it is worth noting that in 2016 a new statute was adopted which significantly decreased the amount of pensions of former officers, which raised justified controversies as to its compliance with constitutional and international human rights requirements.[334]

In cases which do not involve limitations of constitutional freedoms and rights (article 31 para 3—see below), the CT distils the principle of proportionality from article 2.[335]

The principle of the democratic state ruled by law includes also certain requirements concerning the way statutes are to be formulated. In this regard the CT underlines that provisions must be sufficiently clear (i.e. understandable) and precise (i.e. specific enough to be enforceable) allowing individuals to determine the legal consequences of their conduct.[336] However, only provisions which reach a level of ambiguity that renders it impossible to eliminate serious doubts in terms of their content *via* interpretation would violate article 2.[337]

The various ways in which article 2 of the 1997 Constitution has been present in the jurisprudence of the CT and the level of elaboration it has reached therein stands in a stark contrast with the way it has been undermined by the 'United Right' government.

---

[328] Lech Garlicki, *Polskie prawo* (n 85) 77.

[329] See e.g. Wojciech Sokolewicz and Marek Zubik, 'Komentarz do Art. 2' (n 312) 140–3; Piotr Tuleja, 'Komentarz do Art. 2 Konstytucji' (n 315) 226.

[330] See e.g. CT, Judgment of 2 December 2014, Ref. No. P 29/13; CT, Judgment of 9 March 2016, Ref. No. K 47/15.

[331] See e.g. CT, Judgment of 10 February 2015, Ref. No. P 10/11; CT, Judgment of 4 June 2013, Ref. No. SK 49/12.

[332] See e.g. CT, Judgment of 17 November 2003, Ref. No. K 32/02.

[333] See e.g. CT, Judgment of 24 February 2010, Ref. No. K 6/09.

[334] See e.g. Anna Rakowska-Trela, 'Obniżenie emerytur funkcjonariuszy służb mundurowych nabytych począwszy od 1990 r. a standardy konstytucyjne' ('Lowering the pensions of uniformed services officers acquired from 1990 onwards and constitutional standards') (2018) 40 Gdańskie Studia Prawnicze 275.

[335] Ibid, 153–154; Bogusław Banaszak, *Konstytucja* (n 227) 35–38.

[336] See e.g. CT, Judgment of 17 January 2019, Ref. No. K 1/18; CT, Judgment of 28 October 2009, Ref. No. Kp 3/09.

[337] See e.g. Wojciech Sokolewicz and Marek Zubik, 'Komentarz do Art. 2' (n 312) 149; CT, Judgment of 6 October 2015, Ref. No. SK 54/13.

4. The Constitutional Protection of Human Rights: Dignity of the Person, Equality, and Freedom

The Constitution encompasses a substantial catalogue of rights and freedoms which are interlinked with the rule of law concept described above. At their apex stands human dignity which, according to the directly applicable article 30, is 'inherent', 'inalienable', 'inviolable', constituting 'a source of freedoms and rights of persons and citizens'. Human dignity as a concept had no presence in the communist legal system which was instead based on the idea of class struggle.[338] Consequently, it stood—as an antithesis to the oppressive communist system—at the centre of the *Solidarność* movement.[339] The Constitution follows a personalistic dignity concept with roots in natural law ideas. It displays features of Thomism.[340] Its 'meta foundation' can be seen both in Christian as well as humanistic values. Polish legal doctrine elaborated an understanding of dignity which draws both on Catholic thought as well as Kantian philosophy.[341] Dignity plays a role both as a constitutional principle being already invoked by the preamble ('paying respect to the inherent dignity of the person') as well as a subjective right.[342] In its former dimension, it serves as an interpretative guideline and an axiological foundation of the whole legal system.[343] In its dimension as a subjective right, dignity may be enforced by individuals, in particular via constitutional complaints.[344]

While not being defined within the constitutional text, in various judgments the CT identified certain elements which form the essence of dignity.

First, human dignity implies the individual's autonomy and its right to self-determination.[345] The CT referred to this aspect of dignity, for example, in the context of proceedings regarding the constitutionality of provisions which allowed guardians of incapacitated persons to place them in social care homes against their will without any procedural guarantees.[346] Second, human dignity prohibits the depersonalization, instrumentalization and objectification of humans. Human beings must not be—following a variation of *Kant's* second variant of the categorical imperative[347]—treated only as means to achieve some end.[348] That is why the CT held—therein following the FCC—that the provision which authorized state organs to order the shooting down of a passenger aircraft 'when state security reasons require it, and aircraft has been used for illegal purpose, in particular as a measure of terrorist attack' violated the personal dignity of innocent passengers and members of crew due to their instrumentalization.[349] Third, human dignity prohibits the humiliation

---

[338] See Marta Soniewicka and Justyna Holocher, 'Human Dignity in Poland', in Paolo Becchi and Klaus Mathis (eds), *Handbook of Human Dignity in Europe* (Springer International Publishing, Heidelberg, 2019) 698.

[339] Ibid.

[340] Ibid, 702.

[341] Ibid, 704.

[342] Leszek Garlicki, 'Komentarz do Art. 30 Konstytucji' ['Commentary on article 30 of the Constitution'], in Leszek Garlicki and Marek Zubik (eds), *Konstytucja Rzeczypospolitej Polskiej. Komentarz* [*Constitution of the Republic of Poland: A Commentary*], Vol. II (Wyd Sejmowe, Warsaw, 2016) 35–43.

[343] Lech Garlicki, *Polskie prawo* (n 85) 97; Piotr Winczorek, *Komentarz do Konstytucji* (n 278) 80.

[344] Leszek Bosek, 'Komentarz do Art. 30 Konstytucji', ['Commentary on article 30 of the Constitution'] in Marek Safjan and Leszek Bosek (eds), *Konstytucja RP* (n 221) 736–737.

[345] Leszek Garlicki, 'Komentarz do Art. 30' (n 342) 33; Piotr Tuleja, *Stosowanie Konstytucji RP* (n 237) 113.

[346] CT, Judgment of 28 June 2016, Ref. No. K 31/15.

[347] Immanuel Kant, second formulation of the categorical imperative: 'Act so that you use humanity, as much in your own person as in the person of every other, always at the same time as end and never merely as means', Immanuel Kant, *Groundwork for the Metaphysics of Morals* (Allen W Wood (ed, transl) (Yale University Press, New Haven, 2002) 46 [Ak 4:429].

[348] Leszek Garlicki, 'Komentarz do Art. 30' (n 342) 34.

[349] CT, Judgment of 30 September 2008, Ref. No. K 44/07.

of persons and subjecting them to maltreatment[350] (which is also expressed in article 40). Fourth, according to the CT, human dignity also requires the 'existence of a certain material minimum that provides the individual with the possibility of independent functioning in society',[351] which inserts a 'social dimension' into the dignity concept.[352] On that basis the CT ruled, *inter alia*, that provisions which failed to protect evicted tenants against homelessness were inconsistent with article 30.[353]

Human dignity imposes on state authorities not only negative, but also positive obligations ('The respect and protection thereof [i.e. dignity] shall be the obligation of public authorities.'—article 30 clause 3).

Human dignity, as opposed to the majority of other rights and freedoms, is of an absolute character, meaning that an interference with human dignity on the part of state authorities is always unlawful and the proportionality test specified in article 31 para 3[354] does not apply.

Two other provisions which serve both as subjective rights as well as guiding principles within the constitutional system of protecting of individuals rights and freedoms are the right of freedom (article 31) and the right of equality (article 32).[355] Within the internal hierarchy of constitutional norms they rank below human dignity, but nonetheless remain intrinsically linked to it. Both types of principles and rights may be limited in accordance with the principle of proportionality. Within a constitutional complaint the right of equality must be always invoked in conjunction with the specific fundamental right with regard to which an unequal treatment occurred.[356] Due to its accessory nature article 32 of the Constitution resembles article 14 of the ECHR.

This tripartite foundation of the Polish Constitution—dignity of the person, freedom, and equality—is further differentiated and expanded in other Chapters of the Constitution—predominately in Chapter II[357]—which entail specific fundamental rights and freedoms. They can be classified into three categories: personal (e.g. personal liberty, prohibition of maltreatment, right to court, freedom of speech), political (e.g. freedom of assembly, freedom of association, right of access to public information) and economic, social, and cultural (e.g. freedom of occupation, right to health, right to social security) rights. Beyond these explicitly enshrined guarantees, some fundamental rights have been inferred from general constitutional provisions: The CT derived the principle of *ne bis in idem* from article 2 which entails the principle of the 'democratic state ruled by law'[358] and the freedom of contract from article 31 para 1.[359] Fundamental rights and freedoms differ in their personal scopes which allows a further categorization: rights entitling all human beings (for instance, human dignity, personal liberty, freedom of expression, freedom of assembly), rights addressed to citizens (for example, right of access to public information, right to social security, right of

---

[350] See e.g. CT, Judgment of 31 March 2015, Ref. No. U 6/14; Supreme Court, Judgment of 28 February 2007, Ref. No. V CSK 431/06.

[351] See e.g. CT, Judgment of 4 April 2001, Ref. No. K 11/00; CT, Judgment of 28 October 2015, Ref. No. K 21/14.

[352] Wojciech Brzozowski, Adam Krzywoń, and Marcin Wiącek, *Prawa człowieka* (*Human rights*) (Wolters Kluwer, Warsaw, 2019) 122–123.

[353] CT, Judgment of 18 October 2017, Ref. No. K 27/15.

[354] Leszek Bosek, 'Komentarz do Art. 30' (n 344) 741.

[355] Lech Garlicki, *Polskie prawo* (n 85) 109–112.

[356] See e.g. CT, Judgment of 11 June 2013, Ref. No. SK 23/10; CT, Judgment of 29 November 2011, Ref. No. SK 15/09.

[357] For example, the freedom of economic activity is regulated in Chapter I of the Constitution (articles 20 and 22).

[358] See e.g. CT, Judgment of 15 April 2008, Ref. No. P 26/06; CT, Judgment of 1 December 2016, Ref. No. K 45/14.

[359] See e.g. CT, Judgment of 29 April 2003, Ref. No. SK 24/02; CT, Judgment of 27 November 2006, Ref. No. K 47/04.

equal access to public service), rights entitling natural and legal persons (e.g. freedom of speech, right to court, right to protection of privacy) and rights reserved for natural persons (e.g. prohibition of maltreatment, right to social security). A few fundamental rights and freedoms are addressed to specific collective bodies (trade unions in case of the right to strike and other collective forms of workers' protests). Public authorities (including local self-governments) are not protected by constitutional rights and freedoms[360] since the state cannot be simultaneously entitled and obliged.

Constitutional rights and freedoms operate primarily within vertical relations between individuals and the state. The jurisprudence of the CT has remained inconclusive on the question of the applicability of fundamental rights in horizontal, inter-individual relations, whilst scholarship is not completely opposed to this idea, at least in the case of certain rights and freedoms, such as human dignity or the prohibition of discrimination.[361]

The sphere of personal freedom and equality guaranteed by the Polish Constitution is not without limits. Most rights may become subject to limitations in accordance with the principle of proportionality (article 31 para 3). First, every limitation must find its legal basis in a statute. Second, it must be suitable to achieve a legitimate aim enumerated in the Constitution (i.e. public security, public order, protection of the natural environment, public health, public morals, freedoms, and rights of other persons).[362] Third, it must be 'necessary', which means that the objective pursued by the limitation must not be achievable by less restrictive and intrusive measures.[363] The latter condition represents the principle of proportionality *sensu stricto* requiring that a fair balance is struck between the effects of the regulation and the burden imposed on the individual.[364] Furthermore, limitations of rights and freedoms must not violate their essence. Therefore, the proportionality test applied by the CT is to a large extent similar to the proportionality concept as applied by international courts (e.g. ECtHR or CJEU) and foreign constitutional courts (in particular, the FCC) and, indeed, the CT has often used the jurisprudence of international human rights bodies as a point of reference in interpretation of the Constitution (see above).

Constitutional rights and freedoms are not designed merely as (objective) principles, but as enforceable subjective rights. For this reason, the Constitution provides several mechanisms for their protection.

The most important mechanism is undoubtedly the right of access to courts[365]—in itself a subjective right. In this regard the Constitution provides that '[e]veryone shall have the right to a fair and public hearing of his case, without undue delay, before a competent, impartial and independent court' (article 45 para 1) and that '[s]tatutes shall not bar the recourse by any person to the courts in pursuit of claims alleging infringement of freedoms or rights' (article 77 para 2). Furthermore, judicial proceedings should have at least two instances (article 176 para 1).

The CT has held that the right to court is composed of four elements: right of access to court, right to a fair trial, right to judgment, and the right to an appropriate organizational set-up and status of courts, in accordance with the requirements of independence and

---

[360] See e.g. Lech Garlicki, *Polskie prawo* (n 85) 116; Marek Zubik, 'Orzekanie przez TK o przepisie nieobowiązującym dotyczącym jednostek samorządu terytorialnego' ['Constitutional Tribunal adjudicating on non-binding provisions concerning units of local self-government'] (2014) 1 Państwo i Prawo 3, 10–13.

[361] See e.g. Monika Florczak-Wątor, *Horyzontalny wymiar praw konstytucyjnych* (*The horizontal dimension of constitutional rights*) (Wydawnictwo Uniwersytetu Jagiellonskiego, Cracow, 2014) 345–370.

[362] See e.g. CT, Judgment of 16 October 2014, Ref. No. K 20/12.

[363] See e.g. CT, Judgment of 25 July 2013, Ref. Nc. P 56/11.

[364] See e.g. CT, Judgment of 10 December 2013, Ref. No. U 5/13.

[365] Lech Garlicki, *Polskie prawo* (n 85) 135.

impartiality.[366] The latter element allows individuals to question the constitutionality of provisions which may undermine the independence of judges adjudicating their cases. Specific guarantees ensuring the independence of judges, such as life tenure, irremovability, adequate remuneration, and immunity, are provided for in Chapter VIII of the Constitution, although the current government only pays lip service to them.

A further important mechanism to enforce fundamental rights is the constitutional complaint (article 79). The Constitution adopted a narrow model of a complaint—it may be directed only against a normative act which served as a basis for a decision or judgment rendered by a court or an organ of public administration with regard to the complainant's constitutional rights or freedoms. The complaint may be submitted by anyone whose constitutional rights or freedoms were violated—thus, the access to the CT is not limited to citizens. Furthermore, it may be submitted only after ordinary remedies have been exhausted and within three months after a final judgment has been rendered.[367] Complainants— represented by a professional lawyer[368]—are required to claim that their rights and freedoms as enshrined in the Constitution have been infringed for the complaint procedure to be admissible. The complaint may not be based on provisions enshrined in international treaties, even those protecting human rights like the ECHR.[369] A judgment by the CT declaring the unconstitutionality of the provision challenged does not engender an automatic annulment or cassation of a judgment or decision issued on the basis of such law, but merely enables the complainant (and other persons in analogous situation) to reopen the proceedings.

Despite the wide implications of the complaint procedure, it has to be borne in mind that the judicial enforceability of rights and freedoms varies across the different clusters of rights and freedoms. The enforceability question is particularly raised with regard to 'social rights.'[370] Some of these are formulated as programmatic norms, which, according to some scholars, are inept to be invoked directly and independently within a constitutional complaint.[371] However, according to others, in the case that the essence of a social right (formulated as a programmatic norm) is affected, the individual may file a constitutional complaint.[372] While this controversy and its main arguments surface frequently within legal orders protecting social rights, in the Polish socio-economic, historical, and political context it touches—in light of the urgency of the 'social question'—upon a key problem.

There are also constitutional features peculiar to the Polish constitutional system that limit the effectivity of certain social rights: their enforceability finds a further limitation in article 81, according to which '[t]he rights specified in article 65, paras 4 and 5, article 66, article 69, article 71 and articles 74–76, may be asserted subject to limitations specified by statute'. Consequently, individuals cannot base claims solely on the provisions mentioned in

---

[366] See e.g. CT, Judgment of 24 October 2007, Ref. No. SK 7/06; CT, Judgment of 6 November 2012, Ref. No. K 21/11.

[367] Article 77 para 1 ustawy z dnia 30 listopada 2016 r. o organizacji i trybie postępowania przed Trybunałem Konstytucyjnym (*Act of 30 November 2016 on the Organization and the Mode of Proceedings before the Constitutional Tribunal*), Dziennik Ustaw, item 2017 (2016) with further amendments.

[368] Article 44 para 1 ustawy o organizacji i trybie postępowania przed Trybunałem Konstytucyjnym (n 367).

[369] Leszek Bosek and Mikołaj Wild, 'Komentarz do Art. 79 Konstytucji', ['Commentary on article 79 of the Constitution'] in Marek Safjan and Leszek Bosek (eds), *Konstytucja RP* (n 221) 1845.

[370] Janusz Trzciński and Michał Szwast, 'Social and economic rights as fundamental rights', in Biruta Lewaszkiewicz-Petrykowska (ed), *Rapports Polonais. XIXe Congres International De Droit Compare. XIXth International Congress of Comparative Law. Vienne, 20-26 VII 2014* (Wydawnictwo Uniwersytetu Łózkiego Łódź, 2014) 308.

[371] Bogusław Banaszak, *Konstytucja* (n 227) 466.

[372] Janusz Trzciński and Marcin Wiącek, 'Komentarz do Art. 79 Konstytucji' ('Commentary on article 79 of the Constitution'), in Leszek Garlicki and Marek Zubik (eds), *Konstytucja Rzeczypospolitej Polskiej* (n 342) 903–904.

480 MICHAL SZWAST, MARCIN SZWED, AND PAULINA STARSKI

article 81 of the Constitution but will always have to invoke a proper statutory basis.[373] Some interpret article 81 as a norm which prevents the enforcement of the enumerated rights via constitutional complaints,[374] although others have cast doubt on this interpretation (partially).[375] In any case, the Constitution explicitly excludes the possibility of filing a constitutional complaint with regard to article 56 (the right to asylum).

Nevertheless, even if one accepted that social rights could form the basis of a constitutional complaint, the effectiveness of such protection would be severely limited due to two factors. First, the powers of the CT in terms of a constitutional review of legislative omissions are very restricted[376] (see above) and second, authorities enjoy a wide margin of discretion in regulating the implementation and realization of social rights. For these reasons, some judgments of the CT concerning social rights were criticized by politicians and the public opinion. The jurisprudence of the CT has been so far devoid of 'social rights activism'. In particular, the 2014 decision, in which the CT ruled that raising the retirement age of men and women did not violate the Constitution, was often used within the public debate as an example of an unsatisfactory approach of the CT with regard to the protection of citizens' rights and granting the government too extensive discretion.[377] Such a restraint in the realm of social rights is, however, not untypical for European constitutional courts.

With regard to non-judicial measures of human rights protection, the Constitution guarantees everybody 'the right to apply to the Commissioner for Citizens' Rights' (article 80). The Commissioner for Citizens' Rights (or the Ombudsman) is an independent body elected by the *Sejm* (with the consent of the Senate) for a term of five years (articles 209, 210). The Commissioner may assist individuals in the enforcement of their fundamental rights by, for instance, joining, or initiating administrative or judicial proceedings or lodging extraordinary appeals to the Supreme Court or the Supreme Administrative Court. He is also authorized to lodge a motion to the CT to review the constitutionality of statutes. The Constitution also establishes the separate office of the Commissioner for Children's Rights (article 72 para 4). Particularly during the 'constitutional crisis', the 'Ombudsman' has become a key figure within the fight against an unconstitutional recalibration of the Polish state.

The Constitution explicitly guarantees 'the right to compensation for any harm done ... by any action' of public authorities (article 77 para 1) and, separately, the right to compensation

---

[373] Bogumił Naleziński, 'Komentarz do Art. 81 Konstytucji', [Commentary on article 81 of the Constitution] in Marek Safjan and Leszek Bosek (eds), *Konstytucja RP* (n 221) 1862; Piotr Winczorek, *Komentarz do Konstytucji* (n 300) 189.

[374] See e.g. Anna Łabno, 'Skarga konstytucyjna w Konstytucji III RP' (Constitutional complaint in the III Republic of Poland), in Bogusław Banaszak and Artur Preisner, *Prawa i wolności obywatelskie w Konstytucji RP* [*Civic Rights and Freedoms in the Constitution of the Republic of Poland*] (CH Beck, Warsaw, 2002) 768.

[375] Janusz Trzciński and Marcin Wiącek, 'Komentarz do Art. 81 Konstytucji' (Commentary on article 81 of the Constitution), in Leszek Garlicki and Marek Zubik (eds), *Konstytucja Rzeczypospolitej Polskiej* (n 342) 933; Lech Garlicki, *Polskie prawo* (n 85) 135.

[376] Kamil Zaradkiewicz, 'Wolność "słabszego" do samookreślenia gospodarczego w świetle art 76 Konstytucji RP' ['Freedom of the "weaker party" to economic self-determination in the light of art 76 of the Polish Constitution'], in Maria Boratyńska (ed), *Ochrona strony słabszej stosunku prawnego. Księga jubileuszowa ofiarowana Profesorowi Adamowi Zielińskiemu* [*Protection of the Weaker Party within a Legal Relationship: Jubilee Book Offered to Professor Adam Zieliński*] (Wolters Kluwer, Warsaw, 2016) 133.

[377] For example, the President Andrzej Duda, commenting the CT ruling on the retirement age, asked: 'Was this a court that functioned for the Polish society and the Polish state? Or for some narrow ruling caste that had such an interest at that time?'—Marcin Hołubowicz, 'Prezydent Duda: Nie mam żadnych wątpliwości, że naruszono konstytucję także w działalności Trybunału Konstytucyjnego' [President Duda: I have no doubt that the constitution was violated also within the activities of the Constitutional Tribunal] *Wyborcza.pl* (4 July 2019) https://wroc law.wyborcza.pl/wroclaw/7,35771,24962025,prezydent-duda-nie-mam-zadnych-watpliwosci-ze-naruszono-konstytucje.html (last accessed on 23 April 2022).

for an unlawful deprivation of liberty (article 41 para 5). Detailed rules regarding the enforcement of the right to compensation are enshrined in statutes.

The effectiveness of this constitutional system of fundamental rights protection has been significantly weakened by the 'constitutional crisis' that we have been witnessing in the last years: As mentioned above, the CT issues far fewer judgments now than before 2015. The legality of some of its judgments is also more than questionable since they were issued by benches in which unlawfully elected judges participated.[378] Furthermore, a group of CT judges protested in an open letter against the unfair and unclear practice of the President of the Tribunal in terms of the allocation of cases to judges.[379] The effectiveness of the protection of fundamental rights is also threatened by various governmental actions and legislative measures which are detrimental to the independence of judges. Particularly worrisome is the 'reform' of the National Council of the Judiciary, which has led to politicization of this body.[380] NGOs also made some cases public where unjustified disciplinary proceedings were initiated against judges together with other forms of harassment.[381]

5. The Constitution and the Separation of Powers

The 1997 Constitution follows the classical 'liberal' idea of a (horizontal)[382] separation of powers (article 10 para 1) distinguishing between the executive, legislative, and judicial branch in the sense of a modern 'rule of law' concept. Simultaneously, it assumes an obligation of cooperation between these distinct powers as is reflected in the Preamble ('cooperation between the public powers'). At the core of this system stands the idea of 'balancing'. The separateness of, but also the considerable overlap between the three branches are instruments designed to prevent a centralization of power, at the same time serving as a 'mistake-correcting mechanism'.[383] The idea of the separation of powers—while inexistent during the times of communist authoritarian rule and curtailed during Pilsudski's reign, which was shaped by a concentration of presidential powers—is not a new addendum to Polish constitutionalism: It formed already an essential part of the Constitution of 1791, thus rendering it an element of the Polish 'constitutional heritage'.[384]

---

[378] See e.g. Piotr Radziewicz, 'On legal consequences of judgments of the Polish Constitutional Tribunal passed by an irregular panel' (2017) 32 Review of Comparative Law 45; Monika Florczak-Wątor, 'Glosa do wyroku TK z dnia 16 marca 2017 r., sygn. akt Kp 1/17' [Gloss on the judgment of the Constitutional Tribunal of 16 March 2017, Ref. No. Kp 1/17] LEX/el. 2017 (no 324075) http://konstytucyjny.pl/glosa-do-wyroku-tk-z-dnia-16-marca-2017-r-sygn-akt-kp-117-monika-florczak-wator/ (last accessed on 23 April 2022).

[379] Letter of the seven judges of the CT to the President of the CT, 5 December 2018 https://oko.press/images/2018/12/List-Se%CC%A8dzio%CC%81w-TK_5.12.2018-r.pdf (last accessed on 23 April 2022).

[380] See e.g. decision of the European Network of Councils for the Judiciary on suspension of the membership of the Polish National Council of the Judiciary, 17 September 2018 https://www.encj.eu/node/495 (last accessed on 22 April 2022); Mariusz Jałoszewski, 'Sędziowie odmawiają współpracy z nową KRS. Nie będą opiniować awansów' [Judges refuse to cooperate with the new NCJ. They will not give opinions on promotions], OKO.press (26 November 2018) https://oko.press/sedziowie-odmawiaja-wspolpracy-z-nowa-krs-nie-beda-opiniowac-awansow/ (last accessed on 22 April 2022).

[381] Justice Defence Committee (KOS), A country that punishes. Pressure and repression of Polish judges and prosecutors https://komitetobronysprawiedliwosci.pl/app/uploads/2019/02/Raport-KOS_eng.pdf (last accessed on 23 April 2022).

[382] On the 'vertical' separation of powers see more further below.

[383] Hanna Suchocka, 'Checks and Balances' (n 55) 48.

[384] See Jerzy Lukowski, 'Recasting Utopia: Montesquieu, Rousseau and the Polish Constitution of 3 May 1791' (n 20) 1, 69.

Within the constitutional system of 1997 the legislative is given 'the first place ... among other branches'[385] or to the least it is vested 'with a certain advantage over the other powers'.[386] While installing a 'mutual equilibrium' between the different branches, the Constitution does not opt from an 'absolute equality' between them,[387] thus standing in line with the tradition of the Constitution of 1921.[388] Yet, the Constitution installs safeguards in order to prevent a centralization of powers on the horizontal level which would lead back to the 'doctrine of the unity of power' that dominated during the times under authoritarian, communist rule and focused on the idea of the supremacy of the *Sejm*. On the one hand, in light of historical experiences power shifts towards the legislative, which the 1997 Constitution opts for (particularly when the ordinary procedures fail as a 'fall back option'[389]), are seen as potentially dangerous.[390] On the other hand, the Polish people seem to have a traditional preference for a strong legislative.[391] The Polish system of the separation of powers seems to have borrowed in an 'eclectic' manner 'from several models, namely, the chancellery model, the presidential or semi-presidential model and the parliamentary model'.[392]

In interpreting the 'separation of powers' model that underlies the Polish Constitution, the CT has adopted the concept of the 'essence of powers'. This concept provides that the 'essence of powers' must remain unaffected by possible delegations and transfers of competences, which forms also a part of the rationale of the jurisprudence of the FCC.[393] In one of its judgments, the CT quoted the FCC (directly in German), according to which 'the violation of the principle of separation of powers takes place only if the interference of the parliament concerns the very essence of the executive power'.[394] This concept has been repeated several times in the case law of the CT.[395] Various provisions establish the incompatibility of functions—see articles 102, 103—which is a further means to delineate the respective powers from each other.

a) The Legislative

In terms of the legislative branch the Constitution establishes a bicameral system which is shaped by power asymmetries. The legislative is comprised of both the *Sejm* and the Senate (article 10 para 2, article 95 para 1). The competences of the former are considerably stronger. The *Sejm* fulfils a legislative, creative, and controlling function. Its key role is to exercise control over the Council of Ministers (CoM) (Article 95 para 2). Yet, the *Sejm* exercises this function 'within the scope specified by the provisions of the Constitution and statutes' (article 95 para 2). This addition has been regarded as particularly important by the drafters because it prevents the legislature from assuming the status of a 'supreme power' within the

---

[385] Bogusław Banaszak, '§ 1 Concise History of Constitutions', in Bogusław Banaszak and others (eds), *Constitutional Law in Poland* (n 31) 17, 26.

[386] Ibid, 33, para 34.

[387] Ibid.

[388] Ryszard Cholewinski, 'The Protection of Human Rights' (n 40) 242; Leszek L Garlicki, 'The Presidency in the New Polish Constitution' (1997) 6 E. Eur. Const. Rev. 81, 88.

[389] See for example article 154 para 3.

[390] Hanna Suchocka, 'Checks and Balances' (n 55) 60.

[391] See Andrzej Rapaczynski, 'Constitutional Politics in Poland: A Report of the Constitutional Commission of the Polish Parliament' (1991) 58 U. Chi. L. Rev. 595, 623 f.

[392] See Hanna Suchocka, 'Checks and Balances' (n 55) 61.

[393] Krzysztof Wojtyczek, *Sądownictwo konstytucyjne* (n 127) 250–251.

[394] CT, Decision of 22 November 1995, Ref. No. K 19/95: '('Erst wenn zugunsten des Parlaments ein Einbruch in den Kernbereich der Exekutive erfolgt, ist das Gewaltenteilungsprinzip verletzt' – Entscheidungen des Bundesverfassungsgerichts, Band IX (1959), 280)'.

[395] See, for instance, CT, Judgment of 14 April 1999, Ref. No. K 8/99 and CT, Judgment of 24 February 2010, Ref. No. K 6/09.

state. The principle of the separation of powers does likewise form part of the 'provisions of the Constitution', hence limiting the extent of supervision.[396]

The Senate serves as a 'house of reflection'.[397] It lacks control powers over most of the state bodies. Still, it is endowed with some legislative competences as well as competences to participate in the nomination of candidates for state bodies (see e.g. article 209 para 1). It has the right to introduce legislation (article 118 para 1). In terms of its legislative activities its decisions are subject to an overruling decision by the *Sejm*. The Senate's rejection of a bill or its resolution to amend a bill maybe rejected by the *Sejm* 'by an absolute majority vote in the presence of at least half of the statutory number of Deputies' (article 121 para 3).

In some instances, the Senate and the *Sejm* merge into the National Assembly—see article 114—whose competence it is to take the oath of the President after her or his election, to declare the President's incapacity in exercising her/his duties, and it has—according to article 145 para 2—the competence to initiate an indictment proceeding against the President before the Tribunal of the State.

b) The Executive

The executive power manifests in a dual guise being vested in the President and the CoM—a collective body (article 10 para 2, article 146). The qualification of the President as part of the executive has been a major point of controversy during the deliberations on the Constitution since various voices argued for placing the President outside the sphere of the three branches which would allow him to fulfil her/his coordinating function more effectively.[398]

The CoM is presided by the Prime Minister (see articles 89 para 2, 147 para 1). While there exist considerable political links between the *Sejm* and the CoM whose appointment by the President is to be approved by the *Sejm* majority (article 154 para 1),[399] the CoM is not subject to any prerogative powers of the President. The President plays, however, a role in its creation (article 154 para 1 clause 1). The latter marks a significant departure from the communist political order in which the appointment of the government was merely a matter of the *Sejm*. Yet in some special constellations—the President does not appoint a Prime Minister according to article 154 para 1 or the CoM fails to obtain the vote of confidence according to article 154 para 3—the role of the President in terms of appointment becomes purely formal (see article 154 para 3) and it is up to the *Sejm* to choose the Prime Minister and the Members of the CoM as proposed by him.[400] Here the arrangement seems to display features of the 'new' (President as a counterbalance to the *Sejm*) and the 'old' (supremacy of the *Sejm*).[401]

The CoM is politically accountable to the *Sejm*. This political accountability manifests itself in the option of parliamentary votes of no confidence, which have to be constructive in nature (article 158 para 1 clause 1).

While the President is directly elected (article 127 para 1), the 1997 Constitution has limited her/his role. The President serves as an 'arbiter among other state bodies'.[402]

---

[396] Hanna Suchocka, 'Checks and Balances' (n 55) 49.

[397] Izabela J Bista, 'Legislative Branch', in Bogusław Banaszak and others (eds), *Constitutional Law* (n 31) 127, para 121.

[398] Hanna Suchocka, 'Checks and Balances' (n 55) 49.

[399] An 'absolute majority of votes in the presence of at least half of the statutory number of Deputies' is required, see article 154 para 2 cl 2.

[400] Should this option fail, article 155 modifies the appointment procedure further.

[401] See for a critical assessment of this multi-stage appointment procedure: Hanna Suchocka, 'Checks and Balances' (n 55) 56.

[402] See Leszek Garlicki, 'Constitutional Law', in Stanislaw Frankowski (ed), *Introduction into Polish Law* (Kluwer, The Hague-Cracow, 2005) 1, 24.

According to article 126 para 1 the President is the 'supreme representative of the Republic of Poland and the guarantor of the continuity of State authority' and her/his main functions are to 'ensure observance of the Constitution, safeguard the sovereignty and security of the State as well as the inviolability and integrity of its territory' (article 126 para 2).

The validity of most acts issued by the President is subject to the countersignature by the Prime Minister (article 144 para 2, see for exceptions para 3). This countersignature requirement defines the presidency model that the Polish Constitution has opted for and strengthens the role of the Prime Minister vis-à-vis the President. It is the Prime Minister who is accountable for the countersigned acts to the *Sejm* (article 144 para 2). This model forces both the Prime Minister and the President to cooperate and to collaborate, thus realizing the key idea of 'checks and balances'.

One dispute is particularly exemplary of the tension between the President and the role of the Prime Minister within the Polish constitutional order. President Lech Kaczyński and the Prime Minister Donald Tusk fought intensely over the competence to represent Poland at the European Council's meetings. In the period of cohabitation in 2007–2010, both the President and the Prime Minister participated simultaneously in some meetings of the European Council on behalf of Poland and often presented separate positions on issues raised at these meetings. The dispute was settled, at the request of the Prime Minister, by a decision of the CT of 20 May 2009.[403] The CT had to comment on the division of tasks and competences in the field of foreign policy in the context of this 'executive plurality' in Poland. It ruled that the relationship between the President, the CoM and the Prime Minister is steered by the principle of cooperation: authorities shall cooperate in the exercise of their constitutional tasks and competences, which is expressed in the Preamble as well as in article 133 para 3. The President, as the supreme representative of the Republic of Poland, may, pursuant to article 126 para 1, decide on her/his participation in a specific meeting of the European Council, if he/she deems it advisable to carry out the tasks of the President specified in article 126 para 2. The CoM, based on article 146 paras 1, 2, and 4 pt 9, determines the position of the Republic of Poland which is to be presented within a particular meeting of the European Council.[404] The Tribunal made clear that '[t]he participation of the President of the Republic of Poland in a given session of the European Council requires cooperation of the President with the Prime Minister and the competent minister, according to the principles set out in article 133(3) of the Constitution'. The objective of this cooperation is to 'ensure uniformity of actions taken on behalf of the Republic of Poland in relations with the European Union and its institutions'.[405] This cooperation has—in view of the CT—two effects. First, it 'enables the President to refer—in matters related to the exercise of his duties specified in article 126 para 2 of the Constitution—to the stance of the Republic of Poland determined by the Council of Ministers'. Second, it allows 'to specify the extent and manner of the intended participation of the President in a session of the European Council'.[406] This ruling was unprecedented in constitutional practice and is regarded as one of the 'milestones' of CT jurisprudence.[407]

---

[403] CT, Decision of 20 May 2009, Ref. No. Kpt 2/08 (also on the factual background).
[404] Ibid, ruling pt 3.
[405] Here and before ibid, ruling pt 4.
[406] Ibid, ruling pt 5.
[407] Dariusz Dudek, *Autorytet Prezydenta a Konstytucja Rzeczypospolitej Polskiej* [*The authority of the President and the Constitution of the Republic of Poland*] (Catholic University, Lublin, 2013) 229. See also Jerzy Ciapała, 'Komentarz do postanowienia Trybunału Konstytucyjnego z dnia 20 maja 2009 r., sygn. akt Kpt 2/08' [Commentary on the decision of the Constitutional Tribunal of May 20, 2009, Ref. No. Kpt 2/08], in Leszek Garlicki, Marta Derlatka, and Marcin Wiącek (eds), *Na straży państwa prawa* (n 38) 61.

The President is endowed with several powers to influence the legislative process. She or he has the power of legislative initiative (article 118 para 1). Beyond that a statute adopted by the legislative bodies requires for its validity—i.e. for becoming part of the Polish legal order—the signature of the President (article 122 para 1). This signature requirement gives the President two options to prevent a statute of coming into force. First, the President has the right to submit a motion to the CT to review the conformity of a bill with the Constitution (preventive control) (article 122 para 3). Second, the President may exercise her/his right to declare a suspension veto (which can be overridden by a three-fifths majority of the parliament in the presence of at least half of the statutory number of deputies—article 122 para 5). The 1997 Constitution has rendered the veto override easier if compared to the Small Constitution which required a two-thirds majority of deputies. The right to submit a bill to the CT or to exercise a veto forcing the *Sejm* to reconsider a bill are designed as alternative options. The President may not refer a bill to the *Sejm* for reconsideration after it was 'judged by the Constitutional Tribunal as conforming to the Constitution' (article 122 para 3).

Furthermore, the President is also endowed with powers to dissolve the *Sejm* in specific circumstances, which then triggers an automatic dissolution of the Senate (article 98 para 4).[408] The intricate relationship between the legislative and the President evidences that the Polish state displays characteristics of both a presidential as well as parliamentary system, meandering between both of them.

c) The Judiciary

The 'judicial power' is 'vested in courts and tribunals' (see article 10 para 2 and Chapter VIII). Article 173 secures both the separateness of the judicial branch from the other branches of government as well as its independence.

The CT provided for by article 194 marks an essential cornerstone of the system of checks and balances that underlies the Constitution (see more on its competences already above).[409] By making use of signalling resolutions (see above) and thereby commenting on errors in the current legal system,[410] the CT sets points of orientation for the legislators. The monopoly of the CT to declare statutes unconstitutional—on the controversial 'dispersed judicial review' see Section D.1—in a binding manner (with an *ex nunc* effect in terms of their voidness,[411] see article 190 para 3)[412] forms a considerable departure from the previous system in which it was possible for the parliament to overrule a judgment of the CT establishing the non-conformity of a statute with the Constitution by a two-thirds majority.[413] Yet, in the course of the 'constitutional crisis' of 2015 and onwards, such a power appeared to be an attractive option for some political factions. The 'United Right' in the end opted for a de facto neutralization of the CT by its personal reconfiguration. The same applies to the whole judicial branch which has been affected by the 'constitutional crisis' severely (see Section C). While

---

[408] Both chambers fail to adopt a budget within four months (article 225) or *Sejm* fails to accept a cabinet appointed by the President (article 155 para 2 of the Constitution).

[409] Hanna Suchocka, 'Checks and Balances' (n 55) 53.

[410] See Michał Bernaczyk, 'Constitutional Judiciary', in Bogusław Banaszak and others (eds), *Constitutional Law* (n 31) 178, para 189.

[411] A judgment of the CT declaring a statute unconstitutional leads to its voidness.

[412] Ordinary courts have the option to refer questions as to the constitutionality of a statute to the CT, see article 193.

[413] See article 6 para 1 and para 3 of the Ustawa z dnia 29 kwietnia 1985 r. o Trybunale Konstytucyjnym [Law of 29 April 1985 on the Constitutional Tribunal], Dziennik Ustaw, No 22, item 98 (1985); also: Lech Garlicki, 'The Experience of the Polish Constitutional Court', in Wojciech Sadurski (ed), *Constitutional Justice, East and West: Democratic Legitimacy and Constitutional Courts in Post-Communist Europe in a Comparative Perspective* (Kluwer Law International, The Hague, 2002) 265, 265; Hanna Suchocka, 'Checks and Balances' (n 55) 53.

not having been abolished, the 'United Right' sought to subjugate it by different means—most importantly by ways of a re-composition of court benches. The judiciary reacted inter alia by stretching doctrine to its limits ('constitutional self-defence'—see above). While severely injured, the third branch is yet not entirely eradicated.

6. The Constitution and the Form of the State

One of the basic principles within the Polish constitutional order is the principle of the uniformity of the state (article 3). This principle provides that Poland has an integral organization of public authority, comprises a 'Nation' understood as a political unity (community of citizens) as well as a uniform territory, the integrity of which is expressed by the fact that its division is solely administrative.[414] In accordance with the latter, the territory of Poland is indivisible, and no autonomous regions exist. Legislative and executive powers are exercised at the central level.

As a consequence of the principle of the uniformity of the state it is impossible to transform Poland by way of a statute into a federal state in which regions (lands, provinces) could adopt separate constitutions binding on their territory, enjoy relatively extensive autonomy vis-à-vis the central government, possess a separate judiciary and legislature, and whose citizens would have dual citizenship. While such a 'federalization' has not been on the agenda of relevant political forces since 1918, the Constitution of 1997 introduced the decentralization of public power and the transfer of a 'substantial part of public duties' (article 16 para 2) to the local government (articles 15, 16; articles 163 to 172). The vertical separation of powers is vital to the constitutional set-up of Poland also in light of the power centralization that shaped communist state models. The Constitution aims to depart from these models and this departure was a major issue for the *Solidarność* movement.[415]

According to article 15 para 1, '[t]he territorial system of the Republic of Poland shall ensure the decentralization of public power' and the 'territorial division' is to be determined by statute (article 15 para 2). 'The inhabitants of the units of basic territorial division ... form a self-governing community in accordance with law' (article 16 para 1), the local government takes part 'in the exercise of public power' (article 16 para 2). According to the CT,[416] the legislator must not unduly interfere in the sphere of independence granted to local government, depriving its units of both duties, which the local government[417] ought to exercise in accordance with the principle of decentralization, as well as financial resources allocated for the implementation of those duties.[418] Article 163 provides that local governments 'perform public tasks not reserved by the Constitution or statutes to the organs of other public authorities'. This provision implies a presumption of competence for local governments in the field of performing public tasks,[419] which is closely related to the principle of subsidiarity included in the Preamble of the Constitution.

---

[414] Piotr Tuleja, 'Komentarz do Art. 3 Konstytucji', ['Commentary on Art. 3 of the Constitution'] in Marek Safjan and Leszek Bosek (eds), *Konstytucja RP* (n 221) para IV.1.

[415] Maria Kruk, 'The Systematic Order of the Constitution' (n 27) 44.

[416] CT, Judgment of 3 November 2006, Ref. No. K 31/06.

[417] The constitutive and executive bodies of local government units are directly elected within elections which are universal, direct, equal and conducted by secret ballot (article 169 para 2).

[418] CT, Judgment of 31 January 2013, Ref. No. K 14/11.

[419] Andrzej Skoczylas and Wojciech Piątek, 'Komentarz do Art. 163 Konstytucji', ['Commentary on article 163 of the Constitution'] in Marek Safjan and Leszek Bosek, *Konstytucja RP* (n 102) para I.

Units of local government 'possess legal personality', have 'rights of ownership and other property rights' (article 165 para 1), are 'assured public funds adequate for the performance of the duties assigned to them' (article 167 para 1), 'to the extent established by statute, ... have the right to set the level of local taxes and charges' (article 168), 'have the right to associate' (article 172 para 1) and are entitled 'to join international associations of local and regional communities as well as to cooperate with local and regional communities of other states' (article 172 para 2), which thus allows for transnational regulation. Local governments may 'enact local legal enactments applicable to their territorially defined areas of operation' (article 94). The 'legality of actions by a local government [is] subject to review' (article 171 para 1) by 'the Prime Minister and voivods and regarding financial matters—regional audit chambers' (article 171 para 2). Their 'self-governing nature ... [is] protected by the courts' (article 165 para 2).

The Constitution does not enumerate all functioning units of local government, thereby subjecting the structure and types of local government to regulation by statute (article 164 para 2). Article 164 para 1 determines, however, the commune (*gmina*) as the basic unit of local government, which is hence protected against liquidation and an excessive curtailment of competences by legislative action. The *gmina* performs 'all tasks of local government not reserved to other units of local government' (article 164 para 3). Communes were the only local government units (apart from voivodships) that existed at the time of the Constitution's adoption. For these reasons, the authors of the Constitution recognized them as basic units and left it up to the legislator to determine the type and nature of other local government units.

Article 164 para 2 requires that at least one further unit of local government exists beyond the *gmina*, without determining how many units and levels should be established.[420] The Act of 24 July 1998 opted for a three-level territorial division leading to the establishment of poviats (*powiaty*) and voivodships (*województwa*) besides communes.[421] All units act, as a rule, upon separate competences and exercise distinct functions, while only the *gmina* is constitutionally protected.[422] No supervisory relationships exit between these units.[423] While the three-level structure is not constitutionally commanded, one of the questions in the nationwide referendum proposed by the President of Poland in 2018 concerned the constitutional petrification of the current territorial division of Poland.[424]

Currently there are 2477 communes, 380 poviats, and sixteen voivodships in Poland, and no radical changes have been introduced to this system so far.

---

[420] The CT pointed out in the Judgment of 4 March 2014, Ref. No. K 13/11 that the Constitution requires at least a two-level structure of local government.

[421] Communes and poviats are created and liquidated by regulations of the CoM, whereas voivodships were created by the Act of 24 July 1998 on the introduction of the basic three-level territorial division of the state (Dziennik Ustaw, No 96, item 603).

[422] Critically Bogusław Banaszak, *Konstytucja* (n 227) 136; Marian Kallas, *Konstytucja Rzeczypospolitej Polskiej* (*Constitution of the Republic of Poland*) (PWN, Warsaw, 1997) 72.

[423] CT, Judgment of 26 May 2015, Ref. No. Kp 2/13.

[424] The referendum question was: 'Are you in favor of regulating the division of local government units into communes, poviats and voivodships in the Constitution of the Republic of Poland?' See Projekt Postanowienia (20 July 2018) at https://www.prezydent.pl/storage/file/core_files/2021/8/5/722e0101ba72c81fb88d5d6667ca137e/projekt_postanowienia.pdf (last accessed on 7 December 2022).

7. The Constitution and its Identity

Although the 1997 Constitution was explicitly designed to pave the way towards the accession of Poland to the EU—its membership within the EU forming hence part of its constitutional core—the CT has installed bars to an 'Europeanization' and 'integration' that circulate around the concept of 'constitutional identity' (*tożsamość konstytucyjna*).[425] In its Lisbon judgment, that we mentioned above, the CT—referring to Dzialocha and basically following the reasoning of the FCC in its own Lisbon ruling[426]—delineated 'constitutional identity' as 'a concept which determines the scope of excluding—from the competence to confer competences—the matters which constitute ... "the heart of the matter", i.e., are fundamental to the basis of the political system of a given state'.[427] Taking an *ex negativo* approach, the CT has identified as matters that would be subject to a prohibition of conferral based on article 90 of the Constitution 'decisions specifying the fundamental principles of the Constitution and decisions concerning the rights of the individual which determine the identity of the state, including, in particular, the requirement of protection of human dignity and constitutional rights, the principle of statehood, the principle of democratic governance, the principle of a state ruled by law, the principle of social justice, the principle of subsidiarity, as well as the requirement of ensuring better implementation of constitutional values and the prohibition to confer the power to amend the Constitution and the competence to determine competences'.[428] Contrary to the approach of the Czech Constitutional Court,[429] the CT opted here for a catalogue of issues forming part of the 'constitutional identity' despite the non-existence of an eternity clause within the 1997 Constitution.

While the Polish CT has early on referred to international jurisprudence (especially the jurisprudence of the ECtHR), it regards 'the norms of the Constitution within the field of individual rights and freedoms' as 'a minimum and unsurpassable threshold'.[430] This applies also with respect to the EU: The level of protection guaranteed by the Constitution 'may not be lowered or questioned as a result of the introduction of Community provisions'.[431] Fundamental rights form hence the core of 'constitutional identity'.[432]

Therefore, the concept of 'constitutional identity' becomes relevant in the constellation of an explicit transfer of powers governed by article 90 but also if amendments to primary law of the EU effectively result in a transfer of sovereign powers.[433] The Tribunal also followed this line of argument in its judgment of 2013 on the amendment of Article 136 TFEU. It held

---

[425] This concept is applied exclusively with regard to EU law, see Anna Śledzińska-Simon and Michał Ziółkowski, 'Constitutional Identity of Poland: Is the Emperor Putting on the Old Clothes of Sovereignty?' in Christian Calliess and Gerhard van der Schyff (eds), *Constitutional Identity in a Europe of Multilevel Constitutionalism* (Cambridge University Press, Cambridge 2019) 243.

[426] Federal Constitutional Court, Judgment of 30 June 2009, 2 BvE 2/08, para 208. The Tribunal not only analysed the ruling of the FCC extensively, see CT, Judgment of 24 November 2010, Ref. No. K 32/09 (Lisbon Treaty) para 3.3 but also discussed relevant judgments rendered by constitutional courts of other states, see para 3.2 f.

[427] CT, Judgment of 24 November 2010, Ref. No. K 32/09 (Lisbon Treaty).

[428] CT, Judgment of 24 November 2010, Ref. No. K 32/09 (Lisbon Treaty) para 2.1. referring to Krzysztof Wojtyczek, *Przekazywanie kompetencji państwa organizacjom międzynarodowym* (Kraków 2007) 284 f.

[429] Czech Republic Constitutional Court, Decision of 3 November 2009, Pl. ÚS 29/09 (Lisbon Treaty II) para 111.

[430] CT, Judgment of 11 May 2005, Ref. No. K 18/04.

[431] CT, Judgment of 11 May 2005, Ref. No. K 18/04; CT, Judgment of 24 November 2010, Ref. No. K 32/09 (Lisbon Treaty) as translated and reproduced in Selected Rulings of the Polish Constitutional Tribunal concerning the Law of the European Union (2003–2014), Studia i Materiały Trybunału Konstytucyjnego, Vol. LI (Warszawa 2014).

[432] See also Sławomir Dudzik and Nina Półtorak, 'The Court of the Last Word: Competences of the Polish Constitutional Tribunal in the Review of European Union Law' (2012) 15 Y.B. Polish Eur. Stud. 225, 255.

[433] CT, Judgment of 24 November 2010, Ref. No. K 32/09 (Lisbon Treaty) para 2.1.

that '[t]he guarantee of preserving the constitutional identity of the Republic is Article 90 of the Constitution and boundaries of conferral of competences specified therein.'[434]

The CT has suggested that EU law which is incompatible with Poland's constitutional identity is *ultra vires*.[435] An encroachment upon the Polish constitutional identity eradicates the primacy of the relevant (primary) EU law.

Interestingly, the CT regards 'national identity' as found in primary EU Law—*tożsamość narodowa*—as an 'equivalent of the concept of constitutional identity'.[436] In this respect, the Court stresses that the 'idea of confirming one's national identity in solidarity with other nations, and not against them, constitutes the main axiological basis of the European Union, in the light of the Treaty of Lisbon', thereby emphasizing the solidarity aspect in the protection of 'national identity'.[437] Therefore, the aspect of 'national uniqueness' circulating around concepts like tradition and culture remains relevant to determine the constitutional identity of the Polish state,[438] albeit the Tribunal did not directly refer to the cultural dimension in its catalogue of elements forming part of Poland's 'constitutional identity'.

The interrelatedness of 'constitutional identity' and 'national identity' suggested by the CT renders article 6 para 1 potentially significant when delineating the former. Pursuant to this provision the 'Republic of Poland shall provide conditions for the people's equal access to the products of culture which are the source of the Nation's identity, continuity and development'. Accordingly, the constitution presupposes a close relationship between 'culture' and 'national identity'. Article 5 employs the term of the 'national heritage' that the Republic of Poland is obliged to safeguard, article 6 speaks of the national cultural heritage. Scholarship defines 'national heritage' in the sense of article 5 as the sum of 'all substantive and intellectual factors present in the history of the Polish state and society which form the basis of its identity, also in terms of its position to other nations, and also forming the basis of its future development'.[439] Obviously, it is debatable what exactly forms the core of 'national identity'. In that regard the position of Christian values within the Constitution would present a controversial case. While the Preamble does speak of the Polish 'culture rooted in the Christian heritage of the Nation', it combines this statement with a reference to 'universal human values'. Furthermore—as already seen—it includes also those 'not sharing such faith [to God] but respecting those universal values as arising from other sources' into the concept of the Polish Nation. While the argument can hence be elaborated both ways, Christianity and Christian values are considered as integral parts of Polish identity. And this aspect has become an essential part of the narrative purported by the 'United Right': the 'monstrance' is as frequently referred to by the 'United Right' as the Polish flag. This alignment has proven highly politically effective as is the alliance between the 'United Right' and the right-wing, conservative, and Catholic-oriented radio broadcasting channel 'Radio Maryja'.

---

[434] CT, Judgment of 26 June 2013, Ref. No. K 33/12 [Procedure for the Ratification of the European Council Decision 2011/199/EU amending Art 136 of the TFEU], para 6.4.1. translated and reproduced in Selected Rulings of the Polish Constitutional Tribunal concerning the Law of the European Union (2003–2014), Studia i Materiały Trybunału Konstytucyjnego, Vol. LI (Warszawa 2014).

[435] Cf. the rationale of CT, Judgment of 24 November 2010, Ref. No. K 32/09 (Lisbon Treaty).

[436] CT, Judgment of 24 November 2010, Ref. No. K 32/09 (Lisbon Treaty) para 2.1.

[437] CT, Judgment of 24 November 2010, Ref. No. K 32/09 (Lisbon Treaty) para 2.1.

[438] CT, Judgment of 24 November 2010, Ref. No. K 32/09 (Lisbon Treaty) para 2.1. See Anna Śledzińska-Simon, 'Constitutional identity' (n 83) 141.

[439] See Paweł Sarnecki, 'Komentarz do Art. 5 Konstytucji' ('Commentary on article 5 of the Constitution)' in Leszek Garlicki and Marek Zubik (eds), *Konstytucja Rzeczypospolitej Polskiej* (n 221) para 10.

E. Conclusions and Outlook

The Polish Constitution displays all characteristics of modern constitutions of democratic states centred around the protection of fundamental rights and the rule of law. It comprises elements of both the French as well as the German constitution. Yet, the institutional safeguards that it has installed were unable to prevent the 'unconstitutional moment' and the dismantling of the Constitution's foundations that have occurred since 2015. This process culminated in an 'institutional capture' which took as—Sadurski states—'no less than two years'.[440] It appears that we are left with nothing more than a variant of Böckenförde's dictum that a state governed by the rule of law cannot guarantee the conditions its very existence rests upon.[441] These conditions need to be reinstalled. Resilience of a system against illiberal backsliding depends to a large extent on an 'intersubjective agreement' anchored in civil society. Additionally, it depends on individuals in office willing to obey judgments by courts that pose obstacles to their policies. This is nothing more and nothing less than the core of the 'separation of powers' idea. But there are reasons for an optimistic outlook into the future and hope that the era of a detachment of the 'real constitution' from constitutional reality will come to an end. If Poland's constitutional history has proven one thing it is that ruptures are followed by the re-establishment of continuities.

Epilogue

We have finalized this chapter on the '*Gestalt*' of the Polish Constitution in 2019/2020. Since then, various constitutional developments took place—most of them highly disturbing. Most importantly, the 'cordiality' and 'openness' of the Polish constitutional order towards EU law and international law faced a profound attack: the CT—in its unconstitutional composition and in a jurisprudential U-turn—found that it had no obligation to act in conformity with interim measures of the CJEU with regard to the Polish judiciary[442] and declared articles 1, 2, and 19 para 1 subparagraph 2 TEU to be incompatible with the Polish Constitution.[443] This was met with severe criticism by EU institutions[444] and other EU member states.[445] Most importantly, it was met with heavy resistance by retired judges of the CT who pointed to 'many false assertions' to be found in the judgment.[446] The same is true for Polish scholarship.[447] On 22 December 2021 the European Commission initiated an infringement procedure in reaction to this strand of CT case law.[448] After aspects of the rule of law in Poland had also

---

[440] Wojciech Sadurski, *Poland's Constitutional Breakdown* (n 6) 186.

[441] Ernst-Wolfgang Böckenförde, 'Die Entstehung des Staates als Vorgang der Säkularisation' (1967), in Ernst-Wolfgang Böckenförde, *Recht, Staat, Freiheit* (Suhrkamp, Berlin, 1991) 92, 112 f.

[442] CT, Judgment of 14 July 2021, Ref. No. P 7/20.

[443] CT, Judgment of 7 October 2021, Ref. No. K 3/21.

[444] See Statement by European Commission President Ursula von der Leyen (STATEMENT/21/5163), 8 October 2021.

[445] See generally Nettesheim, 'Exclusion from the EU is Possible as a Last Resort', VerfBlog, 11 March 2021, https://verfassungsblog.de/exclusion-from-the-eu-is-possible-as-a-last-resort (last accessed on 23 April 2022).

[446] See Statement of Retired Judges of the Polish Constitutional Tribunal, VerfBlog, 10 November 2021, https://verfassungsblog.de/statement-of-retired-judges-of-the-polish-constitutional-tribunal (last accessed on 23 April 2022).

[447] Resolution No. 04/2021 of the Committee of Legal Sciences of the Polish Academy of Sciences in connection with the settlement of the Constitutional Tribunal of 7 October 2021, Nauka 1/2022, 199 f; see also Lasek-Markey, Poland's Constitutional Tribunal on the status of EU law, European Law Blog 2021, https://europeanlawblog.eu/2021/10/21/polands-constitutional-tribunal-on-the-status-of-eu-law-the-polish-government-got-all-the-answers-it-needed-from-a-court-it-controls/ (last accessed on 23 April 2022).

[448] European Commission, Press Release IP/21/7070.

become the subject of the jurisprudence of the ECtHR,[449] the CT ruled that article 6 para 1 of the ECHR is incompatible with the Polish Constitution in so far it comprises the CT and 'grants the European Court of Human Rights the jurisdiction to review the legality of the process of electing judges to the Constitutional Tribunal'.[450] Recently the CT found article 6 para 1 of the ECHR to be incompatible with Polish constitutional law *inter alia* in so far as it allows the ECtHR to establish standards for the appointment procedure of judges and allows the ECtHR to determine the compatibility of provisions governing the structure of the judiciary with the ECHR.[451] The CT issued the latter judgment at a time when the Russian invasion in Ukraine generated fears within the Polish society in terms of a possible Russian attack on Polish sovereign statehood. One could have expected that the exceptionality of the Russian aggression created a particular momentum of 'belonging' in Poland in which challenging European normative foundations had no space. Yet, the dissonance seems to have become even more pronounced. At this point the conflict between the 'real constitution' and its distorted and politicized reading unfolds again reaching a very sad climax. Yet, we still have not lost hope—this unprecedented disintegration of Poland from the European 'constitutional compound'[452] will not remain the last word.

---

[449] See e.g. ECtHR, *Xero Flor w Polsce sp. z o.o. v Poland*, Judgment of 7 May 2021, App. No 4907/18; *Reczkowicz v Poland*, Judgment of 22 July 2021, App. No 43447/19.

[450] CT, Judgment of 24 November 2021, Ref. No. K 6/21. For an English translation see https://trybunal.gov.pl/en/hearings/judgments/art/11709-art-6-ust-1-zd-1-konwencji-o-ochronie-praw-czlowieka-i-podstawowych-wolnosci-w-zakresie-w-jakim-pojeciem-sad-obejmuje-trybunal-konstytucyjny (last accessed on 23 April 2022).

[451] CT, Judgment of 10 March 2022, Ref. No. K 7/21.

[452] On this term see Matthias Jestaedt, 'Der Europäische Verfassungsverbund – Verfassungstheoretischer Charme und rechtstheoretische Insuffizienz einer Unschärferelation', in Rüdiger Krause (ed), *Gedächtnisschrift für Wolfgang Blomeyer* (Duncker & Humblot, Berlin 2004) 637; Hermann-Josef Blanke, 'Art. 4' in Herman-Josef Blanke and Stelio Mangiameli (eds), *The Treaty on European Union (TEU)* (Springer, Heidelberg 2013) para 86.

10

The Evolution and *Gestalt* of the Romanian Constitution

Bogdan Iancu[*]

A. **Origins of the Current Constitution**	493		b) The 1991 Constitution	511
1. Constitutionalism in Romania: Continuities and Discontinuities	493	B.	**The Evolution of the Constitution**	515
			1. Shifting Contexts: New Conflicts, New Vocabularies	515
2. The Genesis of Constitutionalism in Romania	496		2. The 'Euro-Amendments'	516
a) The Romanian Enlightenment and Early Modernization Projects; The Organic Regulations	496		3. Constitutional Conflicts	521
			4. Anticorruption as a Quasi-constitutional Meta-discourse	524
b) Nineteenth-century Constitutionalism: The Theory of Forms without Substance	500	C.	**Basic Structures and Concepts**	531
			1. The Constitutionalization of Romanian Law	531
c) The Constitution of 1923: Rise and Fall	505		2. Fundamental Rights and the Rule of Law	536
3. Return or New Beginning? The Constitution of 1991	508		3. Separation of Powers	542
a) The Post-Communist Setting	508	D.	**Constitutional Identity**	545

A. Origins of the Current Constitution

1. Constitutionalism in Romania: Continuities and Discontinuities

Normative constitutionalism, as it appeared in the aftermath of the eighteenth-century French and American revolutions, is part of a larger Enlightenment project in which most of the world participated most of the time, if at all, incompletely and fragmentarily. Systems where modernity—as expressed in the achievements of liberal constitutionalism—has not been internalized may encounter difficulties in adapting to multi-layer constitutional postmodernism.

---

[*] The historical research was partly undertaken within the project PN-III-P4-ID-PCE-2016-0013 *Heads of State (Princes, Kings and Presidents) and the Authoritarian Dynamic of Political Power in Romanian Constitutional History*, funded by the Romanian Research Funding Agency (UEFISCDI). I want to thank Professor Armin von Bogdandy for his generous collegial hospitality and the staff at the Max Planck Institute for Comparative Public Law and International Law for superb research support during my July–August 2018 stay in Heidelberg, when a first draft was written. Thanks are due to Dr. Michael Ioannidis, senior Researcher at MPIL, for very useful comments on the draft during a 2019 Heidelberg workshop, and to Dr. Cosmin Văduva and Dr. Károly Benke, Assistant Magistrate and Chief Assistant Magistrate at the Constitutional Court of Romania, respectively, for indicating to me the earlier decisions where the phrase 'national constitutional identity' appeared. The paper was submitted in 2018, revised in 2019 and 2020, and marginally updated in spring 2021. The usual disclaimer applies.

Bogdan Iancu, *The Evolution and* Gestalt *of the Romanian Constitution* In: *The Max Planck Handbooks in European Public Law*. Edited by: Armin von Bogdandy, Peter M Huber, and Sabrina Ragone, Oxford University Press. © Bogdan Iancu 2023.
DOI: 10.1093/oso/9780198726425.003.0010

In Romania, as in many other jurisdictions that emerged from behind the Iron Curtain in the early 1990s, a resiliently shared belief was, at least at the intelligentsia and the political centre-right elite level (the two categories largely overlap), that the collapse of state socialism implied a fall-back on a presumably European and democratic pre-communist past. This return to the golden age, usually located between the two world wars, was to happen after a hopefully brief transition. Emblematic in this respect, a widely read constitutional history tract published with a highbrow Bucharest press in 1992 argued in essence that the entire period from 1947 until December 1989 had been a hiatus. Consequently, the author intimated, since the communist regime had been illegally instituted, a simple parliamentary resolution declaring the 1947 takeover null and void would have been enough to restore the monarchy under the last lawful fundamental charter, that of 1923. Another implication was that the then-recently adopted constitution of 1991 was, in and of itself, an act of dubious legality and legitimacy, confirmatory referendum notwithstanding. The author thus proposed a similar solution to dispose of it.[1] Second and third editions followed until 2003, with the same argument being extended over longer stretches of time. Three decades after the collapse of state socialism, it has however become increasingly clear that the enduring penchant on using the post-communist lens as a conceptual or ideological passe-partout to tackle the vagaries of the transition is oversimplifying to the point of inadequacy. To wit, whereas in the 1990s and early 2000s the aftereffects of the communist past (restitution, lustration/decommunization, and the like) needed to be grappled with for practical reasons, the more distant the events of 1989, the less this proxy is useful to comprehend and practically address deficiencies and path dependencies in a coherent manner. By the same token, the thesis that communist throwbacks are alone to blame for various evils, for instance judicial formalism as a by-product of Marxian theory and practice[2] or the perpetuation of 'dirty togetherness' in law and politics via personnel continuities,[3] is less persuasive after three decades, due to manifold, including biological, reasons. Moreover, Romania, like all the former Eastern Bloc jurisdictions, is 'post-' many other things.[4] Therefore, the post-communist label and germane presuppositions, including that of an abruptly broken liberal-constitutional continuity,

---

[1] 'As far as the 'Constitution of 1991' is concerned, it is non-existent and since it does not have the binding force of a constitution, its inexistence may be taken notice of by an ordinary legislative assembly'. Eleodor Focșeneanu, *Istoria constituțională a României 1859–1991* (Humanitas, Bucharest, 1992), 188. [Unless otherwise indicated, all translations are mine.]

[2] See the more qualified restatement of this position: Zdeněk Kühn, *The Judiciary in Central and Eastern Europe: Mechanical Jurisprudence in Transformation?*, Series: Law in Eastern Europe, vol 61 (Martinus Nijhoff, Leiden, 2011).

[3] I.e. refurbished *nomenklatura*. Compare (in what concerns legal elite continuities) Bernd Rüthers, 'The Functions of Law and Lawyers in Political and Social Transformation Processes', in Bogdan Iancu (ed), *The Law/Politics Distinction in Contemporary Public Law Adjudication* (Eleven Publishing, The Hague, 2009) 117–132; András Sajó's, 'Socialist Law Unaccounted', in Bogdan Iancu (ed), *The Law/Politics Distinction in Contemporary Public Law Adjudication* (Eleven Publishing, The Hague, 2009) 133–136.

[4] This observation was already made in 2006 by Krygier and Czarnota: the states in the region are post many other things as well. Adam Czarnota and Martin Krygier, 'After postcommunism: the next phase' (2006) 2 Annual Review of Law and Social Science 299, 301. Increasing recognition of this reality transpires in comparativist methodologies. See for instance Michael Stolleis, *Konflikt und Koexistenz. Die Rechtsordnungen Südosteuropas im 19. und 20. Jahrhundert Band I, Rumänien, Bulgarien, Griechenland* (Vittorio Klostermann, Frankfurt, 2015), where the common historical denominator framing the comparison of these jurisdictions is the Ottoman past. Also relevant is the collection edited by Michal Bobek, *Central European Judges under the European Influence: The Transformative Power of the EU Revisited* (Hart, Oxford, 2015), is marked by a significant degree of geographical and temporal ambivalence. The focus, as announced by the title is on Central European judges, yet a Bulgarian chapter is thrown in the comparative pool (indicating post-communist commonalities), whereas the positions with respect to the methodological shibboleth of post-communist legal sociology, i.e. 'formalism' as a Communist throwback, are evenly divided (some authors hold fast to this early 1990s explanatory model, whereas a significant number consider it obsolete).

obfuscate a wider palette of influences and complexities, of which the communist period is, albeit important, only a segment.

Furthermore, as the local variant of the 'end of history' discourse went, the apex of this collectively redemptive process would be a 'return to Europe' also in the formalized sense of joining the European Union. Expectations with respect to the transformative powers of 'Europe' have been, until the accession of 2007, immense. Related to this was the understanding that a ceasefire was necessary in order to achieve a national goal, an understanding shared across the full gamut of the ideological and political spectrum. Conversely, whatever changes were either not made or were made deficiently in the pre-accession period became the 'new normality' once post-accession fatigue set in.[5] In this sense, what is often called backsliding nowadays is simply the coming to full fruition of a set of contradictions and tensions that, although momentarily hidden from view, were underlying the local systems all along and now resurface, mixed with new-fangled, supranationally induced antinomies.

In Romania, the rosy trope of the 'return to Europe' has been challenged by recent events. Especially after the accession, an increased polarization of the political life and recurrent constitutional crises cast a shadow over the capacity of the local system to ensure even minimal conditions of stability and predictability. Since January 2017 alone, for instance, the same parliamentary majority brought down two prime ministers (of its own) by motions of censure. A third cabinet received a vote of confidence in January 2018 and lost a confidence vote due to defections and the unravelling of the supporting political alliance in October 2019. Two minority centre-right governments followed (National-Liberal, Orban I and II). In effect, the same prime minister, Ludovic Orban, was redesignated by the president and confirmed by parliament right after a successful motion of censure brought down his first cabinet in February 2020. 'Pandemic politics' resulted in a new government (*Cîțu* Cabinet), supported by a fragile, three-party centre-right coalition. The 2020 elections also generated an opposition that includes, for the first time in more than a decade, a strong right- to far-right parliamentary party. AUR, the Romanian acronym for the Alliance for the Unity of Romanians, means 'gold'. This faction, whose measure of success was wholly unanticipated, competed in national elections for the first time. Fully ignored by the mainstream press, it promoted a stridently conservative and ultranationalist platform exclusively by canvassing tours and on social networks. AUR entered parliament well over the 5 per cent threshold, with 10 per cent of the seats in both chambers, riding on a particularly high percentage of the diaspora poll. For instance, AUR came in first in Italy and second in Spain, both countries with sizeable, over one million strong, Romanian expatriate communities. These vote results openly contradicted a mainstream, longstanding discourse that has regularly resurfaced in both academic commentary[6] and the domestic and Western press,[7] presenting the

---

[5] Michal Bobek, 'Conclusion: Of Form and Substance in Central European Judicial Transitions', in Michal Bobek, *Central European Judges under the European Influence: The Transformative Power of the EU Revisited* (n 4) 391–418.

[6] See e.g. in constitutional law, for an optimistic view concerning the diaspora as a force for the good, an enlightened counter-populist counterweight, Elena-Simina Tănăsescu, 'COVID-19 and Constitutional Law: Romania', in José María Serna de la Garza (ed), *COVID-19 and Constitutional Law. COVID-19 et droit constitutionnel* (Ciudad de México: UNAM, 2020) 191–197 available at https://archivos.juridicas.unam.mx/www/bjv/libros/13/6310/26.pdf and https://biblio.juridicas.unam.mx/bjv/detalle-libro/6310-covid-19-and-constitutional-law-covid-19-et-droit-constitutionnel) (last accessed on 14 March 2022).

[7] See, e.g. Teodor Stan, 'The Romanian Diaspora's Impact on European Stability' (2019) Carnegie Council available at https://www.carnegiecouncil.org/publications/articles_papers_reports/20190627-romanian-diaspora-impact-european-stability (last accessed on 14 March 2022) and Robert Schwartz, 'Proteste in Rumänien: Die Diaspora soll es richten' (2018) DW available at https://www.dw.com/de/proteste-in-rumänien-die-diaspora-soll-es-richten/a-45017998 (last accessed on 14 March 2022). Such examples of 'political romanticism' abound in the media.

Romanian diaspora as a progressive, pro-European force. The turnout, at 31.84 per cent,[8] was the lowest for all national elections held over the last thirty years and, indeed, significantly lower than that of the local elections that had taken place two months earlier, in September.[9]

In the next section, I shall use the pre-1989 history of Romanian constitutional modernization to emphasize a number of continuities, with the stated purpose of doing as little injustice as possible to the minute intricacies of historical phenomena, while still being able in the process to 'identify historical knowledge that can inform current legal scholarship'.[10] The mainstays of the Romanian system are that it is hypothesized, the relative inability of the fundamental law to fulfil an integrative function, the construction of identity almost exclusively via explicit or latent ethnocentric definitions, and pervasive and deep rifts within society and particularly between the elites and society at large. In this latter respect, although the configuration of elites differs, the disconnect, in its various avatars, runs through Romanian political-constitutional history. Admittedly, the categories, although analytically distinct, blend into each other or overlap slightly, since, for instance, the capacity of constitutions to integrate polities relies on minimal preconditions (social homogeneity, common values, etc.).[11] Building political unity through the means of exclusionary forms (i.e. exclusive of ethnic alterity) can substitute and compensate for the lack of deeper kinds of shared commonality only to a limited and superficial degree and reinforces, in turn, cleavages that further subvert the conditions for the possibility of integration by constitution. It should be mentioned in the closing of this subsection that, whereas Romania is, like all jurisdictions, in many respects idiosyncratic, comparisons with other forms of 'peripheral modernity' in Europe or beyond are readily imaginable on a number of dimensions.[12]

2. The Genesis of Constitutionalism in Romania

a) The Romanian Enlightenment and Early Modernization Projects; The Organic Regulations

In the eighteenth century, the two lands that would eventually form the 'Old Kingdom' (i.e. Moldova and Valahia) were under a form of almost direct administration by the High Porte. Although the two principalities north of the Danube were, unlike Greece, Serbia, or Bulgaria, not technically parts of the Ottoman Empire, after 1711 the High Porte ceased to recognize any form of local selection of the princes by the domestic nobility (boyars) and directly appointed Greek rulers recruited from the Fener district of Constantinople (*Phanariotes*). The Phanariote period (1711–1821) is almost universally described in the Romanian historiography as a 'dark age'.[13]

---

[8] See Listă județe (counties of Romania) available at https://prezenta.roaep.ro/parlamentare06122020/romania-counties (last accessed on 14 March 2022).

[9] The municipal elections turnout was 46.2 per cent available at https://prezenta.roaep.ro/locale27092020/romania-counties (last accessed on 14 March 2022).

[10] Armin von Bogdandy and Peter M. Huber, 'Evolution and Gestalt of the German State', in Armin von Bogdandy, Peter M Huber, and Sabino Cassese (eds), *The Administrative State* (OUP, Oxford, 2017) 197–198.

[11] Dieter Grimm, 'Integration by constitution' (2005) 3 International Journal of Constitutional Law 193, 193.

[12] See Marcelo Neves, 'Die Staaten im Zentrum und die Staaten an der Peripherie: Einige Probleme mit Niklas Luhmanns Auffassung von den Staaten der Weltgesellschaft' (2006) 12 (2) Soziale Systeme 247, 247.

[13] Bianca Selejan-Guțan, *The Constitution of Romania - A Contextual Analysis* (Bloomsbury/Hart, London, 2016) 3. Among historians, Nicolae Iorga presented a more benevolent depiction of the Phanariotes, albeit he did so polemically, in order to oppose by the starkest possible contrast modernization by foreign transplant in the nineteenth century (i.e. even the Phanariotes were better).

Towards the turn of the century, some of these Greek princes introduced modern legislation, partly inspired by Austrian codifications[14] (Ipsilanti codes 1775–1777, Calimach Code in Moldova 1817, Caragea Code in the southern country 1818), yet the applicability of such endeavours was limited, not least on account of the fact that they were redacted in Neo-Greek and would be translated into Romanian much later (the Calimach Code, for instance, in 1833). Constantin Mavrocordat (1746, 1749) rescinded the late medieval rule according to which a peasant was tied to the land (*adscriptus glebae*), yet the progressiveness of this change, in the existing context, was ambiguous.[15] Moreover, the selling of offices, including the bidding for appointments by the Phanariotes in Constantinople and the ensuing accumulated burden of the levies on the local population, had rendered the situation for most inhabitants, particularly for the rural population, unbearable. In addition, frequent wars devastated the two countries, whereby the nobility retreated usually to then-Habsburg Transylvania, in order to escape the Turkish or Tatar attacks, whereas the commoners suffered what they had to; the last Tatar inroad into Moldova took place in 1799, while the southern city of Craiova was repeatedly sacked and burned by the Ottoman maverick warlord Osman Pasvantoğlu at about the same time.[16] Towards the end of this period, the Phanariotes increasingly antagonized the local gentry, by conferring on their own countrymen 'empty' functional titles of nobility, by the virtue of which privileges accrued to their 'owner' (e.g. taxation exemptions), without any correlative obligations or the need to prove lineage and land-possession or former service.[17]

By the close of the Phanariote period, rudiments of the Enlightenment reached Moldova and Valahia, so that, for example, the Calimach Code included in the index an entry on the concept of 'reason' and a decree promulgating an educational reform in Țara Românească (1776) declared that the value of education resided in that people would become accustomed to life 'according to reason'. Ioan Tăutu, an early political writer, complained, however, in Voltairian key, that 'nos lumières sont trop peu nombreuses'.[18] Revolutionary ideas from France were apparently also received in the two countries,[19] indirectly, through the intermediary of press, books and French tutors, which some higher *boyars* had begun to employ in their houses.

Reception was however selective, acclimatized in a distorted instrumental 'translation'. The new idea of national sovereignty proved influential, since it directly served the purposes of opposing the Phanariotes and promoting the aspirations to emancipation from direct

---

[14] In the Calimach Code, promulgated in Moldova, it stood written: 'We had decided to change our old ways, proceeding from the newest European codes.'

[15] Vlad Georgescu, *Ideile politice și iluminismul în principatele române, 1750–1831* (Editura Academiei, Bucharest, 1972). Original edition: Vlad Georgescu, *Political Ideas and the Enlightenment in the Romanian Principalities, 1750–1831* (Boulder & Columbia University Press, New York, 1971 cites a contemporary author, the Greek doctor Depasta, who saw the cause of liberation from arbitrary servitude in the fact that most peasants had been deprived of natural freedom from the onset (page 95). The interesting observation is also made by Georgescu (footnote 34, page 94), that freedom implied also the freedom *of the landlord* from any obligations. This was apparently reflected by terminological shifts, the landed gentry seeking to replace the use of the common term 'peasant' (*țăran*, a word that shares a common root with 'land') with neutral designations, such as 'land worker', 'plough-sharer', 'land settler', etc, that underlined an emerging conception regarding the unfettered right of property and the functional character of the peasant's right to be on the land.

[16] Vlad Georgescu, *Ideile politice și iluminismul în principatele române, 1750–1831* (n 15) 23–24.

[17] Ioan C. Filitti, *Les Principautés roumaines sous l'occupation russe (1828–1834)* (Imprimerie de l' 'Indépendence Roumaine', Bucharest, 1904) 32: '*Jusqu'à la fin du XVIIIe siècle, les charges des boyards correspondirent à des fonctions effectives. Ce n'est qu'à partir de cette époque que tous les rangs, même les plus élevés, purent être conférés sans entrainer l'accomplissement des fonctions correspondantes. Ainsi le nombre des boyards augmenti-t-il considérablement.*'

[18] Vlad Georgescu, *Ideile politice și iluminismul în principatele române, 1750–1831* (n 15) 91, 130 respectively.

[19] Violeta-Anca Epure, 'Revoluția franceză și reverberațiile ei în spațiul românesc' [The French Revolution and its echoes in the Romanian Lands] (2017) 9 Terra Sebus Acta Musei Sabesiensis 251, 265.

Ottoman rule, unification, and independence. The rest of revolutionary doctrine, namely the social dimension, individual rights, and functional separation of powers, was downplayed or disregarded. After 1769, peaking in 1821–1831,[20] reform programmes were submitted to various courts (Russia, Austria, even France) but most memoranda were variations on the themes of the 'aristocratic republic', 'aristo-democratic republic', or limited monarchy. The screeds proposed in essence the immediate demotion and expulsion of the Greeks, the return of the principalities to their former privileged status according to older treaties and *hatt-i sharifs* (whereby the High Porte consented to be a neutral suzerain, to collect tribute but not interfere in internal affairs) and either rule by the high nobility alone or the election of a prince restrained in the exercise of his office by the high landowning aristocracy and the high clergy represented in the council. For example, a Moldavian memorandum, written in 1769 and submitted to Russian empress Catherine II, planned a system by which the country would be governed by six high noblemen with legislative attributions and six high nobles that would exercise judicial functions, whereas the administrative apparatus could be staffed by middle and lower nobility. The plan or form of 'aristo-democratic Government' of 1802, authored by the Logothete Dumitrache Sturza, proposed the division of executive and judicial functions between two councils (Divans), each composed of members selected from the upper ranks. Legislative powers were to be exercised jointly, each new law first drafted by a joint committee of six and then adopted in turn by both *Divans*. The progressive element consisted in the fact that fiscal powers were to be entrusted to a Lower Council (*Divanul cel dă jos*), composed of representatives of all classes and summoned every six months.[21] Although higher boyars would in this period begin to complain that the lower gentry was 'possessed by the spirit of French disobedience', this rant has to be put into perspective; the most advanced of the eighteenth-century thinkers, Ioan Tăutu, went only so far as to propose enlargement of the franchise to 'the average citizen [*tout citoyen moyen*], possessing 143 hectares of land or an annual income of 1,000 lei (gold coins)'.[22]

At the same time, the idea began to gain momentum that the best choice in view of independence and nationhood was a hereditary monarchy with a foreign ruler 'from a non-neighbouring dynasty',[23] under Ottoman suzerainty and collective (Russian and Austrian) guarantee. This project was the result of strategic calculation, in the hope that such a system could pit the external players and their interests against each other. Austria had annexed Bukowina in 1774, after the Peace of Kuchuk Kanardji and temporarily (1718–1739) occupied Oltenia (*Lesser Wallachia, Kleine Walachei*) after the Treaty of Passarowitz (1718), Russia had progressively extended its borders southwards, annexing Bessarabia in 1812, through the Treaty of Bucharest.

In cases of stalemate between the powers, foreign influence could be beneficial. Between 1828 and 1834, during the Russo-Turkish wars and in the aftermath of the Peace of Adrianople (1829), the two provinces were under Russian occupation, their two assemblies overseen by the Russian military Governor, Pavel Kiseleff (Kiselyov or Kiseleff, Pavel Dmitrievich). In order to ensure a buffer between the Russian and Ottoman Empires, the

---

[20] Graph and breakdown in Vlad Georgescu, *Ideile politice și iluminismul în principatele române, 1750–1831* (n 15) 34.

[21] Vlad Georgescu, *Ideile politice și iluminismul în principatele române, 1750–1831* (n 15) 113–116.

[22] Vlad Georgescu, *Ideile politice și iluminismul în principatele române, 1750–1831* (n 15) 111.

[23] The German principalities were perceived as respectable but fragmented and remote enough to have no immediate stakes in local politics, whereas, by the system of collective guarantees, the hope was that the directly interested powers would be played against each other. The idea of a foreign dynasty appears as early as 1824, in a petition of the lower-ranking Moldavian noblemen (dubbed *cărvunari*, a *renvoi* to the Italian *Carbonari*) to the High Porte. Ioan Scurtu, *Carol I* (Editura Enciclopedică, Bucharest, 2004) 17.

Russian administration supported a measure of autonomy and reform, introducing what in the local context constituted a step towards modernization. Two largely identical organic statutes (Organic Regulations) were initially drafted locally by committees composed of high noblemen working under the oversight of Russian General Consul ML Minciaky. The drafts were sent for amendment and approval in Saint Petersburg, then referred back to local Extraordinary General Assemblies of Revision and eventually promulgated with minor variations in both countries (Țara Românească (Wallachia) in 1831, Moldova in 1832).

With many caveats,[24] it can be said that these laws introduced, albeit in a very imperfect way, constitutional elements in the territories that would form the nucleus of present-day Romania. In what concerned state organization, the Regulations, in essence mixtures of constitutional and administrative rules, instituted the principle of rulers (Domn, Hospodar) locally elected for life, with Russian and Ottoman imprimatur[25] and removable only on account of demonstrable infringements, with the agreement of both courts, rules concerning the institutional separation of functions (legislation was to reflect the consensual decision of the prince and a general ordinary assembly, of forty-three members in Valahia, thirty-five in Moldavia), the abolition of consular jurisdiction, rules regarding citizenship and naturalization, the principle of stability of definitive judgments (*res judicata*).[26] A guarantee was also given that, except for fiscal changes, where the consent of both the suzerain and the protective power was needed and new laws touching on the vested rights of the two courts vis-à-vis the principalities, local assemblies would enjoy a form of home rule under the Regulations. The Organic Regulation also defined what had been throughout history a relatively fluid category, namely, nobility, who would be recognized thereafter if lineage could be demonstrated or could be created by the prince, by way of nominal proposals to the assembly.

Elements of modernity in terms of separation of powers principles and inchoate institution-building (induced by the Russian administration) were, however, skewed by a strong reactionary undercurrent in terms of social power relations, this being the local contribution to the acts. In this respect, the Regulations transformed feudal relations into a hybrid regime whereby the medieval liens on the boyars' estates diminished significantly, with an inversely proportional increase in the obligations of the peasants towards the new-fangled 'landowners': the estate was converted into land property and, whereas the peasants could claim a right to till two-thirds of it, their claim on the *tiers sage* was foreclosed, yet obligations towards the landlords increased exponentially.[27] The new framework, through which the local nobility tightened the grip on the peasant population, was so oppressive

---

[24] Filitti's doctoral dissertation is on the whole favourable: '*Au point de vue intérieur, la Russie, en imposant aux Turcs le Règlement organique, nous à aide à poser les bases d'une organisation plus moderne*' (253). Yet in Ioan C Filitti, *Domniile române sub Regulamentul Organic, 1834–1848* (Socec & Comp, Bucharest, 1915), Filitti describes how various factions sought to undermine each other by supplications and intercessions through the conduit of local consuls.

[25] These were to be elected by special estate-based assemblies (counting 190 members in the southern principality of Valahia, 132 in the relatively less populous Moldova, out of which twenty-seven and twenty-two members, respectively, were not noblemen.

[26] This was novelty, since, although the Phanariote codifications tried to put an end to the practice (according to the Caragea Code, a judgment was definitive if confirmed by three successive princes), trials could in principle be always reopened. The idea of a modern trial was novel; in 1829 the Russian general Mircovici asked the members of the Divan (Privy Council) of Moldova to hold court sessions 'in the public building, not in their houses, as they are accustomed.' Valentin Al Georgescu and others, *Judecata domnească în Țara Românească și Moldova, 1611–1831* (Editura Academiei Republicii Socialiste România, Bucharest, 1981) 177.

[27] David Mitrany, *The Land and the Peasant in Rumania: The War and Agrarian Reform* (Oxford University Press/Yale University Press, London, 1930) 28: 'The former tithe-owners blossom into full owners of the land; the former full possessors shrink to little more than privileged tenants.'

500 BOGDAN IANCU

that Kiseleff himself, either out of instrumental concerns regarding the future stability of the principalities or perhaps acting out of humanistic instinct, suspended the application of the rules. His attempt to wrest from the local landed nobility better conditions for the peasants was sidestepped as the boyars interceded to Saint Petersburg and Kiseleff had to give way.[28] In 1848, a generation after their adoption, revolutionaries in Bucharest burnt the official copy of the Regulations in the public square, together with the official list of boyar ranks (*Arhondologia*).

A superficial acceptance of Western forms or jargons, used instrumentally, for export purposes, to disguise or legitimate domestic interests, runs like a *fil rouge* through Romanian constitutionalism, all the way up to contemporary rule of law ideologies or original understandings of corruption or judicial independence. A historical example will suffice, also allowing our transition to the next section of the argument. Ad-hoc Divans were convened in 1857 at the request of the Guarantor Powers, in both principalities. In these assemblies, peasants were also represented, following the express request of the Paris Convention signatories to collect the grievances and wishes for reform of all the local classes. The boyars in the Moldavian *Divan* deflected all requests made by the peasant delegates for a rural reform or at least for a lessening of their burdens, calling these, in a deft and timely signal in shorthand to the Western protecting powers, 'communist sophistry' (*o sofismă comunistă*).[29]

b) Nineteenth-century Constitutionalism: The Theory of Forms without Substance

In the aftermath of the 1848 revolutions, the Convention of Balta Liman suspended the Regulations, including the principle of rulers elected for life, but, after the Crimean War, the cards were again reshuffled, and the ensuing Convention of Paris decided to question the inhabitants of the two principalities with respect to their preferred form of government. The treaty also obliged Russia to return three counties (Southern Bessarabia, part of what had been annexed in 1812) to Moldova.

The '*Ad hoc Divans*' (i.e. ad hoc councils, assemblies) made similar requests in both capitals, in essence limiting the powers of the High Porte to what had been stipulated in the medieval capitulations, union as a new country to be called Romania, under a foreign prince from a European dynasty, whose successors were to be raised in the local, Greek Orthodox faith, and a unicameral legislative assembly elected on the basis of a broad franchise. Social requests were deferred and placated within the *Divans* by reference to the higher purpose of union and statehood. The guarantor powers, which met in Paris in 1858 to take a decision, admitted only part of the requests, placing the countries under a common guarantee, providing for two common institutions (on the border, in the city of Focşani, a Central Commission with attributions in the field of harmonizing legislation and a common Court of Cassation, whose judges were to be irremovable) but rejected the idea of foreign monarchy, instead specifying that each of the principalities would have its own ruler, elected by its own assembly for life. Both assemblies successively elected the same person, the Moldavian Colonel Alexandru Ioan Cuza, using a normative gap in the convention and thus putting the European powers in a state of fait accompli.[30] The system rapidly evolved

---

[28] David Mitrany, *The Land and the Peasant in Rumania: The War and Agrarian Reform* (Oxford University Press/Yale University Press, London, 1930) 33–34. At 34: 'But what a trenchant commentary on the indiscriminate exaltation of national government to see Kisselev—an alien Count and general, representative of Europe's most autocratic ruler—fighting to save some of the birthrights of the Rumanian peasants which, at the first opportunity, the native boiars were rapaciously usurping.'

[29] Alexandru D Xenopol, *Istoria partidelor politice in România* (Librăria Stănciulescu, Bucharest, 1910) 368.

[30] Selejan-Guţan, *The Constitution of Romania - A Contextual Analysis* (n 13) 9. See as well Cătălin Turliuc, 'Constitutional Law as a Political Program in Romania 1856–1914', in Michael Stolleis (ed) *Konflikt und*

from a loose confederation to personal union and then to centralized political union (the capital was moved to Bucharest and institutions were merged). Cuza introduced a number of important reforms (modern codification, most importantly the Civil Code of 1859, an extended franchise, the secularization of the so-called dedicated monasteries lands, whose revenues had previously flown to Athos, land reform) but his regime quickly degenerated into personalism, amid allegations of favouritism and maladministration. Cuza eventually pushed through a constitution patterned after that of the French Second Empire, which, adopted by plebiscite, entered into force in 1864. The results were overwhelmingly in his favour, with 682,621 votes to 1307, but widespread illiteracy and administrative haste placed the process under suspicion.[31] The 'Statute Developing the Paris Convention', modelled after the Second Empire, centralized power in the prince, thereby relegating the legislature to a rubber-stamp function (a Senate was created, appointed predominantly by the ruler, as a countervailing body to the elected assembly, whereas legislative initiative was reserved to the prince). Meanwhile, the elites of all factions masterminded a plan to dethrone Cuza, who was eventually forced to resign and fled into exile in 1866.

In a context of uncertainty, especially with regards to the probability of external intervention, the leaders of the coup set out to find a suitable foreign candidate among western Houses. The choice eventually fell on Carol (Karl) I of the Swabian, Sigmaringen Catholic branch of the Hohenzollerns. A constitution was drafted as a local adaptation of the 1831 Belgian blueprint. In the debates, two issues were contentious. The project submitted to the Assembly by the government proposed that naturalization could be obtained by any resident, irrespective of his faith, breaking with the Organic Regulation rule according to which only Christians could obtain citizenship. This article (article 7 of the Constitution of 1866) overwrote and entrenched constitutionally a provision in the Civil Code, which had made the naturalization of the Jews possible, subject to strict conditions. Debates on this provision were extended and radicalized to the point where one delegate proposed a constitutional rule that would have made even the admission of Jewish residents subject to special legislation in each particular case.[32] Multiple and contradictory reasons were provided by the deputies, ranging from the trope of lack of education (the 'uneducated Jew' could not be assimilated), different religion ('their religion is incompatible with any other'), poverty (the 'Jewish proletarian' was alone to blame), excessive wealth (the 'Jewish tycoon' was to be rejected), to run-of-the-mill conspiracy theories, a common consensus being that the government's proposal was unacceptable (and minister Brătianu eventually withdrew it).[33] A provision forbidding 'the colonization of foreign populations' on the territory of the country was also adopted, incidentally a rule in the Constitution of 1866 that found its way into the current 1991 Constitution. Article 7 was eventually amended in 1879, since the Congress of Berlin (article 44 of the Treaty of Berlin (1878)), after the War of 1877–1878,

---

Koexistenz: Die Rechtsordnungen Südosteuropas im 19. und 20. Jahrhundert Band I (n 4) 531–574, for a sympathetic view of fait accompli as a national strategy and for the argument that 'desire for independence and struggle for nationhood' are 'conveniently encapsulated in the balance between internal and external factors that affected constitutional law' (at 574).

[31] Robert W Seton-Watson, *A History of the Roumanians: From Roman Times to the Completion of Unity* (CUP, Cambridge, 1934) 309, calls the plebiscite 'somewhat of a farce'.
[32] Amendment proposed by deputy Lateş. In Alexandru Pencovici, *Desbaterile Adunărei Constituante din anul 1866 asupra Constituţiunei şi Legei electorale din România* (Tipografia Statului, Bucharest, 1883) 120. Out of 363 pages of debate records, the discussion on the Jewish question covers roughly a third (through to page 126).
[33] I discuss this at length in Bogdan Iancu, 'Ambiguïtés Identitaires dans les Constitutions de la Roumanie Moderne: 1866, 1923, 1991' (2016) 7 Romanian Journal of Comparative Law 113.

made the recognition of independence conditional upon this amendment. The demand was perceived as an unacceptable foreign encroachment on the autonomy of the country and as a tragedy similar to the territorial concessions (Russia had re-annexed the southern counties of Bessarabia, whereas the principalities received in exchange Ottoman Dobrogea and thus access to the Black Sea). Dogged resistance in parliament led to the resignation of the prime minister. The king himself had to supplicate the assembly, pointing out both the negative consequences of a refusal and the fact that eliminating the religious bar did not necessarily have to equate collective awards of citizenship to the Jews.[34] Consequently, the form in which article 7 was eventually revised required naturalization bills to be adopted for individual cases. Large-scale naturalization of the Romanian Jews was deferred. At the end of the war, decree-laws of 1918 and 1919 extended political rights to Romanian Jews, whereas the Constitution of 1923 replaced the legislative naturalization procedure with an administrative one.[35] In January 1938, however, the Goga-Cuza government adopted a decree-law on the basis of which 225,222 Romanian Jews would be eventually stripped retroactively of their citizenship by asking them to produce, within a strict timeline, the original documents supporting naturalization.[36]

Another skirmish took place in the Assembly on the issues of parliamentary configuration and elections. The main parties were established later (the Liberal Party—PNL—in 1875, the Conservative Party in 1880) but factions existed and were already defined, dividing the future liberals, whose target electoral base was the slowly emerging urban middle class, and the conservatives, essentially large rural landowners. The conservatives carried the debate, creating a bicameral parliament elected according to extremely restrictive census conditions. For the fourth college of the Chamber of Deputies, encompassing all taxpayers, irrespective of their contributions, the vote was indirect, by delegates. After the amendments of 1884, this college (which became the third) comprised thirty-eight deputies out of 183. The thirty-eight seats constituted in essence a sinecure pool for governmental candidates that could not be elected in the other two colleges, whose voters, affluent and educated, were more difficult to strong-arm than the third-college peasant delegates.[37] In his 1912 Sorbonne doctoral dissertation on the *Electoral and Parliamentary Regime in Romania,* Gheorghe Tătărescu, himself a future prominent liberal politician, twice Prime Minister, paints a burlesque picture of third-college voting. Gendarmes escorted the delegates from their communes to the county seats, the delegates being even ferried on one occasion (as recorded in March 1911, during the parliamentary debates on the Speech from the Throne) with Interior Ministry rail passes, by cattle waggons, as no regular train could be boarded in time. The peasant delegates were billeted in local inns and kept incommunicado by the county officialdom until election day. When they voted for the government's candidate, they were regaled by the latter after the vote count with a barrel of wine and then went back home to their villages.[38]

The Senate, except for the eight members *ex officio* and two representatives of the Universities of Iași and Bucharest (the professorial bodies constituted separate electoral

---

[34] George Nicolescu, *Parlamentul român: 1866–1901* (Ed. Socec, Bucharest, 1903) 342, 356.

[35] The 883 Jewish veterans of the Russo-Turkish War (in Romanian historiography called The Independence War) were naturalized collectively. The total number of Jewish citizens in 1912 was 4,688. Zigu Ornea, *Anii treizeci-Extrema dreaptă românească* (4th edn, Cartea Românească, Bucharest, 2015) 308.

[36] Zigu Ornea, *Anii treizeci-Extrema dreaptă românească* (n 35) 308. 'Wiesel Commission' report available at http://old.presidency.ro/static/ordine/ICHR-2004.pdf (last accessed on 14 March 2022) (at 64).

[37] Gheorghe Tătărescu, *Regimul electoral și parlamentar în România* (Delia Răzdolescu tr, Editura Fundației PRO 2004) 80.

[38] Gheorghe Tătărescu, *Regimul electoral și parlamentar în România* (n 37) 81–85.

colleges), was in essence a landed aristocracy fiefdom.[39] The number of active citizens decreased from the reforms of Cuza to 1866, tenfold (from one voter to eight to ten inhabitants under Cuza to one in eighty-three).[40] Before the amendments of 1884, 1.3 per cent (Chamber) and 0.38 per cent (Senate) of the male adult population had the right to vote directly. The figures increased to 6.1 per cent and 1.5 per cent (elections of 1911) but most of the direct votes for the Chamber were allocated to the third college, where they were trebly diluted, by indirect votes, small number of deputies, and brutal governmental interference in the elections.[41] Admittedly, *Besitz und Bildung* ('Possessions and education') parliamentarism presupposed restrictions in paradigmatic systems as well but the extent, context, and effect of such restrictions were idiosyncratic. To compare, in France (1883) the figure (related to the population) was 26.9 per cent, in Germany 7 per cent, and in Italy 6 per cent.[42] In England, the Reform Acts of 1832, 1867, and 1884 gradually enlarged the electorate to the point when, although the system still did not reflect the 'one person one vote' principle until 1919, it included roughly 60 per cent of the adult male population. In France, universal male franchise is first utilized in 1792 and then firmly established in 1848. Even Belgium, which started with a restrictive electoral system (1 per cent of the population could vote in 1831)[43] extends the franchise significantly at the end of the century, when a form of direct universal male vote is adopted.

The liberals pushed through an amendment to the Constitution in 1884, eliminating one of the four Chamber of Deputies electoral colleges and consequently extending their base in the lower house but the Constitution could function, to the extent that it did, only upon the basis of draconian limitations of the direct suffrage and various other forms of voter suppression. This state of facts subsisted, in spite of the marginal alterations of 1884, for the entire period during which the 1866 Constitution was in force.

Whereas the separation of powers structure presupposed a certain degree of parliamentary control over the executive (by way of providing for impeachment of the ministers,

[39] The Chamber was elected for four years, the Senate for eight-year terms in staggered form (half of the Senate was renewed every four years). In the second college of the Senate commercial and industrial interests played a marginal role, since first and second class commercial and industrial patent holders had the right to vote (representing, namely, big industry and trade). This was a very thin layer of the electorate, due to an insufficient degree of industrialization. The Old Kingdom had a predominantly agrarian economic structure, based, until the land reform of 1921, on large, wheat and corn-producing estates. In 1907, 4,171 large landowners held 3,787,192 hectares, 250,000 peasant families were landless, 423,000 owned less than three ha (the subsistence level for a family was five ha). The latter two categories were forced to resort to sharecropping, which was in turn mediated by large leaseholder firms, a situation that significantly raised the rent paid by the end-user, i.e. the peasant sharecropper. 58 per cent of arable land was leased, 2,400,000 ha. Apostol Stan, *Putere politică și democrație în România: 1859–1918* (Editura Albatros, Bucharest, 1995) 275.

[40] Tudor Drăganu, *Începuturile și dezvoltarea regimului parlamentar în România până în 1916* [The Beginnings and Development of Parliamentarism in Romania: 1866–1916] (Editura Dacia, Cluj-Napoca 1991) 190.

[41] Out of a total population of 5,000,000, as Romania had in 1883, at the elections for the Chamber of Deputies College I had 3,388 voters, College II had 4,814, College III 15,382, College IV, 37,070 indirect voters, Tudor Drăganu, *Începuturile și dezvoltarea regimului parlamentar în România până în 1916* (n 40) 189. In the parliamentary elections of 1911, even if only male suffrage is taken as a hypothetical normative baseline, out of 1,644,302 individuals (male, over twenty-one), the franchise extended only to 6.1 per cent (149,910) for the Chamber, 1.5 per cent (24,921) for the Senate. Alexandru Radu, 'Reforma sistemului electoral-o istorie analitică' (2012) 1 (167) Sfera Politicii 3, 6.

[42] Mattei Dogan, *Analiza statistică a democrației parlamentare în România* (Editura Partidului Social-Democrat, Bucharest, 1946) 9. In the case of Germany, Dogan must be referring to state elections, e.g. the Prussian *Dreiklassenwahlrecht*, rightly dubbed at the time *Klassenwahlunrecht*. In the German Empire (at the federal level) however, universal male franchise is introduced immediately after the *Reichsgründung*, in 1871.

[43] Raoul Charles van Caenegem, *An Historical Introduction to Western Constitutional Law* (CUP, Cambridge, 1995) 195 (on British developments see 196–197). The extension of the franchise in late nineteenth-century Belgium was however diluted by plurality voting; one would cast between one and three votes, in correlation with property and education qualifications.

countersignature of royal decrees, and incompatibilities) and divided legislative power between the king and the parliament, fairly soon the situation diverged from the original constitutional representations. The king established (1871) the dubious custom of deciding when alternation in power should occur, namely, he dismissed the sitting Prime Minister, appointed a new one, and called snap elections (the three royal decrees were issued simultaneously). The new appointee organized the elections and won them amid massive fraud and bribery. This situation resulted in moving the political disputes outside the parliament. The opposition withdrew from the legislature and organized violent protests in front of the Royal Palace, until the king, himself a prisoner of context, yielded. Paradoxically, governments were overthrown while they enjoyed quasi-unanimous parliamentary support. Petre Carp, a nineteenth- century conservative politician, famously told the king 'Give me the power and I shall give you a Parliament'. Tătărescu also described the various forms of enticement, coercion, prevarication, and abuse by virtue of which the 'official candidate' won elections, supported by the entire state apparatus, as 'administrative thuggery'. One form of inducement consisted in enforcing the law to the letter selectively: '[I]n Romania, a voter for the opposition breaks many a regulation … The deputy prefect, the doctor, the police commissioner, the agricultural inspector, the veterinarian, the tax collector, the health inspector, the veterinarian inspector, the fiscal inspector, the gendarme, all cooperate in giving the refractory voter a solid civic education.'[44]

In a work of literary criticism, prominent politician and cultural figure Titu Maiorescu coined the expression 'forms without substance', to which the Romanian discourse on modernization is still tributary. The term immediately became a catchphrase because it had struck a raw nerve. Some interpreted the notion to mean that transplanting Western forms (universities, academy, literary societies, and, indeed, a Western-style constitution) would eventually fill these empty vessels with content, whereas other critics pointed out the underlying hypocrisy and vainglorious pretentions of these forms devoid of substance. In this latter sense, IC Brătianu, the iconic Romanian modernizer and liberal prime minister between 1876 and 1888 noted, in words that are worth quoting at some length: 'It was not enough that they translated French laws word for word, now they had to dress after the French fashion too. This is how we see our judges and barristers clad in borrowed cloaks that in France may signify something, according to their traditions, but here, with us, simply look ridiculous.'[45] For the nationalist arch-historian Nicolae Iorga, in the context of a speech delivered at the Romanian Social Institute in 1923, in the trail of debates on the new constitution, the fundamental law of 1866 itself was a 'borrowed cloak', made by an 'excellent tailor but one accustomed to cut bespoke suits for other kinds of bodies', so that Romanians 'had lived with [their collective] body on one side and the coat fluttering about'.[46] For Iorga, the implication of his sartorial metaphor was that a Romanian tailor had to look at *Romanian* traditions in order to fashion autochthonous, suitable constitutional garments. Brătianu hoped to bridge a gap, whereas Iorga, in the new nationalist spirit of the early twentieth century, already proposed to supersede it.

As regards constitutional evolutions, an optimistic reading can discern a measure of normalization towards the end of the nineteenth century and the onset of the twentieth century. Whatever normalization occurred reached however primarily the skin-deep level of urban

---

[44] Gheorghe Tătărescu, *Regimul electoral și parlamentar în România* (n 37) 57–58.

[45] Tudor Drăganu, *Începuturile și dezvoltarea regimului parlamentar în România până în 1916* (n 40) 354.

[46] Nicolae Iorga, 'Istoricul constituției românești' in N. Iorga and others (eds), *Noua Constituție a României și noile Constituții europene* (Ed. Cultura Națională/Imprimeria Statului, Bucharest, 1923) 5–24.

elite practices. Peasant revolts erupted in 1888 and 1907, the last one being crushed with the help of the army and at the price of thousands of casualties. The king did try however to better approximate the 'mood' of the country in appointing new prime ministers, non-removability of judges was eventually extended downward from the Court of Cassation up until 1909, and in 1912 the Ilfov Tribunal and then the Court of Cassation on appeal instituted the principle of constitutionality control (judicial review), striking down a retroactive statute of 1911 that sought to bring into effect an expropriation under the guise of an interpretive law.

c) The Constitution of 1923: Rise and Fall

In the aftermath of the First World War, a new constitution had to be adopted, especially in view of the needed social transformation and significant territorial changes: franchise was extended to universal male suffrage, in 1918, by decree-law,[47] Jewish residents were naturalized, an agrarian reform was underway (1921).[48] Post-1918 'Greater Romania' was, compared to the Old Kingdom, double in territory, due to territorial extensions recognized by the Treaty of Versailles: Bessarabia, joined in March 1918, somewhat as a windfall,[49] Bukovina and Transylvania, on 1 December 1918. A portion of Bulgarian Dobrogea had already been annexed in the wake of the Balkan Wars.[50] This enlarged kingdom was much more diverse in its ethnic make-up, especially in the cities. The new configuration brought along some 'complications': the Resolution of the National Assembly in Alba Iulia, declaring union with the Kingdom, stipulated expressly in its first recital that 'full national freedom would be guaranteed in the new state to all co-inhabiting peoples', a provision understood until today by the Hungarian minority to imply a form of territorial autonomy.[51]

A window of opportunity for meaningful debate and perhaps beneficial, liberal change was lost, due to the artificial protraction of the state of emergency, whereby extensive use was made, until 1922, of decree-laws and the state of siege. Both instruments were of dubious legality. The institution of the state of siege had been approved by a law of 1916, upon entry into the war on the side of the Triple Entente and authorized 'until the restoration of European peace'. Decree-laws were adopted on the basis of an enabling law passed by the 1918 parliament, whose dissolution, according to the royal decree, entailed the consequence that all its parliamentary acts (thus, presumably, also that particular statute) were null and

---

[47] The rule of universal male suffrage (from the age of twenty-one for the Chamber and forty for senatorial elections) was entrenched in the Constitution of 1923. Art 6 made the extension of political rights to women possible, on the basis of a law adopted by a two-thirds majority. Women received the active right to vote (but not passive electoral rights!) when it no longer mattered, in 1938, according to the 'royal dictatorship' constitution.

[48] Electoral and agrarian changes to the constitution were proposed by the National Liberal Party and a constituent assembly started to debate on these proposals already in 1914. But deliberations were cut short and deferred, due to the onset of the Great War. Towards the end of the war (1917), in a sensitive context (the Government retreated to Iaşi, Romanian, and Russian troops held a fragile front line in Romanian Moldova) the parliament voted amendments preparing the ground for future electoral (1918; first elections in 1919) and land (1921) reforms by eliminating constitutional hurdles. For instance, the takings clause in the fundamental law, art 19, in its initial form allowed for expropriation with just compensation only for the purposes of defence, communications, and public sanitation.

[49] Romania entered the war with a view to eventually securing Transylvania. By the same token, the alliance with Russia against the Central Powers effectively meant a trade-off and the abandonment of the Russian-held Bessarabia (which forms the current Republic of Moldova).

[50] The territory expanded from 139,000 square kilometres to 295,000, the population growth was from over 7 to about 18 million.

[51] The Resolution of the National Assembly in Alba-Iulia on the 18 November/the 1 December, English translation available at: http://www.cimec.ro/Istorie/Unire/rezo_eng.htm (last accessed on 14 March 2022).

void.[52] Such exceptional measures, along with the dissolution by the king of the first freely elected parliament, four months after the elections of 1919, made possible a slow return to pre-war 'normality', adapted to the new context.

The Constitution of 1923 did not reshuffle the constitutional structure, amending it only to bring it into accord with unavoidable realities: out of 138 articles, seventy-six were taken over verbatim from the 1866 Constitution.[53] This was in line with the preferences of the National Liberal Party in power, which did its utmost to preserve the *status quo à l'ancienne* by preventing a genuine constitutional debate. The alternative drafts, supported by the opposition forces, were completely ignored.

In order to stabilize a political system created for and consolidated in a context of restricted franchise within a much smaller country, the electoral legislation of 1926, inspired by the Italian fascist Acerbo Law of 1923, functioned in the logic of reinforced proportionality. A party winning 40 per cent of the national vote would, via redistribution, win a comfortable majority, namely half of the mandates and the corresponding percentage of the remainder. This also was in line with the preferences of the National Liberal Party, which sought indirectly to entrench its predominance in a context in which the influence of its traditional competitor, the Conservative Party, had been effectively eliminated by virtue of the agrarian reforms. In addition, the system of 'government rotation' triggered by the royal decree appointing a care-taker government who would then organize and win elections, thus legitimizing *ex post* its position, was carried over in the context of mass democracy.[54] The National Liberal Party, called by the king to form a government weeks before elections in 1922, wins 60.3 per cent of the national vote, whereas in 1926, this time in opposition, it falls to 7.3 per cent, and, called again to govern, dissolves the parliament, organizes elections, winning 61.7 per cent of the vote, falling once again in 1928, anew in opposition, to 6 per cent.[55] The perpetuation of old-style royal prime-ministerial appointments by 'rotation' in the context of mass democracy made electoral fraud or suasion both harder to achieve and much more necessary to ensure overall stability. There were limits to the extent to which elections could be nudged or doctored using the police, prefects, and local notables, although such limits were, especially in the countryside, lax. According to the census of 1930, illiteracy, as measured for all citizens from ten years of age upwards, reached 43 per cent. It was unevenly distributed, from a high of 66 per cent in Bessarabia, around 40 per cent in the Old Kingdom, to a low of 33–34 per cent in Transylvania, the Banat, and Bukovina.[56] The simulacra of quasi-parliamentary democracy were complemented with frequent recourse to decree-laws (side-stepping the parliamentary procedures), the adoption of special legislation severely curtailing rights, and frequent recourse to the state of siege, an instrument now provided by the Constitution of 1923 (article 128).[57] For instance, following the assassination of Liberal

---

[52] Friedrich E Weinreich, *Die Verfassung von Rumänien von 1923* (Universitätsverlag von Robert Noske, Leipzig, 1933) 223–225.

[53] Hans Christian Maner, *Parlamentarismul în România: 1930–1940* (Adela Moțoc tr, Ed. Enciclopedică, Bucharest, 2004) 32.

[54] Art 95 of the Constitution of 1866, taken over verbatim (as art 90) in the Constitution of 1923, provided that the king could dissolve either or both houses, provided that new elections were held within two months and the newly elected houses would be summoned in session within three months.

[55] Figures quoted after Mattei Dogan, 'Dansul electoral în România interbelică', in Mattei Dogan (ed), *Sociologie politică: Opere alese* (Editura Alternative, Bucharest, 1999) 143.

[56] To compare, illiteracy percentages were at the same time 9 per cent in Hungary, 4 per cent in Czechoslovakia, 5 per cent in France, and 1 per cent in Germany. Cliver Jens Schmitt, 'Hundert Jahre Einsamkeit-Grundzüge der Geschichte Rumäniens' (2019) 6–8 Osteuropa, Durchblick: Politik und Gesellschaft in Rumänien 7, 22–23.

[57] See on the use of emergency legislation in the interwar period, the pertinent parts covered by Bogdan Iancu and C Cercel, respectively, in Manuel Guțan and others (eds), *Șefii de stat. Dinamica autoritară a puterii politice în*

Prime Minister IG Duca by Iron Guard members in 1933, a state of siege was declared in a context where emergency measures were clearly justified, but extended afterwards repeatedly right up until the elections of 1937.[58]

The PNL and the newly-formed National Peasant Party—PNȚ (fusing an agrarian party in the Old Kingdom and Transylvanian unionists under Iuliu Maniu) could for a short while alternate in power 'by rotation', in the old fashion. In 1937, the PNL, eroded by a long stretch in government, no longer reached, in spite of their having organized the elections, the needed 40 per cent threshold (winning only 36.4 per cent of the national vote). This also happened as a consequence of a strange bed-fellowship between the (nominally mainstream left) PNȚ and the emerging Romanian fascist faction (Legion of the Archangel St Michael, which registered in those elections under the political party label 'Everything for the Country'). The two had signed an 'electoral non-aggression pact', which even contemporary observers identified as the death knell of the fragile Romanian constitutional democracy, since, by virtue of this move, Maniu legitimized an upstart fascist movement in order to gain the upper hand on an establishment opponent.[59] The first time voters did not give a mandate to the party in government, the entire system collapsed.

In the aftermath, a minority extreme-right government (deeply anti-Semitic, fascist in nature, but opposed to the hard(er)-line fascists in the Legion) was called to form a government, which lasted from the end of December 1937 to early February 1938. In 1938, as the Goga-Cuza government was beginning to make overtures to the Legion and threatened to cripple the economy through haphazard anti-Semitic economic policies, Carol II suspended the Constitution of 1923 altogether. Political parties were dissolved and replaced with an umbrella 'movement' or 'monopoly party' (the Front of National Rebirth) led by King Carol II. Royal dictatorship under the Constitution of 1938 functioned in a corporatist key, with the new bicameral parliament partly elected by the three recognized corporate bodies (agrarian, merchant-industrial, intellectual). In the confirmatory plebiscite, 4,283,398 approved the Constitution, 5,413 voted against it. The new Constitution of 1938 mixed royal authoritarianism with the contemporarily fashionable corporatism, and ethnocentrism (e.g. only a third-generation Romanian citizen could be appointed minister, article 67). Intellectuals quickly positioned themselves around the new framework, with characteristically calculated passion. As prominent legal philosopher Mircea Djuvara argued at a 1939 conference in Kiel, the arrangement was reflective of wider European tendencies: 'The new

---

istoria constituțională a României (Heads of State and the Authoritarian Dynamic of Political Power in Romanian Constitutional History) (Universul Juridic, București, 2020).

[58] See generally Hans Christian Maner, Parlamentarismul în România: 1930–1940 (n 53) whose essential argument is that the received wisdom in Romanian historiography, according to which the democratic, parliamentary system collapsed at a later point in Romania (relative to other states in the region), is false, since the system was much more authoritarian in its essential logic from the very beginning.

[59] For instance, a prominent politician and future Prime Minister, Armand Călinescu, stated with regard to the pact between Maniu and the Legion leader, Codreanu: 'I believe that in that very moment the fate of the old system was decided.' Quoted in Angela Banciu, Rolul Constituției din 1923 în consolidarea unității naționale: evoluția problemei constituționale în România interbelică (Editura Științifică și Enciclopedică, Bucharest, 1988) 159. To be sure, Călinescu himself was not an impartial or innocent observer. He was instrumental in the extrajudicial killing of the Legion Leader C. Z. Codreanu, who was executed (i.e. murdered) in 1938 while being transferred between prisons. The Legion retaliated, assassinating Călinescu in 1939, whereby in a spiral of violence, the new caretaker government carried out countrywide executions of some three hundred Iron Guard members, the corpses being left for three days on display in public squares. During the short-lived National-Legionary State (September 1940–February 1941), those responsible for this act would be themselves extrajudicially assassinated while interned in the Jilava prison, by a Legion commando. On the intricacies of Romanian fascism see generally the monograph by Roland Clark, Holy Legionary Youth: Fascist Activism in Interwar Romania (Cornell University Press, Ithaca, 2015).

Romanian Constitution is an attempt to translate new ethical currents in positive law … the individual is no longer an end in himself, his value and that of his acts can only be measured against the yardstick of a higher ideal. The individual can be only posited in his organic relation to the social groups to which he belongs and these in turn in their ties to the nation.'[60]

By the Vienna Diktat, Romania lost Northern Transylvania and the Ribbentrop-Molotov pact resulted in the Soviet annexation of Bessarabia. Blamed for this disaster, the king was forced to abdicate as a direct result and a national-legionary state (from September 1940 to the end of January 1941) followed, in the logic of which the Legion and Marshall Ion Antonescu (as 'Leader', *Conducător*) shared power with the Head of Legionary Movement, Horia Sima (appointed Vice-President of the Council of Ministers). This uneasy cohabitation between a more pragmatic warlord and the fanatical and disorderly 'Iron Guard' lasted only four months, followed by direct rule by Antonescu. The young king (Mihai I) remained a figurehead. In 1944, once Romania changed sides and turned against its former allies in the Axis, the Constitution of 1923 was reinstated but with Soviet troops in the country and dies cast at Yalta, it endured only until 1947, when the republic was proclaimed, and the king was forced to abdicate. Three constitutions (1948, 1952, 1965) were adopted under Communist rule, entrenching the common institutional scheme of most communist constitutions: one-party system, formal-functional division of powers, and symbolic-precatory rights provisions. In 1974, the office of the President of the Socialist Republic of Romania was created, in order to merge Party (General Secretary) and State leadership and give in this way legal expression to the consolidation of authority in the person of Nicolae Ceauşescu, underlining his preeminent position over both the Politburo (Central Committee, *Comitetul Central*) and the Communist parliament (Grand National Assembly, *Marea Adunare Naţională*). Towards the end of the Communist regime, Ceauşescu's aggrandizement and stifling of all dissent transformed the system into essentially a personal dictatorship with a pronounced nationalistic undercurrent.

3. Return or New Beginning? The Constitution of 1991

a) The Post-Communist Setting
After the Revolution of 1989, Decree-Law 92/1990 provided for elections and the possibility of the newly elected President to dissolve the Chamber and the Senate, after consulting with both speakers and the Prime Minister, should a new Constitution not be adopted within nine months from the start of the new parliament's first session. Some of the main choices (semi-presidential republic, bicameralism) were therefore predetermined or at least a presumption of legitimacy in their favour was accomplished by post-communist elites as a decision on the proverbial Schmittian exception.

The main ideological fault line was that between the National Salvation Front and the centre-right parties. The National Salvation Front (*FSN*) was established as an 'organic'

---

[60] Mircea Djuvara, *Die neue rumänische Verfassung* (Deutscher Rechtsverlag, Berlin, 1940) 16–17; in the same general spirit see Paul Negulescu, *Étude sur la constitution sociale et politique de Roumanie du 27 fevrier 1938* (Institutul de Arte Grafice 'Mârvan S.R.L.', Bucharest, 1938). Negulescu also noted that unlike the fundamental laws of 1866 and 1923, whose forms of adoption were « legally deficient »: '*La Constitution de 1938 apparaît, ainsi que le Statut de 1864, comme un acte parfait du point de vue de la forme et de la légalité*' (at 8). Throughout the volume the new philosophic spirit is emphasized: rejection of individualism and of the empty form parliamentarism that had 'spread alcoholism and discord in the countryside' (at 76), social regeneration under the authority of the king, etc.

'emanation' of the Revolution. Its leaders favourably depicted it at the time as a political party formed out of the provisional post-revolutionary government (the Council of the National Salvation Front, *CFSN*). Once former dissidents resigned from the Council in order to distance themselves from this act and as the newly created parties protested in the streets, another structure was composed to include also 'outsider' factions, namely, the Provisional Council of National Union (CPUN). The party as such, FSN, metamorphosed over the years, splitting and merging with(in) various factions, with a faction renamed *FDSN* (Democratic Front of National Salvation) in 1992, *PDSR* (Romanian Social Democratic Party) in 1996, *PSD* (Social Democratic Party), the name used since 2001 until today. The formation recycled at the top a fair number of former Communist *nomenklatura* members, starting with its president, who eventually became (1990, 1992, 2000) head of state, Ion Iliescu.[61] Iliescu had been a Communist minister, head of a publishing house, 'first secretary' of two counties; he had been perceived as a Perestroika-type alternative to Ceaușescu. In the centre-right discourse, this continuation of Communist elites from the original sin of the Revolution up to the present days is usually underlined, more recently in tandem with the anticorruption discourse. At the other end of the spectrum, the historic parties (National Liberal Party-PNL, National Peasant Party (as PNȚCD, the addition 'CD' standing for Christian and Democratic)) were re-established in the early 1990s. 'Historic' was of course a euphemism even then, since the former detainees or *emigrés* leading them had had, of necessity, limited governmental experience before 1947. In the initial PNȚ, Corneliu Coposu, who had served as an aide to Iuliu Maniu, was, for instance, an exception. Around these two poles, various splinters gravitated,[62] whereas the Hungarian minority would be represented by UDMR (Democratic Union of the Hungarians in Romania). The UDMR is technically a foundation ('organization representing a national minority') and primarily pursues ethnic interests, which means in practice that its traditional 6–7 per cent representation in parliament functions as a swing vote, allowing it to serve as a kingmaker to ideologically diverse coalitions.[63] A peculiarity of early Romanian politics was the existence of Romanian extreme or virulent nationalist parties, the PUNR (Romanian National Unity Party, with a primarily regional, Transylvanian base, created in 1990) and the Greater Romania Party (PRM, established in 1991).

The strong position of the FSN/PDSR (65 per cent in 1990) and of its leader Iliescu (85.07 per cent in 1990 presidential elections)[64] took a number of traditional transitional issues off

---

[61] The President is expected to be a trailblazer for his party. Paradoxically, the Constitution also requires the President to be a neutral umpire (art 80 para 2), between state and society and between institutions, hovering above political minutiae. On the contradictions between the legal-constitutional and political-constitutional 'bodies' of the Romanian President, see Elena Simina Tănăsecu, 'The President of Romania, or: the slippery slope of a constitutional system' (2008) 4 European Constitutional Law Review 64–97.

[62] The political system has shifted (evolved) from extreme to moderate pluralism. The evolutions were strongly correlated with the role of the President, which is enhanced by or at least varies in direct relation to fragmentation and shifting alliances. See Bogdan Dima, *Conflictul dintre palate: raporturile de putere dintre Parlament, Guvern și Președinte în România postcomunistă* (Hamangiu, Bucharest, 2014) 338–339. The number of parliamentary parties varied from 1990 (sixteen in the Chamber, seven in the Senate) to 2008 (five in both Houses). The number of registered parties differed, from eighty (1990) and 155 (1992) to twenty-eight (2012), see Bianca Selejan-Guțan, *The Constitution of Romania - A Contextual Analysis* (n 13) 69. This downward slope is inversely correlated with the registration conditions, which have been rendered more permissive (now three founding members are required, down from 25,000, no geographical distribution, financial burdens are trivial). The relatively stringent supporting signatures condition that parties must meet for being qualified to run in parliamentary elections has however been maintained.

[63] Bianca Selejan-Guțan, *The Constitution of Romania - A Contextual Analysis* (n 13) 70–71.

[64] For election statistics see http://www.insse.ro/cms/files/statistici/stat_electorale.pdf (last accessed on 14 March 2022).

the table, although the situation as such was not unusual, in comparison with other communist countries. Lustration (de-communization), restitution of confiscated or nationalized property and privatization of state property became subjects of extremely polarized and thus inherently rudimentary debates from the onset. The centre-right advanced radical solutions, such as *restitutio in integrum*, meaning *in natura* of all property, irrespective of consequences and implications (public buildings, good faith tenants), complete lustration and decommunization (the latter demand would have immediately entailed the withdrawal of Iliescu from the run for the presidency), and rapid privatization of all state property. Iliescu notoriously retorted in kind, to the effect that the right to property was a 'trifle' (*moft*) and with public declarations adverse to early restitution judgments.[65] The decision with respect to the new Constitution was burdened by a similar process of polarization, with parts of the urban, centre-right political and intellectual elite promoting the Constitution of 1923 or, rather, grossly embellished reinterpretations of it. As has been described in the previous section, the constitutions of 1866 and 1923 were underpinned by presuppositions and preconditions not necessarily conducive to liberal democracy. At the pragmatic level, the option of building on the better aspects of tradition, taking as a starting point the Constitution of 1923, was foreclosed by virtue of the fact that most structural elements in pre-communist constitutionalism were fused at the hip with a choice for the restoration of monarchy.

The communist past had an influence extending beyond immediate political elite continuities. A note on the impact of communism on legal elites is necessary at this juncture. Whereas the impact of Marxism on lawyers was ideologically limited and albeit its aftereffects three decades later should not be overstated,[66] the rudimentary and much more reduced need for lawyers in communism did have an impact on the availability[67] and quality of legal elites at the onset of the transition. This is especially true in the field of public law (the Civil Code adopted in Romania under Cuza, by contrast, applied—albeit to different degrees and as amended—until 2011, straddling eight constitutions of all possible typologies). This observation is pertinent in respect of all post-communist countries, the impact differed however in correlation with the harshness of the regime and the relative degrees to which dissent was stifled and law was needed as a coordination mechanism.[68] A related note is also necessary at this point to indicate that, due to the overlaps between transitional issues and throwbacks to and carryovers from communism, the conscious choice was made to analyse the impact of communism implicitly, in the following sections, rather

---

[65] These latter statements also led to an impeachment initiative promoted by the opposition against him, in 1994. The proposal was eventually voted down by the parliamentary majority. Bogdan Dima, *Conflictul dintre palate* (n 62) 239.

[66] A quip by Adam Czarnota nicely encapsulates the philosophical influences, 'On Post-Communist Transformation, Structural Corruption, and dealing with the Past as a Constitutional Process', in Bogdan Iancu (ed) *The Law/Politics Distinction* (n 3) 179: 'The dominant type of legal theory under communist was simplistic legal positivism with a thin Marxist sauce.'

[67] There were at the time of Reunification thirty-eight attorneys in the GDR, compared to 902 in the FRG, ninety-four judges compared to 294 (rates per million). Erhard Blankenburg, 'The purge of lawyers after the breakdown of the East German communist regime' (1995) 20 Law & Social Inquiry 223, 238.

[68] Exceptions did exist. Professor Tudor Drăganu, the chair of Constitutional Law in Cluj, authored, among many commentaries, a rather nuanced history of nineteenth-century parliamentary evolutions and served as a sophisticated observer of post-1989 developments Contrariwise, some pre-Second World War authors have remained, for good reasons, controversial. George (Gheorghe) Alexianu, prolific administrative and constitutional law author (e.g. of a standard, two-volume manual of constitutional law (1930, 1933, Editura Casa Şcoalelor, Bucharest) is a good example in this latter respect. He was executed in 1946, following a conviction by the People's Tribunal for war crimes committed as civil governor of occupied Transnistria (the conviction, contested by his son in extraordinary appeal (revision) was confirmed in the 2006 and 2008 by the Court of Appeals of Bucharest and the High Court of Cassation and Justice, respectively).

THE EVOLUTION AND *GESTALT* OF THE ROMANIAN CONSTITUTION   511

than dedicate a separate, chronological sub-chapter to the period between 1947 and 1989 (or to dictatorships/authoritarianism, right and left, 1938–1989). This choice is also justified by virtue of the fact that the tensions and cleavages that dominate Romanian constitutional evolutions nowadays resemble more closely pre-communist evolutions. Latter-day referrals to communism, lustration and decommunization are sometimes instrumentalized for de-legitimation purposes in the current conflicts, primarily by the political right, in tandem with rule of law and anticorruption ideologies. The gaping social rift between the wealthier big urban agglomerations and the significantly poorer countryside and small towns[69] is often a more salient proxy for understanding current Romanian political and constitutional divisions and developments.

b) The 1991 Constitution

The parliament elected in 1990 functioned also as a Constituent Assembly for a term of two years since according to the Decree-Law 92/1990, the newly elected parliament was to be dissolved within a year from the moment the new Constitution would be adopted, whereas the decree-law would lapse once an electoral law was passed on the basis of the new Constitution (articles 80 and 99). President Iliescu was also elected for what turned out to be a two-year term.[70]

A joint committee, formed to draft the constitution bill, reflected in its composition the heavily offset structure of the parliament. The flamboyant personality of the Committee's chair, Antonie Iorgovan, known also by the self-promoted moniker 'Father of the Constitution', dominated the works of this body. Iorgovan, who held at the time the chair for administrative law at the University of Bucharest, had been elected as an independent Senator in 1990, and would serve afterwards for two terms as a PDSR/PSD (2000–2004; 2004–2008 legislatures) Senator, after a stint at the Constitutional Court, to which he was appointed in 1992 and which he left by resigning in 1996. Iorgovan is best-known academically for his solid, two-volume *Administrative Law Treatise*. He also authored/edited the primary source of the debates, a folio-format volume entitled unconventionally *The Odyssey of Elaborating the Constitution: Facts and Documents, Individuals and Personalities; Chronicle and Explanation, Unravelling and Meditation.*[71] The book is an invaluable research source in the intricacies of committee and parliamentary workings and mechanics but is not entirely written as an academic analysis. Interspersed are Professor Iorgovan's somewhat picaresque observations about various individuals, events, feelings, his persona ubiquitously populating the events, imparting accolades and reprimands to the other participants (*suum cuique tribuere*), according to individual desert.[72] Five experts, out of which two constitutional

---

[69] In 2017, GDP per capita in the metropolitan region Bucharest-Ilfov was 144 per cent of EU average. Conversely, Romania's GDP was 63 per cent (in the North-East, 39 per cent, South and South-West, 45 per cent, and 50 per cent, respectively); https://ec.europa.eu/eurostat/documents/2995521/9618249/1-26022019-AP-EN.pdf/f765d183-c3d2-4e2f-9256-cc6665909c80 (last accessed on 14 March 2022) (PPS, EU 28 = 100).

[70] In 1996, when he ran for what the opposition considered to be a third mandate (1990–1992, 1992–1994), Iliescu's candidacy was challenged before the Constitutional Court, which, in Ruling 1/1996, decided that the Constitution of 1991 only applied for the future, so the 1996–2000 term would not be a third constitutional term. Iliescu won before the court, lost however the elections but the ruling helped secure his candidacy in the 2004 elections, which he eventually won. Hotărârea (ruling) 1/8.09.1996, M.Of. nr. 213 din 09.09.1996. The Constitutional Court of Romania issues rulings (*hotărâri*), advisory opinions (*opinii*) and decisions (*decizii*). Decisions will be cited using the standard abbreviation DCC. Due to space limitations, cites are in 'shorthand', indicating only type of act, number, and year and eliding the full Official Journal references.

[71] Antonie Iorgovan, *Odiseea elaborării Constituției-fapte și documente, oameni și caractere; cronică și explicații, dezvăluiri și meditații* (Editura Uniunii Vatra Românească, Târgu Mureș, 1998).

[72] Antonie Iorgovan, ibid, 29: some experts in the committee have 'intrigue, obsequiousness, and duplicity in their blood', instinct tells Professor Iorgovan to 'never turn his back on them, since these are dangerous snakes, especially if their interests are affected' and can easily 'turn into scorpions and cobras'. Prime Minister Petre Roman

law—such as it was—professors of the universities in Cluj (Ioan Deleanu) and Bucharest (Ioan Muraru), were selected as non-voting members, with Deleanu serving also as a liaison member between the two working groups eventually created within the committee (on fundamental rights and state organization, respectively).[73]

The Commission worked under a very tight schedule on the main ideas (the so-called 'theses of the Constitution'), proceeding according to its approved calendar from a documentation stage (1 August–15 September 1990) to principles and a skeleton draft to be already presented on 11 December in the Plenary of the Constituent Assembly/parliament. Once the principles had been adopted by the Assembly, a draft could be worked out, debated in the Constituent Assembly, finally adopted in parliament on 21 November 1991, and then approved by referendum on 8 December 1991.

A number of working trips were organized (to Italy, Spain, and France), contacts with the Venice Commission were initiated, including with its founder and then-president, Antonio La Pergola, and an international conference took place in Bucharest (Constitutional Perspectives and Mutations in Eastern Europe, 19–13 November). Robert Badinter, at the time President of the *Conseil Constitutionnel*, visited with the committee in October of 1990. More informal contacts also existed between the committee and the ABA-CEELI programme, which was, at the time, an industrious legal transplant entrepreneur in the region.[74] The desire to emulate Western practices did result in various additions, for example the institution of the Ombudsman (Advocate of the People, *Avocatul Poporului*), which was introduced in the 1991 Constitution (Title II, Chapter IV, articles 55–57) but could only start to function years later, once its organic law, L. 35/1997 was adopted.[75]

The work of this Committee was even in the preparatory stage constrained by political choices, especially in sensitive areas such as the form of government, where the issue was raised as to whether one should have consulted the people by referendum on the monarchy/republic choice before proceeding to elaborate further in the Committee and, subsequently, in the *Constituante*. Iorgovan mentions direct discussions with Senate President Bârlădeanu and Prime Minister Roman, the latter expressing displeasure that such an option could even be raised and tabled.[76] Political imponderables also mattered since, although the identity-related choices of 1991 follow the well-trodden path of building unity through ethnocentric means, UDMR was already a player. Observations sent by President Iliescu on the 'Theses' Draft clearly rejected a proposed principle according to which 'the only criterion in

---

was however (page 32) 'a good-natured fellow, of my own generation' (at the beginning, before Roman entered into a conflict with Iliescu and was sacked).

[73] Iorgovan's opinion of the experts, *Odiseea elaborării Constituției-fapte și documente, oameni și* (n 71) 22, was that 'some of them only began to decipher the mysteries of public law, whereas others held also public appointments and when they—rarely—attended, stood on needles and let it be known to all that more important engagements awaited them elsewhere.' All experts, including Senator Iorgovan, were eventually appointed to the CCR.

[74] Antonie Iorgovan, *Odiseea elaborării Constituției-fapte și documente, oameni și caractere* (n 71) 65–70. The mention of an ABA-funded delegation to Bucharest, including Georgetown professor [sic!] 'Merk Tushenet' is made on page 383 (from which one may safely infer that the American visit did not make a lasting impression), together with the reproduction of the subsequent courtesy letter of 21 May 1991 signed by a Dr Mark Ellis in the name of the ABA. European contacts prevailed in relevance also on account of the sheer fact that final debates were by that time already well underway.

[75] I discuss this process, the amendments of 2003 and other revision initiatives at length in 'Constitutional revision in Romania: Post-accession pluralism in action', in Paul Blokker (ed), *Constitutional Acceleration within the European Union and Beyond* (1st ed, Routledge, London, 2017) 177–196.

[76] Antonie Iorgovan, *Odiseea elaborării Constituției-fapte și documente, oameni și* (n 71) 31–34.

establishing a political party is the political one' (meaning, a Bulgarian-style solution, forbidding *ab initio* and *in principle* ethnically based parties or factions).[77]

Aside from this concession, the tenor was tilted towards foreclosing any future possibility of territorial autonomy on ethnic bases,[78] the target being the Hungarian minority, concentrated in the middle of the country, especially in two counties where Hungarian Szeklers make up over 90 per cent of the population. Opening the constitution with the title on the *State* (rather than with Fundamental Rights, Freedoms, and Duties (Title II)) was a choice that could be justified in the line of tradition (Constitutions of 1866 and 1923). The State was defined as 'national, sovereign and independent, unitary and indivisible' (Compare with the fundamental law of 1923, article 1: 'The Kingdom of Romania is a national unitary and indivisible state.'). Unlike in 1923, the Constitution of 1991 also contains an eternity clause, according to which, among other values, the republican form of government and the national, unitary, independent, and indivisible character of the state may not form the objects of a revision (article 148 (C. 1991), now article 152 (2003)).[79] The ethnocentric side of the 1991 Constitution, unlike pre-1947 identity building by rejection or suppression of alterity,[80] was however more subdued and, to a certain degree, rhetorical, seeking to substitute the deep polarization on all other issues with the invocation of the national unitary state and its indivisible territory.[81] To wit, even the phrase 'Revolution of 1989', which is used in article 1 para 3 of the Constitution (2003) is subject to deep-seated contestation, many preferring until today to adjectivize the noun (as in *confiscated* revolution) or to use neutral terms such as 'the events of 1989' in its stead.

As regards the institutional structure, the already existing post-revolutionary framework was entrenched: bicameral parliament, semi-presidential system. A Constitutional Court (CCR) was created, after the French *Conseil* model, instead of reinstating the 1912 or 1923 precedents (judicial review by all ordinary courts or by the High Court in Grand Chamber session, respectively). The initial version of the CCR was endowed with weaker powers: unconstitutionality judgments could be overturned by a two-thirds majority vote in parliament. Bicameralism could be regarded prima facie as a nod to tradition but, on closer observation, the post-communist parliament resembles its 1923 predecessor only at the nominal level. The 1866 and 1923 Senates were distinguished from the Chambers either (initially) in the social composition of electors and members as determined by census and qualifications restrictions or (later, after extension of the franchise) due to a relatively high number of *ex officio* and territorially or corporately selected Senators and significantly

---

[77] Antonie Iorgovan, *Odiseea elaborării Constituției-fapte și documente, oameni și* (n 71) 82–83.

[78] See for instance, at page 499, Iorgovan criticizing a proposed and rejected amendment in the plenary debates: 'To maintain in the Constituent Assembly of Romania that the right to identity encompasses a birth right to ancestral land [i.e. to territorial autonomy] is unforgivable.'

[79] In this vein, the opinion of the Venice Commission on the later amendments in 2003 was factually (formally) wrong, in proposing that the word 'national' from art 1 be deleted on revision (Opinion No. 169/2001, of 18 March 2013, on the draft revision of the Constitution of Romania CDL-AD (2003) 4). The Venice Commission noticed the problem (Limits of revision, then art 148, now 152) but declined to comment on it, which, nonetheless, did not make the problem (i.e. unamendability) disappear. The Commission was however right to point out a number of contradictions (as in national state (ethnically defined) vs. national minority/minorities arts 4 para 2, 6, 32 para 3 and 119 para 2).

[80] This did not concern only the Jewish question. The citizens of Dobrogea, territory that had at the time a 'melting pot' composition (and a Turkish and Tatar majority), received Romanian citizenship *en masse* but were denied full political rights (such as they existed, census-based) until 1909. They could only vote for local administration bodies.

[81] See e.g. Manuel Guțan, 'Romanian Tendential Constitutionalism and the Limits of European Constitutional Culture', in Martin Belov (ed.), *Global Constitutionalism and Its Challenges to Westphalian Constitutional Law* (1st ed, Bloomsbury/Hart, London, 2018) 103–129.

higher age qualifications imposed on the electors (over forty years of age). Not being able to decide on a salient distinction, not wanting to copy the French model of the Senate due to its 'territorial' implications, the constitution-makers of 1991 created almost identical chambers (*bicameralismo perfetto*).[82]

A myriad of minute issues were similarly left somewhat open-ended, for instance the problem of separation of powers and checks and balances (especially in the context of presidential and parliamentary terms initially running concurrently) or the configuration of the judiciary. Conversely, grand contours had been decided already in the preparatory stage, even in terms of 'dilatory compromises'.

In respect of this latter category, the solution regarding the place of prosecutors, already crystallized in preparatory stage, is the result of a compromise that straddles two clearly opposed visions. One position recommended a clear choice for ministerial organization as a conscious departure from Soviet-style *Prokuratura*, another advocated preserving the magistrate status, equivalent to judges. The solution was an uneasy synthesis that placed prosecutors within 'judicial authority', as a Public Ministry placed 'under the authority of the Minister of Justice'.[83]

As regards the clarity and coherence of the final document and the many details wherein the proverbial devil lies, the template is hard to trace back either to tradition or to transplant. For instance, in an elegant study on the use of foreign precedents in Romanian constitutional adjudication, the authors argue that the 'grand design and the general structure of the fundamental law belong to national, rather than universal, constitutionalism'.[84] This is true if the word constitutionalism is to be understood in a thin, procedural sense. The Constitution makes reference (article 1 para 2, as amended in 2003) to the 'spirit of the democratic traditions of the Romanian people', yet none of its structural features, from semi-presidential republic to Constitutional Court, reflects constitutional traditions. Sometimes the system, especially in what concerns institutional aspects, is compared with the French model[85] but this is only true should the analogy follow a rudimentary *genus proximum* baseline. The Romanian Constitutional Court, for example, is composed somewhat alike the French *Conseil* (yet without the former Presidents as *ex officio* members) but its powers are very different. The Romanian President has the power to submit questions of national importance to a referendum, like his counterpart in Paris, but the Romanian result has consultative value only. The Constitution provides for the possibility of delegated legislation via ordinances, yet here as well the resemblance is nominal, since delegation in its Romanian form comprises both ordinary delegation (but, unlike France, not in the field of organic law) and Italian-style emergency decrees that may be adopted on a plea of necessity by the Executive (with some exceptions, emergency ordinances may be adopted within the fields of both ordinary and organic law).[86]

---

[82] They differ in the age requirements for Deputies and Senators (23 and 33, respectively) and in the representation ratios (73,000 per Deputy, 168,000 per Senator). See on symmetrical bicameralism, Chapter 6 on Italy by Sabrina Ragone and Giacomo d'Amico in this volume.

[83] Antonie Iorgovan, *Odiseea elaborării Constituţiei-fapte şi documente, oameni şi caractere* (n 71) 43.

[84] Elena Simina Tănăsescu and Ştefan Deaconu, 'Romania: Analogical Reasoning as a Dialectical Instrument', in Tania Groppi and Marie-Claire Ponthoreau (eds), *The Use of Foreign Precedents by Constitutional Judges* (Hart, London, 2013) 325.

[85] E.g. by the Constitutional Court, in DCC 683/2012 (II.5.), referring to 'the Constitution of France, the source of inspiration for the Romanian Constitution'.

[86] Manuel Guţan, 'Transplantul constituţional şi obsesia semiprezidenţialismului francez in România contemporană I and II' (2010) 5 Pandectele Române 30–84; Manuel Guţan, 'Transplantul constituţional şi obsesia semiprezidenţialismului francez in România contemporană I and II' (2010) 7 Pandectele Române 31–67. See also Manuel Guţan, 'The French legal model in modern Romania: An ambition, a rejection. Comments on Sylvain

B. The Evolution of the Constitution

1. Shifting Contexts: New Conflicts, New Vocabularies

The Constitution of 1991, an imperfect document, had the merit of ensuring a framework for the peaceful transition of power by free and fair elections, arguably a first in modern Romanian constitutional history. In 1996, parliamentary elections were won by centre-right parties running under a political coalition umbrella (the Democratic Convention (CDR)), whereas the Convention candidate and Rector of the University of Bucharest, Emil Constantinescu, became President. The Convention years ended in disillusion, whereby Constantinescu pulled out of the run for a second term and the PNȚCD, the Convention flagship party, never again managed to pass the 5 per cent parliamentary threshold. The social-democratic pole won the elections of 2000 in a landslide, and thus a mandate to carry negotiations for the accessions to NATO (2004) and EU (2007) and to revise the Constitution, which was overhauled in 2003, in view of impending accessions.

The political configuration started changing in the 2000s. Extreme nationalist parties gradually exited the scene,[87] whereas the spectrum became as a rule more clearly divided between the PSD on the left (with its allies of various ideological colours) and forms of contestation on the right. PSD, with a strong territorial base, has constantly won around 30–40 per cent of the national vote in parliamentary elections, but, ever since the early 1990s, no absolute majority. It usually needs to form electoral and political coalitions with smaller parties in order to reach the majority needed to form a government. By the same token, since 2004, PSD candidates have lost all presidential elections to the centre-right.[88] The left/right divide reinforces class and territorial cleavages, with the more redistributive PSD drawing its strength from poorer regions, country-side or smaller towns and the right vying primarily for the urban middle class (large cities) and the sizable Romanian diaspora. Thus, territorial, social, and economic divisions reinforce both political and institutional divides.

Political-ideological labels have always been somewhat fluid in Romanian politics. Due to endemic party-switching and aisle crossing, so too are parties and coalitions. To exemplify, the former National Salvation Front (the party from which the current social-democrats split) was redefined as PD, won membership in the Socialist International (1995), exited the International (2005), and then reinvented itself as centre-right. It joined the EPP (2006) and changed its name again in 2007, in fashion with newer times, as PDL (Liberal-Democratic Party), eventually dissolving into the PNL. Conversely, a former president of PNL, Călin Popescu Tăriceanu (Prime Minister 2004–2008), as the leader of a splinter conservative liberal party (ALDE) opposed to the PNL, entered a coalition with the PSD. A confusing string

---

Soleil's Le modèle juridique français dans le monde. Une ambition, une expansion (xvie-xixe siècle)' (2015) 1 Romanian Journal of Comparative Law 120–141.

[87] The ultranationalist right resurfaced in parliamentary form in 2020 (see notes 6–8 and associated text).
[88] The contradiction results from much higher turnouts in the second round of presidential elections (compare the turnout in the 2016 parliamentary elections available at http://prezenta.bec.ro/index.html (last accessed on 19 March 2022) with participation in the second round of the presidential elections, 2014 available at http://bec2 014.roaep.ro/wp-content/uploads/2014/11/ComunicatFinaleProvizorii.tif (last accessed on 19 March 2022) and partly also from the fact that the Romanian diaspora votes overwhelmingly centre-right (89.73 per cent for Klaus Werner Iohannis (338,873 votes), the Liberal candidate in 2014, 10.26 per cent for his competitor, SPD candidate Victor Viorel Ponta). This latter factor had a negligible impact in 2014, when the difference between candidates was significant but diaspora votes have tipped the balance and determined the victory of President Băsescu in 2009.

of political realignments has been a staple of Romanian post-1989 politics.[89] However, since 2004, political divisions have been polarized or reinforced and preconditioned by a number of constitutional decisions taken in 2003, partly reflective of EU conditionalities.

In view of the accession to the EU, the Romanian constitutional system was overhauled. The revision induced a clear tendency towards systemic fragmentation by desynchronizing parliamentary and presidential terms of office (an endogenous choice with a tremendous potentiality for fostering inter-branch conflicts) and as a result of the new, quasi-constitutional discourse of anticorruption (an EU conditionality, reflected by constitutional changes).

Anticorruption has been increasingly appropriated by the centre-right as its dominant political narrative, fused at the hip with simplified or 'sloganized' rule of law or judicial independence ideologies, to which the social democrats responded with equally rudimentary, 'populist' counter-discourses.[90] Neither the rule of law nor judicial independence are, in and of themselves, ideological notions, but these foundational constitutional concepts have been manipulated in order to preserve various *status-quos*. For instance, the rule of law is a term charged with conceptual and contextual presuppositions;[91] using it wholesale for instrumental political purposes inevitably transforms the concept into a slogan.

For the past fifteen years centre-right presidents have cohabitated uneasily with primarily centre-left parliaments. Discourse polarization trickled down into institutional conflicts or rather a vicious circle correlation has entwined the two phenomena.

2. The 'Euro-Amendments'

When the revision of 2003 was submitted to the confirmatory referendum, the poll had to be extended by an additional day by emergency ordinance. In the end, the turn-out requirement was exceeded, with 55.7 per cent of the electorate casting a ballot, 89.7 per cent voting in favour of the revision. The contradiction (lack of interest and approval quasi by acclamation) can be explained as an instantiation of the 'constitutionalism without constitutional moment' which characterized more generally the process of eastward enlargement, arguably EU constitutionalism as such, and certainly the convergence of these two developments.[92] Presented as indispensable to EU and NATO integration, the changes were favourably received by a citizenry that, conversely, did not believe it had much choice and certainly took little interest in the legal minutiae through which the desirable result was to obtain.

---

[89] According to Bogdan Dima, *Conflictul dintre palate* (n 62) 83 the average lifetime of a Cabinet was (1990–2013) 1.6 years, noting also that only three Prime Ministers managed to complete the four-year term for which they received a vote of confidence at the time of investiture (this trend is still ongoing as of 2018, with three Cabinets since the 2016 elections alone).

[90] See Tamás Kiss and István Gergő Székely. 'Populism on the Semi-Periphery: Some Considerations for Understanding the Anti-Corruption Discourse in Romania' (2021) *Problems of Post-Communism*, DOI: 10.1080/10758216.2020.1869907 (arguing persuasively that the anticorruption discourse is itself a (admittedly, peculiar) form of populism, playing divisively on class and geographical stereotypes and displaying selective anti-institutionalism in the form of a deep antiparliamentary hostility). I make a similar argument in Bogdan Iancu, *'Status Quo Hegemony?: Conflicting Narratives about the "Rule of Law"'* (2020) VerfBlog https://verfassungsblog.de/status-quo-hegemony/ (last accessed on 19 March 2022).

[91] Dieter Grimm, 'Stufen der Rechtsstaatlichkeit – Zur Exportfähigkeit einer westlichen Errungenschaft' (2009) 64 (12) Juristen Zeitung 596–600; I touch on the issue of sloganization of judicial independence in the Romanian context in Bogdan Iancu, 'Changed Vocabularies: A Few Semantic Ambiguities of Network Constitutionalism', in Iulia Motoc, Krzysztof Wojtyczek, and Paulo Pinto de Albuquerque (eds), *New Developments in Constitutional Law: Essays in Honour of András Sajó* (Eleven Int'. Publishing, The Hague, 2018) 191–212.

[92] András Sajó, 'Constitution without the constitutional moment: A view from the new member states' (2005) 3 (2–3) International Journal of Constitutional Law 243.

The amendments, albeit perceived and presented as primarily EU-related, are a complex bundle of provisions within which a three-fold taxonomy can be distinguished. First, some articles were introduced as run-of-the-mill Europe (and NATO)-related clauses, e.g. Title VI, Euro-Atlantic integration (primacy, ratification of the institutive treaties and their revisions by a special procedure, namely, a law adopted by a two-thirds majority in a joint session, the obligation of the government to inform parliament with respect to draft regulations or directives, etc.), electoral rights in European parliamentary elections (article 38) and local administration (article 16 para 4), and the like.

A second category of amendments were undertaken as expressions of pre-accession conditionalities. The country is also subject to a *post-accession* conditionality concerning anticorruption and judiciary reforms, under the Cooperation and Verification Mechanism (CVM).[93] The CVM, established by the Commission on the basis of the Act of Accession of Romania and Bulgaria, was supposed to lapse in 2010, three years after the entry of these two countries in the EU, on 1 January, 2007, unless extended.[94] In the meanwhile its application has been expanded in time and scope, apparently for indefinite duration and with a normative capillarity reaching issues often many steps removed from the initial, ostensibly more technical objectives ('benchmarks'). The reforms undertaken before accession resulted in important structural changes with respect to the Superior Council of the Magistracy, which, in the initial version of the Constitution was elected by parliament, for a term of four years, its main attributions being to nominate judges and prosecutors for appointment by the President and to serve as a disciplinary council for judges only. With the 2003 amendments, this weaker institution was in effect replaced by the 'Judicial Council Euro-model'[95] as the application of a more general reform blueprint with a specific Romanian anticorruption twist. In the specific case of Romania, the already existing ambiguity concerning the role of prosecutors intersected the preference of the EU Commission for judiciary reforms in the CEE countries directed towards the creation of constitutionally-entrenched judicial self-government[96] and the newly crystallized consensus on anti-corruption as an element of international constitutional law.[97] The result was the creation of a Superior Council of the Magistracy that goes well beyond the Judicial Council Euro-model template offered to the new Member States in 2004. The current CSM comprises not half (as the international standard would require) but 73.6 per cent judges and prosecutors elected by their peers (the other five members are the President of the High Court of Cassation and Justice (HCCJ), the

---

[93] European Commission, 'Cooperation and Verification Mechanism for Bulgaria and Romania' available at https://ec.europa.eu/info/policies/justice-and-fundamental-rights/effective-justice/rule-law/assistance-bulgaria-and-romania-under-cvm/cooperation-and-verification-mechanism-bulgaria-and-romania_en (last accessed on 22 March 2022). This monitoring also applies to Bulgaria, which is additionally under Commission scrutiny with respect to progress in combatting organized crime.

[94] The legal basis of the Romanian CVM is Commission Decision 2006/928/EC (an almost identical mechanism was instituted for Bulgaria by Decision 2006/929/EC). The decision purports to give expression to arts 37–38 in the Act of Accession, concerning transitional, safeguard clauses, although the CVM as such and the safeguard clauses in the treaty are only very approximately related (art 37 has to do with post-accession market distortions, 38 with failure to transpose civil and criminal law mutual recognition acts).

[95] Michal Bobek and David Kosař, 'Global solutions, local damages: A critical study in judicial councils in Central and Eastern Europe' (2014) 15 (7) German Law Journal 1257, 1261: 'The European Commission went even further in the 2007 enlargement wave by basically requiring Romania and Bulgaria to adopt the JC model 'as it is'.

[96] On this, see the comparative study by David Kosař, *Perils of Judicial Self-Government in Transitional Societies* (CUP, Cambridge, 2016).

[97] Peter W. Schroth and Ana Daniela Bostan, 'International constitutional law and anti-corruption measures in the European Union's accession negotiations – Romania in comparative perspective' (2004) 52 (3) The American Journal of Comparative Law 625; Patrycjia Szarek-Mason, *The European Union's Fight Against Corruption – The Evolving Policy Towards Member States and Candidate Countries* (CUP, Cambridge, 2010).

Prosecutor General, and the Minister of Justice as members *ex officio* and two 'representatives of civil society' selected by the Senate from lists of candidates submitted by NGOs). If one factored in the two high magistrates who sit in the Council by virtue of their office, the percentage of judiciary representatives would be 84 per cent. Civil society members participate only in plenary meetings, meaning that they do not vote in the two sections, where crucial career decisions are made (e.g. disciplinary actions). The term of the Council was extended from four to six years, whereas its presidency is ensured by one of the elected judges and prosecutors for a non-renewable one-year term. Anticorruption constitutional changes included the rethinking of parliamentary immunity rules so that, since 2003, MPs have only been immune from pretrial arrest, search, and detention without the agreement of their House. Ministers are covered by immunity from prosecution, which can be lifted by the President, the House, or the Senate, respectively.

The constitutional changes described in the previous paragraph can only be understood in the context of wider judicial reforms. In view of the accession, three judiciary laws were passed, on the statute on judges and prosecutors, judicial organization, and the CSM, respectively (Laws 303/2014, 304/2004, 317/2004). These are organic laws, meaning that they can only be passed and amended by absolute majorities. According to the CSM law, the Council has to render an advisory opinion on all proposed changes. A Romanian anticorruption watchdog, *Direcția Națională Anticorupție* (DNA), was established by an emergency ordinance as an autonomous unit within the Prosecutor General's office. In effect, it has been autonomous not only from the political branches but also from the General Prosecutor's Office, since both the General Prosecutor and the Chief Prosecutor of the DNA have been appointed in the same way since 2005, namely by the President, upon a nomination by the Minister of Justice, following an advisory opinion by the CSM, for three-year terms, renewable once. The DNA has competence over high- and medium-level corruption, defined in terms of a) the quality of the defendant, according to the list in Law 78/2000 on the prevention, discovery and sanctioning of corrupt acts or b) the value of the bribe (over 10,000 Euro in Romanian Lei) or c) damage to the state (over 200,000). It prosecutes not only classical corruption crimes (passive and active bribery, unlawful gratuities, trafficking in influence) and corruption-related offences (e.g. laundering the proceeds) but also 'assimilated' offences, for instance the abuse of public office.

These constitutional and legislative amendments followed a holistic logic according to which anticorruption could only be pursued vigorously by a fully independent prosecutor's office entrenched within a fully autonomous judiciary and that a change of the generational guard would give full effect to the reform. In this latter respect, the reform of the CSM favoured 'judicial democracy' as lack of hierarchy, implicitly empowering younger, presumably progressive elements of the profession. For example, the constitution provides that nine judges and five prosecutors shall be elected in the Council but does not establish proportions of representation pegged to jurisdictional tiers. According to the CSM law 317/2004, among the five elected prosecutors in the Council, three represent the prosecutors' offices attached to lowest jurisdictional tiers, trial courts and tribunals, as an expression of the 'wind of generational change' paradigm.

A third set of modifications were triggered endogenously, with the ostensible purpose of rendering the constitutional system more 'efficient'. Some endogenous changes are cosmetic or unimportant in nature, such as the reference in article 1 to the 'spirit of the Revolution of 1989' and the 'democratic traditions of the Romanian people'. Some were however intended to substantially alter institutional processes. For instance, the initial constitution provided for a cumbersome legislative process, especially given the threefold classification of legislation (French-, Hungarian-, Spanish-style) in constitutional, organic, and ordinary. Given the symmetrical and congruent bicameralism of 1991 and the *navette parlementaire* and conciliation committee procedures for adopting legislation, the result was (described as) overwrought and slow parliamentary law-making. The revision sought to remedy this deficiency by distinguishing the roles of the two houses according to the subject matter of legislation, into 'first notified' and 'decisional' chambers, which means in effect that a law can be tacitly adopted by the first notified chamber, within forty-five (default) or sixty days (codification or complex legislation). This new procedure applies to organic and ordinary legislation, whereas constitutional amendments still follow the older symmetrical procedure.

The Constitutional Court was significantly reinforced by adding to its powers, most notably in respect of *Organstreit* proceedings (according to article 146(e) the Court solves 'legal conflicts of a constitutional nature between public authorities', at the request of the President of Romania, either of the two Speakers, the Prime Minister or the president of the CSM). The possibility to overturn decisions of unconstitutionality was eliminated, but this tendency towards increased juridification of the Court in terms of its powers was not reflected in the rules on composition, so that the amendments entrenched a clumsily overhauled judicature. The post-2003 CCR combines thus German-style, *Bundesverfassungsgericht* powers (concrete and abstract review, including treaties, solution of conflicts of competence, etc.) with a French, *Conseil*-type composition (three members each are appointed by the President, the Chamber, the Senate, for staggered terms of nine years).

The mandate of the President was extended in 2003 to five years, which made the transplant of French-style cohabitation possible. Paradoxically, this happened three years after France itself gave up its 1958 tradition and abolished the *septennat*, and thus, in practice, cohabitation, drawing this conclusion from a long experience of stalemate and conflict.[98]

The Romanian constitution is relatively rigid. Initiative belongs to the President at the proposal of the government, to 500,000 citizens, provided that territorial dispersion requirements are met (at least 20,000 signatures collected each in at least half of the counties) or to one fourth of the Deputies *or* Senators. An amendment must be passed with two-third majorities in both Houses. If the versions differ and the conference procedure fails, the bill can only be adopted by a three-fourth majority of the total number of Senators and Deputies in a joint session of both Houses. Due to the limits of revision specified by the 'eternity clause' (article 152), constitutionality is verified *suo motu* by the CCR before the bill is tabled *and* after adoption (Law 47/1992, articles 19–23; the presumption of constitutionality can be overturned in this particular case by a two-thirds majority of the justices). After adoption in parliament, a confirmatory referendum must approve the revision; until recently, the turnout validity condition was 50 per cent of the voters.[99] Due to the political polarization that occurred immediately after 2003, as a direct result of cohabitation and given the high majority required to adopt constitutional amendments, all recent attempts to revise the constitution have failed. President Băsescu promoted a revision bill in 2011, starting from the report of an expert commission convened under the auspices of the Presidential Administration

---

[98] See Bianca Selejan-Guțan, *The Constitution of Romania - A Contextual Analysis* (n 13) 106–107, arguing that it was a mistake and picking on this paradox of legal transplant. The change may however have been determined by more mundane and practical considerations, namely, to foster the ambitions of sitting Prime Minister Năstase, who was the PSD presidential candidate at the time.

[99] The Referendum Law 3/2000 was amended in 2013, to provide a common validity threshold, 30 per cent turnout, 25 per cent valid votes for all national referenda (impeachment, confirmatory, consultative). The Constitutional Court decided that the change was constitutional, provided it applied with a one-year delay, this delay being imposed by reference to Venice Commission recommendations, DCC 471/2013.

(out of the initial membership, half resigned in the process, some accusing pressures to conform, and were promptly replaced). The commission report and the bill that selected some its elements both proposed to 'rationalize' the system by tilting it towards a presidentialized form of semi-presidentialism. The parliament retorted with its own project, pursued in 2012 under the auspices of the Senate Speaker. At that time, the USL, Social-Democratic/Liberal political alliance controlled the required parliamentary majority but since the USL (PNL and PSD) coalition eventually came undone, the bill could not be adopted. The parliamentary project was preceded by a wider, albeit rather cursory, consultation of various interests and constituencies (*Constitutional Forum*) and started from the premise that 'rationalization' meant increasing the powers of the government and parliament relative to and at the expense of the President.

More recently, over 3,000,000 signatures were collected by an informal association (*Coalition for the Family*), with the support of the Orthodox Church, to promote an amendment to article 48 that would have defined marriage in heterosexual key, as a union between a man and a woman. The Constitutional Court decision declared the bill in conformity with the fundamental law, using (for the first time) an originalist interpretation.[100] A conservative social consensus on family values cuts almost fully across institutional and ideological divides, thus the constitutional amendment was adopted in parliament with the requisite two-thirds majority. Nonetheless, the amendment failed due to insufficient participation in the confirmatory referendum held in October 2018 (21.1 per cent over two days, 91.56 per cent 'Yes' votes).[101] The participation in the diaspora was higher than that in the previous ballot, the parliamentary elections of 2016,[102] reflecting the traditional conservative centre-right orientation of many Romanians living overseas. Within the country, the low turn-out can be accounted for both as a reflection of the perceived lack of salience of the topic and as a consequence of superimposed political quandaries. The Social-Democrats did not support the referendum more vigorously, in order to toe the ideological line of their European political family. The Right feared that a success would be politically hijacked by the Social-Democratic party and its leader, as he then was, Liviu Dragnea.

Signatures were collected for an amendment promoted by a parliamentary party with a pronounced anticorruption platform, the USR (*Union Save Romania*). The initiative (*No criminals (fără penali) in public office*) seeks to prevent the election to parliament or the Presidency of persons definitively condemned to an imprisonment sentence, for crimes committed with intent, unless legally exonerated.

On 26 May 2019, European parliamentary elections were held in sync with the ballot on a consultative referendum initiated by the President. This referendum contained two questions related to the fight against corruption (and impliedly directed against the Social-Democrats). The first asked the citizens to cast a vote on whether amnesty or pardon should

---

[100] DCC 580/2016; the Court decided that the initiative does not impinge upon art 152 para 2, constituting a suppression of fundamental rights, freedoms and the guarantees thereof, essentially with the argument that relevant texts in the constitution had been understood from the beginning as heterosexual (traditional) marriage and family, so no guarantee existed that could be taken away: 'In 1991, when the Constitution was adopted, marriage was understood in its traditional acceptation, as a union between a man and a woman' (para 42). This decision is not challenged in any way by the admission of the exception of unconstitutionality following the Grand Chamber Judgment in C-673/16 (*Coman and Others*). The exception has been admitted by the Court, once the preliminary reference was answered by the ECJ, on the narrowest of grounds (marriage concluded elsewhere within the EU between an EU citizen and a third country national gives both spouses' citizenship-derived rights to free movement and settlement in Romania, even if the Romanian regulation of marriage differs).

[101] See http://prezenta.bec.ro (last accessed on 19 March 2022).

[102] See 126. 239 (2018) available at http://prezenta.bec.ro/referendum/abroad (last accessed 19 March 2022) and 106. 038 (2016) available at http://prezenta.bec.ro/parlamentare2016/ (last accessed on 19 March 2022).

be used in the area of corruption offenses. The second was a composite query into whether emergency decrees ought to be issued by the government in the fields of criminal law and judicial organization and whether the possibility of seizing the Constitutional Court with complaints of unconstitutionality concerning emergency ordinances ought to be extended.[103] Boosted by the referendum and a sustained campaign orated by the opposition, successfully depicting the PSD as the party of graft, participation in the elections spiked to 45 per cent. The referendum turn-out reached 42.28 per cent,[104] with 80 per cent of the latter voting in favour of the President's position, whereas the PSD percentage halved in comparison to its last results.

3. Constitutional Conflicts

With increased cohabitation, conflicts between governments supported by left-dominated majorities in parliament and consequently hostile to the centre-right Presidents became a commonality of Romanian political life, up until 2021. The President has full liberty to nominate a Prime Minister via negotiations if no party wins an absolute majority (article 103). If the parliament withholds confidence, after two failed nominations taking place within sixty days, the President may dissolve the legislature after consultations with the speakers and parliamentary faction leaders, but dissolution may not occur in the last six months of the presidential term (article 89). These provisions already existed in the initial version of the Constitution but their relevance, against the backdrop of cohabitation in the context of the political and social background mentioned in the previous section, is now enhanced.

In November 2015 a fire occurred during a concert in a crowded Bucharest club, killing dozens and seriously injuring over a hundred patrons. Massive demonstrations followed, under the slogan 'Corruption kills!', asking for the resignation of the PSD Prime Minister Ponta. The implicit chain of reasoning moving the protestors was that the tragedy could occur only as a result of poor administrative enforcement and inadequate legislation, that such deficiencies could only be a consequence of corruption, and that the Social Democratic-dominated coalition in power was the main culprit for corruption and thus for the deaths. The Ponta cabinet was replaced upon the Prime Minister's resignation under the pressure of the street by a caretaker 'technocratic' government formed by the Prime Minister and designated by the President, former EU Agriculture Commissioner Cioloș. Without the Damocles sword of dissolution and snap elections in the middle of a crisis, this could arguably not have happened. In October 2009, when a motion of censure brought down the Boc government, which was politically close to President Băsescu, the latter made two nominations that failed, won the presidential elections in December and immediately re-nominated the recently deposed Prime Minister Boc. In the new context of a re-legitimated President, Boc secured a vote of confidence from a parliamentary majority now in disarray.[105]

---

[103] Currently, only the Ombudsman may raise an exception of unconstitutionality in respect of ordinances, all other exceptions must go the more tortuous, time-consuming course of referrals from ordinary courts, which results in a practical impossibility of challenging such decrees in time.

[104] For the referendum results see https://prezenta.bec.ro/referendum26052019 (last accessed on 19 March 2022).

[105] Bogdan Dima, *Conflictul dintre palate* (n 62) 300 notes that 'although it is practically almost impossible for dissolution to be imposed by the President ... the institution of dissolution can be used as a pressure instrument on the parliamentary majority, determining mutations in the political behavior of majorities'.

Conflicts appear from the very onset of cohabitation and continue in the form of attrition constitutional warfare for the duration of either term or until either of the two branches manages to prevail conclusively. Occasionally, the antagonism may result in presidential impeachments ('suspension from office').[106] According to the procedure provided by article 95, the impeachment is initiated by one fourth of the MPs, adopted by an absolute majority in joint plenary session and submitted to the popular vote in a referendum convened within a month. The Constitutional Court renders an advisory opinion on the articles of impeachment. The Court has established the standard according to which the phrase 'serious acts breaching the Constitution' may only refer to actual deeds, as opposed to political statements, the latter being covered by the freedom of political speech. As mentioned already, the President's ostensible role according to the Constitution is that of an impartial umpire, but the need to seek re-election as well as personal imponderables render this interpretation (of a politically equidistant head of state) untenable.

During the two terms of former President Băsescu, he was subject to the procedure of suspension from office in 2007 and 2012. The second time, impeachment occurred in a highly charged political climate with a parliament dominated by the USL, an alliance between liberals and social democrats *created against Băsescu* and with a population clearly favourable to removing a head of state whose authority had been eroded by austerity politics and various abuses and missteps. Within a very short time-span parliament and the government adopted a flurry of emergency ordinances and legislation with the goal of sacking the incumbent President. The speed and the crude instrumental manner in which this attempt to remove the incumbent from office unfolded were labelled as a legal *coup d'État*, or even as attacks on 'the rule of law', yet such Manichean representations presuppose, to begin with, the existence of realities that may be accurately described by reference to this concept. In the larger context, parties close to the President had committed equally unorthodox breaches of constitutional principle, for equally instrumental purposes. To exemplify, whereas the 2012 coalition sought to remove the quorum condition in the Referendum Law 3/2000 (by emergency ordinance) in order to expedite impeachment, a previous government, close to the President, had recently amended the very same law, in the exact same manner, so that removal could only be carried by the vote of an absolute majority of the registered voters.[107]

In the event, a 2012 reversal of the Court's 2007 jurisprudence,[108] imposing in effect a quorum and a subsequent ruling giving constitutional imprimatur to Băsescu's *volte-face*[109] (he initially asked his supporters to vote, then changed his mind and asked them to boycott the procedure in order to sabotage the quorum) saved the President from removal, allowing him to resume office and complete the rest of his second term. In declaring the abrogation

---

[106] Official translations (e.g. https://www.presidency.ro/en/the-constitution-of-romania (last accessed on 19 March 2022) refer to this procedure as suspension, whereas the suspension/conviction for high treason provided by art 96 is called impeachment. I use the term impeachment to refer to the procedure under art 95 since, like its US equivalent, this is an emphatically political process. In contrast, the high treason conviction under art 96 is a judicial procedure (the High Court convicts or acquits of an actual criminal charge, whereas the Parliament operates there merely as a prosecutorial body, in lieu of the Public Ministry). Art 96 was never applied.

[107] OUG 103/2009, approved by Law 62/212: 'Removal from office takes effect if it is approved by a majority of the citizens registered on the electoral lists.' For a chronology of the 2012 crisis see Bogdan Iancu, 'Separation of Powers and the Rule of Law in Romania: The Crisis in Concepts and Contexts', in Armin von Bogdandy, Pál Sonnevend (eds), *Constitutional Crisis in the European Constitutional Area: Theory, Law and Politics in Hungary and Romania* (Hart/Nomos, Oxford, 2015)164–183; See on the vagaries of the Court's jurisprudence Bianca Selejan-Guțan, *The Constitution of Romania-A Contextual Analysis* (n 13) 123–124. A table comparing the two impeachment referenda (2007, 2012) on page 125 reveals both the inconsistencies and their practical effects.

[108] DCC 731/2012.

[109] Constitutional Court 3/2012.

of the turn-out condition unconstitutional and thus muddling its own precedents, the Court selectively cited the Venice Commission's Code of Good Practice on Referendums, emphasizing the reasonable recommendation to not change rules in the middle of electoral processes, but not the main Venice Commission position on referendum turn-out validity conditions (namely, that they should not be imposed to begin with). A ruling was issued in the middle of a Court-ordered recount and published in the Official Journal with an 'errata' inserted *ex post*, specifying that the electoral lists according to which votes would be recounted were those applying to the law on presidential elections. This meant in effect that the threshold was heightened, including in the computation all Romanian citizens over the age of twenty-one, not just those registered in the then-uninominal parliamentary constituencies. These are exemplifications of wider, problematic trends in constitutional jurisprudence, where Courts composed predominantly of appointees of the president or 'his' parliamentary majorities tend to reinforce presidential prerogatives (and vice versa). Adopted in the same context of the summer conflict, a decision on a constitutional conflict between the government and the President established, for example, the rule of presidential representation of the state in the European Council, using as an argumentative prop the definition of semi-presidentialism according to Maurice Duverger. Somewhat circularly, according to the CCR (citing Duverger), in a semi-presidential system the President *should* be endowed with 'considerable powers', including that of representing the country as 'head of state'.[110]

The crisis of 2012 was solved by the Court with significant help from the European and Venice Commissions, the former issuing a CVM report with a list of commands to the government and the interim President going well beyond the legal basis and specific scope of this instrument. In the July 2012 CVM report, 'point eight' in a decalogue of bullet point-formatted commandments to the interim president read: 'Avoid any presidential pardons during the interim presidency'.[111] This was arguably an overreach, the implication being that the 'corrupt' majority, through the Senate Speaker as acting President, would seek to pardon former PSD leader Adrian Năstase, who was then serving time following a definitive conviction on a corruption charge. The allegation was unsubstantiated and the solution over-inclusive, since pardons may benefit a wide range of inmates. The Venice Commission mustered its own resources, publishing letters of support in defence of the Court (some judges accused various threats) and an after-the-fact opinion which castigated the actions of the parliament and the government over the summer, blotting out the role of the other institutions in fostering conflict and, indeed, the wider context.[112] The partiality of the EU Commission may be accounted for as expressing the anticorruption consensus, the incumbent President Băsescu being still perceived and presenting himself at the time as a champion of judicial independence and anticorruption. Such positions are easy to comprehend in the wider constellation of incentives and risks, whereas, in a united Europe, no state can be an island. Nonetheless, it is difficult to understand how, for instance, the EU Commission's choice to throw its full weight behind a camp, in the middle of this conflict, on the basis of oversimplified, cartoonish representations ('the friends of the rule of law' vs 'its enemies')

---

[110] DCC 683/2012. See also comments in Bogdan Dima, *Conflictul dintre palate* (n 62) 213 ff.

[111] COM (2012) 410 final.

[112] For an overall positive assessment of the Romanian Court's 2012 jurisprudence and of the external reactions to the crisis, see Vlad Perju, 'The Romanian double executive and the 2012 constitutional crisis' (2015) 13 (1) International Journal of Constitutional Law 246, 246–278. The author explains the positional somersaults above as at least partly predetermined by methodological/theoretical underpinnings ('Romanian judges, good old Kelsenians'). The paper, published in 2015, when a new centre-right President had just come to power, salutes the election of Klaus Werner Johannis, German ethnic, Lutheran (elected by an overwhelmingly Orthodox, Romanian ethnic citizenry), with favourable citations to press releases calling the event 'Romania's Obama moment'.

of complex, grey realities is, in the long term, conducive to constitutional virtues. Double standards expressed in mock-constitutional idiom may simply reinforce or breed more sophisticated networks of instrumentalism rather than foster the European and Romanian public good.[113]

4. Anticorruption as a Quasi-constitutional Meta-discourse

The evolution of the Romanian political-constitutional system after 2004 is difficult, if not impossible to comprehend without understanding the impact of anticorruption policies. Anticorruption has in fact become a quasi-constitutional meta-discourse (insofar as myriads of policies are translated, reformulated, linked with anticorruption) or even an informal constitutional change.[114]

The language of anticorruption as such swings back and forth between two dimensions, namely, an ethical side and a quantitative dimension. Corruption means in technical juridical terms, if anything, a set of crimes, each with its usual criminal law dogmatic schemata: definition, *mens rea*/imputability, participation, extenuating, and aggravating circumstances, etc. But once bundles of specific crimes were placed under the policy/ethical desideratum of uprooting political corruption and under the institutional umbrella of an anticorruption watchdog, morally charged, radical friend/enemy distinctions could easily be reinforced or manufactured. The quantitative side relates at the global level of the anticorruption consensus to the familiar standard indicators, most notably the CPI.[115] In the activity of an anticorruption prosecutor, quantification embraces the shape of an inescapable 'tunnel vision', e.g. pie charts, quantifying success as a measure of number of convictions, number of indictments, quality of the defendants, years of imprisonment (suspended sentence or execution), recovered proceeds, etc.

Neither of these two dimensions is easy to reconcile with the essentially normative structure of liberal legal rationality. Yet the need to reconcile the paradigms has been inevitable, in the context of radicalized anticorruption-related conflicts, channeled into legal-constitutional conflicts.

As mentioned, the drive towards anticorruption as a master-key of the reform in the East, a policy crystallized already by 2007, has led the Commission to insist on an extreme Romanian transposition of the 'Judicial Council Euro-model'.[116] It quickly became apparent

---

[113] I discuss this at length, with a focus on Venice Commission opinions, in Bogdan Iancu, 'Quod licet Jovi non licet bovi? The Venice Commission as norm entrepreneur' (2019) 11 (1) Hague Journal on the Rule of Law 189, 221.

[114] Carlos Bernal, 'Foreword: Informal constitutional change: a critical introduction and appraisal' (2014) 62 (3) American Journal of Comparative Law 493, 514. This example would be covered in Bernal's taxonomy by the category of 'infra-constitutional-mutation', namely the appearance by informal or formal sub-constitutional means of new norms and practices, sometimes challenging or displacing formal rules.

[115] According to a study by Ginsburg and Versteeg, rule of law indicators (WB, Freedom House, etc.) converge and correlate saliently only with the CPI, irrespective of the way in which these indicators are normatively conceptualized; the authors wonder, 'whether rule of law indicators capture corruption rather than the rule of law or perhaps a more general concept of government impartiality that encompasses both corruption and the rule of law'; Mila Versteeg and Tom Ginsburg, 'Measuring the rule of law: A comparison of indicators' (2017) 42 (1) Law & Social Inquiry 100, 113.

[116] Local receptivity existed, also or at least less opposition. Bulgaria did not implement the entire set of policies, although it was subject to the same constraints. The EU Commission, interested in stability, however achieved, has turned a blind eye on Bulgarian deficiencies; See Vassileva Radosveta, 'CVM Here, CVM There: The European Commission in Bulgaria's Legal Wonderland' (2019) Verfassungsblog *available at* https://verfassungsblog.de/cvm-here-cvm-there-the-european-commission-in-bulgarias-legal-wonderland/ (last accessed on 19 March 2022).

that the entrenchment of a fully autonomous judicial self-government produced various pathologies, including infighting within the judiciary (between the prosecutors and judges in the CSM, between the CSM and the Judicial Inspection, between structures at the apex of the Public Ministry). The European Commission insisted on even more 'independence' as a panacea, whereas the internal political revision initiatives sought to rethink the structure, by enhancing the political appointee component of the CSM.

An initiative promoted by President Băsescu, to increase the number of 'civil society' (political) appointees from two to six and to further allow these to sit and vote in the two Council sections (on prosecutors and judges) was declared unconstitutional by the CCR, with the credible argument[117] that judicial independence would be imperiled if decisions concerning the careers of magistrates could be taken by a majority of politically appointed members (in the prosecutor's section, the five magistrates would have been in minority).[118] When the subsequent parliamentary proposal to increase the number from the current two to four came before the court, the justices declared that proposed amendment unconstitutional as well, with short ceremony, now citing, in lieu of reasoning, their prior decision. The Court held now, apodictically, that *any increase* in the number of politically appointed Council members would endanger judicial independence if the number of judges and prosecutors elected by their peers were not simultaneously raised in equal proportion.[119] The initial 2011 decision had pointed out that, whereas judicial accountability may not imply political accountability, e.g. via presidential and parliamentary appointments to the Council, other responsibility mechanisms would compensate for this shortfall. The CCR specifically indicated in this sense a recall procedure in the CSM Law 317/2004. The recall procedure allowed a majority of judges and prosecutors corresponding to the jurisdictional tier in respect of which the Council member had been elected to recall 'their' representative.[120] And yet the same Court later (in 2013) declared that procedure unconstitutional, in the course of deciding on an exception raised by two recalled members. The reasoning mixed an analogy with the prohibition of binding parliamentary mandates with arguments drawn from analogies with fair trial guarantees, apparently closing the door on recalls.[121] These holdings are difficult to reconcile with Romanian and comparative law models with international standards and, indeed, with one another. The sloganization of judicial independence by the CCR,

---

[117] Sustainable in the logic of the international good practices and probably in that of Romanian realities. Conversely, one may note that one of the two systems that served as prototype for the good practice, France, no longer follows this model (*Conseil* sections are composed in a balanced way, mixing a minority of elected judges/prosecutors with representatives of other institutions (*Conseil d'État*), of the bar, and with politically appointed personalities. One judge sits in the prosecutorial section and vice versa). This 2008 change gave effect to sustained criticism, including from members of the profession, that the former version was an expression of 'professional endogamy' ('Le CSM et la démocratie', Le Monde, 9 November 1998, page 12).

[118] DCC 799/2011.

[119] DCC 80/2014.

[120] There are currently (excluding the military justice system) 176 trial courts (188 provided by law, twelve disestablished during austerity), forty-two tribunals (one in each of the counties and in Bucharest), four specialized tribunals (commercial; minors, and family), fifteen courts of appeal and the High Court of Cassation and Justice in Bucharest (*Înalta Curte de Casație și Justiție* (ÎCCJ)). The Prosecutor General's Office contains two specialized and autonomous directorates, the DNA and a counterterrorism and organized crime special prosecutor's office, DIICOT and an autonomous special section, recently established (2018) to prosecute crimes committed by magistrates (*Secția Specială pentru Investigarea Infracțiunilor din Justiție-SIIJ*). Proportions of representation in the Council are set forth in the organic law, with the judicial section composed primarily of judges from the higher jurisdictional tiers (High Court, courts of appeal), whereas, by contrast, three out of five elected prosecutors represent lower levels. In 2004 and 2005, as already mentioned, the idea was also to upend generational and hierarchical biases by 'bringing the youth in'.

[121] DCC 196/2013.

which reinforced a problematic trend towards fragmentation,[122] may partly be explained by the institutional cooperation with the Commission, borrowing the latter's path dependencies and preferred policies. The CCR liaised for a while with Commission CVM delegations. The Plenum discontinued this practice in March 2018, with a summarily reasoned press release (need to maintain institutional neutrality, judicial duty of reserve).

Corruption in its many forms (paternalism, nepotism, and the criminal graft type targeted by the DNA) is not a figment of the imagination or a product of international conspiracies, as emerging counter-discourses had it. Romanian politicians do adopt self-serving, private legislation, including mollifications of anti-corruption law in order to evade their criminal responsibility. This happened for instance in 2017, immediately after parliamentary elections, when an emergency ordinance was adopted, which would have redefined the crime of abuse of office, to include a public damage element, namely, a threshold of 200,000 lei (at the time approximately 45,000 euros). The amendment clearly appeared to benefit Liviu Dragnea, the PSD party leader, especially given the way in which this ordinance was adopted (late at night, published after midnight in the Official Journal). Large demonstrations erupted in the capital of Bucharest. spreading to the larger cities. Meetings peaked at an estimated half a million people nationwide, under anticorruption ('Justice is our DNA') and anti-PSD banners ('the Red Pest', this being also a play upon meanings, since the party logo is red, as is, in the view of the demonstrators, its ancestry).[123] Demonstrators also protested against proposed pardon legislation, arguing that 'the [convicted] corrupt' would be thus freed from prisons. This particular measure had been promoted in anticipation of the pilot judgment, which was eventually rendered by the ECtHR on the finding of a structural dysfunction (chronic prison overcrowding) that results in a persistent breach of article 3 ECHR.[124] The Romanian conflict found a way into the Strasbourg court's reasoning, with a majority opinion praising the government's efforts to replace pretrial arrest and full execution of the sentences with alternatives (probation, bail, house arrest, etc.). Conversely, a concurrent opinion by Judge Wojtyczek pointed out that the Convention imposed also positive duties on the state, including repressive measures to protect rights, and that leniency as a partial solution to prison overcrowding had been clearly rejected by the demonstrators in Bucharest.

---

[122] See Cristina E. Parau, 'The Drive for Judicial Supremacy', in Anja Seibert-Fohr, *Judicial Independence in Transition. Beiträge zum ausländischen öffentlichen Recht und Völkerrecht* (Springer, Heidelberg, 2012) 619, arguing that the constitutional and legislative changes of 2003, 2004, and 2005 created judicial supremacy rather than independence. See also Bogdan Dima and Elena Siminia Tănăsescu 'Puterea judecătorească (The judicial power)' (2013) 1 Revista de Drept Public, 121, 123: 'By reforming the SCM in 2003 and adopting Law 317/2004 a transition was made in the functiong of the Romanian legal system from total dependence to complete independence. But, like any other extreme, this absolute independence of the judicial system from the rest of Romanian state structures, including the citizens, is deleterious.'

[123] Rick Lyman and Kit Gillet, 'Romania Protests Simmer Despite Leaders' Promises to Back Down' (2017) The New York Times available at https://www.nytimes.com/2017/02/05/world/europe/romania-protests-corruption-sorin-grindeanu.html (last accessed on 19 March 2022).

[124] ECtHR, 25 April 2017, Application nos. *61467/12, 39516/13, 48231/13 et 68191/13, Rezmiveş and others v Romania* [in French]. The unanimous pilot judgment, analogous in reasoning and context to *Torreggiani v Italy* and *Ananyev v Russia*, finds that structural overcrowding in Romanian prisons (together with other conditions, such as the lack of light, exercise, and hygiene) amounts to inhuman and degrading treatment of the inmates and thus to a form of torture in the sense of Art 3 ECHR. Although pilot judgments leave the defendant country ample room in terms of means (e.g. building new prisons, modifying criminal legislation, offering the possibility of early release to compensate at a ratio of two to three or three to four time already served in inadequate conditions etc.), the majority opinion in *Rezmiveş* strongly implied that alternative means could be found to imprisonment (e.g. a more liberal use of probation or suspended sentences) and to pretrial detention pending a definitive judgment (e.g. bail, house arrest).

Equally problematic as political corruption—in terms of creating or maintaining the conditions for the possibility of building the rule of law state—have been the shortcuts taken by anticorruption in order to meet the lofty goal of ridding the country of political corruption. The crime of abuse of office, used by the DNA in many cases, had been declared by the Constitutional Court constitutional (in a *verfassungskonforme Auslegung*-type procedure) only insofar as the phrase 'executes an act or carries it out defectively' means that the defendant public official must be found to have breached a clear provision of primary law, i.e. a norm in a parliamentary enactment or in an ordinance, as opposed to an internal regulation or guideline. This reasoning was an application of the general principle of legality of incrimination (*nullum crimen, nulla poena sine lege scripta, clara, praevia, stricta*) under article 1 para 5 (legality) of the Constitution.[125] This decision and the observation in the reasoning that criminal law is an *ultima ratio*, whereas responsibility embraces also less dramatic forms (administrative, disciplinary, civil) was implicitly criticized by Laura Codruța Kövesi, then Chief Prosecutor of the DNA, with the argument that many abuses, for instance in the field of acquisitions, where the conditions of public bids are not regulated at the level of primary law, would escape any responsibility '[i]t remains to be seen if society shall be defended in such cases by non-criminal law means'.[126]

By the same token, in a country where administrative law is far from attaining the Fullerian criteria of the rule of law and where informal social practices, not all nefarious or corrupt, allow social cooperation to cope with incoherent or contradictory legislation or the mere lack of resources, vague criminal law permits prosecutors to 'cherry pick'. In a number of instances, high profile indictments ended in acquittals, often with the reasoning that the criminal act, as charged, did not exist. For example, one of the Constitutional Court justices was arrested by the DNA one day after voting to strike down the Cybersecurity Law in abstract review.[127] The bill would have given the Romanian Intelligence Service (*Serviciul Român de Informații*, SRI) a blank cheque over the mining of bulk data retention through the designation of 'cybernetic structures of national interest'. Feigning European respectability, the law purported to 'transpose' the then not yet adopted NIS Directive. Furthermore, the directive requires monitoring by a civilian data protection institution, whereas the Romanian internal intelligence service, by evident contrast, is militarized. The Constitutional Court justice has been in the meanwhile acquitted. The coincidence (unconstitutionality/Justice brought up on charges) raised suspicions, in the context of intense cooperation of the DNA with the SRI. Such cooperation was based on inter-institutional protocols (classified until recently), adopted in turn on the basis of Supreme Council for National Defense decision 17/2005 (still classified), declaring corruption a matter of national security under the National Security Law 51/1991. The Romanian Intelligence Service is a militarized institution, its number of employees is classified, but its budget comfortably exceeds those of affluent Western European counterparts.[128] Until 2016, when the Constitutional Court held that the SRI was

---

[125] DCC 405 din 15.06.2016, M.Of. 517 din 8.07.2016.

[126] See https://www.agerpres.ro/justitie/2018/02/07/kovesi-275-de-dosare-inchise-in-2017-ca-urmare-a-deciz iei-ccr-privind-abuzul-in-serviciu--50740 (last accessed on 19 March 2022).

[127] DCC 17 din 21.01.2015, M.Of. 79 din 30.01.2015.

[128] Yearly budgets have constantly increased, to over 2.3 billion Romanian Lei in 2018 (approximately 492 million euros, at the current exchange rate). The amount compares favourably with the sensibly lower budget of the closest German equivalent of the SRI, the Office for the Protection of the Constitution (*Bundesamt für Verfassungsschutz*, 348,9 million euros in 2017), particularly if raw figures are weighted for relative GDPs (1:17, nominal), populations (1:4), perhaps also security risks see https://www.bundeshaushalt-info.de/#/2017/soll/ausgaben/einzelplan/0414.html (last accessed on 19 March 2022). The Service has by law the authority to operate commercial ventures, which generate revenues that add to its budget (Law 14/1992 on the functioning and organization of the Romanian Intelligence Service). See, on the correlation between the SRI budget spike and the gathering momentum of the fight against corruption (and more generally on the shadowy aspects of Romanian

not a 'criminal investigation body' in the meaning of the Criminal procedure code and could therefore no longer execute surveillance warrants, the cooperation between the institutions had a technical legal basis.[129] To what extent, if any, illegalities have been committed or pressures exerted is unclear. In 2019, the Constitutional Court decided that a conflict of constitutional nature resulted from, one, the conclusion of two such memoranda, in 2016 and 2019, between the Prosecutor General's Office and the SRI and, two, from insufficient parliamentary oversight over the SRI. The CCR consequently held one protocol and specific provisions in another unconstitutional.[130] Over time, problematic statements were made by intelligence high officials,[131] including veiled, implicit threats addressed by the civilian director of the SRI to the CCR.[132] These threats targeted a consistent line of decisions declaring various structures and forms of surveillance unconstitutional on privacy and legality/rule of law grounds. Surveillance as such is a recent, worrisome tendency, including surveillance on the basis of an increasing number of national security warrants, which have been approved by judges at quasi-unanimous rates.[133]

The shadier parts of the fight against corruption have been blotted out completely in CVM country reports, which continued for over a decade to crunch unabated rosy narratives of golden paths to progress (and the selfsame panacea: less politics, more judicial independence, more 'robust' anticorruption). The simplest explanation for this *parti pris* is that such policies (judicial independence and anticorruption) have become an orthodoxy of structural adjustment reforms and *acquis* requirements in current candidate or neighbouring states. Too much is invested in this discourse and credibility would suffer if downsides were emphasized, particularly shortcomings in a country proffered as an anticorruption success story and model to be emulated elsewhere (e.g. Western Balkans, Moldova, or Ukraine). By the same token, the Commission's Romanian policies are now not a top-down process, integrating and echoing, albeit selectively, local (political/ideological and judicial-factional)

---

anticorruption), Martin Mendelski (2021), 'Fifteen years of anti-corruption in Romania: augmentation, aberration and acceleration', 22 (2) European Politics and Society 237, 258 (DOI: 10.1080/23745118.2020.1729051) and Bogdan Iancu (2021), 'Hidden Continuities? The avatars of "judicial lustration" in post-communist Romania', 22 (7), German Law Journal 1209–1230. doi:10.1017/glj.2021.61

[129] DCC 51/2016.

[130] DCC 26/2019.

[131] A scandal erupted, with snowball effect, once General Dumitru Dumbravă, then head of the legal department of the SRI, appeared to have stated, in the course of an interview, that the judicial system constituted 'a tactical field' for the Service, from the moment a complaint was lodged to the rendering of a final judgment: 'Concretely, if a few years ago we considered that the objective was reached once the PNA [the anticorruption prosecutor's office, under its initial name] was notified, for instance if we pulled out of the tactical field once the indictment reached the court, concluding (naively, once could now say) that our mission had ended, we now maintain our interest/attention until each case is definitively solved.' Available at: https://www.juridice.ro/373666/dumitru-dumbrava-sri-este-unul-dintre-anticorpii-bine-dezvoltati-si-echipati-pentru-insanatosirea-societatii-si-eliminarea-corupt iei-v1.html (last accessed on 19 March 2022).

[132] Anca Simina and others, 'INTERVIU Daniel Morar, judecător CCR: „Amenințările SRI la adresa Curții Constituționale au depășit cadrul legal. Așa ceva nu se întâmplă într-o țară civilizată" (2015) available at https://adevarul.ro/news/societate/interviu-daniel-morar-judecator-ccr-amenintarile-sri-adresa-curtii-constitution ale-depasit-cadrul-legal-asa-e-neacceptat-intr-o-tara-civilizata-1_556f20d3cfbe376e35e4060f/index.html (last accessed on 19 March 2022). (*The threats made by the SRI have gone over the limits of legality. This is unacceptable in a civilized country*. Interview with Daniel Morar, Constitutional Court judge). Before his appointment to the Constitutional Court, Mr Morar was the first Chief Prosecutor of the DNA.

[133] According to data collected on wiretap warrants requested by the prosecution and approved by the county courts, tribunals, courts of appeal, and the High Court of Cassation and Justice by human rights and constitutional law professor Radu Chiriță (Babeș-Bolyai University in Cluj-Napoca), the total rate of approval is 93.44 per cent. At the High Court of Cassation, which issues national security warrants, the rate is 99.98 per cent (4,523 requests between 2010 and 2015; 4,522 approved). Available at: http://raduchirita.com/interceptari.pdf (last accessed on 19 March 2022).

centre-right preferences.[134] A tendency to turn a blind eye on uncomfortable segments of reality clearly exists; for example, the only document issued by an international organization where an assessment, albeit cursory, of SRI involvement was even made is a report by the Venice Commission on changes to the judiciary laws.[135]

The last two episodes in the ongoing saga concern amendments to the three judiciary laws and the revocation of the Chief Prosecutor of the DNA. These developments, complex and still unfolding, will be treated in what follows only insofar as they exemplify, in the foundational logic driving this volume, wider local constitutional trends towards sloganization, instrumentalism, and polarization/fragmentation. The changes were promoted with the stated purpose of enhancing the accountability of the judiciary, professionalizing it by added stress on experience, and more clearly separating the career paths between prosecutors and judges. In the first category fall provisions reinstating a version of the recall procedure, a newly introduced procedure of 'interpellation' (by the judicial 'constituency', of the Council member), a 'lustration' provision by virtue of which collaboration with the intelligence services leads to forfeiture of the office, and material liability in the case of a judicial error. The second set of rules heightened for example from four to two and from one to two the traineeship in the National Institute of Magistracy and the probationary period before appointment as definitive magistrate, respectively. Seniority requirements were introduced for prosecutors seconded to the DNA (since recruitment consisted basically in an interview, many DNA prosecutors were seconded at the apex of the Public Ministry hierarchy from the lowest tier, that of trial courts). In the third category, the most contentious issues concerned appointments and revocation rules. Judicial apex appointments have been, until now, made by the President at the proposal of the CSM, whereas the new rules vest responsibility in the judicial section of the Council. In the case of high prosecutorial appointments (General Prosecutor and deputies, Chief Prosecutors of the DNA, and DIICOT and their deputies) the changes significantly diminish the role of the President, who may refuse an appointment only once upon the nomination made by the minister of justice, after the Council renders its advisory opinion. For these positions, ten years of seniority in the profession is now a precondition for the nomination. A new structure was established in 2018 in the Prosecutor General's Office, the Section for the Investigation of Criminal Offences in the Judiciary. The SIOJ (SIIJ) is composed of maximum fifteen prosecutors, its chief prosecutor and his or her deputy to be appointed not by the political branches but by the Plenum of the judicial council.[136]

These modifications can be subject to rational criticism. For instance, the material responsibility of judges for errors committed with bad faith or gross negligence is a well-known red herring of judicial accountability, if narrowly defined: it produces negligible results in systems where it exists.[137] Moreover, if error is understood to be proven by contradictory judgments, as some promoters intimated—notably EctHR judgments—the procedure goes

---

[134] See Cristina E Parau, 'Explaining governance of the judiciary in Central and Eastern Europe: External incentives, transnational elites and parliamentary inaction' (2015) 67 (3) Europe-Asia Studies 409, 428, arguing that a degree of interlocking had existed from the onset, by virtue of the fact that the Commission delegation recruited its Romanian staff and experts from among key political appointees in the centre-right, outgoing Justice Ministry staff, right after the Democratic Convention lost elections to the PSD in 2000: 'Both the Commission and its transnational elite allies became interlocked with certain domestic ideological tendencies, and the political parties that embodied them, and not others.'

[135] CDL-PI (2018)007 available at: http://www.venice.coe.int/webforms/documents/default.aspx?pdffile=CDL-PI(2018)007-e (last accessed on 19 March 2022).

[136] Only some of these amendments have entered into force, since until now only one of the three laws has been promulgated (Law 207/2018 amending Law 304/2004 on judicial organization, M.Of. 636 din 20.07.2018).

[137] Mauro Cappelletti, 'Who watches the watchmen – A comparative study on judicial responsibility' (1983) 31 (1) The American Journal of Comparative Law.

against the grain of the way in which legal hermeneutics operate. A Romanian judge cannot be held accountable only because an adverse judgment was rendered against Romania by the Strasbourg Court. In the same vein, the 'lustration' of collaborators with SRI, in the current form, borders on conspiratorial hysteria. Cooperation was inevitable until 2015 and perfectly legal insofar as it meant execution of wiretap warrants. Whereas scepticism is warranted and in-depth investigations into the entire protocol affair are due, the proposed amendment is not the proper tool and bears potential for abuse. A rational debate, separating the wheat from the chaff, proved impossible in context, as the opposing sides engaged in wholesale attacks or defences of the anticorruption *status quo*. This polarization transpires partly also in the recently issued opinion by the Venice Commission, which cites 'sources from the DNA' according to which only six out of 997 defendants sent to trial by the DNA for high level corruption or assimilated crimes were judges or prosecutors.[138] The Venice delegation inferred from this that no need for such a section existed in the first place, musing as to whether such a structure would not intimidate judges and ruminating that perhaps specialized anticorruption prosecutors would be better trained to tackle corruption in the judiciary. Yet, according to the Judicial Inspection, judges and prosecutors were under investigation in hundreds of DNA case files. These case files do not necessarily need to end in indictments, whereas, should it turn out that many of the files were kept open and dormant artificially and concerned particular judges in criminal panels, the practice may arguably have served as a lever to obtain convictions by latent intimidation.[139]

A recent decision by the Constitutional Court, in the matter of a constitutional conflict between the Presidency and the government, held that the request by the Justice Minister asking the President to remove from office the Chief Prosecutor of the DNA should have been heeded by the latter.[140] The majority reasoned that the preeminent position in the procedure was that of the Minister, flowing from article 132 (placing prosecutors under the authority of the Minister of Justice). This decision was rendered against a peculiar but telling political and social backdrop. Mrs Kövesi, former General Prosecutor of Romania for two terms, serving until recently a second term as chief prosecutor of the DNA, had been feted in the international and parts of the local media as an 'anticorruption rock star',[141] not least due to the intrinsic needs of the discourse for hero/villain dichotomies. The decision imposing

---

[138] CDL-PI (2018)007, paras 79–89. I discuss the role of the Venice Commission in this context, at some length, in Bogdan Iancu, 'Quod licet Jovi non licet bovi?: The Venice Commission as Norm Entrepreneur' (n 113).

[139] See for more information https://www.agerpres.ro/justitie/2018/07/30/inspectia-judiciara-va-efectua-un-control-la-dna-in-legatura-dosarele-in-care-sunt-cercetati-magistrati--153113 (last accessed on 19 March 2022).

[140] DCC Nr. 358 din 30 mai 2018, M.Of. nr. 473 din 07.06.2018.

[141] See https://www.economist.com/leaders/2016/06/02/cleaning-up (last accessed on 19 March 2022); whereas Mrs Kövesi had been lionized in the Western press and in the local centre-right media to the end, chinks in the armor and clumsy attempts to patch them had been visible for a long time. For purposes of limited exemplification, when accusations of plagiarism were made regarding her doctoral dissertation, a committee found that 4 per cent (twenty-some pages) in the dissertation constituted copy-paste plagiarism but recommended that the *Dr. iur.* title was not to be withdrawn, as the sanction would have been disproportionate. The national academic evaluation body, CNATDCU, its members recently appointed by the technocratic government, validated this report and its solution quasi-unanimously (one abstention). Available at http://www.cnatdcu.ro/wp-content/uploads/2016/04/Raport-comun-nesemnat-LCK.pdf (last accessed on 19 March 2022). Another scandal occurred when the Chief Prosecutor, who had for years declared that a magistrate should have no relations with politicians and must interact 'with state institutions only' was accused of spending presidential election evening 2009 in select dinner company, including a prominent politician in the pro-presidential alliance (in whose house the social event took place), the civilian director of the SRI, and an SRI general. She refused to explicitly confirm or deny these allegations and repeatedly ignored parliamentary committee subpoenas, in spite of a CCR decision holding that failure to appear before the committee and explain 2009 whereabouts was a breach of the constitutional duty of loyal cooperation among state institutions. Mrs Kövesi extolled the activity of the territorial DNA section in the city of Ploiești as an 'elite unit', whereas significant irregularities were later discovered (one prosecutor was recorded stating that his only pleasure in life was 'to destroy Romanians (i.e. people, individuals)').

on the President a duty to issue to revocation decree has been adopted with two concurrent and three dissenting opinions, emphasizing contradictions with prior jurisprudence and wider constitutional implications. This ruling, bolstering the role of the minister, vindicates the majority in parliament and government, but diminishes the role of the President with respect to high level prosecutorial appointments and thus upsets the balance of powers. The political discord intensified also within the Court as such, with a Plenum ruling giving the Court President power to decide whether 'irreverent' dissenting opinions would be published in the Official Journal.[142]

C. Basic Structures and Concepts

1. The Constitutionalization of Romanian Law

The role and place of the Constitutional Court of Romania have changed dramatically, especially after the revision of 2003. The Court was created once its organic law 47/1992 was adopted, four months after the Constitution itself entered into force, but, for the first twelve years of its existence, its powers were relatively limited. Constitutional decisions as such were explicitly subordinate to politics by virtue of the initial possibility for the parliament to overturn a verdict by a two-thirds majority vote. This instrument was never used but mere potential served as a reminder of the exact place of the Court in the general constitutional architecture. Furthermore, political actors were more cohesive at the onset of the transition, not least due to the fact of concurrently running presidential and parliamentary terms. Vices of institutional design were thus hidden or offset and conflict could be channeled through political safety valves. Both constitutional rules and context have changed dramatically after the revision of 2003.

As regards the Court, the possibility to overturn unconstitutionality by parliamentary vote was eliminated in 2003 and its jurisdictional competence was significantly extended. Notably, as already mentioned, by virtue of what is now article 146I, the Court was vested with the power to 'solve legal conflicts of a constitutional nature between public authorities'. In an attempt to preserve a measure of control, letter (l) was also added to the enumeration of attributions in article 146, to the effect that amendments to the Court's organic law could add specific powers (and presumably also subtract these). No change was made to the structural-institutional set-up, which appears to have been, in retrospect, a misguided course of (in) action. Although constitutional adjudication by a specialized tribunal always straddles a fine line between law and politics, as a general rule, the more juridified the powers, the more that should reflect in the rules concerning appointments, length of the terms and composition. The French *Conseil*, which by design was meant to police divisions of competence by way of abstract review, is composed as a direct consequence of its role by politically appointed judges, serving for short terms of office. Moreover, although few avails themselves of this possibility (currently, as this was written, only Valéry Giscard d'Estaing), former French presidents may, after completion of their terms, sit in the Council. At the other end of the

---

[142] In the meanwhile, the Plenum (r. 1/2017) was challenged in administrative review by a barrister, with the argument that this particular decision of the Plenum was not an exercise of constitutional jurisdiction –immune from review in ordinary courts—but an administrative act, subject to review. The Court of Appeals of Bucharest, section VIII (fiscal and administrative review) found for the public interest plaintiff, ordering the annulment of the ruling and the *ex post* publication of the censored concurring/dissenting opinions.

spectrum, the significant powers of the German Constitutional Tribunal correlate with longer terms (twelve years), rules to ensure consensual appointments (two-third majorities), and a proportion of career judges seconded to Karlsruhe. As already mentioned in the previous part of this study, this sound lesson of comparative constitutional design was not followed in 2003, with the result that appointments often appear to reflect political rather than jurisprudential considerations. Former career magistrates do sit in the Constitutional Court of Romania but there is no rule in this respect, no established custom[143] and such professional credentials are not necessarily the decisive reason in the appointment process. With increased avenues for political turmoil, many conflicts have found their way to the CCR, which, in turn, has not very often risen to the height of expectations and to the challenge posed by its new, refurbished role.[144]

Although an evident tendency towards heightened sophistication in the way in which decisions are written can be noticed,[145] the frequent reversals of current jurisprudence show through the lengthier reasonings and are increasingly difficult to reconcile. They primarily occur in cases with high political stakes. Admittedly, *stare decisis* is an Anglo-Saxon doctrine, embedded in the logic of common law systems and judicial review by courts of general jurisdiction but jurisprudential stability (or the lack thereof) has a direct influence on the credibility and thus the legitimacy of constitutional courts as well.

For instance, in its own decision on the draft proposal of the 2003 amendments, the Court held that adding to its competence by modifying the organic law of the Court would affect the political neutrality of the institution and recommended that the provision be expunged.[146] In 2010, by an amendment to Law 47/1992, the power to verify the constitutionality of parliamentary resolutions (*hotărâri*) was added, to be exercised under the same procedural preconditions as the control of standing orders (at the request of the Speakers, fifty deputies or twenty-five Senators). During the crisis of 2012, the Speakers of both Houses and the Ombudsman were removed from office by parliamentary resolutions and the competence of the Court was curtailed, eliminating the review of resolutions from its jurisdictional competence. The Court held in response that this particular power, once conferred, could not be retracted[147] but 'in exchange' rejected all exceptions coming to it from the recently dismissed officials. The exceptions raised by the Speakers were deflected with the argument that only those resolutions that directly affect 'constitutional principles and values' may form the object of review.[148] This contradicted however prior jurisprudence, also somewhat idly reasoned, according to which the appointment of the Speakers reflects a constitutional principle, namely that of reflecting 'the political configuration resulting from the elections', meaning they cannot be removed discretionarily whenever a new majority is recomposed within parliament. The Ombudsman, whose complaint was decided on later, received the curt answer that the resolution by which he had been removed from office was an

---

[143] A civilized custom with respect to appointments does however exist, namely, that one of the justices is an ethnic Hungarian.

[144] For an instructive diachronic analysis of the way and reasons why the CCR is increasingly swept into political battles in which it takes clear sides, see Elena Simina Tănăsescu, 'The Romanian Constitutional Judge: Lost in Transition', in Miodrag Jovanović (eds), *Constitutional Review and Democracy* (Eleven Publishing, The Hague, 2015) 223–252.

[145] This may however be primarily the by-product of increased professionalization of the court clerks. The translation is imprecise, since the twenty-one assistant-magistrates are not clerks in the common sense, their status being equated to that of assistant magistrates at the High Court.

[146] DCC 148/2003.

[147] DCC 727/2012.

[148] DCC 728/2012, 729/2012.

'individual act', the novel implication being that the Court only censors *normative* parliamentary resolutions.[149]

Often enough, the CCR is simply a victim of poor institutional design, whose deficiencies show through in the context of the dogged, bare-knuckled political fights of recent years. Judges consequently try to patch up constitutional gaps, usually in an avuncular or Solomonic way, so that no party leaves the forum without some degree of satisfaction. For instance, whereas the rules on the appointment of the Prime Minister at the formation of a Cabinet are relatively clear, by rule and convention, nothing was stipulated with respect to cabinet reshuffles. After the break-up of the *DA* coalition, increasing tension ensued between the Prime Minister and the President, resulting in the refusal by the latter to appoint a newly nominated Justice Minister. The Court set up the rule that the President may refuse a nomination but only once, providing reasons through[150] a formula that eventually became a running diatribe in legal and political circles. The reasoning was that the President may send a law back to parliament for reexamination once (with reasons) and thus similar considerations would prevail in the analogous hypothesis of a Cabinet reshuffle. In the same year, the Court was called to solve a constitutional conflict bearing on the lifting of ministerial immunity. Unlike MPs, whose immunity is limited to inviolability from searches, detention, and pretrial arrest, Ministers are immune from prosecution as such, for acts committed in the exercise of their official functions, unless immunity is lifted by the President, the Chamber, or the Senate. Since this lack of clarity produced in effect a form of forum-shopping by prosecutors, the Court held that only the Houses may lift the immunity of Ministers who are also MPs, whereas in the case of 'independents', prosecutors will go to the President.[151] The Court, however, cannot be blamed for exercising a power misguidedly conferred on it, especially as warnings had been available.[152] Furthermore, provided that this attribution is constrained by stable methodological frameworks of reference and a modicum of jurisprudential consistency, it may in principle contribute to constitutional stability.

Methodological stability is however ensured by many preconditions, including the institutional design choices already mentioned. The CCR rarely cites foreign jurisprudence, a habit which is not necessarily to blame; positions on the proper extent and legitimacy of foreign citations differ, in direct correlation with perspectives on democracy, the law/politics distinction, constitutional supremacy, etc.[153] Nonetheless, in the context of rights provisions and some general principles, bricolaged in the 1990s from Western instruments, addressing the underlying conceptual structures of the borrowings has an emancipatory hermeneutical potential in itself. This is true even if and perhaps precisely when one rejects at the end of this propaedeutic exercise the worldview-representations underlying the practice in the jurisdiction of origin. Among various values proclaimed as supreme by article 1 para 3 already in the initial form of 1991 are 'human dignity' and the 'free development of personality', phrases

---

[149] DCC 732/2012.

[150] DCC 98/2008.

[151] DCC 270/2008.

[152] Opinion No. 169/2001, of 18 March 2013, on the draft revision of the Constitution of Romania CDL-AD (2003).

[153] According to a study by Elena Siminia Tănăsescu and Stefan Deaconu, 'Romania: Analogical Reasoning as a Dialectical Instrument' (n 84), direct citations of foreign judgments can be identified in only fourteen decisions out of 13,234 rulings rendered in the period 1992–2011, as covered by the authors. Most of these concerned rights (eleven out of fourteen) and in ten out of fourteen references are made to support the majority reasoning (nine out of these ten were unanimous rulings). Foreign in this context means other jurisdictions. ECtHR and CJEU caselaw has been cited with increasing frequency since the early 2000s, whereas the Court does refer to soft law documents (e.g. Venice Commission reports), see as well comments in Bianca Selejan-Guțan, *The Constitution of Romania* (n 13) 231–233.

whose Spanish-German filiation is not difficult to divine (the words also appear in the Universal Declaration articles 22–23, but in a social and economic context). Human dignity is understood both in German constitutional law and as a general principle of EU law in the familiar legal restatement of the second formulation of the Kantian categorical imperative.' In a quaint decision striking down a law providing that municipalities had to act with respect to the endemic stray dog population by submitting three alternative choices to the citizens (neuter and release, keep in shelters at public expense or euthanize), the Court reasoned that human dignity was a principle implying 'the harmony of human relations' but also 'harmonious cohabitation with the animal world' and thus collective euthanasia to cull the stray dog population was constitutionally foreclosed.[154] Once a four-year-old was killed by strays in a public park in Bucharest a year later, a new law was passed to deal with the problem, this time providing for euthanasia within a somewhat flexible timeline. The Court reconsidered. It now reasoned that nothing was wrong with euthanizing stray dogs in droves, as long as each case (i.e. stray dog) would be processed individually (rather than by collective decisions).[155]

The Court exercises abstract a priori review of laws, treaties, standing orders and concrete a posteriori review in the case of both laws and ordinances (delegated legislation). Exceptions of unconstitutionality constitute the primary interface between the general legal system and the CCR. Out of the 42,060 procedures with which the Court was seized from its creation until 31 July 2018, 41,059 have been exceptions raised before courts (40,989) or by the Ombudsman (seventy). The number of exceptions increased from twenty-four in 1992 and a few hundred until the early 2000s, peaking at 8,823 in 2009, before then lowering and levelling off at figures in the thousands now.[156] According to the current rule, an exception may be raised by the parties in a case pending before a court or an arbitral tribunal, including prosecutors, referred by the judge or (since 2003) raised directly by the Advocate of the People. From the outset it can be observed that in the case of the Ombudsman the term exception is an obvious misnomer, the Ombudsman being a public body without a direct litigation interest. Over the years, the hybrid nature of this instrument has become a mainstay of Romanian constitutional law, with uncertainties concerning a) whether the procedure is primarily designed to give effect to procedural defence rights, b) what the respective roles of the referring judges and the Court are in the filtering of exceptions, and c) the effect of rulings in concreto.[157] The Constitutional Court law was changed repeatedly to provide for various models of cooperation. Within a short timeframe the exception actually functioned primarily as a defence mechanism, meaning that once the referring (a quo) court relayed the exception to the CCR (as court ad quem), the trial was stayed pending the Constitutional Court answer. This also explains why the number of concrete referrals spiked

---

[154] DCC 1/2012: 'Human dignity, in its constitutional meaning, presupposes two inherent dimensions, namely, the relationships among humans, meaning reciprocal respect for each other's fundamental rights and freedoms, as well as the relation of mankind to the environment, including the animal world, which implies, in what concerns animals, responsibilities to care for these beings in a way illustrating the attained level of human civilization.'

[155] See Elena Simina Tănăsescu, 'Grundrechte in Rumänien', in Detlef Merten and Hans-Jürgen Papier (eds), *Handbuch der Grundrechte in Deutschland und Europa, Band IX (Grundrechte in Ostmittel- und Osteuropa, Mitherausgeber Rainer Arnold)* (C.F. Müller, Heidelberg, 2016) 614: '*Vielmehr – und sehr praxisbezogen ausgedrückt – scheint der rumänische Verfassungsgerichtshof im Jahre 2012 einmal mehr Opfer verschiedener Einflüsse geworden zu sein, da nur ein Jahr später infolge eines auf ein breites Medienecho gestoßenen tragischen Ereignisses der Verfassungsgerichtshof entschieden hat, dass dieselbe Rechtsgrundlage, die dem Verfassungsgerichtshof nun zum vierten Mal ohne wesentliche Änderungen vorgelegt worden war, vollständig mit der Verfassung übereinstimme*'.

[156] See https://www.ccr.ro/Statistici-periodice (last accessed on 19 March 2022).

[157] See Elena Siminia Tănăsescu, 'L'exception d'inconstitutionnalité qui ne dit pas son nom ou la nouvelle sémantique constitutionnelle roumaine' (2013) 4 65–64 Revue internationale de droit comparé 905–939; Bianca Selejan-Gutan, 'Curtea Constituțională și instanțele judecătorești în România: cooperare sau conflict?' (2015) 2 Acta Universitatis Lucian Blaga 186–196.

to almost 9,000 in 2009. With courts basically forwarding anything raised by parties to the CCR without any vetting (acting, as a commentator put it, as 'a mail service')[158] and given the physical impossibility of solving both the backlogs and the piling new reams of cases on the docket, a reasonable expectation could be, especially in criminal cases, that by the time a constitutional decision would be rendered the statute of limitations might well have run out. According to the current rules, the trial at the referring court is not stayed. Should the later constitutional decision have a potential impact on the solution of a case where an already definitive judgment has been pronounced by an ordinary court, the party can seek redress afterwards, invoking the CCR decision in an extraordinary appeal procedure (revision).

Sometimes, the latent tension between the Constitutional Court and ordinary courts is openly vented. This has happened for instance in the context of judicial battles over the decriminalization of insult and defamation. These two crimes, together with an article on the defence of truth, existed in the Criminal Code of 1969 (articles 205–207) but the provisions were abrogated in 2006. The Constitutional Court was seized with an exception and, through an interpretation of the human dignity clause in article 1 para 3, declared the decriminalization of insult and defamation unconstitutional, with the reasoning that absolutes such as dignity deserve heightened constitutional protection, whereas civil actions in damages did not substitute for the lack of incrimination: 'Dishonor is in its nature irreparable, whereas human dignity cannot be either quantified in money or compensated for by damage awards.'[159] This was well enough said in theory, but ordinary courts did not know whether what was called colloquially the 'abrogation of the abrogation' meant the lawmaker needed to re-incriminate or whether the effect of the decision was that insult and slander 'reemerged', as it were, in the Criminal Code. As a direct result, divergent positions ensued in the lower courts, some considering that insult and defamation were as a result of the decision still crimes, some starting from the premise that a finding of unconstitutionality imposes obligations on the lawmaker only and thus civil actions in torts were now the only remedy. Consequently, some trial courts admitted the criminal complaints, while some rejected them as inadmissible. Confusion lingered on for years. In 2010, deciding on an appeal on points of law raised by the General Prosecutor, the HCCJ (High Court of Cassation and Justice) took the latter position, namely, that the decision only concerned the lawmaker and that 'the Parliament's failure to exercise its prerogative and reexamine a legislative provision found unconstitutional cannot lead to a univocal solution to substitute oneself for this essential authority in the rule of law state'.[160] In 2013 the Constitutional Court replied in kind, declaring the provision under which the High Court, in solving appeals on points of law, renders interpretations meant to unify the practice as *ultra vires, unconstitutional* 'insofar as this should be understood to open for that court an avenue allowing it, in this way, on the basis of infra-constitutional law ... to issue binding interpretations contrary to the Constitution and the decisions of the Constitutional Court'.[161] From a practical point of view, this protracted controversy ended

---

[158] See Elena Siminia Tănăsescu, on the implications of what she defines as 'mailbox behaviour', at 924 ff. The author argues in essence that due to a convergence of factors (the lack of acceptance by ordinary judges of this new institution, whose introduction had in their view flaunted tradition, inconsistencies in the CCR jurisprudence, legislation unwittingly relaxing procedural thresholds for raising exceptions), the exception of unconstitutionality has become a procedural interface for judicial battles (ordinary courts vs Constitutional Court), whereby individuals as such and their constitutional rights are often collateral damages in this squabble.

[159] DCC 62/2007.

[160] Recurs în interesul legii, Decizie ICCJ nr. 8 din 18 octombrie 2010 cu privire la consecințele Deciziei Curtii Constitutionale nr. 62 din 18 ianuarie 2007, M.Of. 416/2011.

[161] DCC 206/2013.

with the entry into force in 2014 of the new Criminal Code in which insult and defamation are not incriminated. Hence, the issue became moot.

The entry into force of the new Criminal Code opened however another conflict with respect to the application of the *lex mitior* principle according to article 5 in the new Criminal Code. The penological 'philosophies' of the two laws differ, with, e.g. harsher punishments and lenient rules on repeat offenders in the old code, whereas the newer one applies milder sanctions to first-time offenders and harsher sanctions for repeat-offenders. The HCCJ considered that in determining the most lenient penal law applying to a particular defendant, the judge was to take into consideration provisions from both the 1969 Code and the newer criminal law, insofar as general criminal law rules, e.g. concerning prescription (statute of limitations), concurrence of offences or repeat offence would be 'autonomous institutions'.[162] The courts could therefore, according to the HCCJ guideline decision, combine, for instance, the rules on prescription in the 1969 law and the rules on punishment in the 2014 code, in order to reach the regime most lenient on the specific defendant before them. This guideline preliminary interpretation was in accordance with both ECHR and comparative law and Romanian doctrine and prior practice.[163] The CCR contradicted this by holding that the judge must assess the most lenient criminal law applicable *taking as a whole* either the old or the new criminal code. Otherwise, the CCR reasoning went, any judge would be able to combine provisions into a *lex tertia,* infringing the constitutional provision in article 61 para 1 according to which the parliament is the sole legislative authority of the country.[164] Apex conflicts between the Constitutional Court and the HCCJ are all the more perplexing for the lower judicature as, following a 2012 amendment to Law 303/2004 on the statute of magistrates, disregarding either (both) CCR decisions or guideline judgments of the HCCJ constitute disciplinary offences.

The Constitutional Court of Romania has developed in some areas a consistent and solid case law. In the field of protecting the right to privacy from various forms of surveillance, the pertinent decisions are prudentially and jurisprudentially praiseworthy. To give just one example, its first decision on the national transposition of the Data Retention Directive preceded and partly anticipated the reasoning of the CJEU, whereas the unanimous decision on the Romanian Cybersecurity Law showed undeniable prowess. Nonetheless, systemic problems (as in the case of exceptions); structural deficiencies deriving from institutional design and the immersion of the Court in high politics, swinging back and forth and changing favourites with often visible partiality, have prevented both 'the penetration of constitutional standards into ordinary legislation' and the provision of coherent 'binding guidelines for politics.'

2. Fundamental Rights and the Rule of Law

The concept of the rule of law is mentioned in article 1 para 3 in a modern translation the phrase *stat de drept*—a neologism—has replaced the local, older term *domnia legii* (closer to the *ad litteram* translation of the notion 'the rule of law'): 'Romania is a democratic and

---

[162] ÎCCJ, Decizia 2 din 14 aprilie 2014.

[163] Florin Streteanu, 'Consideraţii privind aplicarea legii penale mai favorabile in cazul legilor complexe' (2014) Juridice available as a blog post at https://www.juridice.ro/317849/consideratii-privind-aplicarea-legii-penale-mai-favorabile-in-cazul-legilor-complexe.html (last accessed on 19 March 2022).

[164] DCC 265/2014.

social state, governed by the rule of law.' The more limited principle of legality is covered by article 1.5: 'In Romania, the observance of the Constitution and its supremacy and of the laws is mandatory.'

The Court has generally shied away from using the rule of law concept as a determinant criterion in reaching results, preferring on the whole to hew closely to the more modest and juridically precise concept of legality in article 1 para 5 with its doctrinal elements (predictability, clarity, etc.). More recently, this may also reflect the political overuse, perhaps abuse, of the notion with interesting semantic dichotomies: whereas in the political discourse of the centre-right the notion *stato di diritto/Rechtsstaat* (*stat de drept*) is embraced wholeheartedly to mean in essence anticorruption by criminal law means, the left preferred the older terminology of *domnia legii* (rule of law) to proffer counter-discourses emphasizing but also instrumentalizing individual rights.

When the phrase appears in constitutional law, a similar ambivalence ensues, although for obvious reasons, it is not reflected at the semantic level. To wit, in the 'abuse of office' decision, the notion is incorporated by reference to a 2005 Lithuanian Constitutional Court ruling, according to which the rule of law would be breached if criminal responsibility attached to deeds that are not dangerous to society or if disproportionately severe punishments were imposed.[165] Criminal law is *ultima ratio* in terms of social regulation. In a follow-up decision concerning a combined exception (with respect to the abuse of office in the 1969 Code, the abuse of office in the current Code, and the special reference norm in the anticorruption law),[166] the Court explained that *ultima ratio* also means an obligation for the law-maker to define the threshold in terms of monetary value (damage to the public, when damage is produced) and, in the case a right is violated, to determine the intensity of the violation. These considerations appear expressed in mandatory form: 'The Court underlines that the lawmaker is under an obligation to establish a threshold and to specify the requisite intensity of the violation when a legitimate interest or a right are affected by the commission of the crime.'[167] This second abuse of office ruling was published without the concurrent opinion of Justice Stanciu. The latter argued, reasonably enough, that it was nonsensical to reject in the *ratio decidendi* one of the heads of a constitutional complaint and simultaneously impose an obligation on the lawmaker in *obiter dicta*. Justice Stanciu's argument is particularly pertinent since a longstanding constitutional doctrine, referred to in the majority opinion, maintains that any decision is mandatory from the moment of publication in terms of both its reasoning (considerations) and holding.[168] The doctrine had been understood as applying to admissions, not to rejections of unconstitutionality exceptions, whereas the majority sought to conflate the contradiction by reading backwards the second set of criteria into the *ultima ratio* mention of the first, unanimous ruling.[169]

---

[165] DCC 405/2016, para 90.

[166] The exception was raised by the former wife of PSD President Dragnea, from a case where both were tried under charges brought by the DNA. In essence, Dragnea was accused of inciting the child protection service director to fictitiously hire two employees in the child protection services of the Teleorman county, whereas the two were in fact working for the PSD country party unit, led by Dragnea at the time. Should a high bar (threshold) have been set in the material definition of the crime, the case would have gone away (*lex mitior*). In the meanwhile, Dragnea has been definitively convicted to an imprisonment sentence. The High Court postponed pronouncement until Monday 27 May 2019, the day after the European parliamentary elections, which the PSD lost. The day after the elections, Dragnea was convicted on appeal.

[167] DCC 392/2017, para 52-6.

[168] DCC (Plenum) 7/1995.

[169] Whereas the decision was published on the Court website and in the Official Journal without the concurrent opinion, the entire text was leaked to the anti-corruption press.

In 2014 the Court had used the concept to obtain, *mutatis mutandis*, a diametrically opposed result. One of the four benchmarks of the CVM required the creation of an autonomous integrity agency that would function, partly on the prevention side, as the administrative alter ego of the DNA, its powers relating to asset declarations (disclosures), unjustified wealth, conflicts of interest in the non-criminal form, and incompatibilities. The National Integrity Agency was established as an autonomous administrative authority to implement the national integrity law 176/2010.[170] In 2014, an exception was brought before the Court concerning a provision in the integrity law according to which an elected official in the case of whom a final determination was made concerning a conflict of interest or an incompatibility could not hold (run for) 'the same office' for a period of disqualification of three years.[171] In this case, the concept of the rule of law was interpreted by the Court in the sense that the legal provision establishing a future disqualification with reference to the same public office *implied* a disqualification for all elective public offices. Therefore, in the context of this judgment, clarity under the rule of law did not operate in favour of the affected right but in support of the needs to combat corruption most efficiently.[172]

These rulings are relevant for a wider tendency of using interpretation instead of the constitutionally more precise course of action, namely, a declaration of unconstitutionality. A decision of unconstitutionality would lead to the automatic abrogation of the impugned provision in forty-five days from the moment of publication in the Official Journal. The two cases also reveal a more general trend in the recent jurisprudence towards methodological laxity in order to reach results, a laxity that translates into frequent procedural shortcuts. In the case of the latter ruling, an original understanding of the principle of proportionality is also evident.[173] Arguably, proportionality under article 53 ought to be applied in the familiar step-by-step methodology, whereas the Court used it in in the 'same office' case in a 'compressed' or 'telegraphed' form to reach the desired result at that particular moment. A broader observation has also been made by commentators to the effect that the general trend of departure from an initial positivistic, restrained stance, replaced more recently by an infatuation with natural law, is not necessarily indicative of a rights- or rule of law-friendly posture.[174] This criticism appears to be validated by facts since, as the same author observes, the rate of admissions with respect to exceptions is very low (overall 2.71 per cent) in comparison with rates of admission in the more politically relevant fields of abstract control or solutions of constitutional conflicts.[175] Moreover, even positive rates of admission may turn

---

[170] One of its initial prerogatives was requesting automatic confiscation of unjust wealth (by injunctions in Appeals Court), meaning differences over 10,000 euros that could not be justified in accordance with the wealth declarations. This power was clipped at an early stage by the CCR, as incompatible with the constitutional presumption of lawful acquisition of property, arts 44 para 8 and 44 para9. DCC 415 din 14 aprilie 2010, M.Of. 294 din 5.05.2010.

[171] DCC 418/2014.

[172] See Bianca Selejan-Guțan, 'Considerații despre Decizia nr. 418/2014 a Curții Constituționale' (2014) 12 Pandectele Romane 44, 51.

[173] The truncated use of proportionality is a perennial problem. Elena Siminia Tănăsescu, 'Grundrechte in Rumänien' (n 155) 605: '*Vom Beginn seines Bestehens hat der Verfassungsgerichtshof die Verhältnismäßigkeit nicht als allgemeines Rechtsprinzip angesehen, das geeignet ist, einen Rahmen für die allgemeinen Leitlinien der öffentlichen Einrichtungen insbesondere im Verhältnis zu den Bürgern zu bilden, sondern als ein Instrument, dessen geringe Bedeutung seinen Anwendungsbereich sehr begrenzt. So erhielt die im Schrifttum als allgemeiner Rechtsgrundsatz bezeichnete Verhältnismäßigkeit durch die Verfassungsrechtsprechung eine sehr bescheidene Rolle zugewiesen, im Sinne eines einfachen Anhaltspunkt für den Grund von Einschränkungen bei der Grundrechtsausübung ...*' [emphasis added].

[174] Ibid 607, arguing that the metamorphosis of the CCR from a defender of rights and freedoms to an activist court embroiled in high politics was made possible by a simultaneous transition from judicial restraint and positivistic methodology to activism and increased use of natural law.

[175] A slight increase in the rates of admissions may be noticed recently (4.7 per cent in 2017, 4 per cent in 2018, compared to 0.74 per cent in 2011 and 1.7 per cent in 2012), yet a combined statistical/sociological and textual

out to incorporate sometimes, as the second abuse of office decision and the constellation of interests and conflicts related to the issue show, considerations that may have more to do with political conflicts ricocheting in constitutional law than with Dworkinian propensities towards 'taking rights seriously'. The changes in the composition of the Court over time (2014 to 2017) appear therefore to transpire also in rights-relevant case law, although, in order to establish clear correlations, a more grounded study would be needed (linking for instance majorities and appointments with reversals of precedents and diametrically opposed interpretations of the same concepts).

Rights and liberties under the Romanian Constitution have been from the outset 'internationalized'. The fundamental law adopted, like many other Eastern European constitutions, the international good practice of providing for a monistic solution with the primacy of international law, albeit limited to the field of fundamental rights.[176] According to the initial formulation of article 20, constitutional provisions concerning rights and liberties were to be interpreted in accord with the Universal Declaration and other human rights conventions ratified by Romania and in the case of a normative conflict, international law would 'trump' domestic law. In 2003 a safeguard clause was added to the effect that the presumption of priority of international human rights law would be rebutted if the Constitution or national legislation provided for a more favourable treatment: 'the international regulations shall take precedence, unless the Constitution or national laws comprise more favourable provisions' (article 20 para 2). This complicates the initial situation, especially in cases of rights collisions, where a more favourable treatment of one right (e.g. freedom of expression) logically results in a less favourable treatment of another (e.g. dignity or privacy). Another implication concerns the determination of which jurisdictional tier should undertake the balancing exercise, namely, whether the constitutionally proper point of ascription is the level of ordinary courts or the Constitutional Court.

The complicated balancing required by article 20 para 2 in its current form does not give rise in practice to significant difficulties. Both the courts of general jurisdiction and the Constitutional Court have started from the early 2000s onward to cite ECtHR judgments but neither the former, nor the latter do this in a structured manner. The CCR does refer for example in the recriminalization of insult and defamation decision (DCC 62/2007) to Strasbourg judgments but selects those concerning the right to an effective remedy (article 13 ECHR) to rationalize its position. In the later decision, whose addressee was the HCCJ (DCC 206/2013), the Strasbourg judgment against Romania in *Cumpǎnǎ and Mazǎre*, finding that imprisonment convictions for insult and defamation as applied to journalists were in breach of article 10 ECHR, was discussed. But the engagement with the doctrinal implications was cursory and instrumental: not punishing journalists with imprisonment sentences does not mean one cannot criminalize insult and defamation, hence one must incriminate. In 'compensation', a flurry of judgments on the limits or article 10 ECHR were cited. As for the general judicature, including the High Court, citations to the ECtHR have become routine, often without a correlative care for enhanced methodology and perhaps also as way of ignoring or deflecting the CCR.[177] This latter phenomenon is not idiosyncratic

---

analysis would be needed to assess the full implications of the fluctuations and recent reversal of the downward slope.

[176] Valentina Volpe, 'Drafting counter-majoritarian democracy: The Venice Commission's constitutional assistance' (2016) 76 Zeitschrift für ausländisches öffentliches Recht und Völkerrecht 811, 843.

[177] Elena Siminia Tǎnǎsescu, 'Grundrechte in Rumänien' (n 155) 600: '*In der Mehrzahl der Fälle zeigen die ordentlichen Gerichte offenbar größere Bereitschaft, sich auf einschlägige europäische und internationale Standards und Urteile zu beziehen als auf die Erkenntnisse der rumänischen Verfassungsrechtssprechung*'.

to Romania and may even embrace more hostile forms of judicial confrontation in other jurisdictions, as the French *Cour de Cassation* reference in *Melki and Abdelli* arguably shows.[178]

Romania has been a member of the Council of Europe since 1993 and has ratified the Convention in 1994 (Law 30/1994). Ever since, the number of applications and that of adverse judgments have constantly increased: Poland, also a former communist country, party to the Convention since 1993, with a population almost double in size, was subject to 958 rulings finding at least one violation, a figure that contrasts with the 1,202 judgments against Romania.[179] ECtHR statistics are consistent in this respect, with a CoE average of 0.76 cases allocated by the Court to judicial formations (complaints per 10,000 inhabitants in 2017), whereas the figure in respect of Romania was 3.31 (4.15 in 2016, the average being then 0.65). To compare and contrast, the respective figures for Poland are 0.64 in 2016 and 0.54 in 2017.[180] Although, given the backlogs and delays in Strasbourg, a conclusion is premature, very few of the adverse judgments rendered thus far intersected the fight against corruption and one of them has to do with a structural problem, namely improper conditions of detention, not the activity of the DNA.[181] Nonetheless, in recent public debates, these cases and the *Rezmiveș* judgment already mentioned were instrumentalized by all sides to justify opposite positions (centre-right: no pardon or amnesty since the convicted corrupt will be otherwise released vs centre-left: material responsibility for judicial errors needs to be imposed since ECtHR cases reveal judicial abuses and pardon legislation must be quickly adopted since otherwise the ECHR 'will sanction us'). The article 3 pilot judgment in *Rezmiveș* is primarily indicative of incoherent legislation and the general administrative weakness of the state, whereas local political and social reactions to these judgments reveal instrumentalism and polarization.

A similarly multi-layered human rights story could be told with respect to the restitution cases, which also culminated in a pilot judgment, *Maria Atanasiu*, regarding the breach of article 1 of the Additional Protocol. Whereas agricultural land was subject to restitution on the basis of a law adopted in 1991 (Law 18/1991), the status of residential buildings confiscated or nationalized after 1947 was unclear for much longer.[182] In the 1990s, some courts admitted restitution claims on the basis of the Constitution (right to property, article 21) and of the Civil Code (*déni de justice*, article 5). Prodded by President Iliescu, the Prosecutor General attacked these judgments in the Supreme Court (now the HCCJ) using the procedure of 'appeal in annulment' (*recurs în anulare*), which was inherited from communist law as extraordinary appeal (*recurs extraordinar*) and democratically rebaptized. This procedure could be used to quash final judgments in both civil and criminal cases and, until 1997, when a term of six months was imposed, the application could be made at any time.

---

[178] Joined Cases C-188/10 and C-189/10 *Melki and Abdeli* [2010] ECR I-05667. The *Cour de Cassation* appears to have conscripted Luxemburg, in order to limit the effects of the newly introduced preliminary constitutional reference (QPC) to the *Conseil Constitutionnel*. See in this sense, Nicolas Molfessis, 'La résistance immédiate de la Cour de cassation à la QPC' (2011) 137 Pouvoirs 83, 99.

[179] Violations by Article and by State available at https://www.echr.coe.int/Documents/Stats_violation_1959_2 017_ENG.pdf (last accessed on 19 March 2022).

[180] European Court of Human Rights, Analysis of statistics 2017 (Council of Europe, 2018) available at https:// www.echr.coe.int/Documents/Stats_analysis_2017_ENG.pdf (last accessed on 19 March 2022).

[181] Case of *Pendiuc v Romania*, Application 1765/15, Judgment (Fourth Section) of 14 February 2017 (violation of art 3; conditions of detention at the Bucharest Police Detention Centre) and *Popoviciu v Romania*, Application 52942/09, Judgment (Fourth Section) of 1 March 2016 (violation of art 5 para 1; complainant deprived of liberty on the basis of an order to appear, from 3pm to 11.30pm, before being heard, charged, and remanded in custody).

[182] Law 112/1995 allowed for restitution to owners or heirs of apartments currently occupied by them or vacant. For all other nationalized properties compensation with a ceiling was possible. Furthermore, lawful tenants could buy the nationalized flats where they lived.

The Court in Strasbourg declared in the *Brumărescu* case[183] that the use of this instrument to challenge final judicial decisions an infringement of access to a court under article 6 para 1 ECHR. The appeal in annulment was undoubtedly a blunt instrument. But, in the wider context, the judicial arrogation of a power to create 'original' remedies in the absence of a restitution law passed by parliament (thus without the possibility of balancing all interests at stake) likewise represented an unusual form of fair trial. And a violation of rights: if a court reprivatizes a building on the basis of rules created *proprio motu* and good faith tenants are as a result thrown by the owner out in the street, their rights may arguably be affected, even though the property rights of the owner may be vindicated. The EU Commission, during pre-accession negotiations, adamantly insisted on the abolition of the appeal in annulment as it considered it an undue political influence on the independence of the judiciary.[184] The provision was scrapped for civil matters in 2003 and for criminal matters in 2004 in order to vindicate prosecutorial (and judicial) independence from politics. Yet, by that time, prosecutors had been emancipated from 'conveyor belt' forms of political control. Furthermore, as was previously argued, the unfolding story of judicial organization/independence in Romania hides a congeries of dizzying complexities, hard to capture in simple formulations. In 2001, a law (10/2001) was finally passed but its contradictions and erratic administration of the law converged in the end in the rendering of the pilot judgment *Maria Atanasiu and Others vs. Romania.*[185] The Strasbourg Court held that the lack of a coherent framework for restitution and/or compensation of nationalized buildings stemmed from a structural deficiency, amounting to a violation of article 1 of the Additional Protocol. Structural deficiencies have continued unabated.[186] In the context of an incoherent legislative definition of 'public affectation' exceptions to restitution and due to the lack of clear, adequate procedures to ensure compensation or reprivatisation from case to case, the buildings of universities, schools, research institutes, museums, etc. were returned to the former owners or their heirs.[187] Often, no countervailing measures were taken by the state to redeem the properties or to build alternative spaces for these institutions. In this way, what András Sajó once appositely called, in Hungarian context, the 'Pepsi feeling' understanding of rights and the rule of law manifested itself in a newly distorted form, with the pendulum swinging from one extreme in the 1990s and early 2000s (i.e. no legislation applying to nationalized and confiscated buildings and actions of annulment systematically used by the Prosecutor General to block restitutions in the 1990s) to the other.[188]

---

[183] Case of *Brumărescu v Romania*, Application 28343/95, Judgment (Grand Chamber) of 28 October 1999.

[184] See Bianca Selejan-Guțan, *The Constitution of Romania - A Contextual Analysis* (n 13) 228–230, for chronology and legal framework. See also Cristina E Parau, 'The Drive for Judicial Supremacy', in Anja Seibert-Fohr (ed), *Judicial Independence in Transition. Beiträge zum ausländischen öffentlichen Recht und Völkerrecht* (Springer, Heidelberg, 2012) 656–662, for an analysis of the social and political, national, and international backdrop against which the use, abuse, and abrogation of the appeal in annulment took place.

[185] *Maria Atanasiu and Others v Romania*, Applications 30767/05 and 33800/06, Judgment (Third Section) of 12 October 2010.

[186] See on the general context of the *Atanasiu* judgment, Radu Chiriță, 'Privatizarea bunurilor devenite proprietatea statului prin naționalizare (Un comentariu al hotărârii *Maria Atanasiu c. România* pronunțată de CEDO)' (2011) 56 Studia Universitatis Babes-Bolyai, 31–39.

[187] An initial version of the law provided for restitution of buildings in public use, as specified in a list annexed to the law, but obliged the owners to both maintain the public use affectation of the buildings for periods of three to five years and pay themselves for all maintenance and repair costs for this duration. Only in 2005 was the law modified to provide also that the owner has a right to receive rent during this period, at rates to be determined by government decisions.

[188] See András Sajó, 'Parks, Dogs, and the Rule of Law: Post-communist Reflections,' in David Dyzenhaus (ed), *Recrafting the Rule of Law: The Limits of Legal Order* (Hart, Oxford, 1999) 238: 'The dignity of loafing around, the comfort without empathy, the Pepsi feeling, is not a Hungarian invention. But it discovered very 'cool' soil here among us.'

3. Separation of Powers

The nature of the Romanian semi-presidential system and its partial interpretations and re-interpretations by the Constitutional Court have already been extensively discussed in the previous junctures of the text.[189] Two phenomena shall be addressed in this section as emblematic of recent separation of powers evolutions, namely the position of the parliament and agencification.

Among the classical branches, the parliament has arguably been the biggest institutional victim of constitutional reforms and evolutions. Partly, this has resulted from political confrontations in the logic of the dual executive. A referendum was for instance initiated by President Băsescu in 2009. Two questions were submitted to the people, namely, the transition to a unicameral parliament and the reduction to 300 of the number of MPs (ostensibly in order to save money and increase efficiency). Since the poll and the first round of presidential elections took place simultaneously, participation exceeded the validation threshold; this appeal to the better part of democratic valour, especially in the context of the crisis, was approved by the voters in trans-partisan consensus, with 72.32 per cent. Referendums initiated by the President on the basis of article 90 have consultative value only but the result and its various interpretations resurface in political debates.[190] In the context of the fight against corruption, the parliament has stood under constant suspicion as a presumptively corrupt institution.[191] It now comprises a newly formed party with an almost single-mindedly focused anticorruption agenda (USR, Union Save Romania). By the same token, counter-discourses emerged: if at the beginning of the fight against corruption immunity from pre-trial detention and searches was lifted in the logic of a generally shared idea that the concerned MPs should have the 'chance to prove their innocence', the discourse of anticorruption as such has been increasingly called into question in recent parliamentary debates.[192]

The weakness of the parliament derives primarily from structural shortcomings. As mentioned, in 1991 two symmetrical houses were created, procedurally linked by the fact that mediation (conference committee) was required for the adoption of any law (ordinary, organic, or constitutional) when the two drafts differed. In order to increase efficiency, this logic was changed in 2003, with mutually exclusive subject-matter competences being attributed to each of the houses. For instance, since treaty ratification falls within the purview of the Senate, the draft bill must be introduced in the first notified house, the Chamber

---

[189] For reasons of space limitation, I shall not address the problem of territorial organization. Romania is a centralized state, territorially organized in forty-one counties. The attributions of the central government in the territory are exercised by prefects, who supervise deconcentrated units of the central government in the territory and oversee the legality of local administration (municipal administrative acts are suspended if the prefect challenges them in administrative court). The Municipality of Bucharest has its own administration, partly analogized to that of a county (e.g. tribunal, prefect). Current political debates with respect to local administration revolve around the election of mayors, now (since 2007) elected in a single ballot. This usually favours the Social Democratic Party; the mayor of Bucharest 2016–2020 was for instance elected on a PSD ticket in 2016, with 42.97 per cent of the vote. The opposition constantly requests the adoption of a two-round system. Recurrent debates about autonomy usually revolve around the request of the Hungarian minority party for territorial autonomy in the Szekler region, which, in view of political opposition and constitutional limitations (art 152), has little if any chance of success. See Bianca Selejan-Guțan, *The Constitution of Romania - A Contextual Analysis* (n 13) 147–161.

[190] See for analyses and critical opinions, Valentin Constantin, 'Referendumul și ficțiunea democrației directe' (2009) 4 Studia Universitatis Babes-Bolyai Iurisprudentia 3–10 available at 0_cuprins (ubbcluj.ro) (last accessed on 19 March 2022); Bogdan Dima, 'Parlament bicameral versus parlament unicameral' (2009) 140 Sfera Politicii 18, 36.

[191] See Tamás Kiss & István Gergő Székely, 'Populism on the Semi-Periphery: Some Considerations for Understanding the Anti-Corruption Discourse in Romania' (n 90) on Romanian anticorruption populism.

[192] Alexandra Alina Iancu, 'Questioning anticorruption in post-communist contexts: Romanian MPs from commitment to contestation' (2018) 66 (3) Südosteuropa Journal of Politics and Society 392, 417.

of Deputies, which has to adopt its version within forty-five days. The new structure made 'tacit' adoption in the first notified chamber possible and increased (an understanding of) efficiency but created, in effect, a situation that goes against the grain of bicameralism. Put more precisely, the enhanced deliberation and thus rationality that are supposed to result from having two houses in a non-federal, unitary state are defeated by design. In the literature, the post-2003 setting was often criticized as producing a strangely disjointed institution and a peculiar form of 'tricameralism' (the House of Deputies, the Senate, and Parliament in Joint Sittings).[193] The Constitutional Court has tried to remedy at least the blatant disregard by the second chamber of the version adopted in the first notified House, particularly using a sort of *sui generis* 'essentialness' theory (essential elements cannot be changed) but 'pinpoint' jurisdictional policing in order to remedy structural deficiencies can only function in limited cases and ad hoc.

A second structural problem, ingrained in the functioning of Romanian constitutionalism, concerns legislative delegation. Simple ordinances may be adopted on the basis of an enabling law (in practice, this procedure is used when parliament is not in session). This rule reproduces locally a more widespread solution to the needs of the administrative state. However, from the beginning, the Constitution has also provided for the adoption of emergency ordinances (*ordonanță de urgență a Guvernului*, OUG). The latter are essentially decree laws issued by the government on a plea of necessity (they must be laid before parliament and published; if the legislature is not in session, it is convened within five days). Emergency delegation is subject to parliamentary ratification. Since the parliamentary approval (ratification) is 'tacit' once sixty days have lapsed from the moment they are submitted to parliament (thirty days per house), sometimes years passed until the legislative branch adopted a formal law, approving and modifying the ordinance.

This perpetual pre-emption of parliament puts the legislature in a continuous situation of fait accompli and is also apt to generate erratic, contradictory practices. In the pandemic context, measures were taken at the beginning on the basis of OUG 1/1999 (on the state of emergency) and OUG 24/2004. Both instruments were inadequate for the tasks at hand. OUG 1/1999, which fleshes out the details for the operation of a constitutional instrument, provides for the adoption of 'military ordinances' as state of emergency normative instrumentalities. This is an atavism from the times before the de-militarization of the Interior Ministry. The latter act, OUG 24/2004, created the infra-constitutional instrument of the state of alert as a form of *ersatz* or 'light' state of emergency. It was adopted in the post-Madrid attacks context of a perceived need to react to the challenge of terrorism with gradual, incremental responses. The state of alert, never before put to the test of constitutionality, was immediately hampered in its functioning by a Constitutional Court decision holding that the exercise of constitutional rights and liberties cannot be restricted on the basis of an ordinance.[194] In response, parliament adopted, with lightning speed (within two days) a dedicated Covid-19 normative act, Law 55/2020, to bridge the normative and practical gaps created by the Court decision and the lapse of the thirty-day time limit of the state of emergency, respectively. Since laws enter into force at the earliest three days after their publication, a state of alert was instituted on the basis of the ordinance to fill the regulatory void between the end of the state of emergency and the entry into force of the new law. As everybody understood the implications of the Constitutional Court decision, namely, that no rights restrictions could

---

[193] Ion Deleanu, *Instituții și proceduri constituționale-în dreptul românesc și cel comparat* (CH Beck, Bucharest, 2006).

[194] DCC 157/2020.

be imposed on the basis of OUG 24/2004, the three-day bridge between 14 May (end of the extended, second thirty-day period of the state of emergency) and the institution of a thirty-day state of alert on the basis of Law 55/2020 on 17 May functioned as a normative vacuum. In practical effect, the three days constituted a Covid-19 restrictions Saturnalia (parties, mass trips the seashore, etc.).[195]

From a political point of view, although criticism is constant, no government would yield control of this instrument. As mentioned, unlike in the case of laws, where procedural hurdles may imply months of delay even in the emergency legislative procedure and which take effect at the earliest three days after publication (article 78), ordinances are of immediate application and their adoption process imposes few procedural preconditions. Furthermore, unless the Ombudsman challenges an ordinance directly, *ex post* constitutional review by regular exceptions of unconstitutionality takes much longer to reach the Constitutional Court. For this reason, the problem resurfaces in constitutional crises, as exemplified by the discussions above on the 2012 conflict and OUG 13/2017, which generated massive anticorruption protests. The EU Commission and the Venice Commission have justly found fault with the habit, yet the needs of EU integration were among the most important catalysts that influenced the spike in emergency ordinances (the DNA itself, a part of the conditionality, has been created by an emergency governmental ordinance; the issue was too important to be abandoned to the vagaries of parliamentary politics). Attempts were made by the CCR to limit the proliferation of this form of 'motorized legislation'. Procedurally, according to the amendments of 2003 to what is now article 115, such acts may only be adopted in 'exceptional situations, the regulation of which cannot be postponed' and the executive must provide reasons for the adoption in the act. Since normatively defining emergency constitutes a delightful Schmittian paradox and since the constitutional definition is necessarily tautological, the Court seldom ventured in the field of 'extrinsic' review of emergency. Substantive limits are also provided, namely that emergency ordinances may not affect rights, take steps towards expropriation, and affect fundamental institutions or electoral rights (article 115 para 5); some decisions of the Court marginally limited extreme forms of emergency 'delegations.'[196] But the practice as such is structural and impossible to control jurisdictionally: For example, 117 emergency ordinances were adopted in 2017 alone. In some years, ordinances surpassed in importance self-standing parliamentary enactments.[197]

---

[195] See the detailed country report on the impact of the pandemic on the Romanian constitutional system, Bogdan Iancu, Bogdan Dima, and Horatius Dumbravă, 'Romania: Legal Response to Covid-19' (Parts I–IV), in Jeff King et al (eds), *The Oxford Compendium of National Legal Responses to Covid-19* (OUP, Oxford, 2021), DOI: 10.1093/law-occ19/e38.013.38, available at https://oxcon.ouplaw.com/view/10.1093/law-occ19/law-occ19-e38?rskey=PzI4kp&result=3&prd=OXCON (last accessed on 14 March 2022).

[196] An emergency ordinance may not be adopted to circumvent a decision of unconstitutionality on a law, by reissuing the same provisions in a different form. Ordinances cannot be issued in order to directly and immediately counter a law adopted by parliament. See Károly Benke, 'Dezvoltări recente în jurisprudența Curții Constituționale a României în privința limitelor de care este ținut Guvernul în adoptarea ordonanțelor de urgență' (2009) 1 Buletinul Curții Constituționale.

[197] In 2008, for instance, 229 ordinances were adopted: http://www.cdep.ro/pls/legis/legis_pck.lista_anuala?an=2008&emi=3&tip=18&rep=0&nrc=200 (last accessed on 19 March 2022), whereas the parliament adopted 308 legislative acts (ordinary and organic laws). Of the latter category, however, a significant part are purely reactive enactments, namely, laws approving (142) or rejecting (twelve) emergency ordinances. A law approving an ordinance is often a rubberstamp, shell enactment, consisting usually of one article (e.g. http://www.cdep.ro/proiecte/2007/900/00/4/leg_pl904_07.pdf (last accessed on 19 March 2022)). A significant part of the remaining statutes are private laws (e.g. establishing communes, chartering universities, and the like) and a handful modified ordinances or enabled the government to adopt simple—ordinary—ordinances outside parliamentary sessions. If one discounts in this way numerical parliamentary outputs, the overall picture is clearer and thus the magnitude of the challenge posed by emergency delegations to the role of the Parliament is readily comprehensible.

Agencification is the by-product of both internally driven institutional design choices and EU conditionalities. The Constitution of 1991 already provided that 'autonomous administrative authorities' can be established outside the hierarchical executive structure of the government (article 116) by organic law (article 117). Some authorities were already internally generated before the 2007 accession, for example the CNSAS (National Council for Studying the Former Securitate Archives) or the CNA (National Telecommunications Council). The number of these institutions has increased and their overall importance in the general separation of powers scheme has grown during negotiations and after the accession, notably by the establishment of the integrity agencies. These latter resulted from direct conditionalities. It is true that EU law as such makes very limited institutional demands in this respect (an exception is the need to establish autonomous data protection bodies) but regulatory interactions have resulted in the 'bolstering' of agencification in older member states as well. In the case of newer members criteria differ significantly, due to a) the relatively open-ended political conditionalities (Copenhagen Criteria); b) the general practice used since 2004, by virtue of which candidates have to adopt the *acquis* before accession; and c) the significant leverage of the EU Commission as 'master of conditionalities' vis-à-vis these countries.[198] The Commission, itself a supranational independent agency of sorts, has a natural propensity towards sectorial replication of its own design. The National Integrity Agency (whose creation is a formal CVM benchmark) falls under the strictly defined Romania constitutional category, yet the phenomenon of agencification (the proliferation of bodies autonomous from direct and visible forms of majoritarian influence) arguably encompasses also the CSM in its current form and the DNA. The anticorruption prosecutor's office has in fact been established initially as an autonomous integrity agency, i.e. a prosecutor's office specialized in corruption crimes and fully insulated from the general hierarchy of the Public Ministry (PNA, *Parchetul Național Anticorupție*). The DNA had to be grafted onto the structure of the General Prosecutor's Office as a result of a CCR decision whose holding would have made it impossible otherwise for the anticorruption watchdog to pursue its mandate in the initial institutional configuration. The current structure uneasily combines full autonomy from the General Prosecutor with an appearance of constitutional conformity.

The CCR encountered significant difficulties to build a coherent doctrine accounting for the new phenomenon of agencification, whereas the effect of the proliferation of autonomous bodies on a political-constitutional system already riddled with institutional dysfunctions is additional fragmentation with sometimes mixed benefits to compensate for it.

D. Constitutional Identity

The Constitutional Court has developed the concept of 'national constitutional identity' in relation to the limits of EU integration, which translate constitutionally in the scope and meaning of article 148 (primacy of EU law, duty of all state institutions to guarantee the fulfilment of obligations undertaken upon accession). Thus far, the notion, which surfaced first in the decision concerning the constitutional conflict between the Prime Minister and the President over European Council representation,[199] has been reiterated on six

---

[198] See the contributions by Jaques Ziller (on agencification and its impact on the administrative structures of the Western member states) and Elena Siminia Tănăsescu (agencification in new MS, exemplified with the creation of integrity agencies in Romania) in Bogdan Iancu and Elena Siminia Tănăsescu (eds) *Governance and Constitutionalism: Law, Politics and Institutional Neutrality* (Routledge, London, 2018).

[199] DCC 683/2012, discussed above.

further occasions. Initially, the Court mentioned identity in a routine manner, specifying that obligations deriving from EU law prevail over national law as per article 148 but not over the Constitution itself, with standard citations to Polish and German case law.[200] The three most recent decisions grapple with the constitutional spillovers of anticorruption. The overarching question in all of them concerned the implications of this conditionality, namely, whether specific extrapolations from the benchmarks in Decision 2006/928/CE establishing this mechanism or if recommendations in the yearly or biannual CVM reports by the EU Commission would be mandatory as a matter of Romanian constitutional law (article 148).[201] The CCR reached its decisions on narrower grounds but tackled the identity issue vis-à-vis the anticorruption conditionality less cursorily. The request by the authors of the objection in the last case (DCC 137/2019) for a preliminary reference to the ECJ, asking the Luxemburg court to interpret the legal nature of the mechanism, was rejected by the Romanian Constitutional Court with the argument that the CVM is obligatory for the state but 'has no *constitutional* relevance'. The Court leaned on the 2012 precedent establishing the doctrine or principle of national constitutional identity but ignored a landmark decision of the same year (DCC 2/2012) which had reached an opposite conclusion concerning this conditionality. It held that EU Commission recommendations, via the conduit of article 148, were mandatory under Romanian constitutional law. Meanwhile, the CVM continued to produce significant political influence, while its nature, scope, procedure, and duration continue to remain in a Romanian and EU (soft?) law limbo.[202]

At a more foundational level, constitutional identity should be understood as encompassing more than exhortations in preambles or the more technical limits in various entrenchment or eternity clauses. More than this, an 'identitary' choice presupposes clear worldview representations at the foundational moment, as reflected in the document. At the very least, the constitution must represent an attempt to acquiesce in a set of social realities and historical ideals (US Constitution, Irish Constitution), depart from a burdensome past (Germany, South Africa) or seek to mould the newly constituted state in accordance with an emancipatory plan (arguably, India).[203]

---

[200] DCC 64/2015 (exception of unconstitutionality, in the context of national legislation curbing the rights of employees to be informed and consulted prior to collective redundancy procedures attached to insolvency proceedings); DCC 857/2015 and DCC 259/2015 (exceptions of unconstitutionality, partly duplicative, in the context of a clash between a Commission state aid investigation/decision, heeded by the Romanian authorities through legislative 'proactive' measures, in order to stop the execution of a contrary ICSID arbitral award).

[201] DCC 104/2018 (objection of unconstitutionality, challenging amendments to an anticorruption law (L. 161/2003) to eliminate from the list of incompatibilities applying to public officials the quality of merchant (natural person); DCC 682/2018 (objection of unconstitutionality, challenging amendments to the 'integrity law' (176/2010) and to the organic law of the National Integrity Agency (L. 144/2007), seeking to set a statute of limitations of three years on the sanctioning of conflicts of interest and incompatibilities); DCC 137/2019 (objection of unconstitutionality to a law approving emergency ordinance 90/2018, adopted to operationalize the newly-established prosecutorial Special Section of Investigation of Crimes Committed by Magistrates-SIIJ).

[202] AG Bobek's 23 September 2020 Opinion in Joined C-83/19, C-127/19 and C-195/19, ECLI:EU:C:2020:746 does little to dispel the confusion in EU law. Whereas AG Bobek opines correctly that the CVM as such is binding, he attributes to the Commission's opinions (the only instruments clarifying the meaning of the cryptic CVM benchmarks) the same legal force (i.e. as purely persuasive authorities) as Immanuel Kant's writings or 'the memorable quotes from Terry Pratchett or *Alice in Wonderland*' (para 167). This stylistic *coup de force* (or hermeneutical sleight of hand) may do away with practical embarrassments (see Iancu 2020, supra note 90) but does little to enhance clarity and predictability. In the meanwhile, the Commission did not issue any CVM report from October 2019 until June 2021, in spite of its express obligation to do so every six months after June 2007, per art 2, Decision 2006/928/CE. SeeBogdan Iancu, 'Goat, Cabbage and Wolf: Primacy in Romania', *VerfBlog* (7 January 2022), https://verfassungsblog.de/goat-cabbage-and-wolf/, DOI: 10.17176/20220107-195122-0 (last accessed on 14 March 2022).

[203] See Gary Jeffrey Jacobsohn, *Constitutional Identity* (Harvard University Press, Cambridge, 2010). According to Jacobsohn's argument (he uses a number of essentialist dichotomies, the most important being arguably that between acquiescent and militant constitutions), there are always disharmonies in the understandings of identity,

The Romanian Constitution of 1991 brought social peace and immediate stabilization only on the surface level and at the price of suppressing and obfuscating significant, deeper value-driven divisions, as the nature and implications of the transition from communism, the form of state or the institutional intricacies of the political system. The violent nature of the break with the communist past and the massive continuation until 1996 of old elites in the new regime made it possible to entrench a fundamental law that, in essence, reproduced in broad strokes minimal elements of the post-communist *status quo* (semi-presidential republic, bicameralism), incorporating swathes of the *status quo* ante (to wit, the basic territorial organization in forty-one counties and the municipality of Bucharest follows the 1968 reform under Ceauşescu), all seasoned with a fair amount of bricolage (e.g. rights provisions, Ombudsman, Constitutional Court).

A measure of essential continuity has continued in the ethnocentric vision of the unitary nation, a ghost that has haunted Romanian state formation, spanning all possible ideological currents, from liberalism to fascism and communism.[204] Yet, as already noted, the invocation of the national unitary indivisible state, albeit it expresses insecurities and apprehensions well enough, cannot alone ensure cohesiveness to the polity. Conversely, the general trend towards gradually deemphasising the ethnic nation as a paramount ideal and value is one of the few positive, liberal evolutions of post-1989 constitutionalism. The other two features of Romanian constitutionalism, poor integration by constitution and deep underlying social divides, continue to mark current arrangements. Their forms alone differ, whereby, for instance, the exclusionary nature of 1866 constitutionalism, when only a splinter of the adult male population could vote directly, has been more recently 'democratized' and replaced by a big-urban right/rural left divide, no less vicious in its manifestations and potentialized by adjunct pathologies.

The weak integrative function of the 1991 document was reinforced rather than alleviated by the revision in 2003, when additional incentives for political and institutional fragmentation were added, in the absence of either a constitutional moment or at least clarity of design. Integration via EU-induced judicial independence plus anticorruption reforms as *passe-partout* modernization has not played an overall positive role in the constitutional and political life of the country. Notably, the rise of the new meta-language of anticorruption became rapidly entwined with older discourses and ideologies under a very thin veneer of normative camouflage. Increasingly more primitive in its manifestations and effects, this development reproduces both older and newer tensions and has found a proper place in the traditional pre-modern arsenal of local instrumentalism and polarization, now hybridized with the multi-layered dimensions of abrupt post-modernity.

which are worked out (negotiated) dialectically: '[C]onstitutional identity develops dialogically and usually incrementally and involves interpretive and political activity that follows from the inevitable disharmonies present in the constitutional condition' (at page 341).

[204] Paul Blokker, 'Modernity in Romania: Nineteenth Century Liberalism and its Discontents' (2003) 2 EUI Working Paper SPS.

11

The Evolution and *Gestalt* of the Spanish Constitution

*Victor Ferreres Comella**

A. Origins of the Current Constitution	549	1. The Position of the Constitution in the Legal and Political System	565
1. Historical Background	549	2. Democracy	566
a) Introduction	549	3. The Rule of Law: General Principles	569
b) The Memory of the Second Republic, the Civil War, and the Dictatorship	550	4. Recognition and Protection of Fundamental Rights	570
c) A Negotiated Transition to Democracy	551	a) The Distinction between Fundamental Rights and Social and Economic Principles	571
2. The Constitutional Spirit: The Politics of 'Consenso'	553	b) The Principle of Proportionality and the Essential Content Guarantee	572
a) The Constitution as the Embodiment of Shared Values	554	c) Fundamental Rights in the Private Sphere	573
b) The Constitution as the Product of a Bargaining Process	555	5. Constitutional Organs and Separation of Powers	575
3. Foreign Influences and the Impact of Constitutional Scholars	558	a) Parliament	576
		b) The Government	581
B. The Evolution of the Constitution	560	c) The Public Administration	583
1. Constitutional Rigidity: The Amendment Procedure	560	d) Ordinary Courts	584
2. Procedural Dualism and Substantive Limits to Amendments	562	e) The Constitutional Court	587
3. Interpretation	564	f) The Territorial Organization of the State	591
4. Influential Personalities in the Development of the Constitution	565	6. Political Unity and the Sovereignty of the Spanish People	594
C. Basic Structures and Concepts	565	**D. Constitutional Identity**	597

A. Origins of the Current Constitution

1. Historical Background

a) Introduction

It is impossible to understand the political process that led to the enactment of the Spanish Constitution without paying attention to the historical background against which the

---

* This contribution draws from some parts of my book, *The Constitution of Spain: A Contextual Analysis* (Hart Publishing, Oxford, 2013). I have developed some new themes and updated information in light of recent events.

Victor Ferreres Comella, *The Evolution and* Gestalt *of the Spanish Constitution* In: *The Max Planck Handbooks in European Public Law.* Edited by: Armin von Bogdandy, Peter M Huber, and Sabrina Ragone, Oxford University Press. © Victor Ferreres Comella 2023.
DOI: 10.1093/oso/9780198726425.003.0011

constitutional framers conducted their parliamentary deliberations in 1977–1978. The Constitution marked a new beginning in political life, after Spaniards suffered the experience of a long dictatorship under General Francisco Franco (1939–1975), which was the upshot of a terrible Civil War (1936–1939).

When Franco died on 20 November 1975, a complex transition to democracy started. During three extraordinary years, Spain faced the challenge of creating a new political order. On 29 December 1978, a Constitution based on democratic and liberal ideas was finally enacted into law. The new charter reflected the agreement the main political parties had reached over certain basic rules and principles. The Constitution obtained the approval of most citizens in a referendum.

For four decades now, people have generally endorsed the Constitution as the fundamental norm of the political system. The governmental structure it lays down, and the rights and principles it designates, are broadly supported by political actors and ordinary citizens of different persuasions. The Constitution has taken root, for it has been able to fix many important matters that have historically divided Spaniards (concerning, for example, the form of government, the role of the Church, the responsibilities of the military, and the economic order). The main issue that remains to be settled, as we will discuss later, concerns the territorial organization of the state, especially considering the emergence of a strong secessionist movement in Catalonia.

It is important to emphasize the relevance of this success from a historical perspective. We must bear in mind that Spain had many constitutions in the past.[1] Unfortunately, the more liberal and democratic charters—those of 1812, 1869, and 1931—were ephemeral. The constitutions that were less committed to the principles of democratic liberalism, in contrast, lasted longer. This is especially true of the Constitutions of 1845 and 1876, which were in effect for various decades.[2]

b) The Memory of the Second Republic, the Civil War, and the Dictatorship

When the current Constitution was being written in 1977–1978, Spanish history was on everybody's mind. Many people recalled the Republican experiment of 1931–1936 (the Second Republic), the Civil War, and the long dictatorship.

The Republican Constitution of 1931, indeed, was a modern and progressive charter, but it died at a very young age. The debate is still open as to the causes of the Second Republic's failure. The international context was certainly not favourable. This was the time of the Great Depression. As a result of the deep social and economic crisis, fascism rose dramatically in Europe. But part of the reason for the downfall of the Second Republic is connected to constitutional defects. The Constitution of 1931 was not written in a conciliatory spirit. It was a partisan document that did not reflect the political heterogeneity of Spanish society. The constituent assembly over-represented the left. When the conservative forces won the general elections in 1933, a tension transpired between their programme and some specific constitutional provisions—concerning, for example, the Church, schools, divorce, and agrarian reform. Life under the Republic would probably have been less polarized if the founding document had been drafted in a different spirit.

---

[1] For a brief description of Spanish constitutionalism, see Joaquín Tomás Villarroya, *Breve historia del constitucionalismo español* (Centro de Estudios Constitucionales, Madrid, 1985).

[2] For a classification of Spanish Constitutions along these lines, see Francisco Tomás y Valiente, 'La Constitución de 1978 y la historia del constitucionalismo español', in Francisco Tomás y Valiente (ed), *Códigos y Constituciones* (Alianza Editorial, Madrid, 1989) 125–151.

Despite its shortcomings, the Republic was still supported by many people when the military rebellion started on 18 July 1936. It is unlikely that General Franco would have won the war without the help of Mussolini and Hitler.

The dictatorship was a long one, however, and it evolved through the years. Until the late fifties, Franco's dictatorship exercised extreme brutality against the opposition. Indeed, large numbers of people went into exile, while others were executed or imprisoned. These were very hard times. This was also the period of Spain's isolation from the rest of the world. The dictatorship became an anomaly after the victory of the Allies in the Second World War. Restoring democracy was the order of the day in Western Europe.

From the late 1950s to 1975, the dictatorship became milder in some respects. In 1953, in the context of the Cold War, the Spanish government signed various economic and military agreements with the United States. It also renewed its relationship with the Vatican through a new Concordat. The economy, moreover, gradually opened itself to the international markets. The gross domestic product grew dramatically in the sixties, causing a substantial expansion of the middle classes. The regime also carved out some spaces for individuals and groups to exercise limited freedoms. A new law enacted in 1966, for example, abolished the prior censorship of the press. Political parties, however, were still illegal.

The dictatorship was not sustainable in the long run. It created the conditions for its own gradual decline. The economic modernization in the sixties led to a great expansion of the middle classes, as has already been noted. Once the years of misery were over, citizens were less eager to accept severe restrictions on their liberties. In particular, the floods of tourists that started to come to Spain every summer helped change prevailing moral attitudes. The influence of the Catholic Church began to diminish because of modernization. In the 1960s, moreover, a generation that had been born after the Civil War came of age. Young citizens looked to the future. Even the Catholic Church started to distance itself from the regime. Since the Second Vatican Council (1962–1965) had embraced human rights and liberties, Franco's dictatorship found itself in an embarrassing position.

In Catalonia and the Basque country, the opposition to the dictatorship was reinforced by nationalist discontent. Franco had dismantled the institutions of self-government that the Second Republic had created in those regions. The local languages were marginalized from public life. The struggle against the dictatorial regime adopted a violent form in the Basque country. A terrorist group was founded in 1959: ETA (*Euskadi ta Askatasuna*, which means 'Basque Homeland and Liberty'). Its criminal activities posed serious problems to the dictatorship. In 1973, for example, ETA killed the President of the government, Luis Carrero Blanco, whom Franco had recently appointed to guarantee the maintenance of the regime in the future.

c) A Negotiated Transition to Democracy

So, the authoritarian government that was in place when Franco died in 1975 lacked legitimacy in the eyes of an increasing number of people. The transition to democracy was not an easy process, however. The leaders of the political groups that had defended the Republic were in exile, distant from the new realities in Spain. The leaders that were emerging in Spain, in turn, were scarcely known by the people. It was difficult, moreover, for the democratic opposition to organize itself effectively in a common front. Citizens were not intensely mobilized. To a large extent, this was a legacy of the dictatorship, which had instilled political apathy among the people.

In such circumstances, the opposition realized that it was too weak to destroy the dictatorship. It needed the complicity of those players within the regime that were in favour of a democratic transformation. Only a gradual and negotiated transition to democracy was feasible.

An important figure came to perform a surprising role in this process: King Juan Carlos. Few people expected that the monarch would serve the democratic cause. We should bear in mind that Juan Carlos was crowned in 1975 by virtue of the laws of the dictatorship. It was Franco himself who had chosen Juan Carlos in 1969 as the future Head of State. The dictator disliked Don Juan de Borbón, Juan Carlos' father, who had been critical of the regime. Yet, against all expectations, King Juan Carlos appointed a new President, Adolfo Suárez, who soon expressed his resolution to make important changes and turned out to be the engine of Spain's successful transition to democracy.

The reform launched by President Suárez was articulated in 1976 in a *Proyecto de Ley para la Reforma Política* (Bill for Political Reform), which sought to amend the fundamental laws of Franco's regime. For the valid amendment of such laws, it was necessary to obtain the approval of the existing legislative assembly (*Cortes*) and of the people themselves in a referendum. The *Proyecto* proclaimed the principle of popular sovereignty and guaranteed fundamental rights. It also established that the legislative power would be bestowed upon a bicameral parliament (*Cortes*), which would consist of a Congress and a Senate to be elected by universal, direct, and secret suffrage. The King, however, was authorized to appoint up to one-fifth of the senators. Moreover, the *Proyecto* provided for the possibility of enacting 'Laws of Constitutional Reform' which could be proposed by the government or by Congress and would be enacted into law if approved by Congress and the Senate and by the citizenry in a referendum.

Fortunately, on 18 November 1976, the old *Cortes* voted for this new Law, which was then submitted to the people. The turn-out in the referendum was 77.72 per cent, and 94.2 per cent voted yes.

The next step was to establish the conditions for the first democratic elections to select the members of the newly created bicameral parliament. President Suárez reached an agreement with the political parties in the opposition concerning the details of the electoral system, the rules for financing political parties, the criteria for having access to public media, etc. Importantly, Suárez agreed to legalize all political groups, including the Communist Party, which had led the opposition to Franco's dictatorial rule. The most conservative forces were appalled by the decision. The Communist Party reacted by appearing in public with the national flag that represented the monarchy, instead of the flag that Spain had had during the Second Republic. This gesture was aimed at convincing public opinion that the Communist Party would act in a moderate and responsible manner.

Once the political parties had been legalized and the electoral rules had been established, the Spanish people were convened to vote on 15 June 1977. A multitude of political parties were created and ran candidates for parliament. The elections witnessed a high level of popular participation: the turn-out was 79.11 per cent. The main parties that emerged from the electoral process were the following: AP (*Alianza Popular*), on the right end of the political spectrum; UCD (*Unión de Centro Democrático*), on the centre; PSOE (*Partido Socialista Obrero Español*), on the moderate left; and PCE (*Partido Comunista de España*), on the left end of the political spectrum. In the elections for Congress, these parties obtained the following results: UCD: 165 seats; PSOE (together with its Catalan branch: PSC): 118 seats; PCE: twenty seats; AP: sixteen seats. Some smaller parties obtained seats too. Importantly, the nationalist parties from Catalonia and the Basque Country were represented in Congress: *Pacte Democràtic per Catalunya*: eleven seats; *Esquerra de Catalunya-Front Electoral Democràtic*: one; *Partido Nacionalista Vasco*: eight; *Euskadiko Ezquera-Izquierda de Euskadi*: one. There was no regional or nationalist party representing Galicia, however, or any other specific territory.

The new parliament was a democratic institution in the middle of a sea of dictatorial power structures. A Constitution would have to be approved to eliminate those structures. Congress thus appointed a special parliamentary commission on constitutional matters. Seven members of the Commission were asked to draft a first version of the constitutional text.[3] These were soon called the *padres de la Constitución*. After a long process of negotiation and discussion in both Congress and the Senate, the Constitution was finally approved on 31 October 1978. It was ratified by the people in a referendum held on 6 December and was finally promulgated by the King. It became part of the legal system on 29 December 1978.

2. The Constitutional Spirit: The Politics of 'Consenso'

There was something special about Spain's 'constitutional moment' of 1977–1978. Political parties were able to reach a broad agreement about the fundamental rules of the new political order, an agreement that was made possible by the enormous spirit of conciliation, generosity, and public service those parties exhibited.[4] Several factors pressed in that direction.

First, both the right and the left, as well as nationalist parties from Catalonia and the Basque Country, were present in the new *Cortes*. The political plurality of Spanish society was thus reasonably mirrored by parliament. The victorious party (UCD), moreover, only garnered a relative majority of the seats (47.14 per cent). To enact a Constitution, therefore, the support of other groups would be needed. Spanish citizens, moreover, expressed their preference for moderation. The majority of voters on the right chose UCD over AP, while those on the left preferred PSOE over PCE. Even the more conservative right (AP) and the more radical left (PCE) avoided extreme positions.

Secondly, history had taught some lessons. Many Spanish people still remembered the Civil War and were aware that no democracy would flourish in an extremely polarized environment. Things had to be worked out in a conciliatory manner. This spirit of accommodation was especially present among the seven members of the special Committee that produced the first constitutional draft.

Thirdly, these were difficult times for Spain. The economy was suffering as a result of the oil crisis that started in 1973. Inflation was high and unemployment was rising. More threatening for the immediate future was the violent actions of terrorist groups, ETA in particular. As the Constitution was being discussed, thirty people were killed in 1977, and ninety-nine in 1978.[5] Most victims were members of the police and the armed forces. This caused all democratic parties to worry that the situation might get out of control. It was imperative to work together to reach a broad consensus on the rules and principles that the new Constitution should embody.

There were, inevitably, moments of tension within the constitutional Committee. At a certain point during the debates, a coalition seemed to emerge around the centre-right (AP,

---

[3] This smaller group (*ponencia*) included three representatives of UCD (Gabriel Cisneros, Miguel Herrero Rodríguez de Miñón, and José Pedro Pérez-Llorca); one of PSOE-PSC (Gregorio Peces-Barba); one of Minoría catalana (Miguel Roca i Junyent); one of PCE-PSUC (Jordi Solé Tura); and one of AP (Manuel Fraga).

[4] In fact, they were able to find common ground, not only for purposes of adopting a Constitution, but also for defining the necessary policies to stabilize the Spanish economy. Such policies were articulated in the *Pactos de la Moncloa* of 1977.

[5] Raymond Carr and Juan Pablo Fusi, *Spain: Dictatorship to Democracy* (HarperCollins, New York, 1981) 237.

UCD and *Minoría Catalana*), against the left (PSOE and PCE). The PSOE's representative, Gregorio Peces-Barba, abandoned the debates in protest. When President Suárez learned about this, he intervened to make sure that, from then onwards, the agreements would shift towards the left.[6] Fortunately, the final text was primarily based on the agreement between UCD and PSOE. The agreement was almost entirely accepted by PCE, and partially so by AP. As a result, the Constitution was supported by the vast majority of the members of parliament, both in Congress (94.2 per cent yes; 1.8 per cent no; 4.1 per cent abstentions) and in the Senate (94.5 per cent yes; 2.3 per cent no; 3.3 per cent abstention).

There was a cost to the process, however, in terms of transparency. The real negotiations and discussions did not take place within parliament, but in restaurants and private offices and homes, where the leaders of the major parties met secretly. The basic agreements were being struck outside parliament.

Not surprisingly, given the broad consensus reached by the political parties, the Constitution was ratified by the vast majority of citizens in a referendum. Of those who turned out, 87.87 per cent voted yes, while 7.83 per cent voted no. The Constitution was a clear success. The turn-out in the referendum was low, however: 67.11 per cent (which was lower than the turn-out of 79.11 per cent in the general elections of June 1977). A section of the citizenry abstained for active political reasons, however. The Basque nationalists of PNV encouraged abstention because they were not happy enough with the degree of self-government they had obtained under the new Constitution. Less than half of the Basque electorate (46 per cent) voted in the referendum. In the rest of Spain, abstention reflected a certain measure of *desencanto* (disenchantment) that prevailed among people who did not like the secret politics of *consenso*.[7]

a) The Constitution as the Embodiment of Shared Values

The Spanish Constitution expresses a widespread commitment to democracy and fundamental rights. These were the values the democratic opposition to Franco had struggled for. And these are also the values that the vast majority of citizens nowadays endorse. The Constitution is not felt by the living generation to be an imposition from the past when it enshrines democracy and basic rights.

To a large extent, what has made it possible for the Constitution to resist the passage of time is its non-partisan character. Because the text adopted in 1978 was not written to serve the programme of one section of the political spectrum but was instead meant to express principles embraced by both the right and the left, the Constitution has not been eroded as a result of the shifts of power in ordinary politics. Indeed, it has proven to be a charter under which both the centre-right (after the general elections of 1979, 1996, 2000, 2011, and 2016) and the centre-left (after the general elections of 1982, 1986, 1989, 1993, 2004, 2008, and 2019) have been able to govern comfortably. This is in contrast to the way things developed under the Second Republic. As has already been pointed out, the Republican Constitution of 1931 was too biased in favour of the political programmes espoused by the left. The framers of the 1978 Constitution agreed that this had been a mistake that should not be repeated.

---

[6] Soledad Gallego-Díaz and Bonifacio de la Cuadra, *Crónica secreta de la Constitución* (Tecnos, Madrid, 1989) 46–62; and Gregorio Peces Barba, *La elaboración de la Constitución de 1978* (Centro de Estudios Constitucionales, Madrid, 1988) 123–133.

[7] On this point, see Francisco Rubio Llorente, 'El proceso constituyente en España', in Francisco Rubio Llorente (ed), *La forma del poder. (Estudios sobre la Constitución)* (Centro de Estudios Constitucionales, Madrid, 1993) 24–5; and José María Maravall, *La política de la transición: 1975-1980* (Taurus, Madrid, 1981) 81.

The constitutional Bill of Rights, in particular, obtained ample support. Except for some clauses that were hard to negotiate, as we will see later, there was a deep commitment to link Spain to the culture of rights prevailing in Europe. It is true that the left was more insistent than the right on including a *long* list of liberties in the constitutional text. But this does not mean that the parties on the right were less committed to their protection. Actually, in 1977, more than one year before the Constitution was enacted, the UCD government signed several international instruments: The International Covenant on Civil and Political Rights; the International Covenant on Economic, Social and Cultural Rights; Conventions number 87 and 98 of the International Labour Organization; and the European Convention on Human Rights. The centre-right was clearly sensitive to the need to safeguard fundamental liberties. The Constitution finally agreed upon embodied values that were then shared, and are still shared, by different political forces and social groups throughout a broad ideological spectrum.

Actually, in order to reinforce the protection of democracy and rights, the Constitution expresses a common will to connect Spain to international organizations. This common will has to be understood against the background of Spain's isolation during the dictatorship. None of the 'fundamental laws' adopted under Franco made any reference to international law. This was in contrast to the very advanced character of the Republican Constitution of 1931 in this regard, article 78 of which had constitutionalized Spain's membership of the League of Nations.[8] The Constitution of 1978 restores this internationalist conception when it mentions the Universal Declaration of Human Rights in article 10 para 2. The Constitution provides that this document must be considered when interpreting the rights and liberties enumerated in the Constitution. It also refers interpreters to the human rights conventions ratified by Spain in the realm of rights. In addition, the framers had the European Community in mind when they wrote article 93, which enables Spain to enter international organizations that exercise powers delegated by member states. Once more, the great value accorded to this provision has to be read as a reaction against the dictatorship. The European Community had closed its doors to Franco's Spain. Democracy was associated with the country being able to participate in European organizations. Both the left and the right agreed about this, and they still do. The Constitution does not really constrain democratic politics in this regard. It expresses a 'supranationalist' commitment that is shared across the nation. It was a unanimous Congress, for example, that on 26 June 1985 voted for the law enabling Spain to enter the European Community. All deputies that were present in Congress that day (309) voted yes. And they rose for a long and strong applause.[9]

b) The Constitution as the Product of a Bargaining Process

We have seen that there was broad agreement on democracy, basic rights, and supranational law among the political parties that wrote the Constitution in 1977–1978. But they were also in deep disagreement concerning certain matters. The framers understood that some historically divisive issues had to be settled. And the settlement had to be respected by future majorities in parliament. A factor that facilitated the conclusion of political deals was connected to the different degree of importance the players attached to the various questions under discussion. For the political right, for example, it was very important to preserve the monarchy. For the left, in contrast, inserting a long list of fundamental rights in the Constitution was more urgent.[10]

---

[8] Antonio Remiro Brotons, *La acción exterior del Estado* (Tecnos, Madrid, 1984) 12

[9] See *Diario de Sesiones, Congreso de los Diputados*, Pleno, núm. 222, 26/06/1985.

[10] Josep M. Colomer, *La transición a la democracia: el modelo español* (Anagrama, Barcelona, 1998) 114–45.

Some examples can be mentioned to illustrate the compromises that were reached at the constitutional table. With respect to the form of government, for instance, there was division of opinion between left and right. The left was mostly republican, while the right was in favour of preserving the monarchy, as has just been noted. A solution was designed that most people found acceptable. On the one hand, the monarchy was maintained. The left agreed that King Juan Carlos had played a crucial role in Spain's transition to democracy, and it concluded that the issue of monarchy versus republic was of secondary importance. On the other hand, democratic qualifications were introduced so that the King would no longer enjoy the powers that he had under Franco's laws. The monarch would have moral authority (*auctoritas*), but no effective political power. This equilibrium was possible because the issue concerning the monarchy was part of a larger constitutional package. Interestingly, polls indicated that if a separate referendum on the preservation of the monarchy had first been held, most people would have voted yes. The republican parties would therefore have lost a bargaining chip at the constitutional table. Because no such referendum was organized, the parties on the left were able to reduce the power of the King (and obtain additional benefits too), in exchange for their acceptance of the Crown.[11]

Similarly, the regional problem was addressed in a conciliatory spirit. Spain had been a centralized polity since the eighteenth century. At the end of the nineteenth century, the two most economically advanced regions in Spain—the Basque Country and Catalonia—expressed their will to be granted some measure of self-government. The Second Republic tried to give an answer to this problem by awarding 'Statutes of Autonomy' to the regions that wished to have them. Franco abolished the Statutes of Autonomy that had been enacted, and for forty years Spain was once again a strongly centralized state.

During Spain's transition to democracy, it was clear that working out an acceptable solution to the regional question was at the very top of the political agenda. Actually, before the Constitution was enacted, President Suárez had already struck a deal with Josep Tarradellas, a seventy-eight-year-old exiled President of the *Generalitat* (the Catalan government that had existed under the Second Republic), to establish a provisional local government in Catalonia. Tarradellas returned in triumph to Barcelona on 23 October 1977 to preside over the reinstalled *Generalitat*. Self-government was also restored in the Basque country, after the deputies and senators from that region negotiated with the government in Madrid. An interim body was created in the Basque Country under the presidency of Ramón Rubial, a historic socialist leader.

So, the constitutional framers had to organize a process of devolution of political power. Article 2 of the Constitution, after announcing that the Spanish nation is one and indivisible, recognizes the right of self-government (*autonomía*) of the different regions and *nacionalidades* that make up Spain. The term *nacionalidades* is rather ambiguous. It seems to refer to territories that are special because of their cultural or linguistic specificities, but which cannot be considered as nations. The inclusion of this expression in the constitutional text is a revealing example of the delicate balances that had to be struck when the Constitution was written. Article 3 is also based on a difficult equilibrium when it provides that *castellano* (Castilian Spanish) is the official language of the state, which all Spanish citizens have the duty to learn and the right to use. The article also establishes, however, that the 'other Spanish languages' will also be official within the respective territories, in accord with their Statutes of Autonomy. All these general principles figure in the Preliminary Title of the

---

[11] Charles Powell, *Juan Carlos of Spain. Self-made Monarch* (Palgrave Macmillan UK, London, 1996) 139–156.

Constitution. Title VIII then specifies the system of norms that regulate the territorial structure of the state, although many issues are left open to future political negotiations.

The Bill of Rights also includes some articles that were the result of a bargaining process. The Constitution, for example, includes the right to private property, but it establishes that the scope of this right is to be defined by the social function private property must serve (article 33). The Constitution protects individuals against takings without just compensation (article 33), but it also imposes a constitutional duty to pay taxes under a system that is based on the principle of fiscal progressiveness (article 31). Likewise, it guarantees the right to free enterprise within a regime of market economy, but it constrains this right by authorizing the government to intervene in the economy in different ways, in order to serve the public interest (articles 38, 40, 128, 129, 130, and 131). Although the differences between the political right and the political left in the economic field are less pronounced now than they were in 1977–1978, the Constitution does rule out certain economic programmes. These constraints have been useful: they have reduced the stakes of ordinary politics when it comes to social and economic issues.

A similar pattern emerges regarding the right to education. Here the left and the right had different views about how to organize schools. The right basically wanted to protect private schools, especially religious ones, while the left defended the centrality of public and secular education. Since they could not agree on any specific solution, they chose to enumerate the relatively specific rights and goals that ought to be accommodated in the future. Article 27 thus provides that parents can decide the kind of moral and religious education their children will receive. The aim of education, however, is the free development of one's personality under the principles of democracy and rights, which means that the right of parents has limits. Similarly, private individuals are granted the fundamental right to create schools, but teachers, parents, and students are entitled to participate in the administration of those schools that are subsidized by the government. The state, moreover, shall inspect and regulate the educational system as a whole. Interestingly, the inclusion of a reference to human rights treaties in article 10 para 2 of the Constitution helped pacify the debates over the school system. The more conservative forces thought that those treaties helped reinforce the protection they wanted private schools to enjoy under the new Constitution.[12]

Similarly, with respect to the position of the Catholic Church, a solution had to be worked out through negotiation. The more conservative parties wanted to secure the central role of the Church, while the left was against this. The framers finally agreed to hammer out the principle of religious neutrality (the state has no religion or church), subject to this qualification: 'the state shall take into account the religious beliefs of Spanish society and shall therefore cooperate with the Catholic Church and the other religions' (article 16). This was not a solution everyone could be fully satisfied with, but it occupied a middle ground between the various positions at war.

It is important to note that the Constitution requires certain matters to be regulated by means of 'organic statutes' (*leyes orgánicas*), whose passage by parliament requires the affirmative vote of an absolute majority (not a simple majority) of members of Congress (article 81). The framers predicted (wrongly) that it would be almost impossible for a single political party to obtain an absolute majority of seats in Congress. So, requiring certain issues to be dealt with by organic statutes was supposed to entail the consequence that the

---

[12] Alejandro Saiz Arnaiz, *La apertura constitucional al Derecho internacional y europeo de los Derechos Humanos. El artículo 10.2 de la Constitución española* (Consejo General del Poder Judicial, Madrid, 1999) 15–34.

spirit of accommodation and compromise that characterized the constitution-making process would be maintained in the future.

In sum, and as a result of these bargaining efforts, the Constitution has performed a pacifying function. Ordinary majorities in parliament are constrained by a collection of fundamental rules that were adopted in 1977–1978. Such constraints have proven to be useful to stabilize the democratic regime. Different political majorities in Parliament can thus pursue their own programmes in the many fields that are left open by the Constitution, while enjoying the stability that such constraints make possible.

3. Foreign Influences and the Impact of Constitutional Scholars

The Spanish Constitution includes a number of rules and institutions borrowed from other countries.[13] In general, Spanish legal culture in the field of public law has traditionally maintained strong links with Western European academic scholarship, especially that produced in Germany and Italy. Even under the dictatorship, Spanish scholars paid attention to developments in other European countries. Therefore, when the Constitution was being written in 1977–1978, the constitutional experiences from abroad were taken into account by the framers in order to shape a Constitution that would be in conformity with general tendencies in Western Europe. Interestingly, the framers were more attentive to comparative law than to Spanish constitutional history when looking for precedents and ideas. Only the Spanish Constitution of 1931 had a significant impact, particularly regarding the territorial organization of the state.

Thus, many Spanish constitutional framers insisted on the need to adopt a long Bill of Rights. As noted, the political parties on the left were strongly supportive of such a Bill. The declaration of rights that figures in Title I of the Constitution mirrors the German Constitution in many respects. It lists 'fundamental rights', a concept that has been especially worked on in German jurisprudence. Article 53 of the Spanish Constitution, moreover, provides that the legislature must respect the 'essential content' of the right that is being regulated, an expression also borrowed from the German Constitution. Spanish scholars have had to interpret this notion considering German theories. A judge on the Spanish Constitutional Court once said, jokingly, that 'essential content' is whatever Germans say it is. The Constitution also includes a human dignity clause (article 10 para 1) similar to that of the German Basic Law.

The German influence is also notable when it comes to institutional arrangements. In order to enhance governmental stability, the Spanish Constitution requires that a 'motion of censure' to bring down the government be 'constructive'. That is to say, the parliamentary opposition must agree on the person that will replace the President of the government that is being targeted through the motion. This modality of vote of no confidence was taken from the German constitutional experience. From Germany as well did the framers draw their ideas about how to regulate the structure and functions of the Constitutional Court. Among other things, they imported with some modifications the 'constitutional complaints'

---

[13] For a general view of foreign influences throughout the history of Spanish constitutionalism, see Joaquín Varela, 'El constitucionalismo español en su contexto comparado' (2010) 13 Documentos de trabajo IELAT (Instituto de Estudios Latinoamericanos-Universidad de Alcalá) 1–26. The particular impact of the German Constitution on the Spanish Constitution of 1978 is described in Pedro Cruz Villalón, 'La recepción de la Ley Fundamental de la República Federal de Alemania', in Pedro Cruz Villalón (ed), *La curiosidad del jurista persa, y otros estudios sobre la Constitución* (Centro de Estudios Políticos y Constitucionales, Madrid, 1999) 55–82.

procedure that allows a private person to file a complaint before the Constitutional Court to challenge a decision by a public authority that is alleged to be in breach of fundamental rights. It should be noted, in this connection, that the Spanish Constitution of 1931 served as a precedent too: Spain had been one of the few countries in Europe that had set up such a tribunal before the Second World War.

The Italian Constitution exerted its own influence on the Spanish text as well. Article 9 para 2 of the Spanish Constitution, for example, which requires public authorities to perform an active role in the social and economic spheres in order to eliminate the existing obstacles to real liberty and equality, was written in the spirit of a similar clause of the Italian Constitution. The Italian Constitution was also influential with respect to the General Council of the Judiciary, an organ whose mission is to govern the judicial power in order to secure its independence from the executive branch. Furthermore, the Italian system had an impact on the articulation of sources of law. In particular, the Spanish Constitution follows in the Italian steps when it regulates the conditions under which the Government is enabled to issue certain norms that have the same rank as parliamentary statutes (*decreto-ley*, and *decreto legislativo*). Importantly, the Italian experience with the devolution of power to the regions, by means of the enactment of Statutes of Autonomy, was also taken into account when the Spanish framers discussed the manner in which Spain should grant self-government to the regions. Interestingly, the Italians had in turn paid attention to the Spanish experience with regionalism under the Constitution of 1931 when they adopted their own Constitution in 1947.

Other constitutions also influenced the content of the Spanish Constitution, but this influence was less significant. The Portuguese Constitution, for example, was taken into account when social and economic principles were included in Title I of the Spanish Constitution. The French Constitution, in turn, inspired the introduction of a special type of statute, the 'organic statute' (*ley orgánica*), which was required to regulate certain important matters. Finally, the Swedish Constitution was the intellectual source of the Ombudsman (*Defensor del Pueblo*), whose main function is to supervise the public administration in the name of fundamental rights.

The operation of all these external influences was facilitated by the fact that some relevant members of parliament that enacted the Constitution had an academic background. Thus, four of the seven 'fathers of the Constitution' that issued the first draft of the constitutional text were experts in the field of public law, and had obtained academic chairs: Jordi Solé Tura, Gregorio Peces-Barba, Miguel Herrero, and Manuel Fraga. Other members of Congress and the Senate were also university professors in that field, such as Enrique Tierno, Raúl Morodo, Óscar Alzaga, Carlos Ollero, Manuel Jiménez de Parga, and Luis Sánchez-Agesta. Knowledge about the constitutional experiences of other countries could be conveyed by these experts during the parliamentary deliberations.

It should be observed that, under Franco's dictatorship, no course entitled 'Constitutional Law' was taught at the universities. The regime had no interest in portraying its fundamental rules and principles as part of the Spanish 'constitutional' tradition, a tradition that was widely associated with political liberalism. What was instead offered was a course on 'Political Law', whose subject matter was not clearly defined. Paradoxically, this vagueness permitted many professors to engage in comparative law research and to instruct students about the constitutional experiences of other countries, all of which was intellectually liberating. So, when parliamentary discussions were undertaken at the constitutional moment of 1977–1978, politicians and experts could draw from the intellectual reservoir of comparative constitutional law that had been accumulated over the years. A prominent figure in this regard was Professor Manuel García-Pelayo, who had been in exile during the dictatorship. He had written an important book on comparative constitutional law that turned out to be quite influential. He later became the first President of the Spanish Constitutional Court that was established in 1980, a fact of great symbolic significance.

B. The Evolution of the Constitution

In order to understand the evolution of the Spanish constitutional order, we must first examine the procedures that the Constitution stipulates for its amendment. As we will see, the Spanish political parties have been reluctant to use the amendment procedure, the consequence being that the evolution of the constitutional order has taken place through judicial interpretation and political practices.

1. Constitutional Rigidity: The Amendment Procedure

The Constitution establishes two different amendment procedures depending on the subject matter. Article 167 establishes the procedure that applies as a general rule. A super-majority of three-fifths of both chambers of the *Cortes Generales* (Congress and the Senate) is initially required. If that super-majority is not obtained, a joint Commission made up of members of Congress and the Senate must try to agree upon a text. If the new text is not approved by three-fifths of each parliamentary chamber, the Congress can enact it by a two-thirds super-majority, provided that at least an absolute majority of senators voted for it. (Absolute majority means that those voting in favour are more than 50 per cent of the total number of representatives).

It is worth stressing that the crucial role that political parties played at the initial constitutional stage is replicated in the amendment context. It is basically a new pact among political parties that can lead to a reform. The Constitution does not allow the people to initiate the process of constitutional amendment: only the government, Congress, the Senate, and the regional parliaments can propose a reform (article 166). A referendum is not necessary, moreover, for the valid adoption of the amendment, unless 10 per cent of members of Congress or 10 per cent of Senators ask for it.

In fact, the only two amendments that have been introduced so far were enacted through this procedure, and no referendum was called. In 1992, the constitutional text was modified to allow citizens of the European Union to stand as candidates in Spanish municipal elections. Without the amendment, it would not have been possible for Spain to validly ratify the Maastricht Treaty, which granted that right. In its original version, the Constitution permitted non-Spaniards the right to vote in municipal elections, but not the right to stand as candidates. Changing the Constitution was thus necessary. Years later, in 2011, a constitutional reform was enacted to impose certain limits on public debt and public deficit. Article 135 of the Constitution was modified to reinforce Spain's compliance with public deficit and public debt limitations established by European Union law. This amendment was introduced in the middle of financial turmoil in Europe to send the message that Spain would be committed to fiscal discipline. Not only were citizens excluded from this constitutional reform, but the two main parties (PSOE and PP) quickly agreed on its terms, and it was enacted by the *Cortes Generales* in just a few days.

Interestingly, during the constitutional debates in 1977–1978, it was the more conservative right (AP) that was in favour of expanding popular participation in the amendment process, making the referendum compulsory in all cases. The other parties (especially those on the left) argued that it was dangerous in Spain to enlarge the institutions of direct democracy, since they might undermine respect for the parliamentary system. They were concerned about the fragility of political parties and representative institutions in a country that had suffered forty years of dictatorship.[14]

The Constitution, however, includes an exceptional rule governing amendment of a special kind. Article 168 stipulates a special procedure to enact a 'total revision' of the Constitution, or a partial one that affects certain clauses: those that figure in the Preliminary Title (which includes some of the most basic principles of the constitutional system), those that guarantee a special subset of fundamental rights (enumerated in articles 15–29), and those that regulate the Crown (Title II). A very onerous procedure needs to be followed in such cases: first, Congress, and the Senate must approve the general proposal by a majority of two-thirds each. Second, parliament must be dissolved immediately, and general elections called for. Third, the new parliament has to ratify the decision to initiate the reform. Fourth, the reform must be approved by two-thirds of the members of each house. Fifth, a referendum must be held, to obtain the support of the majority of citizens.

This is indeed a very burdensome procedure. The framers, apparently, sought to immunize in practice certain constitutional choices against repeal.[15] They were not very careful, however, when it came to identifying the matters deserving this extra protection. They could have said, for example, that the monarchical form of state is protected by the special procedure of article 168. Instead, they covered Title II as a whole, with all its minor details about the structure and functioning of the Crown. In contrast, they left aside the principle of human dignity, which article 10 solemnly proclaims to be one of the foundations of the political order. The framers, moreover, included a sub-group of fundamental rights (enumerated in articles 15–29), but they did not distinguish between restriction and expansion of rights. Article 15 of the Constitution, for example, abolishes the death penalty in general, but allows criminal military law to impose it in the event of war. The law can, of course, decline to establish the death penalty, as is currently the case. But if a proposal is made to reform the Constitution to eliminate the exceptional circumstance where capital punishment is permitted, why should the extraordinary procedure of article 168 be imposed?

In any case, it is important to emphasize that, although there are two procedures of constitutional amendment, the Constitution as a whole has turned out to be very rigid as a political matter. Even if the formal requirements of the easier procedure (regulated in article 167) are not hard to fulfil in theory, a political practice has developed that avoids any real talk about constitutional reforms. Changing the Constitution has become political taboo. The fear exists that any revision of the text—even if the matters involved are relatively marginal—may end up generating big divisions of opinion among citizens and political groups of the kind that the framers of the Constitution tried to settle in 1977–1978. In this regard, it is extremely revealing that the only two amendments that have been adopted so far were 'forced' on Spain by its membership of the European Union. As already indicated, the 1992 amendment was necessary to make it possible for Spain to validly ratify the Maastricht Treaty, while the 2011

---

[14] Javier Pérez Royo, *La Reforma de la Constitución* (Publicaciones del Congreso de los Diputados 1987) 131–135, 142–150, 159–160.

[15] Javier Pérez Royo, *La Reforma de la Constitución* (n 14) 156–157, 190, 202. See as well Pedro de Vega, *La reforma constitucional y la problemática del poder constituyente* (Tecnos, Madrid, 1985) 148.

amendment was required to enshrine the rules on fiscal austerity that were expected from Spain to deal with the crisis of the euro. No 'internally driven' reform has been adopted after four decades since the enactment of the Constitution.

It is worthy of note, in this connection, that the current structure of the system of political parties makes constitutional amendment even more difficult than it was in the past. Until recently, the two main political parties (PSOE and PP) had enough parliamentary votes to adopt constitutional amendments through the ordinary procedure of article 167. It was very hard, moreover, for critics of the amendments to gather the necessary parliamentary votes (10 per cent of Congress or 10 per cent of the Senate) to require the government to hold a referendum on the matter. In recent years, however, new political parties have appeared (*Ciudadanos* and *Vox* on the right, and *Podemos* on the left), while the big parties have lost a significant portion of their popular support. As a result, the agreement of a larger number of players is now needed to pass a constitutional reform. Moreover, it is now easier for a political party that objects to the reform to force the organization of a referendum. It is thus somewhat ironic that as the Constitution of 1978 gets older and is thus more in need of revision, the political conditions for the successful passage of a constitutional amendment have become harder.

2. Procedural Dualism and Substantive Limits to Amendments

The existence of two different avenues to produce a constitutional reform (an easier one regulated in article 167, and a harder one regulated in article 168) can give rise to some problems. How to decide, for example, when a 'total' revision of the Constitution is being entertained, so that the complicated procedure of article 168 needs to be followed? Is it a question of numbers—how many provisions are to be modified? Is it a question of the qualitative importance of the matters under consideration? The claim has been advanced, for example, that eliminating the Constitutional Court would be a total revision—even if article 168 does not explicitly mention Title IX (where that Court is regulated).[16]

And how should one determine whether a partial revision of the Constitution 'affects' the set of clauses that are covered by article 168? The very first time the Constitution was reformed illustrated the complexity of the issue. The Maastricht Treaty that Spain planned to ratify as part of the ongoing process of European integration provided that every European Union citizen would be entitled to vote and to stand as a candidate at the municipal elections in the Member State where he or she resides. As already observed, the Spanish Constitution provided in article 13 para 2 that only Spaniards enjoyed the rights of political participation mentioned in article 23, except that a treaty or a law could extend to foreigners the right to vote (*sufragio activo*) in municipal elections, if this was done in accordance with the principle of reciprocity. Only the right to vote was covered by the exception, not the right to stand as a candidate (*sufragio pasivo*). In order for Spain to validly ratify the Maastricht Treaty, therefore, it was plain that article 13 para 2 had to be amended, to expand the scope of the exception.

The problem was this: article 13 para 2 is not included in the group of clauses that are covered by the more burdensome amendment procedure of article 168, but article 23 is included in this group. Given the connection between the two articles, does the amendment

---

[16] Javier Pérez Royo, *La Reforma de la Constitución* (n 14) 196–197.

of article 13 para 2 'affect' article 23? There was doctrinal controversy about this, and the Constitutional Court was required by the government to address the issue. The Court (in its Declaration 1/1992) held that article 23 had to be conceptually separated from article 13: one defines the substantive right, while the other says who is entitled to enjoy the right. It concluded that the easy procedure was to be followed. And so, it was—which meant, among other things, that parliament was not dissolved, and no referendum was held. It is not obvious that the Court was technically right. It is rather doubtful that one can disconnect article 13 para 2 from article 23 in the way the Court suggested. The Court's prudential approach is understandable, however, given the political stakes involved.

An interesting question concerns the protection to be accorded to the most basic principles the Constitution embodies, such as democracy and human dignity. Is an amendment valid if it infringes upon those values?[17] The Constitutional Court has insisted in its jurisprudence that the Constitution places no substantive barriers to procedurally valid constitutional amendments (STC 48/2003, STC 42/2014, STC 114/2017). Many scholars endorse this position. They argue that, since a 'total revision' of the Spanish Constitution is explicitly permitted, no substantive limits are operative. Other voices counter that the Constitution is best interpreted as implicitly protecting certain core values against repeal. To reinforce this point, it is possible to appeal to Spain's membership of the European Union and the Council of Europe. External limits in the name of democracy and rights are clearly applicable. A constitutional transformation against liberal democracy would be illegal under European supranational norms. The Constitution, which refers to supranational law (article 10 para 2 and article 93), could thus be taken to express an irreversible commitment to democracy and rights.

A different issue is whether the articles regulating constitutional amendments may themselves be amended. There seems to be no a priori reason to deny the possibility of changing the existing amendment rules. There is no logical problem in using a procedure to change the rules that regulate that procedure. The real question is which procedure needs to be followed to modify articles 167 and 168. Since the Constitution has established a general rule (article 167) and an exception (article 168), the argument has sometimes been made that it is possible to use article 167 to change both article 167 and article 168. The argument is based on the observation that neither article 167 nor article 168 is included in the exceptional list that figures in article 168. This textual argument leads to an outcome that sounds plausible when it comes to changing article 167. But with respect to changing article 168, the outcome is counterintuitive. Is it possible to reform the 'difficult' procedure through the 'easy' procedure? Isn't it a constitutional fraud for a super-majority in parliament to overcome the constraints that article 168 imposes on it, through the convenient strategy of using the easy procedure to eliminate those constraints?

For a while, discussing these issues was a sort of pastime for idle professors. But they started to have practical bite some years ago in connection with the proposal made by President José Luis Rodríguez Zapatero to eliminate gender discrimination in the succession to the Crown. This discrimination derives from article 57 of the Constitution. The special procedure regulated in article 168 would have to be followed to implement the proposed change. But it appeared to be politically unreasonable to use such a demanding procedure to enact a relatively marginal change. Was it possible to relax that procedure, or exclude certain matters from it, through a constitutional amendment? If so, which procedure was to be

---

[17] On this issue, see Benito Aláez Corral, *Los límites materiales a la reforma de la Constitución española de 1978* (Centro de Estudios Políticos y Constitucionales, Madrid, 2000).

employed? Most scholars are of the view that the procedure of article 168 needs to be followed in order to introduce such a change.[18] Some dissenting voices were heard, however, suggesting that the easy procedure of article 167 could be used to relax the more burdensome one.[19]

Quite likely, if article 168 is ever modified to soften the rigidity of the procedure it lays down, it will be in the context of a 'total revision' of the Constitution enacted through article 168. In other words, if an ambitious reform of the Constitution is launched in the future in order to modify a number of articles dealing with many different matters, the modification of article 168 may then be put on the table as part of the package. The constitutional amendment process can thus be adjusted in the context of a broader constitutional revision. It is hard to imagine that it will ever be changed in isolation from other matters.

3. Interpretation

The political parties' general reluctance to reform the Constitution has had some repercussions on interpretive practices. The constitutional text has sometimes been read in a very flexible way to accommodate certain changes which, were it not for that reluctance, would normally have triggered the process of constitutional amendment. The Constitution, for example, refers to 'compulsory military service' in article 30 para 2. In 1999, however, a statute passed by parliament eliminated this service. In order to avoid constitutional problems, the statute established that the military service was 'suspended indefinitely', instead of being formally abolished. There is no doubt, however, that the effect is exactly the same as if it had been formally extinguished. Since there was a broad majority in parliament in favour of this legislative change, it would not have been hard to amend the Constitution. Yet, such a constitutional move was out of the question.

Similarly, the Constitution recognizes in article 32 the right of 'a man and a woman' to get married. A law was enacted in 2005 to allow same-sex marriage. The law can persuasively be defended on equality grounds: if we believe that individuals have a right not to be discriminated against on grounds of sexual orientation, it follows that homosexuals should not be excluded from the institution of marriage. Yet, there is a textual dissonance between the 2005 statute and the way the constitutional clause is written. If political parties were more prepared to reform the Constitution, a bill would have been tabled to change article 32. (The Constitutional Court, it should be noted, upheld the validity of the 2005 statute: STC 198/2012.)

The existence of a political taboo when it comes to revising the Spanish Constitution has put the Constitutional Court in a delicate position. The Court knows that none of its rulings will be overridden through a constitutional amendment.[20] In other European countries, such as France and Italy, for example, some changes in the Constitution have been introduced as a response to the jurisprudential position of the Court.[21] This healthy counterweight to the Court's power is totally absent in Spain.

---

[18] See for example Ignacio de Otto, *Derecho constitucional. Sistema de fuentes* (Ariel, Barcelona, 1988) 667.

[19] See Francisco Laporta, 'Las dos vías para la reforma de la Constitución' (2004) 145 Claves de la Razón Práctica 14–23.

[20] Pedro Cruz Villalón, 'Constitución y tiempo: primera década', in Pedro Cruz Villalón (ed), *La curiosidad del jurista persa, y otros estudios sobre la Constitución* (n 13) 114–115.

[21] For references, see Victor Ferreres Comella, *Constitutional Courts and Democratic Values: A European Perspective* (Yale University Press, New Haven, 2009) 104–107.

4. Influential Personalities in the Development of the Constitution

The enactment of the Constitution in 1978 produced a dramatic change in the academic and professional world.[22] The new Constitution, a written document enshrining liberal and democratic principles, soon became the focus of scholarly studies. The Constitution was to be treated as part of the law, it was urged. The Constitution is a special source of law, of course, given its supreme rank and the foundational role it performs in a legal system. But it is law, after all, and must therefore be approached with the tools with which jurists have traditionally made sense of the law in different fields. An emphasis was placed on the 'unity' of the legal method.

The professors of 'administrative law', who had already developed modern legal scholarship during Franco's regime, insisted on the unity of public law and the need to view the Constitution as part of it. The most prominent figure in these efforts at legalization and normalization of the Constitution of 1978 was Eduardo García de Enterría, whose book *La Constitución como norma y el Tribunal Constitucional*[23] soon became a classic in Spain. Other scholars, such as Francisco Rubio Llorente, Ignacio de Otto, Pedro Cruz Villalón, Luis María Díez-Picazo, and Luis López Guerra, just to mention some of the most influential scholars in Spain, basically shared the new approach.

A dialogue between scholars and judges soon developed after the Constitutional Court was created in 1980. The Court had to address new and complex legal issues and looked for ideas and guidance in academic literature. Scholars, in turn, paid attention to the jurisprudence which the Court was working out, which was generally celebrated as quite progressive. The presence of professors of constitutional law and other legal fields in the Court, whether acting as judges or as part of its legal staff, helped create bridges between the Court and the academic world. Implementing the Constitution became a broad collective enterprise. No single scholar stands out in terms of the degree of influence on the evolution of Spanish constitutional law. What was consequential was laying down the foundations for the legalization of the Constitution. Multiple voices have been heard throughout the years engaging in a fruitful dialogue with the Court.

C. Basic Structures and Concepts

1. The Position of the Constitution in the Legal and Political System

In the early years of the Constitution's existence, many ordinary judges in Spain were reluctant to take the Constitution as part of the law they had to interpret and apply to decide controversies. They viewed it as a 'political document' that was external to the legal system they had to adjudicate. As soon as the Constitutional Court was established in 1980 and started to lay down decisions, it had to react against such understanding. It emphasized the 'normative force' of the new fundamental charter. The Constitution is law, the Court insisted, and ordinary judges must apply it directly, without having to wait for the legislature to intervene. If the Constitution recognizes the right to conscientious objection against military service, for

---

[22] For an illuminating overview of Spanish constitutional scholarship since the adoption of the Constitution in 1978, see Luis López Guerra, 'Algunas notas sobre el desarrollo de la doctrina constitucionalista española' (2010) 41 Revista catalana de dret públic 85–116.

[23] Eduardo García de Enterría, *La Constitución como norma y el Tribunal Constitucional* (Madrid, Civitas, 1981).

example, judges must guarantee the core of this right, even if parliament has not yet passed a statute regulating the conditions and the procedures to exercise such right (STC 15/1982).

The Constitution, moreover, enjoys supremacy within the legal system. This is in keeping with the decision to create a Constitutional Court. Title IX regulates this specialized tribunal, the most important function of which is to review the constitutional validity of legislation enacted by parliament. The Court can strike down statutes (or other norms of equivalent rank) that it finds inconsistent with the Constitution. Ordinary judges, in turn, must certify a question to the Constitutional Court, if they believe that a piece of legislation that is applicable to the instant case is unconstitutional.

Given this supremacy, the rest of the law needs to be interpreted in light of the Constitution. Judges must read and apply the relevant law in such a manner that fundamental rights are respected. This requirement to read ordinary legislation 'in conformity with the Constitution' operates in all legal fields, including private law, as we will discuss later.

The Constitution is not only the highest norm in the legal system. It has an additional characteristic: it organizes the sources of law. That is, it establishes which organs, following which procedures, under what kinds of constraints, are authorized to issue which types of norms. And it orders these different sorts of norms into a systematic whole defining the relationships among them.

It is important to stress this structural function of the Constitution given the traditional role of the Spanish Civil Code in this field. Indeed, the Code was for a long time the basic document where the sources of the legal system were defined. This was true in other European countries as well. Article 1 of the Spanish Civil Code provided (and still provides) that the sources of the Spanish legal system are 'laws, customs and general principles of law' (*leyes, costumbres, principios generales del Derecho*). This is a very sketchy definition of the sources of law. There is nothing wrong with it, but it needs to be interpreted in light of the Constitution, which is the most important legal instrument where the elements of the legal system are fixed. The relevance of the Code is that it recognizes two sources (customs and general principles of law) beyond those that the Constitution explicitly mentions. These extra-constitutional sources are legitimate since the Constitution (in article 149 para 1 lit viii) authorizes the central government to 'determine the sources of law', which implies that there may be other sources of law beyond those specified and regulated in the Constitution.[24]

2. Democracy

Because Franco's dictatorship was obviously in breach of democratic principles, the authors of the 1978 Constitution included many references to democratic values in the text. The very first article of the Constitution proclaims that Spain constitutes itself as a 'democratic and social state under the rule of law' (*Estado social y democrático de Derecho*). This is an important clause that points to different dimensions of political morality, which need to be read as forming part of a coherent whole.[25]

Democracy is understood to mean, first, that the different organs of the state owe their existence to the people. The Constitution provides that 'national sovereignty is vested in the Spanish people, from which the powers of the state derive' (article 1 para 2). The fact that

---

[24] Ignacio de Otto, *Derecho constitucional. Sistema de fuentes* (n 18) 86.
[25] For an influential and early treatment of this constitutional clause, see Ángel Garrorena Morales, *El Estado español como Estado social y democrático de Derecho* (Tecnos, Madrid, 1984).

the Constitution was enacted by a popularly elected parliament, and that a referendum was held to obtain the people's approval, makes it possible to assert that all governmental institutions exist by virtue of popular will. The Constitutional Court has insisted on the strong link between popular sovereignty and the principle of constitutional supremacy. The political institutions, even those whose members are elected by citizens, cannot claim to have a democratic mandate to break a constitutional rule since it is the sovereign people itself that has authored the Constitution from which all political institutions derive their existence and limited powers (STC 114/2017).

This idea has some consequences when it comes to the Crown. The King is not elected by the people or by any democratic branch. But the very existence of the Crown as an institution rests on the democratic choice embodied in the Constitution. Because there are no exceptions to the proposition that all state institutions derive their existence from the people, there is no limitation on the power of the people to dismantle the monarchy through a constitutional amendment. The Constitution explicitly provides for the possibility of amending the articles dealing with the Crown—although it imposes a very burdensome procedure, as we have seen.

That Spain is a democratic state means, secondly, that the laws are 'the expression of popular will' (as the preamble of the Constitution announces). There must be an institution, therefore, in charge of legislation, the members of which are elected by citizens. This is the central role of parliament. There is a bicameral legislative assembly at the state level, the *Cortes Generales*, which consists of a Congress and a Senate, and there is a unicameral assembly in each Autonomous Community. The statutes produced by these institutions have a special democratic dignity because of their source.

The Constitutional Court has held that democracy requires that the ordinary parliament enjoy wide latitude to revise previous legislative decisions. Within the framework of the Constitution, which places certain matters outside the sphere of ordinary politics, the principle of 'reversibility' of decisions governs (STC 31/2010).

To make democracy possible, citizens must of course be granted the right to vote and to stand as candidates. Article 23 para 1 of the Constitution establishes that 'citizens have the right to participate in public affairs, directly or through representatives freely elected in periodic elections by universal suffrage'. This right, article 13 para 2 specifies, is reserved to Spanish citizens, except for the possibility of allowing foreign citizens to vote and to stand as candidates at municipal elections, in accordance with the principle of reciprocity.

The Constitution explicitly mentions political parties in article 6 and considers them to be 'fundamental instruments for political participation'. They are expected to provide voters with a diversity of political programmes. It is worth emphasizing that, during the transition to democracy, the understanding prevailed that any political party should be allowed to participate in public life, no matter what its programme or discourse was, provided it was prepared to respect the rules of the game and therefore abstained from using violent means to achieve its goals. That the Communist Party was entitled to be legalized, for example, no matter its programme, was part and parcel of the idea of an open democracy. The Constitution was also thought to protect the parties on the extreme right that might argue in defence of Franco's dictatorship, for instance, or those that are in favour of regional secession. When the Constitution was being framed, proposals establishing some form of 'militant democracy' were rejected.[26] The first statute that regulated political parties, enacted in 1978,

---

[26] Roberto Blanco Valdés, *Los partidos políticos* (Tecnos, Madrid, 1990) 124–141.

reflected this original understanding. Most scholars, moreover, insisted on the open character of the Constitution, which can be amended in many different directions, thus making it possible for political parties to pursue radical programmes.[27] In 2002, a new statute on political parties was adopted, however, which partially deviated from this conception. The new law imposed restrictions that went beyond the prohibition of using violence: certain goals are excluded (those that are incompatible with democracy and rights), and certain forms of speech are prohibited (those that are not sufficiently critical of terrorist actions, for example).[28] Some forms of radical speech might end up being suppressed as a result of this law. The regional government of the Basque Country challenged the statute through an appeal to the Constitutional Court. The Court nevertheless upheld the statute (STC 48/2003), relying in part on the jurisprudence of the European Court of Human Rights.[29]

The Constitution lays down several procedures to permit the direct participation of citizens. Their scope is limited, however. The framers were of the view that it was necessary to strengthen the role of political parties in a scheme of representative democracy, given the legacy of the dictatorship.

One mechanism for citizens to participate in politics is the popular initiative. Citizens are empowered by the Constitution to present legislative proposals to be considered by the national parliament (article 87 para 3). This is a very limited form of participation, however, since a majority of members of Congress can decide at an early stage not to take the proposal into consideration, which means that the proposal will not be discussed any more. The Constitution, moreover, requires that at least 500,000 signatures be collected. This number represents a very large portion of the population, much larger than in Italy, for example, where 50,000 signatures are sufficient.[30] The Constitution also establishes that popular legislative proposals cannot involve certain matters. They cannot deal with taxes, international affairs, and pardons. Nor can they propose an amendment to the Constitution. The Constitution goes so far as to also exclude issues that must be covered by an 'organic statute'. Among the matters that are reserved to organic statutes are the fundamental rights mentioned in articles 15 to 29 of the Constitution. This means that no popular legislative proposal can be advanced that touches upon any of those rights, such as religious freedom, the right to association, the right to life, the right to education, the right to privacy, freedom of speech, the right to judicial protection, to name a few. It is objectionable that citizens have been denied the possibility of triggering the legislative process in such cases.

A different and stronger form of direct democracy is the referendum. The Constitution provides in article 92 that the President of the government, having obtained the authorization of an absolute majority of the members of Congress, may submit 'political decisions of special transcendence' to the people. The question posed to the citizens must be of a general character. No specific statute, therefore, can be submitted to the people.

This form of direct democracy, however, has been cabined to make sure it does not erode representative democracy. First, the referendum is not legally binding. It is merely *consultivo*, as article 92 says. Second, the law that regulates the referendum has organized it in such a

---

[27] The most important doctrinal work in this regard was Ignacio de Otto, *Defensa de la Constitución y partidos políticos* (Centro de Estudios Constitucionales, Madrid, 1985).

[28] For a critical comment on the law, see Victor Ferreres Comella, 'The New Regulation of Political Parties in Spain, and the Decision to Outlaw Batasuna', in András Sajó (ed), *Militant democracy* (Eleven International Publishing, The Hague, 2004) 133–156.

[29] The Constitutional Court explicitly cited the European Court of Human Rights judgment of 31 July 2001 in the *Refah Partisi v Turkey* case.

[30] Art 71 of the Italian Constitution.

way that political parties are the leading voices in the campaign. The referendum has thus been 'rationalized' in order to prevent political parties from losing their centrality.[31]

So far, Spanish citizens have been asked to participate in this type of referendum twice: in 1986, to decide whether Spain should remain in NATO; and in 2005 to approve Spain's ratification of the 'Treaty establishing a Constitution for Europe'. In both cases, the majority of citizens voted 'yes'.

In addition to the non-binding referendum just described, the Spanish Constitution requires referenda in some specific cases and makes the results legally binding. At the national level, referenda are sometimes legally necessary to amend the Constitution, as noted earlier. In the regional sphere, referenda are also sometimes required to enact and amend the Statutes of Autonomy—the legal instruments that organize the political system of each Autonomous Community.[32] These referenda have a 'constitutional nature' to a certain extent since they relate to the basic charters that set up and organize the regional governments.

There is some controversy about the possibility of holding non-binding regional and local referenda. In any event, the Constitution is clear when it establishes that only the central Government can authorize popular referenda (article 149 para 1 lit xxxii). The Constitutional Court has thus stopped regional institutions from organizing popular consultations not authorized by the central state. It has also maintained that no referendum can be held on an issue that has already been settled by the sovereign people through the exercise of its constituent power. If such settlement is to be reconsidered, the procedures of constitutional amendment need to be triggered (STC 103/2008, STC 31/2015, STC 114/2017).

3. The Rule of Law: General Principles

Article 1 proclaims that Spain is a 'state under the rule of law' (*Estado de Derecho*). Article 9 para 1, in turn, provides that 'citizens and public powers are subject to the Constitution and the rest of the law'. Article 9 para 3 then details some of the normative consequences of this basic notion.

When the framers hammered out the principle of the rule of law in the Constitution, they did so against the background of the dictatorship. An underdeveloped form of *Estado de Derecho* had been constructed during the fifties and sixties as part of the efforts undertaken by the Francoist regime to modernize the apparatus of the state. Some new laws had been enacted at that time to allow courts to check the legality of administrative acts in a more or less independent manner.

The Spanish Constitution, of course, embraces a much more ambitious conception of the rule of law. The individual rights to be protected include many rights and liberties that the dictatorship repressed. Title I of the Constitution enumerates those basic rights. All the institutions of the state, moreover, are to be constrained by legal standards. In addition to the public administration, the government and parliament must abide by the law. The Constitution lays down rules and principles that political institutions must observe and that courts are authorized to enforce.

---

[31] For a description and criticism of this 'rationalization' of referenda, see Pedro Cruz Villalón, 'El referendum consultivo como modelo de racionalización constitucional', in Pedro Cruz Villalón (ed), *La curiosidad del jurista persa, y otros estudios sobre la Constitución* (n 13) 255–281.

[32] See arts 151, 152, and *Disposición Transitoria* 4 of the Constitution.

For the rule of law to be realized in practice, certain technical requirements need to be met. The law, for example, must be organized in a hierarchical structure so that the large number of rules that are generated by the institutional machinery of the modern state do not lead to chaos. The rules occupy different ranks and those at the top prevail over those at the bottom (*lex superior derogat inferiori*). Another technical requirement that needs to be satisfied for the rule of law to be honoured concerns the accessibility and the clarity of the law. It is very important that the laws be accessible to the public. Individuals can only plan their actions and check the performance of the state if they have access to the existing laws. Article 9 para 3 of the Constitution proclaims, in this regard, the 'principle of publicity'. The law must be published in an official gazette in order for citizens to learn about it. The basic instrument in Spain for these purposes is the *Boletín Oficial del Estado*.[33] The principle of publicity is connected to another requirement that is not explicitly mentioned in the Constitution but is implicit in it: the law should be expressed with clarity. Citizens must be able to understand what the law provides. The Constitutional Court, following in the steps of the European Court of Human Rights, has held that the clarity requirement is an ingredient of the rule of law idea. It is of special relevance in the area of criminal law.[34]

Another important component of the rule of law concerns the temporal effects of the laws. Article 9 para 3 of the Constitution prohibits the retroactive effects of laws establishing sanctions, unless the new laws are less severe than the ones that existed at the time the relevant facts occurred. This constitutional provision also bans the retroactive application of laws that restrict 'individual rights'. The Constitutional Court has interpreted the expression 'individual rights' narrowly, however. It has said that it primarily refers to the fundamental rights protected in Title I of the Constitution (see STC 112/2006). The expression does not cover, therefore, all rights granted by ordinary legislation. As a result, the democratic branches can introduce new laws to bring about important social transformations. The democratic and social components of the state mentioned in article 1 of the Constitution press here against a broad reading of the non-retroactivity clause.

To make sure that all these requirements that define the rule of law are duly respected by the government, mechanisms of judicial review must be set up. Different courts have different responsibilities in Spain when it comes to checking the actions and omissions of public institutions, as will be explained later.

4. Recognition and Protection of Fundamental Rights

As already mentioned, the rule of law is connected to the recognition and protection of fundamental rights.[35] Title I of the Constitution draws a distinction between 'fundamental rights' properly so-called, which figure in chapter II (articles 14 to 38), and the 'principles on social and economic policy' (*principios rectores de la política social y económica*), which are enumerated in chapter III (articles 39 to 52). The legal regime that applies to each category differs.

---

[33] On the principle of publicity, see Paloma Biglino Campos, *La publicación de la ley* (Tecnos, Madrid, 1993).

[34] On the principle of clarity in criminal law, see Víctor Ferreres Comella, *El principio de taxatividad en material penal y el valor normativo de la jurisprudencia* (Civitas, Madrid, 2002).

[35] For a comprehensive treatment of fundamental rights in Spain see Luis María Díez-Picazo, *Sistema de derechos fundamentales* (Aranzadi, Cizur Menor, 2013).

a) The Distinction between Fundamental Rights and Social and Economic Principles

Regarding fundamental rights, article 53 of the Constitution provides that they are 'binding on all public authorities'. This means that there is no need for ordinary laws to be passed to guarantee a fundamental right: the Constitution directly protects it. Almost all rights have been developed through the pertinent laws, but some of them have not. Article 20 para 1 of the Constitution guarantees the right of journalists to the confidentiality of their sources, for example, but no law has yet been passed to specify this right. Judges have therefore had to apply the Constitution directly and have balanced the interests at stake on a case-by-case basis.

Another rule embodied in article 53 prescribes that only statutes may regulate the exercise of fundamental rights. The popularly elected parliament must therefore necessarily intervene to specify the scope of the right and lay down the pertinent conditions and restrictions. Administrative regulations are only admissible if they play a marginal role in working out the details of the relevant statutes.

The legislature, moreover, must respect the 'essential content' of the right, article 53 says. There has been a complex scholarly discussion about the meaning of this expression, as we will see. But it is plain that the legislature does not have free rein to impose limitations and restrictions on rights.

While fundamental rights are awarded a high level of protection, the social and economic principles included in Chapter III benefit from a less robust legal regime. Article 53 specifies that such principles are to inspire legislation, as well as judicial and administrative practices, but they are not directly enforceable. The Constitution explicitly says that the social and economic principles 'can only be invoked before the ordinary courts in accordance with the laws that develop them'. Note that the implementation of those principles is not reserved to statutory sources of law. Administrative regulations have thus a wider space to occupy, than it is the case when fundamental rights are at stake.

So, the contrast between fundamental rights and social and economic principles is significant. Within the category of fundamental rights, however, further distinctions have been drawn. Thus, only some rights (those enumerated in articles 15 to 29) are covered by the requirement that an 'organic statute' be enacted to develop the contents of the right. As was explained earlier, organic statutes are based on a broader parliamentary consensus than ordinary statutes: an absolute majority of members of Congress (not a simple majority) is needed to approve and modify them. Similarly, only some rights (those that figure in articles 14 to 30 para 2) enjoy a special procedural protection: a constitutional complaint (*amparo*) can be lodged before the Constitutional Court to obtain redress if the right has been breached.

It is debatable whether the complexity of this system is worth the price. One of the problems derives from the presence of strong internal connections between rights that happen to be placed in the different subgroups. The right to conscientious objection to the military service (article 30 para 2), for instance, is not within the list of rights that need to be regulated by organic statute, but it is obviously connected to the right to liberty of conscience (article 16), which is part of that list. The Constitutional Court once had to address the matter. In a rather convoluted opinion, it held that, despite the underlying links, no organic statute is required to regulate the right to conscientious objection to the military service, which appears in the Constitution as an autonomous right (STC 160/1987). The problem is that two years before, the Court had asserted that physicians who object to performing an abortion on conscientious grounds are protected by the constitutional guarantee of liberty of conscience (STC 53/1985). This entails that an organic statute is necessary to govern the conditions for

572   VICTOR FERRERES COMELLA

physicians to object, while an ordinary statute is the appropriate law to govern the conditions for those who refuse to perform military duties. It is difficult to see the justification for this contrast.

b) The Principle of Proportionality and the Essential Content Guarantee

If we turn to the jurisprudence developed by the Constitutional Court when adjudicating fundamental rights, we should observe that the principle of proportionality has achieved high prominence. In order to assess whether a measure restricting a right passes the constitutional test, the Court has basically followed the version of the principle of proportionality developed in Germany, which includes three steps in the analysis: the Court asks, first, whether the restriction is useful to achieve a legitimate goal; second, whether the restriction is necessary, in that no less restrictive measure could be chosen to sufficiently satisfy that goal; and third, whether the costs that the restriction entails are offset by the benefits it achieves (STC 66/1995).[36] It is important to note that the work of Robert Alexy has had a huge impact among Spanish constitutional scholars. The principle of proportionality has been understood, to a large extent, in accordance with the account this German scholar has developed in his writings.[37]

In this context, the role of the 'essential content' guarantee has been a matter of debate. To simplify the discussion, some scholars are of the view that even restrictions that may be justified in order to serve other rights or public interests may be declared unconstitutional if they destroy the heart of the right. The scope of the right, as they conceive it, is composed of two circles: the outer circle defines the 'normal' content of the right, which can be reduced if good reasons are supplied on the basis of the principle of proportionality. The inner circle, however, defines the nucleus of the right, which cannot be eroded or destroyed. Other scholars, by contrast, believe that the 'essential content' does not guarantee anything that is not already guaranteed by the principle of proportionality. What it does is to remind interpreters that, as the restrictions under review get closer and closer to the core of the right, the reasons to justify further restrictions need to be increasingly weighty.[38]

The Constitutional Court, in turn, has defined the 'essential content' through two complementary strategies (STC 11/1981). The first appeals to interests: the essential content is destroyed if the interests protected by the right can no longer be served as a result of unreasonable restrictions. This line of argument easily connects the essential content to the principle of proportionality. After all, the best way to decide whether the restriction is unreasonable is to apply the proportionality test. The second strategy is more conceptual: the Court has said that if the restrictions are such that the right can no longer be recognized as falling under the pertinent category, the essential content has been violated. There are features, in other words, that must be present for the right to be recognized as such and not to be degraded into something else. This line of reasoning detaches the essential content

---

[36] The origin and the evolution of this doctrine in the jurisprudence of the Spanish Constitutional Court are traced in Markus González Beilfuss, *El principio de Proporcionalidad en la jurisprudencia del Tribunal Constitucional* (Aranzadi, Cizur Menor, 2003).

[37] The classic book (in its English version) is Robert Alexy, *A Theory of Constitutional Rights* (Oxford University Press, Oxford, 2002). Carlos Bernal Pulido has further helped increase Alexy's influence in the Spanish-speaking world with his book *El principio de proporcionalidad y los derechos fundamentales* (Centro de Estudios Políticos y Constitucionales, Madrid, 2003).

[38] For a detailed discussion on the essential content guarantee and its connection to the principle of proportionality, see Javier Jiménez Campo, *Derechos fundamentales. Concepto y garantías* (Trotta, Madrid, 1999), and Manuel Medina Guerrero, *La vinculación negativa del legislador a los derechos fundamentales* (McGraw-Hill, Madrid, 1996).

from a proportionality analysis, and refers interpreters to the consensus among jurists, as well as ordinary citizens, as to what are the paradigmatic traits of a right that should always be present (or, what are the paradigmatic instances of a particular right being violated). The Court has not come up with a clear theory on this, but it seems to evolve to an understanding that centres on interests rather than concepts and on the principle of proportionality as the guiding tool. Concepts are necessary to fix the provisional image of a right, but when restrictions are imposed and conflicts emerge, proportionality appears to be the key principle.

We have so far discussed the possibility for rights to be restricted. We should note that article 55 of the Constitution empowers the executive branch to go further: it can 'suspend' certain rights in some special circumstances.[39] First, when the government declares a state of siege or exception (as authorized under article 116 of the Constitution), rights may be suspended. The Constitution enumerates which rights may be affected. It bears emphasizing that if a state of alarm is decreed, as has recently happened to address the Covid pandemic, for example, rights may not be suspended. Rights may be restricted very severely indeed, but not suspended. The distinction between restriction and suspension, however, is hard to specify in practice. (See, for example, STC 148/2021, striking down some Covid-related measures.)

Second, measures involving suspension of rights may also be taken against specific persons in connection with investigations of the activities of 'armed bands or terrorist groups'. We should bear in mind that the constitutional framers did their job in a complicated political and social atmosphere, charged with the anger caused by the actions of diverse groups of terrorists, the most important of which was ETA. Until October 2011, ETA was active and caused many deaths. The laws suspending rights have been in operation to facilitate police investigations. Only three fundamental rights, however, may be suspended when fighting against terrorism: the right of the arrested person to be brought to a judge no later than seventy-two hours since the arrest (article 17 para 2); the right to the inviolability of one's home (article 18 para 2); and the right to the secrecy of private communications (article 18 para 3). The Constitution, moreover, lays down some rules to prevent governmental abuses. First, it requires that the specific types of measures to be enforced by the executive branch be established through an organic statute. Second, courts must intervene to check the validity of the actions taken. Third, appropriate forms of parliamentary control must be organized. Fourth, the unjustified or abusive employment of suspension measures will produce criminal responsibility, as a violation of the rights and liberties recognized by the laws. The Constitutional Court, moreover, has also applied the principle of proportionality to rule out suspension measures deemed to be excessive (see for instance, STC 199/1987).

c) Fundamental Rights in the Private Sphere

A controversial question that has emerged in the Constitutional Court´s jurisprudence is this: are private individuals bound by the constitutional recognition of fundamental rights?

Certain rights are only for the state to honour. So, for example, the right not to be punished for actions that were not defined as crimes when they were committed exclusively applies to the state since only the state exercises the power to punish. The right to be compensated for takings of property for the public interest is also for the state to observe. But many other rights are susceptible to being extended to private individuals—thus acquiring 'horizontal effect', as the expression goes.

---

[39] See Pedro Cruz Villalón, *Estados excepcionales y suspensión de garantías* (Tecnos, Madrid, 1984).

In Spain, there is some scholarly and judicial consensus that fundamental rights play a role in the private sphere. Some constitutional rights must constrain the actions of private individuals, for otherwise they would have a very marginal effect. The rights to reputation and to privacy, which are explicitly referred to in the Constitution as 'limits' on freedom of speech and information (article 20 para 4), are usually mentioned to illustrate the idea that individuals must respect the constitutional rights of other individuals when they exercise their own liberties. In the context of labour relationships, moreover, the Constitution enshrines some rights that workers are entitled to invoke in their interactions with employers. The right to strike, for example, is clearly for employers—and not only for the state—to respect. As the Constitutional Court has held, the employer would violate the right to strike if he sanctioned workers on strike, replaced them with other workers, or resorted to lock-out measures as a response (STC 11/1981).

The more controversial question is this: how differently do rights operate when they are alleged against private individuals as opposed to governmental institutions? The fact that private parties to a relationship may both hold fundamental rights against each other makes the situation special. The constitutionally protected claims of A against B may be weaker when B is a private individual since B may also be shielded by a fundamental right against A. Equality, for example, the Court has said, needs to be harmonized with freedom of contract (STC 177/1988). The academic freedom of professors in private schools must be accommodated with the right of the owners of such schools to define their philosophical or religious programme (STC 47/1985). The right to privacy needs to coexist with the right of the employer to control worker performance (STC 98/2000 and 186/2000). An association may have freedom to choose whom to open its doors to, while a governmental entity is forced to deal with everybody, no matter their race or gender. If that association has a monopoly granted by the state, however, its freedom to exclude potential members is reduced (ATC 254/2001). In general, the Court has tried to strike a balance between the interests at stake in each case, considering the principle of proportionality.[40]

A problem that has some connections to horizontal effect, but is conceptually different, is the role of the state in fostering rights. The Constitutional Court has espoused the idea that the state must actively implement public policies to protect and satisfy rights. It has imported from German law the notion that rights have a double dimension: they are subjective rights that their owners can invoke against the government, and they are also objective values of the legal order that all branches of the state must promote (STC 25/1981). This philosophy fits well with article 9 para 2 of the Spanish Constitution, which requires the state to foster the conditions for real liberty and equality.

With this background, it has been relatively easy for the Court to accept the legitimacy of affirmative action programmes, for example. The Court has thus upheld laws that establish quotas for handicapped people in selection processes for public positions (STC 28/1992, STC 69/1994), as well as measures that grant special benefits to women, to cover nursery school expenses for their children (STC 128/1987). More controversially, it has upheld laws that impose gender parity on the lists of candidates presented by political parties during the elections (STC 12/2008). The Court has thus made it impossible for a feminist party to draw up a list that only comprises female candidates. It has gone so far as to accept the constitutionality

---

[40] For a detailed study of the Constitutional Court's case law on the problem of horizontal effect, see Juan María Bilbao Ubillos, *La eficacia de los derechos fundamentales frente a particulares* (Centro de Estudios Políticos y Constitucionales, Madrid, 1997).

of a law that imposes a higher penalty on men than it imposes on women for committing the same type of crime in the context of domestic violence (STC 59/2008).

The Court has also held that certain rights that the Constitution grants individuals in the private sphere place the state under the duty to enact the pertinent regulations to ensure protection. The right of workers to a sufficient remuneration, which is guaranteed in article 35, for example, requires the legislature to establish a minimum wage (STC 31/1984).

This governmental duty of protection may require in some contexts the enactment of criminal laws. The Constitution includes an explicit duty to criminalize offences to the environment and to cultural goods, as well as to punish officers who abuse their powers to suspend rights in extraordinary cases (articles 45, 46, and 55). The notion that the effective protection of fundamental interests may necessitate in some cases the employment of criminal law is well established in the jurisprudence of the European Court of Human Rights.

The most controversial example of criminalization in Spain concerns abortion. The Constitutional Court (STC 53/1985) held that the foetus is entitled to protection, even though it is not a person. To ensure this protection against private actors, the law must penalize abortion. The Court accepted some exceptions, however, concerning extreme circumstances where prohibiting abortion would be against a woman's fundamental rights. In particular, the Court accepted the three types of situations where the law under review had decriminalized abortion (rape, malformation of the foetus, and health risks for the mother). The Court found that the law was nevertheless deficient, for lack of sufficient safeguards to guarantee that the abortions performed as legal fell in practice under one of those exceptions. The law was modified accordingly and was in effect for many years. A new statute was passed in 2010, however, exempting abortion from the reach of criminal law, if performed within the first fourteen weeks of pregnancy. The PP (*Partido Popular*), then in the opposition, challenged the law on the grounds that abortion can only be permitted in particular cases, in light of the Court's doctrine. The Court has not yet rendered its decision at the time of writing—a rather scandalous delay. It is not to be excluded that the Court will revise its earlier doctrine, which was laid down more than three decades ago, and will uphold the new law.

5. Constitutional Organs and Separation of Powers

The Constitution regulates the structure and functions of the basic institutions that make up the machinery of the state. The political system the Constitution lays down is a 'parliamentary monarchy' (article 1 para 3). The most important features of this system are the following.

First, the Head of the State is a monarch who exercises no political power. Both former King Juan Carlos and his son, King Felipe VI, have performed a merely symbolic function. They have wielded no governmental power. The Constitution expressly provides that no act by the monarch is valid if it is not ratified by the pertinent democratic institution (article 56). In some extraordinary circumstances, such as those that arose in Catalonia in October 2017 leading to the proclamation of an independent Catalan Republic, the monarch can become a very relevant figure as the symbol of the unity of Spain. Thus, King Felipe VI delivered a speech to the nation on 3 October 2017, to strongly criticize the breach of the constitutional order that had been perpetrated by the Catalan institutions. The speech had great political impact.

Second, because the political regime established by the Constitution is of a 'parliamentary' nature, there must be a tight connection between the executive branch and the legislative assembly. Indeed, the appointment of the President of the government requires the affirmative vote of a majority in Congress. Although there is a formal separation of powers between the government and Congress, political power is actually concentrated in the hands of the ruling majority. So, the main political checks on the governing majority come from the parties that are in the parliamentary opposition.

Third, in this parliamentary context, ordinary courts and the Constitutional Court play a major role when it comes to subjecting the political branches to a number of limitations, in the name of the rule of law.

In what follows, we will examine the major political institutions that the Constitution has created at the horizontal level. We will later discuss the distribution of power between the state and the regions (Autonomous Communities).

a) Parliament

The national parliament, the *Cortes Generales*, is the organ that 'represents the Spanish people', as article 66 para 1 of the Constitution states. As already indicated, parliament is a bicameral institution, comprising a Congress and a Senate. The Constitution establishes that the term of both houses is four years. When the term expires, new elections are automatically called. It is possible, however, for parliament to be dissolved before the four-year period has elapsed. Specifically, the President of the government has the authority to dissolve the legislative assembly and call early elections (article 115).[41] This is a powerful weapon in his hands, as we will see. The Constitution also establishes two instances where early dissolution is required as a matter of law: when the special procedure of constitutional amendment is initiated (article 168) and when Congress has been unable to invest a President of the government after a certain period of time has elapsed (article 99 para 5).

Political parties are the key players during the elections. They propose the lists of candidates for citizens to vote for. In the case of Congress, the lists are 'closed' (citizens cannot combine candidates from different parties) and 'blocked' (citizens cannot alter the order of the candidates within a particular list). In the case of the Senate, in contrast, the lists are open: citizens can freely choose the candidates, drawn from all the different lists. In practice, however, citizens very rarely exercise this freedom. Normally, they do not alter the lists made up by the political parties of their choice.

Congress currently consists of 350 deputies. The deputies are not elected in a single, nation-wide district, but in different districts. For these purposes, each of the fifty provinces in Spain is a district. The Constitution requires the system to be based on the principle of proportional representation.

The rules that apply to the Senate are different and strongly deviate from proportionality. Each province counts as an electoral district, entitled to appoint four senators each. In addition to these so-called 'provincial' senators elected by the people, the Constitution establishes that the regional parliaments can appoint some senators. This mixture of provincial and regional senators has attracted criticism. Many scholars have pointed out that, if the Senate is to become 'the chamber of territorial representation' where the voices of the regions

---

[41] The Constitution gives the President discretion to decide whether to dissolve both chambers of parliament, or only one of them. In practice, however, the dissolution has always affected both. As a result, the congressional and the senatorial elections have always been held simultaneously.

can be heard (as article 69 para 1 of the Constitution proclaims), all its members (or at least a large majority of them) should be selected by the Autonomous Communities.

An interesting question concerns the power of political parties over members of parliament. The deputy or senator is technically free to act according to his or her own beliefs. As a matter of fact, though, the laws assume that political parties will play a large role in parliamentary life. Thus, all deputies and senators must necessarily belong to a 'parliamentary group'.[42] Such groups, in practice, mirror the diverse political parties that run in the elections.

The existence of parliamentary groups, which receive facilities and funds, is justified by the need to simplify the workings of the legislative assembly. When debates take place, for example, the participants are not individual deputies or senators, but the spokespeople of the different parliamentary groups. There is strong discipline within the groups, moreover. Members of parliament can be fined by the groups they belong to if they fail to attend the meetings without justification, or if they do not vote according to the party line. These are not state sanctions, but 'private' sanctions imposed by such groups. In the parliamentary commissions, moreover, deputies and senators can be replaced by others at any point in time, according to party wishes.

Individual deputies and senators are also weak as a result of them not having their own staff to help them with their parliamentary activities. They must rely on the services provided by the groups they belong to in order to get the information and the advice they need to deal with the typically complex issues that are discussed in a modern parliament. It is important to note, in this connection, that there is a high level of rotation from legislature to legislature, sometimes reaching levels between 45 per cent and 60 per cent.[43] This lack of continuity is not conducive, of course, to the professionalization of the Spanish parliament.

So parliamentary groups (and the parties they stand for) are of great significance in practice. Now, what happens if a member of parliament is expelled from his party? Should he abandon his seat—which he obtained, after all, because he was included in the electoral list of that party? Or should he keep it? There has been great controversy over this problem. The Constitution explicitly says that the members of the *Cortes Generales* are not subject to *mandato imperativo* (article 67 para 2). The parliamentary mandate is 'free'. The historical meaning of this rule is clear: the members of parliament represent the interests of the nation in its entirety, and they meet in the general assembly in order to deliberate and negotiate. They cannot be subjected, therefore, to instructions issued by their local electors. The question, however, is whether members of parliament can also be immune from the decisions of the political parties, which the Constitution conceives as the main instruments of political participation (article 6). The Portuguese Constitution explicitly provides that deputies will lose their seats if they register as a member of a party other than that for which they stood for election (article 160). The Spanish Constitutional Court, by contrast, has ruled that the representative is entitled to keep the seat (STC 5/1983, STC 10/1983).[44] The Court's holding rests on the view that when citizens cast their votes in the elections, they express their support for individual representatives, and not for a political party. The Court is aware, of course, that— with the exception of the Senate—political parties present electoral lists that are 'closed' and

---

[42] On the legal status and functions of parliamentary groups, see Alejandro Saiz Arnaiz, *Los grupos parlamentarios* (Congreso de los Diputados, Madrid, 1989).

[43] José M Magone, *Contemporary Spanish Politics* (Routledge, London, 2009) 112.

[44] The Court's decision concerned a law that regulated municipal elections, but its holding is clearly applicable to members of the *Cortes Generales*.

'blocked', as explained earlier. Yet, the Court insists that the individual representative is directly connected to the voters, so that it violates the latter's fundamental rights to political participation (as guaranteed in article 23 of the Constitution) for a law to provide that representatives must relinquish their seats if they are expelled from the party. Some judges on the Court filed dissenting opinions, however, and scholars disagree among themselves.

Let us now turn to the functions of the *Cortes Generales*. A first function concerns the selection and control of the government.[45] Because Spain has adopted a parliamentary system, there needs to be a tight relationship between the majority in the legislative assembly and the executive branch. The system works on the assumption that there is a majority in Congress that endorses the political programme and the specific policies that the President of the government and his cabinet are pursuing. Should that parliamentary support cease to exist, several mechanisms are available to overcome the *impasse*, which may lead to the appointment of another President, or to the calling of an early general election. The crucial figure here is the President: since the rest of the cabinet is freely appointed by him and will have to step down if he is removed, it is the President that needs to obtain and retain the parliamentary confidence.

The investiture of the President requires an explicit decision by Congress. Normally, the decision is made when general elections have been held and a new parliament has been formed. But the same procedure must be followed in the more extraordinary cases where the President dies, resigns, or is removed as a result of loss of parliamentary confidence.

The candidate to the presidency is formally proposed by the King, with the countersignature of the President of Congress. The monarch, however, has to act in light of the electoral outcome and the agreements reached by the political parties. The candidate proposed by the King must then proceed to explain his governmental programme to Congress. A debate takes place where the different political groups express their points of view and votes are taken. Deputies are called one by one and are asked to express their vote orally. If an absolute majority of deputies vote in favour, the candidate is appointed President by the King. Otherwise, a second vote is cast forty-eight hours later, and a simple majority of deputies is then sufficient. If the candidate does not obtain a simple majority, the King must make new proposals (which does not necessarily mean new candidates), and the same procedure is followed. If no candidate gets the required majority within two months after the first vote is taken, the Constitution provides that both houses of parliament must be dissolved, and general elections called. This happened for the first time in 2016: the elections that were held on 20 December 2015 generated a parliament that was unable to select a President of the government, so the parliament was dissolved, and new elections took place on 26 June 2016. A new government was finally installed headed by Mariano Rajoy. The same thing happened after the elections of 28 April 2019: parliament had to be dissolved, and new elections were held on 10 November 2019, which finally led to the appointment of Pedro Sánchez as President.

Because a strong connection must exist between the parliamentary majority and the President of the government, the Constitution provides that the latter can be removed if the confidence he initially obtained disappears at a later stage. The Constitution, however, seeks to protect governmental stability by limiting the circumstances under which the President of the government is obliged to step down. The mere fact, for example, that the executive has lost a vote on an important bill does not mean that the government comes to an end. Only

---

[45] Miguel Revenga Sánchez, *La formación del gobierno en la Constitución española de 1978* (Centro de Estudios Constitucionales, Madrid, 1988); Joaquín García Morillo, *El control parlamentario del Gobierno en el ordenamiento español* (Congreso de los Diputados, Madrid, 1985).

specific mechanisms can force a governmental change, according to the Constitution. It is worthy of note, in this connection, that the constitutional framers believed that minority governments would be frequent. It was actually a minority government in the hands of UCD that ruled the country when the Constitution was being written in 1977–1978. The framers thought that it would be extremely rare for a single party to obtain an absolute majority of congressional seats in the following years. Among other things, they had the memory of the very fragmented parliaments that were formed during the Second Republic.[46] For a long while, events developed differently than predicted, since both PSOE (in 1982–1986, 1986–1989, and 1989–1993) and PP (2000–2004 and 2011–2015) obtained absolute majorities. The periods of minority governments were less frequent: those of 1993–1996 and 2004–2008 (under PSOE) and 1996–2000 (under PP).

Things have dramatically changed in recent years, however: as already mentioned, new parties have emerged in Spain with significant popular support (*Ciudadanos* and *Vox* on the right, *Podemos* on the left). The composition of Congress is nowadays more fragmented, so governmental stability is harder to achieve.

The key instrument to force a government down is the so-called *moción de censura* (articles 113 and 114 para 2 of the Constitution). The motion can be brought by at least one tenth of the deputies. Following the German model, the Constitution requires a 'constructive' motion: the challenging deputies must present their own candidate to the Presidency. It is thus not sufficient for the assembly to agree that the current President should step down. It is also necessary to reach an agreement as to who should replace him. The debate in the assembly focuses on the candidate to the Presidency. For the motion to be approved, moreover, an absolute majority is required. Note the asymmetry, in favour of governmental stability: to be invested President, a simple majority is sufficient; for someone to be appointed later, through a 'motion of censure', a larger majority is required. If the motion is successful, the King automatically appoints the alternative candidate to the Presidency. In practice, no motion of censure succeeded for decades. Only recently has such a motion achieved its purpose: Pedro Sánchez (PSOE) brought President Mariano Rajoy down in June 2018. To a large extent, the corruption scandals affecting Rajoy's party made it possible for a very heterogeneous combination of political groups (including Catalan secessionists) to agree to install Sánchez as the new President.

The other mechanism that can lead to the removal of the President is initiated by the President himself, after having listened to his ministers. The Constitution provides that he can submit a so-called *cuestión de confianza* to Congress concerning his governmental programme or a general policy statement (articles 112 and 114 para 1 of the Constitution). The idea is to test the waters in the assembly and press the majority to express clearly whether the government still enjoys parliamentary confidence. The President cannot submit a specific legal proposal and condition his continuance in office upon the parliamentary approval of that proposal. A more general political statement or programme is to be debated. The President survives the motion if a simple majority of the votes in Congress are favourable. Otherwise, the President is removed, and a new President needs to be proposed by the King, following the ordinary procedure that was explained before.

In practice, governments have very rarely used this mechanism. If the President is confronting a difficult situation, the normal reaction is for him to dissolve parliament and call early elections. This is a powerful weapon that the Constitution places in his hands. The mere

---

[46] Lynn M Maurer, *El poder del Parlamento: Congreso y políticas públicas en España* (Centro de Estudios Políticos y Constitucionales, Madrid, 2008) 125.

threat that elections will be held earlier than expected may push the majority in the legislative assembly to be more disciplined. The coalition of parties that support the government may reinforce their ties to prevent the dissolution of parliament. In addition, the dissolution prerogative allows the President to choose the best moment to hold elections, in light of the general interests of the country or, more likely, for partisan reasons.

Regarding these two procedures to bring a government down, the Senate plays no part at all. But there is another way for parliament to check the government, through techniques that do not seek to remove the President and his government, but merely to criticize and control. Here the Senate, as well as Congress, plays a part. In practice, of course, it is the political parties in the opposition that monitor and censure the activities of the executive branch. The parliamentary majority (especially when based on a single party) will tend to be supportive of the government.[47]

In addition to selecting and checking the government, the *Cortes Generales* have the authority to enact legislation. The government, however, has pre-eminence in the legislative process: the vast majority of statutes passed by parliament originate in a proposal drafted by the executive branch. This is consistent with the notion that, in a parliamentary democracy, the government has a political programme that a majority in the legislative assembly endorses and that needs to be translated into new laws that the government is expected to initiate. A study found that the percentage of enacted statutes initiated by the executive branch in the different parliamentary periods was as follows: 76.2 per cent (1979–1982); 85.3 per cent (1982–1986); 88.4 per cent (1986–1989); 73.7 per cent (1989–1993); 80 per cent (1993–1996); and 78.9 per cent (1996–2000).[48] It is important to note that the projects submitted by the executive have priority in the parliamentary agenda (article 89 of the Constitution). The government, moreover, is always entitled to withdraw the legislative proposal it has sent Congress.

Alternatively, the legislative process can begin when Congress or the Senate presents a 'proposition of statute' (*proposición de ley*). Such propositions can only be submitted by fifteen deputies, or by a parliamentary group with the sole signature of its spokesperson (in the case of Congress); or by twenty-five senators or a parliamentary group (in the case of the Senate).

The law takes it for granted that parliamentary groups are the engines of the legislative process, together with the government. Very marginally do other actors initiate the legislative proceedings, such as citizens or regional parliaments. Concerning citizens, we already saw that the Constitution is very restrictive. Proposals must be signed by at least 500,000 citizens, and many matters are excluded. With respect to the regional parliaments, the Constitution allows them to request the national government to submit a 'project of law'. More importantly, the Constitution also permits them to send a 'proposition of law' directly to Congress, and to appoint a group of no more than three regional deputies to defend that proposition before Congress. The number of proposals submitted in this manner has increased throughout the years, but it is still relatively low.

As far as the Senate is concerned, it has a marginal role to play in the legislative process. The Constitution establishes (in article 90) that a statute passed by Congress can be vetoed by the Senate only if an absolute majority of senators are agreed—a simple majority is not

---

[47] Manuel Aragón Reyes, 'Gobierno y forma de gobierno: problemas actuales', in Manuel Aragón and Ángel J. Gómez Montoro (eds), *El Gobierno. Problemas constitucionales* (Centro de Estudios Políticos y Constitucionales, Madrid, 2005) 61–62.

[48] Lynn M Maurer, *El poder del Parlamento: Congreso y políticas públicas en España* (n 46) 59–60.

sufficient. Moreover, the veto can be immediately overcome by Congress if an absolute majority of deputies insists on the initial text. If no such absolute majority obtains, Congress need only wait for two months, and a simple majority is then sufficient to overcome the veto. If, instead of a veto, the Senate seeks to introduce amendments, it can do so by simple majority, but Congress may immediately decide whether to accept them or not, also by simple majority.

As has already been pointed out, the government is the main actor throughout the legislative process. This is not to say, however, that the parliamentary groups have no capacity to influence the legislative outcomes. This influence has varied over time because of several factors. The key factor is whether the government can simply rely on its own party, which has obtained a majority of the seats in Congress, or instead needs the additional support of some other parties. As already mentioned, there have been periods of majority governments (under PSOE: 1982–1986; 1986–1989; 1989–1993; under PP: 2000–2004; 2011–2015), as well as periods of minority governments (under PSOE: 1993–1996; 2004–2008; 2008–2011; under PP: 1996–2000; 2016–2018). Not surprisingly, the capacity of parliamentary groups to influence the legislative agenda is larger in the latter cases. Historically, both the PSOE and the PP minority governments had to negotiate with regional and other smaller parties to have their legislative programmes enacted into law, though no coalition government was ever agreed upon. Recently, PSOE and *Podemos* reached an agreement to install a coalition government, which started to exercise its functions in January 2020. This coalition government, however, still needs the parliamentary support of smaller parties (including the main Catalan secessionist party on the left: ERC, *Esquerra Republicana de Catalunya*).

In addition to producing legislation, parliament has an important responsibility: it approves the general budget of the state. Although it is the government that has the exclusive power to propose the budget, parliament needs to vote for it. It bears emphasizing that the approval of the budget is a crucial moment in political life. It is impossible for the government to implement its legislative choices without getting the parliamentary authorization to spend money for the various programmes. If the government loses that vote, it runs into serious trouble. Even if the previous budget is prorogated, it is harder for the government to go on. This often leads to new elections—as happened in 2019, for example, when the failure of Pedro Sánchez's cabinet to obtain the necessary votes to enact the new budget caused the dissolution of parliament.

b) The Government

The Constitution bestows upon the government the 'directive function' (article 97). The government, indeed, runs the state machinery to reach the public goals that figure in the political programme endorsed by the parliamentary majority. The government has at its disposal the different organs that make up the public administration.

The Constitution establishes that the government comprises the President and the ministers. It can also include vice-presidents and any other members that the laws establish (article 98 para 1). Within the government, the President enjoys clear pre-eminence since the link of support between parliament and the government runs through him. The President is invested by Congress and can be removed by the latter through the two mechanisms we examined previously. The vice-presidents and the ministers, by contrast, get their positions from the President, who freely appoints and removes them.[49]

---

[49] The candidate to the Presidency is not required to announce the composition of his future government when his investiture is discussed and voted upon in Congress. The practice is for the President to reveal the name of his

A feature consistent with the centrality of the President is the fact that the Constitution establishes that all the members of the government lose their positions when the President leaves (article 101). This situation occurs when general elections are held, when the President loses parliamentary support in the manner specified in the Constitution, or when he dies or resigns. The government then becomes a care-taker government (*gobierno en funciones*) that needs to be replaced by a new one. A new President will be chosen, who will then proceed to make the pertinent ministerial appointments. The care-taker government can only administer ordinary matters unless the general interest or an urgent situation justify taking special measures. It is not allowed to call general elections or a referendum, for example, or draft the general budget, or submit legislative proposals to parliament.

The President's formal powers are reinforced when he is the leader of the political party that won the general elections. Although his appointment depends on the votes of a majority of deputies, democratic legitimacy is also transferred to him in a more direct way. Because citizens have in mind the different candidates to the Presidency of the government when they cast their votes in the parliamentary elections, the candidate that belongs to the victorious party can claim to have a mandate from the people.

The Constitution entrusts the President with some specific decisions of great political import, such as deciding whether to submit a parliamentary 'question of confidence' (article 114), calling a referendum (article 92), calling general elections (article 115) or attacking a law through an abstract review challenge brought to the Constitutional Court (article 162). These attributes help reinforce the President's prominence within the executive branch.

We must now turn to an examination of the main tasks the government is charged with. The Constitution provides that the government 'directs domestic and foreign policy, the civil and military administration and the defense of the state' (article 97). The government's directive function is especially salient in the field of foreign affairs. The need for states to deal and negotiate with other states has often led constitutional systems to grant the executive branch more leeway when engaging in foreign policy. The way international treaties are agreed upon, for example, is revealing. Negotiations to enter a treaty can only be entertained by the executive branch. Parliament intervenes later, sometimes to be informed about the treaty, other times to give its consent. Similarly, it is for the government to declare war or peace, though it needs parliament's approval.

In addition to the directive function, the Constitution explicitly provides that the government is authorized to issue regulations (*reglamentos*). These norms have a lower rank than statutes passed by parliament.

The government is also empowered by the Constitution to produce two types of norms that have the same rank as statutes. Because they have the same rank, such norms are capable of repealing or amending any previous statutory provisions. The first type of norm is called *decreto-ley*.[50] Article 86 authorizes the government to issue such a norm in the event of 'an extraordinary and urgent necessity'. The *decreto-ley* produces effects since its promulgation, but it is necessary for Congress to ratify it within thirty days (the Senate does not take part in this procedure). If the decree is validated by Congress, it continues to operate for the indefinite future. If, instead, it is not validated, it is 'repealed', as the Constitution says. The decree

---

ministers after being appointed. An exception occurred in 1982, when Felipe González gave the list of his future Ministers during the parliamentary debates leading to his investiture.

[50] For a systematic examination of this type of norm, see Ana Carmona Contreras, *La configuración constitucional del Decreto-ley* (Centro de Estudios Políticos y Constitucionales, Madrid, 1998).

thus stops producing legal effects. In general, the Constitutional Court has been very deferential in its review of the governmental judgment that an extraordinary or urgent need arises at a particular moment. The government has used this legal instrument quite often. Many important changes in the economic sphere, for example, have been introduced by *decreto-ley*. The fact that the Court has been very deferential towards the government has encouraged the latter to make an active use of this source of law.[51]

The other type of norm is the *decreto legislativo*. The government can be granted by parliament legislative authority to regulate particular matters[52] (articles 82 to 85 of the Constitution regulates this possibility). This is a useful technique to produce more coherent legislative pieces, and to introduce clarity in areas that are governed by scattered texts. Important laws like the Civil Code, and the laws regulating civil and criminal procedures, for example, were historically introduced in Spain through this mechanism, which the Constitution of 1978 preserves.

c) The Public Administration

The government can only exercise its directive function in an effective manner if it can use the public administration (*Administración Pública*) to implement its policies. The administrative apparatus in a 'social state' (as the Constitution proclaims Spain to be) is bound to be large. Beyond exercising traditional police powers, the administration provides many important services and goods to citizens, who are entitled to certain levels of social and economic wellbeing.

The Constitution lists some principles that govern the structure and performance of the administration. Article 103 mentions the principles of hierarchy, decentralization, coordination, objectivity, and efficacy. It also provides that civil servants must be recruited through a system based on merits and ability. In practice, however, political connections have too much weight in the higher echelons of the administration.[53] Some scholars have suggested that the law should require the government to inform Congress of the appointments being considered. Parliament would then be able to scrutinize the technical qualifications of the candidates. Even if no veto power were granted to Congress, at least there would be checks.[54]

Given the politicization at the highest levels of the administrative apparatus, it is not surprising that the reaction, in part, has been to establish independent agencies or authorities in some fields. The need has been felt to create institutions that are detached from the government, to depoliticize certain decision-making processes.[55]

The first such agency was the Council of Nuclear Security. The law drew inspiration from the American and British models. A more important example is the Bank of Spain, which was given an independent status to comply with European Union norms, as laid down in the Maastricht Treaty. Other examples are the National Stock Exchange Commission, the

---

[51] The Court, however, has struck down *decretos-ley* in a few cases. See for instance, STC 55/2005 and STC 137/2011.

[52] On this legal technique, see Ignacio Gutiérrez Gutiérrez, *Los controles de la legislación delegada* (Centro de Estudios Constitucionales, Madrid, 1995).

[53] For a critical view, see Rafael Jiménez Asensio, *Altos cargos y directivos públicos (Un estudio sobre las relaciones entre política y administración en España)* (IVAP, Vitoria-Gasteiz, 1996).

[54] For a proposal along these lines, see Roberto Blanco Valdés, *Las conexiones políticas* (Alianza Editorial, Madrid, 2001) 156–164.

[55] On the constitutional status of these agencies, see Mariano Magide Herrero, *Límites constitucionales de las administraciones independientes* (Instituto Nacional de Administración Pública, Madrid, 2000) and Artemi Rallo Lombarte, *La constitucionalidad de las administraciones independientes* (Tecnos, Madrid, 2002).

Market of Communications Commission, the National Competition Commission, the Data Protection Agency, and the State Council of Audiovisual Media.

Some features tend to be common among these different agencies. First, the government often appoints their members, but it cannot freely remove them. They hold their positions for a limited period (though it is often possible to renew the appointment once). This job security ensures a certain degree of independence. Sometimes, the government is expected, or even required, to fill the vacancies with people that represent different political groups. Other times, parliament has a say in the appointment process. Second, the government cannot issue instructions to the agencies as to how they should perform their task. Third, the agencies are often partially funded out of the fees they charge for their services. This ensures a measure of economic independence. Fourth, many of the decisions made by the agencies cannot be challenged before the government. Instead, they are directly reviewed for their validity by the courts. These and other features secure the autonomy of the agencies, but it is a limited autonomy. The government, after all, does appoint the members of many of these administrative entities. And it is sometimes possible for the government to influence their strategies in informal ways.

Considering the important powers that the executive branch can exercise, it is necessary to secure the right mechanisms to control its actions. As will be discussed later, courts have a crucial responsibility in this regard. In addition, other institutions have been set up. Chief among them is the Ombudsman, who is appointed by the *Cortes Generales* to supervise the administration for purposes of guarding the fundamental rights protected in Title I of the Constitution. The Ombudsman can initiate inquiries on the request of interested individuals. The complaints cannot be anonymous (they must be signed), but no lawyers are required, and no fees are charged. In addition, the deputies, and senators (or the pertinent parliamentary commissions) can ask the Ombudsman to investigate a particular matter. And he may start an inquiry on his own motion.

Public authorities must offer their cooperation to the Ombudsman. The latter is entitled to read administrative documents and files, and to interview the pertinent staff. It is a criminal offense for someone to refuse the cooperation requested. Even documents that are classified as secret can be accessed unless the Council of Ministers decides otherwise. If a judicial decision is pending in a particular case, however, the Ombudsman must abstain from investigating.

When the Ombudsman finishes his investigation concerning a particular affair, he can make proposals. The administration is free to follow them or not. The Ombudsman can also make suggestions of a more general character concerning the norms and practices that need to be changed. In general, the administration tends to agree with the Ombudsman when it answers its suggestions and recommendations.

d) Ordinary Courts

The existence of independent courts is crucial in order to ensure the rule of law and thus subject public institutions to the laws constraining their powers. The Constitution devotes a specific title to the judiciary (Title VI).[56]

Judges are part of a bureaucratic body whose members have tenure until the age of retirement fixed by the law. Judges 'may only be dismissed, suspended, transferred or retired on the grounds, and subject to the guarantees, provided by law', article 117 para 2 of the

---

[56] On the constitutional status of the judiciary, see Ignacio de Otto, *Estudios sobre el Poder Judicial* (Ministerio de Justicia, 1989) and Luis María Díez-Picazo, *Régimen constitucional del Poder Judicial* (Civitas, Madrid, 1991).

Constitution announces. To safeguard judicial independence, moreover, certain delicate decisions concerning the administrative status of judges are placed in the hands of bodies that are insulated from the executive branch. The General Council of the Judiciary plays a key role in this regard, as we will see.

Judicial independence, interestingly, also shields judges against any pressures from their judicial peers. The highest courts can only correct the lower courts' interpretation and application of the law through the system of appeals. No judicial institution can issue instructions on the law for lower courts to follow, though the latter are generally expected to interpret the law in conformity with the jurisprudence produced by the highest courts.[57]

The Constitution also mentions the principle of 'judicial responsibility'. Indeed, independence does not mean that judges are immune from all kinds of legal consequences if they make mistakes or otherwise cause damages. This is, of course, a delicate matter. The laws establish different types of responsibility: disciplinary (when administrative rules are breached), civil (when there has been a judicial error, or damages have been caused some other way), and even criminal. It should be noted, particularly, that judges commit the crime of *prevaricación* if they knowingly render a decision that is clearly illegal or render such a decision through serious negligence or inexcusable ignorance.

The Spanish constitutional framers distrusted the executive power when it comes to governing judges. For this reason, they established a special institution, the General Council of the Judiciary, drawing inspiration from the French and Italian systems.[58]

The Council comprises twenty members, who then appoint the President of the Supreme Court. The latter will also preside over the Council. According to the Constitution (article 122), the twenty members are to be appointed as follows: twelve from amongst judges and magistrates (*entre jueces y magistrados*), four by a three-fifths majority of Congress, and four by a three-fifths majority of the Senate. The law implementing this provision in 1985 established that the first group of twelve members were to be judges, but were not to be elected by judges, but by Congress (six of them) and the Senate (the other six). There was a huge controversy about this law, and objections were raised on constitutional grounds. The Constitutional Court upheld the law against the challenges that were launched (STC 108/1986). An amendment was introduced some years later (in 2001), establishing a mixed solution: the twelve members are still appointed by the parliamentary chambers, but the list of candidates is now drawn by judges.

The members of the Council occupy their offices for a limited five-year period, which is non-renewable. All of them are appointed at the same time, which is not a very reasonable arrangement. Every time a new Council is appointed, too many plans are conceived from scratch. The organ lacks institutional memory.

The Council's most important responsibility is to make a number of administrative decisions that affect courts: selecting and educating judges, making judicial appointments, deciding promotions, inspecting the courts, granting judges administrative permissions for various matters, imposing disciplinary sanctions on those who violate the laws. These are all delicate decisions that it might be too risky to charge the executive branch with. The Council, which is insulated from that branch, seems to be better equipped to handle such matters. Its decisions, moreover, can be reviewed by the Supreme Court by way of an appeal.

---

[57] For a collection of essays on this topic, edited by the General Council of the Judiciary, see *La fuerza vinculante de la jurisprudencia* (Consejo General del Poder Judicial, Madrid, 2001).

[58] On the origin and justification of this institution, see Manuel José Terol Becerra, *El Consejo General del Poder Judicial* (Centro de Estudios Constitucionales, Madrid, 1990).

It should be observed that judicial promotions, though decided by the Council, are almost always the result of the mechanical application of the criteria established by the law. Seniority is the basic standard that is employed. Only exceptionally does the Council have discretion to choose whom to appoint, from amongst the various candidates that meet the legal requirements. This is so, for example, with respect to the appointment of Supreme Court judges.

It is important to emphasize the critical role that the judiciary plays in order to subject the executive branch to the rule of law. In this connection, Spain has followed the European tendency to set up specialized courts for this purpose. 'Administrative courts' are thus bestowed with the authority to control the legality of the actions of the government and the administration. At their summit sits the third chamber of the Supreme Court. In spite of their specialization, these courts belong to the ordinary judicial branch, and are granted the same guarantees of independence that apply to courts in general.[59]

The Constitution is quite categorical when it provides that the administration is 'fully subject to the statutes and the law' (article 103 para 1). This is an important statement. It clarifies that the norms to be observed cannot be reduced to statutes (or regulations). Additionally, there constitutional principles to be considered, as well as 'general principles of law', which have traditionally provided courts with a powerful instrument to curb the excesses of the executive branch.

The full subjection to the law also means that there are no areas of activity that are exempt from the law. Sometimes the content of the decision to be rendered by the executive branch is clearly predetermined in the relevant legal provision. Other times, by contrast, the executive branch has discretion to decide (*discrecionalidad*): the law merely lays down a framework, within which there is ample room for manoeuvre. But even in these cases, legal limits apply. In this connection, the principle of proportionality is increasingly used by courts to test the reasonableness of administrative decisions that affect private interests. Those decisions, courts have held, must attain public goals with the least restrictive means, and must be based on a reasonable balance of the costs and benefits involved.[60] So judges may be more or less deferential when reviewing governmental and administrative acts, but they cannot hold a category of acts to be exempt from judicial review.[61]

Courts are not only empowered to invalidate actions by the executive branch, they are also authorized to fix the compensation the state must pay to indemnify the individuals who have been harmed by its actions or omissions. The Constitution is quite generous in the way it proclaims the principle of state liability for damages. Article 106 para 2 provides that private individuals, under the terms established by law, shall be entitled to compensation for the harm they may suffer in their property or rights, except in cases of *force majeure*, whenever the harm derives from the operation of public services. There is no need for there to be a malfunction of the administration: if an individual suffers a collateral damage that he is not legally obliged to bear, he is entitled to compensation, even if the administration has acted properly. Even the damages caused by the legislature may be indemnified. There has been

---

[59] For a comprehensive treatment of Spanish administrative law, see Eduardo García de Enterría and Tomás-Ramón Fernández, *Curso de Derecho Administrativo* (Civitas, Madrid, 2017).

[60] For a detailed analysis of the application of the principle of proportionality by Spanish courts, see Daniel Sarmiento Ramírez-Escudero, *El control de proporcionalidad de la actividad administrativa* (Tirant lo Blanch, Valencia, 2004).

[61] There has been debate on how deferentially courts should review the discretionary decisions made by the executive branch. For a complete picture of the debate, which was especially passionate in the nineties, see Mariano Bacigalupo Sagesse, *La discrecionalidad administrativa (Estructura normativa, control judicial y límites constitucionales a su atribución)* (Marcial Pons, Madrid, 1997).

debate about the precise limits of this doctrine, however. Some scholars have criticized the Supreme Court for having come too close to a regime of strict liability, which may have undesirable consequences.[62]

e) The Constitutional Court

Given the concentration of power in the hands of the governing political majority, the role of the Constitutional Court is particularly important as an institution that is authorized to test the validity of legislation against the Constitution.[63]

The constitutional framers easily agreed that a Constitutional Court had to be created.[64] This is not surprising. Firstly, various European nations at that time had already established such an institution. Particularly Germany, France, and Italy had done so, which were the three countries whose political systems were most influential in the framing of the Spanish Constitution. The reasons that are usually offered to justify the centralization of judicial review of legislation in a single body were applicable to Spain too: legal certainty is deemed to be better protected if a single tribunal is in charge of checking ordinary law against constitutional norms, instead of conferring that power on all courts. To the extent, moreover, that statutes are enacted by a democratic parliament, the general feeling is that their validity should only be reviewed by a special institution whose members are selected in more democratic ways than ordinary judges are. The justices of the Constitutional Court, moreover, tend to be prestigious jurists who exhibit diverse professional backgrounds. Some of them have served as judges and prosecutors, while others are lawyers, professors, or public servants. This professional diversity is a desirable feature of the membership of a tribunal that must address complex constitutional issues.[65]

Secondly, Spain had already set up a Constitutional Court during the Second Republic. At that time, Spain was one of the few countries (together with Austria, Czechoslovakia, and Liechtenstein) that followed the so-called 'Kelsenian' model of constitutional review.[66] General Franco's dictatorship abolished this republican institution, but it served as a historical precedent for the constitutional framers in 1977–1978.

Thirdly, the ordinary judges that had been appointed under Franco's dictatorial regime were not replaced when democracy came, despite the fact that the liberal–democratic commitments of many of them were rather weak. Given this historical circumstance, it made no sense to grant regular courts the power to check the validity of the laws enacted by the new democratic parliament. The framers preferred to ascribe the task of legislative review to a separate body, whose members would be selected by the political branches.

---

[62] See, for example, Eduardo García de Enterría, *La responsabilidad patrimonial del Estado Legislador en el Derecho español* (Civitas, Madrid, 2007).

[63] The most important commentary on the law that regulates the structure and functions of the Constitutional Court in Juan Luis Requejo (ed), *Comentarios a la Ley Orgánica del Tribunal Constitucional* (Tribunal Constitucional, Madrid, 2001). For an interesting and influential set of studies on the theoretical foundations of this institution, see Francisco Rubio Llorente and Javier Jiménez Campo, *Estudios sobre la jurisdicción constitucional* (MacGraw-Hill, New York, 1998).

[64] See Pablo Pérez Tremps, *Tribunal Constitucional y poder judicial* (Centro de Estudios Constitucionales, Madrid, 1985) 97–109.

[65] For a general discussion of the potential advantages of constitutional courts, see Victor Ferreres Comella, *Constitutional Courts and Democratic Values. A European Perspective* (n 21).

[66] For a general study of the emergence of the 'European model' of judicial review between the First and the Second World Wars, with a specific examination of the Spanish version of it as it operated during the Second Republic, see Pedro Cruz Villalón, *La formación del sistema europeo de control de constitucionalidad (1918–1939)* (Centro de Estudios Constitucionales, Madrid, 1987).

For all these reasons, the framers easily agreed to set up a Constitutional Court in Spain, as part of the new political order.

The Constitutional Court comprises twelve members, all of whom must be prestigious jurists with at least fifteen years of professional experience. Four of them are selected by Congress, four by the Senate, two by the government, and the other two by the General Council of the Judiciary. Parliament has thus an important say in the appointment process: most judges on the Court (eight out of twelve) are chosen by it.[67]

Despite this strong link between the Constitutional Court and parliament, it is impossible for a transient majority to appoint a Court of its liking. A super-majority of three-fifths is necessary for both Congress and the Senate to nominate the justices. This means that the governing majority must negotiate the names of the candidates with the main party (or parties) in the opposition. Unlike ordinary judges, the members of the Constitutional Court do not serve indefinitely until retirement age, but for a fixed period of nine years. Every three years, there is a partial renewal of the Court. For these purposes, the twelve justices are distributed in three different groups, depending on the institution that appointed them (Congress, the Senate, the government, and the General Council of the Judiciary). The justices can only be reappointed after a partial renewal of the Court has taken place.

The Court performs different functions. Most importantly, it controls the constitutionality of statutes (or other types of norms of the same rank). Different procedures can be employed to trigger the Court's review: constitutional challenges, constitutional questions, and preventive control. Constitutional challenges (*recursos de inconstitucionalidad*) can be initiated by the President of the government, the Ombudsman, fifty deputies, or fifty senators. Through this procedure, laws are attacked in the abstract (within three months of their official publication). In practice, the fifty deputies or fifty senators belong to the parliamentary opposition: they disagree with the majority and, since they take the statute to be problematic from a constitutional point of view, they decide to bring an action to the Court.

When the law has been enacted by the national parliament, the regional governments or their legislative assemblies can also file constitutional challenges. Such challenges are normally related to questions concerning the territorial distribution of power. But the Court has interpreted the standing rules broadly: if the law has some connection to the sphere of responsibilities of the regional government, a constitutional attack can be launched on other grounds too (STC 56/1990). So, for example, the regional parliament of Navarra was granted standing to question a law that restricted the fundamental rights of foreign citizens (STC 236/2007).

The effects of the Court's decisions are *erga omnes*: they bind all branches of government. If the statutory provision under examination is found to be unconstitutional, it is declared invalid. Normally, this means that the provision will be eliminated from the legal system. Sometimes, however, the Court thinks it better to 'save' the provision: it establishes the conditions under which it can remain in the legal system (see for example, STC 74/1987). In other cases, the Court has deferred to a future moment the effects of a declaration of unconstitutionality (see for instance, STC 195/1998).

---

[67] With respect to the Senate, the law was reformed in 2007 to permit the legislative assemblies of the Autonomous Communities to propose the names of possible candidates. The Senate was to choose the constitutional justices from among the lists provided by the Communities. The Constitutional Court, however, has introduced an important qualification: if the candidates proposed by the Autonomous Communities fail to obtain the required super-majority of three-fifths, the Senate is then free to select others (STC 49/2008).

A special rule applies to regional Statutes of Autonomy. Given the constitutional importance of these norms, which establish the institutional framework of regional governments, the law provides that it is possible to challenge their constitutional validity before they are enacted, and before a referendum is held to obtain popular ratification of the text. This special rule was introduced in 2015 to avoid the situation that had occurred in 2010 when the Constitutional Court struck down some provisions of the Catalan Statute of Autonomy, which had been approved by Catalan citizens in a regional referendum (see STC 31/2010).

A second avenue to get the Court exercise legislative review is the constitutional question procedure (*cuestión de inconstitucionalidad*).[68] When ordinary judges handling disputes entertain doubts about the constitutionality of the relevant law, or are convinced that the law is unconstitutional, they are required to refer a question to the Constitutional Court. The proceedings in the particular case are stayed until the Court gives an answer. There is thus a division of labour between the Constitutional Court and ordinary judges. The procedures that the Court follows, and the effects of its decisions, are basically the same as those that apply to abstract constitutional challenges.

Interestingly, the law provides that, before an ordinary judge sends a statute to the Constitutional Court for its review, she must try to find an interpretation of that statute that makes it consistent with the Constitution. That is, if the applicable legal provision can be read in different ways, the judge must choose that reading that harmonizes it with constitutional principles. The Court should intervene only when this attempt at *interpretación conforme* has been unsuccessful. This does not mean, of course, that judges are entitled to distort a statutory provision through interpretive means. The constitutionally inspired reading of the statute should not be at odds with its clear textual meaning and the underlying legislative intention. As the Court has held, the judge should not use the Constitution to support an interpretation of the statute that is *contra legem* (STC 138/2005). The problem, however, is that it is not always easy to determine whether a particular reading of the statute is still possible as a fair interpretation of it or is, on the contrary, so strained a reading that it should count as a prohibited, *contra legem* interpretation.

In addition to constitutional challenges and questions, a third procedure exists in order to check international treaties (article 95 para 2 of the Constitution). Once treaties are signed by Spain, but before they are finally consented to, the Court can be requested to determine whether they respect the Constitution. Congress, the Senate, and the government can petition the Court to rule on the issue. A parliamentary minority, however, is not entitled to do so, a feature of the system that has attracted criticism.[69] The justification for this mechanism is that it is particularly useful to clarify the underlying constitutional issue before Spain ratifies a treaty that will affect third parties on the international level. If the Court rules that there is an incompatibility, the treaty cannot be ratified, unless the Constitution is first amended. This procedure has been used twice, in connection with the 1992 Maastricht Treaty (Declaration 1/1992), and the 2004 Treaty establishing a Constitution for Europe (Declaration 1/2004). It should be mentioned, however, that the Court is also entitled to review a treaty after it has been ratified, through an ordinary constitutional challenge or question. The preventive mechanism complements, but does not replace, the general procedures that are available to impugn the validity of statutes and legal norms of equivalent force.

---

[68] For a comprehensive treatment, see Juan Manuel López Ulla, *La cuestión de inconstitucionalidad en Derecho español* (Marcial Pons, Madrid, 2000).

[69] See for instance, Antonio Remiro Brotons, *La acción exterior del Estado* (n 9) 218–220.

A different head of jurisdiction relates to controversies between public institutions. The most important disputes arise in the area of regionalism. So-called 'conflicts of competences' are likely to arise between the two levels of government (or, less often, between different regions). The Court has also been given the authority to settle controversies between various organs at the national level. Only the government, Congress, the Senate, and the General Council of the Judiciary are relevant for these purposes, however. In a parliamentary democracy, it is unlikely that deep tensions will emerge between these institutions. As a matter of fact, only in very few cases have such controversies been filed.

A third kind of conflict, which is also of marginal importance, was introduced in 1999 to protect local autonomy. When municipalities or provinces consider that a statute (or another norm of equivalent rank) enacted by the state or a region violates their constitutionally protected 'local autonomy', a certain number of them can bring an action to the Court.

Another function of the Court is linked to fundamental rights. As already observed, some of these rights (those mentioned in articles 14 to 30 para 2 of the Constitution) benefit from a special procedural guarantee: public actions (or omissions) that violate them can be attacked through a 'complaint' (*recurso de amparo*) that is lodged before the Constitutional Court. The actions that can be impugned in this way may originate in the executive, the judiciary, or a parliamentary assembly.

Standing is given to the persons who claim to have been harmed by the infringement of fundamental rights. The Ombudsman and the Office of the Public Prosecutor are also granted standing, but they rarely bring cases.

An important reform in 2007 introduced a revolutionary change. It granted the Court wide discretion to decide which *amparo* cases to take. Only those that exhibit a 'special constitutional transcendence' are admissible.

Before an *amparo* is filed, the plaintiff must exhaust all judicial remedies. That is, he must first seek legal protection from the ordinary judiciary, if it is available under the pertinent procedural laws. The Constitutional Court therefore acts as 'special court of appeals'. It is the supreme judicial body in Spain, for it can quash the decisions of any other court—including the Supreme Court. It cannot decide, however, all the factual and legal issues that a case poses. Its *amparo* jurisdiction is limited to checking whether the relevant fundamental right has been infringed. If it concludes that there has been such a violation, it so declares, and it normally invalidates the action that has caused the violation. It can also establish measures to restore the right.

It bears emphasizing that, in the vast majority of cases, the action that is found to offend a fundamental right rests on an incorrect interpretation and application of the relevant body of law. The law as such is fine, but the public authorities have not read it in a proper way or have exercised their discretion in the wrong direction. Sometimes, however, it is the applicable statutory provision that is at fault in that it violates a fundamental right. If the Constitutional Court so concludes, it suspends the procedure, and declares the statute's invalidity in a separate decision that will produce general effects.

When thinking about the performance of the Court, the question often arises concerning the political impact of its decisions. It matters, of course, who invokes the Court's jurisdiction. There is a clear contrast in this respect between the parliamentary opposition (fifty deputies or fifty senators) bringing a constitutional challenge against a law, on the one hand, and an ordinary judge certifying an issue to the Court, on the other. In the first case, the Court is closer to the terrain where political battles are fought. A decision upholding the statute will count as a political victory for the government and a defeat for the opposition, while a decision against the statute will be read in the opposite way.

This is not to say, however, that when ordinary judges raise questions to the Constitutional Court, no potential conflict arises with the political branches. The latter may be very upset if an important piece of legislation is struck down, even if the parliamentary minority cannot claim a victory. Actually, ordinary judges have sometimes asked the Court to intervene in connection with statutes which political parties have chosen not to challenge—either because they support the statute, or because it would not be very popular to insist on certain criticisms. Thus, both the majority and the parliamentary opposition were in favour of a legal provision enacted in 1995 that makes it a crime for someone to deny or justify past genocides, or to defend political regimes that committed such acts. When criminal charges were brought against a person who sold books that denied the existence of gas chambers in Nazi concentration camps, the criminal court in Barcelona handling the case decided to certify a question to the Constitutional Court on the grounds that the applicable provision offended freedom of speech. The Court's decision (STC 235/2007) declared the relevant law to be unconstitutional in part. It held that it is possible to criminalize speech that seeks to justify past genocides, but not speech that simply denies their commission.

Similarly, the Criminal Code was amended in 2004 to establish harsher penalties for certain crimes of domestic violence, but it did so in a way that treats the convicted persons differently depending on whether they are men or women—men receive higher penalties than women for the same kind of conduct. The law was voted for unanimously in parliament. Given this unanimity and given that it is not very popular to challenge a law whose explicit goal is to reduce the level of violence against women, no constitutional challenge by political actors was to be expected. Instead, a significant number of ordinary judges in charge of enforcing the new provision concluded that it was unduly discriminatory and chose to petition the Court to review it. In a very controversial decision, however, the Court upheld the new law (STC 59/2008).

f) The Territorial Organization of the State

As already explained, one of the most controversial issues on the constitutional table in 1977–1978 was the definition of the new territorial structure Spain needed. Political parties and public opinion were aware of the need to channel the aspirations of Catalonia and the Basque country—and to a lesser extent Galicia)—(where nationalist sentiment was quite deep), while keeping Spain united around some common structures and principles. The framers knew that this was the hardest task they confronted. Title VIII of the Constitution on the 'territorial organization of the state', together with some other constitutional clauses, is the answer the framers came up with. That political power would have to be decentralized was a shared conviction among the framers. Several options were possible, however, as to the degree and geographical reach of the devolution process. Should all Spain be divided in self-governing communities? Should all such communities have the same number of powers? No completely worked-out solution emerged from the constitutional debates. Title VIII of the Constitution merely established a framework for the creation of Autonomous Communities, through the passage of the pertinent Statutes of Autonomy.[70] Many choices were left open.

---

[70] On the legal nature of Statutes of Autonomy, see César Aguado Renedo, *El Estatuto de Autonomía y su posición en el ordenamiento jurídico* (Centro de Estudios Constitucionales, Madrid, 1996). For a systematic study of the legal system that has been built as a result of the enactment of Statutes of Autonomy, see Santiago Muñoz Machado, *Derecho público de las Comunidades Autónomas* (Iustel, Madrid, 2007).

To a large extent, the territorial question was 'de-constitutionalized'—it was deferred to further processes of political negotiation.[71]

As things developed, the transfer of political power from the state to the regions was finally applied to the whole Spanish territory. Seventeen Communities were created: Andalucía, Aragón, Asturias, Baleares, Canarias, Cantabria, Castilla-La Mancha, Castilla y León, Catalonia, Comunidad Valenciana, Euskadi (Basque Country), Extremadura, Galicia, La Rioja, Madrid, Murcia, and Navarra. In addition, two 'autonomous cities' in African territory were set up: Ceuta and Melilla. These cities are not Autonomous Communities, however, and their powers are more limited. They exercise no legislative authority, for example.

The degree of self-government granted to the Communities was not the same for all, however. Different regions came to enjoy different levels of self-government. In this connection, the Constitution distinguished two ways to achieve autonomy: a 'slow' one (regulated in article 143) and a 'fast' one (regulated in article 151). If the slow path was followed, the Autonomous Community would first achieve a relatively small package of competences (those enumerated in article 148). Only at a second stage (at least five years afterwards), the Statute of Autonomy would be amended to grant the Community additional competences. If, by contrast, the fast path was followed, the Autonomous Community would reach the highest level of self-government in a single step. For the fast path to be taken, however, the procedural hurdles were more complicated than if the slow path was chosen. The idea was to permit those regions in Spain that proved to be more intensely interested in self-government to obtain a higher level of autonomy than the rest—at least for a while.

This dualism was complicated, however, by the existence of a special rule in the Constitution (*Disposición Transitoria 2ª*) that applied to those territories whose citizens had already ratified a Statute of Autonomy in the past through a referendum. This was an implicit but clear reference to Catalonia, the Basque Country, and Galicia, which had held such referenda during the Second Republic. This special rule made things easier for such territories, since they could achieve the highest level of self-government through a procedure that was less complicated than the ordinary one. Obviously, Catalonia, the Basque Country, and Galicia chose to avail themselves of the special rule.

Andalucía, in its turn, wanted to have the highest level of autonomy from the very beginning, so it used the cumbersome procedure of article 151 to get there. Twelve regions (Asturias, Cantabria, La Rioja, Murcia, Comunidad Valenciana, Aragón, Castilla-La Mancha, Castilla y León, Canarias, Extremadura, Baleares, and Madrid) took the slow path outlined in article 143. They did so through a political process that was coordinated from above by the two main parties at the national level: UCD and PSOE. The remaining Community, Navarra, had access to autonomy through a special organic statute that was enacted by the *Cortes Generales*, after negotiation with the *Diputación foral* of that province.

There were thus stark differences in the way the different Communities were formed. In the nineties, however, the Statutes of Autonomy of the regions that had initially been awarded fewer competences were amended to expand their sphere of self-government. This equalization was not complete, as we will see, since some differences inevitably remained. Still, this trend caused the major nationalist parties in the Basque country (PNV), Catalonia (CiU), and Galicia (BNG) to sign the so-called Declaration of Barcelona in July 1998 in order to reaffirm the special character of these three communities. The Declaration was critical of

---

[71] See Pedro Cruz Villalón, 'La estructura del Estado, o la curiosidad del jurista persa', in Pedro Cruz Villalón (ed), *La curiosidad del jurista persa, y otros estudios sobre la Constitución* (n 14) 381–394.

the equalization process.[72] The situation changed again in 2006, when Catalonia obtained a new Statute of Autonomy that expanded its sphere of powers. Some Communities (notably, Andalucía) partially followed in the Catalan steps, and a new contrast was thus introduced.[73]

There has been debate about the pros and cons of this asymmetry.[74] It should be noted, first of all, that symmetry is impossible in some specific areas. The Constitution, for example, provides that Castilian is the official language, and that the other languages in Spain (such as Catalan, Euskera, and Galician) are also official in the respective Autonomous Communities (article 3). Obviously, laws need to be passed to regulate linguistic matters. Both the central government and the Communities have competences to exercise in this area. An asymmetry naturally emerges between those regions where only Castilian is spoken, and those others where another language is also official (Aragon, Catalonia, Comunidad Valenciana, Baleares, the Basque Country, Navarra, and Galicia). The former regions have no legislative powers concerning languages (or only very marginal ones), while the latter do.

Another source of asymmetry concerns private law. Liberalism in Spain triggered a process of codification throughout the nineteenth century. Many fields were subjected to common rules as a result of it, but pockets of private law were partially preserved in some regions and were maintained even under Franco's dictatorship. The Constitution ascribes the power to lay down private law rules to the central government, but it permits the Autonomous Communities to 'preserve, modify and develop' their own laws in the field, if such laws exist (article 149 para 1 lit viii). Obviously, only those regions where local private law was not eliminated in the past are empowered to issue this type of updating legislation.

Another factor that makes complete symmetry impossible concerns the fiscal system and local institutions that have traditionally existed in the Basque Country and Navarra. Since the Constitution includes a clause guaranteeing these special arrangements, which are linked to 'historic rights' (*Disposición Adicional 1ª*), another difference inevitably arises.[75]

Beyond these matters, however, there seems to be flexibility: the Spanish system may develop towards homogeneity, or it may retain asymmetries among the regions in a number of fields. What can be said for or against these different possibilities?

It is sometimes said that all the Communities should have the same legislative powers so that citizens are treated equally. This position seems to rest on a conceptual confusion, however. Whether or not the regions should have the same sphere of powers is not immediately connected to the principle of equality among citizens. Suppose a particular Community prefers to have a lower level of autonomy than the others. It is not obvious why honouring the equality of citizens should mean that a higher level of autonomy should be forced on that Community.

Asymmetry, of course, introduces a measure of complexity. It raises some intricate issues. One of the problems is analogous to the so-called 'West Lothian question' that has become a

---

[72] Richard Gunther, José Ramón Montero, and Joan Botella, *Democracy in Modern Spain* (Yale University Press, New Haven, 2004) 312.

[73] For a general view of the evolution of Spanish regionalism over the years, see Eliseo Aja, *Estado autonómico y reforma federal* (Alianza Editorial, Madrid, 2014), and José Tudela Aranda, *El fracasado éxito del Estado autonómico. Una historia española* (Marcial Pons, Madrid, 2016).

[74] For a comparative perspective on the Spanish debate on asymmetry, see Enric Fossas and Ferran Requejo Coll (eds), *Asimetría federal y estado plurinacional: el debate sobre la acomodación de la diversidad en Canadá, Bélgica y España* (Trotta, Madrid, 1999).

[75] On the constitutional meaning of these 'historic rights', see Miguel Herrero de Miñón, *Derechos Históricos y Constitución* (Taurus, Madrid, 1998), and Francisco J Laporta and Alejandro Saiz Arnaiz, *Los derechos históricos en la Constitución* (Centro de Estudios Políticos y Constitucionales, Madrid, 2006).

constitutional issue in the United Kingdom since the introduction of devolution.[76] Suppose some Autonomous Communities are granted legislative powers over a particular field, while others are not. This means that the regional parliaments in the first group will issue the laws that apply to those territories, while the national parliament will enact the law that will be operative in the rest of the country. The question is: should all the members of the national parliament participate in the decision-making process that leads to the adoption of the national law? If all of them do, the national representatives of the regions that belong to the first group are then given more power than they should get, arguably. The citizens of the Communities they represent have two votes: through their regional representatives, they determine the content of the regional laws that will apply to them; and through their representatives at the national level, they also help shape the national law for the other communities. They govern themselves, and they govern others at the same time. A clear example of this problem concerns fiscal matters: the representatives of the Basque Country and Navarra vote for laws at the national parliament that are not entirely applicable in such territories. There is no easy solution to this problem.

Another problem that asymmetry generates concerns the Senate. Under the current institutional arrangements, the Senate is a very marginal organ, as explained earlier. There has been constant talk about reforming the Senate to transform it into a chamber that represents the interests of the Autonomous Communities. There seems to be an agreement that the Senate is a rather useless institution, if kept in its present form. There is more controversy about the direction the reform should take. A Senate, of course, can operate more smoothly if all the regions represented in the Senate possess the same legislative competences, than if some regions enjoy more competences than others.

To make matters more complex, the nationalist parties are not especially worried about the future of the Senate. Those parties are already present in Congress, where they can play their cards to protect the interests and competences of the Autonomous Communities they represent. When the governing party at the state level needs the support of smaller groups to ensure the passage of legislation, the main nationalist parties from Catalonia, the Basque Country, and Galicia have often been asked to provide the necessary votes. Given the open-ended character of the Spanish Constitution when it comes to the territorial distribution of power, the nationalist parties can use their votes to press for legislative changes that actually expand the sphere of self-government of the Autonomous Communities. What these parties really worry about, therefore, when general elections take place, is whether or not a political party will get an absolute majority of the seats in Congress. To a certain extent, when no party has an absolute majority, Congress becomes a 'territorial' chamber of sorts.

6. Political Unity and the Sovereignty of the Spanish People

The Constitution lays down a number of principles regarding the territorial organization of the state. Article 1, which figures in the Preliminary Title, proclaims that national sovereignty lies with the Spanish people from which the powers of the state derive. Article 2, in turn, establishes the principles of unity, autonomy, and solidarity. 'The Constitution', this article solemnly proclaims, 'is based on the indissoluble unity of the Spanish nation, the

---

[76] See Peter Leyland, *The Constitution of the United Kingdom: A Contextual Analysis* (Hart Publishing, Oxford, 2012) 272–274.

common and indivisible homeland of all Spaniards'. At the same time, it recognizes the 'right to autonomy' of the 'nationalities and regions' that Spain comprises.

The reference to 'nationalities' (*nacionalidades*) is meant to be ambiguous. There was deep disagreement among the framers concerning the nature to be attributed to communities like Catalonia, the Basque Country, and Galicia. There was no doubt that such communities exhibited linguistic and cultural features that made them special. More importantly, the population in the Basque Country and Catalonia was eager to be awarded self-government.[77] It was not plausible to regard such communities as ordinary regions. On the other hand, many people believed that only Spain is genuinely a nation. The expression 'nationality' tries to draw a bridge between these two positions. It captures the special character of some communities, while it preserves Spain as the homeland of all citizens. Interestingly, however, the distinction between regions and nationalities bears no technical legal consequences in the rest of the constitutional document. Title VIII, which lays down the more specific rules to create Autonomous Communities, no longer employs this distinction—though we can interpret the special rule that applied to Catalonia, the Basque Country and Galicia to facilitate their access to self-government (the *Disposición Transitoria 2ª* that was mentioned before) to be somehow related to that distinction.

Inevitably, there has been political controversy about the meaning and consequences of the term 'nationality', as used by the Constitution. Is there really a difference between a 'nation' and a 'nationality'? Could one say that Catalonia, the Basque Country, and Galicia, for example, are genuine nations within a larger Spanish nation? The debate became passionate in 2005 when the Catalan parliament approved a proposal for a new Statute of Autonomy that declared Catalonia to be a nation. The proposal was amended by the *Cortes Generales* in 2006, but the preamble of the finally enacted text still referred to the fact that the Catalan parliament had defined Catalonia as a nation. The PP (*Partido Popular*), then in the opposition, was very critical of the new Statute. By April 2006, it had collected four million signatures from citizens throughout Spain to petition the government to hold a referendum in order to decide whether Spain should continue to be a single nation, based on equal rights. President José Luis Rodríguez Zapatero refused to call such a referendum. The PP then challenged the new Statute before the Constitutional Court. In its decision, the Court reasoned that, legally speaking, the only nation under the Constitution is Spain. It thus held that the Preamble of the Catalan Statute was to be deprived of interpretive force, to the extent that its reference to Catalonia as a nation might be taken to undermine that constitutional assumption (STC 31/2010).

More recently, in the context of the Catalan secessionist challenge, the Court has insisted on the idea that sovereignty is an attribute of the Spanish people. The Court thus declared unconstitutional a resolution passed by the Catalan parliament in 2013 that proclaimed the sovereignty of the Catalan people (STC 42/2014). It was easy for the Court to point out that the Constitution clearly announces in article 1 that national sovereignty is ascribed to the Spanish people. The 'constituent power', from which all structures of the state derive, is exercised by the Spanish people. Article 2, in addition, proclaims that the Constitution rests on the indissoluble unity of Spain. If so, the Catalan people, legally speaking, cannot be sovereign, for its sovereignty would involve the denial of the sovereignty of the Spanish people. The two sovereignties cannot legally coexist.

---

[77] The nationalist movement in Galicia was dormant at that time. No regionalist party from Galicia was represented at the constituent assembly in 1977–1978. It was some years later that a minority nationalist party emerged in Galicia: the *Bloque Nacionalista Galego* (BNG).

One consequence that the Court drew from this conclusion was that a region in Spain 'cannot unilaterally call a referendum of self-determination to decide on its integration in Spain'.[78] In this context, the Court cited in its support the opinion rendered by the Supreme Court of Canada in 1998, on the issue of Quebec's independence.[79] As has been noted by various scholars, however, the Spanish Court failed to distinguish two different issues: whether a region is entitled to secede unilaterally, and whether the region can hold a referendum on secession unilaterally. The Supreme Court of Canada did not question the legality of the two unilateral referenda that Quebec had organized in 1980 and 1995. Instead, it ruled on whether Quebec had a right to secede unilaterally, and the answer was no. The Spanish Court, in contrast, derived two consequences from the idea that the Spanish people is sovereign: Catalonia cannot secede unilaterally, and it cannot convoke a referendum on independence unilaterally. The Spanish Court's reference to the Canadian judicial opinion is therefore confusing in this context.[80]

It is important to observe that the Court was 'legalistic' in an interesting way when it discussed the issue of sovereignty in its decision. It explicitly said that in the same way that the Catalan people, as a legal entity, exists in the legal world because of its recognition in the Constitution, the Spanish people also exists by virtue of the Constitution. This, of course, can give rise to familiar paradoxes in constitutional theory: if the Spanish people is the author of the Constitution, how is it possible to maintain that the Spanish people exists by virtue of the Constitution? This legalism, however, can have the advantage of flexibility. As already noted, the Court has always insisted that the Constitution can be amended in any direction. There are no constitutional principles that are immune against modification through the applicable procedures of revision. Even the principles that establish the unity of Spain and the sovereignty of the Spanish people can be altered in the future through the pertinent amendment. Indeed, if the Spanish people, legally speaking, only exists as a creature of the Constitution, there is no limit to the kinds of transformations that the Spanish people can undergo in the future, including its partial fragmentation. Secession is therefore not excluded as a legal possibility, provided the Constitution is properly amended.

It bears emphasizing that the Court asked itself whether the principle of sovereignty that figured in the Catalan parliamentary resolution under review could be reinterpreted in order to save its constitutional validity. The Court concluded, however, that this remedy was not possible since the parliamentary resolution was very clear when it affirmed that the Catalan people is (already) sovereign. Parliament was not expressing its wish that the Catalan people would be sovereign sometime in the future, after the necessary constitutional reforms had been adopted. It instead stated that it was already sovereign. The Court, in sum, concluded that it had no other option but to strike down the principle of Catalan sovereignty.

Sometime later, the Court also invalidated the Catalan statutes that organized a referendum on independence to take place on 1 October 2017, and that regulated the transition towards the construction of an independent Catalan Republic, should the people vote in favour of independence (STC 114/2017, STC 124/2017). There was no doubt that it was a grave

---

[78] See STC 42/2014, FJ 3.

[79] See opinion of the Supreme Court of Canada, 20 August 1998, 'Reference re Secession of Quebec' [1998] 2 SCR 217.

[80] For a criticism of the Spanish Constitutional Court's reasoning on this point, see Enric Fossas Espadaler, 'Interpretar la política: Comentario a la STC 42/2014, de 25 de marzo, sobre la Declaración de soberanía y el derecho a decidir del pueblo de Cataluña' (2014) 101 Revista Española de Derecho Constitucional 273; and Victor Ferreres Comella, 'The Spanish Constitutional Court confronts Catalonia's "right to decide" (Comment on the Judgment 42/2014)' (2014) 10 European Constitutional Law Review 571.

breach of the Spanish constitutional order for the Catalan parliament to regulate a procedure for Catalonia to unilaterally secede from Spain, and to finally declare independence opening the door to the formation of a new Catalan Republic.[81]

It should be mentioned, in this connection, that article 155 of the Spanish Constitution empowers the central government to use extraordinary measures to react against an Autonomous Community that infringes upon the Constitution and the laws or that acts in a manner that is gravely prejudicial to the general interest of Spain. The measures need to be approved by the Senate by an absolute majority of its members. This instrument was used in 2017 to preserve the constitutional order against the Catalan authorities. President Mariano Rajoy employed this weapon after the Catalan parliament declared the independence of Catalonia on 27 October 2017. The Catalan government and the Catalan parliament were dissolved, and new elections were held on December 2017. In such elections, the secessionists did not get the majority of the popular vote, but they gathered the majority of the parliamentary seats, so they managed to install the new President of the regional government (Quim Torra). The Supreme Court, in turn, tried the secessionist leaders who were responsible for the acts that led to the organization of the referendum and the proclamation of Catalonia's independence from Spain. The Court found them guilty of several crimes, including sedition (STS 459/2019).[82]

D. Constitutional Identity

The Spanish Constitution has an identity that needs to be protected, as we will see, but the Constitution is otherwise quite open to external norms. First, a specific constitutional clause gives normative weight to human rights instruments. Article 10 para 2 provides that the provisions of the Spanish Constitution concerning fundamental rights and liberties shall be interpreted in accordance with the Universal Declaration of Human Rights, as well as the international treaties or conventions ratified by Spain on such matters.[83] The most important document that courts have used to shed interpretive light on the Spanish Bill of Rights is the European Convention on Human Rights. The fact that the European Court of Human Rights in Strasbourg has produced a rich case law in many areas has transformed the Convention into a very important part of constitutional practice in Spain.

Secondly, the Constitution includes a special provision (article 93) dealing with treaties that create international or supranational organizations to which governmental powers derived from the Constitution are granted. What the framers had in mind when they wrote this article was Spain's future membership of the (then) European Communities.[84] The provision was thus used in 1985 to authorize the ratification of the treaty of accession. But it has also been used in another case: to ratify the 1998 Rome Statute of the International Criminal Court.

---

[81] For a discussion of the constitutional crisis generated by the Catalan secessionist movement, see Victor Ferreres Comella, 'Constitutional Crisis in Spain: The Catalan Secessionist Challenge', in Mark A Graber, Sanford Levinson, and Mark Tushnet (eds), *Constitutional Democracy in Crisis?* (Oxford University Press, Oxford, 2018) 227–242.

[82] For a collection of comments on the Supreme Court's decision, El Cronista del Estado Social y Democrático de Derecho (2019) 82–83.

[83] On the role and impact of this clause, see Alejandro Saiz Arnaiz, *La apertura constitucional al Derecho internacional y europeo de los Derechos Humanos. El artículo 10.2 de la Constitución española* (n 12).

[84] Pablo Pérez Tremps, *Constitución Española y Comunidad Europea* (Fundación Universidad Empresa, Madrid, 1994).

Some scholars have criticized article 93, however, on the grounds that it does not require a sufficiently large parliamentary majority. An organic statute needs to be passed, which means that an absolute majority of members of Congress must vote in favour. This is not, in practice, a larger majority than that needed to authorize ordinary treaties.[85] Because a nation takes an almost irreversible decision when it joins a supranational organization, a super-majority should be necessary, these critics claim.[86]

A tricky problem concerns the relationship between the Constitution and Treaties of the European Union (EU). The starting point is that treaties in general can only be validly ratified if they are consistent with the constitutional text. The Constitution can therefore maintain its supremacy over EU law at an early stage. Since the consent of all member states is required to give legal force to a new treaty, Spain can insist on its own Constitution and refuse to ratify it. Most probably, however, the Constitution will be amended, which is another way to preserve its supremacy. This is what happened in 1992, for example, with the regard to the adoption of the Maastricht Treaty, as already explained.

Things get more complicated when laws or acts issued by EU institutions seem to contradict the Spanish Constitution. Should courts be allowed to check those acts and laws in light of the latter? There are good reasons for the European Court of Justice to have rejected this kind of control by national judges. EU law can only be applied uniformly if national judges abstain from using their domestic Constitutions as grounds to block the enforcement of EU law.

The Spanish Constitutional Court was forced to say something about this problem when the failed 'Treaty establishing a Constitution for Europe' was sent to it for its review. The question arose whether the provision establishing the principle of primacy of EU law over national law was consistent with the principle that holds that the Spanish Constitution is the supreme law of the land. In its Declaration 1/2004, the Court saw no inconsistency. It argued, quite powerfully, that a systematic reading of the Spanish Constitution should be conducted. The Constitution is the supreme norm, but Spain is constitutionally authorized by article 93 to become a member of an organization whose decisions and norms are binding. Therefore, a balance needs to be struck. The Court held that, to the extent that the EU respects the same basic principles embedded in the Spanish Constitution (related to the sovereignty of the State, basic constitutional structures, and substantive values, including fundamental rights), and to the extent that the level of protection afforded those principles by the European institutions is similar, Spain can accept the clause that ascribes primacy to EU law. The Court marred its otherwise well-constructed argument with an additional point, drawing a formalistic distinction between supremacy and primacy. It reasoned that the Spanish Constitution is 'supreme', though EU law enjoys 'primacy'. As many commentators have maintained, this additional argument offered no attractive way to harmonize the Spanish Constitution with EU law. It seemed to minimize the importance of the transformations that were going on.[87]

Some years ago, the Constitutional Court had to confront an interesting question, concerning the potential conflict between the European arrest warrant and the Spanish

---

[85] See art 74 para 2 of the Constitution.

[86] Antonio Remiro Brotons, *La acción exterior del Estado* (n 8) 27, 114. The first draft of the Constitution approved by the congressional *Ponencia* in August 1977 required a three-fifths supermajority, which is identical to the supermajority that is needed to amend the constitution through the ordinary procedure of art 167.

[87] See Antonio López Castillo, Alejandro Saiz Arnaiz, and Víctor Ferreres Comella, *Constitución española y Constitución europea* (Centro de Estudios Políticos y Constitucionales, Madrid, 2005).

Constitution (ATC 86/2011).[88] For many years the Court had interpreted the Spanish Constitution to impose very strict limits on the possibility of extraditing someone to another country when the person concerned was not physically present at the trial that led to his criminal conviction. Under the laws regulating the European arrest warrant, however, the warrant has to be served, even if the person was not physically present at trial, provided the absence was voluntary and a lawyer was present at the trial. The Constitutional Court decided to raise a preliminary reference to the Court of Justice of the European Union—the only time it has done so. The question had two parts, basically: are the applicable provisions regulating the European arrest warrant in conformity with the Charter of Fundamental Rights of the European Union? If so, may Spanish judges apply a more generous understanding of the fundamental rights at stake so that the arrest warrant is subjected to stricter judicial review in Spain? The Court of Justice of the European Union held that the pertinent provisions regulating the arrest warrant were in conformity with the Charter, and that Spain could not invoke its own Constitution to block the application of European Union law (*Stefano Melloni*, 26 February 2013, C-399/11). The Spanish Constitutional Court accepted this ruling and modified its case law accordingly (STC 26/2014).

A special case of normative collision would appear if a constitutional amendment were enacted that were at odds with pre-existing EU law. If the Constitution is the supreme law of the land, such an amendment would have to prevail as far as Spain's legal system goes, it would seem. On the other hand, Spain's constitutionally warranted membership of the European Union imposes obligations that need to be honoured by all law-making institutions, including those with the authority to amend the Constitution. There is no doctrinal consensus on how this tension should be resolved. The suggestion has been made for a mechanism of a priori review to be established, thereby permitting the Constitutional Court to scrutinize the validity of constitutional amendments before they are enacted.[89] When deciding this question, the Court should raise a preliminary reference to the European Court of Justice to get the latter's view as to the compatibility of the proposed amendment with EU law.

It is noteworthy that the Court has followed an asymmetric conception when dealing with the question whether there is a normative core in the Constitution that needs to be entrenched against contrary norms. Whereas the Court has affirmed that certain principles are to be protected against international and supranational law, it has not extended that protection against the domestic constitutional amendment power. Indeed, in the context of the secessionist challenge in Catalonia, the Court has repeatedly held that the unity of Spain announced in article 2 of the Constitution can be amended using the procedure regulated in article 168. At the same time, however, it has insisted that Spain is constitutionally disabled from ratifying an international treaty that could be read to empower a region in Spain to unilaterally secede from Spain (STC 114/2017, FJ 2). According to the Court, the principle of state sovereignty would operate as a barrier to that effect. So, whereas the Constitution does not prevent the domestic institutions from amending the Constitution through the appropriate procedures to make it possible for a region to withdraw from Spain, it does prevent international treaties signed by Spain from granting a region the right to secede.

---

[88] For a discussion of this issue see Aida Torres Pérez, 'Constitutional dialogue on the European Arrest Warrant: the Spanish Constitutional Court knocking on Luxembourg's door', (2012) 8 European Constitutional Law Review 105–127.

[89] Pedro Cruz Villalón, *La Constitución inédita* (Trotta, Madrid, 2004) 77–78.

12

The Evolution and *Gestalt* of the Swedish Constitution

Thomas Bull and Ian Cameron

A. Origins of the Current Constitution	601		have had a Special Importance in the Development of the Constitution?	617
1. The Four Constitutional Documents in Sweden	601		4. The Balance Between Rigidity and Flexibility in the Constitution	618
2. Historical Experiences Influencing the Current Instrument of Government	602		**C. Basic Structures and Concepts**	619
3. Major Critical Points During the Constituent Phase of the Instrument of Government and Political Factors Influencing the Outcome	605		1. The Position of the Constitution within the Legal System	619
			2. Democracy	622
			3. Relationship Between Constitutional Law and International Law	624
4. Issues Explicitly Left Open at the Time of the Adoption of the New Instrument of Government and Subsequent Development of These	608		4. Relationship Between Constitutional Law and EU Law	626
			5. Rights and the Rule of Law	628
B. The Evolution of the Constitution	611		6. Constitutional Organs, the Separation of Powers, the Organization of the Courts, and the Independence of the Judiciary	630
1. Major Features of the Constitutional Order	611		7. The Organization of the State	633
2. Foreign Influence and Common Features of Nordic Constitutions	614		8. Citizenship and the 'Political Unity'	635
3. What Personalities (Judges, Academics, Politicians) and Which Legal Texts			**D. Constitutional Identity**	635

A. Origins of the Current Constitution

1. The Four Constitutional Documents in Sweden

When dealing with the historical experiences influencing the 'Swedish constitution' it is necessary to begin by pointing out that there are four documents in Sweden which have constitutional status: the Instrument of Government (*Regeringsformen*, RF),[1] the Freedom of the Press Act (*Tryckfrihetsförordningen*, TF),[2] the Freedom of Expression Act (*Yttrandefrihetsgrundlag*, YGL),[3] and the Succession Act (*Successionsförordningen*, SO).

---

[1] 1974:152 References to the Swedish statute book (*Svensk författningssamling*, SFS) are by year, followed by the relevant number. Translations of the constitution come from the official English edition unless otherwise stated. References to a constitutional provision are by chapter and article number, e.g. RF 11:14.

[2] 1949:105.

[3] 1991:1469.

Thomas Bull and Ian Cameron, *The Evolution and* Gestalt *of the Swedish Constitution* In: *The Max Planck Handbooks in European Public Law*. Edited by: Armin von Bogdandy, Peter M Huber, and Sabrina Ragone, Oxford University Press.
© Thomas Bull and Ian Cameron 2023. DOI: 10.1093/oso/9780198726425.003.0012

These have come into being at different times and have older antecedents dating back to at least the seventeenth century. The oldest constitutional document still in force is the Succession Act from 1810, providing for the line of succession of the monarch, and requiring the monarch to be of the Lutheran faith. The Freedom of the Press Act is from 1949, however, its antecedents date back to 1766. It only applies to printed media. As new forms of publication became common in the modern age, a new act, the Freedom of Expression Act was enacted in 1991, covering media such as TV and radio. Generally speaking, it follows the structure of the Freedom of the Press Act. The acts also go beyond press freedom by providing for public access to official documents.

The Instrument of Government corresponds to what most countries would regard as 'the Constitution'. It was adopted in 1974, completely replacing the earlier version from 1809 but has its oldest roots from 1634. In this chapter, we will mainly deal with the Instrument of Government, although we make occasional reference to the Freedom of the Press and Freedom of Expression Acts. The fifteen chapters of the Instrument of Government set out the basic rules governing parliament and government, their composition, relationship inter se, law-making, budgetary, and treaty-making powers, the functions and competence of the courts and the administrative agencies, constitutional control mechanisms, and emergency powers.

It should be mentioned here that both the Freedom of the Press and Freedom of Expression Acts are quite unusual constitutional documents, providing comprehensive statutes setting out detailed[4] rules on criminal responsibility and court procedure in cases concerning free speech in the covered media. They are in essence constitutionalized criminal law. It must also be pointed out that as far back as the middle of the nineteenth century it was argued that no other constitutional right than 'the right to print' (*tryckfrihet*) was necessary to protect, nor was the constitutional protection of other rights much worth without the right to print freely. The late adoption of a full catalogue of other constitutional rights in Sweden (see below, Sections A.5 and B.3) can partly be explained by this strong emphasis on the constitutional protection of a free press as a bulwark against misuse of power and a perceived lack of need of anything else.

2. Historical Experiences Influencing the Current Instrument of Government

When discussing the historical experiences shaping the present Swedish constitution, a number of things stand out.[5] Firstly, Sweden is an old unitary state established around the fourteenth century with a King as head of state and, since the fifteenth century, a parliament, the *Riksdag*, as a representative body of other influential groups in society. The King traditionally swore an oath to his subjects to uphold their basic rights and this was regarded as binding according to a constitutional document called the Code of the King (*Konungabalken*), even if there was no mechanism, short of revolt, to hold the King to his

---

[4] TF has 122 sections, divided into fourteen chapters. YGL has sixty-five sections, divided into eleven chapters.

[5] The historical antecedents of the Swedish instrument of government are dealt with in more detail in Hans-Heinrich Vogel, 'Grundlagen und Grundzüge staatlichen Verfassungsrecht: Schweden', in Armin von Bogdandy and others, (eds), *Handbuch ius publicum europaeum. Band 1. Grundlagen und Grundzüge staatlichen Verfassungsrecht* (CF Müller, Heidelberg, 2007). Where possible, we have tried to refer to publications in 'world languages', in particular, bearing in mind the present publication, in English.

THE EVOLUTION AND *GESTALT* OF THE SWEDISH CONSTITUTION   603

oath.[6] The idea of a fundamental law is old in Sweden. The conditions for creating the rule of law in Sweden were particularly favourable, as the land-owning yeomanry, and the burghers (in towns) were sufficiently strong to be regarded classes of their own with political influence through the *Riksdag*. These classes often allied themselves with the central power (the King), and against extending the powers of the local aristocracy. The lack of a large landless population (serfs) dependent upon the aristocracy also contributed to a relatively stable balance of power between the social groups in the *Riksdag*. In practice, this meant that there has been a long Swedish tradition that the monarch was under the law, not above it.

Second is the fact that since 1814, Sweden has not been at war and there has been no period of foreign occupation. The third point is that Sweden, since the reign of King Gustav II Adolphus (1611–1632) has had a strong central administration, at the same time as the size of the country also meant a high level of de facto local self-government. A key figure in the history of centralization and effectivization of governance was the chancellor of justice, Axel Oxenstierna, who more or less ruled the country between 1632 and 1654 (and had had a strong influence even before this time). It was Oxenstierna who instigated the first Instrument of Government, in 1634. This Instrument of Government was however more in the nature of an Administration Act than a modern constitution, setting up the running of government in absence of the King.[7] Mainly as a result of effective state administration, during the seventeenth and early eighteenth centuries, Swedish military power was considerable. This power waned after the wars of King Karl XII, which bled human and other resources of the country dry, ending with the King's death and the country's total defeat in 1718.

The forerunner to the present Instrument of Government was adopted in 1809. Just prior to the adoption of the Instrument of Government, King Gustav IV Adolph had been deposed in the wake of the traumatic loss of Finland to Russia in the Napoleonic wars. He was replaced with his uncle, the ageing and childless Karl XIII. A marshal in Napoleon's army, Bernadotte, with little previous connection to Sweden, was quite hastily adopted by Karl XIII—and in effect offered the Swedish crown. He became king in 1814 under the name of Carl XIV Johan. The 1809 constitution was based on the principle of separation of powers in a Swedish context. It was thus a constitutional document inspired by international developments in France and the newly founded USA, as well as build on old national traditions (see further Section B.2). Under the 1809 Instrument of Government, the King was given charge of the executive power, and the legislative power was shared between the King and the parliament, the *Riksdag*. However, since 1720 the administrative agencies of the state had been kept separate from the government. This was maintained in the 1809 Instrument of Government, in order to limit the King's powers over the day-to-day administration of the state.[8] This separation is a special feature of the Swedish constitution which has continued and remained in place until today.[9]

The *Riksdag* had since the fifteenth century been composed of four 'houses' in which different classes of citizens were represented: the aristocracy, the clergy, the yeoman farmers,

---

[6] The Act on Succession (SO) was undoubtedly binding and can also be seen as an attempt to limit foreign influence on the (then) major organ of the state, the monarch. The Code of the King had a less certain legal status, but as political revolt was not uncommon during the fourteenth through sixteenth century and it often was based on the perceived breach of the monarchs oath, it certainly had a practical effect, legitimating revolt.

[7] Gustav II Adolphus died on the battlefield of Lützen and his daughter Kristina was not yet of age, so the realm needed a stable form for government until she could ascend the throne, which Oxenstierna provided.

[8] The 1809 Instrument of Government displays some signs of foreign influences, even if these were packaged as 'national'. See further Section B.2.

[9] See further Section C.6.

and the burghers. This was confirmed in 1809. The parliament strengthened its position towards the King in certain ways, giving it a control function over both the King's advisors (the Cabinet) and the Administration. The most obvious example of this was the creation of a new institution, that of a parliamentary ombudsman. The first incumbent was LA Mannerheim, a prominent member of parliament at the time and a founding father of the new constitution.

However, the *Riksdag* met only once every five years (after 1845, once every three years) and this obviously severely limited the control it could actually exert. Moreover, while the King had to take account of power relationships in the *Riksdag*, he still chose the Cabinet. The 'departmental reform' of 1840 established that the King's advisors had responsibility for a given department, and thus strengthened their position of the vis-à-vis the King, but still did not give them direct control over the administrative agencies.

With industrialization (which came rather late to Sweden) and other significant social changes, the old way of composing the *Riksdag* became less and less tenable and a two-chamber *Riksdag* was created in 1866.[10] The first chamber consisted of representatives sent from the local authorities (a major reform of which had been carried out in 1862). The second chamber was directly elected. Only men with immoveable property or a certain level of taxed income were eligible to vote in second chamber elections. Voting rights in local authority elections were also based on property ownership (meaning that some women were entitled to vote). However, the financial threshold applied was static, meant that, with increasing prosperity and inflation, the franchise to the first chamber gradually expanded. Parallel to this development, the idea that the government should be primarily responsible to the *Riksdag* grew steadily throughout the late nineteenth century.

Liberals and social democrats pushed repeatedly for the introduction of universal suffrage. This was finally accepted in 1919. While Sweden was neutral during the First World War, the disruption of trade caused by the war (in particular, the allied blockade of German ports) led to food shortages and civil unrest. This unrest and the Russian revolution increased the willingness of the King and right-wing politicians to accept universal suffrage. One can also say that, historically speaking, the decision of the Social Democratic Party (SDP) not to follow a revolutionary platform but instead to seek power by peaceful, parliamentary means was of crucial importance in Swedish politics of the twentieth century.

The 1920s were characterized by weak coalition governments. However, with universal suffrage the SDP soon became the dominant party. This party ruled, alone or in coalition with other parties (usually the farmers, later Centre, party) between 1932 and 1976. It was generally in favour of a (strong) social welfare state, and it generally took a sceptical approach to constitutionalism (at least the German idea of constitutionalism as a control on what the state can do). Its ambitious ideas on economic and social reform did not sit well with ideas on restrained political powers.

Constitutional practice and theory in Sweden are deeply affected by this period of SDP rule. During this 'constitution-less half century'[11] the Instrument of Government of 1809 had little importance in political and legal practice. Some of the legal norms of the constitution did not reflect the constitutional reality—particularly concerning the role of the parliament and the King, even if certain legal experts, independent or allied to more conservative political forces, occasionally criticized the tension between the wording of the constitution and constitutional practice. As it was constitutional practice which came to shape the

---

[10] An influential figure in this was the then Minister of Justice, Louis de Geer. See further Section B.3.

[11] Fredrik Sterzel, 'Författning i utveckling', i Författning i utveckling', in Fredrik Sterzel (ed) *Tjugo studier kring Sveriges författning* (Iustus, Uppsala, 2009).

THE EVOLUTION AND *GESTALT* OF THE SWEDISH CONSTITUTION   605

relationships between the organs of the state, the wording of the provisions of the Instrument of Government were not regarded as *law* in the strict sense and certainly not as the 'supreme law of the land'. These provisions were, in any event, regarded by the government and the majority in the *Riksdag* as directed towards the political institutions and not something that the courts had to (or were supposed to) consider. It was regarded more as a technical manual.[12]

As explained in more detail in the next section, partial reforms of the Instrument of Government were carried out in the 1960s and 1970s, ending the long period of a partly obsolete constitution. This process culminated in the adoption of the wholly new Instrument of Government of 1974. This was an explicit and unsentimental[13] modernizing project. Nothing was kept of the old constitution on the basis that it was incompatible with parliamentarism.[14]

As a constitutional reform, this was also unusual in the sense that it explicitly aimed for codifying the already existing changes in 'the living constitution' and not to bring about any real change in how public power was exercised in Sweden. It was thus to a large extent a descriptive constitution that was created, not a normative one. The 1974 Instrument of Government was no 'revolutionary' break with the past, no 'constitutional moment'.[15] The underlying idea was that the constitution should be changed by political decisions by the elected representatives of the people rather than by interpretation by legal experts. The constitution was to be kept 'up to date' so that a 'constitution-less' period would not happen again. This way of looking at the constitution as something that does not legally—or even politically—bind the political actors in how they find it appropriate to decide on issues of policy is rather typical for Swedish constitutional thinking and quite surprising given the otherwise legalistic and formalistic culture of Sweden. As we shall discuss further below however, the heritage of the constitution-less half-century is fading and some would argue that it largely now belongs to history, as membership in the European Union has 'normalized'—or at least is in the process of normalizing—constitutional thinking in Sweden.

3. Major Critical Points During the Constituent Phase of the Instrument of Government and Political Factors Influencing the Outcome

The present Instrument of Government has been amended significantly on a number of occasions in 1976, 1979, 1995, and 2011. In practice, all constitutional amendments are the product of a consensus among the political parties.[16] The most recent significant reform was in 2010, coming into force in 2011.[17]

The normal way of preparing legislation in Sweden is by means of a departmental or parliamentary commission of inquiry and this method is used also for constitutional

---

[12] See further Section C.1.

[13] Contrast the strong Norwegian attachment to the 1814 constitution which is seen much more as constituting the Norwegian nation.

[14] An attempt was made to keep the provision in the Instrument of Government that was the embryo to rights protection (para 9), but the language of this provision was rejected as being too old-fashioned for the needs of a modern administration. Nils Stjernkvist (ed), 'Mellan juridik och politik', in *Skrifter utgivna av Juridiska Föreningen i Lund* (Juristförlaget i Lund, Visby, 1987). The total rejection of the constitution of the past is not a purely Swedish experience. For example, Switzerland replaced its constitution of 1874 in 2000.

[15] Bruce Ackerman, *We the People: Foundations* (Harvard University Press, Cambridge, 1991).

[16] See Section B.4.

[17] The Instrument of Government has been amended fifty times to date (October 2019), probably making it the most frequently amended constitution in the world.

reform. The commissions of inquiry responsible for drafting the partial reforms of the 1809 Instrument of Government, and thereafter, the new 1974 Instrument of Government, were parliamentary commissions, with high-level representation of all the major political parties. These worked in an unhurried fashion. The first of these constitutional commissions of inquiry was appointed in 1954 and reported nine years later in 1963. This inquiry reached the conclusion that it was necessary to adopt a completely new Instrument of Government, and a completely new Act governing the more detailed work of the *Riksdag* (*Riksdagsordning* (RO), which at the time also had constitutional status. The Commission agreed that representative rather than direct (referenda) democracy was primary. It agreed that there should be a special chapter in the new Instrument of Government on rights and freedoms. However, the mechanisms for protecting rights, in particular, the role to be given to the courts, were the subject of disagreement. The Commission also agreed that the courts had a (limited) power of constitutional review and that this should be codified in the new Instrument of Government. The Commission was, however, unable to agree on several central political questions, namely the electoral system, whether the new *Riksdag* should be unicameral or bicameral and the role of the King in the formation of government. The link between national and local elections was also the subject of dispute.

The issues were inter-related, and the political parties pushed for different solutions based partly on ideology and partly on their own (perceived) self-interest in order to maintain, or improve, their own prospects of obtaining and exercising local and national political power. However, there was also a strong desire on the part of all the major parties to obtain a consensus, and an awareness that this could only be obtained by compromise.

The second inquiry was appointed in 1966. On the issue of a unicameral or bicameral parliament some progress could be made. Prior to the 1964 election, the non-socialist parties had agreed to recommend a single-chamber parliament. The SDP was not in favour of this, as it traditionally had strong representation at the local level (and thus a significant proportion in the indirectly elected first chamber). However, the SDP suffered major losses in the local elections of 1966 and could no longer reckon with a majority in the first chamber. The SDP thus became converted to the idea of a single chamber. Views were also converging in the area of electoral system. The SDP had, during its long period of almost total political dominance, been strongly in favour of a first-past-the-post system. Other parties were in favour of a proportional electoral system. Demographic changes meant that the SDP also was won around to the idea of a proportional system. The commission of inquiry eventually recommended a highly proportional system for national elections. This would adjust the number of MPs each party would receive to the overall national votes, assuming the party in question reached a voting threshold of four per cent of the votes throughout the country. The SDP wished to maintain the link between local and national elections, and so the compromise also included a common election day for parliamentary and local government elections. A three-year electoral period was also introduced. This partial reform of the constitution was approved by the *Riksdag* in 1969. Elections to the new unicameral parliament with 350 members[18] took place in the autumn of 1970 and it

---

[18] This is a high figure for a country with a relatively small population. The number of 350 was obtained by simply adding the number of representatives in the first and second chambers. The even number soon caused problems, as the number of MPs after the election 1971 split evenly into two electoral blocks with 175 mandates each, causing some highly controversial issues to be decided by lottery. This was an untenable situation and the number is now 349.

met for the first time in January 1971. The highly proportional electoral system which resulted from this compromise is important in understanding the consensus approach which is often taken in the *Riksdag* to legislation.[19]

During the work of the first and second commissions of inquiry, it became apparent that parliamentarism needs some sort of impartial (i.e. non-political) mechanism in a number of situations, e.g. inviting a political leader with a prospect of building a majority in parliament to form a government, the decision to prorogue parliament and call an election etc. It was natural to think in terms of giving such functions to the head of state, the King. The monarch had, albeit reluctantly, relinquished his power to exercise influence over the composition of the government in 1917. Giving back such a significant power to the monarch was obviously unacceptable—mainly to the SDP, sections of which wanted to abolish the monarchy altogether. The role of the monarchy in the new Instrument of Government was thus not simply a symbolic issue, looking backward to the traditions of the monarchical past, or forward to the democratic future. A compromise was reached in 1971 (the 'Torekov compromise') to maintain the monarchy but limit the King's role in political issues severely. The role of leading the formation of government was given to the Speaker of the *Riksdag*, including sounding out the leaders of the political parties following an election to see which of them were capable of building a majority in parliament to form a government. This function was, until the election of 2018, not particularly significant, as it was until then relatively clear from the election which party, or parties, were capable of forming a government. In 2018 however the process was politically very complicated and put a new focus on the Speaker and his/her role (see Section C.2).

The next section deals with issues left open in 1974, however, this is an appropriate place to note that the issue of electoral reform, which lay at the heart of the compromises underpinning the 1974 constitution, arose again. In 2004 the idea of constitutional change was initiated by the government as an answer to new challenges to Sweden's political system since 1974. Membership in the European Union, changes in civil society, and a number of issues still open since the compromises of the 1960s and 1970s (see below A.4) were the more obvious reasons for this push for change. At the same time, the number of political parties in parliament had gone from five in the 1970s to eight in the 2000, fragmentizing policymaking in the *Riksdag*. Minority government had become the rule, in contrast to the experience of those who constructed the constitution of 1974.

A commission of inquiry came with some proposals in 2008, but it was from a political point of view a rather bland product, that all but one party could agree on. No new solutions on the difficult questions of electoral system or the functions of parliament or government could thus be achieved. However, as noted in the next section, some other important changes were made and the Instrument of Government had a thorough makeover where it came to structure and language, modernizing and simplifying it to a great extent. All in all, the 2010 reform was not the revitalization of Swedish democracy that the government in 2004 had hoped for.

---

[19] Below, Section C.2.

4. Issues Explicitly Left Open at the Time of the Adoption of the New Instrument of Government and Subsequent Development of These

As seen from the above historical presentation, the position of fundamental rights was initially the subject of disagreement, and the present system of rights protection emerged in stages, (1976, 1978, 1994, and 2010). The same can be said of the position of the courts in the constitutional system (1974, 1978, and 2010). These issues were closely linked, and will be treated together, chronologically. A third issue which was largely left unregulated in the Instrument of Government were the powers of the *Riksdag* over the budget. A fourth issue, still left open today, were rules on formation of the government.[20]

As regards the first of these, the parties agreed in 1973 that an all-party commission of inquiry should be appointed to consider the issue of constitutional protection of rights. The existing Chapter 2 in the Instrument of Government in 1974 had simply sketched out a number of fundamental rights and freedoms. Two years later, this commission, the Commission on Rights and Freedoms, proposed major reworking of Chapter 2. The rights were to be increased in both number and scope. A few rights were stated to be unconditional/absolute. However, most rights, such as the freedoms regarded as necessary for democracy, of expression, association, information, assembly etc., were to be framed in relative terms. These rights were only to be limited by a statute, which in turn had to fulfil certain material conditions.[21] The formulating of the material conditions was borrowed from the ECHR. Parliament noted, in the *travaux préparatoires*, that the main job of ensuring that statutes were in conformity with the Instrument of Government was to lie with the parliament itself.

Rights of non-discrimination on the basis of sex and ethnicity were added. Social rights were not to be legally protected, but instead these were to be included in a new 'forward-looking'/goal-based provision setting out constitutional values in the first chapter (RF 1:2).[22]

Aliens present in Sweden were to enjoy, in certain cases, equality of protection with Swedish citizens but in other cases, the protection was either weaker—the material conditions do not apply to laws which apply exclusively to aliens—or did not exist at all (e.g. the right to freedom of movement within the realm was not to apply to aliens). Thus, two parallel systems of protection were provided in Chapter 2: for aliens and Swedish citizens.

It should be noted in this respect that all bills involving limitations in constitutional rights, or otherwise raising issues under the constitution, are sent to the Parliamentary Committee on the Constitution (*Konstitutionsutskottet*, KU) which makes a report on the issue. These reports have importance both in the debate in parliament and in media and (as with opinions of the Council on legislation) in any subsequent legal proceedings in which the constitutionality and interpretation of statutes limiting constitutional rights are at issue.[23]

---

[20] See Section C.2.

[21] Not all relative rights were covered by the new general material conditions. In particular, these did not apply to the right to property. This right was originally formulated in a negative sense, providing only for compensation 'on grounds determined by law' when expropriation occurred. As shown below in this section, the right has been successively strengthened.

[22] This provision thus primarily serves as an interpretative aid, similar to the function of a preamble in other constitutions.

[23] A comparison can be drawn here with the Finnish system for preparation of legislation, which has no equivalent to the Council on Legislation, and which instead puts even more emphasis on the Constitutional Law Committee (*Perustuslakivaliokunta*). As regards the ordinary legislative process, see Section B.1.

As already mentioned, the power of the courts to engage in constitutional review had already been agreed in principle by the first commission of inquiry in the 1960s, however, it had not been written into the text of the 1974 Instrument of Government. Positions on this point divided broadly on left–right lines. The Social Democratic Party, to some extent supported by the Centre party, wanted protection through the political process. They pointed out, quite correctly, that where the political culture was deficient, constitutional protections would be an empty letter. The SDP—with its long experience as the governing party—also wanted strong government, and as few restrictions as possible on the power of the state to make social and economic reforms. The representatives of the other parties wanted better protection for rights.

The proposals of the Commission on Rights and Freedoms were largely implemented in 1976, although constitutional review was not included. The parties agreed that yet another commission of inquiry should be appointed to consider further the issue of rights protection and that of constitutional review. In 1978, this commission of inquiry, the Commission on the Protection of Rights, reached more or less complete agreement. It proposed the introduction of a procedural mechanism in the *Riksdag* for legislation limiting certain, particularly important relative rights (the 'qualified legislative procedure'). A minority of MPs would be able to obtain a one-year delay in the adoption of a statute limiting such rights which could only be overridden by a supermajority of five-sixths of the number of MPs. In addition, there was to be an expansion of the expert preview of proposed legislation which was carried out by the Council on Legislation.[24] The Council performs a quality control function on draft legislation, somewhat akin to the Council of State (*Conseil d'État*) in many countries. However, it was now proposed that it would be able to examine both the constitutionality of draft legislation and whether it complies with the principle of legal certainty.

This commission of inquiry also considered that the right to constitutional review should be affirmed in the constitution. This would be a power exercisable by all courts and, interestingly, all administrative agencies.[25] However, a material limit was placed on it: when it came to legislation passed by the *Riksdag*, or ordinances adopted by the government, courts and administrative agencies should only be able to review these if the violation of the higher norm was 'manifest'.[26] The Commission on the Protection of Rights also proposed the possibility of holding a binding referendum on a pending amendment to a constitutional document. In 1979, the *Riksdag* adopted all of the Commission's proposals. The political compromises thus meant better protection for rights, but that the focus would still be on preventive protection by the legislature, rather than post-hoc protection by the courts applying constitutional review.[27]

The third important series of amendments to Chapter 2 was in 1994, entering into force in 1995. These were largely occasioned by the incorporation of the ECHR into Swedish law and,

---

[24] The Council on Legislation consists of judges from the Supreme Court and the Supreme Administrative Court, temporarily serving on the council. See further below, Section B.1, and Thomas Bull, 'Judges Without a Court: Judicial Preview in Sweden', in Tom Campbell, Keith Ewing, and Adam Tomkins (eds), *The Legal Protection of Human Rights. Sceptical Essays* (OUP, Oxford, 2011).

[25] At this time, certain quasi-judicial functions were still performed by administrative agencies. See further Section C.6.

[26] No such limitation applies to subordinate legislation issued by administrative agencies on delegation by the government which conflicts with higher norms.

[27] There is, however, a link between the two methods of protection. See Thomas Bull and Iain Cameron, 'Legislative Review for Human Rights Compatibility: A View from Sweden', in Murray Hunt, Hailey Hooper, and Paul Yowell (eds), *Parliaments and Human Rights: Redressing the Democratic Deficit* (Hart, London, 2015). See also below, Section C.

indirectly, by Swedish membership of the EU.[28] The reform added certain new rights.[29] These are formulated as 'sub-constitutional' rights, in that their content is defined by statutory law. It also improved the protection of the right to property as to correspond with its formulation in the ECHR and provided for a special status for the ECHR. The ECHR was ratified in 1953 but it was only incorporated into Swedish law (by means of a statute) in 1995.[30] The ECHR was given a quasi-constitutional status by a special provision in Chapter 2.[31]

The fourth important series of amendments to Chapter 2 were adopted in 2010 and entered into force in 2011. The right of personal integrity (RF 2:6) was expanded to cover surveillance and data protection. The reason for this was a report made by a commission of inquiry which had criticized the parliament for giving insufficient weight to issues of personal integrity when adopting statutes, particularly those dealing with criminal procedure and involving an expansion of police powers. A new right to fair trial within a reasonable time was added. The reason for this was the finding by a commission of inquiry that the Swedish courts had been invoking the ECHR more often than they had invoked the Instrument of Government—and in practice this had largely concerned the right of fair trial under article 6 ECHR.[32] The commission of inquiry considered that there was a clear gap in the constitutional protection of rights that should be filled.

The most significant change, at least symbolically, was that the 'manifest' restriction on constitutional review was removed. This represented a change in approach from the SDP and a more general acceptance of the courts as guardians of the constitution (below Section C.1). The parliament, when it adopted the changes, made an important point in the *travaux préparatoires*, by stressing that ensuring conformity of laws with RF is also the responsibility of the courts.[33] At the same time it was stressed that the constitutional protection of rights should be given full effect by courts and administrative agencies, shifting some of the focus from the legislative process in parliament to the practice of law in society.

Finally, it should be noted that, around about the same time, a new element of rights protection (at constitutional level) was added, namely, the EU Charter of Fundamental Rights and Freedoms. This applies as part of Swedish law since the Lisbon treaty entered into force in December 2009. It is, of course, only applicable when Swedish institutions act within the framework of EU law.

The 2010/2011 reform of the Instrument of Government also made some changes to Chapter 8 on legislative competence.[34] This is the chapter of the constitution which has attracted the most case law, and there was a need to update and rationalize it. The 2010/2011 reform also separated into different chapters the provisions dealing with administrative agencies with those dealing with courts. This was an important symbolic change, marking the 'up-grading' of courts in Swedish constitutional thinking. As mentioned above, it also

---

[28] Fri- och rättighetsfrågor SOU 1993:40, del A och B. Public commissions of inquiry are cited from the official series *Statens offentliga utredningar*. Compared to the earlier commissions of inquiry this was a 'rush job'; designed to fix immediate problems and with little in the way of conceptual reasoning. As to why Sweden became a member of the EU, and the relationship between EU law and the constitution, see Sections B.2 and C.4 respectively.

[29] Namely the right to primary and secondary school education (now RF 2:18) and the right to engage in business activity, in particular, the right of the Sami to herd reindeer (RF 2:17).

[30] SFS 1994:1219. Sweden is bound by additional protocols 1, 4, 6, 7 and 13, but not protocol 12. As regards the relationship between international law and constitutional law, see further Section C.4.

[31] See Section C.3.

[32] This was not surprising art 6 is, relatively speaking, detailed and so more easily made 'operative' as compared to, e.g. art 8. It also deals with procedural issues with which the courts are very familiar.

[33] SOU 2008:125, s 380 and Prop. 2009/10:80, s 147. Legislative bills (*propositioner*) are cited by parliamentary year and number.

[34] See Section C.6.

THE EVOLUTION AND *GESTALT* OF THE SWEDISH CONSTITUTION   611

generally simplified the language throughout the document, updating it and making it more 'user-friendly'.

While the most significant changes to the 1974 Instrument of Government have concerned rights protection and constitutional review, one final issue should be mentioned which was unresolved in 1974 but which was later resolved in the early 1990s, namely, parliament's powers over the budget. Chapter 9 of the Instrument of Government sets out parliament's powers in a very summary way. This was done intentionally as a way to not bind the parliament or the government by impractical rules. The original process can be described in the following simplified terms: each administrative agency made an application for funds for the coming year, and these were then processed by the relevant parliamentary committees. The results were then put together in a budget and voted upon. The process was long, complicated, characterized by political compromises and tended to inflate the state budget as parliamentary committees had the power to expand the costs of their respective policy-area.

Sweden experienced a financial crisis in 1990/1991.[35] This provided the impetus to reform the budget process (and de-regulate the provision of certain public services).[36] Major changes were secured, in broad political unity, largely by passing a new Budget Law and changing the mandate period of the *Riksdag* from three to four years (the shorter period having been seen as contributing to stop-go economic cycles).[37] The passing of the Budget Law did not entail any amendment of the constitution, except as regards establishing the autonomy of the central bank (RF 9:13). The new system is that the government now prepares the budget and parliament takes decisions on the total available state expenditure in a certain procedure and through one single decision (RO 5:12). Details are then discussed in the committees, but the single decision binds those committees to the over-all budgetary limits of the state and any increase of costs must be balanced by reductions. The changes made are generally credited with improving the system, overall, for rational budget-planning, improving government steering of administrative agencies and reducing the temptation to inflate public finances. However, it has meant a certain loss in influence for the parliament as well as a stronger position of the government in relation to the parliament.[38] The *Riksdag* has a constitutional role to follow up on policy reforms (RF 4:8). However, in practice, it has tended to delegate this role to a quasi-independent body, the National Audit Commission (*Riksrevision*), which (like the Ombudsman) is an agency under the *Riksdag*, not the government.

B. The Evolution of the Constitution

1. Major Features of the Constitutional Order

To begin with, we refer to the preceding Section A, which deals with many aspects of this topic. We will not repeat what has been said there unless necessary. This section elaborates further on features of Swedish constitutional law and says something about constitutional

---

[35] See also Section B.2.
[36] See also Section C.7.
[37] As amended, 2011:203. The reform process was dominated by political economists, not lawyers.
[38] On the financial power, see generally Fredrik Sterzel, *Finansmakten*, 2 uppl. (Studentlitteratur, Lund, 2018). One issue was left unresolved in 2011, and is still unresolved today, namely the possibility for the political majority in the *Riksdag* to 'break out' an issue from the government's budget proposal.

trends. There is thus an overlap between this section and the final section on constitutional identity.

Firstly, constitutional development in Sweden has generally been peaceful and step-by step and not in revolutionary leaps. Thus, it is misleading to divide the Swedish constitution into a 'creation' and 'evolution' phase, as gradual change under wide political consensus has been the rule.[39]

Secondly, many times, as with the transformation to a parliamentary democracy 1905–1921, changes in practical political life have not always been reflected in changes to the formal constitutional rules until (much) later. Formal change of constitutional rules can thus to a certain extent be seen as the final stage of a process of constitutional change that primarily takes place in parliament or in society at large. The experience of a formal constitution that was very old and partly irrelevant has thus still influenced the role of constitutional law in political life to a certain degree, even after the last vestiges of that constitution ceased to apply in 1975. In that sense, the latest constitutional reform of 2011, even if not very important in substance, may be seen as an important marking of a new attitude towards constitutional law, more than thirty years after the introduction of the Instrument of Government of 1974. The historical legacy of the 1809 constitution is finally starting to fade away.

Thirdly, notwithstanding the old approach to the wording of the constitution, the basic tenant of a society governed by democracy and the 'rule of law' (meaning respect for the principle of legality) is old and, as pointed out in section A, firmly entrenched in Swedish legal and political culture. Public authorities cannot act without clear and specific legal support, courts are independent from political institutions and the media sector is free from intrusive governmental control. The need for substantive constitutional limits of legislative and executive powers is less in such a society, as respect for the principle of legality and a free and critical journalism will have a similar effect.

Legislation is the main way to change society and the process of legislation is slow, open (i.e. inclusive) and deliberative. The process usually begins with a commission of inquiry being given a (published) directive to investigate the need for legislation. The commission can be either departmental or be an independent investigator (often a senior judge). Sole investigators are most common, but experts are almost always appointed from departments, administrative agencies, and others (business, academia) to assist the investigator. Some commissions have a parliamentary component (either members who are MPs, or with a reference group of MPs).[40] The commission then works for a period of time (usually between nine and eighteen months) and publishes its report. There is then a period of public consultation, before a draft law is sent to the Council of Legislation.[41] The opinions given by the Council on Legislation are not binding. However, if critical they tend to draw media attention and give rise to a political debate that in some cases can change the government's mind. Thereafter, the relevant government department drafts a bill. The process means that there are several 'rationality checkpoints', and opportunities to withdraw or reword controversial provisions. Legislation cannot be 'sneaked in' without extensive public debate in

[39] Compare the views of Leonard Besselink on the 'historical' Dutch constitution, 'The Evolution and *Gestalt* of the Dutch Constitution', Chapter 8 in this volume.

[40] During the 1950s, 1960s, and 1970s the corporativist representation in committees—trade unions and employers association—was much stronger.

[41] In accordance with the present wording of RF 8:19, the scrutiny of draft bills of the Council on Legislation is focused on five specific issues: the effect on the constitution, the coherence of the proposal with the existing system of legal regulation, the likely impact on the principle of legal certainty, if the law is constructed in a way that will make it possible to achieve its underlying objectives and, finally, to detect issues that may become problematic in practice.

which fundamental values such as protection of rights and 'legal security' (*rättssäkerhet, Rechtssicherheit*) will be addressed even if this debate does not necessarily occur in legalistic language.

Fourthly, the role of parliament as the most important institution of the state is firmly in the constitutional order since around the turn of the nineteenth century. Although there are elements of the separation of powers in the Instrument of Government, the main feature of it is all public power originates in the people (*folksuveränitet*) and the government is responsible to the representatives of the people: parliament.

Fifthly, as mentioned, minority government has become a very common feature of the Swedish constitutional experience. This is a result of the highly proportional electoral system.[42]

Sixthly, Sweden is a very strong centralistic state, while at the same time exhibiting extensive delegation of powers to regional and local authorities. This is somewhat of a constitutional paradox. The national power of parliament and government is exercised through extensive legislation and national public authorities that supervise regional and local authorities, ombudsmen also have such a role and—as a last resort—there is a wide right for individuals to appeal local authorities' decisions to administrative courts.[43] At the same time, power over huge sectors of public policy has been delegated to regional or local organs, concerning for example issues such as health care, education, and environmental care.[44] These regional and local organs have a weak formal (constitutional) position in relation to national government and its authorities, but in practice most of the political elite of Sweden wish to avoid infringing local autonomy too much. The Swedish political system is a delicate mix of central steering and local action (somewhat like the executive federalism of the EU) and the balance between central and local powers cannot be shifted without far-reaching consequences for the whole of the system. In addition, many of the politicians on the national scene started their political careers there and are still dependent upon their local constituency.[45] This makes it difficult to exercise strong political control from the national perspective. One case in point would be the regional organization of health care in Sweden, for which there are strong arguments to reform, in order to make it more sustainable and effective, but the entrenchment of regional interests make this exceedingly difficult to achieve in practice. In practice this 'soft federalism' is perhaps not much different from systems that have a more formal federal organization, such as Austria for example.[46]

Finally, the constitutional role of courts has not been important in the development of the constitutional system in Sweden until rather recently. Sweden can thus be described as falling into a broad category of countries characterized by political constitutionalism.[47] As the constitution of 1809 had little to say about individual rights and its institutional provisions were partly irrelevant, the courts had very seldom to face constitutional issues in legal practice during the twentieth century. Thus case-law on constitutional issues was rare

---

[42] Below, Section C.2.

[43] See Section C.6.

[44] See further Section C.5.

[45] Moreover, many MPs leave the *Riksdag* after a single mandate period, and return to local politics, often because they feel they can do more at the local level. See Shirin Ahlbäck Öberg, Jörgen Hermansson, and Lena Wängnerud, *Exit riksdagen* (Liber, Solna, 2007).

[46] See Ewald Wiederin, 'The Evolution and *Gestalt* of the Austrian Constitution'.

[47] As some comparative studies do, see e.g. Anneli Albi and Samo Bardutzky, *National Constitutions in European and Global Governance: Democracy, Rights, the Rule of Law: National Reports* (Springer, Berlin, Heidelberg, 2019). See generally on the concept Richard Bellamy, *Political Constitutionalism: A Republican Defence of the Constitutionality of Democracy* (CUP, Cambridge, 2007).

and mostly without any political impact. However, as noted in Sections A.3 and A.4, since Sweden became a member of the EU and since it incorporated the ECHR in 1995 the position of the courts has changed somewhat.[48]

2. Foreign Influence and Common Features of Nordic Constitutions

As mentioned in Section A, Sweden has had a long and independent constitutional development from the Middle Ages on into modern times. There is thus a national historical development that in major parts is dependent upon national political, economic, social, etc., conditions.

Foreign influence was certainly part of the process in the establishment of the Instrument of Government in 1809, the French revolution and its political and philosophical impact was not unknown in Sweden at the time. However, the constitutional solutions at that time were an adaptation of these international trends to national circumstances and needs, especially the long and ongoing battle for power between the King and the different classes represented in the parliament. The extent of these foreign influences on the Instrument of Government of 1809 was the object of controversy in Swedish political science during the early twentieth century with sharply different views being expressed.[49]

Foreign influence on constitutional developments can also be viewed in a wider sense, as events in other countries influencing events in one's own country. As already mentioned, the Russian revolution helped change the Swedish King's opposition to parliamentarism. Sweden managed to keep out of the Second World War, staying neutral while balancing between its traditionally strong cultural connections with Germany and the democratic and economic ideals that brought it closer to the Western allies. At the same time, the democratic political parties in Sweden managed to keep national branches of both Nazism and Communism under control and away from political influence. After the war, Sweden had a unique situation in that it was mostly unharmed by the war and its industry could start exporting much needed goods to the European market without much competition. This set up for a remarkable economic growth in Sweden during the 1950s and 1960s in which the living conditions of citizens in general were bettered, while at the same time the social and economic ambitions of the state grew. A successful export industry became the motor of Swedish economy and the basis for any progressive political programme, establishing a close connection between the SDP and leading persons in Swedish industry in which informal deals were made so as to facilitate their common interests. For this reason, big industries in Sweden had no grave political grievances with the SDP government during this period even if it was pushing for extensive social reforms.

The Swedish dependency on international trade, as well as the internationalization of the financial markets in the late 1980s, resulted indirectly in the Swedish decision in 1991 to seek membership of the (then) European Community. The Swedish economy had, and still has, considerable income from the export of timber and wood products, iron ore and manufactured goods. A well-educated workforce, and the availability of relatively cheap electrical

---

[48] See Sections C.3, C.5, and C.6.

[49] The main protagonists were Bruzewitz, professor in Uppsala, and Lindroth, professor in Lund—which also led to an unfortunate polarization for a while between the two faculties. For the story see Emma Rönström, 'Forskardebatten kring 1809 års regeringsform—Till frågan om grundlagens härkomst' (1997) 100 (4) Statsvetenskaplig tidskrift 448.

power from hydropower, and nuclear power, have also been factors in Swedish economic successes. Swedish manufacturing industries (car manufacture, shipbuilding etc.), produced high-quality but (relatively) high-priced products for which there was a high demand during the 1950s, 1960s, and early 1970s. With successive oil crises and with competition from other states, including Japan and South Korea, Swedish manufacturing industry experienced increasing problems with competitiveness during the 1980s and early 1990s. Government intervention ameliorated the resulting unemployment problems. However, the costs of such economic intervention were considerable, and contributed to a growing interest in encouraging economic growth by means of deregulation.

The Swedish banks ran into a financial crisis in 1990/91, caused by deregulation of credit markets, and a consequent housing and commercial properties bubble. This in turn sparked a currency exchange crisis. The Swedish state again intervened strongly, taking over two banks, introducing guarantees for ordinary people's savings and forcing the banks' shareholders to accept losses.[50] While these measures were successful in restoring confidence in the banking sector, the housing sector took time to recover. This financial crisis, and the realization that the Swedish economy was small, and would remain open to, and so, dependent upon, outside influences, led to a reassessment by the SDP of its opposition to European Community membership. The business community and the centre-right parties were already positive to European Community membership, Swedish industry and agriculture were already aligned with European Community law because of Swedish membership of the European Economic Area, and membership negotiations took only two years. Nowadays, the structure of Swedish industry has changed somewhat: iron ore and timber/wood product exports are still important, there is still manufacturing of niche products, but there is also considerable income from export of services and high technology products, including biotechnology. In many cases since the 1990s, iconic Swedish industry brands have been bought or incorporated into international business corporations. This goes for Volvo, Asea, Pharmacia, and many others. On the structural level, this has meant that the earlier coordination between governmental politics and big industry in Sweden no longer works as it used to do. The industrial actors of USA, China, or other countries do not have the same inclination to do deals with the Swedish government as their national predecessors had. Economic policy—and the room for political reform programmes—has been affected to a large degree by this development, perhaps 'normalizing' Sweden.

As for foreign influence in a narrower sense, meaning constitutional borrowing, there are some examples. As mentioned, the formulation of the rights chapter in the Instrument of Government has been heavily influenced by the ECHR in several stages. A clear example of this is the new (since 2010/2011) provision on a right to a fair trial (RF 2:6), which has a wider scope of application in one respect than article 6 ECHR, as it applies to all court proceedings, although narrower in another, in that it gives no right of access to a court. The Swedish adoption of a '*Solange*' perspective as regards the position of Swedish constitutional law vis-à-vis EU law is another example.[51] In connection with the 2010/2011 reform, the new chapter on the courts, Chapter 11, was influenced by Danish experience and the revised provision on judicial review in the chapter (RF 11:14) was influenced by Norwegian experience. The Commission of Inquiry that prepared the reform also visited the German and Austrian

---

[50] For the background, see Peter Englund, *The Swedish 1990s Banking Crisis: A Revisit in the Light of Recent Experience* (Riksbanken, Stockholm, 2015) http://archive.riksbank.se/Documents/Avdelningar/AFS/2015/Session%201%20-%20Englund.pdf (last accessed on 30 March 2022).

[51] Below, Section C.4.

constitutional courts but decided not to introduce an institution like that in the Swedish system. This can perhaps be seen as an example of 'negative influence', which otherwise is hard to measure.

This section is also a suitable place to take up the question of to what extent the Swedish constitution can be seen as representative for the other Nordic constitutions. To the outside observer, the Nordic states may look very similar. They are economically prosperous, they combine economic and political liberalism with strong welfare states, they all emphasize equality of the sexes, and they are socially progressive (indeed, by some standards, radical). The World Values Survey—a global network of social scientists that investigate human beliefs and values—puts the Nordic states (together with the Netherlands) in a distinct 'post-modern' category.[52] However, even within this category Swedes stand out in terms of being more rational, individualistic, and socially progressive than their Nordic neighbours. We from inside the 'Nordic community' tend to see the differences between us more than the similarities (except when we are confronted with another group of course, then we all tend to find a lot to agree on).

To what extent economic prosperity depends upon the constitution is a large topic, outside the scope of the present article. As far as Sweden is concerned, the economic powers of government are not constitutionally regulated, except at a minimal level, and the constitution does not contain any (expensive) economic and social rights.[53] The prosperity of the Nordic states, indeed, the Western world, or at least, the enjoyment of that prosperity by the majority of the population, is a relatively new phenomenon.

As to the Nordic constitutions, there are some common features.[54] For example, all four states combine strong central institutions with, in practice, strong local government autonomy.[55] All the Nordic parliaments are unicameral, applying highly proportionate electoral methods. All are parliamentary. In some matters, such as the organization of the courts, the powers of the Ombudsman, and ministerial government contra collective government,[56] a distinction can be drawn between the 'East' Nordic states (Sweden and Finland) and the 'West' Nordic states (Denmark, Norway, and Iceland). This is not surprising, bearing in mind their common history and culture; Norway and Iceland were ruled by Denmark, and Finland by Sweden, for almost 500 years (and, more or less, at war with each other, on and off, for most of this period).[57]

There are common Nordic elements in approaches to legal interpretation, which tend to follow the *travaux préparatoires*, and take a more limited view of the judicial function in context of separation of powers—probably in turn born out of a respect for the institutional competence of the legislator, as well as for elected politicians who have, thanks to the highly

[52] See World Value Survey, http://www.worldvaluessurvey.org/WVSContents.jsp (last accessed on 30 March 2022).

[53] Obviously, the absence of strong institutions of the state can hinder economic development. As noted, the electoral cycle and the budgetary process can affect economic prosperity negatively and both these issues were reformed in Sweden after the financial crisis of 1990/1991.

[54] This issue is discussed in detail in Markku Suksi, 'Common Roots of Nordic Constitutional Law? Some Observations on Legal-Historical Development and Relations between the Constitutional Systems of Five Nordic Countries', in Helle Krunke and Björg Thorarensen (eds), *The Nordic Constitutions: A Comparative and Contextual Study* (Hart, Oxford, 2018) 9–42.

[55] Thomas Bull, 'Institutions and Division of Powers', in Helle Krunke and Björg Thorarensen (eds), *The Nordic Constitutions: A Comparative and Contextual Study* (n 54) 43–66.

[56] Björg Thorarensen, 'Mechanisms for Parliamentary Control of the Executive', in Helle Krunke and Björg Thorarensen (eds), *The Nordic Constitutions: A Comparative and Contextual Study* (n 54) 67–106.

[57] The fact that Sweden is the largest state and ruled Finland, and, briefly, Norway, is another reason for caution in finding commonalities. No one likes an overbearing 'big brother' (even if the description prim and proper big sister is probably more accurate nowadays).

proportional systems, a high degree of democratic legitimacy. As Suksi notes, there are commonalities in the absences of certain constitutional elements common in other states, such as a constitutional court, the individual right of constitutional complaint, federalism and presidentialism.[58] However, Suksi's conclusion, overall, is that the reasons for the current similarities in the Nordic states, e.g. in the form of the welfare state, should be sought elsewhere than in the historical commonalities of their constitutions.[59]

3. What Personalities (Judges, Academics, Politicians) and Which Legal Texts have had a Special Importance in the Development of the Constitution?

During the middle part of the nineteenth century, the single most important political figure in Sweden was Louis De Geer. He was instrumental in the abolishment of the old, medieval organization of parliament and introducing new and more modern forms of work. These were reforms that more or less stood until the great constitutional reform in the 1970s. De Geer was Minister of Justice, as well as a judge, and a writer of essays on legal matters. In advocating a bicameral legislature, he had been influenced by legislature in the pre-eminent world power at the time, the United Kingdom.

During the period of democratic transformation of the Swedish political system, several political figures had important roles. Most important was perhaps Hjalmar Branting, the party leader of the Social Democratic Party in 1907 and Prime Minister in 1920. Two influential lawyers that were also Social-democratic politicians were Professor Vilhelm Lundstedt and Professor Östen Undén. The latter was the long-term member of the SDP governments from 1917–1966, most of the time as Foreign Minister, and exercised considerable influence over both domestic and foreign policy. Undén was against restraints on 'strong' government, and dismissive of the very idea of human rights as a legal phenomenon. Allegedly, all reforms in those areas—such as giving individuals the right to complain in accordance with the European Convention on Human Rights—had to wait until Undén had retired. Other highly influential SDP politicians were the Prime Ministers Tage Erlander, Per Albin Hansson, Olof Palme, and the finance minister Gunnar Sträng (who served as minister for thirty consecutive years, and as finance minister for twenty of these).

An important figure in the work leading up to the reform 1975 was the professor of political science Jörgen Westerståhl. Among other things he acted as secretary for the inquiry into the constitutional reform that laid the basic structure of the coming reforms between 1954 and 1963. Sweden's entry into the European Union in 1995 must be regarded as 'constitutional moment'. The professor of political science Olof Ruin played an important role in the work leading up to full membership. The unitary front of both the conservative politician Carl Bildt and the social-democrat leader Ingvar Carlsson won a referendum on the issue of accession, uniting the mainstream parties of the political right and left on this particular issue. As regards the reform in 2011, Johan Hirschfeldt, former Chancellor of Justice and president of the Svea Court of Appeal played an important role as an expert member of the

---

[58] Markku Suksi, 'Common Roots of Nordic Constitutional Law? Some Observations on Legal-Historical Development and Relations between the Constitutional Systems of Five Nordic Countries' (n 54) 39–40.

[59] Markku Suksi, 'Common Roots of Nordic Constitutional Law? Some Observations on Legal-Historical Development and Relations between the Constitutional Systems of Five Nordic Countries' (n 54) 41.

parliamentary inquiry leading up to that reform, as did the secretary of the inquiry, Court of Appeal judge (now, president of the Supreme Court) Anders Eka.

4. The Balance Between Rigidity and Flexibility in the Constitution

The Instrument of Government can be amended by simple majority (RF 8:14), although there must be a general election between the first and second reading of an amendment bill. The first decision must be taken no later than nine months before the elections, unless a five-sixths majority in the parliament's Committee on the Constitution waives this requirement. The nine-months delay is intended to allow for public debate before a constitutional change is made. As noted in Section A.4, a referendum can be called on a pending constitutional change (RF 8:16), if a third of MPs vote for it, but so far this has never yet occurred.[60] Thus, while the Swedish constitution is very flexible, the process of changing it is time-consuming. As already mentioned, the Swedish tradition is to seek consensus among all the major political parties when changing the constitution. The inclusiveness of the process is to some extent guaranteed by the possibility of triggering a referendum. Still, it can be speculated whether the tradition of consensus will continue now that a populist right-wing party is the second largest party (after the 2022 election). A Commission of Inquiry is currently examining whether the procedures for constitutional change be strengthened, in particular, whether a requirement be made that the intervening general election be an ordinary general election, i.e., scheduled after the four-year parliamentary term has expired, rather than an extraordinary, general election, i.e., an election called by the Prime Minister during the period of a parliamentary term.

It is common that there are one or more constitutional changes after every election. This is to some extent because of the rather technical regulation on free speech in mass-media in the Freedom of the Press Act (*Tryckfrihetsförordningen*) and the Freedom of Expression Act (*Yttrandefrihetsgrundlag*). However, it is also a sign of the already mentioned ambition to keep the constitutional regulation 'up to date' and descriptively correct. If there is a need for change, the preferred way is not by constitutional interpretation or evolution, but by a formal change.

As already mentioned, the *Riksdagsordning* (RO) used to have the status of fundamental law, but this was changed in 1974. However, to increase the stability of the rules governing the *Riksdag*, the main provisions of it can only be changed in accordance with the same procedure as applies for changing the constitutional laws. There are two other laws to which the same rule applies, namely the Act on the Swedish Church (1998:1551)[61] and the Act on Religious Communities (1998:1593). This is largely a historical oddity, reflecting the importance religious freedom has had in the past. Otherwise, Sweden does not have 'organic laws'.

Nor does the Instrument of Government have an emergency procedure for passing laws, except in the situation where the country finds itself at war, or on the brink of war. The last constitutional commission of inquiry discussed whether such rules should be introduced but contented itself to making only minor changes to Chapter 15 of the Instrument of Government, which deals with war-powers. This is perhaps an illustration of the peacefulness of Swedish constitutional developments. Sweden's experience during the Covid-19

---

[60] A comparison can be drawn here with the Danish constitution, where a referendum approving a constitutional change is obligatory, and which is thus much more rigid.

[61] The status the Swedish Church had as a state church was removed by this Act.

C. Basic Structures and Concepts

1. The Position of the Constitution within the Legal System

As noted briefly before, the half century of 'being without a constitution' had a strong influence on how the new Instrument of Government was perceived by the parliament, the courts, and the legal profession as a whole. It took time for the parliament to adopt a new mindset. For example, in 1974, the *Riksdag* was aware that the then legislation on the police was not in accordance with the new constitutional rules and therefore enacted a transitional clause. It took another ten years before a new, constitutionally correct, Police Act was enacted.[62] Even when it began to be taken more seriously, the Instrument of Government was for a long time seen as being an instrument for regulating the relations between government and legislature. As such its norms were still not seen as being 'real law'.

How the courts have been organized has played a role in this respect (see further Section C.4). It was only in the late 1960s that the precedent creating character of the Supreme Court became dominant, and that the style and extent of judicial reasoning in the cases decided changed accordingly. Similar points can be made as regards the Supreme Administrative Court: it only became a proper precedent-creating court when a complete system of lower administrative courts was put in place in the 1970s.

The legal technique of loyally following the *travaux préparatoires* and a general 'positivistic' attitude in the legal profession are other parts of the explanation for the slow adaption to the new constitutional document as 'law' relevant to courts and lawyers in general. Swedish constitutional interpretation has been 'bottom-up' not 'top-down'. If there are more specific and concrete provisions, these are to be applied in preference to vaguer, more general provisions of more 'principle' character, even if the latter might be in higher norms. It is, even today, still not usual for Swedish administrative agencies and first instance courts to begin their reasoning with whatever provisions in the Instrument of Government might be applicable. As courts themselves did not generally refer to the rights in the Instrument of Government, then advocates did not do so either. This is changing, but slowly.

One must, however, note that a quite different approach was taken to the constitutional rights in the Freedom of the Press Act, even in times preceding the reforms of the 1970s. These rights were treated as 'real law' and as a living part of the Swedish legal order. This can probably be explained by the detailed, concrete, formulation of these rights, the long familiarity with the legislation (the 1949 Act had predecessors going much further back in time), wide political entrenchment of a legalistic approach to these constitutional documents, and a powerful pressure group—the press—which insisted that these legal rights be respected.

As already noted, the post-war period in Sweden was a time of economic prosperity and greatly increased standards of living for ordinary people. This enabled generous social welfare programmes. Economic and social rights were enacted, but at the level of statutory, not constitutional, law. The state was 'good'. In such a state, democratic and stable, the courts

---

[62] This can be contrasted with the approach taken thirty-six years later, when constitutional protection against surveillance/data processing was enacted, RF 2:8 para 2, above. The Security Police requested such a transitional clause but this was refused.

have more of a role as technical helping hand to the political power than as a controlling mechanism for the protection of individual rights.

Another explanation for the self-restraint exercised by the courts is the strong Swedish attachment to democracy—largely interpreted as parliamentary supremacy—as the main governing principle of society, both national and local (see Section C.2). The SDP had both ideological and pragmatic reasons to desire not to be overly hindered by higher norms when it adopted social and economic reforms, and this is the most important aspect of this. However, there is a historical element to this too. Sweden's parliamentary democracy had not collapsed in the 1930s under the threat from the left and the right, and Sweden had not been occupied or otherwise involved during the Second World War. The consequent interest in individual rights, and in binding or constraining parliamentary sovereignty which had arisen in other European states in the post war years largely passed Sweden by.[63] Still, even twenty years previous to the 1974 constitution, i.e. 1954, Sweden would probably have been in the European mainstream in this respect: it is first with the rise of the constitutional courts in the major European powers (France, Germany, Italy) that constitutions began to be generally regarded as being justiciable.[64]

The relative absence of constitutionally conforming interpretation and constitutional review in court practice should not be seen as equivalent to there being no respect for constitutional rights at all. As already mentioned, the emphasis in the Swedish system has been (and today, the main emphasis still is) on the legislative process and the content of ordinary law. Where commissions of inquiry correctly identify potential rights concerns at an early stage and build safeguards into the draft legislation in the first place, the room for problems to emerge in later application of this legislation is much less.

Legal academic constitutional scholarship—being almost non-existent during the 'constitution-less half century'—began re-emerging first in the early 1990s and received a major boost with Sweden joining the EC (EU) and incorporating the ECHR in 1995. At the same time, the practice of the Council on Legislation and the courts gradually changed due to this change in the legal environment. It became more common for the Council on Legislation and the courts to interpret lower Swedish norms against the standards of European norms and even to set aside the Swedish norms. It became more common to refer to the ECHR, especially, as noted above, the right to a fair trial which (until 2011) did not exist as a constitutional right in Swedish law. So, the experience of engaging in EU, and ECHR-conform interpretation influenced the Swedish courts and lawyers in general to engage more in constitutional-conform interpretation.[65] And the experience of engaging in 'constitutional' review against EU and ECHR norms made it much easier for the Swedish courts to overcome their hesitation to engage in constitutional review of legislation and ordinances against the standards of the Instrument of Government. Moreover, the experience of awarding damages for violation of EU law and the ECHR led to another 'spill-over' effect: the courts found

---

[63] Jan-Werner Müller, Contesting Democracy: Political Ideas in Twentieth-Century Europe (Yale University Press, New Haven, 2011).

[64] Among many authorities, see Lech Garlicki, 'Constitutional Courts Versus Supreme Courts' (2007) 5 (1) ICON 44. Garlicki refers to a 'European tradition [that] national constitutions were regarded mainly as political instruments rather than as the supreme law of the land' (at 47). It is first when these constitutions began incorporating individual rights catalogues, and a dedicated judicial mechanism (the constitutional court) was created that this changed.

[65] See e.g. NJA 2004 s 336, NJA 2012 s 400 (Manga), NJA 2014 s 79, HFD 2015 ref 61. Cases from the Supreme Court (*Högsta domstolen*) are cited from the semi-official Supreme Court Reports, NJA, and of the Supreme Administrative Court (*Högsta förvaltningsdomstolen*, HFD) from the official reports are cited from the official series (HFD, and its forerunner, *Regeringsrättens Årsbok*, RÅ).

it possible to award damages for violations of constitutional rights even if no clear constitutional provision supported such a conclusion.[66] These developments have been gradual. The judgments placing greater emphasis on the Instrument of Government have most often been from the Supreme Court and the Supreme Administrative Court, but the cases obviously have been filtered through the lower courts. Today, also lower courts can be seen engaging in constitutional interpretation in a way that would have been almost unthinkable thirty years ago.

As noted in Section A.4, the 2011 reform on constitutional review could be made only after the dominant political party in Sweden, the SDP, had changed its traditionally sceptical attitude towards constitutional review. The SDP lost political power in 2006 after twelve years of being in government. It realized that it was no longer the—guaranteed—party of government. This change of heart concerning constitutional review fits in with the theory that such review is easier to accept for a political party which knows it runs the risk of losing governmental power (a form of 'insurance' policy for politicians).[67] Moreover, growing societal complexity led the SDP gradually to modify its stance towards judicial power. When in government in the 1990s, the SDP had handed over significant power to determine disputes in several areas to the administrative courts, such as migration law and environmental planning. These steps were taken partly out of a desire to improve legal certainty, partly out of a desire to reduce the workload of the government and partly to avoid having to take governmental decisions in areas where there was a lot of media attention and little political goodwill to be won. In the end of the 2010s the SDP was no longer against constitutional review on ideological grounds and had come around to even favour it as a balancing instrument of power in both national and international contexts.

Another element in this development concerning the role of courts relates to the quality of preparation of legislation. Paradoxically, while EU membership and ratification of the ECHR have boosted awareness of the constitution in some respects, they have also made the process of preparation of legislation more hurried, and more complex. Less stable coalition governments, and their vulnerability to media pressure and sudden shifts in public opinion, has also led to hastily and deficient draft legislation more often being presented, notwithstanding the constitutional duty on the government to prepare legislation carefully.[68] If this trend continues, it is likely to force the courts to be more active.

Still, even today it cannot be said that the Swedish constitution has penetrated popular consciousness.[69] The press publicizes when the Council on Legislation considers that a draft bill has not sufficiently taken into account constitutional matters, but the angle taken on this is often the (implicit) criticism this entails of the government. Judgments of the Supreme Courts referring to the constitution are noted only rarely and seldom if ever analysed in the

---

[66] Below Section C.5.

[67] See e.g. Tom Ginsburg, 'Economic analysis and the design of Constitutional Courts' (2002) 3 Theoretical Inquiries in Law 20.

[68] RF 7.2 provides that 'In preparing Government business the necessary information and opinions shall be obtained from the public authorities concerned. Information and opinions shall be obtained from local authorities as necessary. Organizations and individuals shall also be given an opportunity to express an opinion as necessary.' Government business includes preparing legislative bills. The Supreme Court case NJA 2018 s 743 dealt with an amendment to a criminal statute which had been prepared very speedily, and which had been criticized by the Council on Legislation for this reason. The court found that even if not very satisfactory, the legislative process had in essence not been in breach of the formal rules of the constitution.

[69] Although see Section D below. Even here one can say that Sweden is in no way unique. See for example, the similar Dutch experience, in particular the (largely unsuccessful) attempts to make public opinion aware of the Dutch constitution, during the 200-year 'celebrations'.

press. The Swedish quality media are a long way from their German counterparts who have specialist correspondents in Karlsruhe.

Finally, on this point, although Sweden is 'special' in many ways, the Swedish approach to constitutional review in particular does not stick out much if put in Nordic perspective. The Norwegian courts have a slightly more activist approach, but constitutional review by courts is very rare indeed in Finland and Denmark.[70]

2. Democracy

There are a number of dimensions to the role given to democracy in the Swedish constitution. The first point which can be made is that democracy is mentioned in the very first provision in the Instrument of Government. RF 1:1 provides that, 'All public power in Sweden proceeds from the people. Swedish democracy is founded on the free formation of opinion and on universal and equal suffrage. It is realized through a representative and parliamentary form of government and through local self-government.' Thus, RF 1:1 links democracy to the basic freedoms of expression, information, and association. On the other hand, the Swedish view of democracy is primarily procedural—input legitimacy in Scharpe's term[71]— the views of the political majority in the *Riksdag* ought to prevail. The 'output' aspect: that government is effective, and that necessary societal reforms actually get passed and put into place, tends to be taken for granted.

In the view of the present authors, the legitimacy of judicial power over constitutional matters is connected to the legitimacy of the political power, which in turn, to a large extent depends upon the 'fairness' of the electoral system. The Instrument of Government is not very detailed on these rules that make democracy work in practice. There are some basic provisions in Chapter 3 on elections, the right to vote, and on how the electoral system and mandates are distributed, but they presuppose a detailed regulation in law and ordinance. The constitution also provides (in RF 6:3) that two weeks after an election, the *Riksdag* must vote on whether a candidate for Prime Minister proposed by the Speaker has the support of the *Riksdag*. If he or she is rejected by a majority of MPs, then the proposal fails. Sweden can thus be said to employ a form of negative parliamentarism, making it fairly easy to form minority governments.

The electoral system of Sweden is highly proportional, and the threshold of representation is set at 4 per cent. The combined effect of this is that it is possible for a relatively large number of parties to achieve representation in the *Riksdag*. However, the system has surprisingly often managed to produce stable governments, perhaps due to the willingness to find compromises that has been part of Swedish political culture. Today there are eight parties represented—from the smallest to the largest—of around 5 per cent to around 28 per cent. No single political party dominates the political scene as the Social Democrats used to do during most of the twentieth century.

---

[70] See Eivind Smith, 'Judicial Review of Legislation' in Helle Krunke and Björg Thorarensen (eds), *The Nordic Constitutions: A Comparative and Contextual Study* (n 54) 107–132. See also Jens Elo Rytter and Marlene Wind, 'In need of juristocracy? The silence of Denmark in the development of European legal norms' (2011) 9 (2) ICON 470; Juha Lavapuro, Tuomas Ojanen and Martin Scheinin, 'Rights-based Constitutionalism in Finland and the development of pluralist Constitutional review' (2011) 9 (2) ICON 505. An interesting attempt at comparative discussion and analysis can be found in Ran Hirschl 'The Nordic counternarrative: Democracy, human development, and judicial review' (2011) 9 (2) ICON 449.

[71] Fritz W Scharpfe, Governing in Europe: Effective and Democratic (OUP, Oxford, 1999).

Voter turnout is generally high: 87.2 per cent at the 2018 election and 84.12 per cent in 2022. In Sweden, politicians still have a, by international standards, high level of legitimacy. Having said this, Sweden is not free from the wave of disenchantment with established political parties which appears to have swept through Western democracies. This is shown by the steep rise since 2010, in the people voting for a populist party, the Swedish Democrats. They are, in many ways, a 'single issue' party, focusing on migration as the source of most societal problems. In a Nordic perspective it can be noted that Sweden is following Norway and Denmark, where similar parties established themselves some ten or twenty years earlier. The rise of this kind of political movement is a challenge for many of the established political parties in Western Europe, as elections around the continent in 2018 and 2019 have shown. The attractiveness of their rather simplistic message is a fact as well as a puzzle. Here is not the place to discuss this further, but it must be noted that the idea of an 'illiberal democracy' that some of these populist movements are inspired by is probably the antithesis of the constitutional and limited form of democratic governance that we have in focus in this work.

In the general election of September 2014, the result was a centre/right and a social democratic/green/left block of more or less equal size, with the populist right-wing party, the Swedish Democrats, holding the balance of power. A minority government was formed between the SDP and the green party, with the tacit support of the left party. There was a similar election result in 2018. A minority government was eventually formed between the SDP and the green party, with the tacit support of the centre and liberal parties, and with the left party not voting against it. The process of negotiations etc. took 143 days, the longest period of a caretaker government yet in modern Swedish history. In 2022, the four centre/right parties formed a minority government with the support of the Swedish democrats.

In any event, for most of the last fifty years of Swedish political history, the government has not had a clear majority in parliament, but rather has been dependent upon cutting deals with one or more small parties for support. This situation is now so established that it seems to be the natural order of Swedish politics. There is a debate among political scientists as to whether the Swedish political system can be described, following Lijphart's taxonomy,[72] as 'majoritarian' with consensus elements, or as 'consensuses with majoritarian elements,[73] but it is clear that a consequence of the party system has been that negotiations and political solutions that cross party lines are common in political life in Sweden. This fits well with a political culture that is also very consensus-oriented in other aspects, such as labour market relations and economic policy. The desire to build consensus is usually a strength. However, where there is an equal power-relationship between the 'left' and the 'right' blocks, and there is consequently less interest in compromise, then the desire for consensus can be a weakness, in that it can block necessary reforms (e.g. of the housing market, which according to many economists, is an overdue fundamental reform). The willingness to compromise increases when one is in an actual crisis. As mentioned in Section A.4, during the financial crisis of 1990/91, the political parties quickly reached agreement on a parcel of major reforms of the budgetary system that probably could not have been reached otherwise.

So, Sweden can be said to have mainly a procedural approach to democracy. The Swedish constitutional discussion has not had to formulate substantive limits to democracy. As noted

---

[72] Arend Lijphart, Patterns of Democracy Government Forms and Performance in Thirty-Six Countries (Yale University Press, New Haven, 1999).

[73] Magnus Isberg, 'Is Sweden Going Majoritarian?' in, Torbjörn Persson and Matti Wiberg (eds), *Parliamentary Government in the Nordic Countries at a Crossroads: Coping with Challenges from Europeanisation and Presidentialisation* (Santerius, Stockholm, 2011).

above in Section A.4 (and further discussed below, Section C.3) the main safeguards for rights are still the parliamentary process and the transparent public administration together with the established media serving as public watchdogs.[74] The procedure for constitutional amendment (above Section B.4) and the 'qualified legislative procedure' is based on the—perhaps quaint—idea that, should a majority of the people's representatives try to enact a statute which goes too far in limiting relative rights, then this can be delayed by a minority. The delay is to enable the people to 'wake up' and exercise their democratic rights to protest. Sweden has not yet had to cope with the fact the majority of the people may be enthusiastically for a law which restricts their own rights, e.g. in the name of security (or, more likely, restricts the rights of an ethnic minority).

The final aspect of this issue is the balance between direct and representative democracy and can be dealt with very briefly. National referendums are a very limited exception to the representative form of government set out in RF 1:1 and they can be held only in two cases: as binding on a matter of constitutional change (RF 8:16) and as consultative on any other question put to the people. As noted in Section A.4, the first of these was introduced in 1980, as part of a package of constitutional reforms designed to strengthen rights protection. RF 8:16 provides for clear turnout and approval quorum rules for binding referendums, whereas consultative referendums are governed by a statute passed for each referendum.

There has never been a binding referendum. However, there have been two consultative referendums in modern times, on EU membership (1994) and on joining the euro (2003). The fact that the political parties agreed in advance that the result of these referendums would be treated as 'politically binding' has blurred the distinction made in the constitution between binding and non-binding referendums.

3. Relationship Between Constitutional Law and International Law

The issue of whether treaties could be self-executing was in fact unresolved until the early 1970s, just before the adoption of the new RF, when the Swedish courts ruled that, in the absence of legislation converting it to Swedish law, the ECHR did not create direct rights capable of being invoked before national courts.[75] Thus, the dualism of the Swedish legal order is a creation of case law, something which is an exception to what we have said before, that all constitutional issues of importance have been decided by politicians.[76] The RF still does not say anything explicitly about the domestic legal effect of treaties. Nonetheless, dualism is implicit in the structure of RF, particularly the provisions dealing with transfer of legislative power (RF 10:6, 7, and 8), which are based on a conceptional distinction between the realm of international law, and domestic law—a distinction which all international lawyers know is increasingly difficult to sustain.

In Sweden, the first argument against letting a ratified but unincorporated treaty create rights for individuals is not so much democracy in the sense of parliamentary control over

---

[74] The decline in importance of the established media, and the rise in importance of social media thus has implications for Swedish democracy, and rights protection.

[75] AD 5/1972, s 75; NJA 1973, s 423; and RÅ 197, s 121. Decisions from the Labour Court (*Arbetsdomstolen*, AD) are from the official series, AD. On the issues discussed in this section, see generally Iain Cameron, 'Swedish parliamentary participation in the making and implementation of treaties' (2005) 74 (3–4) Nordic Journal of International Law 429.

[76] Of course, one can counter this by saying that, at the time, international law was not a significant source of domestic law, and so the issue was not regarded as very important.

the government, but constitutional notions of the domestic division of powers between parliament and government on the one hand and the courts on the other. The second argument relates to legal certainty (*rättssäkerhet*). This involves not simply the foreseeability of particular norms but also, in need of a better term, 'system coherence' naturally enough something which is particularly important in codified legal orders.

It can, of course, be argued that legal certainty is not a good reason for denying a right to an individual exercisable vis-à-vis the state, as opposed to another individual. On the other hand, allowing unincorporated/untransformed treaties to create rights would still mean that the Swedish courts would have to decide which rights in a treaty were sufficiently clear, complete etc. to be self-executing. This would, in the Swedish legal tradition, be regarded as a usurpation of the role of parliament.[77] After all, most rights cost money, and in the end, it is the taxpayer who pays. Even if arguments could be found that the Swedish courts should take such a power, it is clear that this would lead to costs to society in the form of litigation, ineffective use of scarce judicial resources, and risks of conflicting findings in the administrative and ordinary courts. Human rights treaties also mean infringing on the autonomy of local authorities.

Partly as a result of this, Sweden has traditionally incorporated relatively few of the many human rights treaties it is bound by. The recent decision to incorporate the UN Convention on the Rights of the Child in consequence drew considerable criticism from legal institutions and legal scholars. In particular it was pointed out that as the *Riksdag* did not accompany the incorporation decision by providing, in the bill, any detailed guidance for administrative agencies and the courts in applying the vague and result-oriented provisions of the Convention. Consequently, it posed a risk of being a large transfer of power from specialized administrative agencies and local authorities to the courts.

Legislation, or delegated legislation, is almost invariably required when an international treaty is to be given effect in some way in Sweden. At what constitutional level the norm is passed is something which is regulated in Chapter 8 of the Instrument of Government.[78] However, the practice which has developed requiring conversion of international treaties to national law is somewhat wider than simply covering treaties creating rights or, naturally, duties for individuals. Treaties which require the enactment of rules governing the activity of government departments, administrative agencies, or local authorities, especially this activity vis à vis individuals, should also be converted, if the rules in question have no existing national equivalent, or conflict with existing national rules.[79]

Negotiation of treaties is an exclusive matter for the government, as in most constitutional systems. However, RF 10:3 provides that the government may not conclude an international agreement binding upon the Realm without the approval of the *Riksdag*, if the agreement presupposes the amendment or abrogation of a law or the enactment of a new law, or if it otherwise concerns a matter which it is for the *Riksdag* to determine. Thus, when approving a treaty involves the need to enact or amend a statute, the *Riksdag* must take two separate parliamentary decisions. Approval can come first, or enactment of the statute can come first. However, both are usually expressed in one and the same bill.

---

[77] Similar reasons are invoked for not incorporating, but rather transforming, treaties containing vague provisions.

[78] Below, Section C.6.

[79] See e.g. Government bill (Proposition, Prop.) 1990/91:113, 13–14 (concerning mutual assistance in criminal matters).

The Swedish courts do apply the principle of treaty conform construction. However, in practice, this is mainly used in regard to the ECHR and some very technical but important treaties on international taxation.[80] As already mentioned, the ECHR is also a special case constitutionally speaking, as RF 2:19 provides that, 'a law or other regulation may not be issued in conflict with [the Convention]'. This provision means that if a norm violates the ECHR (as interpreted by the ECtHR), it also violates the constitution and so, in accordance with the provision on constitutional review in (RF 11:14) should not be applied. This provision is, however, primarily directed to the legislature and pre-legislative scrutiny of statutes is supposed to be the primary mechanism for avoiding conflicts with either the constitution or the ECHR. However, if, for some reason, this scrutiny has failed to detect a conflict, or a conflict has later arisen as a result of later case law, the Swedish courts have the power, and the duty, to refuse to apply the offending norm. In the—unlikely—event that a provision in the constitution conflicts with the ECHR, and the conflict between the two provisions cannot be solved by giving the constitutional provision an ECHR-conform interpretation, then the Swedish courts must apply the constitutional provision.

As already noted, the Swedish courts have become used to applying the ECHR, and it has had an impact on a number of areas of Swedish law, primarily administrative law and the law of criminal procedure.[81] However, constitutional review of statutes based on ECtHR case law is still rare. This can partly be explained by the fact that draft legislation is supposed to take the ECHR into account. Another reason is the fact that the highest Swedish courts, while encouraging the lower courts to engage in ECHR-conform interpretation, have formulated a test requiring there to be 'clear support' in the case law of the ECtHR before going so far as to engage in constitutional review.[82] This clear support test can be seen as a recognition that the Court's principles are at times vague, that there are five different chambers in the Court, and they do not always agree and that errors can easily be made in the process of 'translating' a judgment concerning another state into the Swedish context. As already noted, there is no longer a 'manifest' rule in RF 11:14, and the ECJ rejects the idea that EU law should be subject to such a test. This means that there are different constitutional review tests to be applied, depending on the catalogue of rights in question (Chapter 2 RF/EU Charter/ECHR). On the other hand, the confusion caused by the ECtHR's case law on ne bis in idem[83] confirms the need for something like the 'clear support' test.

4. Relationship Between Constitutional Law and EU Law

Nowadays, the coherence of the Swedish dualist position vis-à-vis international law is undermined by the wholescale incorporation of EU law through the Act (1994:1500) in connection with Swedish membership of the EU. The Act provides that EU law governs the effect that EU norms have in the national legal order. Thus, the primary treaties, EU regulations, some EU directives, and some EU treaties with third states can now have direct effect in Swedish law.

---

[80] See e.g. NJA 1992 s 532. See further Iain Cameron and Thomas Bull, 'Sweden', in Jannecke Gerards and Joseph Fleuren (eds), *Implementation of the European Convention on Human Rights and of the Judgments of the ECtHR in National Case Law, A Comparative Analysis* (Intersentia, Cambridge, 2014).

[81] See Iain Cameron and Thomas Bull, 'Sweden' (n 80). See also Section C.6.

[82] See NJA 2000 s 622 and NJA 2013 s 502.

[83] The ECtHR's judgment in *Sergey Zolotukhin v Russia* [GC], No. 14939/03, 10 February 2009, caused considerable litigation in Sweden, culminating in judgments in the Supreme Court (sitting in plenary) and Supreme Administrative Court, and then legislative changes to the system of tax surcharges. Following this, the ECtHR then backtracked, to some extent, in *A and B v Norway* [GC], Nos. 24130/11 and 29758/11, ECHR 2016.

We have already touched upon the decision of Sweden to become an EU member. In this section we say something about the relationship between the concept of 'sovereignty' in the Instrument of Government, and how this it connected to the democratic principle.[84]

The Swedish state has existed in (more or less) the same borders for more than 500 years. Consequently, Swedish sovereignty has been taken for granted. It was first in connection with membership of the EC/EU that the Swedish parliament had to think about the question of national (as opposed to popular) sovereignty. The first proposal which was made by a commission of inquiry to enable Swedish membership of the (then) European Community (EC) was to provide that EC law took precedence over all national law, including national constitutional law. This was described in the political context as a 'walk-over' solution and rejected out of hand. Instead, a new, hastily appointed, commission of inquiry borrowed a solution from the German Federal Constitutional Court (*BVerfG*), namely the *Solange II* case.[85] After the referendum approving Swedish membership in November 1994, parliament definitively approved a legislative proposal to amend the provision which allows the transfer of legislative power to the EU. The relevant part of (what is now RF 10:6) reads: 'Within the framework of EU cooperation, the *Riksdag* may transfer decision-making authority which does not affect the basic principles by which Sweden is governed. Such transfer presupposes that protection for rights and freedoms in the field of cooperation to which the transfer relates corresponds to that afforded under this Instrument of Government and the ECHR.'

What the exact 'basic principles by which Sweden is governed' are, was not set out in the constitution. Instead, there was a discussion of these in the *travaux préparatoires*, where protecting the position of parliament as the main actor when it comes to legislation and use of public power, the protection of constitutional rights and the fundamental parts of the special constitutional protection of the media (Freedom of the Press Act and Freedom of Expression Act YGL), including the principle of transparency were mentioned as examples.[86] This provision is not an 'eternity clause', but there is a certain overlap in function with such a clause.

Originally, the parliament considered that it itself had the final word on whether a transfer of sovereignty had in fact occurred. However, this was based on a misunderstanding of the nature of the EU treaty. As the EU treaty is a 'framework' treaty, it is first when the EU legislates on a particular topic that one can say whether or not it has acted within the delegated area. Later it was noted in the *travaux préparatoires* of the reform of 2010, that the ultimate responsibility for policing the boundaries set out by the Swedish parliament in RF 10:6 must be given to the Swedish courts.[87] Parliament has indicated that, normally, the courts should accept that the EU norm falls within the area of legislative competence delegated to the EU and so give it precedence over Swedish laws.[88] The creation of the subsidiarity mechanism in the Lisbon treaty (Article 5 TEU, and the Protocol on the Role of national parliaments in the EU) means that in practice, the room for such conflicts is limited in practice.[89] For its

---

[84] For more detail on the relationship between the EU and the Swedish constitution, see Joakim Nergelius, 'The Constitution of Sweden and European Influences: The Changing Balance Between Democratic and Judicial Power', in Anneli Albi and Samo Bardutzky, *National Constitutions in European and Global Governance: Democracy, Rights, the Rule of Law: National Reports* (n 47).

[85] See BVerfGE 73, 339—*Solange II*.

[86] 1993/94: KU21 s 27. See also the more detailed discussion in 2001/02: KU18 s 42. For analysis see Joachim Åhman, *Överlåtelse av beslutanderätt* (Iustus, Uppsala, 2015).

[87] See SOU 2008:125, s 500.

[88] Prop. 2001/02:72, s 34–35.

[89] Sweden differs from Denmark and Finland in not having created a powerful parliamentary committee which can bind the government in its negotiations in the EU Council. Instead, the Committee on EU affairs (*EU-nämnden*) coordinates the substantive committees' consideration of draft EU legislation and can make

part, the Swedish Supreme Court has taken the approach that, as far as compliance with the ECHR is concerned, where the ECJ has examined the issue (a preliminary ruling had been sought and obtained in the case in question) there is a presumption that the ECJ will comply with the ECHR, and that the room for the Swedish courts coming to another conclusion was limited.[90]

The fact that the EU Charter on Fundamental Rights has become binding law means that the same—more or less—human rights standards apply for the EU as legislator, as do for the Swedish *Riksdag*. However, the extent of the protections for freedom of the press and freedom of expression in the Freedom of the Press Act and the Freedom of Expression Act means that Sweden has to be careful to secure exceptions when negotiating a range of EU regulations and directives, e.g. as regards the prohibition of any form of censorship. There is an ongoing debate in Sweden as regards whether there is a 'price' that is being paid for maintaining the Freedom of the Press Act—Freedom of Expression Act, and if so, whether this price is still worth paying. Nonetheless, even in areas covered by qualified majority voting, national fundamental interests can usually be accommodated. The situation is different if an issue is left, accidentally or by design, to the ECJ to decide. The ECJ may balance competing rights differently from the Swedish *Riksdag*. Indeed, it has done so in several areas, which has caused considerable headaches for the Swedish legislator.[91]

5. Rights and the Rule of Law

We have already dealt with the evolution of the rights chapter in the Instrument of Government and how these rights have, since 1995, and increasingly, since 2011, been treated by the courts as enforceable rights. The main body responsible for drawing balances between constitutional rights and other interests is still the parliament. As already mentioned, the category of relative rights set out in Chapter 2 can be restricted by an ordinary statute, passed by simple majority in the parliament, although certain substantive conditions have to be fulfilled. This category includes the freedoms from search, seizure, telecommunications, and mail interception and other major restrictions in personal integrity (section 6), from deprivation of liberty (section 8), and the right of access to court to challenge detention (section 9), and the right to a fair trial (section 11).[92] Three rights included in Instrument of Government Chapter 2 are of the kind that demand constitutional amendment to effect any limitation: the prohibitions of the death penalty (section 4), inhuman or degrading punishment (section 5), and retroactive criminal law (section 10). Rights under the Freedom of the Press and Freedom of Expression Acts require constitutional amendment to change.

---

recommendations to the government. The Swedish system has been compared unfavourably to the Danish and Finnish systems.

[90] NJA 2014 s 79.

[91] See, in particular, Case C-341/05 *Laval* (ECLI EU:C:2007:809). More recently, problems have been caused by Cases C-157/15 *Samira Achbita and Centrum voor gelijkheid van kansen en voor racismebestrijding v G4S Secure Solutions NV* (ECLI:EU:2017:203) and C-188/15 *Asma Bougnaoui Association de défense des droits de l'homme (ADDH) v Micropole SA* (ECLI:EU:C:2017:204) and Joined Cases C 203/15 and C 698/15, *Tele2 Sverige AB* (C 203/ 15) *v Post- och telestyrelsen, and Secretary of State for the Home Department* (C 698/15) *v Tom Watson, Peter Brice and Geoffrey Lewis* (ECLI:EU:C:2016:970).

[92] As already noted, the procedural safeguard the 'qualified legislative procedure' applies. This is very seldom invoked, but its existence (in particular, when, as is usual the government is a minority government) serves to encourage careful preparation of the legislation, as well as political compromise.

We have also dealt with the quasi-constitutional status of the ECHR (above Section C.3) and the position of the EU Charter (above Section C.4). As noted in Section C.1, one particularly interesting development since 2011 is the recognition by the Supreme Court of a right to damages for violations of the constitutional rights of individuals in certain cases.[93] This is a 'spill over' effect of national case law recognizing a right to damages for violation of ECHR rights (article 13).[94] It can be seen as an exception to what we have written earlier, that the legislator is the main driver of constitutional developments, and can be explained partly by the creative role the general courts have traditionally had in the area of tort law. Even here, however, the exception is temporary. The legislator has later 'retaken' control over the process. A commission of inquiry investigated a general right of damages for violation of the (incorporated) ECHR and legislation was introduced, amending the Tort Liability Act (1972:207) in the 2010s.[95] The government has recently introduced a bill providing for a right of damages for violation of constitutional rights.[96]

We have also dealt with the role of the Council on Legislation in the legislative process. When it scrutinizes draft legislation from the perspective of the constitution, the Council on Legislation is engaging in a form of abstract constitutional preview, and thus acting as a substitute for a constitutional court. The other mechanism, which to some degree substitutes for the function of constitutional complaints (*Verfassungsbeschwerde*) in the German system is individual complaints to the parliamentary ombudsman (*Riksdagens ombudsman, justitieombudsmannen*), and this mechanism can suitably be dealt with in this section.

The task of the ombudsman—which is regulated in a special law—is to watch over the public administration so that it follows the law and respects the rights of individuals. Any person can complain to the ombudsman about administrative actions or decisions. The ombudsman will however not deal with a case where the same situation is tried in court or where there is a more suitable public authority that the person could approach. In that sense the ombudsman is an extra-ordinary legal remedy. The ombudsman will examine any complaint and if accepted an inquiry will be made, involving a more or less ambitious investigation according to the need of the case.

The ombudsman decides around 400 cases yearly in substance.[97] Many decisions are taken in a simplified form that only reminds the authority in question that it has made a (formal) mistake of some kind. Other decisions are made public and contain criticism of one or more civil servants for mistakes or negligence in the line of service. In rare cases the ombudsman can act as a public prosecutor, bringing civil servants before the courts for criminal acts.

The critical decisions of the four Parliamentary Ombudsmen in the Swedish system are not binding. This has resulted in certain authors not regarding the Ombudsman as a 'protection' of constitutional rights.[98] However, criticism from the ombudsman has, generally speaking, serious consequences for the career of the civil servant concerned.[99] The decisions

---

[93] See NJA 2014 s 323; NJA 2014 s 332; NJA 2015 s 374; NJA 2018 s 103.

[94] See NJA 2005 s 462; NJA 2005 s 726; NJA 2007 s 584; NJA 2007 s 891. The process began with the ECtHR judgment in *Kudla v Poland*, No. 30210/96, 26 October 2000.

[95] SOU 2010:87, Tort Liability Act 3:4.

[96] Prop 2021/22:229, Grundlagsskadestånd.

[97] Out of around 8500 complaints. Decisions can be found at https://www.jo.se/sv/Om-JO/Ambetsberattelser/ (last accessed on 01 July 2022).

[98] It should be noted here that the Swedish Ombudsman is not, generally speaking, regarded as a remedy within the meaning of Article 13 ECHR. The government also has an official with wide supervisory (and prosecution) powers over the administration (the Chancellor of Justice). While important as a means of constitutional control, this institution cannot generally be described as an independent remedy for individuals.

[99] In practice, a distinction can sometimes be drawn between the impact of the Ombudsman's decisions on state authorities and on local authorities. The principle of local government autonomy, enshrined in RF 14:2, occasionally makes it easier for a local government civil servant, where he or she has been acting in accordance with

of the ombudsman are usually also well-reasoned. They are thus influential in maintaining and improving standards of good public administration and we consider that a wider approach to the Swedish 'legal culture' of constitutional rights should take them into account.

Having said this, they can be dealt with fairly briefly in the present article because, while many cases concern alleged infringements of rights (especially in the area of police powers) relatively few decisions explicitly take up rights under the Instrument of Government or the ECHR.[100] The ombudsman slightly more frequently criticises public authorities for not complying with the right of public access to documents, or limiting civil servants' right of access to the press, and other issues under the Freedom of the Press and Expression Acts.

Turning now to the 'rule of law' in the Swedish constitutional system, RF 1:1 para 2 provides that: 'public power is exercised under the law'. This expresses the principle of legality, the first part of the rule of the law. Any exercise of public power must be based on a legal authority—in statute, a government ordinance, or a binding administrative. There are many examples of Ombudsman criticism, and judgments of the administrative courts, finding that such legal authority has been lacking, rendering any consequent decisions null and void. Equality before the law/non-discrimination is protected by the constitutional principle of objectivity (*sakligkeit*). The constitutional provision in question, RF 1:9, states that all courts and public authorities 'shall observe in their work the equality of all persons before the law and shall maintain objectivity and impartiality'.[101] The principle of objectivity is an important adjunct to constitutional rights protection and was, before the introduction of the explicit protection of rights in Chapter 2 of the Instrument of Government, one of the only ways to argue legally against the arbitrary use of public powers. It is still an essential mechanism for reconciling the administrative flexibility necessary for a complex social welfare state with the rule of law and strengthens the legitimacy of the public administration (and social capital). Other essential elements of the rule of law are dealt with in the next section.

6. Constitutional Organs, the Separation of Powers, the Organization of the Courts, and the Independence of the Judiciary

Parliamentarism and not separation of powers is the defining political feature of the Swedish constitution and, as has been pointed out above, the central constitutional institution is thus the *Riksdag*. Historically speaking this focus on parliament is due to the struggle of power between parliament and the King in early twentieth century. 'Separation of powers' has in the historical Swedish context come to be associated with a political role for the King and is for this reason something to be avoided. We have already covered the importance given to parliamentary legislation and the slowly emerging acceptance of the courts as a separate state power in its own right. With the constitutional reform in 2011 the full acceptance of such a 'normal' concept of separation of powers—legislators legislate, governments govern, and courts decide according to law—was symbolically heralded in by devoting a full chapter of the Instrument of Government to the role of the courts.

the wishes of the elected local authority, to shrug off such criticism. As explained below (C.7), many of the public functions of the state are handled by local government.

[100] Like the courts, the Ombudsman has a natural preference for concrete norms over abstract norms.
[101] Under the Ombudsman Act (1986:765) one of the particular functions of the Ombudsman is 'to ensure compliance with this principle and that citizens' basic human rights are not infringed'.

When it comes to executive powers, RF 1:6 states that the government governs the country and is accountable to the *Riksdag*. Under RF Chapter 6, the Prime Minister appoints the cabinet and distributes tasks to ministers as s/he sees fit. Members of the cabinet cannot at the same time hold a seat in parliament. Sweden does not have a ministerial government, as is common in many states. Instead, RF 7:3 stipulates that all government decisions (with a few exceptions) are collective cabinet decisions, even if they are prepared within specific ministries. Individual ministers of government thus wield little formal public power and the government is characterized by formal decision-making in the cabinet as a whole. Constitutionally, there is no such thing as ministerial government in Sweden as the government can only, with only a few exceptions, act as a collective.[102]

As mentioned, the Swedish system separates the administration from the government. Only a relatively small number of people (around 3,800) are employed in government departments. The bulk of the state public administration is performed by national administrative agencies (though as noted in the next section, most delivery of public services is in fact at local and regional level). These central administrative agencies have a duty to obey government directives. They can be steered by government in a number of different ways; however, they have a rather unique constitutionally protected freedom to interpret and apply the law in individual cases (RF 12:2) without the interference of government. This constitutionally protected independence applies except in the—relatively—rare cases where a law specifies that the government itself is the final administrative decision-making body. The administrative agencies in Sweden are thus not exercising their powers per delegation from the minister of a particular ministerial department but are seen as acting only on the basis of legal provisions granting them power in specific areas. Ministers—and the government—are therefore not legally responsible for actions taken by the administration in concrete cases of exercises of public power. Instead, public officials have criminal responsibility for their acts in the line of duty and are precluded from blaming instruction from 'above'.[103] The practical effect of this is that public officials are formally immune to political influence in their decision-making, while politicians are formally unaccountable for faults by the administration. In the context of a legalistic and (relatively) stable legal and political culture this has worked out quite well. This set-up means inter alia that there is not the same need for the courts to intervene to prevent the government from steering the administrative system (and the distribution of benefits) for party political reasons. The separation of the government from the every-day decisions of the administration also explains the (in international comparison) unusual scope of judicial review applied by the administrative courts, i.e. not simply of legality but also of appropriateness. As the minister is not responsible, even in theory, for the decisions of civil servants in an administrative agency, it is not an interference with a ministerial prerogative for the courts to replace it with the 'correct' decision.[104] Of course, the administrative courts are mindful of the technical expertise of civil servants, and do not, in fact, always exercise their power to amend an administrative decision, choosing instead to refer it back for a new decision.

---

[102] In practice individual ministers of government can of course have more or less influence and have informal ways of exercising influence.

[103] In practice, prosecution is very rare: the courts have set the threshold of the offence of 'misuse of office' very high.

[104] The exception being decisions of elected local and regional bodies. Due to the idea that it is political mechanisms of accountability which should be primary, these decisions are only subject to appeal on legality grounds. See also Sections C.5 and C.7.

As mentioned above, even parliamentary systems provide for division of state functions, and, regarding the exercise of legislative powers, Chapter 8 of the Instrument of Government specifies that the enactment of rules involving the creation of duties for individuals requires authority in the form of a statute. It is moreover stated that certain areas of law, among these, civil law, criminal law, and procedural law, are generally to be regulated by statute. In principle, any norms entailing obligations for natural or legal persons vis-à-vis the state must also be in statute form, as must the rules concerning the basic structure and competence of local authorities. However, both of these main rules are subject to a large number of exceptions where the parliament may, by statute, delegate power to the government to issue ordinances and/or to sub-delegate this power to administrative agencies or local authorities. Under the rules in Chapter 8, the government also has an independent power to issue ordinances in areas not specifically reserved for statutes and may sub-delegate this power to administrative agencies.

This section is also an appropriate place to say something about the third branch of government, the judiciary. Sweden has a dual court system common to many continental countries, with one kind of courts for private and criminal law issues (general courts) and one kind of courts for administrative law issues (general administrative courts). Some specialized courts also exist, i.e. the Labour Court. The general court system is old, with the Svea Court of Appeal (*Svea Hovrätt*), established in 1614, acting as a court of last instance until the Supreme Court was established in 1789. The Supreme Administrative Court was established as recently as 1909 as a way of relieving the government from the legal complaints that individuals by tradition always could bring before the 'King' (the government). A complete administrative three-tier court system was however not in place until the 1970s. Even after that time, many issues were still appealed not to the administrative courts but to hierarchically superior administrative agencies. As a result of Europeanization, beginning with the case law of the ECtHR and then EU membership, the right of appeal to the administrative courts has been expanded, and this is now the rule (though there are still exceptions, where appeals lie to quasi-judicial bodies).[105]

There is, as already mentioned, no constitutional court, in Sweden. The constitutional power of judicial review is instead given to all courts, rather like the decentralized systems of the United States of America and Norway. However, the constitutional changes in 2011 opened the way for the two Supreme Courts to co-opt members from the other court, when a case arises which raises issues 'straddling' administrative law and private or criminal law. Such issues can arise as a consequence of Europeanization, and a factor behind this change is the increased 'weight' such a combined court composition would have, in a situation of 'dialogue' between the Swedish courts and the ECtHR or ECJ.

Judges are appointed by the government which (since 2009) follows the recommendations of an independent commission on judicial appointments (*domarnämnden*), consisting of judges, lawyers, prosecutors, and some members of parliament. It has yet not happened that the government has appointed anyone not recommended by the commission.

Lawyers wanting to become judges follow a rather strict career, starting as junior judges in local courts and then serving alternatively in courts of appeal and in local court until they can obtain a tenure position. There is no 'automatic' promotion based solely on length of service. On paper, the protection of judicial independence for the large category of not-yet

---

[105] An individual can apply to the Supreme Administrative Court for review on points of law (*rättsprövning*) against decisions of the government.

tenured judges in Sweden is weaker than in many other countries.[106] Junior judges tend to spend a relatively long period (ten to fifteen years) before they can apply for a post with 'full' tenure, although the ordinary employment protection rules apply (i.e. dismissal only for personal deficiencies/good cause). Therefore, judicial appointments are not politically motivated and even judges without strong tenure behave with full independence from the executive. Having said this, the long period judges tend to spend without full tenure may serve to make them generally more cautious, not wanting to make any mistakes that will make it more difficult to obtain a full tenured post. This tends to make for ambitious junior judges, but also for a somewhat restrictive attitude to finding creative solutions to some legal problems, for example in the area of human rights and constitutional law. Lay judges sit in all first instance courts, and even in appeal courts, where, however, they are in a minority.[107]

It is likely that the level of detail in which the courts are regulated at the constitutional level will increase in the future, as a Commission of Inquiry has been appointed to propose such changes. It should be noted that there is an administrative agency, the Courts Administration, which deals with common administrative issues for the courts. However, the dividing line between administration and judging is not always clear, thus providing a—at present, it should be stressed theoretical—power for the government to steer the courts through this agency. Thus, an important part of the background to this new inquiry was the 'rule of law backsliding' in EU states such as Hungary and Poland. While no 'entrenchment' can protect against a determined assault on judicial independence, a requirement that changes in court procedure, funding etc. must be in the form of a statute would make quick, and quiet, changes much more difficult, and may consequently make it easier to mobilize public pressure to withdraw draft changes.

7. The Organization of the State

As noted before (in Section B.1), Sweden is a unitary state, but there is a relatively high level of local self-government. The state is represented at the regional level by twenty-one county boards (*länsstyrelsen*) which amongst other things, supervise certain administrative decisions taken by local authorities within the county. The bulk of the public administration is performed by, or through, the 290 communes and, in the areas of transport and health care, by twenty[108] county health/transport authorities (*regioner*). Each local authority and each region is based on a democratic mandate and have an elected assembly from which the governing body is chosen. Basically, the same proportional methods of election as for national elections apply: the electorate is all residents in the area (including foreign citizens). The decentralized delivery of public services meant that Sweden's response to the Covid-19 pandemic was somewhat fragmented, with no one taking a holistic responsibility.[109]

Although most delivery of public services is local, or regional, most of the local authorities and regions tasks are regulated in some detail in national statutes. These include social

---

[106] For a (very) critical approach see Joakim Nergelius and Dominik Zimmermann, 'Judicial Independence in Sweden', in Anja Seibert-Fohr (ed), *Judicial Independence in Transition: Strengthening the Rule of Law in the OSCE Region* (Springer, Heidelberg, 2012) 185.

[107] Jury trial exists only for cases under the Freedom of the Press and Freedom of Expression Acts.

[108] The island of Gotland has a local authority which is also responsible for regional health/transport issues.

[109] See Iain Cameron and Anna Jonsson Cornell, 'Sweden and Covid-19: A (Mainly) Recommendary Approach', in Nadav Morag (ed), *Impacts of the Covid-19 Pandemic: International Laws, Policies, and Civil Liberties* (Wiley, NY, 2022).

services (Social Services Act 2001:453), health and medical services (Health Services Act 2017:30), the environmental and health protection (Environmental Code 1998:808), planning (Planning and Building Act 2010:900), as well as legislation on pre-, basic, and upper secondary school (School Act 2010:800). The Administration Act (2017:900) provides general rules for administrative agencies and local authorities on the administration dealings with individuals.[110]

During the late 1980s and early 1990s, a wave of deregulation of public services occurred, and many public services are nowadays provided by private actors which have been procured by the local authorities, instead of by the local authorities themselves. This rather radical change in the public sector was achieved without constitutional change[111] and may be surprising for some outside observers who associate the Swedish welfare state with some sort of 'socialism'. The performance of these procured services is usually monitored by central administrative agencies, to which individual complaints can often be made.

Local authorities vary widely in size, the largest being Kiruna (19,447 km^2) and the smallest being Sundbyberg (9 km^2) as well as population, the largest being Stockholm (approximately 794,000) to Bjurholm (approximately 2,600). Thirteen of the country's local authorities have more than 100,000 inhabitants. A trend in Sweden (as in most of the rest of the Western world) is urbanization, leading to a shrinking population in rural local authorities and consequent problems for delivery of public services. The huge variations in size and population of local authorities cause problems when it comes to ensuring a satisfactory minimal level of technical and administrative competence for local authority civil servants. Nonetheless, the quality of administration in Sweden (and, in the Nordic countries as a whole) tends to be relatively high.[112] An important element in this is a constitutional principle, not included in the Instrument of Government but in the Freedom of the Press Act, namely, the principle of transparency of public documents.[113] Combined with the right to leak public information,[114] a strong media. and the investigative powers of the Ombudsman, this facilitates the uncovering of maladministration.

The territorial organization of the state is only to some extent regulated in the constitution. This is deliberate, in order to leave flexibility for future changes. The 2011 reform of the Instrument of Government gathered together most of the provisions dealing with local authorities in a single chapter, Chapter 14. This is another example of the tendency we identified (Section B.1) of the constitution being amended to reflect social realities.

---

[110] We will not go into the relationship between administrative law and constitutional law, beyond noting that they have previously lived quite separate lives, but that a degree of constitutionalization (and 'Europeization') of general administrative law can now be detected. See, inter alia, Lena Marcusson, 'Grundzüge des Verwaltungsrechts in gemeineuropäischer Perspektive: Schweden', in Sabino Cassese, Armin von Bogdandy, and Peter Huber (eds), *Handbuch Ius Publicum Europaeum. Band V: Verwaltungsrecht in Europa: Grundzüge* (CF Müller, Heidelberg, 2014) 631 ff and Luc Heuschling, 'The Complex Relationship Between Administrative and Constitutional Law: A Comparative and Historical Analysis', in Sabino Cassese, Armin von Bogdandy, and Peter Huber (eds), *The Max Planck Handbooks in European Public Law: Volume i: The Administrative State* (OUP, Oxford, 2017) 493 ff.

[111] RF 12:4 provides that 'Administrative functions may be delegated to local authorities. Administrative functions may also be delegated to other legal entities or to individuals. If such a function involves the exercise of public authority, it may only be delegated in accordance with law.' This last sentence means that a statute passed by the *Riksdag* must provide for the possibility of delegation.

[112] As already noted, respect for the principle of objectivity, and the general effectiveness of the social welfare system, appears to have a strong positive effect on social capital. See Sören Holmberg and Bo Rothstein, *Good Government—The Relevance of Political Science* (Edward Elgar Publishing, Cheltenham, 2012).

[113] TF 2:1, 2:2, which should be read together with the Openness and Secrecy Act (2009:400) which sets out the detailed exceptions, and procedures, for keeping official documents secret.

[114] TF 1:1.

THE EVOLUTION AND *GESTALT* OF THE SWEDISH CONSTITUTION   635

Local authorities have a constitutionally recognized power to set local income tax rates (RF 14:4). This is of course an important part of the independence of local authorities in the Swedish constitutional system; they have financial muscles. At the same time, RF 14:5 provides, that local authorities may be obliged to contribute to costs incurred by other local authorities, if necessary, to achieve an equal financial base. The framework for redistributing income tax is set out in a statute.

Local self-government is given a weak level of protection in RF 14:3 which provides that, 'Any restriction in local self-government should not exceed what is necessary regarding the purpose of the restriction.' This provision is, according to the *travaux préparatoires*, non-judicially reviewable. RF 14:6 provides that regulations regarding grounds for changes in the division of the realm into local authorities are to be laid down in law, giving local institutions some protection against governmental control.[115]

8. Citizenship and the 'Political Unity'

Relatively little need be said about this issue. The term used to describe the state in the Instrument of Government is '*riket*', the Realm. This is despite the fact that the state is, to all intents and purposes, a republic. Little is said about citizenship in the Instrument of Government. RF 3:4 provides that 'Every Swedish citizen who is currently domiciled within the Realm or who has ever been domiciled within the Realm, and who has reached the age of eighteen, is entitled to vote in an election to the *Riksdag*. Only a person who is entitled to vote may be a member or alternate member of the *Riksdag*. The question of whether a person has the right to vote is determined on the basis of an electoral roll drawn up prior to the election.'

RF 2:7 provides, that Swedish citizens may not be deprived of their citizenship, nor refused entry into the realm. There has been a small amount of case law interpreting this provision.

More detailed regulation of citizenship is set out in a statute, the Act (2001:82) on Swedish Citizenship. It is relatively easy to become a Swedish citizen: eligibility comes more or less automatically after five years of residence. Since 2004, dual citizenship is possible. There has been a perception that Sweden was, historically, a homogenous country. Of course, from the beginning of the Swedish nation-state, it has included minorities, of which the indigenous Sami people and immigrants from Finland were the largest groups. Now, more than one million of the 10.5 million Swedish population have a foreign origin, meaning birth abroad, or one or both parents having been born abroad. The concept of 'constitutional patriotism' may become more important in the future as Sweden is no longer an ethnically homogenous country.[116] In the wake of the migration crisis of 2015, there is an ongoing discussion on whether material conditions (in particular, some degree of proficiency in the Swedish language) should be introduced to qualify for citizenship.

D. Constitutional Identity

Little or nothing is said about constitutional identity in the constitutional texts in Sweden. The Instrument of Government contains no ringing (emotional) declarations of principles, nation, or religion. Sweden has, compared to many other countries, felt less need to (re)

---

[115] See also Section C.4.
[116] Jan-Werner Müller, *Constitutional Patriotism* (Princeton University Press, Princeton, 2007).

invent itself in the constitution. This has, of course, to do with the 500 years of rather un-broken history of statehood. As already noted (Section C.4) in the section on international cooperation, some limits are set for transfer of legislative power to international organizations and in that context the 'basic principles by which Sweden is governed' are mentioned as something that must not be affected by such a transfer. So, here is a hint of a legally defined constitutional identity. No case law has evolved that would make this rule more concrete, so it is still somewhat unsure what it means in practice. The parliament has not, so far, taken the view that any EU norm oversteps this boundary, although it has (quite frequently) objected to draft EU norms being adopted on the basis of the principle of subsidiarity.

So, we need to look elsewhere to find the constitutional identity of Sweden. Three features stand out and shall be presented below.

The first attribute we would single out as part of a Swedish constitutional identity on the level of political and legal culture has already been mentioned: namely the strong striving towards consensus in Swedish society generally. This has also had effects on how politics are conducted in Sweden, as political solutions that include rather than exclude are preferred.[117] To a certain extent this striving for a common understanding also has to do with a rational and technical approach to societal problems as problems that can be met by (more) know-ledge and the right tools to implement the solutions that this knowledge reveals. One can note in this respect that there is a case for Sweden being a country far less like other countries than one would be inclined to think as a Swede.[118] As a constitution can only reflect the so-ciety in which it operates (if not a facade), it is at least likely that a society that stands out like this would also have a constitutional identity that is unusual in a comparative perspective.

Secondly, the 'constitution-less half century', to which we have referred several times above has had two interesting effects on constitutional thinking in Sweden, the first being the embracing of a highly descriptive constitution and the second being a very sceptical view on the law's relationship to politics. Both of these traits have had long-term effects on ap-proaches to constitutional issues that we can see still today.

Thirdly, as for constitutional rules that hold a special place in the political and legal prac-tice and in the mind of citizens, the Swedish constitution does not have the norms like the German Basic Law's fundamental provision on human dignity (article 1 Basic Law) or the Fourteenth Amendment on the right to equal treatment of the US Constitution. In this sense, the Swedish constitution is not 'socially embedded'. However, as already noted in Section B.1, the idea of constitutionalism is firmly established in Swedish constitutional tradition: that the government of the country is under the law, and that these laws are to be drafted, slowly, by consensus if possible and taking into account certain important values. And if you look a bit closer at the Swedish system there are in fact some candidates for this type of particular position as a value-laden symbol of the constitutional system as such.

The first such candidate would be the above-mentioned constitutional regulation of free speech in the media, covered by the Freedom of the Press and Freedom of Expression Acts. Their history goes back to 1766 and they have over the centuries taken on an almost mythical

---

[117] See Leif Lewin, *Bråka inte! Om vår tids demokratisyn* (SNS, Stockholm, 2002) [*Don't fight! On the approach to democracy in our times*].

[118] Henrik Berggren and Lars Trädgårdh, *Är svensken människa? gemenskap och oberoende i det moderna Sverige* (Norstedts, Stockholm, 2009) [*Is the Swede Human? Collectivity and Self-sufficiency in Modern Sweden*]. A short version is available in English: Henrik Berggren and Lars Trädgårdh, 'Social Trust and Radical Individualism', in *The Nordic Way: Equality, Individuality and Social Trust* (Svenska institutet, Stockholm, 2012) 13. As already noted, the World Value Survey also indicates that Sweden stands out even from close neighbours in the attitudes and values of the population.

significance as a symbol of a free society. When Sweden joined the EU in 1995, one of the few legal issues discussed politically was the impact this would have on free press and access to public documents.

The other candidate would be the special regulation of the area of labour law in Sweden. This legal field evolved around strong trade unions and strong employers' organizations. It was deemed better to let them negotiate solutions to the problems of the labour market rather than to legislate. In this way labour law became an area of little legislation and only one strong actor representing the state (but with corporativistic elements)—the Labour Court. Otherwise, the public policy was very hands-off when it came to labour law, no laws were necessary on issues such as minimum wages or working hours; they were settled in negotiations. This tradition has been very strong and very successful and every threat to it is opposed in strong terms. This is part of the Swedish constitutional identity, even if it is not actually mentioned more than cursorily in the Instrument of Government (RF 2:14). Instead, they are an unwritten part of our fundamental understandings of law and what should and should not be subject to legislation.

13

The Evolution and *Gestalt* of the Swiss Constitution

Giovanni Biaggini

A. **Origins of the Swiss Constitutional System: The Creation of the Federal Constitutions of 1848, 1874, and 1999** 640
  1. Foundation of the Confederation: The Federal Constitution of 1848 641
     a) The Creation of the First Federal Constitution 641
     b) Major Contentions and Content 642
  2. Expansion of the Constitutional Order of the Confederation: The Fully Revised Constitution of 1874 645
     a) The Creation of the Second Federal Constitution 645
     b) Innovations 646
  3. Constitutional Renewal: The Federal Constitution of 1999 647
     a) Background History 647
     b) Reform Concept and Creation of the Third Federal Constitution 649
     c) Interfaces with Tradition and Innovations 650

B. **The Evolution of the Constitution: Milestones and Formative Factors** 653
  1. Main Types of Procedure of Constitutional Amendment 653
     a) Partial Revision of the Federal Constitution in Ordinary Procedure 653
     b) Popular Initiative for Partial Revision of the Federal Constitution 653
     c) Limitations to Constitutional Revision 655
  2. Milestones in the Development of the Constitution 656
     a) Democracy 656
     b) Federalism 658
     c) Rule of Law 659
  3. Actors and 'Neglected Issues' of Constitutional Development 661

C. **Basic Structures and Concepts** 663
  1. The Federal Constitution as a Basis for and Object of Politics 663

  2. On the Significance of Structure-establishing Constitutional Principles 664
  3. Democracy and the Understanding of Democracy 665
     a) Overview of the Political Rights 665
     b) Instruments of Direct Democracy in the Confederation 667
     c) On the Significance of the People's Rights for the Political System and the Understanding of Democracy 668
  4. The Rule of Law and the Understanding of Fundamental Rights 670
     a) Fundamental Rights and Rule of Law 670
     b) Constitutional Jurisdiction: System and Gaps 671
  5. Organ Make-up and Understanding of the Separation of Powers 673
     a) The System of the Supreme Federal Authorities 673
     b) Federal Assembly 674
     c) Federal Council 676
     d) Federal Supreme Court and Other Judicial Authorities 677
     e) Interaction of the Powers 678
  6. Federalism and the Understanding of Federalism 680
     a) Basic Questions 680
     b) Organizational, Task-related, and Financial Autonomy of the Cantons 681
     c) Participation of the Cantons in the Decision-making Process of the Confederation 683
     d) Interaction of the Levels 684

D. **Constitutional Identity: Characteristics and Identity-creating Elements** 685
  1. Citizens and People, Nation and State in the Light of the Federal Constitution 685
  2. Balancing Out of Equality and Inequality as a Never-ending Task 687

Giovanni Biaggini, *The Evolution and* Gestalt *of the Swiss Constitution* In: *The Max Planck Handbooks in European Public Law.*
Edited by: Armin von Bogdandy, Peter M Huber, and Sabrina Ragone, Oxford University Press. © Giovanni Biaggini 2023.
DOI: 10.1093/oso/9780198726425.003.0013

A. Origins of the Swiss Constitutional System: The Creation of the Federal Constitutions of 1848, 1874, and 1999

On 1 January 2000, the third Federal Constitution, approved by the People and the Cantons on 18 April 1999, came into force in Switzerland. It replaced the second Federal Constitution of 1874, which in turn had replaced the first Constitution of 1848. The Constitution of 1848 created the principles of the Swiss Federal State that largely still apply today. The Constitution of 1874 brought about the substantial expansion of the constitutional system of the Confederation. Despite numerous innovations, the newest constitutional reforms brought with them no profound change but rather, first and foremost, the consolidation and cautious modernization of that which had come before. For understanding the present constitutional system, it is important to trace the creation of the Constitutions of 1848 and 1874 as well as their underlying development. Moreover, it would appear useful to establish beforehand some of the non-legal factors shaping the constitutional system.

One of Switzerland's outstanding characteristics is its four languages. German is by far the most widely spoken, with a share of around 62.1 per cent (or around 5.2 million people). French is in second place with 22.8 per cent (around 1.9 million), followed by Italian with 8.0 per cent (around 673,000).[1] The fourth language, Romansh (*Rumantsch*), is under threat of disappearing and is represented by a mere 0.5 per cent (around 42,000 speakers). Unlike German, French, and Italian, it lacks direct connection with a larger linguistic area in a neighbouring country. German, French, and Italian are official languages of the Confederation; for Romansh, this applies only when communicating with people who speak Romansh (article 70 Federal Constitution of the Swiss Confederation (BV)). Further, it is important that the traditional political units are not the linguistic regions but rather twenty-six cantons, which are very different in many respects. The populations of these cantons currently range from 16,000 (Appenzell Innerrhoden) to 1.56 million (Zurich) (2021). With the exception of the canton of Jura, which was first established in 1979, the cantons all existed as separate political entities even before the establishment of the Confederation. Therefore, it is significant that the linguistic borders do not correspond precisely with the borders of the cantons. Aside from three bilingual cantons (Bern/Berne, Fribourg/Freiburg, Valais/Wallis), there is also a trilingual canton (Graubünden/Grischun/Grigioni). In denominational terms Switzerland is not homogenous either. The two traditional main denominations (Catholic and Protestant[2]) experienced a somewhat tense coexistence for a long time. With increasing immigration and domestic migration, they have mixed geographically. The cities of Zurich and Geneva, once two strongholds of the reformation (Zwingli, Calvin), are today home to more Catholics than Protestants. It is the experience of many Swiss that, in linguistic, cultural, and confessional terms—from a local, regional, and national viewpoint—they are simultaneously a member of the majority but also of a minority. It is no coincidence that a tradition and culture of compromise and proportional representation accompanies such diversity.

---

[1] Federal Statistical Office, 'Inhabitants by main language' (Sprachen, 2021), see www.bfs.admin.ch/bfs/de/home/statistiken/bevoelkerung/sprachen-religionen/sprachen.html (last accessed on 7 April 2022).

[2] Roman Catholic: 35.1 per cent, Protestant: 23.1 per cent. Today, the third-largest group are Muslims (5.4 per cent). Around 20 per cent indicate no affiliation with a church or religious community; Federal Statistical Office, 'Religionszugehörigkeit, 2017–2019' (Religionen, 2021), see https://www.bfs.admin.ch/bfs/de/home/statistiken/bevoelkerung/sprachen-religionen/religionen.html (last accessed on 7 April 2022).

1. Foundation of the Confederation: The Federal Constitution of 1848

a) The Creation of the First Federal Constitution

The formation of the federal state in the European revolutionary year of 1848 was preceded by a deep internal crisis. The Swiss Federation amalgamated by a federal treaty since 1815—originally a complex system of alliances and, after the invasion of French troops, a unitary state for a short while (Helvetic Republic, 1798–1803[3])—threatened to break apart. Following the unsuccessful attempt at a 'federal reform', whose legacy includes two unrealized draft constitutions (1832/33),[4] the tensions between the progressive and the conservative powers intensified. Seven Catholic, conservative cantons formed a '*Sonderbund*' (separate alliance), which was initially kept secret (1845). It was abolished in November 1847 by federal enforcement using military means (the so-called *Sonderbund* War). The military operations lasted just under four weeks and claimed just over 100 lives.

The road to a legal reorganization of the Confederation was now clear.[5] With the participation of delegates from twenty-three (of twenty-five) cantons, a reform commission (set up in August 1847) began drafting a federal constitution (February 1848). Time was of the essence given the uncertain developments in Europe. The revision commission was able to draw on the constitutional drafts of 1832/33 and presented a draft for a federal constitution as early as 8 April 1848. Shortly thereafter the so-called *Tagsatzung*, the main organ of the confederation, began deliberations. On 27 June 1848, the *Tagsatzung* adopted the text of the new Federal Constitution by a majority vote after two readings and with a few amendments to the commission's version and disseminated it to the cantons.[6] These now had to decide on the acceptance of the new Constitution in accordance with their constitutional provisions. Between 5 August and 3 September 1848, referendums or '*Landsgemeinden*' (i.e. decisions in the framework of meetings of the electorate in the open air) took place in all cantons except for Fribourg, where the cantonal parliament took the final decision. On 12 September 1848, the *Tagsatzung* ascertained that seventeen cantons,[7] which represented the prevailing majority of the Swiss population, had spoken in favour of the Federal Constitution. Eight cantons had rejected the Constitution; six of these eight also later rejected the constitutions of 1874 and of 1999, i.e. never consented to a federal constitution.[8]

On 12 September 1848, the *Tagsatzung* declared the new Federal Constitution as accepted by majority vote and put it into effect for the entire Confederation. The *Tagsatzung* majority was able to rely on a 'transitional provision' included in the draft of the Constitution, which stipulated that the voting results 'shall be communicated to the *Tagsatzung*, which will decide if the new Federal Constitution is adopted'. However, this decision clearly represented a break with the confederative contractual legal bases up until then—a 'little revolution'

---

[3] On the Constitution of the Helvetic Republic—'*une et indivisible*' (art 1 of the Constitution of 12 April 1798)—and on the foundation of the Federal State: Alfred Kölz, *Neuere schweizerische Verfassungsgeschichte*, vol I (Stämpfli, Bern, 1992) 98 ff, 547 ff.

[4] As Chairman of the then Reform Commission, Italian law professor Pellegrino Rossi (1787–1848), who had emigrated to Geneva in 1815, had a significant share of the work.

[5] For detail, Alfred Kölz, *Neuere schweizerische Verfassungsgeschichte*, vol I (n 3) 547 ff.

[6] The only major point of contention was the question of the configuration of the Federal Parliament (bicameral system).

[7] Including three of the six so-called 'half-cantons' (for the term, see n 208). Thanks to special decision procedures, the two *Sonderbund* cantons Fribourg (parliamentary decision) and Lucerne also voted in favour of the Federal Constitution (abstentions were counted as endorsing votes).

[8] These are the cantons of Uri, Schwyz, and Wallis and the half-cantons of Obwalden, Nidwalden, and Appenzell Innerrhoden.

(Kölz).[9] The dissenting cantons fell into line, albeit in part reluctantly, and ultimately sent members to the two chambers of the Federal Assembly, which met for the first time on 6 November 1848 in Bern. On 16 November 1848, the Federal Assembly elected the seven members of the Federal Government (*Bundesrat*); six of those elected had been part of the revision commission. Looking back, it was not only the break with the legal continuity that was problematic. The process from which the first Federal Constitution emerged in 1848 is also flawed, certainly by today's democratic standards, and is not a perfect example of how the constituent power of a nation should be articulated. In Switzerland, however, the opinion that certain 'birth defects' of a constitution can heal seems to have prevailed.

b) Major Contentions and Content

The constitutional fathers of 1848 had a pioneering feat to accomplish. A rather loose confederation of states was to be replaced by an effective structure with a more rigid legal bond which would, however, not constrict too much the individual cantons as still-independent communities. A tight unitary (centralist) state solution was never a serious contender given the unwelcome experience with the imposed Helvetic Republic. An important source of inspiration was the model of the United States of America, although the constitutional fathers did not simply mimic this. In addition, one drew from the experiences and achievements of the cantonal constitutional struggles of the first half of the nineteenth century and from the core principles of the French Revolution (equality, individual freedom, democratic participation). The result was a structure that was without precedent on the old continent: the first European *Bundesstaat* or federal state. However, the term '*Bundesstaat*' does neither appear in the Federal Constitution of 1848, nor later in the constitutions of 1874 and 1999.[10] The text of the Constitution was not free of confederative reminiscences either—they have in part remained to this day. Thus, the official name of the state in the national languages of Latin origin: *Confédération suisse*, *Confederazione svizzera*, *Confederaziun svizra*, i.e. 'Swiss Confederation'.[11] Despite such uncertainties, Switzerland was spared altercations concerning the legal nature of the new federation, unlike the United States.

The Federal Constitution of 1848 was divided into three sections: 'General Provisions' (articles 1–59), 'Federal Authorities' (articles 60–110), 'Revision of the Federal Constitution' (articles 111–114), supplemented by seven 'Transitional Provisions'. The fundaments then achieved were designed to prove durable in the further course of the development of the Federal State. The main points of contention on the drafting of the Constitution of 1848 included the scope of the powers of the federation (especially in the areas of the economy, the military, and civil law) as well as the structure and design of the federal organs. Disputed was also the scope to which the federation should guarantee fundamental rights, such as the freedom of establishment or freedom of religion. The question of language, on the other hand, prompted no debate.[12] The 'capital question' remained excluded from the Constitution. It was to be regulated by parliament. On 28 November 1848, the Federal Assembly established

---

[9] Alfred Kölz, 'Zur Staatenbildung im 19. Jahrhundert mit besonderer Berücksichtigung der Schweiz' (1998) Der Staat 172. Older scholars such as Fritz Fleiner, *Die Gründung des Schweizerischen Bundesstaates im Jahre 1848* (Schwabe, Basel, 1898) 14 ff are more restrained in their view.

[10] Unlike later constitutions such as the Austrian Federal Constitution Act (art 2), the German Basic Law (art 20), or the coordinated Belgian Constitution of 1994 (art 1: 'Federal State').

[11] The official Latin name *Confoederatio helvetica* (abb: CH) was first introduced after the establishment of the Federal State. It is found, for example, on coins (since 1879), principally so as not to favour any one national language.

[12] The naming of the 'three main languages' of German, French, and Italian (art 109 BV 1848) was to express their parity. Technical, financial issues (translation costs) were in the foreground.

Bern as the seat of the federal authorities (*Bundesstadt*, 'Federal City').[13] Switzerland still has no real capital city to this day. It was clear to the proponents of stronger political unity that a compromise had to be found with the defenders of 'cantonal sovereignty' in order to avoid endangering the reform altogether. The concessions included dropping the original stipulation for a single-chamber parliament, which would have embodied the idea of the unity of the Swiss nation, in favour of a bicameral system based on the American model.[14] The sovereignty issue could be glossed over with a compromise formula, according to which the cantons 'are sovereign except to the extent that their sovereignty is limited by the Federal Constitution' (article 3 BV 1848). This passage was carried over word for word into the Constitution of 1874 and into the present Federal Constitution (article 3 BV).

One of the most important organizational specifications of 1848 was the creation of two new political authorities, the Federal Assembly (Federal Parliament) and the Federal Council (Government). Essentially, the basic structures of these two main organs have survived until today. In accordance with article 60 BV 1848, the Federal Assembly was 'the supreme authority of the Confederation'. It was (and still is today) not only responsible for legislation and budget but also for the election of the members of the Federal Council and the members of the Federal Supreme Court. The Federal Assembly consists of two chambers of equal standing: the National Council (*Nationalrat*) and the Council of States (*Ständerat*). The National Council as the representation of the people comprised 111 members (today 200) who were elected according to the simple majority system (today proportional representation). The Council of States, which was formed on the model of the US Senate, had forty-four members (two per canton, one per half-canton; today: forty-six). The members of the Council of States exercise a free mandate just like the National Council members (but unlike the earlier *Tagsatzung* envoys) (article 79 BV 1848). The cantons were (and still are) responsible for the regulation of the Council of States elections.

As the supreme executive authority, the Federal Council comprised seven members in accordance with article 83 BV 1848; these were each elected by the United Federal Assembly (i.e. the National Council and Council of States in a joint session) for a fixed tenure of three years (since 1931, four years) with unlimited possibility of re-election. The Federal Council was designed as a collegiate body with equal members and a presidency that changed annually. A head of government in a true sense was not foreseen. The President of the Confederation (chairman of the Federal Council) was (and is) *primus inter pares*. A strict separation of powers for personnel was laid down in the relationship between parliament and government: the members of the Federal Council could not belong to the Federal Assembly at the same time. The early dismissal of the government or its individual members by the Federal Assembly was (and is) not possible, nor was the early dissolution of parliament by government or parliamentary decision.

The cantons remained generally responsible for the judiciary. According to an old Swiss tradition, certain powers of arbitration in disputes in the public law area were assigned to the Federal Government and the Federal Parliament. The Constitution of 1848 provided for a federal court. However, until 1874, this was a non-permanent body which had only very few competences in the area of private and criminal law (but not in public law). The Federal Supreme Court only had jurisdiction over the assessment of complaints regarding the violation of the new fundamental rights guaranteed by the Federal Constitution if the Federal

---

[13] Bern prevailed against Zurich and Lucerne not least of all due to support from western and southern Switzerland.
[14] For detail, Alfred Kölz, *Neuere schweizerische Verfassungsgeschichte*, vol I (n 3) 554 ff.

Assembly concluded not to decide on the matter itself but rather to transfer it to the Federal Supreme Court (article 105 BV 1848), which happened only once until 1874.[15]

The federal order created in 1848 was essentially based on three—still existent—pillars. The separation of powers and tasks between the Confederation and the cantons followed the principle of conferral (article 3 BV 1848; today article 3 and article 42 BV). The Confederation was only responsible if and to the extent that the Federal Constitution assigned a competence to it. Transfer of competence had to be decided on a federal level ('*Kompetenz-Kompetenz*' of the Confederation). The basic configuration of federal competences in 1848 was rather modest. The Confederation was responsible primarily for foreign policy (conclusion of inter-state treaties), customs, the postal system, parts of the military, and coinage ('*Münzregal*'—the sovereign right of coinage). The Swiss franc was introduced by law in 1850 as the single currency; it would be decades, however, before the creation of a national bank and the issuance of uniform banknotes. The Confederation was also given the authority to establish a Federal Polytechnic Institute, which opened its doors in Zurich in 1855 (today the Swiss Federal Institute of Technology, ETH) as well as a Federal University, which does not exist until today. The cantons held on to authority for the police, schools, and taxes, continued to maintain their own troops and remained responsible for important areas such as private and criminal law, the judiciary and health, labour, trade, and banks. A second pillar of the Federal State was the involvement of the cantons in the formation of the Federal Will. The basic configuration of 1848 included the requirement of the double majority for amendments to the Constitution: Not only the 'majority of voting Swiss citizens' but also the 'majority of the cantons' had to agree (so-called '*Ständemehr*', cantonal majority; article 114 BV 1848), which afforded (and continues to afford) additional political weight to the more sparsely populated cantons.[16] The Federal Constitution also granted each canton the right of proposal on a federal level (the so-called *Standesinitiative* or cantonal initiative). The third pillar is formed by various principles regarding the relationships between the federal stakeholders (in particular, a duty of consideration and support, compliance with federal law).

The Federal Constitution of 1848 is rightly considered a successful 'combination of the national principle with respect for the cantons'.[17] The fundamental organizational structures created in 1848 are in essence still in place today. In the eyes of the constitutional fathers, however, the work of 1848 was in some respects left incomplete. The aspired-to unity of the law was still very far away, as was the goal of a national army. A federal jurisdiction worthy of the name was still lacking. The systematic guarantee of fundamental rights by the Confederation had been dispensed with. In the area of the protection of fundamental rights, there was initially a certain distribution of tasks between the Confederation and the cantons. Federal law guaranteed, namely, equality before the law (article 4 BV 1848), a limited right of establishment for Swiss nationals (article 41 BV 1848), inter-cantonal freedom of trade (article 29 BV 1848), freedom of faith and conscience, even if only for members of Christian denominations for the time being (article 44 BV 1848), freedom of the press (article 45 BV 1848), and freedom of association (article 46 BV 1848). The selection taken at that time creates the impression that what mattered to the constitutional fathers was not least of all the

---

[15] Decision of the Federal Supreme Court of 3 July 1852 in the matter *Dupré* (reprinted in Zeitschrift für Schweizerisches Recht (1853) 41 ff).

[16] For the relativization of the principle of democratic majority by means of the bicameral system, see below Sections C.5.b and D.2.

[17] Jean-François Aubert, 'Geschichtliche Einführung', in Jean-François Aubert and others (eds), *Kommentar zur Bundesverfassung der Schweizerischen Eidgenossenschaft vom 29. Mai 1874* (Helbing und Lichtenhahn, Basel, Schulthess, Zurich, 1987–1996) (loose leaf) para 110.

nationwide enforcement of minimum standards in legal fields with a lacking federal competence. Even today, some fundamental rights play a role as a means of federal integration.

The Federal Constitution of 1848 established an almost purely representative democracy on the federal level on the basis of universal (male) suffrage and the simple majority system (first-past-the-post system). Of the direct democratic instruments that characterize the Swiss political system today, only two go back to the foundation of the Federal State in 1848: the mandatory constitutional referendum (that was first used in 1866) and the (nonspecific) popular initiative for the revision of the Federal Constitution, which is of no practical significance for the time being, however.

2. Expansion of the Constitutional Order of the Confederation: The Fully Revised Constitution of 1874

a) The Creation of the Second Federal Constitution

In the 1860s, supporters of an extension of the democratic rights of the people and advocates for unification of the law grew in strength. In 1865, the Federal Parliament passed a package of nine decisions amending the Constitution, which aimed at supplementing the 'unfinished' regime of 1848 (expansion of federal powers and in the area of fundamental rights). The bills failed, however, with one exception,[18] in the referendum of 14 January 1866. Soon, the Federal Council worked out proposals for several specific constitutional amendments (1870). The government bill was reshaped in parliament into an actual total revision of the Federal Constitution. The main objective was to strengthen federal powers.[19] The debates in parliament (1871/72) were marked by the contrast between centralist and federalist positions. As compensation for the aspired-to substantial expansion of the federal powers, the introduction of the optional referendum on laws was decided: Eight cantons or 30,000 voters were to be able to demand that a law passed by the Federal Assembly is presented to the people for a ballot. The new Federal Constitution failed in the popular vote of 12 May 1872, if only by the narrowest of margins,[20] due to the united resistance of the Catholic conservative forces and the western-Swiss federalists.

A second attempt was undertaken immediately. This led to success. The liberal radical forces gave in to centralization demands in areas such as civil law, the military, and education. As a result, the western-Swiss federalists were won over to total revision. In the deepening 'cultural battle', it was believed that there was no need to be considerate of the Catholic conservative forces. The anti-Catholic articles of the Constitution contained in the failed bill of 1872 were even intensified. Approval for the new Federal Constitution—readily characterized in the voting campaign (with a view to western Switzerland) as a 'work of reconciliation'—was relatively clear in the referendum of 19 April 1874.[21] It entered into force on 29 May 1874. Unlike in 1848, it was not an act of genuine constitutional creation but rather a derived constitution in accordance with the procedures laid down in article 111 ff BV 1848. Many provisions were carried over word-for-word from the Constitution of 1848.

---

[18] Equality of Swiss non-Christian (in particular Jewish) faiths through amendment of art 41 and 48 BV.

[19] On the total revision of 1872/74, see Alfred Kölz, *Neuere schweizerische Verfassungsgeschichte*, vol I (n 3) 599 ff; Rainer J Schweizer, 'Die Totalrevision der Bundesverfassung von 1872 und 1874', in Piermarco Zen-Ruffinen (ed), *De la constitution. Études en l'honneur de Jean-François Aubert* (Helbing und Lichtenhahn, Basel, 1996) 101 ff.

[20] With approximately 255,000 votes in favour to 260,000 votes against and nine to thirteen cantonal votes.

[21] With approximately 340,000 votes in favour to 200,000 votes against and 14.5 to 7.5 cantonal votes.

b) Innovations

The Federal Constitution of 1874 resulted above all in a strengthening of the Confederation vis-à-vis the cantons, an expansion of the democratic rights, and a strengthening of the state over the church. With respect to the federal order, there were substantial changes in the area of the 'left-overs' of 1848. The Confederation obtained the competence for the unification of significant parts of private law (article 64 BV 1874). Omitted were, however, important areas such as marriage, family and inheritance law, procedural law, and judicial organization. Armed conflicts in neighbouring countries (1870/71) had clearly demonstrated the need for the centralization of the armed forces (article 19 ff BV 1874); however, the last cantonal powers and cantonal troops disappeared only at the beginning of the twenty-first century. The goal of establishing a unified economic area was served by various new federal powers as well as the guarantee of the fundamental right of freedom of trade and commerce (article 31 BV 1874). With regard to fundamental rights, the focus was on the right to marry, an extension of the freedom of establishment, and the expansion of freedom of faith and conscience to followers of all confessions. At the same time, two confession-related special provisions were included in the Constitution (both revoked in 1973): article 51 BV 1874 banned the Jesuits from establishing themselves in Switzerland and forbade members of the Order to participate in any activity in churches and schools; article 52 BV 1874 declared the establishment of new and the restoration of repealed monasteries or religious orders to be unlawful.[22]

In the institutional area, the basic structures of the political authorities (Federal Assembly, Federal Council) were unchanged. However, the Federal Supreme Court was expanded to become a permanent supreme court and was entrusted with the role of guarantor of the unity of law and certain (limited) constitutional-judicial functions[23] (article 113 and 114 BV 1874). Thanks to an exempting clause, the federal legislature could continue to lay the assessment of certain constitutional violations in the hands of the Federal Council (as appellate authority), with the possibility to appeal to the Federal Assembly (article 85 No 12 BV 1874). It was said, as the main reason for this solution, that, in some regulatory matters, 'the legal frameworks were still unstable',[24] so certain fundamental rights were of increased political as well as legal importance. In the still-young federal state, these were considered to include, in particular, freedom of establishment, freedom of faith and conscience, and freedom of trade and commerce. In this regard, judicial responsibility was only at a later date gradually transferred to the Federal Supreme Court.[25]

In the area of citizens' rights, there was a 'democratization' of the cantonal majority: Under federal law, the result of the referendum in each canton (article 121 BV 1874) now counted as the so-called cantonal vote; this meant that the cantons could no longer stipulate that the cantonal vote would be determined by the cantonal parliament. The optional referendum on federal acts was rightly considered the 'showpiece of the revision' (*Aubert*). Henceforth

---

[22] Art 75 BV 1874 (which limited the right to be elected (passive electoral rights) in the Confederation to persons of 'secular standing'; in effect until the end of 1999) and art 50 para 4 BV 1874 (which required the approval of the Confederation for the establishment of dioceses; repealed in the referendum of 10 June 2001 by deleting the original art 72 para 3 BV 1999) also had anti-Catholic motivation.

[23] Comprehensively vis-à-vis the cantons; in limitation in relation to federal powers. On the 'immunity' of the federal laws (art 113 para 3 Federal Constitution of the Swiss Confederation of 1874 and today art 190 BV: mandatory application clause), see below Section C.4.b, and Giovanni Biaggini, 'Constitutional Adjudication in Switzerland', in Armin von Bogdandy, Peter M Huber, and Christoph Grabenwarter (eds), *The Max Planck Handbooks in European Public Law*, vol III (Oxford University Press, Oxford, 2020), 779 ff, 793 ff, 832 ff.

[24] Thus, the Federal Council's clarifications on the revision of the Federal Constitution, BBl 1870 II 700.

[25] First steps were taken in 1893 and 1911; for individual fundamental rights (including the right to sufficient, free-of-charge primary education) only at the end of 1999.

the Federal Assembly would no longer have the last word in legislation, except in cases of an 'urgent nature' (article 89 BV 1874). This innovation was to have profound long-term consequences for the political system.[26]

The push towards centralization triggered by the total revision of 1874 was considerable, but, in retrospect, had a rather modest effect in comparison to the developments in the twentieth century. However, in the upcoming competence extensions, the Confederation no longer focussed on the rapid but conflict-prone and high-risk reform method of the total revision, as seen in 1872/74, but rather on a step-by-step approach in the form of partial revision; 125 years would elapse before the next total renewal of the Federal Constitution.

3. Constitutional Renewal: The Federal Constitution of 1999

a) Background History

Under the Federal Constitution of 1874, a heavily agrarian, resource-poor Switzerland transformed itself from a land of emigration into a prosperous community with an internationally oriented national economy. What motivated the Federal Council to submit the draft for a new Federal Constitution in November 1996?[27] What prompted the Federal Assembly to discuss the draft with the usual meticulousness but very rapidly and to adopt it on 18 December 1998? There had been no profound upheaval or national crisis. The constitutional structures were generally considered to have proven themselves. The Federal Assembly had taken recourse in 1914 and 1939 to the means of extra-constitutional decision and granted the Federal Council sweeping special powers. And in the 1930s and 1940s, the use of the so-called urgent legislation ('*Dringlichkeitsrecht*') had increased (legislation under exclusion of the referendum; article 89 para 2 BV 1874 old version).[28] After the end of the Second World War, however, it had been possible to restore constitutional normalcy and to democratize the institute of urgent legislation by subjecting it to a subsequent referendum.[29]

In the official statements of the 1990s,[30] the necessity of constitutional renewal was justified with substantive and formal defects of the Constitution. Thanks to numerous partial revisions, the Constitution was up to date in most matters,[31] but, over the years, it had become a confusing, incomplete, and sometimes barely understandable patchwork.[32] The orientation, control, and limiting functions of the Constitution could only be strengthened

---

[26] For the significance of the referendum on the emergence of the so-called *consociational democracy* (*Konkordanzdemokratie*), see Section C.3.c.

[27] The draft for a new Federal Constitution and the Federal Council's 'Message on a new Federal Constitution' (both from 20 November 1996) are reproduced in Federal Gazette of the Swiss Confederation (BBl) 1997 I ff and 589 ff (also available at https://www.bj.admin.ch/bj/de/home/staat/gesetzgebung/archiv/bundesverfassung.html) (last accessed on 7 April 2022).

[28] On the so-called regime of full powers (*Vollmachtenregime*) and the urgent legislation, see Alfred Kölz, *Neuere schweizerische Verfassungsgeschichte*, vol I (n 3) 665 ff, 763 ff, 823 ff (where the controversy between Zaccaria Giacometti and Dietrich Schindler senior is also discussed).

[29] The new art 89bis BV 1874 (today art 165 BV) was the result of a successful popular initiative (1949).

[30] Representative of this are the statements in the Federal Council's 'Message on a new Federal Constitution' (n 27) Federal Gazette of the Swiss Confederation (BBl) 1997 I 19 ff.

[31] See, for example, the provision created in May 1992 on reproductive medicine and gene technology (art 24[novies] BV 1874, today arts 119 and 120 BV).

[32] Often mentioned were old-fashioned constitutional terms such as '*Verkommnis*' (covenant) (art 7 BV 1874), '*Brauteinzugsgebühr*' (bridal moving-in fee) (art 54 BV 1874), or '*Abzugsrecht*' (emigration fee) (art 62 BV 1874). Some gaps were filled by the Federal Supreme Court through recognition of unwritten fundamental rights. See below Section B.2.c.

648 GIOVANNI BIAGGINI

by means of a general overhaul. All of this is certainly true but still does not explain why the total revision of the Constitution could become such a primary political issue. At the beginning, there was no list of defects but rather a diffuse 'unease in the small state' that had begun to spread in the 1960s. Basel-based constitutional law professor and politician Max Imboden (1915–1969) aptly spoke of a 'Helvetic malaise' (1964) and advocated for a 'revision of the Constitution as a path to the future' (1965).[33] The idea took root in parliamentary circles. The Federal Council set up a small expert commission, which recommended total revision of the Constitution in its detailed final report of 1973.[34] In 1977, after a good two-and-a-half years of work, a forty-six-member expert commission presented an Expert Draft for a new Federal Constitution together with the accompanying report.[35] The constitutional draft received a great deal of attention, also beyond Swiss borders, but proved to be too ambitious. In particular, the openly formulated provisions on the economic and social system and the division of powers between the Confederation and the cantons were met with criticism.

In its 'Report on the total revision of the Federal Constitution' presented on 6 November 1985, the Federal Council outlines various options for further action without committing to any.[36] Scepticism was rife in parliament. Basel-based constitutional law professor Kurt Eichenberger (1922–2005) became the 'saviour' of the revision idea. In an essay entitled 'Reality-based revision of the Constitution' which was published on 12 May 1986 in the *Neue Zürcher Zeitung*, Eichenberger argued for a revision of the Constitution that would be limited to the 'politically feasible' and which would focus on 'bringing order to the Constitution, reducing its list of defects ..., i.e., on updating it'.[37] The idea of an updating of the Constitution ('*Nachführung*', *mise-à-jour*) was received positively in the parliament. The process of a total revision of the Constitution was formally initiated by federal decree on 3 June 1987 after a prelude of more than twenty years. As a content-related guideline, the Federal Assembly established that the constitutional draft presented by the Federal Council was to 'update the applicable written and unwritten constitutional law, to present it in an understandable way, order it systematically, and unify conciseness and language'.[38] The sense of reality of the 1980s had replaced the slightly too euphoric sense of possibility of the early 1970s. But the project soon ground to a halt. The main reason for this were the negotiations begun in 1989 on inclusion of the EFTA states in the EC single market (European Economic Area—EEA). Work on the total revision was effectively discontinued. The presentation of a 'Europe-compatible' draft constitution would be desirable in due time.

---

[33] Titles of two pieces of writing by Max Imboden, both in id. (ed), *Staat und Recht* (Helbing und Lichtenhahn, Basel, 1971) 279 ff and 309 ff.

[34] Working group for the preparation of a total revision of the Federal Constitution (also called the 'Wahlen Working Group' after its chairman, former Federal Councillor Friedrich Traugott Wahlen), final report of 6 September 1973, Bern 1973.

[35] Report of the expert commission for the preparation of a total revision of the Federal Constitution (under the chairmanship of Federal Councillor Kurt Furgler, head of the Federal Department of Justice and Police), Bern 1977.

[36] Reprinted in Federal Gazette of the Swiss Confederation (BBl) 1985 III 1 ff. In the annex is the 'model study' developed from the expert drafts of 1977 by the Federal Department of Justice and Police (FDJP).

[37] More details on this, with references, Heinrich Koller, 'Die Nachführung der Bundesverfassung', in Yvo Hangartner and Bernhard Ehrenzeller (eds), *Reform der Bundesverfassung* (Dike, Zurich, 1995) 51 ff.

[38] Art 3 of the federal decree of 3 June 1987 on the total revision of the Federal Constitution, Federal Gazette of the Swiss Confederation (BBl) 1987 II 963.

b) Reform Concept and Creation of the Third Federal Constitution

After the very tight rejection of EEA membership in the referendum of 6 December 1992,[39] the conviction gained ground that before working on any major integration policy measures it was first important to strengthen the capacity to act of Switzerland as well as of its institutions. This is where the project for the total revision of the Federal Constitution could step in. What was required now was no longer a mere 'constitutional update' but rather a reform that would also encompass institutional innovation. The Federal Council developed the concept of constitutional reform 'in stages' in the years 1993–1994. The updates of the applicable constitutional law commissioned by the Federal Assembly in 1987 would serve as a basis. Building on this but in formally separate proceedings, further reforms were to be carried out step by step. Accordingly, the Federal Council provided its draft for a new Federal Constitution (of 20 November 1996) with two 'reform packages'—a first 'reform package' on the topic of citizens' rights (instruments of direct democracy) and a second 'reform package' concerning reforms in the area of the judiciary.[40] The prospect of further 'reform packages' concerning the areas of government ('*Staatsleitungsreform*'), parliament ('*Parlamentsreform*'), and federalism ('*Föderalismusreform*') was presented. Thanks to speedy debates—first in the two constitutional commissions (1997) set up by the National Council and the Council of States, then parallel in the plenary of the National Council and the Council of States—it was possible to have the final vote on the new Federal Constitution in parliament—as hoped—in December of 1998, the Jubilee Year.[41] The results of the vote were clear in both the National Council and the Council of States.[42] The referendum scheduled for 18 April 1999 was anticipated with confidence, especially since there seemed to be no substantial opposition. The mandatory referendum results were surprisingly tight but positive.[43]

The Federal Assembly, too, aligned itself with the 'update concept', which aimed first and foremost at consolidation and systemization. This meant that the substantive debates in parliament were held within limits. Parliamentary debates were marked not by a main point of contention but by many small controversies. As was already the case in 1848 and 1874, the 'art of exclusion' was practiced with success now, too. This was facilitated by the fact that the reform packages were already ready and available for institutional innovations. After all, the Federal Assembly did not have a narrowly conceived idea of the 'constitutional update'. It was open to specific innovations. In this, the criterion of consensus played an important role: Broadly-based reform proposals, which were assumed not to endanger the acceptance of the new Constitution by the People and the Cantons, were integrated into the total revision. This was legally acceptable since, notwithstanding the federal decree of 1987, this was a fully fledged total revision, meaning that the entire contents of the Constitution were

---

[39] The distribution of votes was 49.7 per cent to 50.3 per cent (difference: approximately 24,000 votes). Seven cantons approved, sixteen rejected. At 78.7 per cent, turnout was very high by Swiss standards.

[40] See Federal Council, Message on a new Federal Constitution (n 27) Federal Gazette of the Swiss Confederation (BBl) 1997 I 1 ff, 436 ff, 487 ff, 589 ff. Corresponding pre-drafts were previously subject to broad-based public consultation (so-called people's discussion).

[41] The plenary deliberations are documented in the official bulletin of the Federal Assembly (National Council and Council of States) of 1998. However, in accordance with general regulations, the commission deliberations were confidential.

[42] In the National Council with 134 Yes votes against fourteen No votes (with thirty-one abstentions); in the Council of States, unanimously.

[43] Around 970,000 Yes votes (59.2 per cent) against approximately 670,000 No votes (40.8 per cent) as well as thirteen to ten cantonal votes, at a voter turnout of 35.3 per cent which was low even by Swiss standards. As far as can be ascertained, the specific content of the constitutional template was less responsible for the tight result than diffuse fears.

on the table. There were also various proposals aimed at undoing constitutional achievements in the areas of social policy or environmental protection, for example. Such attempts at 'turning back the clock' were unsuccessful, however. The contentious question of the relationship of Switzerland to the European process of integration was deliberately omitted. The new Federal Constitution was to be cosmopolitan but 'Europe-neutral'.[44] Furthermore, it turned out time and again that the constitutional position that was to be updated was less clear than hoped. Legal ambiguities and controversies grew here and there into hardened political confrontation, for example in connection with the regulation of the constitutional status of strikes and lock-outs (occasionally highly stylized as 'a question of fate').[45]

The fates of the procedurally separate reform packages were varied. The parliamentary discussions on the reform of the judiciary were completed in 1999, albeit with some curtailments on the government's bill. Namely, the expansion of constitutional jurisdiction on federal laws (judicial review in application) advocated by the government was rejected in parliament. The constitutional bill was clearly approved in the referendum of 12 March 2000.[46] The government bill concerning citizens' rights ('*Reform der Volksrechte*') did not find the necessary support in parliament. As a result, the Federal Assembly worked out its own reduced bill, which was then successfully approved on 4 October 2002 and adopted in the referendum of 9 February 2003.[47] In late autumn 2001, the Federal Council provided parliament with another two major 'reform packages': the bill concerning the Reform of Fiscal Equalization and Task Allocation between the Confederation and the Cantons (NFA), which touched on around two dozen constitutional provisions;[48] and the bill concerning the so-called '*Staatsleitungsreform*' (*Reform of the Government*), which centred on innovations of the governmental organ (Federal Council).[49] The Reform of the Government was temporarily halted in the National Council in March 2004 and finally abandoned in 2012/2013. In contrast, in the referendum of 28 November 2004, both the People and the Cantons approved the NFA bill which had been adopted on 3 October 2003 by the Federal Assembly.[50]

c) Interfaces with Tradition and Innovations

The new Federal Constitution, which came into force on 1 January 2000,[51] is—despite a slightly higher number of articles—leaner, shorter and more structured than its predecessor.

---

[44] See Federal Gazette of the Swiss Confederation (BBl) 1997 I 543 f.

[45] Amongst other things, certain sibylline statements in recent judgments of the Federal Supreme Court had an impact on the debates (BGE 111 II 245, X. AG [1985]). For details of the compromise formula found at the last minute (art 28 para 4 BV), see Giovanni Biaggini, 'Vereinigungsfreiheit und Koalitionsfreiheit', in Detlef Merten and others (eds), *Handbuch der Grundrechte in Deutschland und Europa, Band VII* (Dike/C.F. Müller, Zurich, 2007) para 33 ff.

[46] Parts of the bill came into force on 1 April 2003 (Official Compilation of Federal Legislation 2002 3147); the rest followed on 1 January 2007.

[47] Parts of the bill came into force on 1 August 2003 (Official Compilation of Federal Legislation 2003 1949); the reform was concluded with the referendum of 27 September 2009 (see Section B.2.a).

[48] See Federal Council, Message on the Reform of Fiscal Equalization and Task Allocation between the Confederation and the Cantons (NFA) of 14 November 2001, Federal Gazette of the Swiss Confederation (BBl) 2002, 2291 ff.

[49] See Federal Council, Message on the Reform of the Government of 19 December 2001, Federal Gazette of the Swiss Confederation (BBl) 2002 2295 ff.

[50] The constitutional amendments consolidated in Federal Decree of 3 October 2003 on the NFA (Federal Gazette of the Swiss Confederation [BBl] 2003, 6591) entered into force in 2008.

[51] See in particular René Rhinow, *Die Bundesverfassung 2000—eine Einführung* (Helbing und Lichtenhahn, Basel, 2000); Ulrich Zimmerli, *Die neue Bundesverfassung* (Stämpfli, Bern, 2000); Peter Gauch and Daniel Thürer (eds), *Die neue Bundesverfassung* (Schulthess, Zurich, 2002) (with an appraisal 'from the outside' by Klaus Stern); Giovanni Biaggini, 'Verfassungsreform in der Schweiz – Die neue schweizerische Bundesverfassung vom 18. April 1999 im Zeichen von "Verfassungsnachführung" und Verfassungspolitik' (1999) Austrian Journal of Public Law 433 ff; Martin Kayser and Dagmar Richter, 'Die neue schweizerische Bundesverfassung' (1999) 59 Heidelberg

Some 'General Provisions', which form the first Title (articles 1–6 BV) are followed by a comprehensive body of fundamental rights as the main part of the second Title ('Fundamental rights, citizenship, and social goals', articles 7–41 BV). The third Title ('Confederation, cantons, and communes', articles 42–135 BV) governs the relationship of the federal levels to each other and sets out powers and duties of the Confederation. The fourth Title ('The People and the Cantons', articles 136–142 BV) deals primarily with the instruments of direct democracy. The fifth Title ('Federal authorities', articles 143–191 BV) maps the basic structures of the highest federal bodies. The sixth and final Title (articles 192–196 BV, today articles 192–197 BV) contains provisions concerning the 'Revision of the Federal Constitution and Transitional Provisions'. In terms of content, the new Constitution ties in with proven basic structures. Textual 'interfaces with tradition' (*Traditionsanschlüsse*) were consciously sought, as in article 3 BV ('Sovereignty' of the cantons) for example. Although, inherent to the concept, the consolidation of what had already been achieved was in the foreground, there are numerous innovations to be pointed out, which may appear unspectacular but should not be underestimated. Many of these innovations would have hardly had a chance of rapid realization outside the total revision of the Constitution (in the absence of sufficient pressure for reform). Worth highlighting is the consolidation and supplementing of the fundamental rights, which were previously somewhat scattered, in a catalogue of fundamental rights (articles 7–36 BV), which includes a general prohibition of discrimination—new for Switzerland—(article 8 para 2 BV), a fundamental rights provision on the 'Protection of children and young people' (article 11 BV), an explicit guarantee of the protection of journalistic sources (article 17 BV), and a commitment to the constitutive function of the fundamental rights (article 35 BV). The key maxims of Swiss federalism are set down in text, in part for the first time, and newly collated in a general constitutional chapter on the 'Relations between the Confederation and the cantons' (articles 42–53). The innovations also include the constitutionalization of fundamental principles of environmental law (precautionary and polluter pays principle as well as the principle of sustainability, articles 73 and 74 BV). There were specific extensions here and there in the responsibilities of the Confederation. In the structure of the supreme federal authorities, there have been no major changes. However, the Federal Assembly took the opportunity to conclude long-discussed 'reforms for its own end'.[52] The influence of constitutional comparison and international law (notably the ECHR) is particularly noticeable in the fundamental rights chapter (articles 7–36 BV).[53] Even more than foreign constitutions, the most recent cantonal constitutions served as a source of inspiration. Previous constitutional drafts such as the expert draft of 1977, the model study of 1985, and the private draft by the two constitutional law professors Alfred Kölz and Jörg Paul Müller of 1984 played a role that should not be underestimated.[54]

The history of the total revision of the Federal Constitution can, depending on the point of view, be told as a short story of success, beginning in 1993/94, or, as a long tale of woe, with its beginnings in the 1960s. Both versions have a happy ending, which, again depending

---

Journal of International Law 985 ff; Rainer J Schweizer, 'Die erneuerte schweizerische Bundesverfassung vom 18. April 1999' (2000) 48 Jahrbuch des öffentlichen Rechts der Gegenwart N.F. 263 ff.

[52] Enlargement of the chamber chairmanships (art 152 BV), strengthening of the role of parliament in the areas of foreign policy (art 166 BV), state planning (art 173 para 1g BV), parliamentary oversight over the Federal Council and the Federal Administration (art 169 BV), etc.

[53] See in particular art 13 BV (protection of privacy) and art 29–32 BV (general and special procedural guarantees).

[54] Alfred Kölz and Jörg Paul Müller, *Entwurf für eine neue Bundesverfassung (1984)* (3rd edn, Stämpfli, Bern, 1995).

on the point of view, can be dated to 1999 (referendum on the new Federal Constitution), 2000 (referendum on judiciary reform), 2003 (referendum on the reform of citizens' rights), 2004 (referendum on the new fiscal equalization, NFA), or 2007/2008 (full enactment of the reform of the judiciary and the reform of the NFA).[55] These references again highlight the procedural peculiarities of the most recent constitutional reform. With the reform concept elected in 1993/94, there was a break away from the popular understanding of 'total revision' being an overall renewal of the constitutional system in a single, one-time legislative act. This was replaced by an understanding of constitutional reform as an open renewal process in terms of time and content, which takes place in several procedurally independent steps. The traditional 'art of exclusion' was refined into the 'art of constitutional renewal'.[56] This goes hand in hand with a blurring of the distinction between total and partial revision of the Constitution that is characteristic of Swiss constitutional law but not often seen elsewhere.[57] This is seen, for example in the bill on the reform of fiscal equalization and task allocation between the Confederation and the cantons (NFA). This was formerly classified by the government and parliament as a total revision bill within the meaning of article 193 BV but the parties behaved as if it were rather a somewhat broader partial revision.[58]

The particularities of the history of the Constitution's origins are not without significance for the interpretation of the new Federal Constitution.[59] According to the prevailing case law and doctrine the constitutional provisions are interpreted 'in accordance with the same methodological rules ... that were developed for the interpretation of ordinary statute law'.[60] Based on the wording, the Federal Supreme Court determines the meaning and purpose of a provision pursuant to all accepted methods of interpretation. According to the Federal Supreme Court itself, it is led in this by a 'pragmatic pluralism of methods' and it rejects the idea of a 'hierarchical order of priority of the methods of interpretation'.[61] The weight of each element may vary, depending on whether it is an organizational provision or a fundamental right.[62] Case-law and doctrine in general tend towards a contemporary, teleological interpretation. Furthermore, according to the 'updating idea', one must often rely on doctrine, practice, and materials on the previous provisions of the Federal Constitution of 1874. There is no threat of a 'petrification' of constitutional law and its interpretation in its version as of the end of 1999. The parliamentary debates clearly show that the Federal Supreme Court is to have the option in the future to continue the development of the catalogue of fundamental rights in accordance with the principles of previous case-law[63] in line with the times.

---

[55] The failure of the 'Staatsleitungsreform' is not considered here.
[56] In reference to the title of a collection of essays (1968–1996) published in 1998 by Peter Saladin *Kunst der Verfassungserneuerung* (Helbing und Lichtenhahn, Basel).
[57] The Austrian Federal Constitution Law (art 44 para 3) and the Spanish Constitution of 1978 (art 168) are also familiar with the institute of total revision. See also below Section B.1.a.
[58] See Federal Council, Message NFA (n 48), BBl 2002 2323. The adoption of the Federal Decree of 3 October 2003 on the NFA thus resulted in neither a new dating of the Constitution nor renumbering or similar.
[59] See Pierre Tschannen, 'Die Auslegung der neuen Bundesverfassung', in Ulrich Zimmerli (ed), *Die neue Bundesverfassung* (n 51) 223 ff; Giovanni Biaggini, 'Verfassungsauslegung', in Oliver Diggelmann and others (eds), *Verfassungsrecht der Schweiz*, vol I (Schulthess, Zurich, 2020) 235 ff. See also Verwaltungspraxis der Bundesbehörden (Administrative Practices of the Federal Authorities) (VPB) 65 (2000), No 2 (Bundesamt für Justiz, 29 June 2000).
[60] BGE 116 Ia 359 (367), *Theresa Rohner* [1990]. See also Pierre Tschannen, 'Verfassungsauslegung', in Daniel Thürer and others (eds), *Verfassungsrecht der Schweiz* (Schulthess, Zurich, 2001) 149 ff.
[61] Thus, expressly BGE 128 I 34 (41), *Rudolf Hausherr* [2002]. See also BGE 139 I 16 (24), *X.* [2012].
[62] See BGE 116 Ia 359 (367), *Theresa Rohner* [1990]; BGE 112 Ia 208 (213), *Kritisches Forum Schwyz* [1986]. See also Hans Huber, 'Der Formenreichtum der Verfassung und seine Bedeutung für ihre Auslegung' (1971) 107 Zeitschrift des Bernischen Juristenvereins 172 ff.
[63] See below Section B.2.c.

B. The Evolution of the Constitution: Milestones and Formative Factors

Looking at the sequence of the constitutional documents, the development of the Swiss Constitution presents itself as a three-step process: foundation (1848), expansion (1874), renewal (1999). No less important for the understanding of the Swiss constitutional system are the numerous smaller and larger development steps that took place between the total revisions of 1874 and 1999 and thereafter, mostly in the process of partial revision, in part outside formal amendment procedures (evolutionary constitutional interpretation through practice by the courts and authorities). Whereas the Federal Constitution of 1848 underwent only one partial revision in just under twenty-six years (1866), in its 125 years of applicability, the Federal Constitution of 1874 went through over 140 amendments. The new Federal Constitution, too, has already been revised several times. According to the standards of constitutional theory, the Federal Constitution should be categorized as a 'rigid' constitution. In practice, it has however proven to be very open and prone to change. Following a short explanation of the basic concepts of the revision process, the most important developments will be dealt with thematically.

1. Main Types of Procedure of Constitutional Amendment

a) Partial Revision of the Federal Constitution in Ordinary Procedure

In accordance with article 192 BV, the Federal Constitution can be revised at any time in whole or in part. Revision is made 'by the legislative process' unless otherwise stipulated (article 192 para 2 BV).[64] A distinction is made between the processes of total revision (article 193 BV) and of partial revision (article 194 BV).[65] In the partial revision that is of greater interest here, there are two main types: the ordinary procedure (article 192 BV) and the process of popular initiative for partial revision of the Federal Constitution (article 139 BV).

The ordinary procedure is arranged in two stages: the constitutional amendment is discussed and decided by the Federal Assembly, on request by the government or (rarely) a canton, or on its own initiative. A referendum follows a few months later. The referendum is mandatory (mandatory constitutional referendum; article 140 BV). The amendment can only come into force when it has been accepted by the people and the cantons (so-called double majority; article 195 BV). Hallmarks of the ordinary process are the low hurdles in the parliamentary process—a qualified majority is not required—and relatively high hurdles in the post-parliamentary process, which are not unsurmountable, however.

b) Popular Initiative for Partial Revision of the Federal Constitution

A partial revision of the Federal Constitution can also be requested by 100,000 citizens—today just a little over 2 per cent of the electorate (article 139 BV). The subject of a popular initiative can generally be any issue that can be clothed in a constitutional provision. The lists with the required signatures must be submitted no later than eighteen months after the publication of the text of the initiative in the Federal Gazette. The main type that is of particular

---

[64] In this sense arts 118, 119, and 121 BV 1874 as well as arts 111 and 112 BV 1848.
[65] On criteria and scope of differentiation, see for example Pierre Tschannen, *Staatsrecht der Schweizerischen Eidgenossenschaft* (5th edn, Stämpfli, Bern, 2021) 554 ff.

interest here is the popular initiative for a partial revision in the form of a specific draft. In addition, the Federal Constitution knows the popular initiative in the—less attractive and seldom used—form of the general proposal.[66]

The popular initiative in the form of specific draft is characterized by the following features:[67] The authors of the initiative submit a text, which includes the enactment, the modification, or the repeal of a provision of the Constitution, and, if need be, of several factually related norms. Following official verification of the signature lists and the title of the initiative, the title and text as well as the name of the authors of the initiative are published in the Federal Gazette. After expiry of the collection period, the Federal Chancellery (general administrative office of the government) establishes whether or not the popular initiative has the required number of valid signatures. If the popular initiative is achieved (and is not declared void by the Federal Assembly or withdrawn by the authors), a nationwide referendum must be held, the results of which are binding. Just as in the ordinary procedure, the double majority (people and cantons; article 142 BV) is required.

It is of great importance for the functioning of the political system that the Federal Assembly (like the Federal Council) has only limited response options to constitutional initiatives in the form of a specific draft. The authors have the constitutionally guaranteed right for popular initiatives to be submitted to the vote of the people 'as they stand'.[68] The Federal Assembly has no influence on the text of the initiative. It can prevent the referendum only by declaring the successfully requested popular initiative invalid. But this is only possible when certain grounds that are listed in the Federal Constitution apply (article 139 BV; see Section B.1.c.). The popular initiative is not only a 'request from the people but also one to the people', as Fritz Fleiner (1867–1937) aptly put it.[69] The fate of the initiative is decided at the ballot box (referendum), not in parliament. The role of the Federal Assembly is not purely passive, however. It has the right and the duty to comment on the content of the initiative and to recommend to the voters either to accept or—and this is the norm—to reject it (article 139 BV). Furthermore, the Federal Assembly may present, at the request of the government or on its own initiative, a so-called counterproposal ('*Gegenentwurf*', alternative draft).[70] Not infrequently, the authors end up withdrawing their initiative in favour of a parliamentary alternative draft which sufficiently meets their demands. If there is no withdrawal, a double vote takes place on the popular initiative and the alternative draft, in which the voters state their preference (since 1988) in a tie-break question in case both the initiative and the alternative draft are approved by a double majority of the people and the cantons (articles 139b para 2 and 3 BV). The success rate for constitutional initiatives is a good 10 per cent, even slightly higher in recent years (from 2002–2018: around 14.3 per cent).[71]

---

[66] In the context of the reform of citizens' rights, the People and the Cantons (referendum of 9 February 2003) approved introduction of a so-called general popular initiative (art 139a BV). The new initiative form was to replace the popular initiative in the form of general proposal. It would have made it possible to regulate a political issue on a legislative level (rather than on a constitutional level, as with the popular initiative in accordance with art 139 BV). In view of the complicated procedure, the People and the Cantons decided not to introduce the General popular initiative (referendum of 27 February 2009).

[67] For more detail, see art 68 ff Federal Act on Political Rights (*Bundesgesetz über die politischen Rechte*; BPR) and art 97 ff Federal Act on the Federal Assembly (*Parlamentsgesetz*; ParlG).

[68] Thus art 99 ParlG.

[69] Fritz Fleiner, *Schweizerisches Bundesstaatsrecht* (JCB Mohr, Tübingen, 1923) 398.

[70] Some important constitutional provisions can be traced back to official alternative drafts, for example the reorganization of the treaty referendum (1977) The direct alternative draft must be differentiated from the (frequently used) *indirect* alternative draft: a parliamentary bill on a *legislative level* (art 74 BPR), which is subject only to an optional referendum.

[71] Since the introduction of the popular initiative on the partial revision of the Federal Constitution (1891), 23 of more than 220 initiatives have been approved by the People and the Cantons (March 2021). These included

Not to be underestimated, though, are the indirect effects (such as influencing the parliamentary and government agenda, change in the legislation or authority practice under the pressure of popular initiatives). Frequently addressed topics have in recent years been social policy, transport and energy policy, immigration and asylum policy, and criminal law policy. Hardly present are federal and constitutional concerns.

c) Limitations to Constitutional Revision

The Federal Constitution can be revised at any time but there are certain limitations to be noted. Three limitations are mentioned expressly in the Federal Constitution. For one, popular initiatives for partial revision as well as proposals submitted by the Federal Assembly may, in the interest of genuine decision-making, only have factually related issues as a subject (maintaining the unity of subject matter, '*Einheit der Materie*'; articles 139 and 194 BV as well as article 75 para 2 BPR). Popular initiatives which mix different forms of initiative (specific draft, general proposal) are not permitted either (maintaining the unity of form, '*Einheit der Form*'). Popular initiatives and proposals by the authorities must then comply with the mandatory provisions of international law. The scope of this barrier—initially unwritten (since 1996), now constitutionally established—has still not been completely clarified.[72] 'Eternity clauses' after the model of the Italian Constitution of 1947 (article 139) or the German Basic Law (article 79 para 3) are unknown in the Swiss Federal Constitution. If a popular initiative violates the unity of form, the unity of subject matter, or the mandatory provisions of international law, the Federal Assembly must declare it (wholly or partially) invalid (article 139 BV). The declaration of invalidity by the Federal Assembly is final. There is no right of appeal.

State practice and jurisprudence acknowledge an unwritten, fourth ground for invalidation: the feasibility of a popular initiative.[73] The recognition of further limitations is repeatedly called for in legal doctrine.[74] The Federal Assembly has rightly not given in to these demands and also in general handles the recognized limitations generously[75]—not least of all when it is a question of the unity of subject matter in its own proposals.

the popular initiative concerning the switch to proportional representation in the National Council (1918; art 73 BV 1874, today art 149 BV); concerning the banning of the liqueur of the absinthe plant (1908; 1999 'deconstitutionalized', abolished as of 1 March 2005); concerning the ban on gambling establishments (1920 and 1928; abolished 1993); concerning the protection of the Alpine region from the negative effects of transit traffic (1994; art 36[sexies] BV 1874, today art 84 BV); concerning Switzerland's entry into the UNO (2002; art 197 no 1 BV); concerning the lifelong incarceration of certain sexual and violent offenders (2004; art 123a BV); concerning GMO-free agriculture (2005; art 197 no 2 BV); most recently, the popular initiative concerning the ban on the construction of minarets (2009; art 72 para 3 BV); concerning the extradition of criminal foreigners (2010; art 121 para 3 ff and 197 no 8 BV); concerning the limitation of the construction of second homes (2012; art 75b and 197 no 9 BV); concerning mass immigration (2014; art 121a BV); concerning the permanent loss of the right to work with minors or dependent persons for persons convicted of harming the sexual integrity of a child or of a dependent person (2014; art 123c BV); and concerning the ban on covering the face (2021; art 10a BV).

[72] Cited as an example: the essence of the humanitarian law of war, the non-derogable guarantees of the ECHR, the prohibition of genocide, slavery, and torture. See for example, René Rhinow, Markus Schefer, and Peter Uebersax, *Schweizerisches Verfassungsrecht* (3rd edn, Helbing und Lichtenhahn, Basel, 2016) 704 ff (with further references).

[73] Practical difficulties in the implementation of an initiative are not sufficient grounds. The only precedent dates from 1955. See Ulrich Häfelin and others, *Schweizerisches Bundesstaatsrecht* (10th edn, Schulthess, Zurich, 2020) para 1758.

[74] Immutability of essential core values and/or 'fundamental standards' of the Federal Constitution; Invalidity of popular initiatives with retroactive effect, etc. Overview in Yvo Hangartner and Andreas Kley, *Die demokratischen Rechte in Bund und Kantonen der Schweizerischen Eidgenossenschaft* (Schulthess, Zurich, 2000) 200 ff.

[75] The last three initiatives declared invalid date from 1996 (popular initiative 'for a reasonable asylum policy': violation of the non-refoulement principle), 1995 (popular initiative 'for less military spending and more peace policy': unity of subject matter), and 1977 (popular initiative 'against rising prices and inflation': unity of subject matter).

2. Milestones in the Development of the Constitution

Federal Constitutional law experienced numerous smaller and larger developmental steps in the time between the two total revisions of 1874 and 1999. Even though the development of the Constitution was not based on a uniform plan, some major threads can be identified: the expansion of the instruments of direct democracy, progressive centralization—albeit still with considerable autonomy of the cantons—and the strengthening of the rule of law (with certain counter-movements in recent years; see Sections B.2.c and C.3.c).

a) Democracy

One development that has been of extraordinary importance for the constitutional system altogether is the gradual construction and expansion of the citizens' rights that today characterize the system (instruments of direct democracy). An important impulse was (and is) the development in the cantons, which could be described as actual experimental labs for direct democracy.[76] The first Federal Constitution had created an essentially representative system at a federal level. With the Federal Constitution of 1874, the optional referendum on federal acts ('*fakultatives Gesetzesreferendum*') was introduced. Further important development stages followed in the form of partial revisions:

- Introduction of the popular initiative for partial revision of the Federal Constitution (1891) in the form of a specific draft (article 121 BV 1874, today article 139 BV): this innovation, which was requested not least of all by opposition forces (Catholic conservatives, social democrats), found the necessary majority in the Federal Assembly and in the referendum thanks to the support of the reform-oriented wing of the majority forces (so-called '*Freisinn*', today FDP).[77]
- Introduction of the optional referendum on international treaties ('*Staatsvertragsreferendum*'; 1921): the trigger for the new citizens' rights created by way of the popular initiative (article 89 para 3 BV 1874 old version; today article 141 BV) was the conclusion of a non-cancellable treaty between Switzerland, Germany, and Italy with regard to the Gotthard railway (1909) with some highly controversial clauses (maximum tariffs).
- Democratization of the so-called urgent federal acts ('*Dringlichkeitsrecht*'; 1949): The option used often by the Federal Assembly in the years of war and crisis to pass a legislative act without a referendum by declaring it as urgent (article 89 para 2 BV 1874 old version) was abolished by way of popular initiative. Now, urgent decrees are subject to a subsequent referendum (article 89[bis] BV 1874; today article 165 BV).
- *Extension* of the optional referendum on international treaties and introduction of the mandatory referendum concerning accession to supranational communities (e.g. the EU) or organizations for collective security (1977): This development step is based on a successful direct alternative draft to a popular initiative (article 89 para 3–5 BV 1874; today articles 140 and 141 BV).

---

[76] See Alfred Kölz, 'Geschichtliche Grundlagen', in Daniel Thürer and others (eds), *Verfassungsrecht der Schweiz* (n 60), 122 ff; Yvo Hangartner and Andreas Kley, *Die demokratischen Rechte und Kantonen der Schweizerischen Eidgenossenschaft* (n 74) 534 ff.

[77] See Jean-François Aubert, *Bundesstaatsrecht der Schweiz*, vol I (Helbing und Lichtenhahn, Basel, 1991) para 162 f.

In the framework of the already-mentioned reform of the citizens' rights (2003), the treaty referendum was refined (article 141 BV).

The 1918 switch to proportional representation in the National Council elections, as decided by popular initiative, had very significant impact on the political system (article 73 BV 1874; today article 149 BV). Two failed initiatives preceded (1900 and 1910). However, the repeatedly requested introduction of the popular election of members of the Federal Council (government) has secured no majority thus far. Several amendments to the Constitution concerned the composition of the circle of people with full citizen's rights. General (male) voting and electoral rights had already existed in Switzerland since 1848. In 1966, this was extended to include Swiss citizens living abroad, then in 1971 to women, and in 1991 to eighteen- and nineteen-year-olds. Various cantons had already introduced women's suffrage in cantonal and communal affairs before 1971; the others were to follow shortly—with the exception of the canton of Appenzell Innerrhoden, which the Federal Supreme Court eventually had to force into taking action in the startling *Rohner* decision (1990).[78] The increase in the population and the introduction of women's suffrage were occasion for the increase in the number of signatures required for referenda (50,000 instead of 30,000) and popular initiatives (100,000 instead of 50,000) decided in 1977.

The way from representative democracy to Swiss-style half-direct democracy was so far a 'one-way street': citizens' rights were introduced, further developed, and, where necessary, adapted to changing circumstances (signature numbers), but so far there has been no reform that would abolish a citizens' right without substitution. For this reason, in particular, proposals for extensions of the instruments of direct democracy are examined carefully regarding their effects on the political system. The People and the Cantons have already rejected an extension to their own rights several times.[79]

Although the success rate for popular initiatives is low and although a referendum is adopted against only a small fraction of all parliamentary decisions requiring a referendum,[80] the participation rights of the people are of enormous significance for the functioning of the constitutional institutions and the political system due to their multi-level indirect effects.[81] The referendum, which acts as a 'brake' in the political process, and the popular initiative, which usually serves as a 'motor' for legal development, contribute significantly to the gradual emergence of the consociational democracy which today characterizes political Switzerland and which looks for compromise solutions on as broad a base as possible.[82]

---

[78] BGE 116 Ia 359, *Theresa Rohner* [1990]. See Giovanni Biaggini, 'Die Einführung des Frauenstimmrechts im Kanton Appenzell I.Rh. kraft bundesgerichtlicher Verfassungsinterpretation' (1992) 10 recht (Zeitschrift für juristische Weiterbildung und Praxis) 65 ff.

[79] For example, a popular initiative was rejected which sought the introduction of the so-called constructive referendum (24 September 2000), a hybrid of referendum and initiative known in only a few cantons. The suggestion of framework permits of the Confederation for nuclear facilities under the optional referendum, rejected by the people and cantons in 1979, was recently introduced via legal amendment (art 48 of the Nuclear Energy Act of 21 March 2003; Systematic Compilation of Federal Law 732.1).

[80] According to Bernhard Ehrenzeller and Roger Nobs, 'Vorbemerkungen zu Art. 136–142 BV', in Bernhard Ehrenzeller and others (eds), *Die schweizerische Bundesverfassung. St. Galler Kommentar* (3rd edn, Dike and Schulthess, Zurich, 2014) para 36, between 1978 and 2013, 5.9 per cent of all parliamentary proposals (1602) resulted in a referendum.

[81] See (from a legal perspective) René Rhinow, Markus Schefer, and Peter Uebersax, *Schweizerisches Verfassungsrecht* (n 72) 383 ff; (from a political perspective) Wolf Linder and Sean Mueller, *Schweizerische Demokratie* (4th edn, Haupt, Bern, 2017) 293 ff.

[82] See below Section C.3.c.

b) Federalism

The development of the federal system has been based since 1848 on the expansion of the federal powers. This is not the place to look at the assignments of competences individually.[83] Aside from the central (initial and continuing) concern of the single Swiss economic area, needs in the area of infrastructure as well as social and environmental issues emerged increasingly. The individual development steps did not follow a fixed plan but rather were attuned to the respective requirements and political feasibility. It is striking that a comprehensive constitutional basis for the unification of the material civil and criminal laws has been in place only since 1898 and exploited by the Confederation only since 1912 (Swiss Civil Code) and 1942 (Swiss Criminal Code). The legal basis for the unification of the civil and criminal procedural law itself has only existed since 2007. The competence for the regulation of residence and establishment of foreigners was first transferred to the Confederation in 1925 (article 69[ter] BV 1874, today article 121 BV). Formal constitutional bases for today's two greatest sources of income for the Confederation—the direct federal tax (formerly defence tax) and VAT (formerly purchase turnover tax), were created only in the post-war period. In both cases, the Confederation's power of collection was and is limited in time, meaning that the People and the Cantons have to be called to the ballot box from time to time to decide on an extension.[84]

In this process of centralization, the problematic US method of creative-extensive constitutional interpretation is usually not used, but rather the more arduous path to formal constitutional amendments is taken, meaning that almost the entire economic and social state development of the twentieth century is reflected in the different layers of text of the Federal Constitution from 1874. The increasing internationalization of the law, the levelling effect of constitutional jurisdiction, and a certain 'federalism blindness' of the administrative law of the Confederation are also contributing to centralization.[85] Despite these developments, the Swiss cantons still have a great degree of autonomy in comparison to the member states of other federal states. There is no cause for concern but certainly an occasion for increased attention. In the early 1990s, efforts were made for a renewal of federalism. The trigger was, for one thing, the rapprochement of Switzerland to the European integration process that was envisaged at the time; for another, the increasingly obvious need for reform of the federal fiscal equalization system. One part of the reforms was addressed in the context of the total revision of the Federal Constitution. A project organization borne by both the Confederation and the cantons was created for the reform of fiscal equalization and task allocation between the Confederation and the cantons.[86] The objective was four-fold: simplification of the equalization of financial resources and burdens through reduction of the formerly three dozen or so financial equalization mechanisms to three; unbundling of tasks and financing in around twenty fields; improvement of coordination between the Confederation and the cantons in the areas not unbundled; promotion of the horizontal cooperation between the cantons and of the inter-cantonal equalization of burdens. The federal decree of

---

[83] See René Rhinow and others, *Öffentliches Wirtschaftsrecht* (2nd edn, Helbing und Lichtenhahn, Basel, 2011) 32 ff.

[84] Most recently in the referendum of 4 March 2018 (extension until end of 2035). See art 196 No 13 and 14 BV.

[85] See Walter Kälin, Verfassungsgerichtsbarkeit in der Demokratie - Funktionen der staatsrechtlichen Beschwerde (Stämpfli, Bern, 1987) 177 ff; Giovanni Biaggini, *Theorie und Praxis des Verwaltungsrechts im Bundesstaat* (Helbing und Lichtenhahn, Basel, 1996) 308 ff.

[86] On this project sometimes referred to as the 'second phase' of a federalism reform, see Federal Council, Message NFA (n 48), Federal Gazette of the Swiss Confederation (BBl) 2002 2291 ff; Giovanni Biaggini, 'Föderalismus im Wandel' (2002) Austrian Journal of Public Law 359 ff.

3 October 2003 which combined the around two dozen affected constitutional provisions[87] also included an express commitment to the federal principle of subsidiarity (article 5a BV, in force since 1 January 2008), a concern of the cantons that had not yet been heard in the context of the parliamentary deliberations on total revision of the Federal Constitution (1998), shortly before.[88]

Reform proposals with territorial or institutional reference had so far had a hard time.[89] A singular occurrence was the founding of the canton of Jura which took effect on 1 January 1979. The 26th canton could thank a series of referendums for its existence; after long and not always peaceful discussions, these made possible the separation of three French-speaking, traditionally Catholic districts from the largely German-speaking and Protestant canton of Bern. The People and the Cantons approved the formation of the canton on 24 September 1978 and further smaller territorial amendments in two subsequent votes.[90]

c) Rule of Law

Due to the circumstances, the constitutional fathers of 1848 focused their attention more on the federal and state-organizational, democratic bases of the new community-in-waiting rather than on the development of the rule of law, which—compared to today's standards— initially remained somewhat underdeveloped on a federal level.[91] With the total revision of 1874 came two further guarantees of fundamental rights and, with regard to cantonal sovereign acts, a true constitutional jurisdiction. However, there was still a stronger focus on democratic control than on judicial review. Only the developments after 1874 (which were only partially translated into the Constitution itself) truly made the constitutional system of the Confederation flourish in regard to the rule of law. Some characteristics (not to say: rule-of-law 'anomalies') have survived until the present.

A formal constitutional amendment in 1914 initiated a strengthening of the rule of law. The inclusion of article 114[bis] BV 1874 created the basis for an (initially limited) administrative jurisdiction in the Confederation, exercised by the Federal Supreme Court. For many issues, legal action could only be taken within the administration itself for the time being. Even today, the Federal Council has the last word on certain administrative disputes.[92] With the coming into effect of the guarantee of access to the courts adopted in the course of the reform of the judiciary (article 29a BV, in force since 1 January 2007) and the reorganization of

---

[87] Federal Decree of 3 October 2003 on the NFA (Federal Gazette of the Swiss Confederation [BBl] 2003 6591), adopted in the referendum of 28 November 2004 (in force since 1 January 2008).

[88] A few substance-poor economic doctrines were also admitted ('Principles for the assignment and fulfilment of governmental tasks': art 43a BV), which—like the subsidiarity principle—were considered not justiciable. See Federal Council, Message NFA (n 48), BBl 2002 2458, 2460, 2339.

[89] E.g. the fusion of cantons, the weighting of cantons according to population size in the determination of the cantonal majority, the restructuring of the Council of States into a 'chamber of federal states' after the German model.

[90] Switch of the Laufental district from the canton of Bern to the canton of Basel-Landschaft (1994) and transfer of the commune of Vellerat from the canton of Bern to the canton of Jura (1996). An appeal against the validity of the popular vote on the switch of the city of Moutier from the canton of Bern to the canton of Jura was approved in August 2019 (Decision of the Administrative Court of the Canton of Bern, 100 2018 388 of 23 August 2019). The vote was repeated on 28 March 2021 and Moutier decided to switch to the canton of Bern. Today, on federal level such territorial changes are subject merely to the optional referendum (art 53 BV). See Ulrich Häfelin and others, *Schweizerisches Bundesstaatsrecht* (n 73) para 997 ff.

[91] The cantonal constitutional systems require separate assessment.

[92] See art 187 para 1 (d) BV as well as art 72 VwVG. On the development, see Benjamin Schindler, 'Verwaltungsgerichtsbarkeit in der Schweiz', in Armin von Bogdandy, Peter M Huber, and Sabino Cassese (eds), *IPE vol VIII* (CF Müller, Heidelberg, 2019) 601 ff; Heinrich Koller, 'Die Verwaltungsrechtspflege des Bundesrates als Residuat', in Walter Schluep (ed), *Recht, Staat und Politik am Ende des zweiten Jahrtausends: Festschrift zum 60. Geburtstag von Bundesrat Arnold Koller* (Haupt, Bern, 1993) 359 ff.

the judiciary in the Confederation, an important stage in the development of the rule of law was concluded.[93] Through formal amendments to the Constitution, the guarantee of ownership went from being an unwritten fundamental right to being a written fundamental right in the Confederation in 1969 (article 22[ter] BV 1874; today article 26 BV). However, this step was mostly about providing a liberal counterpart to the simultaneously created competence of the Confederation for framework legislation in the area of spatial planning (article 22[quater] BV 1874, today article 75 BV). The protection of fundamental rights was further extended in 1973, when both articles about confessional exemption of 1874[94] were revoked, as well as in 1981, when equality for men and women was enshrined in the Constitution (article 4 para 2 BV 1874, today article 8 para 3 BV).

For the development of the rule of law, trends outside the Constitution are equally important, namely the evolutionary constitutional interpretation in the case-law of the Federal Supreme Court. Encouraged by statements in the constitutional legal doctrine,[95] the Federal Supreme Court gradually recognized several unwritten fundamental rights. The first step took place covertly: in a decision of 11 May 1960 (not recorded in the official compilation),[96] the Federal Supreme Court referred to two unpublished decisions from the previous year, wherein it had classified the guarantee of ownership as a right protected under the Federal Constitution. This changed little for the protection of property rights since the Federal Supreme Court had already developed a 'common federal' protective standard from the cantonal guarantees of ownership. In contrast, the consequences for the general development of fundamental rights were profound because the Federal Supreme Court soon recognized, now in officially published decisions, a series of further unwritten fundamental rights of the Confederation:[97] first, in an *obiter dictum*, the freedom of expression (1961), then, shortly afterwards, personal freedom (1963) and freedom of speech (1965), then later freedom of assembly (1970), and finally, as a late-comer, the right to assistance when in need (1995), which grants individuals in hardship a claim to state aid and care and provides the means required for a decent standard of living (today article 12 BV). After initial uncertainty, the Federal Supreme Court developed a standing formula, whereby individual rights not mentioned in the Constitution can be recognized as unwritten fundamental rights of the Confederation, if these constitute a prerequisite for the exercise of another freedom (mentioned in the Constitution) or otherwise appear to be essential to the democratic and constitutional order of the Confederation; with a view to the 'limitations imposed on constitutional judges', it must in the opinion of the Federal Supreme Court be investigated further 'as to whether the guarantee in question already corresponds to a widespread constitutional reality in the

---

[93] Central are the Federal Supreme Court Act (BGG), which replaced the Federal Judicial Code of 1943 (Federal Act on the organization of federal administration of justice of 16 December 1943), and the Administrative Court Act (VGG), which merged numerous smaller special administrative courts into a federal administrative court of first instance. These laws, both from 17 June 2005, came into force on 1 January 2007.

[94] Art 51 and 52 BV 1874 (Jesuit ban, ban on establishment of new monasteries). See above Section A.2.b). The adoption of the popular initiative regarding a ban on the construction of minarets (art 72 para 3 BV) in the referendum of 29 November 2009 created a new discrimination.

[95] Worth mentioning by name is *Zaccaria Giacometti* (1893–1970), professor of constitutional law in Zurich with roots in the Italian-speaking part of Graubünden, related to the artist Alberto Giacometti. See in particular his rectorate speech: Zaccaria Giacometti, 'Die Freiheitsrechtskataloge als Kodifikation der Freiheit' (1955), in Alfred Kölz (ed), *Ausgewählte Schriften* (Schulthess, Zurich, 1994) 23 ff.

[96] Excerpts reproduced in Schweizerisches Zentralblatt für Staats- und Verwaltungsrecht (ZBl) 1961 69.

[97] BGE 87 I 114 (117), *Sphinx-Film S.A.* [1961]; BGE 89 I 92 (98), *Kind X.* [1963]; BGE 91 I 480 (486), *Association de l'Ecole française* [1965]; BGE 96 I 219 (224), *Nöthiger und Pinkus* [1970]; BGE 121 I 367 (371), *V.* [1995].

cantons and is supported by a general consensus'.[98] The formula retains its importance even under the new Federal Constitution.

Before the recognition of unwritten fundamental rights, the Federal Supreme Court had already 'derived' a variety of rule of law-motivated guarantees and principles from the general principle of equality of article 4 BV 1874 (today article 8 para 1 BV) over many years of creative case-law.[99] These include the protection against arbitrary conduct, various procedural guarantees (such as the right to be heard, entitlement to free legal aid in cases of need, the prohibition of excessive formalism), the right to be treated by state authorities in good faith, the principle of legality, and the principle of non-retroactivity. In the framework of the total revision of the Federal Constitution, most of these 'derivations' from article 4 BV 1874 were independently codified.[100]

Through selective amendments to the constitutional text and, especially thanks to innovative constitutional interpretation, to which practice by the political authorities also contributed,[101] Switzerland evolved step by step into a well-developed constitutional state. Against this background, the comparatively late accession of Switzerland to the ECHR (1974) and some of the initial difficulties are more easily understandable.[102] On the other hand it is striking that the Federal Supreme Court used the first possible opportunity to emphasize the constitutional nature of the ECHR guarantees and to procedurally equate these with the fundamental rights of the Federal Constitution.[103] The total revision of the Federal Constitution brought about an important consolidation in terms of rule of law[104] but it was not the end of its development, especially since old and new tensions continue to emerge in the relationship between rule of law and democracy.[105]

3. Actors and 'Neglected Issues' of Constitutional Development

One characteristic of Swiss constitutional development is the diversity of actors and processes. In addition to the political bodies (Federal Assembly, Federal Council), the Federal

---

[98] BGE 121 I 367 (370 f), *V.* [1995]; see also BGE 100 Ia 392 (400 f), *Komitee für Indochina* [1974] (where the recognition of an independent freedom of demonstration beyond the freedom of expression and assembly was rejected).

[99] See Arthur Haefliger, *Alle Schweizer sind vor dem Gesetze gleich* (Stämpfli, Bern, 1985); Georg Müller, 'Kommentierung zu Art. 4', in Jean-François Aubert and others (eds), *Kommentar aBV* (n 17) para 48 ff.

[100] See in particular art 5 (Rule of law), art 9 (Protection against arbitrary conduct and principle of good faith), art 29–32 BV (general and specific procedural guarantees). An exception is the principle of non-retroactivity. However, it can still claim validity. See Ulrich Häfelin, Georg Müller, and Felix Uhlmann, *Allgemeines Verwaltungsrecht* (8th edn, Dike, Zurich, 2020) para 266 ff.

[101] Thus, for example 1996, when the Federal Assembly recognized mandatory international law as an unwritten barrier to constitutional change in the assessment of the validity of a popular initiative (see above Section B.1.c).

[102] See Michel Hottelier, Hanspeter Mock, and Michel Puéchavy, *La Suisse devant la Cour européenne des droits de l'homme* (2nd edn, Schulthess, Zurich, 2011); Mark E Villiger, *Handbuch der europäischen Menschenrechtskonvention* (3rd edn, Schulthess, Zurich, 2020).

[103] BGE 101 Ia 67 (69), Diskont- und Handelsbank AG [1975].

[104] Not least of all thanks to various provisions based on ECHR guarantees. See for example art 13 BV (art 8 ECHR), art 31, and art 32 BV (art 5 and 6 ECHR), as well as art 17 para 3 BV (Protection of sources) as a direct reaction to the Strasbourg judgment in the case *Goodwin v the United Kingdom*, App no 17488/90, 27 March 1996.

[105] See art 190 BV (lack of constitutional jurisdiction vis-à-vis federal laws); BGE 129 I 217, *A. und Mitb.* [2003], as well as BGE 129 I 232, *Schweizerische Volkspartei der Stadt Zürich* [2003] (*discrimination in naturalizations*). For a résumé after ten years of the new Federal Constitution, see Giovanni Biaggini, 'Entwicklungen und Spannungen im Verfassungsrecht—Versuch einer Standortbestimmung zehn Jahre nach Inkrafttreten der Bundesverfassung vom 18. April 1999' (2010) Schweizerisches Zentralblatt für Staats- und Verwaltungsrecht (ZBl) 1 ff.

Supreme Court plays a significant role, despite limited constitutional jurisdiction, namely in questions of the rule of law. Within the framework of the citizens' rights, the electorate (including women since 1971) participates directly in the development and amendment of the Constitution. Namely, the instrument of popular initiatives requesting a partial revision of the constitution ensures that 'established' politics (Federal Assembly, Federal Council, political parties) receive impetus from 'outside'. The significance of individual persons is not naturally so clearly apparent in the Swiss system of many collegially organized authorities and bodies. The contribution (and influence) of legal scholars is not to be underestimated,[106] whether in the form of *de constitutione ferenda* opinions in constitutional commentaries, constitutional law monographs and essays, in the form of policy consulting (participation in expert commissions, expertise on behalf of the government or parliament), or in the context of political office.

For many years, the cantons played a subordinate role in the development of the Constitution, despite their constitutionally documented participation rights. This perhaps surprising finding can be explained in particular by the fact that the cantons (or the governments acting for them) have very few effective active instruments on the federal level, and they do not have an actual veto position. However, the cantonal governments have succeeded recently in engaging in the important early phase of significant reform processes, for example in the development of the draft for a new Federal Constitution,[107] and even more intensively in the reform of fiscal equalization and task allocation between the Confederation and the cantons (NFA). The indirect influence of the cantons should not be underestimated: the constitutional development in the Confederation traditionally receives many impulses from cantonal law development, thus also in the area of citizen's rights.

The 'neglected issues' of constitutional development also include certain questions of a general nature. Thus systematic 'constitutional care' regarding the supreme constitutional bodies came up short until the latest total revision of the Federal Constitution; individual problems and selective reforms blocked an encompassing view of the whole. For a long time, the fundamental rights and rule-of-law principles could not count on a sufficiently strong 'codification lobby'. It is hardly surprising that the Federal Supreme Court chose to develop case-law for this neglected area. However, it is noteworthy that the criticism directed at the Federal Supreme Court by politics was less concerned with ('undemocratic') constitutional case-law but rather, first and foremost, decisions in which the Federal Supreme Court essentially only fulfilled its task as guardian of the Constitution (albeit also in politically sensitive areas) without contributing particularly creatively to the evolutionary interpretation of the Constitution.[108]

---

[106] On the role of constitutional jurisprudence, see the article by Rainer J Schweizer, 'Schweiz', in Armin von Bogdandy, Pedro Cruz Villalón, and Peter M Huber (eds), *IPE vol II* (2008) section 36.

[107] See Federal Council, Message on a new Federal Constitution (n 27), Federal Gazette of the Swiss Confederation (BBl) 1997 I 1 ff, in particular 78 ff and 205 ff, as well as Konferenz der Kantonsregierungen (ed), *Verfassungsreform als Föderalismusreform* (Schulthess, Zurich, 1997).

[108] Examples here are the 'crucifix decision', BGE 116 Ia 252, *Comune di Cadro* [1990] (in which the Federal Supreme Court decided that placing a crucifix in the classrooms of a primary school was not compatible with the state's commitment to confessional neutrality), and BGE 129 I 232, *Schweizerische Volkspartei der Stadt Zürich* [2003] (discriminatory naturalization process).

C. Basic Structures and Concepts

1. The Federal Constitution as a Basis for and Object of Politics

According to the prevailing constitutional understanding, the Federal Constitution should assume not only a constitutive function (order and organizational function) and a limiting function (function of guaranteeing freedom and limiting power) as the 'fundamental legal order of the state' (*Werner Kägi*[109]), but also a *guiding* function. The newer doctrines[110] add various other constitutional functions to these main functions, namely the function of promoting integration and unity as well as an embedding or bridging function in the sense of a positioning of Switzerland and its constitutional system in the international law environment.[111] The characterization of the Constitution as the 'fundamental legal order of the state' requires two clarifications in the case of Switzerland. In federal terms, it must be emphasized that the constitutions of the cantons are not derived from the Federal Constitution, even if they must meet certain minimum requirements and need guarantee by the Federal Assembly (articles 51 and 172 BV).[112] Important requirements for the legislative process are also taken more and more directly from the international norms with constitution-like function—thanks to the commitment of the Swiss constitutional system to international law.[113] The Federal Constitution must thus be more precisely outlined than the fundamental legal order of the Confederation which is increasingly influenced by international law.

The Federal Constitution does not want to be only an organizational and procedural framework. This can be seen in various constitutional provisions which formulate binding guidelines for action in politics and the law implementation process. These include numerous general and specific purpose and goal provisions of various abstraction levels.[114] A material understanding of the Constitution is then also based on article 35 BV, which determines in a novel way that the fundamental rights must 'be upheld throughout the legal system' (para 1). The legislature and all other state authorities are urged to contribute to the

---

[109] Werner Kägi, Die Verfassung als rechtliche Grundordnung des Staates (Polygraphischer Verlag, Zurich, 1945).

[110] See the detailed, varying catalogue of functions in Kurt Eichenberger, 'Verfassungsrechtliche Einleitung', in Jean-François Aubert and others (eds), *Kommentar aBV* (n 17) para 79 ff; René Rhinow, Markus Schefer, and Peter Uebersax, *Schweizerisches Verfassungsrecht* (n 72) 9 ff; Pierre Tschannen, *Staatsrecht der Schweizerischen Eidgenossenschaft* (n 65) 49 ff.

[111] Serving this purpose are, for example, regulations concerning the relationship between international law and national law or aims for foreign policy (see arts 5, 54, 139 BV). See Giovanni Biaggini, 'Die Öffnung des Verfassungsstaates als Herausforderung für Verfassungsrecht und Verfassungslehre', in Bernhard Ehrenzeller and others (eds), *Der Verfassungsstaat vor neuen Herausforderungen—Festschrift für Yvo Hangartner* (Dike, Zurich, 1998) 967 ff.

[112] This is attested by the Constitution de la République et Canton de Genève du 24 mai 1847, which originated in the time *before* the founding of the Confederation (1848) and was still in force until 31 May 2013 (today: Constitution de la République et canton de Genève du 14 octobre 2012; Systematic Compilation of Federal Law 131.234).

[113] See Ernst-Ulrich Petersmann, 'Die Verfassungsentscheidung für eine völkerrechtskonforme Rechtsordnung als Strukturprinzip der Schweizer Bundesverfassung' (1990) 115 Archiv des öffentlichen Rechts 537 ff; Helen Keller, *Die Rezeption des Völkerrechts* (Heidelberg, Springer, 2003) 285 ff, 711 f. From case-law, see the two—not uncontroversial—decisions BGE 139 I 16 [2012] (Precedence of the European Convention on Human Rights and the case-law of the European Court of Human Rights itself vis-à-vis the national constitution, *obiter dictum*) and BGE 142 II 35 [2015] (Precedence of the Switzerland-EU Agreement on the Free Movement of Persons vis-à-vis national law, *obiter dictum*).

[114] These include a general purpose article (art 2 BV, similar to art 2 BV 1848, art 2 BV 1847), a general social goal provision (art 41 BV), as well as subject-related objectives for example for foreign policy (art 54 BV), general economic policy (art 94 and 100 BV), or agricultural policy (art 104 BV). The neutrality of Switzerland is anchored in the Federal Constitution only as a means, not as a goal of foreign policy (see arts 173 and 185 BV).

implementation of the fundamental rights (para 2) and to ensure that 'fundamental rights, where appropriate, apply to relationships among private persons' (para 3).[115] The penetration of the values embodied in the fundamental rights into ordinary legislation serves not least of all the recognized and regularly practiced method of interpretation in conformity with the Constitution.[116]

The Federal Constitution does not only set out substantive parameters for politics. It is, as shown in the comments on constitutional development, itself the subject matter of politics to a great extent. In the course of the twentieth century, it has become customary to assign new tasks to the Confederation in two political steps, each with a different level of detail: in the constitutional provision that establishes the competence, important corner points of content are set down constitutionally and, in the next step, the details are worked out on a legislative level.[117] The result is that the policies pursued by the Confederation are democratically legitimized to a high degree in many legislative areas (mandatory constitutional referendum). The flipside is that there are many competence and task provisions that are detailed[118] and can sometimes greatly restrict the scope of action of the legislature.[119] Delays in the legislative implementation may under some circumstances entail a longer-lasting, unconstitutional state of uncertainty, such as in the case of the constitutional mandate of 1945 concerning the creation of a maternity insurance that was implemented only in 2005 (article 34^{quinquies} BV 1874, today article 116 BV).[120]

2. On the Significance of Structure-establishing Constitutional Principles

In the description and characterization of the constitutional system of the Confederation, the terms democracy, rule of law, federalism, and the welfare state come up regularly.[121] These four 'core values' (so called in Ulrich Häfelin and others, *Schweizerisches Bundesstaatsrecht*, see n 73) or 'constitutionally formative principles' (so called in René Rhinow, Markus Schefer and Peter Uebersax, *Schweizerisches Verfassungsrecht*, see n 72) of the Federal Constitution are supplemented by further principles, depending on the author: the 'nation state principle', the 'economic state principle', the 'subsidiarity principle', the 'sustainability principle', and the 'principle of the cosmopolitan and cooperative constitutional state'.[122] It can only

---

[115] See Jörg Paul Müller, *Verwirklichung der Grundrechte nach Art. 35 BV* (Stämpfli, Bern, 2018).

[116] For example, BGE 116 Ia 359 (369), *Rohner* [1990]. See also BGE 129 II 249 (263) *A.X.* [2003]; BGE 128 V 20 (24 f), *E.* [2002].

[117] Example: the constitutional norm concerning reproductive medicine (art 24^{novies} BV 1874, today art 119 BV) was approved in the referendum of 17 May 1992; the executive federal law (Reproductive Medicine Act; Systematic Compilation of Federal Law 810.11) was adopted in Parliament on 18 December 1998 and entered into force on 1 January 2001.

[118] Chapter 2 'Powers' (arts 54–125 BV) is more similar to Part three of the Treaty on the Functioning of the European Union ('Union Policies and Internal Actions', Arts 26–197 TFEU) than the catalogue of competences of the German Basic Law (arts 73–75 GG).

[119] The exceptions include, not incidentally, two older federal competences concerning social health insurance (1890) and immigration policy (1925). See today arts 117, 121, and 121a BV.

[120] The legislation serving the implementation was approved in the referendum of 26 September 2004.

[121] See for example Andreas Auer, Giorgio Malinverni, and Michel Hottelier, *Droit constitutionnel suisse*, vol I (3rd edn, Stämpfli, Bern, 2013) para 1442 ff; René Rhinow, Markus Schefer, and Peter Uebersax, *Schweizerisches Verfassungsrecht* (n 72) 31 ff; Pierre Tschannen, *Staatsrecht der Schweizerischen Eidgenossenschaft* (n 65) 82 ff.

[122] For the first two mentioned, see Philippe Mastronardi, *Strukturprinzipien in der Bundesverfassung?* (Helbing und Lichtenhahn, Basel, 1988); for the rest, René Rhinow, Markus Schefer, and Peter Uebersax, *Schweizerisches Verfassungsrecht* (n 72) 36 ff.

be a question of time before the principle of self-responsibility, which is mentioned several times in the new Federal Constitution,[123] is elevated to the rank of a core value or structural principle. But there is still no definitive clarity on the legal significance of such structural principles. The constitutional text itself shies away from (structural) principles. The term 'principle' appears here and there but not in connection with the four core values. The words 'federal state' and 'welfare state' are completely absent in the constitutional text. The term 'rule of law' is found only once in the heading to article 5 BV (*Grundsätze rechtsstaatlichen Handelns*'; 'rule of law'). The term 'democracy/democratic' is mentioned three times but not in provisions that are of central importance for the political system on federal level.[124] This is no coincidence but rather the result of a deliberate waiver by the constitutional lawmakers of 1999 of a distinct self-characterization of the Confederation.[125] It was believed that the new Constitution already sufficiently demonstrated the democratic, liberal, social, and federal character of the Swiss Confederation in its individual provisions. Furthermore, the risk of a hasty 'derivation' from abstract principles was to be avoided.[126]

Swiss legal practice is also characterized by the same stance. Although it happily applies legal principles and constitutional principles of lesser to medium levels of abstraction,[127] it holds back on referring to the aforementioned structure-establishing principles. For example, the term 'democratic principle/principle of democracy' appears only occasionally and incidentally in the case-law of the Federal Supreme Court without playing a decisive role in the decision-making process.[128] Even less present is the '*Rechtsstaatsprinzip*' (principle of rule of law).[129] Upon closer inspection, constitutional legal doctrine also predominantly resonates with this scepticism regarding principles. The 'constitutionally formative principles' are primarily understood in the sense of guiding principles or general construction principles. There have only been isolated attempts to use the 'core principles' as a starting point for substantial legal derivations.

3. Democracy and the Understanding of Democracy

a) Overview of the Political Rights

There is no doubt about the democratic character of the Swiss Confederation, even if the Federal Constitution is lacking a formal commitment to the 'principle of democracy'.[130] The most striking features are the highly developed, direct democratic possibilities for citizens to

---

[123] See in particular arts 6 and 41 para 1 BV. See also Peter Saladin, *Verantwortung als Staatsprinzip - Ein neuer Schlüssel zur Lehre vom modernen Rechtsstaat* (UTB, Stuttgart, 1984).

[124] Preamble (the strengthening of democracy as a goal of constitutional renewal), art 51 (requirements for the cantonal constitutions), art 54 BV (promotion of democracy as a goal for foreign policy).

[125] Unlike some recent cantonal constitutions, such as that of the canton of Bern of 6 June 1993 (Systematic Compilation of Federal Law 131.212) in art 1.

[126] See *Heinrich Koller*, 'Die Aufnahme staatsgestaltender Grundsätze in die neue Bundesverfassung', in Solothurnischer Juristenverein (ed), *Solothurner Festgabe zum Schweizerischen Juristentag* (1998) 27 ff.

[127] See above Section B.2.c.

[128] See BGE 129 I 232 (232 and 248), *Schweizerische Volkspartei der Stadt Zürich (SVP)* [2003]; BGE 125 I 289 (293 and 296 f), *Esther Bucher Helfenstein* [1999]; BGE 103 Ia 369 (383 and 390), *Wäffler* [1977].

[129] In BGE 128 I 113 (126), *Verein des Bündner Staatspersonals* [2002], the 'general rule-of-law principle' is mentioned in passing (in connection with a literature reference). See also BGE 130 I 388 (392), *K.* [2004].

[130] See Andreas Auer, 'Problèmes fondamentaux de la démocratie suisse' (1984) II Zeitschrift für Schweizerisches Recht 1 ff; Etienne Grisel, *Initiative et référendum populaires* (3rd edn, Stämpfli, Bern, 2004); Pierre Tschannen, *Stimmrecht und politische Verständigung* (Helbing und Lichtenhahn, Basel, 1995).

participate, also on a national level. The collective term '*Volksrechte*' or 'people's rights' has become commonly used for these in literature and practice.[131] The Federal Constitution uses the somewhat wider-ranging term of 'political rights'. In addition to participation in voting and the launching and signing of popular initiatives and referenda, this also includes participation in elections (article 136 para 2 BV). Taking account of the wide range of political rights, one does not usually speak in Switzerland of electors (the electorate) but of voters (the people).

On the one hand, the Federal Constitution lays the foundation for the political rights in the Confederation, the details of which are the responsibility of federal legislation.[132] On the other hand, the Federal Constitution also establishes the minimum requirements for the system of political rights in the cantons: the cantons must provide 'a democratic constitution'; the cantonal constitution 'requires the approval of the People and must be capable of being revised if the majority of those eligible to vote so request' (article 51 BV). With a view to the cantonal constitutional systems, the Federal Constitution thus, quite 'un-Swiss', takes on a narrow understanding of the term 'democratic' in that it is satisfied, aside from the requirements mentioned, with representative (parliamentary) forms.[133] Today all cantons go far beyond these minimums required by the Federal Constitution. Thus, the referendum on legislative acts, the legislative initiative, the popular election of the cantonal government,[134] and the so-called finance referendum are known everywhere these days.[135] In establishing the minimum voting age, the cantons are not bound by the solution on the federal level (today, eighteen years of age). They can also grant foreigners political rights on a communal or cantonal level, which some cantons have in fact done in recent years. According to the Federal Supreme Court, the cantons may generally 'decide freely as to whether they elect their parliament according to the proportional or the majority principle'; however, the Federal Supreme Court is very critical of the first-past-the-post electoral system (majority).[136] In nearly all cantons, the proportional system is practiced in different variants today.

Democracy is protected by a specific fundamental right. Article 34 BV ('political rights') protects the active and passive right to vote, the electoral equality and the right of initiative and of referendum. The 'freedom of the citizen to form an opinion and to give genuine expression to his or her will' is guaranteed specifically (article 34 para 2 BV). Key issues of the latest Supreme Court case-law include questions on the design of the proportional representation system, the verification of the validity of popular initiatives, and the influencing of opinion by authorities ahead of popular votes.[137] At first such cases concerned only political rights on a cantonal level, but in the course of the reform of the judiciary, (federal) judicial

---

[131] The term does not appear in the text of the Constitution. See anyway arts 2 and 148 BV ('Rights of the People').

[132] See art 16 ff BPR (National Council elections), art 58 ff BPR (referendum), art 68 ff BPR, and art 96 ff ParlG (popular initiative). Cantonal law applies to the elections to the Council of States (art 150 BV).

[133] Therefore, there is no federal legal obligation to subject acts of cantonal legislation to referendum: BGE 126 I 180 (182), *X.* [2000].

[134] This involves collegiate authorities, today with five or seven members, depending on the canton.

[135] The finance referendum covers decisions of parliament on uncommitted spending that exceeds a certain amount. Notes on other instruments in Yvo Hangartner and Andreas Kley, *Die demokratischen Rechte in Bund und Kantonen der Schweizerischen Eidgenossenschaft* (n 74) 525 ff.

[136] BGE 140 I 394, 398 f. E. 7.1 [2014] (Canton of Appenzell Ausserrhoden). See also BGE 143 I 92 [2016] (Canton of Uri; mixed system); BGE 145 I 259 [2019] (Canton of Grisons). Critical on the case-law of the Federal Supreme Court: Giovanni Biaggini, *Kommentar: Bundesverfassung der Schweizerischen Eidgenossenschaft* (2nd edn, Orell Füssli, Zurich, 2017) art 34, para 9a ff.

[137] See BGE 129 I 185, *X. und Y. gegen Stadt Zürich* [2003]; BGE 130 I 185, *ASLOCA* [2004]; BGE 130 I 290, *Zürcher Anwaltsverband* [2004]; BGE 138 I 61, *Kiener Nellen* [2011]; BGE 143 I 78, *Muster* [2016]; BGE 145 I 207, *Béglé* [2019] (with further references in each case).

review of direct democracy was enabled selectively also on the federal level (see article 189 BV in the version of 12 March 2000).[138] In 2019 the Federal Supreme Court for the first time annulled the result of a federal vote. It considered that, prior to the vote on a popular initiative for the partial revision of the Federal Constitution (*Volksinitiative 'Für Ehe und Familie—gegen die Heiratsstrafe'*), the government had misinformed voters and that this could have an influence on the 'general state of information' available to the voters. In the opinion of the Federal Supreme Court the outcome of the ballot could have been different, had it not been for the incomplete and non-transparent information.[139] Considering the fact that acts of the Federal Assembly or the Federal Council may not be challenged in the Federal Supreme Court (article 189 para 4 BV), it is quite surprising that the Supreme Court, without further explanation, considered itself competent to annul an act of the 'sovereign' (the People and the Cantons), even though the Constitution does not expressly mention such a competence.

b) Instruments of Direct Democracy in the Confederation

In addition to the right to participate in the national elections, the political rights in the Confederation include (article 138 ff BV): the mandatory constitutional referendum (see Section B.1.a); the mandatory referendum in the case of accessing an organization for collective security or a supranational community (mandatory treaty referendum; see Section B.2.a); the subsequent mandatory referendum in the case of urgent federal laws that have no constitutional basis (see Sections A.3.a and B.2.a); the optional referendum on federal acts (see Sections A.2.a and B.2.a); the optional referendum in the case of certain international treaties (see Section B.2.a); the popular initiative requesting the total revision of the Federal Constitution (see Section B.1.a); the popular initiative for the partial revision of the Federal Constitution in the form of a specific draft (see Section B.2.a); the popular initiative for the partial revision of the Federal Constitution in the form of a general proposal (see Section B.1.b). It is important for an understanding of Swiss democracy that these are constitutionally guaranteed (participation) rights of the citizens. It is not at the discretion of the federal authorities to arrange a referendum or a poll via a popular initiative or not. The voting results are always binding. The term 'plebiscite', which suggests an instrumentalization of direct democracy by governments or parliaments, has a negative connotation in Switzerland and is usually avoided. In view of the extensive range of tools available in Switzerland, one occasionally tends to underestimate the significance of the parliamentary-representative structures on which the constitutional system of the Confederation is based. The instruments of direct democracy are to be understood as corrective and supplementary to parliamentary action (or non-action). They would not be workable without the parliamentary 'substructure'.

The extensive rights of participation of the people in questions of foreign policy are particularly conspicuous. In Switzerland, foreign policy is not only traditionally subject to intense parliamentary participation (article 166 BV) but also to extensive direct-democratic control.[140] The rights of the people contribute on the one hand to the broad democratic

---

[138] From the case-law, see BGE 138 I 61 [2011] (Misinformation on the part of the Federal Council in prior to the referendum of 24 February 2008 on a corporate tax reform); BGE 143 I 78 [2016] (official statements before the referendum of 25 September 2016 on the Intelligence Service Act); BGE 145 I 207 [2019] (Misinformation on the part of the Federal Council prior to the referendum of 28 February 2016).

[139] BGE 145 I 207 [2019]. See also Giovanni Biaggini, 'Eine Premiere mit begrenzter präjudizieller Tragweite. Zur Aufhebung der Volksabstimmung vom 28. Februar 2016 über die Volksinitiative «Für Ehe und Familie – gegen die Heiratsstrafe» durch das Bundesgericht' (2019) Schweizerisches Zentralblatt für Staats- und Verwaltungsrecht (ZBl) 531 ff.

[140] See also Luzius Wildhaber, 'Kontrolle der auswärtigen Gewalt' (1997) 56 Veröffentlichungen der Vereinigung der Deutschen Staatsrechtslehrer (VVDStRL) 67 ff.

668   GIOVANNI BIAGGINI

support and legitimization of foreign policy; on the other hand, they have had a not insignificant part to play in the slow-moving, repeatedly halted opening up of Switzerland to the world. A glance at the now rich voting practice shows, however, that the voting public understand quite well how to express their differing opinions when it comes to foreign policy. Thus, the People and the Cantons approved the entry of Switzerland into the UNO in 2002 after a first negative vote in 1986.[141] The 'No' from the People and the Cantons regarding the treaty on the European Economic Area (1992) was followed in May 2000 by a 'Yes' from voters on a number of complex agreements that create internal market-like structures in relations to the European Union (the so-called Bilateral Treaties I). On 5 June 2005, the voters—unimpressed by the 'No' from the French and Dutch to the EU Constitutional Treaty a few days earlier—approved Switzerland's entry into the Schengen and Dublin systems, on 25 September 2005 the expansion of the freedom of movement to citizens of ten new EU member states, and, on 8 February 2009, its expansion to Romania and Bulgaria.

c) On the Significance of the People's Rights for the Political System and the Understanding of Democracy

As a result of the people's rights, the Swiss voters can exercise direct influence on the course of politics even between parliamentary elections; in the context of three to four federal voting weekends per year, during which usually several matters are to be decided.[142] Of the 728 popular votes that took place around the world in the period between 1900 and 1993 on a national level, 357 were held in Switzerland.[143] Whereas popular initiatives rarely meet with approval, federal acts of parliament are rejected time and again at the ballot box. In addition, the people's rights also have many indirect effects. Thus, it is part of Swiss everyday political life to threaten to seize a referendum or to announce a popular initiative. To avoid the risks and delays associated with referendums, government and parliament tend to design laws and other bills as 'referendum-safe' as possible. Broadly supported compromise solutions should be inclusive towards potential political opposition. Furthermore, the people's rights influence the party-political composition of the seven-member government. In the early days of the Confederation, one political force, the 'Freisinn' (today FDP), dominated federal politics and formed the government alone. With the introduction of the referendum as a political 'weapon' in 1874 and the popular initiative for the partial revision of the Federal Constitution in 1891, the pressure grew to elect representatives of other major parties to the seven-member government, too. This happened from 1891 onwards in several stages until, finally in 1959, the so-called 'magic formula' was found, according to which the Federal Council is made up of representatives of the four major parties in a ratio of 2:2:2:1.[144] Another

---

[141] Formally, it was a popular initiative (art 139 BV) which called for the inclusion of art 197 No 1 BV.

[142] Usually one to five bills (in May 2003: nine). This number is usually supplemented by cantonal and communal bills. Voting turn-out varies. Between 1971 and 2018, it was 43 per cent on average, which so far has not diminished the legitimacy and acceptance of the decisions made. It has reached more than 70 per cent in only a few rare cases (around 78 per cent in the referendum of 6 December 1992 concerning entry into the EEA). Occasionally it has dipped below 30 per cent (around 28.7 per cent in the referendum of 9 February 2003 on the reform of the people's rights!). In comparison: Turn-out in the *national elections* in recent years was between 42 per cent and just under 49 per cent (2015: 48.5 per cent). It was last over 70 per cent in 1955.

[143] See Alexander H Trechsel, 'Volksabstimmungen', in Ulrich Klöti and others (eds), *Handbuch der Schweizer Politik* (3rd edn, NZZ Verlag, Zurich, 2002) 558 (based on David Butler and Austin Ranney, *Referendums Around the World* (AEI Press 1994)).

[144] On the (legally non-binding) 'magic formula', see René Rhinow, Markus Schefer, and Peter Uebersax, *Schweizerisches Verfassungsrecht* (n 72) 478. The ratio of 2:2:2:1 still continues to apply, with a short interruption (2008–2015); however, there was a change in the role of the 'junior partner' (with a win of just one seat in government) at the end of 2003.

facet of this development in the direction of consociational democracy[145] is the absence of a parliamentary opposition in the traditional sense. In the legislature 2015–2019, the representatives of the four government parties had 168 out of 200 seats in the National Council; the largest non-government party occupied only eleven seats. In the Council of States, the four government parties occupied forty-three out of forty-six seats. Between 2003 and 2007, all forty-six members of the Council of States belonged to a governing party. This does not mean, however, that there is no opposition in the Swiss political system. It is, occasionally and specifically in certain areas, exercised to great effect: be it through parliamentary members of the government parties (the discipline of party and faction is not particularly strong in Switzerland), be it through a government party as a whole which distances itself from a governmental bill, perhaps even actively opposing it by means of a referendum or initiative (without having to fear exclusion from the government), or be it through the voting public in the context of direct democracy (opposition function of the people's rights).[146]

Although there is no need to idealize the instruments of direct democracy as a shield against party rule and a guarantor of the public interest, the people's rights enjoy high esteem in Switzerland, also in constitutional legal doctrine (which is by no means a given in a comparative perspective).[147] The question of whether direct or indirect democracy should be seen as the 'actual' form of democracy[148] would appear to have no particular emotional effect in Switzerland. In the legal science in particular, the people's rights are discussed under the title of 'democracy'. The parliamentary-representative component of the constitutional system, which is not of lesser importance on the federal level, is sometimes a little neglected. However, the question of the rule of law limits to democracy is regularly paid the necessary attention; this stands in contrast to political practice, where the tendency is on occasion to put the 'people' (the 'sovereign') above the rule of law and the fundamental rights. Tensions emerged recently, in particular, regarding the relationship between direct democracy (people's initiative) and Switzerland's duties under public international law.[149] The Federal Supreme Court may count on the support of constitutional scholars if—as in two decisions handed down in July 2003 concerning the naturalization process, for example[150]—it limits

---

[145] On consociational democracy, see (from a legal science perspective) René Rhinow, 'Grundprobleme der schweizerischen Demokratie' (1984) II Zeitschrift für Schweizerisches Recht 237 ff; from a political science perspective see, Wolf Linder and Sean Mueller, *Schweizerische Demokratie* (n 81) 363 ff.

[146] See René Rhinow, 'Grundprobleme der schweizerischen Demokratie' (n 145) 207 ff; Leonhard Neidhart, *Die politische Schweiz* (NZZ Verlag, Zurich, 2002) 326 ff.

[147] Fundamental criticism comes primarily from economic science, where there are also dedicated supporters of the people's rights. See for example, Bruno S Frey and Gebhard Kirchgässner, *Demokratische Wirtschaftspolitik* (3rd edn, Vahlen, Munich, 2002); Gebhard Kirchgässner, Lars Feld, and Marcel Savioz, *Die direkte Demokratie* (Vahlen, Munich, 1999).

[148] See Ernst-Wolfgang Böckenförde, 'Mittelbare/repräsentative Demokratie als eigentliche Form der Demokratie', in Georg Müller and others (eds), *Staatsorganisation und Staatsfunktionen im Wandel: Festschrift für Kurt Eichenberger* (Helbing und Lichtenhahn, Basel, 1982) 301 ff.

[149] See Giovanni Biaggini, 'Die schweizerische direkte Demokratie und das Völkerrecht—Gedanken aus Anlass der Volksabstimmung über die Volksinitiative „Gegen den Bau von Minaretten" (2010) Austrian Journal of Public Law 325 ff; Walter Haller, *The Swiss Constitution in a Comparative Context* (2nd edn, Dike, Zurich, 2016), 265 ff; Roger Nobs, *Volksinitiative und Völkerrecht* (Dike, Zurich, 2006); Johannes Reich, 'Direkte Demokratie und völkerrechtliche Verpflichtungen im Konflikt' (2008) Heidelberg Journal of International Law 979 ff; see also Federal Council, Das Verhältnis von Völkerrecht und Landesrecht, Report from 5 March 2010, Federal Gazette of the Swiss Confederation (BBl) 2010 2263 ff; Federal Council, Message of 5 July 2017 on the popular initiative 'Swiss law instead of foreign judges (Self-determination initiative)', Federal Gazette of the Swiss Confederation (BBl) 2017 5355 ff.

[150] BGE 129 I 217, *A. und Mitb.* [2003]; BGE 129 I 232, *Schweizerische Volkspartei der Stadt Zürich* [2003]. According to the Federal Supreme Court, it is incompatible with the claim to the substantiation of individual decisions (art 29 BV) and the prohibition of discrimination (art 8 para 2 BV) to decide on naturalization in the framework of a ballot box vote.

670 GIOVANNI BIAGGINI

direct democracy in favour of the rule of law. In Switzerland, too, the people are not always granted the 'last word'.[151] Most recently the Federal Supreme Court even went one step further and annulled the result of a federal vote (an act of the People and Cantons, article 142 BV) as it considered that the freedom of vote had been violated.[152]

4. The Rule of Law and the Understanding of Fundamental Rights

a) Fundamental Rights and Rule of Law

One of the most important results of the latest total revision of the Federal Constitution is the consolidation and selective supplementation of the achievements of the nineteenth and twentieth centuries regarding the rule of law. Without going into detail, reference will be made here to some aspects that serve a better understanding of the Swiss constitutional system or that are among its special features, compared to 'common European constitutional law' (*Häberle*). In addition to today's usual guarantees, the extensive catalogue of fundamental rights (articles 7–36 BV),[153] one of the most striking innovations of the total revision, also encompasses an express prohibition of discrimination on the basis of 'way of life' (which can be invoked by homosexuals, for example[154]), a right to assistance when in need (article 12 BV), an express guarantee of the (previously unwritten) freedom of language (article 18 BV), and a constitutional protection of political rights (article 34 BV).[155] Special features include the two final provisions of the fundamental rights catalogue. Under the titles 'Upholding of fundamental rights' (article 35 BV) and 'Restrictions on fundamental rights' (article 36 BV), important aspects of the general doctrine on fundamental rights developed in legal doctrine and case-law are codified here.[156] The fundamental rights should accordingly 'be upheld throughout the legal system' (article 35 para 1 BV). They not only guarantee enforceable individual rights, but they are also to be understood as basic ordering principles and objective fundamental standards, which—in particular in the form of the indirect third-party effect that is conveyed through legislation and the application of statute law in conformity with the Constitution[157]—affect the legal relationships between private individuals

---

[151] For notes on further fundamental problems and current questions of Swiss democracy, see René Rhinow, 'Grundprobleme' (n 145) 111 ff; Giovanni Biaggini, 'Ausgestaltung und Entwicklungsperspektiven des demokratischen Prinzips in der Schweiz', in Hartmut Bauer, Peter M Huber, and Karl-Peter Sommermann (eds), *Demokratie in Europa* (Mohr Siebeck, Tübingen, 2005) 107 ff.

[152] BGE 145 I 207 [2019]. See Section C.3.a.

[153] See Jörg Paul Müller and Markus Schefer, *Grundrechte in der Schweiz* (4th edn, Stämpfli, Bern, 2008).

[154] See BGE 126 II 425 (433), *P. and C.* [2000].

[155] The catalogue of fundamental rights still leaves some space for additional guarantees by the cantons. This is used variously. See for example arts 11–18 of the constitution of the canton of Zürich of 27 February 2005 (Systematic Compilation of Federal Law 131.211), whereas the constitution of the canton of Graubünden of 18 May/14 September 2003 (Systematic Compilation of Federal Law 131.226) deliberately does not have its own guarantees.

[156] Important preparatory work was provided by Peter Saladin, *Grundrechte im Wandel* (1970) (3rd edn, Stämpfli, Bern, 1982), and Jörg Paul Müller, *Elemente einer schweizerischen Grundrechtstheorie* (Stämpfli, Bern, 1982). See also Markus Schefer, *Die Kerngehalte von Grundrechten* (Stämpfli, Bern, 2001); Jörg Paul Müller, *Verwirklichung der Grundrechte* (n 115).

[157] On this already BGE 86 II 365, *Witwe Alfred Giesbrecht Söhne gegen Vertglas* [1960]; thoroughly BGE 111 II 245 (254), *X. AG* [1985]—A *direct* third-party effect of fundamental rights is recognized only in a few very special cases. Art 8 para 3 cl 3 BV, in which men and women are entitled to an equal wage for work of the same value, is the chief example.

(so-called horizontal effect).[158] The 'limitation of fundamental rights' must, according to article 36 BV, fulfil four conditions: first, it must be based on a sufficient legal basis; second, it must be justified by public interest or the protection of the fundamental rights of a third party; third, it must be proportionate; and fourth, it must uphold the sacrosanct essence of the fundamental rights. Although article 36 BV codifies long-standing, proven case-law, some questions remain open.[159] Apart from very few exceptions, one can invoke the fundamental rights of the Federal Constitution irrespective of nationality. The issue of legal persons as recipients of fundamental rights is not systematically regulated.

In the context of constitutional jurisdiction, the Federal Supreme Court is called upon to hear 'disputes concerning violations of constitutional rights' (article 189 BV in the original version applicable until the end of 2006).[160] Neither the Constitution nor the legislation define this term. In addition to the traditional fundamental rights of the Federal Constitution (articles 7–34 BV) and the cantonal constitutions, the Federal Supreme Court also counts a number of other constitutional norms, which protect individual rights as constitutional rights. These include the primacy of federal law over cantonal law (article 49 BV), the principle of separation of powers contained in article 51 BV, the prohibition of inter-cantonal double taxation (article 127 para 3 BV), as well as the principle of legality under tax law and the principle of legality under criminal law.[161] Outside these areas of law, the principle of legality is a constitutional principle (article 5 BV), the violation of which in the context of constitutional jurisdiction may be challenged not independently but rather only together with a constitutional right. The same applies for other principles of the rule of law, such as the principle of proportionality or the principle of good faith in accordance with article 5 BV.[162]

b) Constitutional Jurisdiction: System and Gaps

As the supreme court of the Confederation (article 188 BV), the Federal Supreme Court occupies a key position in the system of legal protection. Not only is it an appellate court in civil and criminal matters and the supreme administrative court for the Confederation, but it also exercises important functions in the area of constitutional jurisdiction.[163] A few of the

---

[158] Art 35 para 3 BV lays down that: 'the authorities shall ensure that fundamental rights, where appropriate, apply to relationships among private persons'. 'Authorities' means here the courts as well as legislative and executive authorities.

[159] This includes application to fundamental rights that are not among the classic freedom rights. See BGE 129 I 12 (20), V. [2002]: analogous (partial) application of art 36 BV in the right to primary education (art 19 BV); BGE 142 I 1 (7) [2016]: analogous (partial) application of art 36 BV in the right to assistance when in need (art 12 BV).

[160] This passage is missing in art 189 BV in the version from 12 March 2000 (in force since 1 January 2007). The figure of 'constitutional right' continues to be legally relevant, however (see art 189 para 1(d) BV in the version from 12 March 2000 as well as art 116 of the Federal Supreme Court Act (n 93).

[161] See, for example, BGE 130 I 82 (86), *Sozialdemokratische Partei des Kantons Zürich* [2004] (principle of precedence of federal law); BGE 130 I 1 (5), *D. and B. X.* [2003] (Separation of powers); BGE 130 I 205 (210), *A.* [2004] (prohibition of inter-cantonal double taxation); BGE 128 I 317 (321), *A.X. and B.X.* [2002] (Tax law); BGE 118 Ia 137 (139), *B.* [1992] ('*nulla poena sine lege*').

[162] See Beatrice Weber-Dürler, 'Zur neusten Entwicklung des Verhältnismässigkeitsprinzips', in Benoît Bovay and Minh Son Nguyen (eds), *Mélanges en l'honneur de Pierre Moor* (Stämpfli, Bern, 2005) 593 ff; Beatrice Weber-Dürler, 'Neuere Entwicklungen des Vertrauensschutzes' (2002) Schweizerisches Zentralblatt für Staats- und Verwaltungsrecht (ZBl) 281 ff.

[163] See Walter Kälin, 'Verfassungsgerichtsbarkeit', in Daniel Thürer and others (eds), *Verfassungsrecht der Schweiz* (n 60) 1167 ff; Giovanni Biaggini, 'Constitutional Adjudication in Switzerland', in Armin von Bogdandy and others (n 23), 779 ff. Until the end of 2006, it was especially the '*Staatsrechtliche Beschwerde*' (constitutional appeal; art 84 Federal Act on the Organization of federal administration of justice of 16 December 1943) and partly also the '*Verwaltungsgerichtsbeschwerde*' (administrative law appeal; art 97 Federal Act on the Organization of federal administration of justice of 16 December 1943) that were relevant. These two legal remedies were replaced as of 1 January 2007 by the appeal in public law matters (art 82 ff Federal Supreme Court Act) and the thereto subsidiary constitutional appeal (art 113 ff Federal Supreme Court Act).

originally extensive jurisdiction powers of the supreme political federal bodies in constitutional matters have survived. Thus, it is the Federal Assembly and not the Federal Supreme Court that is responsible for hearing conflicts of jurisdiction between the highest federal authorities (article 173 para 1(i) BV).[164]

The *constitutional jurisdiction* does not form an independent court branch in the Swiss legal system. The question of constitutionality can generally come up in front of all judicial powers. The courts are called upon to review the relevant legal provisions on a preliminary basis with regard to their compatibility with higher-ranking law, in particular with the Federal Constitution, and, if necessary, to refuse to apply them (judicial review). A special preliminary ruling procedure for bills or provisions (as there is in the EU or the German model) is not known in the Swiss legal protection system (diffuse system).

A very significant constraint in practice is found in article 190 BV: 'The Federal Supreme Court and the other judicial authorities apply the federal acts and international law.' Federal acts[165] must, in other words, be applied even when they turn out to be unconstitutional— which of course does not give a carte blanche to the federal legislature for disregard of the Constitution.[166] All previous attempts to extend constitutional jurisdiction to federal acts have failed.[167] Case-law and legal doctrine have developed various strategies (such as, in particular, the interpretation in conformity with the Constitution) that allow the alleviation of certain consequences of the 'immunization' of federal acts.[168] The problem is also somewhat mitigated through the general precedence of international law over national law in cases of conflict (article 5 para 4 BV), according to the Federal Supreme Court, especially when the international law norm serves the protection of human rights.[169] Consequently, the Federal Supreme Court would have to deny application of ECHR-adverse provisions in federal laws.[170] Whether this will happen consistently in the future is uncertain, given that there is no unanimous position on the question of the relationship between the ECHR and federal law within the Federal Supreme Court.[171] A popular initiative which wanted to establish the

---

[164] The competence plays hardly any role in practice. The Federal Assembly exercises a sort of abstract review of statutes in the verification of the validity of federal popular initiatives (art 139 BV; see above Section B.1.c) and in the guarantee of cantonal constitutions (art 51 and 172 BV).

[165] In regulations of the Federal Council, the preliminary control is not subject to any restriction, unless a possible constitutional violation is 'covered' by a federal act. See BGE 129 II 249 (263), *A.X.* [2003].

[166] Art 190 BV lays down an order of application, not a prohibition of assessment. A statement on the federal law – international law relationship cannot be derived from art 113 BV 1874 or art 190 BV. See BGE 129 II 249 (263), *A.X.* [2003]; Giovanni Biaggini, 'Constitutional Adjudication in Switzerland', in Armin von Bogdandy and others (n 23), 832 ff.

[167] Most recently in the context of the reform of the judiciary (Federal Gazette of the Swiss Confederation [BBl] 1997 I 505 ff) and of Federal Decree of 3 October 2003 on the NFA (Federal Gazette of the Swiss Confederation [BBl] 2002 2464; limited to disputes of competence in the cantons-Confederation relationship). The proposals of the Federal Council found no majority in parliament.

[168] See Andreas Auer, *Die schweizerische Verfassungsgerichtsbarkeit* (Helbing und Lichtenhahn, Basel, 1984) 85 ff; Giovanni Biaggini, *Verfassung und Richterrecht* (Helbing und Lichtenhahn, Basel, 1991) 426 ff; Walter Kälin, *Das Verfahren der staatsrechtlichen Beschwerde* (2nd edn, Stämpfli, Bern, 1994) 11 ff.

[169] BGE 125 II 417 (424 f), *A.* [1999] (concerning the confiscation of propaganda material of the Kurdistan Workers' Party, so-called PKK decision); see also BGE 139 I 16 (28 ff) [2012]. On the complex regulation of the relationship between international law and national law in the new Federal Constitution, see Giovanni Biaggini, *Kommentar: Bundesverfassung* (n 136) art 5 para 26 ff.

[170] The situation thus remains unsatisfactory, particularly in the case of fundamental rights that are not covered or not fully covered by the ECHR and the additional protocols (Switzerland has not ratified the first, fourth, and twelfth additional protocols in particular), such as the general principle of equality before the law (art 8 para 1 BV), the guarantee of ownership (art 26 BV) and economic freedom (art 27 BV).

[171] See BGE 125 II 417 (425 f), *A.* [1999] (First Public Law Division), BGE 117 Ib 367 (373), *Eidg. Steuerverwaltung* [1991] (Second Public Law Division) on the one hand, BGE 120 II 384 (387), *E. and B.* [1994] (Second Civil Law Division) on the other. See also Stefan Schürer, 'Hat die PKK-Rechtsprechung die Schubert-Praxis relativiert?' (2015) Schweizerisches Zentralblatt für Staats- und Verwaltungsrecht (ZBl) 115 ff and BGE 142 II 35 [2015] (concerning the relationship between the Switzerland-EU freedom of movement agreement and federal law). As far as

general primacy of constitutional law vis-à-vis international law (*Volksinitiative 'Schweizer Recht statt fremde Richter [Selbstbestimmungsinitiative]'*) was rejected in November 2018.

5. Organ Make-up and Understanding of the Separation of Powers

a) The System of the Supreme Federal Authorities

The Federal Constitution provides for three supreme federal authorities: the Federal Assembly, which—'[s]ubject to the rights of the People and the Cantons'—exercises 'the supreme authority of the Confederation' (article 148 BV), the Federal Council as 'the supreme governing and executive authority of the Confederation' (article 174 BV), and the Federal Supreme Court as 'the supreme judicial authority of the Confederation' (article 188 BV). The Constitution nominates the voters ('people') or the People and the Cantons as further decision-makers (article 136 ff BV). Although the term 'sovereign' is often used in this context, 'the People' or 'the People and the Cantons' act in the framework of constitutionally established powers and procedures and thus as instituted powers. The term '*Verfassungsorgan*' (constitutional organ) is not used in Switzerland, neither for the three highest federal authorities nor for the People and the Cantons or other bearers of tasks and decisions mentioned specifically in the Constitution, such as the Swiss National Bank (article 99 BV), the Federal Administration (article 178 BV), or the Federal Chancellery as the general administrative office of the Federal Council (article 179 BV). There is no actual head of state. The representation of the Confederation domestically and abroad is the task of the Federal Council as a body (articles 174, 184, and 186 BV). State visits are received by the Federal Council *in corpore*. Since it is impractical to send the entire government on visits abroad, the President of the Confederation carries these out alone. Despite the fine-sounding title (article 176 para 1 BV), the President of the Confederation is basically only, and only for one year (article 176 para 2 and 3 BV), Chairman of the Federal Council, i.e. (Federal) Council President. For the records, the highest-ranking Swiss person is the President of the National Council who also changes annually (article 152 BV).

In contrast to most of the newer cantonal constitutions, the new Federal Constitution foregoes express mention of the principle of separation of powers. The trinity of the supreme authorities and the constitutional structure make it easy to recognize that the organization of the authorities in the Confederation is built on the idea of the separation of powers.[172] However, as it did for the constitutional fathers of 1848 and 1874, this fundamental organizational principle[173] served the constitutional legislators of 1999 only as a general guideline. Only personal or subjective separation of powers is performed strictly. Membership in parliament and government office are incompatible (article 144 BV).

The Swiss political system (*Regierungssystem*) defies classification in common typology. Compared with the British or continental European-style systems, parliament and the government each have a very independent position. After successful election, the Federal

the ECHR-Federal Constitution relationship is concerned, the Federal Supreme Court has advocated the primacy of the ECHR (and the case-law of the European Court of Human Rights) in an *obiter dictum* (BGE 139 I 16, 29 ff [2012]).

[172] See Pascal Mahon, 'Le principe de la séparation des pouvoirs', in Daniel Thürer and others (eds), *Verfassungsrecht der Schweiz* (n 60), 1011 ff; Hansjörg Seiler, *Gewaltenteilung* (Stämpfli, Bern, 1994).
[173] See art 16 of the Declaration of Human and Civil Rights of 26 August 1789.

Council is not dependent on the support of the Federal Assembly. Neither the Federal Council nor individual members of government can be forced to withdraw prematurely. Unlike in the American presidential system, the executive is not installed monocratically; at the top there is a collegial body with seven[174] equal members. The Swiss political system is sometimes referred to as being a directorial system,[175] which says very little, however. If one looks for its closest relatives, they will be found most likely—despite all the differences— in the USA (if one focusses on the independence of the first and second powers) and in Liechtenstein (if one thinks of the expanded people's rights and ignores the monarchical elements). There are certain parallels in the EU system, too.

b) Federal Assembly

The Federal Assembly (articles 148–173 BV) consists of two chambers: the National Council and the Council of States. The two councils have equal standing (article 148 BV). As the representative body of the people, the National Council represents the principle of democratic equality; as the representative body of the cantons,[176] the Council of States embodies the federative principle of the equality of the cantons. The fact that the Council of States consists of twenty-six members, although Switzerland has twenty-six cantons, is due to the fact that the six historical 'half-cantons' do not have two members in the Council, like the other cantons, but only one.[177] Although the Council of States is part of the federal authorities, elections are based on cantonal law (article 150 BV). The formerly common election of the Council of States members by the cantonal parliament has given way today to popular vote (most recently in 1977 in Bern). Elections are according to the majority system (first-past-the post) with two exceptions (cantons of Jura and Neuchâtel).

The *National Council* consists of 200 members,[178] who are elected for a fixed term of four years. Elections are based on the system of proportional representation that was introduced as the result of a popular initiative in 1918 (article 73 BV 1874; today article 149 BV), replacing the original majority system.[179] The legislature has opted for the system of variable lists in the election procedure for proportional representation without being obliged to do so by the Constitution: the voters can delete candidates (in French called '*latoiser*'), list them twice (cumulate), or enter candidates from another list on the preferred lists (split one's vote).[180] This strengthens the individual members vis-à-vis the party leaders or parliamentary group leaders. The members of the National Council are representatives of the entire people (article 149 BV), whereas the members of the Council of States represent their cantons (article 150 BV). However, this difference is practically of little importance since, in the National Council elections, the cantons form the constituencies on the basis of constitutional law, meaning that there is a particularly close relationship to a canton, too. The seats in the National Council are allocated to the cantons according to their population size;

---

[174] The number 'seven' is fixed in the Federal Constitution (art 175 para 1 BV).

[175] See Pascal Mahon, 'Remarques liminaires', in Jean-François Aubert and Pascal Mahon (eds), *Petit commentaire de la Constitution fédérale de la Confédération suisse du 18 avril 1999* (Schulthess, Zurich, 2003) fifth title para 10.

[176] The common term is misleading because the members of the Council of States also exercise free mandate (art 161 BV).

[177] Art 150 BV: Obwalden, Nidwalden, Basel-Stadt, Basel-Landschaft, Appenzell Ausserrhoden, Appenzell Innerrhoden.

[178] From 1848 to 1963, the number of members varied, since they were decided in relation to the population: originally one member per 20,000 inhabitants (for a total of 111), most recently one member per 24,000 inhabitants (just under 200).

[179] An exception applies in the (now six) cantons with one member (simple majority system; art 47 BPR).

[180] Detailed provisions can be found in art 21 ff BPR.

each canton is guaranteed a seat (article 149 BV). In nineteen of the twenty-six cantons, the number of seats is eight or fewer, meaning that natural quorums (or 'de facto thresholds') of 11.1 per cent and more are formed there, which, according to the standards usually set by the Federal Supreme Court in the assessment of the parliamentary elections in the cantons, would not be consistent with the principle of equal success value for each vote ('*Erfolgswer tgleichheit*').[181] The five most populous cantons provide more than half of the members of the National Council. Conversely, half of the seats in the Council of States go to cantons that altogether make up just under a fifth of the Swiss population as a whole. Formally, only the National Council has a legislative term (of four years today, three years until 1931). In the Council of States, the term of office and election dates are aligned with the respective cantonal law.[182]

The Federal Assembly plays a significant role in leading the Confederation at the highest level ('*Staatsleitung*'). In addition to legislation (including constitutional legislation) and the fixing of the federal budget, its competences include the approval of international law agreements, carrying out certain elections (in particular for the members of the Federal Council and the Federal Supreme Court), and oversight over the Federal Council and the Federal Administration, the federal courts, and other bodies entrusted with the tasks of the Confederation (articles 163 ff BV).[183] Because of the expanded people's rights, the Federal Assembly does not have 'the last word' in many matters. In Switzerland, the idea that the Federal Assembly is a '*Milizparlament*' with representatives serving as part-time members (citizen legislature or semi-professional parliament) is still very common. In fact, many members of the Councils do indeed have another 'main' profession in addition to their parliamentary seat. The time requirements and the statutory compensation scheme would suggest calling it a 'semi-professional parliament'.[184] The Councils do not meet constantly but rather in four annual sessions, each of which lasts for three weeks (not counting committee meetings). The individual members have a relatively strong position (right to submit individual initiatives and motions). Collective minority rights are, by contrast, rather weak, as is the faction discipline. The size difference (200 to forty-six) as well as other election and recruitment mechanisms explain the different working and deliberation culture in the two Councils: the Council of States is reputed to be a *chambre de réflexion*, where not only party political views, but also arguments guided by state policy are exchanged.

Both chambers have the same competences and have the same powers in exercise of these. They generally deliberate and decide separately. For decisions of the Federal Assembly, the agreement of both Councils is always required (article 156 para 2 BV). The detailed procedure for the resolution of differences between the Chambers (article 89 ff ParlG) increases the chance of concurring decisions coming about. The disadvantage of the complex

---

[181] BGE 131 I 74 (83), *Grüne Aargau* [2004], as well as BGE 131 I 85 (90), *Hugo-Lötscher* [2004]: The limit is 10 per cent when there is no pronounced 'special case'. From the latest case-law BGE 143 I 92 (98 f), *Infanger* [2016].

[182] Today the term of office is four years everywhere, and the elections take place everywhere at the same time as the National Council elections. An exception is Appenzell Innerrhoden, where the election takes place at the '*Landsgemeinde*' assembly at the end of April of the election year.

[183] See also art 22 ff ParlG (Systematic Compilation of Federal Law 171.10) as well as the Standing Orders (*Geschäftsreglemente*) of the National Council and the Council of States (Systematic Compilation of Federal Law 171.13 and 171.14).

[184] According to René Rhinow, Markus Schefer, and Peter Uebersax, *Schweizerisches Verfassungsrecht* (n 72), 467 f, Council members spend an average of 56 per cent of their working time on parliamentary work and receive annual remuneration of around 133,000 Swiss francs (members of the National Council) or 151,000 Swiss francs (members of the Council of States). The parliamentary groups ('*Fraktionen*') receive modest financial support from the Federal Treasury. Party financing by the state does not exist on the federal level, however. See Wolf Linder and Sean Mueller, *Schweizerische Demokratie* (n 81) 246 f.

decision-making process is easily offset by the *advantages of the bicameral system*: preventing the smaller cantons and their populations of being voted out, intra-organ control, and promotion of the rationality of deliberations and the quality of the decisions. Derogation from *'Bicamérisme parfait'* (*Aubert*) occurs only when the two Councils convene together under the chairmanship of the President of the National Council in order to exercise certain functions listed exhaustively in the Constitution (in particular, elections) as the *United Federal Assembly* (article 157 BV). Because of the smaller number of members, the Council of States carries less weight here.

c) Federal Council

The Federal Council (articles 174–187 BV) is the 'supreme governing and executive authority' and thus the government (article 1 RVOG) of the Confederation. It is a collegial organ (article 177 BV) without an actual Head of Government, and it consists of seven equal members as a matter of constitutional law (article 175 BV). The annually changing President of the Confederation, who is the chairperson of the Federal Council, is merely *primus inter pares*. The members of the government are elected individually by the United Federal Assembly (National Council and Council of States in joint proceedings) for a fixed term of four years. The Federal Assembly is obliged to ensure that 'the various geographical and language regions of the country are appropriately represented' (article 175 para 4 BV). This obligation is not legally enforceable, which is similar to the *constitutional conventions* of British constitutional law. There is no possibility of early dismissal of the government or individual members. It is extremely rare that Federal Council members who run for a new term are not elected.[185] Effectively it is left to the individual Federal Council members to decide the timing of their stepping down. Thanks to the mechanism of consociational democracy, the government is highly stable. There is, however, neither a formal coalition agreement nor an actual government programme. Despite comfortable majorities in numbers in both chambers of the Federal Assembly, the Federal Council, almost like a minority government, must constantly struggle for new majorities. Defeats in Parliament or in popular votes are not rare, but they do not entail any direct consequences in terms of personnel. The thinking in terms of legislative periods is less pronounced than in other systems of government.

According to the constitutional catalogue of its tasks and powers (articles 180–187 BV), the Federal Council also plays a significant role in leading the Confederation at the highest level ('*Staatsleitung*'). In addition to the enforcement of legislation and the budget, it is also responsible for determining the goals and means of government policy. It has comprehensive powers of initiative. The law drafts dealt with in parliament are generally government bills. The Federal Council is empowered to adopt ordinances, provided the Constitution or a federal act authorize it to do so (article 182 BV).[186] It handles foreign affairs but must uphold the participation rights of the Federal Assembly when doing so (article 166 BV). In addition, it is responsible for maintaining relations with the cantons and ensuring their compliance with federal law (article 186 BV). The Federal Council directs and supervises the

---

[185] There was one such 'vote out' on 10 December 2003, the first in decades. The reason was primarily weight shifts in the party system. See n 144. Another 'vote out' took place on 12 December 2007.

[186] The Federal Council has the power to enact temporary ordinances based directly on the constitution in order to safeguard foreign-policy interests or in order to counter existing or imminent threats of serious disruption to public order or internal or external security (art 184 and 185 BV). See for example Verordnung 3 über Massnahmen zur Bekämpfung des Coronavirus (Covid-19) of 19 June 2020 (Official Compilation of Federal Law [AS] 2020 2195) (based on art. 185 BV); see also Giovanni Biaggini, '«Notrecht» in Zeiten des Coronavirus – Eine Kritik der jüngsten Praxis des Bundesrats zu Art 185 Abs. 3 BV' (2020) Schweizerisches Zentralblatt für Staats- und Verwaltungsrecht (ZBl) 239 ff.

Federal Administration, which is divided into departments. Each department (or 'ministry') is headed by a member of the Federal Council (article 178 BV). Government decisions are made by the Federal Council as a collegial body (collegiality principle, article 177 BV). For its preparation and execution, government business is distributed to the individual members of the Federal Council according to their department. The departments may also be equipped with independent decision-making powers. The individual members of the Federal Council have a dual role. They are both members of the collegial government body and head of a department at the same time. As heads of department, they are subject to the guidance and supervision by the government college to which they themselves belong. This juxtaposition of the 'Kollegial- und Departementalprinzip' ('Principle of collegiality and allocation to departments'), as it says in the heading of article 177 BV, is a source of permanent tension and system-typical problems (responsibility).[187] In practice, there is a tendency towards the 'departmentalization' of politics. The strengthening of the government college vis-à-vis the departments is one of the enduring themes of the latest discussions on reform.

d) Federal Supreme Court and Other Judicial Authorities

The Federal Supreme Court (article 188 ff BV), based in Lausanne, is the Supreme Court of Appeal in the areas of civil law, criminal law, and federal administrative law, and is entrusted with the exercise of certain constitutional-judicial tasks. Today it comprises thirty-eight regular federal judges elected by the United Federal Assembly.[188] Election is for a term of six years (article 145 BV) with the possibility of re-election. At the federal level, there is also a Federal Criminal Court (since April 2004) for the first-instance hearing of criminal cases that are assigned to the jurisdiction of the Confederation, as well as a Federal Administrative Court (with fifty to seventy judges), which, as of 2007 has sat in place of the various special administrative courts (article 191a para 2 BV). In 2012, a Federal Patent Court was added as the patent court of first instance of the Swiss Confederation (article 191a para 3 BV). The focus of the third power lies on the cantonal level. The administration of justice in civil matters and in criminal cases, including the organization of the courts, is a responsibility of the cantons, unless the law provides otherwise (articles 122 and 123 BV). The assessment of disputes in the area of cantonal and, to the extent applied by the cantons (article 46 BV), federal administrative law is also the task of the cantonal courts. The right of appeal to the Federal Supreme Court is generally available against decisions of the cantonal courts. The organization of the judiciary varies significantly from canton to canton.

Judicial independence is constitutionally guaranteed.[189] For the Federal Supreme Court, the Federal Constitution lays down an explicit self-governance guarantee (article 188 para 3 BV). Like the other federal courts, the Federal Supreme Court is also subject to supervision by the Federal Assembly (article 169 BV).[190]

---

[187] Illustrative is the Parliamentary Investigation Commission report on organizational and governance problems in the Federal Pension Fund and the role of the Department of Finance (from 7 October 1996), Federal Gazette of the Swiss Confederation (BBl) 1996 V 153 ff, in particular 412 f.

[188] Including the ten members of the two social law divisions located in Lucerne. The law sets a framework of thirty-five to forty-five members (art 1 Federal Supreme Court Act); the exact number is determined through an ordinance by the Federal Assembly.

[189] Art 191c BV determines: 'The judicial authorities are independent in the exercise of their judicial powers and are bound only by the law.' See also art 30 BV (as well as art 6 ECHR).

[190] Parliamentary oversight over the federal courts deals with the proper course of business and not with the control of the content of the judicial decisions (see art 26 para 4 ParlG).

With regard to the appointment and status of the judges, there is a colourful picture of federal diversity in Switzerland.[191] The election of the cantonal judges is usually the responsibility of the parliaments,[192] special election committees on occasion, rarely the Executive,[193] and sometimes the electorate for the election of first-instance judges (ballot box). Election is generally for a rather short term of four to six years with the possibility of re-election. Even today, in most cantons, legal training is not formally required for the office of judge. This is explained by the tradition of lay judges. This even applies to the Federal Supreme Court in that, according to the Constitution, any person eligible to vote may be elected (article 143 BV). In practice, however, virtually all judges of upper instance have a degree in law. Part-time judges, even in the Federal Supreme Court, remain very common. The strongly democratic system of the selection/election of judges has, in addition to its advantages, certain weaknesses (e.g. the politicization of judge elections, ensuring professional qualification), but seems to have proven its worth by and large.

Codifying the existing practice, the Federal Supreme Court Act foresees that the members of the Federal Supreme Court leave office at the end of the year in which they reach the age of sixty-eight. There is no provision in the Constitution or in statute law for the premature dismissal or removal from office.[194] This is different in the Federal Criminal Court and the Federal Administrative Court. Their members can be removed from office by the Federal Assembly before the expiry of their term if they have wilfully or through gross negligence committed serious breaches of their duties of office or have permanently lost the ability to perform their official duties.[195] This has, however, not happened in practice so far.

e) Interaction of the Powers

In its basic structures, the Federal Constitution follows the idea of separation of powers in that it creates three supreme federal authorities separated in terms of organization and personnel. However, it does not schematically allocate the classic state functions (legislation, execution, judiciary) to the supreme federal authorities. This means that some legislative and judicial powers are also vested in the Federal Council (articles 182 and 187 BV), and certain administrative competences (article 188 BV) and individual legislative tasks in the Federal Supreme Court.[196] In good democratic tradition, the Constitution emphasizes the special position of the Federal Assembly by allocating to it the role of 'supreme authority' (article 148 BV). The passage in question may not create any additional competences for the Federal Assembly but other provisions do foresee a certain primacy in relation to the other

[191] See Walter Kälin, 'Justiz', in Ulrich Klöti and others (eds), *Handbuch der Schweizer Politik* (n 143) 187 ff; Regina Kiener, *Richterliche Unabhängigkeit* (Stämpfli, Bern, 2001).

[192] The election of members of the Federal Supreme Court, the Federal Criminal Court, the Federal Administrative Court, and the Federal Patent Court is the duty of the United Federal Assembly (art 168 BV; art 135 ParlG).

[193] The members of the earlier Federal Appeals Commissions (special administrative courts; replaced by the Federal Administrative Court as of 1 January 2007) were elected by the Federal Council (art 71b VwVG in the version valid until the end of 2006).

[194] Highly problematic were certain hasty reactions in Parliament (2003) in the case of a federal judge (who stepped down voluntarily in the end), whose behaviour had received criticism. See René Rhinow, Markus Schefer, and Peter Uebersax, *Schweizerisches Verfassungsrecht* (n 72) 448 f.

[195] Thus art 49 of the Criminal Authority Organization Act of 19 March 2010 (StBOG; Systematic Compilation of Federal Law 173.71) and art 10 of the Administrative Court Law of 17 June 2005 (Systematic Compilation of Federal Law 173.32).

[196] E.g. Regulations of the Federal Supreme Court of 11 September 2006 concerning the supervision of the Federal Criminal Court, the Federal Administrative Court, and the Federal Patent Court (AufRBGer; Systematic Compilation of Federal Law 173.110.132).

two highest authorities: election of members of the government and of the Federal Supreme Court (article 168 BV), supervision of the Federal Council and the federal courts (article 169 BV), the authority to allocate orders to the Federal Council and thus (with limitations) influence the areas of competency of the Federal Council (article 171 BV), decisions on certain important individual acts (where a federal act expressly so provides) and on certain public-law disputes (article 173 BV), and lack of constitutional jurisdiction vis-à-vis the federal legislator (article 190 BV). However, article 148 BV also foresees limitations for the Federal Assembly: Its powers are expressly '[s]ubject to the rights of the People and the Cantons' (article 148 BV); it *is* not the supreme power in the Confederation but rather merely exercises it, as a trustee in a certain sense. In doing so, it is committed to the Constitution and international law (article 5 BV) and involved in a network of democratic checks and balances.

The many deviations from the theoretical ideal scheme of separation of powers used to be termed 'breaches' (*Durchbrechungen*) by older legal scholars.[197] In more recent doctrine, there is an increasing move away in favour of a terminology that emphasizes the collaboration of the powers and aims at expressing a cooperative understanding of the separation of powers.[198] However, a common terminology has yet to establish itself. The widespread complaints about a loss of significance of the parliament stand in clear contrast to the wording of the Constitution. The main reason for this is, aside from the internationalization of the law, the de facto advantage of the executive in terms of resources and information. Although this is a common phenomenon in Western democracies, it is felt more strongly and criticized more loudly in Switzerland, where (not least of all in the text of the Constitution) the image of a strong parliament is maintained. Citing a cooperative understanding of the separation of powers, the Federal Assembly has recently, sometimes against fierce opposition from the government, undertaken various measures to strengthen the parliamentary rights to information and the planning, control, and supervisory instruments. These measures are reflected in part in the text of the new Federal Constitution and in part in the legislation.[199]

The more or less symmetrically structured catalogues of constitutional tasks and responsibilities of the Federal Assembly (articles 163 ff BV) and Federal Council (articles 180 ff BV) clearly illustrate the necessity of the cooperation of both institutions in the division of tasks. There is nothing wrong with a cooperative understanding of the separation and limitation of powers that is more strongly aligned with the realities of the political process. This requires, however, that the key concern of clarity in the allocation of responsibilities is maintained, as it is crucial to the rule of law and democracy. Particularly sensitive areas have proven time and again to be the parliamentary oversight over the Federal Council and the Federal

---

[197] See for example, Ulrich Häfelin and Walter Haller, *Schweizerisches Bundesstaatsrecht* (6th edn, Schulthess, Zurich, 2005) title before para 1420 (today: Ulrich Häfelin, Walter Haller, Helen Keller, and Daniela Thurnherr, *Schweizerisches Bundesstaatsrecht* (n 73): 'Abweichungen von der organisatorischen Gewaltenteilung in der Bundesverfassung'). See also Giovanni Biaggini, ,Gewaltenteilung im Verfassungsstaat', in Giovanni Biaggini, Thomas Gächter, and Regina Kiener (eds), *Staatsrecht* (3rd edn, Dike, Zurich, 2021) 205 ff.

[198] See for example, Philippe Mastronardi and Benjamin Schindler, 'Vorbemerkungen zu Art. 143-191c', in Bernhard Ehrenzeller and others (eds), *Die schweizerische Bundesverfassung. St. Galler Kommentar* (n 80) para 36; René Rhinow, Markus Schefer, and Peter Uebersax, *Schweizerisches Verfassungsrecht* (n 72) 430 ff (who prefer to speak of '*Gewaltengliederung*' ['structure of powers'] instead of '*Gewaltenteilung*' ['separation of powers']).

[199] See in particular arts 153 para 4 and 169 para 2 BV as well as art 150 ff ParlG (right to information), art 166 BV, as well as arts 24 and 152 ParlG (shaping of foreign policy), art 173 BV, as well as arts 28 and 146 ff ParlG (planning). Since 1966, the instrument of the Parliamentary Investigation Committee, which is not specifically mentioned in the Constitution and which is equipped with certain special powers, has been regulated by law (today art 163 ff ParlG).

Administration (article 169 BV) as well as foreign policy (articles 166 and 184 BV), both of which not surprisingly have been the subject of extensive monographs.[200]

In the similarly conflict-ridden area of legislation, collaboration based on the division of tasks seems to have established itself more or less. This is probably also thanks to the fact that there are effective controls in place through constitutional and administrative jurisdiction. The Federal Constitution allows for a transfer of legislative powers to the Executive branch under certain conditions. However, such a delegation is excluded for all important legal norms based on reasons of democracy and the rule of law. According to the non-exhaustive enumeration in article 164 para 1 BV, the 'fundamental provisions' on the exercise of political rights, on the restriction of constitutional rights (see also article 36 BV), on the organization of the federal authorities, and in some other areas must be mandatorily enacted in the form of a federal act. This codification of the notion of legislation has not brought about the level of clarification of the unresolved issues that some had hoped for. The application of article 164 BV is likely to remain controversial, no different from the handling of the unwritten principles of the delegation of legislation which were the inspiration for article 164 and continue to play a role in the case-law of the Federal Supreme Court.[201]

6. Federalism and the Understanding of Federalism

a) Basic Questions

Since the founding of the Federal State, the Federal Constitution has devoted its first article to the Federal State and its composition. Article 1 of the new Constitution, which aims at updating the previous Constitutions in a modern way, adopts the following approach: 'The People and the Cantons [listed by name in the original] form the Swiss Confederation'. This peculiar double formulation, in which the entire population (the Swiss 'People') and twenty-six political entities ('Cantons') would seem to merge into one unit, should of course not be taken literally and should also not be understood as a definitive statement on the concept of the Federal State, but rather first and foremost as a confirmation of the traditional double structure used by the originators of the constitution ('The People and the Cantons'). The Federal Constitution also manages in other respects to avoid appropriation by any one particular theory of federalism by means of ambiguity. Even the name is idiosyncratic: in the Latin-based national languages, Switzerland still calls itself 'Confederation'.[202] This formula dating back to 1848, according to which the cantons are 'sovereign except to the extent that their sovereignty is limited by the Federal Constitution' (article 3 BV), would appear to assume, together with de Tocqueville, the notion of a sovereignty 'shared' by the Confederation and the cantons, but is, however, basically just a consolation prize for the irrevocable loss of sovereignty suffered more or less voluntarily by the cantons in 1848. Elsewhere, the Federal Constitution then appears to place sovereignty clearly with the Confederation. The fact that the Constitution does not juxtapose only the 'Federal State' ('*Bund*') and the 'cantons' (articles 42 ff BV) but also speaks of the 'Swiss Confederation' ('*Schweizerische Eidgenossenschaft*')

---

[200] See in particular Bernhard Ehrenzeller, *Legislative Gewalt und Aussenpolitik* (Helbing und Lichtenhahn, Basel, 1993); Philippe Mastronardi, *Kriterien der demokratischen Verwaltungskontrolle* (Helbing und Lichtenhahn, Basel, 1991); in detail also Hansjörg Seiler, *Gewalterteilung* (n 172).

[201] In detail, BGE 118 Ia 305 (310), *X*. [1992]; from more recent case-law, see, for example, BGE 141 V 688 (691 ff), *A*. [2015] (with references).

[202] See Section A.1.b above and Section D.1 below.

THE EVOLUTION AND *GESTALT* OF THE SWISS CONSTITUTION   681

formed by the Swiss people and the twenty-six cantons (article 1 BV), suggests the tripartite federal model of Kelsen.[203] Only the doctrine of the cantons as mere 'self-governing bodies of the Confederation'[204] would appear to be inconsistent with the terms of the Federal Constitution. The cantons each have a complete state organization (parliament, government, justice), see themselves as independent communities (see also article 47, headed: 'Autonomy of the Cantons'), and generally proclaim this very clearly in their own constitutions. In recent literature, the cantons have rightly been attested 'statehood', albeit a 'limited' and 'non-sovereign' one.[205]

Given the difficulties of classifying the Swiss Confederation in the outdated categories of federal state theory, a pragmatic, functional approach would be appropriate. A starting point could be the distinction of three or five 'pillars' (depending on how they are counted) of the Federal State, namely: (1) a substantial autonomy of the cantons (see article 47) as regards (a) their organization, (b) their tasks, and (c) their finances; (2) participation in the decision-making process of the Confederation (see article 45 BV); (3) the loyal collaboration of the federal actors (see article 44 BV).[206] The principle of the equality of the cantons, which is recognized in practice and jurisprudence, is not specifically mentioned in the text of the Federal Constitution;[207] it leaves room for certain differentiations, for example according to financial capacity. The Federal Constitution itself stipulates that the six historical 'half-cantons' each have only half of a cantonal vote and only one seat in the Council of States (articles 142 and 150 BV).[208] In addition to the traditional term 'canton' (which has French origins), the old term '*Stände*' has also survived, particularly in connection with the second chamber of parliament (*Ständerat*) and with the requirement of the double majority ('*Volks- und Ständemehr*', meaning 'a majority of those who vote and a majority of the Cantons', article 142 BV). The communes, as an important third level of the federal state,[209] are addressed only sporadically in the Federal Constitution. Their position and autonomy are derived from cantonal law (article 50 BV). The Confederation provides them with the right of appeal to the Federal Supreme Court for violations of autonomy by the cantonal authorities (article 189 BV).

b) Organizational, Task-related, and Financial Autonomy of the Cantons

The Federal Constitution grants the cantons extensive discretion in matters concerning their constitutions and the organization of their authorities (article 51 BV; constitutional and organizational autonomy).[210] In the choice of their governmental systems, the cantons

---

[203] See Hans Kelsen, *Allgemeine Staatslehre* (Springer, Berlin, 1925) 199 f.

[204] See Fritz Fleiner and Zaccaria Giacometti, *Schweizerisches Bundesstaatsrecht* (Polygraphischer Verlag, Zurich, 1949) 47.

[205] See for example, Tobias Jaag, 'Die Rechtsstellung der Kantone in der Bundesverfassung', in Daniel Thürer and others (eds), *Verfassungsrecht der Schweiz* (n 60) 477 f.

[206] Pioneering work by Peter Saladin, 'Bund und Kantone' (1984) II Zeitschrift für Schweizerisches Recht 443 ff (where organizational autonomy, task-related autonomy, and financial autonomy are counted separately).

[207] See Ulrich Häfelin and others, *Schweizerisches Bundesstaatsrecht* (n 73) para 963 ff; Dietrich Schindler, 'Differenzierter Föderalismus', in Walter Haller and others (eds), *Festschrift für Ulrich Häfelin* (Schulthess, Zurich, 1989) 371 ff.

[208] The usual conceptual distinction under the Constitutions of 1848 and 1874 of (full) cantons on the one hand and 'split' cantons (art 80 BV 1874) or 'half-cantons' (art 72 BV 1874) on the other was dropped in 1999.

[209] In 1850, there were around 3,200 autonomous communes in Switzerland. Today, around 2,200 still exist (as the result of mergers).

[210] See Vincent Martenet, *L'autonomie constitutionnelle des cantons* (Helbing und Lichtenhahn, Basel, 1999); Tobias Jaag, 'Die Rechtsstellung der Kantone in der Bundesverfassung' (n 205) 479 ff. On possible restrictions on organizational autonomy in connection with the enforcement of federal administrative law by the cantons see Giovanni Biaggini, *Verwaltungsrecht* (n 85) 129 ff, 330 ff.

can settle for an essentially representative democracy (which no canton does anymore), select one of the varieties of direct democracy (referendum democracy), or keep the time-honoured form of cantonal citizens' assembly (as do Appenzell Innerrhoden and Glarus). Despite broad autonomy and pronounced cantonal consciousness, the cantonal constitutions[211] demonstrate some similarities in the area of state organization. Thus, all cantons know a well-developed system of citizens' rights. Everywhere, the members of the cantonal governments are elected directly by the people.

In the division of competences and tasks between Confederation and cantons, the Federal Constitution proceeds according to the system of individually conferred powers (article 3 BV): the Confederation fulfils the duties that are assigned to it by the Federal Constitution (article 42 BV). Otherwise, the cantons remain responsible (article 43 BV). Exclusive federal competences are rare. Usually, it is a question of so-called competitive competences ('konkurrierende Kompetenzen'), which nullify cantonal regulations only if and to the extent that the federal legislator makes use of the federal competence. There are also parallel competences, including, in particular, competences for promotion measures (e.g. in the fields of higher education, research, and culture). Despite progressive centralization, the cantons today still have significant areas of responsibility, for example in the field of schools and education (including universities) and in healthcare. As before, they also continue to have authority in the areas of culture, church, roads, and police, always within the limits of federal law (namely the fundamental rights). There is even an allowance for 'minor' foreign policy by the cantons (article 56 BV).[212] The implementation and enforcement of federal administrative law is generally the responsibility of the cantons, according to the Constitution and the law (administrative federalism). The Confederation is obligated to allow the cantons 'all possible discretion' in this duty (article 46 BV).[213]

Substantial financial autonomy is rightly considered to be the 'backbone of federalism',[214] since autonomy regarding tasks remains an empty phrase without adequate financial means. According to the general rule (article 3 BV), the Confederation only has those tasks and powers in the area of state finances (including taxes and other charges), which the Federal Constitution assigns to it. The Confederation essentially is entitled to the collection of indirect taxes (VAT, special consumption taxes, tariffs, etc.) and the collection of direct taxes on the incomes of natural persons and on the net profit of legal entities.[215] Within the jurisdiction of the cantons remain income and earnings taxes (parallel to the competences of the Confederation), taxes on assets, inheritance and gifts, property transaction taxes, land property gain taxes, vehicle taxes, etc. The cantons have their own tax laws and tax rates. The Confederation lacks the competence for a material harmonization of taxes. The effect of

---

[211] The constitutional texts can be found under Systematic Compilation of Federal Law 131.211–131.235. The most recent constitution is currently (2021) that of the canton of Geneva; as of 1 June 2013, it replaced the earlier Geneva Constitution, which originated in 1847 in the time before the founding of the Federal State and for a long time was by far the oldest of the cantonal constitutions. Essentially, Zaccaria Giacometti, Das Staatsrecht der schweizerischen Kantone (Polygraphischer Verlag, Zurich, 1941); Andreas Auer, Staatsrecht der schweizerischen Kantone (Stämpfli, Bern, 2016); see also Denise Buser, Kantonales Staatsrecht (2nd edn, Helbing und Lichtenhahn, Basel, 2004).

[212] See Thomas Pfisterer, 'Auslandbeziehungen der Kantone', in Daniel Thürer and others (eds), Verfassungsrecht der Schweiz (n 60) 525 ff; Giovanni Biaggini and Julia Haas, 'Verfassungsrechtliche Grundlagen der Grenzüberschreitenden Zusammenarbeit in der Schweiz', in Hans Martin Tschudi and others (eds), Die Grenzüberschreitende Zusammenarbeit der Schweiz (Dike, Zurich, 2014) 139 ff.

[213] See Giovanni Biaggini, 'Allgemeine Pflichten und Rechte bei der Umsetzung von Bundesrecht durch die Kantone', in Peter Hänni (ed), Mensch und Staat—Festschrift für Thomas Fleiner (Schulthess, Zurich, 2003) 3 ff.

[214] Markus Reich, 'Grundzüge der föderalistischen Finanzverfassung', in Daniel Thürer and others (eds), Verfassungsrecht der Schweiz (n 60) 1203.

[215] Art 128 para 1 BV sets the maximum rates, in particular for the conservation of the cantonal tax substrate.

this pronounced 'tax federalism' is that the tax burden for natural persons is very different depending on the place of residence; it can be more than twice as much in some cantons than in the canton with the lowest tax rate. These disparities are a constant theme in politics but, until now, have barely come up as a question of (constitutional) law. A lessening of the differences can be expected as the result of the reform of fiscal equalization and task allocation between the Confederation and the cantons (NFA), established in 2008. The Confederation controls just under a third of the public finances, with the cantons controlling around 40 per cent and the communes the rest. The Federal Constitution obligates the cantons and communes to a revenue and expenditure policy that is in line with the economic situation (article 100 BV) but, remarkably, does not provide the Confederation with the instruments required to enforce this obligation.

c) Participation of the Cantons in the Decision-making Process of the Confederation

The characteristics of Swiss federalism include the participation of the cantons 'in the federal decision-making process, and, in particular, in the legislative process' (article 45 BV). The list of the relevant instruments[216] is very impressive at first glance. But when one analyses them in terms of the effective representation of the interests of the cantons, the assessment is in fact rather modest. The requirement of the cantonal majority in mandatory constitutional and treaty referenda (article 142 BV; see Section B.1.) constitutes a special type of collective participation right which is not in the power of disposition of the cantonal governments or parliaments. The cantonal referendum (article 141 BV; see Section B.2.a), which only was first used around 130 years after it had been introduced,[217] grants the cantons the right to hold a referendum, but not an actual veto position. Unlike the popular initiative, the cantonal initiative (article 160 BV; see Section B.1.a)) establishes only a referral obligation of the Federal Assembly, which can therefore block the matter submitted with little effort. The consultation and participation rights of the cantons in the preparation of important legislation and other projects of the Confederation of substantial impact (article 147 BV) and in the preparation of certain foreign policy decisions that affect their powers or their essential interests (article 55 BV)[218] do not prevent the Confederation from embarking on a different path, even in the case of cantonal unanimity. The members of the Council of States (article 150 BV) are representatives with a free mandate (article 161 BV), not cantonal delegates bound by instructions.

It is no surprise that demands for more effective participatory options (not least of all from cantonal executive politicians) are raised time and again, going as far as to call for the restructuring of the Council of States into an upper chamber based on the German '*Bundesrat*' model. Such reforms ought to be considered carefully because they could easily lead to a situation in which the political levels of 'Confederation' and 'Cantons', which today—to the country's advantage—are merely very loosely coupled together, interlock and tendencies of a power shift towards the executive continue to intensify. In addition, the instruments mentioned really do have their practical significance in that they contribute to the disciplining

---

[216] See for example, Ulrich Häfelin and others, *Schweizerisches Bundesstaatsrecht* (n 73), para 949 ff; Pierre Tschannen, *Staatsrecht* (n 65) 349 ff.

[217] The subject of the referendum demanded by eleven cantons (16 May 2004) was a fiscal package put forward by the federal legislator that would have meant greater tax losses for the cantons. The voters rejected the legislative proposal by 34.1 per cent to 65.9 per cent.

[218] In more detail, Peter Hänni (ed), *Schweizerischer Föderalismus und europäische Integration* (Schulthess, Zurich, 2000).

of federal power and, in the interest of the protection of minorities, detract from the democratic majority principle.

d) Interaction of the Levels

Mutual respect is the 'drop of oil' that the 'legal workings' need if 'such a complicated mechanism as the Swiss federal state is to be kept in gear and the collaboration of Confederation and cantons is to lead to a fruitful result' (*Walther Burckhardt*).[219] The new Federal Constitution dedicates several provisions to the question of the collaboration of the Confederation and cantons. At the heart of these is article 44 BV: the Confederation and cantons owe each other consideration, support, and mutual assistance—somewhat like in a marriage;[220] disputes should be resolved, according to the culture of dialogue, through negotiation and mediation. This means that disputes between the Confederation and cantons or between cantons before the Federal Supreme Court (article 189 BV) are rather rare.[221] The Federal Council, whose responsibility it is to ensure compliance with federal law by the cantons (articles 49 and 186 BV), exercises so-called federal supervision, traditionally with great restraint.[222] Under the Federal Constitution of 1874, the principle of federal loyalty was in general recognized as an unwritten constitutional principle, but was never truly at home in legal doctrine and case-law.[223] With article 48 BV, the Federal Constitution provides an even slightly more canton-friendly framework for the traditional horizontal cooperative federalism[224] between the cantons. At the request of interested cantons, the Confederation may declare inter-cantonal agreements to be generally binding in certain areas of duty or to require resistive cantons to participate in inter-cantonal agreements (article 48a BV). Thus, in addition to voluntary co-operation, the rather autonomy- and democracy-unfriendly forced cooperation appears as a new legal institute; while this has never been used to date and will probably seldom be decreed in reality, it is likely to have an impact as a possible means of leverage. In recent times, a progressive institutionalization of cooperative federalism can be observed. An important role in this is played by the so-called conferences, in which the cantonal governments as such (Conference of the Cantonal Governments, KdK) or the respective cantonal ministers (e.g. for justice, for finance, for education, for health) come together to coordinate cantonal policy horizontally or establish common positions vis-à-vis the federal authorities. This institutionalization occasionally also includes the Confederation and occasionally creates hybrid structures, such as the joint bodies of Confederation and cantons in the field of higher education

---

[219] Walther Burckhardt, *Kommentar der schweizerischen Bundesverfassung vom 29. Mai 1874* (3rd edn, Stämpfli, Bern, 1931) 17. See also Peter Saladin, in Jean-François Aubert and others (eds), *Kommentar aBV* (n 17), art 3 para 33 ff.

[220] See art 159 para 3 of the Civil Code (Systematic Compilation of Federal Law 210): 'They [the spouses] owe each other loyalty and support.'

[221] See for example, BGE 125 II 152, *Canton of St. Gallen vs Swiss Confederation* [1999] (Delimitation of competences in the licensing of slot machines); BGE 118 Ia 195, *Canton of Bern vs Canton of Jura* [1992] (Validity of a cantonal popular initiative which questioned the territorial integrity of the neighbouring canton); BGE 117 Ia 202, *Swiss Confederation vs Canton of Basel-Landschaft* [1991] (Handling of state security files of the Confederation). Slightly more frequent are court-referred disputes *between the cantons* under constitutional or administrative law.

[222] On the instruments and legal framework conditions, see Giovanni Biaggini, *Verwaltungsrecht* (n 85) 134 ff; Verwaltungspraxis der Bundesbehörden (Administrative Practices of the Federal Authorities) (VPB) 69 (2005), No. 1 (Bundesamt für Justiz, 31 August 2004).

[223] See Alfred Kölz, 'Bundestreue als Verfassungsprinzip?' (1980) Schweizerisches Zentralblatt für Staats- und Verwaltungsrecht (ZBl) 145 ff. Cautiously also BGE 125 II 152 (163 f), *Kanton St. Gallen* [1999]. See also BGE 118 Ia 195, *Canton de Berne* [1992].

[224] See Ulrich Häfelin, 'Der kooperative Föderalismus in der Schweiz' (1969) II Zeitschrift für Schweizerisches Recht 549 ff; René Rhinow, Markus Schefer, and Peter Uebersax, *Schweizerisches Verfassungsrecht* (n 72) 158 ff.

(article 63a para 4 BV) and for implementing the legislation on gambling. Intertwining like this leads to new challenges and tests for accountability and control of government action.

D. Constitutional Identity: Characteristics and Identity-creating Elements

1. Citizens and People, Nation and State in the Light of the Federal Constitution

A federalism deeply rooted in tradition with very independent members of the Confederation and the gradually formed institutions of direct democracy are system-defining fundamental elements of the constitutional system of the Swiss Confederation. They have already been described in detail so the attention here will be on some other characteristic elements that are important for the understanding of the Swiss constitutional system and idea of state, but which may not be obvious to the outside observer.

Switzerland has triple citizenship[225] which is built in the old tradition from the bottom to the top and shaped by diversity. The Federal Constitution determines that 'any person who is a citizen of a commune and of the Canton to which that commune belongs is a Swiss citizen' (article 37 para 1 BV). Swiss citizenship is thus based on the citizenship of a canton, and this in turn is generally based (in accordance with cantonal law) on citizenship of a commune. A definitive national regulation exists for the cases of citizenship through descent, marriage, and adoption mentioned in the Constitution (article 38 para 1 BV) but not for so-called ordinary naturalization. In this case, the Confederation is limited to establishing *minimum requirements* and to monitoring compliance with these (article 38 para 2 BV).[226] Otherwise, ordinary naturalization is a matter for the cantons. The cantons—and depending on the canton, also the communes—may establish further requirements (e.g. in relation to the duration of residence, language skills, integration), which makes a real national naturalization policy impossible.[227] In practice, the decision on naturalization at a communal level is the 'eye of the needle' in applying for Swiss citizenship. The decision can be the responsibility of an executive authority or of the communal parliament. In many cases, especially in smaller communes, it is the duty of the voters who come together in the (citizens') communal assembly.[228] In the self-conception of many decision-makers, inclusion into citizenship is a political act[229] in which the commune's citizens indicate their will to accept an applicant into

---

[225] See René Schaffhauser, 'Bürgerrechte', in Daniel Thürer and others (eds), *Verfassungsrecht der Schweiz* (n 60) 317 ff.

[226] See arts 9 ff of the Federal Act of 20 June 2014 on Swiss Citizenship (*Bürgerrechtsgesetz*, BüG; Systematic Compilation of Federal Law 141.0). In addition to minimum requirements, there are occasionally also 'maximum requirements' in the Swiss Citizenship Act (art 18: length of residence; art 35: fees) whose constitutionality is doubtful. See Giovanni Biaggini, *Bundesverfassung Kommentar* (n 136) art 38, para 13.

[227] A specific shift in competence to the Confederation regarding so-called second and third-generation foreigners (Federal Gazette of the Swiss Confederation [BBl] 2003 6599 ff) failed in the referendum of 26 September 2004. Through an amendment to art 38 para 3 BV in the popular vote of 12 February 2017, the possibility of an easier naturalization of third-generation foreigners now exists.

[228] In two decisions of 9 July 2003, the Federal Supreme Court declared the decision in the form of a ballot box vote to be inadmissible (BGE 129 I 217, *A. und Mitb.* [2003]; BGE 129 I 232, *Schweizerische Volkspartei der Stadt Zürich* [2003]). See above Section C.3.c, at the end.

[229] Which does not exempt from the observance of the fundamental rights, which the Federal Supreme Court has occasionally had to remind of. See the decisions cited in the previous footnote as well as BGE 130 I 140 (150 ff), *A. und Mitb.* [2004] (Municipal Assembly).

their circle and make him or her the bearer of extensive political participation rights in the commune, the canton, and the Confederation.

Switzerland is often described as a 'nation of will' because its cohesion is not based on a common culture but rather on the will, constantly updated in a long, common history, to form a nation.[230] In actual fact, at the time of the formation of the state (and even yet today), there was no Swiss people in the traditional ethno-linguistic, cultural sense. However, this did not prevent the founding fathers of the Constitution from evoking the 'Unity ... of the Swiss nation' in the Preamble of the Constitution (which survived in this form until the end of 1999). Democratic institutions and procedures were also set up immediately on a federal level although a pan-Swiss public existed at best in part at that time. From today's perspective, national cohesion is ensured not least of all by constitutional institutions such as the Federal Assembly, the Federal Council, the referendum, and the popular initiative (as well as the popular votes arising from these), which means that Switzerland could also be described as a 'constitutional nation'. Bringing about a renewal of the national basic consensus is a political achievement of the total revision process of the 1990s that should not be underestimated. The (not so many) 'flaws' of the new Federal Constitution include the fact that the term 'nation' has disappeared from the Preamble of the Constitution.[231] Here and in the text of the Federal Constitution (article 1 BV) now the hitherto uncommon term 'Swiss people' appears.[232] The term 'people', which was already multifaceted, in the Constitution sometimes meaning the entirety of the citizens, sometimes only the voters, sometimes the entire population,[233] was given yet another facet. The lack of a Swiss people in the ethno-linguistic, cultural sense remains unchanged by this, however.

There is no doubt that Switzerland is a democratic federal state. And yet, when contemplating the Constitution, the question arises as to whether the Confederation really wants to be a state. The naming of the state in French, Italian, and Rumantsch (*Confédération, Confederazione, Confederaziun*), which sounds like a confederation of states, and the attribute 'sovereign' (article 3 BV), with which the Federal Constitution bestows the cantons, have already been discussed, as have the characteristics of the three-fold citizenship. It is also striking that the Federal Constitution has always addressed its intended task of integration without any reference to national symbolism (such as flag, coat of arms, currency, motto, national anthem);[234] despite the great need for the establishment of a common identity, it delegates the area of symbolism to the cantonal constitutions (without causing any harm to national unity). One would almost be given the impression that the 'Swiss Confederation', as it is officially known, were a 'state against wills'. The naming of the state in German ('*Eidgenossenschaft*') is also revealing in that the community is described as a 'cooperative' ('*Genossenschaft*')—in the common definition, a corporately organized association 'of an unlimited number of persons' who pursue certain purposes 'by way of collective self-help'

---

[230] See for example, René Rhinow, Markus Schefer, and Peter Uebersax, *Schweizerisches Verfassungsrecht* (n 72) 116.

[231] Already in 1996, the German term '*Nationalsprachen*' (art 116 Federal Constitution of the Swiss Confederation of 1874 old version) was re-termed '*Landessprachen*' (see today art 4 BV). The terms '*Nationalrat*' (National Council), '*Nationalbank*' (National Bank) and '*Nationalstrassen*' (national highways) remain.

[232] On the function of the term (as a confirmation of the double structure of the constitutional legislator), see above Section C.3.a. In the Constitutions of 1848 and 1874, only the 'peoples' (plural) of the cantons were mentioned (art 1).

[233] Thus in the preamble, in arts 2 para 1 and 149 para 1 BV. See René Rhinow, Markus Schefer, and Peter Uebersax, *Schweizerisches Verfassungsrecht* (n 72) 45 f; Giovanni Biaggini, 'Das 'Problem' des fehlenden europäischen Volkes', in Benoît Bovay and Minh Son Nguyen (eds), *Mélanges Pierre Moor* (n 162) 3 ff.

[234] Only the (non-working) 'National Day' of 1 August is constitutionally ordained, even though at a late stage (1993/94) and (today) a little bashfully in the last paragraph of the provision on 'Labour' (art 110 BV).

and thus in principle are subject to 'equal rights and obligations'.[235] In fact, much *cooperative thinking* traditionally resonates in the idea of the Swiss state and constitution (whereas—unlike in very many Western constitutions—a monarchical heritage is completely lacking). Mentioned here are only: the tradition of the '*Zweckartikel*' (article of purpose; article 2 BV: Aims), the procedure of naturalization, the same political rights and duties (article 136 BV), the militia principle ('In principle, the armed forces shall be organized as a militia.'; article 58 BV), the emphasis on solidarity and personal responsibility. Concerning personal responsibility, not only the constitutional appeal of article 6 BV is to be considered, but also, in particular, the people's rights.

The people's rights have a 'downside' which benefits those in power. If the potential vested in the people's rights (as real participation rights) is not used to control parliament and government, responsibility for the conduct of politics cannot simply be laid at the feet of those in power alone. This means that the people's rights form an important element in a greater context of responsibility. The people's rights in the Swiss direct democracy undoubtedly have an important legitimizing function. Their main significance could well be seen in a corrective function, however. In Switzerland, the processing of discontent with politics is not primarily the taking to the streets (as is the case in France) or going before a constitutional court (as in Germany), but rather the use of the people's rights. In contrast to other constitutional systems, the accent in Switzerland lies a little less on the rule of law than on the democratic controls (which can partly explain the hesitant development and expansion of administrative jurisdiction). Only by considering the corrective function of the people's rights does it become understandable why the chronically low turn-out in popular votes—'poison' for democracy from a purely legitimizing point of view—has led to no serious problems of acceptance thus far. Switzerland's difficulties in clarifying its relationship with the European Union have not least of all to do with the fact that the people's rights would suffer a noticeable loss of significance as a (direct) democratic corrective in the case of accession to the EU[236] (currently not under consideration).

2. Balancing Out of Equality and Inequality as a Never-ending Task

The idea of 'democratic equality' is an integral part of the Swiss constitutional system: 'All citizens have the same political rights and duties.' (article 136 para 1 clause 2 BV). However, a hallmark of the constitutional system is also that democratic equality and the principle of majority closely associated with it are 'broken' by federalism several times at the federal level. Half of the representatives in the Council of States, the second parliamentary chamber, come from smaller cantons, which comprise only a fifth of the overall Swiss population. In the elections for the National Council, there are considerable distortions of the equal success value for each vote because the very differently sized cantons form the constituencies (article 149 BV). The requirement of the cantonal majority (article 142 BV) gives the less-populated

---

[235] The quotations are taken from two central provisions of the cooperative legislation: art 828 and 854 OR (Federal Act of 30 March 1911 on the Amendment of the Swiss Civil Code, Part Five: The Code of Obligations; Systematic Compilation of Federal Law 220).

[236] See, for example, Pascal Mahon and Christoph Müller, 'Adhésion de la Suisse à l'Union européenne et démocratie directe', in Thomas Cottier and Alwin R Kopše (eds), *Der Beitritt der Schweiz zur Europäischen Union* (Schulthess, Zurich, 1998) 449 ff.

cantons more weight in the mandatory (constitutional) referendum.[237] To see in this only an erosion of the idea of democratic equality would be a one-dimensional point of view, as this is above all a question of the elementary protection against majorization in a federal state tailored to the peculiarities of Switzerland.

These relativizations of democratic equality are the expression of a general and essential feature of the Swiss constitutional system which allows for a *high degree of inequality* and sometimes even requires it. Characteristic examples of this are the lack of an actual federal 'homogeneity clause',[238] the conscious renunciation of a federal competence for substantive tax harmonization,[239] unequally high hurdles in the ordinary naturalization procedure depending on the canton and communes and the comparatively high tolerance threshold in the varying strictness of the enforcement of federal law from canton to canton.[240] In the implementation of the aspired '*Vielfalt in der Einheit*' or 'diversity in unity' (German wording of the Preamble to the Constitution), the accent usually lies more on 'diversity'. Drawing on their still considerable competences, the cantons adopt regulations that are not always compatible with free movement within Switzerland and the goal of a unified economic area (Article 95 BV). Such drawbacks of a 'living' federalism[241] are generally accepted for the sake of the considerable advantages. A certain degree of competition between the cantons helps to promote innovation and to keep the complicated federal machinery in gear. Thanks to the strong federalist structures, the protection of minorities in Switzerland relies to a high extent on general institutions (self-determination on a cantonal and communal level, fundamental rights, legal protection). Specific provisions to protect minority groups are rather rare.

The readiness to accept disparities is not without limits. The Federal Constitution refrains from giving the Confederation a general mandate for 'creating equivalent living conditions' throughout Switzerland, for example. Since the beginnings of the Federal State, the Constitution has assigned the Confederation a certain responsibility in the area of the provision with certain basic public services, however.[242] The issue of securing equal basic services is likely to gain in importance[243]—and with it the task of balancing diversity and unity, inequalities and equality. In addition to the tried and tested art of compromise, the art of constitutional renewal will be required since, in Switzerland, the Federal Constitution is not only the basis and framework, but also to a large extent the object of politics.

---

[237] In the (theoretical) extreme case, 9 per cent of Swiss voters from eleven and a half small cantons could cause a proposal that is subject to the cantonal majority to fail in the popular vote. In practice, the people's and the cantonal majorities rarely diverge.

[238] Art 51 BV is satisfied with requiring a 'democratic constitution'. See above Section C.3.a.

[239] Art 129 BV (despite large fiscal disparities, particularly in income taxes). See above Section C.6.b.

[240] See Benjamin Schindler, 'Rechtsanwendungsgleichheit in Mehrebenensystemen' (2019) 78 Veröffentlichungen der Vereinigung der Deutschen Staatsrechtslehrer (VVDStRL) 167 ff.

[241] Rainer J Schweizer, 'Homogenität und Vielfalt im schweizerischen Staatsrecht', in Daniel Thürer and others (eds), *Verfassungsrecht der Schweiz* (n 60) 164 ff.

[242] Thus, in art 33 BV 1848 and art 36 BV 1874 for the postal system; in art 92 BV expressly also for telecommunications services.

[243] See art 43a para 4 BV: 'Universally provided services must made be available to every person in a comparable manner.'

14

The Evolution and *Gestalt* of the British Constitution

Martin Loughlin

A. Introduction	689	2. Main Controversies	709
B. Origins of the Current Constitution	692	a) Democracy and the Second Chamber	709
1. Historical Experiences	692	b) The Growth of Administrative Law	709
a) The Crown	692	c) Ministerial Overload	710
b) The Reformation	693	d) New Public Management	711
c) Conflict between Crown and Parliament	694	e) Local Government	712
d) Restoration	694	f) Ireland	712
e) The Glorious Revolution	694	g) Northern Ireland	712
2. International Influences	695	h) Devolution	713
3. Major Debating Points	697	i) Britain and European Convention on Human Rights	714
a) Parliamentary Government	697	j) Britain and the European Union	714
b) Parliamentary Sovereignty	697	k) Prime Ministerial Government	715
c) The Rule of Law and Civil Liberty	698	l) Status of Parliament	716
d) Extension of the Franchise	698	3. Flexibility of the Constitution	717
4. Defining Moments	699	**D. Basic Structures and Concepts**	719
a) Habeas Corpus Act 1679	699	1. Constitutional Law and Politics	719
b) Act of Settlement, 1701	699	2. Sovereignty and Democracy	721
c) Acts of Union 1707, 1801	699	a) The Idea of Sovereignty	722
d) Reform Acts 1832, 1867	700	b) Judicial Independence	724
e) Municipal Corporations Act 1835	700	c) Dicey and the Rule of Law	725
f) Northcote–Trevelyan Reforms	700	d) The Rule of Law and Judicial Review	726
5. Influential Texts	701	e) Human Rights Act 1998	726
C. The Evolution of the Constitution	704	3. Institutions of Government	727
1. The Evolving Constitution	704	a) The Monarchical Constitution	727
a) Basic Principles	704	b) Parliamentary Standards	728
b) The Role of Conventions	704	c) Ministerial Conduct	729
c) Conventional Understandings	705	d) Role of Civil Servants	729
d) Representative Government	705	e) The Supreme Court	730
e) Cabinet Government	706	f) Towards a Separation of Powers?	730
f) Responsible Government	706	4. State, Nation, and Citizen	731
g) Club Government	706	a) The State	731
h) The Parliamentary Function	707	b) People and Nation	732
i) Permanent and Neutral Civil Service	707	c) Citizenship and Nationality	732
j) The Waning of Constitutional Understanding	708	**E. Constitutional Identity**	733

A. Introduction

Britain and Europe. It is often said that Britain is of Europe but not in Europe. It is particularly tempting to adopt that adage when examining its constitutional arrangements,

Martin Loughlin, *The Evolution and* Gestalt *of the British Constitution* In: *The Max Planck Handbooks in European Public Law.* Edited by: Armin von Bogdandy, Peter M Huber, and Sabrina Ragone, Oxford University Press. © Martin Loughlin 2023. DOI: 10.1093/oso/9780198726425.003.0014

and not only because of recent developments that see Britain exiting from the European Union of which it has been a member state since 1973. From a longer historical perspective, Britain's constitutional evolution evidently falls within the mainstream of European constitutional traditions.[1] The British system offers a distinctive variant of the European way of governing.[2] During the eighteenth and nineteenth centuries, it was widely praised as having established a constitutional form that not only had been able to reconcile order with liberty but also to make a successful transition to political modernity.[3] Being almost the only advanced nation not to possess a foundational constitutional text, the British constitution is now perceived as an unusual specimen. But this is mainly because its historic success in being able to accommodate modern governing arrangements with traditional constitutional forms, together with its comparative success in the European theatre of war and diplomacy.

British system of government. The legacy of those historic achievements now presents major problems which are not confined to the evident difficulties we face in being able to present a concise and coherent account of the constitutional framework of the British state. In their essential characteristics, the traditional constitutional arrangements reflect the terms of an ambiguous settlement that was forged in the century following the Glorious Revolution of 1688. But these basic arrangements were embellished, especially with Britain's emergence as an imperial power, and for much of the twentieth century seemed to reflect a Victorian conception of government. Being anti-rationalist in style and aristocratic in form, this style of government could be adapted to modern ideas of democracy and equality only with some difficulty. The resulting ambiguities have created a considerable degree of uncertainty about the essential characteristics of the British system, and with the recent trend towards greater transparency, formality, and rationality within government, these ambiguities and uncertainties are now exposed for scrutiny.

Form and practice. For those seeking a juristic account, then, the British constitution remains an enigma. The adjustment required by the emergence of democracy has been a political achievement. But the legal form of the British constitution remains medieval, originating in the belief that the Crown remains the source of governmental authority. Many of the constitutional forms thus appear to have been bequeathed as an exercise of majesty. But operating within the shadows of these legal forms is continuous political struggle over the exercise of governmental authority. Behind the 'dignified version' of pageantry and ritual that has its symbolic importance in generating a sense of a people, lies an 'efficient version' by which governmental power is actually exercised.[4] Constitutional lawyers have been obliged to negotiate their way through these contrasting versions, and the resulting dynamic offers a clue to the most basic method of the discipline. One complication is that today constitutional lawyers, keen to present a legal account of the British constitution, sometimes fail to acknowledge that the logic of British governmental practice runs contrary to a modern juristic

---

[1] See Raoul C van Caenegem, *An Historical Introduction to Western Constitutional Law* (CUP, Cambridge, 1995).

[2] See Thomas Ertman, *Birth of the Leviathan: Building States and Regimes in Medieval and Early Modern Europe* (CUP, Cambridge, 1997).

[3] See e.g. Émile Boutmy, *The English Constitution* (Macmillan, London, 1891); Rudolph Gneist, *The History of the English Constitution* (William Clowes & Sons, London, 1886); Josef Redlich and Francis W Hirst, *Local Government in England* (Macmillan, London, 1903); Elie Halévy, *A History of the English People in the Nineteenth Century* (Benn, London, 1913).

[4] The formulation is that of Walter Bagehot in his classic nineteenth century study, *The English Constitution* (HS King, London, 1872).

logic. We seem to have reached a situation in which all clear accounts seem false, yet complicated ones seem confused and unhelpful.

Constitutional legacy. Many scholars have argued that Britain's constitutional heritage now presents a barrier to continuing successful adaptation.[5] Some even contend that constitutional modernization is a pre-condition for continuing economic development.[6] This type of argument influenced the establishment of a programme of constitutional reform promoted by the Labour government, 1997–2010. But that programme relied heavily on continuing European integration, not least because of the formal, law-driven character of the European Union project and withdrawal from the EU throws up a significant number of constitutional issues that now need to be addressed.

European constitutionalism. At the beginning of the twentieth century, British governing practices formed part of the European mainstream. One consequence of the European conflicts of the twentieth century, however, has been to bring about a realignment of the constitutional frameworks of many of the states of Europe. Following the models of revolutionary settlements of late-eighteenth century USA and France, modern constitutional regimes have been established at critical points in the recent development of European states. These settlements have invariably been expressed in the form of texts that have the status of fundamental law and they operate on the assumption that the constituent power of the state is vested in the people, rather than being reflected through the concept of the Crown. The institutionalization throughout Europe of liberal democratic constitutional forms left Britain as the only state within the European Union seeking to maintain liberal democratic governing arrangements through the workings of an ancient constitution. The British constitution may thus be presented as one that remains fixed at a particular stage of development of the European state form.

Structure of presentation. Given these peculiarities, this account cannot focus on a fundamental text. Instead, it will be argued that the basic characteristics of the British constitution were shaped in the century following the Glorious Revolution of 1688 and formalized in the nineteenth century (Section B). The development of the constitution during the twentieth century—in response to the emergence of representative democracy, the growth of administrative government, and the rise of disciplined political parties—will next be examined with a view to revealing the logic of constitutional practice within the British system (Section C). Finally, an account of the main juristic ideas that currently are influencing discourse on the British constitution will be presented (Section D). This should indicate why the attempt to provide a juristic interpretation of the British constitution can never be straightforward and that, in the words of one of the greatest of our constitutional historians, 'the more we study our constitution whether in the present or the past, the less do we find it conforms to any such plan as a philosopher might invent in his study'.[7]

---

[5] Nevil Johnson, *In Search of the Constitution* (Pergamon, Oxford, 1977).

[6] On constitutional modernization thesis see David Marquand, *The Unprincipled Society: New Demands and Old Politics* (Cape, London, 1988); Will Hutton, *The State We're In: Why Britain is in Crisis and How to Overcome It* (Vintage, London, 1996).

[7] Frederic W Maitland, *The Constitutional History of England* (CUP, Cambridge, 1908) 197.

B. Origins of the Current Constitution

1. Historical Experiences

The problem of origins. Since there is no basic text, there can be no moment that provides a fixed point against which to identify origins. But the fundamentals of British constitutional arrangements are undoubtedly to be found in the practices of parliamentary government. Parliamentary government is the product of a historical struggle between the Crown and the communities of the realm, with the Crown operating to maintain the discretionary character of its prerogatives of governing against those who sought to define these powers and encase them within fixed institutional forms. This ceaseless process has led to the emergence of a composite sovereign authority, that of the Crown in parliament. This was achieved only after a civil war (1642–1649), the execution of Charles I (1649), the formation of the Commonwealth and Protectorate (1649–1660), the restoration of the king (1660), and a revolution which led to the removal of James II and, at the instigation of a convention parliament, the installation on the throne of William and Mary (1688). After the Glorious Revolution of 1688, the conditions were set for the emergence of the principles of parliamentary sovereignty and government by law. The workings of this system of parliamentary government evolved during the eighteenth century and came to be formulated by legal scholars mainly in the nineteenth century.

a) The Crown

The account must begin with the concept of the Crown. Although the origins of the distinction between king and Crown lie buried in the medieval juristic thought, the distinction was well understood by the fourteenth century when the coronation oath of the period required kings to swear to maintain unimpaired the rights of the Crown.[8] The concept of the Crown provides the basis for differentiating between private and public, and between lordship and office. These are the key terms by which the historic significance of Magna Carta of 1215 can be assessed. The importance of Magna Carta was to limit the power of the Crown as *dominus* and thereby to strengthen it as *rex*: the king's authority to govern was not questioned, but the king was required to exercise that authority only through his council. Stubbs both exaggerated and misconstrued its significance in his comment that 'the whole of the constitutional history of England is little more than a commentary on Magna Carta'.[9] But by acknowledging that acts of the king have an official character that must be exercised through certain forms, the charter constitutes a landmark in the emergence of English governing arrangements. Although the subsequent history is messy, with no consistent differentiation being made in law between the king and the Crown,[10] it is from this idea of the Crown that our understanding of the office of government evolves.

The Crown in Parliament. This work of the 'Crown in Council' was gradually amplified through the formation of a parliament that came into existence as an act of royal will and as an instrument of royal government. Although parliament is often presented as an institution that operates as a counterbalance to government, parliament's origins lie in its perceived

---

[8] Gaines Post, *Studies in Medieval Legal Thought: Public Law and the State, 1100–1322* (Princeton University Press, Princeton NJ, 1964) 415–433.

[9] William Stubbs, *The Constitutional History of England in its Origins and Development* (Clarendon Press, Oxford, 1880) 597–598. See as well James C Holt, *Magna Carta* (2nd edn, CUP, Cambridge, 1992).

[10] Martin Loughlin, 'The State, the Crown, and the Law', in Maurice Sunkin and Sebastian Payne (eds), *The Nature of the Crown: A Legal and Political Analysis* (OUP, Oxford, 1999) 33–76.

value to the king in assisting him in the activity of governing. In order to appreciate the institution's strength, it is essential to recognize that the king's council was centrally embedded within his parliament. When we talk of the establishment of sovereign authority, then, we should in strictness refer to the work undertaken by the 'Crown in Council in Parliament'.

b) The Reformation

The role of parliament in forging a national state is seen most clearly in relation to the innovative work of the Reformation parliament which, using the authority of the Crown in Parliament to the full, sought to eliminate those medieval liberties or privileges which had acted as encumbrances on the complete exercise of sovereign authority. The greatest of these medieval privileges belonged to the church. The revolutionary act of breaking with the church in Rome was one in which Henry VIII made full use of the instrumentality of parliament: Crown and parliament united to challenge any rival jurisdictions. Consequently, while making full use of his regal powers of kingship, Henry also accepted that 'we at no time stand so highly in our estate royal as in the time of parliament; wherein we as head and you as members are conjoined and knit together into one body politic'.[11]

Changing conception of law. The process by which an absolute legislative power was established marks a critical stage both in the formation of the modern state and in the extension in the apparatus of government. In the medieval period, legislation was regarded as a declaratory process and therefore as an aspect of judicial procedure. This is indicated by the historic references to parliament as a high court.[12] All governmental action was understood to involve the interpretation and application of the law. The activity of legislation, and hence its differentiation from adjudication, came about as the result of the growing acceptance of law as an expression of the command of the sovereign rather than as a reflection of an unchanging pattern of custom. But of equal importance is the recognition that this power of command is impersonal and institutional. Sovereign authority resides not so much in the personal power of the king as in the institutional power of the Crown in Council in Parliament.

Changing role of government. Of comparable importance is the acknowledgement that executive government itself is a public office. In addition to establishing a modern conception of legislative sovereignty, Henry's reign saw the creation of a 'revised machinery of government whose principle was bureaucratic organization in place of the personal control of the king, and national management rather than management of the king's estate'.[13] Notwithstanding the transformation of central government from household to bureaucratic methods, however, appointments to governmental offices remained subject to the exercise of patronage. Yet the basis had been laid for the challenge to patrimonial government, and for the eventual establishment during the eighteenth and nineteenth centuries of a more impersonal public administration.[14]

---

[11] *Ferrers' case* (1543), excerpted in Geoffrey R Elton (ed), *The Tudor Constitution: Documents and Commentary* (CUP, Cambridge, 1960) 270.

[12] Charles H McIlwain, *The High Court of Parliament and its Supremacy: An Historical Essay on the Boundaries between Legislation and Adjudication in England* (Yale University Press, New Haven, 1934).

[13] Geoffrey R Elton, *The Tudor Revolution in Government* (CUP, Cambridge, 1953) 4.

[14] Sir Norman Chester, *The English Administrative System 1780–1870* (Clarendon Press, New York, 1981); Richard A Chapman and John R Greenaway, *The Dynamics of Administrative Reform* (Croom Helm, London, 1980).

c) Conflict between Crown and Parliament

The tensions between Crown and parliament in the early modern period centred on the government's need for revenues to meet the escalating costs of government and parliament's traditional control over the voting of supply, which would be voted only if there were redress of grievances. These came to a head in the early seventeenth century, when parliament sought to limit the discretion of the Stuart kings, and they responded by dissolving parliament and generating revenues through innovative use of their prerogative powers. Parliament had asserted its authority through the Petition of Right (1628), but Charles dissolved the parliament in 1629 and ruled without parliament till forced to recall it in 1640 because of the need to raise an army against a rebellion of the Scots who were objecting to his religious policies. With the parliamentary and royalist factions unable to reach a settlement, civil war broke out in 1642 and the parliamentary forces eventually claimed the victory.

Commonwealth. After the execution of the king in 1649, England became a republic and the office of the king—along with the House of Lords (the aristocratic chamber of parliament) and the established (Anglican) Church—was abolished. The parliament remained, but real power vested in the army and in 1653 the army effectively seized control and Oliver Cromwell was proclaimed Lord Protector. In the same year, the Instrument of Government—England's first and only written constitution (and the first written constitution in Europe)—was drafted. But as the Puritan revolution unravelled, parliament in 1658 was dissolved and then, following the death of Cromwell, in 1660 the monarchy—along with parliament and the church—was restored.

d) Restoration

With the restoration of the monarchy under Charles II, son of the executed king, the balance between Crown and parliament was also restored. But in 1685 Charles was succeeded by his Catholic brother, James II. The Whigs had sought to have James excluded from the succession on account of his religion, and this had led to a rupture within the ruling elite between Whigs and Tories. When James proceeded to rule without parliament, the old tensions resurfaced, especially when James tried to repeal both the penal laws against Catholic worship and the Test Acts (which excluded Catholics from holding public office or being Members of Parliament). After applying pressure on the judges to rule that he was able to use his dispensing power to permit the employment of Catholics in government,[15] he sought to extend his prerogative powers and suspend all penal laws forbidding Catholic worship. These actions threatened the protestant ruling elite and challenged the constitutional role of parliament, and after James' queen gave birth to a son in June 1688, the die was cast.

e) The Glorious Revolution

In November 1688, and at the instigation of members of the English ruling elite, William of Orange—who was married to James' Protestant daughter, Mary—landed in England with an army. William pledged to uphold a free parliament and was willing to negotiate terms that enabled James to maintain the throne with reduced powers. In December, however, James fled the country. The ruling elite determined that James had forfeited his right to the crown, held a convention parliament (without a king who should have summoned it) and, in a compromise between adherence to the hereditary principle and the deployment of reason of state thinking, invited William and Mary to reign jointly. Parliament determined that the

---

[15] *Godden v Hales* (1686) 11 St Tr 1165: see John P Kenyon, *The Stuart Constitution 1603–11714* (2nd edn, CUP, Cambridge, 1986) 439.

crown would pass first to Mary and heirs, then to Anne (Mary's sister) and heirs, and then to William and heirs. The main terms of the constitutional settlement were expressed in the Bill of Rights, 1689.

The basic settlement. The constitutional settlement made after the Glorious Revolution affirmed the Protestantism of the English state. It established a constitutional monarchy, imposed limitations on the prerogative powers of the Crown, provided the basis for maintaining free parliaments, led to the formulation of the legal doctrine of parliamentary sovereignty, and promoted a balanced constitution—between monarch, lords, and commons—that sought to reconcile authority and liberty. The circumstances in which the settlement was made led to a Whig supremacy in government for the following eighty years, during which period the main conventional practices of constitutional government were shaped and Britain itself was transformed from an insular society with a largely agricultural economy to an industrial and commercial nation underpinned by a fiscal-military state of considerable imperial might.[16]

2. International Influences

The ancient constitution. Owing to its evolutionary character, English constitutional scholarship has been susceptible to a particular type of historical reasoning. This method, the use of the past for the purpose of bolstering present political concerns, has been called 'the Whig interpretation of history'.[17] This method of reasoning employs two related tropes that draw on foreign influences. The first is that of the Gothic bequest: the belief that there existed an ancient, pre-feudal, and law-observing Anglo-Saxon constitution that preserved liberty.[18] As Montesquieu, following Tacitus, put it: 'the English have taken their idea of political government from the Germans. This fine system was found in the forests'.[19] Aligned to this myth of the ancient constitution is that of the Norman Yoke: that the Normans, by imposing an alien feudalism on an existing structure of English government, had corrupted the original Anglo-Saxon constitution.[20]

Immemorialism. The ideas of the Gothic bequest and the Norman Yoke gave rise to a particular form of constitutional reasoning: that all struggles for liberty are to be interpreted as appeals for the restoration of our ancient, immemorial liberties. In this vein, the great constitutional documents of Magna Carta (1215), the Petition of Right (1628), and the Bill of Rights (1689) did not enact anything new. In the words of a leading nineteenth-century constitutional historian: 'All claimed to set forth ... those rights of Englishmen which were already old. In all our great political struggles the voice of the Englishmen has never called for the assertion of new principles, for the enactment of new laws; the cry has always been for the better observance of the laws which were already in force, for the redress of grievances which had arisen from their corruption or neglect.'[21]

---

[16] John Brewer, *The Sinews of Power: War, Money and the English State, 1688–1783* (Unwin Hyman, London, 1989).

[17] Sir Herbert Butterfield, *The Whig Interpretation of History* (Bell, London, 1931).

[18] See John G A Pocock, *The Ancient Constitution and the Feudal Law* (CUP, Cambridge, 1957).

[19] Charles Louis de Secondat, Baron de Montesquieu, *The Spirit of the Laws* (CUP, Cambridge, 1989), Book 11, chapter 6; Tacitus, *Germania* (Clarendon Press, Oxford, 1999), chapter 11.

[20] Christopher Hill, 'The Norman Yoke', in Christopher Hill, *Puritanism and Revolution* (Secker and Warburg, London, 1958) 50 ff.

[21] Edward A Freeman, *The Growth of the English Constitution* (3rd edn, Macmillan, London, 1876) 57.

Protestantism. Although the main themes of the ancient revolution resurfaced during the contemporary debates over the significance of the Glorious Revolution,[22] there was a more immediate and direct foreign aspect. While there was widespread concern among the ruling elite about James II's actions, the aristocracy did not maintain private armies; military support for the policy of removing James from the throne had therefore to come from abroad. And although William of Orange acted in part to protect his wife's rights of succession, his main objective in mounting an invasion was to bring England into a European war in the protestant cause against France. William was convinced that Louis XIV sought the eradication of Protestantism and was intending to invade the Low Countries; his action in supporting the protestant character of English government may have had the benefit of restoring a balanced constitution, but it was mainly driven by the exigencies of European foreign policy. The invasion marked the first steps towards a second hundred-years war against the French that was to last until Waterloo in 1815.

Hanoverian rule. The determination to maintain a protestant monarch created complications. It was believed that once James and William had died, the monarchy could revert to its normal course. This was frustrated by the death of Anne's last surviving child in 1700: since Mary had died in 1694, and William and Mary had been childless, the Protestant line would end with Anne (Mary's sister, who assumed the throne in 1702), leaving a choice between James II's son (raised as a Catholic in France) and a more remote protestant relative, Sophia, Electress of Hanover (who descended from James I's daughter). The Act of Settlement 1701 made provision for the latter, putting the final nails in the coffin not only of divine right but also of hereditary monarchy. This legislation also placed restrictions on the power of foreign monarchs. By the time George I assumed the throne in 1714, his powers had been curtailed. Although the prerogatives of government remained vested in the Crown, the king was obliged to appoint ministers who could manage parliament and it was the king's ministers who directed the administration. And because of the emergence of party divisions, party leaders were able to use more effectively the power of parliament to control the Crown's exercise of its prerogatives. Having German kings accelerated this process. George I did not withdraw from Cabinet meetings, as legend has it, because of his inability to speak English: the king withdrew because he recognized that he lacked authority. The circumstances in which he obtained the crown became an important factor in the shift in the focus of governmental authority.

The British Isles. There is a final factor to consider in noting 'foreign' influences. As the most powerful and populous nation on the islands, the English had long sought to dominate for the purpose of maintaining the security of their state. Wales was absorbed into the English state by conquest, a process that was completed by the Statute of Wales, 1535. But throughout modern history, the Scots and Irish have used, and have been used by, other European powers as part of an island struggle. Ireland has been the target of English internal colonization throughout much of the course of development of modern history, a process that became exacerbated as a result of religious differences.[23] With respect to the Scots, there was a union of the crowns in 1603 (James VI of Scotland becoming James I of England), and although there were discussions during the seventeenth century, Scotland joined with England only by the Treaty of Union of 1707 to create the United Kingdom of Great Britain.

---

[22] John Locke's *Two Treatises of Government* (Awnsham Churchill, London, 1690) (but written in 1680) can be read, for example, as a vindication of the principles of the ancient constitution, albeit in a more theoretical and rationalistic (rather than traditional legal-historical) form.

[23] Union eventually was imposed in 1800: see *Ireland*, Section C.2.f.

3. Major Debating Points

The basic character of the British constitution was settled during the eighteenth century. This was the century in which the practices of parliamentary government evolved, and the basic concepts of parliamentary sovereignty and the rule of law were formulated. Once settled, the outstanding issue to have a major impact on these governing arrangements was the question of the franchise: this was addressed only during the nineteenth century.

a) Parliamentary Government

The Act of Settlement not only settled the succession, but also established the principle of judicial independence and prohibited placemen from sitting in the Commons. It therefore went a considerable way towards prescribing in law a constitutional framework governed by the principle of the separation of legislative, executive, and judicial functions. However, although the exclusion of those holding an office of the Crown ensured that the Crown could not corrupt parliament, it was quickly recognized to be contrary to the traditions of English government. The provision was therefore repealed in 1706. This was done because parliament had found a more informal means of ensuring ministerial responsibility to parliament for the conduct of government. During the early eighteenth century, then, a battle arose between the Crown's use of patronage to seduce leaders from their parliamentary parties, and the parties' use of parliament to acquire control over this power of patronage. In this struggle, parliamentary censure of ministers replaced parliamentary impeachment, and political accountability replaced legal responsibility. From this struggle, the conventions of individual ministerial responsibility to parliament for the conduct of affairs of his department and, underpinned by the practice of Cabinet government, that of collective responsibility of the entire ministry itself to parliament were forged. Thereafter, the traditional notion of balanced government—consisting in a balance between monarchy, aristocracy, and commons—was replaced by a balance between the political parties for the purpose of ensuring that government was kept within certain boundaries.

b) Parliamentary Sovereignty

In the modern period, legislation came to supplant the common law as the primary source of law. Rather than being viewed as a reflection of the customary ways of a people, law came increasingly to be treated as the product of human will and parliament was established as the critical law-making agency. The seventeenth century constitutional language that made appeals to the 'fundamental laws of the realm' a reference to the traditional ways of operating[24] gave way during the eighteenth century to the idea that no legal limitation could be placed on the power of the Crown in parliament to legislate. The Crown in Parliament thus came to wield a sovereignty that legally and constitutionally was recognized to be absolute. In 1765, Sir William Blackstone gave an exhaustively comprehensive account of this sovereign power of the King in parliament, which 'hath sovereign and uncontrollable authority in making, confirming, enlarging, restraining, abrogating, repealing, reviving, and expounding of laws', this being 'the place where that absolute despotic power, which must in all governments reside somewhere, is entrusted by the constitution of these kingdoms.' This sovereign power, Blackstone continued, 'can change and create afresh even the constitution of the kingdom and of parliaments themselves.'[25]

---

[24] John W Gough, *Fundamental Law in English Constitutional History* (Clarendon Press, Oxford, 1955).
[25] William Blackstone, *Commentaries on the Laws of England Book 1* (Clarendon Press, Oxford, 1765) 156.

c) The Rule of Law and Civil Liberty

Because of the ideological sway of the sovereignty principle, law in the British system has commonly been regarded as a species of command. Since law was therefore assumed generally to impose constraints, the liberal conviction grew up that the less law there is, the freer we are likely to be. This conviction lies at the root of the British tradition of civil liberty, in which an appeal is made to our ancient liberties to protect us from the rigours of the law. The price of liberty is eternal vigilance, and civil liberty is preserved primarily through the maintenance of a vibrant political discourse. But the fulcrum of these arrangements is parliament, and this receives institutionalized recognition in the retention of extensive parliamentary privileges.[26] The judiciary performs two main roles in protecting these constitutional values and these are often not in harmony. First, they ensure that the Crown is unable to make broad prerogative claims; we see this in the landmark case of *Entick v Carrington* (1795) 19 St. Tr. 1030, in which the judges rejected the argument that the minister's warrant was sufficient to authorize the search of premises and seizure of papers. Rebuffing the argument of state necessity, the court claimed that, 'the common law does not understand that kind of reasoning'. 'If it is law', the judges maintained, 'it will be found in our books. If it is not found there, it is not law.' In this mode, the judiciary are conceived as the precision instruments for implementing the will of parliament. But this did not entirely supplant their more ancient role of acting as the guardians of the common law. In this latter role, the judiciary—drawing on the myth of the ancient constitution—presented the common law not as the expression of the governing will, but as the law of a free people. This is the image of the common law as an ideal constitution 'comprising those fundamental rules of Common Law which seem essential to the liberties of the subject and the proper government of the country', which rules 'cannot be repealed but by direct and unequivocal enactment' and 'in the absence of express words or necessary intendment, statutes will be applied subject to them'.[27] The tensions between these roles of the judiciary as the implementers of sovereign will (expressed in Acts of Parliament) and of guardians of traditional constitutional values (expressed in the common law) was to resurface in the latter half of the twentieth century.

d) Extension of the Franchise

The late-eighteenth century reaction in Britain to the French revolution put back the cause of reform for almost half a century. The breakthrough eventually came with the Reform Act 1832, which had the effect of reducing the power of the aristocracy in the Commons and enabled the Whigs to maintain their influence in government for much of the following fifty years. In giving just over 5 per cent of the population the franchise, the 1832 Act was scarcely a democratic measure. It marked a great turning point precisely because, being a compromise measure, which was devoid of principle, it paved the way for the gradual democratization of the Commons. This was achieved in stages over the following one hundred years. With the establishment of universal adult suffrage, we see also the institutionalization of disciplined political parties charged with the task of representing the interests of sections of the population in the arrangements of government.

---

[26] These parliamentary privileges include freedom of speech, freedom from arrest, ability of the House to regulate its own proceedings and the right to punish for breach of these privileges or for contempt of parliament, see Stanley de Smith and Rodney Brazier, *Constitutional and Administrative Law* (8th edn, Penguin, London, 1998) chapter 16.

[27] David L Keir and F H Lawson, *Cases in Constitutional Law* (OUP, Oxford, 1928) 3.

4. Defining Moments

Care needs to be taken in highlighting certain 'defining moments', since doing so might convey a false impression about the evolutionary nature of these constitutional arrangements. Some of the more important statutes to the end of the nineteenth century might nevertheless be noted.

a) Habeas Corpus Act 1679

The writ of habeas corpus acquired its fame mainly because of its role in the constitutional struggles of the seventeenth century. It existed to ensure the protection of the value expressed in the Petition of Right 1628 that 'no freeman may be taken or imprisoned ... but by the lawful judgment of his peers or by the law of the land' (s 3). But the practice of the king ordering detentions without legal authorization (i.e. 'by the special command of the king') was abolished only after the Habeas Corpus Act of 1640. Even then, it was replaced by legislation giving the king extensive powers of detention, and it was only after the 1679 Act that the modern law was framed. During the eighteenth century the writ was discussed in elevated tones, Bolingbroke referring to 'that noble badge of liberty, which every subject of Britain wears, and by which he is distinguished so eminently, not from the slaves alone, but even from the freeman of other countries'.[28] Habeas corpus provided the basis for judicial protection against executive arrest, detention, and imprisonment and in the nineteenth century. Dicey felt able to assert that, 'the securities for personal freedom are in England as complete as the laws can make them'. The Habeas Corpus Acts, he declaimed, 'declare no principle and define no rights, but they are for practical purposes worth a hundred constitutional articles guaranteeing individual liberty'.[29]

b) Act of Settlement, 1701

As has been seen, the Act of Settlement sets out a Protestant line of succession to the throne and establishes the principle of judicial independence. But, as noted, it also included provisions that could have resulted in a more formalized separation of legislative and executive membership, and therefore have prevented the emergence of the modern system of parliamentary government. These provisions were, however, repealed a few years later.

c) Acts of Union 1707, 1801

In 1707, the union of the English and Scottish crowns that occurred in 1603 was extended by the construction of a unitary state of Great Britain, based on the establishment of a common legislative, executive, fiscal—though not judicial—framework. Although some recent Scottish jurists have argued that the Treaty of Union should be seen as providing a form of modern constitutional settlement,[30] it seems 'idle to deny that Scotland was swallowed up in an Anglo-centric Britain, instead of England being absorbed into a polycentric one' and, more generally, that 'a large part of medieval and modern "British" history can be seen as a process of conquest and forcible Anglicization'.[31] Union with Ireland in 1801, it

---

[28] Henry St John, Viscount Bolingbroke, 'A Dissertation upon Parties' in Henry Bolingbroke, *Political Writings* (CUP, Cambridge, 1997) 107–108.

[29] Albert V Dicey, *Introduction to the Study of the Law of the Constitution* (8th edn, Macmillan, London, 1915) 195; see as well, Paul D Halliday, *Habeas Corpus: From England to Empire* (Belknap Press, Cambridge, MA, 2010).

[30] Thomas B Smith, 'The Union of 1707 as fundamental law' (1957) 2 Public Law 99; Neil MacCormick, 'Does the United Kingdom have a constitution?' (1978) 29 Northern Ireland Legal Quarterly 1; Michael Upton, 'Marriage vows of the elephant: The Constitution of 1707' (1989) 105 Law Quarterly Review 79–103.

[31] Gerald Aylmer, 'The peculiarities of the English State' (1990) 3 Journal of Historical Sociology 91, 94.

would appear, was the final stage in a process of institutionalizing the principle of parliamentary sovereignty during the eighteenth century. In the words of JCD Clark, 'Whig regimes after 1688 progressively destroyed adjacent assemblies in the name of unified authority: the Edinburgh Parliament with the Union of 1707; Convocation, the Church of England's representative assembly, in 1717; the Dublin Parliament in the Union of 1801.'[32]

d) Reform Acts 1832, 1867

Although an admirer of the ability of the way in which the English constitution had made adjustments to reconcile order and liberty, in 1831 Hegel argued that British constitutional development had become stultified. The reason was because of the relative weakness of the monarchical element in the eighteenth-century constitution, and consequent hegemony of the privileged landed class who dominated parliament. The governing class, he contended, was displaying an indifference to the propertyless workers and this threatened the unity and stability of the state.[33] The Reform Act of 1832 thus marked the beginning of modern electoral reform. The 1832 Act itself was modest in its aims, and the Representation of the People Act 1867, in doubling the electorate, was much more radical. Significantly, the latter Act was introduced by the Tories in the belief that they could still win elections on an expanded franchise. This strategy was later consolidated by the creation of Tory working class voters maintaining a loyalty to the Crown, and which became a decisive factor in twentieth-century elections.[34] After 1867, there followed a struggle to establish universal suffrage, marked by significant reforms in 1884, 1918, and the eventual realization of that goal in 1928.

e) Municipal Corporations Act 1835

The 1832 Reform Act led directly to the reform of local government. A system of modern local government was thus created following the reform of the municipal corporations in the 1835 Act. This imposed a uniform constitution on the municipal corporations, most of which had lost their sense of public purpose. The reform process was later extended to the rural areas of England by the Local Government Act 1888, which created elected county councils to undertake local government functions previously exercised by justices of the peace.[35] Modernization was required to ensure that local authorities were able to respond to the public challenges presented by rapid industrialization and urbanization. These reforms were achieved incrementally, and it was only in the Local Government Act 1933 that it became possible to lay down in legislation a common set of organizational rules governing all local authorities.

f) Northcote–Trevelyan Reforms

In his 1831 essay, Hegel had suggested that a second factor undermining the unity of the British constitution was the lack of a class of professional administrators who were trained to act in the public interest and maintained at public expense.[36] This reform took a little longer in coming. The foundation of the modern civil service originates in the proposals of

---

[32] Jonathan CD Clark, *The Language of Liberty 1660–1832* (CUP, Cambridge, 1993) 8.
[33] Georg WF Hegel, 'On the English Reform Bill' (1831), in Laurence Dickey and Hugh B Nisbet (eds) *Political Writings* (CUP, New York, 1999) 234.
[34] Iain McLean, *Rational Choice and British Politics: An Analysis of Rhetoric and Manipulation from Peel to Blair* (OUP, Oxford, 2001) chapter 3, 58–88.
[35] Josef Redlich and Francis W Hirst, *Local Government in England* (n 3).
[36] Georg Hegel, 'On the English Reform Bill' (n 33).

the Northcote–Trevelyan report of 1854.[37] The report sought to eliminate the link between patronage and the exercise of administrative power by promoting the formation of a non-political administrative class educated in liberal values and assessed for administrative competence through open, competitive examination. Insofar as the extension of governmental capacity rested on a competent bureaucracy, then its roots lie in the reforms that were introduced following this report.[38]

5. Influential Texts

The status of texts. It has often been noted that 'the characteristic virtue of Englishmen is their power of sustained practical activity, and their characteristic vice a reluctance to test the quality of that activity by reference to principles.'[39] These traits—often the motivation for self-congratulation—offer an indication of the apparent unwillingness of the English clearly to explain their basic principles of constitutional government. As a consequence, we often find that, notwithstanding errors and idiosyncrasies, the works of foreign scholars curious about the nature of British governmental arrangements have been able to offer clearer insight into basic principles than native writers. In the eighteenth century, Montesquieu's work proved to be highly influential, and in the nineteenth/early twentieth century the works of von Gneist, Boutmy, Redlich, and Halevy exhibit greater effort to understand the motivational springs of British government than most of the laudatory and self-congratulatory British works.[40] The general difficulty is that British government operates mainly through procedure and precedent rather than principle.

Blackstone's Commentaries. The most influential of the eighteenth-century English texts that elaborated the basic precepts of British constitutional law was Blackstone's *Commentaries on the Laws of England*.[41] Blackstone is an institutional work: written in the vernacular and influenced in organization by Justinian's *Institutes*, this type of work seeks to explain an entire system of law as a system of national law. The genre is associated with the introduction into the European universities of the teaching of national—as distinct from canon and civil—law,[42] and this movement has obvious connections to a more general ideology of nationalism. Given the 'common accusations that the civilians and civil law supported royal absolutism', the movement bolstered 'the representation of the common law as national law, protecting the liberties of English men and women'.[43] Blackstone argued that the common law was uniquely English, that it formed a system of national law,[44] and that the common law was superior to all other systems of law. At the heart of Blackstone's scheme was a principle of parliamentary sovereignty that was unitary, absolute and based on divine authority. JCD Clark notes that, 'Where the early-eighteenth century Whigs had employed a false rhetoric

---

[37] For the report see The Fulton Committee, *The Civil Service* (Report of the Committee, Cmnd 3638, 1963), vol 1, Appx B.

[38] See Peter Hennessy, *Whitehall* (Fontana, London, 1989), chapter 1.

[39] Richard H Tawney, *The Acquisitive Society* (G Bell, London, 1921) 1.

[40] See above, n 19 and n 3 respectively.

[41] William Blackstone, 'Commentaries on the Laws of England' (Clarendon Press, Oxford, 1765–1769) Books 1–4.

[42] In 1758 Blackstone became the first holder of the Vinerian Chair of English Law at Oxford University.

[43] John W Cairns, 'Blackstone, an English institutionalist: Legal literature and the rise of the nation state' (1984) 4 Oxford Journal of Legal Studies 318, 332.

[44] Note that English law did not exist at that time as a unified system, since differences existed between common law, equity, and admiralty.

to claim checks and balances as the characteristics of the Constitution, Blackstone candidly emphasized sovereignty, the unity of King, Lords and Commons in Parliament.[45] Law was command rather than custom, and Blackstone presented a Hobbesian account of law as an orderly arrangement underpinned by a constitution founded on an Anglican conception of sovereign power whose enemy was Dissent.[46]

Whig constitutional history. Blackstone had written to educate 'the guardians of the English constitution; the makers, repealers and interpreters of the English laws'.[47] But although the *Commentaries* were influential amongst lawyers, it was not the dominant approach to the study of the constitution. That mantle was assumed by the Whig constitutional historians: Stubbs, Freeman, Macaulay, and Hallam. These writers conceived the English constitution as forming an elaborate cultural heritage, the historical study of which provided a boundless source of prescriptive wisdom and told a 'story of the triumph of constitutional liberty and representative institutions'.[48] The historians regarded the lawyer's interpretation of the constitution with some distaste, arguing that 'our constitutional history has been perverted at the hands of lawyers'.[49] The legal mind, they contended, seemed unable to grasp ambiguity, uncertainty, and heterogeneity, and was thus incapable of sensitive historical understanding. These failings, together with the fact that 'the natural tendency of the legal mind is to conservatism and deference to authority',[50] rendered the lawyer's account of the constitution deficient. This was nowhere more evident than in relation to the apparently foundational concept of sovereignty. '[T]he whole ideal conception of the Sovereign', wrote Freeman, 'is a purely lawyer's conception and rests upon no ground whatever in the records of our early history'.[51]

Dicey's Law of the Constitution. During the latter half of the nineteenth century, however, the lawyer's view assumed a higher degree of authority. This was mainly the result of the work of AV Dicey. Bentham had sought to remove the Anglicanism and natural law ethos from Blackstone's account of sovereignty,[52] and the fruits of his efforts were seen in Austin's more austere account of sovereignty.[53] Building on this type of legal positivism, Dicey tried to rescue the constitution from the historians' grasp and to lay bare the legal fundamentals of the constitution.[54] In his highly influential text on the law of the constitution, Dicey cut through the ambiguities, nuances and absurdities of the constitution to present an account of the legal fundamentals of the constitution which was both elegant and simple. The foundational legal principle of the constitution is that of parliamentary sovereignty. But this must be interpreted in conjunction with the central importance of the rule of law and the ways in which those two basic principles are rendered harmonious in the working practices of the British constitution is through the operation of certain precepts of political morality that Dicey called 'constitutional conventions'.[55] Dicey, a successor of Blackstone in the Vinerian

---

[45] Jonathan Clark, *The Language of Liberty* (n 32) 83.
[46] Ibid, 83–84.
[47] William Blackstone, *Commentaries on the Laws of England* (n 25) 9.
[48] John W Burrow, *A Liberal Descent: Victorian Historians and the English Past* (CUP, Cambridge, 1981) 3. See also PBM Blaas, *Continuity and Anachronism: Parliamentary and Constitutional Development in Whig Historiography and in the Anti-Whig Reaction between 1890 and 1930* (Martinus Nijhoff, The Hague, 1978) chapter 2, 72–195.
[49] Edward A Freeman, *The Growth of the English Constitution* (n 21) x.
[50] Ibid, 128.
[51] Ibid, 128–129.
[52] Jeremy Bentham, *An Introduction to the Principles of Morals and Legislation* (T Payne & Son, London, 1789).
[53] John Austin, *Lectures on Jurisprudence* (John Murray, London, 1885).
[54] Albert V Dicey, *Introduction to the Study of the Law of the Constitution* (Macmillan, London, 1885).
[55] Ibid.

Chair, became the first law professor to apply the juridical method to the study of the British constitution.

Bagehot's English Constitution. If Dicey founded the scholarly discipline of constitutional law, then Bagehot—although in certain respects the last of the Whigs—provided the foundations of a political science of British government.[56] His work on *The English Constitution* (1867) was written for the purpose of rescuing the constitution from the hands of constitutional lawyers. Its main objective was to challenge two erroneous interpretations of the British constitution: the separation of powers, and the idea that British government operated through some balance between monarchy, aristocracy, and commons. Bagehot argued that it was necessary to distinguish between 'dignified' and 'efficient' versions of the constitution. The dignified parts are the ancient, complex and ceremonial aspects, 'which excite and preserve the reverence of the population' and thereby 'attract its motive power'.[57] The efficient parts are modern, simple and functional; these are the aspects which deploy that power and authority, the parts 'by which it, in fact, works and rules'.[58] Bagehot suggested that, even though it was the professional politicians who operate the 'efficient' machinery of government, 'the use of the Queen, in a dignified capacity, is incalculable'.[59] In effect, the dignity of the Queen masked the real workings of government which, rather than being based on a separation of powers, was characterized by 'the close union, the nearly complete fusion of the executive and legislative powers'.[60] This, he claimed, was the 'efficient secret of the English constitution' and its fulcrum was the institution of the Cabinet, 'a committee of the legislative body selected to be the executive body'.[61] Thus, while the Queen is head of the dignified part of the constitution, the Prime Minister is at the head of the efficient part. The Crown may be the fountain of honour, but the Treasury is 'the spring of business.'[62]

Textual interpretation. Bagehot's framework reveals how aristocratic government— government by elites—is perpetuated in an era of democracy. The dignified elements, 'august with the Gothic grandeur of a more imposing age', are able to exercise their 'imaginative attraction upon an uncultured and rude population',[63] while preserving the club practices of parliamentary government. The British state maintains the trappings of a monarchy but is, in reality, a 'disguised republic'.[64] And crucial to this achievement was the formation in the eighteenth century of political parties within a parliamentary structure of government and opposition and underpinned by a common loyalty to the state.[65] Bagehot's work warns against any attempt to offer an account of the British constitution that seeks to separate law from practice.

---

[56] Stefan Collini, Donald Winch, and John W Burrow, *That Noble Science of Politics: A Study in Nineteenth-Century Intellectual History* (CUP, Cambridge, 1983) chapter 5, 161–182.

[57] Walter Bagehot, *The English Constitution* (first printed 1867, OUP, Oxford, 2001) 7.

[58] Ibid, 7.

[59] Ibid, 38.

[60] Ibid, 11.

[61] Ibid, 11.

[62] Ibid, 11–12.

[63] Ibid, 11.

[64] Ibid, 48.

[65] Ibid, 16: 'It has been said that England invented the phrase 'Her Majesty's Opposition', that it was the first government which made a criticism of administration as much a part of the polity as administration itself.'

C. The Evolution of the Constitution

1. The Evolving Constitution

Dignified and efficient elements. For the purpose of explaining the British constitution, Bagehot deployed a method that exploited the tensions between ideal and actuality—between thought and action. This method, involving the utilization of paradox, came to be widely embraced by twentieth century British commentators, causing irritation among certain foreign scholars.[66] After all, an explanation of the British constitution that is required to fall back on tensions between 'dignified' and 'efficient'—between the traditional and the rational—and through which the paradox of stability (of outward forms) and change (in real workings) is to be expressed, does not make for easy scientific analysis. This problem is compounded when one attempts a legal account since many of the positive constitutional laws belong to the dignified sphere, with the real workings being shrouded from legal view by changing political practices. Further, this dynamic between the dignified and efficient workings of the constitution altered during the twentieth century and caused many in the latter decades to present a case for fundamental constitutional reform. In this Part, developments affecting the 'working constitution' during the twentieth century will be outlined, leaving a more basic legal analysis to Part D.

a) Basic Principles

The centrality of the dynamic between dignity and efficiency is thrown into relief by noting that the two key constitutional principles identified by Dicey—parliamentary sovereignty and the rule of law—do not sit harmoniously with one another. How then are they to be reconciled? Bagehot had argued, rather provocatively, that 'the most essential mental quality of a free people' is 'stupidity'.[67] What he called stupidity, however, is in reality 'steadiness of conduct and consistency of opinion'.[68] This explains how Dicey's formal principles could be reconciled. To the extent that they are reconciled in practice, the work is undertaken by evolving customs, practices, and understandings about how government ought to be conducted. An appreciation of the nature of these practices—what Dicey called constitutional conventions—is central to an understanding of constitutional development in the twentieth century.

b) The Role of Conventions

Constitutional conventions evolve to adjust the formal allocation of governmental powers to reflect the realities of the evolving constitution. The British system possesses no clear legal concept of the state; the nearest equivalent being that of the Crown, which serves both as a symbol of governmental authority and of the power and majesty of the nation. The prerogatives of the Crown are extensive. In purely formal terms, for example, it is the King's fiat that makes laws, it is his sentence which condemns, and it is his judgments which determine the rights and liabilities of her subjects. The King, as head of the executive, appoints his ministers, who are servants of the King and do not stand in any legal relation to parliament.

---

[66] See Giovanni Sartori, 'Constitutionalism: A preliminary discussion' (1962) 56 Amer. Pol. Sci. Rev. 823, 854.

[67] Walter Bagehot, 'French coup d'état', in F Morgan (ed), *Collected Works* (Routledge, London, 1995) 50–51. Bagehot argued that the French do not possess this quality: 'nations ... may be too clever to be practical, and not dull enough to be free' 53.

[68] Ibid, 52.

Further, this parliament, which assembles in the royal palace at Westminster, is summoned, prorogued, and dissolved by the King. Justice is said to emanate from His Majesty. All jurisdiction is exercised in his name and all judges derive their authority from his commission. Every breach of the peace is a transgression against the King. He alone has the authority to prosecute criminals; when sentence is passed, he alone can remit the punishment. And as the fountain of honour, the King maintains the power of dispensing honours and dignities. Each of these formal attributes of the King's public powers is now strictly regulated by convention.

c) Conventional Understandings

The King may remain the keystone of the constitutional architecture but in the exercise of his prerogative powers he is advised, directed, and controlled by others. The King may be the source of justice but at least since the reign of Henry III (1216–1272), the monarch has not been able to disturb the fountain or divert the stream from its proper channel except through the agency of his judges.[69] Legislation may formally require the royal assent but not since the reign of Queen Anne (1702–1714) has a monarch sought to exercise that power. The King may appoint ministers, but conventions dictate that the leader of the political party best able to command the confidence of the House of Commons must be invited to form a ministry and that the King must be advised by that person—the Prime Minister—in the appointment of ministers. Similarly, the King is obliged to follow advice from the Prime Minister in the exercise of such prerogative powers as proroguing or dissolving parliament and conferring honours.[70] These conventions remain 'vague and slippery' and 'cannot be understood "with the politics left out"'.[71] But their general objective is clear: it is to accommodate the ancient governmental powers to the political requirements of representative and responsible government. As Lord Browne-Wilkinson expressed the situation, 'The constitutional history of this country is the history of the prerogative powers of the Crown being made subject to the overriding powers of the democratically elected legislature as the sovereign body.'[72]

d) Representative Government

The conventions of representative government operate to transfer decision-making power from the monarch to representative ministers. This is why convention requires the monarch to call the leader of the party most likely to command the support of the House of Commons to form a ministry. And by convention, the other members of the ministry are appointed (and dismissed) by His Majesty solely on the recommendation of the Prime Minister (an office more or less unknown to law).[73] The prerogative powers of government are by convention

---

[69] For the most celebrated formulation see Sir Edward Coke, *Twelfth reports, prohibitions del Roy* (1607) 12 Co Rep 63.

[70] See Geoffrey Marshall, *Constitutional Conventions: The Rules and Forms of Political Accountability* (Clarendon Press, Oxford, 1984). This advice is, however, subject to judicial review. In *R (Miller) v Prime Minister/R(Cherry) v Advocate General* [2019] UKSC 41, the Prime Minister's advice to prorogue parliament was found to infringe the principles of parliamentary sovereignty and parliamentary accountability without reasonable justification. The advice was ruled unlawful, and the prorogation quashed.

[71] Godfrey HL LeMay, *The Victorian Constitution* (St Martin's Press, New York, 1979) 21.

[72] *R v Secretary of State for the Home Department, ex parte Fire Brigades Union* [1995] 2 WLR 464, 474.

[73] Sidney Low, *The Governance of England* (revised edn, Fisher Unwin, London, 1904) xx–xi notes that since a royal proclamation of 2 December 1905 gave precedence to 'Our Prime Minister' after the two Archbishops (of Canterbury and York), 'the Prime Minister is no longer officially "unknown to the constitution" or known only as a privy councillor placed at the Head of the Treasury or some other department of State. ... [H]e has a titular dignity which raises him above his colleagues, and above all non-royal personages except the two great ecclesiastics and the quasi-ecclesiastical Lord Chancellor.'

exercised entirely by ministers whose authority is exercised through a representative office and who owe this authority ultimately to their party's success in the electoral poll.

e) Cabinet Government

At the centre of these representative arrangements sits Cabinet government. The Cabinet, an institution not known to law,[74] emerged as the most powerful committee of the leading ministers. As Jennings expressed it, 'The Cabinet is the core of the British constitutional system. It is the supreme directing authority. It integrates what would otherwise be a heterogeneous collection of authorities exercising a vast variety of functions. It provides unity to the British system of government.'[75] The Cabinet is the institution where unity is forged from potential diversity of policies of the main government departments. It operates on the principle of Cabinet solidarity, which is underpinned by the convention of collective responsibility. This convention has three main dimensions: *confidence*, which requires a government to resign or advise dissolution of parliament if it loses the confidence of the House of Commons; *unanimity*, requiring all members of the government to speak with one voice in support of government policy; and *confidentiality*, which ensures that the business of government in conducted in strict confidence.[76]

f) Responsible Government

By convention, ministers must be members of one or other of the Houses of Parliament and are obliged to assume responsibility to parliament for government decision-making, with the role of officials being solely to advise ministers and to implement their decisions. This leads to a simple, linear conception of accountability: agencies and officials are accountable to ministers who in turn account to parliament. This accountability trail has also shaped executive form. In the Victorian era, the practice was adopted of having all governmental tasks either directly undertaken or closely supervised by a central Department of State headed by a minister who sat in parliament.[77] The policy of allocating governmental powers to independent boards and agencies was thus reversed, in favour of centralized departments. Aneurin Bevan explained the linkage between form and accountability: 'It is not proper that a Member of Parliament should be expected to defer to a non-elected person. The minister, by divesting himself of parliamentary responsibilities, disenfranchises the House of Commons; and that means he disenfranchises the electorate as well.'[78] These conventions ensure the functioning of the system of parliamentary government.

g) Club Government

In order for this intricate set of conventions, customs, understandings, and practices to operate harmoniously, it was essential that that their spirit would be shared amongst members of the governing class. This is what Gladstone, one of the great Victorian Prime Ministers, meant when he claimed that, 'the public schools of England are part of the constitution.'[79] These arrangements led to the formation of a regime that Bagehot labelled club government: 'Nobody will understand Parliament[ary] government who fancies it an easy thing, a

---

[74] But see *Attorney-General v Jonathon Cape* [1976] QB 752 (on the basis of the convention of collective responsibility, the court ruled that there was a relationship of confidence amongst members of the Cabinet).

[75] Ivor Jennings, *Cabinet Government* (CUP, Cambridge, 1969) 1.

[76] See Geoffrey Marshall, *Constitutional Conventions* (n 70).

[77] William C Lubenow, *The Politics of Government Growth* (David and Charles, Newton Abbot, 1971).

[78] Aneurin Bevan, *In Place of Fear* (Heinemann, London, 1952) 127.

[79] Cited in Colin Turpin, *British Government and the Constitution* (Weidenfeld and Nicolson, London, 1985) 16.

natural thing, a thing not needing explanation. You have not a perception of the first elements of this matter till you know that government by a *club* is a standing wonder.'[80] Elaborating on this theme, David Marquand has argued that the atmosphere was one in which office-holders 'trusted each other to observe the spirit of the club rules' and 'the notion that the principles underlying the rules should be clearly defined and publicly proclaimed was profoundly alien'.[81] Club government is based on a habitual distrust of abstract principle and a high degree of cohesion within the governing class; having all been educated in a common tradition of rule, there was no need formally to specify these rules of conduct. The practice of club government bolsters the convictions underpinning parliamentarism: that governing is a practical art rooted in tacit knowledge and is best conducted through relatively closed, informal and private arrangements.

h) The Parliamentary Function

Bagehot identified five main functions of the House of Commons. The first, and most important (though one often overlooked), is to act as an electoral chamber: 'it is the assembly which chooses our president [i.e. the prime minister]'. The second is the expressive function, of 'express[ing] the mind of the English people on all matters which come before it'. The third is its teaching function: this 'great and open council' must inevitably alter society, he argues, and 'ought to alter it for the better'. It must 'teach the nation what it does not know'. Fourthly, it has an informing function, of laying before the Crown the grievances and complaints of sections of society. And finally, there is the function of legislation.[82] In mentioning legislation—which many might regard as being the most important—last, Bagehot was making a point. In an efficient sense, parliament does not play a major role in the making of legislation. The responsibility for proposing and drafting the great bulk of legislation rests the government which, because of its parliamentary majority, is generally able to ensure its enactment into law. This practice reflects a deeply held conviction that a committee is not the best law-making vehicle,[83] and during the twentieth century this message was reinforced by the growth of party discipline. The practice of government-sponsored legislation has prevented parliament from becoming the site of pork-barrel or log-rolling politics and the enormous size of the House of Commons (with over 600 members) ensures that Members of Parliament cannot be captured by vested interests.[84] But there is one important function of parliament that Bagehot underplays, and this is their ability to test ministers through debates, questions, and other forms of scrutiny. In this role, parliament is able both to promote standards of ministerial probity and competence and to provide a nursery of ambitious Members of Parliament who themselves aspire to become ministers. It is this function of parliament that underpins the ritualized arrangements of government and opposition through which much of the business of parliament is conducted.[85]

i) Permanent and Neutral Civil Service

The institutionalization of tensions between government and parliament—which had been clearly expressed in the work of John Locke[86]—created a binary separation of power as a

---

[80] Walter Bagehot, *The English Constitution* (n 57) 156.
[81] David Marquand, *The Unprincipled Society* (n 6) 178.
[82] Walter Bagehot, *The English Constitution* (n 57) 100–102.
[83] Walter Bagehot, *The English Constitution* (n 57) 119.
[84] Christopher Foster, *British Government in Crisis* (Hart Publishing, Oxford, 2005) 11–12.
[85] This point—the necessity of maintaining the tensions to prevent the corruption of parliament—was made by Henry Bolingbroke, *A Dissertation on Parties* (R Franklin, London, 1733–1734).
[86] John Locke, *Second Treatise of Government* (Awnsham Churchill, London, 1690) § 159.

distinctive feature of the British system.[87] To the extent that a tripartite system of checks was introduced, this was not achieved by the independent judiciary (whose influence remained 'sporadic and peripheral'[88]) but instead by the emergence of a permanent and impartial civil service. In the British system, ministers are given a vast range of responsibilities for which they must account. Initiating legislation and taking it through its parliamentary stages, policymaking, making decisions on all aspects of their remit, making appointments, handling complaints, managing their departments, and contributing to the formation of collective government policy. With the growth of governmental functions, this would have imposed an impossible burden without the formation of a permanent and neutral civil service that ensured the seamless continuity of governmental business through changes not only in ministries but also in ministers (who on average held their posts for only two or three years). The formation of a career civil service based on competitive examination owes its origins to the Northcote–Trevelyan reforms of 1854 and consolidated in the Haldane report, which highlighted the need for fusion between the politically accountable minister and his alter ego, the independent official charged with the duty to offer advice and guidance and faithfully implement all policy decisions.[89] For this to take place, all meetings and decisions had to take place with officials present, who minuted decisions and maintained the files, thus operating government in accordance with precedents and as an extension of the common law mentality. These precedents in turn generated the standards of probity, consistency and impartiality in the conduct of governmental business.

j) The Waning of Constitutional Understanding

The power of Victorian constitutional convention 'was precisely the result of a belief that it was founded on habits and traditions expressive of the genius of the people which, like the rock of ages, would endure.'[90] However, with the extension of democracy, the entrenchment of party discipline and the growth of the governmental responsibilities, the traditions of club government became strained. During the twentieth century, the emergence of disciplined political parties that were promoting ideological (rationalist) politics has tended to erode the authority of many of these conventional (anti-rationalist) constitutional arrangements. To the extent that the assumptions of the club have been challenged or undermined, there has been a 'waning of constitutional understanding.'[91] Conventions of individual ministerial responsibility have been eroded as a consequence of ministers owing their primary allegiance to party rather than the Constitution, and collective responsibility, which evolved as a method of holding government to account by parliament, has been used by governments commanding majorities to shield ministers from criticism. Some have argued that we now have a system of party government, in which the main restraints on government conduct are forged through party mechanisms, or even a regime of 'elective dictatorship', in which there exist few constitutional limitations on what a majority is able to do.[92] Nevil Johnson argues that, 'the disease manifests itself in the atrophy of any language in which we can talk of constitutional issues, of rules, or of principles of public law' and 'we are left floundering in a

---

[87] John S Mill, *Considerations on Representative Government* (Parker, Son and Bourn, London, 1861) chapter 5, 86–107; Adam Tomkins, *Public Law* (Clarendon Press, Oxford, 2003) chapter 2.

[88] Stanley A de Smith, *Judicial Review of Administrative Action* (3rd edn, Stevens, London, 1973) 3.

[89] Viscount Haldane, *Report of the Committee on the Machinery of Government* (Cd 9230, 1918). The legal doctrine that reflects this constitutional understanding is laid out in *Carltona Ltd v Commissioners of Works* (1942) 2 All ER 560.

[90] Nevil Johnson, *In Search of the Constitution* (n 5) 33.

[91] Nevil Johnson, *In Search of the Constitution* (n 5) chapter 3.

[92] Lord Hailsham, *The Dilemma of Democracy: Diagnosis and Prescription* (Collins, London, 1978) chapter 20.

world of pure pragmatism'.[93] John Griffith expressed it more pithily when he suggested that, being reduced to a collection of habits, 'the constitution is what happens'.[94]

2. Main Controversies

a) Democracy and the Second Chamber

The traditional constitutional balances between monarch, aristocracy, and the people could not easily survive the extension of the franchise. The issue came to a head when the House of Lords—the hereditary chamber—rejected the Liberal government's budget in 1909. The ensuing crisis was eventually resolved by the Parliament Act 1911, which removed the House of Lords' power of veto over legislation. The second chamber's consent to money bills was entirely removed and bills approved by the House of Commons in each parliamentary session but rejected by the Lords under the Act's procedure could receive the royal assent after a delay of around two years. Although the Parliament Act was designed as a temporary measure, pending proposals to establish a new chamber not based on the hereditary principle, reform proposals were not forthcoming until after 1997.[95] These proposals led to the House of Lords Act 1999, which removed the right of hereditary peers to sit in the second chamber and required the hereditary peers to elect from amongst their number ninety-two who sit in the Lords to represent their views. Thereafter, the House of Lords consisted of the ninety-two hereditary peers, over 500 life peers appointed by the Queen on the advice of the Prime Minister (most of whom represent the main political parties, but who until reforms introduced in the Constitutional Reform Act 2005 included twenty Law Lords who sat as the Judicial Committee and acted as the final court of appeal), and up to twenty-six archbishops and bishops of the Church of England. The 1999 Act was to be the first step in a more comprehensive reform of composition that would include a directly elected element, remove hereditary peers entirely, and have other members appointed by an independent statutory Appointments Commission. In 2003 the two Houses debated a number of options and failed to reach a majority on any and subsequent proposals from the Coalition Government of 2010–2015 for a mainly elected second chamber also failed.[96] Since then the issue of further reform of the House has remained in abeyance, which suits government who have little desire to enhance the legitimacy of an institution that can act as a restraint on its power.

b) The Growth of Administrative Law

Dicey had claimed that the rule of law meant 'the equal subjection of the ordinary law of the land administered by the ordinary Law Courts'[97] and this amounted to a rejection of administrative law, understood as a special body of law that might evolve to deal with the extraordinary challenges presented by the growth of the administrative state. This argument, a defence of the methods of the common law, reinforced the practices of club government.

---

[93] Nevil Johnson, *In Search of the Constitution* (n 5) 33.

[94] John AG Griffith, 'Comment' (1963) Public Law 401.

[95] The Parliament Act 1949 had reduced the period of delay over Commons bills to effectively one year, and in the Life Peerages Act 1958, non-hereditary personal peerages were created, thereby facilitating the appointment of senior party figures to the second chamber to assist with the conduct of governmental business in that chamber.

[96] Martin Loughlin and Cal Viney, 'The Coalition and the Constitution', in Anthony Seldon and Mike Finn (eds), *The Coalition Effect, 2010–2015* (CUP, Cambridge, 2015) 71–75.

[97] Albert V Dicey, *Introduction to the Study of the Law of the Constitution* (n 29) 198.

After the First World War, however, the legislature bequeathed extensive powers to the executive, which provoked the Lord Chief Justice, as head of the common law courts, to complain that, by acquiring delegated legislative powers and administrative adjudicative powers, the executive was undermining the principles of the constitution.[98] The government responded by establishing a committee of inquiry, whose report resulted in some modifications to the practices concerning delegated legislative powers.[99] The most influential inquiry concerning administrative adjudication, however, was not established until the mid-1950s, and this report sought to bring administrative tribunals more clearly within the framework of the judicial branch of the state.[100] Commencing in the 1960s, the judiciary began in earnest on the project of integrating this growing body of administrative law within the framework of the common law by developing the principles and procedures of judicial supervision of administrative action. This has resulted in the articulation of more formal principles of judicial review, more streamlined procedures, the establishment of a specialized Administrative Division of the High Court, and—inevitably—the drawing of a conceptual distinction between private law and public law.[101]

c) Ministerial Overload

As government assumed responsibility for the management of the economy and the welfare of its citizens, an administrative state emerged. Big government led to more centralized government, and club government ensured that this would be an informal world of government. But these arrangements did not necessarily lead to more effective government. The gathering sense of dissatisfaction first came to be expressed as a problem of ministerial overload, as the extension of governmental responsibilities highlighted the extent of the gulf between 'doctrinal simplicity' and 'administrative complexity' within the British parliamentary system.[102] Given twentieth-century ministerial workloads, the conviction that ministers could sensibly take all critical decisions seemed implausible. But because of the importance of the conventions of ministerial responsibility (and its corollary of civil servant anonymity), they lived on as myths, casting a veil around a secretive, informal, and private world of governmental decision-making. The first response of successive Conservative administrations since 1979 was to abolish a number of the non-departmental public bodies that had evolved.[103] But this failed to eliminate many bodies and the policy was soon overtaken by a more radical agenda of privatization, including telecommunications (1984), gas supply (1986), electricity generation and supply (1989), water (1991), and the railways (1996). By 1991, privatization had transferred over 50 per cent of the public sector to the private sector.[104] But privatization of these major public services has often resulted simply in the transfer from public to private monopoly and has therefore required the establishment of new regulatory offices to protect the public interest. This in turn has led to a growth in the use of regulation as an instrument of government, a trend that has been strongly reinforced as a result of the extending influence of European Union regulatory measures encompassing such fields as competition policy, consumer protection, environmental protection, and financial services. Since the

[98] Lord Hewart, *The New Despotism* (Ernest Benn, London, 1929).
[99] Donoughmore, *Report of the Committee on Ministers' Powers* (Cmd 4040, 1932).
[100] Franks, *Report of the Committee on Administrative Tribunals and Inquiries* (Cmnd 218, 1957).
[101] The leading text is Stanley A de Smith, Harry Woolf, and Jeffrey Jowell, *Judicial Review of Administrative Action* (5th edn, Sweet & Maxwell, London, 1995).
[102] Nevil Johnson, 'Accountability, control and complexity: moving beyond ministerial responsibility', in Anthony Barker (ed), *Quangos in Britain* (Macmillan, London, 1982) 206, 216.
[103] Leo Pliatsky, *A Review of Non-Departmental Public Bodies* (Cmnd 7797, 1980).
[104] David Marsh, 'Privatisation under Mrs Thatcher' (1991) 69(4) Public Administration 459, 464.

parliamentary system fosters the belief that all regulation in the public interest should be either performed or supervised by a minister answerable to parliament, the British system has avoided the emergence of the independent regulatory commission which in jurisdictions like the United States acquired the status of a fourth branch of government. But it has resulted in an uncertain role for these new regulatory agencies of government.

d) New Public Management

The growing influence of regulatory techniques in government has been further strengthened as a consequence of two general reform movements. The first is a rolling programme for subjecting public sector programmes to market testing and associated with this programme, forms of organizational restructuring that entrench a distinction between purchaser and provider.[105] This has resulted in the recasting of governmental arrangements away from an administrative and towards a managerial ethos. The second is the managerial revolution in the civil service which has resulted from the separation between policy and executive functions of government, and the hiving off of executive tasks to newly formed agencies.[106] With over three-quarters of civil servants now working in agencies, these reforms constitute 'the most far-reaching since the Northcote–Trevelyan reforms in the nineteenth century'.[107] The cumulative impact of these reforms has been such that we are now seeing the emergence of what might be called a 'regulatory state'.[108] The emerging regulatory state raises significant constitutional questions, mainly because its practices run counter to those of club government. Regulation replaces tacit knowledge with explicit rules, closed arrangements with transparency, traditional ways with standardized arrangements, and the reliance on experience (civil service precedents) with adherence to formal codes of conduct. The challenge to traditional British constitutional practice is evident: formalization leads to more precise specification of official roles in governmental decision-making; managerialism leads to the identification of officials who bear executive responsibilities for aspects of decision-making; and ministers no longer carry the same degree of constitutional responsibility for all action taken within the ambit of their portfolios. Parliamentary methods are thus exposed as being of demonstrably limited value as techniques of accountability, and the rule of law tradition has ensured that we do not have the means to think systematically about these accountability issues in juridical terms.[109] The emergence of the regulatory state has therefore not led, as might have been supposed, to juridification—i.e. the predominant use of law as a precise instrument for defining, controlling and evaluating governmental action.[110] Instead of placing a heavy reliance on law, an alternative technique has been used to fill the gap in arrangements for constitutional accountability: the technique of performance auditing.[111]

---

[105] Christopher Foster and Francis Plowden, *The State Under Stress* (Open University Press, Buckingham, 1996) chapters 3–6.

[106] Christopher Foster and Francis Plowden, *The State Under Stress*, chapters 8–10 (n 105).

[107] Treasury and Civil Service Committee, *Civil Service Management: The Next Steps* (HC 1987–1988, 494) § 1.

[108] Christopher Hood and others, *Regulation Inside Government: Waste-Watchers, Quality Police and Sleaze-Busters* (OUP, Oxford, 1999); Michael Moran, *The British Regulatory State: High Modernism and Hyper-Innovation* (OUP, Oxford, 2003).

[109] John DB Mitchell, 'The causes and effects of the absence of a system of public law in the United Kingdom' (1965) 9 Public Law 95.

[110] See Gunther Teubner (ed), *Juridification of Social Spheres* (De Gruyter, Berlin, 1987). The juridification argument is made in Dawn Oliver, *Constitutional Reform in the United Kingdom* (OUP, Oxford, 2003).

[111] See Michael Power, *The Audit Society: Rituals of Verification* (OUP, Oxford, 1997).

e) Local Government

The pivotal importance of parliament in accountability structures has also contributed to the growth in central supervision of local government action. During the nineteenth century, the existence of a robust system of local government formed a central plank in the constitutional arrangements, mainly by linking with parliamentary interests to limit central government supervision of local administration and to ensure that a system of administrative law, with local authorities operating in a subordinate relationship to the centre, could not emerge.[112] During the first half of the twentieth century, this tradition of local government was retained largely because of the emergence of conventional understandings about the conduct of central-governmental relations.

However, although local government grew to the point at which it absorbed around one-quarter of total public expenditure, much of this growth had been financed by central government grants. When severe public expenditure restraints were imposed from the late 1970s onwards, the compact dissolved as ministers acted to forge a hierarchical relationship between central and local government. The conventional understandings about the appropriate roles of the centre and localities disintegrated, and the parties turned to law as the determinant of their authority. Within a centralized system founded on the principle of sovereignty, this inevitably led to the assertion of a hierarchical relationship.[113] After 1997, the Labour government took action to reinvigorate local government, but only within the parameters of centralized strategic controls. By this point, the constitutional status of local government had been all but destroyed.[114] Recently, however, some attempt at reinvigoration of local government has emerged with the election of 'metro Mayors' in six combined authorities across the UK. These combined authorities are groups of councils working together on matters such as transport, housing, planning, skills and economic development.

f) Ireland

Although Ireland had been formally united with Britain only by the Act of Union of 1801, throughout the nineteenth century there had been struggles—rooted in ethnic and religious divisions—for Irish home rule. Legislation providing for this had been passed in 1914—under the Parliament Act provisions—but was suspended during the war and after the Easter rising in Dublin in 1916 was defeated the pressure for independence increased. This prospect caused a strong reaction by the Protestant Unionist minority, mainly located in six counties of Ulster, and the British proposed an accommodation: home rule was to be provided with separate parliaments for Ireland (in Dublin) and Ulster (in Belfast).[115] But civil war broke out in southern Ireland over home rule or independence, and in 1925 a parliament with devolved powers of home rule from Westminster was established for Northern Ireland, with the rest of Ireland acquiring independence.

g) Northern Ireland

As with other settlements in the context of decolonization, the Northern Ireland parliament was intended to replicate the practices of the Westminster parliament. This failed: despite statutory prohibitions on discrimination, the Unionist governments—against

---

[112] Josef Redlich and Francis W Hirst, *Local Government in England* (n 3).

[113] See Martin Loughlin, *Legality and Locality: The Role of Law in Central-Local Government Relations* (Clarendon Press, Oxford, 1996).

[114] Martin Loughlin, 'The Demise of Local Government', in Vernon Bogdanor (ed), *The British Constitution in the Twentieth Century* (OUP, Oxford, 2004) chapter 13.

[115] Government of Ireland Act 1920.

the background of a difficult security situation making extensive use of emergency powers—ran the province to the benefit of the Protestant majority. When the Catholic minority grievances emerged in the 1960s in the form of civil rights campaigns, tensions became heightened, the British government (and army) became increasingly involved in the domestic affairs of the province, and in 1972 the Northern Ireland parliament was suspended and responsibility for governing the province transferred to London.[116] This remained the case for most of the following period until, after intense discussions involving also the representatives of the Irish government, the Northern Ireland Act 1998 restored devolved government under elaborate power-sharing arrangements between unionist and nationalist parties. These arrangements, however, have not always worked smoothly; they were, for example, suspended from October 2002 to May 2007 and from January 2017 to January 2020 because of disputes between the power-sharing parties.

h) Devolution

The United Kingdom is a multi-national state, and this has been reflected in its territorial governing arrangements. Schemes for administrative devolution of governmental functions have existed in relation to Scotland and Wales, and schemes for devolution of legislative and executive powers of government (respectively) were promoted by the Labour government in the 1970s, but not implemented. After four successive terms of Conservative administration—implementing policies in Scotland and Wales which had not been voted for by their majority populations—there was considerable support for the reconsideration of these arrangements on the election of a Labour government in 1997. In the Scotland Act 1998, an initial scheme of devolved legislative powers was enacted through the establishment of a Scottish parliament in Edinburgh.[117] In the Government of Wales Act 1998 a scheme of devolved executive powers was enacted through the establishment of a National Assembly for Wales in Cardiff.[118] Within these arrangements, it had been explicitly enacted that the existence of legislative powers within defined spheres of competence does not affect the sovereignty of the United Kingdom parliament.[119] Under the 2010 Coalition government, these spheres of competence were further extended. After a positive vote in a referendum, in 2011 the powers of the Welsh Assembly were expanded.[120]

The Scotland Act 2012 conferred greater fiscal powers upon the Scottish parliament, which came into effect in 2016. Meanwhile, in the election of 5 May 2011, the Scottish National Party was returned with an overall majority for the first time in the Scottish parliament's short history. This provided a mandate for a referendum on Scottish independence which was agreed by the Westminster parliament. The 2014 independence referendum, on a turnout of around 85 per cent, yielded a majority vote against independence (55.3 per cent to 44.7 per cent). The three main UK parties had already issued a joint statement pledging to strengthen

---

[116] See Northern Ireland Constitution Act 1973; Christopher McCrudden, 'Northern Ireland and the British Constitution', in Jeffrey Jowell and Dawn Oliver (eds), *The Changing Constitution* (3rd edn, Clarendon Press, Oxford, 1994) chapter 12, 323–378; John F McEldowney, *Public Law* (2nd edn, Sweet & Maxwell, London, 1998) chapter 19.

[117] See Noreen Burrows, *Devolution* (Sweet & Maxwell, London, 2000).

[118] See Richard Rawlings, *Delineating Wales: Constitutional, Legal and Administrative Aspects of National Devolution* (University of Wales Press, Cardiff, 2003).

[119] Northern Ireland Act 1998, s 5(6); Scotland Act 1998, s 28(7).

[120] On 9 February 2010, Assembly Members voted in favour of a referendum on further law-making powers: the UK government enacted legislation enabling a referendum to be held on 3 March 2011, which resulted in 63.5 per cent voting in favour. The Assembly acquired its new powers on 5 May 2011 under the Government of Wales Act 2006, Pt. IV and Schedule 7.

further the powers of the Scottish parliament; this became the Scotland Act 2016, which also recognizes in law the existence of the Sewel Convention, under which Westminster will not normally legislate on devolved matters without the consent of the Scottish parliament.[121] Though this might appear to elevate this cornerstone of the devolution arrangements to the status of law, the UK Supreme Court in 2017 reaffirmed its status as a 'political restriction on the activity of the UK parliament'.[122] The most recent statute on devolution is the Wales Act 2017, which shifted Wales from its 'conferred powers' model to the 'reserved powers' model used by Scotland, reducing some of the asymmetry in the devolution arrangements.

i) Britain and European Convention on Human Rights

Citizens do not possess basic rights that can be protected from incursion by Act of Parliament (this being a corollary of the principle of parliamentary sovereignty), and the liberties of the subject derive from the fact that we may do as we please provided, we do not break the law or infringe the rights of others. The importance of these liberties was signalled by the fact that the United Kingdom became, in 1951, the first country to ratify the European Convention on Human Rights. Initially, this was on the assumption that it would not accept the right of individual petition, but in 1966, this was accepted by the Labour government. Between 1966 and 2015, the European Court has made 305 judgments that found violations by the UK,[123] many of which have been serious, and have led to amendments to domestic law. Owing to our dualist tradition between domestic law and international law, Convention rights are unable to confer rights to individuals that are enforceable in our own legal order. Convention rights had played a marginal interpretative role in the development of domestic judicial review, but they could be directly enforced in British courts only through authorization conferred by legislative enactment. This was eventually achieved in the Human Rights Act 1998, which came into effect in October 2000, and is discussed further in Section D.3. below. There have been recent calls from within the Conservative party for the UK to withdraw from the European Convention and protect citizens' rights directly through a 'British Bill of Rights' but this has not been acted on by the current Conservative government.[124]

j) Britain and the European Union

Britain was not a founder member of the European Economic Community; having a significant colonial legacy and close trading ties to the British Commonwealth countries, in the 1950s it did not see that its primary economic relations lay within Europe. But it was also felt that membership could entail an unacceptable loss of sovereignty. By the 1960s, a revision had taken place, but de Gaulle, the French President, vetoed two applications by Britain. After de Gaulle's resignation in 1969, negotiations recommenced, and Britain acceded in January 1973. This was a Conservative government initiative and subsequent concern about the implications of membership caused the Labour government in 1975 to undertake a novel constitutional experiment and hold a referendum on whether the UK should remain in the Community; 67.2 per cent answered in the affirmative. Concerns about the loss of political independence—'the end of a thousand years of history'—have permeated political debate ever since. The European Communities Act 1972, which was enacted for the purpose of

---

[121] Scotland Act 2016, s 2.
[122] *R (Miller) v Secretary of State for Exiting the European Union* [2017] UKSC 5, [2018] AC 61, § 145.
[123] European Court of Human Rights, 'State Violations 1959–2015' https://www.echr.coe.int/Documents/Stats_violation_1959_2015_ENG.pdf (last accessed on 6 January 2022).
[124] Conservatives, *Protecting Human Rights in the UK* (Conservative Party, London, 2014) 5.

THE EVOLUTION AND *GESTALT* OF THE BRITISH CONSTITUTION   715

giving effect in domestic law to the 'new legal order' of Community law, was a masterpiece of concise legislative drafting, the implications of which were understood by few at the time. The implications of Union law on parliamentary sovereignty are discussed below, but the general question of Britain's relationship with the European Union (EU) has come to dominate British politics since the election of a majority Conservative government in 2015.

In response to the rise of the UK Independence Party, which had the highest vote share in the 2014 European Parliament elections,[125] the Conservatives promised to renegotiate the terms of Britain's membership and hold a referendum on the continuation of that membership.[126] The European Council largely agreed to Britain's demands for greater protection for non-eurozone countries, increased emphasis on cutting red tape, an opt-out from the Union's goal of 'ever closer union'[127] and changes to end the abuse of free movement provisions which would enable greater restrictions on immigration.[128] The in-out referendum on 23 June 2016 had the question 'Should the United Kingdom remain a member of the European Union or leave the European Union?'.[129] On a turnout of 72.2 per cent, leave prevailed, by 51.9 per cent to 48.1 per cent. A Notification under Article 50 TEU to initiate the process by which Britain would leave the EU was made on 29 March 2017, with an expectation that the UK would formally withdraw ('Brexit') on 29 March 2019. Due to the internal politics of the Conservative party, however, which by late 2017 had formed a minority government operating in a confidence-and-supply arrangement with Members of Parliament from Northern Ireland's Democratic Unionist Party, the initial Withdrawal Agreement negotiated with the European Commission was not ratified by parliament, and three extensions to the Article 50 TEU period were granted by the European Council. The UK formally left the EU on 31 January 2020 and the transition period, during which the existing arrangements remained in place, ended on 31 December 2020.

k) Prime Ministerial Government

The Prime Minister had always been *primus inter pares* in the Cabinet system but in 1963, Richard Crossman, later to become a minister in the Labour government, maintained that because of the growth of big government and because of the disciplinary power of modern political parties Cabinet government had been relegated to the dignified version of the constitution. The Prime Minister, he argued, was now 'the apex of a pyramid of power' and after the Second World War we see the final transformation of the system into one of prime ministerial government:

> His right to select his own Cabinet and dismiss them at will; his power to decide the Cabinet's agenda and announce the decisions reached without taking a vote; his control … over patronage—all this had already before 1867 given him near-Presidential powers. Since then, his powers have been steadily increased, first by the centralization of the party machine under his personal rule, and secondly by the growth of a centralized

---

[125] European Parliament, 'Results of the 2014 European elections' http://www.europarl.europa.eu/elections2014-results/en/country-results-uk-2014.html (last accessed on 6 January 2022). This marked the first time that a party other than the Conservatives and Labour had garnered the most popular support at any British election since 1906.

[126] Conservatives, *The 2015 Conservative Party Manifesto* Conservatives.pdf (lancs.ac.uk) (last accessed on 6 January 2022).

[127] Art 1 TEU.

[128] *Decision of the Heads of State or Government, meeting within the European Council, concerning a New Settlement for the United Kingdom within the European Union*, EUCO 1/16 (Brussels, 19 February 2016).

[129] EU Referendum Act 2015, s 1 (4).

bureaucracy, so vast that it could no longer be managed by a Cabinet behaving like the board of directors of an old-fashioned company.[130]

This decline, Crossman argued, has been concealed from the public eye even more successfully than its emergence was in the eighteenth and nineteenth centuries. Crossman's thesis provoked debate over the coming decades,[131] but reached its apotheosis as a consequence of the experience of the administrations of Thatcher (1979–1991) and Blair/Brown (1997–2010). The decline in the Cabinet system was particularly pronounced under Blair, with Cabinets having met less frequently, for shorter periods, and with fewer papers than under any period in the twentieth century. Government policy is often made by the Prime Minister in informal, bilateral, and unminuted meetings with ministers, advised by his own special advisers rather than career civil servants.

As a former Foreign Secretary in the Labour government noted, the Prime Minister normally 'avoids having discussions in Cabinet until decisions are taken and announced to it'.[132] The informality of executive decision-making at the centre presents its difficulties in ensuring accountability in the system, as was especially evident in the reviews on decision-making in relation to the Iraq war in which serious weaknesses in the presentation of the evidence and the taking of minutes of decisions were revealed.[133] On occasions, this can appear to be closer to the re-appearance of a monarchical court rather than the evolution of a presidential style of government. The experience of the Coalition government (2010–2015) had not much modified that analysis, with business being operated through 'the Quad'—the regular meetings between the Prime Minister, Deputy Prime Minister, Chancellor of the Exchequer, and Chief Secretary to the Treasury—rather than the Cabinet.[134]

l) Status of Parliament

During recent decades there has been a gathering sense that the institution of parliament has suffered a decline in status. In part, this is because of party dominance and the organization of parliamentary business between government and opposition. Reforms designed to improve parliamentary scrutiny, such as select committees of the House of Commons which since 1979 have shadowed the work of the main departments of state, should have improved ministerial accountability, though there is little evidence to suggest that it has made a substantial difference.[135] During the same period, parliamentary scrutiny of government bills seems to have declined, especially since many bills are badly prepared and introduced before fully developed, and bills are increasingly being subject to a specific allocation of time.[136]

After the 1997 election a Modernization Committee was established for the House of Commons, which has sought to modernize procedures, to make sitting hours more convenient, and to improve timetabling by, for example, enabling uncompleted bills to be carried

---

[130] Richard HS Crossman, 'Introduction' to Walter Bagehot, *The English Constitution* (Collins, London, 1963) 51–52.

[131] Peter Hennessy, *Cabinet* (Wiley-Blackwell, London, 1986).

[132] Robin Cook (2003): cited in Christopher Foster, *British Government in Crisis* (n 84) 165.

[133] Lord Hutton, *Report of the Inquiry into the Circumstances Surrounding the Death of Dr David Kelly CMG* (HC 2003–2004, 247); Baron Butler of Brockwell, *Review of Intelligence on Weapons of Mass Destruction* (HC 2003–2004, 898). See Walter G Runciman (ed), *Hutton and Butler: Lifting the Lid on the Workings of Power* (OUP, Oxford, 2004).

[134] Martin Loughlin and Cal Viney, 'The Coalition and the Constitution' (n 96).

[135] See Hansard Society, *The Challenge for Parliament: Making Government Accountable* (Vacher Dod, London, 2001).

[136] See Hansard Society, *Making the Law* (Hansard Society for Parliamentary Government, London, 1992).

over from one session to the next.[137] Such reforms may make Members of Parliament better equipped to carry out their various responsibilities, but they do so at the cost of blunting the old instruments—threats to continue debates until late into the night, or to filibuster a bill so that it cannot get through its various stages in the session—that have been available to force governments to listen to their concerns.

3. Flexibility of the Constitution

The flexible constitution. The British constitution is recognized to be a highly flexible constitution. Since there is no entrenched constitutional law of higher status than ordinary law, there is no aspect of British constitutional law not susceptible to change through the ordinary processes of legislation. Statutes dealing with such constitutional questions as the right to a fair trial or the basic arrangements of the key institutions of state, or landmark statutes like the Habeas Corpus Acts or the Parliament Acts, may in principle be amended or repealed in much the same way as legislation concerning any sphere of ordinary life. Furthermore, since so much of constitutional significance is regulated through practice (i.e. conventions) rather than law, constitutional change can often appear to occur simply as a consequence of behavioural change amongst the key governmental actors. In any formal classification of constitutions along the spectrum of rigidity–flexibility, the British constitution would appear to be located at one extreme pole.

The traditional constitution. This flexibility claim cannot be authoritatively resolved, however, until the idea of the traditional constitution is brought into the frame. The idea of the traditional constitution highlights the extent to which constitutional authority is generated by appeal to the customary ways of governing. These customary ways can range from appeals to the ideals of the ancient constitution through to the claim that precedent—the habitual way of acting—itself provides a source of authority. Before concluding that the British constitution is actually a flexible constitution one must first inquire into the authority of appeals to history in British constitutional discourse; if the traditional way of doing things is accepted as being authoritative, then this limits the degree of constitutional flexibility. If the traditional way of doing things is accepted at face value, the British constitution, which in theory appears highly flexible, may in fact be rigid.

Reason and experience. This argument takes the inquiry into a difficult area, requiring an assessment to be made about the relative importance of reason and experience in the conduct of British government. The importance of experience—what Burke called 'untaught feelings' and others label 'character'—tends to be accentuated by those who believe that government, and especially constitutional government, requires the perpetuation of aristocracies of political talent. And the institutional arrangements that have evolved to achieve the general objective of good government in the British system do not easily lend themselves to rationalistic analysis. There is a tension between theory and practice, reflecting Bagehot's distinction between dignified and efficient versions of the Constitution. But it is also captured by Maitland's distinction between 'jurist-law' and 'folk-law', especially as Maitland had argued that the intricacy of the connections between these two concepts meant that public lawyers were unable to venture too far into 'legal metaphysics'.[138] Consequently, although the issue

---

[137] Modernization Committee, *A Reform Programme* (HC 2001–2002, 1168).
[138] Frederic W Maitland, *Township and Borough* (CUP, Cambridge, 1898) 14.

of rigidity-flexibility is symptomatic of this tension, the questions that it raises are extensive, touching ultimately on the epistemological foundations of constitutional understanding.

The logic of constitutional practice. The argument being made here is that British constitutional practice operates according to a different logic to that of the rationalist discourse of modern constitutional law. This suggests that those who evaluate British constitutional practice against modern precepts of liberal democratic systems may be making a categorical mistake. Take, for example, the role of parliament. As the legislative institution of a modern democracy, parliament has evident deficiencies: the first-past-the-post (i.e. simple majority) electoral system leads to an obvious skewing of its representational function, the adversarial mode of parliamentary operations—institutionalized through the organization of business between the government and 'His Majesty's Opposition'—ensures executive dominance of the legislature's timetable, the extreme pressure on the parliamentary timetable together with the apparent inefficiencies in scheduling of parliamentary meeting times seems to diminish the opportunities for deliberative scrutiny, and even the cramped working conditions of Members of Parliament would appear militate against the promotion of informed debate. But reforms designed to bolster the position of parliament as a deliberative legislative assembly, and to remedy these ostensible deficiencies, may well have the effect only of eroding existing safeguards within the British system. Thus, proportional methods of parliamentary representation would destroy the two party adversarial system that provides the basis on which many of the existing constitutional safeguards are based; less adversarial methods of scrutiny might improve the quality of discussion on policy proposals but only at the expense of removing the means for testing the competence of government ministers under pressure; more family-friendly meeting times might attract higher calibre Members of Parliament, but only at the price of Members of Parliament losing a blunt power (keeping busy ministers in parliament long into the night) by which they are able to register their grievances; and improved office accommodation for Members of Parliament might improve their constituent grievance-handling role but only at the price of losing opportunities for ministers and Members of Parliament to thrash out differences in the informal atmosphere of the Commons' bars and tearooms. The peculiarities of British parliamentary practice are not easily tinkered with without the law of unintended consequences taking effect.

Institutional tension. The logic of British constitutional practice is not easily grasped precisely because it is a relational logic. By this I mean that each element of practice derives its meaning and function only by grasping the significance of an overall system of 'conductorless orchestration'.[139] The system of constitutional practice holds institutions in a relationship of mutual tension. The logic applies not just to an understanding of parliamentary practice; a similar tension can be seen between the permanent, neutral, and ubiquitous civil service and transient ministers, an arrangement that enables an extensive, complex, modern government machine to function continuously and effectively while being responsive to popular pressures and changing policies.[140] It also lies at the core of the twentieth century compact between central and local government, where the inefficiencies and apparent logicalities in

---

[139] Pierre Bourdieu, *The Logic of Practice* (Polity, Cambridge, 1990) 59.

[140] Note that some have argued that the recent reforms under the New Public Management initiative mark the end of the Northcote–Trevelyan tradition, which was 'an attempt to ensure that two sets of people, with different motivations, unable to influence each other's promotion prospects, worked together on everything of importance, to ensure enough truth and objectivity for ministers' decisions, policies and bills to be as open and carefully explained as to make their underlying reasoning, and the evidence for it, reasonably transparent and clear.' Christopher Foster, *British Government in Crisis* 222 (n 84).

the structure of duties and powers formed important elements of the constitutional settlement. John Griffith explained this logic in these terms:

> At the heart of the constitution of the United Kingdom is a tension, a tautness, that ultimately determines all the institutional relationships within the state. It can be expressed in many ways: as an aspect of the sovereignty of Parliament, a reflection of party politics, an incident in the relationship between frontbenchers and backbenchers, a pressure on the judicial process, a facet of representative democracy, a fundamental part of the notion of legality itself. It touches on individual freedom, on ministerial accountability, on the redress of grievances, on voting supply, on the limits of authority, on the stability of the state itself.[141]

Or, in Maitland's lapidary words, the British 'are not logical enough to be elementary'.[142]

The waning of constitutional understanding revisited. The problem today is that this logic of British constitutional practice is no longer widely understood. Or, if it is understood by those who seek to change it, then the difficulties of 'modernizing' these practices are being underestimated. The programme of constitutional modernization after 1997 has created evident difficulties for those seeking to understand the logic of constitutional arrangements. Making civil servants responsible for decisions within the sphere of their operations leads to a confusion in the structuring of accountability mechanisms. Bringing in special advisers to ministers with the status of civil servants to assist in the process of policy formation blurs the critical distinction between official and politician. Requiring local authorities to measure up against centrally determined prescriptive targets destroys the power of local variety that lies at the heart of the justification for local government (as contrasted with local administration). Asking judges to rule on the fundamentals of the constitution when the traditional logic of constitutional practice has dictated that they be kept at the margins of governmental action compounds the difficulties of constitutional understanding. All this means that we are obliged to be tentative when we turn to the final part of the account: a legal analysis of British constitution.

D. Basic Structures and Concepts

1. Constitutional Law and Politics

The influence of legal positivism. In the British system, constitutional law stands outside the general stream of jurisprudence. The reasons are various. Perhaps the most important has been the predominant influence since the early nineteenth century of legal positivism. If by law is meant positive law, then in a governing regime based on the legal doctrine of sovereignty there is little to be said as a matter of law in relation to the constitutional structure of the state: this mode of ordering would appear to be essentially circumstantial.[143]

---

[141] John AG Griffith, 'Foreword', in Martin Loughlin and others (eds), *Half A Century of Municipal Decline, 1935–1985* (Allen & Unwin, London, 1985) xi.

[142] Frederic W Maitland, 'Moral Personality and Legal Personality', in Frederic W Maitland, *Collected Papers*, vol 3 (CUP, Cambridge, 1911) 311.

[143] Thomas Hobbes, *Leviathan* (first published 1651) chapter 26: 'The sovereign of a commonwealth, be it an assembly, or one man, is not subject to the civil laws. For having the power to make, and repeal laws, he may when he pleaseth, free himself from that subjection, by repealing those laws that trouble him, and making of new; and consequently, he was free before.'

The influence of the common law. Another reason for the lack of interest in the juristic aspects of the constitution of the state is because of the continuing influence of a common law mentality. The very idea of the common law suggests that no binary distinction can be drawn between public law and private law.[144] That is, the body of ordinary law is assumed to regulate all legal relations within the state and the ordinary courts acquire a universal jurisdiction to determine all questions of civil and political obligation that raise an issue of law. This mode of thought yields the principle of equality before the law: legal claims are subject to common rules whether the claimant be an ordinary subject or a Minister of the Crown. But common law ideology also suggested that powers and duties are to be interpreted according to private law relationships and then simply extended to the field of public law, and this did not always yield sensible results.[145] Nevertheless, common law ideology has also remained a repository of natural law ideas, especially given the belief that custom is tantamount to 'second nature'. This left the field of constitutional law ripe for periodical applications of the vestiges of natural law theories to the subject.[146] It also meant that the discourse of constitutional law was remarkably flexible, as may be illustrated by the way in which the protection of civil liberty could be conceptualized. Do such liberties simply represent the space for free action which is left over as a product of the circumstantial silence of the law (legal positivism), or are they part of a customary inheritance (reminiscence of the doctrine of the ancient constitution and immemorialism), or are they to be viewed as the fundamental rights of 'the freeborn Englishman' (natural rights) that yield the core values of British constitutionalism?

Law and social change. In the hands of a small cadre of senior judges recruited from a narrow social elite, this flexibility presented problems for those who viewed the emergence of democracy and the extending responsibilities of government as progressive developments. Critics contended that once judges moved beyond narrow methods of interpretation and 'looked for the philosophy behind the Act', they invariably found 'a Victorian Bill of Rights, favouring (subject to the observance of accepted standards of morality) the liberty of the individual, the freedom of contract, and the sacredness of property, and which was highly suspicious of taxation'.[147] This caused public lawyers concerned about the potentially reactionary use of common law techniques to embrace a strict positivism that sought to keep matters of government policy and its implementation free from common law controls.[148] This strict separation of matters of law and politics became a distinctive feature of twentieth century British constitutional practice.[149] It also led scholars to draw a peculiar distinction between the 'political constitution' and the 'legal constitution', as though somehow the two could be kept apart.[150]

---

[144] See John WF Allison, *A Continental Distinction in the Common Law: A Historical and Comparative Perspective on English Public Law* (Clarendon Press, New York, 1996).

[145] See e.g. *Malone v Metropolitan Police Commissioner* [1979] Ch 344.

[146] See argument above on the common law as an 'ideal constitution': Keir and Lawson, *Cases in Constitutional Law* (n 27).

[147] Lord Devlin, 'The judge as lawmaker' (1976) 39 Modern Law Review 1, 14. See generally, John AG Griffith, *The Politics of the Judiciary* (5th edn, Fontana, London, 1997).

[148] See Martin Loughlin, *Public Law and Political Theory* (Clarendon Press, Oxford, 1992) chapter 8.

[149] Most recently, this has been challenged in Lord Sumption, 'Judicial and Political Decision-Making: The Uncertain Boundary' (FA Mann Lecture, London, 8 November 2011). See further Nicholas Barber, Richard Ekins and Paul Yowell (eds), *Lord Sumption and the Limits of the Law* (Hart, Oxford, 2016).

[150] See: John AG Griffith, 'The political constitution' (1979) 42 Modern Law Review 1–21; Vernon Bogdanor, *Politics and the Constitution* (Dartmouth, Aldershot, 1996) chapter 1; Adam Tomkins, 'In defence of the political constitution' (2002) 22(1) Oxford J. of Legal Studies 157–175; Tom Hickman, 'In defence of the legal constitution' (2005) 55(4) University of Toronto Law Journal 981–1022; David Dyzenhaus, *The Constitution of Law* (CUP, Cambridge, 2006).

Constitutional modernization. During the last forty or so years, there has been a gathering sense of dissatisfaction about the conceptual division between legal and political matters within British constitutional arrangements. One reason has been because of a belief that, under the pressure of the disciplinary mechanisms of political parties, the authority of conventional understandings has diminished. The lack of formal institutional safeguards caused Lord Hailsham in 1977 to argue that the British system has become one of 'elective dictatorship'[151] and such unease about the workings of traditional constitutional arrangements is one of the factors contributing to an extension in the power and scope of judicial review. This is exemplified in Lord Mustill's speech in *R v Secretary of State for the Home Department, ex parte Fire Brigades Union* [1995] 2 AC 513 (at 567–568), which bears extensive quotation:

> It is a feature of the peculiarly British conception of the separation of powers that Parliament, the executive and courts have each their distinct and largely exclusive domain. Parliament has a legally unchallengeable right to make whatever laws it thinks right. The executive carries on the administration of the country in accordance with the powers conferred on it by law. The courts interpret the laws and see that they are obeyed. This requires the courts on occasion to step into the territory which belongs to the executive, to verify not only that the powers asserted accord with the substantive law created by Parliament, but also that the manner in which they are exercised conforms with the standards of fairness which Parliament must have intended. Concurrently with this judicial function Parliament has its own special means of ensuring that the executive, in the exercise of its delegated functions, performs in a way which Parliament finds appropriate. Ideally, it is these latter methods which should be used to check executive errors and excesses; for it is the task of Parliament and the executive in tandem, not of the courts, to govern the country. In recent years, however, the employment in practice of these specifically Parliamentary remedies has on occasion been perceived as falling short, and sometimes well short, of what was needed to bring the performance of the executive into line with the law, and with the minimum standards of fairness implicit in every Parliamentary delegation of a decision-making function. To avoid a vacuum in which the citizen would be left without protection against a misuse of executive powers the courts have had no option but to occupy the dead ground in a manner, and in areas of public life, which could not have been foreseen thirty years ago.

Such concerns culminated in a rejuvenation of interest in constitutional matters and with the election of the Labour government in 1997 on a programme of constitutional modernization programme, a range of institutional reforms were introduced. In this section, the key elements of this modernizing movement will be reviewed and set in the context of recent constitutional debates.

2. Sovereignty and Democracy

Constitutionalization. Political regimes in the European tradition have invariably been constructed from above and the history of constitutional government has been one of struggle to impose limitations on this absolutist, top-down conception of authority. There have been

---

[151] Lord Hailsham, *The Dilemma of Democracy* (n 92).

three main landmarks in this development. The first involves recognition of the essentially representative character of the office of government: those maintaining governmental positions hold them on trust for the public good. Although there were extensive debates about the institutional implications of this claim, this principle lies at the core of the distinction between ownership and rulership, between private and public. The second involves recognition of its composite character: given the complexity of the tasks of government, there was a need for institutional differentiation of its various functions—law-making, law-enforcing, and law-interpreting. This has led to the evolution of elaborate structures of government and, as the balance of political forces alters, to the rearrangement of the relative positions of the partners in authority.

The final stage has been to effect a basic change in the constitution of authority. This is achieved by establishing a constitutional framework that recognizes that, rather than being yielded as a concession from above, the constitution of governmental authority is generated from below. One reason for the ambiguity of the British arrangements is that, although British practices reflected the first two landmarks of representation and differentiation at a relatively early stage, the final stage has been achieved mainly through political accommodation rather than juristic reconstruction. This causes difficulties in presenting a legal account of sovereignty in the British system.

a) The Idea of Sovereignty

One of the complications concerning the concept of sovereignty is that, while its etymological roots lie in the medieval idea of suzerainty (or lordship), it is in a legal sense a modern concept that comes into existence only with the idea of a state equipped with an absolute and impersonal apparatus of rule. In a strict sense, sovereignty was not wrested from the king, since the Crown never possessed sovereignty as such; sovereignty was achieved through the workings of the Crown in Parliament. This legal concept of sovereignty is itself expressed through an absolute power to make law.

The legal doctrine of sovereignty. As an attribute of the state, sovereignty suggests not only unity but also the possession of absolute legal authority. To impose a legal limitation on sovereign power is therefore to destroy it. In the British system, this absolute legal authority is vested in the Crown in Parliament. The legal doctrine of sovereignty means that there can be no legal limitation on the power of parliament to enact legislation. Tocqueville expressed the point when stating that the British parliament is at once a legislature and a constituent assembly.[152] Through the ordinary processes of legislation, parliament not only passes laws regulating civil conduct, but also is able to alter the constitutional framework of the state. Parliament has thus passed laws to extend its own life,[153] to alter the line of succession to the throne,[154] to reform the composition of Houses of Parliament,[155] and even to alter the meaning of what constitutes an Act of Parliament.[156] The doctrine also means that the authority of an Act of Parliament may not be called into question by any other institution of the state. The judiciary, in particular, have a constitutional duty to give full and faithful effect to the provision of an Act of Parliament. In the words of Lord Reid in *Madzimbamuto v Lardner-Burke* [1969] 1 AC 645 (at 723):

---

[152] Alexis de Tocqueville, *Democracy in America*, vol 1 (first published 1835) chapter VI, 128–132.

[153] See e.g. Septennial Act 1716 repealing the Triennial Act 1694 and extending the duration of parliament from two to seven years. The period is now five years: Parliament Act 1911, s 7.

[154] See e.g. Act of Settlement of 1700; Abdication Act 1936.

[155] See e.g. Reform Acts 1832, 1867; Life Peerages Act, 1958; House of Lords Act 1999.

[156] Parliament Acts 1911–1949, which enabled Bills to become Acts without the assent of the House of Lords.

It is often said that it would be unconstitutional for the United Kingdom Parliament to do certain things, meaning that the moral, political and other reasons against doing them are so strong that most people would regard it as highly improper if Parliament did these things. But that does not mean that it is beyond the power of Parliament to do such things. If Parliament chose to do any of them the courts could not hold the Act of Parliament invalid.

The Act of Parliament is, in short, the highest form of law.

Continuing sovereignty. The one rule that presents itself as a limitation on parliamentary sovereignty, but which is an exemplification of that doctrine, is the rule that an Act of Parliament cannot bind later parliaments. The reason is straightforward: to attempt to limit the sphere of legislative action of future parliaments—by, for example, seeking to provide special protection for a statute against subsequent repeal—would be to impose a restriction on parliament's competence and thus destroy its sovereign authority. There are, however, evident qualifications when dealing with constitutional legislation (i.e. legislation that results from parliament acting as a constituent assembly). Legislation that alters the component parts of the Crown in Parliament can be subsequently amended only by a parliament constituted by those altered forms: if the House of Lords were abolished and replaced by an elected Senate whose assent was required to legislation, then subsequent modifications to this constitutional arrangement would require that Senate's approval. And in the case of legislation that has conferred independence on former colonies, any subsequent legislation that purported to extend to that territory would have no legal authority within the jurisdiction of the former colony, for the reason that a new state with its own source of ultimate authority had come into existence. But the general rule is that the 'legislature cannot, according to our constitution, bind itself as to the form of subsequent legislation'[157] and that, if there exists a conflict between two Acts of Parliament, the Act that is later in time prevails. It being assumed that the later Act must be assumed to have impliedly repealed the earlier, this is sometimes referred to as the doctrine of implied repeal.

Sovereignty and the European Union. Britain acceded to what is now the EU in 1972. By the European Communities Act 1972, parliament made provision for ensuring that Union law would have direct effect within the United Kingdom and required all legislation, whether existing or to be passed in the future, to take effect subject to the rules of Union law. Since the legal order of the EU is built on the principle of the primacy of Union law, this was an essential aspect of accession. But it seemed to be plainly contrary to rules elaborating the doctrine of parliamentary sovereignty. Nothing in the Act affects, and would be capable of affecting, the ability of a future parliament repealing the European Communities Act 1972 and withdrawing from the EU. But what would be the position if legislation enacted after 1972 were found to be contrary to a provision of EU law (which law is part of domestic law only by virtue of the 1972 Act)? The basic principle of the EU's legal order requires EU law to prevail, while the principle of sovereignty requires the Act that is later in time to prevail. After some years of seeking to avoid the sovereignty question by use of techniques of legal interpretation, the issue was resolved in *R v Secretary of State for Transport, ex parte Factortame (No 2)* [1991] 1 AC 603. In this judgment, the House of Lords ruled that while the United Kingdom remains part of the EU, the legislation of parliament must give way to the principle of the supremacy of EU law. In 2003, the courts declared that the European Communities Act was a

---

[157] *Ellen Street Estates v Minister of Health* [1934] 1 KB 590, 597 (Maugham LJ).

'constitutional statute' and was not subject to the principle of implied repeal.[158] A caveat was added by the UK Supreme Court in 2014, which ruled that the primacy of EU law was qualified by fundamental constitutional legislation and principles.[159]

Sovereignty and common law constitutionalism. In his speech in the *Fire Brigades Union* case (see Section D.1 above), Lord Mustill had indicated that for the purpose of maintaining a sense of constitutional balance the judiciary had been engaging more actively in the exercise of judicial review of governmental decision-making. In doing so, however, it became more difficult to sustain the argument that this was justified on the basis of ensuring that the executive remained faithful to parliament's intention in passing legislation. In the process of developing an active judicial review jurisdiction, the judiciary was obliged to breathe new life into the common law as the repository of the fundamental values of the Constitution—to restore the idea of the 'ideal constitution' (see Section D.1. above) An illustration of the type of reasoning at work is found in the writing of Sir John Laws. Laws argues that sovereignty must rest 'not with those who wield governmental power, but in the conditions under which they are permitted to do so', and therefore that 'the constitution, not the Parliament, is in this sense sovereign'. In Britain, he continued, 'these conditions should now be recognized as consisting in a framework of fundamental principles', and that 'judicial power in the last resort rests in the guarantee that this framework will be vindicated'.[160] Using this type of argument, in his judicial capacity Laws LJ promoted the idea that the British Constitution is a common law constitution and that judges act as the ultimate guardians of its most basic values. Its logic may be seen in his Court of Appeal judgment in *Thoburn v Sunderland City Council* [2003] QB 151, in which he stated that:

> We should recognize a hierarchy of Acts of Parliament: as it were 'ordinary' statutes and 'constitutional' statutes. The two categories must be distinguished on a principled basis. In my opinion, a constitutional statute in one which (a) conditions the legal relationship between citizen and State in some general, overarching manner, or (b) enlarges or diminishes the scope of what we would now regard as fundamental constitutional rights … Ordinary statutes may be impliedly repealed. Constitutional statutes may not.

Sovereignty and democracy. The doctrine of parliamentary sovereignty can be seen to express the democratic principle of ensuring that the will of the majority, once transposed into enacted law, is to be given full legal effect. The articulation of common law constitutionalism leads to a more nuanced conclusion. Although representative democracy is one of the basic values on which the British constitution rests, the judiciary is now suggesting that the constitution means more than that of permitting a government, through its management of parliamentary procedures, to pass any edict it desires into law without deliberation over its likely consequences.

b) Judicial Independence

The principle of legality within the Constitution is underpinned by the principle of judicial independence. Parliament plays no role in appointments to the judiciary: traditionally, judges were appointed by the Crown on the advice of the Prime Minister and the Lord Chancellor, though since 2005 the procedure involves assessment by a Judicial Appointments

---

[158] *Thoburn v Sunderland City Council* [2003] QB 151.
[159] *HS2 Action Alliance v The Secretary of State for Transport* [2014] UKSC 3, [2014] 1 WLR 324.
[160] Sir John Laws, 'Law and democracy' (1995) 2 Public Law 72, 92.

Commission.[161] But judges have had security of tenure since 1701; they hold office 'during good behaviour', and may be removed only on the presentation of an address passed by both Houses of Parliament to the Crown.[162] However, although judicial independence underpins the principle of legality, this principle is only one facet of the idea of the rule of law. Working out what the rule of law means is important, not least because section 1 of the Constitutional Reform Act 2005, which replaced the Judicial Committee of the House of Lords as our highest court with a newly established Supreme Court, states that this Act 'does not adversely affect ... the existing constitutional principle of the rule of law, or ... the Lord Chancellor's existing constitutional role in relation to that principle'.

c) Dicey and the Rule of Law

In the classic (if somewhat opaque) formulation provided by Dicey, the rule of law has three main meanings.[163] First, it involves the rule of regular law as opposed to the influence of arbitrary power of the Crown. By challenging the existence of broad prerogative powers, this aspect of the concept bolsters the doctrine of parliamentary sovereignty. And by its reference to 'regular' law, it suggests that law-making concerns the establishment of general rules of conduct rather than a conferral of broad discretionary powers. Secondly, the rule of law expresses the principle of equality before the law, or 'the universal subjection of all classes to one law administered by the ordinary Courts'.[164] Thirdly, the rule of law is an expression of the conviction that, in the British system, the constitution is the result of the ordinary law of the land. The 'law of the constitution', wrote Dicey, is 'not the source but the consequence of the rights of individuals'.[165] This third formulation expresses the British tradition of civil liberties; liberties have been won through a process of struggle which are recorded in particular decisions of courts and are protected by specific remedies underpinned by a general culture of liberty. Dicey's conception of the rule of law thus comprises certain principles of classical liberalism as refracted through the singular practices of English judicial procedure.

The rule of law and civil liberty. In Dicey's formulation, civil liberties are residual liberties— the sphere of freedom left over after parliamentary legislation has imposed restraints in the public interest. As a modern statement, however, his account underplays the importance of legislation both in defining and limiting the basic rights of the citizen. Many civil liberties, such as freedom from discrimination on grounds of race or sex, have been laid down by statute rather than having been recognized through the common law.[166] And many restrictions on such liberties as freedom of expression and liberty of the person have been imposed by modern statutory powers that authorize public bodies to regulate processions and assemblies,[167] to stop and search individuals,[168] or to arrest and detain.[169] If the modern practice of civil liberty protection is dependent on those holding governmental office being willing

---

[161] See Constitutional Reform Act 2005, Part IV, on the role of an independent Judicial Appointments Commission in this process.

[162] Act of Settlement 1701; see also Constitutional Reform Act 2005, s 3, which imposes a duty on the Lord Chancellor and other ministers to uphold the principle of judicial independence.

[163] Albert V Dicey, *Introduction to the Study of the Law of the Constitution* (8th edn, Macmillan, London, 1915) chapter 4, 179–202.

[164] Ibid, 189.

[165] Ibid, 199.

[166] See e.g. Race Relations Act 1976, Sex Discrimination Act 1975.

[167] See e.g. Criminal Justice and Public Order Act 1994.

[168] See e.g. Police and Criminal Evidence Act 1984.

[169] See e.g. Terrorism Act 2000; Anti-Terrorism, Crime and Security Act 2001; Prevention of Terrorism Act 2005.

726 MARTIN LOUGHLIN

to exercise their powers in accordance with a spirit of liberty, this would appear to place too great a burden on an inchoate sense of trust.

d) The Rule of Law and Judicial Review

The recent period of activism in judicial review is motivated by the desire to reinvigorate the idea of the rule of law in the context of the modern state. Lord Steyn has argued that the rule of law 'enforces minimum standards of fairness, both substantive and procedural', and that it is for the judiciary to unpack the requirements of fairness to ensure that government keeps within the bounds of its powers.[170] This more abstract and potentially all-encompassing conception of the rule of law has close affinities to the argument Sir John Laws makes on the relationship between democracy and law.[171]

In effect, the judiciary is asserting that the rule of law is not simply a political aspiration: it is itself a juridical principle. The rule of law, it suggests, is not a secondary feature of a constitution anchored by the doctrine of parliamentary sovereignty: it is a coordinate legal principle of the constitution. More precisely, it is the meta-principle of a juridical conception of the British Constitution. This is made plain by Lord Bridge's statement in *X v Morgan-Grampian* [1991] AC 1, at 48:

> The maintenance of the rule of law is in every way as important in a free society as the democratic franchise. In our society the rule of law rests upon twin foundations: the sovereignty of the Queen in Parliament in making the law and the sovereignty of the Queen's courts in interpreting and applying the law.

Although this statement was made in the context of a case in which the court was not concerned with governmental power as such but with the balancing of two competing rights of confidentiality and freedom of expression, it has been taken up as the basis of a constitutional argument about the bi-polar nature of the British constitution.[172] The reference to sovereignty in this context may not make much sense since sovereignty divided is sovereignty destroyed. But the general thrust of the argument is clear: there is a perceived need to assert a juridical basis to the British constitution. In this light, the constitution is presented as a common law constitution, the judiciary acts as the guardian of the common law, and the judiciary 'has both the capacity and the obligation to move in the next generation towards a principled constitutional order'.[173] The prominence given to the rule of law in this presentation of the constitution has been reflected in recent case law, in which the UK Supreme Court maintained that the rule of law was as fundamental to the constitution as parliamentary sovereignty.[174]

e) Human Rights Act 1998

The rights-based approach to judicial review that the courts had been developing during the 1990s was reinforced by the enactment of the Human Rights Act 1998. The Act, which came into force on 2 October 2000, made provision for the direct enforcement in domestic

---

[170] *R v Secretary of State for the Home Department, ex parte Pierson* [1998] AC 539 575. For scholarly elaboration see Trevor RS Allan, *The Sovereignty of Law: Freedom, Constitution, and the Common Law* (OUP, Oxford, 2015).

[171] See above n 160.

[172] Sir Stephen Sedley, 'The sound of silence: Constitutional law without a Constitution' (1994) 110 Law Quarterly Review 270, 289.

[173] Sir Stephen Sedley, 'The Sound of Silence' 273 (n 172). See also Sir John Laws, above [text at n 160].

[174] *R (Evans) v Attorney-General* [2015] UKSC 21 (Lords Neuberger, Kerr and Reed).

law of the rights guaranteed by the European Convention on Human Rights. The Act makes it 'unlawful for a public authority to act in a way which is incompatible with a Convention right'.[175] Section 3 requires all legislation to be interpreted 'in a way which is compatible with the Convention rights'. This imposes a powerful interpretative obligation on the judiciary, one that runs contrary to the 'plain meaning' interpretation adopted by the courts for much of the twentieth century. But the Act seeks to preserve the formal principle of parliamentary sovereignty. Consequently, if legislation cannot be interpreted in such a manner as to render it compatible with Convention rights, the courts are not authorized to strike down the legislation. Instead, under section 4, they may issue a declaration of incompatibility, the effect of which is simply to signal incompatibility. The relevant provision remains in force, though under section 10 the government is authorized to use a fast-track procedure for bringing forward legislation to ensure compatibility.[176]

Given that the Human Rights Act strengthens the capacity of the courts to protect basic rights, it is clearly of constitutional significance. More generally, however, the Act is of constitutional significance in signalling a fundamental shift that was already taking place in the legal reconstruction of constitutional arrangements. Since the court is a public authority for the purpose of the Act, judges are now obliged to develop the common law in conformity with those rights; and this provides a further impetus to a general rights approach that the courts had been developing over the previous decade or so.[177] It might therefore be said that the Human Rights Act is not the source of our rights, but (in part at least) the consequence of the judiciary's reworking of the common law on a rights foundation.

3. Institutions of Government

a) The Monarchical Constitution

From a legal perspective, constitutional development in Britain remains within the framework of a monarchical constitution. A distinction is drawn between the king and the Crown, but—in part because of the pervasive culture of the common law—it has proven difficult to differentiate the private (monarch) from the public (Crown) so as to enable the Crown to emerge as a legal symbol of the state.[178] The prerogative powers of the Crown have partly been curtailed or superseded by statute and responsibility for exercising them transferred by convention to ministers, but the core of such powers remain available for ministers to operate as a type of intrinsic governmental power that owes nothing to delegation from below. And in general, the logic of constitutional practice within the British system is a form of political reason that does not easily lend itself to legal translation. The programme of constitutional modernization, driven by formalization, differentiation, and separation, presents a major challenge for those seeking to offer an account of the legal logic of contemporary arrangements.

---

[175] Human Rights Act 1998, s 6(1).

[176] See e.g. the House of Lords' ruling in December 2004 in *A v Secretary of State for the Home Department* [2004] UKHL 56, in which the court declared that s 23 of the Anti-Terrorism, Crime and Security Act 2001 (authorizing the Home Secretary to detain suspected international terrorists who—for legal or practical reasons—could not be deported from the UK) was incompatible with art 5 ECHR. The judgment led to the enactment in March 2005 of a new Prevention of Terrorism Act, which effectively replaced the arrangements in Part IV of the 2001 Act with a new system of control orders.

[177] See Murray Hunt, *Using Human Rights Law in English Courts* (Hart Publishing, Oxford, 1997).

[178] See Martin Loughlin, 'The State, the Crown, and the Law' (n 10).

Formalization of conventional understandings. One powerful aspect of modernization has been the attempt to formalize a number of conventional understandings. This process has a relatively long history. An early illustration is offered by the Parliament Act 1911, in which the tacit assumption that the House of Lords, comprising hereditary peers, would exercise their legislative powers in a cautious fashion and give way to the clear will of the House of Commons, was transformed into a statutory formula. But this process of codifying understandings either in statutory enactments or into official documents has recently become more common.[179] The exercise in part is born of an attempt to bolster the authority of these understandings by reformulating them as prescriptive rules and in part it is motivated by a desire to draw a clearer separation of responsibilities among the main institutions of government. To the extent that the latter objective is influential, we may be witnessing an attempt to demonstrate—250 years after Montesquieu claimed it to be the case—that the British system is indeed built on a separation of powers. This process may be illustrated by reference to its impact on the main institutions of government: parliament, ministers, civil servants, and the judiciary.

b) Parliamentary Standards

Members of Parliament are expected to act independently to raise matters of public concern and are accorded powerful parliamentary privileges to support their role. Recently, concerns have been expressed about the outside interests of Members of Parliament, including sponsorship and consultancy arrangements. Although these arrangements are not unlawful, provided they are registered, the sense that some have been using their positions of public trust for private advantage is gaining ground. This concern reached a critical stage during the mid-1990s, when it came to light that certain Members of Parliament had been accepting cash and other benefits in return for asking parliamentary questions. Since parliamentary arrangements were underpinned by trust and honour, it became evident that the rules were ambiguous, less than comprehensive, and that effective mechanisms for enforcing them were lacking. These revelations led to the establishment of a Committee on Standards in Public Life, which reiterated seven principles of public life: selflessness, integrity, objectivity, accountability, openness, honesty, and leadership.[180] These principles were codified, taking form in documents such as the Code of Conduct implemented by the House of Commons.[181] This Code is monitored by a newly established independent officer of the House, the Parliamentary Commissioner for Standards, backed by the Select Committee for Standards and Privileges.[182] Then, in 2009, in the wake of the Members of Parliament expenses scandal, the ability of Members of Parliament to set their own expenses regime was removed and transferred to a new Independent Parliamentary Standards Authority, which is given authority by statute to draft and police the new rules.[183]

In 2011 the Government published the *Cabinet Manual*, a 110-page document that provides 'a source of information on the laws, conventions and rules that affect the operation and procedures of the Government'.[184] These developments illustrate the extent to which

---

[179] For illustrations see Dawn Oliver, *Constitutional Reform in the UK* (n 110) 17–18.
[180] Committee of Standards in Public Life, *Standards in public life* (Cm 2850, 1995).
[181] Committee on Standards in Public Life, *Code of Conduct* (HC 1995–1996, 688).
[182] See further Dawn Oliver, *Constitutional Reform in the United Kingdom* (n 110) 182–186.
[183] Parliamentary Standards Act 2009, s 3.
[184] Cabinet Office, *Cabinet Manual* (Cabinet Office, 2011) iv https://assets.publishing.service.gov.uk/governm ent/uploads/system/uploads/attachment_data/file/60641/cabinet-manual.pdf (last accessed on 6 January 2022).

THE EVOLUTION AND *GESTALT* OF THE BRITISH CONSTITUTION

a cart-and-horses has been driven through the traditionally informal and trust-based arrangements of the constitution.

c) Ministerial Conduct

A similar story can be told with respect to ministerial conduct. Since 1945, new ministers had been supplied with a cabinet paper that distilled from precedents certain guides relating to appropriate ministerial behaviour. This document remained unpublished until in 1992, when it was declassified by the then Prime Minister.[185] Publication transformed its significance: from being a guide or code of etiquette, it took the form of a rulebook against which ministerial behaviour could be judged, and not only in parliament but also in the media and public generally. But does the code lay down a set of constitutional conventions? Apparently not, since it is issued by the Prime Minister (not the Cabinet) and could be freely amended or dispensed with by the Prime Minister; but parts of it do in fact codify principles of constitutional significance.[186] There is, however, little doubt that the Ministerial Code is being regularly used as the rulebook against which the acceptability of ministerial conduct is measured. The Ministerial Code was added to in 1997: following a period of uncertainty about the conventions of ministerial responsibility in the era of 'new public management', parliamentary resolutions were passed that restated these conventions in rulebook form.[187] Most recently, in the Constitutional Reform and Governance Act 2010, these values, together with management arrangements for the civil service, were placed on a statutory foundation.

d) Role of Civil Servants

The 'new public management' initiative has also affected the role of civil servants, not least because those who run executive agencies remain civil servants but are expected to assume public responsibility for agency operations. Such changes have required adjustments to the standard accountability rules.[188] But political pressures at the apex of modern government have also strained certain aspects of relations between ministers and civil servants. The question of whether civil servants owe their duties entirely to the minister, or whether they are subject to a more general public duty that may define the boundaries of appropriate ministerial-official interaction is one such controversial issue.[189] In certain highly charged situations, relations between ministers and officials have become strained,[190] and the codes of conduct do not easily operate when, especially in the case of special advisers, there is a close political relationship between ministers and officials.[191]

---

[185] The document, then called Questions of Procedure for Ministers and now called the Ministerial Code, is available online: https://assets.publishing.service.gov.uk/government/uploads/system/uploads/attachment_data/file/826920/August-2019-MINISTERIAL-CODE-FINAL-FORMATTED-2.pdf (last accessed on 6 January 2022).

[186] See further Peter Hennessy, *The Hidden Wiring: Unearthing the British Constitution* (Gollancz, London, 1995) chapter 1.

[187] HC Deb 19 March 1997, vol. 292, cols 1046–1047.

[188] For details see Dawn Oliver, *Constitutional Reform in the United Kingdom* (n 110) 220–230.

[189] See Sir Robert Armstrong, *The Duties and Responsibilities of Civil Servants in Relation to Ministers* (Note by the Head of the Civil Service, 1985): 'Civil servants are servants of the Crown. For all practical purposes the Crown in this context ... is represented by the Government of the day.' Cf the Civil Service Code 1996, s 2: 'Civil servants are servants of the Crown. Constitutionally, the Crown acts on the advice of Ministers and, subject to the provisions of this Code, civil servants owe their loyalty to the duly constituted Government.'

[190] See e.g. prosecution of a civil servant for releasing documents to an MP concerning a ministerial answer in relation to the Falklands conflict (*R v Ponting* [1985] Crim. L. Rev. 318) and ministerial decision-making in relation to the Westland affair in the mid-1980s: Defence Committee, *Westland plc: The Government's Decision-Making* (HC 1985–1986, 519).

[191] See e.g. Public Administration Committee, *These Unfortunate Events* (HC 2001–2002, 303).

Such difficulties led to calls for the enactment of a Civil Service Act that would formalize the relationship in statutory rules. In 1998, the Labour government committed itself to such a measure,[192] but it took until November 2004 for a draft bill to be published,[193] and a further six years for it to reach the statute book as the Constitutional Reform and Governance Act 2010. This re-establishes the Civil Service Commission, requires the publication of a Civil Service Code and sets limits on the powers of special advisers. Yet in 2013, the Public Administration Select Committee recommended the creation of a Parliamentary Commission on the Civil Service to discuss solutions to the deteriorating relationships between ministers and officials,[194] a suggestion to which the government gave short shrift and eventually ignored.[195] Though conventional understanding has been formalized in this field, there remain calls for the codification of the new rules to clarify the current relationship between ministers and officials.[196] Most recently, attention has turned towards the role of ministers in improving these relationships,[197] though no substantive reform has taken place for some years.

e) The Supreme Court

As has been indicated, the principle of judicial independence has been a vital aspect of British constitutional practice. Nonetheless, now that judges have become routinely involved in the review of governmental action, it seemed anachronistic to many that our highest court (the Appellate Committee of the House of Lords) remained a committee of a legislature, and that its judges (the Law Lords), as members of that House, could have played some role in debating the legislation lying at the heart of a dispute.[198]

Although distance from government and parliament is ensured through the workings of conventional understandings, in 2003 the government, recognizing the need for greater formal differentiation (and perhaps with an eye on article 6 of the European Convention of Human Rights), announced a proposal to establish a new Supreme Court.[199] This proposal was enacted in Part III of the Constitutional Reform Act 2005, which in Part II also took the opportunity to specify certain of the conventions on judicial independence in statutory form. The new UK Supreme Court was opened in 2009.

f) Towards a Separation of Powers?

The process of formalization of relations between the various institutions of government may be viewed as an attempt to devise a more precise definition of the separate tasks and

---

[192] See The Government, *Response to the Report from the House of Lords Select Committee on the Public Service* (Cm 4000, 1998).

[193] Cabinet Office, *A Draft Civil Service Bill* (Cm 6373, November 2004).

[194] Public Administration Select Committee, *Truth to power: how Civil Service reform can succeed* (HC 2013–2014, 74).

[195] Public Administration Select Committee, *Truth to Power: How Civil Service reform can succeed: Government Response to the Committee's Eighth Report of Session 2013–14* (HC 2013–2014, 955) Appendix 1.

[196] Public Administration and Constitutional Affairs Committee, *The Work of the Civil Service: key themes and preliminary findings* (HC 2016–2017, 253) § 31.

[197] Public Administration and Constitutional Affairs Committee, *The Minister and the Official: The Fulcrum of Whitehall Effectiveness* (HC 2017–2019, 497) 3.

[198] With respect to disputes over devolution legislation, the relevant court was the Judicial Committee of the Privy Council, technically a committee of the executive.

[199] This proposal coincided with the announcement of the abolition of the office of the Lord Chancellor. The Lord Chancellor embodied the lack of a separation of powers, since the officeholder was formal head of the judiciary, a member of the Government and the chair of proceedings in the House of Lords. The Constitutional Reform Act 2005 removed the judicial and legislative roles, though the Lord Chancellor remains involved in the process of judicial appointments.

responsibilities of the institutions and therefore to demonstrate more clearly how governmental power in the British system is subject to constitutional checks and balances. It remains a rather haphazard exercise, however, not least because the programme is entirely subject to the control of the government of the day. As part of the modernization programme, for example, concern has been expressed in parliament about the breadth of, and also the ambiguities pervading the exercise of, prerogative powers.[200] But the government has shown little enthusiasm for placing these powers—which remain subject to governmental control and which include a range of powers extending from appointment of the Prime Minister and the dissolution of parliament to the declaration of war—on to a clearer statutory foundation.[201] Constitutional modernization in the British system remains subject to government policy.

4. State, Nation, and Citizen

State, nation, and citizen. The terms state, nation and citizen are three of the most ambiguous concepts that fog the subject of British constitutional law. In part, this is because of the lack of a modern, comprehensive restatement of the basic precepts of constitutional law. But it is also because constitutional law remains fixed within the frame of a monarchical conception of authority and has thus been unable to articulate a modern legal concept of the state, or of the British nation, or of a concept of a British people who act as the repository of popular sovereignty.

At the beginning of the twentieth century, Maitland noted that: 'We cannot get on without the State, or the Nation, or the Commonwealth, or the Public, and yet that is what we are proposing to do'.[202] The issue was not much clearer at the beginning of the twenty-first century.

a) The State
The general concept of the state is itself uncertain since sometimes it is used as an expression of the entire community that comprises an independent political unity (the body politic), and sometimes the term is intended to be limited to the centralized apparatus of governmental authority.[203] In English law, the Crown is the nearest legal symbol we possess of the state in each of these senses. The concept of the Crown signifies the monarchy in its public capacity[204] and although it has also been used as a symbol of the entire public realm,[205] the

---

[200] See Public Administration Select Committee, *Taming the Prerogative: Strengthening Ministerial Accountability to Parliament* (HC 2003–2004, 422).

[201] Although war powers have not been placed onto a statutory footing, a convention seems now to have evolved that requires parliament to authorize to deployment of troops in any armed conflict. This was reflected in the 2011 Cabinet Manual: see Cabinet Office, *The Cabinet Manual: A Guide to Laws, Conventions and Rules on the Operation of Government* (HMSO, London, 2011) 44. The government's positive response to the vote against intervention in Syria in 2013 highlights its effective operation.

[202] Frederic W Maitland, 'The Crown as Corporation', in Frederic W Maitland, *Collected Papers* 253 (n 143).

[203] This is not a problem confined to British discourse, see Jürgen Habermas, 'The European nation state. Its achievements and its limitations. On the past and future of sovereignty and citizenship' (1996) 9 Ratio Juris 125, 126: 'In the German tradition "state" is a legal term that refers simultaneously to *Staatsgewalt*, an executive branch securing internal and external sovereignty, to *Staatsgebiet*, a clearly delimited territory, and to *Staatsvolk*, the totality of citizens.'

[204] This in turn has its origins in the medieval idea of the king's two bodies (personal and political/king and crown): see Ernst H Kantorowicz, *The King's Two Bodies: A Study in Mediaeval Political Theology* (Princeton University Press, Princeton, 1957).

[205] This usage extends back to the Middle Ages: see e.g. *Calvin's Case* (1608) 7 Coke Report 1, 11b: the Crown 'is an hieroglyphic of the laws' and what it signifies is 'to do justice and judgment, to maintain the peace of the land, etc, to separate right from wrong, and the good from the ill'.

lawyers have not systematically carried out the juristic work required.[206] We do not even have a clear ruling on whether in law the Crown in a corporation sole or a corporation aggregate.[207] The roots of these difficulties reach back to the medieval idea of the king's two capacities, which have not been unravelled. And in a monarchical frame, perhaps they cannot be. As Francis Bacon said in the early seventeenth century, the belief that this distinction could be carried through is 'a damnable and damned opinion' which, being tantamount to treason, would lead to 'execrable and detestable consequences'.[208] The jurisprudence on the concepts of both Crown and state thus remains replete with ambiguity.

b) People and Nation

Deriving from the idea of the state as the body politic, there has emerged the idea of 'the people'.[209] In modern constitutional discourse, 'the people' is an expression of a political unity and, as a matter of legal analysis, the concept should not be confused with the idea of a group drawn together by bonds of race, language, history, or culture.

As in all issues concerning the constitution of the British state, matters are not so straightforward. As befits a multinational state, a strong sense of nationhood has never permeated constitutional discourse; there certainly exists no equivalent of the French sense that the right to rule ultimately vests in the Nation. But there does exist a powerful stream of thought promoted by judges and jurists that appeals to the idea that the English common law not as the law of the state but as the law of a freedom-loving people.[210] It is with these strands of thought that those judges and jurists who have recently been promoting the idea of common law constitutionalism are seeking a reconnection.[211]

c) Citizenship and Nationality

This confusion in the relation between state, Crown, and king permeates the law of citizenship. In English law, citizenship is tied to the ancient bonds of allegiance, by which subjects owed fealty to their king. Political continuity and the ambiguity between king and Crown ensured that the modern law imported the idea of a personal relationship between subject and king,[212] and as a consequence we lack any clear concept of citizenship or nationality.[213]

One further reason was that nationality within the British Empire was not addressed in a systematic way: in imperial law, all peoples of the empire became subjects of the king. Consequently, the recent laws relating to citizenship have become entangled with the law on

---

[206] See e.g. *Town Investments Ltd. v Department of the Environment* [1978] AC 359; Martin Loughlin, 'The State, the Crown, and the Law' (n 10) esp. 56–64.

[207] See *M v Home Office* [1993] 3 All ER 537, 566 (Lord Woolf): the Crown 'can be appropriately described as a corporation sole or a corporation aggregate'

[208] Francis Bacon, *Works*, vol 7 (A Hart, Philadelphia, 1852) 651.

[209] See Thomas Hobbes, *De Cive* (first published 1647) chapter 12.8: '[M]en do not make a clear enough distinction between a people and a crowd. A people is a single entity, with a single will; you can attribute an act to it. None of this can be said of a crowd. In every commonwealth the People reigns, for even in Monarchies the People exercises power; for the people wills through the will of one man. But the citizens, i.e., the subjects, are a crowd. In a Democracy and in an Aristocracy the citizens are the crowd, but the council is the people; in a Monarchy the subjects are the crowd and (paradoxically) the King is the people.'

[210] This strand of discourse is tied to the idea of the ancient Anglo-Saxon constitution as the constitution founded on the right of the Saxon people to elect their king and appoint their own judges (above, p 9).

[211] Albert V Dicey, *Introduction to the Study of the Law of the Constitution* (see above n 163); Sir Stephen Sedley, 'The Sound of Silence' (n 173); Trevor Allan, *The Sovereignty of Law* (n 170).

[212] See *Calvin's Case* (1608) 7 Coke Report 1, in which the judges held that those born in Scotland after the accession of James VI (of Scotland) to the throne of England (as James I) were naturalized in England and entitled to the full protection of its law. Allegiance, it was held, was a personal bond of subject to the king.

[213] Clive Parry, *Nationality and Citizenship Laws of the Commonwealth and the Republic of Ireland* (Stevens, London, 1957) 5: 'There is not and never has been any domestic concept of British nationality as such.'

immigration. The resulting position is complicated. The Immigration Act 1971 had divided the main citizenship status categories—Citizen of the United Kingdom and Colonies, British subject without citizenship of any Commonwealth country, and British Protected Person— between partials and non-patrials, with only the former category having the right of abode in Britain. In 1981, the British Nationality Act then established five categories: British Citizen, British Dependent Territories Citizen, British Overseas Citizen, British Subject and British Protected Person—with only the first category carrying with it a right of abode. But other citizenship rights are not defined with respect to this category.

The right to vote or to stand for office is vested not only in most categories of British people but also in citizens of the Republic of Ireland and the British Commonwealth. Finally, for the purposes of the EU the definition of a British national 'includes British citizens, about 30,000 out of 3.3 million Dependent Territories' citizens, and a handful of British subjects as defined in 1981. No other British passport-holders and no other Commonwealth citizens qualify.'[214]

E. Constitutional Identity

A challenging period. As the UK grappled with its departure from the EU after the Brexit vote of 2016, the British constitution underwent one of the most challenging periods in its modern history. Many of the traditional assumptions about its manner of operation have been tested by post-referendum events. The traditional allegiance to the two-party system that underpins parliamentary government has waned, with people's political loyalties increasingly defined by their views on Brexit.[215] A crisis of political representation followed, given that the great majority of Members of Parliament voted to remain but also pledged, ambiguously, to respect the referendum result. And the convention of government control of parliament has been challenged by a minority Conservative Government that grew even more unstable under Johnson's first premiership, with twenty-one Conservative Members of Parliament losing the party whip after voting against the Government in September 2019 on a Bill that mandated the Prime Minister to seek a further extension to exit day. In another blow to this convention, that Bill had been introduced under an emergency debate motion that allowed opposition and backbench Members of Parliament to take control of the House of Commons order paper.[216] Even the courts, which have traditionally given 'political' questions a wide berth in judicial review,[217] have been drawn further into this field; most recently, in a ruling that marks a paradigmatic shift, the Prime Minister himself was found by the UK Supreme Court to have unlawfully advised the Queen to prorogue parliament.[218]

The European question. The British have long maintained a distinctive constitutional identity. Though the modern constitutional settlement has been based on a system of

---

[214] Ann Dummett and Andrew Nicol, *Subjects, Citizens, Aliens and Others: Nationality and Immigration Law* (Weidenfeld and Nicolson, 1990) 3.

[215] John Curtice, 'A nation of remainers and leavers? How Brexit has forged a new sense of identity' (UK in a Changing Europe, 22 October 2018) https://ukandeu.ac.uk/a-nation-of-remainers-and-leavers-how-brexit-has-forged-a-new-sense-of-identity (last accessed on 6 January 2022).

[216] The EU (Withdrawal) (No.2) Act 2019 was introduced under the House of Commons Standing Order No. 24.

[217] *R v Secretary of State for Education and Employment, ex parte Begbie* [2000] 1 WLR 1115, §§ 80–81 (Laws LJ). See as well: Lord Sumption, 'Judicial and Political Decision-Making: The Uncertain Boundary' (FA Mann Lecture, London, 8 November 2011).

[218] *R (Miller) v Prime Minister/R(Cherry) v Advocate General* [2019] UKSC 41. For critical analysis see Martin Loughlin, 'The Case of Prorogation' (Policy Exchange, 15 October 2019) https://policyexchange.org.uk/publicat ion/the-case-of-prorogation/ (last accessed on 6 January 2022).

parliamentary government underpinned by the legal principle of parliamentary sovereignty, the meaning of the rules is dependent on practice, usage and experience, or what might be called a 'tradition of conduct'. It might even be said that the meaning of the rule was embedded in, or constituted by, the practice.[219] And because of the character of the English common law, the legal elements of the settlement are not entrenched in the same way as the provisions of a modern constitution. Consequently, the United Kingdom had always been an outlier among the constitutional orders of member states of the EU. Although EU membership and the ratification of the European Convention on Human Rights brought the UK closer to the European model, during the last decade the tide has decidedly turned. In 2014, the Conservatives formally called for the UK to withdraw from the European Convention, citing the 'mission creep' of the Strasbourg court and its apparent claim of supremacy over the British courts.[220] Under their proposed plans for a British Bill of Rights, pride of place in human rights law was to be restored to parliament and the British courts. Less than two years later, the Leave campaign in the 2016 referendum on EU membership won with its slogan of 'take back control'. Both episodes suggest a desire for the distinctive British constitutional identity to be reasserted after decades of treading the path of European integration.

The future of the Union. In contrast to the federal systems adopted in North America and on the European continent, British devolution arrangements are marked by their asymmetry and flexibility, reflecting once again this distinctive constitutional identity. Despite this, Brexit threatens to destabilize rather than bolster existing devolution arrangements. The status of Northern Ireland has proved a major issue in the Brexit debate. The Good Friday Agreement 1998, which enabled peace, stability, and reconciliation on the island of Ireland, was made when both the UK and Ireland were EU member states, and it drew its efficacy from these common overarching arrangements. The need for creative solutions such as the 'Irish backstop'[221] to avoid a hard border between Northern Ireland and the Republic of Ireland has highlighted the extent to which Northern Ireland's place in the UK has been dependent on EU membership. In Scotland, Remain prevailed over Leave in the 2016 referendum by around 62 per cent to 38 per cent. In response, the SNP Government voted in March 2017 to open talks for a second independence referendum that would allow an independent Scotland to rejoin the EU after Brexit. The continuation of Scotland's place in the UK has therefore become bound up with the UK's membership of the EU.[222] Even in Wales calls for independence have increased as 'exit day' has grown closer.[223] These responses to the reassertion of a distinctive British constitutional identity in the constituent nations of the United Kingdom suggests that the more Westminster diverges from the continent, the greater the challenges presented to the future of the Union. Yet, to this point, little work has

---

[219] See Ludwig Wittgenstein, *Philosophical Investigations* (first published 1953, Basil Blackwell, Oxford, 1958) Part I, §§ 198–208.

[220] Conservatives, *Protecting Human Rights in the UK* (n 126) 3, 5. These plans have been put on hold since 2017. See also Jonathan Sumption, *Trials of the State: Law and the Decline of Politics* (Profile Books, London, 2019) chapter 3.

[221] *Agreement on the withdrawal of the United Kingdom of Great Britain and Northern Ireland from the European Union and the European Atomic Energy Community, as endorsed by leaders at a special meeting of the European Council on 25 November 2018, Protocol on Northern Ireland*. This has since been superseded by a new agreement dated 19 October 2019 which relies on a 'democratic consent mechanism' to uphold the Good Friday Agreement.

[222] See the comments of SNP Westminster Leader Ian Blackford on the possibility of Scottish independence as a response to Brexit: HC Deb 19 October 2019, vol 666, col 623.

[223] Jac Larner, 'How Brexit reinvigorated the Welsh independence movement' (LSE Brexit Blog, 27 September 2019) https://blogs.lse.ac.uk/brexit/2019/09/27/how-brexit-reinvigorated-the-welsh-independence-movement/ (last accessed on 6 January 2022).

been undertaken on the challenge of rebuilding the authority of representative democracy in the post-Brexit state.

No longer a 'tradition of conduct'? The British constitutional settlement has long been characterized by its 'tradition of conduct' in which important matters have been left to be resolved by political understanding and practice rather than codified legal rules. In recent decades, however, greater numbers of these conventional understandings have become codified. At the same time, the status of important political conventions appears to have waned. The significance of ministerial responsibility to parliament, for example, seems diminished, not least with two Secretaries of State and the Prime Minister himself having failed to resign in the aftermath of political controversy.[224] The efficacy of collective Cabinet responsibility seems also to have declined following its suspension during campaigning for the 2016 referendum.[225] And in this unsettled state, the judiciary has extended its remit by making important—and controversial—rulings in cases concerning conventions. The scope of the 'education convention' that allows confidential correspondence between the heir to the throne and government ministers to prepare the next monarch for office was, for example, crucial in resolving an important information rights case.[226] And in 2019 the Supreme Court in the *Miller/Cherry* case appears to have converted the convention of parliamentary accountability into a judicially enforceable constitutional principle.[227] The long-standing 'tradition of conduct' that has been a marker of the distinctiveness of the Britain's constitutional identity is gradually being worn away. With the British constitutional settlement now facing one of the most challenging periods in its history, it edges closer to an 'identity crisis': it is at once European and something distinct; it is grounded in unwritten practices yet becomes ever more rule based; and its underpinning principle of parliamentary supremacy is now subjected to challenge on the basis of an ambiguous principle of constitutional supremacy. The United Kingdom evidently stands on the threshold of one of its most constitutionally significant moments.

---

[224] The Secretary of State for International Development, Liz Truss, remained in post despite her department granting export licences in contravention of the Court of Appeal's judgment in *R (Campaign Against Arms Trade) v Secretary of State for International Development* [2019] EWCA Civ 1020. On 1 May 2019, the then Secretary of State for Defence, Gavin Williamson, was sacked upon refusing to resign after leaking information from a National Security Council meeting. The Prime Minister unlawfully advised the Queen to prorogue parliament: see *Miller/Cherry* case, above n 218.

[225] See Robert B Taylor, 'Brexit and collective cabinet responsibility: why the Convention is still working' (LSE Brexit Blog, 20 May 2019) https://blogs.lse.ac.uk/brexit/2019/05/20/brexit-and-collective-responsibility-why-the-convention-is-still-working/ (last accessed on 6 January 2022). Though party discipline has been scant, the convention remains in operation in modified form.

[226] *Evans v Information Commissioner* [2012] UKUT 313 (AAC). The issue of whether the Attorney-General could veto disclosure under the Freedom of Information Act 2000, s 53 was litigated in *R (Evans) v Attorney-General* [2015] UKSC 21, though the UK Supreme Court's reasoning was not based on the convention.

[227] See above n 218.

Index

For the benefit of digital users, indexed terms that span two pages (e.g., 52–53) may, on occasion, appear on only one of those pages.

absolutism 701–2

acts of government 85, 99, 110, 175, 192, 207, 234, 247, 250–51, 261, 283–84, 322–23, 345, 365, 367–68, 371, 389–90, 393, 395, 406–7, 417, 602, 603, 605–6, 618–19, 629, 645, 676–77, 682–85, 700

administration

administration bound by law 30, 37, 41, 42, 43, 44–45, 47, 48–49, 50, 85, 87, 90, 92, 166, 170, 181, 188, 190, 196, 214, 404, 410, 420, 455–56, 573, 609–10, 625, 677, 734–35

civil service *see* civil service

competences 5, 8, 9–10, 11, 14, 15, 17–18, 21, 22, 23–24, 30–31, 32–35, 37, 40, 42–43, 51, 60, 70, 71, 215–16, 244, 259, 260, 261, 287, 288–89, 372–73, 442, 454, 458, 467, 469–70, 472, 482–83, 484, 485–86, 487, 488–89, 542–43, 590, 592, 593, 594, 643–44, 658, 664, 675, 678–79, 682, 688

concept of 9, 28, 36–37, 39, 53, 70, 71, 72, 83, 84, 85, 86–87, 91, 93, 94–95, 96, 102, 104, 122, 131, 184, 197, 220, 237–38, 260, 266, 304–5, 307, 316, 376, 381, 394–95, 415, 420, 427, 431, 443–44, 446–47, 455, 463, 465–66, 469–70, 471, 472–73, 488–89, 536–37, 538, 545–46, 626–27, 649, 702, 704–5, 722, 731–32

discretion, concept of 458, 464–65

executive federalism 613

function of 16, 114, 237–38, 277, 291, 304–5, 334, 367, 369, 449, 453, 459–60, 547, 566, 590, 629, 650–51, 663, 668–69, 687, 707

lawfulness, principle of 9–10, 23, 31, 204, 337, 408, 702–3

legislation *see* legislation

principles/guidelines 10, 14, 28–29, 34–35, 37, 40, 41, 135, 203–4, 311, 316–17, 336–37, 348–49, 361–62, 406, 425, 567, 612–13, 722

private/non-state actor 12, 31, 50, 163, 178–79, 189–90, 234, 250–51, 292, 347, 364, 413, 549, 558–59, 573, 575, 634, 663–64, 670–71

privileges/special rights 44–45, 46–47, 123, 134, 174, 273, 339–40, 358, 367, 370, 475, 497, 693, 698, 728

reform 5, 17–18, 23, 35, 68, 139–40, 148, 156, 157, 177, 183, 189, 287, 288, 291–92, 296–97, 299–300, 327–28, 379, 381, 389–91, 392, 393, 394, 395–97, 401, 403–4, 409, 429, 434–35, 462–63, 475, 481, 498–99, 500–1, 502–3, 505, 517–18, 524–25, 547, 550, 552, 560, 561–62, 563, 564,

590, 594, 604, 605, 606–7, 609–10, 611, 612, 613, 615–16, 617–18, 621, 627–28, 630, 634, 639, 641, 642–43, 647, 649, 650, 651–52, 657, 659, 662, 666–67

relation to politics 2, 15, 16, 25–26, 59, 62–63, 68, 117, 120, 159, 170, 172–73, 177, 179, 180, 185, 189, 190–91, 193, 195–96, 197–99, 201–2, 210, 212, 216, 294, 300–1, 302–3, 312, 315, 381, 415, 418, 438–39, 464–65, 468–69, 531–32, 533–34, 540–41, 549, 553, 554, 567, 568, 604, 615, 623, 636, 639, 661–62, 663–64, 705, 715, 719, 720

relation to the citizen/subject 70–71, 126, 128–29, 131, 439, 666–67, 685–86, 731

structure/hierarchy 3, 7, 23, 37, 40, 53–54, 57, 82, 85, 86, 103, 128–29, 147, 151, 160, 161, 170, 180, 209–10, 219, 224–25, 234–35, 238, 239–40, 251–52, 275, 276, 303, 309–10, 313–14, 332, 354–55, 356, 362, 366, 377, 406–7, 409, 411, 430, 434–35, 445–46, 447, 449, 468, 472–73, 487, 490–91, 506, 508–9, 511–12, 513–14, 518, 529–30, 542–43, 545, 550, 558–59, 562, 575, 583, 602, 617–18, 624, 632, 639, 642, 650–51, 664–65, 673, 680–81, 695, 703, 718–19, 724

supervision of 33, 53, 136, 204, 205, 395, 427, 449, 676–77, 678–79, 684–85, 709–10, 712

administrative law 67, 155–56, 184–85, 194, 389–90, 413, 419, 425, 511–12, 527–28, 565, 632, 677, 709–10, 712

relation to constitutional law 3, 7, 10–12, 17–21, 22–23, 27–35, 37–45, 140–41, 196, 243–44, 298–99, 382–83, 390–91, 395–96, 400, 408–10, 413, 414, 415, 454–55, 534–35, 545, 611, 685–86, 702, 704, 713, 719, 724–25, 732

administrative organization 2, 7, 11, 17–18, 22, 23, 24–25, 26, 27, 30–31, 33, 34–35, 38–39, 40, 42, 43, 44–46, 48–49, 50, 53–54, 67, 72, 83*f*, 94, 97, 109–55, 116, 117–18, 128–29, 130–31, 135, 155–56, 158, 194, 204, 207–8, 218–19, 234–35, 243, 274, 283, 284, 287–88, 289, 297, 307, 313, 314, 333, 340–41, 352, 356, 364–65, 372, 374, 375, 407, 413, 419, 425, 441–42, 450–51, 456, 458–59, 480, 497–98, 499, 503–4, 508–9, 511–12, 514, 518, 521, 527–28, 538, 540–41, 543, 547, 550, 558, 565, 569, 571, 584, 585, 586, 593, 594–95, 601, 602, 603, 604, 609, 610–11, 612–13, 616, 619, 620–21, 625, 626, 629, 630, 631, 632, 633, 634, 639, 671–72, 673, 677, 678–79, 680, 691, 709–10, 711, 712, 713, 718

738 INDEX

administrative state 543, 709–11
Advocate-General 72, 363–64, 414–15
appropriateness 631
    see also proportionality, principle of
arbitrariness/prohibition of arbitrary action 47, 66,
    87, 93–94, 95, 99, 101–2, 195, 450, 458, 661
army see military
asylum, right to 183, 184, 447
Austro-Hungarian Compromise 3, 7
autarchy/self-sufficiency 336–37, 636
Autonomous Communities 576–77, 588, 591–94,
    595, 597
    see also Cantons; Land/Länder
autonomy 21, 30–31, 32, 36, 95, 98, 101, 122, 147–48,
    243, 249, 260, 287–89, 298–99, 311, 313, 325,
    340, 346–47, 352, 357, 397–98, 410, 412, 427,
    476–77, 486, 498–99, 501–2, 513, 545, 556, 559,
    569, 584, 588, 589, 591, 592, 593, 594–95, 611,
    613, 625, 656, 658–59, 680–82, 684–85
    see also self-government

banking/banking supervision 63, 73–74, 75–76, 180,
    213, 214, 216, 224, 231, 347, 359, 366, 583–84,
    611, 615, 644, 673
Bundesrat 8, 9, 30, 35–36, 170, 175, 201, 641–
    42, 683–84
bureaucracy/bureaucratization 315, 700–1, 715–16

Cantons 137, 639, 640, 643, 644, 646–47, 653, 657,
    659, 663, 664–65, 666, 674–75, 677, 681–
    83, 684–86
    see also Land/Länder; regions/Autonomous
    Communities
cardinal law (Hungary) 225, 227, 228, 231,
    243, 264–65
care for the poor 144, 171, 201, 205–6, 207–3, 213,
    235, 476–77, 613
    poor relief see social security
    see also welfare state
cartography/land register 39, 296, 359, 497–98, 499–
    501, 502–3, 540–41, 602–3
censorship 386, 551, 628
census 8, 187–88, 502, 506–7, 513–14
census voting right 29–30
centralism/central state/centralization 64, 98, 130–
    31, 135, 165, 221–22, 288–89, 389, 428–29, 481,
    486, 569, 587, 603, 645–46, 647, 656, 658–59,
    682, 715–16
Charter of Fundamental Rights of the European
    Union 55, 70–71, 193–94, 214, 215, 249, 291,
    309, 317, 364–65, 430, 452–53, 598–99, 610,
    626, 628
    see also European Union; European Convention on
    Human Rights
child labour 49–50, 278, 423, 452–53, 480
church(es)/religious communities 46–47, 130, 134,
    146, 170, 182, 188–89, 208–10, 223, 225, 226–
    28, 231, 267, 279–80, 439, 440–42, 520, 550,
    551, 557, 560, 640, 645, 646, 682, 693, 694, 709

freedom of religion see freedom of religion under
    freedom
influence on administrative law 52–53, 107,
    135, 168–69, 170, 178, 187, 188–89, 193–94,
    208–10, 225, 229, 279, 394–95, 422, 568, 574,
    618, 646
Islam 188–89, 201, 208–9, 267
Judaism 165–66, 177, 188–89, 208, 247–48, 264–65,
    501–2, 505, 513, 645
secularism/separation between state and
    church 52–53, 170, 172–74, 208, 221–22,
    429, 659
citizens/citizenship 51, 70–71, 126–27, 144, 145, 168–
    69, 178, 190, 198, 200, 205, 215–16, 223, 236–37,
    243, 246–47, 250, 314–15, 333, 337, 356–57,
    358–59, 370, 419, 420, 427, 428, 434–35, 439,
    448, 455, 470, 486, 497–98, 499, 501–2, 507–8,
    513, 520, 562, 601, 607, 608, 635, 650–51, 666–
    67, 685–87, 689, 694, 721, 724, 725–26, 731–33
city/cities 97, 107, 190, 201, 234, 315, 332, 471, 497,
    500–1, 505, 515, 526, 530–31, 592, 640, 642–43
    see also municipalities
civil servants/state officials 27–28, 127, 178, 236,
    315, 395–96, 425, 583, 629, 631, 711, 716, 719,
    728, 729
civil service 30, 130, 175–76, 177, 188, 203–4, 458,
    689, 700–1, 707–8, 711, 718–19, 729, 730
civil society 129, 164–65, 174, 176–77, 179, 226, 353,
    359, 361–62, 394–95, 413, 415, 418, 419, 517–
    18, 525–26, 607
    see also participation
civil war 18–19, 269, 271, 272, 273, 549–50, 551, 553,
    692, 694, 712
    see also war/warfare
clergy 127, 129, 399, 497–98, 603–4
    see also church(es)/religious communities
coercion/power of coercion 23, 182–83, 229, 230,
    503–4, 610
collectivism 66, 176–77, 363, 539
collegiate agencies 666
collegiate bodies 38, 44–45, 173, 643
colonies/colonial empire/colonialization 129,
    166–67, 179, 384–85, 391–92, 397–98, 696,
    714–15, 723
commercial law 158
common good 133, 194–95, 202, 353, 356, 378, 442,
    446–47, 463, 470–71
common law 95, 173–74, 430, 532, 697–98, 701–2,
    707–8, 709–10, 720, 724, 726, 727, 732, 733–34
communism 105, 164, 179, 206, 254, 267, 326, 441–
    42, 462, 472–73, 510–11, 547, 614
comparative law 239–40, 269, 274–76, 443–44, 479,
    481, 501–2, 517–18, 525–26, 529–30, 536,
    558, 559–60
compensation/redress 32–33, 89–90, 190, 199–200,
    205, 224–25, 230, 354–55, 421, 430, 480–81,
    505, 534–35, 539–41, 571, 586–87, 608, 645,
    675, 694, 695
    see also state liability

INDEX 739

competition law/regulation guarantee by
    agencies 583–84, 614–15, 688, 710–11
concordat 551
conditionality 59, 443, 516, 517–18, 545–46
confederation 320, 428–29, 500–1, 643
    old Swiss confederacy 9, 640, 641–42, 644, 646,
        647–48, 649, 650–52, 658–61, 662, 663, 664–
        65, 666, 667, 668–69, 671–72, 673, 675, 676,
        677, 680–81, 682–87, 688
confiscation 103, 509–10, 540–41
conflict of interest/partiality/prohibition 66, 87, 93–
        94, 95, 177, 197–98, 206–7, 232, 257, 306–7,
        313, 324, 325, 386, 399. 401, 404, 407–8, 421,
        477–78, 488, 536, 538, 671–72
conflicts of jurisdiction 671–72
constitutional law 3, 4, 6–7, 8, 9, 10, 11–23, 25,
        26, 27–29, 30–31, 32–54, 57, 78, 80, 82,
        83–84, 86–88, 90, 92, 96, 97, 110, 112, 120,
        123, 126, 127, 155–56, 157–58, 163–65,
        170–72, 178–79, 180–81, 184, 187–88,
        189, 190–91, 192, 193–94, 195, 197, 202,
        206, 209–10, 213, 214, 215–16, 266, 278,
        281–82, 289–90, 297, 329, 333, 336–37,
        338, 340–42, 352, 367–68, 382–83, 392,
        395–96, 401, 404, 405–7, 408–409, 410,
        411, 413, 415, 430, 432–33, 446, 450–51,
        468, 490–91, 517–18, 533–36, 537, 538–
        39, 545–46, 559–60, 565, 611–12, 615–16,
        624–26, 627, 632–33, 647–49, 650–52,
        656, 661–62, 670–71, 676, 689, 690–91,
        701–2, 703, 717, 718, 719–20, 731
constitutional rights see fundamental rights
constitutionalization 26, 73–74, 84, 157–58, 184,
        210, 297, 302–4, 410, 413–15, 464, 531–36,
        650–51, 721–22
construction law 34, 52–53, 633–34
consumer protection 710–11
continuity 7, 51–52, 92–93, 111, 142, 149, 158, 232,
        247, 266, 324, 326–27, 328–29, 362, 383, 386,
        387, 404, 435, 470, 489, 494–95, 547, 577,
        641–42, 732
cooperation 22, 183, 207–8, 215, 222, 226–27, 231,
        247–48, 259, 260, 264, 265, 340, 344–45, 370–
        71, 372, 397, 414, 416, 481, 484, 517–18, 525–
        26, 527–28, 529–30, 534–35, 584, 627, 658–59,
        679–80, 684–85
coordination 201–2, 361–62, 416, 510–11, 658–59
corporations 129, 134, 222, 271, 689, 700
    private law corporations 190
corporatism 507–8
corruption 220–21, 284, 293, 304, 500, 524, 529–30,
        545, 579, 695
    fight against 517–18, 520–21, 526, 527–29, 538,
        540, 542
Council of Europe 59, 107, 181, 205, 223, 226, 230–
        31, 243–44, 341, 423, 540, 563
    see also European Convention on Human Rights;
        European Union
Council of Ministers see government

see also European Union: Council of the European
    Union/European Council
Council of State 143, 313, 402, 413, 425, 643, 649,
    668–69, 674–76
Conseild'État 130, 155–56, 157, 263, 609
county/district 11, 17–18, 30, 43, 135, 224–25, 245,
    266–67, 300, 372, 374–75, 415, 462, 496, 502,
    633, 700
criminal law 23, 172–73, 177, 193–94, 216, 341, 474–
    75, 520–21, 524, 527–28, 536, 537, 570, 575,
    602, 628, 632, 643–44, 654–55, 677
criminal procedure 448, 527–28, 610
Crown 232, 266, 270, 279, 399, 561, 563–64, 567, 603,
    690–91, 692–95, 696, 697–98, 700, 703, 704–5,
    707, 720, 723, 724–25, 727, 731–32
    King-/Queen-in-Parliament 120–21, 692–93, 697,
        701–2, 722, 723, 726
culture 112–13, 117–18, 121–22, 126, 127, 131, 141,
    146, 155–56, 157, 159, 172, 174, 179, 186, 201–
    2, 233, 234, 235, 247, 266, 268, 304, 314–15,
    325–26, 336–37, 356, 387, 404, 413, 418–19,
    427–28, 429, 433, 442, 470–71, 489, 558, 605,
    609, 612, 616, 622, 623, 629–30, 631, 636, 686,
    719, 732
    academic culture 184
    legal culture 121–22, 172, 184, 336–37, 558, 629–
        30, 636
currency/currency system 347–48, 351, 615, 644
customary law 17, 391, 404
    see also common law
customs/customs administration 44, 135, 358, 566,
    644, 704, 706–7

data protection 46, 50, 245, 527–28, 545, 583–84, 610
decentralization 55, 97–99, 130–31, 276, 286, 287,
    288, 297, 301, 313, 389, 427, 486, 583
    see also federalism
Déclaration des droits de l'homme et du citoyen of
    26 August 1789 128–29, 138–39
defence 26, 232, 233, 255, 257, 267, 372, 399, 408, 410,
    465–66, 485–86, 534–35
democracy 7, 8, 10, 18–19, 24–25, 26–31, 36, 52–53,
    62–63, 65, 67, 72, 74–75, 81, 88, 90, 91, 93, 100,
    101, 103–4, 108, 137–38, 144, 145–46, 147,
    159–60, 164–65, 166, 167, 172, 174–75, 176–
    77, 178, 180, 189, 191–92, 193–94, 195–201,
    204, 212, 213, 215, 216, 219–22, 229, 230, 245,
    247, 252–53, 254, 255–56, 266, 272, 273, 279,
    280–81, 286, 294, 304–7, 320, 345–46, 353,
    354–55, 356–57, 359, 360–62, 366, 367–68,
    369, 378, 379, 383, 393–95, 415–19, 420, 428,
    430, 435–37, 445, 459, 463, 469, 471–74, 506–7,
    509–10, 518, 533–34, 550, 551–52, 553, 554,
    555, 556, 557, 563, 566–69, 580, 587, 605–6,
    607, 608, 612, 620, 622–24, 649, 650–51, 656,
    657, 664–65, 666–70, 679–80, 681–82, 684–85,
    687, 690, 703, 708–9, 718, 719, 720, 721–
    27, 734–35
departmental principle/system 604, 605–6, 612–13,

740   INDEX

deregulation 614–15, 634
devolution 288–89, 291, 556–57, 559, 591, 713–
    14, 734–35
  see also federalism
dictatorship 140, 198, 216, 229, 230, 247, 254–56,
    507–8, 549–50, 551, 552, 555, 558, 559–60, 566,
    567–68, 569, 587, 593, 708–9
Directorate General *see* European Union; European
    Commission
directorial system 673–74
disaster/civil protection 145
discretion 25, 361–62, 408, 458, 464–65, 480, 586,
    590, 681–82
  abuse of 590, 667, 694
  margin of appreciation 42, 44, 343
discrimination 82, 95, 166–67, 168, 169, 193–94,
    195, 206–7, 209–10, 211, 325, 421, 630, 650–
    51, 712–13
  equality/equal treatment, 423, 608, 669–71
  racial and other 49–50, 179–80, 186, 235–36, 249,
    423, 725–26
  religious 165–66, 225, 231, 393, *see also* freedom
    of religion
  against women 165–66, 407–8
  see also equal treatment of men and women
due process 49, 170–71, 193–94, 205, 230, 362

economic crisis 19, 20–21, 45, 220–21, 226, 232, 233–
    34, 235–36, 240–41, 257, 258–59, 261, 265, 266,
    344–45, 350–51, 403, 454, 469–70, 471, 489,
    495, 507–8, 551, 553, 560, 562, 563, 598–99,
    689–90, 710–11, 715
  see also European Union
economy 51, 59, 101, 164, 222, 278, 356, 362, 395, 418,
    557, 614–15, 642–43, 647, 695, 710–11
education/education system 11–12, 17–18, 21–
    22, 142–43, 144, 145, 155–56, 158, 160–61,
    169, 170, 201–2, 206–7, 209, 220–21, 222,
    228, 243, 304, 325, 391, 393, 400, 421,
    450, 464–65, 497, 501–4, 557, 568, 613,
    682, 684–85
efficiency, effectiveness 39, 45, 47, 86, 147, 198–99,
    202, 250, 346–47, 354–55, 431, 434–35, 480,
    481, 542–43, 704
elections 8, 9–10, 16, 18–19, 29–30, 44, 64, 65, 75–
    101, 102, 131, 142–43, 149, 151, 152, 154–55,
    159, 170, 203–4, 210, 212, 213, 225–26, 245,
    246, 252, 270–71, 272, 274, 279, 281, 284,
    287, 288–89, 290, 294–96, 300, 301–2, 305,
    306–7, 311, 312, 314, 320–21, 326, 327–28,
    331–32, 370–71, 372–74, 375, 391–92,
    393–94, 395–96, 399, 400, 401–2, 403, 417,
    434–35, 437, 438–39, 447–48, 450, 455, 457,
    458, 460, 467, 468, 471, 472–73, 483, 495–96,
    497–98, 522–23, 542, 552–53, 554, 560–61,
    562, 567, 574–75, 577–78, 604, 605–7, 633,
    635, 643, 657, 665–66, 667, 668–69, 673–76,
    677, 678, 687–88, 700, 712, 713–14, 716–
    17, 721

parliamentary 28, 67–4, 73, 105–6, 107, 163, 196–
    200, 218, 219, 220–21, 222–23, 233, 234–35,
    236, 247, 255–56, 258, 265, 285, 286, 405, 416,
    421, 439, 502–4, 505–7, 508, 509–10, 515,
    517, 520–21, 526, 532–33, 549–60, 576–77,
    578–80, 581, 594, 597, 607, 618, 622, 623, 674–
    75, 714–15
  see also right to vote
employment 46–48, 160–61, 189, 192, 209–10, 421,
    432, 573, 575, 632–33, 694, 721
energy 114, 121, 190–91, 261–62
  see also electricity; infrastructure
enlightenment 321–22, 496–500
environment 69, 112, 157, 181, 212–13, 221–22,
    292–93, 305, 328–29, 331–32, 385, 395, 397,
    419, 620–21
  environmental law 138, 155, 159–60, 190–91, 299,
    613, 621, 633–34, 649–51, 658, 710–11
  protection of 63, 179–80, 421, 470–71, 478
equality, principle of 47–48, 49–50, 135, 142, 161,
    168, 169, 177–78, 186, 193–94, 195, 209–10,
    211, 249, 250, 260, 276–77, 291, 294–95, 297,
    303, 307, 321–22, 325, 361–62, 367, 442, 477–
    78, 482, 559, 564, 574, 630, 642, 644–45, 661,
    666–67, 674, 681, 687–688, 690, 720, 725
  equal treatment of men and women 59–60, 73–74,
    95, 102–3, 135, 145, 160–61, 165–66, 171, 177–
    78, 179–80, 184–85, 198, 472–73, 593, 608,
    616, 659–60
estates 321, 499–500
Euro *see* currency
European Community/European Communities *see*
    European Union
European Convention on Human Rights 21–22, 23,
    26, 41, 46, 48–50, 56, 60, 88, 89–90, 173, 176,
    178, 200, 214, 215, 226, 291–92, 308–9, 333,
    338, 340–43, 348, 364–65, 382, 403, 414, 415,
    422, 430, 443, 451–53, 490–91, 526, 536, 539–
    40, 555, 608, 609–10, 613–14, 615–16, 620,
    621, 624, 626–29, 650–51, 661, 672–73, 714,
    726–27, 733–34
European Law/Europeanization 69, 172, 226, 298–
    99, 412, 488, 632
  see also European Union
European Union 2, 15–16, 19, 23, 34, 52, 55, 57,
    59, 65, 68, 69–70, 71–72, 80, 86, 90, 105,
    107, 156–57, 161–62, 172, 205, 216, 223,
    226, 232, 233–34, 235–36, 240–41, 249,
    257, 258–59, 261, 266, 292, 344–46, 348–
    49, 403, 430, 454, 469–70, 484, 489, 495,
    560, 561–62, 563, 583–84, 598–99, 605,
    607, 617–18, 673–74, 687, 689–90, 691,
    710–11, 714–15, 723–24
  European constitutional law 21, 23, 32–33, 34, 46,
    52–53, 80, 83–84, 86, 90, 172, 180–81, 192,
    197, 215, 216, 266, 333, 341–42, 352, 367–68,
    382–83, 396, 409, 411, 430, 446, 472, 490–91,
    517–18, 537, 627, 670–71, 726
  history 105, 172, 495, 605, 714–15

INDEX 741

institutions 180, 232, 255–56, 262, 347, 360–61, 363–64, 484, 500–1, 523–24, 558, 598

Council of the European Union/European Council 367–68, 372–73, 484, 523–24, 545–46, 715

Court of Justice of the European Union 55, 72, 78, 209–10, 224–25, 231, 246, 249, 259, 262, 263–64, 292, 316–17, 340–41, 396, 398, 412, 598–99

European Commission 167–68, 224–25, 228, 235–36, 367–68, 462–63, 490–91, 517–18, 524–25, 715

European Parliament 73, 185, 222–23, 226–27, 230–31, 255–56, 266, 360–61, 715

treaties/primary law 33, 71, 83–84, 86–87, 90, 156–57, 226, 291–92, 308, 316, 339–40, 348–49, 382–83, 398, 428

see also Charter of Fundamental Rights of the European Union

executive 8, 18–19, 40, 45, 50, 51, 55, 61, 63, 64, 66, 67, 73, 75–77, 86, 95, 105, 111, 118, 124, 126, 139–40, 143, 146, 148, 150, 151, 158, 175–76, 182, 202, 203–4, 219, 270, 275, 283, 284–86, 288, 292–93, 295–96, 307, 309–10, 311, 313, 321–22, 325, 365, 366, 367–68, 370, 372–73, 375, 406, 407, 411, 418, 424, 425, 426, 430, 436–37, 440–41, 448, 457–58, 481–82, 483–85, 486, 497–98, 503–4, 514, 542, 544, 559, 573, 576, 578, 580, 582, 584–85, 586–87, 590, 603, 612, 631, 643, 673–74, 676, 679, 680, 683–84, 685–86, 693, 697, 699, 703, 704–5, 709–10, 713, 716, 718, 721, 724, 729

see also administration

fascism 163–64, 166–67, 177, 180, 188, 194–95, 200, 216, 270–75, 279, 280, 282, 284, 290–91, 293, 302–3, 304, 306, 418, 472–73, 506–8, 547, 550

federal court

Germany

Bundesverfassungsgericht 55, 172–73, 175, 176–77, 185, 197, 212, 482, 519,

Bundesverwaltungsgericht 23

Switzerland

Bundesgericht/Tribunal fédéral/Tribunale federale 642–44, 646, 649–50, 652, 657, 659–61, 662, 665, 666–124, 669–70, 671–73, 674–75, 677–80

federal state 3, 10–12, 32, 51, 486, 640–41, 642–43, 644–45, 646, 664–65, 680–81, 684–85, 686, 687, 688

see also federalism

federalism 7, 8, 9, 10, 14, 22, 32, 34–35, 53, 164–65, 166–67, 170, 172, 175, 179–80, 183, 189, 193, 195–96, 201–2, 206–7, 212, 216, 287–88, 427, 616–17, 649, 650–51, 658–59, 664–65, 680–85, 687–88

executive federalism 613

see also decentralization; devolution

federation 9, 10, 11, 18–19, 21, 22, 27, 29, 32–36, 38, 40, 43, 45–46, 51, 53, 170, 179, 195–96, 201–2, 203, 218, 397–98, 641, 642

see also federal state

feudalism/feudal state 499–500, 695

finance/financial system 23, 170, 206–7, 224, 231, 287–88, 313, 486, 611, 614–15, 635, 658–59, 666, 681–83, 684–85, 712

see also taxes

First World War *see* World War

food, control of 422–23, 604

foreign policy/foreign affairs 109–10, 139, 202, 367–68, 372, 392, 408, 410, 484, 582, 617, 644, 667–68, 676–77, 679–80, 682, 683

foreigners 107, 127, 207–8, 210–11, 212, 232, 233–34, 257, 258, 314–15, 338, 342–43, 359, 374–75, 562, 654–55, 658, 666

see also asylum, right to; citizenship; removal; right of residence

formalism 66, 163–64, 494–95, 661

fragmentation 2, 3, 16–17, 133, 198–99, 271, 275, 284, 310, 331–32, 516, 525–26, 529, 545, 596

framework legislation 8, 659–60

freedom

of action 46–48, 49, 136, 160–61, 190, 193–95, 208–9, 234, 236–37, 250, 303, 361–62, 363–64, 413, 453, 462–63, 473, 476, 477–78, 522, 539, 602, 622, 631, 660–61, 666–67, 725–26

of assembly 2, 25, 91, 92, 119, 178, 190, 233, 234, 292, 378, 473, 477–78

of association 49–50, 66–67, 92, 119, 146, 155, 158, 193–94, 265–66, 472–73, 477–78, 522, 622, 644–45

of information 91, 168–69, 223, 267, 477–78, 574, 622

of movement 46–47, 228, 477–78, 608, 622, 646, 667–68, 688, 715

of the press/media 89, 109, 160–61, 178, 193–95, 214, 359, 414, 421, 477–78, 602, 618, 628, 644–45, 660–61, 726

see also censorship

of religion 11, 168–69, 188–89, 208–9, 228, 236–37, 260, 421, 442, 568, 644–45, 646

of trade/free trade 48, 168–69, 644–45, 646, 720

see also fundamental rights

French Revolution 115, 128–29, 131, 134–35, 137, 141, 145, 387, 388, 408–9, 419, 427, 428–29, 614, 642, 698

fundamental rights 11, 25–26, 37, 46–50, 52–53, 55, 62–63, 65–67, 70–71, 83, 88–90, 92, 101–3, 106, 145, 154–55, 161, 163–64, 166–67, 170, 171, 175–76, 177, 178, 181, 182–83, 184–85, 186, 187–88, 189–90, 191, 193–95, 200, 203–5, 206, 209–11, 212, 214, 215–16, 219, 222, 233, 245, 246, 248, 249–51, 256–60, 263–64, 265–66, 268, 281, 302, 304, 308–9, 316–17, 325, 333, 342–43, 361–65, 375, 403, 408–9, 411, 413–14, 420, 421–23, 429, 430, 435, 441–43, 451, 452–53, 464–65, 477–78, 479, 480–81, 488, 490, 513,

742 INDEX

fundamental rights (*cont.*)
536–41, 552, 555, 558–59, 561–62, 566, 568, 570, 571–72, 573, 574, 577–78, 584, 588, 590, 597, 598–99, 608, 610, 628, 642–48, 650–51, 652, 659–61, 662, 663–64, 669–73, 682, 685–86, 688, 720
see also human rights

globalization 71, 167, 172, 181, 211–12, 323
glorious revolution 141–42, 690, 691–92, 694–95, 699–700
good faith, principle of 671
government 8, 9–10, 12, 27–28, 52–53, 81–82, 106–7, 116, 125–26, 128, 147–49, 154, 160, 161. 173, 175, 178, 179–80, 182–83, 184–85, 192–93, 198, 200–1, 218, 244, 255–56, 257, 290, 299–301, 306, 316, 360, 365, 408–9, 495–96, 497–98, 500, 501–2, 507–9, 515, 517–18, 519–20, 521, 523–24, 530–31, 555, 602–3, 654–55, 668–70
  competences/tasks 20–21, 22, 35, 61–64, 74–75, 80, 86, 91, 96, 117, 118, 143, 150–51, 207, 224, 226–29, 230–38, 246–47, 252–53, 260, 261–62, 271–77, 282, 292–96, 297, 344–45, 346, 394, 398–99, 403–5, 406–7, 410, 411, 413, 415, 432, 433–34, 437, 439, 480, 558–59, 560, 562, 576, 578–84, 592–94, 604–6, 610–17, 625–1, 628–30, 635–37, 645, 653, 692–95, 714–15, 724–27
  relation to other administrative institutions 18, 130–31, 136–37, 164–65, 243, 250–51, 365, 367–69, 370, 371–72, 373–74, 408, 417, 418–19, 551, 608, 712–632, 727–29
  structure of 17–19, 38, 43–45, 65, 67–68, 69, 75–77, 83–84, 85, 94–95, 97–99, 102, 110, 113–14, 128–29, 131–33, 146, 198–99, 201–2, 219, 220–22, 241–42, 253–55, 283–89, 301–2, 303–4, 309–11, 313, 389–94, 395–97, 400–1, 402, 403, 416, 424, 429, 430, 440, 441–42, 483, 485, 486–87, 506–7, 550, 551, 552, 556–57, 567–68, 569, 586–90, 595–97, 606–7, 617–24, 631–33, 641–42, 643–10, 649, 650, 662, 666, 676–79, 681–82, 683, 684–85, 690–91, 697–99, 700–2, 704–12, 715–19, 720–22, 730–31, 733–31
  see also ministers
governors 15, 34–35, 75–76, 126–27, 391–92, 498–99
guardianship/guardianship systems 399–400

Habsburg family/Habsburg monarchy 3, 20–21, 59–60, 497
harmonization/standardization 369, 426, 682–83, 688
healthcare 189, 206–7, 209–10, 682
  see also welfare state
hierarchy of norms 3–4, 21–22, 25, 36–37, 53–54, 83*f*, 302, 409
homogeneity 2, 29–30, 261–62, 496, 593 688
House of Lords 694, 709, 722, 723, 724–25, 728
human rights 23, 24, 45–46, 66, 86–87, 88–90, 101, 103–4, 106, 134, 142–43, 144, 146, 155, 156–57, 164–65, 166, 167, 169, 172, 174–75, 178–79, 181,

188, 192–94, 209–10, 212, 216, 223, 230–31, 245, 250, 267, 328–29, 353, 354–55, 361–62, 435, 446–47, 458–59, 462, 463, 539, 540–41, 551, 555, 557, 597, 624–25, 628, 632–33, 634, 730
  see also Charter of Fundamental Rights of the European Union; European Convention on Human Rights; fundamental rights

impartiality 312, 362, 450, 458–59, 470–71, 630, 707–8
industrialization 604, 700
industry 399, 418, 502–3, 614–15
infrastructure 658
inheritance/succession 130, 132, 293, 387–88, 394, 401, 410–11, 563–64, 602, 646, 682–83, 697, 699, 720
inspections 524–25, 529–30,
instructions 10, 30–31, 33, 38, 41, 44–45, 145, 577–78, 584, 585, 683
internal market 648
international law 8, 9–10, 21, 22, 52, 166, 169, 181, 239–40, 291, 326–27, 337, 340–42, 346–47, 357, 362, 383, 406, 408, 412, 428, 430, 441–42, 448, 452–53, 490–91, 539, 555, 626–27, 650–51, 655, 663, 669–70, 672–73, 675, 714
international organizations interpretation 14, 34, 48, 57, 59–60, 66–67, 69, 70, 71, 75–76, 84, 89–90, 91, 98, 100, 103, 106, 154–55, 158–59, 181, 195, 206–7, 214, 233, 234, 240–41, 249, 257, 258, 259–60, 261, 262, 264–65, 283–84, 290–92, 297–98, 308, 317, 335–38, 341–43, 345, 347–48, 350–51, 354–55, 362–63, 374–75, 377, 389–90, 398, 404, 407, 408, 411, 412, 414–15, 426, 432, 438, 444, 446–47, 450, 451, 452–53, 454–56, 465–66, 475, 478, 479–80, 510–11, 520, 522, 535–36, 538–39, 542, 555, 560, 564, 589, 590, 605, 608, 616–17, 618, 619, 620–21, 626, 652–53, 658–59, 660–61, 662, 663–64, 672–73, 691, 693, 695, 703, 720, 726–27
interventionism/state intervention 32–33, 48, 147–48, 152, 158, 167, 201–2, 297, 302–4, 306, 391, 408, 446–47, 614–15
Islam 188–89, 201, 208–9, 267
ius commune 315
ius publicum Europaeum 3, 163–64, 180, 602–3, 605

Judaism 165–66, 177, 188–89, 208, 247–48, 264–65, 501–2, 505, 513, 645
judicial review 10, 26, 109, 122, 123–27, 155, 166–67, 170–71, 172–73, 183, 191, 192–93, 198–99, 204, 205, 209–11, 212, 217, 236–44, 250, 335, 401, 404, 423, 425, 456, 460–61, 465–66, 485–86, 504–5, 513–14, 532, 570, 598–99, 615–16, 631, 632, 650, 659, 672, 689, 721, 724, 726
justices of the peace 700

king *see* monarch/monarchy

labour 133, 142, 145, 280–81, 356, 363, 470–71, 574, 589, 623, 644
  labour law 158, 224–25, 637

land reform 296, 500–1

Land/Länder 9–10, 11–12, 14, 15, 17–19, 21, 23, 27, 29–30, 32–37, 38–39, 43, 45–46, 51, 53, 113, 122, 160, 164–65, 166, 189, 201, 267, 296, 322–23, 336–37, 353, 358, 497, 499–500, 540–41, 598, 599, 604–5, 647, 682–83, 699, 709–10, 725
   see also Cantons; regions/Autonomous Communities

language 2, 51, 100, 112, 134, 168, 248, 264, 280, 314–15, 322–23, 324–25, 327–28, 332, 340–41, 356, 358, 396–97, 407, 414, 424, 426, 428, 432, 435, 524, 547, 551, 556–57, 593, 607, 610–11, 612–13, 640, 642, 648, 670–71, 676, 680–81, 685–86, 697, 708–9, 732

legal certainty, principle of 37, 53–54, 92–94, 361, 362, 425–26, 455–56, 609, 612–13

legal history 172, 321

legal principles 92, 239–40, 298–99, 320–21, 357, 361, 377, 425–26, 449, 452–53, 665, 702–3, 733–34

legal protection 23, 36–37, 38–39, 167, 205, 275, 590, 671–72, 688

legality, principle of 28–29, 41, 93–94, 307, 316–17, 397, 407, 527–28, 536–37, 612, 630, 661, 671, 724–25

legislation 8, 10, 12–13, 14, 16, 17–18, 20–21, 27–28, 32–36, 37, 39–41, 50–51, 53–54, 69, 74, 79, 84–85, 86–87, 120–21, 126, 135, 139–40, 147–48, 153, 156, 166, 170–71, 177, 183, 191, 192–93, 201–2, 203–4, 205–6, 211, 214–15, 219, 230, 236–37, 239, 244, 247, 257, 262, 288, 289–90, 292, 293, 297, 302–3, 304, 305–6, 307, 308, 309–10, 311, 313, 314, 316–17, 326, 328–29, 330, 334, 335, 336–37, 341–43, 347, 349–50, 354–55, 361–62, 367–69, 371, 398, 400, 405–6, 407–8, 410, 413, 417–18, 419, 425, 426, 427, 428, 430, 432, 435, 473, 483, 499, 500–2, 506–7, 514, 518–19, 521, 522, 526, 527–28, 534–35, 539–41, 544, 546, 566, 567, 570, 571, 580, 581, 587, 591, 593, 594, 605–6, 607, 608, 609, 612–13, 619, 620–21, 624, 625–26, 627, 629, 630, 633–34, 637, 643, 646–47, 654–55, 659–60, 663–64, 666, 670–71, 675, 676–77, 678–79, 680, 683, 684–85, 693, 696, 697, 699, 700, 705, 707–9, 712, 717, 722, 723–24, 725–27, 730

legislative decrees/ordinances 9–10, 22, 28–29, 32, 37, 40–41, 53–54, 97, 98–99, 123, 128–29, 234, 272–73, 311, 514, 520–21, 522, 526, 534–35, 543–44, 630, 632, 676–77

legitimacy 2, 3, 27–28, 93, 125–26, 137, 151, 155, 162, 174–75, 179–80, 196–97, 203–4, 215, 239, 255–56, 287, 290, 294, 308, 321–22, 323, 342–43, 345–46, 353, 356–57, 372–73, 438–39, 449–50, 458–59, 494–95, 508, 532, 533–34, 574–75, 582, 616–17, 622, 630, 709

legitimate expectations, protection of 335, 337–38, 339–40, 354–55, 361, 362, 363–64, 475

liberalism/liberalization 108, 222, 254, 256, 273, 547, 550, 558, 559–60, 593, 725

local government 130–31, 234, 276, 393, 455, 486–87, 556, 606–7, 616, 700, 718–19

magistrate *see* municipality

majorities/majority rule 76, 102, 110, 149, 151, 273, 281, 289, 290, 297–98, 306, 309–10, 393, 401–2, 444–45, 518, 522–23, 558, 579, 676, 708–9

margin of appreciation *see* discretion

market 184–85, 211–12, 350, 557, 614, 623, 648, 673–74
   internal market 648
   market economy 62–63, 101, 363–64
   single market 648
   supervision of the market 335, 381

mayors 30, 149–50, 215–16, 243, 287, 301–2, 400, 712
   see also cities; municipalities

media 91, 238, 256, 306–7, 330–31, 359, 602, 618, 623–24, 627, 636–37

middle ages 135, 614, 731–32

military/military state 18–19, 32, 34–35, 57, 64, 66–67, 166–67, 172, 180, 182–83, 208–9, 211–12, 230, 264, 272, 292–93, 351, 390, 442, 543–44, 550, 551, 561, 564, 565–66, 571–72, 582, 603, 641, 644, 645, 695

military jurisdiction 32, 64, 66–67, 164–65, 166–67, 182–83, 208–9, 264, 313, 390, 525–26, 543–44, 561, 642–43, 695

ministers/secretaries of state 43, 44–45, 139, 148, 283, 291, 300, 310, 371, 373, 390, 391, 416, 439, 503–4, 508, 533, 579, 584, 696, 706, 718, 721, 723–24, 726–27, 735

minority rights/protection of minorities 91, 102, 675, 683–84, 688

modernization 321–22, 384, 390–91, 498–99, 547, 551, 640, 691, 700, 716–17, 719, 721, 727–28, 730–31

monarch/monarchy 3–5, 7, 10, 13, 26, 42, 53, 116, 118, 120, 121, 122, 123, 125, 128, 132, 138–39, 146, 266, 269–70, 271–72, 273, 279, 307, 320, 321–22, 388, 389, 390, 391, 392, 396, 399–400, 405, 424, 428–29, 433–35, 494–95, 497–98, 501–2, 503–4, 505–8, 510–11, 512–13, 552, 553, 567, 575, 578–79, 602–4, 605–6, 607, 614, 630, 692–93, 694–95, 696, 697, 699, 701–2, 703, 705, 709, 722, 727, 731–33, 735

monopoly on the use of force 197–98, 465–66

morals, public 133, 478

multilevel governance/multilevel system 80, 192, 309, 488

municipal law 21

municipalities 11, 21, 29, 30–31, 35–36, 85, 98–99, 234, 276, 287, 315, 389, 400, 427, 533–34, 590
   see also cities; self-government

National Catholicism (Spain) 551, 557

National Socialism 26–27

nationalism 180–81, 200–1, 216, 221–22, 267–68

nationalization 164, 304, 539

744 INDEX

nation-state 58, 59–60, 72, 105, 106, 131, 147, 160–61,
180–81, 197, 247, 257, 267, 268, 305, 315, 324,
325–26, 329, 353, 356, 357–59, 361, 366, 367,
370, 427, 454, 470–72, 489, 498–99, 594, 635,
664–65, 686–87
natural law 115, 127, 476, 538–39
natural resources 164, 195–96
networks 495–96, 523–24
neutrality 20–21, 52–53, 75–76, 177, 209, 315, 361–
62, 392, 525–26, 532–33, 557
new public management 689, 711, 718–19, 729
nobility/aristocracy 386, 387–88, 433–35, 496–98,
499–500, 502–3, 602–3, 696, 697, 698, 703, 709
non-governmental organization (NGO) 62, 250

occupation 52, 168–69, 171, 319–20, 327–29, 332,
395, 427
Ombudsman 23, 40, 45–46, 82, 227, 244, 245,
399–400, 467, 480, 512, 532–33, 534–35, 544,
547, 559, 562–63, 588, 590, 603–4, 611, 516,
629–30, 634
Ottoman Empire 496

Parliament
Austria 6–7, 8, 10, 12, 18–19, 23, 27–31, 40–41,
43–45, 52–53
Crown in see under Crown
Czech Republic 64, 72, 75–76, 78–79, 85, 86, 87,
91, 94–95
elections see under elections
France 120–21, 123, 127, 129, 133–34, 139–40, 146,
147–49, 151
Germany 166, 175, 177, 182, 191, 192, 196–200,
201, 202–4
Hungary 217–21, 223, 224–27, 230–31, 234,
238, 242–43, 244, 245–46, 247–48, 251, 253,
256, 266
Italy 270–71, 280, 281, 283–84, 285, 286, 288, 290,
292, 294, 296, 300, 301–2, 303, 309–10, 311
Lithuania 321–22, 323, 325, 326, 353, 365
Netherlands 389–90, 391–48, 396–95, 398–99, 400,
401–3, 404–8, 410–13, 417, 421–24, 425–27,
428, 429
Poland 432, 444–45, 457, 459, 460–61, 464–65,
472, 473
Romania 495–96, 502, 503–4, 505–8, 511, 512,
513–14, 517–18, 519–24, 530–36, 542–44
Spain, 552, 553–54, 561, 564, 566–67, 576–81, 582–
83, 587–88, 595, 596
Sweden 602–3, 606–8, 610–2, 612, 613, 614, 619,
627–28, 630
Switzerland 641, 642–43, 645–47, 648–49, 650,
651–52, 654–55, 661–62, 668–69, 674, 675–76,
681, 685–86, 687
United Kingdom 692, 693–95, 696, 697–700, 702,
706, 707, 709, 712–15, 716–19, 721, 722, 724,
726, 728–29, 730–31, 733–35
participation 15, 19, 30, 40, 132, 147, 271–72, 284,
303, 344, 360–61, 370, 408, 415, 419, 460,

464–65, 484, 520, 524, 561, 567–568, 577–78,
657, 661–62, 667, 681, 683, 687
see also democracy
parties 4–6, 16, 20, 49–50, 58, 61–62, 63, 65–66,
67–68, 76–77, 81, 90, 102, 109, 166, 182, 192,
197–200, 222, 236, 246, 250, 253, 254–55, 272,
278–79, 284, 293, 295–96, 297–98, 305–7, 315,
367, 370, 394–95, 402, 416, 468–73, 502, 507–8,
515–16, 534–35, 552, 553, 556, 557, 558, 560,
567–68, 569, 574, 576–78, 581, 594, 605–9,
614–15, 618, 622, 623, 624, 661–62, 668–69,
691–98, 703, 709, 712–13, 715, 721
peace/peace treaties 4–5, 169, 180, 498–99, 505–
6, 547
pension insurance see social security
see also welfare state
pensions 72, 230, 252, 364, 475
People's Republic, Poland 436–38, 442, 474
petition, right to 46–47, 421
pluralism 155, 160, 188–89, 209, 215, 293, 305, 306–7,
312, 473, 652
political rights see fundamental rights
political science 155–56, 614, 617–18, 703
positivism 702–3, 719–720
precedent 234, 242, 558–59, 587, 619, 642–43,
701, 717
prefect/prefecture 503–4, 506–7
priority/precedence/supremacy of the law 18–19, 37,
84, 87, 166–67, 213, 363, 413, 451–52, 454, 469,
539, 580, 627–28, 652
see also lawfulness, principle of private law; legality,
principle of
private law 50, 190, 210–11, 410, 413, 414–15, 593,
646, 709–10, 720
relation to constitutional law 25, 41, 43, 382–83,
413, 719
see also administrative law
private sector 710–11
privatization 221, 509–10, 710–11
privileges 44–45, 46–47, 123, 134, 174, 175–76, 273,
358, 367, 370, 433–35, 475, 497, 693, 698, 728
of the administration 123, 273, 367, 370, 461, 475,
497, 693, 698, 728
of social groups 134, 358
Privy Council 499, 730
procedural guarantees 249–50, 435, 590, 650–51, 661
procedural law 243–44, 450–51, 604, 646, 658
see also administrative law; administrative
procedure; civil procedure
procedural/formal requirements 47, 239,
244, 561–62
property 46–48, 74–75, 103, 141, 142, 145, 369, 427,
435, 441–42, 486, 660–61
private property 230, 328–29
public property 278, 499–500, 509–10
proportionality, principle of 47, 49–50, 66, 95, 178,
183, 184–85, 187, 188, 204, 362, 364, 422, 425,
443–44, 446–47, 475, 477, 478, 538–39, 572–
73, 576–77, 586, 671

provinces 129, 287, 313, 315, 384, 387–89, 400, 408–9, 427, 428–29, 486, 498–99, 576, 590
public authorities 34–35, 36, 45, 99, 190, 203–4, 248, 259, 322, 419, 421–22, 486, 558–59, 629, 726–27
    administration of 34–35, 45–46, 559
public law, concept of 17–18, 35, 40, 52, 129, 131, 155–56, 260, 282, 415, 510–11, 558, 643–44, 692, 720
public order 99, 142, 155, 228–29, 234, 478
public services 152, 297, 586–87, 611, 631, 633–34, 688, 710–11
public use 540–41

rationalism/rationalization 292
Rechtsstaat 36, 37, 53–54, 65–67, 88, 91–95, 203–5, 409, 420–23, 443–44, 664–65
referendum 14–16, 28, 44, 52–53, 69, 80, 83–84, 90, 138, 151–53, 158–59, 179, 218, 220–21, 232, 233, 255–56, 272, 273, 284, 294, 296–97, 301–2, 305–6, 314–15, 322, 330–32, 359, 363, 378, 416–17, 429, 439, 441, 447–48, 454, 487, 494–95, 512–13, 514–16, 520–22, 542, 550, 552, 554, 556, 562, 568–69, 582, 589, 595, 596, 597, 618, 627, 645–48, 649–57, 664, 666–669, 683, 686, 713–15, 733–34
reformation 59–60, 141–42, 267, 640
regional development/regional planning 34
regions/Autonomous Communities 97, 98, 201, 269–70, 272, 274, 276, 278, 286–89, 291–92, 298–99, 301–2, 313–15, 389, 486, 515, 551, 556, 559, 576–77, 591–95, 640, 676
    see also Cantons; *Land/Länder*
removal 28, 77–78, 102, 230, 247–48, 343, 370, 522–23, 556–57, 678, 692
    see also asylum, right to
restoration 53, 116, 139–40, 185–86, 273, 320, 327–28, 330, 505–6, 509–10, 646, 692, 694, 695
reunification 168, 179, 182
revolution 58, 59, 105–6, 114, 115, 120–21, 128, 134–35, 141, 145, 217–18, 222, 264–65, 387, 388, 391, 428–29, 441, 508, 513, 604, 642, 690, 691–92, 694, 695, 696
right of residence 46–47, 314–15, 428, 635, 658, 685–86
    see also foreigners
right to be heard (*audiatur et altera pars*) 193–94, 661
right to vote 19, 29–30, 132, 193–94, 198, 213, 215–16, 246–47, 292, 305, 330–31, 393–94, 396–97, 400, 417, 421, 455, 502–3, 560, 562, 567, 622, 635, 666–67, 733
    see also elections
Roman law 210
rule of law
    Austria 3, 9, 14, 24–25, 27, 28–29, 36–37, 39, 52–54
    Czech Republic 63, 69–70, 86, 91–92, 93–94, 95, 96, 99, 100–1, 102–4
    France 155, 162
    Germany 165–66, 172, 177, 179, 189, 191, 192, 193, 195–96, 197–98, 200–1, 203, 204–5, 212, 216
    Hungary 217–18, 220, 222, 223, 229, 230–31, 239–41, 244, 248, 255, 256

Italy 307–8, 316–17
Lithuania 320–21, 322, 325, 334, 336–37, 339, 349–50, 353, 361, 362–63, 379
Netherlands 420
Poland 431, 432–37, 446–47, 459, 460, 462–63, 469, 471, 473, 474, 476, 481, 490–91
Romania 500, 510–11, 516, 522, 523–24, 527–28, 536–41
Spain 566, 569–70, 576, 586
Sweden 602–3, 612, 630, 633
Switzerland 656, 659–62, 664–65, 669–71, 679–80, 687
United Kingdom 697, 698, 702–3, 704, 709–10, 711, 724–26

Schmitt, Carl 150–51, 174–75, 210, 276
Second World War *see* World War
secularization 395, 418, 429, 500–1
security/safety 34–35, 46–47, 142, 160–61, 169, 183, 205, 235, 241, 303–4, 345, 369, 400, 417, 453, 472, 475, 476–77, 483–84, 527–28, 583–584, 612–13, 623–24, 656, 667, 696,
    external/internal 18–19, 34, 188, 209, 370
    public 43, 228–29, 234, 478
self-government 52–53, 63, 64, 95, 96–100, 116, 118, 128–29, 131–33, 136–37, 138, 146, 160, 161, 313, 441–42, 472–73, 524–25, 551, 556–57, 571–72, 595, 603, 622, 633, 635
    see also autonomy
separation of powers
    Austria 10, 40–43, 51, 52–50
    Czech Republic 77, 88, 95–98, 102
    France 118, 131, 138–40, 146, 154–55
    Germany 195–96, 201, 202
    Hungary 241
    Italy 302, 310, 311, 313, 315
    Lithuania 346, 356, 361–62, 365–68
    Netherlands 408, 426, 430
    Poland 432, 433–35, 437–38, 446–47, 459, 463, 471, 481, 482–83, 486, 490
    Romania 497–98, 499–500, 503–4, 514, 542
    Spain 576
    Sweden 603, 613, 616–17, 630
    Switzerland 643, 644, 678–79
    United Kingdom 703, 721, 728
single market 648
social justice 59–60, 73–74, 378, 437, 471, 473, 488
social rights 11, 73–74, 77–78, 144, 155, 160–61, 164, 169, 170, 494–95, 605–6
social security 17–18, 160–61, 170, 189, 206–7, 278, 303–4, 425, 477–78
    see also welfare state
solidarity 276–77, 281, 315, 363–64, 369, 489, 594–95, 686–87, 706
sovereign act/sovereign power/sovereign state 38–39, 63, 71, 114, 119–22, 139–40, 152, 156, 169, 177, 188, 260, 281, 307, 323, 328–29, 356–59, 389, 410, 454–55, 469–70, 472, 488–89, 490–91, 513, 596, 642–43, 644, 680–81, 692, 693, 698, 701–2, 723

746   INDEX

sovereignty 20–21, 23, 70, 71, 80, 90, 100, 102, 115, 116, 118, 119, 120–22, 133, 137, 146, 147, 151–52, 237–38, 254, 255–56, 259–60, 261–62, 263–64, 277, 278, 305, 313–14, 322, 356, 357, 359, 383, 388, 397, 419–21, 435, 463, 469–70, 552, 595–96, 599, 626–28, 642–43, 695, 697–98, 702–3, 712, 714–15, 723–26, 731

standing 45, 165–66, 174–75, 191, 199, 203–4, 215–16, 404, 590

state/statehood 3, 56, 59–60, 103–4, 180, 201, 208, 232, 247, 321, 322, 324, 325, 326–27, 328–29, 330, 332, 351–52, 356, 376, 377, 378, 469–70, 488, 490–91, 500–1, 608, 663–64, 680–81

  concept of 100, 103–4, 107, 212, 215, 266, 376, 378, 469–70, 488–89, 635

  demise/loss of 188–89, 321, 322, 324

  inclusion in/cooperation with supranational and international organizations 79, 121–22, 156–57, 161–62, 308, 344–47, 360–61, 412, 426, 442, 452–53, 454, 469–70, 472, 528–29, 597–98, 656, 667

  objectives 25–26, 51, 303–4, 442, 464–65

  origins 3–4, 58–60, 65, 101, 320–21, 357–59, 433–37, 640, 692–93, 731

  see also administration

state church 208

state liability 586–87

state organs 84–85, 170–71, 192–93, 202, 220, 411, 420, 474, 476–77

strike, right to 145, 278, 477–78, 551

  see also fundamental rights

subject *see* citizen

subsidiarity, principle of 99, 367–69, 486, 488, 658–59

taxes 35–36, 201–2, 231, 320–21, 427, 487, 557, 568, 644, 682–83

  tax law 158, 671

telecommunications 46–47, 253, 545, 710–11

  see also infrastructure

territorial entities 11–12, 36, 51, 301–2, 314, 315

  see also federation; *Land/Länder*; Cantons; municipalities; corporations

territorial reforms 287–88

terror/terrorism 138, 182–83, 188, 192, 231, 319–20, 495–96, 573

  see also dictatorship

Third Reich *see* National Socialism

trade unions 134, 145, 278, 289–90, 439, 637

transparency 175, 199–200, 223, 554, 627, 634, 690, 711

ultra vires **doctrine** 72, 73, 77–78, 98, 257, 258–60, 261, 263–64, 489, 535–36

unification 180, 188–89, 269–70, 386, 497–98, 645, 646, 658

  see also reunification

unitary state 3, 10, 20, 63, 85–86, 100, 101, 322, 360, 389, 427, 428–29, 513, 602–3, 633, 699–700

United Nations 26–27, 52, 167–68, 179, 365

universities 174, 182–83, 243, 418, 502–3, 512, 559–60, 701–2

war/warfare 164, 166, 179, 185, 189, 206, 236, 269, 271, 272, 273, 279, 328–29, 382, 392, 394, 397, 398, 500–2, 549–50, 551, 553, 557, 603, 618–19, 641, 692, 694, 696, 712, 716, 730–31

  World War *see* World War

welfare state 73–74, 106, 169, 170, 205–6, 207, 212, 216, 275, 276–77, 281, 460, 604, 617, 630, 634, 664–65

  see also social security

Wesentlichkeitstheorie 203–4, 209

World War

  First 4, 56, 76, 270, 324, 393, 505–11, 604, 709–10

  Second 10, 14, 23–24, 44, 47–48, 93, 103, 104, 145, 163–64, 167, 169, 182, 205–6, 210, 211–12, 216, 230, 269, 271–72, 273, 279, 282–84, 296, 307, 326–27, 328–29, 357, 382, 384–85, 395, 397, 412, 551, 558–59, 614, 620, 647, 715